THE
DIRECTORY OF
EU INFORMATION
SOURCES

THE DIRECTORY OF EU INFORMATION SOURCES

14th edition

Routledge
Taylor & Francis Group

LONDON AND NEW YORK

First published 1989
Fourteenth edition 2005

© **Routledge 2005**
Haines House, 21 John Street,
London, WC1N 2BP, United Kingdom
(a member of the Taylor & Francis Group)

ISBN 1 85743 284 3
ISSN 1025-6733

Typeset in 8.5 on 9.5 pt. Century Schoolbook

Typeset by AJS Solutions, Huddersfield ● Dundee
Printed and bound by Polestar Wheatons, Exeter

FOREWORD

With the enlargement of the European Union to 25 Member States in May 2004, many new outlets have become available offering information about the Union to the general public.

The fourteenth edition of the Directory of EU Information Sources, which forms part of the Europa Publications EU Information Series, brings together a wide range of information sources, comprising not only the various constituent institutions of the European Union, their personnel, publications, information offices, websites and representations in Europe and the rest of the world, but also diplomatic representation in Brussels, European-level trade and professional associations and NGOs, consultants and lawyers specializing in EU affairs, Press Agencies, EU grants and loans programmes, and universities offering courses in European integration.

Much attention has been given to page layout in the new edition, with the result that the presentation of most sections of the directory has been thoroughly overhauled. We hope that our readers will find the changes beneficial and, as always, would be delighted to receive suggestions for further improvements, both to layout and to content.

The Editor
February 2005

CONTENTS

CONTENTS

CONTENTS

FOREIGN, REGIONAL AND INSTITUTIONAL REPRESENTATION IN BRUSSELS

PRESS AGENCIES, CONFERENCE ORGANIZERS AND THINK TANKS SPECIALIZING IN EU AFFAIRS

CONSULTANTS SPECIALIZING IN EU QUESTIONS

LAWYERS AND LEGAL ADVISERS SPECIALIZING IN EU LAW

TRADE AND PROFESSIONAL ASSOCIATIONS, INTEREST GROUPS, NGOs AND CHURCH ASSOCIATIONS

STUDIES IN EUROPEAN INTEGRATION

EU GRANTS AND LOANS

OTHER USEFUL SOURCES OF INFORMATION

(On 31 December 2004 the European Commission ceased to support the activities of the networks Info Points Europe and Carrefours. It was announced that a new, unified Europe Direct Information Network would be established in all EU Member States in the course of 2005.)

THE EUROPEAN COMMISSION

THE EUROPEAN COMMISSION: OVERVIEW

Following the radical overhaul undertaken by former President, Romano Prodi, the European Commission is now made up of the following Directorates-General and dependent entities:

- Secretariat-General
- Group of Policy Advisers
- European Anti-Fraud Office
- Legal Service
- Press and Communication DG
- Interpretation DG
- Eurostat
- Translation DG
- Agriculture and Rural Development DG
- Competition DG
- Economic and Financial Affairs DG
- Education and Culture DG
- Employment, Social Affairs and Equal Opportunities DG
- Energy and Transport DG
- Enterprise and Industry DG
- Environment DG
- Fisheries DG
- Health and Consumer Protection DG
- Information Society and Media DG
- Internal Market and Services DG
- Justice, Freedom and Security DG
- Regional Policy DG
- Joint Research Centre
- Research DG
- Taxation and Customs Union DG
- Development DG
- Enlargement DG
- EuropeAid Co-operation Office
- External Relations DG
- Humanitarian Aid Office – ECHO
- Trade DG
- Budget DG
- Informatics DG
- Office for Infrastructure and Logistics
- Internal Audit Service
- Personnel and Administration DG
- Publications Office

As the instigator of EU Policy, the European Commission produces an enormous amount of information and has naturally developed a series of channels to disseminate it: Commission Offices, the Press and Communication Service, the Office for Official Publications of the European Communities, Euro-Info-Centres and a large number of relays and networks. (Each of these channels is covered in depth in this section of the Directory.) The European Commission's Directorate-General for Education and Culture is responsible for promoting the EU's image and for informing the outside world about EU activities and life in the European Union. Information offices, falling under the aegis of that Directorate-General, are maintained in each of the EU's Member States.

Outside the EU, information offices are maintained within three of the Commission's external delegations: in Geneva, Washington and Tokyo. There is also a branch of the Washington office in New York.

External delegations are maintained in third countries and are supervised by the Directorate-General for External Relations. One or more persons are responsible, within these delegations, for providing information to interested parties.

The role of the information officer varies a great deal, according to the size of the delegation, but the officer is, in principle, in a position to supply all information on the European Union or to request it from Brussels, should an immediate reply not be possible.

OFFICES OF THE EUROPEAN COMMISSION IN MEMBER STATES

The European Commission has maintained Offices in the Member States for many years and their basic role has been to inform the press and the public about Commission initiatives in those countries in which they are located.

The Commission's Offices are the sole centres of de-centralized information which the European Commission maintains outside Brussels. They are located in each Member State, as well as in three non-member states, and some have branch offices in major towns.

The offices systematically receive all the EU documentation published by the Office for Official Publications of the European Communities, along with some bulletins specially intended for them. In addition, they receive all the press notes or dossiers drafted by the European Commission's Press and Communication service. They naturally have access to all the databases managed by the Commission.

The offices may also refer questions to the Brussels centre, or directly contact officials from the Commission's relevant services when faced with a technical or tricky question.

Commission Offices' Own Publications

The Press and Information Services of the Commission Offices produce a certain number of publications tailored more specially to the countries for which they are intended. The publications may be periodical, and therefore general in character, or one-off and deal with a specific subject.

It is worth remembering, however, that the Offices are European Commission services and that their publications automatically toe the Commission's line. The offices are competent solely in respect of the country to which they are attached.

Details are provided about the publications of most of the Offices over the next few pages. The publications are free, unless otherwise indicated. Where there is a charge, it is generally to cover mailing costs.

Users of the Commission's Offices

The task of the offices is to inform primarily the media and, secondarily, administrations, organizations, companies and other information seekers. A large part of the information sought from the Commission's offices can be obtained from the 'information relays' which the European Union sponsors in the Member States, such as European Documentation Centres for students and researchers, certain libraries, Euro-Info Centres for SMEs, and EU information centres for consumers.

Offices of the European Commission in Member States

AUSTRIA

Vienna: Kärtner Ring 5–7, 1010 Vienna, Austria; tel (1) 51618-0; fax (1) 51342-25; e-mail burvie@cec.eu.int; internet www.europa.eu.int/austria; includes a library (Head of Information, Documentation and Publications Bernard Kühr); Head of Representation: Karl Doutlik; publications: *EU-Direkt*, regional brochures on Austria, *Almanach*, *The Union, Austria and the European Union*, *The European Union and Enlargement*.

BELGIUM

Brussels: 73 rue Archimède, 1000 Brussels, Belgium; tel (2) 295-38-44; fax (2) 295-01-66; e-mail represent-bel@cec.eu.int; internet www.europa.eu.int/comm/represent/be; no library, but the documentalist can receive visitors by appointment; Head of Representation: Guy Vandebon; publications: bulletins *EURinfo* in French, *EUROPA-bericht* in Dutch and *EURO-Info* in German (10 a year, containing items of general interest, details of research programmes and a list of new publications), brochures and leaflets.

CYPRUS

Nicosia: Iris Tower, 8th Floor, 2 Agapinor St, 1076 Nicosia, Cyprus; POB 23480, 1683 Nicosia; tel (22) 81-7770; fax (22) 76-8926; e-mail press-rep-cyprus@cec.eu.int; internet www.delcyp.cec.eu.int; includes press and information service (Press and Information Officer Katerina Yennari); Head of Delegation: Adriaan van der Meer.

CZECH REPUBLIC

Prague: Jungmannova 24, POB 811, 111 21 Prague 1, Czech Republic; tel 22412835; fax 224312850; e-mail press-rep-czech@cec.eu.int; internet www.evropska-unie.cz; includes a press information service (Press Officer Jaromír Leviček); Head of Delegation (acting): Christian Bourgin.

DENMARK

Copenhagen: Højbrohus, Østergade 61, POB 144, 1004 Copenhagen K, Denmark; tel 33-14-41-40; fax 33-11-12-03; e-mail eu@europa-kommissionen.dk; internet www.europa-kommissionen.dk; includes information department (Head of Press and Information Michael Vedsø); Head of Representation: Thomas A. Christensen; publication *Europa* (monthly magazine for the general public).

ESTONIA

Tallinn: Kohtu 10, 10130 Tallinn, Estonia; tel 626-44-00; fax 626-44-39; e-mail pille.vaher@cec.eu.int; internet www.europaliit.ee; includes a press information service (Press Officer Pille Vaher) and a European Union Information Centre (e-mail info@euroopaliit.ee); Head of Representation John Kjaer.

FINLAND

Helsinki: Pohjoisesplanadi 31, POB 1250, 00101 Helsinki, Finland; tel (9) 6226544; fax (9) 656728; e-mail burhel@cec.eu.int; internet www.eukomissio.fi; includes press information service (Press Officer Marjatta Hautala; e-mail marjatta.hautala@cec.eu.int); Head of Representation (acting): Marjatta Hautala; publications: *Europa* (magazine in Finnish), weekly factsheet and background sheets (in Finnish and Swedish) on main decisions and events in the EU, brochures on EU policies.

FRANCE

Paris: 288 blvd Saint-Germain, 75007 Paris, France; tel 1-40-63-38-00; fax 1-45-56-94-17; e-mail burpar@cec.eu.int; internet europa.eu.int/france; includes Documentation Centre (contacts Mrs Touttou, Mrs Messai); Head of Representation: Sixtine Bouygues; publications:

7 Jours Europe (weekly newsletter for subscribers), *MiniTel* (database with EU news, information about Europe, regions of France, the Communities' publications etc.; accessible via the code 36 15 CEE).

Marseilles: 2 rue Henri-Barbusse, 13241 Marseille Cedex 01, France; tel 4-91-91-46-00; fax 4-91-90-98-07; e-mail antmar@cec.eu.int; internet www.europa.eu.int/france; includes documentation facility (Documentalist Mrs Espel); Head of Representation: Jacques Huchet.

GERMANY

Berlin: Unter den Linden 78, 10117 Berlin, Germany; tel (30) 22802000; fax (30) 22802222; e-mail eu-de-kommission@cec.eu.int; internet www.eu-kommission.de; Head of Representation: Dr Gerhard Sabathil.

Bonn: Bertha-von-Suttner-Platz 2–4, 53111 Bonn, Germany; tel (228) 53009-0; fax (228) 53009-50; e-mail eu-de-bonn@cec.eu.int; Head of Representation: Barbara Gessler; publications: *EU Kommunal* (handbook on European issues for local authorities and local media), *EU Almanach* (databases on European issues in Germany), *EU-Nachrichten/Thema* (thematic compilation of information about the EU), *EU-Nachrichten* (weekly newsletter for journalists), *Europäische Gespräche* (text of speeches given in the Representation in Bonn), *Regionalbroschüren* series (brochures about the 16 Bundesländer), *Europa-Pässe* (for particular regions and Bundesländer), *Rednerteam Europa* (portraits of speakers on European topics), *Jahresbericht* (annual report of the Commission's representation).

Munich: Erhardstr. 27, 80331 Munich, Germany; tel (89) 242448-0; fax (89) 242448-15; e-mail eu-de-muenchen@cec.eu.int; Head of Representation: Jochen Kubosch.

GREECE

Athens: Vassilissis Sofias 2, POB 11002, 106 74 Athens, Greece; tel (1) 7272100; fax (1) 7244620; e-mail burath@cec.eu.int; internet www.europa.eu.int/hellas; includes library (e-mail eu-gr-documentation@cec.eu.int; Head of Documentation Service Olympia Papayanakopoulou); Head of Representation: George Markopouliotis; publications: *Evropaiki Epikairotita* (review published in Greek every 2 months), Last Week (weekly newsletter in Greek), brochures in Greek.

HUNGARY

Budapest: Bérc utca 23, 1016 Budapest, Hungary; tel (1) 209-9700; fax (1) 466-4221; e-mail press-rep-hungary@cec.eu.int; internet www.eudelegation.hu; Head of Representation: Jürgen Köppen.

IRELAND

Dublin: European Union House, 18 Dawson St, Dublin 2, Ireland; tel (1) 6341111; fax (1) 6341112; e-mail eu-ie-info-request@cec.eu.int; internet www.euireland.ie; includes reference library (Head of Information Harry O'Connor); Head of Representation: Peter Doyle; publications: *Regional Brochure Ireland*, *In Search of Europe* school pack, *Team Europe* leaflet.

ITALY

Rome: Via IV Novembre 149, 00187 Rome, Italy; tel (06) 699991; fax (06) 6791658; internet www.comeur.it; includes a Documentation Centre (head Eulalia Martinez de Alos-Moner); Heads of Representation: Lucio Battistotti, Fabrizio Grillenzoni; publications: *News Europa* (monthly news summary), *Europa* (monographs, 2 a year).

Milan: Corso Magenta 59, 20123 Milan, Italy; tel (2) 4675141; fax (2) 4818543; internet www.uemilano.it; includes a library (Documentalists Annalisa Affer, Rosalia Bodega); Head of Representation: Roberto Santaniello.

LATVIA

Riga: Jacob's Barracks, Block 1c, Tornu 4, 1050 Riga, Latvia; tel 732-5270; fax 732-5279; e-mail delegation-latvia-news@cec.eu.int; internet www.eiropainfo.lv; includes a press information service (Press Officer Inese Stepiņa); Head of Representation: Andrew Rasbash.

LITHUANIA

Vilnius: Naugarduko g. 10, 01141 Vilnius, Lithuania; tel (5) 231-31-91; fax (5) 231-31-92; e-mail delegation-lithuania@cec.eu.int; internet www.eudel.lt; includes a Press and Information Section (Press and Information Officer Laimutė Pilukaitė); Head of Representation: Michael Graham.

LUXEMBOURG

Luxembourg: Bâtiment Jean Monnet, rue Alcide de Gasperi, 2920 Luxembourg, Luxembourg; tel 4301-32925; fax 4301-34433; internet www.europa.eu.int/luxembourg; Head of Representation: Fons Theis; publication: *Echos de l'Europe* (newsletter covering topics relating to EU integration).

MALTA

Ta'Xbiex: Villa 'The Vines', 51 Ta'Xbiex Seafront, Ta'Xbiex, MSD 11, Malta; tel (21) 344891; fax (21) 344897; e-mail delegation-malta@cec.eu.int; internet www.delmlt.cec.eu.int; includes a press and information service (Press and Information Officer Agnes Borg); Head of Representation: Ronald Gallimore.

NETHERLANDS

The Hague: Korte Vijverberg 5, 2513 AB The Hague, Netherlands; POB 30465, 2500 GL The Hague; tel (70) 3135300; fax (70) 3646619; e-mail burhay@cec.eu.int; internet www.eu.nl; includes documentation department (head Judit Wessel); Head of Representation: Henk Beereboom; publications: *Europa van Morgen* (fortnightly information bulletin), brochures.

POLAND

Warsaw: Warsaw Financial Centre, 29th Floor, Emilii Plater 53, 00-113 Warsaw, Poland; tel (22) 5208200; fax (22) 5208282; e-mail delegation-poland@cec.eu.int; internet www.europa.delpol.pl; includes an Info Point (Director Robert Połkowski) and a Press and Reporting service (Press Officer Hanna Jeziorańska); Head of Representation: Bruno Dethomas.

PORTUGAL

Lisbon: Largo Jean Monnet 1 (10°), 1069-068 Lisbon, Portugal; tel (21) 3509800; fax (21) 3509801; e-mail burlis@cec.eu.int; internet www.ce.pt; includes a library (Librarian José Antonio Martins) and information service (Head of Information Margarida Marques); Head of Representation: Ricardo Charters d'Azevedo.

SLOVAKIA

Bratislava: Palisády 29, 811 06 Bratislava, Slovakia; tel (7) 5443-1718; fax (7) 5443-2980; e-mail mailto@delsvk.cec.eu.int; internet www.europa.sk; includes a press information service (Press Officer Branislav Slyčko); Head of Representation: Eric van der Linden.

SLOVENIA

Ljubljana: Dalmatinova 4, 1000 Ljubljana, Slovenia; tel (1) 438-2270; fax (1) 438-2360; e-mail info@evropska-unija.si; internet www.evropska-unija.si; Head of Representation: Erwan Fouère.

SPAIN

Madrid: Paseo de la Castellana 46, 28046 Madrid, Spain; tel (91) 4238000; fax (91) 5760387; internet www.europa .eu.int/spain; includes library (Librarian Teresa Frontan); Head of Representation: José Luis González Vallvé; publications: newsletters, information notes, statistical notes, external relations, diary and analysis, *Single Market* and *Research & Development* fact sheets (all with circulation restricted to the press and other relevant organizations), and for the general public *The EC: What Is It?* and *UE Digame* (directory of Community correspondents in Spain).

Barcelona: Passeig de Gràcia 90, 08008 Barcelona, Spain; tel (93) 4677380; fax (93) 4677381; includes documentation service; Head of Representation: Josep Coll i Carbó.

SWEDEN

Stockholm: Nybrogatan 11, POB 7323, 103 90 Stockholm, Sweden; tel (8) 562-444-11; fax (8) 562-444-12; e-mail bursto@cec.eu.int; internet www .eukomm.se; includes a documentation facility (Documentalist Charles Murelius); Head of Representation: Hans Allden; publication: *Europa Posten*.

UNITED KINGDOM

London: Jean Monnet House, 8 Storey's Gate, London, SW1P 3AT, United Kingdom; tel (20) 7973-1992; fax (20) 7973-1900; e-mail ian.barber@cec.eu.int; internet www.cec.org.uk; includes a library (visits by appointment); Head of Representation (acting): Ian Barber; publications: *The Week in Europe* (weekly summary of EU events), press releases.

Belfast: Windsor House, 9–15 Bedford St, Belfast, BT2 7EG, United Kingdom; tel (28) 9024-0708; fax (28) 9024-8241; e-mail eddie.mcveigh@cec.eu.int; internet www.europe.org.uk/info/ni; includes a reference library; Head of Office: Eddie McVeigh; publications *EU Weekly* (weekly review of main EU issues for the Northern Ireland press), *Info-Point* information leaflet, *Northern Ireland in Europe* (EC regional brochure outlining the relationship between Northern Ireland and the EU), gateway site at www.europe.org.uk/info/ni with details of all EU information providers in Northern Ireland and regular news updates and hyperlinks to websites related to Northern Ireland, the United Kingdom and the European Union).

Cardiff: 2 Caspian Point, Caspian Way, Cardiff, CF10 4QQ, United Kingdom; tel (29) 2089-5020; fax (29) 2089-5035; e-mail ian.barber@cec.eu.int; internet www.cec.org.uk; includes a library; Head of Office (acting): Ian Barber; publications: *Wales in the European Union*, *Cymru yn undeb Europeaidd*, *The European Commission Representation in Wales*.

Edinburgh: 9 Alva Street, Edinburgh, EH2 4PH, United Kingdom; tel (131) 225-2058; fax (131) 226-4105; e-mail elizabeth.holt@cec.eu.int; internet www .europe.org.uk/info/scotland; includes a library; Head of Office: Elizabeth Holt; publications: *Scotland in Europe* (regional brochure), *A Guide to the Funding Process – Scotland*, *European Information in Scotland* (directory of information providers).

External Delegations of the European Commission in Non-Member States

Albania: Rruga Donika Kastrioti, Villa No 42, Tirana; tel (42) 28320; fax (42) 30752; e-mail mailto@delalb.cec.eu.int; Head of Delegation: Lutz Salzmann.

Algeria: Domaine Benouadah, chemin du Val d'Hydra, El Biar, Algiers; tel (21) 92-36-41; fax (21) 92-36-81; internet www.dz-eudel.com; Head of Delegation: Lucio Guerrato.

Angola: 6 rua Rainha Jinga 45, 3°, CP 2669, Luanda; tel (2) 391339; fax (2) 392531; e-mail delago@uniao-europeia .netangloa.com; Head of Delegation: Glauco Calzuola.

Anguilla: (see Barbados).

Antigua and Barbuda (Sub-office of Delegation to Barbados): Alpha Bldg, 2nd Floor, Upper St George's St, POB 1392, St John's; tel 462-2970; fax 467-8687; e-mail mailto@delbrb.cec.eu.int; Resident Adviser: (vacant).

Argentina: Ayacucho 1537, c1112aaa Buenos Aires; Casilla de Correo 2892, 1000 Buenos Aires; tel (11) 4805-3759; fax (11) 4801-1594; e-mail mailto@ delarg.cec.eu.int; internet www.delarg .cec.eu.int; Head of Delegation: Angelos Pangratis.

Armenia: (see Georgia).

Aruba: (see Trinidad and Tobago).

Australia: 18 Arkana St, Yarralumla, POB 609, Canberra, ACT 2600; tel (2) 6271 2777; fax (2) 6273 4445; e-mail australia@delaus.cec.eu.int; internet www.delaus.cec.eu.int; Head of Delegation: Piergiorgio Mazzocchi (also responsible for New Zealand).

Azerbaijan: (see Georgia).

Bahamas: (see Jamaica).

Bangladesh: Plot 7, Road 84, POB GN 6086, Gulshan, Dhaka 1212; tel (2) 8824730; fax (2) 8823118; e-mail mailto@ delbgd.cec.eu.int; internet www .eudelbangladesh.org; Head of Delegation: Esko Kentrschynskyj.

Barbados: Mervue House, Marine Garden, Hastings, Christ Church; POB 654c, Bridgetown; tel 427-4362; fax 427-8687; e-mail mailto@delbrb.cec.eu.int; internet www.delbrb.cec.eu.int; Head of Delegation: Amos Tincani (also responsible for Anguilla, Antigua and Barbuda, the British Virgin Islands, Dominica, French Guiana, Grenada, Guadeloupe, Martinique, Montserrat, St Christopher and Nevis, St Lucia, and St Vincent and the Grenadines).

Belarus: (see Ukraine).

Belize (Sub-office of Delegation to Jamaica): Blake Bldg, 3rd Floor, cnr Hutson and Eyre Sts, POB 907, Belize City; tel (2) 32070; fax (2) 72785; e-mail mailto@delblz.cec.eu.int; Resident Adviser: (vacant).

Benin: Bâtiment Administratif, ave Clozel, BP 910, Cotonou; tel 31-30-99; fax 31-53-28; e-mail mailto@delben.cec .eu.int; Head of Delegation: Franco Nulli.

Bolivia: Calle 15 Obrajes 406, Casilla 10747, La Paz; tel (2) 2782244; fax (2) 2784550; e-mail delegation-bolivia@ cec.eu.int; Head of Delegation: (vacant).

Bosnia and Herzegovina: Union Bank Bldg, 4th Floor, 71000 Sarajevo, Dubrovacka 6; tel (71) 666044; e-mail delegation-bih@cec.eu.int; Head of Delegation: Michael Humphreys.

Botswana: Plot 68, North Ring Rd, POB 1253, Gaborone; tel 314455; fax 313626; e-mail eudelbwa@delbwa.cec.eu.int; Head of Delegation: Claudia Wiedey-Nippold.

Brazil: SHIS QI 11, Conj. 5, Casa 13, Lago Sul, 71615-570 Brasília, DF; tel (61) 248-3122; fax (61) 248-0700; e-mail europa@comdelbra.org.br; internet www .comdelbra.org.br; Head of Delegation: Rolf Timans.

British Antarctic Territory: (see Trinidad and Tobago).

British Virgin Islands: (see Barbados).

Brunei: (see Indonesia).

Bulgaria: 9 Moskovska Ul., BG 1000 Sofia, POB 668; tel (2) 97-33-240; fax (2) 97-33-872; e-mail mailto@delbgr.cec .eu.int; internet www.evropa.bg; Head of Delegation: Demetre Kourkoulas.

Burkina Faso: ave Kwame Nkrumah, opp Sonatur, BP 352, Ouagadougou; tel 30-73-85; fax 30-89-66; e-mail delegation -burkina-faso@cec.eu.int; Head of Delegation: Antonio García Velázquez.

Burundi: ave du 13 octobre, BP 103, Bujumbura; tel 223426; fax 224612; e-mail hdel@delbdi.cec.eu.int; Head of Delegation: Georges André.

Cambodia (Sub-office of Delegation to Thailand): 1 St 21, Tonlé Bassac, Chamcarmon, POB 2301, Phnom Penh; tel (23) 216-996.

Cameroon: 105 rue 1770, quartier Bastos, BP 847, Yaoundé; tel 21-00-28; fax 20-21-49; e-mail eudelcmr@delcmr.cec .eu.int; Head of Delegation: Peter Hughes (also responsible for Equatorial Guinea).

Canada: 45 O'Connor St, Suite 1900, Ottawa, K1P 1A4; tel (613) 238-6464; fax (613) 238-5191; e-mail mailto@delcan .cec.eu.int; internet www.delcan.cec .eu.int; Head of Delegation: Eric Hayes.

Cape Verde: Achada de Santo António, CP 122, Praia; tel 62-13-93; fax 62-13-91; e-mail eudelcpv@mail.cvtelecom.cv; Head of Delegation: Eduardo Sorribes Manzana.

Cayman Islands: (see Jamaica).

Central African Republic: rue de Flandre, BP 1298, Bangui; tel 61-30-53; fax 61-65-35; e-mail eudelrca@intnet.cf; Head of Delegation: Josep Lloveras.

Chad: Concession Caisse Coton, route de Farcha, BP 552, N'Djamena; tel 52-72-76; fax 52-71-05; e-mail eudeltcd@intnet.td; Head of Delegation: Joël Fessaguet.

Chile: Torre Paris, Av Ricardo Lyon 222-3er piso Providencia, Casilla 10093, Santiago 9; tel (2) 335-17-79; fax (2) 335-24-50; e-mail mailto@delch.cec .eu.int; internet www.deluechile.org; Head of Delegation: Wolfgang Plasa.

China, People's Republic: 15 Dong Zhi Men Wai Dajie Sanlitun, Beijing 100600; tel (10) 65324443; fax (10) 65324342; e-mail mailto@delchn.cec.eu.int; internet www.delchn.cec.eu.int; Head of Delegation: Klaus-Dieter Ebermann (also responsible for Mongolia).

Colombia: Calle 97, No 22-44, AP Aéreo 94046, 114 Santafé de Bogotá 8, DC; tel (1) 621-6043; fax (1) 610-0059; e-mail ecco.eudelcol@cable.net.co; internet www .delcol.cec.eu.int; Head of Delegation: (vacant) (also responsible for Ecuador).

Comoros: blvd de la Corniche, BP 559, Moroni; tel (762) 657797; fax (73) 2494; e-mail eudelcom@snpt.km; Resident Adviser: (vacant).

Congo, Democratic Republic: Immeuble BCDC, Blvd du 30 Juin, Gombra, CD Kinshasa I, Gombe; tel (88) 41878; fax (12) 34546; e-mail mailto@delcod.cec.eu .int; Head of Delegation: Carlo de Filippi.

Congo, Republic: ave Lyautey, opp Italian Embassy, BP 2149, Brazzaville; tel 81-31-34; fax 81-18-45; e-mail eudelcog@ congonet.cg; Head of Delegation: Jean-Eric Holzapfel.

Costa Rica: Ofiplaza del Este, Edif D, 3°, De Rotonda de la Bandera, 5m Oeste, Centro Colón, Apdo 836, 1007 San José;

tel 283-2959; fax 283-2960; e-mail mailto@delcri.cec.eu.int; Head of Delegation: (vacant—also responsible for Panama).

Côte d'Ivoire: Immeuble Azur, 18 rue du Dr Crozet, 01 BP 1821, Abidjan 01; tel 20-31-83-50; fax 21-40-89; e-mail mailto@delciv.cec.eu.int; Head of Delegation: Friedrich Nagel (also responsible for Liberia).

Croatia: 10000 Zagreb, Masarykova 1; tel (1) 4896500; fax (1) 4896555; e-mail delegationcroatia@cec.eu.int; Head of Delegation: Jacques Wunenburger.

Cuba: (see Mexico).

Djibouti: 11 blvd du Maréchal Joffre, BP 2477, Djibouti; tel 352615; fax 350036; e-mail eudeldj@internet.dj; Head of Delegation: Pierre Philippe.

Dominica: (see Barbados).

Dominican Republic: Edif Plaza JR, 7°–9°, Avda Tirandentes esq Roberto Pastoriza, Ensanche Naco, AP 226-2, Santo Domingo, DN; tel 540-5837; fax 227-0510; e-mail eudeldom@codetel .net.do; Head of Delegation: Miguel Amado.

Ecuador: (see Colombia).

Egypt: El Fouad Office Bldg, 11th Floor, 37 Gamaet el Dowal el Arabeya, Mohandessin, Giza, Cairo; tel (2) 749-46-80; fax (2) 749-53-63; e-mail delegation-egypt@ cec.eu.int; Head of Delegation: Ian Boag.

El Salvador: (see Nicaragua).

Equatorial Guinea (Sub-office of Delegation to Cameroon): route de l'Aéroport, BP 779, Malabo; tel (9) 29-44; fax (9) 32-75; e-mail cemalab@intnet.gq; Head of Delegation: Rafael Senan Llarena.

Eritrea: 1 Gainer St, Zone 4, Admin 02, POB 5710, Asmara; tel (1) 126566; fax (1) 126578; e-mail mailto@deleri.cec.eu.int; Head of Delegation: Carl Lostelius.

Ethiopia: off Bole Rd, POB 5570, Addis Ababa; tel (1) 612511; fax (1) 612877; e-mail mailto@deleth.cec.eu.int; Head of Delegation: Yves Gazzo.

Falkland Islands: (see Trinidad and Tobago).

Fiji: (see Pacific).

French Guiana: (see Barbados).

French Polynesia: (see Pacific).

French Southern and Antarctic Territories: (see Trinidad and Tobago).

Gabon: Bas de Gué-Gué, Lotissement des Cocotiers, BP 321, Libreville; tel 73-22-50; fax 73-65-54; e-mail eudelgab@ delgab.cec.eu.int; Head of Delegation: Jochen Krebs (also responsible for São Tomé and Príncipe).

The Gambia: 10 10th St South, POB 512, Banjul; tel 495146; fax 497848; e-mail ec@qanet.gm; Resident Adviser: Thierry Mathisse.

Georgia: 38 Nino Chkheidze St, Tbilisi; tel (32) 94-37-63; fax (32) 94-37-68; e-mail mailto@delgeo.cec.eu.int; Head of Delegation: Torben Holtze (also responsible for Armenia and Azerbaijan).

Ghana: Kotoka Int Airport, The Round House, 81 Cantonments Rd, POB 9505, Accra; tel (21) 774201; fax (21) 774154; e-mail mail@delcomgh.org; Head of Delegation: Stefan Frowein.

Grenada (see Barbados).

Guadeloupe and Dependencies: (see Barbados).

Guatemala: Edif Murano, 14 Calle 3-51, Zona 10, Nivel 14 OF 1401, Guatemala City; tel 366-5812; fax 366-5816; e-mail adas.eudelgtm@ue.guate.org; internet www.ueguate.org; Resident Adviser: Philippe Combescot.

Guinea: rue MA 752, Matam, BP 730, Conakry; tel 40-48-70; fax 66-35-25; e-mail mailto@delce.org.gn; Head of Delegation: Dominique David.

Guinea-Bissau: Bairro da Penha, CP 359, 1113 Bissau Cedex; tel 251469; fax 251044; e-mail eu@sol.gtelecom.gw; Head of Delegation: Antonio Moreira Martins.

Guyana: 11 Sendall Place, Stabroek, POB 10847, Georgetown; tel (2) 62667; fax (2) 62615; e-mail delegation-guyana@ delguy.cec.eu.int; internet www.delguy .cec.eu.int; Head of Delegation: Vincent de Visscher.

Haiti: c/o Hotel Montana, Delmas 60, impasse Brave No 1, BP 15.588, Petion Ville, Port-au-Prince; tel 260-05-44; fax 260-05-41; e-mail mailto@delhti.cec .eu.int; Head of Delegation: Marcel Van Opstal.

Honduras: Calle Gemma 2121, colonia Loma Linda, Apartado 557, HO-Tegucigalpa; tel (239) 9991; fax (239) 9994; e-mail eudelhon@compunet.hn; Head of Delegation: (vacant).

Hong Kong: 19/F St John's Bldg, 33 Garden Rd, Central, Hong Kong; tel 2537-6083; fax 2522-1302; e-mail adas@ delhkg.cec.eu.int; internet www.delhkg .cec.eu.int; Head of Delegation: David Ting (also responsible for Macao).

India: 65 Golf Links, New Delhi 110 003; tel (11) 4629237; fax (11) 4629206; e-mail eudelind@giasd101.vsnl.net.in; internet www.delind.cec.eu.int; Head of Delegation: Michael Caillouet.

Indonesia: Wisma Dharmala Sakti Bldg, 16th Floor, Jalan Jendral Sudirman 32, Jakarta 10220; POB 6454, Jakarta 10064; tel (21) 570-6076; fax (21) 570-6075; e-mail delegation-indonesia@cec.eu.int; internet www.delidn.cec.eu.int; Head of

Delegation: Sabato Della Monica (also responsible for Brunei and Nepal).

Israel: Paz Tower, 15th Floor, 31–35 Betzalel St, Ramat Gan 52521; POB 3513, Ramat Gan 52136; tel (3) 6137799; fax (3) 6137770; e-mail delegation-israel@ cec.eu.int; internet www.eu-del.org .il; Head of Delegation: Giancarlo Chevallard.

Jamaica: 8 Olivier Rd, POB 463, Constant Spring, Kingston 8; tel 924-6333; fax 924-6339; e-mail delegation -jamaica@cec.eu.int; Head of Delegation: Gerd Jarchow (also responsible for the Bahamas, Belize, the Cayman Islands and the Turks and Caicos Islands).

Japan: Europa House, 9–15 Sanbancho, Chiyoda-ku, Tokyo 102–0075; tel (3) 3239-0441; fax (3) 3261-5194; e-mail deljapan@deljpn.cec.eu.int; internet www.jpn.cec.eu.int; Head of Delegation: Bernhard Zepter.

Jordan: 15 Al Jahez St, Shmeisani, opposite Arab Potash Co, POB 926794, Amman; tel (6) 5668191; fax (6) 5686746; e-mail mailto@deljor.cec.eu.int; internet www.deljor.cec.eu.int; Head of Delegation: Robert Van Der Meulen (also responsible for Yemen).

Kazakhstan: 480100 Almaty, 20a Kazybek bi; tel (3272) 63-62-655; fax (3272) 91-07-49; e-mail eudel@delkaz.cec.eu.int; internet www.delkaz.cec.eu.int; Head of Delegation: Alan Waddams (also responsible for Kyrgyzstan and Tajikistan).

Kenya: Union Insurance House, Ragati Rd, POB 45119, Nairobi; tel (2) 713020; fax (2) 716481; e-mail delegation -kenya@cec.eu.int; Head of Delegation: Gary Quince (also responsible for Somalia).

Kiribati: (see Pacific).

Korea, Republic: Sean Bldg, 16th Floor, Shinmoonru 1 Ka 116, Chongro-Ku, POB 911, Seoul 110-700; tel (2) 735-1101; fax (2) 735-1211; e-mail mailto@delkor.cec .eu.int; Head of Delegation: Frank Hesske.

Kyrgyzstan: (see Kazakhstan).

Laos: (see Thailand).

Lebanon: 490 Harbour Drive, Charles Helou Saifi, RL-Beirut; tel (1) 56-94-00; fax (1) 56-94-15; e-mail delegation -lebanon@cec.eu.int; internet www .dellbn.cec.eu.int; Head of Delegation: Bernard Patrick Renauld.

Lesotho: 167 Constitutional Rd, POB MS 518, Maseru 100; tel 313726; fax 310193; e-mail mailto@dellso.cec.eu.int; Head of Delegation: Robert Collingwood (also responsible for Swaziland).

Liberia: UN Drive, Mamba Point, Monrovia; tel 226273; fax 226274; e-mail euliberia@liberia.net; Head of Delegation: (vacant).

Macao: (see Hong Kong).

Macedonia, Former Yugoslav Republic of: Paleta Makedonia, 1000 Skopje, Maršal Tito 12; tel (2) 122032; fax (2) 123213; Head of Delegation: José Pinto Teixeira.

Madagascar: Immeuble Ny Havana, 67 ha, BP 746, Antananarivo; tel (20) 2224216; fax (20) 2264562; e-mail delegation-madagascar@delmdg.cec.eu .int; Head of Delegation: Pierre Protar.

Malawi: Europa House, POB 30102, Capital City, Lilongwe 3; tel (1) 773743; fax (1) 773382; e-mail eudelmwi@malawi .net; Head of Delegation: Wiepke van der Goot.

Malaysia: (see Thailand).

Maldives: (see Sri Lanka).

Mali: Immeuble UATT, quartier du Fleuve, BP 115, Bamako; tel and fax 22-23-70; e-mail delegation-mali@cec.eu.int; Head of Delegation: Francesc Gosetti di Sturmeck.

Martinique: (see Barbados).

Mauritania: Ilot V, Lot No 24, BP 213, Nouakchott; tel (2) 525-27-24; fax (2) 525-35-24; e-mail delcemau@compuserve .com; Head of Delegation: Dominique Pavard.

Mauritius: St James Court Bldg, 8th Floor, St Denis St, POB 1148, Port Louis; tel 207-1515; fax 211-6624; e-mail mailto@delmus.cec.eu.int; Head of Delegation: Juan Carlos Ray Salgado (also responsible for Mayotte, Réunion and the Seychelles).

Mayotte: (see Mauritius).

Mexico: Paseo de la Reforma 1675, Lomas de Chapultepec, 11001 México, DF; tel (5) 540-3345; fax (5) 540-6564; e-mail mailto@delmex.cec.eu.int; internet www.delmex.cec.eu.int; Head of Delegation: Nigel Evans (also responsible for Cuba).

Moldova: (see Ukraine).

Mongolia: (see China, People's Republic).

Montserrat: (see Barbados).

Morocco: Riad Business Centre, Aile Sud, blvd Er-Riad, BP 1302, Rabat; tel (7) 76-67-61; fax (7) 76-11-56; e-mail delegation-morocco@cec.eu.int; internet www.delmar.cec.eu.int; Head of Delegation: Sean Doyle.

Mozambique: Avda Julius Nyerere, CP 2820, MOC-Maputo; tel (1) 481000; fax (1) 491866; e-mail delegation -mozambique@delmoz.cec.eu.int; Head of Delegation: Jose Manuel Pinto Teixeira.

Myanmar: (see Thailand).

Namibia: Sanlam Bldg, 4th Floor, 154 Independence Ave, 9000 Windhoek; tel (61) 2026224; fax (61) 2026000; e-mail

mailto@delnam.cec.eu.int; internet www.delnam.cec.eu.int; Head of Delegation: Antonius Brueser.

Nepal: (see Indonesia).

Netherlands Antilles: (see Trinidad and Tobago).

New Caledonia (Sub-office of Delegation to Pacific): 19 ave du Maréchal Foch, 6è, BP 1100, 98845 Nouméa; tel 27-70-02; fax 28-87-07; e-mail mailto@ delncl.cec.eu.int; Resident Adviser: (vacant).

New Zealand: (see Australia); e-mail newzealand@delaus.cec.eu.int.

Nicaragua: Carretera a Masaya, del Colegio Teresiano 1 cuadra al Este, Apdo 2654, Managua; tel (2) 70-4499; fax (2) 70-4484; e-mail delegation-nicaragua@cec .eu.int; Head of Delegation: Giorgio Mamberto (also responsible for El Salvador, Honduras and Guatemala).

Niger: BP 10388, Niamey; tel 73-23-60; fax 73-23-22; e-mail delnig@intnet.ne; Head of Delegation: Irene Horejs.

Nigeria: Plot 63, Usuma St, Maitama District, Abuja; tel (9) 413348; fax (9) 413347; e-mail delegation-nigeria@cec .eu.int; Head of Delegation: Leonidas Tezapsidis.

Norway: Håkon Vll's gate 10, 9th Floor, 0161 Oslo; POB 1643, Vika, 0119 Oslo; tel 22-83-35-83; fax 22-83-40-55; e-mail delegation-norway@cec.eu.int; internet www.europakommisjonen.no; Head of Delegation: Gerhard Sabathil.

Pacific (Fiji): Devt Bank Centre, 4th Floor, Victoria Parade, Suva, Fiji; PMB, GPO, Suva, Fiji; tel 313633; fax 300370; e-mail eudelfidji@eu.org.fi; Head of Delegation: David Macrae (also responsible for French Polynesia, Kiribati, New Caledonia, Pitcairn Islands, Samoa, Tonga, Tuvalu, Vanuatu and Wallis and Futuna Islands).

Pakistan: No 9, St No 88, Sector G 6/3, POB 1608, Islamabad; tel (51) 2271828; fax (51) 2822604; e-mail mailto@delpak .cec.eu.int; Head of Delegation: Ilkka Uusitalo.

Panama: (see Costa Rica).

Papua New Guinea: The Lodge, 3rd Floor, Bampton St, POB 76, Port Moresby; tel 3213544; fax 3217850; e-mail admin@eudelpng.org; internet www .eudelpng.org; Head of Delegation: Anthony Crasner (also responsible for Solomon Islands).

Paraguay: (see Uruguay).

Peru: Calle Manuel González Olaechea 247, San Isidro, Lima 27; CP 18-0792, Lima 18; tel (1) 422-87-78; fax (1) 415-08-00; e-mail delegation-peru@cec.eu.int; internet www.delper.cec.eu.int; Head of Delegation: Mendel Goldstein.

Philippines: Doña Salustiana Dee Ty Tower, 7°, 104 Paseo de Roxas, cnr Parea St, Legaspi Village, Makati, Metro Manila; tel (2) 8126421; fax (2) 8126687; e-mail delegation-philippines@ cec.eu.int; internet www.delphl.cec.eu .int; Head of Delegation: Johannes de Kot.

Pitcairn Islands: (see Pacific).

Réunion: (see Mauritius).

Romania: Rue Jules Michelet, RO-71297 Bucharest; tel (1) 2035400; fax (1) 2128808; e-mail mailto@delrom.ce c.eu.int; internet www.infoeuropa.ro; Head of Delegation: Jonathan Scheele.

Russian Federation: Kadashevskaya Nab., 14/1, 109017 Moscow; tel (95) 7212000; fax (95) 7212020; e-mail delegation-russia@cec.eu.int; internet www.eur.ru; Head of Delegation: Richard Wright.

Rwanda: 14 rue Député Kamuzinzi, BP 515, Kigali; tel 575586; fax 574313; e-mail eudelrwa@delrwa.cec.eu.int; Head of Delegation: Jeremy Lester.

St Christopher and Nevis: (see Barbados).

St Helena and Dependencies: (see Trinidad and Tobago).

St Lucia: (see Barbados).

St Pierre and Miquelon: (see Trinidad and Tobago).

St Vincent and the Grenadines: (see Barbados).

Samoa (Sub-office of Delegation for the Pacific—Fiji): Ioane Viliamu Bldg, 4th Floor, POB 3023, Apia; tel 24622; fax 20070; e-mail euoffice@lesamoa.net.

São Tomé and Príncipe (Sub-office of Delegation to Gabon): Bairro 3 de Fevereiro, BP 132, São Tomé; tel (12) 21780; fax (12) 22683; e-mail ceestp@cstome.net; Resident Adviser: Mario Tomasello.

Senegal: 12 ave Albert Sarraut, BP 3345, Dakar; tel 823-13-34; fax 823-68-85; e-mail delegation-senegal@cec.eu.int; internet www.delsen.cec.eu.int; Head of Delegation: Thierry de Saint-Maurice.

Serbia and Montenegro: Paje Adamova 4, 11050 Belgrade; tel (11) 3672411; fax (11) 3671143; e-mail delegation@cec.eu .int; Head of Delegation: Geoffrey Barrett.

Seychelles: (see Mauritius).

Sierra Leone: Wesley House, 4 George St, POB 1399, Freetown; tel (22) 227319; fax (22) 225212; e-mail eudelsle@ ecdsl.org; Head of Delegation: Jeremy Tunnacliffe.

Solomon Islands (Sub-office of Delegation to Papua New Guinea); City Centre Bldg, 2nd Floor, POB 844, Honiara; tel 21575; fax 23318; e-mail ecsol@welkam .solomon.com.sb; Resident Adviser: (vacant).

Somalia: (see Kenya).

South Africa: 1–2 Green Park Estate, 27 George Storrar Dr, Groenkloof, Pretoria 0181; POB 945, Pretoria 0027; tel (12) 4525200; fax (12) 4609923; e-mail delegation-s-africa@cec.eu.int; Head of Delegation: Michael Lake.

South Georgia and the South Sandwich Islands: (see Trinidad and Tobago).

Sri Lanka: 26 Sir Marcus Fernando Mawatha, Colombo 7; tel (1) 674413; fax (1) 678860; e-mail mailto@dellka.cec.eu.int; Head of Delegation: (vacant).

Sudan: Block 1b, Plot 10, Gamhoria St, POB 2363, Khartoum; tel (11) 775158; fax (11) 775393; e-mail eudelsud@hotmail.com; Head of Delegation: Kent Degerfelt.

Suriname (Sub-office of Delegation to Guyana): Dr Sophie Redmondstraat 239, POB 484, Paramaribo; tel 499322; fax 493076; e-mail delsur@sr.net; internet www.delsur.cec.eu.int; Resident Adviser: Jacques Roman.

Swaziland (Sub-office of Delegation to Lesotho): Lilunga House, 4th Floor, Gilfillan St, POB A36, Mbabane; tel 4042908; fax 4046729; e-mail mailto@delswz.cec.eu.int; Head of Delegation: Aloysius Lorkeers.

Syria: Chakib Arslane St, Abou Roumaneh, BP 11269, Damascus; tel (11) 3327640; fax (11) 3320683; e-mail mailto@delsyr.cec.eu.int; Head of Delegation: Frank Hesske.

Tajikistan: (see Kazakhstan).

Tanzania: 38 Mirambo St, POB 9514, Dar es Salaam; tel (22) 2117473; fax (22) 2113277; e-mail delegation-tanzania@cec.eu.int; Head of Delegation: William Hanna.

Thailand: Kian Gwan House II, 19th Floor, 140/1 Wireless Rd, Bangkok 10330; tel (2) 255-9100; fax (2) 255-9113; e-mail delegation-thailand@cec.eu.int; internet www.deltha.cec.eu.int; Head of Delegation: Klauspeter Schmallenbach (also responsible for Cambodia, Laos, Malaysia and Myanmar).

Togo: 37 ave Nicolas Grunitzky, BP 1657, Lomé; tel 255-91-00; fax 21-13-00; e-mail eu@deltgo.cec.eu.int; Head of Delegation: (vacant).

Tonga (Sub-office of Delegation for the Pacific—Fiji): Maile Taha, Taufa'ahau Rd, Private Mail Bag No 5, Nuku'alofa; tel 23-820; fax 23-869; e-mail eutonga@candw.to.

Trinidad and Tobago: Mutual Centre, 16 Queen's Park West, POB 1144, Port of Spain; tel 622-6628; fax 622-6355; e-mail mailto@deltto.cec.eu.int; Head of Delegation: Sari Suomalainen (also responsi-

ble for Aruba, the British Antarctic Territory, the Falkland Islands, the French Southern and Antarctic Territories, the Netherlands Antilles, St Helena and Dependencies, St Pierre and Miquelon, and South Georgia and the South Sandwich Islands).

Tunisia: Immeuble Europe, Berges du Lac Nord, croisement rue du Lac Malâren-rue du Lac Oubeira, BP 150, 1053 Tunis; tel (1) 96-03-30; fax (1) 96-03-02; e-mail delegation-tunisia@cec.eu.int; internet www.ce.intl.tn; Head of Delegation: Marc Pierini.

Turkey: 88 Ugur Mumcu Caddesi, 4th Floor, 06700 Gaziosmanpasa Ankara; tel (312) 4465511; fax (312) 4466737; e-mail mailto@deltur.cec.eu.int; internet www.deltur.cec.eu.int; Head of Representation: Hansjoerg Kretschmer.

Turks and Caicos Islands: (see Jamaica).

Tuvalu: (see Pacific).

Uganda: Rwenzori House, 5th Floor, Plot 1, Lumumba Ave, POB 5244, Kampala; tel (41) 233303; fax (41) 233708; e-mail mailto@deluga.cec.eu.int; Head of Delegation: Sigurd Illing.

Ukraine: vul Kruhlouniversitetska 10, 01024 Kiev; tel and fax (44) 462-00-10; e-mail mail@delukr.cec.eu.int; internet www.delukr.cec.eu.int; Head of Delegation: Norbert Jousten (also responsible for Belarus and Moldova).

USA (New York): 3 Dag Hammarskjöld Plaza, 305 East 47th St, New York, NY 10017; tel (212) 371-3804; fax (212) 688-1013; e-mail delegation-new-york-euinfo@cec.eu.int; internet www.europa-eu-un.org/index.asp.

USA (Washington, DC): 2300 M St, NW, 3rd Floor, Washington, DC 20037-1434; tel (202) 862-9500; fax (202) 429-1766; e-mail delegation-washington@cec.eu.int; internet www.eurunion.org; Head of Delegation: Gunter Burghardt.

Uruguay: Blvd Artigas 1257, 11200 Montevideo; tel (2) 19440101; fax (2) 19440122; e-mail eudelury@delury.cec.org.uy; Head of Delegation: Styliani Zervoudaki (also responsible for Paraguay).

Vanuatu (Sub-office of Delegation for the Pacific—Fiji): Moore Stephens House, Ground Floor, Kumul Highway, Rue Higginson St, POB 422, Port Vila; tel 22501; fax 23282; e-mail mailto@delvut.cec.eu.int; Resident Adviser: (vacant).

Venezuela: Edif Comision Europea, Plaza Las Américas 1061a, Avda Orinoco, Las Mercedes, Apdo 67076, Caracas; tel (2) 991-5133; fax (2) 993-5573; e-mail mailto@delven.cec.eu.int; internet www.comisioneuropea.org.ve; Head of Delegation: Cesare De Montis.

Viet Nam: Metropole Centre, 56 Ly Thai To St, Hanoi; tel (4) 9341300; fax (4) 9341361; e-mail mailto@delvnm.cec.eu.int; Head of Delegation: Frederic Baron.

Wallis and Futuna Islands: (see Pacific).

West Bank and Gaza Strip 5 Sheikh Hussam Eddin Jarrallah St, POB 22207, East Jerusalem, Israel; tel (2) 541-58-88; fax (2) 541-58-48; e-mail mailto@delwbg.cec.eu.int; internet www.delwbg.cec.eu.int; Head of Delegation: Jean Breteche.

Yemen: (see Jordan).

Zambia: Plot 4899, Los Angeles Blvd, POB 34871, Lusaka; tel (1) 251140; fax (1) 250906; e-mail mailto@delzmb.cec.eu.int; Head of Delegation: Henri Sprietsma.

Zimbabwe: Construction House, 6th Floor, 110 Leopold Takawira St, POB 4252, Harare; tel (4) 701915; fax (4) 725360; e-mail hod.ecdelzwe@delzwe.cec.eu.int; Head of Delegation: Francesca Mosca.

External Delegations of the European Commission to International Organizations

Geneva: 37–39 rue de Vermont, CP 195, 1211 Geneva 20, Switzerland; tel (22) 9182211; fax (22) 7342236; e-mail delegation-geneva@cec.eu.int; Head of Delegation: Carlo Trojan.

New York: 3 Dag Hammarskjöld Plaza, 305 East 47th St, New York, NY 10017, USA; tel (212) 371-3804; fax (212) 758-2718; e-mail mailto@delusny.cec.eu.int; Head of Delegation: John Richardson.

Paris: 12 ave d'Eylau, 75116 Paris Cedex 16, France; tel 1-44-05-31-60; fax 1-44-05-31-79; Head of Delegation: John Maddison.

Rome: Via IV Novembre 149, 00187 Rome; tel (06) 6793729; fax (06) 6799830; e-mail delegation-roma@cec.eu.int; Head of Delegation: Vilma du Marteau-Verdiani.

Vienna: Argentinierstrasse 26/10, A-1040 Vienna, Austria; tel (1) 505-84-11; fax (1) 505-84-117; e-mail delegation-vienna@cec.eu.int; Head of Delegation: Ulrich Knüppel.

EUROPE DIRECT

Launched in June 1998, Europe Direct is a one-stop information shop designed to provide EU citizens with easy access to information about their rights and opportunities within the European Union. The service operates via a call centre (telephone 00 800 67891011 from an EU Member State or +32 2-2999696 from other countries). If a correspondent is unable to provide an answer, the question is referred to a special European Commission unit which then seeks out the answer. The most frequently asked questions relate to funding, travelling, working and studying. For further information, visit the website at http://europa.eu.int/ europedirect.

A further extension of Europe Direct is the Dialogue with business website (http://europa.eu.int/business/en/ index.html). The site covers such themes as public procurement, product certification, business partner search, Internal Market rules, funding opportunities, environment, technical harmonization and social security.

INFORMATION FOR THE PRESS

The EU's institutions have always been keen to affirm their role as players on the world and European stage. They have therefore, from the start, facilitated the tasks of media likely to report on this role.

The European Commission has a Press and Communication Service (previously entitled Spokesman's Service) and press services in the Member States and in some non-member countries.

The former Spokesman's Service has been radically restructured. Whereas each Commissioner previously had his own spokesperson, a pool of spokespersons, working under the direct authority of the President, has now been set up.

PRESS AND COMMUNICATION SERVICE

The basic mission of the Press and Communication Service (DG Press) is to:

- inform the media and citizens of the activities of the Commission and to communicate the objectives of its policies and actions;
- inform the Commission of the evolution of opinion in the Member States.

To fulfil this mission, DG Press :

- co-ordinates the activities of the representations in the Member States;
- centralises all contacts with the media;
- seeks to ensure a coherent approach to communication and information issues within the Commission. This involves contact with Directorates-General and Services within the Commission that have information units responsible for sectoral information. The DGs responsible for external relations provide information to citizens of third countries including information for the general public in Applicant States.

The service is at the disposal of journalists accredited to the European Communities, and visiting or national journalists. The latter may also obtain information from the Commission offices located in each of the EU's Member States, as well as in Washington, Tokyo and Geneva.

A database was brought into service in 1990 which supplies the notes and press releases issued by the Press and Communication Service (see the 'Rapid' database, in the section on databases). A summary of the most important press releases is available on the Europa website under the heading 'Midday Express'. URL: http://europa.eu.int/comm/press_room.

Press and Communication Service

(45 ave d'Auderghem, 1049 Brussels, Belgium; tel (2) 299-11-11; fax (2) 295-01-43; e-mail forename.surname@cec.eu.int; internet www.europa.eu.int/comm/dgs/press_communication/index_en.htm)

Spokesman: Reijo Kemppinen; tel (2) 295-33-58.

Deputy Spokesman: Marco Vignudelli; tel (2) 299-45-60.

Administration and Forward Planning: Gerassimos Thomas, tel (2) 299-34-42; Michael Mann (Forward Planning), tel (2) 299-97-80; Pia Ahrenkilde Hansen (Co-ordination), tel (2) 295-30-70.

Relations with the Media—Press Room

Spokespersons: Jean-Christophe Filori (Enlargement), tel (2) 296-56-60; Emma Udwin (External Relations), tel (2) 295-95-77; J. C. Ellerman-Kingombe (Development and Humanitarian Aid), tel (2) 295-60-53; Pietro Petrucci (Justice and Home Affairs), tel (2) 298-94-92; Arancha Gonzalez (Trade), tel (2) 296-15-53; Eric Mamer (Administrative Reform, Budget, Anti-Fraud), tel (2) 299-40-73; Frédéric Vincent (Education and Culture), tel (2) 298-71-66; Michael Mann (Enterprise and the Information Society), tel (2) 299-97-80; Jonathan Todd (Internal Market, Taxation and Customs), tel (2) 299-41-07; Amelia Torres (Competition), tel (2) 295-46-29; Amador Sanchez Rico (Transport and Energy), tel (2) 299-24-59; Gerassimos Thomas (Economic and Monetary Affairs), tel (2) 299-34-42; Antonia Mochan (Employment and Social Affairs), tel (2) 296-48-96; Gilles Gantelet (Regional Policy), tel (2) 299-48-96; Gregor Kreuzhuber (Agriculture, Rural Development and Fisheries), tel (2) 296-65-65; Beate Gminder (Health and Consumer Protection, especially Food Safety), tel (2) 296-56-94; Thorsten Muench (Health, Consumer Protection and Agriculture), tel (2) 296-10-63; Ewa Hedlund (Environment), tel (2) 299-12-23; Fabbio Fabbi (Research), tel (2) 296-41-74

DIRECTORATE A

(Interinstitutional Relations, Information Policy, Representations)

Director: Panos Carvounis (acting); tel (2) 295-21-73; fax (2) 295-24-69.

Units

1 Relations with the European Parliament and other Institutions, and Information Policy.

Head of Unit: Benoît Woringer; tel (2) 296-34-98.

2 Representations: Information Campaigns, Relays and Networks.

Head of Unit: Fabrizia De Rosa; tel (2) 299-37-39.

3 Representations: Co-ordination and Analysis.

Head of Unit: Linda Corugedo-Steneberg; tel (2) 299-63-83.

DIRECTORATE B

(Communication, Media and Services)

Director: Niels Thøgersen; tel (2) 299-90-99; fax (2) 299-92-07.

Units

1 Opinion Polls, Press Reviews, Europe Direct.

Head of Unit: Antonis Papacostas; tel (2) 295-99-67.

2 Europa, SCAD+ and Publications.

Head of Unit: Lindsey Armstrong; tel (2) 299-90-17.

3 TV/Radio Services and Studios.

Head of Unit: Alain Dumort; tel (2) 295-38-49.

DIRECTORATE C

(Resources)

Director: Jean Pierre Vandersteen; tel (2) 298-61-70.

Units

1 Personnel and Administration.

Head of Unit: Alberto Hasson; tel (2) 295-58-00.

2 Budget and Finances.

Head of Unit: Giuseppe Menchi; tel (2) 296-11-93.

3 Informatics.

Head of Unit: Jose Torcato; tel (2) 296-35-37.

OFFICE FOR OFFICIAL PUBLICATIONS OF THE EUROPEAN COMMUNITIES (EUR-OP)

EUR-OP is the official publisher of all the organs of the European Union. Based in Luxembourg, EUR-OP systematically publishes about 15 000 monographs and around 100 periodicals a year, as well as an important number of CD-ROMs, databases, videos, etc.

EUR-OP's products

Newsletter: up-to-date information on all EUR-OP's products

Previously entitled EUR-OP News, the Newsletter is published twice a year and is a periodical in which the most recent EU publications are listed with their catalogue numbers, prices and a brief description of their contents. Introductory articles on recent developments of EU policy in different fields provide a handy overview of the political background against which the EU publications can be placed. The newsletter is available free of charge online and as a paper subscription. To subscribe, go to the website http://publications.eu.int/general/newsletter_en.html.

Catalogues

All available traditional EUR-OP publications are listed in annual catalogues; a regularly updated directory of public databases keeps customers informed on the various online data sources that have been produced by the EU institutions. All these catalogues can be obtained free of charge at EUR-OP or from EUR-OP sales agents.

In addition to traditional publications, such as the Official Journal, EUR-OP focuses on European Union developments in a variety of fields such as environment, social policy, education, economy, research and culture. A wide range of audiovisual products illustrate the different policies and objectives of the European Union, and the changes brought about by the process of European unification, while a series of databases provide information on a wide range of subjects, such as EU law, press releases, references, public tenders and statistics.

In order to further facilitate access to the online services, the EUR-OP maintain a system of national gateway distributors.

TED licensed products and services. TED is the abbreviation for Tenders Electronic Daily and refers to the tenders listed in the 'S' series of the Official Journal. As TED is available free on the Internet, the former TED-ALERT service has been disbanded and the data is now available under licence to third parties who may offer a service similar to that of TED-ALERT. The licence may cover the whole or part of the data, and the licence-holder may deliver the licensed information as a product or a service. A complete list of licence-holders is available on request from the Office for Official Publications (e-mail: info-copyright-opoce@cec.eu.int).

Europe on the Internet

With a view to providing EU citizens with clear, comprehensive and up-to-date information on the objectives, institutions and policies of the EU, the EUROPA internet server contains general information on the EU, the Commission (tasks, composition, speeches by the President or Commissioners, organizations, guide to document access), an 'ABC' on EU policies providing access to broad public information emanating from the Directorates-General and information on access to the Commission's databases such as I'M-GUIDE, CORDIS and IDEA. The access code for EUROPA is http://europa.eu.int. It also provides information on EUR-OP and its services. The newsletter is available on the Internet. The address is http://publications.eu.int/index_en.html.

CD-ROMs produced by the institutions of the EU

EUR-OP also produces a considerable number of CD-Roms, some of the better known being the Combined Nomenclature, Europe in Figures, Dobris Assessment, Integrated Tariff of the EC, IUCLID and Panorama of EU Business.

Contact and information

EUR-OP: 2 rue Mercier, 2985 Luxembourg, Luxembourg; tel (+352) 29291; fax (+352) 292942758.

How to obtain EUR-OP's priced publications

EUR-OP has appointed sales agents to make sure that all EUR-OP's paper and audiovisual products can be obtained easily throughout the world. Following the principle of subsidiarity, all EUR-OP publications have to be purchased through these agents. Clients living in countries in which EUR-OP has not yet appointed a sales agent can contact the EUR-OP sales agent of their choice.

EUR-OP publications can also be ordered in leading bookshops.

Electronic publications (e.g. CD-ROMs, online access to databases) can be obtained via the network of decentralized dissemination agents for electronic products. A list of sales agents is available at http://publications.eu.int/index_en.html. The office has also introduced a new online catalogue system CATDIFF.

Euro-Bookshops

To offer better access to its publications, EUR-OP has initiated a new bookshop scheme. Euro-Bookshops, which display EUR-OP publications in a separate section or window, are obliged to keep a permanent stock of the most important EUR-OP publications and have access to a direct online ordering system for publications that are out of stock. The Euro-Bookshops' staff are trained to advise customers on EU affairs and publications and to direct them to the appropriate institutions and information sources.

Document delivery

To comply with the increasing demand for concise information on specific aspects of EU law, EUR-OP has set up a document delivery service designed to provide tailor-made information rapidly and to assure the necessary follow-up.

At the moment, the service focuses primarily on EU law and the resolutions and opinions of the different EU institutions but, in the future, it will also provide other types of information, eg. documents on research and development. Information can be supplied on various supports and delivered by mail, fax or e-mail. A list of document delivery agents is provided below.

Free publications

Free publications are not available at EUR-OP or at its sales agents, but have to be ordered directly from the author services or institutions that initiated the publication. To obtain free publications of the European Commission, contact the nearest Commission office.

Info-Points Europe, which offer a display of free information leaflets on the different aspects of EU policy, also have access to EU databases and a staff trained to answer questions of general interest.

Students, researchers and the public in general can consult all EUR-OP publications at European Documentation Centres (EDCs). EDCs, usually located in universities and large public libraries, can receive the complete range of EU publications (see the section on European Documentation Centres for a full list of these centres).

EUR-OP general contact details

Office for Official Publications of the European Communities: 2 rue Mercier, 2985 Luxembourg, Luxembourg; tel (+352) 29291; tel (general information) (+352) 292942224; tel (Helpdesk) (+352) 292942777;fax (+352) 292942758; e-mail opoce-info-info@cec.eu.int.

Document Delivery Agents

AUSTRIA

Wirtschaftskammer Österreich: Euro Info Centre, Wiedner Hauptstrasse 63, Postfach 150, 1045 Vienna; tel (+43 1) 501 05 42 06; fax (+43 1) 501 05 297; e-mail euroinfo@wko.at; internet http://wko.at/eu.

BELGIUM

EIC Brussels Airport: Medialaan 26, 1800 Vilvoorde; tel (+32 2) 255 20 21; fax (+32 2) 255 20 30; e-mail eic@ccihv.be.

Kamer voor Handel en Nijverheid: 500 Avenue Louise, 1050 Brussels; tel (+32 2) 648 50 02; fax (+32 2) 640 93 28; e-mail info.ccib@ccib.irisnet.be; internet www.ccib.be.

BULGARIA

InterClip Ltd: Shipchenski Prohod 69A, P.O. Box 303, 1113 Sofia; tel (+359 2) 73 10 14; fax (+359 2) 73 02 46; e-mail docdel@daxy.com; internet www.daxy.com.

CANADA

Euroline Inc.: EU Info, 165 Sparks Street, Suite 300, Ottawa, Ontario K1P 5B9; tel (+1 613) 294 22 05; fax (+1 613) 230 22 09; e-mail info@euros.ch; internet www.euros.ch.

DENMARK

J. H. Schultz Information A/S: Herstedvang 4, 2620 Albertslund; tel (+45) 43 63 23 00; fax (+45) 43 63 62 45; e-mail hr@schultz.dk; internet www.schultz.dk.

FRANCE

EMCA Editions & Conseil: Immeuble "Las Maradas", 1 Boulevard de l'Oise, 95030 Cergy Pontoise Cedex; tel (+33) 1 30 38 27 27; fax (+33) 1 30 38 28 27; internet www.emca.fr.

GERMANY

ICC Hofmann: Am Stockborn 16, 60439 Frankfurt am Main; tel (+49 6082) 91 01 01; fax (+49 6082) 91 02 00; e-mail khofmann@icc-hofmann.com.

Nomos Verlagsgesellschaft: Waldseestrasse 3-5, 76530 Baden-Baden; tel (+49 7221) 21 04 47; fax (+49 7221) 21 04 27; e-mail beierwaltes@nomos.de; internet www.nomos.de.

GREECE

Helketek SA: D. Aeginitou Street 7, 11528 Athens; tel (+30 210) 723 52 14; fax (+30 210) 729 15 28; e-mail helketec@techlink.gr; internet www.techlink.gr/elketek.

HUNGARY

Euro Info Service: Szt. István krt. 12 - III emelet 1/A, P.O. Box 1039, 1137 Budapest; tel (+36 1) 264 82 72; fax (+36 1) 264 82 75; e-mail euroinfo@euroinfo.hu; internet www.euroinfo.hu.

IRELAND

Eurotext Research: Kilbeg, Kilbeggan, Co. Westmeath; tel (+353 506) 32 882; fax (+353 506) 32 882; e-mail michaelmartyn@eircom.net.

Lendac Data Systems Ltd: Unit 6, IDA Enterprise Centre, Pearse Street, Dublin 2; tel (+353 1) 677 61 33; fax (+353 1) 671 01 35; e-mail lendata@lendac.ie; internet www.lendac.ie.

ITALY

Contea Marketing S.R.L.: Via Febo 21/A, 10133 Turin; tel (+39) 011 660 61 06; fax (+39) 011 660 61 06; e-mail eurocontea@eurocontea.com; internet www.eurocontea.com.

Starter S.R.L.: Via Cartiera 47, 33080 Porcia; tel (+39) 04 34 55 52 95; fax (+39) 04 34 55 51 28; e-mail starter@dedalus.it.

LUXEMBOURG

DBIT SA: 7 Route des Trois Cantons, 8399 Windhof; tel (+352) 49 24 20; fax (+352) 49 24 20 50; e-mail docdel@dbit.lu; internet http://docdel.dbit.lu.

PF Consult SARL: 8 Grand Rue, 8372 Hobscheid; tel (+352) 24 17 99; fax (+352) 26 10 80 99; e-mail info@pfconsult.com; internet www.pfconsult.com.

NETHERLANDS

Ellis Publications BV: Wilhelminasingel 105, Postbus 1059, 6201 BB Maastricht; tel (+31 43) 321 53 13; fax (+31 43) 325 39 59; e-mail document@ellispub.com; internet www.ellispub.com.

Europe Consult: Horstacker 20-38, Postbus 38325, 6546 AH Nijmegen; tel (+31 24) 373 72 41; fax (+31 24) 373 67 89; e-mail docdel@europeconsult.nl; internet www.europeconsult.nl.

SPAIN

Europroa: Escultor Garcia Màs 8, pta. 19, 46015 Valencia; tel (+34 9) 632 73 110; e-mail info@europroa.com; internet www.europroa.com.

Greendata: Tuset 19, 2°-7a, 08006 Barcelona; tel (+34) 90 211 83 98; fax (+34) 93 202 10 77; e-mail info@greendata.es; internet www.greendata.es.

SWEDEN

BTJ AB: Traktorvägen 11-13, 221 82 Lund; tel (+46 46) 18 00 00; fax (+46 46) 30 79 47; e-mail ingela.olsson@btj.se; internet www.btj.se.

Kommerskollegium: Box 6803, 113 86 Stockholm; tel (+46 8) 690 48 00; fax (+46 8) 30 67 59; e-mail registrator@kommers.se.

UNITED KINGDOM

Lawtel EU, Sweet & Maxwell: 100 Avenue Road, London NW3 3PF; tel (+44 207) 393 76 05; fax (+44 207) 393 74 85; e-mail al.keve@sweetandmaxwell.co.uk; internet www.sweetandmaxwell.co.uk.

UNITED STATES OF AMERICA

European Document Research: 2220 Wyoming Avenue NW, Washington, DC 20008; tel (+1 202) 785 85 94; fax (+1 202) 785 85 89; e-mail ghl@europeandocuments.com; internet www.europeandocuments.com.

THE EUROPEAN COMMISSION'S MAIN PUBLICATIONS

This section provides details of the major periodicals, newsletters and brochures produced by the European Commission's individual Directorates-General.

Over the past three years, there has been a major shift towards electronic information and many newsletters are now available only online. A great deal of material can now be downloaded in pdf format at each Directorate-General's website, although paper versions still exist in a good number of cases.

Website Addresses of the Directorates-General and Depending Entities

Agriculture DG (AGRI): http://europa.eu.int/comm/dgs/agriculture/index_en.htm

Budget DG (BUDG): http://europa.eu.int/comm/dgs/budget/index_en.htm

Competition DG (COMP): http://europa.eu.int/comm/dgs/competition/index_en.htm

Development DG (DEV): http://europa.eu.int/comm/dgs/development/index_en.htm

Economic and Financial Affairs DG (ECFIN): http://europa.eu.int/comm/dgs/economy_finance/index_en.htm

Education and Culture DG (EAC): http://europa.eu.int/comm/dgs/education_culture/index_en.htm

Employment DG (EMPL): http://europa.eu.int/comm/dgs/employment_social/index_en.htm

Energy and Transport DG (TREN): http://europa.eu.int/comm/dgs/energy_transport/index_en.htm

Enlargement DG (ELARG): http://europa.eu.int/comm/dgs/enlargement/index_en.htm

Enterprise DG (ENTR): http://europa.eu.int/comm/dgs/enterprise/index_en.htm

Environment DG (ENV): http://europa.eu.int/comm/dgs/environment/index_en.htm

EuropeAid Cooperation Office: http://europa.eu.int/comm/dgs/europeaid/index_en.htm

European Anti-Fraud Office (OLAF): http://europa.eu.int/comm/dgs/olaf/index_en.htm

Eurostat: http://europa.eu.int/comm/dgs/eurostat/index_en.htm

External Relations DG (RELEX): http://europa.eu.int/comm/dgs/external_relations/index_en.htm

Fisheries DG: http://europa.eu.int/comm/dgs/fisheries/index_en.htm

Health and Consumer Protection DG (SANCO): http://europa.eu.int/comm/dgs/health_consumer/index_en.htm

Humanitarian Aid Office (ECHO): http://europa.eu.int/comm/dgs/humanitarian_aid/index_en.htm

Information Society DG (INFSO): http://europa.eu.int/comm/dgs/information_society/index_en.htm

Internal Market DG (MARKT): http://europa.eu.int/comm/dgs/internal_market/index_en.htm

Joint Interpreting and Conference Service (SCIC): http://europa.eu.int/comm/dgs/interpretation/index_en.htm

Joint Research Centre: http://www.jrc.cec.eu.int/jrc/index.asp

Justice, Freedom and Security DG (JAI): http://europa.eu.int/comm/dgs/justice_home/index_en.htm

Legal Service (SJ): http://europa.eu.int/comm/dgs/legal_service/index_en.htm

Personnel and Administration DG (ADMIN): http://europa.eu.int/comm/dgs/personnel_administration/index_en.htm

Press and Communication DG (PRESS): http://europa.eu.int/comm/dgs/press_communication/index_en.htm

Publications Office (OPOCE): http://eur-op.eu.int/general/en/index.htm

Regional Policy DG (REGIO): http://europa.eu.int/comm/dgs/regional_policy/index_en.htm

Research DG (RTD): http://europa.eu.int/comm/dgs/research/index_en.htm

Secretariat-General (SG): http://europa.eu.int/comm/dgs/secretariat_general/index_en.htm

Taxation and Customs Union DG (TAXUD): http://europa.eu.int/comm/dgs/taxation_customs/index_en.htm

Trade DG (TRADE): http://europa.eu.int/comm/dgs/trade/index_en.htm

Translation DG (DGT): http://europa.eu.int/comm/dgs/translation/index_en.htm

The Secretariat-General

The European Commission's Secretariat-General is responsible for producing two major publications: the general report on the activities of the European Communities and the monthly bulletin of the European Union, both of which are invaluable reference works. It also manages SCAD (the automated central documentation service).

General Report on the Activities of the European Communities

Reviews the work of the European Union and policy developments of the previous year. The report is an interesting reference document but is not critical in nature. From February 2005, there were to be two separate parts:

- *General Report,* highlighting the year's major developments and the main achievements in the different areas of Community activity. Available in all the official languages of the EU.
- *General Report – Technical Annex,* which describes in more detail, in the publication's traditional manner, the material presented in the *General Report.* Available in English, French and German.

Author: the European Commission's Secretariat-General. Tel (+32) 2-2953914. Fax (+32) 2-2960554.

Frequency: annual.

How to obtain: the publication is expected to become available in pdf format as well as in a paper version. Order from the Office for Official Publications of the European Communities at 2985 Luxembourg or from sales offices in the Member States. E-mail europapp@sg.cec.be. Consult websites http://publications.eu.int and www.bookshop.eu.int for further information.

Bulletin of the European Union

The bulletin reports on EU activities and policies. The main headings are as follows:

- The single market and the European economic and social continuum.
- The EU's role in the world.
- Intergovernmental co-operation.
- Financing of Community activities.
- Statistical activities.
- EU institutions and organizations

The bulletin is, in this respect, a valuable document for people who want to be informed regularly about decisions and events in the European Union.

Author: the European Commission's Secretariat-General. Tel: (+32) 2-2953914. Fax (+32) 2-2960554.

Frequency: monthly in paper format; updated several times a month for an online version.

Languages: in English, French and German.

How to obtain: It is expected that the publication will be available online in 2005, as well as in a paper format. Order from the Office for Official Publications of the European Communities at 2985 Luxembourg or from sales offices in the Member States. E-mail eurobull@sg.cec.be.

DG Press and Communication

Europe by Satellite

Europe by Satellite (EbS) is the European Commission's satellite information service, whicht officially began transmission on 4 September 1995. EbS is part of the Commission's ongoing policy for greater openness and transparency. The service is available to television companies – local, regional and national – within the Union, the Mediterranean area and in Central and Eastern Europe, as well as to national and regional EU institutions.

EbS provides a daily Monday-to-Friday service supplying pictures illustrating Commission and European Union news, both live and pre-recorded in some or all of the EU's official languages. Footage on the activities of the European Union institutions and other major events is broadcast by satellite to television stations all over Europe to illustrate daily news programmes or to be filed for later transmission.

The live coverage of events is supported by relevant thematic video files with international sound track transmitted the day before the event in question. Supplementary information is available on teletext, e-mail and by fax.

During interactive conferences between the Commission's studios and the Commission's Representations and Delegations across the world, opinion leaders, journalists and information relays can question representatives from EU institutions on decisions taken, projects envisaged and current negotiations.

Between and during programmes, the EbS's teletext service provides a continuous up-to-date link, offering, among other things, daily news, the programme schedule and the institutional agenda.

The service is entirely free of charge and free of rights for non-commercial use, (i.e. for information purposes). The general e-mail address is europe-by-satellite@cec.eu.int.

Technical information: Satellite Eutelstat II F2 at 10° E. Transponder 21. Down link frequency 11,080,000 Mhz. Polarisation: Horizontal 19 Mhs/Volt.

News: EbS 1: 11h30; EbS2: 16h00; EbS3: 19h00.

Interactive conferences: 10h00 to 11h00, 14h30 to 15h30.

Dossiers and documentaries: before 10h00 and after 16h30.

Editor in Chief: Diederik Bangert. Tel (+32) 2-2968868. Fax (+32) 2-2990309. E-mail diederik.bangert@cec.eu.int.

European Documentation

Published in DIN C5 (16.2 x 22.9 cm) form, the works from this collection comprise some 40–50 pages and are valuable reference documents. Although the brochures are factual and descriptive, and generally objective in tone, it must be remembered that they come from the Commission and that, in this respect, they are not critical in character and conform to the Commission's positions.

Typical of the institutional questions addressed:

- The European Union: still enlarging.
- The European Union and the world.
- Seven key days in the making of Europe.
- Treaty of Amsterdam: What has changed in Europe.
- Europe's Agenda 2000: Strengthening and widening the EU.

Author: earlier the responsibility of the Directorate-General for Education and Culture, the series is now managed by the Press and Communication Service.

Addressees: all interested persons.

Languages: the EU's official languages.

How to obtain: contact the Commission's offices in the Member States. They are responsible for distributing the publication in their own language. For versions in other languages, contact the Office for Official Publications of the European Communities at 2985 Luxembourg or the sales agents.

Europe on the Move

A series of booklets and leaflets on policies of the European Commission. The principle is to publish a brochure for each theme, along with several leaflets to illustrate certain aspects of the brochure.

Booklets and leaflets:

- A Community of Cultures: The European Union and the Arts
- A World Player – The European Union's External Relations
- Choices for a Green Future: The European Union and the Environment.
- eEurope: An Information Society for All
- eLearning: Designing Tomorrow's Education
- Enlarging the European Union
- Europe: An Area for Research
- Europe Direct: *series of leaflets and practical data sheets on Europeans' rights in each Member State, published in the context of a dialogue*

with citizens and businesses; 2 or 3 issues per year, available in national editions.

- Europe's Agenda 2000: Strengthening and Widening the EU
- European Employment and Social Policy: A Policy for People.
- European Solidarity with the Victims of Humanitarian Crises
- From Farm to Fork – Safe Food for Europe's Consumers
- Going for Growth – The Economy of the EU
- Healthy food for Europe's citizens – The European Union and Food Quality.
- How the European Union Works – A Citizen's Guide to the EU Institutions
- It's a Better Life – How the EU's Single Market Benefits You
- It's Your Europe – Living, Learning and Working Anywhere in the EU
- Living in an Area of Freedom, Security and Justice: Justice and Home Affairs in the European Union
- Looking beyond Tomorrow – Scientific Research in the European Union
- Making Globalisation Work for Everyone – The European Union and World Trade
- More Unity and More Diversity – The European Union's Biggest Enlargement
- Passport to Mobility: Learning Differently Learning Abroad
- Regions of Europe
- Serving the People of Europe – How the European Commission Works
- Tax Policy in the European Union
- The budget of the European Union.
- The Customs Policy of the European Union
- The European Union and the World
- The European Union and World Trade
- The European Union: Still Enlarging
- Toward a Knowledge-Based Europe – The European Union and the Information Society
- Working for the Regions

How to obtain: from the Publications Unit of the Press and Communication Service. Tel (+32) 2-2960980. Fax (+32) 2-2999208.

Group of Policy Advisers

The Group of Policy Advisers, an internal service of the European Commission, provides timely, informed and impartial advice to the President and Commissioners on issues relating to the future policy of the European Union. The Group has replaced the Forward Studies Unit.

The Advisers' role is to concentrate on issues which are multi-disciplinary and which tend to have longer time horizons than those commonly dealt with by Commission services. Typically such issues have several dimensions, including political and institutional, economic, social, scientific and technological.

The Group of Policy Advisers focuses on the earlier stages within the policy development cycle, that is the collection of information, analysis and the development of policy options for consideration by the President and Commissioners. As such, the activities of the Group are clearly distinguished from operational and policy implementation activities. It plays the role of a catalyst for new ideas emerging within the Commission. In practice, the work concentrates on four different fields: economic and social issues, political and institutional issues, external relations, dialogue with religions and humanisms.

The Group of Policy Advisers organizes the 'European Lectures' on topical issues of economics and politics and also provides the secretariat of the European Group on Ethics in Science and new Technologies.

The archives of the Forward Studies Unit – a series of working papers – are available on the website of the Policy Advisers Group.

Working Paper Series

The Working Paper Series was launched in 1999 and includes documents like Reports, Conference Papers and Interim Reports of the Forward Studies Unit. They are intended to stimulate debate but they are also a way of submitting the unit's work to detailed, constructive outside criticism.

Published Working Papers include:

- Scenarios Europe 2010, Five Possible Futures for Europe.
- The Union we Need.
- Project on European Integration Indicators.
- Evolutions in Governance: What Lessons for the Commission? A first Assessment.
- The Future of European Regulation *(Workshop review)*.
- Improving the Effectiveness and Legitimacy of EU Governance.
- Compétitivité européenne, comportement des entreprises et cohésion sociale *(in French only)*.
- The Social Impact of Electronic Money: A Challenge to the European Union.
- Opening the World to Omnilateralism.
- A learning Organization for a Society: Proposals for Designing Tomorrow's Commission.
- Civilisation and Governance (Seminar report).
- Some Unpleasant Arithmetics of Regional Unemployment in the EU.
- Organized Criminality.

- Survey of National Identity and Deep-Seated Attitudes towards European Integration in the Ten Applicant Countries of Central and Eastern Europe.
- Tool box, Extracts from Official Speakers (1950–1996).
- Developing New Modes of Governance, Notis Lebessis. *John Paterson (full text, pdf)*.
- Citoyenneté. Droits et devoirs. Société civile. Réflexions et contributions des religions et des humanismes. *Win Burton, sous la direction de Thomas Jansen (full text, in French only, pdf)*.
- European Competitiveness and Business, *Alexis Jacquemin (full text, pdf)*.
- Ressources immatérielles et Compétitivité, *Alexis Jacquemin*.
- Harnessing Differentiation in the EU – Flexibility after Amsterdam. A Report on Hearings with Parliamentarians and Government Officials in Seven European Capitals. *Christian Deubner, edited by T. Jansen (full text, pdf)*.
- La Pauvreté. Premières réflexions sur les moyens de lutte et pistes pour l'action. *B. Caremier, I. Ioannides, F. Milner (full text, French only, pdf)*.
- Theories of Industrial Organisation and Competition Policy: What are the links? *A. Jacquemin (full text, pdf)*.
- A Global Strategy for the Promotion of Sustainable Economic and Social Development. *L. Pench (full text, pdf)*.
- Reflexions on European Identity. *Thomas Jansen (full text, pdf)*.
- Globalization and Social Governance in Europe and in the United States. *Wolfgang Bücherl and Thomas Jansen (full text, pdf)*.
- Generating Public Space for our Common Futures: Models of Integration in Asia and Europe. *Wolfgang Pape (full text, pdf)*.
- Le(s) service(s) public(s) dans la société de l'information. *Bénédicte Caremier (full text, French only, pdf)*.
- Reconciling the Welfare State with Sound Public Finances and High Employment. *M. Buti, D. Franco, L.R. Pench (full text, pdf)*.
- How to make Use of Closer Cooperation. The Amsterdam Clauses and the Dynamics of European Integration. *Francesco Milner, Alkuin Kölliker (full text, pdf)*.

DG Economic and Financial Affairs

Since the late 1970s, the Directorate-General for Economic and Financial

Affairs have published a series of reports and studies under the 'European Economy' heading, grouped in the following series: European Economy; European Economy – Special Reports; European Economy – Economic Papers; and European Economy – Enlargement Papers.

European Economy

This publication contains important reports and communications from the Commission to the Council and the European Parliament on the economic situation and developments. In 2002 the various reports, studies and analyses produced under the general title *European Economy* were grouped in the following series:

- *European Economy*. Contains important reports and communications from the Commission to the Council and the European Parliament on the economic situation and developments. Six issues a year in online and paper versions.
- *European Economy – Economic Papers*. Provides information about the technical work done by the staff of the DG and seeks comments and suggestions for further analyses.
- European Economy – Enlargement Papers. Provides overviews and forecasts of economic developments, and reports on the progress of reform in the Candidate Countries.
- European Economy – Occasional Papers. The papers are intended to increase awareness of the technical work done by the staff of the DG. They cover a wide range of subjects.

For further information: contact Robert Gangl (tel +32 2-2993342) or the EUR-OP sales agents.

European Economy published prior to 2002

European Economy – main edition: this publication series appeared twice a year. It contained important reports and communications from the Commission to the Council and the European Parliament on the economic situation and developments.

European Economy – Reports and Studies: 'Reports and Studies' provided reports, analyses and studies on specific macro-economic aspects, including several country reports on Member States and Central and Eastern European Countries. Up to seven issues were produced each year. All these issues were published in English. Country reports were also published as paper versions in the language of the country concerned.

European Economy – Supplement A: economic trends & macro-economic forecasts. This series described the most recent trends in industrial production, consumer prices, unemployment, the balance of trade, exchange rates, and other indicators. This supplement also presented the Commission staff's Macroeconomic Forecasts and Commission communications to the Council on economic policy.

European Economy – Supplement B: business and consumer survey results. This series gave the main results of opinion surveys of industrial chief executives (orders, stocks, production outlook, etc.) in the Community, and other business cycle indicators.

European Economy – Supplement C: brief overviews of the economic situation and economic reform in Candidate Countries, Economic Reform Monitor.

Economic Papers

Economic studies and research papers conducted by Commission officials or external experts.

Addressees: universities, administrations which can prove that they need such studies. The papers are not distributed via the Office for Official Publications.

Author: the Economic and Financial Affairs DG, which entrusts the drafting of the papers to experts.

Frequency: irregular. In principle, some 10 publications a year.

Languages: the language in which the study is conducted (most frequently English).

How to obtain: by writing to Robert Gangl, European Commission, ECFIN – 01, Rue de la Loi 200, 1049 Brussels, Belgium; tel: (+32) 2-2993342; fax: (+32) 2-2969428. A list of titles available may be obtained from the same address.

Enlargement Papers

This bulletin provides information on the economies of the candidate countries and on the progress of reform.

Author: services of the European Commission or experts working in association with them.

Frequency: irregular.

Languages: English.

How to obtain: contact Robert Gangl, European Commission, ECFIN – 01, Rue de la Loi 200, 1049 Brussels, Belgium; tel (+32) 2-2993342; fax (+32) 2-2969428.

DG Enterprise

The Acquis of the European Union under the Management of the Enterprise DG

This publication, known also as the 'Pink Book', covers the provisions in industrial policy and small and medium-sized enterprises, and legislation in the field of industrial products, including more than 482 directives. It is updated annually to take account of legislative developments.

Author: Enterprise DG.

Frequency: annual.

How to obtain: download from http://europa.eu.int/comm/dgs/enterprise/acquis.htm.

For further information: European Commission, Enterprise DG, Unit G.1, 1049 Brussels, Belgium; fax (+32) 2-2998031; e-mail entr-regul-coord-mra@cec.eu.int.

European Competitiveness Report 2002

Analytical contribution to the policy debate on how to make Europe a more dynamic and competitive economy. The first part deals with the European Union's economic performance vis-à-vis the United States and Japan. The second part takes stock of recent structural changes and emphasizes the services sector, underlining its role as a source of growth and competitive performance. The last section takes stock of B2B e-commerce development and the policy issues which it raises.

Addressees: SMEs, financial analysts, administrators, researchers, journalists.

Author: European Commission.

Frequency: annual.

Languages: English.

How to obtain: contact the Office for Official Publications of the European Communities.

Enterprise Europe

Enterprise Europe is a free newsletter. It aims to show how fostering enterprise, innovation and entrepreneurship can help create a Europe of sustained economic growth, with more and better jobs and greater social cohesion. The newsletter is supplemented by an E-mail alert service.

Frequency: quarterly.

Languages: Community languages.

How to obtain: European Commission, Enterprise Directorate-General, Enterprise Europe, Rue de la Loi 200 (SC-15 6/49), 1049 Brussels, Belgium; fax (+32) 2-2991926. The electronic version is available at http://europa.eu.int/comm/enterprise/library.

CORDIS Focus

Based on information taken from the CORDIS News Service, CORDIS focus includes the latest developments in all aspects of EU research activities including calls for proposals, programme implementation and comprehensive information on general policy, legislation, publications, events and much more.

Frequency: every two weeks.

Languages: German, English, French, Italian and Spanish.

How to obtain: Innovation Helpdesk; tel (+352) 43013161; fax (+352) 430132084; e-mail innovation@cec.eu.int; internet www.cordis.lu/focus/en/home.html.

CORDIS Focus / RTD-Results Supplement

These supplements are mainly based on the CORDIS Results Service and contain a snapshot of the most representative exploitable research results and technology offers. Entries are compiled so that the contributing organization may highlight potential market applications as well as the kind of collaboration sought (licensing opportunities, manufacturing agreements, etc.). Subscribers to CORDIS Focus will automatically be put on the mailing list for any supplement issues.

Frequency: quarterly.

Languages: English.

Innovation and Technology Transfer

Innovation and Technology Transfer is published by the European Commission's Innovation and SMEs programme, which promotes innovation and encourages the participation of small and medium-sized enterprises (SMEs) in the Community research framework programme.

Frequency: six times a year.

Languages: German, English, Spanish, French, Italian.

How to obtain: Innovation Helpdesk; tel (+352) 430133161; fax (+352) 430132084; e-mail innovation@cec.eu.int; internet www.cordis.lu/itt/itt-en/home.html.

Euroabstracts

Euroabstracts is published by the European Commission's Innovation and SMEs programme. The magazine encourages the dissemination of research-oriented publications across Europe. Each edition features book reviews, ordered by theme, as well as a major feature article and interview.

Frequency: six issues a year.

How to obtain: Innovation Helpdesk; tel (+352) 430133161; fax (+352) 430132084; e-mail innovation@cec.eu.int; internet www.cordis.lu/euroabstracts/en/home.html.

DG Competition

EC Competition Policy Newsletter

Launched in 1994, the *Competition Policy Newsletter* contains articles from Commission officials and external authors about competition law both within and outside the European Union. The articles cover a wide range of themes and sectors and examine most important recent developments.

Author: Competition DG.

Frequency: 2 or 3 issues a year.

Languages: multilingual, depending on the author's mother tongue, but English is the predominant language.

How to obtain: Linda Jones, Information Unit, DG IV (Competition) – J/70 00/122, Rue de la Loi 200, 1049 Brussels, Belgium; tel (+32) 2-2955938; fax (+32) 2-2955437; e-mail: infocomp@cec.eu.int. The full text of the newsletter may be downloaded in pdf format at http://europa.eu.int/comm/competition/publications/cpn.

Report on Competition Policy

The report provides an overall view of the past year's policy, its application to companies, state aids, the reorganization of commercial or public national monopolies and corporate merger trends.

Author: Competition DG in conjunction with the Secretariat-General of the European Commission.

Frequency: annual.

Languages: all the EU's official languages.

How to obtain: order from the Office for Official Publications of the European Communities at 2985 Luxembourg or from sales offices in the Member States.

DG Employment, Social Affairs and Equal Opportunities

Gender Equality

This magazine replaces the former 'Equal Opportunities' magazine.

Frequency: quarterly.

Languages: English, French, German.

European Social Dialogue

Reports on the results of the social dialogue between social partners in different sectors.

Frequency: 5 issues a year.

Languages: All EU official languages.

How to obtain: online at http://europa.eu.int/comm/employment_social/soc-dial/social/index_en.htm.

EWON – Work Organisation in Europe

A newsletter produced by the European Work Organisation Network. A specific edition is published for each Member State. The first two pages, edited by the European Commission, address developments in the EU. EWON members produce the last two pages which focus on national issues.

How to obtain: online at http://europa.eu.int/comm/employment_social/soc-dial/workorg/ewon/nlet_en.htm.

Family Observer

Published by the European Observatory for Family Affairs, this new magazine looks at family issues, the development of European families and solidarity between the generations.

Frequency: irregular.

Languages: German, French, English.

How to obtain: online at http:europa.eu.int/comm/employment-social/family/observatory/publications.html

Missoc Info

This newsletter analyses social protection in the EU Member States (MISSOC = Mutual Information System on Social Protection). The first part of the newsletter examines developments at EU level, while the second part focuses on developments in each of the Member States in turn.

Frequency: two issues a year.

Languages: English, French, German.

How to obtain: online at http://europa.eu.int/comm/employment_social/MISSOC2001/MISSOC-info-en.htm.

Further information from: Documentation Centre of the Employment and Social Affairs DG; tel (+32) 2-2954988; fax (+3) 2-2962393; e-mail empl-info@cec.eu.int.

Social Agenda

The magazine provides information on European employment and social policies.

Frequency: quarterly.

Languages: English, French, German.

How to obtain: e-mail: empl-info@cec.eu.int.

ES Mail

This electronic newsletter is published in English, French and German and may be ordered electronically from empl-esmail@cec.eu.int.

DG Agriculture and Rural Development

The Directorate-General for Agriculture has a large library intended primarily for the European Commission's internal needs but also open to the public: European Commission, Directorate-General for Agriculture, Library – Loi 130/6-21, Rue de la Loi 200, 1049 Brussels, Belgium; tel (+32) 2-2953240; fax (+32) 2-2957540; e-mail agri-library@cec.eu.int. The Directorate produces a number of reports, studies and documents, of which some of the major ones are listed below.

The Agricultural Situation in the European Union

The report contains analyses and general statistics on production factors, the structures and state of the market for different agricultural products, barriers to the common agricultural market, the position of consumers and producers, and financial aspects. The general outlook and markets for agricultural products are also examined.

Addressees: all interested persons.

Author: Agriculture DG in conjunction with the European Commission's Secretariat-General.

Frequency: annual.

Languages: the EU's official languages.

How to obtain: order from the Office for Official Publications of the European Communities at 2985 Luxembourg or from sales offices in the Member States.

The Agriculture Newsletter

Launched in 1998, the monthly agricultural newsletter looks at background information and recent developments in European agriculture and rural development. The newsletter concentrates on a specific theme and is backed up sometimes by a special edition.

Further information from: Information Unit; tel (+32) 2-2952963.

Frequency: monthly.

Languages: all the EU's official languages.

How to obtain: Mary Brown; tel: (+32) 2-2953270; fax (+32) 2-2957540; e-mail: agri-library@cec.eu.int.

Fact Sheets

Several fact sheets are normally published each year. Some examples of the topics recently covered are The Meat Sector in the European Union, New Perspectives for EU Rural Development, Agriculture and the Environment, EU and Enlargement, Agricultural Committees, Clearance of Accounts Procedure,

CAP Reform: Milk and Milk Products, Olive Oil: Implementing Rules, Environment, The Euro and the Reform of the Agri-monetary System, CAP reform: The wine sector, CAP reform: Rural development.

Prospects for Agricultural Markets 2001–2008

A CAP Report which can be downloaded in pdf format from http://europa.eu.int/comm/agriculture/publi/index_en.htm.

Agenda 2000 CAP Reform Decisions: Impact Analyses

A CAP Report which can be downloaded in pdf format from http://europa.eu.int/comm/agriculture/publi/index_en.htm.

DG Energy and Transport

Energy and Transport in Europe Digest

Published since April 2002, this newsletter looks at background information and recent developments in the fields of energy and transport.

Frequency: weekly.

Languages: English.

How to obtain: online at http://europa.eu.int/comm/energy-transport/mm-dg/index-en.html.

Annual Energy Review

A key publication of the DG Energy and Transport.

EU Energy and Transport in Figures

Compiled in conjunction with Eurostat.

Energy

Covers European Energy issues to 2020.

Languages: French, English, German.

How to obtain: online at http://comm/energy/en/etf-2-en.html.

DG Environment

DG Environment maintains a comprehensive website which provides regularly updated information on policy areas, publications, press releases, etc. The website can be consulted at http://europa.eu.int/comm/environment/index_en.htm.

The Communications and Civil Society Unit (ENV 3) manages an Information Centre which deals with enquiries on EU environmental policy from interested outside parties – local and regional authorities, NGOs, trade associations, etc. The Centre is open to students and other researchers 13.00–17.00 on weekdays and is located at BU 9 0/17, Avenue de Beaulieu 9, 1160 Brussels, Belgium; fax (+32) 2-2996198; e-mail at envinfo@cec.eu.int.

The DG Environment publications catalogue is available online at: http://europa.eu.int/comm/environment/pubs/home.htm. Free publications listed in the catalogue can be ordered from the Information Centre.

Environment for Europeans

This magazine, which is available in both paper and online versions, is produced to keep EU citizens up to date with European environmental issues. *Environment for Europeans* has incorporated the *Enlargement Newsletter* since August 1999.

Frequency: quarterly.

Languages: Spanish, German, English, French, Italian.

How to obtain: online at http://www.europa.eu.int/comm/environment/news/efe/index/htm.

Natura 2000

This newsletter provides regular updates on the implementation of the EU's Habitats and Birds Directives and the establishment of the Natura 2000 network. The newsletter is divided into five sections – Editorial, In Focus, On Site, NATURA Barometer, News Round-up.

Frequency: 3 issues a year.

Languages: German, English, French, Spanish, Italian.

How to obtain: online at http://www.europa.eu.int/comm/environment/news/natura/index-en.htm

EU Eco-Label Newsletter

The EU Eco-Label award is a voluntary market instrument that allows manufacturers whose products have received the Eco-Label to demonstrate to the public that their products meet the high environmental standards that have been set. It also helps consumers to make an informed choice before making a purchase.

Frequency: two issues a year.

How to obtain: contact Alexa Servante, European Commission – DG ENV, Rue de la Loi 200, 1049 Brussels, Belgium; tel: (+32) 2-2958924; e-mail ecolabel@cec.eu.int.

Further information on the EU Eco-Label can be found on the EU Eco-Label homepage at http://europa.eu.int/en/comm/environment/ecolabel/index.htm.

ETAP Newsletter

The newsletter presents news about the Environmental Technologies Action Plan (ETAP) and initiatives in the field of environmental technology in Member States.

How to obtain: subscribe at http://europa.eu.int/comm/coreservices/mailing/index.cfm?serviceid=2395.

Newsflash

Newsflash is a monthly newsletter which provides information about the various projects, events and new publications of the DG's LIFE Unit.

WFD Newsletter

The newsletter, published several times a year, provides information about the work done under the WFD (Water Framework Directive) Common Implementation Strategy, which is a joint strategy for improving, protecting and enhancing the quality of rivers, lakes, transitional and coastal waters and groundwater. The newsletter is available online through the WFD webpage of the Environment DG.

DG Research

Numerous EU-funded research programmes have been established since the beginning of a common research and development policy. Consequently, a need for information has arisen, basically from research centres, companies and other organizations interested in EU financial support for their co-operative projects.

As the EU is now committed to moving towards a genuine 'European Research Area' (ERA), policy issues play an increasingly important role in the DG's overall strategies and actions, not least since the role of research for the development of society and the well-being of individual citizens has become increasingly evident.

The DG's Information and Communication Unit provides a focus for the dissemination of such information, as well as being the central contact point for all interested parties from the research community, industry, the scientific press or the public at large. The Unit can be contacted at European Commission, SDME 2/85, Rue de la Loi 200, 1049 Brussels; tel (+32) 2-2969028; fax (+32) 2-2958220.

The following is a key publication of the DG Research.

RTD Info

RTD Info is a magazine on research and technological development supported by the European Union. It covers general aspects of Community research such as project results and research policy, as well as practical information, including dates of calls for proposals, events, conferences, publications, and so on.

Addressees: not only current and potential participants in Community research programmes, but also a wider public of industrialists, decision-makers, students and others who are interested in developments in European research.

Author: Information and Communication Unit, DG Research.

Frequency: quarterly.

Languages: English, French, German.

How to obtain: online at http://europa .eu.int/comm/research/rtdinfo.html or from DG Research – European Commission, Square de Meeûs 8 – SDME 2-85, 1049 Brussels, Belgium; tel (+32) 2-2959971; fax (+32) 2-2958220; e-mail research@cec.eu.int.

DG Information Society

The Information office offers general information and guidance and has been merged to incorporate the INFSO library. INFSO-Desk: tel (+32) 2-2955997; fax (+32) 2-2999499; e-mail infso-desk@cec .eu.int.

ISPO

The Information Society Promotion Office (ISPO) no longer exists, but its website does. The IS (Information Society) website, at http://europa.eu.int/ ispo/welcome.html, is a one-stop online source on Information Society issues and is managed by the Information and Communication Unit of the European Commission's Information Society DG.

IS News

IS News is an online daily or weekly news service. Subscribers may choose from a variety of themes – education and training, economy and work, industry, research, quality of life, regions/world, society and culture. Subscriptions may be taken out at http//europa.eu.int/ information-society/services/subscribe/ index-en.htm.

Head of Unit Communication and Information: Pierrette Pelhate, European Commission, DG Information Society, BU 24-1/3, Rue de la Loi 200, 1049 Brussels, Belgium; tel (+32) 2-2969633; fax (+32) 2-2969037.

DG Fisheries

Fishing in Europe

Launched in February 2000, Fishing in Europe replaces *Pesca Info*, a newsletter which ran from 1996 to 1998 in conjunction with the PESCA Programme. *Fishing in Europe* is a glossy A4 publication, and is available online in pdf format.

Editor: outside author working under the aegis of the Fisheries DG.

Frequency: five issues a year.

Languages: all official languages of the EU.

How to obtain: online at http://europa.eu.int/comm/fisheries/doc-et-publ/ magaz/fishing-en.htm.

Selected Publications

- The Common Fisheries Policy
- Green Paper – the CFP after 2002 – 'A chance to have your say'
- Regional socio-economic studies on employment and the levels of dependency on fishing
- Forward Study of Community Aquaculture – Summary Report (pdf format)
- Summary Report on the Study 'Evaluation of the Fisheries Agreements concluded by the European Community' (pdf format)
- Facts and figures on the CFP
- Agriculture in the European Union (map)
- TACS and quotas
- European distant water fishing fleet.
- Report on market perpectives for European freshwater aquaculture
- Evaluation of the state of knowledge concerning by-catches of cetaceans.
- Dissemination of the results of 153 biological studies
- Synopsis of selected R&D projects in the field of fisheries and aquaculture
- Fisheries research organizations and research programmes in the European Union, Iceland, Israel and Norway.

DG Internal Market and Services

Single Market News

This newsletter covers the latest developments relating to the internal market and financial services. Each newsletter contains a special insert on a specific theme and the publication also reports on company law, free movement and intellectual and industrial property. Latest judgments of the Court of Justice are reported, while there is a diary of forthcoming conferences or events.

Frequency: 5 issues a year.

Languages: English, French, German.

How to obtain: contact Suzanne Fischer, European Commission – DG Internal Market, Unit A-4, Rue de la Loi 200, C 107 4/39, 1049 Brussels, Belgium; fax (+32) 2-2954351; e-mail markt-a4@cec .eu.int.

Dialogue with Business

This new service is designed to provide the business community with a one-stop Internet shop. The website, at http://europa.eu.int/business/en/index.html, has been established to help businesses make the best use of the Internal Market and brings together data, information and advice from multiple sources. The home page provides access to information on a variety of key issues, including public procurement, intellectual property rights, technical harmonization, funding opportunities, the Euro, social security, internal market rules and practical business information.

DG Regional Policy

The Regional Policy DG may be contacted on the Internet at www.inforegio.org.

Inforegio News

This monthly newsletter provides an account of recent activities in the field of regional policy. The bulletin examines latest programmes and projects and details recent regional funding developments. Forthcoming conferences are also announced. The complete archives of the Inforegio newsletters are available in all the official languages of the EU as from January 1994.

Frequency: monthly.

Languages: all the official languages of the EU.

How to obtain: contact DG Regional Policy – CSM2, Avenue Tervuren 41, 1040 Brussels, Belgium; tel (+32) 2-2960634; fax (+32) 2-2966003; e-mail regio-info@ cec.eu.int.

Inforegio Fact Sheet

The fact sheet summarizes official documents and covers a specific theme. It is published each time that there is a significant development in terms of regional policy.

Frequency: irregular.

Language: depends on the subject.

For further information: contact DG Regional Policy – CSM2, Avenue Tervuren 41, 1040 Brussels, Belgium; tel (+32) 2-2960634; fax (+32) 2-2966003; e-mail regio-info@cec.eu.int.

Inforegio – Panorama

Launched in October 2000, the magazine is a glossy publication which allows local authorities to discuss the projects that they have conducted under the Structural Funds or ERDF.

Frequency: quarterly.

Languages: all official EU languages.

How to obtain: contact DG Regional Policy – CSM2, Avenue Tervuren 41, 1040 Brussels, Belgium; tel (+32) 2-2960634; fax (+32) 2-2966003; e-mail regio-info@cec.eu.int.

DG Taxation and Customs Union

The Key

Informs on the Commission's policy in the fields of taxation and customs union; the publication is also available on the Internet. The newsletter ceased in 2001. Copies of previous editions are available at http://www.europa.eu.int/comm/taxation-customs/publications/publications.htm.

Frequency: 5 issues a year.

Languages: multilingual English, French, German.

Other Publications

Apart from reports and studies, working papers and information documents, the DG has produced the following publications and brochures, some of which are available online.

- TARIC – the Integrated Tariff of the Community (online).
- European Customs Inventory of Chemical Substances – ECIS (online).
- Evolution of the Tax Systems in the European Union (online).
- The Structures of the Taxation Systems in the EU (1970–1997).
- Guide to Community Customs Legislation.
- Customs Policy of the EU: brochure aimed at the general public. Available online in all EU official languages or from EU Member States' representations.
- The taxation policy of the EU: brochure aimed at the general public. Available online in all EU official languages or from EU Member States' representations.
- User's guide to the rules of preferential origin.
- New customs transit systems for Europe.

Library and Information Officer: F. de Buysscher; tel (+32) 2-2969630; fax (+32) 2-2963306; e-mail: librarian-information@cec.eu.int.

DG Education and Culture

Following internal reorganization, much of the Education and Culture DG's publishing activity (inherited from the former DG X) has moved to the Press and Communication Service. The DG's information policy is 'under construction' and other publications series may be developed, but in future sources are likely to be:

- more Internet-based;
- more decentralized, involving EAC contacts in the Member States and applicant countries;
- carried out in partnership with external contractors.

The central website has been developed considerably. It can be visited at http://europa.eu.int/comm/dgs/education_culture/index_en.htm

DG Health and Consumer Protection

The Health and Consumer Protection DG has been publishing its quarterly magazine *Consumer Voice* and the magazine *Prevention* for several years, but has now decided to concentrate its efforts on electronic rather than printed tools. A new electronic newsletter, in English, French and German, may be downloaded on the Directorate-General's website at http://europa.eu.int/comm/dgs/health-consumer/index-en.htm. The newsletter will focus on events and developments in the areas of health, consumer protection and food safety. A series of other publications may also be downloaded covering such subjects as air passenger rights, consumer credit, legal aid, BSE, consumer law and the Food and Veterinary Office.

DG Justice, Freedom and Security

The Directorate does not produce any periodicals but details of programmes can be found on the Internet at www.europa.eu.int/comm/justice-home/index-en.htm.

Press releases and documents can be downloaded from http://www.europa.eu.int/comm/justice_home/news_en.htm.

DG Trade

DG Trade does not produce any periodicals but has some documents and information packs which may be downloaded from http://trade-info.cec.eu.int/europa/index-en.php.

An e-mail information service has been launched by the DG Trade providing news about the following subjects: bilateral trade relations, world trade and the WTO, trade in goods, trade in services, multilateral issues, trade and development, intellectual property, trade policy instruments, market access, sustainable trade, and procurements and grants. Subscribers may select their areas of interest at http://europa.eu.int/comm/trade/misc/register.htm.

DG Development

This Directorate-General plays a very important role on account of the close relations which the EU maintains with the African, Caribbean and Pacific countries (ACP). The Directorate contains an information unit which provides the general public with information on development, and produces *The Courier*, a bimonthly magazine in English and French on ACP–EU issues. The contact details of this unit are as follows: Leonidas Antonakopoulos, European Commission – DG Development, Rue de la Loi 200, 1049 Brussels, Belgium; tel (+32) 2-2963748; fax (+32) 2-2993002.

The Commission also maintains a network of overseas offices, known as delegations. There is a delegation or sub-office in nearly every ACP country. Although the primary function of the delegations is to facilitate the execution of projects financed by the European Development Fund, they are also responsible for answering requests for information on the European Union.

The Courier ACP–EU

The Courier ACP–EU is the co-operation review of the European Union and the African, Caribbean and Pacific States party to the Cotonou Agreement. The review is disseminated in more than 150 countries and has a circulation of about 80,000.

The review traces the story of the Lomé Convention and its successor, the Cotonou Agreement. It basically contains interviews, reports on ACP countries, dossiers on specific subjects, reports on ACP–EU Council of Ministers' decisions, etc. *The Courier* is a good reference document on EU–ACP relations but does not contain any critical theses on these relations or their functioning. At the end of the review, there are the so-called 'blue pages', which give a picture of how EU development initiatives are progressing prior to their execution. This section covers not only ACP projects but also projects financed in the Mediterranean countries and Asian and Latin American developing countries. The following indications are provided in principle for each development initiative and for each beneficiary country: name of the initiative; responsible authority in the ACP country; estimated cost or amount financed; brief description of the planned project (construction work, supply of equipment, technical assistance, etc.); possible execution details; state of the project.

Author: the Commission's Division for Communications, Publications and the Courier ACP–EU, under the aegis of a European editor.

Frequency: 6 issues a year.

Languages: French, English.

How to obtain: download from http://europa.eu.int/comm/development/publicat/courier/index_en.htm Alternatively, contact the Commission's Offices in the Member States, or contact Courier ACP–EU, European Commission, 1049 Brussels, Belgium; fax (+32) 2-2992525. Always mark your full address details.

Partnership

This bulletin is published by the Centre for Industrial Development (CID) whose role is to promote industrial co-operation between the countries of the European Union and ACP countries (Cotonou Agreement countries). The bulletin provides information about all the CID's activities (contacts with the development banks, institutions representing ACP countries or the European Union for example), in-depth articles, industrial opportunities, ideas for projects etc.

Addressees: institutional bodies, SMEs.

Frequency: 6 issues a year.

Languages: French, English.

How to obtain: contact the Centre for Industrial Development, Avenue Hermann Debroux 52, 1160 Brussels, Belgium; tel (+32) 2-6791811; fax (+32) 2-6752603; e-mail info@cdi.be; internet www.cdi.be. N.B. *Partnership* is inserted in the *The Courier*.

Europe Information: Development

The *Europe Information* documents are, along with the ACP–EU Courier, the main European Commission publications on the European Union's relations with the developing countries. The documents are about 10 pages long and deal with either a general subject, or a specific issue, concerning the question of development and, in particular, co-operation with the African, Caribbean and Pacific countries (ACP).

Examples of general subjects:

- The European Development fund in a few words
- Compendium on co-operation strategies 2001
- Fighting hunger – food security at the heart of poverty reduction
- ACP–EU Partnership Agreement signed in Cotonou on 23 June 2000
- The European Community's Development Policy – Statement by the Council and the Commission
- EU–ACP co-operation in 1998 – Towards a new long-term partnership agreement
- The European Union and the developing world (Map)
- InfoFinance 2000
- 20 questions and answers: the Lomé Convention between the EU and the ACP
- Lomé IV Convention (revised text)
- Peace-Building and Conflict Prevention in Africa

Sectoral subjects:

- The EU Tropical Forestry Sourcebook
- Energy as a tool for sustainable development for African, Caribbean and Pacific countries
- Proceedings of the Conference on Sustainable Use of Aquatic Biodiversity: Data, Tools and Co-operation – Lisbon, Portugal, 3–5 September 1998
- ACP-EU Fisheries Research Report nr 5. Proceedings of the EXPO'98 Conference. Ocean Food Webs and economic productivity – Lisbon, Portugal, 1–3 July 1998
- Sysmin and mining development
- Development co-operation to improve health in the ACP Countries
- EU food aid and food security programme

Geographical subjects:

- The South Pacific and the European Union
- European Union, Latin America, Caribbean – Advancing together
- Partners in Progress – The EU/South Africa Trade, Development and Co-operation Agreement for the 21st century
- The European Union, the Countries of West Africa and WAEMU
- Zimbabwe and the European Union
- The European Union and the overseas countries and territories
- Cameroon and the European Union
- Southern Africa and the European Union

Other subject areas:

- Regionalism and Development – Report of the European Commission and World Bank Seminar
- The European Community External Co-operation programmes

- EC Co-operation on Oceans and Seas
- Eurobarometer: Europeans and development aid
- Collection of Communications from the Commission to the Council and the European Parliament and of relevant Resolutions, Declarations and Conclusions of the Councils of Ministers. Development co-operation policy in the run-up to 2000
- Development: Studies and Research. Safe blood in developing countries. Principles and organization
- Development: Studies and Research. Safe blood in developing countries. The lessons of Uganda

Manuals:

- The Rules of Origin – Manual for the use of officials, exporters and producers
- Guidelines for water resources development co-operation – Towards sustainable water resources management
- Transport sector guidelines – Towards sustainable transport infrastructure: a sectoral approach in practice
- Forests in sustainable development – Guidelines for forest sector development co-operation.
- Financial and Economic Analysis of Development Projects.
- Microfinance –Methodological considerations.

Author: The Directorate-General for Development, Unit VIII/1 and specialized journalists.

Frequency: irregular.

Languages: various, depending on the issue; but, generally speaking, all the brochures are published in at least French and English.

Contact: Elke Martin, Documentation Service; tel: (+32) 2-2993062; fax (+32) 2-2992525; internet http://europa.eu.int/comm/development/publication_en.htm.

Newsletters

Published by some European Commission Delegations in ACP or Mediterranean Countries.

The European Union has delegations in most countries with which it has concluded specific co-operation agreements: African, Caribbean and Pacific (ACP) countries tied to the EU under the Cotonou Agreement and southern Mediterranean countries linked to the EU by individual agreements which follow a standard format. Nearly all the Mediterranean delegations and a good number of the ACP delegations publish newsletters which report on initiatives undertaken in the countries concerned under co-operation agreements or the Cotonou Agreement: development projects, the functioning of the agreement and generally the overall relations between these countries and the European Union.

In order to subscribe to these publications, contact the delegation concerned.

DG Enlargement

Enlargement is naturally a major issue and the Directorate-General produces a sizeable amount of information. The DG publishes progress reports on the applicant countries as well as a series of key documents (see below). The Phare programme is an instrument of the Enlargement process and falls under the aegis of the Directorate for Enlargement.

Phare finances and produces a wide variety of publications ranging from the Phare Address Book to topical newsletters. Gradually, all of them will be put online.

The publications below can be obtained from both the EC's Phare & Tacis Information Centre (phare-tacis@cec.eu.int) and the DG Enlargement Information Unit (phare-info@cec.eu.int) upon simple request.

Enlargement Weekly

This newsletter provides an overview of where European Union enlargement has got to, who's doing what in the EU, in the institutions and candidate countries, and how the main challenges are being met.

Enlargement Research Bulletin

This monthly bulletin provides abstracts of publications concerning the enlargement of the European Union. The abstracts are selected from a database of 300 organizations based in Member States, Candidate Countries and elsewhere. The bulletin is available online through the DG's website as well as in a paper format.

Recent key documents include:

- The Enlargement Address Book (September 2004)
- Commission proposes comprehensive measures to end isolation of Turkish Cypriot community (July 2004)
- Proposal for a Council Regulation establishing an instrument of financial support for encouraging the economic development of the Turkish Cypriot community (July 2004)
- Proposal for a Council Regulation on special conditions for trade with those areas of the Republic of Cyprus in which the Government of the Republic of Cyprus does not exercise effective control (July 2004)

- Draft Commission Regulation (EC) laying down specific rules concerning goods arriving from the areas not under the effective control of the Government of Cyprus in the areas in which the Government exercises effective control (July 2004)
- Proposal for a Commission Decision on the authorization of the Turkish Cypriot Chamber of Commerce according to Article 4 (5) of Council Regulation (EC) No. 866/2004 (July 2004)
- Phare National Programmes Highlights VI (in English, December 2003)
- EU Support for Roma Communities in Central and Eastern Europe (May 2002; versions in several languages October 2003)
- An enlarged Europe of solidarity with the regions (in all EU official languages, June 2003)
- Enlarging the European Union – A well-regulated market place (June 2003)
- Phare National Programmes Highlights V (in English, June 2003)
- European Union Enlargement – An historic opportunity (in English, German French, May 2003)
- What can enterprises in the new Member States expect? Questions and answers (in English, May 2003)
- Practical Guide – Free movement of persons (versions in several languages, May 2003)
- Key indicators on Member States and Candidate Countries (April 2003)

Enlargement weekly and key documents can be found at http://europa.eu.int .comm/enlargement/docs/index.htm.

For further information: Phare and Tacis Information Centre, Rue Montoyer 19, 1000 Brussels, Belgium; tel (+32) 2-5459010; fax (+32) 2-5459011; e-mail: phare-tacis@cec.eu.int; opening hours Monday to Friday 9.30–18.00.

DG External Relations

The Directorate-General does not produce any periodicals for general release but offers a weekly news digest. To subscribe, go to http://europa.eu.int/comm/external-relations/feedback/weekly.htm.

Other publications, many of which may be downloaded electronically from http://europa.eu.int/comm/external-relations/library/publication.htm, include:

- The European Union and the World (in all EU official languages)
- Small Arms and Light Weapons: the response of the European Union (in English and French)

- The European Union Mine Actions in 2000 (in English, French and Spanish)
- European Union – Canada relations (in English and French)
- The Europe–Mediterranean partnership (in English, French and Spanish)
- Union Europea–Mercosur: Una asociación para el futuro (in Spanish)
- The European Union, Latin America and the Caribbean (in English, French, Spanish and Portuguese)
- Democratisation and human rights in Latin America
- The European Union and Latin America: Towards a strengthening of the partnership
- European Union Aid to uprooted people
- EU–ASEAN Relations – A Growing Partnership
- European Union and Latin America: Caribbean – Advancing together

Inter-institutional Documents

Official Journal of the European Communities

The Official Journal of the Communities is the reference work par excellence for all those who wish to keep a close eye on changes in Regulations and EC life. It is an inter-institutional document recording the official texts of all the institutions. It consists of two series along with a further series entitled 'Supplement to the EC's Official Journal'.

The subscription covers the two aforementioned series, while a separate subscription is required for the supplement. The Official Journal L + C series can be consulted free of charge on the Internet for at least 45 days from the date of publication, at http://europa.eu.int/eur-lex.

The **L series 'Legislation'** contains all the legislative acts and regulations whose publication is obligatory under the Treaties establishing the European Communities, as well as a large number of acts that do not carry a statutory obligation to publish.

The **C series 'Information and Notices'** covers a wide range of Union information: Commission proposals for legislation, reports of the progress of cases before the Court of Justice, written questions put by the European Parliament to the Council and the Commission together with their relative answers, the current exchange rate of the euro, invitations to tender for agricultural and animal products, the annual report of the Court of Auditors, competition notices for job vacancies in the EU institutions, opinions of the Economic and Social Committee, etc.

The S Series 'Invitations for Public Tenders'. Since the advent of the single market, all invitations to tender for public works, services and supply contracts must be promulgated throughout the EU if they are valued above a certain amount (depending upon the type of contract). Due to the considerable increase in the number of tenders, presentation in the Supplement to the OJ takes the following patterns: *Section 1:* Various tenders translated in their entirety; *Section 2:* Notices by the institutions of the EU in their entirety; *Section 3:* Contract award tenders; *Section 4:* Translated summaries of EU and EEA pre-information and contract notices; *Section 5:* The entire text (in the original language) of the translated summaries given in section 4 in their original language; *Section 6:* The GATT notices in English. This new structure enables readers to examine the full text of the notice in its original language (only the original text being authentic) without having to consult other editions of the Supplement. The 'S' series is also available online via the database at http://ted.eur-op.eu.int/ojs/html/index2.htm.

Indexes to the OJ

Monthly and annual chronological indexes, as well as the annual *Directory of Community legislation in force*, are automatically provided to Official Journal subscribers. The monthly and annual indexes consist of two volumes: Volume I is an Alphabetical Index, and Volume II comprises Methodological Tables (numerical index). *The Directory of Community legislation in force* is a subject index in two volumes of current legislation, one alphabetical and the other chronological. It is updated and re-issued every six months.

The L and C series, plus the indexes and the directory, also appear on microfiche, but the microfiche editions are published in monthly batches some two or three months after the paper edition. EUR-OP ceased production of the OJ on microfiche at the end of 1999.

As a result of an increasing number of people interested in receiving, on a regular basis, only those Official Journals containing open competition announcements, EUR-OP has introduced a subscription, set to cover the running costs and postal charges of such a service.

Frequency: five days a week (Tuesday to Saturday).

Languages: all the EU's official languages.

Documents

This catalogue contains bibliographical references on three series of documents: the COM Documents of the European Commission; the Opinions and Reports of the European Economic and Social Committee; the Opinions of the Committee of the Regions.

The catalogue is divided into three parts: a thematic index classifying the bibliographical references for each subject under 19 headings; a cumulative alphabetical index containing all the keywords and key expressions in relation to the documents' titles; a cumulative numerical index containing all the document numbers in ascending order and the corresponding microfiche number.

Frequency: catalogues are updated and published on a regular basis and an annual catalogue, covering the period July to June, complements the monthly lists which only contain the thematic index.

Languages: all the EU's official languages.

How to obtain: order from the Office for Official Publications of the European Communities at rue Mercier, OP A4B, 2985 Luxembourg, Luxembourg, or from sales agents in the Member States.

EuropeAid Co-operation Office

The EuropeAid Co-operation Office, which is a department of the Commission, has a website containing full details of contract procedures and all the relevant documentation. Interested parties can download the documents directly. The website further contains final evaluation reports on projects and programmes carried out with European Commission funding and will soon provide information on projects under way.

The following reports and publications may also be downloaded, from http://europa.eu.int/comm/europeaid/reports/index-en.htm:

- External aid programmes – Financial trends
- Annual Report
- External Aid: A new policy, a new management structure
- Human Rights, environment and other issues
- South-Eastern Europe: The Balkans
- The Partner States of Eastern Europe and Central Asia
- South Mediterranean, Near and Middle East
- Africa, Caribbean, Pacific
- Asia
- Latin America
- Financial Tables and Annex
- Report on the Implementation of the European Commission External Assistance
- The European Community External Cooperation Programmes. Policies, Management and Distribution

- Annual Report of the Meda programme

Headquarters: EuropeAid H/5 (Information & Communication), Rue de la Loi 41 – 7/52, 1040 Brussels, Belgium; tel (+32) 2-2991111; fax (+32) 2-2996407; internet europa.eu.int/comm/europeaid.

For correspondence: European Commission, EuropeAid H/5 L41 7/52, Rue de la Loi 200, 1049 Brussels, Belgium; e-mail europeaid-info@cec.eu.int.

The 'Documents' Series of the Commission, the European Economic and Social Committee, and the Committee of the Regions

The European Union publishes, through the Office for Official Publications of the European Communities, three series of documents covering the regulatory related issues which might be adopted by the Council of Ministers of the European Union, and might therefore have a direct impact on the activity of Member States and of their partners from third countries.

The documents reflect the position of three EU institutions: COM Documents, which contain the European Commission's finalized proposals to the Council; the Opinions and Reports of the European Economic and Social Committee on the proposals of the Commission to the Council after they have been adopted by the ESC in plenary session; the Opinions of the Committee of the Regions.

Several such documents are published in the course of a year and their subscription cost is high. It is possible to take out a selective subscription, however.

COM Documents

COM Documents comprise Commission proposals, communications and reports to the Council.

The bulk of EC Regulation is adopted by Member-State Ministers on a proposal from the European Commission. These proposals are highly important, as they lie at the origin of EC law, and they come in the form of communications to the Council – COM Documents. The COM Documents may also contain other Commission texts, such as reports to the Council. They are greatly appreciated reference documents as they are available rapidly and contain the 'explanatory memorandum' – an explanation of the reasons which inspired the Commission to propose the Regulation in question.

Author: all the European Commission's services.

Frequency: almost daily.

Languages: all the EU's official languages.

How to obtain: order from sales agents.

ESC Documents

ESC Documents comprise opinions and reports of the European Economic and Social Committee.

The documents are generally the Committee's opinions on Commission proposals or communications to the Council. They are exactly the same as those published in the OJ but are available more quickly.

Author: the Committee's different sections.

Frequency: irregular.

Languages: all of the EU's official languages.

How to obtain: order from sales agents.

Committee of the Regions Documents

The documents are generally opinions of the Committee of the Regions of the European Communities on Commission proposals or communications to the Council. They are exactly the same as those published in the OJ but are available more quickly.

Author: the Committee's different sections.

Frequency: irregular.

Languages: all of the EU's official languages.

How to obtain: order from sales agents.

OFFICE FOR OFFICIAL PUBLICATIONS OF THE EUROPEAN COMMUNITIES (EUR-OP): CATALOGUE OF THE OFFICE'S PUBLICATIONS

The Office for Official Publications of the European Communities (EUR-OP) is the editor of all the EU's institutions and their bodies. The Office markets all EU publications on sale and distributes those which form part of free series. Some publications, however, including brochures and newsletters, are distributed direct by the Directorates-General and are not included in the Office's catalogue.

The following list is taken from the 2004 catalogue of the Office's publications. The entries provide practical information that potential purchasers need.

The catalogue comprises both the main and most recent publications of EUR-OP (which are on sale at the Office for Official Publications, 2 rue Mercier, 2985 Luxembourg) and the most popular publications for general information (which may be obtained from various of the European Commission's Directorates-General and from the Commission's offices in the Member States and elsewhere).

Publications appearing in the catalogue under the heading 'General Information Publications' are nearly all free. The subscriber is usually charged mailing costs.

Publications available in English are listed only in that language. Important titles that are not available in English are listed in one other language version in the following order of choice: German (DE), French (FR). The following abbreviations denote language versions in which publications are available:

- CS: Czech
- DA: Danish
- DE: German
- EL: Greek
- EN: English
- ES: Spanish
- ET: Estonian
- FI: Finnish
- FR: French
- HU: Hungarian
- IT: Italian
- LT: Lithuanian
- LV: Latvian
- MT: Maltese
- NL: Dutch
- PL: Polish
- PT: Portuguese
- SK: Slovak
- SL: Slovene
- SV: Swedish

List of Publications

Official Journal of the European Union L and C series

The Official Journal of the European Union is a fundamental publication containing Community legislation and is available in various formats: paper, CD-ROM and online access.

It consists of two series: the L series 'Legislation' and the C series 'Information and Notices'.

The L series contains legislation, regulations, directives, decisions, recommendations and opinions. The C series includes summaries of judgments of the Court of Justice and the Court of First Instance, minutes of European Parliament part-sessions and reports of the Court of Auditors.
Edition 2004
Daily
Available in the official languages of the European Union
Theme: 6

Paper edition (700-800 issues)
Edition 2004
Daily
21 x 29.7 cm
Cat. No: FX-AC-04-000-EN-C (1725-2423)
Cat. No: FX-AL-04-000-EN-C (1725-2555)
Subscription code: VJA
Annual subscription price (excluding VAT): € **1000**

CD-ROM edition
The monthly edition is derived from the EUR-Lex database and provides a connection to the EUR-Lex Internet site. This cumulative, monolingual version provides the contents page in HTML format and the content of the OJ in PDF format (portable document format image files). The annual collection contains every issue of the OJ for the year in question.
Edition 2004
Monthly
ISSN 1725-4191
Cat. No: FX-AX-04-000-EN-Z
Subscription code: OCDJML
Annual subscription price (excluding VAT): € **400**

EUR-Lex (http://europa.eu.int/eur-lex)
The new EUR-Lex portal site offers access to all legal texts and documents of the European Union including the treaties, legislation, legislation in preparation, case-law, parliamentary questions and documents of public interest. These texts and documents are available in HTML, PDF and TIFF format.

The EUR-Lex portal offers harmonised search functions, an explanation of the legislative procedures of the EU, and provides links to other legislative sites of the EU institutions.

Debates of the European Parliament

The compilation of texts of speeches by Members of the European Parliament in plenary sitting is known as the Verbatim report of proceedings (Compte Rendu in Extenso – CRE- in French). It contains all the texts in the original languages and is also published on the Parliament's Internet site. These texts are all translated into the official languages of the European Union and are published under the same address on the site. This version is known as Debates. Since the beginning of the fifth parliamentary term, the debates have also been published on CD-ROM.
Edition 2003
A series of multilingual CD-ROMs offering the 11 official languages of the European Union as at 1 January 2004
ISSN 1609-1213
Subscription code: OCVII
Annual subscription price (excluding VAT): € **200**
Theme: 1

Supplement to the Official Journal of the European Union: S series

The CD-ROM edition is published for the period from Tuesday to Saturday and contains over 1000 invitations to tender for public works and supplies contracts issued by the Member States of the European Union, by the ACP countries (African, Caribbean and Pacific States) associated with the EU, by non-associated countries carrying out projects funded by the European Development Fund, and by the EFTA States.
Edition 2004
A multilingual CD-ROM in the official languages of the European Union
ISSN 1725-3357

Subscription of two issues a week
Cat. No: FX-AS-04-000-IF-Z
Subscription code: OCDJOS
Price (excluding VAT): € 6
Annual subscription price (excluding VAT): € 300
Theme: 4

Online version TED
In addition to the current invitations to tender, available in the official languages, this database allows easy access to all the archives of the S series for the previous five years in English. Access to TED is free of charge.

Integrated tariff of the European Communities (TARIC): Official Journal of the European Communities C 103 and C 103 A

TARIC is used by the Commission and the Member States for the purpose of applying Community measures relating to imports and exports, and – where necessary – to trade between Member States. TARIC also serves as a basis for the working tariffs and tariff files in the Member States.
Edition 2003
Annual
A series of multilingual CD-ROMs in the 11 official languages of the European Union as at 1 January 2004
ISBN 92-78-40155-2
ISSN 1725-2199
Cat. No: FX-AM-03-103-1F-Z
Price (excluding VAT): € 50
Theme: 2

Paper version
Available in the 11 official languages of the European Union as at 1 January 2004
2003 – 3829 pp. – 21 x 29.7 cm
ISSN 1725-2423
Cat. No: FX-AC-03-103-EN-C
Cat. No: FX-AM-03-103-EN-C
Price (excluding VAT): € 184

Combined nomenclature: OJ L 281 of the European Communities

As published in the Official Journal of the EC L 281 of 30 October 2003, this CD-ROM contains the combined nomenclature for 2004, explanatory notes and different classification regulations published between 1 January 1988 and 31 October 2003 on the tariff and statistical nomenclature and on the Common Customs Tariff.
Edition 2003
Annual
A series of multilingual CD-ROMs in the 11 official languages of the European Union as at 1 January 2004
ISSN 1562-9236
Cat. No: FX-AL-03-281-1F-Z
Price (excluding VAT): € 50
Theme: 2

Paper version
Available in the 11 official languages of the European Union as at 1 January 2004
2003 – 894 pp. – 21 x 29.7 cm
ISSN 1725-2563
Cat. No: FX-AL-03-281-EN-C
Price (excluding VAT): € 86.50

European Union: Selected instruments taken from the Treaties

Available in the 11 official languages of the European Union as at 1 January 2004
Theme: 6

Book I – Volume I: Treaty on European Union and Treaty establishing the European Community
This edition of Selected instruments taken from the Treaties (Book I – Volume I) includes the Treaty of Amsterdam for the first time. It contains the complete texts of the Treaty of Amsterdam, the Treaty on European Union and the Treaties establishing the European Communities and the amendments to them.
Available in the official languages of the European Union
1999 – 1045 pp. – 11.5 x 17 cm
ISBN 92-824-1661-5
Cat. No: FX-22-99-337-EN-C
Price (excluding VAT): € 20

Book I – Volume II: Treaties ECSC and EAEC
The second volume of the series contains the complete texts of the Treaties establishing the European Coal and Steel Community, the European Communities and the European Atomic Energy Community.
Available in the official languages of the European Union
1995 – 591 pp. – 11.5 x 17 cm
ISBN 92-824-1180-X
Cat. No: FX-85-94-430-EN-C
Price (excluding VAT): € 23

Volume II: Documents concerning the accessions to the European Communities
Available in the official languages of the European Union
1988 – 693 pp. – 21 x 29.7 cm
ISBN 92-771-9304-2
Cat. No: FX-80-86-002-EN-C
Price (excluding VAT): € 81

Book II – Volume II: Documents concerning the accession of the Republic of Austria, the Republic of Finland and the Kingdom of Sweden to the European Communities
Available in the official languages of the European Union
1995 – 368 pp. – 21 x 29.7 cm
ISBN 92-824-1405-1
Cat. No: FX-92-95-651-EN-C
Price (excluding VAT): € 23

The 2003 accession Treaty

On 16 April 2003 in Athens, the 15 existing Members of the European Union and the 10 acceding countries – Cyprus, the Czech Republic, Estonia, Hungary, Latvia, Lithuania, Malta, Poland, Slovakia and Slovenia – signed the Treaty on their accession to the Union. The Treaty has been published in the Official Journal of the European Union L 236 and C 227 E of 23 September 2003.
Contents OJ L236:
– The Treaty proper, comprising a preamble and three articles
– The Act concerning the conditions of accession of the 10 acceding countries and the adjustments to the Treaties on which the European Union is founded, comprising five parts and 62 articles
– 18 annexes setting out the detailed conditions of negotiation for the accession, including the various transitional periods (colour illustrations)
– 10 protocols on specific questions
– A Final Act containing, among other things, a number of declarations by the plenipotentiaries.
Contents OJ C 227 E:
– The appendices to the annexes to the Act
Theme: 6

Official Journal L 236
Available in the official languages of the European Union
2003 – 996 pp. – 21 x 29.7 cm
Cat. No: FX-AL-03-236-EN-C
Price (excluding VAT): € 89.50

Official Journal C 227 E (paper version)
Available in the 11 official languages of the European Union as at 1 January 2004
Cat. No: OA-15-03-000-EN-C
Price (excluding VAT): € 110.50

Official Journal L 236 + Official Journal C 227 E (combined product)
Available in the official languages of the European Union
Cat. No: OA-4V-03-000-EN-C
Price (excluding VAT): € 200

CD-ROM version
Multilingual edition in English (EN), Czech (CS), Estonian (ET), Latvian (LV), Lithuanian (LT), Hungarian (HU), Maltese (MT), Polish (PL), Slovakian (SK), Slovene (SL)
2004
ISBN 92-78-40192-7
Cat. No: OA-57-04-815-1N-Z
Price (excluding VAT): € 70

Consolidated Treaties (February 2003)

This publication contains the consolidated versions of the Treaty on the European Union and the Treaty establishing the European Communities, incorporating the amendments made by the Treaty of Nice, signed on 26 February 2001.

*Available in the 11 official languages of
the European Union as at 1 January 2004
2003 – 184 pp. – 17.6 x 25 cm
ISBN 92-78-40125-0
Cat. No: FX-49-02-288-EN-C
Price (excluding VAT): € **20**
Theme: 6*

Treaty of Nice

The Treaty of Nice was signed on 26 February 2001. The main focus of the Nice Treaty was the reform of the EU's internal operating mechanisms, in order to allow an enlarged Union of around 27 members to operate efficiently. During the longest summit ever in EU history, the Heads of State or Government of the 15 Member States finally reached an agreement on the size and composition of the Commission, the re-weighting of votes in the Council, qualified-majority voting, the distribution of seats in the European Parliament and enhanced cooperation. The Treaty was also published in the Official Journal of the European Communities (OJ C 80, 10.3.2001).
*Available in the 11 official languages of
the European Union as at 1 January 2004
2001 – 90 pp. – 17.6 x 25 cm
ISBN 92-824-1977-0
Cat. No: FX-36-01-338-EN-C
Price (excluding VAT): € **10**
Theme: 6*

Treaty of Amsterdam

The Treaty of Amsterdam modified the Treaty on European Union, the Treaties establishing the European Communities and certain related acts. Signed in Amsterdam on 2 October 1997, it came into force on 1 May 1999.
*Available in the 11 official languages of
the European Union as at 1 January 2004
1997 – 144 pp. – 17.6 x 25 cm
ISBN 92-828-1652-4
Cat. No: FX-08-97-468-EN-C
Price (excluding VAT): € **10**
Theme: 6*

The Schengen acquis integrated into the European Union

When the Treaty of Amsterdam entered into force on 1 May 1999, cooperation measures hitherto in the Schengen framework were integrated into the European Union framework, including the detailed arrangements for that integration process. This collection presents the Schengen acquis chronologically and according to topic.
*Available in the 11 official languages of
the European Union as at 1 January 2004
2001 – 577 pp. – 17.6 x 25 cm
ISBN 92-824-1776-X
Cat. No: BX-26-99-651-EN-C
Price (excluding VAT): € **66**
Theme: 6*

The Financial Regulation applicable to the general budget of the European Communities and its implementing rules – synoptic presentation

This publication combines the texts of the Financial Regulation and the rules for its implementation. These two Regulations have constituted the regulatory framework for the management of Community finances since 1 January 2003. The synoptic presentation of the Financial Regulation and the implementing rules will enhance the transparency, accessibility and above all the understanding of the financial and budgetary rules. It will therefore be of everyday practical use both for the managers of Community funds and for readers from outside the institutions who are interested in financial and budgetary management in the European Institutions.

The possibility of easy Internet access to the updates that will be produced whenever changes are made to these two Regulations will also contribute to more precise knowledge of the rules in question.
*Available in German (DE), English (EN) and French (FR)
2003 – 160 pp. – 23 x 32 cm
ISBN 92-894-4759-1
Cat. No: KV-47-02-608-EN-C
Price (excluding VAT): € **25**
Theme: 1*

European Union public finance

This third edition takes on board the impact of the Agenda 2000 financial framework adopted at the Berlin European Council in March 1999. A coherent set of measures was taken to pave the way for the impending enlargement and major reforms have been introduced in the biggest areas of Union expenditure – the common agricultural policy and structural operations.

The purpose of this publication is to provide an insight into Community public finances that, if not exhaustive, is at least wide-ranging and accurate. With its division into separate chapters and the inclusion of a detailed summary, it can also serve as a reference work.
*Available in the 11 official languages of
the European Union as at 1 January 2004
2002 – 410 pp. – 16.2 x 22.9 cm
ISBN 92-894-1620-3
Cat. No: KV-39-01-336-EN-C
Price (excluding VAT): € **20**
Theme: 9*

CD-ROM version
*A multilingual CD-ROM offering the 11 official languages of the European Union as at 1 January 2004
2003
ISBN 92-894-1627-0
Cat. No: KV-39-01-336-1F-Z
Price (excluding VAT): € **20**

European governance: A White Paper

The White Paper on European governance contains the Commission's propositions for opening up the policy-making process to get more people and organisations involved in shaping and delivering EU policy, in an effort to bridge the gap between the citizens of Europe and the EU institutions.

The paper also launched a consultative process, running until the end of March 2002 on the need for action by the other institutions and Member States. By the end of 2002, the Commission was to report on the progress it had made and to have drawn lessons from the White Paper consultation, establishing a basis for taking the governance agenda forward with the other institutions.
*Available in the 11 official languages of
the European Union as at 1 January 2004
2001 – 71 pp. – 17.6 x 25 cm
ISBN 92-894-1061-2
Cat. No: KA-06-01-001-EN-C
Price (excluding VAT): € **8**
Theme: 1*

European governance – Preparatory work for the White Paper

The working group's objectives were to provide helpful suggestions on how to transform the citizens of the European Union into actors in the European political process. This involved them looking at how to improve the flow of information on European matters and to make it more accessible. Among the questions they asked themselves were how to make communications a strategic tool of governance for the Commission and how to inject relevant European aspects into political debates still dominated by national discourses, concerns and actors.
*Available in English (EN), French (FR)
2002 – 412 pp. – 17.6 x 25 cm
ISBN 92-894-1072-8
Cat. No: KA-06-01-002-EN-C
Price (excluding VAT): € **20**
Theme: 1*

General Report on the Activities of the European Union 2003

This publication offers a general overview of Community policy in 2003, covering the measures taken to implement the single market and Community policies on industry, competition, the environment, the regions, agriculture, education, social affairs and transport. Other chapters deal with enlargement, the Community economic and social area, financing of Community activities, resource management, and protection of the Communities' financial interests.
*Annual
Available in the 11 official languages of
the European Union as at 1 January 2004*

2004 – XIV, 564 pp. – 16.2 x 22.9 cm
ISBN 92-894-7018-6
ISSN 1608-7321
Cat. No: KA-AD-04-001-EN-C
Price (excluding VAT): € **38**
Theme: 1

Bulletin of the European Union

This publication is an indispensable source of information on all Community activities. A clear structure allows rapid access to the information the reader requires, and, in order to assist the reader in their research, precise references of the legal base for all summaries of policies and decisions are given, including related texts that have already been published.

You will also find information on the role of the European Union in the world.
Edition 2004
Monthly
Available in the 11 official languages of the European Union as at 1 January 2004
ISSN 1025-4005
Cat. No: KA-AA-04-000-EN-C
Subscription code: VLA
Price per copy (excluding VAT): € **18**
Annual subscription price (excluding VAT): € **152**
Theme: 1

Publishing in the nine new official languages is foreseen at a later stage

XXXIInd Report on competition policy 2002

This report analyses the principal measures and decisions taken by the Commission to ensure that EU competition rules (Articles 81 to 86 of the Consolidated Treaties) are followed. It includes the judgments of the Court of Justice in this field and a description of competition policy and State aid.
Annual
Available in the 11 official languages of the European Union as at 1 January 2004
2003 – 350 pp. – 16.2 x 22.9 cm
ISBN 92-894-6028-8
ISSN 0259-3157
Cat. No: KD-AC-03-001-EN-C
Price (excluding VAT): € **32.50**
Theme: 6, 8

XXXIII Report on competition policy 2003
Next edition was expected in 2004

The Agricultural Situation in the European Union: 2001 Report

This report, which is the 27th annual agricultural situation report, is published in conjunction with the 2001 General Report on the Activities of the European Union. The format of the report has been changed from previous years, and this volume no longer contains a statistical annex. The annex is available as a separate publication: Agriculture in the

European Union – Statistical and economic information 2001. It is free of charge and available in EN only.
Annual
Available in the 11 official languages of the European Union as at 1 January 2004
2003 – 164 pp. – 16.2 x 22.9 cm
ISBN 92-894-5232-3
ISSN 1025-6660
Cat. No: KF-BC-02-001-EN-C
Price (excluding VAT): € **18.50**
Theme: 3

The Agricultural Situation in the European Union: 2002 Report
Next edition was expected in 2004

Progress achieved by the European Union 1995–99

As laid down by Article 4 of the Treaty on European Union, the European Council has to submit to the European Parliament a report after each of its meetings, and a yearly written report on the progress achieved by the Union. This title, produced by the General Secretariat of the Council of the European Union provides detailed information on both the internal and external policies of the Union.
Available in the 11 official languages of the European Union as at 1 January 2004
2001 – 206 pp. – 21 x 29.7 cm
ISBN 92-824-1944-4
Cat. No: BX-26-99-853-EN-C
Price (excluding VAT): € **62**
Theme: 1

Basic texts on transparency concerning the activities of the Council of the European Union: February 2000

This publication contains all the legislative texts related to the policy of transparency of the Council of the European Union.
Available in the 11 official languages of the European Union as at 1 January 2004
2000 – 173 pp. – 17.6 x 25 cm
ISBN 92-824-1831-6
Cat. No: BX-26-99-611-EN-C
Price (excluding VAT): € **22**
Theme: 6

Council's Rules of Procedure – Rules for the organisation of the proceedings of the European Council – July 2002

In order fully to exercise its role of providing impetus and defining the general political guidelines of the Union in accordance with Article 4 of the Treaty on European Union, the European Council has set up its procedure's rules and rules for the preparation, conduct and conclusions of its proceedings.

This edition contains the Council Decision of 22 July 2002 (2202/682/EC, Euratom), replacing the Council Decision

of 5 June 2000 (2000/396/EC, ECSC, Euratom).
2002 edition
Available in the 11 official languages of the European Union as at 1 January 2004
2003 – 48 pp. – 14.8 x 21 cm
ISBN 92-824-2166-X
ISSN 1725-1257
Cat. No: QC-46-02-290-EN-C
Price (excluding VAT): € **7**
Theme: 1

Rules of Procedure – European Parliament – 15th edition

The European Parliament's Rules of Procedure are published periodically in booklet form and in the Official Journal of the European Union. The European Parliament may, however, amend its Rules of Procedure from time to time. The version in force is available on the European Parliament's web site (http://www.europarl.eu.int).
Available in the 11 official languages of the European Union as at 1 January 2004
2003 – 237 pp. – 14.8 x 21 cm
ISSN 1682-8836
Cat. No: QA-42-02-545-EN-C
Price (excluding VAT): € **25**
Theme: 1

Rules of Procedure – European Parliament

Next edition in the 20 official languages of the European Union was expected in 2004

European Parliament – List of Members

List of Members of the Bureau, Parliament, political groups, committees and interparliamentary delegations
Multilingual edition in the 11 official languages of the European Union as at 1 January 2004
2003 – 218 pp. – 21 x 29.7 cm
ISSN 0256-243X
Cat. No: QA-AE-03-003-1F-C
Price (excluding VAT): € **15**
Theme: 1

Who's who in the European Union? 2003/04 edition

The Interinstitutional directory is a guide to the administrative structure of the European institutions and a reliable source of information concerning the names and addresses of high-ranking civil servants. Based on the IDEA database (http://europa.eu.int/idea/en/index.htm), the directory is published once a year.
Annual
Available in the 11 official languages of the European Union as at 1 January 2004
2003 – XXXV, 401 pp. – 21 x 29.7 cm
ISBN 92-78-40160-9
ISSN 1680-3698
Cat. No: FX-WW-03-001-EN-C
Price (excluding VAT): € **50**
Theme: 1

Corps diplomatique: Vade-mecum

This book includes: a list of the Brussels-based heads of mission of the non-EU countries, together with the dates on which they took office; the missions accredited to the European Commission, with names of the members of the teams; the representatives of international organizations accredited to the European Commission and the names of the members of their teams; the dates of the national holidays of the non-EU countries; and the diplomatic corps' protocol teams.

Semestrial
Bilingual edition in English (EN) and French (FR)
2003 – 295 pp. – 14.8 x 21 cm
ISSN 0591-2156
Cat. No: KA-AG-03-002-2A-C
Price (excluding VAT): € 15
Theme: 11

Directory of Community legislation in force and other acts of the Community institutions

The 41st edition of the Directory of Community legislation in force published by the institutions of the European Communities contains all Community legislation set out in the Official Journal of the European Union up to 1 July 2003.

The directory is compiled from the CELEX database, the interinstitutional computerised documentation system for Community law, which has been open to the public since 1981.

With regard to the range of documentation covered, it was felt that the directory should include not only current Community legislation as such but also other instruments reflecting the activities of the European Union (EU, ECSC, EEC, EC and Euratom) such as policy instruments and decisions taken in individual cases but of more interest.

The directory therefore covers:

(a) agreements and conventions concluded by the Communities in connection with their external relations;

(b) binding secondary legislation (regulations, decisions, ECSC general decisions and recommendations, EEC/EC/Euratom directives) under the Treaties establishing the European Union and the European Communities, with the exception of day-to-day administrative acts;

(c) supplementary legislation, in particular decisions of representatives of the Governments of the Member States meeting within the Council;

(d) certain non-binding acts considered by the institutions to be important.

The directory appears in two volumes:
Volume I, the main body of the directory, consists of 20 chapters with acts arranged according to subject,

Volume II contains chronological and alphabetical indexes of the acts appearing in Volume I.

41st edition
Semestrial
Available in the 11 official languages of the European Union as at 1 January 2004
2003 – 21 x 29.7 cm
ISSN 1608-4551
Cat. No: OA-09-03-000-EN-C

Price (excluding VAT): € 125 (Volumes I and II are not sold separately.)
Theme: 6

Volume I: Analytical register

Volume II: Chronological index and alphabetical index

Official Journal of the Office for Harmonisation in the Internal Market

The mission of the OHIM, Office for Harmonisation in the Internal Market (trade marks and designs), is to register applications of brands from within the European Union and to grant uniform and legal protection.

Edition 2004
Monthly
Multilingual edition in Spanish (ES), German (DE), English (EN), French (FR) and Italian (IT)
21 x 29.7 cm
ISSN 1025-5494
Cat. No: TB-AA-04-000-5D-C
Subscription code: VWJO
Price per copy (excluding VAT): € 20
Annual subscription price (excluding VAT): € 200
Theme: 6

Community trade marks bulletin

This CD-ROM provides information in the official languages of the European Union, with an interface in five languages on the Office for Harmonisation in the Internal Market (trade marks and designs) as well as useful data on the Nice and Vienna nomenclatures. It also contains a cumulative index covering most of the areas studied.

Edition 2004
± 52 issues per year
A multilingual CD-ROM offering the 11 official languages of the European Union as at 1 January 2004
ISSN 1606-2116
Cat. No: TB-AB-04-000-1F-Z
Subscription code: OCOHB1
Price per copy (excluding VAT): € 50
Annual subscription price (excluding VAT): € 1500
Theme: 8

Selected instruments relating to the Community trade mark

Community Trade Mark Regulation and related texts (Implementing Regulation, Fees Regulation, Rules of procedure of the Boards of Appeal, Joint Statements

entered in the Council Minutes; Decisions and Communications of the President of the Office.

Second edition
Available in Spanish (ES), German (DE), English (EN), French (FR) and Italian (IT)
2002 – 297 pp. – 14.8 x 21 cm
ISBN 92-9156-066-9
Cat. No: TB-45-02-434-EN-C
Price (excluding VAT): € 15
Theme: 6

Official Gazette of the Community Plant Variety Office

Every two months the Office publishes an Official Gazette including extracts from its registers. It also publishes an annual report listing valid Community plant variety rights, the names of their holders and the dates on which they were granted and will expire.

Edition 2004
Multilingual edition in the 11 official languages of the European Union as at 1 January 2004
21 x 29.7 cm
ISSN 1025-4471
Cat. No: TG-AB-04-000-1F-C
Subscription code: VST
Price per copy (excluding VAT): € 15
Annual subscription price (excluding VAT): € 80
Theme: 3

Reports of the cases before the Court of Justice

This series contains all the cases dealt with by the Court of Justice and Court of First Instance, including the opinions of the Advocates-General and the texts of the judgments covering the period from 1954 to 2003.

Annual
Available in the 11 official languages of the European Union as at 1 January 2004
Theme: 6
ISSN 1022-842X
Subscription code: VZI

Volume 2004
Cat. No: QD-AB-04-000-EN-C
Annual subscription price (excluding VAT): € 170

Volume 2003
Cat. No: QD-AB-03-000-EN-C
Price (excluding VAT): € 170

Volume 2002
Cat. No: QD-AB-02-000-EN-C
Price (excluding VAT): € 170

Volume 2001
Cat. No: QD-AB-01-000-EN-C
Price (excluding VAT): € 170

Volume 2000
Cat. No: QD-AB-00-000-EN-C
Price (excluding VAT): € 170

Volume 1999
Cat. No: DX-AB-99-000-EN-C
Price (excluding VAT): € **170**

Volume 1998
Cat. No: DX-AB-98-000-EN-C
Price (excluding VAT): € **170**

Volume 1997
Cat. No: DX-AB-97-000-EN-C
Price (excluding VAT): € **170**

Volume 1996
Cat. No: DX-AB-96-000-EN-C
Price (excluding VAT): € **170**

Volume 1995
Cat. No: DX-AB-95-000-EN-C
Price (excluding VAT): € **170**

Volumes 1954–1994
These volumes are sold separately (price depends on volume)

Index A – Z

This index consists of three parts: a numerical list of cases, an alphabetical list of parties, and a list of courts that have referred questions to the Court for a preliminary ruling.
Available in English (EN) and French (FR)
Theme: 6

Volume I: Numerical and alphabetical index of cases before the Court of Justice of the European Communities from 1953 until 1988
2000 – 489 pp. – 21 x 29.7 cm
ISBN 92-829-0599-3
Cat. No: QD-31-00-013-EN-C
Price (excluding VAT): € **11**

Volume II: Numerical and alphabetical index of cases before the Court of Justice and the Court of First Instance of the European Communities since 1989: Situation on 31 March 2000
2000 – 837 pp. – 21 x 29.7 cm
ISBN 92-829-0601-9
Cat. No: QD-31-00-021-EN-C
Price (excluding VAT): € **18**

Notes: Références des notes de doctrine aux arrêts de la Cour de justice et du Tribunal de première instance des Communautés européennes

In this two-volume publication, judgments are ordered by number, while the references in the notes are given in chronological order. At the end of each volume, a chronological table of all the acts noted allows the reader to find the judgment which he is seeking by date.
Annual
Available only in French (FR)
Theme: 6

Volume I: Notes aux arrêts de la Cour prononcés dans les affaires introduites avant le 1er janvier 1989

2000 – 453 pp. – 21 x 29.7 cm
ISBN 92-829-0539-X
Cat. No: QD-51-00-001-FR-C
Price (excluding VAT): € **22**

Volume II: Notes aux arrêts de la Cour et du Tribunal de première instance prononcés dans les affaires introduites à partir du 1er janvier 1989
2003 – 781 pp. – 21 x 29.7 cm
ISBN 92-829-0689-2
Cat. No: QD-51-03-366-FR-C
Price (excluding VAT): € **28**

Economic policy-making in the European Union – Proceedings of the first four meetings of the Group of Economic Analysis

The Group of Economic Analysis (GEA) gathers some 25 top EU and non-EU economists in meetings three to four times a year under the chairmanship of President Romano Prodi, together with other relevant commissioners, with the aim of discussing selected economic issues. Each meeting of the GEA is divided into two parts: first a specific theme is discussed, followed by an exchange of views on the current economic situation.

The content of this publication consists of the meetings held by the GEA between December 2001 and January 2003.

One of the topics (research, patents and financing of ideas) is prospecting for answers concerning the low EU growth potential.

Other interesting themes brought up by the GEA meetings are economic policy coordination, industrial policy in an enlarged Europe, and corporate governance.
Available only in English (EN)
2003 – 252 pp. – 17.6 x 25 cm
ISBN 92-894-61810
Cat. No: KA-49-02-280-EN-C
Price (excluding VAT): € **25**
Theme: 8, 9, 10

Economic portrait of the European Union 2002 – Data up to 2001

This publication brings together a wide range of macroeconomic data on the European Union and its Member States and provides a statistical analysis of these data. In addition to economic aspects, the report examines the structural differences between the Member States and the way in which they are developing.
2002 edition
Available in German (DE), English (EN) and French (FR)
2003 – 167 pp. – 21 x 29.7 cm
ISBN 92-894-3771-5
ISSN 1680-1687
Cat. No: KS-AI-02-001-EN-C
Price (excluding VAT): € **30**
Theme: 10, 17

Business demography in Europe – Results for 10 Member States and Norway – Data 1997–2000

The first publication aims to provide extensive information on enterprise births and deaths, as well as survival rates. It also includes data in relation to employment and turnover generated by newly born enterprises. The data covers the period 1997–2000, across a full range of business activities.
Edition 2003
Available only in English (EN)
2003 – 97 pp. – 21 x 29.7 cm
ISBN 92-894-5708-2
Cat. No: KS-53-03-104-EN-C
Price (excluding VAT): € **15**
Theme: 8, 17

European Economy

European Economy is a series of publications consisting of important reports and communications from the Commission to the Council and the Parliament on the EU economic situation and future development.
Available only in English (EN)
21 x 29.7 cm
ISSN 0379-0991
Cat. No: KC-AR-04-000-EN-C
Subscription code: VED
Price per copy (excluding VAT): € **50**
Annual subscription price (excluding VAT): € **150**
Theme: 10

Economic and monetary union: Compilation of Community legislation

This publication groups together all the Community legislation relating to economic and monetary union, as published in the Official Journal.
Available in the 11 official languages of the European Union as at 1 January 2004
1999 – 258 pp. – 17.6 x 25 cm
ISBN 92-828-4310-6
Cat. No: CM-15-98-900-EN-C
Price (excluding VAT): € **20**
Theme: 1

Eurostatistics: Data for short-term economic analysis

The purpose of this publication is to supply, as quickly as possible, the most recent sets of statistics on the European Union and the euro zone for the Member States and their main partners outside the European Community (the United States of America and Japan).
Monthly
Available only in English (EN)
2004 – 21 x 29.7 cm
Subscription code: VHI
Price per copy (excluding VAT): € **20**
Annual subscription price (excluding VAT): € **180**
Theme: 17

European Union foreign direct investment yearbook 2001: Data 1992–2000

The direct investment yearbook provides users with analytical aspects of the foreign direct investment position, flow and income for the European Union. It aims to provide political and corporate decision-makers with high-quality statistical information on direct investment by providing internationally comparable figures through close cooperation with the Member States and the OECD.
2002 edition
Available only in English (EN)
2002 – 132 pp. – 21 x 29.7 cm
ISBN 92-894-3319-1
ISSN 1605-2935
Cat. No: KS-BK-02-001-EN-C

Price (excluding VAT): € 30 (Paper and CD-Rom are not sold separately)
Theme: 17

European Union international transactions: Analytical aspects – Detailed tables on CD-ROM – Data 1991–2001

The publication gives the most recent portrait (2001) of EU international transactions, focusing on analytical aspects and providing statistical tables. It mainly covers international exchanges (exports and imports) in services (53 items) and other balance of payments items, including goods, income received on capital invested abroad or paid on foreign capital invested on EU territory; salaries earned abroad by EU residents or salaries paid to non-residents on EU territory; and current transfers such as international aid and migrant workers' remittances. The publication emphasises the EU's geographical trading partners (50). Its annex provides more detailed statistical tables containing harmonised and internationally comparable current account data. The CD-ROM also includes methodological explanations and a short description of the harmonisation work undertaken.
Edition 2003
Available only in English (EN)
2003 – 99 pp. – 21 x 29.7 cm
ISBN 92-894-5216-1
ISSN 1680-225X
Cat. No: KS-AP-03-001-EN-C
Price (excluding VAT): € 45
Theme: 2, 9, 17

Working papers

These working papers from the European Parliament offer important information and insights on the EU policies and activities.

Impact of world commodity prices on developing countries
Available only in English (EN)
2001 – 48 pp. – 21 x 29.7 cm
ISBN 92-823-1572-X

Cat. No: QA-36-01-774-EN-C
Price (excluding VAT): € 7

The euro as 'Parallel currency' 1999–02
Multilingual edition in the 11 official languages of the European Union as at 1 January 2004
2001 – 182 pp. – 21 x 29.7 cm
ISBN 92-823-1570-3
Cat. No: QA-35-01-182-1F-C
Price (excluding VAT): € 16

Depleted uranium: Environmental and health effects in the Gulf war, Bosnia and Kosovo
Available only in English (EN)
2001 – 38 pp. – 21 x 29.7 cm
ISBN 92-823-1584-3
Cat. No: QA-38-01-746-EN-C
Price (excluding VAT): € 7

European ombudsman and national ombudsmen or similar bodies – Comparative tables
Available in English (EN), French (FR)
2001 – 102 pp. – 21 x 29.7 cm
ISBN 92-823-1581-9
Cat. No: QA-38-01-415-EN-C
Price (excluding VAT): € 16

Le droit de pétition dans les pays de l'Union européenne
Available only in French (FR)
2001 – 185 pp. – 21 x 29.7 cm
ISBN 92-823-1593-2
Cat. No: QA-39-01-837-FR-C
Price (excluding VAT): € 28

A Single market in financial services: Effects on growth, employment and the real economy
Available only in English (EN)
2001 – 128 pp. – 21 x 29.7 cm
ISBN 92-823-1588-6
Cat. No: QA-38-01-988-EN-C
Price (excluding VAT): € 17.50

Tax coordination in the European Union
2001 – 108 pp. – 21 x 29.7 cm
ISBN 92-823-1567-3
Cat. No: QA-36-01-160-EN-C
Price (excluding VAT): € 16

The WTO negotiations in the field of agriculture and food: Strategic positions of the US and China
Available in English (EN) and French (FR)
2001 – 94 pp. – 21 x 29.7 cm
ISBN 92-823-1612-2
Cat. No: QA-41-01-769-EN-C
Price (excluding VAT): € 14.50

Structures of the taxation systems in the European Union – Data 1995–2001

The 2003 edition of this publication presents for the first time a global overview of this corpus of ESA95 statistics and lays particular emphasis on tax indicators in national accounts, the classification of taxes, and methodology for calculating

harmonised implicit tax rates on labour, capital and consumption. A large section of the publication is also devoted to a comparative analysis of recent developments in the taxation systems of EU Member states.
Available only in English (EN)
2003 – 277 pp. – 30 x 42 cm
ISBN 92-894-5149-1
Cat. No: KS-51-03-124-EN-C
Price (excluding VAT): € 35.50
Theme: 17

Company taxation in the internal market

The report concludes that there are potentially significant benefits to be derived from providing, via a genuinely comprehensive solution, companies with a common consolidated tax base for the EU-wide activities. However, its findings are based mainly on the current stage of development of the research and further work would be necessary to implement any of the comprehensive approaches. Any solution going in this direction must obviously also take into account the competition rules laid down in the EC Treaty, in particular those concerning State Aids. Moreover, as already noted, the results of the quantitative analysis suggests that that the overall national tax rate is an important factor in determining the effective tax rate, and it is clear that a single or common base without further adaptations in practice would almost 'mechanically' accentuate this.
Available in English (EN) and French (FR)
2002 – 772 pp. – 17.6 x 25 cm
ISBN 92-894-1695-5
Cat. No: KP-39-01-869-EN-C
Price (excluding VAT): € 31
Theme: 9

CosmetLex: The rules governing cosmetic products in the European Union

Cosmetics Directive 76/768/EEC was adopted on 27 July 1976. One of its main objectives was to give clear guidance on the requirements a safe cosmetic product should have in order to circulate freely within the EU without pre-market authorisation (i.e. labelling, packaging, and safety regulations). The three-volume series of CosmetLex covers all the EU-related legislation and other material.
Available only in English (EN)
Theme: 5

Volume 1: Cosmetic legislation. Cosmetic products
This volume includes the legislation applicable to cosmetic products: Council Directive 76/768/EEC on the approximation of the laws of the Member States relating to cosmetic products and Commission Directive 95/17/EC laying down

detailed rules for the application of Council Directive 76/768/EEC.
2000 – 74 pp. – 21 x 29.7 cm
ISBN 92-828-8545-3
Cat. No: NB-26-99-958-EN-C
*Price (excluding VAT): € **14.50***

Volume 2: Cosmetics legislation. Cosmetic products: Methods of analysis
This volume incorporates the seven Commission directives on the approximation of the laws of Member States relating to the analysis necessary for checking the composition of cosmetic products.
2000 – 187 pp. – 21 x 29.7 cm
ISBN 92-828-8546-1
Cat. No: NB-26-99-966-EN-C
*Price (excluding VAT): € **31***

Volume 3: Cosmetics legislation. Cosmetic products: Notes of guidance for testing of cosmetics ingredients for their safety evaluation
This volume includes the notes of guidance prepared by the Scientific Committee on Cosmetic Products and Non-Foodstuff Products Intended for Consumers (SCCNFP) of the European Commission. The notes are not legally binding but can be of assistance for those responsible for consumer health protection and take into consideration the new concepts incorporated into the cosmetics directive.
2000 – 84 pp. – 21 x 29.7 cm
ISBN 92-828-8547-X
Cat. No: NB-26-99-974-EN-C
*Price (excluding VAT): € **16***

*Price (excluding VAT): € **52** (Volumes 1, 2 and 3)*

Eudralex: The rules governing medicinal products in the European Union

Theme: 5

Volume 1: Pharmaceutical legislation: Medicinal products for human use
Available in Spanish (ES), German (DE), English (EN), French (FR) and Italian (IT)
1998 – 312 pp. – 21 x 29.7 cm
ISBN 92-828-2032-7
Cat. No: CO-08-97-856-EN-C
*Price (excluding VAT): € **44.50***

Volume 2A: Notice to applicants. Medicinal products for human use: Procedure for marketing authorisation
Available in English (EN) and French (FR)
1998 – 204 pp. – 21 x 29.7 cm
ISBN 92-828-2060-2

Volume 2B: Notice to applicants. Medicinal products for human use: Presentation and content of the dossier
Available only in English (EN)
1998 – 235 pp. – 21 x 29.7 cm
ISBN 92-828-2061-0
Cat. No: CO-41-97-000-EN-C

*Price (excluding VAT): € **70** (Volumes 2A and 2B are not sold separately.)*

Volume 3A: Guidelines. Medicinal products for human use: Quality and biotechnology
Available only in English (EN)
1998 – 422 pp. – 21 x 29.7 cm
ISBN 92-828-2437-3
Cat. No: CO-54-97-001-EN-C
*Price (excluding VAT): € **60***

Volume 3B: Guidelines. Medicinal products for human use: Safety, environment and information
Available only in English (EN)
1998 – 250 pp. – 21 x 29.7 cm
ISBN 92-828-2438-1
Cat. No: CO-54-97-002-EN-C
*Price (excluding VAT): € **34***

Volume 3C: Guidelines. Medicinal products for human use: Efficacy
Available only in English (EN)
1998 – 410 pp. – 21 x 29.7 cm
ISBN 92-828-2439-X
Cat. No: CO-54-97-003-EN-C

*Price (excluding VAT): € **122** Volumes 3A, 3B and 3C*

Volume 4: Good manufacturing practices. Medicinal products for human and veterinary use
Available in Spanish (ES), German (DE), English (EN) and French (FR)
1998 – 153 pp.
ISBN 92-828-2029-7
Cat. No: CO-08-97-977-EN-C
*Price (excluding VAT): € **22***

Volume 5: Pharmaceutical legislation: Veterinary medicinal products
Available in Spanish (ES), German (DE), English (EN), French (FR) and Italian (IT)
1998 – 300 pp. – 21 x 29.7 cm
ISBN 92-828-2037-8
Cat. No: CO-08-97-864-EN-C
*Price (excluding VAT): € **40***

Volume 6A: Notice to applicants: Veterinary medicinal products, procedures for marketing authorisation
Available only in English (EN) and French (FR)
1998 – 178 pp. – 21 x 29.7 cm
ISBN 92-828-4340-8

Volume 6B: Notice to applicants: Veterinary medicinal products, presentation and contents of the dossier
Available only in English (EN)
1998 – 331 pp. – 21 x 29.7 cm
ISBN 92-828-4341-6
Cat. No: CO-05-98-000-EN-C

*Price (excluding VAT): € **52** (Volumes 6 A and 6 B are not sold separately)*

Volume 7A: Guidelines. Veterinary medicinal products: General, efficacy and environmental risk assessment
Available only in English (EN)
1999 – 331 pp. – 21 x 29.7 cm

ISBN 92-828-5745-X
Cat. No: CO-30-98-001-EN-C

Volume 7B: Guidelines. Veterinary medicinal products: Immunologicals and quality
Available only in English (EN)
1999 – 195 pp. – 21 x 29.7 cm
ISBN 92-828-5746-8
Cat. No: CO-30-98-000-EN-C

*Price (excluding VAT): € **70** (Volumes 7A and 7B are not sold separately)*

European business – Facts and figures: Data 1991–2001

European business – Facts and figures – Data 1991–2001 provides a standard set of information for industrial and service activities within the European Union. The data provided in European business traces the major developments of output, employment and external trade. The commentaries concentrate largely on the 3-digit level of the NACE Rev.1 classification of economic activities. For the first time, European business now includes data on the EU accession countries.
Annual
Available in German (DE), English (EN) and French (FR)
2003 – 434 pp. – 21 x 29.7 cm
ISBN 92-894-5444-X
ISSN 1681-2050
Cat. No: KS-BW-03-001-EN-C
*Price (excluding VAT): € **50***
Theme: 2, 8, 17

CD-ROM version
European business – Facts and figures – Data 1990–2002 (CD-ROM) provides a standard set of information for industrial and service activities within the European Union. The data provided in European business traces the major developments of output, employment and external trade. The commentaries concentrate largely on the 3-digit level of the NACE Rev.1 classification of economic activities. For the first time, European business now includes data on the EU accession countries. The CD-ROM version (Data 1990–2002) of the publication contains all three language versions (EN/FR/DE) of the commentary, tables and figures, and a database containing many additional series, including longer time series and breakdowns by Member State, plus a large amount of background information.
Trilingual edition in German (DE), English (EN) and French (FR)
2003
ISBN 92-894-5726-0
Cat. No: KS-BZ-03-001-3A-Z
*Price per copy (excluding VAT): € **300***

Quarterly panorama of European business statistics

The Quarterly Panorama of European Business is a tool to follow the evolution

of the short-term trends of the European economy as a whole as well as from the perspective of a broad range of individual industrial, construction trade and other service sectors. The split into sectors follows roughly the 2-digit level of detail of the NACE classification. A commentary on the European and Eurozone economy and each sector is accompanied by graphs and tables for a range of economic indicators. The picture is completed by a comparison of the economy with the United States and Japan. A special feature treats a particularly relevant and actual topic in depth.
Edition 2004
Quarterly
Available only in English (EN)
21 x 29.7 cm
Cat. No: KS-DL-04-000-EN-C
Subscription code: VPA000
Price (excluding VAT): € **30**
Annual subscription price (excluding VAT): € **100**
Theme: 17

E-commerce and the Internet in European businesses – Data 2001–2002

This publication reports on the results of the second enterprise survey. The survey was undertaken by all Member States and Norway. The surveys were generally carried out during the first half of 2002. The surveys concentrated on the measurement of e commerce in terms of sales and purchases by enterprises via Internet and other computer mediated networks, as well as looking at the use of key information and communication technologies.
Edition 2003
Available only in English (EN)
2004 – 113 pp. – 21 x 29.7 cm
ISBN 92-894-6219-1
Cat. No: KS-54-03-889-EN-C
Price (excluding VAT): € **20**
Theme: 8, 17

Business in candidate countries – Facts and figures – Data 1995–1999

Business in candidate countries — Facts and figures is the first comprehensive publication on structural business statistics in the candidate countries, providing standardised data on a wide range of economic activities within these countries. Like its counterpart dealing with the EU countries, European business — Facts and figures, this publication provides a wealth of information on the economies, the development patterns and the state of the different economic sectors of the countries covered. These are Bulgaria, Cyprus, the Czech Republic, Estonia, Hungary, Latvia, Lithuania, Poland, Romania, the Slovak Republic and Slovenia. Presenting economic activity, with 20 separate chapters covering the main industries and

services, and an overview of enterprises and country-specific situations, Business in candidate countries — Facts and figures gives the detailed data necessary for an accurate analysis of key business areas in the candidate countries.
Available in German (DE), English (EN) and French (FR)
2002 – 143 pp. – 21 x 29.7 cm
ISBN 92-894-4190-9
Cat. No: KS-45-02-975-EN-C
Price (excluding VAT): € **30**
Theme: 17

European competitiveness report 2003

The present report continues the analysis of productivity developments initiated with the 2001 edition and continued in the 2002 report. The present edition consists of four topics. First, there is a comparison and decomposition of productivity growth in Europe and the USA. Second, recent evidence suggests that the combination of organisational capital with other types of enterprise modernisation measures constitute an essential characteristic of those firms that have experienced robust productivity growth. Third, the report also examines empirically some hypotheses derived from recent developments in economic geography. Fourth, it examines various aspects of the enlargement process and discusses the likely impact of the enlargement on economic structures in a wider Europe.
Annual
Available only in English (EN)
2003 – 190 pp. – 21 x 29.7 cm
ISBN 92-894-6305-3
Cat. No: NB-AK-03-001-EN-C
Price (excluding VAT): € **35**
Theme: 8, 10, 14

Next edition was expected in 2004

EU productivity and competitiveness: an industry perspective – Can Europe resume the catching-up process ?

This report consists of a summary chapter, five chapters making up the main body of the analysis and a chapter describing sources and methods for the underlying industry results. Chapter I begins with a discussion of the overall productivity picture comparing the EU with the US. Chapter II describes industry structure in the EU and US. Chapter III presents the main results on industry productivity performance. Chapter IV examines the argument that cyclical developments affect the comparability of the EU–US comparisons. Chapter V employs company accounts data which allows estimation of the direct effect of RandD on performance at the firm level.
Available only in English (EN)
2003 – 273 pp. – 16.2 x 22.9 cm

ISBN 92-894-6303-1
Cat. No: NB-55-03-035-EN-C
Price (excluding VAT): € **35**
Theme: 3, 8, 10

Glossary of business statistics

This CD-ROM contains the glossary of business statistics of companies. Each version is presented as a collection of files in HTML format.
Trilingual edition in German (DE), English (EN) and French (FR)
2000
ISBN 92-828-6511-8
Cat. No: CA-22-99-927-3A-Z
Price (excluding VAT): € **35**
Theme: 17

Prodcom: List 2001

In accordance with Article 2(2) of Council Regulation 3924/91 (text included in publication), production is to be recorded according to the product headings of the Prodcom list. The current version of Prodcom was completed in September 2000 and is based on the Union's external trade nomenclature [2001 Combined Nomenclature (CN)], which came into force on 1 January 2001.
2000 – 524 pp. – 21 x 29.7 cm
ISBN 92-894-0185-0
ISSN 1606-2485
Cat. No: KS-32-00-928-EN-C
Price (excluding VAT): € **88**
The paper version is only available in English (EN).
Theme: 17

Distributive trades in Europe: Data 1995–99

The distributive trades Panorama publication provides an overview of the importance of the distributive trades sector and its different economic activities (motor trade, wholesale trade and retail trade) in Europe. It contains an analysis of the data on distributive trades delivered in the frame of the regulation on structural business statistics (Council Regulation n°58/97) by the EEA countries. Furthermore special themes are analysed in self-standing thematic chapters (e.g. electronic commerce, internationalization and concentration). A chapter with a triad comparison for distributive trades as well as a large table part and methodological information is added.
Available in German (DE), English (EN) and French (FR)
2002 – 235 pp. – 21 x 29.7 cm
ISBN 92-894-1426-X
Cat. No: KS-AJ-01-001-EN-C
Price (excluding VAT): € **32.50**
Theme: 17

CD-ROM version
Trilingual edition in German (DE), English (EN) and French (FR)
ISBN 92-894-1756-0
Cat. No: KS-AL-01-001-3A-Z
Price (excluding VAT): € **60**

Distributive trades in Europe. Pocketbook: Key indicators
Trilingual edition in German (DE), English (EN) and French (FR)
2001 – 141 pp. – 10.5 x 21 cm
ISBN 92-828-9978-0
Cat. No: KS-AK-01-001-3A-C
Price (excluding VAT): € **10**

External and intra-European Union trade – Statistical yearbook – Data 1958–2002

The yearbook on external and intra-European Union trade sets out to provide data on long-term trends in the trade of the European Union and its Member States. It contains data on the trade flows, broken down by major product group, of the EU with its main trading partners on the one hand and between the Member States on the other. In view of the impending enlargements of the European Union and taking into account the importance of trade by members of the European Free Trade Association (Iceland, Liechtenstein, Norway and Switzerland) with the Union, a description of trade with the candidate countries and the EFTA has been added to that usually given for Member States only.
Edition 2003
Available in German (DE), English (EN) and French (FR)
2003 – 249 pp. – 21 x 29.7 cm
ISBN 92-894-4302-2
ISSN 1606-3481
Cat. No: KS-CV-03-001-EN-C
Price (excluding VAT): € **29.50**
Theme: 2, 17

Enterprises in Europe: Data 1987–97

This publication is divided into several parts, presenting the information gathered by Eurostat. Each part has been designed for easy consultation and rapid reference to the main facts. The reader is presented with detailed information by sector and by country. For further analysis a CD-ROM containing the SME database can be ordered.
Available in German (DE), English (EN) and French (FR)
2001 – 199 pp. – 21 x 29.7 cm
ISBN 92-828-3005-5
ISSN 1681-6137
Cat. No: KS-27-00-815-EN-C
Price (excluding VAT): € **30**
Theme: 17

CD-ROM version
2001 edition
Multilingual edition in German (DE), English (EN) and French (FR)
2001
ISBN 92-894-1099-X
ISSN 1681-5661
Cat. No: KS-AD-01-001-3A-Z
Price (excluding VAT): € **300**

SMEs in Europe – Competitiveness, innovation and the knowledge-driven society

This publication is the first in a series focusing on topics relevant to small and medium-sized enterprises. It contains a wide range of up-to-date information from diverse Eurostat and Commission databases. Inter alia, the publication: deals with the structure, performance and conduct of SMEs in Europe; provides detailed information and a reality-based understanding for needs and evolutions of European enterprises; gives a clear picture of the needs and opportunities of SMEs in Europe. SMEs in Europe is of particular interest to active economic actors but also to anyone wanting to understand and take part in future economic developments.
Available only in English (EN)
2002 – 70 pp. – 21 x 29.7 cm
ISBN 92-894-4252-2
Cat. No: KS-CJ-02-001-EN-C
Price (excluding VAT): € **14.50**
Theme: 17

Services in Europe: 1995–97 data

This report presents a detailed picture of the services sector in Europe. Taken as a whole, Services in Europe essentially provides a comprehensive descriptive analysis of the structure of services activities in the European Union.
Available in German (DE), English (EN) and French (FR)
1999 – 223 pp. – 21 x 29.7 cm
ISBN 92-828-8016-8
ISSN 1606-2337
Cat. No: CA-24-99-736-EN-C
Price (excluding VAT): € **27.50**
Theme: 17

Services in Europe 1999: 1995–1997 data (CD-Rom)
Available in German (DE), English (EN) and French (FR)
1999
Cat. No: CA-24-99-744-3A-Z
Price (excluding VAT): € **100**

Business in Europe: Statistical pocketbook – Data 1995–2002

This publication is a compendium of Eurostat's business statistics — it is intended for the general reader as a showcase for the activities of the Business Statistics Directorate. The vast majority of data is from official sources and is presented according to sectoral themes covering: the business enterprise population, manufacturing, construction, distributive trades, information and communication society and other services. A double-page spread is given over to topics such as industrial specialisation of the EU Member States, slow and fast growth industries within the EU, a breakdown of retail trade by product — who buys what, hotel capacity in the EU and household Internet connection rates.
Second edition
Available only in English (EN)
2003 – 110 pp. – 10.5 x 21 cm
ISBN 92-894-5222-6
Cat. No: KS-DH-03-001-EN-C
Price (excluding VAT): € **10**
Theme: 17

Employment in the market economy in the EU – An analysis of the structural business statistics

The Structural Business Statistics (SBS) represent the most complete source of data on business in the EU which is at present available. The main aim of this publication is to present the SBS data, particularly those which relate to employment, and to show how these data are capable of increasing knowledge and understanding of employment and related issues across the EU.
Available only in English (EN)
2003 – 65 pp. – 21 x 29.7 cm
ISBN 92-894-4832-6
Cat. No: KS-51-03-318-EN-C
Price (excluding VAT): € **20**
Theme: 17

European employment & industrial relations glossary: Finland

Employers, employees and their representatives working at a European level are faced by complex problems of industrial relations, the relevant legislation and the different labour markets in the Member States. The Dublin-based European Foundation for the Improvement of Living and Working Conditions has produced for each Member State a glossary of industrial relations.

There are two series: one in English only and one in the language of each Member State (except France where only the English edition exists).

Further information is available on the EMIRE database (http://www.eurofound.ie/emire/emire.html).
Edition 2003
Available only in English (EN)
2004 – 406 pp.
ISBN 92-827-0217-6
Cat. No: TJ-52-03-263-EN-C
Price (excluding VAT): € **35**
Theme: 4

Statistics on innovation in Europe: Data 1996–97

The second Community innovation survey (CIS2) was launched in the European Economic Area (EEA) Member States in 1997/98 for the reference year 1996. This publication focuses on the main results from this survey giving an overview of the situation of innovation activities within the EEA. The main topics covered are the number of innovating enterprises, innovation activities and expenditures, turnover of new and significantly improved products, the reasons why enterprises are innovative, their sources of information and the barriers the enterprises are facing in their innovation activity. The survey covers the manufacturing sector and subset of service industries.

In the publication the results are broken down by country, activity sector and size-class. A special chapter is devoted to innovation activity according to the level of technology (high-tech sectors and other sectors). The main target group for this publication is policy-makers responsible for strengthening the scientific and technological basis for European businesses, both within the European Commission and in the Member States. Other target groups are economic operators, professional associations, researchers and the general public.
Available in German (DE), English (EN) and French (FR)
2001 – 131 pp. – 21 x 29.7 cm
ISBN 92-894-0173-7
Cat. No: KS-32-00-895-EN-C
Price (excluding VAT): € **35**
Theme: 17

Cinema, TV and Radio in the EU – Statistics on audiovisual services – Data 1980–2002

This publication Cinema, TV and radio in the EU – Statistics on Audiovisual Services – Data 1980 – 2002 is the new renamed edition of the publication Statistics on audiovisual services and is, as before, based on the data collected via the AUVIS questionnaire from EU Member States, candidate countries and EFTA countries (the results of the 2002 enquiry have been taken into consideration). The aim of this publication is to provide a statistical overview of the audiovisual sector, based on the statistical work carried out at Eurostat.
Edition 2003
Available only in English (EN)
2003 – 164 pp. – 21 x 29.7 cm
ISBN 92-894-5709-0
ISSN 1725-4515
Cat. No: KS-BT-03-001-EN-C
Price (excluding VAT): € **17.50**
Theme: 8, 17

Third European survey on working conditions 2000

This report presents the main findings of the third European survey on working conditions. The survey, carried out simultaneously in each of the 15 Member States of the European Union in March 2000, aims to provide an overview of the state of working conditions in the EU, as well as indicating the nature and content of changes affecting the workforce and the quality of work.

2001 edition
Available in German (DE), English (EN) and French (FR)
2001 – XI, 72 pp. – 21 x 29.7 cm
ISBN 92-897-0130-7
Cat. No: TJ-39-01-764-EN-C
Price (excluding VAT): € **25**
Theme: 4

Working conditions in the acceding and candidate countries

This new publication provides the first important benchmark of the situation in all acceding and candidate countries (ACCs) as they moved towards membership of the European Union. Gauging the status on issues ranging from stress in the workplace to types of employment or working hours, the report attempts to portray a realistic picture of the working environment of these countries as they were taking this important step towards an enlarged Europe.
Available in English (EN) and French (FR)
2003 – 119 pp. – 21 x 29.7 cm
ISBN 92-897-0224-9
Cat. No: TJ-54-03-809-EN-C
Price (excluding VAT): € **25**
Theme: 4, 5

Recent trends in employee financial participation in the European Union

This report describes recent developments in financial participation, looking in particular at the reasons for its take-up and its impact on the employment relationship. It presents an overview of recent research into the subject and highlights the success and failure, advantages and disadvantages of various schemes in operation in Member States. Special attention is given to the different types of employee share ownership and their relationship with the three other pillars of employee participation – direct participation, representative participation and participation via collective bargaining.
Available in German (DE), English (EN) and French (FR)
2001 – 124 pp. – 21 x 29.7 cm
ISBN 92-897-0087-4
Cat. No: TJ-37-01-477-EN-C
Price (excluding VAT): € **22**
Theme: 4

Government support programmes for new forms of work organisation

Major changes are taking place in the way in which work is organised within companies: they are based on a new model of 'high skill' and extensive employee involvement in decision-making.

This publication looks at new forms of work organisation, public policy and new forms of work organisation, government programmes, lessons learnt and good

practices. Three annexes include a database of government programmes, case studies and literature review.
Available only in English (EN)
2000 – 87 pp. – 21 x 29.7 cm
ISBN 92-828-9326-X
Cat. No: KE-28-00-672-EN-C
Price (excluding VAT): € **15**
Theme: 4

Legal aspects of standardisation in the Member States of the EC and EFTA

The European Commission and the European Free Trade Association present the results of a study that sets out to contribute to a better understanding of standardisation. Consisting of 18 reports and a comparative analysis, it presents for the first time a comprehensive overview of legal aspects of standardisation in all countries of the European Economic Area.

The study is an invaluable tool for lawyers, authorities, standards bodies and other parties engaged in standardisation.
Cat. No: CO-37-99-000-EN-C (for the 3 volumes)
Theme: 6

Volume 1: Comparative report
Available only in English (EN)
2000 – 289 pp. – 17.6 x 25 cm
ISBN 92-828-8907-6
Cat. No: CO-37-99-001-EN-C
Price (excluding VAT): € **15**

Volume 2: Country reports
Bilingual edition in English (EN) and French (FR)
2000 – 1005 pp. – 17.6 x 25 cm
ISBN 92-828-8908-4
Cat. No: CO-37-99-002-2A-C
Price (excluding VAT): € **35**

Rechtliche Aspekte der Normung in den EG-Mitgliedstaaten und der EFTA – Band 3: Deutschland
Available only in German (DE)
2000 – 598 pp. – 17.6 x 25 cm
ISBN 92-828-8909-2
Cat. No: CO-37-99-003-DE-C
Price (excluding VAT): € **32**

European trends in the development of occupations and qualifications

This reference book is addressed to all those interested in the principal tendencies in the development of occupations and qualifications in the light of demographic, social, economic, technological, ecological and cultural challenges.
Theme: 4

Volume 1
Available in German (DE), English (EN) and French (FR)
1999 – 76 pp. – 21 x 29.7 cm
ISBN 92-828-7192-4
Cat. No: HX-22-99-741-EN-C
Price (excluding VAT): € **8.50**

Volume 2: Findings of research, studies and analyses for policy and practice
Available only in English (EN)
2000 – 364 pp. – 21 x 29.7 cm
ISBN 92-828-7414-1
Cat. No: HX-22-99-749-EN-C
Price (excluding VAT): € 19

Internationalisation and changing skills needs in European small firms – Synthesis report

The creation of a single market in Europe builds on the well grounded belief that the removal of constraints on economic activity between Member States will serve to boost economic prosperity. European businesses, even small ones and those that operate locally, need to understand and even respond to the impact of European Union integration. The survey, whose results are contained in this Cedefop publication, was carried out in seven EU countries and covered a sample of small firms employing fewer than 50 persons from various industries. The countries covered were: Greece, Spain, Ireland, Italy, the Netherlands, Austria and the UK. The analysis attempts to provide answers to crucial questions related to the required competences for small firms' efficient internationalisation and the extent to which such firms do in fact possess them or the types of initiatives that could contribute to an improvement of the situation.
Available in Spanish (ES), English (EN) and French (FR)
2003 – 112 pp. – 17.5 x 25 cm
ISBN 92-896-0101-9
ISSN 1608-7089
Cat. No: TI-41-01-713-EN-C
Price (excluding VAT): € 8.50
Theme: 4, 5, 16

Early identification of skill needs in Europe

In March 2000, at the Lisbon European Council, the European Union committed itself to making Europe 'the most competitive and dynamic knowledge-based economy in the world, capable of sustainable economic growth, better jobs and greater social cohesion'; and outlined the initial targets by launching the eEurope initiative. The e-Europe plans place great weight on education and training. A highly skilled workforce is needed to achieve this commitment. This report offers an overview about European policies, initiatives, strategies and the connection between e-learning and economics. Its purpose is to provide accurate and reliable information on the strengths and potentials of e-learning markets outside traditional education. A great deal of information in this report goes far beyond Europe and has been collected in the United States and other

countries where data have been available. A comparative analysis is made between Europe and other countries, where sufficient and consistent information has been available.
Available only in English (EN)
2003 – VI, 334 pp. – 17.5 x 25 cm
ISBN 92-896-0202-3
ISSN 1608-7089
Cat. No: TI-49-02-353-EN-C
Price (excluding VAT): € 25
Theme: 4, 5, 16

Perspectives for European e-learning businesses – Markets, technologies and strategies

In this report you will find information, supported by charts and graphs, on:
– developments in Europe, the United States and other countries where data are available;
– the most promising segments of the global e-learning market, including K-12, higher education, corporate training, customer training and higher education for non-traditional students;
– strategies for e-learning companies, including the construction of virtual communities around their products and services and criteria for successful e-learning products;
– key technologies including wired and wireless LANs, VPNs, mobile learning, network computers, e-books, artificial intelligence, streaming video, copyright protection, web-based multimedia presentations, CD-ROM-based interactive, collaborative computing tools and simulation software;
– e-learning companies and the products and services they offer, including reviews of many e-learning firms and the content of the courses they provide, as well as enrolment percentages.
Available only in English (EN)
2003 – 207 pp. – 17.5 x 25 cm
ISBN 92-896-0215-5
ISSN 1608-7089
Cat. No: TI-49-03-886-EN-C
Price (excluding VAT): € 25
Theme: 16

Regions: Statistical yearbook 2003

This new edition provides the most recent statistics on the European Union's regions, focusing on the following fields: agriculture, population, regional gross domestic product, the labour force survey, research and development, tourism, and transport and unemployment at regional level.
Edition 2003
Annual
Available in German (DE), English (EN) and French (FR)
2003 – 169 pp. – 21 x 29.7 cm

ISBN 92-894-5366-4
ISSN 1681-9306
Cat. No: KS-AF-03-001-EN-C

Price (excluding VAT): € 60 (Paper and CD-ROM are not sold separately.)
Theme: 17

Next edition was expected in 2004

The Structural Funds in 2001 — Thirteenth annual report

This report is compiled in accordance with Article 45(2) of Regulation (EC) No 1260/1999 laying down general provisions on the Structural Funds. It sets out the work of the Structural Funds and the activities undertaken to coordinate their work with that of the other financial instruments during 2001.
Annual
Available in the 11 official languages of the European Union as at 1 January 2004
2002 – 116 pp. – 21 x 29.7 cm
ISBN 92-894-4642-0
Cat. No: KN-AC-02-001-EN-C
Price (excluding VAT): € 17.50
Theme: 13

Portrait of the regions

Portrait of the regions offers a comparison between the 200 regions of the European Union. Each region is presented with the aid of maps, graphs, tables and commentaries. The descriptions cover territory, the structure and evolution of the population, strengths and weaknesses of the region, intraregional imbalances, lists of regions showing similar characteristics, the economic structure, statistical data on employment and unemployment, labour costs, what is produced in that area and levels of productivity, and the environment. Maps indicate the geographical location of the region and its subdivisions, the main sites of interest and the road and waterway networks.
Available in German (DE), English (EN) and French (FR)
Theme: 17

Volume 1: Germany, Benelux, Denmark
1993 – 291 pp. – 21 x 29.7 cm
ISBN 92-826-3322-9
Cat. No: CA-74-91-001-EN-C
Price (excluding VAT): € 100

Volume 2: France, United Kingdom, Ireland
1993 – 307 pp. – 21 x 29.7 cm
ISBN 92-826-3223-7
Cat. No: CA-74-91-002-EN-C
Price (excluding VAT): € 100

Volume 3: Portugal, Spain, Italy, Greece
1993 – 335 pp. – 21 x 29.7 cm
ISBN 92-826-3224-5
Cat. No: CA-74-91-003-EN-C
Price (excluding VAT): € 100

Volume 4: Austria, Finland, Sweden, Iceland, Liechtenstein, Norway, Switzerland
1996 – 227 pp. – 21 x 29.7 cm
ISBN 92-827-0058-5
Cat. No: CA-85-94-389-EN-C
Price (excluding VAT): € **70**

Volumes 1-4
ISBN 92-827-8735-4
Cat. No: CA-74-95-000-EN-C
Price (excluding VAT): € **300**

Volume 5: Hungary
1996 – 172 pp. – 21 x 29.7 cm
ISBN 92-827-8021-X
Cat. No: CA-95-96-293-EN-C

Price (excluding VAT): € **32** *(This volume is sold individually)*

Portugal
Special edition published for the 1998 Lisbon Expo.
Available as well in Portuguese (PT)
1998 – 120 pp.
ISBN 92-828-2883-2
Cat. No: CA-12-98-110-EN-C
Price (excluding VAT): € **25**

Portrait of the regions

These new volumes of the Portrait of the regions series cover central and eastern Europe. Each volume examines demographic and economic issues, including the labour market, education, resources and the particular strengths and weaknesses of each region. Maps, diagrams and statistical tables back up the written analysis.
Available only in English (EN)
Theme: 17

Volume 6: Czech Republic and Poland
2000 – 207 pp. – 21 x 29.7 cm
ISBN 92-828-4395-5
Cat. No: CA-17-98-281-EN-C
Price (excluding VAT): € **50**

Volume 7: Slovakia
2000 – 40 pp. – 21 x 29.7 cm
ISBN 92-828-4393-9
Cat. No: CA-17-98-273-EN-C
Price (excluding VAT): € **20**

Volume 8: Estonia, Latvia and Lithuania
2000 – 136 pp. – 21 x 29.7 cm
ISBN 92-828-9404-5
Cat. No: KS-29-00-795-EN-C
Price (excluding VAT): € **25**

Volume 9: Slovenia
2000 – 80 pp. – 21 x 29.7 cm
ISBN 92-828-9403-7
Cat. No: KS-29-00-779-EN-C
Price (excluding VAT): € **25**

Volume 10: Bulgaria
2000 – 136 pp. – 21 x 29.7 cm
ISBN 92-828-9405-3
Cat. No: KS-29-00-787-EN-C
Price (excluding VAT): € **45**

Volume 11: Romania
2001 – 138 pp. – 21 x 29.7 cm
ISBN 92-894-1802-8
Cat. No: KS-41-01-034-EN-C
Price (excluding VAT): € **30**

Portrait of the islands

The rich diversity of the European Community encompasses 440 inhabited islands, which make up almost 5 % of its total land mass. Islands, which are host to a national capital and are linked to the mainland by a bridge, are not dealt with in this publication. Portrait of the islands therefore locates and describes all the remaining inhabited islands using maps, statistical indicators and commentary.
Available in German (DE), English (EN) and French (FR)
1994 – 201 pp. – 21 x 29.7 cm
ISBN 92-826-6259-4
Cat. No: CA-75-92-300-EN-C
Price (excluding VAT): € **30**
Theme: 17

Regional and local powers in Europe

This study gives an overview of the powers of local and regional authorities in the Union in areas in which the Committee of the Regions has for the first time been given a consultative role, i.e. education and youth, culture, public health, trans-European networks and regional policy. It emphasises the diversity of local and regional bodies in the European Union, and national or regional differences in the implementation of these policies.
2001 edition
Available in the 11 official languages of the European Union as at 1 January 2004
2002 – 362 pp. – 16 x 23 cm
ISBN 92-895-0016-6
Cat. No: QG-36-01-168-EN-C
Price (excluding VAT): € **35**
Theme: 13

Trans-European cooperation between territorial authorities

This study pinpoints the strengths and weaknesses of trans-European cooperation, attempts to clarify the imprecise terminology often used in this field and proposes concrete measures which would provide a new Europe-wide legal framework for cooperation between regional and local authorities.
Available in the 11 official languages of the European Union as at 1 January 2004
2002 – 222 pp. – 16 x 23 cm
ISBN 92-895-0094-8
Cat. No: QG-42-02-909-EN-C
Price (excluding VAT): € **35**
Theme: 13

The social situation in the European Union — 2003

This report aims at giving a general description of the social situation in Europe on the basis of harmonised information. The publication contains three sections: section one presents an executive summary of the key social and economic developments in Europe, section two provides a more detailed examination of developments in social trends related to health, and section three presents a set of harmonised social indicators for each Member State.
Available in German (DE), English (EN) and French (FR)
2003 – 210 pp. – 21 x 29.7 cm
ISBN 92-894-5263-3
ISSN 1681-1658
Cat. No: KE-AG-03-001-EN-C
Price (excluding VAT): € **25**
Theme: 5, 17

Disability and social participation in Europe

Aiming to respond to information needs on the situation of people with disabilities throughout Europe, this pocketbook contains comparisons on the social situation and participation of three population groups: people with severe disabilities, people with moderate disabilities, people without disabilities, as defined by a 'global disability question' in the European Community household panel (ECHP).
Available only in English (EN)
2001 – 81 pp. – 10.5 x 21 cm
ISBN 92-894-1577-0
Cat. No: KS-AW-01-001-EN-C
Price (excluding VAT): € **7**
Theme: 5

Integrated approaches to active welfare and employment policies

This report presents an analysis of initiatives in all EU-15 Member States that aim to achieve better coordination of employment activation measures. It describes the role of the different agencies and actors involved in the planning, implementation and delivery of services. It shows the approach taken in some countries and localities towards better coordination through a range of new institutions and mechanisms.
Available in English (EN), Spanish (ES), French (FR)
2002 – 120 pp. – 21 x 29.7 cm
ISBN 92-897-0160-9
Cat. No: TJ-43-02-018-EN-C
Price (excluding VAT): € **19**
Theme: 5

The life of women and men in Europe — A statistical portrait — Data 1980–2000

This report describes women and men at different stages of their lives. It begins by covering children and education and

initial training, as well as possible differences between women and men in the age at which they leave the family home and in their lifestyles. It then examines women and men in working life, focusing on their differing career paths, the respective positions they occupy and their abilities – and strategies – for reconciling the pursuit of a working career with family responsibilities. The final analytical part is a review of women and men beyond retirement age, including the income they receive from pensions and other sources, whether or not they are still working, their household circumstances, their health and social relations.
2002 edition
Available in German (DE), English (EN) and French (FR)
2002 – 197 pp. – 21 x 29.7 cm
ISBN 92-894-3568-2
Cat. No: KS-43-02-680-EN-C
Price (excluding VAT): € **30**
Theme: 17

European social statistics — Social protection: Expenditure and receipts 1991–2000

The data presented in this publication cover the 15 Member States of the European Union, Iceland, Norway, Slovakia, Slovenia and Switzerland and generally relate to the years 1991 to 2000.
Annual
Available in German (DE), English (EN) and French (FR)
2003 – 284 pp. – 21 x 29.7 cm
ISBN 92-894-4894-6
ISSN 1681-9365
Cat. No: KS-DC-03-001-EN-C
Price (excluding VAT): € **45**
Theme: 17

New edition was expected in 2004

European social statistics — Income, poverty and social exclusion: 2nd report — Data 1994–1997

This report gives a picture of income poverty and social exclusion in the European Union during the mid-1990s. The publication includes an executive summary and a detailed explanation of the conceptual and methodological framework. There are chapters dealing with income distribution, income poverty and the dynamics of income poverty. Appendices include detailed statistical tables.
2002 edition
Available in German (DE), English (EN) and French (FR)
2003 – 174 pp. – 21 x 29.7 cm
ISBN 92-894-4333-2
Cat. No: KS-BP-02-008-EN-C
Price (excluding VAT): € **28**
Theme: 5, 17

European social statistics — Demography — 2002 edition

Not only does this Eurostat publication present demographic statistics on the European Union and its 15 pre-May 2004 Member States, it also covers the other countries in the European Economic Area and also provides data on Switzerland and central and east European countries, plus Cyprus and Malta.
2002 edition
Available in German (DE), English (EN) and French (FR)
2002 – 171 pp. – 21 x 29.7 cm
ISBN 92-894-4324-3
Cat. No: KS-BP-02-005-EN-C

Price (excluding VAT): € **50** *(Paper version and CD-ROM are not sold separately.)*
Theme: 17

European social statistics — Migration

This publication presents statistics on the main international migration topics collected by Eurostat. The tables in the volume are mainly based on data for 1999 and 2000. One new development since the previous edition is the inclusion of short introductory texts on migration and population change, immigration and emigration, asylum applicants, acquisition of citizenship and population composition (by nationality). The second innovation is the provision of detailed tables in spreadsheet format on CD-ROM.
2002 edition
Available in German (DE), English (EN) and French (FR)
2003 – 73 pp. – 21 x 29.7 cm
ISBN 92-894-4327-8
Cat. No: KS-BP-02-006-EN-C
Price (excluding VAT): € **43**
Theme: 5, 17

European social statistics — Labour market policy — Expenditure and participants — Data 2001

This publication is the result of data collected by Eurostat as part of the 'Labour Market Policy' database project undertaken in collaboration with DG-Employment, all EU Member States and Norway. It is based upon a collection of information from administrative sources, relating to public expenditure and to participants, covering both stocks and flows. It also includes much qualitative information concerning labour market measures, which may be found useful for analysis purposes.
Edition 2003
Available in German (DE), English (EN) and French (FR)
2003 – 144 pp. – 21 x 29.7 cm
ISBN 92-894-6062-8
Cat. No: KS-DO-03-001-EN-C
Price (excluding VAT): € **17.50**
Theme: 4, 5, 17

European social statistics — Labour force survey results 2002 — Data 2002

This publication presents the detailed results of the 2002 (2nd quarter for countries having a quarterly survey or yearly results) Labour Force Survey conducted in the Member States of the European Union in accordance with Council Regulation (EC) No 577/98 and in the following EFTA countries: Iceland, Norway and Switzerland. It contains 4 chapters: Population and households, Employment, Unemployment, Inactivity. At the end of every chapter a table presents the main indicators at NUTS 2 level.
Edition 2003
Available in German (DE), English (EN) and French (FR)
2003 – 227 pp. – 21 x 29.7 cm
ISBN 92-894-5662-0
Cat. No: KS-BP-03-001-EN-C
Price (excluding VAT): € **34**
Theme: 4, 5, 17

European social statistics — Continuing vocational training survey (CVTS2)

This publication provides comparable statistical results on continuing vocational training in enterprises in the fifteen pre-May 2004 Member States of the European Union, Norway and nine Accession Countries (Bulgaria, Czech Republic, Estonia, Hungary, Latvia, Lithuania, Poland – Pomorskie region only, Romania, Slovenia). The source of the data is the second Continuing Vocational Training Survey (CVTS2) that was conducted in 2000/2001. The reference year was 1999. The survey covered enterprises with 10 and more employees in the NACE sections C to K and O. A total of some 76 000 enterprises took part in the survey and provided comparable statistical data on the volume and content of continuing vocational training at work as well as background information on training policy and training management.
2002 edition
Available in German (DE), English (EN) and French (FR)
2002 – 160 pp. – 21 x 29.7 cm
ISBN 92-894-4330-8
Cat. No: KS-BP-02-007-EN-C
Price (excluding VAT): € **25**
Theme: 17

European social statistics — Accidents at work and work-related health problems — Data 1994–2000

This publication presents in detail, for the first time, the large statistical information and data series collected by Eurostat over the period 1994–2000 concerning health and safety at work out-

comes, namely accidents at work and other work-related health problems.
2002 edition
Trilingual edition in German (DE), English (EN) and French (FR)
2003 – 236 pp. – 21 x 29.7 cm
ISBN 92-894-3601-8
Cat. No: KS-BP-02-002-3A-C
Price (excluding VAT): € 34
Theme: 17

Health statistics — Atlas on mortality in the European Union

This atlas describes the situation regarding mortality in the Member States of the European Union. The 1994–96 mortality data in this publication come from the national statistical institutes and the competent government agencies in the 15 pre-May 2004 Member States of the European Union. They are analysed at NUTS 2 level for all the Member States as mortality in the EU Member States is rarely uniform. There can be extreme differences between the regions of a particular country while the regions of other countries may all have very similar mortality rates. The factors which determine the pattern of mortality are intrinsic (age, sex), extrinsic (biological or social collective factors, living or working conditions) and individual (lifestyle, smoking, alcoholism, driving behaviour, sexual behaviour) and are to some extent cultural or economic. These factors lead to specific causes of death, and this publication looks at their frequency and distribution in the various Member States and regions of the European Union. The figures are subjected to a two-tier analysis: (i) general mortality broken down by age group and sex; (ii) the medical causes of death. Additionally, a short publication, in the Statistics in focus series (2/2004 — 'Mortality in the European Union 1997–1999), that updates some main results of the atlas over the period 1997–99 accompanies the publication.
2002 edition
Available in German (DE), English (EN) and French (FR)
2004 – 119 pp. – 21 x 29.7 cm
ISBN 92-894-3727-8
Cat. No: KS-AC-04-000-EN-C
Price (excluding VAT): € 30
Theme: 17

Health statistics — Key data on health 2002 — Data 1970–2001

This second edition of Key Data on Health responds to the growing demand of EU health policy for a comprehensive, consistent and internationally comparable set of health data and indicators, highlighted in a new programme of Community action in the field of public health (2003–2008); this programme was adopted by the European Parliament and the Council on 23 September 2002 in the framework for action in the field of public health. A strong feature of this report is the fact

that Eurostat brings together information on a wide range of health topics from the most relevant data-sources available around the world: New Cronos of Eurostat, Ecosante from OECD, Health for All from WHO, FAO, International Agency for Cancer, Euro HIV, specific epidemiological studies, etc. Information on the Health Status of the population, the main Diseases as well as the statistical description of Health Care systems are at the core of this publication; however, Key Data on Health also addresses the issues of life styles (nutrition, smoking, drinking, physical activity, drug use), mortality (infant, causes of death) and health risks associated with environment, work, leisure and traffic. Key Data on Health covers the 15 pre-May 2004 EU Member States, as well as Iceland, Norway, Liechtenstein and Switzerland. Tables and graphs provide, where possible, data from 1970 onwards disaggregated by gender and age. Eurostat considers this publication to be a first step in the long process of building a comprehensive statistical information system on Health and Safety, within the main body of socio-economic statistics. The objective is to make Key Data on Health a valuable tool for EU health policy planners, the medical community, health economists and researchers, the media and the public at large.
2002 edition
Available in German (DE), English (EN) and French (FR)
2004 – 457 pp. – 21 x 29.7 cm
ISBN 92-894-3730-8
Cat. No: KS-08-02-002-EN-C
Price (excluding VAT): € 45
Theme: 5, 17

Quality in social public services

This report examines the impact of quality improvement initiatives on both services to clients and working conditions. It represents a synthesis of studies from field research in 10 pre-May 2004 EU Member States with supplementary research from the remaining five. It documents and assesses service improvements which aim to meet the needs of client groups who typically have multiple needs. The report focuses in particular on measures for coordinated and integrated service delivery for user empowerment and for quality assurance. It examines how these changes can lead to better quality services, and also looks at the implications for workers. Finally, the report presents recommendations and strategies for the future development of social public services in the EU.
Available in German (DE), English (EN) and French (FR)
2001 – xii, 138 pp. – 21 x 29.7 cm
ISBN 92-897-0066-1
Cat. No: TJ-36-01-378-EN-C
Price (excluding VAT): € 20.50
Theme: 4

Inventory of socioeconomic costs of work accidents

Accidents at work and occupational injuries represent a considerable economic burden to employers, employees and to society as a whole. Some of these costs, like lost workdays or lost income, are clearly visible and can readily be expressed in monetary value. For a large part, however, economic consequences of accidents are somewhat hidden or cannot be priced. Administrative activities following an accident for example may be forgotten, damage to the company image is hard to quantify and pricing suffering and health damage is subject to discussion.
Available only in English (EN)
2002 – 46 pp. – 21 x 29.7 cm
ISBN 92-95007-67-0
Cat. No: TE-37-01-623-EN-S
Price (excluding VAT): € 7
Theme: 4

Evaluation of the state of OSH in the EU — Pilot study

The findings presented in this report are a first measurement with respect to the opinions and experiences of those involved with the state of occupational safety and health in the EU-report 2000–. They represent qualitative opinions and have no statistical signifiance.
Available only in English (EN)
2002 – 94 pp. – 21 x 29.7 cm
ISBN 92-95007-69-7
Cat. No: TE-44-02-634-EN-S
Price (excluding VAT): € 14.50
Theme: 4

Learning about occupational safety and health — Proceedings

This publication covers the proceedings of a seminar oganised in Bilbao (4 and 5 March 2002) by the European Agency for Safety and Health. The aim of the seminar was to provide an EU pespective on integrating – or 'mainstreaming' – occupational safety and health (OSH) into education.
Available only in English (EN)
2002 – 80 pp. – 21 x 29.7 cm
ISBN 92-9191-010-4
Cat. No: TE-46-02-452-EN-S
Price (excluding VAT): € 8.50
Theme: 4

How to convey OSH information effectively: the case of dangerous substances

Within the EU's legislative framework, worker information and consultation about hazardous chemical agents occurring in the workplace, health and safety risks and protective and preventive measures are legal obligations of the employer.

This report describes 19 initiatives addressing the existing information gap. These cases cover not only worker information, but also the management and all the other relevant players at company level, occupational safety and health (OSH) experts, preventive services or worker representatives. Moreover, they also include actions taken by suppliers and their organisations and interventions of third parties such as trade unions, employers' organisations, or authorities. The programmes described range from company to sectoral, regional, national or even supranational level.
Available only in English (EN)
2003 – 157 pp. – 16.2 x 22.9 cm
ISBN 92-9191-044-9
Cat. No: TE-52-03-837-EN-C
Price (excluding VAT): € 25
Theme: 4, 5

Recognition schemes in occupational safety and health

The promotion and exchange of good safety and health practice at the workplace level is one of the key objectives of the European Agency for Safety and Health at Work. A classic way to support the improvement of occupational safety and health (OSH) at the workplace level is to provide employers and other stakeholders with detailed information on 'good practice' on how to implement OSH legislation, and/or provide information on 'best practices' that go even beyond the legislative minimum level of OSH.
Available only in English (EN)
2002 – 81 pp. – 21 x 29.7 cm
ISBN 92-9191-011-2
Cat. No: TE-46-02-872-EN-S
Price (excluding VAT): € 13
Theme: 4

Improving occupational safety and health in SMEs: examples of effective assistance

SMEs are important contributors to European competitiveness, with most new jobs in Europe being created by micro-enterprises with up to six employees. However, they also face particular difficulties, including effective management of safety and health, and Member States have set up measures to assist entrepreneurship. The Agency has carried out several important projects to improve occupational safety and health in SMEs, including special funding schemes of good safety and health practice in SMEs initiated by the European Parliament and the European Commission. As part of these efforts, the Agency has also made a study of practical examples of successful occupational safety and health assistance services to SMEs.
Available only in English (EN)
2003 – 142 pp. – 16.2 x 22.9 cm
ISBN 92-9191-043-0

Cat. No: TE-52-03-829-EN-C
Price (excluding VAT): € 25
Theme: 4, 5

A review and analysis of a selection of OSH systems

This project set out to review and analyse a representative selection of occupational safety and health (OSH) monitoring systems currently used in the European Member States. The first chapter of this report sets the background for the project by reviewing the major developments that have taken place in recent years in the field of OSH monitoring. Subsequent chapters give an overall analysis of the monitoring systems, highlighting interesting elements and pointing out shortcomings in the existing schemes. In addition to the analysis, the report makes suggestions about the content of a possible OSH monitoring system at European level.
Available only in English (EN)
2003 – 61 pp. – 21 x 29.7 cm
ISBN 92-9191-046-5
Cat. No: TE-51-03-932-EN-C
Price (excluding VAT): € 25
Theme: 4, 5

Gender issues in safety and health at work

The Agency for Safety and Health at Work has produced a report examining gender differences in workplace injury and illness, gaps in knowledge and the implications for improving risk prevention. The aim of this report is not only to give an overview of gender differences in safety and health at work and how they arise, but also to provide information about what this means for prevention and how a gender-sensitive approach can be taken in occupational safety and health.
Available only in English (EN)
2003 – 222 pp. – 16.2 x 22.9 cm
ISBN 92-9191-045-7
Cat. No: TE-51-03-786-EN-C
Price (excluding VAT): € 25
Theme: 4, 5

How to tackle psychosocial issues and reduce work-related stress

The 15 cases presented here on tackling psychosocial issues and stress at work, from Member States, give detailed information about the way these approaches were implemented and the experiences gained along the way. They show that these issues can be successfully tackled. The aim of this publication is to stimulate stress prevention at the workplace by providing examples of successful prevention programmes.
Available only in English (EN)
2002 – 127 pp. – 16.2 x 22.9 cm
ISBN 92-9191-009-0
Cat. No: TE-45-02-967-EN-C

Price (excluding VAT): € 23.50
Theme: 4

European Union legal texts on drugs

This CD-ROM, produced in response to the growing interest in drug legislation and policies in Europe, provides the European Union Member States, their EU partners, other institutions, practitioners in the drugs field and the general public with a practical overview of Community strategies and policies on drug and related legislation passed since the late 1980s.
Available only in English (EN)
1999
ISBN 92-828-2641-4
Cat. No: AO-06-97-723-EN-Z
Price (excluding VAT): € 70
Theme: 6

Scientific monograph series

The series aims to ensure greater visibility for the European Monitoring Centre for Drugs and Drugs Addiction Agency as a scientific authority in the drugs field. Topics cover a wide range of issues, from science, policy, theory and methods to practical cases and facts and are aimed at specialists and practitioners in the drugs field, including scientists and academics (primary target), policy-makers and their advisers.
ISSN 1606-1691
Theme: 15

Estimating the prevalence of problem drug use in Europe
Available in English (EN) and French (FR)
1998 – 271 pp. – 16 x 24 cm
ISBN 92-9168-006-0
Cat. No: AO-06-97-763-EN-C
Price (excluding VAT): € 28

Evaluating drug prevention in the European Union
Available only in English (EN)
1999 – 144 pp. – 16 x 24 cm
ISBN 92-9168-050-8
Cat. No: AO-11-98-964-EN-C
Price (excluding VAT): € 17.50

Evaluating the treatment of drug abuse in the European Union
Available only in English (EN)
1999 – 136 pp. – 16 x 24 cm
ISBN 92-9168-051-6
Cat. No: AO-14-98-590-EN-C
Price (excluding VAT): € 16.50

Understanding and responding to drug use: The role of qualitative research
Available only in English (EN)
2000 – 350 pp. – 16 x 24 cm
ISBN 92-9168-088-5
Cat. No: AO-24-99-776-EN-C
Price (excluding VAT): € 18

Evaluation: A key tool for improving drug prevention
Available only in English (EN)
2000 – 184 pp. – 16 x 24 cm
ISBN 92-9168-105-9
Cat. No: TD-28-00-656-EN-C
Price (excluding VAT): € 16.50

Modelling drug use: Methods to quantify and understand hidden processes
Available only in English (EN)
2001 – 245 pp. – 16 x 24 cm
ISBN 92-9168-056-7
Cat. No: AO-18-98-655-EN-C
Price (excluding VAT): € 18

Insights

The EMCDDA's 'Insights' publications are thematic volumes conveying the findings of studies and research carried out by the Agency on topical issues in the drugs field. They are designed to meet the needs of policy-makers and their advisers, specialists and practitioners in the drugs field.
Available only in English (EN)
ISSN 1606-1683
Theme: 5

No 1. New trends in synthetic drugs in the European Union: Epidemiology and demand-reduction responses
1998 – 140 pp. – 21 x 14.8 cm
ISBN 92-9168-030-3
Cat. No: AO-10-97-219-EN-C
Price (excluding VAT): € 20.50

No 2. Outreach work among drug users in Europe: Concepts, practice and terminology
1999 – 196 pp. – 21 x 14.8 cm
ISBN 92-9168-062-1
Cat. No: AO-21-99-666-EN-C
Price (excluding VAT): € 28

No 3. Reviewing current practice in drug-substitution treatment in the European Union
2000 – 196 pp. – 21 x 14.8 cm
ISBN 92-9168-104-0
Cat. No: AO-25-99-374-EN-C
Price (excluding VAT): € 28

No 4. Injecting drug use, risk behaviour and qualitative research in the time of AIDS
2001 – 126 pp. – 14.8 x 21 cm
ISBN 92-9168-110-5
Cat. No: TD-34-01-964-EN-C
Price (excluding VAT): € 21

No 5. Prosecution of drug users in Europe
2002 – 378 pp. – 14.8 x 21 cm
ISBN 92-9168-124-5
Cat. No: TD-40-01-359-EN-C
Price (excluding VAT): € 28

European Energy and Transport — Trends to 2030

Expanding on the issues raised in the Annual Energy Review this detailed publication looks at long term energy and transport developments for the European Union post 2004. It states that an integrated approach encompassing both supply and demand of transport and energy resources will be necessary for Europewide sustainable development. Increases in demand will surely have detrimental effects on the environment.

The findings conclude that a structured commitment to the environment is required, and that this policy for reform will even result in lower prices for customers.
Available only in English (EN)
2003 – 220 pp. – 21 x 29.7 cm
ISBN 92-894-4444-4
ISSN 1683-142X
Cat. No: KO-AC-02-001-EN-C
Price (excluding VAT): € 45
Theme: 12

World energy, technology and climate policy outlook — WETO

This publication shows the world energy, technology and climate policy outlook (WETO) positions in Europe in a global context. It provides a coherent framework to analyse the energy, technology and environment trends and issues over the period now to 2030. In this way, it supports long-term European policymaking, particularly considering the questions related to (i) the security of energy supply; (ii) the European research area; (iii) Kyoto targets and beyond.
2002 edition
Available only in English (EN)
2003 – VI, 137 pp. – 21 x 29.7 cm
ISBN 92-894-4186-0
Cat. No: KI-NA-20-366-EN-C
Price (excluding VAT): € 20
Theme: 12

Energy, transport and environment indicators — Data 1990–2000

This edition is the first to combine facts and figures from the energy, transport and environment sectors in a single volume. The purpose of the publication is to provide an overview of the most relevant indicators on energy, transport and the environment, with particular focus on sustainable development. It presents data for the EU pre-May 2004 Member States as well as for the 13 candidate countries and the EFTA countries.
Edition 2003
Available only in English (EN)
2003 – 183 pp. – 10.5 x 21 cm
ISBN 92-894-5396-6
ISSN 1725-4566
Cat. No: KS-DK-03-001-EN-C

Price (excluding VAT): € 13
Theme: 7, 12, 17

Energy efficiency indicators

This publication contains the priority energy efficiency indicators by sector – macro, households, services, industry, transport and transformation for EU-15, the Member States and Norway. It responds to the Commission's communication COM(2000)247 (action plan to improve energy efficiency in the European Community) to the Council, the European Parliament, the Economic and Social Committee and the Committee of the Regions, where the European Commission invites Eurostat and the Member States to work closely together on the development of energy efficiency indicators.
2002 edition
Available only in English (EN)
2003 – 59 pp. – 21 x 29.7 cm
ISBN 92-894-4886-5
Cat. No: KS-49-02-789-EN-C
Price (excluding VAT): € 20
Theme: 12

Renewable energy sources statistics in the EU, Iceland and Norway — Data 1989–2000

The aim of this publication is to give an overview of the evolution of the contribution of renewable energy sources in the European Union from 1989 to 2000, the period during which surveys and studies were carried out in the Member States on behalf of Eurostat, co-financed by Altener.
Available only in English (EN)
2002 – 80 pp. – 10.5 x 21 cm
ISBN 92-894-4251-4
Cat. No: KS-46-02-080-EN-C
Price (excluding VAT): € 10
Theme: 17

Energy prices Data 1990 – 2002

Eurostat collects and publishes a wide range of information on energy prices in the Member States. The aim of this statistical document is to summarise as succinctly as possible the recent price information for all the principal energy sources. It is therefore deliberately confined to trends up to the date at which information for all these energy sources is available. More recent prices for particular sources can be found in the specialist press and notably in the Commission's weekly Oil Bulletin
Edition 2003
Trilingual edition in German (DE), English (EN) and French (FR)
2003 – 163 pp. – 21 x 29.7 cm
ISBN 92-894-4887-3
ISSN 1609-4158
Cat. No: KS-AB-03-001-3A-C
Price (excluding VAT): € 26.50
Theme: 17

Energy: Yearly statistics — Data 2001

This statistical document groups in a single publication an extensive volume of statistical information relating to the energy economy of the Community and the Member States, particularly for the most recent year available. The first chapter covers the characteristic data of energy economics in recent years. The second chapter gives an overall view of the trends for the principal aggregates, taken from the 'energy supplied' balance-sheets of the Community in tonnes of oil equivalent. The third chapter gives historical series for each energy source for the principal aggregates characterising the structure of energy economics.
Edition 2003
Trilingual edition in German (DE), English (EN) and French (FR)
2003 – 231 pp. – 21 x 29.7 cm
ISBN 92-894-6042-3
ISSN 1609-4190
Cat. No: KS-CN-03-001-3A-C
Price (excluding VAT): € 20
Theme: 17

Electricity prices — Data 1990–2003

In addition to providing electricity prices in national currencies/100 kWh with updating for January 2003 for five domestic and nine industrial consumers in over 30 locations within the European Union, the study also contains comparative tables expressed in ECU or euro/100 kWh and PPS/100 kWh and the 'marker prices'. The years 1990, 1995 and 1999 to 2003 are shown.
Edition 2003
Trilingual edition in German (DE), English (EN) and French (FR)
2003 – 220 pp. – 21 x 29.7 cm
ISBN 92-894-6222-1
ISSN 1725-1648
Cat. No: KS-CO-03-001-3A-C
Price (excluding VAT): € 37
Theme: 12, 17

Electricity prices — Price systems 2001

Eurostat collects and publishes a wide range of information on energy prices in the Member States. The aim of this publication is to summarize, every two years, as succintly as possible the information about the price systems in force in the European Union, according to the Directive on the transparency of gas and electricity prices charged to the end-user. Data on prices can be found in specific publications such as the semestrial 'Statistics in focus' and the annual 'Electricity prices' publication.
Trilingual edition in German (DE), English (EN) and French (FR)
2002 – 104 pp. – 21 x 29.7 cm
ISBN 92-894-4335-9

ISSN 1609-414X
Cat. No: KS-46-02-056-3A-C
Price (excluding VAT): € 17.50
Theme: 17

Competition indicators in the electricity market: EU, Norway and candidate countries — Data 1999–2001

This publication provides basic quantitative information on the electricity markets of the European Union Member States and Norway from 1999 to 2001. It is particularly focused to show the results of a questionnaire-based data collection to monitor competition in the electricity market as a result of the ongoing liberalisation process. In addition, following the enlargement process, data from the candidate countries for the same period have been added to this publication, especially focused on the structure of their electricity markets.
Edition 2003
Available only in English (EN)
2003 – 122 pp. – 21 x 29.7 cm
ISBN 92-894-5771-6
Cat. No: KS-53-03-403-EN-C
Price (excluding VAT): € 17
Theme: 12, 17

Gas prices — Data 1990–2003

In addition to providing gas prices in national currencies/GJ for a wide range of both domestic and industrial consumers in over 30 locations within the EU, the study also contains comparative tables expressed in ECU or euro/GJ and PP/GJ. The years 1990, 1995 and 1999 to 2003 are shown.
Edition 2003
Trilingual edition in German (DE), English (EN) and French (FR)
2003 – 221 pp. – 21 x 29.7 cm
ISBN 92-894-6229-9
ISSN 1609-4182
Cat. No: KS-CP-03-001-3A-C
Price (excluding VAT): € 37
Theme: 12, 17

Gas prices — Price systems 2001

EUROSTAT collects and publishes a wide range of information on energy prices in the Member States. The aim of this publication is to summarize, every two years, as succintly as possible the information about the price systems in force in the European Union, according to the Directive on the transparency of gas and electricity prices charged to the end-user. Data on prices can be found in specific publications such as the semestrial 'Statistics in focus' and the annual 'Gas prices' publication.
Trilingual edition in German (DE), English (EN) and French (FR)
2002 – 76 pp. – 21 x 29.7 cm
ISBN 92-894-4336-7

ISSN 1609-4174
Cat. No: KS-46-02-064-3A-C
Price (excluding VAT): € 14.50
Theme: 17

ECSC investments — Investment in the Community coal and steel industries — Report on the 2001 survey

This report has been prepared on the basis of the results of the 2001 survey of investments in the Community coal and steel industries. The survey, which is conducted annually, collects information on actual and forecast capital expenditure and production potential of coal and steel enterprises.
Annual
Trilingual edition in German (DE), English (EN) and French (FR)
2002 – 126 pp. – 21 x 29.7 cm
ISBN 92-894-4456-8
ISSN 1680-3469
Cat. No: KC-AG-02-001-3A-C
Price (excluding VAT): € 25
Theme: 10

Environment statistics: Yearbook 2001

This yearbook on CD-ROM presents the best available data on the main pressures on the environment in such areas as air emissions, water use, waste production or land use, and on responses such as water treatment. waste management. and more generally, environmental expenditures. It includes also data on other policy fields such as agriculture, transport and energy, to the extent that it is relevant for environmental policy. Data are available either through user-friendly html-pages or through a database system with download facilities. System Requirements: PC Pentium 233 MHz; 32 Mb RAM; CD-ROM, 4X; Windows NT, 2000, 95 or 98; Netscape 4.X (or higher) or Internet Explorer 4.X (or higher).
Trilingual edition in German (DE), English (EN) and French (FR)
2001
ISBN 92-894-1823-0
ISSN 1681-2077
Cat. No: KS-40-01-658-3A-Z
Price (excluding VAT): € 180
Theme: 17

Environment statistics. Pocketbook 2001: Data 1980-99
This booklet summarises the most important figures collected or calculated by Eurostat in the field of environment statistics. It explains the figures by giving background information on related environmental problems, and by indicating the most important political objectives. Eurostat's statistics on environment concern the link between environment and economy. This booklet gives information on the pressure of the economy on the environment, such as the emissions of various

pollutants, the consumption of natural resources, and the production of waste.
Available in English (EN) with summary and table of contents in German (DE) and French (FR)
2001 – 80 pp. – 10.5 x 21 cm
ISBN 92-894-1860-5
Cat. No: KS-41-01-074-EN-C
Price (excluding VAT): € 10

Europe's environment: the third assessment

This 341-page report, Europe's environment: the third assesment, is the most comprehensive overview currently available on the state of the environment on this continent. It covers, for the first time, the whole of the Russian Federation and central Asia. The report also analyses how the main economic driving forces put pressure on the European environment and identifies other key areas where further action is needed.
Third edition
Available only in English (EN)
2003 – 341 pp. – 21 x 29.7 cm
ISBN 92-9167-574-1
Cat. No: TH-51-03-681-EN-C
Price (excluding VAT): € 30
Theme: 14

Environmental pressure indicators for the EU

This second edition of 'Environmental pressure indicators for the EU' sets out the available data in a number (48) of indicators covering the most important human pressures on the environment, showing trends and, as far as possible, a breakdown of the contribution which the different sectors of the economy make to these pressures. The principal goal of this publication is to give a comprehensive description of the most important human activities that have a negative impact on the environment, such as emissions of pollutants, waste production, land use and noise.
Available only in English (EN)
2001 – 161 pp. – 21 x 29.7 cm
ISBN 92-894-0955-X
Cat. No: KS-36-01-677-EN-C
Price (excluding VAT): € 36
Theme: 17

Measuring progress towards a more sustainable Europe. Proposed indicators for sustainable development: Data 1980–99

This publication comprises 63 indicator sheets with tables and graphs designed to provide the reader with as much complementary information as possible on the social, environmental and economic dimensions of a more sustainable Europe. A brief report on the experiences and ongoing programmes of the Member States – Austria, Belgium, Finland,

France and Germany – which took part in the UN testing phase is also included. Additional information on current projects for sustainable development at international level can also be found.
Available only in English (EN)
2001 – 167 pp. – 21 x 29.7 cm
ISBN 92-894-1101-5
Cat. No: KS-37-01-203-EN-C
Price (excluding VAT): € 35
Theme: 17

Environmentally sound transport planning in Europe

The aim of this publication is to contribute to the debate on tourism, transport and sustainable development in Europe. It identifies good practices in the tourist regions of Principado de Asturias (Spain), Dresden/Oberes Elbtal (Germany) and the eastern Alps (Austria) in the field of environmentally sound regional transport planning, in order to disseminate these practices to other European regions experiencing similar problems caused by excessive tourist traffic on their roads.
2002 edition
Available in the 11 official languages of the European Union as at 1 January 2004
2002 – 203 pp. – 16 x 23 cm
ISBN 92-895-0083-2
Cat. No: QG-42-02-901-EN-C
Price (excluding VAT): € 20
Theme: 7, 14

Panorama of transport — Statistical overview of transport in the European Union — Data 1970–2000

This publication sets out to describe, via annual statistics, the most important features of transport in the European Union. This third edition covers, for the first time, all main modes of transport as it also includes maritime transport, a domain in which intra-EU trade has experienced spectacular development.
2002 edition
Available in German (DE), English (EN) and French (FR)
2003 – 104 pp. – 21 x 29.7 cm
ISBN 92-894-4845-8
ISSN 1725-275X
Cat. No: KS-DA-02-001-EN-C
Price (excluding VAT): € 25
Theme: 7, 17

Everything on transport statistics — Data 1970–2001

This DVD is a repository of all public documents and data related to transport statistics in Europe and main partner countries. It contains about 20 million statistical data and more than 850 documents, mostly produced by Eurostat's transport unit. Some documents related to transport statistics are also issued from other units of Eurostat (environment, business statistics, regional data,

etc.) or from other DGs of the European Commission, such as the Directorate-General for Energy and Transport. This work relies on the European statistical system, which for transport statistics is mainly represented by the statistical Institutes and the ministries of transport of the European Union Member States plus Norway and Switzerland. This second edition gives access to many new data, publications and legal acts related to transport statistics, in particular in the fields of aviation, maritime and road transport. Much more information related to candidate or Mediterranean countries can also be found.
Edition 2003
Trilingual edition in German (DE), English (EN) and French (FR)
2003
ISBN 92-894-6002-4
ISSN 1725-3136
Cat. No: KS-53-03-944-3A-Z
Price (excluding VAT): € 700
Theme: 7, 17

Transport in the Euro-Mediterranean region — Data 1990–2001

This publication attempts to respond to data needs by providing an updated statistical overview of transport for the 12 Mediterranean partners (Algeria, Cyprus, Egypt, Israel, Jordan, Lebanon, Malta, Morocco, Palestinian Authority, Syria, Tunisia and Turkey).
Edition 2003
Available in English (EN) and French (FR)
2003 – 93 pp. – 21 x 29.7 cm
ISBN 92-894-4606-4
Cat. No: KS-CY-02-001-EN-C
Price (excluding VAT): € 15
Theme: 7, 17

Transport by air — National and international intra- and extra-EU — Data 1993–2001

This CD-ROM presents air passenger and freight figures derived from a voluntary transmission to Eurostat of data by the Member States of the European Union and Norway and Switzerland. The periodicity of the data is in most cases annual. Nevertheless, some quarterly and even monthly data can also be found. Apart from these data, several documents of interest for aviation statistics, in Acrobat PDF format, are also available on the CD-ROM, such as historical publications, legal acts, glossaries and the Energy and Transport DG White Paper. It contains about 5 million statistical data and hundreds of documents or publications mainly available in three languages (German, English and French). It also contains some publications related to transport but issued by other Eurostat units (environment, business, regional data, etc...) and some

publications issued by the European Commission, in particular by the Directorate-General Energy and Transport.
Edition 2003
Trilingual edition in German (DE), English (EN) and French (FR)
2004
ISBN 92-894-6278-7
ISSN 1725-146X
Cat. No: KS-DG-03-001-3A-Z
Price (excluding VAT): € 60
Theme: 7, 17

Paving the way for EU enlargement — Indicators of transport and environment integration

This third report developed under the EU's transport and environment reporting mechanism (TERM) is the first to include the accession countries (ACs). This comparative analysis of the EU and the ACs should contribute to the continuing debate on how to achieve more sustainable transport within an enlarged EU.
Available only in English (EN)
2002 – 64 pp. – 21 x 29.7 cm
ISBN 92-9167-517-2
ISSN 1725-2172
Cat. No: TH-AJ-02-001-EN-C
Price (excluding VAT): € 15
Theme: 7, 14

Environmental statistics in the Mediterranean countries — Compendium 2002

This publication presents the data and the meta-data collected within the twelve Mediterranean countries in the framework of the MEDSTAT-Environment project. It contains, on the one hand, a whole set of general indicators and, on the other hand, more specific indicators concerning soils, forests, water, biodiversity, atmospheric pollution and production and treatment of solid wastes. Certain tables are presented in a way which helps the comparison at a regional level, while other tables illustrate a historical evolution at a national level. Regardless of the country and the indicator, data from 1960 to 2000 appear in these tables.
2002 edition
Available in English (EN), French (FR)
2003 – 136 pp. – 21 x 29.7 cm
ISBN 92-894-4860-1
Cat. No: KS-49-02-628-EN-C
Price (excluding VAT): € 30
Theme: 17

The use of plant protection products in the EU — Data 1992 – 1999

This report presents an update of the publication of 2000 Plant Protection in the EU, consumption of plant protection products in the EU. It provides statistical information on plant protection products (PPPs), broken down by Member State, treated crops and chemical classes and, when confidentiality rules allow, on the level of active ingredient.
Available only in English (EN)
2003 – 130 pp. – 21 x 29.7 cm
ISBN 92-894-4818-0
Cat. No: KS-49-02-830-EN-C
Price (excluding VAT): € 25
Theme: 3, 14, 17

Agriculture and the environment in the EU accession countries — Implications of applying the EU common agricultural policy

Agriculture is very important for the environment in the 13 EU accession countries (pre-May 2004). Large areas of farmland of high nature value are present, but at the same time farming may cause serious pollution and environmental stress. Most of these countries are also remarkable for the extent to which policies and socio-economic conditions have changed in recent decades. EU entry will bring further policy changes.

The structure of the report follows key policy questions that provide an insight into the relationship between agriculture and environment in the accession countries.
Available only in English (EN)
2004 – 56 pp. – 21 x 29.7 cm
ISBN 92-9167-637-3
Cat. No: TH-57-04-936-EN-C
Price (excluding VAT): € 15
Theme: 14

Environmental protection expenditure in Europe 2001

Environmental protection is now being integrated into all policy fields with the general aim of ensuring sustainable development. 'Environmental protection expenditure in Europe' includes statistics on the money spent to protect the environment, any associated revenues or cost-savings, and information about the financing of environmental protection activities (subsidies, payments for services). The publication further contains indicators of the response of society to reduce pollution. The data is the basis for analysis of the 'polluter pays' principle, for the effects on enterprise competitiveness, for cost-effective analysis of proposed new regulations and policies, and for estimates of the size of the environmental goods and services industry. Spending on environmental protection occurs in all sectors of the economy: the public sector, industry, other businesses (including enterprises which specialise in waste and wastewater treatment) and households.

Available only in English (EN)
2001 – 238 pp. – 21 x 29.7 cm
ISBN 92-894-1522-3
Cat. No: KS-39-01-320-EN-C
Price (excluding VAT): € 35.50
Theme: 17

Waste generated and treated in Europe — Data 1990–2001

The purpose of this publication is to offer a set of official European statistics on waste, which are relevant for Community action on the environment, providing the basic data required for the assessment of the environmental impact of waste generation and management. After an introductory section describing the general framework of the report, the statistical source and the methodology applied, results are presented in Sections 2 to 6. Annexed tables include time series for western Europe, east European candidate countries and Malta and Cyprus.
Edition 2003
Available only in English (EN)
2003 – 140 pp. – 21 x 29.7 cm
ISBN 92-894-6355-4
Cat. No: KS-55-03-471-EN-C
Price (excluding VAT): € 20
Theme: 14, 17

Mapping the impacts of recent natural disasters and technological accidents in Europe

This is the first EEA publication to address the impacts of different natural disasters and technological accidents across Europe. Focusing on major events over the past five years, the report adds value to existing studies by bringing together available information on their human and economic costs and adding the environmental perspective. The report provides to the readers a large number of maps, illustrations and case studies to document the impacts of these events in a highly accessible way.
Available only in English (EN)
2004 – 54 pp. – 21 x 29.7 cm
ISBN 92-9167-630-6
Cat. No: TH-55-03-229-EN-C
Price (excluding VAT): € 17.50
Theme: 14

Natlan: Nature/land cover information package

This CD-ROM is an information package designed for distributing information, data and applications on land cover and nature in a comprehensive and easy-to-use way for a wide range of users.
Available only in English (EN)
2000
ISBN 92-9167-297-1
Cat. No: GH-27-99-087-EN-Z
Price (excluding VAT): € 50
Theme: 14

EC-sponsored research on safety of genetically modified organisms

Recent decades have seen massive growth in our knowledge in life sciences. This presents many new opportunities for applications, some of them raising issues for public policy and/or public interest and concern. European Community policy since the start of its framework programmes for research and technological development has been to accompany life sciences research with research on safety aspects of the new technology generated.

Of particular importance in this context is the use of genetically modified organisms (GMO) outside contained facilities.

Available only in English (EN)
2001 – 246 pp. – 17.5 x 24.5 cm
ISBN 92-894-1527-4
Cat. No: KI-NA-19-884-EN-C
Price (excluding VAT): € 37
Theme: 15

European guidelines for quality assurance in mammography screening

These European guidelines are based upon experience gained through the national screening programmes; the Europe against Cancer-funded European network for breast cancer screening and EUREF. Topics covered include quality assurance guidelines in mammography screening, radiography and radiology. This third edition also includes a summary table of key indicators and annexes reflecting current status and activity.

Third edition
Available only in English (EN)
2001 – 366 pp. – 21 x 29.7 cm
ISBN 92-894-1145-7
Cat. No: ND-36-01-540-EN-C
Price (excluding VAT): € 15
Theme: 5

European network on HIV/AIDS and hepatitis prevention in prisons

This publication gives an overview of the network activities in 1998/99 and the current situation regarding HIV/AIDS and hepatitis in European prisons.

Available only in English (EN)
2001 – VIII, 251 pp. – 21 x 29.7 cm
ISBN 92-894-0926-6
Cat. No: ND-31-00-877-EN-C
Price (excluding VAT): € 10
Theme: 5

Statistics on the information society in Europe — Data 1996–2002

This is the second edition of Statistics on the information society in Europe. It aimes to provide detailed information on the information society in the European economic area, Switzerland and the candidate countries. This publication uses data from the recent pilot enterprise survey on e-commerce. It uses, for the first time, data from the information society questionnaire which is a collection of data provided by Member States and candidate countries on a voluntary but less harmonised basis. The publication also brings together extracts from several general Eurostat data sources in so far as they concern information and communication technologies, notably structural business statistics, external trade and the labour force survey. A number of other sources covering specific issues complete the picture.

Edition 2003
Available only in English (EN)
2004 – 103 pp. – 21 x 29.7 cm
ISBN 92-894-5888-7
Cat. No: KS-DP-03-001-EN-C
Price (excluding VAT): € 17
Theme: 8, 17

Information society statistics — Data 1997–2002

This is the third edition of the statistical pocketbook on the information society. It aims to provide a statistical overview of key data on the information society in the European Union and in other European countries. The publication presents aggregated figures of the extent to which information and communications technologies (ICT) have impacted on the business sector and individuals. It now also includes data on candidate countries.

Edition 2003
Available only in English (EN)
2003 – VI, 106 pp.
ISBN 92-894-6429-1
Cat. No: KS-56-03-093-EN-C
Price (excluding VAT): € 10
Theme: 8, 17

Third European report on science and technology indicators — 2003

The Third European report on science and technology indicators presents a quantitative picture of where the European Union stands in relation to research and innovation at the start of the 21st century. With more than 450 pages of graphs, tables and comparative analyses, the report relates current trends in European S & T to recent policy developments at EU level and in the Member States and compares the European Union's performance with that of its main partners. The primary focus of the report is on Europe's transition to the knowledge-based economy.

Third edition
Available only in English (EN)
2003 – XVII, 451 pp. – 21 x 29.7 cm
ISBN 92-894-1795-1
Cat. No: KI-NA-20-025-EN-C
Price (excluding VAT): € 77
Theme: 15

Statistics on science and technology — Data 1991–2001

This publication, intended for both generalists and specialists, is organised as follows. Part I presents an analysis of the recent trends in research and development and patenting. In Part II, the accompanying methodological information is provided in some detail for more specialist users. Part III presents tables containing both original data and derived indicators, providing users with the opportunity to conduct their own analyses on the research and development situation in Europe and beyond.

Edition 2003
Trilingual edition in German (DE), English (EN) and French (FR)
2003 – 180 pp. – 21 x 29.7 cm
ISBN 92-894-4446-0
ISSN 1725-1583
Cat. No: KS-CT-02-001-EN-C
Price (excluding VAT): € 29.50
Theme: 15, 17

Statistics on science and technology — Data 1980–2002

The CD-ROM 'Statistics on science and technology' contains the most updated data at Eurostat in the fields of government budget appropriations or outlays for R & D (GBAORD), R1D expenditure and personnel, human resources in science and technology (HRST) and employment in high tech (EHT). Data are available for the Member States of the EU, Iceland, Norway and other countries, such as Japan or the US at national level. HRST and EHT data are also available for the candidate countries. The time-series covered goes from 1980 to 2002, with differences depending on the indicator. These data are compiled from official national sources and the Community labour force survey (CLFS) and, in general, they use internationally agreed concepts and definitions as recommended in the 'Frascati family' of manuals ('Frascati manual', 'Patent manual' and 'Canberra manual') and Eurostat's 'Regional manual'.

Edition 2003
Trilingual edition in German (DE), English (EN) and French (FR)
2004
ISBN 92-894-6216-7
Cat. No: KS-CG-03-001-3A-Z
Price (excluding VAT): € 140

Science and technology in Europe — Statistical pocketbook — Data 1991–2001

This second edition presents the key indicators describing science and technology in Europe and its main competitors. The publication contains a selection of tables and figures in the fields of government budget appropriations or outlays on research and development (GBAORD); research and development expenditure

and personnel, patents, innovation, high-tech trade, and human resources in science and technology (HRST); and employment in high-technology and knowledge-intensive sectors. The data focus is on the 15 EU pre-May 2004 Member States. However, so as to allow for international comparisons, data for Iceland, Japan, Norway and the USA are also considered when available.
Edition 2003
Available only in English (EN)
2003 – 84 pp. – 10.5 x 21 cm
ISBN 92-894-5807-0
ISSN 1725-5821
Cat. No: KS-43-03-500-EN-C
Price (excluding VAT): € 10
Theme: 15, 17

Statistics on science and technology in Europe — data 1991–2002

This edition of 'Statistics on Science and technology in Europe' presents key data and indicators describing science and technology developments in Europe, also compared to other areas of the world. It contains chapters on government appropriations or outlays on R&D (GBAORD), R & D expenditure and personnel, patents, high-tech trade, human resources in science and technology and on other indicators related to high tech and knowledge intensive sectors.
Edition 2003
Available only in English (EN)
2004 – 173 pp. – 21 x 29.7 cm
ISBN 92-894-6823-8
Cat. No: KS-57-03-104-EN-C
Price (excluding VAT): € 35
Theme: 15, 17

Key data on education in Europe — 2002

The fifth edition of Key Data on Education in Europe provides an exceptionally wide-ranging overview of the functioning of education systems and the participation of young people at all levels of education in 30 European countries (the 15 pre-May 2004 Member States of the European Union, the three EFTA/EEA countries and 12 candidate countries).

It contains 145 indicators. Besides the wide variety of information contained in five chapters structured by level of education, the report also adopts a subject-oriented approach in three chapters devoted to such important issues as the teaching of foreign languages, teaching staff and the financing of education.
Fifth edition
Available in Spanish (ES), German (DE), English (EN) and French (FR), Greek (EL)
2002 – 298 pp. – 21 x 29.7 cm
ISBN 92-894-4635-8
ISSN 1725-1621
Cat. No: NC-AF-02-001-EN-C
Price (excluding VAT): € 18
Theme: 16

Training in Europe: Second report on vocational training research in Europe 2000

The second research report, published by Cedefop (European Centre for the Development of Vocational Training) in 2001, covers six main fields: VET (vocational and training) systems, coordination with the labour market and steering; lifelong learning; training and employment from a company perspective; employment, economic performance and skills mismatch; individual performance, transition to working life and social exclusion; and, research activities in non-EU countries.
Theme: 4

Training in Europe. Second report on vocational training research in Europe 2000: background report (3 volumes)

Available only in English (EN)
2001 – 1500 pp. – 21 x 29.7 cm
ISBN 92-896-0034-9
Cat. No: TI-44-00-000-EN-C

Price (excluding VAT): € 21 (The 3 volumes are not sold separately.)

Training and learning for competence. Second report on vocational training research in Europe: synthesis report

Available in Spanish (ES), German (DE), English (EN) and French (FR)
2001 – 441 pp. – 21 x 29.7 cm
ISBN 92-896-0029-2
Cat. No: TI-33-00-857-EN-C
Price (excluding VAT): € 19

The transition from education to working life: Key data on vocational training in the European Union

This third edition of the Key Data series attempts to answer questions on the dynamics of transition from education to working life for young people. It presents statistical information from the European labour force survey, and analyses the pathways taken by young people on leaving the educational system and seeking to enter the labour market. Statistical indicators have also been provided for the central and east European countries (Bulgaria, the Czech Republic, Estonia, Hungary, Latvia, Lithuania, Poland, Romania, Slovakia and Slovenia) applying for accession to the European Union.
Available in German (DE), English (EN) and French (FR)
2001 – 172 pp. – 21 x 29.7 cm
ISBN 92-896-0012-8
Cat. No: TI-32-00-984-EN-C
Price (excluding VAT): € 11
Theme: 4

Learning through work experience for the knowledge economy: issues for educational research and policy

The publication identifies the achievements and limitations of successive European policy reforms and addresses future challenges in relation to work experience. It describes a new analytical tool – a typology for conceptualising different models of work experience in terms of learning, rather than the traditional approach of treating work experience as a social institution. The new typology of learning through work experience places the question of what is learnt, how it is learnt and how it is used at the centre of research and policy discourse in vocational and general education and also by extension in the wider domain of lifelong learning.
Available only in English (EN)
2004 – 136 pp. – 17.6 x 25 cm
ISBN 92-896-0268-6
ISSN 1608-7089
Cat. No: TI-57-03-467-EN-C
Price (excluding VAT): € 25
Theme: 4, 5, 16

An age of learning: Vocational training policy at European level

This report presents a global overview of the changes in policy related to vocational and continuing education at the European level, and aims to stimulate the debate amongst a large number of interested groups throughout Europe.
Available in German (DE), English (EN), French (FR) and Portuguese (PT)
2000 – 146 pp. – 21 x 29.7 cm
ISBN 92-828-8051-6
Cat. No: HX-25-99-075-EN-C
Price (excluding VAT): € 19
Theme: 4

Vocational education and training

This Cedefop series covers all the EU Member States, Iceland and Norway.

Each volume describes the initial and continuing vocational education and training (VET) in the country concerned. The contents cover background information, a brief description of the education system and its historical development, the vocational education and training system, the administrative and financial framework, qualitative aspects, and trends and perspectives. The annexes include a list of abbreviations and acronyms, the major organisations involved, a bibliography, a glossary of terms, and a list of vocational training qualifications available.

Each country is, or will be, published in the language of that country (with the exception of Sweden, Iceland and Norway) and German, English and French.
Theme: 4

Vocational education and training in the United Kingdom
Second edition
Available only in English (EN)
1998 – 156 pp. – 21 x 29.7 cm
ISBN 92-828-2720-8
Cat. No: HX-12-98-271-EN-C
Price (excluding VAT): € **18.50**

Vocational education and training in Austria
Available in German (DE), English (EN) and French (FR)
2000 – 127 pp. – 21 x 29.7 cm
ISBN 92-828-3552-9
Cat. No: HX-07-97-684-EN-C
Price (excluding VAT): € **18.50**

Vocational education and training in Sweden
Available in German (DE), English (EN) and French (FR)
2000 – 139 pp. – 21 x 29.7 cm
ISBN 92-827-4031-5
Cat. No: HX-06-97-593-EN-C
Price (excluding VAT): € **18.50**

Vocational education and training in Finland
Available in German (DE) and English (EN)
1997 – 135 pp. – 21 x 29.7 cm
ISBN 92-828-1912-4
Cat. No: HX-06-97-577-EN-C
Price (excluding VAT): € **18.50**

Vocational education and training in Norway
Available only in English (EN)
1997 – 153 pp. – 21 x 29.7 cm
ISBN 92-828-2476-4
Cat. No: HX-09-97-842-EN-C
Price (excluding VAT): € **18.50**

Vocational education and training in Luxembourg
Available in English (EN) and French (FR)
2003 – 101 pp. – 21 x 29.7 cm
ISBN 92-828-7481-8
Cat. No: HX-22-99-854-EN-C
Price (excluding VAT): € **18.50**

Vocational education and training in France
Second edition
Available in German (DE), English (EN) and French (FR)
2000 – 134 pp. – 21 x 29.7 cm
ISBN 92-828-2433-0
Cat. No: HX-10-97-453-EN-C
Price (excluding VAT): € **18.50**

Vocational education and training in Spain
Second edition
Available in Spanish (ES), German (DE), English (EN) and French (FR)
2002 – 166 pp. – 21 x 29.7 cm
ISBN 92-828-7454-0
Cat. No: HX-22-99-830-EN-C
Price (excluding VAT): € **18.50**

Vocational education and training in Italy
Second edition
Available in German (DE), English (EN), French (FR) and Italian (IT)
2002 – 158 pp. – 21 x 29.7 cm
ISBN 92-828-7369-2
Cat. No: HX-22-99-822-EN-C
Price (excluding VAT): € **18.50**

Vocational education and training in Belgium
Available in English (EN) and French (FR)
2001 – 140 pp. – 21 x 29.7 cm
ISBN 92-896-0042-X
Cat. No: HX-25-99-067-EN-C
Price (excluding VAT): € **18.50**

Vocational education and training in the Netherlands
Available only in English (EN)
1999 – 112 pp. – 21 x 29.7 cm
ISBN 92-828-7626-8
Cat. No: HX-22-99-862-EN-C
Price (excluding VAT): € **18.50**

Vocational education and training in Denmark
Second edition
Available only in English (EN)
1999 – 144 pp. – 21 x 29.7 cm
ISBN 92-828-2258-3
Cat. No: HX-21-99-795-EN-C
Price (excluding VAT): € **18.50**

Vocational training — European Journal

The journal is published by CEDEFOP (the European Centre for the Development of Vocational Training) and aims to contribute to debate on the development of vocational education and training, in particular by introducing a European perspective. The journal is looking to publish articles which set out ideas, report on research results and report on experience at national and European levels. It also publishes position papers and reaction statements on issues in the field of vocational education and training.
Edition 2004
Available in German (DE), English (EN), Spanish (ES), French (FR), Portuguese (PT)
21 x 29.7 cm
ISSN 0378-5068
Cat. No: TI-AA-04-000-EN-C
Subscription code: VFI
Price per copy (excluding VAT): € **10**
Theme: 4
Annual subscription price (excluding VAT): € **20**

Quality of agricultural products and protection of the environment: training, knowledge dissemination and certification

The main objective of the study is to examine existing environmental education and agricultural practices friendly to the environment. The main findings of the study are that education, training, innovation transfer, and information on producing and distributing certified organic products are important for all the bodies involved in the chain, regardless of educational level.
Available only in English (EN)
2003 – 191 pp. – 17.5 x 25 cm
ISBN 92-896-0174-4
ISSN 1608-7089
Cat. No: TI-49-02-361-EN-C
Price (excluding VAT): € **25**
Theme: 4

Dictionnaire de l'Union européenne

The new edition of this bilingual dictionary contains 3,000 legal definitions used in more than 500 Acts of Community law. A list of these Acts, which is presented in German and French, allows the reader to trace the origin of each definition.

There are also a German-language index by subject and an index of acronyms and abbreviations in German and French.
    Volume I (A – F)
    1999 – 536 pp. – 17.6 x 25 cm
    Volume II (G – Z)
    1999 – 536 pp. – 17.6 x 25 cm
Fourth edition
Available in German (DE) and French (FR)
Theme: 16
ISBN 92-824-1669-0
Cat. No: BX-07-99-000-2B-C
Price (excluding VAT): € **70**

Version CD-ROM
Multilingual edition in German (DE) and French (FR)
2001
Cat. No: BX-23-99-015-2B-Z
Price (excluding VAT): € **40**

Eurovoc

Eurovoc is a multilingual thesaurus (11 languages) which covers all the fields in which the European Union is active and provides a means of indexing the documents in users' documentation systems. This documentation product is currently used by the European Parliament, the Office for Official Publications of the European Communities, national and regional parliaments in Europe, national government departments and certain European organisations.

Since the last paper edition containing version 3 was produced in 1995, Eurovoc has been extended to cover two new languages (Finnish and Swedish) and has been updated several times. The thesaurus is available on the Internet. A new paper edition containing version 4.1 of the Eurovoc thesaurus in two volumes – a thematic presentation and a permuted alphabetical presentation – was expected to be available from May 2004. The

Internet site (http://europa.eu.int/celex/ eurovoc) also offers a multilingual list.
Fourth edition
Available in the 11 official languages of the European Union as at 1 January 2004
Theme: 16
2004
Cat. No: FY-04-04-000-EN-S
Price (excluding VAT): € 150

Permuted alphabetical presentation
Available in the 11 official languages of the European Union as at 1 January 2004
21 x 29.7 cm
ISBN 92-78-40237-0
Cat. No: FY-04-04-001-EN-S
Price (excluding VAT): € 95

Thematic presentation
Available in the 11 official languages of the European Union as at 1 January 2004
21 x 29.7 cm
ISBN 92-78-40248-6
Cat. No: FY-04-04-002-EN-S
Price (excluding VAT): € 55

Stat-Lex — 1998–2002 legislation — Secondary Community legislation relating to statistics

The CD-ROM 'Stat-Lex 1998–2002' aims to give an overview of the texts (in 11 languages) of all Community legislation relating to statistics for the years 1998 to 2002. This represents about 35 legislative acts per year. This publication is intended to be a practical and handy tool for all actors involved in the field of statistics at European level: national statistical offices, other public bodies producing official statistics, organisations and businesses complying with responding obligations in the field of statistics, users of Community statistics both in the public and private sectors and, finally, the European citizens themselves.
Edition 2003
A multilingual CD-ROM offering the 11 official languages of the European Union as at 1 January 2004
ISBN 92-894-4731-1
ISSN 1725-2164
Cat. No: KS-CW-02-001-1F-Z
Price (excluding VAT): € 100
Theme: 17

50 years of figures on Europe

The pocketbook '50 years of figures on Europe' invites its readers on a statistical journey through the last 50 years of European history. It helps to compare data for a broad range of indicators across individual countries, evaluate the effects of successive enlargements as well as developments in between. The data are illustrated by graphs. The pocketbook was written for the occasion of Eurostat's 50th anniversary in May 2003. The figures cover most of the areas Eurostat provides data for: Area and population, Economy, Employment and labor costs, Sectors of the economy, Transport, Tourism, External trade.
Trilingual edition in German (DE), English (EN) and French (FR)
2003 – 151 pp. – 10.5 x 21 cm
ISBN 92-894-5261-7
Cat. No: KS-49-02-264-3A-C
Price (excluding VAT): € 10
Theme: 17

Eurostat yearbook 2003: The statistical guide to Europe. Data 1991–2001

This 8th edition of the Eurostat yearbook offers a wide choice of harmonised and comparable data on the European Union, the euro-zone and the Member States. The candidate countries and principal non-European nations are also given prominence in the 2003 edition.

Two new chapters have been added: 'The European Union in the global context' that shows the EU's position in the world, often compared to the USA and Japan, and 'In the spotlight:...' relating to a different, important topic each year. In 2003, this was the 'Candidate countries'.

The 2003 edition is available as a combined paper and CD-ROM edition. The CD-ROM has considerable content (1000 tables), about two thirds of which are not available in the paper version, and it allows the user to extract data to create customised tables. An electronic version (PDF-format) of the Yearbook, with the same content as the printed version, can be downloaded free of charge from Eurostat's Internet web site.
Annual
Available in German (DE), English (EN) and French (FR)
2003 – 330 pp. – 21 x 29.7 cm
ISBN 92-894-4209-3
ISSN 1681-4789
Cat. No: KS-CD-02-001-EN-C

Price (excluding VAT): € 50 (Paper and CD-ROM are not sold separately.)
Theme: 17

Eurostat yearbook 2004
Edition was expected in September 2004

Monographs of official statistics — Variance estimation methods in the European Union

This report examines the issue of variance estimation of simple statistics under several sampling designs and estimation procedures. It especially focuses on two representative examples of household and business surveys: the labour force survey (LFS) and structural business statistics (SBS) respectively.
2002 edition
Available only in English (EN)
2002 – 69 pp. – 21 x 29.7 cm
ISBN 92-894-4432-0
ISSN 1725-1567

Cat. No: KS-CR-02-001-EN-C
Price (excluding VAT): € 17
Theme: 15, 17

EC economic data pocketbook

The EC Economic data pocket book is a complete, regular and handy reference for all who need to know about and compare the short-term economic aspects in the EU Member States. The publication is the result of cooperation between Eurostat and DG ECFIN, the Directorate General of economic and financial affairs. It offers long chronological series as well as forecasts for 2003 and 2004.
Edition 2004
Quarterly
Trilingual edition in German (DE), English (EN) and French (FR)
ISSN 1026-0846
Cat. No: KS-CZ-04-000-3A-C
Subscription code: VBO
Price per copy (excluding VAT): € 12
Annual subscription price (excluding VAT): € 40
Theme: 17

Living conditions in Europe: Statistical pocketbook

This pocketbook offers statistical information on the EU Member States and Iceland, Liechtenstein, Norway and Switzerland and their populations, households and families, education and training, labour markets, earnings incomes, social protection, consumption and housing, health and safety, social participation and crime.
Available only in English (EN)
2000 – 123 pp. – 10.5 x 21 cm
ISBN 92-828-9349-9
Cat. No: KS-28-00-842-EN-C
Price (excluding VAT): € 10
Theme: 17

New edition was expected in 2004

Consumers in Europe – Facts and figures. Data 1996–2000

The aim of this publication is to present, for the first time, a comprehensive collection of the most important data available from different sources on consumption patterns, including expenditure, and on consumer attitudes and quality indicators in the European Union. It provides an essential source of information to policy-makers concerned with the impact of European and national policies on consumers; to advertisers and other businesses interested in Europe-wide markets; indeed, to anybody interested in Europe's spending patterns and consumption habits.
Available only in English (EN)
2001 – 290 pp. – 21 x 29.7 cm
ISBN 92-894-1400-6
ISSN 1681-5041
Cat. No: KS-39-01-134-EN-C
Price (excluding VAT): € 30
Theme: 17

Comext — Intra- and extra-EU trade data

This CD-ROM is published monthly. It contains statistics of trade of Members States, classifications of countries and products, methodological notes, notes on the state of data availability, and the user manual. It includes data of the acceding countries and the database prodcom (previously europroms CD-ROM). As from Issue 8/2004, it was to be available only on a DVD.

Edition 2004
Monthly
Trilingual edition in German (DE), English (EN) and French (FR)
ISSN 1017-6594
Cat. No: KS-CK-04-000-3A-Z
Subscription code: OCDR00
Price per copy (excluding VAT): € **700**

Annual subscription price (excluding VAT): € **4020** *(Tariffs for local area network (LAN) are available on request.)*
Theme: 17

Agriculture – Statistical yearbook 2002 — Data 1992–2001

This yearbook presents an overview of the main figures from Eurostat's special publications on agriculture, forestry and fisheries. It describes the general developments in agriculture during the period from 1992 to 2001. The data were produced by the national statistics institutes of the Member States on the basis of harmonised methodologies.

2002 edition
Annual
Trilingual edition in German (DE), English (EN) and French (FR)
2003 – 210 pp. – 21 x 29.7 cm
ISBN 92-894-4374-X
ISSN 1681-4711
Cat. No: KS-AQ-03-001-3A-C
Price (excluding VAT): € **31**
Theme: 17

Agricultural statistics — Quarterly bulletin

This publication contains monthly data on crop production, animal production and agricultural prices plus commentary. The source of this publication is the database system FAME/New Cronos (domains ZPA1 and PRAG) where Eurostat collects its data since 1955. The publication now includes also a CD-ROM.

Edition 2003
Quarterly
Trilingual edition in German (DE), English (EN) and French (FR)
21 x 29.7 cm
ISSN 1607-2308
Cat. No: KS-NT-04-000-3A-C
Subscription code: VXAS00
Price (excluding VAT): € **40**
Annual subscription price (excluding VAT): € **140**
Theme: 17

Farm structure – 1999/2000 survey (paper + CD-ROM)

This publication reports the results of the farm structure survey carried out in the European Union in 1999 and 2000. The results, by Member State and for the EU as a whole, cover, in particular, land use, livestock farming and the agricultural labour force. The results are discussed in comparison with those of previous surveys. The attached CD-ROM (in English only) explains the methodology used in each Member State and contains the data in Excel format.

Trilingual edition in German (DE), English (EN) and French (FR)
2003 – 238 pp. – 21 x 29.7 cm
ISBN 92-894-5618-3
Cat. No: KS-52-03-756-3A-C
Price (excluding VAT): € **40**
Theme: 3, 17

Area under vines — Third basis community survey — Analysis of the results — Data 1989–1999

The purpose of this publication is to offer a synthesis of the results of the last basic statistical survey covering the total areas under vines which was conducted throughout the European Union in 1999. To this end, the most relevant data collected by Member States have been selected from the 'VITIS' database and have been used to draw up a series of summary tables, graphics and maps in order to give a concise overview of the European vineyard. Whenever possible, a comparison between the results of the 1989 and 1999 EU basic surveys has also been elaborated.

Trilingual edition in German (DE), English (EN) and French (FR)
2002 – 82 pp. – 21 x 29.7 cm
ISBN 92-894-4723-0
Cat. No: KS-49-02-191-3A-C
Price (excluding VAT): € **17**
Theme: 17

A panorama of rural development

Rural development has become a crucial part of the European Union's agricultural policy. Since the early 1990s, the EU has increased its financial commitment to supporting projects aimed at improving the quality of the countryside and the prospects for people living in rural areas. In this publication you will find beautiful landscapes, from fertile fields to rocky mountains, wild flowers and domestic animals, farm produce and tourist activities, the natural and historic heritage of our relationship with the land.

2002 edition
Trilingual edition in German (DE), English (EN) and French (FR)
2003 – 156 pp. – 29.7 x 21 cm
ISBN 92-894-3184-9

Cat. No: KF-38-01-803-3A-C
Price (excluding VAT): € **38.50**
Theme: 3

Fisheries — Yearbook 2003

This statistical document contains fishery statistics for the Member States of the European Union, the candidate countries and for other important countries in this economic sector. This volume is divided into sections on catches by fishing region, catches of principal species, the fishing fleet and foreign trade in fishery products.

Edition 2003
Annual
Trilingual edition in German (DE), English (EN) and French (FR)
2003 – 67 pp. – 21 x 29.7 cm
ISBN 92-894-6338-4
ISSN 1609-4085
Cat. No: KS-AX-03-001-3A-C

Price (excluding VAT): € **40** *(Paper and CD-ROM are not sold separately.)*
Theme: 17

Tourism – Europe, central European countries, Mediterranean countries: Key figures 2001–2002

This publication gives an overview of recent trends and key figures in the EU Member States, the EFTA countries, the candidate countries and the MED partner countries. It is defined to give information to a broader public, but can also be seen as a first approach for information to people working in the tourism sector.

Edition 2003
Available only in English (EN)
2003 – 48 pp. – 21 x 29.7 cm
ISBN 92-894-6340-6
Cat. No: KS-55-03-318-EN-C
Price (excluding VAT): € **20**
Theme: 10, 17

Tourism statistics — Yearbook — Data 1990, 1995, 1998–2002

This CD-ROM contains data for EU Member States' statistics in the field of tourism. These data have been collected by the national authorities under Directive 95/57/EC on the collection of statistical information in the field of tourism. They comprise mainly the following parts: capacity of collective accommodation, occupancy in collective accommodation establishments and tourism demand – domestic and outbound tourism. Data go up to 2002.

Edition 2003
Trilingual edition in German (DE), English (EN) and French (FR)
2003
ISBN 92-894-6621-9
ISSN 1725-1192
Cat. No: KS-DS-03-001-3A-Z
Price (excluding VAT): € **120**
Theme: 10, 17

Next edition was expected in 2004

Tourism trends in the Mediterranean countries

This title confirms the importance of international tourism in the Mediterranean region and reflects progress made towards the implementation of the Euro-Mediterranean cooperation programme on tourism statistics, Medtour, adopted in June 1997. It also reflects the value of sharing knowledge, expertise and relevant information among the 27 EU Member States partner countries on the basis of a coherent framework of reference established at Community level.
2001 edition
Available only in English (EN)
2001 – VI, 236 pp. – 21 x 29.7 cm
ISBN 92-894-0066-8
Cat. No: KS-40-01-666-EN-C
Price (excluding VAT): € **35.50**
Theme: 17

Statistical yearbook on candidate countries — Data 1997–2001

This extensive yearbook on candidate countries should serve as a working tool for all interested in the enlargement process. Covering the years 1997 to 2001, the yearbook contains detailed tables on demography, education, research and development, social conditions and the labour force, national accounts and finance, agriculture, energy, industry and construction, retail and tourism, transport, telecommunications and the information society, as well as external trade and environment. The yearbook

contains most of the structural indicators that were adopted by the European Council to monitor the Lisbon competitiveness strategy. These indicators were integrated into the respective thematic chapters of the yearbook and are highlighted by a specific logo.
Edition 2003
Available only in English (EN)
2003 – 219 pp. – 21 x 29.7 cm
ISBN 92-894-5523-3
Cat. No: KS-AG-03-001-EN-C
Price (excluding VAT): € **30**
Theme: 17

New enterprises in central European countries in 1998

This report examines the structure of approximately 670,000 newly-created enterprises in 1998, excluding agricultural enterprises, in 11 central European countries. It compares this with information from previous surveys on enterprises which were newly created between 1995 and 1997, and all active enterprises in the business registers in each of the participating countries in January 1995.
Available only in English (EN)
2000 – 45 pp. – 21 x 29.7 cm
ISBN 92-828-9412-6
Cat. No: KS-29-00-812-EN-C
Price (excluding VAT): € **7**
Theme: 17

Communication in the candidate countries — Data 1995–2001

Communication in the candidate countries describes recent developments in

the telecommunications and postal sectors in the 10 acceding and three other candidate countries. This CD-ROM publication highlights some of the most important features, with figures and analytical texts. Comparison with the EU-15 is made, when possible. Detailed data are presented in tables on another part of the CD-ROM, for downloading and further processing. Aspects like economy, employment, traffic, infrastructure and quality of service are covered on a rather aggregate level.
Edition 2003
Available only in English (EN)
2003
ISBN 92-894-6080-6
Cat. No: KS-53-03-871-3A-Z
Price (excluding VAT): € **30**
Theme: 8, 17

Map — The European Union: Member States, new Member States due to join in 2004 and candidate countries

This political map offers basic statistics of the Member States, the new Member States which were due to join the EU in 2004, and the candidate countries.
Available in the 11 official languages of the European Union as at 1 January 2004
2003 – 96.5 x 110 cm
Cat. No: NA-47-02-834-EN-P
Price (excluding VAT): € **20**
Theme: 1

New edition was expected in 2004

After starting out with a description of EUROPA, the Commission's website which plays host to a series of databases, we have covered the other databases available on the Internet produced by the European Commission's different services or by the other EU institutions. Section II provides details of other online databases distributed by the gateways appointed by EUR-OP, while Section III lists some of the major offline bases available on CD-Rom or diskette.

Useful address

Office for Official Publications of the European Communities (EUR-OP), 2 rue Mercier, 2985 Luxembourg, Luxembourg; tel (+352) 292942001; fax (+352) 292942025.

Section I: Databases Accessible via the Internet

EUROPA

Contents

Europa was developed by the Directorate-General for Information, Communication, Culture and Audiovisual Media in co-operation with a number of other EC services. It was launched in February 1995 and was designed as a means of providing up-to-date information on the objectives, institutions and policies of the European Union.

The database contains some 500,000 documents and receives more than one million hits per day.

EUROPA plays host to several major databases:

- RAPID – up-to-date information on European Union activities;
- CELEX – computerized documentation system for European Community law;
- ECLAS – European Commission Library Automated System;
- EUR-LEX – European Union law;
- SCADPlus – a multi-faceted database covering programmes, policies, documentary information and Treaties; and it is the gateway to all policies, legislation and institutions of the EU.

The EUROPA site operates in all the official languages, and interactive services (mail box, charts) are being developed and improved continuously.

Access

Online, free of charge at http://europa.eu.int.

ARCHISPLUS
Database of the Historical Archives

Contents

ARCHISplus contains details of the references of files and organizational structures of various European institutions.

Access

Free of charge on the Internet at http://europa.eu.int/comm/secretariat-general/archisplus/htdocs/en/htm/home.htm.

AUDIOVISUAL LIBRARY
Audio, Photo, Video and Multimedia

Contents

This database offers the press and media a wide range of audiovisual material (audio, photo, video, multimedia). The contents may be used free of charge as long as the copyright is acknowledged. The audio section contains a selection of speeches, while photos of Commission members, European institutions' Presidents, and maps may be downloaded. Special press packs are also available.

Access

Free of charge on the Internet at http://europa.eu.int/comm/mediatheque/contact_en.html.

Further information

Mr De Bruyne (Co-ordination – Médiathèque); European Commission, DG Press and Communication, Audiovisual Library, BREY 04/176, 1049 Brussels, Belgium; tel (+32) 2-2999005; fax (+32) 2-2999012; e-mail mediatheque@cec.eu.int.

CELEX
Computerized documentation system for European Community law

Contents

CELEX is a comprehensive and authoritative information source on European Community law. It offers multilingual and full-text coverage of a wide range of legal acts including the founding treaties, binding and non-binding legislation, opinions and resolutions issued by the European Union institutions and consultative bodies, and the case law of the European Court of Justice and the Court of First Instance.

The CELEX website ceased to be updated on 1 January 2005 but can still be used to search for documents dated up to 31 December 2004. Users are invited to go to the new EUR-LEX website, which incorporates the CELEX features and provides free and easy access in twenty languages to the largest documentary database on EU law.

Access

Via the Internet at http://www.europa.eu.int/celex.

Related products and services

Directory of Community legislation in force (published every six months), which is available through the sales agents of the Office for Official Publications of the European Communities.

CITIZENS FIRST

Contents

This database is designed to help EU citizens who relocate to another Member State for the purposes of studying, working, job-seeking, travelling, buying goods or services or living. It offers highly practical information in respect of citizens' rights, access to employment, recognition of diplomas, administrative formalities (driving licences, etc.).

Access

Online, free of charge at http://citizens.eu.int.

Further information

Emmanuel Economon (Markt A-4); tel (+32) 2-2995804; fax (+32) 2-2954351; e-mail markt-a4@cec.eu.int;

CORDIS
Community Research and Development Information Service

Contents

Cordis is an acronym for the Community Research and Development Information Service, which provides information on all research and technological development (RTD) activities of the European Union. It is a central source of information, important to all organizations wishing to participate in EU research programmes or to exploit their results. It is also important for all researchers in academic and industrial establishments who wish to have knowledge of research trends and details of projects.

Access

Online, free of charge, and offline on CD-ROM.

Related products and services

Via Internet/World Wide Web, document delivery service for major R&D documents, general information and input of expressions of interest for some EU R&D programmes.

CORDIS R&D – ACRONYMS

Contents

RTD-Acronyms is the Cordis database covering acronyms and abbreviations relating to EU research programmes and /projects as well as to organizations carrying out R&D activities.

Access

Via the Internet at www.cordis.lu and on CD-ROM.

CORDIS R&D – COMDOCUMENTS

Summaries of the Commission's Initiatives on Research Matters

Contents

RTD-Com Documents provides details of Com (Commission) and SEC (Secretariat-General) documents. These are documents sent by the Commission to the Council, the European Parliament and other European Union bodies as part of the Union's decision-making and legislative processes.

Access

Via the Internet at www.cordis.lu and on CD-ROM.

CORDIS R&D – CONTACTS

Main Contact Points of the Cordis Database

Contents

R&D – Contacts is the Cordis database covering all main contact points (named individuals) able to provide information, advice or assistance on R&D activities at both national and European levels.

Access

Via the Internet at www.cordis.lu and on CD-ROM.

CORDIS R&D – NEWS

Latest News Announcements of EU R&D Activities

Contents

R&D – News is the Cordis database giving the latest news announcements on all aspects of EU RTD activities, including future and actual calls for proposals, calls for tender, events, publications, activities under preparation, Commission proposals, legislation and policies on R&D issues, progress and results of R&D programmes.

Access

Via the Internet at www.cordis.lu and on CD-ROM.

Related products and services

Cordis Focus is the fortnightly printed version of the files.

CORDIS R&D – PARTNERS

Partner Search Service

Contents

RTD – Partners enables researchers to identify partners either for participation in Community R&D programmes or for other types of collaboration.

Access

Via the Internet at www.cordis.lu and on CD-ROM.

CORDIS R&D – PROGRAMMES

Information on All EU-Funded Research and Research-Related Programmes

Contents

R&D – Programmes is the Cordis database containing information on all EU-funded research and research-related programmes.

Access

Via the Internet at www.cordis.lu and on CD-ROM.

CORDIS R&D – PROJECTS

Contents

R&D – Projects is the Cordis database covering various EU-funded programmes. Details are given for both completed and ongoing projects.

Access

Via the Internet at /www.cordis.lu and on CD-ROM.

CORDIS R&D – PUBLICATIONS

Abstracts of Reports, Publications and Scientific Papers

Contents

R&D – Publications is the Cordis database containing bibliographical information and abstracts on publications, reports and scientific papers arising from EU research activities as well as other scientific and technical documents published by the Commission.

Access

Via the Internet at www.cordis.lu.

Related products

Euroabstracts is the bimonthly printed version of this service.

CORDIS R&D – RESULTS

Information on Results and Prototypes

Contents

R&D – Results contains information on results and prototypes arising from EU and other R&D research projects that are awaiting commercial exploitation. It also contains information on research projects needing further development.

Access

Via the Internet at www.cordis.lu and on CD-ROM.

ECDIN / PHATOX

Environmental Chemicals Data and Information Network

Pharmacological and Toxicological Data and Information Network

The ECDIN database covers chemical products liable to react with the environment. Information is gathered on all chemical compounds manufactured and marketed on a large scale in the European Community, the United States and Japan.

Access

Online on the Internet at http://ecdin .etomep.net. Also available on CD-ROM with a reduced section of ECDIN containing 7,500 compounds.

Further information

Mrs Engelmanntel (+39) 0332-785409.

ECLAS

European Commission Library Automated System – Database of the central library of the European Commission

Contents

ECLAS covers the Union's official publications and documentation as well as the publications and documents of many intergovernmental organizations, commercial, academic and government presses, and selected journal articles of lasting interest.

Access

Online, free of charge, at http://europa .eu.int/eclas.

EIRO

European Industrial Relations Observatory

The EIRO database provides an up-to-date account and analysis of the most important events and issues in the field of industrial relations in the EU Member States, Norway and at EU level. Information may be accessed chronologically or by country.

Access

On the Internet at www.eurofound.ie.

Further information

e-mail information@eurofound.ie.

ELCID

Contents

European Living Conditions Information Directory (ELCID) is an information source on living conditions in Europe.

Further information

e-mail information@eurofound.ie.

Access

Online, free of charge.

EMIRE

European Employment and Industrial Relations Glossaries

Contents

The EMIRE database is the online version of the European employment and industrial relations glossaries, a set of 12 volumes published in English in co-operation with Sweet and Maxwell (UK) and the Office for Official Publications of the European Communities (Luxembourg).

Access

Online, free of charge.

Further information

e-mail information@eurofound.ie.

EURHISTAR

European Historical Archives

Contents

Since 1985 the originals of European Union archives (e.g. annual reports, notes, minutes of meetings and the like) created by the European Union institutions in Brussels and Luxembourg have been deposited centrally at the European University Institute in Florence, Italy. In addition to these central holdings, the University Institute is continuously acquiring private deposits from European politicians and officials, along with documentation from European movements and organizations. The European University Institute in Florence produce the EURHISTAR database.

Access

Online at www.arc.iue.it/ECArchives.

EUR-LEX

The original EUR-Lex facility was established in October 1997 by the Office for Official Publications at the request of the institutions in order to make European Union law available to members of the public. On 1 November 2004 the Publications Office launched an improved and completely free portal to EU law, integrating the former EUR-Lex portal and the CELEX database. CELEX is the European Union's legal database for expert users, while the EUR-Lex portal offered free access to the Official Journal and the collections of EU legal texts. Access to CELEX used to be subject to

payment but is now completely free of charge.

The new site presents the Official Journal online and gives a central access point, with powerful search functions and thematic indexing, for all legal texts, including full coverage of archived documents. It is updated continuously with new texts and is available in all the 20 official languages of the enlarged European Union. The documents – Treaties, legislation, international agreements, preparatory acts, case law of the Court of Justice, Commission documents, parliamentary questions, the collection of consolidated legislation, information and notices from the Official Journal, etc., – can be found in a variety of formats (HTML, PDF and TIFF). As with the old EUR-Lex portal, it is possible to gain direct access to all legal document repositories managed by the Publications Office. There are useful links (PreLex and OEIL as well as to the Court of Justice's website). Explanatory texts on EU procedures and institutions, a glossary and descriptions of the decision-making process are also provided.

In addition to containing all the advantages of EUR-Lex and CELEX, the new site will gradually add additional features such as LexAlert, a new alert service, facilities to search national legislation and a revised expert service.

Access

Online, free of charge, at http://europa .eu.int/eur-lex/lex.

EURODICAUTOM

Dictionary of Terminology

Contents

Terminological database explaining terms, expressions, acronyms and abbreviations.

Access

Online at http://europa.eu.int/ eurodicautom/controller.

Related products and services

Thematic glossaries, on sale through the sales agents of the Office for Official Publications of the European Communities.

EURO-OMBUDSMAN

Multilingual Web Server of the European Ombudsman, Designed to Inform European Citizens about the Ombudsman's Activities

Access

On line, free of charge, at www.euro -ombudsman.eu.int.

Further information

Ben Hagardtel (+33) 3-88-17-24-24; fax (+33) 3-88-17-90-62; e-mail euro -ombudsman@europarl.eu.int;

EUROPARL

European Parliament Multilingual Web Server

Contents

A wide range of vital and timely information about the European Parliament and its work.

Access

On-line, free of charge, at www.europarl .eu.int.

EUROPE DIRECT

Contents

Europe Direct is a one-stop information shop designed to provide EU citizens with easy access to information about their rights within the European Union.

Access

Online, free of charge, at www.europa .eu.int/europedirect.

EUROVOC

Thesaurus

Contents

EUROVOC Thesaurus is a multilingual thesaurus which is currently available in 11 languages and will soon be available in 19 languages. It covers all the fields in which the European Union is active and provides a means of indexing the documents in users' documentation systems. Since the last paper edition was produced, containing version 3, in 1995, EUROVOC has been extended to cover two new languages (Finnish and Swedish) and has been updated several times. The thesaurus is now available on the Internet. A new paper edition contains version 4.1 of the EUROVOC Thesaurus in two volumes – a subject-oriented version and a permuted alphabetical version.

Access

Online at http://europa.eu.int/celex/ eurovoc.

EWC

European Works Council Agreements

Contents

The EWC database contains information on the provisions of the agreements establishing European Works Councils (EWCs), concluded under Article 6 and Article 13 of the Directive on EWCs.

Access

Online at www.eurofound.ie/ewc.

IDEA

Interinstitutional Directory of European Administrations

Contents

Covers European institutions, bodies and agencies, including the European Commission, European Parliament, Council of the European Union, Court of Justice, European Economic and Social Committee, European Investment Bank, Court of Auditors and Committee of the Regions.

Access

Online, free of charge, at http://europa .eu.int/idea/en/index.html.

I*M GUIDE

Information Market Guide

The I*M GUIDE database distribution aims to help the information user to find a way through the maze of online products and services offered by the European information services market.

Access

Online at www.cordis.lu.

PRELEX

Monitoring of the Decision-Making Process between Institutions

Access

Online, free of charge, at: http://europa .eu.int/prelex/apcnet.cfm.

PRESS-ROOM

Contents

The Press-Room site offers access to the latest news and press releases from the EC and the European Union. The site includes the latest headlines and releases (many available in multiple languages), a weekly archive and a searchable database of press releases since 1985.

Access

Online, free of charge, at http://europa .eu.int/comm/press_room/index.htm.

PROSOMA

Turning Innovation into Business

Contents

The Prosoma service provides a means for companies who are looking for innovative solutions to their needs to identify relevant R&D results.

Access

Online, free of charge, at www.prosoma .lu.

RAPID

Daily European Union News Briefings

Contents

A monitoring tool par excellence, RAPID also provides a rich source of background information on Community affairs and offers flexible searching on multiple search criteria.

Access

Online at www.europa.eu.int/en/comm/ spp/rapid.html.

RAPID NEW GENERATION (RAPID NG)

Press Releases mainly of the European Commission and the Council of the European Union

Contents

The Commission's DG Press launched its new RAPID NEW GENERATION (RAPID NG) database on 19 May 2004 in order to allow the storage of documents in all the languages of the enlarged European Union. The RAPID NG database contains all the Press Releases of the Commission since 1985, the great majority of them in at least two languages. It also contains Press releases of some of the other European Institutions, particularly the Council of the European Union. Press releases of the Commission are available at least in English and French, while many of the Press Releases are available in all EC languages. The main goal of RAPID NG service is to provide users with the most flexible way of searching and retrieving the documents in different formats.

All documents within RAPID NG are publicly available without using a personal username. However, users may obtain and use a personal username in order to personalize their working environment within RAPID NG, to subscribe to Press Releases and receive notifications via email or SMS messages.

Access

Online at http://europa.eu.int/rapid.

REM

Radioactivity Environmental Monitoring

Contents

The REM database contains the results of radioactivity readings in the environment taken in several European countries following the Chernobyl accident.

Access

Online, free of charge, at http://java.ei.jrc .ithttp://rem.jrc.cec.eu.int.

RISC

Chemicals, Plastics, Rubber

Contents

RISC is an online database comprising four databases (LégiChim, ComLégi, ChimEre and ChimStat) relating to the economic, commercial, legislative and statistical aspects of chemicals.

LégiChim

LégiChim is a database relating to those chemical substances cited in European legislation (Official Journal of the European Communities, Legislation series), whatever the field of the legislation (classification and labelling, cosmetics, food additives, worker protection, toys, etc.)

and includes data starting from the first publication of the Official Journal.

ComLégi

ComLégi is a database relating to the economic and commercial legislative aspects of the chemical sector (mainly NACE 24 and 25).

ChimEre

ChimEre is a database relating to the production, consumption and trade – in volume and in value – of approximately 400 chemicals in Europe, from upstream (raw materials) to downstream (final applications).

ChimStat

ChimStat is an economic statistical database covering the various subsectors of the chemicals, plastics and rubber industries, and other linked activities in the EU (NACE Rev. 1, Chapters 24 and 25).

Access

Available through EUR-OP agents.

SCADPlus

Practical Information for European Citizens

SCADPlus is a World Wide Web information service which includes the former INFO 92 and SCAD databases. It contains background information which helps provide a better understanding of European Union policies, as well as practical information for European citizens.

Access

On-line, free of charge, at http://europa .eu.int/scadplus.

Further information

Lindsay Armstrong (Database Manager tel (+32) 2-2999017; fax (+32) 2-296-26-95; e-mail lindsay.armstrong@cec.eu.int;

TED

Tenders Electronics Daily – Public Contract Tenders

More than 5,000 users rely on TED as a means of keeping informed of new business opportunities offered by public procurement markets around the world. TED is the online version of the S series supplement to the Official Journal of the European Communities. It is updated daily and it offers users a range of services designed to meet their individual needs.

Access

Online, free of charge, at www.ted.eur-op .eu.int.

Section II: Other Online Databases

AGREP

Permanent Inventory of Agricultural Research Products in the European Communities

Contents

AGREP is a database containing the titles of publicly financed research projects in agriculture, forestry, fisheries and foodstuffs.

Access

Access, against payment: DATACENTRALEN – tel (+45) 43-71-81-22; fax (+45) 43-71-33-12.

BACH

Database for the Accounts of Companies Harmonized

Contents

BACH contains statistical data on aggregate company accounts for 22 sectors and three size categories of companies in 10 countries (Germany, France, Italy, United Kingdom, Belgium, Netherlands, Spain, Portugal, Japan and the United States of America).

Access

Offline, against payment.

COMEXT2

Intra- and Extra-European Union Trade

Contents

Database of statistics on the European Union's external trade with some 300 non-Member countries and trade between the Member States.

A new service, called EASY COMEXT was launched in October 2004.

Access

Online, or offline on CD-Rom, against payment. Contact the EUR-OP information desk.

Online access to EASY COMEXT is free of charge at http://fd.comext.eurostat.cec.eu.int/xlweb or via the Eurostat website at www.europa.eu.int/comm/eurostat.

Information service

Luxembourg: tel (+352) 43352251; fax (+352) 433522221. Brussels: tel (+32) 2-2311414; fax (+32) 2-2311617.

NEW CRONOS

Macroeconomic statistical database

New Cronos is a macroeconomic and social database covering the living conditions and the economic situation of the EU Member States, as well as, in many cases, those of the United States, Japan, non-Member Central European countries

(CECs) and the main economic partners of the European Union.

Access

Online and by extraction, against payment. Contact Luxembourg (tel: (+352) 43352251; fax: (+352) 433522221) or Brussels (tel: (+32) 2-2311414; fax: (+32) 2-2311617).

REGIO

Regional Statistics

Contents

Eurostat's database for regional statistics covers the main aspects of economic and social life in the Community: demography, economic accounts, employment, unemployment, etc.

Access

Online and by extraction, against payment. Contact Luxembourg (tel: (+352) 43352251; fax: (+352) 433522221) or Brussels (tel: (+32) 2-2311414; fax: (+32) 2-2311617).

Section III: Offline Information

ACP-ALA-MED – CD-ROM

A Compendium of Country Snapshots

Contents

Demographic and labour force data for the years 1960, 1970, 1980, 2000 and (projection) 2025.

Health, education, economic, monetary and financial, public development aid and foreign trade data for the years 1980, 1990, 1991, 1992, 1993 and 1994.

Encyclopaedic data: year of independence, capital city, population of major cities, area, official languages, region, currency, main productions, main imports and exports.

For each of the six regions (ACP/Africa; ACP/Caribbean; ACP/Pacific; Mediterranean; Latin America; Asia) there are summary tables, graphs and charts for each country covering the main demographic, social and financial indicators.

Access

Offline on CD-Rom (latest edition 1998).

Distribution

Available through official offline agents and distributors. For details, refer to the list of gateways, agents and distributors in this directory, or consult the list of distribution points on Europa at http://europa.eu.int.

ALLOYS DB

Alloys Database

Contents

Previously entitled HTM-DB, ALLOYS DB is a factual database comprising a databank on the mechanical and physical properties of alloys for elevated and high-temperature applications, such as turbines, pressure vessels and heat exchangers, and methods of assessing these properties (evaluation program library).

Access

Offline, against payment, on application to the Joint Research Centre, Institute for Advanced Materials, Petten.

Further information

Dr H.H. Overtel (+31 22) 4465256; fax (+31 22) 4465222.

BTI – CD-ROM

Binding Tariff Information

Contents

The BTI CD-ROM contains official decisions on tariff classification of products using the Common Customs nomenclature, issued by a Member State's Customs Administration at the request of an economic operator.

Distribution

Available through official offline agents and distributors. For details, refer to the list of gateways, agents and distributors in this directory, or consult the list of distribution points on Europa at http://europa.eu.int.

COMEXT2 – CD-ROM

See section II.

COMPETITIVENESS INDICATORS – CD-ROM

Competitiveness of Manufacturing Industries

Contents

More than 100 variables, covering performance, business environment, cost, price and infrastructure.

Distribution

Available through official offline agents and distributors. For details, refer to the list of gateways, agents and distributors in this directory, or consult the list of distribution points on Europa at http://europa.eu.int.

CORDIS – CD-ROM

See section I.

CORDIS R&D – ACRONYMS CD-ROM

See section I.

CORDIS R&D – COMDOCUMENTS CD-ROM

See section I.

CORDIS R&D – CONTACTS CD-ROM

See section I.

CORDIS R&D – NEWS CD-ROM

See section I.

CORDIS R&D – PARTNERS CD-ROM

See section I.

CORDIS R&D – PROGRAMMES CD-ROM

See section I.

CORDIS R&D – PROJECTS CD-ROM

See section I.

CORDIS R&D – PUBLICATIONS CD-ROM

See section I.

CORDIS R&D – RESULTS CD-ROM

See section I.

ECDIN / PHATOX – CD-ROM

See section I.

ECICS

European Customs Inventory of Chemical Substances

Contents

Approximately 35,400 chemical names; 1,000 to 2,000 chemical substances added each year.

Distribution

Available through official offline agents and distributors. For details, refer to the list of gateways, agents and distributors in this directory, or consult the list of distribution points on Europa at http://europa.eu.int.

EUROPROMS

Output and Market Statistics

Europroms is the only source of information in Europe that supplies detailed and comparable data on output, external trade and markets of several thousand industrial products.

For further information

Statistical Office of the European Communities, Jean Monnet Building, , 2920 Luxembourg, Luxembourg; tel (+352) 430134567; fax (+352) 430132649; internet http://europa.eu.int/eurostat.html.

GISCO

Geographic Information System of the European Commission

Contents

The GISCO database contains geographic information on a wide variety of subjects, from topographic data over administrative regions to data on environment and natural resources.

HTCOR-DB

High-Temperature Corrosion Database

Contents

HTCOR-DB is a factual database comprising a databank on the corrosion properties of alloys for elevated and high-temperature applications such as turbines, pressure vessels and heat exchangers.

Access

Offline, against payment, on application to the Joint Research Centre, Institute for Advanced Materials, Petten.

Further information

Dr H.H. Overtel (+31 22) 4465256; fax (+31 22) 4465222.

IUCLID – CD-ROM

International Uniform Chemicals Information Database

Contents

Iuclid is a database on chemical substances created as an essential tool in the implementation of Council Regulation (EEC) No 793/93 on the evaluation and control of existing substances. The data comprise four main sections: Properties; Environmental Fate; Toxicity; Ecotoxicity.

Access

Data on CD-ROM, Iuclid-software on diskette, obtainable free of charge on request.

Further information

Mr Hanssentel (+39) 0332-785884; fax (+39) 0332-789963.

NUCLIDES 2000 – CD-ROM

Contents

Radionuclides have many applications in agriculture, medicine, industry and research. For basic information on such radioactive materials, the Chart of the Nuclides has proved to be an indispensable tool for obtaining data and qualitative information on decay schemes and reaction paths.

Further information

Mrs Engelmann JRC Ispra, tel (+39) 0332-785409.

PANORAMA CD-ROM

Panorama of European Business

Contents

Panorama-CD provides an extensive review of the situation and outlook of the manufacturing and service industries of the European Union, company profiles of the 500 largest European private companies and more than 15,000 Eurostat macroeconomic time series.

Access

Offline on CD-ROM, against payment. Available in two versions through the offline distribution network of the Office for Official Publications of the European Communities. The value version contains 5,025 time-series, while the new pro version contains 60,000 time-series.

REGIO – CD-ROM

See section II.

INDEX OF EU DATABASES BY SUBJECT

OFFICIAL GATEWAY AGENTS

Access to online databases

In 1995 a significant shift took place in the database distribution policy of EUR-OP. To better cope with an expanding line of commercial databases and a rapidly growing user base, online database dissemination activities were transferred to a group of specially selected agents.

National gateway agents provide access to important online databases (CELEX, EUDOR, RISC) and offer their users related administrative and user-support services.

In line with the principle of subsidiarity, the transfer of this activity aims to strengthen the role of local service providers in the distribution of European Union databases while creating more favourable access conditions for the information user. The system of national gateways allows access to all information through one single entry point without having to deal with numerous script files. Furthermore, users are able to pay in their own currency and receive the necessary technical support in their own language.

Sales Offices

ARGENTINA

World Publications SA: Av. Córdoba 1877, C1120 AAA Buenos Aires; tel (+54 11) 48 15 81 56; fax (+54 11) 48 15 81 56; e-mail wpbooks@infovia.com.ar; internet www.wpbooks.com.ar.

AUSTRALIA

Hunter Publications: PO Box 404, Abbotsford – Victoria 3067; tel (+61 3) 94 17 53 61; fax (+61 3) 94 19 71 54; e-mail admin@tekimaging.com.au.

AUSTRIA

Gesplan GmbH: Pachmüllergasse 15, 1120 Vienna; tel (+43 1) 712 54 02; fax (+43 1) 715 54 61; e-mail wrsvoboda@gesplan.com; internet www.gesplan.com.

BELGIUM

Jean de Lannoy: Avenue du Roi 202, 1190 Brussels; tel (+32 2) 538 43 08; fax (+32 2) 538 08 41; e-mail jean.de.lannoy@infoboard.be; internet www.jean-de-lannoy.be.

La Librairie Européenne: Rue de la Loi 244, 1040 Brussels; tel (+32 2) 295 26 39; fax (+32 2) 735 08 60; e-mail mail@libeurop.be; internet www.libeurop.be.

Moniteur Belge: Rue de Louvain 40-42, 1000 Brussels; tel (+32 2) 552 22 11; fax (+32 2) 511 01 84; e-mail eusales@just.fgov.be.

BRAZIL

Livraria Camões: Rua Bittencourt da Silva 12C, 20043-900 Rio de Janeiro; tel (+55 21) 262 47 76; fax (+55 21) 262 47 76; e-mail livraria.camoes@incm.com.br; internet www.incm.com.br.

BULGARIA

Europress Euromedia Ltd: Blvd Vitosha 59, 1000 Sofia; tel (+359 2) 980 37 66; fax (+359 2) 980 42 30; e-mail Milena@mbox.cit.bg; internet www.europress.bg.

CANADA

Euroline Inc.: 165 Sparks Street, Suite 300, Ottawa, Ontario K1P 5B9; tel (+1 613) 294 22.05; fax (+1 613) 230 22 09; e-mail info@euros.ch; internet www.euros.ch.

Les Editions La Liberté Inc.: 3020 Chemin Sainte-Foy, Sainte-Foy, Québec G1X 3V6; tel (+1 418) 658 37 63; fax (+1 800) 567 54 49; e-mail liberte@mediom.qc.ca.

Renouf Publishing Co. Ltd: 5369 Chemin Canotek, Road Unit 1, Ottawa, Ontario K1J 9J3; tel (+1 613) 745 26 65; fax (+1 613) 745 76 60; e-mail order.dept@renoufbooks.com; internet www.renoufbooks.com.

CROATIA

Mediatrade Ltd: Strohalov Prilaz 27, 10000 Zagreb; tel (+385 1) 660 08 40; fax (+385 1) 660 21 65; e-mail mediatrade@hi.hinet.hr.

CYPRUS

Cyprus Chamber of Commerce and Industry: PO Box 21455, 1509 Nicosia; tel (+357 22) 88 97 52; fax (+357 22) 66 10 44; e-mail stalo@ccci.org.cy.

DENMARK

J. H. Schultz Information A/S: Herstedvang 4, 2620 Albertslund; tel (+45) 43 63 23 00; fax (+45) 43 63 19 69; e-mail schultz@schultz.dk; internet www.schultz.dk.

EGYPT

The Middle East Observer: 41 Sherif Street, 11111 Cairo; tel (+20 2) 392 69 19; fax (+20 2) 393 97 32; e-mail meo@soficom.com.eg; internet www.meobserver.com.eg.

ESTONIA

Eesti Kaubandus-Tööstuskoda: Toom-Kooli 17, 10130 Tallinn; tel (+372) 646 02 44; fax (+372) 646 02 45; e-mail einfo@koda.ee; internet www.koda.ee.

FINLAND

Suomalainen Kirjakauppa Oy: Koivuvaarankuja 2, 01640 Vantaa; tel (+358 9) 85 27 51; fax (+358 9) 85 27 900; e-mail apr@suomalainenkk.fi; internet www.suomalainen.com.

FRANCE

Encyclopédie Douanière: Rue Barbès 6, BP 157, 92304 Levallois-Perret Cedex; tel (+33) 1 47 59 09 00; fax (+33) 1 47 59 07 17; e-mail edinfo@editions-ed.fr; internet www.editions-ed.fr.

Institut National de la Statistique et des Etudes Economiques: Rue de Bercy 195, 75582 Paris Cedex 12; tel (+33) 1 53 17 88 44; fax (+33) 1 53 17 88 22; e-mail datashop@insee.fr; internet www.insee.fr.

Journal Officiel: Service des Publications des CE, Rue Desaix 26, 75727 Paris Cedex 15; tel (+33) 1 40 58 77 31; fax (+33) 1 40 58 77 00; e-mail europublications@journal-officiel.gouv.fr; internet www.journal-officiel.gouv.fr.

GERMANY

Bundesanzeiger Verlag GmbH: Amsterdamer Strasse 192, 50735 Cologne; tel (+49 221) 97 66 80; fax (+49 221) 97 66 82 78; e-mail vertrieb@bundesanzeiger.de; internet www.bundesanzeiger.de.

Carl Heymanns Verlag KG: Luxemburger Strasse 449, 50939 Cologne; tel (+49 221) 943 73 0; fax (+49 221) 943 73 901; e-mail vertrieb@heymanns.com.

DSI Data Service and Information GmbH: Kaiserstege 4, Postfach 11 27, 47495 Rheinberg; tel (+49 2843) 32 20; fax (+49 2843) 32 30; e-mail dsi@dsidata .com; internet www.dsidata.com.

GREECE

G. C. Eleftheroudakis SA: International Bookstore, Panepistimiou 17, 105 64 Athens; tel (+30) 21.03.25 84 40; fax (+30)21 03 25 84 99; e-mail elebooks@ books.gr; internet www.books.gr.

Helketek SA: D. Aeginitou Street 7, 11528 Athens; tel (+30 210) 723 52 14; fax (+30 210) 729 15 28; e-mail helketec@ techlink.gr; internet www.techlink.gr/ elketek.

HUNGARY

Euro Info Service: Szt. István krt. 12, III Emelet 1/A, PO Box 1039, 1137 Budapest; tel (+36 1) 329 21 70; fax (+36 1) 349 20 53; e-mail euroinfo@euroinfo.hu; internet www.euroinfo.hu.

ICELAND

Bokabud Larusar Blöndal: Engjateigi 17-19, 105 Reykjavik; tel (+354) 552 55 40; fax (+354) 552 55 60; e-mail bokabud@ simnet.is.

IRELAND

Alan Hanna's Bookshop: 270 Lower Rathmines Road, Dublin 6; tel (+353 1) 496 73 98; fax (+353 1) 496 02 28; e-mail hannas@iol.ie.

Lendac Data Systems Ltd: Unit 6, IDA Enterprise Centre, Pearse Street, Dublin 2; tel (+353 1) 677 61 33; fax (+353 1) 677 01 35; e-mail lendata@lendac.ie; internet www.lendac.ie.

ITALY

Licosa SpA: Via Duca di Calabria 1/1, Casella postale 552, 50125 Florence; tel (+39) 055 64 83 1; fax (+39) 055 64 12 57; e-mail licosa@licosa.com; internet www .licosa.com.

LUXEMBOURG

Messageries du Livre SARL: 5 Rue Raiffeisen, 2411 Luxembourg; tel (+352) 40 10 20; fax (+352) 49 06 61; e-mail mail@mdl.lu; internet www.mdl.lu.

Messageries Paul Kraus: 11 Rue Christophe Plantin, 2339 Luxembourg; tel (+352) 49 98 88-8; fax (+352) 49 98 88-444; e-mail mail@mpk.lu; internet www.mpk.lu.

PF Consult SARL: 8 Grand Rue, 8372 Hobscheid; tel (+352) 24 17 99; fax (+352) 26 10 80 99; e-mail info@pfconsult.com; internet www.pfconsult.com.

MALAYSIA

EBIC Malaysia: Suite 47.01, Level 47, Bangunan AmFinance (Letter box 47), 8 Jalan Yap Kwan Seng, 50450 Kuala Lumpur; tel (+60 3) 21 62 62 98; fax (+60 3) 21 62 61 98; e-mail eumcci@tm.net .my.

MALTA

Miller Distributors Ltd: Malta International Airport, PO Box 25, LQA 05 Luqa; tel (+356) 21 66 44 88; fax (+356) 21 67 67 99; e-mail info@millermalta.com.

MEXICO

Mundi-Prensa México SA de CV: Río Pánuco 141, Colonia Cuauhtémoc, 06500 México DF; tel (+52 5) 533 56 58; fax (+52 5) 514 67 99.

NETHERLANDS

Nedbook International BV: Asterweg 6, Postbus 37600, 1030 BA Amsterdam; tel (+31 20) 634 08 16; fax (+31 20) 634 09 63; e-mail info@nedbook.nl.

SDU Klantenservice: Postbus 20014, 2500 EA The Hague; tel (+31 70) 378 98 80; fax (+31 70) 378 97 83; e-mail sdu@ sdu.nl; internet www.sdu.nl.

Swets Blackwell BV: Heereweg 347 B, Postbus 830, 2160 SZ Lisse; tel (+31 252) 43 51 11; fax (+31 252) 41 58 88; e-mail info@swetsblackwell.com; internet www .swets.nl.

NORWAY

Swets Blackwell AS: Hans Nielsen Hauges gt. 39, Boks 4901 Nydalen, 0423 Oslo; tel (+47) 23 40 00 00; fax (+47) 23 40 00 01; e-mail info@no.swetsblackwell .com.

POLAND

Ars Polona: Krakowskie Przedmiescie 7, Skr. Pocztowa 1001, 00 950 Warsaw; tel (+48 22) 826 12 01; fax (+48 22) 826 62 40; e-mail books119@arspolona.com.pl.

PORTUGAL

Distribuidora de Livros Bertrand Lda: Rua das Terras dos Vales 4-A, Apartado 60037, 2700 Amadora; tel (+351) 214 95 87 87; fax (+351) 214 96 02 55; e-mail dlb@ip.pt.

Imprensa Nacional-Casa da Moeda SA, Sector de Publicações Oficiais: Rua da Escola Politécnica 135, 1250-100 Lisbon Codex; tel (+351) 213 94 57 00; fax (+351) 213 94 57 50; e-mail spoce@ incm.pt; internet www.dr.incm.pt.

SLOVAKIA

Centrum VTI SR: Námestie Slobody 19, 81223 Bratislava 1; tel (+421 2) 54 41 83 64; fax (+421 2) 54 41 83 64; e-mail europ@ tbb1.cvtisr.sk; internet www.cvtisr.sk.

SLOVENIA

GV Zalozba d.o.o.: Dunajska cesta 5, 1000 Ljubljana; tel (+386) 13 09 1800; fax (+386) 13 09 1805; e-mail europ@ gvzalozba.si; internet www.gvzalozba.si.

SOUTH KOREA

The European Union Chamber of Commerce in Korea: Suite 2004, Kyobo Bldg, 1 Chonro 1-Ga, Chongro-Gu, Seoul 110-714; tel (+82 2) 725 98 80/5; fax (+82 2) 725 98 86; e-mail euop@ eucck.org; internet www.eucck.org.

SPAIN

Boletín Oficial del Estado: Trafalgar 27, 28071 Madrid; tel (+34) 91 538 21 11; fax (+34) 91 538 21 21; e-mail clientes@ com.boe.es; internet www.boe.es.

Greendata: Tuset 19, 2°-7a, 08006 Barcelona; tel (+34) 93 265 34 24; fax (+34) 93 202 10 77; e-mail hugo@greendata.es; internet www.greendata.es.

Mundi Prensa Libros, SA: Castelló 37, 28001 Madrid; tel (+34) 91 436 37 00; fax (+34) 91 575 39 98; e-mail libreria@ mundiprensa.es; internet www .mundiprensa.com.

SRI LANKA

EBIC Sri Lanka: Trans Asia Hotel, 115 Sir Chittampalam, A. Gardiner Mawatha, Colombo 2; tel (+94 1) 074 71 50 78; fax (+94 1) 44 87 79; e-mail ebicsl@ sltnet.lk.

SWEDEN

BTJ AB: Traktorvägen 11-13, 221 82 Lund; tel (+46 46) 18 00 00; fax (+46 46) 30 79 47; e-mail btjeu-pub@btj.se; internet www.btj.se.

SWITZERLAND

Euro Info Center Schweiz, c/o OSEC Business Network Switzerland: Stampfenbachstrasse 85, PF 492, 8035 Zürich; tel (+41 1) 365 53 15; fax (+44 1) 365 54 11; e-mail eics@osec.ch; internet www.osec.ch/eics.

TAIWAN

Tycoon Information Inc.: PO Box 81-466, 105 Taipei; tel (+886 2) 87 12 88 86; fax (+886 2) 87 12 47 47; e-mail eiutpe@ms21.hinet.net.

UNITED KINGDOM

Abacus Data Services (UK) Ltd: Causeway House, 876 North Row, Central Milton Keynes MK9 3NS; tel (+44 1908) 24 07 95; fax (+44 1908) 24 06 49; e-mail info@abacusuk.co.uk; internet www.abacusuk.co.uk.

DataOp Alliance Ltd: PO Box 2600, Eastbourne BN22 0QN; tel (+44 1323) 52 01 14; fax (+44 1323) 52 00 05; e-mail sales@dataop.com; internet www.ojeu.com.

The Stationery Office Ltd: Customer Services, PO Box 29, Norwich NR3 1GN; tel (+44 870) 60 05 522; fax (+44 870) 60 05 533; e-mail book.orders@tso.co.uk; internet www.tso.co.uk.

UNITED STATES OF AMERICA

Bernan Associates: 4611-F Assembly Drive, Lanham, MD 20706-4391; tel (+1 800) 274 44 47; fax (+1 800) 865 34 50; e-mail query@bernan.com; internet www.bernan.com.

EUR-OP's Official Gateways: CELEX, EUDOR, RISC

BELGIUM

PF Consult SARL: Avenue des Constellations 2, 1200 Brussels; tel (+32 2) 771 10 04; fax (+32 2) 771 10 04; e-mail paul.feyt@tvd.be; internet http://pfconsult.com.

CANADA

Advanced Information Databases Inc.: 361 Dundas St, PO Box 248, Woodstock, Ontario N4S 7W8; tel (+1 519) 539 12 97; fax (+1 519) 539 31 76; e-mail adinfo@adinfo.com; internet www.adinfo.com.

DENMARK

J.H. Schultz Information A/S: Herstedvang 4, 2620 Albertslund; tel (+45) 43 63 23 00; fax (+45) 43 63 19 69; e-mail schultz@schultz.dk; internet www.schultz.dk.

FINLAND

TietoEnator Corporation Oyj Information Service: PO Box 406, 02101 Espoo; tel (+358 9) 86 25 23 31; fax (+358 9) 86 25 35 53; e-mail markku.kolari@tietoenator.com; internet www.tietoenator.com/tietopalvelut.

GREECE

Helketek SA: D. Aeginitou Street 7, 115 28 Athens; tel (+30 210) 723 52 14; fax (+30 210) 729 15 28; e-mail helketec@techlink.gr; internet www.techlink.gr/elketek.

NETHERLANDS

EG-Adviescentrum: Pettelaarpark 10, 5201 DZ 's-Hertogenbosch; tel (+31 73) 680 66 00; fax (+31 73) 612 32 10; e-mail info@egadvies.nl; internet www.egadvies.nl.

NORWAY

Euro Info Centre Vestlandsforsking: Postboks 163, 6851 Sogndal; tel (+47) 57 67 61 50; fax (+47) 57 67 61 90; e-mail eic@vestforsk.no; internet http://eic.vestforsk.no.

PORTUGAL

Telepac: Rua Dr. A. Loureiro Borges 1, Miraflores, 1495 Algés; tel (+351) 21 790 70 00; fax (+351) 21 790 73 87; e-mail eurobases@mail.telepac.pt; internet www.telepac.pt.

SPAIN

Sarenet: Parque Tecnologico, Edificio 103, 48016 Zamudio (Vizcaya); tel (+34) 94 420 94 70; fax (+34) 94 420 94 65; e-mail info@sarenet.es; internet www.sarenet.es.

SWEDEN

Sema Group InfoData AB: Fyrverkarbacken 34–36, PO Box 34101, 100 26 Stockholm; tel (+46 8) 738 50 00; fax (+46 8) 618 97 78; e-mail infotorg@infodata.sema.se; internet www.infodata.sema.se.

UNITED KINGDOM

Context Electronic Publishers: Grand Union House, 20 Kentish Town Road, London NW1 9NR; tel (+44 20) 72 67 89 89; fax (+44 20) 72 67 11 33; e-mail enquiries@context.co.uk; internet www.justis.com.

UNITED STATES OF AMERICA

Advanced Information Databases Inc.: 23205 Gratiot Ave, Eastpointe MI 48021; tel (+1 519) 539 12 97; fax (+1 519) 539 31 76; e-mail adinfo@adinfo.com; internet www.adinfo.com.

INFORMATION NETWORKS

The term 'information network' does not refer to a telecommunications or informatics network, but to a coherent set of information on a given theme or sector.

Information may take different forms: electronic (databases for example), written (periodicals, brochures, dossiers, directories), various services, etc.

Access to such networks is sometimes confined to certain categories of user.

Individual sections follow for the Information Networks listed below:

- Euro-Info-Centres
- EBN/BIC Network
- EURYDICE: information network on education in Europe
- European Consumer Information Centres
- EURES: European employment services network
- European Observatory on the Social Situation, Demography and Family
- Innovation Relay Centres
- Urban Forums for Sustainable Development
- Eurolibraries
- ECSA-NET: interactive communication network for academics working in the field of European integration studies
- Network of National Academic Recognition Information Centres (NARIC)
- Eurodesk

As Small and Medium-Sized Enterprises (SMEs) play a major role in economic growth and job creation, a special action programme was implemented to assist them.

One of the primary objectives of the programme was to place at the disposal of SMEs an information system tailored to their needs and directly accessible in the Member States. The result has been the establishment of Euro Info Centres (EICs).

The Euro Info Centres offer companies statistical, legal and regulatory information on the EU. The information is available either immediately, if the Euro Info Centres have it in stock, or within a few days if it has to be sought from the European Commission in Brussels or in Luxembourg.

The Euro Info Centres make it possible to obtain the documents and brochures disseminated by the Office for Official Publications of the European Communities in Luxembourg. They also supply online information via the databases managed by EUROBASES, the European Commission's host: CELEX, RISC.

Following the European Commission's reorganization, the Euro Info Centres are now managed by the DG Enterprise.

Euro Info Centres (EICs) are integrated within existing economic information structures in the Member States so as to enable them to be more accessible. They are spread throughout the whole of the European Union.

Euro Info Centres (EICs) in Member States

AUSTRIA

Eisenstadt: Regionalmanagement Burgenland, Technologiezentrum, 7000 Eisenstadt; tel (2682) 704240; fax (2682) 7042410; e-mail office@rmb.co.at; internet www.rmb.co.at; Contact: Georg Schachinger.

Graz: Wirtschaftskammer Steiermark, Körblergasse 111–113, Postfach 1038, 8021 Graz; tel (316) 60-16-00; fax (316) 60-15-35; e-mail eic@wkstmk.at; internet www.wko.at/stmk/eic; Contact: Claudia Weyringer.

Innsbruck: Wirtschaftskammer Tirol, Meinhardstr 14, 6021 Innsbruck; tel (512) 53-10-12-93; fax (512) 53-10-12-75; e-mail eic@wktirol.at; internet www.wko.at/tirol/eic; Dept Head: Gregor Leitner.

Linz: Wirtschaftskammer Oberösterreich, Mozartstr 20, Postfach 253, 4010 Linz; tel (732) 780-04-79; fax (732) 780-06-42; e-mail eic@wkooe.at; internet wko.at/ooe/eic; Contact: Robert Leitner.

Salzburg: Wirtschaftskammer Salzburg, Julius-Raab-Platz 1, 5027 Salzburg; tel (662) 8888-0; fax (662) 8888-582; e-mail wirtschaftskammer@sbg.wk.or.at; internet wko.at/sbg; Contacts: Dr Christian Möller, Ursula Felser.

Vienna: Wirtschaftskammer Österreich, Wiedner Hauptstr 63, Postfach 152, 1045 Vienna; tel (1) 501-05-42-06; fax (1) 501-05-29-7; e-mail euroinfo@wko.at; internet wko.at/eu; Head of Centre: Heinz Kogler.

Vienna: Wiener Wirtschaftsförderungsfonds, Ebendorferstr 2, 1010 Vienna; tel (1) 40-00-86-173; fax (1) 40-00-70-70; e-mail eic@wwff.gv.at; internet www.europaservice.cc; Head of Centre: Dagmar Tomschitlz; European Dept Head: Monika Unterholzner.

BELGIUM

Antwerp: Kamer van Koophandel en Nijverheid van Antwerpen, 12 Markgravestraat, 2000 Antwerp; tel (3) 232-22-19; fax (3) 233-64-42; e-mail eic@kknaw.be; internet kknaw.be; Dir: Luc Van Looveren.

Brussels: Chambre de Commerce et d'Industrie de Bruxelles, 500 ave Louise, 1050 Brussels; tel (2) 648-58-73; fax (2) 640-93-28; e-mail eic@ccib.irisnet.be; internet www.ccib.be; Head of Centre: Michel Jadot.

Brussels: Ministerie van de Vlaamse Gemeenschap, Administratie voor Economie, 1 Markiesstraat, 5e ver, 1000 Brussels; tel (2) 553-38-77; fax (2) 502-47-02; e-mail euro.infocentrum@ewbl.vlaanderen.be; internet www.vlaanderen.be/net/sites; Contact: Leen De Smet.

Ghent: GOM Oost-Vlaanderen, Huis van de Economie, Seminariestraat 2, 9000 Ghent; tel (9) 267-86-30; fax (9) 267-86-96; e-mail eic@gomov.be; internet www.gom.oost-vlaanderen.be; Contact: Johan Declerck.

Hainaut: rue P. J. Duménil 4, 7000 Mons; tel (65) 200360; fax (65) 220387; e-mail beesh.eic@hainaut.be; Contact: Anne Pagani.

Hasselt: Kamer voor Handel en Nijverheid van Limburg, 51 Gouverneur Roppesingel, 3500 Hasselt; tel (11) 56-02-32; fax (11) 56-02-09; e-mail eic@khnl.be; internet www.khnl.be; Head of Centre: Hilde Nuyts.

Kortrijk: Unizo International, 10 Lange Steenstraat, 8500 Kortrijk; tel (56) 26-44-88; fax (56) 26-44-89; e-mail eic.kortrijk@kmonet.be; www.unizo.be; Dir Christine Faes.

Libramont: Chambre de Commerce et d'Industrie du Luxembourg Belge, 1 Grand Rue, 6800 Libramont; tel (61) 29-30-40; fax (61) 29-30-69; e-mail am.barbette@ccib.be; internet www.ccilb.be; Centre Man: Anne-Michèle Barbette.

Liège: SPI, rue du Vertbois 11, 4000 Liège; tel (42) 20-11-11; fax (42) 30-11-20; e-mail info@spi.be; internet www.ipeliege.be; Head of Office: Monique Rover; Attaché: Sylvie Collard.

Namur: Bureau Economique de la Province de Namur (BEPN), Palais des Expositions, 2 ave Sergent Vrithoff, 5000 Namur; tel (81) 71-71-44; fax (81) 71-71-00; e-mail mdh@bep.be; internet www.namur.be; Contact: Marc Dehareng.

Vilvoorde: Kamer voor Handel en Nijverheid Halle-Vilvoorde, Medialaan 26, 1800 Vilvoorde; tel (2) 255-20-21; fax (2) 255-20-30; e-mail eic@ccihv.be; internet www.ccihv.be/eic; Head of Centre: Frederik Vanden Bulcke; Administration Officer: Nahid Noyen.

CYPRUS

Nicosia: Cyprus Chamber of Commerce and Industry, POB 21455, 38 Grivas Dighenis Ave and 3 Deligiorgis St, Nicosia 1509; tel (2) 2889752; fax (2) 2668691; e-mail chamber@cciorg.cy; internet www.ccci.org.cy; Centre Head: Demetra Palaonda; Information Officer: Stalo Demosthenous.

CZECH REPUBLIC

Brno: Chamber of Commerce, Vystaviste 1, Areal BVV, 64804 Brno; tel (5) 41159082; fax (5) 41153055; e-mail eicbrno@ohkbrno.cz; internet www.ohkbrno.cz; Contact: Magda Drholcova.

Hradec Kralove: Komercni Banka, Osvoboditelu 798, 50216 Hradec Kralove; tel (49) 5815705; fax (49) 5815712; e-mail h_hruba@kb.cz; internet www.kb.cz; Contact: Veronika Rychlovska.

Liberec: Regional Development Agency, nám Dr E. Benese 26, U Jezu 2, 46001 Liberec 1; tel (48) 5226278; fax (48)

5226273; e-mail info@arr-nisa.cz; internet www.arr-nisa.cz; Centre Head: Martina Prokopova.

Most: Usti Regional Development Agency, Budovatelu 2830, 434 37 Most; tel (35) 6206619; fax (35) 7706331; e-mail eic@rra.cz; internet www.rra.cz; Man: Leo Steiner; Project Mans: Tomas Tucek, Kveta Mala.

Ostrava: Regional Development Agency, Na Jizdarne 7, 70200 Ostrava; tel (59) 56912312; fax (59) 56912004; e-mail eic@rdaova.cz; internet www.rdaova.cz; Man.: Gabriela Kalocova.

Plzen: Plzen Business Innovation Centre, Riegrova 1, 30625 Plzen; tel (19) 7235379; fax (19) 7235320; e-mail eic@bic .cz; internet www.bic.cz; Contact: Eva Beranova.

Prague: Korespondencni Stredisko, Regional Development Agency of the Czech Republic, Vinohradska 46, 12000 Prague 2; tel (2) 21580203; fax (2) 21580292; e-mail euroinfo@crr.cz; internet www.crr.cz; Contact: Marie Pavlu.

DENMARK

Aabenraa: Sønderjyllands Erhvervsråd, Bjerggade 4c, 6200 Aabenraa; tel 73-62-10-10; fax 73-62-10-11; e-mail eicdk053@ sjec.dk; internet www.sjec.dk/eic.htm; Contact: Egon Sveistrup.

Aarhus: Aarhus Amts Kommune, Haslegårdsvænget 18–20, 8210 Aarhus V; tel 86-15-25-77; fax 86-15-43-22; e-mail eic@ cvu.dk; internet www.cvu.dk; EU Consultant: Knud Chr. Pedersen.

Copenhagen: Det Danske Handelskammer, Børsen, 1217 Copenhagen; tel 33-95-05-00; fax 33-32-52-16; e-mail eic@ commerce.dk; www.eic-commerce.dk; Contact: Bo Green.

Copenhagen: Danish Agency for Trade and Industry, Rådhuspladsen 14, 1550 Copenhagen; tel 33-32-72-78; fax 33-32-74-78; e-mail eurocenter@schultz.dk; internet www.eurocenter.schultz.dk; Contact: Annette Borchsenius.

Herning: Herning Erhvervsråd, Birk Centerpark 7, 7400 Herning; tel 97-12-92-00; fax 97-12-92-44; e-mail euc@eu -center.dk; internet www.eu-center.dk; Head of Centre: Jette Rendboll.

Odense: Euro Info Centre Fyn, Fyns Erhversrådv, Blangstedgaardsvej 1, 5220 Odense; tel 70-21-18-50; fax 70-21-18-51; e-mail ask@fec.dk; internet www .eufyn.dk; Contact: Erik Helmer Hansen.

Viborg: Håndværksrådet International, Nytorv 1, 8800 Viborg; tel 87-27-47-47; fax 87-27-47-57; e-mail eic@hvri.dk; internet www.hvri.dk; Contact: Finn Kungstad.

Vordingborg: Storstrøms Erhvervscenter, Marienbergvej 132, 4760 Vordingborg; tel 55-34-01-55; fax 55-34-03-55; e-mail eic@eic-storstrom.dk; internet www.eic-strostrom.dk; Contact: Jens Simonsgaard.

ESTONIA

Narva: Business Advisory Services Foundation, Peetri 1, 20308 Narva; tel 35-99-259; fax 35-99-255; e-mail nbas@ nbas.ee; internet www.nbas.ee; Man: Anne Veevo.

Tallinn: Estonian Chamber of Commerce and Industry, 10130 Tallinn, Toom-Kooli 17; tel 644-8079; fax 646-0245; e-mail kristina@koda.ee; internet www.koda.ee; Contact: Kristina Tshistova.

FINLAND

Helsinki: Chamber of Commerce, Kalevankatu 12, 00100 Helsinki; tel (9) 228601; fax (9) 22860228; e-mail taisto .sulonen@helsinki.chamber.fi; internet www.helsinki.chamber.fi; Head of Centre: Taisto Sulonen.

Kuopio: Kuopio Chamber of Commerce, Kasarmikatu 2, 70110 Kuopio; tel (17) 2822228; fax (17) 2823304; e-mail eic .kuopio@iwn.fi; internet www.iwn.fi/ kuopionkauppakamari/eic; Contact: Hannele Holopainen.

Lahti: Lahti Chamber of Commerce, Rauhankatu 10, 15110 Lahti; tel (3) 8216020; fax (3) 8216030; e-mail eiclahti@lahtichamber.fi; internet www .euroneuvontakeskus.com; Contact: Tapani Kasso.

Oulu: Employment and Economic Development Centre for Northern Finland, Viestikatu 1, POB 86, 90101 Oulu; tel (8) 5369007; fax (8) 5368031; e-mail riitta.lumiaho@te-keskus.fi; internet www.euroneuvontakeskus; Contact: Riitta Lumiaho.

Turku: EIC Turku, Employment and Economic Development Centre for Varsinais-Suomi, Business Department, Ratapihankatu 36, POB 523, 20100 Turku; tel (2) 2100400; fax (2) 2100521; e-mail eero.kokkonen@te-keskus.fi; internet www.euroneuvontakeskus.com; Contact: Timo Metsa-Tokila.

Vaasa: EIC Botnia, Ostrobothnia Chamber of Commerce, Raastuvankatu 20, 65100 Vaasa; tel (6) 3186400; fax (6) 3186490; e-mail eicbotnia@multi.fi; internet www.multi.fi/eic-botnia; Contact: Juha Häkkinen.

FRANCE

Ajaccio: Chambre de Commerce et d'Industrie d'Ajaccio et de la Corse, Hôtel Consulaire, quai l'Herminier, 20090 Ajaccio; tel 4-95-51-55-80; fax 4-95-21-23-89; e-mail philippe.bonnefont@ corse-du-sud.cci.fr; Contact: Philippe Bonnefont.

Amiens: 36 rue des Otages, 80037 Amiens Cedex 01; tel 3-22-82-80-93; fax 3-22-82-80-65; e-mail eic@picardie.cci.fr; internet www.picardie.cci.fr; Contact: Marie-Françoise Duée.

Besançon: Chambre Régionale de Commerce et d'Industrie de Franche-Comté, Valparc, ZAC de Valentin, 25043 Besançon; tel 3-81-47-42-13; fax 3-81-80-70-94; e-mail eic@franche.comte.cci.fr; Head: Jean-Michel Chauvin.

Bordeaux: EIC Bordeaux–Aquitaine, 2 place de la Bourse, 33076 Bordeaux Cedex; tel 5-56-79-44-34; fax 5-56-79-44-38; e-mail wtc-eic@mailcity.com; Dir: Sebastien Mounier.

Caen: Chambre Régionale de Commerce et d'Industrie de Basse Normandie, 21 place de la République, 14052 Caen Cedex; tel 2-31-38-31-67; fax 2-31-85-76-41; e-mail eic-fr260@basse-normandie .cci.fr; Contact: Remy Dufour.

Châlons-sur-Marne: EIC Champagne-Ardenne, 10 rue de Chastillon, BP 537, 51011 Châlons-sur-Marne; tel 3-26-69-33-65; fax 3-26-69-33-69; e-mail marie .eic@champagne-ardenne.cci.fr; Contact: Jean-Bernard Massee.

Charenton-le-Pont: Forum Francophone des Affaires, BP 98, 94223 Charenton-le-Pont; tel 43-96-26-06; fax 43-53-41-80; e-mail gimac-ffe@wanadoo.fr; Head of Centre: Jacques Colignon.

Clermont-Ferrand: Euro Info Centre Auvergne, Chambre de Commerce et d'Industrie de Clermont-Ferrand/Issoire, 148 blvd Lavoisier, 63037 Clermont-Ferrand; tel 4-73-43-43-32; fax 4-73-43-43-25; e-mail eic@clermont-fd.cci.fr; internet www.clermont-fd.cci.fr/euro/ euro.htm; Contact: Elke Mayr-Rivière.

Dijon: Chambre Régionale de Commerce et d'Industrie de Bourgogne, Parc de l'Europe, place des Nations Unies, BP 87009, 21070 Dijon Cedex; tel 3-80-60-40-63; fax 3-80-60-40-21; e-mail a .simard@bourgogne.cci.fr; Contact: Robert Guyon.

Grenoble (satellite unit of Lyons Euro Info Centre): EIC Grenoble/Grex, 5 place Robert Schuman, BP 1509, 38025 Grenoble Cedex 1; tel 4-76-28-28-40; fax 4-76-28-28-35; e-mail olivier.bozon@ grex.fr; internet www.grex.fr; Man: Olivier Bozon.

Limoges: Chambre Régionale de Commerce et d'Industrie Limousin/Poitou-Charentes, blvd des Arcades, 87038

Limoges; tel 5-55-04-40-25; fax 5-55-04-40-40; e-mail eic.limousin@pc1.cci.fr; internet www.eiclimousin.fr; Contact: Martin Forst.

Lyons: Chambre de Commerce et d'Industrie de Lyon, place de la Bourse, 69289 Lyons Cedex 02; tel 4-72-40-57-46; fax 4-78-37-94-00; e-mail jamon@lyon.cci.fr; Contact: Catherine Jamon-Servel.

Marcq-en-Baroeul: Euro Info Centre Nord-Pas de Calais, 40 rue Eugène Jacquet, 59708 Marcq-en-Baroeul; tel 3-20-99-45-08; fax 3-20-99-47-59; e-mail www.eic-npdc.or; internet www.eic-npdc.or; Man: Dominique Chaussec de Lecour.

Marseilles: Maison de l'International WTC Marseille, 2 rue Henri-Barbusse, 13241 Marseilles Cedex 01; tel 4-91-39-33-77; fax 4-91-39-33-77; e-mail euro-info-centre@marseille-provence.cci.fr; internet www.marseille-provence.cci.fr; Contact: Martine Liogier-Coudoux.

Metz: Conseil Régional de Lorraine, place Gabriel Hocquard, BP 81004, 57036 Metz Cedex 1; tel 3-87-33-60-80; fax 3-87-32-89-33; e-mail eic@cr-lorraine.fr; Contact: Isabelle Letellier.

Montpellier: Euro Info Centre Montpellier Languedoc-Roussillon, 273 ave de la Pompignane, Résidence 'Majestic', Bâtiment 1, 34961 Montpellier Cedex 2; tel 4-67-13-68-51; fax 4-67-13-68-22; e-mail contact@eic-lr.org; internet www.eic.lr.org; Dir: Nicholas Mouetaux.

Nantes: EIC Pays de la Loire, 16 quai Ernest Renaud, BP 70515, 44105 Nantes Cedex 04; tel 2-40-44-63-75; fax 2-40-44-63-20; e-mail eic@pdl.cci.fr; Contact: Jean-Paul Moulin.

Nice (satellite unit of Marseilles Euro Info Centre): Chambre de Commerce et d'Industrie Nice/Côte d'Azur, 20 blvd Carabacel, BP 1259, 06005 Nice Cedex 1; tel 4-93-13-74-22; fax 4-93-13-75-71; e-mail delphine.foucaud@cote-azur.cci.fr; internet www.ccinice-cote-azur.com; Contact: Delphine Foucaud.

Orléans: Région Centre Chambre Régionale de Commerce et d'Industrie, 6 rue Pierre et Marie Curie, rond-point Parc d'Activités d'Ingré, 45142 Saint-Jean de la Ruelle-Orléans; tel 2-38-25-25-50; fax 2-38-43-00-39; e-mail eic@centre.cci.fr; internet www.eic.centre.cci.fr; Head of Service: Bernard Cottin; Documentalist: Nathalie Angibaud.

Paris: Agence Française pour le Développement International des Entreprises, 14 ave d'Eylau, 75116 Paris; tel 1-44-34-50-70; fax 1-53-70-06-61; e-mail ghivertmes@ubifrance.com; internet www.ubi-france.com; Head of Centre: Gisèle Hivert-Messeca.

Paris: Assemblée Permanente des Chambres de Métiers, 12 ave Marceau, 75008 Paris; tel 1-44-43-10-14; fax 1-47-20-34-48; e-mail eic@apcm.fr; internet www.apcm.com; Contact: Fiona Gerente.

Paris: Comité de Liaison des Comités de Bassin d'Emploi, 10–16 rue Brancion, 75016 Paris; tel 1-53-86-11-65; fax 1-53-86-11-51; e-mail clcbe@wanadoo.fr; internet www.clcbe.com; Contact: Farbod Khansari.

Paris: Chambre de Commerce et d'Industrie de Paris (CCIP), 27 ave de Friedland, 75382 Paris Cedex 08; tel 1-55-65-73-13; fax 1-55-65-73-06; e-mail eicfr274@ccip.fr; internet www.ccip.fr/eic; Contact: Daniel Gassmann.

Paris: EIC MEDEF International, 31 ave Pierre 1er de Serbie, 75784 Paris Cedex 16; tel 1-40-69-96-03; fax 1-40-69-43-66; e-mail pgautier@medef.fr; Contact: Clement Laloux.

Paris: Groupe Banques Populaires, Le Ponant de Paris, 5 rue Leblanc, 75511 Paris; tel 1-40-39-69-48; fax 1-40-69-43-66; e-mail laurence.bertranddespannet@bfbp.banquepopulaire.fr; internet www.banquepopulaire.fr; Enterprises Dept Man: Laurence Bertrand-Espannet.

Paris: Centre Français du Commerce Extérieur, 10 ave d'Iéna, 75783 Paris; tel 1-40-73-32-20; fax 1-40-73-37-48; e-mail fr272.paris@fcis.cec.eu.int; internet www.cfce.fr; Man: Edith Launey-Heymann; Delegate: Laurence Alphandery.

Paris: Secrétariat d'Etat à l'Industrie, de la Poste et des Télécommunications (MINEFI), 20 ave de Ségur, 75353 Paris Cedex 07; tel 1-43-19-28-16; fax 1-43-19-60-37; e-mail denis.lagniez@industrie.gouv.fr; internet industrie/eic; Contact: Denis Lagniez.

Paris: Union Professionnelle Artisanale, 79 ave de Villiers, 75017 Paris; tel 1-47-63-31-31; fax 1-47-63-31-10; e-mail upa@wanadoo.fr; Contact: Armand de Bernières.

Poitiers: Association Poitou-Charentes-Europe, Immeuble Antarès, 4 ave du Téléport, BP 50110, 86961 Futuroscope Chasseneuil Cedex; tel 5-49-49-63-30; fax 5-49-49-07-70; e-mail apce@apce.org; internet www.apce.org; Contact: Laurence Matas.

Rennes: EIC Bretagne, 1 rue du Général Guillaudot, CS 14422, 35044 Rennes; tel 2-99-25-41-57; fax 2-99-25-41-10; e-mail eic@bretagne.cci.fr; internet www.industrie.gouv.fr/eic; Contact: Alexandre Colomb.

Rouen: EIC de Haute Normandie, 9 rue Robert Schuman, BP 124, 76000 Rouen; tel 2-35-88-44-42; fax 2-35-88-06-52; e-mail fr277.rouen@fcis.cec.eu.int; Contact: Véronique Tetu.

Strasbourg: Chambre de Commerce et d'Industrie de Strasbourg et du Bas Rhin, Maison du Commerce Int de Strasbourg (MCIS), 4 quai Kléber, 67080 Strasbourg Cedex; tel 3-88-76-42-24; fax 3-88-76-42-00; e-mail u.gori.kaminski@strasbourg.cci.fr; internet www.strasbourg.cci.fr; Contact: Ursula Gori Kaminski.

Toulouse: Chambre Régionale de Commerce et d'Industrie Midi-Pyrénées, 5 rue Dieudonné Costes, BP 32, 31701 Toulouse-Blagnac; tel 5-62-74-20-32; fax 5-62-74-20-20; e-mail eic@midi-pyrenees.cci.fr; internet www.midi-pyrenees.cci.fr; Contact: Jean-Michel de Bellerive.

Versailles: Euro Info Centre Versailles/Ile-de-France, 21 rue d'Angiviller, BP 3541, 78035 Versailles; tel 1-39-20-58-50; fax 1-39-20-58-78; e-mail eicfr271@iledefrance.cci.fr; Contact: Geraldine Mouellic.

FRENCH OVERSEAS DEPARTMENTS

Cayenne, French Guiana: Chambre de Commerce et d'Industrie de Guyane Française, place de l'Esplanade, BP 49, 97321 Cayenne Cedex, French Guiana; tel 29-97-11; fax 29-96-45; e-mail k.nerin@guyane.cci.fr; Contact: Alain-Georges Habran.

Fort-de-France, Martinique: Chambre de Commerce et d'Industrie de la Martinique, 50 rue Ernest Deproge, 97241 Fort-de-France, Martinique; tel 55-28-25; fax 71-66-80; e-mail moutoucoumaro@martinique.cci.fr; www.martinique.cci.fr; Contact: Cémiane Moutoucoumaro.

Pointe-à-Pitre, Guadeloupe: Chambre de Commerce et d'Industrie de Pointe-à-Pitre, Complexe World Trade Center, blvd de la Pointe Jarry, 97122 Baie-Mahault, Guadeloupe; tel 25-06-16; fax 25-06-06; e-mail eic@pointe-a-pitre.cci.fr; internet www.cci-pap.org/euroinfocentre; Centre Head: Vasanta Venchard; Technical Assistant: Carole Theobald; Researcher/Sec: Sandrine Soubdhan.

Saint-Denis, Réunion: Chambre de Commerce et d'Industrie de la Réunion, Maison de l'Entreprise, 13 rue Pasteur, 97400 Saint-Denis, Réunion; tel 94-21-64; fax 94-22-90; e-mail teci.eic@reunion.cci.fr; internet www.reunion.cci.fr; Contact: Ludovic Serre.

GERMANY

Aachen: EU Beratungsstelle, Industrie- und Handelskammer zu Aachen, 52007 Aachen, Theaterstr 6–10, Postfach 650; tel (241) 44600; fax (241) 4460259; e-mail eic@aachen.ihk.de; internet www.aachen.ihk.de; Dir: Frank Malis.

Augsburg: Industrie- und Hamelskammer für Augsburg und Schwaben, 86150

Augsburg, Stettenstr 1–3; tel (821) 3162285; fax (821) 3162171; e-mail brbara.klause@augsburg.ihk.de; Contact: Axel Sir.

Berlin: BAO Berlin Marketing Service GmbH, 10623 Berlin, Fasanenstr 85; tel (30) 31510240; fax (30) 31510316; e-mail kub@berlin.ihk.de; internet www .baoberlin.de; Centre Head: Monika Schulz-Strelow; Senior Consultants: Eckhard Behrendt, Dr Petra Münch.

Berlin: Deutsches Informationszentrum für Technische Regeln (DITR) im Deutsche Inst für Normung eV, 10787 Berlin, Burggrafenstr 6; tel (30) 26012605; fax (30) 2628125; e-mail eic@ din.de; internet www.din.de; Contact: Bärbel Zimmermann.

Berlin: Bundesverband der Deutschen Industrie, Breite Str 29, 10178 Berlin; tel (30) 20-28-16-23; fax (30) 20-28-26-23; e-mail eic@bdi-online.de; internet www.bdi-online.de; Contact: Fabian Wehnert.

Berlin: Deutscher Sparkassen- und Giroverband, Behrenstr 31, POB 110180, 10831 Berlin; tel (30) 20-22-53-12; fax (30) 20-22-53-13; e-mail eic@dsgv.de; internet www.dsgv.de/dsgv/euservle.usf; Dir: Bertram Reddig.

Berlin: Deutscher Industrie- und Handelskammertag, Abteilung Aussenwirtschaft, Breite Str 29, 10178 Berlin; tel (30) 20-30-82-30-6; fax (30) 20-30-82-33-3; e-mail muenker.jochen@berlin .dihk.de; internet www.ihk.de/dihk; Contact: Jochen Münker.

Berlin: Zentralverband des Deutschen Handwerks, Mohrenstr 20–21, 10117 Berlin; tel (30) 20-61-93-33; fax (30) 20-61-94-55; e-mail zanzig@zdh.de; internet www.handwerk.de; Centre Head: Klauspeter Zanzig.

Bremen: AXON Technologie Consult GmbH, 28359 Bremen, Hochschulring 6, POB 347076; tel (421) 201560; fax (421) 2015690; e-mail eic@axon-technologie.de; internet www.eic-bremen.de; Contact: Robert Redlarski.

Chemnitz: Industrie- und Handelskammer Südwestsachsen, 09111 Chemnitz, Str der Nationen 25; tel (371) 6900230; fax (371) 6900222; e-mail hofmann@ chemnitz.ihk.de; internet www.chemnitz .ihk.de; European Officer: Barbara Hofmann.

Cologne: Arbeitsgemeinschaft Industrieller Forschungsvereinigung 'Otto von Guericke', Bayenthalgürtel 23, 50968 Cologne; tel (221) 3768038; fax (221) 3768027; e-mail eu@aif.de; internet www.aif.de; Contact: Thomas Klein.

Cologne: Bundesagentur für Aussenwirtschaft, Agrippastr 87–93, 50676 Cologne; tel (221) 2057273; fax (221)

2057212; e-mail westeuropa@bfai.com; internet www.bfai.com; Contact: Elfi Schreiber.

Dresden: Industrie- und Handelskammer Dresden, 1239 Dresden, Langer Weg 4; tel (351) 2802185; fax (351) 2802280; e-mail service@dresden.ihk.de; internet www.dresden.ihk.de; Centre Head: Ronny Leskiewicz.

Erfurt: EU-Beratungsstelle für Unternehmen der Landesbank Hessen-Thüringen, 99084 Erfurt, Bonifaciusstr 16, Postfach 100444; tel (361) 2177230; fax (361) 2177233; e-mail euroinfocentreerfurt@t-online.de; internet www.eic.de; Centre Head: Wilbert Somers; Information Experts: Petra Räder, Eva-Maria Nowak.

Frankfurt am Main: Kreditanstalt für Wiederaufbau, Palmengartenstr 5–9, 60325 Frankfurt am Main; tel (69) 74313573; fax (69) 74313505; e-mail stephan.opitz@kfw.de; internet www .kfw.de; Contact: Stephan Opitz.

Frankfurt an der Oder: Industrie- und Handelskammer Frankfurt an der Oder, 15203 Frankfurt an der Oder, Puschkinstr 12b, Postfach 1366; tel (335) 5621287; fax (335) 5621285; e-mail eic@ ffo.ihk24.de; internet www.ffo.ihk24.de; Contacts: Sabine Anders, Frank Kutschke, Heike Trusch.

Hanover: Niedersächsische Agentur für Technologietransfer und Innovation GmbH (NATI), 30165 Hanover, Vahrenwalder Str 7; tel (511) 9357121; fax (511) 9357439; e-mail eic@nati.de; internet www.eic-hannover.de; Man: Uda Ouakidi.

Kassel: Euro Info Centre Kassel, Teichstr 16, 34130 Kassel; tel (561) 9789770; fax (561) 9789780; e-mail info@eic-kassel.de; internet www.eic -kassel.de; Contact: Jorg Stoecker.

Kiel: EU-Beratungsstelle Investitionsbank Schleswig-Holstein/RKW Landesgruppe Nord-Ost, 24103 Kiel, Fleethörn 29–31; 24100 Kiel, Postfach 1128; tel (431) 9003445; fax (431) 9003207; e-mail eic@ibank-sh.de; internet www.ibank -sh.de; Centre Head: Annegret Meyer-Kock.

Lahr: Industrie- und Handelskammer Südlicher Oberrhein, 77933 Lahr, Lotzbechstr 31; 77905 Lahr, Postfach 1547; tel (7821) 2703690; fax (7821) 2703777; e-mail eic@lr.freiberg.ihk.de; internet www.suedlicher-oberrhein.ihk.de; Dir: Petra Steck.

Leipzig: EU-Beratungsstelle für Unternehmen in der Industrie- und Handelskammer zu Leipzig, 04109 Leipzig, Goerdelerring 5; tel (341) 1267325; fax (341) 1267425; e-mail info@leipzig .ihk.de; internet www.leipzig.ihk.de; Dir: Christa Friedrich.

Magdeburg: Handwerkskammer Magdeburg, 39104 Magdeburg, Bahnhofstr 49a; 39005 Magdeburg, Postfach 1568; tel (391) 565000; fax (391) 5650099; e-mail info@eic-magdeburg.de; internet www.eic-magdeburg.de; Contact: Heinz-Dieter Dömland.

Mannheim: Industrie- und Handelskammer Rhein-Neckar, 68016 Mannheim, Postfach 101661, L1–2; tel (621) 1709227; fax (621) 1709219; e-mail eic@ mannheim.ihk.de; internet www .mannheim.ihk.de; Contact: Michael Neuerbrug.

Mülheim an der Ruhr: EU-Beratungsstelle für Unternehmen, Zentrum in Nordrhein-Westfalen für Innovation und Technik (ZENIT) GmbH, 45468 Mülheim an der Ruhr, Dohne 54, Postfach 102264; tel (208) 3000421; fax (208) 3000429; e-mail mk@www.zenit.de; internet www.zenit.de; Contact: Silvia Besse.

Munich: EU-Beratungsstelle für Unternehmen, Industrie- und Handelskammer München und Oberbayern, 80333 Munich, Max-Joseph-Str 2; tel (89) 5116360; fax (89) 5116615; e-mail eic@ muenchen.ihk.de; internet www .muenchen.ihk.de; Contact: Dr Manfred Gössl.

Nuremberg: EU-Beratungsstelle, Landesgewerbeanstalt Bayern (LGA), 90431 Nuremberg, Tillystr 2; tel (911) 6554933; fax (911) 6554935; e-mail eic@ lga.de; internet www.lga.de; Contact: Edwin Schmitt.

Osnabrück: Fachhochschule Osnabrück, 49009 Osnabrück, Postfach 1940, Albrechtstr 30; tel (541) 9692924; fax (541) 9692990; e-mail egbuero@fh -osnabrueck.de; internet www.fh -osnabrueck.de; Contact: Friedrich Uhrmacher.

Potsdam: Zukunftsagentur Brandenburg, Steinstr 104–106, 14480 Potsdam; tel (331) 9675224; fax (331) 9675122; e-mail marzella.gernand@zab .brandenburg.de; internet www.zab -brandenburg.de; Contact: Stefan von Senger und Etterlin.

Rostock: Industrie- und Handelskammer Rostock, Geschäftsbereich Industrie und Außenwirtschaft, 18055 Rostock, Ernst-Barlach-Str 1–3; tel (381) 338820; fax (381) 338617; e-mail deiss@rostock .ihk.de; internet www.rostock.ihk.de; Contact: Willi Deiss.

Saarbrücken: Zentrale für Produktivität und Technologie Saar eV, 66119 Saarbrücken, Franz-Josef-Röder-Str 9; tel (681) 9520453; fax (681) 5846125; e-mail eic@zpt.de; internet www.zpt.de/inhalt/ eic.htm; Contact: Ellen Dienert.

Stuttgart: EU-Beratungsstelle für Unternehmen bei der Handwerkskammer Stuttgart, 70191 Stuttgart,

Heilbronner Str 43; 70017 Stuttgart, Postfach 102155; tel (711) 1657280; fax (711) 1657300; e-mail eic@hwk-stuttgart .de; Dir: Jürgen Schäfer.

Trier: Euro Info Centre Rheinland-Pfalz, 54209 Trier, Postfach 1930, Bahnhofstr 30–32; tel (651) 975670; fax (651) 9756733; e-mail info@eic-trier.de; internet www.eic-trier.de; Contact: Silke Brüggebors.

Wiesbaden: Euro Info Centre Wiesbaden, Leipziger Str 43, 65191 Wiesbaden; tel (611) 50661388; fax (611) 50661550; e-mail mail@eic-vr.de; internet www.eic-vr.com; Contact: Dieter Stasch.

Wiesbaden: EU-Beratungsstelle, Wirtschaftsförderung Hessen Investitionsbank AG—HLT, 65189 Wiesbaden, Abraham-Lincoln-Str 38–42; tel (611) 774257; fax (611) 774385; e-mail eic@ibh -hessen.de; internet www.ibh-hessen.de; Centre Head: Dr Khaled Snouber.

GREECE

Athens: Athens Chamber of Commerce and Industry, Akadimias St 7, 106 71 Athens; tel (1) 3627337; fax (1) 3607897; e-mail eurocntr@acci.gr; internet www .acci.gr/~eurocntr/start.htm; Man: Vassilios Georgiadis.

Athens: EOMMEX, Xenia St 16, 115 28 Athens; tel (1) 7794229; fax (1) 7778694; e-mail eicgr152@eommex.gr; internet www.forthnet.gr/eommex; Contact: Aspa Brati.

Corfu: Prefecture of Corfu, 13 Samara St, POB 425, 49100 Corfu; tel (661) 89208; fax (661) 36485; e-mail eic@ kerkyra.gr; internet www.kerkyra.gr; Dir: Konstantinos Provatas.

Ioánnina: Chamber of Commerce of Ioánnina, X. Trikoupi and Opl. Poutetsi St 14, 453 32 Ioánnina; tel (651) 76589; fax (651) 025179; e-mail eicgr163@ otenet.gr; internet www.eic.gr; Unit Head: Yannis Daskalopoulos; Information Officer: Anna Zerva.

Iráklion: Chamber of Commerce and Industry of Iráklion, Koronaeou St 9, 712 02 Iráklion; tel (81) 285829; fax (81) 225730; e-mail eicm156@ebeh.gr; Centre Head: Maria Petraki; Information Officer Lena Stenadounaki; Education and Training Man: George Kokkinis.

Kavala: Chamber of Kavala, Omonias St 50, 653 02 Kavala; tel (51) 833964; fax (51) 835946; e-mail eic157@mail.otenet .gr; Contact: Soultana Mavrommati.

Komotini: Prefectural Local Government of Rodopi—Evros, Ap Souzou 14, 691 00 Komotini; tel (531) 37031; fax (531) 37061; Office Head: Damianos Stathakis.

Kozani: Regional Development Agency—West Macedonia, Fon

Karayanni St 1–3, 501 00 Kozani; tel (461) 024022; fax (461) 049210; e-mail eic_gr167@anko.gr; Contact: Ioanna Tsatalbasidou-Papaterpou.

Piraeus: Piraeus Chamber of Commerce and Industry, Loudovicou St 1, Pl Odissou, 185 31 Piraeus; tel (10) 4170529; fax (10) 4174601; e-mail evepeic@ath .forthnet.gr; Contact: Mando Savva.

Rhodes: Chamber of Dodecanese, Gr Lambraki St 8, 85100 Rhodes; tel (241) 34840; fax (241) 34755; e-mail ccirho@ otenet.gr; Contact: Ilias Ouzounidis.

Thessaloniki: Association of Industries of Northern Greece, Morihovou Sq 1, 546 25 Thessaloniki; tel (31) 539817; fax (31) 541491; e-mail root@eic153.the .forthnet.gr; internet www.euroinfo.gr; Contact: Suzana Isaakidou.

Tripolis Arkadia: Chamber of Arkadia, 21 Panos and 25th March Sts, 221 00 Tripolis Arkadia; tel (71) 227141; fax (71) 233738; e-mail info@arcadianet.gr; internet www.arcadianet.gr; Contact: Matina Tzimouri-Roussou.

Volos: Association of Industries in Thessaly and in Central Greece, El Venizelou Rd 4, 382 21 Volos; tel (421) 028111; fax (421) 026394; e-mail sbtke@otenet.gr; Centre Head: Stella Vaina; Information Officer: Stella Vaina.

HUNGARY

Budapest: Euro Info Correspondence Centre, Investment and Trade Development Agency in Hungary (ITDH), Alkotmány u. 3, Dorottya U. 4, POB 222, 1364 Budapest; tel (1) 472-8130; fax (1) 472-8131; e-mail euroinfo@itd.hu; internet www.itd.hu/itdheuro.htm; Contact: Judith Lamperth.

Nyíregyháza: Primom Foundation Consultancy and Information Network: Viz St 21/B, 4400 Nyíregyháza; tel and fax (42) 414188; e-mail primomth@ broadband.hu; internet www.users .broadband.hu/primomth; Centre Head: Andrea Haraszti.

Pecs: Chamber of Commerce and Industry, Majorossy l. u. 36, 7625 Pecs; tel (72) 507162; fax (72) 507171; e-mail eic@ pbkik.hu; internet www.pbkik.hu/eic; Centre Head: György Kota.

Salgotarjan: Chamber of Commerce and Industry in Nograd County, Alkotmány u. 9/A, 3100 Salgotarjan; tel (32) 520860; fax (32) 520862; e-mail eurocenter@ nkik.hu; internet www.ccinograd.com; Centre Head: Olga Sztanek; Information Officers: Dóra Ferencz, Gábor Zólyomi.

Szeged: Csongrád County Chamber of Commerce and Industry, Tisza Lajos Körút 2–4, 6701 Szeged; tel (62) 486987; fax (62) 426149; e-mail eicszeged@ scmkik.hu; internet www.csmkik.hu/eic; Centre Head: Csilla Juhasz.

Szekszard: Tolna County Chamber of Commerce and Industry, Arany János u. 23–25, 7100 Szekszard; tel (7) 4411661; fax (7) 4411456; e-mail eic@ tmkik.hu; internet www.tmkik.hu; Head of Centre and Service Dept: Agnes Schweitzer.

Szolnok: Jasz-Nagykun-Szolnok County Chamber of Commerce and Industry, Verseghy Park 8, 5000 Szolnok; tel (56) 510610; fax (56) 370005; e-mail eic@ jnszmkik.hu; internet www.jnszmkik.hu; Contact: Péter Racz.

IRELAND

Cork: Cork Chamber of Commerce, Summerhill North, Cork; tel (21) 4509968; fax (21) 4508568; e-mail eic@corkchamber.ie; internet www.corkchamber.ie/euro_ info.htm; Contact: Kate Geary.

Galway: Galway Chamber of Commerce and Industry, Commerce House, Merchants Rd, Galway; tel (91) 562624; fax (91) 561963; e-mail elaine@ galwaychamber.com; internet www .galwaychamber.com; Contact: Carol Brady.

Sligo: Sligo Chamber of Commerce and Industry, 16 Quay St, Sligo; tel (71) 61274; fax (71) 60912; e-mail sligoeic@ tinet.ie; internet homepage.tinet.ie/ ~sligochamber; European Information Man: Laura Caslin; Chief Executive Officer: Mark Macsharry.

Waterford: Waterford Chamber of Commerce, 8 George's St, Waterford; tel (51) 872639; fax (51) 876002; e-mail eic@indigo.ie; internet www .waterfordchamber.ie; Man: Frank O'Donoghue.

ITALY

Aosta: Centro Sviluppo SPA, Regione Borgnalle 10/L, 11100 Aosta; tel (0165) 239134; fax (0165) 239320; e-mail eic@ centrosviluppo.it; internet www .centrosviluppo.it; Contact: Claudia Carnevali.

Ascoli Piceno: Eurosportello, Camera di Commercio Industria Artigianato e Agricoltura (CCIAA) di Ascoli Piceno, Via L. Mercantini 23–25, 63100 Ascoli Piceno; tel (0736) 279233; fax (0736) 246406; e-mail eurosportello@ ap.camcom.it; internet www.ap.camcom .it; Contact: Annamaria di Patrizio.

Bari: Istituto Finanziario Regionale Pugliese (Finpuglia), Via Lenin 2, 70125 Bari; tel (080) 5016735; fax (080) 5016809; e-mail info-eic@finpuglia -eic357.it; internet www.finpuglia -eic357.it; Contact: Alessandra De Luca.

Bologna: Eurosportello, Associazione degli Industriali della Provincia di

Bologna, Via San Domenico 4, 40124 Bologna; tel (051) 529648; fax (051) 2913448; e-mail eic355@assibo.it; internet www.assibo.it; Contact: Alessandro Baldi.

Bologna: Comitato Impresa Donna, Viale Aldo Moro 22, 40127; tel (051) 6094229; fax (051) 6099474; e-mail valentini@ecipar.it; internet www.cid.er .cna.it; Contact: Mirella Valentini.

Bolzano/Bozen: Handels-, Industrie-, Handwerks- und Landwirtschaftskammer Bozen, Via Perathoner 10, 39100 Bolzano/Bozen; tel (0471) 945645; fax (0471) 945620; e-mail eic@hk-cciaa.bz.it; internet www.kh-cciaa.bz.it/eic; Contact: Dr Petra Seppi.

Cagliari: Eurosportello, Coofcooperative Sardegna, Viale Bonaria 98, 09127 Cagliari; tel (070) 673042; fax (070) 6403842; e-mail floris@economiasociale .it; internet www.economiasociale.it; Centre Head: Fabrizio Floris.

Campobasso: Unione Regionale delle Camere di Commercio del Molise, Piazza della Vittoria 1, 86100 Campobasso; tel (0874) 471220; fax (0874) 90034; e-mail faicb@tin.it; Contact: Marco Zollo.

Catania: Osservatorio Europeo della Provincia Regionale di Catania, Via N. Coviello 15/A, 95128 Catania; tel and fax (095) 508582; e-mail eicit386.catania@ email.it; internet www.provincia.ct.it; Contact: Carmelo Messina.

Cosenza: Bic Calabria, Gruppo Sviluppo Italia, Via Alberto Serra 46, 87100 Cosenza; tel (0984) 391455; fax (0984) 391507; e-mail info@biccal.it; internet www.biccal.it; Contact: Carlo Di Noia.

Florence: Consorzio Eurosportello Confesercenti, Via Pistoiese 155, 50145 Florence; tel (055) 315254; fax (055) 310922; e-mail info@infoeuropa.it; internet www.infoeuropa.it; Contact: Dr Lucio Scognamiglio.

Florence: EIC Promofirenze International Business Centre, Via Por Santa Maria, Palazzo Borsa Merci, 50122 Firenze; tel (055) 2671620; fax (055) 2671404; e-mail promofirenze@ promofirenze.com; internet www .promofirenze.com; Contact: Luigi Boldrin.

Genova: Via Garibaldi 6, 16124 Genova; tel (010) 2704296; fax (010) 2704297; e-mail raffaella.bruzzone@tiscali.be; internet www.ig.camcom.it/eicliguria; Centre Head: Raffaella Bruzzone; Information Officer: Federica Vassallo.

Gorizia: Euro-Info Centre Friuli-Venezia Giulia, c/o Informest, Via Cadorna 36, 34170 Gorizia; tel (0481) 597411; fax (0481) 537204; e-mail eicit388@ informest.it; internet www.informest.it; Contact: Michela Lanzutti.

Matera: Centro Estero Camere di Commercio della Basilicata, Via Lucano 82, 75100 Matera; tel (0835) 338443; fax (0835) 330689; e-mail euroinfocentre@ centroestero.basilicata.it; internet www .centroestero.basilicata.it; Centre Head: Vito Signati.

Milan: Azienda Speciale della Camera di Commercio Industria Artigianato e Agricoltura (CCIAA) di Milano, Via Camperio 1, 20123 Milan; tel (02) 85155244; fax (02) 85155308; e-mail eic@mi.camcom.it; internet www.eurosportello.com; Contact: Attilio Martinetti.

Naples: Camera di Commercio Industria Artigianato e Agricoltura (CCIAA) di Napoli, Corso Meridionale 58, 80143 Naples; tel (081) 5536106; fax (081) 287675; e-mail eicna@tin.it; internet www.eic-it352.it; Contact: Riccardo De Falco.

Palermo: Mondimpresa/Unioncamere Sicilia/Confindustria Sicilia, Via Emerico Amari 11, 90139 Palermo; tel (091) 580444; fax (091) 321703; e-mail palermo@mondimpresa.it; Contact: Gianni Contino.

Pesaro: Eurosportello, Associazione 'Compagnia delle Opere', Via Barignani 30, 61100 Pesaro; tel (0721) 376287; fax (0721) 370713; e-mail euro@cdopesaro .com; internet www.cdo.it/eurosportello; Contact: Stefano Fabbrini.

Ravenna: Eurosportello, Azienda Speciale 'Sportello di Informazione e Documentazione per le Imprese', Viale L. C. Farini 14, 48100 Ravenna; tel (0544) 481443; fax (0544) 218731; e-mail euroinfo@ra.camcom.it; internet www .ra.comcom.it/eurosportello; Pres: Pietro Baccarini; Man: Giovanni Casadei Monti.

Rome: Confederazione Generale Italiana del Commercio e del Turismo, Piazza G. Gioacchino Belli 2, 00153 Rome; tel (06) 5898973; fax (06) 5814984; e-mail eic@confcommercio.it; internet www .confcommercio.it; Contact: Caterina Calafiore.

Rome: Istituto per la Promozione Industriale, Viale Maresciallo Pilsudski 124, 00197 Rome; tel (06) 80972216; fax (06) 80972212; e-mail martini@ipi.it; internet www.ipi.it; Contact: Giorgio Martini.

Rome: Rete Artigianato per l'Europa, Via di S. Giovanni in Laterano 152, 00184 Rome; tel (06) 772675507; fax (06) 77202872; e-mail rae@euroinfopmi .org; internet www.euroinfopmi.org; Centre Head: Bruno Panieri; Information Officers: Giulia Mazzoleni, Natalia Gil-Lopez.

Rome: Eurosportello, Unioncamere/ Mondimpresa, Viale Pasteur 10, 00144 Rome; tel (06) 549541; fax (06) 54954409; e-mail eic374@mondimpresa .it; internet www.mondimpresa.org; Contact: Antonella Marras.

Sardinia: c/o Promocamera, Via Predda Niedda 18, 07100 Sassari, Sardinia; tel (079) 2638813; fax (079) 2638810; e-mail eicss@ss.nettuno.it; internet www .promocmera.com/eicss; Contact: Alessia Bacchiddu.

Teramo: Unione Regionale delle Camera di Commercio Industria, Artigianato Agricoltura d'Abruzzo, Via F. Savini 50, 64100 Teramo; tel (0861) 335212; fax (0861) 246142; e-mail cciaa@webzone.it; internet www.eicabruzzo.com; Contact: Giustino di Carlantonio.

Turin: Camera di Commercio Industria Artigianato e Agricoltura (CCIAA) di Torino, Via San Francesco da Paola 37, 10123 Turin; tel (011) 5716342; fax (011) 5716346; e-mail eic@to.camcom.it; internet www.to.camcom.it; Contact: Paolo Veneruso.

Turin: Federazione delle Associazioni Industriali del Piemonte (Federpiemonte), Corso Vittorio Emanuele II 103, 10128 Turin; tel (011) 549246; fax (011) 5175204; e-mail euroinfocentre@ federpiemonte.org; Contact: Dr Ermanno Maritano.

Venice (Mestre): Eurosportello Veneto, Centro Estero delle Camere di Commercio del Veneto, Via Sansovino 9, 30173 Venice (Mestre); tel (041) 2581666; fax (041) 2581600; e-mail europa@ eicveneto.it; internet www.eicveneto.it; Dir: Gian Angelo Bellati; Centre Officers: Beatrice De Bacco, Michela Oliva.

LATVIA

Rīga: Latvian Development Agency, 1442 Rīga, 2 Perses St; tel 7039430; fax 7039431; e-mail eic@lda.gov.lv; internet www.lda.gov.lv; Contact: Gints Ozols.

LITHUANIA

Kaunas: Chamber of Commerce, Industry and Crafts, K. Donelaicio St 8, 3000 Kaunas; tel (3) 7201491; fax (3) 7208330; e-mail eic@chamber.lt; internet www.chamber.lt; Contact: Gintare Blaziene.

Vilnius: Lithuanian Development Agency Export Dept, Sv. Jono St 3, 2600 Vilnius; tel (5) 2649072; fax (5) 2120160; e-mail lda@lda.lt; internet www.lda.lt; Centre Head: Audrone Masandukaite.

LUXEMBOURG

Luxembourg: Chambre de Commerce du Grand-Duché de Luxembourg, blvd Konrad Adenauer 31, 2981 Luxembourg-Kirchberg; tel 423-93-93-33; fax 43-83-26; e-mail eic@cc.lu; Contact: Sabrina Sagramola.

Luxembourg: Chambre des Métiers du Grand-Duché de Luxembourg, 2 circuit de la Foire Internationale, 1347 Luxembourg; BP 1604, 1016 Luxembourg; tel 426-76-72-30; fax 42-67-87; e-mail eic@chambre-des-metiers.lu; internet www.eic.lu; Contact: Christiane Bram.

MALTA

San Gwann: Malta Export Trade Corporation (METCO), POB 08, Trade Centre, 09 San Gwann; tel 843211; fax 441106; e-mail info@eicc.metco.net; internet eicc.metco.net; Dir: Brigitte Tanti; Information Officers: Dorothy Calleja, Philo Meli.

THE NETHERLANDS

Amsterdam: Kamer van Koophandel en Fabrieken voor Amsterdam, de Ruyterkade 5, POB 2852, 1013 AA Amsterdam; tel (20) 5314439; fax (20) 5314497; e-mail eic@amsterdam.kvk.nl; internet www.kvk.nl; Contact: Linda van Eerden.

The Hague: Senter EG-Liaison, Grote Markstraat 43, POB 30732, 2500 GS The Hague; tel (70) 3610250; fax (70) 3562811; e-mail info@egl.nl; internet www.egl.nl; Contact: Trudy Millenaar.

's-Hertogenbosch: Stichting EG-Adviescentrum Zuid-Nederland, Kamer van Koophandel/INDUMA/BOM, Pettelaarpark 10, POB 70060, 5201 DZ 's-Hertogenbosch; tel (73) 6806600; fax (73) 6123210; e-mail info@egadvies.nl; internet www.egadvies.nl; Centre Head: Hans Aben; Project Man: Gérard Van Den Broek.

Leek: Stichting EIC Noord-Nederland, Lorentzpark 7, POB 97, 9350 AB Leek; tel (594) 555055; fax (594) 555059; e-mail info@eic.nl; internet www.eic.nl; Contact: Sjoerd Stienstra.

POLAND

Bialystok: Podlaska Regional Development Foundation. ul Starobojarska 15, 15-073 Bialystok; tel (85) 7410070; fax (85) 7323821; e-mail euroinfo@pfrr .bialystok.pl; internet www.prr.bialystok .pl; Centre Head: Bartosz Sokoi.

Gdansk: 'Free Entrepreneurship' Association, Gdansk Regional Dept, ul Matejki 6, 80-232 Gdansk; tel (58) 3470340; fax (58) 3470341; e-mail hutyra@euroinfo .gda.pl; internet www.euroinfo.gda.pl; Contact: Anna Hutyra.

Kalisz: Fundacja Kaliski Inkubator, ul Czestochowska 25, 62-800 Kalisz; tel (62) 7672343; fax (62) 7645016; e-mail euroinfo@kip.kalisz.pl; internet

www.kip.kalisz.pl; Centre Head: Omar Saoudi; European Information Officer: Piotr Olichwer.

Katowice: Upper Silesian Regional Development Agency, ul Wita Stwosza 31, 40-042 Katowice; tel (32) 2579540; fax (32) 2579529; e-mail euroinfo@ garr.com.pl; internet www.euroinfo -silesia.pl; Contact: Lucyna Sikora.

Kielce: Chamber of Industry and Commerce 'Staropolska', ul Sienkiewicza 53, 25-002 Kielce; tel (41) 3680278; fax (41) 3680278; e-mail eickielce@siph.com.pl; internet www.siph.com.pl; Man: Dorota Tekieli-Bisinska.

Krakow: Chamber of Commerce and Industry, ul Florianska 3, 31-019 Krakow; tel (12) 4228907; fax (12) 4225567; e-mail jozweg@bci.krakow.pl; internet www.euroinfo.org.pl; Contact: Izba Przemyslowo-Handlowa.

Lublin: Development Foundation, Rynek 7, 20-111 Lublin; tel (81) 5345002; fax (81) 5345002; e-mail eic@ lfr.lublin.pl; internet www.lfr.lublin.pl/ eic; Man: Malgorzata Galczynska; Consultant: Malgorzata Potiopa.

Rzeszow: Entrepreneurship Promotion Association, ul Stowackiego 7a, 35-060 Rzeszow; tel (17) 8524975; fax (17) 8524975; e-mail euro@intertele.pl; internet www.euroinfo.org.pl; Contact: Marta Cisek-Babiarz.

Szczecin: West Pomerania Economic Development Association, Kolumbastr 86, 71-035 Szczecin; tel (91) 4330220; fax (91) 4330266; e-mail euroinfo@ aci.com.pl; internet www.zsrg.szczecin .pl; Man: Hanna Rojek.

Torun: Regional Development Agency, ul Kopernika 4, 87-100 Torun; tel (56) 6635433; fax (56) 6635433; e-mail eic_torun@gapp.pl; internet www .tarr.org.pl; Contact: Zbigniew Baranski.

Walbrzych: Dolnoslaska Agencja Rozwoju Regionalnego, ul Wysockiego 10, 58-300 Walbrzych; tel and fax (74) 8434912; e-mail eic@darr.pl; internet www.darr.pl; Centre Head: Barbara Buryta.

Warsaw: Co-operation Fund, Gornoslaska 4a, 00-444 Warsaw; tel (22) 6228405; fax (22) 6220378; e-mail euroinfo@cofund.org.pl; internet www.euroinfo.org.pl; Contact: Andrzej Szewczyk.

PORTUGAL

Aveiro: Associação Industrial do Distrito de Aveiro, Cais da Fonte Nova (Antigo Edif Fáb. Jeronimo P. Campos), Alçado Sul, 3°, 3801-954 Aveiro; tel (34) 378551; fax (34) 424093; e-mail c.vieira@aida.pt; internet www.ccr-c.pt/eic; Contact: Carla Moura Vieira.

Coímbra: Eurogabinete para a Região Centro, Comissão de Coordenação da Região Centro, rua Bernardim Ribeiro 80, 3000-069 Coímbra; tel (39) 400190; fax (39) 400194; e-mail eic@ccr-c.pt; internet www.ccr-c.pt/actores/eurogabinete; Contact: Nuno Nascimento Almeida.

Évora: Eurogabinete Pequenas e Médias Empresas, Instituto de Apoio às Pequenas e Médias Empresas e ao Investimento, Rua de Velasco 19c, 7000-878 Évora; tel (66) 739700; fax (66) 739701; e-mail eicpme@iapmei.pt; internet www .eic.iapmei.pt; Centre Head: Vanda Narciso.

Faro: Comissão de Coordenação da Região do Algarve, Edif Ninho de Empresas, Horta das Laranjeiras, 8000-489 Faro; tel (89) 880840; fax (89) 806687; e-mail euroalgarve@mail.telepac.pt; internet www.ccr-alg.pt/eic; Dir: Antonio Vairinhos; Co-ordinator: Paulo Bota.

Funchal: Euro Info Centre da Madeira, Associação Comercial e Industrial do Funchal, Câmara de Comércio e Indústria da Madeira, Rua dos Aranhas 24–26, 9004-507 Funchal, Madeira; tel (91) 206800; fax (91) 206868; e-mail eic@acif-ccim.pt; internet www.acif-ccim.pt; Contact: Dr Isabel Vieira de Freitas.

Leça da Palmeira (Porto): Associação Empresarial de Portugal Exponor, 4450-617 Leça da Palmeira (Porto); tel (2) 9981580; fax (2) 9957017; e-mail eurog@ mail.telepac.pt; Contact: Maria Helena Ramos.

Lisbon: Associação Industrial Portuguesa-Câmara de Comércio e Indústria, Praça das Indústrias, Apdo 3200, 1301-965 Lisbon Codex; tel (1) 3639458; fax (1) 3646786; e-mail eic@aip.pt; internet www.aip.pt/eic; Man: Carla Sequeira.

Lisbon: Caixa Geral de Depósitos, Av João XXI 63, 3°, 1000-300 Lisbon; tel (1) 7905389; fax (1) 7905097; e-mail euroglis@mail.telepac.pt; internet www .cgd.pt; Contact: Maria Sofia Geraldes.

Lisbon: Instituto António Sérgio de Sector Cooperativo (INSCOOP), Rua D. Carlos Mascarenhas 46, 1070-083 Lisbon; tel (1) 3878046; fax (1) 3858823; e-mail inscoop@inscoop.pt; internet www .inscoop.pt; Contact: Miguel Carneiro.

Lisbon: Silicon, Electrónica e Telemática, Praça de Alvalade 6, 4°, A1, 1700-036 Lisbon; tel (1) 7958585; fax (1) 7958588; e-mail silicon@silicon-et.pt; internet www.silicon-et.pt; Centre Head: Marisa Gonçalves.

Ponta Delgada: Câmara do Comércio e da Indústria dos Açores, Rua Ernesto do Canto 13, 9500-312 Ponta Delgada, Azores; tel (96) 305000; fax (96) 305050; e-mail eurogab.acores@mail.telepac.pt; Dir: David Fernando Ferreira de Almeida.

Porto: Associação Nacional de Jovens Empresários (ANJE), Casa do Farol, Rua Paulo da Gama, 4169-006 Porto; tel (2) 0108000; fax (2) 0108010; e-mail ricardolavrador@anje.pt; internet www.anje.pt; Centre Head: Gonçalo Andresen Leit.

Viana do Castelo: Associação Industrial do Minho, Centro Empresarial de Viana do Castelo, Campo N. Sra Agonia, 4900-360 Viana do Castelo; tel (53) 202500; fax (53) 276601; e-mail eicminho@aiminho .pt; internet www.aiminho.pt; Contact: Aurea Cardoso.

SLOVAKIA

Bratislava: Euro Info Centrum Korespondencne, National Agency for Development of Small and Medium-sized Enterprises, Prievozska 30 2, 821 05 Bratislava 2; tel (2) 53417328; fax (2) 53417339; e-mail szabo@nadsme.sk; internet www.nadsme.sk; Contact: Henrich Hipca.

Presov: Regional Advisory and Information Centre, Nám Mieru 2, 080 01 Presov; tel (51) 7733552; fax (51) 7733552; e-mail eicsk673@rpicpo.sk; internet www .rpicpo.sk; Man: Maria Dirgova; Information Man: Helena Kundratova.

SLOVENIA

Koper: Science and Research Centre of Slovenia, Santorijeva 7, 6000 Koper; tel (5) 6279610; fax (5) 6279615; e-mail eic.kp@zrs-kp.si; internet www.zrs-kp.si; Contact: Ales Lipnik.

Ljubljana: Small Business Development Centre, Ljubljana 1000, Dunajska 156; tel (1) 5891890; fax (1) 5891885; e-mail eic@pcmg.si; internet www.pcmg.si/eic/ sindex.htm; Centre Head: Lara Cernetic.

Maribor: Mariborska Razvojna Agencija, Glavni trg 17, 2000 Maribor; tel (2) 2345072; fax (2) 2345077; e-mail eic@mra.si; internet eic.mra.si; Contact: Vladimir Rudl.

SPAIN

Albacete: Confederación Regional de Empresarios de Castilla-La Mancha, Calle Rosario 29, 02001 Albacete; tel (967) 217300; fax (967) 240202; e-mail fedaeuro@feda.es; internet feda.es; Contact: María Victoria López Valcarcel.

Alicante: Confederación Empresarial de la Provincia de Alicante, Plaza Ruperto Chapi 3, 03001 Alicante; tel (96) 5212560; fax (96) 5213581; e-mail eic@coepa.es; internet www.coepa.es; Man: Isabel Garcia Luis.

Barcelona: Cámara Oficial de Comercio, Industria y Navegación, Avda Diagonal 452–454, 08006 Barcelona; tel (93) 4169391; fax (93) 4160735; e-mail pcobos@mail.cambrabcn.es; internet www.cambrabcn.es/euroinfo; Contact: Paola Cobos.

Barcelona: Agence Catalane de la Petite Entreprise, Provença 339, 08037 Barcelona; tel (93) 4767210; fax (93) 4767215; e-mail info@cidem.gencat.es; internet www.cidem.com; Contact: Diego Guri.

Bilbao: Cámara Oficial de Comercio, Industria y Navegación de Bilbao, Alameda de Recalde 50, 48008 Bilbao (Vizcaya); tel (94) 4706504; fax (94) 4446324; e-mail coopeic@ue-empresas .org; internet www.camaranet.com; Contact: Enrique Velasco-Ruiz de Olalla.

Cáceres: Ayuntamiento de Cáceres, Edif 'La Chicuela', Calle Sánchez Herrero 2, 10004 Cáceres; tel (927) 217183; fax (927) 217059; e-mail euroinfo@mail-ayto .caceres.es; www.ayto-caceres.es; Contact: Rebeca Dominguez-Cidoncha.

Cordovilla-Pamplona: EIC de Navarra, San Cosme y San Damián s/n, 31191 Cordovilla-Pamplona; tel (948) 421109; fax (948) 421100; e-mail mherias@ain.es; internet www.ain.es/ europa; Contact: Mae Herias Oscariz.

Las Palmas de Gran Canaria: Gobierno de Canarias, Consejería de Economía, Hacienda y Comercio, Calle Leon y Castillo 431, 2pta, 35007 Las Palmas de Gran Canaria, Canary Islands; tel (928) 307167; fax (928) 307181; e-mail eiclpa@gobiernodecanarias.org; internet www.gobiernodecanarias.org; Contact: José Ramon Funes Toyos.

Llanera: Instituto de Fomento Regional del Principado de Asturias, Parque Tecnológico de Asturias, 33420 Llanera; tel (985) 980020; fax (985) 264455; e-mail euro@idepa.es; internet www.idepa.es; Centre Head: Paz Palacio Fernández.

Logroño: Federación de Empresarios de la Rioja, Calle Hermanos Moroy 8, 4°, 26001 Logroño; tel (941) 257022; fax (941) 262537; e-mail euroventanilla@ fer.es; internet www.fer.es; Pres: Julián Doménech Reverté; Centre Head: Eva Tobias.

Madrid: Cámara de Comercio e Industria de Madrid, Plaza de la Independencia 1, 28001 Madrid; tel (91) 5383610; fax (91) 5383643; e-mail eur1@ camaramadrid.es; internet www .camaramadrid.es; Contact: Carmen Verdera.

Madrid: Centro Europeo de Información Empresarial, Dirección General de Política de la PYME, Maria de Molina 50, 28006 Madrid; tel (91) 5450902; fax (91) 5450930; e-mail elemo@ipyme.org; internet www.ipyme.org; Contact: Elena de Rivera Tapia-Ruano.

Madrid: Consejo General de Colegios Oficiales de Graduados Sociales de España, Calle Rafael Calvo 7, 28010 Madrid; tel (91) 2152018; fax (91) 4488571; e-mail info@graduadosocial .com; internet www. graduadosocial.com; Centre Head: Andreu Palomo Peláez.

Madrid: Confederación Española de Organizaciones Empresariales, Diego de León 50, 28006 Madrid; tel (91) 5663400; fax (91) 5640135; e-mail eic@ceoe.es; internet www.ceoe.es; Contact: Carmen García Cossio.

Madrid: Consejo Superior de Cámaras de Comercio, Industria y Navegación de España, Calle Velázquez 157, 1a planta, 28002 Madrid; tel (91) 5906900; fax (91) 5906908; e-mail euroventanilla@ cscamaras.es; internet www.camaras .org; Contact: Cristina Moreno Moya.

Madrid: IMADE, José Abascal 57, 28003 Madrid; tel (91) 3997468; fax (91) 3997464; e-mail eic@imade.es; internet www.comadrid.es/economia -internacional; Contact: Carlos Alberto Martins.

Madrid: Confederación Empresarial Española de la Economía Social (CEPES), Calle Vallehermoso 15, 28015 Madrid; tel (91) 5930412; (91) 4487393; e-mail c.comos@cepes.es; Contact: Carmen Comos Tovar.

Madrid: Federación Española de Organizaciones Empresariales de la Industria del Mueble (FEOEIM), Calle Sagasta 24, 3°, 28004 Madrid; e-mail mj.vazquez@ feoeim.es; internet www.feoeim.es; Centre Head: Ivan Moran.

Málaga: Proyecto Europa-Banesto, Centro Europeo de Información, Plaza de la Constitución 9, 29008 Málaga; tel (95) 2220959; fax (95) 2220936; e-mail proeurop@banesto.es; internet www .banesto.es; Contact: Nuria Toucet Alvarez.

Murcia: Instituto de Fomento de la Región de Murcia, Avda de la Fama 3, 30006 Murcia; tel (968) 362818; fax (968) 362868; e-mail eic-murcia@info.carm.es; internet www.euroinfo-murcia.com; Contact: María Jesús Cachorro Sánchez.

Palma de Mallorca: Centro Baleares Europa, Ramon Llull 2, Edif 'Sa Nostra', 07001 Palma de Mallorca; tel (971) 719877; fax (971) 714681; e-mail ffeliu@ cbe.caib.es; internet www.cbe.es; Contact: Francisco Feliu de Oleza.

San Sebastián: Fundación Euroventanilla del País Vasco, Ramón Maria de Lili 6, 5°, 20002 Donostia/San Sebastián; tel (943) 272288; fax (943) 271657; e-mail fundacion@euroventanilla.org; internet www.euroventanilla.com; Man: Amalur Anguiozar.

Santander: Sociedad para el Desarrollo Regional, Eduardo Benot 5, 39003 Santander; tel (94) 2312100; fax (94)

2217011; e-mail eic@cantabria.org; internet www.eic.cantabria.org; Contact: Ignacio Abaitua.

Santiago de Compostela: Confederación de Empresarios de Galicia, Rúa do Villar 54, 15705 Santiago de Compostela; tel (981) 555888; fax (981) 555882; e-mail euroinfo@ceg.es; internet www.ceg.es/quines/index.htm; Contact: Araceli de Lucas Sanz.

Seville: Confederación de Empresarios de Andalucía, Isla de la Cartuja s/n, 41092 Seville; tel (95) 4488900; fax (95) 4488911; e-mail internacional@cea.es; internet www.cea.es/cgi-bin/asp/international/default.asp; Man: Mercedes León Lozano.

Toledo: Cámara de Comercio e Industria de Toledo, Plaza de San Vicente 3, 45001 Toledo; tel (925) 280112; fax (925) 280007; e-mail eictoledo@camaras.org; internet ccitoledo.camerdata.es/ccitoledo/eic.htm; Contact: Manuel Gómez Martín.

Valencia: Cámara Oficial de Comercio, Industria y Navegación de Valencia, Calle Poeta Querol 15, 46002 Valencia; tel (96) 3103900; fax (96) 3516349; e-mail ce@camaravalencia.com; internet www.camaravalencia.com; Contact: Vicente Mompo.

Valladolid: Parque Tecnológico de Boecillo, 47151 Boecillo, Valladolid; tel (983) 548015; fax (983) 548057; e-mail eic@ceical.cict.jcyl.es; internet www.ceical.es/eic; Contact: Ana Hernandez Pastora.

Zaragoza: Confederación Regional de Empresarios de Aragón, Plaza Roma F-1, 1°, 50010 Zaragoza; tel (976) 460066; fax (976) 327508; e-mail eborobio@crea.es; internet www.crea.es; Dir: Jorge Alonso Vallejo.

SWEDEN

Falun: Företagarnas Riksorganisation (Federation of Private Enterprises), POB 282, 781 26 Falun; tel (23) 794930; fax (23) 794910; e-mail eic@falun.euroinfo.se; internet www.euroinfo.se; Centre Head: Marie Ericson.

Gothenburg: EIC West Sweden, Trade and Industry Development Agency in Gothenburg, Norra Hamngatan 14, 411 14 Gothenburg; tel (31) 612418; fax (31) 612401; e-mail info@brg.goteborg.se; internet www.euroinfo.se; Contact: Leif Norlin.

Jönköping: Jönköping Chamber of Commerce, Elmiavägen 11, 554 54 Jönköping; tel (36) 301460; fax (36) 301469; e-mail eic@euroinfocentre.se; internet www.euroinfocentre.se; Contact: Carl-Gustaf Björstrand.

Malmö: SYD, Lugna Gatan 84, POB 50502, 202 50 Malmö; tel (40) 102140; fax (40) 102145; e-mail euinfo@eicsyd.se; internet www.eicsyd.se; Contact: Anna Hugberg.

Örebro: EIC East and Central Sweden, Almi Företagspartner Örebro AB (ALMI), POB 8023, 700 08 Örebro; tel (19) 174880; fax (19) 174885; e-mail info@orebro.euroinfo.se; internet www.euroinfo.se; Man: Ulla Renström.

Stockholm: Nutek—Swedish National Board for Industrial and Technical Development, Liljeholmsvägen 32, 117 86 Stockholm; tel (8) 681-95-00; fax (8) 744-40-45; e-mail eic@nutek.se; internet www.nutek.se; Contact: Christina Fors.

Västerås: EIC—Mälar Region, Europa Institutet i Västerås, Stora Gatan 16, 722 12 Västerås; tel (21) 107860; fax (21) 107869; e-mail christina@eiv.u.se; Man Dir: Christina Söderström.

Växjö: Almi Företagspartner Kronoberg AB (ALMI), Västra Esplanaden 5, POB 1501, 351 15 Växjö; tel (47) 023044; fax (47) 027937; e-mail eic@almi.se; Contacts: Ulla Rolf, Andreas M. Schroff.

UNITED KINGDOM

Belfast: Invest Northern Ireland, Upper Galwally, Belfast BT8 6TB; tel (90) 239090; fax (90) 542100; e-mail eic@investni.com; internet www.investni.com; Contact: Claire Gadd.

Birmingham: Birmingham Chamber of Commerce and Industry, Chamber of Commerce House, 75 Harborne Rd, Birmingham B15 3DH; tel (121) 455-0268; fax (121) 455-8670; e-mail c.davies@birminghamchamber.org.uk; Contact: Cathy Davies.

Bradford: West Yorkshire Euro Info Centre, Olicana House, Chapel St, Little Germany, Bradford BD1 5RE; tel (1274) 454262; fax (1274) 432136; e-mail eic@bradford.gov.uk; internet www.bradford.gov.uk/euroinfocentre; Contact: Jenny Lawson.

Bristol: Bristol Chamber of Commerce and Initiative, Business Link West, 16 Clifton Park, Bristol BS8 3BY; tel (117) 973-7373; fax (117) 923-8024; e-mail eic@blw.westec.co.uk; Contact: Sarah Harris.

Cardiff: Wales Euro Info Centre, Univ of Wales College of Cardiff (UWCC), Guest Bldg, POB 430, Cardiff CF10 3XT; tel (2920) 229525; fax (2920) 229740; e-mail wilcoxb@weic.demon.co.uk; internet www.waleseic.demon.co.uk; internet www.waleseic.org.uk; Contact: Brian Meredith.

Chelmsford: Essex Euro Info Centre, Essex County Council, Environmental Services Directorate, Enterprise Division, County Hall, Chelmsford, CM1 1QH; tel (1245) 437617; fax (1245) 437789; e-mail eic@essexcc.gov.uk; internet www.essexcc.gov.uk; Contact: Michelle Hutchinson.

Coventry: EPI Centre, Coventry University TechnoCentre, Puma Way, Coventry, West Midlands, CV1 2TT; tel (24) 7623-6284; fax (24) 7623-6024; e-mail j.cornbill@coventry.ac.uk; internet www.epi-centre.org.uk; Contact: Alex Mauser.

Durham: North of England EIC, One North East, The Rivergreen Centre, Aykley Heads, Durham DH1 5TS; tel (191) 383-7319; fax (191) 383-7319; e-mail eic@onenortheast.co.uk; internet www.eeic-northofengland.com; Contact: Graham Wilson.

Exeter: Southwest Euro Info Centre, Exeter Enterprises Innovation Centre, Univ of Exeter, Exeter EX4 4RN; tel (1392) 214085; fax (1392) 264375; e-mail europa@exeter.ac.uk; Contact: Susan Lawrie.

Glasgow: Scottish Enterprise, 150 Broomielaw Atlantic Quay, Glasgow G2 8LU; tel (141) 228-2700; fax (141) 221-3217; e-mail euroinfocentre@scotent.co.uk; internet www.euro-info.org.uk/centres/glasgow; Contact: Walter Murray.

Hull: Humberside European Business Information Centre (HEBIC), Univ of Hull, Brynmor Jones Library, Cottingham Rd, Hull HU6 7RX; tel (1482) 465940; fax (1482) 466488; e-mail euro-info-centre@hull.ac.uk; internet www.eichumberside.demon.co.uk; Centre Head: Sue Arundale-Scott.

Inverness: European Business Services, 81a Castle St, Inverness IV10 8TJ; tel (1463) 715400; fax (1463) 715600; e-mail eic@euro-info.co.uk; internet www.euro-info.co.uk; Contact: Michelle Hardie.

Knutsford: The Forum of Private Business, FPB Rusking Chambers, Drury Lane, WA16 6HA Knutsford; tel (1565) 634467; fax (1565) 650059; e-mail neilmarrs@fpb.co.uk; internet www.fpb.co.uk; Contact: Neil Marrs.

Leicester: Business Link, 10 York Rd, Leicester LE1 5TS; tel (116) 255-9944; fax (116) 258-7333; e-mail enquiries@leicestershire.businesslink.co.uk; Contact: Sarah Wilson.

Liverpool: North West Euro Info Centre, 1 Old Hall St, Liverpool L3 9HG; tel (151) 298-1928; fax (151) 224-2401; e-mail info@eicnw.u-net.com; internet www.eicnew.co.uk; Contact: John Hope.

London: London Chamber of Commerce and Industry, 33 Queen St, London EC4R 1AP; tel (20) 7489-1992; fax (20) 7203-1812; e-mail europe@londonchamber.co.uk; internet www.londonchamber.co.uk; Information Man: Marita Ewins; European Information Officers: Mette Lorentzen, Laura Veart.

Manchester: Chamber Business Enterprises, Churchgate House, 56 Oxford St, Manchester M60 7HJ; tel (161) 237-4020; fax (161) 236-1341; e-mail eic@c-b-e.co.uk; internet www.tvc.org.uk/services.information; Contact: Lynn Shaw.

Norwich: EIC East Anglia, Norfolk and Norwich, Millennium Plain, Norwich NR2 1AW; tel (141) 228-2700; fax (141) 221-3217; e-mail euro.lib@norwich.gov.uk; internet www.euro-info.org.uk; Information Officer: Eileen Wallace; European Projects Officer: Jo Wright.

Nottingham: Nottinghamshire Chamber of Commerce and Industry, 309 Haydn Rd, Nottingham NG5 1DG; tel (115) 962-4624; fax (115) 985-6612; e-mail info@nottschamber.co.uk/gettingadvice/euroinfo.shtml; Centre Head: Graham Birkett; Contact: Esther Carter.

Slough: Thames Valley Chamber of Commerce and Industry, Commerce House, 2–6 Bath Rd, Slough SL1 3SB; tel (1753) 577877; fax (1753) 524644; e-mail enquiries@thamesvalleychamber.co.uk; internet www.thamesvalleychamber.co.uk; Contact: Barbara Moye.

Southampton: Southern Area Euro Info Centre, Northguild Civic Centre, Southampton SO14 7LW; tel (2380) 832866; fax (2380) 231714; e-mail southarea.eic@southampton.gov.uk/education/libraries/eic.htm; Man: Richard Hall; Information Officer: Kerrie Prowting.

St Albans: Hertfordshire Euro Info Centre, Business Link Hertfordshire, 45 Grosvenor Rd, St Albans, Herts, AL1 3AW; tel (1727) 813693; fax (1727) 813404; e-mail info@hertseic.co.uk; Contact: Sue Hugues.

West Malling: Kent EIC, 26 Kings Hill Ave, Kings Hill, West Malling ME19 4AE; tel (1732) 878044; fax (1732) 841109; e-mail eic@businesslinkkent.com; internet www.euro-info.org.uk/centre/kent; Contact: Linda Bennet.

Euro Info Centres (EICs) and Correspondence Centres in Non-Member States

BULGARIA

Dobrich: Chamber of Commerce and Industry, Bulgaria St 3, Office 102, POB 182, 9300 Dobrich; tel (58) 601472; fax (58) 601434; e-mail eicbg809@cci.dobrich.net; internet www.cci.dobrich.net; Centre Head: Tatyana Gicheva; Sec-Gen: German Germanov.

Plovdiv: Chamber of Commerce and Industry, Samara St 7, 4003 Plovdiv; tel (32) 652645; fax (32) 652647; e-mail bg807eic@evro.net; internet www.kamara.evro.net; Dir: Angel Hronev.

Rousse: Business Support Centre for Small and Medium-sized Enterprises, Tzarkovna Nezavisimost St 16, POB 262, 7000 Rousse; tel (82) 224108; fax (82) 230173; e-mail eic@rousse.bg; internet www.eic.rousse.bg; Contact: Christina Kasparian.

Sandanski: Business Information and Consulting Centre, Bulgaria Sq. 1, 2800 Sandanski; tel (746) 30549; fax (359) 74632403; e-mail eicbg806@sani.net; internet www.galia-online.com/eicbg806; Man: Ani Simeonova.

Sofia: Bulgarian Chamber of Commerce and Industry, Parchevich Str 42, 1000 Sofia; tel (2) 9885067; fax (2) 9885067; e-mail eic@bcci.bg; Contact: Beata Papazova.

Stara Zagora: Chamber of Commerce and Industry, George S. Rakovski St 66, 6000 Stara Zagora; tel (42) 26297; fax (42) 26033; e-mail eic@chambersz.com; internet www.chambersz.com; Contact: Krassimira Sokolova.

Vratsa: Chamber of Commerce and Industry, Hristo Botev Str 24, POB 267, 3000 Vratsa; tel (92) 60273; fax (92) 26308; e-mail cci-vr@bitex.com; internet cci-eic-vratsa.bitex.com; Contact: Iliana Philipova.

Yambol: Chamber of Commerce and Industry, Rakovski St 1a, POB 291, 8600 Yambol; tel (46) 62939; fax (46) 34790; e-mail ycci@bsbg.net; internet www.bourgas.net/business; Contact: Neli Kadieva.

EMERGING PALESTINIAN AUTONOMOUS AREAS

East Jerusalem, the Gaza Strip and the West Bank: Development Resource Center (DRC), Industrial Area Erez, POB 74, 79150 Erez; tel (72) 824275; fax (72) 863301; e-mail ot841.gaza@fcis.cec.eu.int; Contact: Michelle Barrett.

ICELAND

Reykjavík: Trade Council of Iceland, Hallveigarstigur 1, POB 1000, 121 Reykjavík; tel 5114000; fax 5114040; e-mail euroinfo@icetrade.is; internet www.icetrade.is; Contacts: Sigrun Lilja, Erna Björnsdóttir, Ingólfur Sveinsson.

Reykjavík: Trade Council of Iceland, Bogartún 35, POB 1000, 121 Reykjavík; tel 5114000; fax 5114040; e-mail euroinfo@icetrade.is; internet www.icetrade.is; Contact: Sigrún Lilja Gudjartsdóttir.

ISRAEL

Tel Aviv: Israel Export Institute, 29 Hamered St, POB 50084, Tel-Aviv 68125; tel (3) 5142879; fax (3) 5142852; e-mail library@export.gov.il; www.export.gov.il; Contact: Alain Mendoza.

JORDAN

Amman: Jordan Export Devt and Commercial Centres Corporation (JEDCO), Shmeisani i Akrama Al-Karashi, POB 7704, 11118 Amman; tel (6) 5603507; fax (6) 5684568; e-mail eicc@jedco.gov.jo; internet www.jedco.gov.jo; Contact: Kamil Madanat; correspondence centre.

LEBANON

Beirut: Chamber of Commerce and Industry, 1 Justinien St, 2100 Sanayeh, POB 11-1801, Beirut; tel (1) 744163; fax (1) 349615; e-mail eicc@ccib.org.lb; internet www.ccib.org.lb; Contact: Albert Nasr; correspondence centre.

NORWAY

Kristiansand: Agder Research Foundation, Serviceboks 415, 4604 Kristiansand; tel 38-14-22-00; fax 38-14-22-01; e-mail eicsor@agderforskning.no; internet www.agderforskning.no; Contact: Oyvind L. Laderun.

Narvik: North Norwegian Institute of Technology and Innovation, VINN, Teknologiveien 10, 8512 Narvik; tel 76-96-72-00; fax 76-96-72-01; e-mail eicnord@vinn.no; internet www.vinn.no; Centre Head: Ingrid Martenson-Bortne.

Oslo: Norwegian Trade Council, Drammensveien 40, 0243 Oslo; tel 22-92-65-70; fax 22-43-16-40; e-mail eic@@ntc.no; internet www.eic.ntc.no; Contact: Per Niederbach.

Sogndal: Vestlandsforsking (Western Norway Research Institute), Fossetunet 3, POB 163, 6851 Sogndal; tel 57-67-61-50; fax 57-67-61-90; e-mail taa@vestforsk.no; internet eic.vestforsk.no; Contact: Terje Aaberge.

Trondheim: Sør-Trøndelag Næringsservice, Sluppenveien 12e, POB 6018 Sluppen, 7434 Trondheim; tel 73-82-54-50; fax 73-82-54-40; e-mail euroinfocentre@ti-trondelag.no; Contact: Lisbeth Vassaas.

ROMANIA

Baia Mare: 'Maramures' Development Foundation for Small and Medium-sized Enterprises, Traian Blvd 9/16, 4800 Baia Mare; tel (62) 224870; fax (262) 224870; e-mail euroinfo@cdimm.org; internet euroinfo.cdimm.org; Centre Head: Mirel Mihali; Information Officer: Mihai Patrascu.

Brasov: Chamber of Commerce and Industry, Mihail Kogalniceanu St 20, 2200 Brasov; tel (68) 474170; fax (68) 474170; e-mail eicbv@ccibv.ro; internet eic.ccibv.ro; Contact: Marinella Margi Manea.

Bucharest: Chambre de Commerce et d'Industrie de Roumanie et de Bucarest, 74244 Bucharest, 2 blvd Octavian Goga; tel (1) 3229532; fax (1) 3229541; e-mail euroinfo@ccir.ro; internet euro-info .ccir.ro; Contact: Ioan Ciuperca.

Constanta: Chamber of Commerce, Industry, Shipping and Agriculture, Mircea cel Batrân 84 MF1, 8700 Constanta; tel (2) 41550960; fax (2) 41619454; e-mail eic@ccina.ro; internet www.ccina.ro; Contact: Petronela Rodica Belteu.

Timisoara: Chamber of Commerce, Industry and Agriculture, Piata Victoriei 3, 1900 Timisoara; tel (56) 219172; fax (56) 219173; e-mail euroinfo@cciat.ro; internet www.cciat.ro; Contact: Rodica Jurcut.

SWITZERLAND

Zurich: Office Suisse d'Expansion Commerciale (OSEC), Euro Info Centre Schweiz, Stampfenbachstr 85, 8035 Zurich; tel (1) 3655443; fax (1) 3655411; e-mail eics@osec.ch; internet www.osec .ch/eics; Contact: Lucia Dobeli; correspondence centre.

SYRIA

Damascus: Syrian European Business Centre, Immeuble 34/A, rue Farabi, POB 36453, East Mezzeh, Damascus; tel (11) 6115772; fax (11) 6133866; e-mail sebc@syriatel.net; internet www .syriatel.org; Contact: George Catinis.

TUNISIA

Tunis: Agence de Promotion de l'Industrie (API), 63 rue de Syrie, Belvédère, 1002 Tunis; tel (1) 792-144; fax (1) 782-482; e-mail api@api.com.tn; Contact: Fadhel El Amri; correspondence centre.

TURKEY

Adana: Adana Euro Info Centre, Adana; tel (322) 3513911; e-mail eu-info@adana-to.org.tr; internet www.adanaeic.org; Contact: Alpar Baykozi.

Ankara: KOSGEB, Small and Medium-sized Industry Development Organization (SMIDO), MKEK Binasi, Kat 11, Tandogan, Cankaya, 06330 Ankara; tel (312) 2122382; fax (312) 2238769; e-mail abm@kosgeb.gov.tr; internet www .kosgeb.gov.tr/eic; Contact: Ercan Tuncer; correspondence centre.

Bursa: European Information Centre for Bursa, Bursa; tel (224) 2428704; e-mail eicbursa@btso.org.tr; Contact: Aytaç Coskun.

Denizli: EU Information Centre for Denizli SMEs, Oğuzhan Caddesi No. 1 Kat; 4 20100 Denizli; tel (258) 2411737; e-mail eic@denizlito.tobb.org.tr; internet www.eicdenizli.tobb.org.tr; Contact: Ali Ihsan Karaalp.

Konya: Euro Information Centre for Konya, Konya; tel (322) 2510670; e-mail mcu@eic.org.tr; Contact: Seyfi Suna.

Samsun: Samsun Chamber of Commerce and Industry, Samsun; tel (362) 4323626; e-mail eic@samsuntso.org.tr; internet http://eic.samsuntso.org.tr; Contact: Okan Gümüs.

European Business and Innovation Centre Network (EBN)

The European Business and Innovation Centres Network (EBN) was created in 1984. It is an international non-profit seeking association gathering together the Business & Innovation Centres (BICs) – a European Commission regional policy initiative to detect and support new and existing innovative SMEs – and their partner organizations (science parks, universities, regional development agencies, financial institutions, etc.).

By January 2005 the EBN had some 230 members, including 160 BICs (full members) in 21 European countries and 70 associate members from across the continent and further afield.

EBN is now the leading network gathering BICs and similar organizations in Europe. It has become a reference point when talking about innovation, entrepreneurship, SMEs and regional economic development, in the EU as well as in partner countries.

Information available: regular E-newsletter (send an e-mail to ebn@ebn.be to register); documentation on the EBN (mission, structure, members, services, etc.); documentation and technical guidance on the BIC instrument; information on thematic seminars, congresses, and other events within the network.

For further information, or to obtain a list of EBN members, please contact: European BIC Network, Avenue de Ter-vueren 168, Bte 25, 1150 Brussels, Belgium; tel (+32) 2-7728900; fax (+32) 2-7729574; e-mail ebn@ebn.be; internet www.ebn.be. Philippe Vanrie is the Managing Director.

Full Members

AUSTRIA

BIC Burgenland GmbH: Technologie-zentrum, 7000 Eisenstadt; tel (+43 2682) 704-220; fax (+43 2682) 704-2210; e-mail office@bice.at; contact Johann Binder.

RIZ NÖ: Prof. Dr. Stephan Koren Strasse, 10, 2700 Wiener Neustadt; tel (+43 2622) 26326; fax (+43 2622) 26326 99; e-mail office@riz.co.at; contact Karin Platzer.

BELGIUM

Bureau Economique de la Province de Namur (BEP): Parc Scientifique, Rue Phocas Lejeune 30, 5032 Gembloux (Les Isnes); tel (+32 81) 71 71 71; fax (+32 81)-71 71 00; e-mail jbo@bep.be; contact Jean Bouvry.

CEEI Héraclès: Avenue Général Michel 1E, 6000 Charleroi; tel (+32 71) 27-03-11; fax (+32 71) 31-67-35; e-mail heracles@heracles.be; contact Philippe Chevremont.

CEEI ID: Avenue Léon Champagne 3 boite 6, 1480 Saintes-Tubize; tel (+32 2) 390-92-72; fax (+32 2) 390-93-86; e-mail info@agenceid.be; contact Michel Preud'homme.

Centre de Développement de Projets (CDP): Dreve de l'Arc-en-Ciel 98, 6700 Arlon; tel (+32 63) 23 18 11; fax (+32 63) 23 18 95; e-mail idelux.aive@idelux.be; contact Daniel Gheeza.

Centre de Technologie et de Gestion des Affaires (CTGA): Rue de l'Industrie 20, 1400 Nivelles; tel (+32 67) 88-36-11; fax (+32 67) 88-36-88; e-mail jcetting@ulb.ac.be; contact Jean-Claude Ettinger.

Innotek: Cipalstraat 3, 2440 Geel; tel (+32 14) 57-05-70; fax (+32 14) 57-05-60; e-mail innotek@innotek.be; contact Luc Peeters.

Maison de l'Entreprise S.A.: Parc Scientifique Initialis, Rue Descartes 2, 7000 Mons; tel (+32 65) 36-11-15; fax (+32 65) 36-17-46; e-mail patrice.thiry@idea.be | me.thibaut@skynet.be; contact Patrice Thiry.

SOCRAN: Parc Industriel du Sart-Tilman, Avenue Pré Aily, 4031 Angleur; tel (+32 4) 367-83-11; fax (+32 4) 367-83-00; e-mail socran@pophost.eunet.be; contact Robert Frederic.

CZECH REPUBLIC

BIC Brno: Prikop 4, CP 2, 60200 Brno; tel (+420 5) 4517-61-30; fax (+420 5) 4517-61-20; e-mail bicbrno@iqnet.cz; contact Jaroslav Chaloupka.

BIC Ostrava: Mostarenska 1, 700300 Ostrava; tel (+420 692) 92-6902; fax (+420 692) 92-6751; e-mail bicova@ostra-va.czcom.cz; contact Josef Barabas.

BIC Plzen: Riegrova 1, 30625 Plzen; tel (+420 19) 723-53-79; fax (+420 19) 723-53-20; e-mail bic@bic.cz; contact Jana Klementova.

BIC Prague CTU: Plzenska 221/130, 15000 Prague, 5; tel (+420 2) 572-12-873; fax (+420 2) 572-12-340; e-mail komarek@bic.cvut.cz; contact Pavel Komarek.

Technology Centre of the Academy of Science: Academy of Sciences of Prague, Rozvojova 135, 16502 Prague, 6; tel (+420 2) 20-390-203; fax (+420 2) 33-321-607; e-mail zbroz@tc.cas.cz; contact Dr. Karel Klusacek.

DENMARK

BIC Nord: Niels Jernes Vej 10, 9220 Aalborg O; tel (+45 96) 35-44-30; fax (+45 96) 35-44-25; e-mail bic@bic-nord.dk; contact Freddy Rano.

FRANCE

Aditec pas de Calais CEEI: Techno-parc Futura, Rue de l'Université, 62400 Béthune; tel (+33 3) 21-63-15-15; fax (+33 3) 21-63-15-16; e-mail aditec@etnet.fr; contact Jean-Pierre Filiatre.

AGECA: 166 Rue Ponsardin, 51100 Reims; tel (+33 3) 26 82 78 78; fax (+33 3) 26 82 78 80; e-mail info@ageca.com; contact Dominique Leboeuf.

Association du Technopole de Brest-Iroise: Rue Jim Sévellec 40 BP4, 29608 Brest Cedex; tel (+33 2) 98-05-44-51; fax (+33 2) 98-05-47-67; e-mail ebntbi@attmail.com; contact Jacques Jestin.

Bordeaux Unitec: 162 Avenue Schweit-zer, 33600 Pessac; tel (+33 5) 56 15 80 00; fax (+33 5) 56 15 11 50; e-mail dbirot@bordeauxunitec.com; contact Daniel Birot.

CAP ALPHA: Avenue de l'Europe – Clapiers, 34940 Montpellier Cedex 9; tel (+33 4) 67-59-30-00; fax (+33 4) 67-59-30-10; e-mail wozniak@mlrt.fr; contact Alain Cottet.

Cap Delta: Parc Technologique Delta Sud, BP 24, 09120 Varilhes; tel (+33 5) 616 79 230; fax (+33 5) 616 79 249; e-mail michel-delau@ariege-expansion.asso.fr; contact Didier Kuss.

Carrefour Entreprise Sarthe: Techno-pole NOVAXIS II, 75, Bld Alexandre Oyon, 72100 Le Mans; tel (+33 2) 43-57-72-72; fax (+33 2) 43-87-01-02; e-mail ces@cybercable.tm.fr; contact Joel Bruneau.

CCI de Lyon Equipe d'Animation NOVACITE: BP 2131, 69603 Villeur-banne; tel (+33 4) 78 94 56 61; fax (+33 4) 78 94 56 06; e-mail gaquere@lyon.cci.fr; contact Gilles Gaquere.

CEEI 47: Agropole Entreprise, BP 112, 47931 Agen Cedex 9; tel (+33 5) 53-77-20-47; fax (+33 5) 53-77-21-00; e-mail agropole@agropole.com; contact Gilles Recour.

CEEI d'Ille et Vilaine CREAT'IV: Espace Performance, Bâtiment C1, 35769 Saint-Grégoire Cedex; tel (+33 2) 99-23-79-00; fax (+33 2) 23-25-08-35; e-mail creativ35@aol.com; contact Jean-Luc Hannequin.

CEEI de Nîmes: Rue de la République 12, Parc Georges Besse, 30032 Nîmes; tel (+33 4) 66-76-33-04; fax (+33 4) 66-04-73-24; e-mail ceei@nimes.cci.fr; contact Frédéric Escojido.

CEEI Gers-Gascogne: Rue Roger Salengro 6, Z.I. de l'Hippodrome, 32000 Auch; tel (+33 5) 62 60 68 68; fax (+33 5) 62 60 68 60; e-mail ceei.gers.gascogne@wanadoo.fr; contact Jean-Michel Justumus.

CEEI Provence: Domaine du Petit-Arbois, BP 88, 13545 Aix en Provence Cedex 4; tel (+33 4) 42-97-18-18; fax (+33 4) 42-97-18-19; e-mail info@ceei-provence.com; contact Claude le Foulgoc.

CEEI Pyrénées: Izarbel, Maison du Parc, 64210 Bidart; tel (+33 5) 59-41-53-55; fax (+33 5) 59-41-53-59; e-mail ceeipyrene@aol.com; contact Alain Estrade.

CEEI Quimper-Cornouaille: 160, Bld de Créac'h Gwen, 29000 Quimper; tel (+33 2) 98-10-02-00; fax (+33 2) 98-10-02-01; e-mail technopole@tech-quimper.fr; contact Christian Flecher.

CEEI Synergia – La Technopole Caen-Normandie: Unicité, 12, rue Alfred Kastler, 14000 Caen Cedex; tel (+33 2) 31-46-73-78; fax (+33 2) 31-46-73-74; e-mail pascal.hurel@synergia.fr; contact Pascal Hurel.

CEEI Théogone: Parc Technologique du Canal, Avenue de l'Europe 10, 31525 Ramonville Saint Agne; tel (+33 5) 61-28-56-56; fax (+33 5) 61-28-56-00; e-mail theogone@wanadoo.fr; contact Daniel Blonde.

CICOM Organisation: 2229, route de Cretes, Sophia Antipolis, 06560 Valbonne; tel (+33 4) 92 94 20 00; fax (+33 4) 92 94 20 20; e-mail meyer@cica.fr; contact Alain Andre.

Futura Corse Technopole: Maison du Parc Technologique, 20601 Bastia Cedex; tel (+33 4) 95 30 96 00; fax (+33 4) 95 30 96 01; e-mail futura.technopole@wanadoo.fr; contact Miguèle Fabiani.

Nantes Atlanpole: Château de la Chantrerie, BP 90702, 44307 Nantes Cedex 03; tel (+33 2) 40-25-13-13; fax (+33 2) 40-25-10-88; e-mail balducchi@atlanpole.fr; contact Jean-François Balducchi.

PROMOTECH Nancy: 6, Allée Pelletier Doisy, 54603 Villers-les-Nancy; tel (+33 3) 83-50-44-44; fax (+33 3) 83-44-04-82; e-mail direction.promotech@wanadoo.fr; contact Jacky Chef.

Régie Départementale des Ruches d'Entreprises: 54-56 rue Jean sans Peur, BP 1291, 59014 Lille; tel (+33 3) 20-63-57-59; fax (+33 3) 20-63-58-85; e-mail reseau.ruches@wanadoo.fr; contact Francois-Louis Billon.

Synergie: Rue Claude Chappe, Technopole 2000, 57070 Metz; tel (+33 3) 87-76-36-36; fax (+33 3) 87-76-23-03; e-mail ejoli@synergie-ceei.com; contact Lionel Navarro.

FINLAND

BIC Botnia: PO Box 810, 65101 Vaasa; tel (+358 6) 282-82-80; fax (+358 6) 282-82-99; e-mail yrjo.halttunen@merinova.fi; contact Yrjo Halttunen.

BIC Carelia: Lansikatu 15, Carelian Science Park, 80110 Joensuu; tel (+358 13) 263-72-10; fax (+358 13) 263-71-11; e-mail pirkka.aula@carelian.fi; contact Pirkka Aula.

BIC Kareltek: Laserkatu 6, 53850 Lappeenranta; tel (+358 5) 624-30-60; fax (+358 5) 624-30-62; e-mail kalle.riihimaki@carel.net; contact Marjut Hannelin.

BIC Kymi: Kotka – Hamina Region, PO Box 198, 48101 Kotka; tel (+358 5) 218-41-57; fax (+358 5) 213-007; e-mail jukka.vakeva@kotka.fi; contact Jukka Vakeva.

Culminatum BIC / Helsinki Region Centre of Expertise: Tekniikantie 12 (Innopoli), Innopoli, 02150 Espoo; tel (+358 9) 435-420-00; fax (+358 9) 502-28-70; e-mail kari.ruohu@culminatum.fi; contact Kauko Huhtinen.

Oulu Tech BIC: Technologiantie 1, 90570 Oulu; tel (+358 8) 551-56-30; fax (+358 8) 551-56-32; e-mail pasi.anttila@oulutech.otm.fi; contact Pasi Anttila.

Western Finland BIC: Hermiankatu 6-14, 33720 Tampere; tel (+358 3) 316-55-50; fax (+358 3) 316-55-52; e-mail olli.niemi@hermia.fi; contact Heidi Huhtamella.

GERMANY

BIC Frankfurt (Oder) GmbH: Im Technologiepark 1, 15236 Frankfurt (Oder); tel (+49 335) 557-11-00; fax (+49 335) 557-11-10; e-mail info@bic-ffo.de; contact Uwe Hoppe.

BIC GIZ & Tele-Service: Obermarkt 24, 63671 Gelnhausen; tel (+49 6051) 828 0; fax (+49 6051) 828 20; e-mail arb3@tele-service-center.de; contact Renate Ciba.

BIC Kaiserslautern: Opelstrasse 10, 67661 Kaiserslautern; tel (+49 6301) 7030; fax (+49 6301) 703-119; e-mail frank.klein@bic-kl.de; contact Mannfred Beisel.

BIC Zwickau GmbH: Lessingstrasse 4, 08058 Zwickau; tel (+49 375) 54-10; fax (+49 375) 54-13-00; e-mail bic@bic-zwickau.de; contact Hans-Jürgen Uhlmann.

IGZ BIC Altmark GmbH: Arneburger Strasse 24, Technologiepark, 39576 Stendal; tel (+49 3931) 681-440; fax (+49 3931) 681-444; e-mail bic@altmark.de; contact Georg Naumann.

GREECE

BIC Attika: Stadiou Street 7, 8th Fl., 10562 Athens; tel (+30 1) 331-42-30; fax (+30 1) 331-42-32; e-mail bicofattika@hol.gr; contact Dimitris Karachalios.

BIC Larissa: Papakiriazi Street 44, 41222 Larissa; tel (+30 415) 34-917; fax (+30 415) 34-919; e-mail bic@bee.gr; contact Dimitrios Stylopoulos.

BIC of Epirus: Domboli 30, 45332 Ioannina; tel (+30 651) 44-447; fax (+30 651) 44-457; e-mail bicepirus@ioa.forthnet.gr; contact Dimitris Skalkos.

BIC Patras: Michalakopoulou Street 58, 26221 Patras; tel (+30 61) 622-711; fax (+30 61) 277-830; e-mail ksmme@patrascc.gr; contact Andreas Papavlasopoulos.

Serres EC-BIC: Amynta Str. 9, 62124 Serres; tel (+30 321) 49 229; fax (+30 321) 45 716; e-mail bic@bic.the.forthnet.gr; contact Christos Karaghiannis.

HUNGARY

Innostart Hungary National Business and Innovation: Fehervari ut 130, 1116 Budapest; tel (+36 1) 382-15-00; fax (+36 1) 382-15-10; e-mail garab@innostart.hu; contact Kinga Garab.

IRELAND

Cork Business and Innovation Centre: Enterprise Centre, North Mall, Cork; tel (+353 21) 39 77 11; fax (+353 21) 85 31 28; e-mail postmaster@corkbic.com; contact Michael O'Connor.

Dublin Business Innovation Centre: The Tower, IDA Enterprise Centre, Pearse Street, Dublin 2; tel (+353 16) 71-31-11; fax (+353 16) 71-33-30; e-mail info@dbic.ie; contact Desmond C.W. Fahey.

Innovation Centre Limerick: National Technological Park, Limerick; tel (+353 61) 33-81-77; fax (+353 61) 33-80-65; e-mail morgana@shannon-dev.ie; contact Alice Morgan.

South-East Business and Innovation Centre: Industrial Park, Unit 1B, Cork Road, Waterford; tel (+353 51) 35-44-10; fax (+353 51) 35-44-15; e-mail director@sebic.ie; contact Declan Carroll.

West BIC: Hardiman House, Eyre Square 5, Galway; tel (+353 91) 56 79 74; fax (+353 91) 56 79 80; e-mail bicgwy@iol.ie; contact Joe Greaney.

ITALY

Agenzia Lumetel: Via Mazzini 92, 25065 Lumezzane (BS); tel (+39 030) 82-51-010; fax (+39 030) 89-21-420; e-mail consolati@lumetel.it; contact Luciano Consolati.

BIC Calabria: Corso d'Italia 166, 87100 Cosenza; tel (+39 0984) 39-14-55; fax (+39 0984) 39-15-07; e-mail info@biccal.it; contact Francesco Samengo.

BIC Emiglia Romagna: Via Morgagni 6, 40122 Bologna; tel (+39 051) 23-11-07; fax (+39 051) 23-29-03; e-mail staff@bic-emigliaromagna.it; contact Paola Maccani.

BIC Friuli Venezia Giulia SpA: Via Flavia 23/1, 34148 Trieste; tel (+39 04) 08-99-21; fax (+39 04) 08-99-22-57; e-mail info@bic.fvg.it; contact Bruno Jurcev.

BIC GELA / Agenzia per lo Sviluppo del Golfo – CEII: Via Filippo Morello 3, 93012 Gela; tel (+39 0933) 92-56-97; fax (+39 0933) 92-56-97; e-mail bicgela@tin.it; contact Antonino Iozza.

BIC La Fucina: Largo Lamarmora 17, 20099 Sesto San Giovanni; tel (+39 02) 26-26-65-07; fax (+39 02) 26-26-65-08; e-mail grandi@asnm.com; contact Maurizio Grandi.

BIC Lazio: Viale Parioli 39b, 00197 Roma; tel (+39 06) 807-94-35; fax (+39 06) 807-88-39; e-mail bic@biclazio.it; contact Luigi Campitelli.

BIC Liguria SpA: Via Greto di Cornigliano 6, 16152 Genova; tel (+39 10) 65-63-1; fax (+39 10) 651-87-52; e-mail genova@bic.liguria.it; contact Filippo Gabbani.

BIC Marche: Z.I. Marino del Tronto, 63100 Ascoli Piceno; tel (+39 0736) 34-21-60; fax (+39 0736) 34-21-70; e-mail eurobic@topnet.it; contact Franco Acciarri.

BIC Omega: ZI Ancarano, 64010 Ancarano; tel (+39 0861) 80-561; fax (+39 0861) 86-246; e-mail omegasrl@tin.it; contact Ing. Francesco di Pietrantonio.

BIC Puglia Sprind SpA: Corso Vittorio Emmanuele 52, 70122 Bari; tel (+39 080) 521 61 66; fax (+39 080) 579 41 30; e-mail bicpuglia@tno.it; contact Enrico Intini.

BIC Salerno: Via Giacinto Vicinanza 11, 84129 Salerno; tel (+39 089) 23-40-06; fax (+39 089) 23-40-25; e-mail bicmngt@bicsalerno.it; contact Antonio de Blasio.

BIC Sardegna: c/o Centro Servizi CASIC, VI. Strada Ovest, Agglomerato Industriale Macchiareddu, 09010 Uta (Calgiari); tel (+39 070) 201 621; fax (+39 070) 20-16-22-36; e-mail bicsardegna@sentieroimpresa.it; contact Giuseppe Matolo.

BIC Sicilia: Zona Industriale, Pantano d'Arci, Contrada Torre Allegra, Stradale Primosole, 95030 Catania; tel (+39 09) 552-32-11; fax (+39 09) 55-23-298; e-mail segrbic@tin.it; contact Giorgio Chimenti.

BIC Umbria: Strada delle Campore 13, Zona Industriale Sabbione, 05100 Terni; tel (+39 0744) 80-60-11; fax (+39 0744) 80-07-60; e-mail bicumbria@tin.it; contact Enrico Muscare.

BIC Varese: Polo Scientifico e Tecnologico Lombardo, Via Volta 11 bis, 21052 Busto Arsizio (Varese); tel (+39 0331) 63 79 59; fax (+39 0331) 63-94-87; e-mail polo@pstl.it; contact Marco Bossi.

CEII Calabria: Via XX Settembre 62, 88100 Catanzaro; tel (+39 0961) 72-25-92; fax (+39 0961) 79-43-78; e-mail eurobic@eurobic-ceii.org; contact Rosario Palaia.

CEII Trentino: Via Pietrastretta 1, 38100 Trento; tel (+390 461) 42-05-30; fax (+390 461) 42-88-42; e-mail ceiitn@tin.it; contact Claudio Zamatteo.

Centro Europeo di Impresa e di Innovazione Toscana – Sud: Via San Gimignano 69/71, 53036 Poggibonsi (Siena); tel (+39 0577) 93-82-27; fax (+39 0577) 98-32-19; e-mail ammbic@dada.it; contact Daniele Cappellini.

Centro Tecnofin Servizi SpA: Via Fortunato Zeni 8, 38068 Rovereto; tel (+39 0464) 44-31-11; fax (+39 0464) 44-31-12; e-mail t.strutture@tecnofin.it; contact Aldo Costa.

C.I.I. Pistoia: Via Tripoli 19, 51100 Pistoia; tel (+39 0573) 96-44-82; fax (+39 0573) 96-44-86; e-mail ciipt@tin.it; contact Francesco Baicchi.

CISI Campania SpA: Via A. Olivetti 1, 80078 Pozzuoli (NA); tel (+39 081) 525-51-11; fax (+39 081) 525-51-20; e-mail socodat@technapoli.interbusiness.it; contact Eduardo Vestiti.

CISI Puglia SpA: Via del Traturello Tarantino 6, Quartier Paolo VI – CP 100, 74100 Taranto; tel (+39 0994) 73-51-11; fax (+39 0994) 73-54-33; e-mail cisipuglia@mediatech.it; contact Francesco Ruggieri.

Creazione d'impresa – Tecnopolis: St. Prov. per Casamassima Km.3, 70010 Valenzano (Ba); tel (+39 080) 467-03-21; fax (+39 080) 87-705-95; e-mail tecnopolis@tno.it; contact Pasquale Orlando.

CSP – BIC Livorno: Via dell'Artigianato 55, 57121 Livorno; tel (+390 586) 42-66-69; fax (+390 586) 42-67-41; e-mail csp-bic@biclivorno.it; contact Dario Luchetti.

Euro-BIC Abruzzo e Molise: Via Po 83, 66020 St Giovanni Teatino (CH); tel (+39 085) 446-50-40; fax (+39 085) 446-11-62; e-mail m.lombardi@eurobic.it; contact Roberto Di Vincenzo.

Euro-BIC Adige PO: Via Umberto I 37, 45100 Rovigo; tel (+390 425) 42-32-93; fax (+390 425) 42-33-17; e-mail eurobicadigepo@bicadigepo.it; contact Alessandro Stefanello.

Euro-BIC – Agenzia per lo Sviluppo del Territorio: Viale Lincoln, Zona Industriale, 81100 Caserta; tel (+39 0823) 35-16-10; fax (+39 0823) 35-46-46; e-mail eurobic@iname.com; contact Maurizio Clemente.

Euro-BIC Dolomiti: Viale C. Rizzarda 21, 32032 Feltre (BL); tel (+39 0439) 30-52-06; fax (+39 0439) 30-52-04; e-mail bicdolomiti@sunrise.it; contact Giuliano Turcato.

Euro-BIC Vallée D'Aoste / Centro Sviluppo: Regione Borgnalle 10L, 11020 Aosta; tel (+39 01) 65-23-91-34; fax (+39 01) 65-23-93-20; e-mail centro.sviluppo@interbusiness.it; contact Paolo Anselmo.

Euroimpresa Legnano: Via Pisacane 46, 20025 Legnano; tel (+39 0331) 48-72-10; fax (+39 0331) 52-29-70; e-mail euroimpresa@aen.ansaldo.it; contact Franco Guglielmina.

Innova BIC SpA: Strada San Giacomo 19, 98122 Messina; tel (+39 090) 66-33-13; fax (+39 090) 66-32-27; e-mail bic@innovabic.it; contact Pietro Franza.

Parco Scientifico e delle Telecomunicazioni in Valle Scrivia: Str. Comunale Savonesa 9, 15050 Rivalta Scrivia-Tortona (AL); tel (+39 0131) 86-01-15; fax (+39 0131) 86-06-56; e-mail pst@pst.it; contact Alessandro Scaccheri.

Systema BIC Basilicata: Via Vaccaro 127, 85100 Potenza; tel (+39 0971) 57-386; fax (+39 0971) 58-479; e-mail bicbasilicata@nts.it; contact Raffaele Ricciuti.

LUXEMBOURG

Centre de Recherche Public Henri Tudor: 6, rue de Coudenhove-Kalergi, 1359 Luxembourg; tel (+352) 42-59-91-1; fax (+352) 43-65-23; e-mail claude.wehenkel@crpht.lu; contact Claude Wehenkel.

NETHERLANDS

BIC Noord-Nederland: Zernikepark 4, 9747AN Groningen; tel (+31 50) 57-45-750; fax (+31 50) 57-36-247; e-mail info@zernikegroup.com; contact Bob Hiemstra.

BIC Twente: Hengelosestraat 705, PO Box 545, 7500 AM Enschede; tel (+31 53) 483-63-53; fax (+31 53) 433-74-15; e-mail info@btc-twente.nl; contact Gijs Van Driem.

NORWAY

Forskningsparken As: Gaudstadalleen 21, 0371 Oslo; tel (+47 22) 35-85-33; fax (+47 22) 60-44-27; e-mail svenning.torp@ sposlo.no; contact Torp Svenning.

POLAND

Olsztyn Incubator: Ul. Warszawska 98, 10702 Olsztyn; tel (+48 89) 535 1780; fax (+48 89) 535 17 84; e-mail incubator@ incubator.prv.pl; contact Jacek Bloniecki.

PORTUGAL

AIMINHO: Av. Dr. Francsesco Pires Goncalves 45, 4700 Braga; tel (+351-253) 20-25-19; fax (+351-253) 27-66-01; e-mail af@aiminho.pt; contact Victor Sa Carneiro.

BIC Algarve Huelva: Av. Dr. Bernardino da Silva 65-2 Dto., 8700 Olhao; tel (+351 289) 70-79-20; fax (+351 289) 78-11-21; e-mail geral@bic-ah.com; contact Dario Dias.

BIC Santarem: Rua Conde da Ribeira Grande, Lote 2, Apdo 445, 2002 Santarem Codex; tel (+351 243) 359-150; fax (+351 243) 359-160; e-mail canela@ det.pt; contact Fernando Soares Canela.

CEISET Centro de Empresa e de Inovaçao de Setubal: Avenida Luisa Todi 375, 2900 Setubal; tel (+351 265) 53-52-42; fax (+351 265) 53-53-56; e-mail ceiset@ip.pt; contact Vasco Lemos Vieira.

Centro de Empresas e Innovaçao – BIC Madeira: Madeira Tecnopolo, Caminho da Penteada, 9000 Funchal – Madeira; tel (+351 291) 72-30-00; fax (+351 291) 72-00-30; e-mail ceim@ madinfo.pt; contact Joao Luis Lomelino de Freitas.

Centro Promotor de Innovaçao e Negocios (CPIN): Taguspark, Nucleo Central, Sala 331, 2780-920 Porto Salvo (Lisbonne); tel (+351 21) 422-04-50; fax (+351 21) 422-04-59; e-mail cpin@ taguspark.pt; contact Pedro Almeida.

CIEBI Centro de Innovaçao Empresarial de Beira Interior: Estrada do Sineiro 54, 6200 Covilha; tel (+351 275) 319-150; fax (+351 275) 324-750; e-mail ciebi.bic@mail.tel.epac.pt; contact Joao Carvalho.

N.E.T. S.A. Novas Empresas Tecnologias: Rua De Salazares 842, 4100 Porto; tel (+351 22) 617-05-79; fax (+351 22) 617-76-62; e-mail net@net-sa.pt; contact José Martins.

NIT-Negocios Inovacao e Tecnologias – BIC Viseu: Edificio Expobeiras, Parque Industrial de Coimbroes, 3500 Viseu; tel (+351 232) 470-200; fax (+351 232) 470-201; e-mail bicviseu@mail.tel .epac.pt; contact Carlos Rua.

Spidouro: Rua Cidade de Espinho 24, 5000 Vila Real; tel (+351 2) 59 30 98 10; fax (+351 2) 59 30 98 19; e-mail spidouro@ mail.tel.epac.pt; contact Rodrigo Sarmento de Beires.

SLOVAKIA

BIC Banska Bystrica: Severna 5, 97401 Banska Bystrica; tel (+421 88) 412-42-24; fax (+421 88) 412-42-20; e-mail bicbb@ psgnetbb.sk; contact Miroslav Ursiny.

BIC Bratislava: Zochova 5, 81103 Bratislava; tel (+421 7) 544-11-195; fax (+421 7) 544-17-522; e-mail lindy@bicba.sk; contact Roman Linczenyi.

BIC Prievidza: Hviezdoslavova 3, 97101 Prievidza; tel (+421 8625) 42-41-01; fax (+421 8625) 42-67-33; e-mail bicpd@bb .tel.ecom.sk; contact František Vrtak.

BIC Spisska Nova Ves: Zimna 72, 05201 Spisska Nova Ves; tel (+421 965) 44-26-254; fax (+421 965) 44-26-254; e-mail bicsnv@spisnet.sk; contact Katarina Krotakova.

Cassovia BIC: Napajadla 2, 04012 Kosice; tel (+421 95) 749-378; fax (+421 95) 740-911; e-mail bicke@napri.sk; contact Ivan Pezlar.

SPAIN

Barcelona Activa: Llacuna 162, 08018 Barcelona; tel (+34 93) 401-98-00; fax (+34 93) 300-90-15; e-mail mbasora@-mail.bcn.es; contact Pau Jorda.

Beaz: Alameda Recalde 18-6, 48009 Bilbao; tel (+34 94) 423 92 28; fax (+34 94) 423 10 13; e-mail javier.barcina@beaz .net; contact José Ignacio Izurieta Mendieta.

BIC Berrilan: C/Barrenengua 3, 20600 Eibar; tel (+34 94) 320 07 26; fax (+34 94) 320 11 07; e-mail karmele.arozena@ bicberrilan.com; contact Maria-Luisa Arriola.

BIC Euronova: Parque Tecnologico de Andalucia, Avda Juan Lopez Penalver 21, 29590 Campanillas (Malaga); tel (+34 951) 010 504; fax (+34 951) 010 527; e-mail info@bic.es; contact Alvaro Simon De Blas.

BIC Galicia: Avda Citroen s/n, Edf. Zona Franca 2, 36210 Vigo; tel (+34 9) 86 20 98 49; fax (+34 9) 86 20 78 82; e-mail bicgalic@jet.es; contact Santiago Gonzalez-Babe.

CEEI Alcoy: Plaza Emilio Sala 1, 03801 Alcoy; tel (+34 96) 554-16-66; fax (+34 96) 554-40-85; e-mail cmiro@ceei-alcoy.com; contact Manuel Rios Perez.

CEEI Aragon: Maria de Luna 11, 50015 Zaragoza; tel (+34 976) 73-35-00; fax (+34 976) 73-37-19; e-mail ceei@ceeiaragon.es; contact Javier Sanchez Asin.

CEEI Bahia de Cádiz: Centro de Lanzamiento Economico, C/Delta 1, Poligono Industrial Las Salinas, 11500 El Puerto de Santa Maria-Cadiz; tel (+34 95) 686-06-54; fax (+34 95) 686-00-27; e-mail ceei@ceeibahia.com; contact Julio Gomez Pastrana.

CEEI Balears: Centre BIT-RAIGUER, C/ Selleters 25, 07300 Inca; tel (+34 97) 18-87-000; fax (+34 97) 18-87-001; e-mail ceeib@bitel.es; contact Trias Auli.

CEEI Burgos: Avenida General Yague 29, entreplanta, 09004 Burgos; tel (+34 947) 24-43-32; fax (+34 947) 24-42-66; e-mail info@ceeiburgos.es; contact José Vicente Orden.

CEEI Castellon: C/Ginjols n.1 (Esquina Avda del Mar), 12003 CASTELLON DE LA PLANA; tel (+34 964) 72-20-30; fax (+34 964) 23-88-89; e-mail ceei@ceei-castellon.com; contact Felix Lafuente.

CEEI de Asturias: Parque Tecnologico de Asturias, 33420 Llanera; tel (+34 985) 98-00-98; fax (+34 985) 26-57-40; e-mail joseluis@ceei.es; contact Jose Luis Suarez.

CEEI de Cartagena: Poligono Industrial Cabezo Beaza, C/Berlin, Parcela 3-F, 30395 Cartagena (Murcia); tel (+34 96) 85 21 017; fax (+34 96) 85 00 839; e-mail ceeicartag@sarenet.es; contact Angel Martinez-Conde Garcia.

CEEI de Castilla y León: Parque Tecnologico de Boecillo, 47151 Boecillo (Valladolid); tel (+34 983) 54-80-15; fax (+34 983) 54-80-57; e-mail ceiva@ceical .cict.jcyl.es; contact Francisco Barredo Avellon.

CEEI de Ciudad Real: C/Pedro Munoz 1, Pol. Larache., 13005 Ciudad Real; tel (+34 926) 27-30-34; fax (+34 926) 21-63-98; e-mail ceei@ceeicr.es; contact Eduardo Escudero.

CEEI de Navarra: Carretera Estacion s/n, Poligono Industrial Elorz, 31110 Noain (Navarra); tel (+34 94) 842-60-00; fax (+34 94) 842-60-10; e-mail mjbernal@ cein.es; contact Javier Catalan.

CEEI de Valencia: Calle Benjamin Franklin 12, Parque Tecnologico de Paterna, 46980 Paterna (Valencia); tel (+34 96) 199-42-00; fax (+34 96) 199-42-20; e-mail informacion@ceei.net; contact Jesus Casanova Paya.

CEEI Elche: Ronda Vall d'Uxo, 125 Pol. Carrus, 03205 Elche (Alicante); tel (+34 96) 666-10-17; fax (+34 96) 666-10-40; e-mail ceei@ceei-elche.com; contact Joaquin Alcazar Cano.

Centre d'Iniciatives Empresarials de Rubi: Rambleta Joan Miro, s/n, 08191 Rubi (Barcelona); tel (+34 93) 588-41-30;

fax (+34 93) 588-61-95; e-mail impes@impes.es; contact Olga Gonzalez Cerezales.

Centro de Empresas e Innovacion de Alava: C/Tecnologico 11, N. 15 area PT-1, Parque Tecnologico de Alava, 01510 Miñano (Alava); tel (+34 94) 529-82-82; fax (+34 94) 529-87-10; e-mail ceia.spri@jet.es; contact Luis del Teso.

EUROCEI Centro Europeo de Empresas e Innovacion: Autovia Sevilla-Coria, s/n, Apdo de Correos 76, 41920 San Juan de Aznalfarache (Sevilla); tel (+34 95) 417-92-10; fax (+34 95) 417-11-17; e-mail eurocei@eurocei.com; contact Enrique Piriz.

SWEDEN

BIC Mid Sweden AB: Midlanda Airport, 86030 Sorberge; tel (+46 60) 19-09-00; fax (+46 60) 19-09-09; e-mail info@bicmid.se; contact Tomas Noreen.

BIC Norr: PO Box 7954, 90719 Umea; tel (+46 90) 15-49-80; fax (+46 90) 15-49-85; e-mail bicnorr@bicnorr.se; contact Tore Sjodin.

BIC Sweden West AB: Kurodsvagen 1, 45155 Uddevalla; tel (+46 522) 65-66-40; fax (+46 522) 39-93-0; e-mail o.halbert@bic.se; contact Olof Halbert.

SWITZERLAND

RET (Recherches Economiques et Techniques): ZI Allee du Quartz 1, 2300 La Chaux de Fonds; tel (+41 32) 92-59-825; fax (+41 32) 92-59-835; e-mail pierre-andre.maire@ne.ch; contact Pierre-Andre Maire.

UNITED KINGDOM

Barnsley BIC: Innovation Way, South Yorkshire, S75 1JL; tel (+44 1226) 249-590; fax (+44 1226) 249-625; e-mail postbox@bbic.co.uk; contact Tim Milburn.

Birmingham BIC: Aston Science Park, Love Lane, Aston Triangle, Birmingham, B7 7BJ; tel (+44 121) 359-0981; fax (+44 121) 359-0433; e-mail dharris@astonsciencepark.co.uk; contact Derek Harris.

East Lancashire Technology Management Centre: St James' Square, Accrington, Lancashire, BB5 0RE; tel (+44 125) 4385522; fax (+44 125) 4231715; e-mail langley.d@enterprise.plc.uk; contact Dennis Langley.

Greater Manchester BIC: Churchgate House, 56 Oxford Street, Greater Manchester, M60 7HJ; tel (+44 161) 245-4742; fax (+44 161) 236-4160; e-mail linda.mickleburgh@c-b-e.co.uk; contact Linda Mickleburgh.

Innovation Centre NORIBIC: 9, Shipquay Street, Londonderry, North Ireland, BT48 6DJ; tel (+44 1504) 264-242; fax (+44 1504) 269-025; e-mail noribic@freeserve.co.uk; contact Gerald McGuckin.

Kent Technology Transfer Centre: Research & Development Building, University of Kent, Canterbury, CT2 7PD; tel (+44 1227) 478580; fax (+44 1227) 763424; e-mail chris.luton@lbl.co.uk; contact Peter G. Parsons.

London BIC: Innova Park, Mollison Avenue, Enfield, Middlesex, EN3 7XU; tel (+44 20) 8350-1350; fax (+44 20) 8350-1351; e-mail gosborne@londonbic.com; contact Gareth Osborne.

North East of England BIC: Sunderland Enterprise Park, Wearfield, Sunderland, SR5 2TA; tel (+44 191) 516-6020; fax (+44 191) 516-6143; e-mail arnold.raine@ne-bic.co.uk; contact Arnold Raine.

Pronovus Ltd.: Howitt Building, Lenton Boulevard, Nottingham, NG7 2BG; tel (+44 115) 952-9320; fax (+44 115) 952-9321; e-mail admin@pronovus.org.uk; contact Bryan Jenkins.

St Johns Innovation Centre Ltd.: Cowley Road, Cambridge, CB4 4WS; tel (+44 1223) 420252; fax (+44 1223) 420844; e-mail wjherriot@stjohns.co.uk; contact Walter Herriot.

Staffordshire and Black Country BIC: Staffordshire Technology Park, Beaconside, Stafford, ST18 0AR; tel (+44 1785) 226598; fax (+44 1785) 220302; e-mail bic@staffs.ac.uk; contact Brian Goddard.

Tapton Park Innovation Centre: Brimington Road, Tapton, Chesterfield, Derbyshire, S41 0TZ; tel (+44 1246) 231234; fax (+44 1246) 230055; e-mail admin@tapton.co.uk; contact Dave Goucher.

Satellites

BELGIUM

Business Centre de Binche: Rue de Pastures 95, 7130 Binche; tel (+32 64) 34-09-51; fax (+32 64) 34-11-03; e-mail me.libert@skynet.be; contact Stephanie Libert.

Business Centre de Tournaisis: Chaussee d'Ath 242, 7850 Enghien (Marcq); tel (+32 2) 397 02 20; fax (+32 2) 395 62 12; e-mail me.herpelinck@skynet.be; contact Philippe Geerkens.

FINLAND

Lieksa Development Agency: Kerantie 22, 81720 Lieksa; tel (+358 13) 520-2239; fax (+358 13) 523-165; e-mail markku.vuorenmaa@lieksa.fi; contact Markku Vuorenmaa.

FRANCE

Association Grand Luminy: Case 922, Parc Scientifique et technologique de Luminy, 13288 Marseille Cedex, 09; tel (+33 4) 91 82 63 12; fax (+33 4) 91 82 91 02; contact Didier Plegat.

C.E.E.I. Synergie, Moselle Nord: Z.I. Ste Agathe, Rue du Lavoisier, 57190 Florange; tel (+33 3) 82-59-32-00; fax (+33 3) 82-59-32-29; contact Ronald Heim.

CEEI Théogone (Martres Tolosanes): Zone d'Activités, Route de Mondavezan | BP 18, 31220 Martres Tolosane; tel (+33 5) 61-90-80-80; fax (+33 5) 61-98-83-00; e-mail theogone-martres@wanadoo.fr; contact Daniel Blonde.

Centre Initia (Antenne d'Aditec): Parc de la Porte Nord, 62700 Bruay-La-Buissière; tel (+33 3) 21-64-69-70; fax (+33 3) 21-69-89; e-mail initia.bruay@wanadoo.fr; contact Pierre Maerten.

Chambre de Commerce et d'Industrie d'Arras: 8 Rue du 29 Juillet, BP 540, 62008 Arras Cedex; tel (+33 3) 21 23 24 24; fax (+33 3) 21 23 84 84; e-mail ciarrasindustrie@wanadoo.fr; contact Marc Poignant.

Chambre de Commerce et d'Industrie de Saint-Omer: 16 Place Victor Hugo, BP 94, 62502 Saint Omer Cedex; tel (+33 3) 21 98 46 22; fax (+33 3) 21 98 01 66; e-mail ccistomer.doc@wanadoo.fr; contact Jean Betremieux.

Comité de Developpement Economique de Liévin: Rue du Chevalier de la Barre 18, BP 161, 62803 Liévin Cedex; tel (+33 3) 21-78-11-11; fax (+33 3) 21-78-24-00; e-mail chconstant@nordnet.fr; contact Christine Constant.

Creamanche: Zone Industrielle de la Liane 50, 62200 Boulogne-sur-Mer; tel (+33 3) 21-80-44-45; fax (+33 3) 21-80-55-77; e-mail jacqueline.danger@wanadoo.fr; contact Jacqueline Danger.

Icem: I.M.T. Technopole de Château Gombert, 13451 Marseille Cedex 20; tel (+33 4) 91-05-44-36; fax (+33 4) 91-05-43-67; e-mail rey@marseille-innov.org; contact Christian Rey.

Les 7 Vallées (Antenne d'Aditec): Route Nationale 39, BP 18, 62990 Beaurainville; tel (+33 3) 21-06-77-77; fax (+33 3) 21-06-77-78; e-mail Les7vallées@wanadoo.fr; contact Jean-Marie Fauvel.

Ruche d'Entreprise de Denain: Rue Arthur Brunet 350, BP 17, 59721 Denain

Cedex; tel (+33 3) 27-21-44-44; fax (+33 3) 27-21-44-45; e-mail ruche.denain@nordnet.fr; contact Anne-Sophie Baey.

Ruche d'Entreprises de Roubaix: 258 rue Ingres, 59100 Roubaix; tel (+33 3) 20-89-44-00; fax (+33 3) 20-75-66-89; e-mail ruche.roubaix@nordnet.fr; contact Jean-Jacques Ferron.

Ruche d'Entreprises de Tourcoing: 31 rue de la Fonderie, BP 2000, 59203 Tourcoing Cedex; tel (+33 3) 20-27-61-61; fax (+33 3) 20-36-67-67; e-mail ruchetg@nordnet.fr; contact Dominique Delzenne.

Ruche des 2 Lys: ZI 8 avenue Pierre Brosselette, 59280 Armentières; tel (+33 3) 20-10-91-20; fax (+33 3) 20-77-50-19; e-mail ruche.deuxlys@nordnet.fr; contact Luc Desmettre.

Ruche du Douaisis: Rue Becquerel – ZI Douai – Dorignies, BP 340, 59531 Douai Cedex; tel (+33 3) 27-08-08-60; fax (+33 3) 27-08-08-61; e-mail ruche.douaisis@nordnet.fr; contact Thierry Montaigne.

Ruche du Littoral: 27 rue Watteau, 59430 Saint-Pol-sur-Mer; tel (+33 3) 28-61-90-00; fax (+33 3) 28-61-55-07; e-mail ruche.littoral@wanadoo.fr; contact Paul Staelen.

Ruche Sambre Avesnois: ZI de la Petite Savate, Route de Mairieux, 59600 Maubeuge; tel (+33 3) 27-53-04-53; fax (+33 3) 27-53-04-79; e-mail ruche.maubeuge@wanadoo.fr; contact Anne-Sophie Baey.

Ruche Technologique du Nord: 121 rue Chanzy, 59260 Hellemmes; tel (+33 3) 20-67-59-59; fax (+33 3) 20-67-59-95; e-mail rtn@ruche-technologique.fr; contact Denis Leroy.

Syndival (Antenne d'Aditec): Rue Ferdinand Buisson 56, Centre Directionnel-6ème Etage, 62327 Boulogne-sur-Mer Cedex; tel (+33 3) 21-99-44-44; fax (+33 3) 21-99-44-45; e-mail D.Fauquet.synd-bd@wanadoo.fr; contact Daniel Fauquet.

IRELAND

Guinness Enterprise Centre: Taylor's Lane, Dublin; tel (+353 16) 70 93 89; fax (+353 16) 70 93 99; e-mail damedbic@indigo.ie.

WESTBIC: Business Park, Weir Road, Tuam – Galway; tel (+353 93) 281-81; fax (+353 93) 280-56; e-mail bictuam@iol.ie; contact John Brennan.

WESTBIC Donegal: Ionad Forbatha Gno, Kilcar, Donegal; tel (+353 73) 383-33; fax (+353 73) 383-42; e-mail bicdongl@iol.ie; contact Eunan Cunningham.

WESTBIC Letterkenny: Letterkenny Institute of Technology, Port Road, Letterkenny, Donegal; tel (+353 74) 643-69; fax (+353 74) 643-50; e-mail westbic@lyit.ie; contact Ultan O'Fatharta.

WESTBIC Mayo: Meitheal Mhaigheo, Lower Main Street, Foxford, Mayo; tel (+353 94) 567-45; fax (+353 94) 567-49; e-mail bicmayo@iol.ie; contact Seamus McCormack.

WESTBIC Roscommon: Roscommon Enterprise, Racecourse Road, Roscommon; tel (+353 903) 251-96; fax (+353 903) 274-07; e-mail bicros@iol.ie; contact James Donlon.

ITALY

BIC Emiglia Romagna Unita di Forli: Via Carlo Seganti 103, 47100 Forli; tel (+39 0543) 47-35-63; fax (+39 0543) 47-35-64; contact Claudio Sirri.

BIC Gorizia – Seed: Autoporto di Gorizia – Mag. A, 34170 Gorizia; tel (+39 0481) 52-77-11; fax (+39 0481) 52-27-79; e-mail bicgo@seed.it; contact Antonio Sviligoj.

BIC Lazio – Acropoli: Via Casilina, 68300 Ferentino; tel (+39 0775) 75-24-59-58; fax (+39 07) 75-20-25-03; e-mail bic@biclazio.it; contact Domenico Silvestri.

BIC Liguria – Imperia: c/o Camera di Commercio, Viale Matteotti 48, 18100 Imperia; tel (+39 01) 83793260; fax (+39 01) 83275021; contact Marco Laurent.

BIC Liguria – La Spezia: Via Melara 12, 19100 La Spezia; tel (+39 01) 87502066; fax (+39 01) 87510862; e-mail genova@bic.liguria.it; contact Marco Salerno.

CISI Campania-Centro di Marcianise: Area ASI Marcianise Sud, 81025 Marcianise; tel (+39 0823) 63-91-11; fax (+39 0823) 63-91-23; contact Le Directeur.

Centro Servizi Incubatore di Settingiano: Localita Campo, 88040 Settingiano (CZ); tel (+39 0961) 99-89-37; fax (+39 0961) 99-86-26.

Sportello di Reggio Calabria: Corso Garibaldi 154, Galeria Caminiti, 89100 Reggio Calabria; tel (+39 0965) 81-87-36; fax (+39 0965) 33-82-52.

SPAIN

CEEI Aragon – Huesca: Carretera de Zaragoza – Km 67, 22197 Cuarte (Huesca); tel (+34 974) 21-19-21; fax (+34 947) 21-35-26; e-mail ceei.hu@ceeiaragon.es; contact Daniel Valles Turmo.

CEEI Aragon – Teruel: Avenida de Sagunto 116, Poligono La Fuenfresca, 44002 Teruel; tel (+34 97) 86-10-812; fax (+34 97) 86-10-966; e-mail ceei.te@ceeiaragon.es; contact Antonio Martinez Algilaga.

SWEDEN

BIC Norr-Skelleftea: Expolaris Center, 93178 Skelleftea; tel (+46 910) 77-08-88; fax (+46 910) 121-20.

UNITED KINGDOM

London BIC – Stratford: 339 High Street, Stratford, E15 2TF; tel (+44 20) 8519-4888; fax (+44 20) 8522-1333; e-mail info@londonbic.com; contact Derek Levy.

EURYDICE: INFORMATION NETWORK ON EDUCATION IN EUROPE

In February 1976, the Council of Ministers of Education adopted an education action programme. They acknowledged that the dissemination of information on EU educational developments needed to be expanded and improved. In 1980, the Eurydice Network was set up. In 1990 and 1992, the Council of Ministers of Education adopted a Resolution and conclusions aimed at strengthening the function and role of Eurydice in the preparation of comparative analyses on themes of common interest to the Member States, in the exchange of information between policy-makers and in the dissemination of the network's information to a broad public. Eurydice is now an action which is part of the Socrates programme. In 1994, the network was opened to the countries of EFTA/EEA and progressively to Central and Eastern Europe. It now covers 31 European countries.

Each Member State has designated at least one National Unit to take part in the network, in accordance with its own educational structures. The Units are generally located within national Ministries of Education, or act in close collaboration with them. The European Commission has set up the Eurydice European Unit which is the driving force behind the network's activities and the production of comparative analyses.

There are three major types of information:

- Comparative analyses and documents on education systems and on themes of common concern to the Member States. The addressees are education bodies in the European Union, policy-makers, research workers, education specialists, etc. Through dissemination of these products on the Internet, Eurydice also reaches the wider education world.
- Indicators on all levels of education and on specific themes ('Key Data on education in Europe': joint biennial Eurydice/Eurostat report).
- Eurybase, a database on the education systems of Europe.

For information about Eurydice initiatives, contact the European Unit in Brussels: Eurydice European Unit, Avenue Louise 240, 1050 Brussels, Belgium; tel (+32) 2-6005353; fax (+32) 2-6005363; e-mail info@eurydice.org; internet www.eurydice.org. This office can also provide details of contact points in the other Member States.

EUROPEAN CONSUMER INFORMATION CENTRES

One of the priorities of the European Union's consumer policy is to provide citizens with the necessary information and advice to exploit for themselves the potential of the internal market. The Commission is therefore promoting consumer information across the borders. More specifically, it supports organizations in the private or public sector with experience in consumer affairs so that they can provide pertinent advice to citizens on the opportunities and possible problems associated with consumption.

The primary aims of the Consumer Information Centres are:

- to disseminate information about relevant Community and Member-State legislation and jurisprudence, and the results of comparative tests, and to prepare transboundary studies.
- to assist and advise in cases of litigation, to provide procedural information, to offer initial legal assistance and to guide consumers to other authorities.

European Consumer Information Centres

AUSTRIA

Europaïsche Verbraucherberatung: Mariahilferstr. 81, 1060 Vienna; tel (+43 1) 58877342; fax (+43 1) 5887771; e-mail info@europakonsument.at; internet www.europakonsument.at.

BELGIUM

Centre Européen des Consommateurs: Rue des Chevaliers 18, 1050 Brussels; tel (+32) 2-5171790; fax (+32) 2-5171799; e-mail info@cec-ecc.be; internet www.cec-ecc.be.

FINLAND

European Consumer Centre of Helsinki: City of Helsinki Environment Centre, P.O. Box 500, 00099 Helsinki; located at: Helsinginkatu 24, 00530 Helsinki; tel (+358 9) 7312 2920 - fax (+358 9) 7312 2727; e-mail eu-kuluttajaneuvonta@hel.fi; internet www.hel.fi/eu-kuluttajaneuvonta.

GERMANY

Europäisches Verbraucherzentrum: Mintropstr. 27a, 40215 Düsseldorf; tel (+49 211) 3809-231; fax (+49 211) 3809-216; e-mail info@evz-duesseldorf.de; internet www.europaeischesverbraucherzentrum.de.

Europäisches Beratungszentrum: Enschede-Str. 362, 48599 Gronau; tel (+49 2562) 70217; fax (+49 2562) 70247; e-mail info.gronau@evz.de; internet www.europaeischesverbraucherzentrum.de.

Europäisches Verbraucherzentrum der Verbraucherzentrale Schleswig-Holstein eV: Willestr. 4–6, 24103 Kiel; tel (+49 431) 9719350; fax (+49 431) 9719360; e-mail evz@evz.de; internet www.evz.de.

GREECE

European Consumer Centre of Athens: 7 Akadimias Street, 10671 Athens; tel (+30) 210-3632443; fax (+30) 210-3633976; e-mail info@ecca.gr; internet www.ecca.gr.

IRELAND

European Consumer Information Centre: 13A Upper O'Connell Street, Dublin 1; tel (+353 1) 8090600; fax (+353 1) 8090601; e-mail info@eccdublin.ie; internet www.eccdublin.ie; Manager Tina Leonard.

ITALY

Centro Europeo dei Consumatori: Via Brennero 3, 39100 Bolzano; tel (+39) 0471-980939; fax (+39) 0471-980239; e-mail info@euroconsumatori.org; internet www.euroconsumatori.org.

LUXEMBOURG

Centre Européen des Consommateurs: Rue des Bruyères 55, 1274 Howald; tel (+352) 2684641; fax (+352) 26845761; e-mail info@euroguichet.lu; internet www.euroguichet.lu; Director Karin Basenach.

PORTUGAL

Centro Europeu do Consumidor: Parça Duque de Saldanha 31 - 3°, 1069-013 Lisbon; tel (+351 21) 3564600; fax (+351 21) 3564719; e-mail ic@ic.pt; internet www.consumidor.pt/cec.

SPAIN

Centre Europeu del Consumidor: Gran Via Carles III 105 Iletra B-1, 08028 Barcelona; tel (+34) 93-556-60-10; fax (+34) 93-411-06-78; e-mail cec@icconsum.org; internet www.cecbarcelona.org/cec.

Centro Europeo del Consumidor: Donostia-San Sebastian 1, 01010 Vitoria-Gasteiz; tel (+34) 945-01-99-48; fax (+34) 945-01-99-47; e-mail cec@ej-gv.es; internet www.euskadi.net/consumoinfo.

SWEDEN

Konsument Europa: Rosenlundsgatan 9, 118 87 Stockholm; tel (+46 8) 429-07-80; fax (+46 8) 429-07-89; e-mail info@konsumenteuropa.se; internet www.konsumenteuropa.se; Director Agneta Gillback.

UNITED KINGDOM

European Consumer Centre: P.O. Box 3308, Wolverhampton, WV10 9ZS; tel (+44 1902) 310568; fax (+44 1902) 710068; e-mail consumer.euro@citizensadvice.org.uk; internet www.nacab.org.uk.

EURES: EUROPEAN EMPLOYMENT SERVICES NETWORK

EURES (EURopean Employment Services) provides a service in support of mobility and employment. It is a co-operation network which brings together the European Commission and the public employment services of the countries belonging to the EEA (European Economic Area), along with other regional and national bodies concerned with employment issues, such as trades unions, employers' organizations, and local and regional authorities. These organizations co-operate to facilitate and promote the mobility of workers within the EEA. EURES aims to inform, advise and assist European citizens who want to work in another country, and employers to recruit from abroad.

A comprehensive human network

EURES has developed a human network of advisers to provide the information required by job-seekers and employers through personal contact. There are more than 500 EURES advisers located throughout the EEA in all member countries.

EURES advisers are trained specialists who provide the three basic EURES services of information, guidance and placement, to both job-seekers and employers interested in the European job market. They have developed specialized expertise in practical, legal and administrative matters related to mobility.

EURES advisers have a number of information tools at their disposal, one of which is a database that contains details on living and working conditions in each of the Member States. Included in this database is information on labour markets, accommodation, education, cost of living, health, social legislation, taxation, training opportunities, comparability of qualifications, etc. This service provided by EURES allows job-seekers and employers to make informed decisions about mobility.

Jobs and CVs databases: europa.eu.int/eures

To match up the needs of job-seekers and employers, EURES has developed a jobs database that lists selected vacancies available throughout Europe and open to non-nationals. This database is available for all on the EURES website. The jobs database is also gradually being integrated into the mainstream systems provided by the various public employment services in the EEA in order to allow even greater accessibility.

Employers are given the opportunity to advertise their vacancies internationally in EEA member countries via this database. Likewise, job-seekers can search for employment in any one of the EEA countries. The number of available vacancies on the jobs database numbers thousands at any given time and is steadily increasing.

In addition to the jobs database there is also a CV search database. Job-seekers can use CV search to make their CVs available to a wide range of employers, who can access the database to look for suitable applicants and get in touch with them directly.

Creating a one-stop job mobility site on the internet

In order to further enhance the EURES web site and to make it a single entry point for job-related mobility information, it will be further enhanced with the database on living and working conditions mentioned above, as well as a database on labour needs in the regional labour markets. The new website will also contain links to other useful information on mobility issues from the Commission and the Member States.

Breaking down the barriers in border regions

EURES has a particularly effective role to play in cross-border regions. These are employment catchment areas in which there are significant degrees of cross-border commuting. People who live in one country and work in another have to cope with different national practices and legal systems. They may come across administrative, legal or tax obstacles to mobility on a daily basis.

In these cross-border regions EURES brings together partner organizations such as public employment services, trades unions and employers and local bodies to actively promote common and open regional labour markets. These partnerships aim to meet the need for information and can act as a forum for consultation on local labour markets.

Cross-border EURES advisers help to find practical solutions to mobility problems and to customize their services to the needs of regional customers. EURES is working towards improving transparency in these local labour markets through the exchange of local vacancies across borders and the distribution of information on vocational training opportunities.

There are currently around 20 cross-border partnerships in EURES, spread geographically throughout the network and located in several EEA countries. The Commission is constantly looking to establish new partnerships with a view to covering all relevant border regions where labour mobility can be supported.

Further information

For more information about EURES, contact: Employment and Social Affairs DG, A.3. EURES, European Commission, Rue de la Loi 200, 1049 Brussels, Belgium; e-mail empl-eures@cec.eu.int; internet http://europa.eu.int/eures.

List of Members

AUSTRIA

Gerhard Bogensperger: *organization:* EURES-INTERALP (DE-AT), AMS, Arbeitsmarktservice; *address:* Kuenburgstr. 634, 5580 Tamsweg; tel (+43 6474) 84845130; fax (+43 6474) 84845090; e-mail gerhard.bogensperger@505.ams.or.at; *languages spoken:* English, Deutsch.

Silvia Casotti: *organization:* EURES-INTERALP (DE-AT), AMS, Arbeitsmarktservice; *address:* Oskar-Pirlo-Strasse 13, 6333 Kufstein; tel (+43 5372) 6489160; fax (+43 5372) 61963; e-mail silvia.casotti@705.ams.or.at; *languages spoken:* Français, English, Deutsch.

Ingrid Dimai: *organization:* AMS, Arbeitsmarktservice; *address:* Eures/AMS Graz, Niesenbergergasse 67-69, 8020 Graz; tel (+43 316) 70809401; fax (+43 316) 70809222; e-mail Ingrid.Dimai@607.ams.or.at; *languages spoken:* English, Deutsch.

Rudof Fischer: *organization:* AMS, Arbeitsmarktservice; *address:* Daniel-Gran-Strasse 12, 3100 St Pölten; tel (+43 02742) 3092013; fax +43 02742) 3092404; e-mail Rudolf.Fischer@326.ams.or.at; *languages spoken:* English, Deutsch.

IdMaria Gasparotto: *organization:* AMS, Arbeitsmarktservice; *address:* Neubaugasse 43, 1070 Vienna; tel (+43 1) 87871-30008; fax (+43 1) 87871-30289; e-mail IdMaria.Gasparotto@970.ams.or.at; *languages spoken:* Français, English, Italiano, Deutsch.

Holger Gärtner: *organization:* Wirtschaftskammer (Chamber of Commerce) Tirol, EURES-INTERALP (DE-AT); *address:* Meinhardstr 14, 6020 Innsbruck; tel (+43 512) 5310-1379; fax (+43 51) 5310-1327; e-mail holger.gaertner@wktirol.at; *languages spoken:* Deutsch.

Otto Hosp: *organization:* TransTirolia (IT-AT-CH), AMS, Arbeitsmarktservice,

EURES-INTERALP (DE-AT); *address:* Schöpfstrasse 5, 6010 Innsbruck; tel +43 512 5903 724; fax +43 512 5903 20; e-mail otto.hosp@702.ams.or.at; *languages spoken:* English, Deutsch.

Karl Lenzhofer: *organization:* EURALP (IT-AT), AMS, Arbeitsmarktservice; *address:* Rudolfsbahngürtel 42, 9020 Klagenfurt; tel (+43 0463) 3831163; fax (+43 0463) 3831192; e-mail Karl.Lenzhofer@200.ams.or.at; *languages spoken:* Français, English, Italiano, Deutsch.

Monika Moser: *organization:* OGB, Österreichischer Gewerkschaftsbund, EURALP (IT-AT); *address:* Bahnhofstrasse 44, 9020 Klagenfurt; tel (+43 5787) 82043; fax +43 5787) 82099; e-mail mmoser@bfkaernten.or.at; *languages spoken:* English, Deutsch.

Dietmar Müller: *organization:* Bodensee (DE-AT-CH), AMS, Arbeitsmarktservice; *address:* Bahnhofstrasse 1b, 6700 Bludenz; tel (+43 5552) 6237127; fax (+43 5552) 66298; e-mail dietmar.mueller@801.ams.or.at; *languages spoken:* English, Deutsch.

Robert Popovits: *organization:* AMS, Arbeitsmarktservice; *address:* Neubaugasse 43, 1070 Vienna; tel (+43 1) 87871-30222; fax (+43 1) 87871-30289; e-mail Robert.Popovits@970.ams.or.at.

Petra Rosenstingl: *organization:* AMS, Arbeitsmarktservice, EURES-INTERALP (DE-AT); *address:* Europaplatz 9, 4021 Linz; tel (+43 0732) 6963-20136; fax (+43 0732) 6963-20290; e-mail Petra.Rosenstingl@400.ams.or.at; *languages spoken:* Français, English, Italiano, Deutsch.

Martina Vodrazka: *organization:* AMS, Arbeitsmarktservice; *address:* Hohenstaufengasse 2, 1010 Vienna; tel (+43 1) 53136315; fax (+43 1 53136322; e-mail Martina.Vodrazka@300.ams.or.at; *languages spoken:* Français, English, Deutsch.

Günther Wilfinger: *organization:* AMS, Arbeitsmarktservice; *address:* Permayerstrasse 10, 7000 Eisenstadt; tel (+43 2682) 692169; fax (+43 2682) 692179; e-mail guenther.wilfinger@100.ams.or.at; *languages spoken:* English, Deutsch.

Harald Wurzer: *organization:* AMS, Arbeitsmarktservice; *address:* Hietzinger Kai 139, 1130 Vienna; tel (+43 1) 87871-26222; fax (+43 1) 87871-26289; e-mail harald.wurzer@966.ams.or.at; *languages spoken:* English, Deutsch.

BELGIUM

Hilde Ameye: *organization:* VDAB, Vlaamse Dienst voor Arbeidsbemiddeling, EuresChannel (BE-FR-UK); *address:* Rijselsestraat 57, 8500 Kortrijk; tel (+32) 56 24 74 15; fax (+32) 56 24 74 16; e-mail hameye@vdab.be; *languages spoken:* Nederlands, Français, English.

Fernand Backaert: *organization:* ORBEM / BGDA, Office Régional Bruxellois de l'Emploi / Brusselse Gewestelijke Dienst voor Arbeidsbemiddeling; *address:* Boulevard Anspach 65, 1000 Bruxelles; tel (+32) 2 505 78 17; fax (+32) 2 505 14 22; e-mail fbackaert@orbem.be; *languages spoken:* Nederlands, Français, English.

Valérie Beghain: *organization:* UCM, EuresChannel (BE-FR-UK); *address:* Quai Notre Dame 3/5, 7500 Tournai; tel (+33) 3-69343640; fax (+33) 3-69343649; e-mail valerie.beghain@mons.ucm.be; *languages spoken:* Français.

Sylvie Couvreur: *organization:* FOREM, l'Office wallon de la formation professionnelle et de l'emploi, EuresChannel (BE-FR-UK); *address:* Bd. Gendebien 16, 7000 Mons; tel (+32) 65 32 45 45; fax (+32) 65 32 45 25; e-mail Sylvie.Couvreur@forem.be; *languages spoken:* Français, English.

Gert De Buck: *organization:* VDAB, Vlaamse Dienst voor Arbeidsbemiddeling; *address:* St Maartenstraat 5, 3000 Leuven; tel (+32) 16 29 86 26; fax (+32) 16 22 91 97; e-mail Gdbuck@vdab.be; *languages spoken:* Nederlands, English.

Gerda Debacker: *organization:* ORBEM / BGDA, Office Régional Bruxellois de l'Emploi / Brusselse Gewestelijke Dienst voor Arbeidsbemiddeling; *address:* Boulevard Anspachlaan 65, 1000 Bruxelles; tel (+32) 2 505 1420; fax (+32) 2 505 1422; e-mail gdebacker@orbem.be; *languages spoken:* Nederlands, Français, English.

Cynthia Deman: *organization:* FGTB/ABVV, Fédération Générale du Travail de Belgique / Algemeen Belgisch Vakverbond, EURES Maas-Rhin (BE-DE-NL); *address:* Grote Markt 48, 2300 Turnhout; tel (+32) 14 40 03 14; fax (+32) 14 42 94 71; e-mail cynthia.deman@abvv.be; *languages spoken:* Nederlands, Français, English, Deutsch.

Agnès Dion: *organization:* P.E.D. (BE-FR-LUX), Chambre de Commerce et de l'Industrie, Belgique; *address:* Grand rue 1, 6800 Libramont; tel (+32) 61-293050; fax (+32) 61-293069; e-mail agnes.dion@ccilb.be; *languages spoken:* Français, English.

Anne-Marie Dory: *organization:* FGTB/ABVV, Fédération Générale du Travail de Belgique / Algemeen Belgisch Vakverbond, P.E.D. (BE-FR-LUX); *address:* Rue des Martyrs 80, 6700 Arlon; tel (+32) 63-226169; fax (+32) 63-226432; e-mail anne-marie.dory@fgtb.be; *languages spoken:* Français, English.

Elisabeth Finet: *organization:* FGTB/ABVV, Fédération Générale du Travail de Belgique / Algemeen Belgisch Vakverbond, EURES Maas-Rhin (BE-DE-NL); *address:* Place St-Paul 9-11, 4000 Liège; tel (+32) 4 221 9583; fax (+32) 4 221 9626; e-mail elisabeth.finet@fgtb.be; *languages spoken:* Français, English.

Romuald Geury: *organization:* ACV-CSC, Algemeen Christelijk Vakverbond / Confédération des Syndicats Chrétiens, P.E.D. (BE-FR-LUX); *address:* 37 Avenue de la Gare, 6700 Arlon; tel (+32) 63 24 20 40; fax (+32) 63 24 20 60; e-mail csc@skynet.be; *languages spoken:* Français.

Bruno Gonsette: *organization:* FOREM, l'Office wallon de la formation professionnelle et de l'emploi; *address:* Boulevard Tirou 104, 6000 Charleroi; tel (+32) 71 206412; fax (+32) 71 206598; e-mail Bruno.Gonsette@forem.be; *languages spoken:* Nederlands, Deutsch.

Frank Heylen: *organization:* ACV-CSC, Algemeen Christelijk Vakverbond / Confédération des Syndicats Chrétiens, Scheldemond (BE-NL); *address:* Mgr. Broekxplein 6, 3500 Hasselt; tel (+32) 11 29 17 22; fax (+32) 11 29 17 13; e-mail frank.heylen@acv-csc.be; *languages spoken:* Nederlands, Français.

Florence Lamoline: *organization:* FOREM, l'Office wallon de la formation professionnelle et de l'emploi, EURES Maas-Rhin (BE-DE-NL); *address:* Carrefour Emploi et Formation, Val Benoît, Quai Banning 4, 4000 Liège; tel (+32) 4 229 11 82; fax (+32) 4 254 40 19; e-mail florence.lamoline@forem.be; *languages spoken:* Nederlands, Français, English.

Wilfrid Laschet: *organization:* FOREM, l'Office wallon de la formation professionnelle et de l'emploi, EURES Maas-Rhin (BE-DE-NL); *address:* Carrefour Emploi et Formation, Quai Banning 4, 4000 Liège; tel (+32) 4 229 11 83; fax (+32) 4 254 40 19; e-mail wilfrid.laschet@forem.be; *languages spoken:* Français, English, Deutsch.

Colette Maertens: *organization:* FOREM, l'Office wallon de la formation professionnelle et de l'emploi; *address:* Rue Clideric 53, 7500 Tournai; tel (+32) 69 88 29 73; fax (+32) 69 88 29 73; e-mail colette.maertens@forem.be; *languages spoken:* Français, English.

Léon Martens: *organization:* VDAB, Vlaamse Dienst voor Arbeidsbemiddeling, EURES Maas-Rhin (BE-DE-NL); *address:* Pastorijstraat 7, 3620 Lanaken; tel (+32) 89 73 92 72; fax (+32) 89 71 83 24; e-mail lmartens@vdab.be; *languages spoken:* Nederlands, Français, English, Deutsch.

Richard Menu: *organization:* FOREM, l'Office wallon de la formation professionnelle et de l'emploi; *address:* Boulevard Tirou 104, 6000 Charleroi; tel (+32) (0)71 206463; fax (+32) (0)71 206198; e-mail

Richard.Menu@forem.be; *languages spoken:* Nederlands, Français.

Patrick Mertens: *organization:* Scheldemond (BE-NL), FGTB/ABVV, Fédération Générale du Travail de Belgique / Algemeen Belgisch Vakverbond; *address:* Vrijdagmarkt 9, 9000 Gent; tel (+32) 9 265 5292; fax (+32) 9 265 5298; e-mail pmertens@abvvmetaal.org; *languages spoken:* Nederlands, Français, English.

Valérie Oosterlinck: *organization:* ACV-CSC, Algemeen Christelijk Vakverbond / Confédération des Syndicats Chrétiens, EuresChannel (BE-FR-UK); *address:* Rue St-Pierre 52, 7700 Mouscron; tel (+32) 56 330303; fax (+32) 56 347612; e-mail valerieoosterlinck@acv-csc.be; *languages spoken:* Nederlands, Français, English.

Michèle Op 't Eijnde: *organization:* VDAB, Vlaamse Dienst voor Arbeidsbemiddeling, EURES Maas-Rhin (BE-DE-NL); *address:* Pastorijstraat 7, 3620 Lanaken; tel (+32) 89 73 92 72; fax (+32) 89 71 83 24; e-mail mopteynd@vdab.be; *languages spoken:* Nederlands, Français, English, Deutsch.

Jos Poukens: *organization:* ACV-CSC, Algemeen Christelijk Vakverbond / Confédération des Syndicats Chrétiens, EURES Maas-Rhin (BE-DE-NL); *address:* Mgr. Broekxplein 6, 3500 Hasselt; tel (+32) 11 290942; fax (+32) 11 291713; e-mail jos.poukens@acv-csc.be; *languages spoken:* Nederlands, Français, English.

Marie-Rose Pétry: *organization:* ORBEM / BGDA, Office Régional Bruxellois de l'Emploi / Brusselse Gewestelijke Dienst voor Arbeidsbemiddeling; *address:* Boulevard Anspachlaan 65, 1000 Bruxelles; tel (+32) 2 505 1421; fax (+32) 2 505 1422; e-mail mrpetry@orbem.be; *languages spoken:* Nederlands, Français, English.

Marco Schaaf: *organization:* EURES Maas-Rhin (BE-DE-NL), ADG, Arbeitsmarkt und Beschäftigung in der Deutschsprachigen Gemeinschaft; *address:* Hütte 79, 4700 Eupen; tel (+32) 87 63 89 00; fax (+32) 87 55 70 85 (+32) 87 85 32 04; e-mail marco.schaaf@adg.be; *languages spoken:* Nederlands, Français, English, Deutsch.

Frie Teppers: *organization:* ACV-CSC, Algemeen Christelijk Vakverbond / Confédération des Syndicats Chrétiens, EURES Maas-Rhin (BE-DE-NL); *address:* Place de l'Eglise 6, 4720 La Calamine; tel (+32) 87 659113; fax (+32) 87 653479; e-mail FTeppers@acv-csc.be; *languages spoken:* Nederlands, Français, Deutsch.

Geert Van Autenboer: *organization:* FGTB/ABVV, Fédération Générale du Travail de Belgique / Algemeen Belgisch Vakverbond, Scheldemond (BE-NL); *address:* Grote Markt, 2300 Turnhout; tel (+32) 14 400375; fax (+32) 14 439876; e-mail gvautenboer@bbtk-abvv.be; *languages spoken:* Nederlands, Français, Deutsch.

Urbain Van Heyghen: *organization:* ACV-CSC, Algemeen Christelijk Vakverbond / Confédération des Syndicats Chrétiens, Scheldemond (BE-NL); *address:* Oostveldstraat 23, 9900 Eeklo; tel (+32) 9 376 92 24; fax (+32) 9 376 92 34; e-mail u.vanheyghen@acv-csc.be; *languages spoken:* Nederlands, Français, English.

Antoni Van der Veen: *organization:* VDAB, Vlaamse Dienst voor Arbeidsbemiddeling, Scheldemond (BE-NL); *address:* Somersstraat 22, 2018 Antwerpen; tel (+32) 32 02 18 77; fax (+32) 32 02 18 76; e-mail avdveen@vdab.be; *languages spoken:* Nederlands, English, Deutsch.

Brigitte Vandeleene: *organization:* UNIZO, EuresChannel (BE-FR-UK); *address:* Lange Steenstraat 10, 8500 Kortrijk; tel (+32) 56 26 44 44; fax 32 56 26 44 65; e-mail brigitte.vandeleene@kmonet.be; *languages spoken:* Nederlands, Français, Deutsch.

Rik Vandevenne: *organization:* ACV-CSC, Algemeen Christelijk Vakverbond / Confédération des Syndicats Chrétiens, EuresChannel (BE-FR-UK); *address:* President Kennedy Park 16 8500 Kortrijk; tel (+32) 56 235525; fax (+32) 56 235523; e-mail rvandevenne@acv-csc.be; *languages spoken:* Nederlands, Suomi.

Nadine Vanhove: *organization:* FGTB/ABVV, Fédération Générale du Travail de Belgique / Algemeen Belgisch Vakverbond, EuresChannel (BE-FR-UK); *address:* Rue des Maux 26, 7500 Tournai; tel (+32) 69 88 18 10; fax (+32) 69 222 492; e-mail nadine.vanhove@fgtb.be; *languages spoken:* Nederlands, Français, English.

Bart Vanpoucke: *organization:* FGTB/ABVV, Fédération Générale du Travail de Belgique / Algemeen Belgisch Vakverbond, EuresChannel (BE-FR-UK); *address:* A. Debunnestraat 49-51, 8930 Menen; tel (+32) 56 52 02 01; fax (+32) 56 51 82 62; e-mail eur.hnfk.ivr.abvv@skynet.be; *languages spoken:* Nederlands, Français, English.

Annie Vanseveren: *organization:* Scheldemond (BE-NL), VDAB, Vlaamse Dienst voor Arbeidsbemiddeling; *address:* Kongostraat 7, 9000 Gent; tel (+32) 92 65 47 31; fax (+32) 92 33 04 16; e-mail avsevere@vdab.be; *languages spoken:* Nederlands, Français, English.

Gisèle Vatriquant: *organization:* P.E.D. (BE-FR-LUX), FOREM, l'Office wallon de la formation professionnelle et de l'emploi; *address:* Rue de la Meuse 14, 6700 Arlon; tel (+32) (0)63 24 29 17; fax (+32) (0)63 23 47 61; e-mail Gisele.Vatriquant@forem.be; *languages spoken:* Français, English, Deutsch.

Kyra Veldkamp: *organization:* VDAB, Vlaamse Dienst voor Arbeidsbemiddeling, Scheldemond (BE-NL); *address:* Somersstraat 22, 2018 Antwerpen; tel (+32) 32 02 18 27; fax (+32) 32 02 18 76; e-mail kveldkam@vdab.be; *languages spoken:* Nederlands, Français, English.

CYPRUS

Savoulla Alexandrou; *address:* 9, Klimentos str., 1480 Nicosia; tel (+357) 22400836; fax (+357) 22400932; e-mail salexandrou@dl.mlsi.gov.cy; *languages spoken:* English, Ellinika.

Georgios Spyrou; *address:* 9, Klimentos str., 1480 Nicosia; tel (+357) 22400817; fax (+357) 22400809; e-mail gspyrou@dl.mlsi.gov.cy; *languages spoken:* English, Ellinika, Deutsch.

CZECH REPUBLIC

Božena Lešková: *organization:* MPSV-Správa služeb zaměstnanosti; *address:* Úřad práce Hradec Králové, Na Okrouhlíku 1371, 502 67 Hradec Kralove; tel +420 49 5868 303; fax +420 49 5213 244; e-mail eures.hk@up.mpsv.cz; *languages spoken:* Français, English, Čeština.

Marcel Navrátil: *organization:* MPSV-Správa služeb zaměstnanosti; *address:* Úřad práce ve Zlíně, Čiperova 5182, Zlin 76042; tel +420 577 577 326; fax +420 577 432 318; e-mail eures.zl@up.mpsv.cz; *languages spoken:* English, Čeština.

Martina Němcová: *organization:* MPSV-Správa služeb zaměstnanosti; *address:* Úřad práce ve Vsetíně, Pod Žamboškou 1024, 755 01 Vsetin; tel +420 571 498 610; fax +420 571 417 200; e-mail eures.vs@up.mpsv.cz; *languages spoken:* English, Čeština.

Hana Pořízková: *organization:* MPSV-Správa služeb zaměstnanosti; *address:* Úřad práce Brno-venkov, Šujanovo nám. 3, 660 35 Brno; tel +420 543 160 329; fax +420 543 211 093; e-mail eures.bo@up.mpsv.cz; *languages spoken:* English, Čeština.

Petra Slezáková: *organization:* MPSV-Správa služeb zaměstnanosti; *address:* Úřad práce v Ostravě, Tř. 30. dubna 2c, 70160 Ostrava; tel +420 595 132 643; fax +420 596 111 023; e-mail eures.ot@up.mpsv.cz; *languages spoken:* English, Čeština, Deutsch.

Miroslava Vlčková: *organization:* MPSV-Správa služeb zaměstnanosti; *address:* Úřad práce v Karlových Varech, Svahová 24, 360 01 Karlovy Vary; tel +420 353 239 570; fax +420 353 225 544; e-mail eures.kv@up.mpsv.cz; *languages spoken:* Slovenčina, English, Čeština.

Radka Vojtíšková: *organization:* MPSV-Správa služeb zaměstnanosti; *address:* Úřad práce v Pardubicích, Boženy Vikové-Kunětické 2011, 530 02 Pardubice; tel +420 466 751 121; fax +420 466 310 039; e-mail eures.pa@up .mpsv.cz; *languages spoken:* English, Čeština.

DENMARK

Robert Andersen: *organization:* AF, Arbejdsformidlingen Public Employment Services; *address:* Nørregade 44, 7400 Herning; tel +45 96 27 34 00/71; fax +45 96 27 34 01; e-mail ra@eures.dk; *languages spoken:* English, Dansk, Deutsch.

Louise Bach-Nielsen: *organization:* AF, Arbejdsformidlingen Public Employment Services; *address:* Værkmestergade 3-5, 8000 Århus; tel +45 89 34 66 16/13; fax 45 89 34 66 17; e-mail lbn@eures.dk; *languages spoken:* English, Dansk, Deutsch.

Lise Lotte Brandt: *organization:* AF, Arbejdsformidlingen Public Employment Services; *address:* Arbejdsformidlingen, Ramsherred 12, 5700 Svendborg; tel +45 62 17 60 66; fax +45 62 17 60 70; e-mail R07llb@adk.dk; *languages spoken:* English, Dansk.

Hanne Christensen: *organization:* AF, Arbejdsformidlingen Public Employment Services; *address:* Kultorvet 17, 1175 København K; tel +45 33 55 17 16/20; fax +45 33 55 17 00; e-mail r01hch@ adk.dk.

Helga Gökcen: *organization:* Ledernes Hovedorganisation; *address:* Vermlandsgade 65, 2300 København S; tel +45 32 83 32 74; fax +45 32 83 32 84; e-mail hcg@ lederne.dk; *languages spoken:* English, Dansk, Deutsch.

Hanne Haarding: *organization:* AF, Arbejdsformidlingen Public Employment Services; *address:* Kultorvet 17, 1175 København K; tel +45 33 55 17 17/20; fax +45 33 55 17 00; e-mail R01hha@adk .dk; *languages spoken:* English, Dansk, Deutsch.

Søren Jensen: *organization:* AF, Arbejdsformidlingen Public Employment Services; *address:* Tornegade, 5 Postboks 119, 3700 Rønne; tel +45 56 94 39 00 / 03; fax +45 56 95 51 09; e-mail sj@eures.dk; *languages spoken:* English, Dansk, Deutsch.

Grete Kerrn-Jespersen: *organization:* AF, Arbejdsformidlingen Public Employment Services; *address:* Helsingørsgade 10, 3400 Hillerød; tel +45-4822-8500 +45-4822-8528; fax +45-4822-8510; e-mail ahil@post1.tele.dk; *languages spoken:* English, Dansk.

Line Kjeldsen: *organization:* AF, Arbejdsformidlingen Public Employment Services; *address:* Skiveegnens Arbejdsmarkedscenter, Posthustorvet 2 A, 7800 Skive; tel +45 9615 2200; fax +45 9615 2266; e-mail r13lk@adk.dk; *languages spoken:* Français, English, Dansk.

Anne-Marie Kjerulff: *organization:* AF, Arbejdsformidlingen Public Employment Services; *address:* Kultorvet 17, 1175 København K; tel +45 33 55 17 09/20; fax +45 33 55 17 00; e-mail r01amk@adk .dk; *languages spoken:* English, Dansk.

Kirsten Melbye: *organization:* AF, Arbejdsformidlingen Public Employment Services; *address:* Jernbanegade 12 Postboks 639, 4000 Roskilde; tel +45 46 38 11 00/16; fax +45 46 38 11 09; e-mail kme@ eures.dk; *languages spoken:* English, Dansk, Deutsch.

Kirsten Mohr: *organization:* AF, Arbejdsformidlingen Public Employment Services; *address:* Værkmestergade 3-5, 8000 Århus; tel +45 89 34 66 16/61 07; fax +45 89 34 66 17; e-mail km@eures.dk; *languages spoken:* English, Dansk.

Claus Bang Møller: *organization:* AF, Arbejdsformidlingen Public Employment Services; *address:* Værkmestergade 3-5, 8000 Århus; tel +45 89 34 66 16/11; fax +45 89 34 66 17; e-mail claus.bang@ eures.dk; *languages spoken:* English, Dansk, Deutsch.

Lydia Nansen: *organization:* LO, Landsorganisationen; *address:* Bjerggade 4 L, 6200 Aabenraa; tel +45 74 62 53 44; fax +45 74 62 73 10; e-mail lydia@net.dialog .dk; *languages spoken:* Dansk.

Karin Nielsen: *organization:* AF, Arbejdsformidlingen Public Employment Services; *address:* Exnersgade 33, 6701 Esbjerg; tel +45 79 12 33 44; fax +45 75 13 38 38; e-mail kn@eures.dk; *languages spoken:* Dansk.

Jonni Sørensen: *organization:* AF, Arbejdsformidlingen Public Employment Services; *address:* Arbejdsmarkedscenter Øresund, Jernbanevej 7, 3000 Helsingør; tel +45 4928 3481; fax +45 4074 3145; e-mail js@eures.dk; *languages spoken:* English, Dansk.

Kis Toft: *organization:* AF, Arbejdsformidlingen Public Employment Services; *address:* Vestensborg Allé 8, DK 4800 Nykøbing Falster; tel +45 54 88 05 42; fax +45 54 88 05 55; e-mail r05kto@adk .dk; *languages spoken:* English, Dansk.

Jorgen Uldall-Ekman: *organization:* AF, Arbejdsformidlingen Public Employment Services; *address:* Smedelundsgade 16, 4300 Holbæk; tel +45 59 48 13 27/70 33 07 07; fax +45 59 48 13 10; e-mail euresjue@post6.tele.dk; *languages spoken:* English, Dansk, Deutsch.

Betty Wurlitzer: *organization:* AF, Arbejdsformidlingen Public Employment Services; *address:* Fiskergade 1, 7100 Vejle; tel +45 70 10 26 26; fax +45 75 72 56 89; e-mail bw@eures.dk; *languages spoken:* English, Dansk, Deutsch.

ESTONIA

Gerli Mets: *organization:* TTA, Tööturuamet; *address:* Ringi 12, Parnu; tel +372 4420511; fax +372 4472183; e-mail gerli .mets@tta.ee; *languages spoken:* English, Eesti.

Kersti Papson: *organization:* TTA, Tööturuamet; *address:* Riia Street 35, Tartu; tel +372 7427154; fax +372 7427158; e-mail kersti.papson@tartu.tta .ee; *languages spoken:* English, Eesti.

Marta Traks: *organization:* TTA, Tööturuamet; *address:* Endla 4, Tallinn; tel +372 6263243; fax +372 6263241; e-mail marta.traks@tta.ee; *languages spoken:* English, Eesti.

FINLAND

Kati Ahonen: *organization:* MOL,Työministeriö/Arbetsministeriet (Ministry of Labour); *address:* Tampere employment office, Hämeenkatu 16, P.O. box 587, 33101 Tampere; tel +358 10 60 45430; fax +358 10 60 45400; e-mail kati.ahonen@mol.fi; *languages spoken:* Svenska, Suomi, Deutsch.

Taru Asikainen: *organization:* MOL,-Työministeriö/Arbetsministeriet (Ministry of Labour); *address:* Joensuu region employment office, P.O. Box 93, 80101 Joensuu; tel +358 10 60 40722 +358 50 396 2039; fax +358 10 60 40762; e-mail Taru.Asikainen@mol.fi; *languages spoken:* Suomi.

Mirja Huttula: *organization:* Confederation of Finnish Industry and Employers, Tornedalen (SV-SF); *address:* Länsipohjan Yrittäjät, Valtakatu 5, 94100 KEMI; tel +358 16 221 701; fax +358 16 221 713; e-mail mirja.huttula@lansipohjanyrittajat .fi; *languages spoken:* Svenska, English, Suomi.

Tuula Kinnunen: *organization:* MOL, Työministeriö/Arbetsministeriet (Ministry of Labour); *address:* Kluuvi employment office, P.O Box 293, 00101 Helsinki; tel +358 10 60 70863; fax +358 10 60 70805; e-mail Tupu.Kinnunen@mol .fi; *languages spoken:* English, Suomi, Deutsch.

Aila Mackel: *organization:* MOL,Työministeriö/Arbetsministeriet (Ministry of Labour); *address:* Kluuvi employment office, P.O. Box 293, 00101 Helsinki; tel +358 10 60 70862; fax +358 10 60 70805; e-mail aila.mackel@mol.fi; *languages spoken:* English, Suomi.

Tuula Matikainen: *organization:* MOL,Työministeriö/Arbetsministeriet (Ministry of Labour); *address:* Turku employment office, P.O. Box 235, 20101 Turku; tel +358 10 60 43137 +358 50 396 0880; fax +358 10 60 43185; e-mail Tuula .Matikainen@mol.fi; *languages spoken:* Svenska, Suomi, Deutsch.

Leena Nyman: *organization:* MOL,Työministeriö/Arbetsministeriet (Ministry of Labour); *address:* Pori employment office, P.O.Box 208, 28101 Pori; tel +358 10 60 43693 +358 50 396 2793; fax +358 10 60 43685; e-mail Leena.Nyman@mol.fi; *languages spoken:* Svenska, English, Suomi.

Pirkko Nyström: *organization:* MOL,-Työministeriö/Arbetsministeriet (Ministry of Labour); *address:* Employment Office of Mikkeli Porrassalmenkatu 29, P.O. Box 74, 50101 Mikkeli; tel +358 10 60 416 31; fax +358 10 60 416 03; e-mail Pirkko.Nystrom@mol.fi; *languages spoken:* Svenska, English, Suomi.

Oili Nätynki: *organization:* MOL,Työministeriö/Arbetsministeriet (Ministry of Labour); *address:* Oulu region employment office, Torikatu 34-40, 90100 Oulu; tel +358 10 60 44272; fax +358 10 60 44315; e-mail Oili.Natynki@mol.fi; *languages spoken:* English, Suomi, Deutsch.

Hannele Ojalehto: *organization:* MOL, Työministeriö/Arbetsministeriet (Ministry of Labour); *address:* Kajaani employment office, P.O. Box 70, 87101 Kajaani; tel +358 10 60 4405 +358 50 396 2207; fax +358 10 60 44009; e-mail hannele .ojalehto@mol.fi; *languages spoken:* English, Suomi.

Leena Pellikka: *organization:* MOL, Työministeriö/Arbetsministeriet (Ministry of Labour); *address:* Kuopio employment office, P.O. Box 62, 70101 Kuopio; tel +358 10 60 42092 +358 50 396 1925; fax +358 10 60 42120; e-mail Leena.Pellikka@mol.fi; *languages spoken:* English, Suomi, Deutsch.

Tomi Puranen: *organization:* MOL,Työministeriö/Arbetsministeriet (Ministry of Labour); *address:* Turku employment office, P.O. Box 235, 20101 Turku; tel +358 10 60 43090 +358 50 396 0899; fax +358 10 60 43104; e-mail tomi.puranen@ mol.fi; *languages spoken:* English, Suomi.

Kristina Rönnblom: *organization:* MOL,Työministeriö/Arbetsministeriet (Ministry of Labour); *address:* Vaasa employment office, P.O. Box 66, 65101 Vaasa; tel +358 10 60 46310; fax +358 10 60 46300; e-mail Kristina.Ronnblom@ mol.fi; *languages spoken:* Svenska, English, Suomi.

Aija Sievänen: *organization:* MOL, Työministeriö/Arbetsministeriet (Ministry of Labour); *address:* Päijät-Häme employment office, P.O. Box 84, 15141 Lahti; tel +358 10 60 45037 +358 50 396 3037; fax +358 10 60 45147; e-mail aija .sievanen@mol.fi; *languages spoken:* Français, English, Suomi.

Suzanne Sjölund: *organization:* MOL, Työministeriö/Arbetsministeriet (Ministry of Labour); *address:* Åland employment office, Ålandsvägen 31, P.O Box 1060, 22111 Mariehamn-Åland; tel +358 18 25 122; fax +358 18 22 622; e-mail suzanne.sjolund@mol.fi; *languages spoken:* Svenska, English, Suomi.

Hannele Soirila: *organization:* MOL, Työministeriö/Arbetsministeriet (Ministry of Labour); *address:* Hämeenlinna employment office, P.O. Box 105, 13101 Hämeenlinna; tel +358 10 60 45294 +358 50 396 3103; fax +358 10 60 45300; e-mail Hannele.Soirila@mol.fi; *languages spoken:* Svenska, English.

Tarja Somervalli: *organization:* MOL, Työministeriö/Arbetsministeriet (Ministry of Labour), Tornedalen (SV-SF); *address:* Suensaarenkatu 2, 95400 Tornio; tel +358 10 60 46897 +358 50 396 2682; fax +358 10 60 46906; e-mail Tarja .Somervalli@mol.fi; *languages spoken:* Svenska, English, Suomi, Deutsch.

Helena Sommarberg: *organization:* MOL,Työministeriö/Arbetsministeriet (Ministry of Labour); *address:* Kouvola employment office, P.O. Box 50, 45101 Kouvola; tel +358 10 60 40225; fax +358 10 60 40297; e-mail Helena.Sommarberg@ mol.fi; *languages spoken:* Svenska, English, Suomi.

Tuula Suihko: *organization:* MOL,Työministeriö/Arbetsministeriet (Ministry of Labour); *address:* Tampere employment office, P.O. Box 587, 33101 Tampere; tel +358 10 60 45563; fax +358 10 60 45400; e-mail tuula.suihko@mol.fi; *languages spoken:* English, Suomi.

Tina Sundqvist: *organization:* MOL, Työministeriö/Arbetsministeriet (Ministry of Labour); *address:* Oulu region employment office, Torikatu 34-40, 90100 Oulu; tel +358 10 60 44292; fax +358 10 60 44315; e-mail tina.sundqvist@ mol.fi; *languages spoken:* English, Suomi.

Irma Tervo: *organization:* MOL,Työministeriö/Arbetsministeriet (Ministry of Labour); *address:* Rovaniemi employment office, Valtakatu 21, 96200 Rovaniemi; tel +358 10 60 46597; fax +358 10 60 46641; e-mail irma.tervo@mol.fi; *languages spoken:* Svenska, English, Suomi.

John Watson: *organization:* MOL,Työministeriö/Arbetsministeriet (Ministry of Labour); *address:* Kluuvi employment office, P.O. BOX 293, 00101 Helsinki; tel +358-20 587 0861; fax +358-20 587 0805; e-mail john.watson@mol.fi; *languages spoken:* English, Suomi.

Terttu Wirzenius: *organization:* MOL, Työministeriö/Arbetsministeriet (Ministry of Labour); *address:* Jyväskylä employment office, 55 Vapaudenkatu, P.O Box 400, 40101 Jyväskylä; tel +358 10 60 41131; fax +358 10 60 41222; e-mail Terttu.Wirzenius@mol.fi; *languages spoken:* English, Suomi, Deutsch.

FRANCE

Georges Ahtiel: *organization:* PYR-EMED/PIRIME (FR-ES), CGT, Confédération Générale du Travail; *address:* 46, Place Rigaud, 66026 Perpignan; tel +33 4 68 34 33 71; fax +33 4 68 34 84 49; e-mail udcgt66@wanadoo.fr; *languages spoken:* Français, English.

Alex Alix: *organization:* ANPE, Agence Nationale Pour l'Emploi; *address:* EEI, 48 Boulevard de la Bastille, 75012 Paris; tel +33 1 53 02 25 50; fax +33 1 53 02 25 95; e-mail alex.alix@anpe.fr; *languages spoken:* Français, English.

Marie-Odile Antonini: *organization:* ANPE, Agence Nationale Pour l'Emploi; *address:* EEI Réunion, 6 bis route de Savanna, BP 74, 97862 Saint Paul Cedex, LA REUNION; tel +262 262 22 02 10; fax +262 262 22 88 04; e-mail mo.antonini@anpe.fr; *languages spoken:* Français, English, Português.

Marie-Catherine Bertrand: *organization:* CFDT, Confédération Française Démocratique du Travail, EURAZUR (FR-IT); *address:* 12 Boulevard Delfino, 06302 Nice; tel +33 4 90 88 18 68; fax +33 4 42 38 60 10; e-mail cfdt-urpaca@ wanadoo.fr; *languages spoken:* Français, English, Italiano.

Jean-Marc Bianchi: *organization:* EURAZUR (FR-IT), ANPE, Agence Nationale Pour l'Emploi; *address:* ANPE, Point Emploi International, 6 rue de Orestis, 06300 NICE; tel +33 4 92 00 26 00; fax +33 4 92 00 26 09; e-mail jmarc.bianchi@anpe.fr; *languages spoken:* Français.

Christian Blicq: *organization:* EURAZUR (FR-IT), CGT, Confédération Générale du Travail; *address:* 4 Place St François, 06300 Nice; tel +33 4 93 85 05 93; fax +33 4 93 80 19 59; e-mail blicq_ ch@hotmail.com-ud6@cgt.fr; *languages spoken:* Français.

Alain Buriot: *organization:* ANPE, Agence Nationale Pour l'Emploi; *address:* EEI, 8 Avenue Normandie-Sussex, 76202 Dieppe; tel +33 2 35 06 95 69; fax +33 2 35 06 02 46; e-mail alain.buriot@anpe.fr; *languages spoken:* Français, English.

Isabelle Calaciura: *organization:* UPV, Union Patronale du Var, EURAZUR (FR-IT); *address:* 20 rue de l'argentière, 83600 Fréjus; tel; e-mail isabelle.calaciura@ wanadoo.fr; *languages spoken:* Français, English, Italiano.

Didier Camensuli: *organization:* ANPE, Agence Nationale Pour l'Emploi; *address:* EEI, 48 Bd. de la Bastille, 75012 Paris; tel +33 1 53 02 25 50; fax +33 1 53 02 25 95; e-mail didier.camensuli@anpe .fr; *languages spoken:* Français.

Joël Charron: *organization:* ANPE, Agence Nationale Pour l'Emploi; *address:* 10, rue Camille St-Saëns, 86035 Poitiers;

tel +33 5 49 38 01 15; fax +33 5 49 38 01 15; e-mail joel.charron@anpe.fr; *languages spoken:* Français.

Elisabeth Cheneval: *organization:* OMI, Office des Migrations Internationales; *address:* EEI, 13 Rue Gilibert, 69002 Lyon; tel +33 478 42 34 40; fax +33 478 42 34 41; e-mail e.cheneval@ext .anpe.fr; *languages spoken:* Français, English, Português, Castellano.

Carline Chevallier: *organization:* ANPE, Agence Nationale Pour l'Emploi; *address:* EEI, Centre Commercial Ozanam Batelière, 97233 Schoelcher (Martinique); tel +33 596 61 40 61; fax +33 596 61 86 46; e-mail carline.chevallier@anpe .fr; *languages spoken:* Français, English, Castellano.

Rachel Collignon: *organization:* ANPE, Agence Nationale Pour l'Emploi, Saar-Lor-Lux-Rheinland/Pfalz (DE-FR-LUX), P.E.D. (BE-FR-LUX); *address:* 2 place saint Nicolas B.P. 428, 57008 Metz Cedex 1; tel +33 387759260; fax +33 387759270; e-mail rachel.collignon@anpe .fr; *languages spoken:* Français, English, Deutsch.

Elise Coubray: *organization:* ANPE, Agence Nationale Pour l'Emploi; *address:* 5 rue de Cercle-Roissytech, 95709 Roissy CDG; tel +33 1 48 62 12 40; fax +33 1 48 64 72 81; e-mail elise.coubray@anpe.fr; *languages spoken:* Français, English, Deutsch.

Henri Coupet: *organization:* TRANS-ALP (FR-IT), CFTC, Confédération Française des Travailleurs Chrétiens; *address:* 214 Avenue Félix Faure, 69441 Lyon Cédex 03; tel +33 4 72 91 29 50; fax +33 4 72 33 15 51; e-mail henri.coupet@ wanadoo.fr; *languages spoken:* Français.

Gilles De Beaulieu: *organization:* ANPE, Agence Nationale Pour l'Emploi; *address:* 48 bd de la Bastille, 75012 Paris; tel +33 153022571; fax +33 153022571; e-mail gbeaulieu.omi@anpe.fr; *languages spoken:* Français, English.

Patrice De Cambourg: *organization:* ANPE, Agence Nationale Pour l'Emploi; *address:* EEANPE, 22 rue de la Chalotais, BP 80605, 35106 Rennes Cedex 03; tel +33 2 99 78 81 50; fax +33 2 99 50 88 11; e-mail patrice.decambourg@anpe.fr; *languages spoken:* Français, English, Deutsch.

Jocelyne De Julis: *organization:* ANPE, Agence Nationale Pour l'Emploi; *address:* Maison de l'Ardenne, 18A Ave. Goerges Corneau, 08000 Charleville-Mézieres; tel +33 3 24 56 67 60; fax +33 3 24 33 44 10; e-mail jocelyne.dejulis@ anpe.fr; *languages spoken:* Français.

Graziano Del Treppo: *organization:* CFDT, Confédération Française Démocratique du Travail, TRANSALP (FR-IT); *address:* INAS, 77 rue A. Croizat, BP 357, 73003 Chambéry; tel +33 4 79 62 01 63; fax +33 4 79 62 91 47; e-mail inasfrance@wanadoo.fr; *languages spoken:* Français, Italiano.

Meriame Deniau: *organization:* ANPE, Agence Nationale Pour l'Emploi; *address:* EEI, 31C Ave. De Paris, 45000 Orléans; tel +33 2 38 77 86 92; fax +33 2 38 77 86 99; e-mail meriame.deniau@anpe.fr; *languages spoken:* Français.

Hugues Dequick: *organization:* ANPE, Agence Nationale Pour l'Emploi, Eures-Channel (BE-FR-UK); *address:* EEI, 12 rue de Jemmapes, 59009 Lille; tel +33 3 28 52 20 20; fax +33 3 28 52 20 21; e-mail hugues.dequick@anpe.fr; *languages spoken:* Français.

Michel Etur: *organization:* ANPE, Agence Nationale Pour l'Emploi; *address:* Espace Cadres de Rouen, 4 rue de Fontenelle, 76005 Rouen; tel +33 2 35 07 54 90; fax +33 2 35 07 45 95; e-mail michel.etur@ anpe.fr; *languages spoken:* Français, English, Deutsch.

Fanny Feller: *organization:* MEDEF, Mouvement des Entreprises de France, P.E.D. (BE-FR-LUX); *address:* Maison de l'Entreprise, Site technologique St. Jacques II, 8 rue A. Kestler, 54524 Laxou Cedex; tel +33 3 83956509/08; fax +33 3 83956511; e-mail ffeller@medemeurthe -moselle.fr; *languages spoken:* Français, English, Deutsch.

Line Fernandez: *organization:* PYREMED/PIRIME (FR-ES), ANPE, Agence Nationale Pour l'Emploi; *address:* EEI, Immeuble le Windsor, 6A Place Occitane, 31000 Toulouse; tel +33 5 61 12 59 59; fax +33 5 61 12 59 79; e-mail line.fernandez@ anpe.fr; *languages spoken:* Français.

Annie Florin: *organization:* ANPE, Agence Nationale Pour l'Emploi, Eures-Channel (BE-FR-UK); *address:* EEI, 12 rue de Jemmapes, 59009 Lille; tel +33 3 28 52 20 20; fax +33 3 28 52 20 21; e-mail annie.florin@anpe.fr; *languages spoken:* Français.

Bernadette Fouquet: *organization:* ANPE, Agence Nationale Pour l'Emploi; *address:* EEI, 48 Bd. de la Bastille, 75012 Paris Cédex; tel +33 1 53 02 25 65; fax +33 1 53 02 25 95; e-mail bfouquet.omi@anpe .fr; *languages spoken:* Français.

Catherine Galharret: *organization:* ANPE, Agence Nationale Pour l'Emploi; *address:* EEI, Tour 2000, 1 Ter Front du Medoc, 33076 Bordeaux; tel +33 5 56 90 85 10; fax +33 5 56 99 21 31; e-mail cath .galharret@anpe.fr; *languages spoken:* Français.

Antonio Garcia: *organization:* Eures-Channel (BE-FR-UK), CGT, Confédération Générale du Travail; *address:* 2 Rue Colliez, 59300 Valenciennes; tel +33 3 27 46 33 17; fax +33 3 27 33 21 77; e-mail uls.cgt.onnaing@wanadoo.fr.

Caroline Garnier: *organization:* OMI, Office des Migrations Internationales, Oberrhein (FR-DE-CH); *address:* EEI, 4 rue Gustave Doré, 67000 Strasbourg; tel +33 3 88 23 41 70; fax +33 3 88 23 41 69; e-mail caroline.garnier@anpe.fr; *languages spoken:* Français, Deutsch.

Colette Gaven: *organization:* ANPE, Agence Nationale Pour l'Emploi, PYREMED/PIRIME (FR-ES); *address:* EEI / ANPE Espace Cadres, ZAC La Fontaine, Quai Louis le Vau, 34184 Montpellier Cedex; tel +33 4 67 84 51 00; fax +33 4 67 04 50 70; e-mail colette .gaven@anpe.fr; *languages spoken:* Français, English.

Lucette Gouy: *organization:* TRANS-ALP (FR-IT), ANPE, Agence Nationale Pour l'Emploi; *address:* ANPE Espace Cadres, 89, Avenue General Mangin, 38100 Grenoble; tel +33 4 76 40 76 72; fax +33 4 76 33 81 61; e-mail lucette.gouy@ anpe.fr; *languages spoken:* English.

Marie-Jeanne Guillaume: *organization:* ANPE, Agence Nationale Pour l'Emploi; *address:* ANPE, Av. du Mont Thabor, BP 937, Centre commercial St-Joseph, 20090 Ajaccio; tel +33 4 95 23 74 00; fax +33 4 95 23 74 09; e-mail mjeanne .guillaume@anpe.fr; *languages spoken:* Français.

Dominique Guéret: *organization:* ANPE, Agence Nationale Pour l'Emploi; *address:* EEI/ANPE, Rue Fred Scamaroni BP 295, 14014 Caen; tel +33 2 31 15 27 27; fax +33 2 31 86 89 05; e-mail dominique.gueret@anpe.fr; *languages spoken:* Français.

Michel Hauman: *organization:* FO, Force Ouvrière, EuresChannel (BE-FR-UK); *address:* 111 Bd. Victor Hugo, 59000 Lille; tel +33 3 28 55 30 44; fax +33 3 20 88 22 13; e-mail fo.eureshnfk@free.fr; *languages spoken:* Français, Português.

Catherine Hertzler: *organization:* OMI, Office des Migrations Internationales; *address:* Espace Emploi International, 7/9 rue Jean Mermoz, 13272 Marseille; tel +33 4 91 32 83 61; fax +33 4 91 328368; e-mail c-hertzler.omi@anpe .fr; *languages spoken:* Français, English.

Claude Hubert: *organization:* P.E.D. (BE-FR-LUX), CGT, Confédération Générale du Travail; *address:* Foyer SNCF, Impasse Blanche Castille, 54440 Herserange; tel +33 3 82 24 30 48; fax +33 3 82 25 17 69; e-mail eurescgt.claudehubert@ wanadoo.fr; *languages spoken:* Français.

Brigitte Lapierre: *organization:* TRANSALP (FR-IT), ANPE, Agence Nationale Pour l'Emploi; *address:* ANPE Point relais cadres, ESC Savoie Techno-Lac, 73381 Le Bourget du Lac Cedex; tel +33 4 79 60 24 70; fax +33 4 79 60 46 88; e-mail brigitte.lapierre@ anpe.fr; *languages spoken:* Français.

Patrick Le Gall: *organization:* CGT, Confédération Générale du Travail, TRANSALP (FR-IT); *address:* 3 Rue

Ronde, 73003 Chambery; tel +33 4 79 62 27 26; fax +33 4 79 96 35 18; e-mail ud73@cgt.fr; *languages spoken:* Français.

Patrice Lopez: *organization:* ANPE, Agence Nationale Pour l'Emploi; *address:* EEI, 48 Bd. de la Bastille, 75012 Paris; tel +33 1 53 02 25 72; fax +33 1 53 02 25 97; e-mail patrice.lopez@anpe.fr; *languages spoken:* Français, English, Italiano, Castellano.

Gilbert Luciani: *organization:* FO, Force Ouvrière, EURAZUR (FR-IT); *address:* Le Solimar B1, 655 Ch. des Combes, 06600 Antibes; tel +33 6 60 92 22 45; fax +33 4 49 39 53 59; e-mail giluciani@airfrance.fr; *languages spoken:* Français.

Serge Marcozzi: *organization:* ANPE, Agence Nationale Pour l'Emploi; *address:* EEI, 48 Bd. de la Bastille, 75011 Paris; tel +33 1 53 02 25 62; fax +33 1 53 02 25 97; e-mail serge.marcozzi@anpe.fr; *languages spoken:* Français, English.

Agnès Martorello: *organization:* ANPE, Agence Nationale Pour l'Emploi, PYREMED/PIRIME (FR-ES); *address:* EEI, 6 Place Occitane, 31001 Toulouse Cédex 6; tel +33 561 12 59 73; fax +33 561 12 59 79; e-mail agnes.martorello@anpe.fr; *languages spoken:* Français, English, Castellano.

Fabien Maurizi: *organization:* P.E.D. (BE-FR-LUX), ANPE, Agence Nationale Pour l'Emploi; *address:* ANPE, 25 du du Maréchal Foch, BP 51, 54190 Villerupt; tel +33 3 82 25 98 40; fax +33 3 82 26 33 13; e-mail fabien.maurizi@anpe.fr; *languages spoken:* Français.

Lamine Mohammedi: *organization:* CGT, Confédération Générale du Travail, Saar-Lor-Lux-Rheinland/Pfalz (DE-FR-LUX); *address:* CGT Lorraine, 5, rue du Moulin, 57385 Teting sur Nied; tel +33 3 87 66 31 12; fax +33 3 87 76 38 33; e-mail secec@telephonie.lu; *languages spoken:* Français, English.

Dominique Moreau: *organization:* ANPE, Agence Nationale Pour l'Emploi; *address:* 78, rue Blaise Pascal, 37000 Tours; tel +33 2 47 60 66 60; fax +33 2 47 60 66 69; e-mail dominique.moreau@anpe.fr; *languages spoken:* Français, English, Italiano.

Claire Moreau: *organization:* TRANS-ALP (FR-IT), ANPE, Agence Nationale Pour l'Emploi; *address:* ANPE Seynod, Parc des regains Nord, 3 rue Blaise Pascal, BP 139, 74607 Seynod; tel +33 4 50 10 91 92; fax +33 4 50 52 11 14; e-mail cl.moreau@anpe.fr; *languages spoken:* Français, English.

Jean-Claude Moulin: *organization:* ANPE, Agence Nationale Pour l'Emploi; *address:* Espace Emploi International, 7/9 rue Jean Mermoz, 13272 Marseille; tel +33 4 91 32 83 60; fax +33 4 91 32

83 68; e-mail jclaude.moulin@anpe.fr; *languages spoken:* Français.

Marie-Françoise Moysan: *organization:* ANPE, Agence Nationale Pour l'Emploi; *address:* EEI, 4 rue de Printemps, 44703 Orvault; tel +33 2 40 59 52 78; fax +33 2 40 94 18 92; e-mail mfrancoise.moysan@anpe.fr; *languages spoken:* Français.

Chantal Pelosse: *organization:* TRANS-ALP (FR-IT), ANPE, Agence Nationale Pour l'Emploi; *address:* EEI, 13 rue Gilibert, 69002 Lyon; tel +33 4 78 42 34 40; fax +33 4 78 42 34 41; e-mail chantal.pelosse@anpe.fr; *languages spoken:* Français, Deutsch.

Patrick Picandet: *organization:* CFTC, Confédération Française des Travailleurs Chrétiens, Saar-Lor-Lux-Rheinland/Pfalz (DE-FR-LUX); *address:* 15, rue de l'Abbé Henrion, 54400 Longwy; tel +33 3 82 24 96 83; fax +33 3 82 24 95 33; e-mail batmat-tp-cftc-europe@wanadoo.fr; *languages spoken:* Français, English.

Daniel Piccinelli: *organization:* FO, Force Ouvrière, P.E.D. (BE-FR-LUX); *address:* 15, rue de l'Abbé Henrion, 54400 Longwy; tel +33 382251669; fax +33 382251669; e-mail piccinelli.eures.FO@wanadoo.fr; *languages spoken:* Français.

Chantal Pilandon: *organization:* ANPE, Agence Nationale Pour l'Emploi; *address:* 67 Bd. Lafayette, 63000 Clermont Ferrand; tel +33 4 73 98 04 37; fax +33 4 73 90 51 45; e-mail chantal.pilandon@anpe.fr; *languages spoken:* Français, English.

François Pétré: *organization:* ANPE, Agence Nationale Pour l'Emploi; *address:* Espace Emploi International, 19, rue Millevoye, 80043 Amiens Cédex; tel +33 3 22 33 82 10; fax +33 3 22 33 82 07; e-mail francois.petre@anpe.fr; *languages spoken:* Français, English, Deutsch.

Albert Riedinger: *organization:* Oberrhein (FR-DE-CH), CGT, Confédération Générale du Travail; *address:* 16 Bd. de la Victoire, 67000 Strasbourg; tel +33 3 88 25 39 54; fax +33 3 88 25 39 59; e-mail walch.riedinger@wanadoo.fr; *languages spoken:* Deutsch.

Brigitte Sala: *organization:* CFDT, Confédération Française Démocratique du Travail, PYREMED/PIRIME (FR-ES); *address:* BP 40, 66290 Cerbere; tel +33 4 68 62 19 37; fax +33 4 68 62 19 37; e-mail cfdt.lr.eures.pyremed@wanadoo.fr; *languages spoken:* Français, English, Castellano.

Jean Jacques Schneider: *organization:* Saar-Lor-Lux-Rheinland/Pfalz (DE-FR-LUX), ANPE, Agence Nationale Pour l'Emploi; *address:* 26 Avenue St. Rémy, 57600 Forbach; tel +33 3 87 84 72 84; fax +33 3 87 84 69 89; e-mail

jjacques.schneider@anpe.fr; *languages spoken:* Français, English, Deutsch.

Jean-Paul Schoeser: *organization:* ANPE, Agence Nationale Pour l'Emploi; *address:* 162, rue de Pont à Mousson BP 30111, 57950 Montigny les Metz; tel +33 3 87 74 63 39; fax +33 3 87 75 75 83; e-mail jpaul.schoeser@anpe.fr; *languages spoken:* Français, English, Deutsch.

Nadine Schwenck: *organization:* Saar-Lor-Lux-Rheinland/Pfalz (DE-FR-LUX), UPIM, Union Patronale Interprofessionnelle Moselle; *address:* 48 Place Mazelle, 57000 Metz; tel +33 3 87 74 33 65; fax +33 3 87 74 96 66; e-mail medef.moselle@wanadoo.fr; *languages spoken:* Français.

Brigitte Stein: *organization:* CFTC, Confédération Française des Travailleurs Chrétiens, Saar-Lor-Lux-Rheinland/Pfalz (DE-FR-LUX); *address:* I.S.L. 69, rue Mazelle, BP 90243, 57006 Metz Cedex 1; tel +33 387047208; fax +33 387047503; e-mail cftc-etam.hbl@wanadoo.fr; *languages spoken:* Français, English, Deutsch.

Marie-Thérèse Thiebaut: *organization:* CFDT, Confédération Française Démocratique du Travail, P.E.D. (BE-FR-LUX); *address:* 9 rue Colonel Merlin, 54400 Longwy; tel +33 3 82 25 17 06; fax +33 3 82 25 17 18; e-mail mtthiebaut@wanadoo.fr; *languages spoken:* Français.

Pascal Thil: *organization:* ANPE, Agence Nationale Pour l'Emploi, Saar-Lor-Lux-Rheinland/Pfalz (DE-FR-LUX); *address:* 12, rue du Général de Gaulle, 57500 Saint-Avold; tel +33 3 87939030; fax +33 3 87911487; e-mail pascal.thil@anpe.fr; *languages spoken:* Français, Deutsch.

Paul Wiesser: *organization:* MEDEF, Mouvement des Entreprises de France, Oberrhein (FR-DE-CH); *address:* 1 Quai Jacques Sturm, 67004 Strasbourg Cédex; tel +33 3 88 35 40 63; fax +33 3 88 35 12 68; e-mail paul.wiesser@medef67.com; *languages spoken:* Français, English, Deutsch.

Rosy Zabala: *organization:* ANPE, Agence Nationale Pour l'Emploi; *address:* Point Relais Cadres, 66 Allées Marines, 64100 Bayonne; tel +33 5 59 52 86 57; fax +33 5 59 52 86 64; e-mail rosy.zabalarrien@anpe.fr; *languages spoken:* Français, Castellano.

GERMANY

Eta Abasow: *organization:* Bundesverwaltungsamt, Diakonisches Werk; *address:* Morusstr. 18 A, 12053 Berlin; tel +49 30 68 24 77 20; fax +49 30 68 24 77 12; e-mail eta.abasow@debitel.net; *languages spoken:* English, Polski, Deutsch.

Sonja Adamsky: *organization:* BA, Bundesagentur für Arbeit, EURES-EUREGIO Gronau/Enschede(DE-NL); *address:* Enscheder Strasse 362, 48599 Gronau; tel +49 02562 702-013; e-mail s.adamsky@euregio.de; *languages spoken:* English, Deutsch.

Katia Amthor: *organization:* BA, Bundesagentur für Arbeit; *address:* Max-Reger-Str. 1, 99096 Erfurt; tel +49 03641 379307; fax +49 03641 379600; e-mail jena.europaservice@arbeitsagentur.de; *languages spoken:* English, Deutsch.

Albert Bachinger: *organization:* EURES-INTERALP (DE-AT), BA, Bundesagentur für Arbeit; *address:* Innstr. 30, 94032 Passau; tel +49 851 508 285; fax +49851508447; e-mail Albert.Bachinger@arbeitsagentur.de; *languages spoken:* Français, English, Deutsch.

Karl-Joachim Besteck: *organization:* BA, Bundesagentur für Arbeit; *address:* Grüner Weg 46, 34117 Kassel; tel +495617012066; fax +495617012958; e-mail Joachim.Besteck@arbeitsagentur.de; *languages spoken:* English, Deutsch.

Thomas Birlenberg: *organization:* BA, Bundesagentur für Arbeit; *address:* Berliner Platz 10, 45116 Essen; tel +49 2011 811 240; fax +492011811450; e-mail Thomas.Birlenberg@arbeitsagentur.de; *languages spoken:* Français, English, Deutsch.

Ulrich Blome: *organization:* EUREGIO Rhein-Waal (DE-NL), BA, Bundesagentur für Arbeit; *address:* Steegerstr. 49, 41334 Nettetal; tel +492153918721; fax +492153918740; e-mail Ulrich.Blome@ arbeitsagentur.de; *languages spoken:* Deutsch.

Heike Borgmann: *organization:* BA, Bundesagentur für Arbeit; *address:* Agentur für Arbeit Bremen, Doventorsteinweg 48-52, 28195 Bremen; tel +49 421 1781250; fax +49 421 1781564; e-mail Bremen.Europaservice@Arbeitsagentur.de; *languages spoken:* English, Deutsch.

Magrit Braun: *organization:* BA, Bundesagentur für Arbeit; *address:* Luxemburger Str. 121, 50939 Köln; tel +49 2219 429 1913; fax +49 221 9429 1994; e-mail Magrit.Braun@arbeitsagentur.de; *languages spoken:* English, Deutsch.

Hartmut Daub: *organization:* Bundesverwaltungsamt, Raphaels-Werk; *address:* Kantstr. 14, 66111 Saarbrucken; tel +49 681 309 060; fax +49 681 309 0618; e-mail hartmut.daub@raphaels-werk.de; *languages spoken:* Français, English, Deutsch.

Ludwin Debong: *organization:* EURES-INTERALP (DE-AT), DGB, Deutscher Gewerkschaftsbund; *address:* Kramer Str. 7-9, 87700 Memmingen; tel 49 8331 2421; fax 49 8331 4945; e-mail ludwin.debong@dgb.de; *languages spoken:* Deutsch.

Helmut Demeter: *organization:* Bodensee (DE-AT-CH), EURES-INTERALP (DE-AT), Arbeitsamt Kempten (Labour office Kempten); *address:* Rottachstr. 26, 87439 Kempten; tel +49 (0831) 2056116; fax +49 (0831) 2056160; e-mail helmut.demeter@arbeitsagentur.de; *languages spoken:* English, Deutsch.

Katrin Distler: *organization:* Oberrhein (FR-DE-CH), DGB, Deutscher Gewerkschaftsbund; *address:* Hauptstrasse 26, 77652 Offenburg; tel +49 7819320933; fax +49 7819320934; e-mail katrin.distler@dgb.de; *languages spoken:* Français, English, Deutsch.

Sabine Ebbert: *organization:* BA, Bundesagentur für Arbeit; *address:* Wohldkamp 1, 23669 Timmendorfer Strand; tel +49 4503 8701-32; fax +49 4503 8701-40; e-mail Sabine.Ebbert@ arbeitsagentur.de; *languages spoken:* English, Deutsch.

Günther Eichkorn: *organization:* Oberrhein (FR-DE-CH), BA, Bundesagentur für Arbeit; *address:* Brombacher Str. 2, 79539 Lörrach; tel +49 7621178519; fax +49 7621178505; e-mail Loerrach.Europaservice@arbeitsagentur.de; *languages spoken:* Français, English, Deutsch.

Jochen Fietz: *organization:* BA, Bundesagentur für Arbeit; *address:* Adol Westphal-Str. 2, 24143 Kiel; tel +49 4317091250; fax +49 4317091130; e-mail Jochen.Fietz@arbeitsagentur.de; *languages spoken:* English, Deutsch.

Ursula Fischenich: *organization:* Bundesverwaltungsamt, Raphaels-Werk; *address:* Norbertstr. 27, 50670 Köln; tel +49 221 283 620; fax +49 221 283 62 14; e-mail koeln@raphaels-werk.net; *languages spoken:* English, Polski, Deutsch.

Susanne Gast: *organization:* BA, Bundesagentur für Arbeit; *address:* Bergerstrasse 30, 16225 Eberswalde; tel +49 3334 37 3165; fax +49 3334 37 4903169; e-mail susanne.gast@arbeitsagentur.de; *languages spoken:* English, Deutsch.

Gerhard Gericks: *organization:* EURES-EUREGIO Gronau/Enschede (DE-NL), BA, Bundesagentur für Arbeit; *address:* Bahnhofstr. 39, 48599 Gronau; tel +49 2562 933438; fax +49 2562 933440; e-mail Gerhard.Gericks@ arbeitsagentur.de; *languages spoken:* Deutsch.

Eugenia Gilge: *organization:* Bundesverwaltungsamt, Deutsches Rotes Kreuz; *address:* Alleestr. 5, 14469 Potsdam; tel +49 331 286 4123; fax +49 331 286 4124; e-mail gilge@debitel.net; *languages spoken:* Français, English, Italiano, Deutsch.

Margot Gille: *organization:* Bundesverwaltungsamt, Diakonisches Werk; *address:* Gerokstr. 17, 70184 Stuttgart; tel +49 711 215 95 34; fax +49 711 215 91 30; e-mail wanderung@diakonie.de; *languages spoken:* Français, English, Deutsch.

Angela Griem: *organization:* BA, Bundesagentur für Arbeit; *address:* Norderstr. 103, 20097 Hamburg; tel +49 40 24 85 19 84; fax +49 40 24 85 19 87; e-mail Angela.Griem@arbeitsagentur.de; *languages spoken:* Français, English, Deutsch.

Birgit Guse: *organization:* BVA, Bundesverwaltungsamt; *address:* Lenaustrasse 41, 40470 Düsseldorf; tel +49 2116398248; fax +49 2116398299; e-mail bguse@dw-rheinland.de; *languages spoken:* English, Italiano, Deutsch.

Hans-Joachim Haesler: *organization:* BA, Bundesagentur für Arbeit; *address:* Georg-Schumann-Str. 150, 04159 Leipzig; tel +49 341 913 12251; fax +49 341 913 12259; e-mail Joachim.Haesler@ arbeitsagentur.de; *languages spoken:* English, Deutsch.

Artur Hansen: *organization:* EURES Maas-Rhin (BE-DE-NL); *address:* Theaterstr. 67, 52062 Aachen; tel +49 241 56 861 0; fax +49 241 56 861 61; e-mail hansen@regioaachen.de; *languages spoken:* Nederlands, Français, English, Deutsch.

Alexander Hennemann: *organization:* Bundesvereinigung der Deutschen Arbeitgeberverbände BDA (Federation of German Employers Organisations), EURES-INTERALP (DE-AT); *address:* Max-Joseph-Str. 5, 80333 München; tel 49 89 55 17 82 34; fax 49 89 55 17 82 33; e-mail alexander_hennemann.vbw@ hbw.de; *languages spoken:* Français, English, Deutsch.

Lore-Elisabeth Hentze: *organization:* Bundesverwaltungsamt, Deutsches Rotes Kreuz; *address:* RudolBreitschei-Str 6, 06110 Halle (Saale); tel +49 345 500 85 32; fax +49 345 202 31 41; e-mail lore-elisabeth.hentze@sachsen-anhalt.drk.de; *languages spoken:* English, Deutsch.

Peter Hiery: *organization:* Oberrhein (FR-DE-CH), BA, Bundesagentur für Arbeit, Saar-Lor-Lux-Rheinland/Pfalz (DE-FR-LUX); *address:* Karlstr. 18, 76437 Rastatt; tel +497275955013; fax +497275955033; e-mail peter.hiery@ arbeitsagentur.de; *languages spoken:* Deutsch.

Sabina Hoffmann: *organization:* Bundesverwaltungsamt, Raphaels-Werk; *address:* Vorderer Schöneworth 10, 30167 Hannover; tel +49511713237; fax +49511713239; e-mail sabina.hoffmann@ debitel.net; *languages spoken:* Français, English, Polski, Deutsch.

Sabine Hohloch: *organization:* Bodensee (DE-AT-CH), BA, Bundesagentur für Arbeit; *address:* Eugenstr. 41, 88045 Friedrichshafen; tel +49754130910; fax +49754130933; e-mail Sabine.Hohloch@ arbeitsagentur.de; *languages spoken:* Deutsch.

Harald Hopf: *organization:* BA, Bundesagentur für Arbeit; *address:* Max-Reger-Str. 1, 99096 Erfurt; tel +49 361 302 1794; fax +49 361 302 2951; e-mail erfurt .europaservice@arbeitsagentur.de; *languages spoken:* English, Deutsch.

Anfried Horbach: *organization:* BA, Bundesagentur für Arbeit, Saar-Lor-Lux-Rheinland/Pfalz (DE-FR-LUX); *address:* Hafenstr. 18, 66123 Saarbrücken; tel +496819441181; fax +496819445011; e-mail Anfried .Horbach@arbeitsagentur.de; *languages spoken:* Français, Deutsch.

Thomas Jacobi: *organization:* BA, Bundesagentur für Arbeit, Saar-Lor-Lux-Rheinland/Pfalz (DE-FR-LUX); *address:* Dasbachstr. 9, 54292 Trier; tel +49 651 2053003; fax +49 651 2053041; e-mail Thomas.Jacobi@arbeitsagentur.de; *languages spoken:* Français, English, Deutsch.

Ilona Jaudzims: *organization:* BA, Bundesagentur für Arbeit; *address:* Kopernikusstr. 1a, 18057 Rostock; tel +49 3818041240; fax +49 3818041504; e-mail Ilona.Jaudzims@arbeitsagentur .de; *languages spoken:* English, Deutsch.

Elisabeth Kieniewicz: *organization:* Bundesverwaltungsamt, Raphaels-Werk; *address:* Landwehrstr. 26, 80336 München; tel +49 89 23 11 49 60; fax +49 89 23 11 49 61; e-mail elisabeth .kieniewicz@debitel.net; *languages spoken:* English, Polski, Italiano, Deutsch.

Ingrid Kuchler: *organization:* EURES-INTERALP (DE-AT), BA, Bundesagentur für Arbeit; *address:* Wittelsbacherstr. 57, 83022 Rosenheim; tel +49 8031202297; fax +49 8031202551; e-mail Rosenheim.Europaservice@ arbeitsagentur.de; *languages spoken:* Deutsch.

Wilfried Kullmann: *organization:* EUREGIO Rhein-Waal (DE-NL), BA, Bundesagentur für Arbeit; *address:* Wiesenstr. 44, 47574 Goch; tel +49 2823933913; fax +49 2823933937; e-mail Wesel.Europaservice@ arbeitsagentur.de; *languages spoken:* Deutsch.

Helga Kunkel-Müller: *organization:* Bundesverwaltungsamt, Evangelische Auslandsberatung e.V./Diakonisches Werk; *address:* Rautenbergstr. 11, 20099 Hamburg; tel +4940244836; fax +4940244809; e-mail kunkel-mueller@ debitel.net; *languages spoken:* English, Castellano, Deutsch.

Ingrid Lang: *organization:* Saar-Lor-Lux-Rheinland/Pfalz (DE-FR-LUX), VSK, Vereinigung des Saarländischen Unternehmensverbände *address:* Harthweg 15, 66119 Saarbrucken; tel +49 681 954 34 36; fax +49 681 954 34 66; e-mail lang@mesaar.de; *languages spoken:* English, Deutsch.

Gerlinde Lang: *organization:* Bundesverwaltungsamt, Diakonisches Werk; *address:* Gerokstr. 17, 70184 Stuttgart; tel +49 711 215 95 41; fax +49 711 215 91 30; e-mail wanderung@diakonie.de; *languages spoken:* English, Castellano, Deutsch.

Eicke Lenz: *organization:* EURES-INTERALP (DE-AT), BA, Bundesagentur für Arbeit; *address:* Kapuzinerstr. 26, 80337 München; tel +49 89 51 54 30 46; fax +49 89 51 54 64 99; e-mail Eicke .Lenz@arbeitsagentur.de; *languages spoken:* Português, Deutsch.

Silke Löblein: *organization:* Agentur für Arbeit Stuttgart (Labour office Stuttgart); *address:* Jägerstr. 14-18, 70174 Stuttgart; tel +49 711 941 1429; fax +49 711 920 4288; e-mail Stuttgart-ZAV .Europaservice@arbeitsagentur.de; *languages spoken:* English, Deutsch.

Christina Löhrer Kareem: *organization:* EURES Maas-Rhin (BE-DE-NL); *address:* Theaterstr. 67, 52062 Aachen; tel +49 241 56 861 20; fax +49 241 56 861 61; e-mail loehrer@regioaachen.de; *languages spoken:* English, Deutsch.

Martina Lüdeke: *organization:* Bundesverwaltungsamt, Raphaels-Werk; *address:* Kaninenberghöhe 2, 45136 Essen; tel +49 201 810 28-7 39; fax +49 201 810 28-8 36; e-mail martina.luedeke@ debitel.net; *languages spoken:* English, Deutsch.

Grit Lüderitz-Gerth: *organization:* BA, Bundesagentur für Arbeit; *address:* Hohepfortestr. 37, 39085 Magdeburg; tel +49 3912 571206; fax +49 3912 57 1207; e-mail Grit.Lueditz-Gerth@ arbeitsagentur.de; *languages spoken:* English, Deutsch.

Anneliese Maier: *organization:* Oberrhein (FR-DE-CH), BA, Bundesagentur für Arbeit; *address:* Karlstr. 18, 76437 Rastatt; tel +497221211036; fax +497221211070; e-mail anneliese .maier@arbeitsgentur.de; *languages spoken:* Français, English, Deutsch.

Norbert Mattusch: *organization:* Oberrhein (FR-DE-CH), BA, Bundesagentur für Arbeit; *address:* Lehenerstr. 77, 79106 Freiburg; tel +497612710462; fax +497612710669; e-mail freiburg .europaservice@arbeitsagentur.de; *languages spoken:* Français, English, Deutsch.

Wilhelm Merkl: *organization:* EURES-INTERALP (DE-AT), BA, Bundesagentur für Arbeit; *address:* Karwendelstr. 1, 82362 WEilheim; tel +49 881 991 224; fax +49881991240; e-mail Wilhelm.Merkl@ arbeitsagentur.de; *languages spoken:* Deutsch.

Doris Mohn: *organization:* BA, Bundesagentur für Arbeit; *address:* Friedrichstr. 39, 10969 Berlin; tel +49 228 7131110; fax +49 228 7131284; e-mail Bonn-ZAV .Europaservice@arbeitsagentur.de; *languages spoken:* English, Deutsch.

Helmut Mors: *organization:* Saar-Lor-Lux-Rheinland/Pfalz (DE-FR-LUX), DGB, Deutscher Gewerkschaftsbund; *address:* Herzogen Buscher Str. 52, 54292 Trier; tel +49 651991 4747; fax +49 651 991 4799; e-mail helmut.mors@ dgb.de; *languages spoken:* English, Deutsch.

Sylvia Müller: *organization:* Oberrhein (FR-DE-CH), BA, Bundesagentur für Arbeit; *address:* Brauerstr. 10, 76135 Karlsruhe; tel +49 721 823 1075; fax +49 721 823 2405; e-mail karlsruhe .europaservice@arbeitsagentur.de; *languages spoken:* Français, English, Deutsch.

Sigrid Müller: *organization:* Arbeitsamt Nordrhein-Westfalen (Labour office Nordrhein-Westfalen); *address:* Thoméstr. 17, 53879 Euskirchen; tel +49 2251797178; fax +49 2251797240; e-mail sigrid.mueller2@arbeitsagentur .de; *languages spoken:* English, Deutsch.

Eberhard Niklas: *organization:* BA, Bundesagentur für Arbeit; *address:* Fischerfeldstr. 10-12, 60311 Frankfurt am Main; tel +49 69 21712115; fax +49 6921712139; e-mail Frankfurt-Main .Europaservice@arbeitsagentur.de; *languages spoken:* English, Deutsch.

Ingo Ostermann: *organization:* BA, Bundesagentur für Arbeit; *address:* Villemombler Str. 76, 53123 Bonn; tel +49 22 87 131145; fax +49 22 87 131460; e-mail Bonn-ZAV.Europaservice@ arbeitsagentur.de; *languages spoken:* Deutsch.

Iljana Patzig: *organization:* BA, Bundesagentur für Arbeit; *address:* Eisenbahnstr. 171, 15517 Fürstenwalde; tel +49 3361 569120; fax +49 3361 569299; e-mail Frankfurt-Oder .Europaservice@arbeitsagentur.de; *languages spoken:* English, Deutsch.

Andreas Pfeuffer: *organization:* Bodensee (DE-AT-CH), DGB, Deutscher Gewerkschaftsbund; *address:* Beyerlestr. 1, 78462 Konstanz; tel +49 7531 45719911; fax +49 7531 8926317; e-mail andreas.pfeuffer@dgb.de; *languages spoken:* Français, English, Deutsch.

Gudrun Pieper: *organization:* BA, Bundesagentur für Arbeit; *address:* Seminarstr. 7, 01796 Pirna; tel +49 371 5671424; fax +49 371 5671425; e-mail Gudrun.Pieper@arbeitsagentur.de; *languages spoken:* English, Deutsch.

Elisabeth Popken: *organization:* Ems-Dollart (NL-DE), DGB, Deutscher Gewerkschaftsbund; *address:* Jahnstraße 6, 26789 Leer; tel +49-(0)491-91 21 311; fax +49-(0)491-91 21 315; e-mail elisabeth.popken@dgb.de; *languages spoken:* Nederlands, Deutsch.

Sabine Raab: *organization:* SønderjyllanSchleswig (DE), DGB, Deutscher Gewerkschaftsbund; *address:* Rote Str. 1, 24937 Flensburg; tel +49 4611444010; fax +49 4611444019; e-mail sabine.raab@gmx.de; *languages spoken:* English, Deutsch.

Detlef Rau: *organization:* Ems-Dollart (NL-DE), BA, Bundesagentur für Arbeit; *address:* Jahnstraße 2, 26789 Leer; tel +49-(0)491-92 70 232; fax +49-(0)491-92 70 800; e-mail Detlef.Rau@arbeitsagentur.de; *languages spoken:* Nederlands, Deutsch.

Helmut Rechenauer: *organization:* EURES-INTERALP (DE-AT), BA, Bundesagentur für Arbeit; *address:* Münchener Str. 3, 83395 Freilassing; tel +49 8654476413; fax +49 8654476429; e-mail Helmut.Rechenauer@arbeitsagentur.de; *languages spoken:* English, Deutsch.

Ina Rosenow: *organization:* BA, Bundesagentur für Arbeit; *address:* Friedrichstr. 39, 10969 Berlin; tel +49-30-555599-6756; fax +49-30-555599-6700; e-mail Berlin-ZAV.europaservice@arbeitsagentur.de; *languages spoken:* English, Deutsch.

Bernd Ruppert: *organization:* BA, Bundesagentur für Arbeit; *address:* Richard Wagner Platz 5, 90443 Nürnberg; tel +49 911/242-2149; fax +49 911/242-2552; e-mail bernd.ruppert@arbeitsagentur.de; *languages spoken:* Français, English, Deutsch.

Renate Scheel: *organization:* Bundesverwaltungsamt, Deutsches Rotes Kreuz; *address:* Wismarsche Str. 298, 19055 Schwerin; tel +49 385 59 147 52; fax +49 385 59 147 19; e-mail renate.scheel@debitel.net; *languages spoken:* Français, English, Deutsch.

Simona Schiemenz: *organization:* BA, Bundesagentur für Arbeit; *address:* Straße der Einheit 2, 02943 Weißwasser; tel +49 3576 270108; fax +49 3576 270103; e-mail simona.schiemenz@arbeitsagentur.de; *languages spoken:* English, Deutsch.

Alphons Schoolkate: *organization:* EURES-EUREGIO Gronau/Enschede(DE-NL), DGB, Deutscher Gewerkschaftsbund; *address:* Enschederstr. 362, 48572 Gronau; tel +49 2562 7020; fax +49 2562 70259; e-mail f.schoolkate@euregio.de; *languages spoken:* Nederlands, Deutsch.

Gisela Schrodin: *organization:* BA, Bundesagentur für Arbeit; *address:* Stromeyersdorfstr. 1, 78467 Konstanz; tel +49 7531 585 310; fax +49 7531 585169; e-mail Gisela.Schrodin@arbeitsagentur.de; *languages spoken:* English, Deutsch.

Claudia Seiler: *organization:* BA, Bundesagentur für Arbeit; *address:* Brühlstr. 4, 30169 Hannover; tel +495119191921; fax +495119191960; e-mail Claudia.Seiler@arbeitsagentur.de; *languages spoken:* English, Deutsch.

Claudia Silvestroni: *organization:* BA, Bundesagentur für Arbeit; *address:* Villemombler Str. 76, 53123 Bonn; tel +49 2287 131235; fax +49 2287 131460; e-mail Claudia.Silvestroni@arbeitsagentur.de; *languages spoken:* Français, English, Deutsch.

Sabine Sklenarz: *organization:* BA, Bundesagentur für Arbeit; *address:* Karl-Harr-Str. 5, 44263 Dortmund; tel +49 231 8421149; fax +49 231 8422843; e-mail Dortmund.Europaservice@arbeitsagentur.de; *languages spoken:* English, Deutsch.

Jan Sladek: *organization:* Bundesverwaltungsamt, Raphaels-Werk; *address:* Vilbeler Str. 36, 60313 Frankfurt am Main; tel +49 69 91 30 65 52; fax +49 69 91 30 65 55; e-mail jan.sladek@debitel.net; *languages spoken:* Français, English, Polski, Castellano, Deutsch.

Peter Sokoll: *organization:* EUREGIO Rhein-Waal (DE-NL), DGB, Deutscher Gewerkschaftsbund; *address:* Hombergerstr. 73, 47441 Moers; tel +49 2841 144495; fax +49 2841 144496; e-mail sokoll@malz.de; *languages spoken:* Deutsch.

Volker Steinmetz: *organization:* BA, Bundesagentur für Arbeit, Saar-Lor-Lux-Rheinland/Pfalz (DE-FR-LUX); *address:* Tholeyer Str. 2, 66822 Lebach; tel +49 6881 9350 35; fax +49 6881 9350 50; e-mail volker.steinmetz2@arbeitsagentur.de; *languages spoken:* Français, English, Deutsch.

Walter Stephan: *organization:* Saar-Lor-Lux-Rheinland/Pfalz (DE-FR-LUX), DGB, Deutscher Gewerkschaftsbund; *address:* Brennender-Berg-Str. 10, 66280 Sulzbach; tel +49 68 974445; fax +49 68 14000120; e-mail walter.stephan@dgb.be; *languages spoken:* Deutsch.

Elmar Symanowski: *organization:* BA, Bundesagentur für Arbeit; *address:* Villemombler Str. 76, 53123 Bonn; tel +49 228 7131010; fax +49 228 7131460; e-mail Bonn-ZAV.Europaservice@arbeitsagentur.de; *languages spoken:* English, Deutsch.

Pietro Turri: *organization:* Oberrhein (FR-DE-CH), BA, Bundesagentur für Arbeit; *address:* Weingartenstr. 3, 77654 Offenburg; tel +49 781 9393-147; fax +49 781 9393-148; e-mail offenburg.europaservice@arbeitsagentur.de; *languages spoken:* Français, English, Deutsch.

EvElisabeth Weber: *organization:* BA, Bundesagentur für Arbeit; *address:* Villemombler Str. 76, 53123 Bonn; tel +49 228 71 31 491; fax +49 228 71 31 111; e-mail EvElisabeth.Weber@arbeitsagentur.de; *languages spoken:* English, Deutsch.

Thorsten Weber: *organization:* Ems-Dollart (NL-DE), BA, Bundesagentur für Arbeit, EURES-EUREGIO Gronau/Enschede(DE-NL); *address:* Stadtring 9-15, 48527 Nordhorn; tel +49 5921 870 422; fax +49 5921 870 683; e-mail thorsten.weber@arbeitsagentur.de; *languages spoken:* Nederlands, Deutsch.

Ute Weisenburger: *organization:* SønderjyllanSchleswig (DE), DGB, Deutscher Gewerkschaftsbund; *address:* Waldstr. 2, 24939 Flensburg; tel +49 461 17427; fax +49 461 17428; e-mail Ute.Weisenburger@eures-kompas.org; *languages spoken:* Deutsch.

Franziska Wenzl: *organization:* EURES-INTERALP (DE-AT), BA, Bundesagentur für Arbeit; *address:* Max-Breiherr-Str. 3, 84347 Pfarrkirchen; tel +49 856 1982103; fax +49 856 1982131; e-mail Franziska.Wenzl@arbeitsagentur.de; *languages spoken:* English, Deutsch.

Heinz Jürgen Werner: *organization:* EURES Maas-Rhin (BE-DE-NL), BA, Bundesagentur für Arbeit; *address:* Roermonder Str. 51, 52072 Aachen; tel +49 241 897 1269; fax +49 241 897 1598; e-mail Heinz-Juergen.Werner@arbeitsagentur.de; *languages spoken:* Nederlands, English, Deutsch.

Eugen Wette-Köhler: *organization:* EURES-INTERALP (DE-AT), BFZ, Berufliche Fortbildungszentren der Bayerischen Wirtschaft; *address:* Maximilianstrasse 18 a, 83278 Traunstein; tel +49 (0861) 98 65 115; fax +49 (0861) 98 65 130; e-mail wette-koehler.eugen@ts.bfz.de; *languages spoken:* English, Deutsch.

Uta Witte: *organization:* Bundesverwaltungsamt, Evangelische Auslandsberatung e.V./Diakonisches Werk; *address:* Rautenbergstr. 11, 20099 Hamburg; tel +49 40 24 48 36; fax +49 40 24 48 09; e-mail kunkel-mueller@debitel.net; *languages spoken:* English, Deutsch.

Romy Zeiler: *organization:* BA, Bundesagentur für Arbeit; *address:* Budapesterstr. 30, 01069 Dresden; tel +49 351 4751639; fax +49 351 4751951; e-mail Romy.Zeiler@arbeitsagentur.de; *languages spoken:* Deutsch.

Tom Zielasko: *organization:* BA, Bundesagentur für Arbeit, SønderjyllanSchleswig (DE); *address:* Waldstr. 2, 24939 Flensburg; tel +49 46 1819 507; fax

+49461819430; e-mail Tom.Zielasko@ arbeitsagentur.de; *languages spoken:* English, Dansk, Deutsch.

Daniela Zink: *organization:* Oberrhein (FR-DE-CH), BA, Bundesagentur für Arbeit; *address:* Karlstr. 18, 76437 Rastatt; tel +49 7222 930 171; fax +49 7222 930 158; e-mail rastatt.europaservice@ arbeitsagentur.de; *languages spoken:* Français, English, Deutsch.

GREECE

Olga Akrivou: *organization:* OAED; *address:* Dodekanisou 10 A, 54626 Thessaloniki; tel +30 231 0 55 44 17; fax +30 231 0 55 43 38; e-mail gr01ea2@hellasnet .gr; *languages spoken:* English, Ellinika.

Panagiotis Alexandridis: *organization:* OAED; *address:* Mantzagriotaki St. 57, 17672 Kalithea; tel +30 210 956 88 87; fax +30 210 95 68 887; e-mail gr01ea6@hellasnet.gr; *languages spoken:* English, Ellinika, Deutsch.

Maria Antoniou: *organization:* OAED; *address:* Dimitriados 3, PO Box 115, 38333 Volos; tel +30 24 21 03 05 33; fax +30 24 210 30 533; e-mail gr01ea12@ hellasnet.gr; *languages spoken:* English, Ellinika.

Vivian Chatzdaki: *organization:* OAED; *address:* Diktinis 7, 73100 Chania; tel +30 28 210 88 920; fax +30 28 210 93 173; e-mail gr01ea17@hellasnet.gr; *languages spoken:* English, Ellinika.

Maria Danilopoulou: *organization:* OAED; *address:* Eth. Antistasis 8, 17456 Alimos; tel +30 210 99 89132; fax +30 210 99 89139; e-mail gr01ea1@ hellasnet.gr; *languages spoken:* Français, English, Ellinika.

Zografia Dogoy: *organization:* OAED; *address:* Kimoloy 5, 84100 Syros; tel +30 228 1088 000-609; fax +30 228 10 83757, 81018; e-mail gr01ea5@hellasnet .gr; *languages spoken:* English, Ellinika.

Kalliopi Froudaki: *organization:* OAED; *address:* Mauromichali 21 & Methonis 19, 18545 Piraeus; tel +30 210 41 72 453; fax +30 210 41 24 476; e-mail gr01ea19@hellasnet.gr; *languages spoken:* English, Ellinika.

Anastasia Geraki: *organization:* OAED; *address:* Ermogenous 10, 41447 Larissa; tel +30 241 0 255 228; fax +30 241 0 537 388; e-mail gr01ea13@hellasnet.gr; *languages spoken:* English, Ellinika.

Georgios Kaskanis: *organization:* OAED; *address:* 3oKm Ethnikis Odou Athinon-Ioanninon, 45500 Ioannina; tel +30 2651 0 20 675; fax +30 2651 0 39 677; e-mail gr01ea15@hellasnet.gr; *languages spoken:* English, Ellinika, Deutsch.

Vithleem KatsavounMichelaraki: *organization:* OAED; *address:* Arxiepiskopou Makariou & Faitaki 2, PO Box 1854, 71110 Heraklion; tel +30 281 0 34 15 67; fax +30 281 0 88 558; e-mail gr01ea16@hellasnet.gr; *languages spoken:* Français, English, Ellinika.

Archontoula Kinami: *organization:* OAED; *address:* Mauromichali 21 & Methonis 19, 18545 Athens; tel +30 210 52 45 158; fax +30 210 524 83 69; e-mail gr01ea4@hellasnet.gr; *languages spoken:* Français, English, Ellinika.

Spyridon Klironomos: *organization:* OAED; *address:* K. Zavitsianou 17, 49100 Corfu; tel +30 2661020270; fax +30 2661039879; e-mail gr01ea9@ hellasnet.gr; *languages spoken:* English, Italiano, Ellinika.

Maria KokkotKafourou: *organization:* OAED; *address:* Vass. Alexandriou 69, 12131 Peristeri; tel +30 210 57 81 444; fax +30 210 57 39 740; e-mail gr01ea21@ hellasnet.gr; *languages spoken:* English, Ellinika.

Georgia Mantazi: *organization:* OAED; *address:* Perigiali 2, P.O Box 1326, 65110 Kavala; tel +30 251 0 22 44 10; fax +30 251 0 83 67 73; e-mail gr01ea18@hellasnet .gr; *languages spoken:* English, Ellinika.

Irini Marinou: *organization:* OAED; *address:* Agiou Andreou 45 Parodos Gerakari 4, 26222 Patra; tel +30 261 0 31 3002; fax +30 261 0 32 89 98; e-mail gr01ea11@hellasnet.gr; *languages spoken:* English, Ellinika.

Stavroula Nikolopoulou: *organization:* OAED; *address:* Farron 170, 24110 Kalamata; tel +30 224 10 32 65; fax +30 224 10 79 17; e-mail gr01ea22@hellasnet .gr; *languages spoken:* Français, English, Ellinika.

Amalia Papadopoulou: *organization:* OAED; *address:* Th. Sofouli 93, 85100 Rodhes; tel +30 241 0 23 265; fax +30 241 0 289 10; e-mail gr01ea7@hellasnet.gr; *languages spoken:* Français, English, Ellinika.

Kyriaki Tektonidou: *organization:* OAED; *address:* Dodekanisou 10 A, 54012/19466 Thessaloniki; tel +30 231 0 545 929; fax +30 231 0 554 415; e-mail gr01ea10@hellasnet.gr.

Sofia Tselepidou: *organization:* OAED; *address:* Tadalou 32 & Afroditis 21, 54629 Thessaloniki; tel +30 231 0 31 79 98; fax +30 231 0 48 67 93; e-mail gr01ea8@hellasnet.gr; *languages spoken:* English, Ellinika, Deutsch.

Ntina Zografou: *organization:* OAED; *address:* Lachanokipon 2, 67100 Xanthi; tel +30 2541 0 70 550; fax +30 2541 0 20 175; e-mail gr01ea14@hellasnet.gr; *languages spoken:* Français, Ellinika.

HUNGARY

Mónika Czéh: *organization:* Állami Foglalkoztatási Szolgálat (State Employment Service); *address:* Városház tér 3., 9021 Győr; tel +36 96529910; fax +36 96319399; e-mail cmonika@lab.hu; *languages spoken:* Magyar, English, Deutsch.

Zoltán Friss: *organization:* Állami Foglalkoztatási Szolgálat (State Employment Service); *address:* FÖ u 37-39, 7400 Kaposvar; tel +36 82 505 523; fax +36 82 505 550; e-mail frissz@lab.hu; *languages spoken:* Magyar, English, Deutsch.

Ágnes Gárgyán: *organization:* Állami Foglalkoztatási Szolgálat (State Employment Service); *address:* Bocskai U. 10-12, 6721 Szeged; tel +36 62555580; fax +36 62555581; e-mail gargyana@lab.hu; *languages spoken:* Français, Magyar, English.

András Kalmár: *organization:* Állami Foglalkoztatási Szolgálat (State Employment Service); *address:* József A. u. 34, 8200 Veszprém; tel +36 88 328 504; fax +36 88 328 504; e-mail kalmarandras@ lab.hu; *languages spoken:* Magyar, English.

Andrea Kocsis: *organization:* Állami Foglalkoztatási Szolgálat (State Employment Service); *address:* Kalvaria ter 7, 1089 Budapest; tel +36 1 303 0810 126; fax +36 1 303 0824; e-mail kocsisa@lab .hu; *languages spoken:* Magyar, English.

Ildikó Pap: *organization:* Állami Foglalkoztatási Szolgálat (State Employment Service); *address:* Kálvária tér 7, 1089 Budapest; tel +36 1 303 0822 130; fax +36 1 303 0824; e-mail pappi@lab.hu; *languages spoken:* Magyar, Deutsch.

Géza Surányi: *organization:* Állami Foglalkoztatási Szolgálat (State Employment Service); *address:* Kossuth Lajos U. 9, 3300 Eger; tel +36 36 410 032; fax +36 36 413 372; e-mail suranyig@lab.hu; *languages spoken:* Magyar, English, Deutsch.

Nóra VargLengyelné: *organization:* Állami Foglalkoztatási Szolgálat (State Employment Service); *address:* Kalvaria ter 7, 1089 Budapest; tel +36 13039300/ 1555; fax +36 12103902; e-mail lengyeln@ lab.hu; *languages spoken:* Magyar, English.

Krisztina Árok: *organization:* Állami Foglalkoztatási Szolgálat (State Employment Service); *address:* 54, Piac Utca, Debrecen 4025; tel +36 52 507 442; fax +36 52 507 229; e-mail tomakrisztina@lab .hu; *languages spoken:* Magyar, English.

ICELAND

Dröfn Haraldsdottir: *organization:* Vinnumalastofnun; *address:* Vinnumidlun hofudborgarsvaedisins, Engjateigur

11, 105 Reykjavik; tel +354 554 7600; fax +354 554 7601; e-mail drofn .haraldsdottir@svm.is; *languages spoken:* Svenska, English.

Jon S Karlsson: *organization:* Vinnumalastofnun; *address:* Vinnumidlun hofudborgarsvaedisins, Engjateigur 11, 105 Reykjavik; tel +354 554 7600; fax +354 554 7600; e-mail jon.s.karlsson@ svm.is; *languages spoken:* Svenska, English, Dansk, Deutsch.

IRELAND

Frances Dunne: *organization:* FAS, Training and Employment Authority; *address:* Industrial Estate, Waterford; tel +353-513-01557; fax +353-51-301517; e-mail frances.dunne@se.fas.ie; *languages spoken:* English.

Carmel Gargan: *organization:* FAS, Training and Employment Authority; *address:* Brookfirls Enterprise Centre, Tallagh, Dublin 24; tel +353 1 462 2950; fax +353 1 462 2950; e-mail carmel .gargan@fas.ie; *languages spoken:* English.

Patrick Gibney: *organization:* FAS, Training and Employment Authority; *address:* Island House, Cathedral Square, Galway; tel +353 91 53 44 00; fax +353 91 56 27 18; e-mail pat.gibney@ wr.fas.ie; *languages spoken:* English.

Tom Hannigan: *organization:* Northern Ireland/Ireland (IE-UK), FAS, Training and Employment Authority; *address:* Ballraine Ind. Est., Donegal-Letterkenny; tel +353 74 22200; fax +353 74 24840; e-mail tom.hannigan@nw.fas.ie; *languages spoken:* English.

Tria McCarthy: *organization:* FAS, Training and Employment Authority; *address:* 27-33 Upper Baggot Street, Dublin 4; tel +353 1 607 0500; fax +353 1 607 0610; e-mail tria.mccarthy@fas.ie; *languages spoken:* Français, English.

Anne McCormack: *organization:* FAS, Training and Employment Authority; *address:* 42 Parnell Street, Co Clare-Ennis; tel +353 65 682 9213; fax +353 65 682 8502; e-mail anne.mccormack@ mw.fas.ie; *languages spoken:* English.

Tom McEnroe: *organization:* FAS, Training and Employment Authority; *address:* Garrycastle, Co. Westmeath, Athlone; tel +353 903 26802; fax +353 903 25399; e-mail tom.mcenroe@ml.fas .ie; *languages spoken:* English.

Geoff McEnroe: *organization:* Northern Ireland/Ireland (IE-UK), IBEC-Irish Business and Employers Confederation; *address:* Confederation House, 84-86 Lower Baggot Street, Dublin 2; tel +3531 6051540; fax +3531 6381540; e-mail Geoff.McEnroe@ibec.ie; *languages spoken:* English.

Sheila McIntyre: *organization:* FAS, Training and Employment Authority; *address:* 34 Main Street, Dublin, Swords; tel +353-16-124800; fax +353-16-798240; e-mail sheila.mcintyre@fas.ie; *languages spoken:* English.

Mary Penny: *organization:* FAS, Training and Employment Authority; *address:* Perry Court-Upper Mallow Street, Limerick; tel +353 61 487 944; fax +353 61 412 977; e-mail mary.penny@mw.fas.ie; *languages spoken:* English.

Fionnuala Smyth: *organization:* FAS, Training and Employment Authority; *address:* 27-33 Upper Baggot Street, Dublin 4; tel +353 1 607 09 03; fax +353 1 607 06 11; e-mail fionnuala.smyth@fas .ie; *languages spoken:* English.

Bernadette Smyth: *organization:* Northern Ireland/Ireland (IE-UK), FAS, Training and Employment Authority; *address:* FÁS Employment Services Office, Adelphi Court, Long Walk, Co Louth, Dundalk; tel +353 42 939 3400; fax +353 42 939 3401; e-mail bernadette .smyth@ne.fas.ie; *languages spoken:* English.

George Wilson: *organization:* FAS, Training and Employment Authority; *address:* 17 Lower Castle Street, Kerry, Tralee; tel +353 66 22155; fax +353 66 23065; e-mail george.wilson@sw.fas.ie; *languages spoken:* English.

Dónal Ó Maoldhomhnaigh: *organization:* FAS, Training and Employment Authority; *address:* 14 North Quay, Drogheda; tel +353 41 983 7646; fax +353 41 983 8120; e-mail donal .omaoldhomhaigh@ne.fas.ie.

ITALY

Cosimo Andriulo: *organization:* MLPS, Ministero del lavoro e delle politiche sociali; *address:* Via Salento 3, 74100 Taranto; tel +39 099 735 0745; fax +39 099 735 12779; e-mail cosimo.andriulo@ tiscalinet.it; *languages spoken:* English, Italiano.

Ingrid Avanzolini: *organization:* Unione Artigiani e Piccole e Medie Imprese, Confartigianato (Union of industrialists and small and medium enterprises), EURALP (IT-AT); *address:* Via del Pozzo 8, 33100 Udine; tel +39 0432 26309, +39 0432 516743; fax +39 0432 515756; e-mail iavanzolini@uaf.it; *languages spoken:* English, Italiano, Deutsch.

Gianfranco Badami: *organization:* MLPS, Ministero del lavoro e delle politiche sociali; *address:* Via Imperatore Federico 70, 90149 Palermo; tel +39 091 696 85 16; fax +39 091 696 84 64; e-mail badami@tiscalinet.it; *languages spoken:* English, Italiano.

Angela Bandiera: *organization:* MLPS, Ministero del lavoro e delle politiche sociali; *address:* Servizio EURES, Via Caserma Borrace, 67, 89100 Reggio Calabria; tel +39 0965 890344; fax +39 0965 890344; e-mail angela.bandiera@ tiscalinet.it; *languages spoken:* Français, English, Italiano.

Adele Bianco: *organization:* MLPS, Ministero del lavoro e delle politiche sociali; *address:* Via S. Carocci, 8, 02100 Rieti; tel +39 33 32 67 60 40; e-mail adelebianco@tiscali.it; *languages spoken:* English, Italiano, Deutsch.

Raffaele Caiazzo: *organization:* MLPS, Ministero del lavoro e delle politiche sociali; *address:* Centro Commerciale Gran Affi, 37100 Canove (Verona); tel +39 045 6261056; fax +39 045 6261094; e-mail linoc@tiscalinet.it; *languages spoken:* English, Italiano.

Pier Giorgio Cattini: *organization:* MLPS, Ministero del lavoro e delle politiche sociali; *address:* Piazza Libertà 16, 50129 Firenze; tel +39 055 43 820 77; fax +39 055 43 820 80; e-mail g.cattini@mail .regione.toscana.it; *languages spoken:* Français, English, Italiano.

Katia Ceré: *organization:* MLPS, Ministero del lavoro e delle politiche sociali; *address:* Via del Borgo di San Pietro 90/ G, 40126 Bologna; tel +39 051 659 8940; fax +39 051 659 8593; e-mail katia.cere@ nts.provincia.bologna.it; *languages spoken:* English, Italiano.

Lorenzino Cestari: *organization:* UIL, Unione Italiana del Lavoro, TRANSALP (FR-IT); *address:* Via Bologna 11, 10152 Torino; tel +39 112417190; fax +39 112417191; e-mail urpiemonte@uil.it; *languages spoken:* Français, English, Italiano.

Giorgio Costabiei: *organization:* MLPS, Ministero del lavoro e delle politiche sociali, TransTirolia (IT-AT-CH); *address:* Arbeitsamt Bezirk Pustertal, Gross Gerau Promenade 6, 39031 Bruneck (Bolzano); tel +39 0474539971; fax +39 0474539979; e-mail giorgio .costabiei@provinz.bz.it; *languages spoken:* English, Italiano, Deutsch.

Federica D'Angela: *organization:* EURALP (IT-AT), MLPS, Ministero del lavoro e delle politiche sociali; *address:* Viale Duodo 3, 33100 Udine; tel +39 0432 205980-73; fax +39 0432 231011; e-mail ari.udine@regione.fvg.it; *languages spoken:* English, Italiano, Castellano.

Guglielmina De Simone: *organization:* MLPS, Ministero del lavoro e delle politiche sociali; *address:* Centro Direzionale Isola C5, 80132 Napoli; tel +39 081 5973111; fax +39 081 5535083; e-mail guglielmina.desimone@poste.it; *languages spoken:* English, Italiano.

Angela Maria Deidda: *organization:* MLPS, Ministero del lavoro e delle politiche sociali; *address:* Via Vittorio Bottego, 07100 Sassari; tel +39 079 25 93 105; fax +39 079 25 93 105; e-mail servizio.eures.sardegna@virgilio.it; *languages spoken:* English, Italiano.

Rosalinda Di Pasca: *organization:* MLPS, Ministero del lavoro e delle politiche sociali; *address:* Via Viggiani 9, 85100 Potenza; tel +39 0971 35407; fax +39 0971 34533; e-mail rosalinda .dipasca@regione.basilicata.it; *languages spoken:* Français, Italiano.

Francesca Fadda: *organization:* MLPS, Ministero del lavoro e delle politiche sociali; *address:* Via Passolanciano 75, 65100 Pescara; tel +39 085 20552243; fax +39 085 20552277; e-mail fadda .eures@virgilio.it; *languages spoken:* Français, Italiano.

Giuseppe Fama: *organization:* CGIL, Confederazione Generale Italiana del Lavoro; *address:* Via Scottoconvento 48, 18039 Ventimiglia (Imperia); tel +39 184 35 11 70; fax +39 184 35 52 03; e-mail cgil.ventimiglia@tin.it.

Mauro Filippi: *organization:* TRANSALP (FR-IT), CISL, Confederazione Italiana Sindacati Lavoratori; *address:* Via Zimmerman 7, 11100 Aosta; tel +39 0165 279611; fax +39 0165 36 33 55; e-mail eurescisl@tiscalinet.it; *languages spoken:* Français, English, Italiano.

Luisa Anna Fiore: *organization:* MLPS, Ministero del lavoro e delle politiche sociali; *address:* Via Corigliano 1, 70100 Bari; tel +39 080 540 75 09; fax +39 080 582 20 29; e-mail eures.bari@regione .puglia.it; *languages spoken:* Français, Italiano.

Marinella Gallo: *organization:* MLPS, Ministero del lavoro e delle politiche sociali; *address:* Via Cardano 10, 20124 Milano; tel +39 02 667432 45; fax +39 02 66984652; e-mail marinella.gallo@ agenzialavorolombardia.it; *languages spoken:* English, Italiano.

Giovanni Gardi: *organization:* CISL, Confederazione Italiana Sindacati Lavoratori, TRANSALP (FR-IT); *address:* Via S. Anselmo 11, 10133 Torino; tel +39 011 660 4750; fax +39 011 660 3575; e-mail operatori.usr.piemonte@ cisl.it; *languages spoken:* Français, English, Italiano.

Luciano Guillone: *organization:* UIL, Unione Italiana del Lavoro, EURAZUR (FR-IT); *address:* Piazza Cassini 16, 18038 San Remo (Imperia); tel +39 018 457 00 89; fax +39 018 457 00 59; e-mail uilsanremo@rosenet.it; *languages spoken:* Français, Italiano.

Paola Lanari: *organization:* MLPS, Ministero del lavoro e delle politiche sociali; *address:* Via M. Angeloni 61, 06124 Perugia; tel +39 075 504 54 36; fax +39 075 505 59 54; e-mail paolalanari@tiscalinet .it; *languages spoken:* Français, Italiano.

Alessandra Lorenzi: *organization:* MLPS, Ministero del lavoro e delle politiche sociali, EURAZUR (FR-IT); *address:* Via Nino Lamboglia 13, 18039 Ventimiglia (Imperia); tel +39 0184 254822; fax +39 0184 254823; e-mail a.lorenzi@tiscalinet.it; *languages spoken:* Français, Italiano.

Patrizia Lucchi: *organization:* MLPS, Ministero del lavoro e delle politiche sociali; *address:* Via Ca' Venier 8, 30172 Venezia; tel +39 041 2501310; fax +39 041 2501312; e-mail patrizia.lucchi@ provincia.venezia.it; *languages spoken:* Français, English, Italiano.

Salvatore Maio: *organization:* CISL, Confederazione Italiana Sindacati Lavoratori, EURAZUR (FR-IT); *address:* Piazza Cesare Battisti 8, 18039 Ventimiglia (Imperia); tel +39 0184 231512; fax +39 0184 237217; e-mail euremaio@ libero.it; *languages spoken:* Français, Italiano, Castellano.

Graziella Massi: *organization:* MLPS, Ministero del lavoro e delle politiche sociali; *address:* Piazzale Morandi 41, 60019 Senigallia (Ancona); tel +39 0717939626; fax +39 0717939626; e-mail cif.senigallia@provincia.ancona.it.

Anna Melinelli: *organization:* MLPS, Ministero del lavoro e delle politiche sociali; *address:* Via Fornovo 8, 00192 Roma; tel +39 06 36 754 720; fax +39 06 320 8824; e-mail amelinelli@welfare.gov .it; *languages spoken:* English, Italiano.

Patrizia Mercuri: *organization:* MLPS, Ministero del lavoro e delle politiche sociali; *address:* Via Bertola 28, 10122 Torino; tel +39 011 861 4927; fax +39 011 861 3974; e-mail mercuri@provincia .torino.it; *languages spoken:* Italiano.

Giuseppe Minichino: *organization:* MLPS, Ministero del lavoro e delle politiche sociali; *address:* Piazza Mazzini 1, 85025 Melfi (Potenza); tel +39 0972238185; fax +39 0972238185; e-mail gminichino@virgilio.it; *languages spoken:* English, Italiano.

Nadja Karin Moriggl: *organization:* MLPS, Ministero del lavoro e delle politiche sociali, TransTirolia (IT-AT-CH); *address:* Arbeitsamt Bezirk Vinschgau, Schlandersburgstrasse 6, 39028 Schlanders; tel +39 0473 736 194; fax +39 0473 736 199; e-mail nadja.moriggl@provinz .bz.it; *languages spoken:* English, Italiano, Deutsch.

Maria Giovanna Nastasi: *organization:* MLPS, Ministero del lavoro e delle politiche sociali; *address:* Via Cesarea 14, 16121 Genova; tel +39 010 5497509; fax +39 010 5497570; e-mail nastasi.g@ provincia.genova.it; *languages spoken:* Français, English, Italiano, Deutsch.

Giovanni Pensabene: *organization:* MLPS, Ministero del lavoro e delle politiche sociali; *address:* Via Caserma Borrace 67, 89100 Reggio Calabria; tel +39 0965 33 27 51; fax +39 0965 89 03 44

Ugo Petroni: *organization:* MLPS, Ministero del lavoro e delle politiche sociali; *address:* Servizio Lavoro Regione Toscana, Piazza della Libertà 16, 50129 Firenze; tel +39 055 4382356; fax +39 055 4382055; e-mail u.petroni@mail.regione .toscana.it; *languages spoken:* Français, Italiano.

Laura Pitteri: *organization:* MLPS, Ministero del lavoro e delle politiche sociali; *address:* Via Maccani 76, 38100 Trento; tel +39 0461 494551-2; fax +39 0461 827016; e-mail eures@agenzialavoro.tn .it; *languages spoken:* English, Italiano.

Gian Carlo Politano: *organization:* TRANSALP (FR-IT), MLPS, Ministero del lavoro e delle politiche sociali; *address:* Viale Partigiani 18, 39100 Aosta; tel +39 0165 237811; fax +39 0165 31426; e-mail giancarlo.politano@libero.it; *languages spoken:* Français, English, Italiano.

Michele Renzulli: *organization:* MLPS, Ministero del lavoro e delle politiche sociali; *address:* Piazza Molise 65, 86100 Campobasso; tel +39 0874 69121; fax +39 0874 698476; e-mail renzullieures@ hotmail.com; *languages spoken:* English, Italiano.

Lucilla Ricci: *organization:* MLPS, Ministero del lavoro e delle politiche sociali; *address:* Via Rosa Raimondi Garibaldi 7, 00147 Roma; tel +39 06 51607085; fax +39 06 51607077; e-mail lucillaricci@ hotmail.com; *languages spoken:* Français, English, Italiano.

Laura Robustini: *organization:* MLPS, Ministero del lavoro e delle politiche sociali; *address:* Via Soderini, 24, 20146 Milano; tel +39 02 77 40 64 16; fax +39 02 7740 50 94; e-mail laura.robustini@ tiscalinet.it; *languages spoken:* Français, Italiano.

Giovanni Rotta: *organization:* EURALP (IT-AT), CISL, Confederazione Italiana Sindacati Lavoratori; *address:* Via Roma 138, 33013 Gemona del Friuli (Udine); tel +39 0348 444 8002; fax +39 0432 971206; e-mail giorotta@libero.it; *languages spoken:* Français, English, Italiano.

Alba Lina Sacchi: *organization:* MLPS, Ministero del lavoro e delle politiche sociali; *address:* 321 Via Tiburtina, 03100 Frosinone; tel +39 0775 826 230/ 231; e-mail alba.lina@libero.it; *languages spoken:* Français, English, Italiano, Deutsch.

Giorgio Santarello: *organization:* MLPS, Ministero del lavoro e delle politiche sociali; *address:* Via Torino 105, 30175 Mestre (Venezia); tel +39 041 2795314-5326; fax +39 041 2795948;

e-mail giorgio.santarello@regione.veneto.it; *languages spoken:* English, Italiano, Deutsch.

Francesco Siano: *organization:* MLPS, Ministero del lavoro e delle politiche sociali; *address:* Via Trento 98, 84131 Salerno; tel +39 089 253777; fax +39 089 254277; e-mail eures.salerno@libero.it; *languages spoken:* Français, Italiano.

Ilaria Sicilia: *organization:* MLPS, Ministero del lavoro e delle politiche sociali, EURALP (IT-AT); *address:* Via Alfieri, 34, 34170 Gorizia; tel +39 0481 533745; fax +39 0481 536229; e-mail ilaria.sicilia@tiscalinet.it; *languages spoken:* English, Italiano, Deutsch.

Fiorella Sisto: *organization:* TRANSALP (FR-IT), MLPS, Ministero del lavoro e delle politiche sociali; *address:* Via Magenta 12, 10100 Torino; tel +39 011 4322 423; fax +39 011 4324 229; e-mail fiorella.sisto@regione.piemonte.it; *languages spoken:* Français, English, Italiano.

Rosalba Sorice: *organization:* MLPS, Ministero del lavoro e delle politiche sociali; *address:* Rue XXV Luglio, 82100 Benevento; tel +39 08 243 26 149; fax +39 08 242 24 676; e-mail rosalbasorice@libero.it; *languages spoken:* Français, Italiano.

Lamine Sow: *organization:* CGIL, Confederazione Generale Italiana del Lavoro; *address:* Via Pedrotti 5, 10152 Torino; tel +39 011 244 2229; fax +39 011 244 2210; e-mail Lsow@mail.pmt.cgil.it; *languages spoken:* Français, English, Italiano.

Carmen Tanasi: *organization:* MLPS, Ministero del lavoro e delle politiche sociali, EURAZUR (FR-IT); *address:* Via Fieschi 15, 16122 Genova; tel +39 010 548 4868; fax +39 010 590205; e-mail euroconsigliere@regione.liguria.it; *languages spoken:* Français, Italiano.

Giuseppe Trotta: *organization:* MLPS, Ministero del lavoro e delle politiche sociali; *address:* Via Tiziano 44, 60125 Ancona; tel +39 071 8063795; fax +39 071 8063018; e-mail giuseppe.trotta@regione.marche.it; *languages spoken:* Italiano.

Monica Ukmar: *organization:* EURALP (IT-AT), CGIL, Confederazione Generale Italiana del Lavoro; *address:* Via Vidali 1, 34129 Trieste; tel +39 040 375 41 11; fax +39 040 768 844; e-mail ukmarm@hotmail.com; *languages spoken:* English, Italiano.

Vincenza Ursino: *organization:* MLPS, Ministero del lavoro e delle politiche sociali; *address:* Via del Borgo di S. Pietro 90/G, 40126 Bologna; tel +39 051 6598640; fax +39 051 6598593; e-mail eures@nts.provincia.bologna.it; *languages spoken* Français, English, Italiano.

Vincenza Zaccardo: *organization:* MLPS, Ministero del lavoro e delle politiche sociali, EURAZUR (FR-IT); *address:* Piazza Roma 2, 18100 Imperia; tel +39 0183 704471; fax +39 0183 704431; e-mail vincenza.zaccardo@tiscalinet.it; *languages spoken:* Français, Italiano.

LATVIA

Rudīte Martinsone: *organization:* Nodarbinātības valsts aģentūra; *address:* Bērzaines iela 15, 410 Cēsis; tel +371 4120690; fax +371 4122026; e-mail RuditeM@nva.lv; *languages spoken:* English, Latviski.

Žanna Ribakova: *organization:* Nodarbinātības valsts aģentūra; *address:* Akadēmijas laukums 1, 1050 Rīga; tel +371 7210189; fax +371 7222993; e-mail ZannaR@nva.lv; *languages spoken:* English, Latviski.

Līga Ruļuka: *organization:* Nodarbinātības valsts aģentūra; *address:* Varšavas iela 18, 5404 Daugavpils; tel +371 5435460; fax +371 5435266; e-mail LigaR@nva.lv; *languages spoken:* English, Latviski.

Andris Segliņš: *organization:* Nodarbinātības valsts aģentūra; *address:* Tirgus iela 15, 3401 Liepāja; tel +371 3429422; fax +371 3422404; e-mail AndrisS@nva.lv; *languages spoken:* English, Latviski.

LITHUANIA

Karolina Gorodnicenko: *organization:* Lietuvos darbo birža; *address:* Tilzes str. 152, 76351 Siauliai; tel +370 69929230; fax +370 41525053; e-mail karolina@siauliai.ldb.lt; *languages spoken:* Lietuviškai, English.

Vaida Kamanduliene: *organization:* Lietuvos darbo birža; *address:* Vilnius 21, 62112 Alytus; tel +370 315 55554; fax +370 315 55554; e-mail vaika.kamanduliene@ldb.lt; *languages spoken:* Lietuviškai, English.

Asta Milvydiene: *organization:* Lietuvos darbo birža; *address:* Naikupes str. 27A, 93202 Klaipeda; tel +370 46 404313; e-mail astam@klaipeda.ldb.lt; *languages spoken:* Lietuviškai, English.

Birute Ruksenaite: *organization:* Lietuvos darbo birža; *address:* J. Kubiliaus str.2/S.Zukausko str. 22, 08234 Vilnius; tel +370 52636005; fax +370 52636005; e-mail biruter@vilnius.ldb.lt; *languages spoken:* Lietuviškai, English.

Živile Stankeviciute: *organization:* Lietuvos darbo birža; *address:* E. Ozeskienes str. 37, 44003 Kaunas; tel +370 37409869; fax +370 37225605; e-mail ziviles@kaunas.ldb.lt; *languages spoken:* Lietuviškai, English, Deutsch.

LUXEMBOURG

Colette Chollot: *organization:* P.E.D. (BE-FR-LUX), ADEM, Administration de l'Emploi; *address:* 10 rue Bender, 1229 Luxembourg; tel +352 478 53 25; fax +352 40 61 41; e-mail colette.chollot@adem.etat.lu; *languages spoken:* Français.

Romain Clees: *organization:* Saar-Lor-Lux-Rheinland/Pfalz (DE-FR-LUX), CGT, Confédération Générale du Travail Luxembourgeoise; *address:* 31 Ave. Grande Duchesse Charlotte, 3441 Dudelange; tel +352 26 51 14 15; fax +352 51 50 05 29; e-mail euresrc@pt.lu; *languages spoken:* Français, Deutsch.

Mario Della Schiava: *organization:* ADEM, Administration de l'Emploi, Saar-Lor-Lux-Rheinland/Pfalz (DE-FR-LUX), P.E.D. (BE-FR-LUX); *address:* Administration de l'Emploi (ADEM), 57 rue du Château, 9515 Wiltz; tel +352 958384-23; fax +352 958611; e-mail mario.dellschiava@adem.etat.lu; *languages spoken:* Deutsch.

Vincent Jacquet: *organization:* P.E.D. (BE-FR-LUX), OGBL, Onofhängege Gewerkschafts-Bond Lëtzebuerg LCGB, Lëtzebuerger Chrëschtleche Gewerkschaftsbond; *address:* 11 rue du Commerce, 1012 Luxembourg; tel +352 499 424238; fax +352 499 42449; e-mail vjacquet@lcgb.lu; *languages spoken:* Français.

Georges Kirsch: *organization:* P.E.D. (BE-FR-LUX), ADEM, Administration de l'Emploi; *address:* 10 rue Bender, 1229 Luxembourg; tel +352 478 53 33; fax +352 40 61 41; e-mail Georges.Kirsch@adem.etat.lu; *languages spoken:* Français.

Emmanuelle Mathieu: *organization:* Saar-Lor-Lux-Rheinland/Pfalz (DE-FR-LUX), FEDIL; *address:* 7 rue Alcide Gasperi, BP 1304, 1013 Luxembourg; tel +352 43 55 66-1; fax +352 43 23 28; e-mail emmanuelle.mathieu@fedil.lu; *languages spoken:* Français, English, Deutsch.

Yvon Moinet: *organization:* P.E.D. (BE-FR-LUX), OGBL, Onofhängege Gewerkschafts-Bond Lëtzebuerg LCGB, Lëtzebuerger Chrëschtleche Gewerkschaftsbond; *address:* 72 Avenue Dr. Gaasch, 4818 Rodange; tel +352 50 73 86; fax +352 50 44 81; e-mail euresrr@pt.lu; *languages spoken:* Français, English, Deutsch.

Marcel Schneider: *organization:* ADEM, Administration de l'Emploi, P.E.D. (BE-FR-LUX); *address:* ADEM, Siège central, 10 rue Bender, 1229 Luxembourg; tel + 352 478 5334; fax + 352 40 61 41; e-mail marcel.schneider@adem.etat.lu; *languages spoken:* Français, English, Deutsch.

Jean-Claude Thilmany: *organization:* P.E.D. (BE-FR-LUX), ADEM, Administration de l'Emploi; *address:* 21 rue Pasteur, 4003 Esch-Alzette; tel +352 54 10 54 218; fax +352 54 91 96; e-mail jean-claude .thilmany@adem.etat.lu; *languages spoken:* Français, English, Deutsch.

Edmond Zinnen: *organization:* Saar-Lor-Lux-Rheinland/Pfalz (DE-FR-LUX), P.E.D. (BE-FR-LUX), OGBL, Onofhängege Gewerkschafts-Bond Lëtzebuerg LCGB, Lëtzebuerger Chrëschtleche Gewerkschaftsbond; *address:* 11, Rue du Commerce, BP 1208, 1012 Luxembourg; tel +352 49 942 42 22; fax 352 49 942 44 29; e-mail ezinnen@lcgb.lu; *languages spoken:* Français, Deutsch.

MALTA

Olivia Bilocca: *organization:* Korporazzjoni ghax- Xoghol u t- Tahrig; *address:* Hal Far BBG 06; tel +356 22201228; fax +356 22201812; e-mail oliviab@etc.org .mt; *languages spoken:* Lietuviškai, Malti, English.

Claire Chetcuti: *organization:* Korporazzjoni ghax- Xoghol u t- Tahrig; *address:* Hal Far BBG 06; tel +356 22201 206; fax +356 22201 812; e-mail clairec@etc.org .mt; *languages spoken:* Malti, English.

NETHERLANDS

Gabby Barreveld: *organization:* CWI, Centrum voor Werk en Inkomen; *address:* Stadsring 75, Postbus 3000, 3800 DQ Amersfoort; tel +31 33 75 17 664; fax +31 33 46 41 585; e-mail gabby .barreveld@cwinet.nl; *languages spoken:* Nederlands, Français, English.

Willie Berentsen: *organization:* FME CWM, Federatie voor Metaal en Electrotechnische industrie, Contactgroep voor Werkgevers in de Metaalnijverheid, Scheldemond (BE-NL); *address:* 40 Boerhaavelaan, Postbus, 2700 AD Zoetermeer; tel +31 79 353 11 00; fax +31 79 353 13 65; e-mail wbe@fme.nl; *languages spoken:* Nederlands.

Frans Buter: *organization:* CWI, Centrum voor Werk en Inkomen, Scheldemond (BE-NL); *address:* Rosegracht 2, Postbus 8, 4530 AA Terneuzen; tel +31 (0)115 75 10 75; fax +31 (0)115 75 10 71; e-mail Frans.Buter@cwinet.nl; *languages spoken:* Nederlands, English, Deutsch.

Rob Damhuis: *organization:* EURES-EUREGIO Gronau/Enschede(DE-NL), CWI, Centrum voor Werk en Inkomen; *address:* Hoedemakerplein 2, Postbus 3433, 7500 DK Enschede; tel +31 74 255 7219; fax +31 74 255 7320; e-mail rob .damhuis@cwinet.nl; *languages spoken:* Nederlands, English, Deutsch.

Hans van den Eijnden: *organization:* EUREGIO Rhein-Waal (DE-NL), CWI, Centrum voor Werk en Inkomen; *address:* Mariënburg 30, Postbus 9120, 6500 HZ Nijmegen; tel +31 24-3293700; fax +31 24-3293750; e-mail hans.vanden .eijnden@cwinet.nl; *languages spoken:* Nederlands, English.

Hannie Eilers: *organization:* EURES-EUREGIO Gronau/Enschede(DE-NL), CWI, Centrum voor Werk en Inkomen; *address:* Terborgseweg 20, 7005 BA Doetinchem; tel +31 (0)314 787179 +31 (0)6-21 598 389; fax +31 (0)314 787171; e-mail hannie.eilers@cwinet.nl; *languages spoken:* Nederlands, English, Deutsch.

Dirk van Gestel: *organization:* MHP, Vakcentrale voor Middengroepen en Hoger Personeel, Scheldemond (BE-NL); *address:* Noord Brabantlaan 66, 5605 Eindhoven; tel +31 (0)345- 851 055; fax +31 (0)345-851 755; e-mail gst-d@unie.nl; *languages spoken:* Nederlands, English.

Barbara Gorter-Zahuta: *organization:* CWI, Centrum voor Werk en Inkomen; *address:* Oosterkerkstraat 1, Postbus 12, 2300 AA Leiden; tel +31 71 750 38 81; fax +31 71 750 38 31; e-mail Barbara.Zahuta@ cwinet.nl; *languages spoken:* Nederlands, English, Deutsch.

Els Hollander: *organization:* Ems-Dollart (NL-DE), CWI, Centrum voor Werk en Inkomen; *address:* Gedempte Zuiderdiep 31, Postbus 30008, 9700 RK Groningen; tel +31 58-2977728; fax +31 58-2977798; e-mail els.hollander@cwinet.nl; *languages spoken:* Nederlands, English, Deutsch.

John Kerkhoff: *organization:* EURES Maas-Rhin (BE-DE-NL), CWI, Centrum voor Werk en Inkomen; *address:* Het Bat 12A, Postbus 1952, 6201 BZ Maastricht; tel +31 43 750 6148; fax +31 43 329 1331; e-mail John.Kerkhoff@cwinet.nl; *languages spoken:* Nederlands, Français, English, Deutsch.

Hinrich Kuper: *organization:* Ems-Dollart (NL-DE); *address:* Postbus 43, 9393 ZG Nieuweschans; tel +31 597521818; fax +31 597522511; e-mail edr@edr.org; *languages spoken:* Nederlands, English, Deutsch.

Els Lugtenberg: *organization:* CWI, Centrum voor Werk en Inkomen; *address:* Prinsessesingel 30, Postbus 1927, 5900 BX Venlo; tel +31 77-3551512; fax +31 77- 3551536; e-mail els .lugtenberg@cwinet.nl; *languages spoken:* Nederlands, Français, English, Deutsch.

Arend Mud: *organization:* Ems-Dollart (NL-DE), CWI, Centrum voor Werk en Inkomen; *address:* Tesselschadestraat 35, Postbus 2200, 8901 Leeuwarden; tel +31 58 297 77 43; fax +31 58 212 03 57; e-mail Arend.Mud@cwinet.nl; *languages spoken:* Nederlands, English, Deutsch.

Tjerk Mulder: *organization:* Ems-Dollart (NL-DE), CWI, Centrum voor Werk en Inkomen; *address:* Kloekhorststraat 29, Postbus 20, 9400 AA Assen; tel +31 (0)592 788680 +31 (0)592-788681; fax +31 (0)6-20619746; e-mail tjerk.mulder@ cwinet.nl; *languages spoken:* Nederlands, English, Deutsch.

Vera Peek: *organization:* CWI, Centrum voor Werk en Inkomen; *address:* Claudius Prinsenlaan 14, Postbus 3296, 4800 DG Breda; tel +31 767 51 14 60; fax +31 76 751 1437; e-mail Vera.Peek@ cwinet.nl; *languages spoken:* Nederlands, English, Deutsch.

Truus Roelofs: *organization:* EUREGIO Rhein-Waal (DE-NL), CWI, Centrum voor Werk en Inkomen; *address:* Telefoonweg 123, Postbus 9050, 6710 HZ Ede; tel +31 318 787280; fax +31 318 787281; e-mail truus.roelofs@cwinet.nl; *languages spoken:* Nederlands, English, Deutsch.

Cindy Sijmonsma: *organization:* CWI, Centrum voor Werk en Inkomen; *address:* Nijverheidsstraat 3, Postbus 131, 1740 AC Schagen; tel +31 224 783200; fax +31 224 783191; e-mail cindy .sijmonsma@cwinet.nl; *languages spoken:* Nederlands, English, Deutsch.

Henk Smolders: *organization:* Scheldemond (BE-NL), CWI, Centrum voor Werk en Inkomen; *address:* Besterdring 235, Postbus 322, 5000 AH Tilburg; tel +31 (0)13-7504241; fax +31 (0)13-7504240; e-mail Henk.Smolders@cwinet.nl; *languages spoken:* Nederlands, Deutsch.

Karin Staal: *organization:* CWI, Centrum voor Werk en Inkomen; *address:* Cornelis Troostplein 23, Postbus 75571, 1070 AN Amsterdam; tel +31 20 577 3230; fax +31 20 577 3224; e-mail karin .staal@cwinet.nl; *languages spoken:* Nederlands, English.

Herman Talsma: *organization:* CWI, Centrum voor Werk en Inkomen; *address:* Amsterdamse Veerkade 66, Postbus 16713, 2500 BS Den Haag; tel +31 7085 03500; fax +31 7085 03501; e-mail Herman.Talsma@cwinet.nl; *languages spoken:* Nederlands, English.

Yvonne Voskamp: *organization:* CWI, Centrum voor Werk en Inkomen; *address:* Schiekade 830, P.O. Box 37035, 3005 LA Rotterdam; tel +31 10 850 22 86; fax +31 10 850 20 41; e-mail yvonne .voskamp@cwinet.nl; *languages spoken:* Nederlands, Français, English.

Marly Westerburgen: *organization:* CWI, Centrum voor Werk en Inkomen; *address:* Jansweg 15, P.O. Box 1165, 2001 BD Haarlem; tel +31 23 5532309; fax +31 23 5323864; e-mail marly.westerburgen@ cwinet.nl; *languages spoken:* Nederlands, Français, English.

Pamela Will: *organization:* CWI, Centrum voor Werk en Inkomen; *address:* Claudius Prinsenlaan 14, P.O. Box 3296, 4800 DG Breda; tel +31 767511479; fax +31 767511437; e-mail pamela.will@cwinet.nl; *languages spoken:* Nederlands, Français, English, Deutsch.

NORWAY

Paul Asantcheeff: *organization:* AETAT, Arbeidsmarkedsetaten; *address:* P.O Box 8168 Dep., 0034 Oslo; located at: Øvre Slottsgt.11, 0034 Oslo; tel +47 22 86 22 65; fax +47 22 86 22 60; e-mail pas@a0379.aetat.no; *languages spoken:* Français, English.

Sandrine Beaudoin: *organization:* AETAT, Arbeidsmarkedsetaten; *address:* Torgenskjoldsgt. 26, 3044 Drammen; tel +47 32 27 75 57; fax +47 32 27 75 01; e-mail sab@a0605.aetat.no; *languages spoken:* Français, English.

Elisabeth Bomo: *organization:* AETAT, Arbeidsmarkedsetaten; *address:* P.O Box 610, 8801 Sandnessjøen; tel +47 75 06 38 27; fax +47 75 06 38 21; e-mail ebo@a1850.aetat.no; *languages spoken:* English.

Carmen Dahl: *organization:* AETAT, Arbeidsmarkedsetaten; *address:* Aetat Molde, Romsdalsgate 7, 6415 Molde; tel +47 71 20 26 25; fax +47 71 20 26 12; e-mail cid@f1501.aetat.no; *languages spoken:* English, Deutsch.

Fred Gundersen: *organization:* AETAT, Arbeidsmarkedsetaten; *address:* Statens park, P.O Box 2093, 3103 Tønsberg; tel +47 33 37 43 00; fax +47 33 37 43 01; e-mail fg@a0705.aetet.no; *languages spoken:* English.

Melanie Hill: *organization:* AETAT, Arbeidsmarkedsetaten; *address:* Statens Hus, 7734 Steinkjer; tel +47 74 14 75 12; fax +47 74 14 75 01; e-mail mh@a1705.aetat.no; *languages spoken:* English.

Catherine Holter: *organization:* AETAT, Arbeidsmarkedsetaten; *address:* P.O Box 1012, 3905 Porsgrunn; tel +47 35 57 33 21; fax +47 35 57 33 41; e-mail cah@a0810.aetat.no; *languages spoken:* English.

Kristin Kvanvig: *organization:* AETAT, Arbeidsmarkedsetaten; *address:* P.O.Box 8127 Dep., 0032 Oslo; tel +47 23352578; fax +47 23352488; e-mail kkv@adir.aetat.no; *languages spoken:* English.

Anne Live Nævdal: *organization:* AETAT, Arbeidsmarkedsetaten; *address:* P.O Box 8168 Dep., 0034 Oslo; tel +47 22 86 22 67; fax +47 22 86 22 61; e-mail aln@a0379.aetat.no; *languages spoken:* English, Deutsch.

Lena Pedersen: *organization:* AETAT, Arbeidsmarkedsetaten; *address:* Statens Hus, 7468 Trondheim; tel +47 73 83 13 00; fax +47 73 83 13 01; e-mail lp@a1660.aetat.no; *languages spoken:* English.

Inger Sagen: *organization:* AETAT, Arbeidsmarkedsetaten; *address:* Øvre Slottsgt. 11, P.O Box 8168 Dep., 0034 Oslo; tel +47 22 86 22 66; fax +47 22 86 22 60; e-mail is@a0379.aetat.no; *languages spoken:* Français, English.

Ragnhild Synstad: *organization:* AETAT, Arbeidsmarkedsetaten; *address:* P.O Box 412, 2303 Hamar; tel +47 625 38 100; fax +47 625 38 101; e-mail rs@f0401.aetat.no; *languages spoken:* English, Castellano.

Eugenia Tecusan: *organization:* AETAT, Arbeidsmarkedsetaten; *address:* P.O Box 8168 Dep., 0034 Oslo; tel +47 22 86 22 63; fax +47 22 86 22 61; e-mail tec@a0379.aetat.no; *languages spoken:* Français, English.

POLAND

Beata Chrościńska: *organization:* Polskie Publiczne Służby Zatrudnienia; *address:* ul. Pogodna 22, 15-354 Białystok; tel +48 85 7497235; fax +48 85 7497209; e-mail biwueures@praca.gov.pl; *languages spoken:* English, Polski.

Tomasz Dobroczynski: *organization:* Polskie Publiczne Służby Zatrudnienia; *address:* ul. Grunwaldzka 200, 60-166 Poznań; tel +48 61 863 02 54; fax +48 61 868 99 49; e-mail powueures1@praca.gov.pl; *languages spoken:* English, Polski.

Anna Janczewska: *organization:* Polskie Publiczne Służby Zatrudnienia; *address:* ul. Ciołka 10a, 10-402 Warszawa; tel +48 22 532 22 35; fax +48 22 532 22 05; e-mail wawueures1@praca.gov.pl; *languages spoken:* English, Polski.

Malgorzata Kociuba: *organization:* Polskie Publiczne Służby Zatrudnienia; *address:* ul. Wojska Polskiego 18, 58-500 Jelenia Góra; tel +48 0757647967; fax +48 0757522754; e-mail wrwujeeu@praca.gov.pl; *languages spoken:* Polski, Deutsch.

Alicja Konkol: *organization:* Polskie Publiczne Służby Zatrudnienia; *address:* Okopowa street 21/27, 80-810 Gdansk; tel +48 583056468; fax +48 583056466; e-mail a_konkol@wup.gdansk.pl; *languages spoken:* English, Polski.

Marcin Lewandowski: *organization:* Polskie Publiczne Służby Zatrudnienia; *address:* ul. Wolczanska 49, 90-608 Lodz; tel +48 42 6320112 ext 120; fax +48 42 6334909 ext 120; e-mail lowueures2@praca.gov.pl; *languages spoken:* Nederlands, English, Polski, Deutsch.

Anna Nowak: *organization:* Polskie Publiczne Służby Zatrudnienia; *address:* pl. Na Stawach 1, 30-107 Kraków; tel +48 12 4240723; fax +48 12 4229785; e-mail eures@wup-krakow.pl; *languages spoken:* English, Polski.

Marta Russek: *organization:* Polskie Publiczne Służby Zatrudnienia; *address:* Ul. Lisa Kuli 20, 35-025 Rzeszów; tel +48 17 8509223; fax +48 17 8524457; e-mail mrussek@wup-rzeszow.pl; *languages spoken:* English, Polski.

Jolanta Tkaczyk: *organization:* Polskie Publiczne Służby Zatrudnienia; *address:* ul. Okopowa 5, 20-022 Lublin; tel +48 81 5315634; fax +48 81 5315634; e-mail luwueures1@praca.gov.pl; *languages spoken:* Français, English, Polski.

Tamara Zegis: *organization:* Polskie Publiczne Służby Zatrudnienia; *address:* Ul. Glowackiego 28, 10-448 Olsztyn; tel +48 895227940; fax +48 895227901; e-mail olciz@praca.gov.pl; *languages spoken:* English, Polski.

PORTUGAL

Susana Maria Andre e Melo: *organization:* ACISAT, Associação de Comércio, Indústria, Serviços e Agrícola do Alto Tâmega, Galicia/Região Norte (ES-PT); *address:* Associação Empresarial do Alto Tâmega, ACISAT, Rua Corenel Bento Roma, 5400-114 Chaves; tel +351 276 332115; fax +351 276 332115; e-mail acisat@mail.telepac.pt; *languages spoken:* English, Português, Castellano.

Natalia Carvalho Correia: *organization:* IEFP, Instituto do Emprego e Formação Profissional; *address:* Rua Dr. Candido Guerreiro 45 1°, 8000 Faro; tel +351 289 89 01 65; fax +351 289 89 01 02; e-mail ncorreia.dralg@mail.iefp.pt; *languages spoken:* Français, English, Português.

Maria Jose Comenda: *organization:* IEFP, Instituto do Emprego e Formação Profissional; *address:* Rua de Menino Jesus 43-45, 7000-601 Evora; tel +351 266 760 591; fax +351 266 760 584; e-mail mariaj.comenda.dra@iefp.pt; *languages spoken:* Français, English, Português.

Maria Bárbara Correia da Cruz: *organization:* IEFP, Instituto do Emprego e Formação Profissional; *address:* Catarina Eufemia 53A, 8900 Vila Real de Santo António; tel +351 281 51 17 52; fax +351 281 51 11 33; e-mail bcruz.dralg@mail.iefp.pt; *languages spoken:* Français, English, Português.

Margarida Costa: *organization:* IEFP, Instituto do Emprego e Formação Profissional; *address:* Rua das Picoas n.° 14, 1069-003 Lisboa; tel +351 213307525; fax +351 213307610; e-mail margarida.costa.drl@iefp.pt; *languages spoken:* Português.

Sonia Maria Esteves Trancoso: *organization:* Galicia/Região Norte (ES-PT), IEFP, Instituto do Emprego e Formação Profissional; *address:* Avenida de Espanha, 4930 Valença; tel +351 25 18 26 105; fax +351 25 18 26 106; e-mail sonia.trancoso.eures@iefp.pt; *languages spoken:* English, Português, Castellano.

Paula Freitas: *organization:* IEFP, Instituto do Emprego e Formação Profissional; *address:* Rua Eng. Ezequiel Campos 480-488, 4149-004 Porto; tel +351 22 615 92 71; fax +351 22 615 92 85; e-mail pfreitas@iefp.pt; *languages spoken:* English, Português.

Manuel Tomas Gonçalves: *organization:* IEFP, Instituto do Emprego e Formação Profissional; *address:* Rua Bispo Idacio n° 50, 5400-303 Chaves; tel +351 276 326 770; fax +351 276 340 338; e-mail mtomas.goncalves.drn@iefp.pt; *languages spoken:* Français, Português.

Helena Gouveia: *organization:* IRE, Instituto Regional de Emprego, Madeira (Regional Employment service); *address:* Rua da Boa Viagem 36, 9060-027, Funchal; tel +351 291 213268; fax +351 291 220014; e-mail eures-madeira@netmadeira.com; *languages spoken:* Français, English, Português.

Bertina Maria Machado: *organization:* IEFP, Instituto do Emprego e Formação Profissional; *address:* Av. Fernão Magalhães 660, 3000-174 Coimbra; tel +351 239 860 836; fax +351 239 860 801; e-mail bertina.machado.drc@mail.iefp.pt; *languages spoken:* Français, English, Português.

Luisa Martins: *organization:* IEFP, Instituto do Emprego e Formação Profissional; *address:* Rua de Xabregas 52-2°, 1949-003 Lisboa; tel +351 21 861 41 45; fax +351 21 861 46 04; e-mail luisa.martins@iefp.pt; *languages spoken:* Français, English, Português.

Maria Helena Rodrigues Cruz: *organization:* IEFP, Instituto do Emprego e Formação Profissional; *address:* Rua de Xabregas n°52-2°, 1949-003 Lisboa; tel + 351 21 861 41 34; fax + 351 21 861 46 04; e-mail helena.cruz@iefp.pt; *languages spoken:* English.

Pedro Santos: *organization:* IEFP, Instituto do Emprego e Formação Profissional; *address:* Av. Valbom n° 17-1°, 2750-508 Cascais; tel +351 21 481 20 39; fax +351 21 481 20 12; e-mail pedro.miguel.santos.drl@iefp.pt; *languages spoken:* English, Português, Castellano.

Dora Silva: *organization:* IEFP, Instituto do Emprego e Formação Profissional; *address:* Av. Fernão de Magalhães 660, 3000-174 Coimbra; tel +351 239 860 800 ext 5047; fax +351 239 86 08 01; e-mail dora.silva.drc@iefp.pt; *languages spoken:* Français, English, Português, Deutsch.

Carlos Valente: *organization:* IEFP, Instituto do Emprego e Formação Profissional; *address:* Av. Vasco da Gama / Edificio Coimbra 1, 4490-410 Póvoa do Varzim; tel +351 252 61 50 08; fax +351 252 61 21 48; e-mail carlos.valente.drn@iefp.pt; *languages spoken:* Français, English, Português.

SLOVAKIA

Lubica Cibulova: *organization:* Úrad práce sociálnych vecí a rodiny (Labour, Social Affairs and Family Office); *address:* Stefanikova 88, 949 01 Nitra; tel +421 37 6926 258; fax +421 37 6926 284; e-mail lubica.cibulova@upsvar.sk; *languages spoken:* Slovenčina, English.

Marek Derzsi: *organization:* Úrad práce sociálnych vecí a rodiny (Labour, Social Affairs and Family Office); *address:* Mileticova 21, 831 03 Bratislava; tel +421 2 5057 2927; e-mail Marek.Derzsi@upsvar.sk; *languages spoken:* Slovenčina, English, Deutsch.

Alica Dobra: *organization:* Úrad práce sociálnych vecí a rodiny (Labour, Social Affairs and Family Office); *address:* Adorska 41, 929 01 Dunajska Streda; tel +421 31 590 4438; fax +421 31 590 4454; e-mail alica.dobra@upsvar.sk; *languages spoken:* Slovenčina, Magyar, English.

Slavka Fulekova: *organization:* Úrad práce sociálnych vecí a rodiny (Labour, Social Affairs and Family Office); *address:* DLHY Rad 17, 085 01 Bardejov; tel +421 544746822; fax +421 544723366; e-mail Slavka.Fulekova@nup.sk; *languages spoken:* Slovenčina.

Iveta Hluchá: *organization:* Úrad práce sociálnych vecí a rodiny (Labour, Social Affairs and Family Office); *address:* Hurbanova 16, 010 01 Zilina; tel +421 41 5119 212; fax +421 41 5624 953; e-mail iveta.hlucha@upsvar.sk; *languages spoken:* Slovenčina, English.

Renata Mesarosova: *organization:* Úrad práce sociálnych vecí a rodiny (Labour, Social Affairs and Family Office); *address:* M.R.Stefanika 20, 911 01 Trencin; tel +421 32 74 15 364; fax +421 32 74 31 758; e-mail renata.mesarosova@upsvar.sk; *languages spoken:* Slovenčina, English.

Peter Mika: *organization:* Úrad práce sociálnych vecí a rodiny (Labour, Social Affairs and Family Office); *address:* Saleziánov 1, 071 01 Michalovce; tel +421 5616860317; e-mail peter.mika@nup.sk; *languages spoken:* Slovenčina, English.

Ingrid Mitterpachova: *organization:* Úrad práce sociálnych vecí a rodiny (Labour, Social Affairs and Family Office); *address:* Popradské nábrezie 16, 058 01 Poprad; tel +421 527721017; fax +421 52 77 25 021; e-mail ingrid.mitterpachova@nup.sk; *languages spoken:* Slovenčina, English.

SLOVENIA

Darja Kapun-Grauf: *organization:* ZRSZ, Zavod Republike Slovenije za zaposlovanje; *address:* Gregorčičeva ulica 37, 2000 Maribor; tel +386 2 2527714; e-mail darja.grauf@ess.gov.si; *languages spoken:* Slovenščina, English, Deutsch.

Vanja Nardin: *organization:* ZRSZ, Zavod Republike Slovenije za zaposlovanje; *address:* Ulica tolminskih Puntarjev 4, 5000 Nova Gorica; tel +386 53350232; fax +386 53350250; e-mail vanja.nardin@ess.gov.si; *languages spoken:* Slovenščina, English, Italiano.

Mirela Pekica: *organization:* ZRSZ, Zavod Republike Slovenije za zaposlovanje; *address:* Kmečka ulica 2, 6000 Koper; tel +386 56135000; fax +386 56271511; e-mail mirela.pekica@ess.gov.si; *languages spoken:* Slovenščina, English, Italiano.

Katarina Zajec: *organization:* ZRSZ, Zavod Republike Slovenije za zaposlovanje; *address:* Parmova ulica 32, 1001 Ljubljana; tel +386 14729762; fax +386 14363203; e-mail katarina.zajec@ess.gov.si; *languages spoken:* Slovenščina, English.

SPAIN

José Antonio Acerete Martín: *organization:* INEM, Instituto Nacional de Empleo; *address:* C/ Pintor León Abadiás, 22005 Huesca; tel +34 974 228011; fax +34 974 230201; e-mail eures-huesca.acerete@inem.es; *languages spoken:* Français, Castellano.

Manuel Angel Alia Alia: *organization:* INEM, Instituto Nacional de Empleo; *address:* C/ Calvo Sotelo 27-29, 26071 Logroño; tel +34 941 263199; fax +34 941 250137; e-mail eures-rioja.alia@inem.es; *languages spoken:* English, Castellano.

Mª Teresa Alonso-Vega Alvarez: *organization:* INEM, Instituto Nacional de Empleo; *address:* C/ General Elorza, 27, 33001 Oviedo; tel +34 985 10 63 96; fax +34 985 10 63 94; e-mail eures-asturias.alonso@inem.es; *languages spoken:* Français, English, Castellano.

Daniel Bellon Serrano: *organization:* INEM, Instituto Nacional de Empleo; *address:* C/ Suarez Naranjo 78, 35004 Las Palmas de Gran Canaria; tel +34 928 445064; fax +34 928 445071; e-mail eures-palmas.bellon@inem.es; *languages spoken:* English, Castellano.

Marisa Carmona Urda: *organization:* INEM, Instituto Nacional de Empleo; *address:* C/ Tomé Cano 12, 38005 Sta. Cruz de Tenerife; tel +34 922 21 35 55; fax +34 922 20 81 35; e-mail eures-tenerife.carmona@inem.es; *languages spoken:* English, Castellano, Deutsch.

Luis Miguel Castañeda Palau: *organization:* INEM, Instituto Nacional de Empleo; *address:* C/ Condesa de Venadito 9, 28027 Madrid; tel +34 91 58 59 912; fax +34 91 37 71 301; e-mail eures-estatal.castaneda@inem.es; *languages spoken:* English, Castellano.

Mª Antonia Castellanos Cicuendez: *organization:* INEM, Instituto Nacional de Empleo; *address:* C/ Gremi Teixidors 38, 07009 Palma de Mallorca; tel +34 971 176300 (4548); fax +34 971 176301; e-mail eures-baleares.castellanos@inem.es; *languages spoken:* Français, Castellano.

Concha Cerdeira Gutiérrez: *organization:* INEM, Instituto Nacional de Empleo; *address:* C/ Condesa de Venadito 9, 28027 Madrid; tel +34 91 58 52 915; fax +34 91 58 52 924; e-mail eures.cerdeira@inem.es; *languages spoken:* Français, Castellano.

Tomàs Chicharro Manero: *organization:* PYREMED/PIRIME (FR-ES), CCOO, Comisiones Obreras; *address:* Via Laietana 16, 08003 Barcelona; tel + 34 93 481 28 92; fax + 34 93 310 27 54; e-mail tchicharro@conc.es; *languages spoken:* Français, Castellano.

Carmen De Eguilior Alvarez de Ribera: *organization:* INEM, Instituto Nacional de Empleo; *address:* Vía Lusitana 21, 28025 Madrid; tel +34 91 42 07 369; fax +34 91 58 02 718; e-mail eures-madrid.eguilior@inem.es; *languages spoken:* English, Castellano, Deutsch.

Manuel De San Mateo Gil: *organization:* INEM, Instituto Nacional de Empleo; *address:* ECYL (Servicio Publico de Empleo) – Edificio Europa, Avda Reyes Leoneses 14, 24008 Leon; tel +34-987297855; fax +34-987297849; e-mail eures-leon.sanmateo@inem.es; *languages spoken:* English, Castellano.

Maria Teresa Delgado Fernandez: *organization:* INEM, Instituto Nacional de Empleo; *address:* C/ San Benito 19, 42001 Soria; tel +34 975222150; fax +34 975228761; e-mail eures-soria.delgado@inem.es; *languages spoken:* Français, Castellano.

Guadalupe Díaz Martin: *organization:* INEM, Instituto Nacional de Empleo; *address:* C/ Badalona 8-10, 10002 Cáceres; tel +34 927 62 62 50; fax +34 927 21 50 92; e-mail eures-caceres.diaz@inem.es; *languages spoken:* Français, Castellano.

Rocío Erena del Pino: *organization:* INEM, Instituto Nacional de Empleo;

address: Avda Andalucia 36 bj., 23006 Jaén; tel +34 953 25 25 29; fax +34 953 22 25 29; e-mail eures-jaen.erena@inem.es; *languages spoken:* English, Castellano.

Angeles Eseverri Asin: *organization:* PYREMED/PIRIME (FR-ES), INEM, Instituto Nacional de Empleo; *address:* C/ Dr. Joaquin Pou 8, 2ª planta, 08002 Barcelona; tel +34 93 301 0935; fax +34 93 317 0418; e-mail eures-barcelona.eseverri@inem.es; *languages spoken:* Castellano.

Teresa Esteban Gasanz: *organization:* INEM, Instituto Nacional de Empleo; *address:* C/ Condesa de Venadito 9, 28027 Madrid; tel +34 91 58 52 915; fax +34 91 58 52 924; e-mail eures.teresa@inem.es; *languages spoken:* English, Castellano.

Estanislao Esteller Viciana: *organization:* INEM, Instituto Nacional de Empleo; *address:* C/ Altamira 19/21, 04005 Almeria; tel +34 950 22 82 63; fax +34 950 22 76 64; e-mail eures-almeria.esteller@inem.es; *languages spoken:* English, Castellano.

Isabel Farre Vega: *organization:* INEM, Instituto Nacional de Empleo, PYREMED/PIRIME (FR-ES); *address:* C/ San Antoni Mª Claret 19, 43002 Tarragona; tel +34 977 21 27 33; fax +34 977 245180; e-mail eures-tarragona.farre@inem.es; *languages spoken:* Français, Castellano.

Juan Miguel Fernández Rosales: *organization:* INEM, Instituto Nacional de Empleo; *address:* C/ Alameda de Mazarredo 39, 48009 Bilbao; tel +34 94 424 5494; fax +34 94 423 1153; e-mail eures-vizcaya.fernandez@inem.es; *languages spoken:* English, Castellano.

Fernando Garbín Hernández: *organization:* INEM, Instituto Nacional de Empleo; *address:* C/ Segovia 25, 05005 Avila; tel +34 920 35 58 07; fax +34 920 85 58 07; e-mail eures-avila.garbin@inem.es; *languages spoken:* English, Castellano.

Yolanda García Enriquez: *organization:* INEM, Instituto Nacional de Empleo; *address:* Avda Casado del Alisal 2, 34001 Palencia; tel +34 979 75 18 80; fax +34 979 74 63 49; e-mail eures-palencia.garcia@inem.es; *languages spoken:* Français, Castellano.

Mª Isabel García Hernández: *organization:* INEM, Instituto Nacional de Empleo; *address:* C/ Herrero 29, 12005 Castellón; tel +34 96 425 5137; fax +34 96 425 3608; e-mail eures-castellon.garcia@inem.es; *languages spoken:* Français, English, Castellano.

Consuelo García Luján: *organization:* INEM, Instituto Nacional de Empleo; *address:* C/ Cid 29, 02002 Albacete; tel +34 967 59 91 36; fax +34 967 59 91 36;

e-mail eures-asturias.alonso@inem.es; *languages spoken:* Français, Castellano.

Carmen Gómez García: *organization:* INEM, Instituto Nacional de Empleo; *address:* C/ Condesa Venadito 9, 28027 Madrid; tel +34 91 58 52 914; fax +34 91 58 52 924; e-mail eures.carmen.gomez@inem.es; *languages spoken:* Français, English, Castellano.

Mª Teresa Hernández Lorenzo: *organization:* INEM, Instituto Nacional de Empleo; *address:* Dr. Fleming 6-8, 49026 Zamora; tel +34 980 521582; fax +34 980 510115; e-mail eures-zamora.hernandez@inem.es; *languages spoken:* Français, English, Castellano.

Mª Belén de los Reyes Hernández Martín: *organization:* INEM, Instituto Nacional de Empleo; *address:* C/ Hilario Goyenechea 2-40, 37008 Salamanca; tel +34 923 216870-266842; fax +34 923 267106; e-mail eures-salamanca.hernandez@inem.es; *languages spoken:* Français, Castellano.

Manuel Iglesias Suarez-Neguerol: *organization:* Galicia/Região Norte (ES-PT), INEM, Instituto Nacional de Empleo; *address:* C/ Progreso 11 Baixo, 32003 Ourense; tel +34 988 222 636; fax +34 988 222 641; e-mail eures-ourense.iglesias@inem.es; *languages spoken:* Français, English, Castellano.

Benjamín Jiménez López: *organization:* INEM, Instituto Nacional de Empleo; *address:* Nicanor Villarta 22, 44002 Teruel; tel +340978601250; fax +34978603104; e-mail eures-teruel.lopez@inem.es; *languages spoken:* Castellano.

Gonzalo Lamas Alonso: *organization:* INEM, Instituto Nacional de Empleo; *address:* Avda Andalucia 23, 29003 Málaga; tel +34 952 13 40 54; fax +34 952 36 66 68; e-mail eures-malaga.lamas@inem.es; *languages spoken:* English, Português, Castellano.

Pilar Leal Bravo: *organization:* INEM, Instituto Nacional de Empleo; *address:* C/ Condesa de Venadito 9, 28027 Madrid; tel +34 91 585 29 14; fax +34 91 585 29 24; e-mail eures.pilarleal@inem.es; *languages spoken:* English, Português, Castellano.

Covadonga López López: *organization:* Galicia/Região Norte (ES-PT), INEM, Instituto Nacional de Empleo; *address:* Pza. Rafael Dieste s/n, 15008 La Coruña; tel +34 981 29 12 44; fax +34 981 29 08 52; e-mail eures-coruna.lopez@inem.es; *languages spoken:* English, Castellano.

Cristina Marañón Prat: *organization:* INEM, Instituto Nacional de Empleo; *address:* C/ Calzadas 36, 09004 Burgos; tel +34 947 27 84 54; fax +34 947 25 04 32; e-mail eures-burgos.maranon@inem.es; *languages spoken:* English, Castellano.

Manuela Martinez Jimenez: *organization:* INEM, Instituto Nacional de Empleo; *address:* Placeta de Villamena s/n, 2ª Planta, 18071 Granada; tel +34 958 02 99 51; fax +34 958 02 95 68; e-mail eures-granada.martinez@inem.es; *languages spoken:* Français, English, Castellano.

Carlos Mogro Remolina: *organization:* INEM, Instituto Nacional de Empleo; *address:* C/ Menéndez Pelayo 45, 39600 Maliaño (Santander); tel +34 942 251358; fax +34 957 25 51 05; e-mail eures-cantabria.mogro@inem.es; *languages spoken:* Français, Castellano.

Violeta Morcillo Narciso: *organization:* INEM, Instituto Nacional de Empleo; *address:* C/ Oquendo, 16-1°, 2004 Donostia-San Sebastian; tel +34 943 44 01 08; fax +34 943 366118; e-mail eures-guipuzcoa.morcillo@inem.es; *languages spoken:* Français, Castellano.

María del Socorro Moreno Alarcón: *organization:* INEM, Instituto Nacional de Empleo; *address:* Avda Gran Capitan 12, aª planta, 14001 Cordoba; tel +34 957 49 62 13; fax +34 957 47 61 20; e-mail eures-cordoba.moreno@inem.es; *languages spoken:* Castellano.

Silvia Nacenta Castarlenas: *organization:* INEM, Instituto Nacional de Empleo, PYREMED/PIRIME (FR-ES); *address:* Mossen Reig 3, 25008 Lleida; tel +34 973 23 05 50; fax +34 973 24 54 52; e-mail eures-lleida.nacenta@inem.es; *languages spoken:* Français, Castellano.

Ana Narro Gómez: *organization:* INEM, Instituto Nacional de Empleo; *address:* C/ Vila Barberá 8, 46007 Valencia; tel +34 96 380 82 98; fax +34 96 641 99 73; e-mail eures-valencia.narro@inem.es; *languages spoken:* Français, Castellano.

Carmen Navarro Felipe: *organization:* INEM, Instituto Nacional de Empleo; *address:* Camino de las Torres 24, 50008 Zaragoza; tel +34 976 421232; fax +34 976 496714; e-mail eures-zaragoza.navarro@inem.es; *languages spoken:* Français, Castellano.

Ricardo Panzuela Santiago: *organization:* INEM, Instituto Nacional de Empleo; *address:* Avda Muñoz de Vargas, 21071 Huelva; tel +34 959 54 36 45; fax +34 959 54 35 69; e-mail eures-huelva.panzuela@inem.es; *languages spoken:* English, Castellano.

Jesús Manuel Perea Saiz: *organization:* INEM, Instituto Nacional de Empleo; *address:* C/ Princesa Zaida 6, 16002 Cuenca; tel +34 969 23 29 01; fax +34 969 23 28 80; e-mail eures-cuenca.perea@inem.es; *languages spoken:* Castellano.

Juan Angel Piqueras Cabanillas: *organization:* INEM, Instituto Nacional de Empleo; *address:* C/ Echegaray 3, 13004 Ciudad Reál; tel +34 926 23 25 60; fax +34 926 23 24 81; e-mail eures-ciudadreal.piqueras@inem.es; *languages spoken:* Castellano.

Teresa Prieto Amez: *organization:* INEM, Instituto Nacional de Empleo; *address:* SEFCARM; Avda Infante D. Juan Manuel, 14, 30011 Murcia; tel +34 968 35 75 52; fax +34 968 35 73 72; e-mail eures-murcia.prieto@inem.es; *languages spoken:* Français, Castellano.

Isabel Pérez García: *organization:* INEM, Instituto Nacional de Empleo; *address:* Avda Blas Infante, 4-5°, 41011 Sevilla; tel +34 955 06 56 72; fax +34 955 06 56 82; e-mail eures-sevilla.perez@inem.es; *languages spoken:* English, Castellano.

Susana Ramirez de Val: *organization:* PYREMED/PIRIME (FR-ES), Fomento del Trabajo Nacional de Catalunya (Employers Confederation); *address:* Via Laietana 32-34, 08003 Barcelona; tel +34 998 387 088; fax +34 388 387 165; e-mail sramirez@foment.com; *languages spoken:* Français, Castellano.

Juan Antonio Reques Plaza: *organization:* INEM, Instituto Nacional de Empleo; *address:* C/ General Santiago 6, 40005 Segovia; tel +34 921 42 52 61; fax +34 921 42 52 45; e-mail eures-segovia.reques@inem.es; *languages spoken:* Français, Castellano.

Carmen Santalla Novo: *organization:* INEM, Instituto Nacional de Empleo; *address:* Ronda da Muralla 70, 27071 Lugo; tel +34 982 29 42 85; fax +34 982 29 42 82; e-mail eures-lugo.santalla@inem.es; *languages spoken:* English, Castellano.

Maria Soledad Santamaría Cid: *organization:* INEM, Instituto Nacional de Empleo; *address:* Granja San Ildefonso s/n 3ª planta dcha, 11007 Cádiz; tel +34 956 24 13 11; fax +34 956 24 13 57; e-mail eures-cadiz.santamaria@inem.es; *languages spoken:* Français, English, Castellano.

Magdalena Saura Saura: *organization:* INEM, Instituto Nacional de Empleo; *address:* Oficina de Empleo, C/ Regino Pradillo 3, 19004 Guadalajara; tel +34 949 21 52 23; fax +34 949 21 51 26; e-mail eures-guadalajara.saura@inem.es; *languages spoken:* Français, Castellano.

Emília Seoane Pérez: *organization:* Galicia/Região Norte (ES-PT), Universidad de Vigo (Vigo University); *address:* Vicereitorado de Relacións Institucionais, Campus Universitário As Lagoas s/n, Unidade Administrativa, 32004 Ourense; tel +34 647 343 069; fax +34 988 387 165; e-mail eures.universidade.emilia@uvigo.es; *languages spoken:* Français, Castellano.

Estela Simons Alvarez: *organization:* Galicia/Região Norte (ES-PT), INEM, Instituto Nacional de Empleo; *address:* C/ López Mora 50, 36211 Vigo; tel +34 986 231746; fax +34 986 296116; e-mail eures-pontevedra.simons@inem.es; *languages spoken:* English, Português, Castellano.

Margarita Soler Barris: *organization:* FOEG-Federació d'Organitzacions Empresarials de Girona (Confederation of business organisation), PYREMED/PIRIME (FR-ES); *address:* Calle Bonastruc de Porta 15, 17001 Girona; tel +34 972 426 184; fax +34 972 215 016; e-mail msoler@foeg.es; *languages spoken:* Français, English, Castellano.

Pilar Sánchez Pérez: *organization:* INEM, Instituto Nacional de Empleo; *address:* C/ San Juan Bosco 15, 3ª planta, 03005 Alicante; tel +34 96 598 44 18; fax +34 96 598 52 30; e-mail eures-alicante.sanchez@inem.es; *languages spoken:* Français, Castellano.

Mercedes Talavera Zamora: *organization:* PYREMED/PIRIME (FR-ES), INEM, Instituto Nacional de Empleo; *address:* C/ Dr. Joaquin Pou 8, 2ª planta, 08002 Barcelona; tel +34 93 301 0935-94; fax +34 93 317 0418; e-mail eures-barcelona.talavera@inem.es; *languages spoken:* English, Castellano.

Mario Valderrama Alberola: *organization:* INEM, Instituto Nacional de Empleo; *address:* c/Alvaro de Bazán 14-16, 5205 Melilla; tel +34 952 67 33 52; fax +34 952 67 60 02; e-mail eures-melilla.valderrama@inem.es; *languages spoken:* English, Castellano.

Cinta Vallespin Fuste: *organization:* INEM, Instituto Nacional de Empleo, PYREMED/PIRIME (FR-ES); *address:* Avda Lluis Pericot 86-90, 17003 Girona; tel +34 972 48 72 80; fax +34 972 41 20 28; e-mail eures-girona.vallespin@inem.es; *languages spoken:* Français, Castellano.

Mª José Vegas Sillero: *organization:* INEM, Instituto Nacional de Empleo; *address:* Avda Otero s/n, 51002 Ceuta; tel +34 9 56 50 97 90; fax +34 9 56 50 78 11; e-mail eures-ceuta.vegas@inem.es; *languages spoken:* English, Castellano.

Mª Mercedes Vilches Plaza: *organization:* INEM, Instituto Nacional de Empleo; *address:* Arcadio María Larraona 1, 1ª, 2ª y 3ª planta, 31008 Pamplona; tel +34 848 42 44 20; fax +34 848 42 44 70; e-mail eures-navarra.vilches@inem.es; *languages spoken:* Français, Castellano.

SWEDEN

Jihad Adlouni: *organization:* AMV, Arbetsmarknadsverket; *address:* Norrtullsgatan 6, Box 6046, 113 29 Stockholm; tel +46 84 06 57 23; fax +46 84 06

57 01; e-mail jihad.adlouni@lanab.amv
.se; *languages spoken:* Svenska, Français,
English.

Margareta Appell: *organization:* AMV,
Arbetsmarknadsverket; *address:* Kristinegatan 28, Box 183, 791 60 Falun; tel
+46 23 937 92; fax +46 23 937 96; e-mail
margareta.appell@lanw.amv.se; *languages spoken:* Svenska, Français,
English.

Arne Arvidsson: *organization:* AMV,
Arbetsmarknadsverket; *address:* Box
173, 461 24 Trollhättan; tel +46 520
491987; fax +46 (520 491870; e-mail
arne.arvidsson@lano.amv.se; *languages
spoken:* Svenska, English.

Marie-Louise Chardet: *organization:*
AMV, Arbetsmarknadsverket; *address:*
Norrtullsgatan 6, Box 6046, 11329 Stockholm; tel +46 84 06 57 22; fax +46 84 06 57
01; e-mail marie-louise.chardet@lanab
.amv.se; *languages spoken:* Svenska,
Français, English.

David Cluer: *organization:* AMV,
Arbetsmarknadsverket; *address:* Kristinegatan 28, Box 183, 79160 Falun; tel
+46 23 937 94; fax +46 23 937 96; e-mail
david.cluer@lanw.amv.se; *languages spoken:* English, Deutsch.

Linda Daugaard: *organization:* AMS,
Arbetsmarknadsstyrelsen; *address:* Bangårdsgatan 9, Box 66, 75103 Uppsala; tel
+46 18683599; fax +46 18683511; e-mail
linda.daugaard@lanc.amv.se; *languages
spoken:* Svenska, English, Castellano.

Tomas Davidson: *organization:* AMV,
Arbetsmarknadsverket; *address:* St
Larsgatan, Box 337, 58103 Linköping;
tel +46 13 20 28 86; fax +46 13 20 28
80; e-mail tomas.davidson@lane.amv.se;
languages spoken: Svenska, English,
Deutsch.

Madeleine Deland: *organization:* AMV,
Arbetsmarknadsverket; *address:* Norrtullsgatan 6, BOX 6046, 102 31 Stockholm; tel +46 8 406 5724; fax +46 8
4065701; e-mail madeleine.deland@
lanab.amv.se; *languages spoken:*
Svenska, English.

Gunnel Ericsson: *organization:* AMV,
Arbetsmarknadsverket; *address:* Kron-
bergsgatan 18-20, Box 199, 351 04
Växjö; tel +46 470 70 37 80; fax +46 470
70 37 31; e-mail gunnel.ericson@lang
.amv.se; *languages spoken:* Svenska,
English, Deutsch.

Rob Floris: *organization:* AMV, Arbetsmarknadsverket; *address:* Norra vägen
50 A, Box 763, 39125 Kalmar; tel +46
480 49 50 34; fax +46 480 49 50 50;
e-mail rob.floris@lanh.amv.se; *languages
spoken:* Svenska, Nederlands, English.

Lena From: *organization:* AMV, Arbetsmarknadsverket; *address:* Stora gatan
33, Box 560, 721 10 Västerås; tel +46 21
15 31 07; fax +46 21 15 31 09; e-mail

lena.from@lanu.amv.se; *languages spoken:* Svenska, Français.

Kenneth Hake: *organization:* AMS,
Arbetsmarknadsstyrelsen; *address:*
P.O.Box 25, 374 21 Karlshamn; tel
+46(0)454-306824 +46(0)70-6664824; fax
+46(0)454-306860; e-mail kenneth
.hake@lank.amv.se; *languages spoken:*
Svenska, English, Deutsch.

Östen Harila: *organization:* Tornedalen
(SV-SF), LO, Landsorganisationen;
address: Skomakargatan 1, Box 133,
353 31 Haparanda; tel +46-922-14135;
fax +46-922-12012; e-mail osten.harila@
telia.com; *languages spoken:* Svenska,
Suomi.

Håkan Hermansson: *organization:* LO,
Landsorganisationen; *address:* Olof
Palmes plats 1, 214 44 Malmö; tel +46-
40-664 53 90; e-mail hakan.hermansson@
lo7.lo.se; *languages spoken:* Svenska,
English, Deutsch.

Eva Holmberg-Tedert: *organization:*
AMV, Arbetsmarknadsverket; *address:*
Nygatan 31, Box 477, S-80106 Gävle; tel
+46 26 13 84 46; fax +46 26 13 85 80;
e-mail eva.holmberg-tedert@lanx.amv
.se; *languages spoken:* Svenska, English,
Deutsch.

Margaretha Holmer: *organization:*
AMV, Arbetsmarknadsverket; *address:*
Norra Hamngatan 20, Box 11114, 404
23 Göteborg; tel +46 31 61 93 21; fax
+46 31 61 93 15; e-mail margaretha
.holmer@lano.amv.se; *languages spoken:*
Svenska, English, Deutsch.

Ivar Jönsson: *organization:* AMV,
Arbetsmarknadsverket; *address:* Brogatan 8, Box 1042, 301 10 Halmstad; tel +46
35 15 50 15; fax +46 35 15 50 30; e-mail
ivar.jonsson@lann.amv.se; *languages
spoken:* Svenska, English, Deutsch.

Nancy Kumpula: *organization:* AMV,
Arbetsmarknadsverket; *address:* Arbetsförmedlingen Stortorget, Box 6009, 200
11 Malmö; tel +46 (0)40 20 71 26; fax +46
(0)40 20 73 60; e-mail nancy.kumpula@
lanm.amv.se; *languages spoken:*
Svenska, Français, Deutsch.

Ramona Källström: *organization:*
AMV, Arbetsmarknadsverket; *address:*
Bangårdsgatan 9, Box 66, 751 03
Uppsala; tel +46 18 68 35 08; fax +46 18
68 35 22; e-mail ramona.kallstrom@lanc
.amv.se; *languages spoken:* Svenska,
Français, English.

Mikael Lindbom: *organization:* AMV,
Arbetsmarknadsverket; *address:* Kriebsensgatan 4, 632 20 Eskilstuna; tel +46
16 176354; fax +46 16 176351; e-mail
mikael.lindbom@land.amv.se; *languages
spoken:* Svenska, English.

Maria Marklund: *organization:* AMV,
Arbetsmarknadsverket; *address:* Drottninggatan 10, 651 14 Karlstad; tel +46
54 19 67 12; fax +46 54 19 67 01; e-mail

maria.marklund@lans.amv.se; *languages spoken:* Svenska, English.

Lars Nilsson: *organization:* AMV,
Arbetsmarknadsverket; *address:* Skep-
paregatan 7, Box 752, 851 22 Sundsvall;
tel +46 60 18 79 92; fax +46 60 18 79 41;
e-mail lars.nilsson@lany.amv.se; *languages spoken:* Svenska, English.

Lilian Nilsson-Tiberg: *organization:*
AMV, Arbetsmarknadsverket; *address:*
Arbetsförmedlingen Utland, Box 923,
971 07 Luleå; tel +46 920 395 42; fax
+46 920 395 49; e-mail lilian.nilsson
-tiberg@lanbd.amv.se; *languages spoken:*
Svenska, Deutsch.

Britt-Inger Olsson: *organization:* AMV,
Arbetsmarknadsverket; *address:* Stad-
sportsgatan 9, Box 25, 374 21 Karl-
shamm; tel +46 454-306808; fax +46
454-306860; e-mail britt-inger.olsson@
lank.amv.se; *languages spoken:* Svenska,
English, Deutsch.

UllBritt Palmborg: *organization:* AMV,
Arbetsmarknadsverket; *address:* Olaiga-
tan 4, Box 353, 701 47 Örebro; tel +46 19
601 52 45; fax +46 19 601 50 71; e-mail
ullbrit.palmborg@lant.amv.se; *languages
spoken:* Svenska, English, Deutsch.

Ylva Papp: *organization:* AMV, Arbetsmarknadsverket; *address:* Box 752, 851
22 Sundsvall; tel +46-60-187806; fax +46-
60-187941; e-mail ylva.papp@lany.amv
.se; *languages spoken:* Svenska, English,
Deutsch.

Linda Schön: *organization:* AMV,
Arbetsmarknadsverket; *address:* Bar-
narpsgatan 40, 551 11 Jönköping; tel
+46 36 15 12 34; fax +46 36 15 12 75;
e-mail linda.schon@lanf.amv.se; *languages spoken:* Svenska, English.

Annika Sund: *organization:* AMV,
Arbetsmarknadsverket; *address:* Nygatan 25, Box 423, 901 09 Umeå; tel +46
90 15 17 43; fax +46 90 15 15 46; e-mail
annika.sund@lanac.amv.se; *languages
spoken:* Svenska, English, Suomi.

Monica Walkenfors: *organization:*
AMV, Arbetsmarknadsverket; *address:*
Ö Storgatan 21, Box 243, 291 23 Kristianstad; tel +46 (0)44 193000, +46 (0)44
193072; fax +46 (0)44 193230; e-mail
monica.walkenfors@lanm.amv.se; *languages spoken:* Svenska, English,
Deutsch.

Hans-Anders Westlund: *organization:*
AMV, Arbetsmarknadsverket; *address:*
Norrtullsgatan 6, Box 6046, 113 29 Stockholm; tel +46 84 06 57 26; fax +46 84 06 57
01; e-mail hans.a.westlund@lanab.amv
.se; *languages spoken:* Svenska, English,
Deutsch.

Margareta Wetterberg: *organization:*
AMV, Arbetsmarknadsverket; *address:*
Petter Heléns gata 2, Box 405, 541 28
Skövde; tel +46 500 47 70 95; fax +46 500

47 70 97; e-mail margareta.wetterberg@ lano.amv.se; *languages spoken:* Svenska, Deutsch.

Dieter Zippert: *organization:* AMV, Arbetsmarknadsverket; *address:* Södra Promenaden 69, Box 4236, 203 13 Malmö; tel +46 40 207050; fax +46 40 207070; e-mail dieter.zippert@lanm.amv .se; *languages spoken:* Svenska, English, Deutsch.

SWITZERLAND

Chiara Barberis: *organization:* ORP-Offices régionaux de placement (FR); *address:* Rue des Glacis de Rive, 1207 Genève; tel +41 22 3276908; fax +41 223276899; e-mail chiara.barberis@etat .ge.ch; *languages spoken:* Français, English, Castellano.

Beat Britt: *organization:* Oberrhein (FR-DE-CH), RAV-Regionales Arbeitsvermittlungszentrum (DE); *address:* Hochstrasse 37, 4002 Basel; tel +41 61 267 5028; fax +41 61 267 5080; e-mail beat .britt@bs.ch; *languages spoken:* Français, English, Deutsch.

Anne Fava: *organization:* ORP-Offices régionaux de placement (FR); *address:* Rue du Parc 119, 2300 La Chaux-de-Fonds; tel +41 32 9197834; fax +41 32 919 6271; e-mail anne.fava@ne.ch; *languages spoken:* Français, English, Castellano.

Kurt Müller: *organization:* Bodensee (DE-AT-CH), RAV-Regionales Arbeitsvermittlungszentrum (DE); *address:* Unterstrasse 4, 9001 St. Gallen; tel +41 71 229 2564; fax +41 71 229 2536; e-mail kurt.mueller@sg.ch; *languages spoken:* Français, English, Deutsch.

Anita Scherrer: *organization:* Bodensee (DE-AT-CH), RAV-Regionales Arbeitsvermittlungszentrum (DE); *address:* Mühlentalstrasse 105, 8200 Schaffhausen; tel +41 52 632 7028; fax +41 52 632 7023; e-mail anita.scherrer@ktsh.ch; *languages spoken:* Français, English, Deutsch.

Agatha Thürler: *organization:* Trans-Tirolia (IT-AT-CH), RAV-Regionales Arbeitsvermittlungszentrum (DE); *address:* Grabenstrasse 15, 7000 Chur; tel +41 81 257 3123; fax +41 81 257 2023; e-mail Agatha.Thuerler@kiga.gr .ch; *languages spoken:* English, Italiano, Deutsch.

Denise Z'graggen Zimmermann: *organization:* RAV-Regionales Arbeitsvermittlungszentrum (DE); *address:* Zentralstrasse 63, 2502 Biel; tel +41 32 3294537; fax +41 32 3294555; e-mail denise.zgraggenzimmermann@vol.be.ch; *languages spoken:* Français, English, Castellano, Deutsch.

UNITED KINGDOM

Siobhan Burns: *organization:* Northern Ireland/Ireland (IE-UK), Department for Employment & Learning (DEL) Northern Ireland; *address:* Gloucester House, Chichester Street, Belfast, BT1 4RA; tel +44 28 9025 2225; fax +44 28 9025 2288; e-mail siobhan.burns@delni .gsi.gov.uk; *languages spoken:* English.

Alison Carmichael: *organization:* Jobcentre Plus; *address:* 11-13 South Saint Andrew Street, Edinburgh, EH2 2BT; tel +44 131 456 3359; fax +44 131 456 3325; e-mail Alison.Carmichael@ jobcentreplus.gsi.gov.uk; *languages spoken:* Français, English, Castellano.

Les Ford: *organization:* TUC, Trade Unions Congress; *address:* Flat 1, 3 Lewis Road, Eastbourne, BN21 2BY; tel +44 1323 737 317; fax +44 1323 732 204; e-mail lford@tgwu.org.uk; *languages spoken:* Français, English.

Helen Giles: *organization:* Jobcentre Plus; *address:* The Pithay, Bristol, BS1 2NQ; tel +44 117 945 6767; fax +44 117 945 6960; e-mail helen.giles1@ jobcentreplus.gsi.gov.uk; *languages spoken:* Français, English, Italiano, Deutsch.

Jomo Ladepon-Thomas: *organization:* Jobcentre Plus; *address:* Snowden House, Meridian Gate, 223 Marsh Wall, London, E14 9PG; tel +44 20 7506 4019; fax +44 20 7506 4001; e-mail jomo.ladepon-thomas@ jobcentreplus.gsi.gov.uk; *languages spoken:* Français, English.

Karen Lambert: *organization:* Jobcentre Plus; *address:* Newtown House 7th floor, Maid Marion Way, Nottingham, NGI 6GG; tel +44 115 9895792; fax +44 115 9895706; e-mail karen.lambert@ jobcentreplus.gsi.gov.uk; *languages spoken:* Français, English.

Lorraine Morris: *organization:* Jobcentre Plus; *address:* 2 Duchesse Place, Hagley Road, Birmingham, B16 8NS; tel +44 121 452 5410; fax +44 121 452 5507; e-mail lorraine.morris1@jobcentreplus .gsi.gov.uk; *languages spoken:* Français, English.

Kevin Oakes: *organization:* Northern Ireland/Ireland (IE-UK), ICTU, Irish Congress of Trade Unions; *address:* 45-47 Donegal Street, Belfast, BT1 2FG; tel +44 28 90 96 11 11; fax +44 28 90 96 11 10; e-mail kevin.oakes@burc.org; *languages spoken:* English.

Jane Osborne: *organization:* Jobcentre Plus; *address:* 1 Barnbury Road, Islington, London, N1 0EX; tel +44 20 7301 5219; fax +44 20 7301 3885; e-mail jane .osborne1@jobcentreplus.gsi.gov.uk; *languages spoken:* English, Castellano.

Susan Oyston: *organization:* Jobcentre Plus; *address:* Kent House, Station Road, Ashford, TN23 1YS; tel +44 1233 203 356; fax +44 1233 203 309; e-mail susan .oyston@jobcentreplus.gsi.gov.uk; *languages spoken:* English.

Anne-Marie Pickles: *organization:* Jobcentre Plus; *address:* Whitehall II, Whitehall Quay, Leeds, LS1 4HR; tel +44 113 307 8094; fax +44 113 307 8213; e-mail anne-marie.pickles@jobcentreplus.gsi .gov.uk; *languages spoken:* Français, English.

Brian Renville: *organization:* Jobcentre Plus; *address:* Phoenix Building, 32 West Street, Brighton, BN1 2RZ; tel +44 1273 366031; fax +44 1273 366190; e-mail brian.renville@jobcentreplus.gsi.gov.uk; *languages spoken:* Français, English.

Naomi Sinharay: *organization:* Jobcentre Plus; *address:* Companies House, Crown Way, Maindy, Cardiff, CF14 3UW; tel +44 292 038 0781; fax +44 292 034 3944; e-mail naomi.sinharay@ jobcentreplus.gsi.gov.uk; *languages spoken:* Français, English, Deutsch.

Jose Vigo: *organization:* Jobcentre Plus; *address:* 3 Denmark Street, London, WC2H 8LR; tel +44 20 7853 3219; fax +44 20 7853 3235; e-mail jose.vigo@ jobcentreplus.gsi.gov.uk; *languages spoken:* Français, English, Castellano.

Nicola Whatmuff: *organization:* Jobcentre Plus; *address:* Whitehall II, Whitehall Quay, Leeds, LS1 4HR; tel +44 113 307 8098; fax +44 113 307 8213; e-mail nicola.whatmuff@jobcentreplus.gsi.gov .uk; *languages spoken:* Français, English.

Paul Whittle: *organization:* Jobcentre Plus; *address:* Whitehall II, Whitehall Quay, Leeds, LS1 4HR; tel +44 113 307 8096; fax +44 113 307 8213; e-mail paul .whittle@jobcentreplus.gsi.gov.uk; *languages spoken:* English, Deutsch.

EUROPEAN OBSERVATORY ON THE SOCIAL SITUATION, DEMOGRAPHY AND FAMILY

The European Observatory on the Social Situation, Demography and Family is a multi-disciplinary network of independent experts established upon the request of the European Commission. As its main tasks, the Observatory:

- monitors political developments in Europe which have an impact on the social situation, demography and family;
- analyses political activities and the impact of family policies;
- monitors demographic, socio-economic and political changes which have an impact on families;
- stimulates academic debate on social, demographic and family issues as well as on related policies;
- organizes annual seminars of the Observatory experts and invited speakers for a specialized audience;
- organizes two closed meetings per year for the Observatory members.

The European Observatory has established a network of 15 National Experts from various EU Member States. These National Experts monitor and report on developments regarding the social situation, demography and family in the light of the Observatory's annual research focus. The monitoring reports are published on the Observatory's website.

The European Observatory on the Social Situation, Demography and Family was established by European Commission in 1989, on the basis of the conclusions of the Council of Ministers responsible for Family Affairs meeting within the Council on 29 September 1989 as well as on the basis of Communication COM(89) 363 final on Family Policies adopted by the Commission.

The Austrian Institute for Family Studies (ÖIF) in Vienna (Austria) has co-ordinated the Observatory since 1998. It is headed by Brigitte Cizek, Managing Director of the ÖIF, who also chairs the ÖIF-based Co-ordination Team. The Observatory work is documented on its website. Every other month, the Observatory publishes *sdf-puzzle*, an electronic newsletter offering scientific contributions on selected key topics. Information on conferences, other events and topical family issues is circulated via the fortnightly newsletter *puzzleweise*. To order the newsletters *sdf-puzzle* and *puzzleweise* write to puzzle@oif.ac.at.

Co-ordination Team

Head of the Co-ordination Team, and Contact for Psychology: Brigitte Cizek, Austrian Institute for Family Studies, Gonzagagasse 19/8, 1010 Vienna, Austria; e-mail brigitte.cizek@oif.ac.at.

Management and Organization: Sylvia Trnka, Austrian Institute for Family Studies, Gonzagagasse 19/8, 1010 Vienna, Austria; e-mail sylvia.trnka@oif.ac.at.

Public Relations: Rudolf Karl Schipfer, Austrian Institute for Family Studies, Gonzagagasse 19/8, 1010 Vienna, Austria; e-mail rudolf.schipfer@oif.ac.at.

Demography: Wolfgang Lutz, IIASA, Schlossplatz 1, 2361 Laxenburg, Austria; e-mail lutz@iiasa.ac.at.

Sociology: Christiane Rille-Pfeiffer, Austrian Institute for Family Studies, Gonzagagasse 19/8, 1010 Vienna, Austria; e-mail christiane.rille-pfeiffer@oif.ac.at.

Sociology and Migration: Johannes Pflegerl, Austrian Institute for Family Studies, Gonzagagasse 19/8, 1010 Vienna, Austria; e-mail johannes.pflegerl@oif.ac.at.

Sociology: Rudolf Richter, University of Vienna, Institute for Sociology, Rooseveltplatz 2, 1090 Vienna, Austria; e-mail rudolf.richter@univie.ac.at.

Members of the Team

AUSTRIA

Rudolf Richter: University of Vienna, Institute for Sociology, Rooseveltplatz 2, 1090 Vienna; e-mail rudolf.richter@univie.ac.at.

BELGIUM

Wilfried Dumon: Katholieke Universiteit Leuven, Faculteit Sociale Wetenschappen, Département Sociologie, E. van Evenstraat 2B, 3000 Leuven; tel (+32) 16-323188; fax (+32) 16-323365; e-mail wilfried.dumon@soc.kuleuven.ac.be.

DENMARK

Jens Bonke: Social Forsknings Instituttet, Herluf Trolles Gade 11, 1052 København K; tel (+45) 33-48-08-86; fax (+45) 33-48-08-33; e-mail jeb@sfi.dk.

FINLAND

Sirpa Taskinen: National Research Centre for Welfare and Health, Siltasaarenkatu 18, PO Box 220, 00531 Helsinki; tel (+358 9) 39672148; fax (+358 9) 39672201; e-mail sirpa.taskinen@stakes.fi.

FRANCE

Claude Martin: CNRS, Centre de recherches administratives et politiques, Institut d'études politiques de Rennes, 104 bld de la Duchesse Anne, 35700 Rennes; tel (+33) 2-99-02-28-38; fax (+33) 2-99-02-28-66; e-mail cmartin@ensp.fr.

GERMANY

Walter Bien: Deutsches Jugendinstitut e.V., Sozialberichterstattung, Nockherstrasse 2, 81541 München; tel (+49 89) 62306234; fax (+49 89) 62306162; e-mail bien@dji.de.

GREECE

Christos Bagavos: Panteion University, Department of Social Policy and Social Anthropology, Leof. Syngrou 136, 176 71 Athens; tel (+30) 210-9201036; fax (+30) 210-9238290; e-mail bagavos@panteion.gr.

IRELAND

Valerie Richardson: University College Dublin, Department of Social Policy & Social Work, Belfield Campus, Dublin 4; e-mail valerie.richardson@ucd.ie.

ITALY

Giovanni B. Sgritta: Universita degli Studi di Roma La Sapienza, Dipartimento di Scienze Demografiche, Via Nomentana 41, 00161 Roma; tel (+39) 06-49919550; fax (+39) 06-85303374; e-mail sgritta@uniroma1.it.

LUXEMBOURG

Monique Borsenberger: CEPS – INSTEAD, Bâtiment Administratif ARBED, 44 rue Emile Mark, 4501 Differdange; tel (+352) 585855528; fax (+352) 585588; e-mail monique.borsenberger@ceps.lu.

NETHERLANDS

Hans-Joachim Schulze: Vrije Universiteit, Faculteit der Psychologie en Pedagogiek, Van der Boechorststraat 1, 1081 BT Amsterdam; tel (+31 20) 4448884; fax (+31 20) 4448745; e-mail hj.schulze@psy.vu.nl.

PORTUGAL

Karin Elisabeth Wall: Universidade de Lisboa, Instituto de Ciências Sociais, Av. das Forças Armadas, 1600 Lisbon; tel (+351 21) 7995048; fax (+351 21) 7964953; e-mail karin.wall@ics.ul.pt.

SPAIN

Juan Antonio Fernández Cordón: Instituto de Estadística de Andalucía, Pabellón de Nueva Zelanda, C/ Leonardo da Vinci s/n, Isla de la Cartuja, 41092 Seville; e-mail jantonio.fernandez.cordon@juntadeandalucia.es.

SWEDEN

Eva Bernhardt: Stockholm University Demography Unit, Center for Women's Research, 10691 Stockholm; e-mail eva.bernhardt@sociology.su.se.

UNITED KINGDOM

Ceridwen Roberts: , C/o 96 North Road, London, N6 4AA; e-mail ceridwen.roberts@btopenworld.com.

INNOVATION RELAY CENTRES

The Network of European Innovation Relay Centres (IRC) aims to promote innovation by bringing research and technology closer to European companies, especially small and medium-sized enterprises (SMEs), and to encourage the participation of research centres and universities in Community RTD programmes.

Created under the Third Activity ('The Innovation Programme') of the Fourth Community Framework Programme (1994–1998) in the field of research and technological development and demonstration, a prime objective of the IRCs is to promote the transfer of research results and technologies to regional environments which have identified both a demand and a capacity for the absorption of new technologies. The ultimate goal is to improve the competitiveness of European industry through innovation.

The Network consists of 71 regional Innovation Relay Centres in the Member States, Bulgaria, Chile, Iceland, Israel, Norway, Romania, Switzerland and Turkey. Most of the Relay Centres are consortia of organizations and nearly 220 partner organizations are involved.

Innovation Relay Centre Network members are signatories to a contract with the Commission, which covers their rights and obligations regarding their activities in the network. All the centres undertake to respect a code of ethics which lays down the principles of their relations with the Commission, between themselves as network members, and especially with their clients – principles such as confidentiality, independence and impartiality are naturally safeguarded.

The Innovation Relay Centres are coordinated by the Commission Services in Brussels and Luxembourg (DG Enterprise). For more information, visit the website www.cordis.lu or contact:

IRC Secretariat (Innovation Relay Centres): 2b rue Nicolas Bové, 1253 Luxembourg, Luxembourg; (+352) 441012-2200; fax (+352) 441012-2055.

Promotion of Entrepreneurship and SMEs: European Commission, Unit B5 – Innovation Networks, Rue de la Loi 200, 1049 Brussels, Belgium; Head of Unit Renate Weissenhorn.

Promotion of Entrepreneurship and SMEs: European Commission, Unit B5 – Innovation Networks, Euroforum, Office 2270, Rue Alcide de Gasperi, 2920 Luxembourg, Luxembourg; Project Officer Michael Busch.

Regional Innovation Relay Centres

AUSTRIA

IRC Austria: Bureau for International Research & Technology Cooperation (BIT), Donau City Strasse 1, 1220 Wien; tel (+43 5) 7755 4701; fax (+43 5) 7755 4099; e-mail kurt.burtscher@ffg.at; internet www.irca.at; contact Kurt Burtscher.

BELGIUM

BIRC for Europe: ABE: The Brussels Enterprise Agency, Rue Gabrielle Petit 4 Bte 12, 1080 Bruxelles; tel (+32 2) 422 00 21; fax (+32 2) 422 00 43; e-mail ban@bea.irisnet.be; internet www.abe.irisnet.be; contact Jacques Evrard.

IRC Flanders: IWT – Instituut voor de Aanmoediging van Innovatie door Wetenschap en Technologie in Vlaanderen, Bischoffsheimlaan 25, 1000 Bruxelles; tel (+32 2) 209 09 39; fax (+32 2) 223 11 81; e-mail irc@iwt.be; internet www.iwt.be/irc; contact Tania De Roeck.

IRC for Wallonia: DGTRE – Direction Générale des Technologies, de la Recherche et de l'Energie, Ministère de la Région Wallonne, DGTRE-CRIW, Avenue Prince de Liège 7, 5100 Jambes (Namur); tel (+32 81) 33 55 50; fax (+32 81) 30 66 00; e-mail jc.disneur@mrw.wallonie.be; internet http://mrw.wallonie.be/dgtre/CRIW.htm; contact Jean-Claude Disneur.

BULGARIA

IRC Bulgaria: Applied Research and Communications Fund (ARC Fund), 5 Alexander Zhendov Str., 1113 Sofia; tel (+359 2) 986 7557; fax (+359 2) 980 1833; e-mail angel.milev@online.bg; internet www.irc.bg; contact Angel Milev.

CHILE

IRC Chile: Fundacion Empresarial Comunidad Europea – Chile, Hernando de Aguirre 1549, Providencia, 650926 Santiago; tel (+56 2) 7878 420; fax (+56 2) 2741 511; e-mail gfacino@eurochile.cl; internet www.eurochile.cl; contact Giuseppe Facino.

CYPRUS

IRC Cyprus: Cyprus Institute of Technology (CIT), PO Box 20783, Ionion Nison 1, 7th floor, 1663 Lefkosia; tel (+357 2) 813 114; fax (+357 2) 317 333; e-mail think@cy.net; internet www.technology.org.cy; contact Costas Konis.

CZECH REPUBLIC

IRC Czech Republic: Technology Centre AS CR, Rozvojova 135, 16502 Prague, 6; tel (+420 2) 203 90 700; fax (+420 2) 209 22 698; e-mail klusacek@tc.cas.cz; internet www.tc.cas.cz; contact Eva Kudrnova.

DENMARK

IRC Denmark: EuroCenter – Ministry for Science, Technology and Innovation, c/o Teknologisk Institut, Indgang 8 Gregersensvej, Postboks 141, 2630 Taastrup; tel (+45) 7220 2964; fax (+45) 7220 2979; e-mail pej@eurocenter.info; internet www.eurocenter.info; contact Peter Ole Jensen.

ESTONIA

IRC Estonia: Tartu Science Park Foundation, Riia 185, 51014 Tartu; tel (+372 7) 383005; fax (+372 7) 383041; e-mail rene@ibs.ee; internet www.park.tartu.ee; contact Rene Tonnisson.

FINLAND

IRC Finland: Tekes – The National Technology Agency, Kyllikinportti 2, PO Box 69, 00101 Lansi-Pasila Helsinki; tel (+358 10) 521 5732; fax (+358 10) 521 5908; e-mail hannu.juuso@tekes.fi; internet www.tekes.fi/eng/co-operation/europe/irc.html; contact Hannu Juuso.

FRANCE

Centr'Atlantic: Bretagne Innovation, Place de la Gare 18, CS 26927, 35069 Rennes; tel (+33 2) 99 67 42 00; fax (+33 2) 99 67 60 22; e-mail cri@bretagne-innovation.tm.fr; internet http://cri.bretagne-innovation.tm.fr; contact Helene Morvan.

IRC Grand-Est: Chambre Régionale de Commerce et d'Industrie de Bourgogne, Parc de l'Europe, Place des Nations-Unies, BP 87009, 21070 Dijon; tel (+33

3) 80 60 40 95; fax (+33 3) 80 60 40 23; e-mail l.volle@bourgogne.cci.fr; internet www.euro-innovation.org; contact Laurent Volle.

IRC MedIN (French Mediterranean): Méditerranée Technologies, Les Docks Atrium 10.2, Place de la Joliette 10, 13002 Marseille; tel (+33 4) 88 66 01 00; fax (+33 4) 88 66 01 01; e-mail irc@ mediterranee-technologies.com; internet www.mediterranee-technologies.com/cri; contact Nicolas Chehanne.

IRC Paris–Ile-de-France: Chambre de Commerce et d'Industrie de Paris, Rue de Viarmes 2, 75040 Paris Cedex 01; tel (+33 1) 55 65 35 71; fax (+33 1) 55 65 39 84; e-mail cri@ccip.fr; internet www.irc -paris-idf.net; contact Gilles Wurmser.

IRC SOFRAA: Chambre Régionale de Commerce et d'Industrie de Rhône-Alpes, Cours Albert Thomas 75, 69447 Lyon Cedex 03; tel (+33 4) 72 11 43 21; fax (+33 4) 72 11 43 23; e-mail marino@ rhone-alpes.cci.fr; internet www.arist .rhone-alpes.cci.fr; contact Sylvie Marino.

IRC South West France: Agence Nationale de Valorisation de la Recherche – Aquitaine, 44 rue du General de Larminat, BB77, 33035 Bordeaux; tel (+33 5) 57 01 65 55; fax (+33 5) 57 01 65 59; e-mail cdubarry@anvar.fr; internet www.cri-sud -ouest.net; contact Christian Dubarry.

GERMANY

IRC Bavaria: Bayern Innovativ Gesellschaft für Innovations- und Wissenstransfer mbH, Gewerbemuseumplatz 2, 90403 Nürnberg; tel (+49 911) 20671-310; fax (+49 911) 20671-722; e-mail eu@bayern-innovativ.de; internet www.irc-bavaria.de; contact Karl-Heinz Hanne.

IRC Hessen/Rhineland-Pfalz: TechnologieStiftung Hessen GmbH, Abraham-Lincoln-Str. 38-42, 65189 Wiesbaden; tel (+49 611) 774 633; fax (+49 611) 774 620; e-mail albert@tsh-hessen.de; internet www.irc-hessen.de; contact Kathrin Albert.

IRC Lower Saxony/Saxony-Anhalt: Investitions-und-Foerderbank Niedersachsen GmbH (NBANK), Guenther-Wagner-Allee 12-14, 30177 Hannover; tel (+49 511) 30031 360; fax (+49 511) 30031 11 360; e-mail stefan.austermann@ nbank.de; internet www.irc-innsa.de; contact Stefan Austermann.

IRC North Rhine-Westphalia/Malta: Zentrum für Innovation & Technik in Nordrhein-Westfalen GmbH, Bismarckstrasse 28, PO Box 102264, 45470 Muelheim; tel (+49 208) 3000 431; fax (+49 208) 3000 461; e-mail wo@www.zenit.de; internet www.zenit.de; contact Peter Wolfmeyer.

IRC Northern Germany: VDI/VDE – Innovation + Technik GmbH, Rheinstr. 10 B, 14513 Teltow – Berlin; tel (+49 3328) 435 173; fax (+49 3328) 435 216; e-mail irc@vdivde-it.de; internet www .irc-norddeutschland.de; contact Thomas Koehler.

IRC Saxony: Agentur fuer Innovationsfoerderung & Technologietransfer GmbH Leipzig, Chamber of Commerce, Goerdelerring 5, 04109 Leipzig; tel (+49 341) 1267 1469; fax (+49 341) 1267 1464; e-mail drbilling@irc-sachsen.de; internet www.irc-sachsen.de; contact Ronald Billing.

IRC Stuttgart-Efurt-Zuerich: Steinbeis-Europa-Zentrum der Steinbeis Stiftung für Wirtschaftsförderung, Haus der Wirtschaft Willi-Bleicher-Str. 19, 70174 Stuttgart; tel (+49 711) 123 4018; fax (+49 711) 123 4011; e-mail puechner@ steinbeis-europa.de; internet www .steinbeis-europa.de; contact Petra Puechner.

GREECE

IRC Hellenic: National Documentation Centre, Hellenic Innovation Relay Centre, Vas. Konstantinou Ave. 48, 11635 Athens; tel (+30 210) 727 39 21; fax (+30 210) 724 68 24; e-mail akarah@ ekt.gr; internet www.hirc.gr; contact George Aargyro Karahaliou.

IRC Help-Forward: Help-Forward Network (PRAXI), Zalokosta 4, 10671 Athens; tel (+30 210) 36 07 690; fax (+30 210) 36 36 109; e-mail vtsak@help -forward.gr; internet www.help-forward .gr; contact Vassilios Tsakalos.

HUNGARY

IRC Hungary: Budapest University of Technology and Economics, National Technical Information Centre and Library, OMIKK, Gyorskocsi utca 5-7, 1011 Budapest; tel (+36 1) 457 5365; fax (+36 1) 457 5341; e-mail nyerges@info .omikk.bme.hu; internet http://irc.info .omikk.bme.hu; contact Gyula Nyerges.

IRELAND

IRC Republic of Ireland: Enterprise Ireland, Old Finglas Road, Glasnevin, Dublin 9; tel (+353 1) 808 23 05; fax (+353 1) 808 23 76; e-mail irc@enterprise -ireland.com; internet www.irc-ireland .ie; contact Kevin Burke.

ISRAEL

IRC Israel: MATIMOP – The Israeli Industry Center for R&D, Hamered St 29, POB 50364, 61500 Tel-Aviv; tel

(+972 3) 517 5905; fax (+972 3) 517 7655; e-mail sterna@matimop.org.il; internet www.irc.org.il; contact Aaron Stern.

ITALY

ALPS IRC: Camera di Commercio Industria Artigianato e Agricoltura di Torino, Via San Francesco da Paola 24, 10123 Torino; tel (+39 011) 5716 320; fax (+39 011) 5716 324; e-mail alps@to .camcom.it; contact Marco Mangiantini.

IRC CIRCE: Consiglio Nazionale delle Ricerche – DAST – Servizio IV, Piazzale Aldo Moro 7, 00185 Roma; tel (+39 06) 49 93 25 38; fax (+39 06) 49 93 25 84; e-mail circe@dcas.cnr.it; internet http://circe .dcas.cnr.it; contact Sara Di Marcello.

IRC IRENE: Ente per le Nuove Tecnologie, l'Energia e l'Ambiente, ENEA – IRC IRENE, Via Don Fiammelli 2, 40129 Bologna; tel (+39 051) 609 8 321; fax (+39 051) 609 8 084; e-mail irene@ bologna.enea.it; internet www.irc-irene .org; contact Diego Santi.

IRC IRIDE: Tecnopolis Csata Novus Ortus s.c.r.l., Parco Scientifico Tecnopolis Novus Ortus, S.P. per Casamassima Km3, 70010 Valenzano (Bari); tel (+39 080) 467 02 38; fax (+39 080) 467 03 61; e-mail www.centroirideit; internet www .centroiride.it; contact Adriana Agrimi.

IRC Lombardia: CESTEC Spa – Centro Lombardo per lo Sviluppo Tecnologico e Produttivo dell'Artig, Via G.Fara 35, 20124 Milano; tel (+39 02) 6673 7307; fax (+39 02) 6693 147; e-mail dominoni@ cestec.it; internet www.cestec.it; contact Guido Dominoni.

IRC MED.I.A.: Consorzio Catania Ricerche, Piazza Falcone 12, 95131 Catania; tel (+39 095) 535606; fax (+39 095) 313763; e-mail media@mediainnovation .it; internet www.mediainnovation.it; contact Francesco Cappello.

IRC RECITAL: Consorzio Pisa Ricerche, Piazza Alessandro d'Ancona 1, 56127 Pisa; tel (+39 050) 97 23 11; fax (+39 050) 54 00 56; e-mail recital@cpr.it; internet www.recital.it; contact Cinzia Giachetti.

LATVIA

IRC Latvia: Latvian Technological Center, Aizkraukles 21, 1006 Riga; tel (+371) 754 0703; fax (+371) 754 0709; e-mail irc@edi.lv; internet www.innovation.lv/ irc; contact Gundega Lapina.

LITHUANIA

IRC Lithuania: Lithuanian Innovation Centre, T. Sevcenkos 13, 2600 Vilnius; tel (+370 5) 235 6116; fax (+370 2) 213 2781;

e-mail ircLT@ktl.mii.lt; internet www
.lic.lt; contact Kastytis Gecas.

LUXEMBOURG

IRC Luxembourg-Trier-Saar-brucken: Luxinnovation GIE, Agence
nationale pour la promotion de l'innova-
tion et de la recherche, 7 rue Alcide de
Gasperi Kirchberg, 1615 Luxembourg;
tel (+352) 436263-671; fax (+352)
438120; e-mail bertrand.dessart@
luxinnovation.lu; internet www
.luxinnovation.lu; contact Bertrand
Dessart.

NETHERLANDS

IRC NL: SenterNovem, Juliana van Stol-
berglaan 3, Postbus 93144, 2509 AC Den
Haag; tel (+31 70) 373 5 263; fax (+31 70)
373 51 00; e-mail irc@senternovem.nl;
internet www.ircnederland.nl; contact
Giel Dubbeld.

NORWAY

IRC Norway: SINTEF Industrial Management, S.P. Andersens vei 5, 7465
Trondheim; tel (+47) 73 59 25 96; fax
(+47) 73 59 12 99; e-mail hans.j.flor@
sintef.no; internet www.sintef.no; contact
Hans Jorgen Flor.

POLAND

IRC Central Poland: OPI – Information
Processing Center, Orodek Przetwarza-
nia Informacji, Niepodleglosci 188 B,
00608 Warsaw; tel (+48 22) 825 12 48;
fax (+48 22) 825 12 48; e-mail irc@opi
.org.pl; internet www.irc-centralpoland
.org.pl; contact Robert Podgorzak.

IRC North-East Poland: Warsaw University, Krakowskie Przedmiescie 26/28,
00927 Warsaw; tel (+48 22) 55 40 730; fax
(+48 22) 55 40 730; e-mail uott@uott.uw
.edu.pl; internet www.uw.edu.pl; contact
Tomasz Cichocki.

IRC South Poland: Cracow University
of Technology, Warszawska 24, 31155
Krakow; tel (+48 12) 628 2845; fax (+48
12) 632 47 95; e-mail ircpk@transfer.edu
.pl; internet www.transfer.edu.pl; contact
Tomasz Maczuga.

IRC West Poland: Wroclaw Centre for
Technology Transfer, ul. Smoluchows-
kiego 48, 50372 Wroclaw; tel (+48 71)
320 39 12; fax (+48 71) 320 39 48;
e-mail g.gromada@wctt.pl; internet www
.wctt.pl; contact Grzegorz Gromada.

PORTUGAL

IRC Portugal (CPI): Agencia de Inovacao S.A., Edf. IDIT Rua do IDIT Espargo,
4520-102 Santa Maria da Feira; tel (+351
256) 330820; fax (+351 256) 332 891;
e-mail bdantas@adi.pt; internet www
.Port-inova.com; contact Bibiana Dantas.

ROMANIA

Romanian IRC 4D: Asocciatia Romana
Pentru Industria Electronica Si Software, 1 Serbota, tel (+4021) 22 49 354;
fax (+4021) 22 48 276; e-mail borcea@
aries.ro; internet www.aries.ro; contact
Alexandru Silviu Borcea.

IRC Romania: The Foundation Romanian Center for Small and Medium Sized
Enterprise, Ion Campineanu 20 – et. 3
sector 1, 70709 Bucharest; tel (+40 21)
311 995/6; fax (+40 1) 312 69 66; e-mail
ltachiciu@imm.ro; internet www.imm.ro;
contact Laurentiu Tachiciu.

SLOVAKIA

IRC Slovakia: BIC Bratislava, Zochova
5, 81103 Bratislava; tel (+421 2) 5441
7515; fax (+421 2) 5441 7522; e-mail
vratny@bicba.sk; internet www.bicba.sk;
contact Stefan Vratny.

SLOVENIA

IRC Slovenia: Josef Stefan Institute,
Jamova 39, 1001 Ljubljana; tel (+386 1)
477 3311; fax (+386 1) 251 9385; e-mail
miroslav.gregoic@ijs.si; internet www
.irc.si; contact Miroslav Gregoric.

SPAIN

IRC Catalonia: Centre d'Innovacio i
Desenvolupament Empresarial, Passeig
de Gracia 129, 08008 Barcelona; tel (+34
93) 567 48 87; fax (+34 93) 476 72 14;
e-mail irc@cidem.gencat.es; internet
www.cidem.com/irc; contact Monica
Duran.

**IRC CENEMES – East and South-
East Spain:** Universidad de Alicante –
OTRI, Campus Universitario de San
Vicente del Raspeig, Edificio German
Bernacer, Ctra de Alicante s/n, 03080
Alicante; tel (+34 965) 903 488; fax (+34
965) 903 803; e-mail cenemes@ua.es;
internet www.cenemes.es; contact
Penhataro Chelo.

IRC CENEO: Instituto Tecnologico de
Aragon, C/ Maria de Luna 7-8, Poligono
Actur, 50018 Zaragoza; tel (+34 976) 71
62 94; fax (+34 976) 71 62 98; e-mail
cgomez@ita.es; internet www.ita.es; contact Ignacio Hernandez.

IRC Galactea: Fundacion para el
Fomento en Asturias de la Investigacion
Cientifica Aplicada y la Tecnologia, C/
Cabo Noval 11, 1C, 33007 Oviedo; tel
(+34 985) 207 434; fax (+34 985) 207
433; e-mail galactea@ficyt.es; internet
www.ficyt.com; contact Suarez Elena.

IRC Madrid: Fundacion para el Conoci-
miento Madrid, C/ Velazquez no 76 Bajo
Izquierda, 28001 Madrid; tel (+34 91) 781
6577; fax (+34 91) 576 6052; e-mail
meugeniagarces@madrimasd.org; internet www.madrimasd.org; contact Arturo
Menendez Abella.

IRC Southern Europe: Instituto de
Fomento de Andalucía, Torneo 26,
41002 Sevilla; tel (+34 95) 503 07 00;
fax (+34 95) 503 07 75; e-mail aramirez@
ceseand.cica.es; internet www.ceseand
.cica.es; contact Antonio Ramirez Mejias.

IRC-SPRI/Basque IRC: Sociedad para
la Promocion y Reconversion Industrial,
S.A. – SPRI, C/ Gran Via 35-3, 48009
Bilbao; tel (+34 94) 403 70 34; fax (+34
94) 403 70 22; e-mail jgabilondo@spri.es;
internet www.spri.es; contact Javier
Gabilondo.

SWEDEN

IRC Anatolia: ODTU Teknokent (Middle East University Technopolis), Odtu
Teknokent (Metu-Technopolis) Idari
Bina Ankara, 06531 Ankara; tel (+903)
122 106 400; fax (+903) 122 106 104;
e-mail ugur.yuksel@metutech.metu.edu
.tr; internet www.metutech.metu.edu.tr;
contact Ugur Yuksel.

IRC Central Sweden: Acreo AB,
Electrum 236, Isafjordsgatan 22, 16440
Kista; tel (+46 8) 632 77 73; fax (+46 8)
750 54 30; e-mail stellan.granstrom@
acreo.se; internet www.acreo.se; contact
Stellan Granström.

IRC-EGE: Ege Universitesi Bilim-
Teknoloji Uygulama ve Arastirma, Bornova, 35100 Izmir; tel (+90) 533 480 2973;
fax (+90) 232 374 4289; e-mail ircege@
ebiltem.ege.edu.tr; internet http://irc.ege
.edu.tr; contact Cagdas Sungur.

IRC Northern Sweden: Stiftelsen
CENTEK, Centrum for Teknologibaserad
Affarsutveckling vid Lulea, Tekniktorget
4, 97187 Lulea; tel (+46 920) 49 11 98;
fax (+46 920) 990 20; e-mail monika
.brynefall@centek.se; internet www
.centek.se; contact Monika Brynefall.

**IRC Western and Southern Sweden/
Iceland:** IVF Industrial Research and
Development Corporation, Argongatan
30, 43153 Mölndal – Göteborg; tel (+46
31) 706 60 00; fax (+46 31) 27 61 30;
e-mail max.maupoix@ivf.se; internet
http://extra.ivf.se/irc/; contact Max
Maupoix.

UNITED KINGDOM

EEIRC: St John's Innovation Centre Ltd, Cowley Road, Cambridge, CB4 0WS; tel (+44 1223) 42 11 17; fax (+44 1223) 42 08 44; e-mail relaycentre@stjohns.co.uk; internet www.innovation-east.co.uk; contact Andrew Goldsbrough.

SWIRC: South West of England Regional Development Agency, 4th floor, 100 Temple Street, Bristol, BS1 6EA; tel (+44 117) 933 0277; fax (+44 117) 933 0240; e-mail swirc@southwestrda.org.uk; internet www.southwest-irc.org.uk; contact Chris Pinnell.

IRC North-Nord Manche: RTC North Ltd, 1 Hylton Park, Wessington Way, Sunderland, SR5 3HD; tel (+44 191) 516 44 00; fax (+44 191) 516 44 01; e-mail mikel.echevarria@rtcnorth.co.uk; internet www.rtcnorth.co.uk; contact Mikel Echevarria.

IRCINVESTNI: Invest NI, 17 Antrim Road, Lisburn, BT28 3AL; tel (+44 28) 9262 3181; fax (+44 28) 9049 0490; e-mail irc@investni.com; internet www.investni.com/irc; contact Marshall Addidle.

IRC Scotland: Targeting Innovation, Third Floor, Atrium Court, 50 Waterloo Street, Glasgow, G2 6HQ; tel (+44 141) 572 1609; fax (+44 141) 572 1608; e-mail caroline@targetinginnovation.com; internet www.ircscotland.net; contact Caroline Gray-Stephens.

London IRC: London Technology Network, 17 Linhope Street, London, NW1 6HT; tel (+44 870) 765 7602; fax (+44 870) 765 7606; e-mail z.bowers@ltnetwork.org; internet www.london-irc.org; contact Zoe Bowers.

MIRC: Coventry University Enterprises Ltd, The Technocentre, Puma Way, Coventry, CV1 2TT; tel (+44 24) 7623 6236; fax (+44 24) 7623 6024; e-mail mirc@coventry.ac.uk; internet www.mirc.org.uk; contact Steve Shorthouse.

SEEIRC: Technology Enterprise Kent Ltd, Research and Development Building, University of Kent, Canterbury, Kent, CT2 7PD; tel (+44 1227) 824 308; fax (+44 1227) 763 424; e-mail john.miller@technologyenterprise.co.uk; internet www.technologyenterprise.co.uk; contact John Miller.

WIRC: Welsh Development Agency, Plas Glyndwr, Kingsway, Cardiff, CF10 3AH; tel (+44 29) 20 82 87 39; fax (+44 29) 20 82 82 29; e-mail walesrelay@wda.co.uk; internet www.walesrelay.co.uk; contact Sandra Lopes.

NETWORK OF URBAN FORUMS FOR SUSTAINABLE DEVELOPMENT (NUFSD)

The purpose of this European Commission experiment, started by the former DG X and DG XI, is to investigate how information about European Union policy can contribute to the sustainable development of cities. An urban forum for sustainable development has been set up in some twenty cities and the forums act as relays, obtaining information directly from the European Commission, tailoring it to the needs of their particular city and passing it on to the operators and individuals with whom they are in contact.

The Network has three main objectives:

- to facilitate communication between citizens and the EU by exchanging information between different levels of society;
- to network and learn from Forum members by sharing lessons learned through practical projects in each city involved;
- to help to change behaviour and to encourage action within each of our societies by assessing the sustainable development issues in each city; raising awareness and fostering debate on sustainable development; increasing public participation; and influencing planning processes.

The Network carries out the following activities to help meet its objectives:

- development and implementation of joint projects with the EU, as well as involvement in local projects;
- information exchange through the Internet, printed media, meetings and other means in order to share best practice and ideas;
- co-operation in the formulation and implementation of policies (EU, national, regional and local) aimed at improving the urban environment;
- organization of events and conferences to provide a platform for parties with an interest in the environment and sustainable development to share experiences and discuss and debate current European issues.

NUFSD Secretariat: ERM, 8 Cavendish Square, London, W1G 0ER, United Kingdom; tel (+44 20) 7465-7375; fax (+44 20) 7465-7350; e-mail environetworks_ secretariat@erm.com; internet www .europa.eu.int/comm/environment/ networks/nufsd/index_en.htm.

A further useful link is the European Environment Agency, whose website can be found at http://eea.eu.int.

Participants involved in the Experiment

AUSTRIA

Die Umweltberatung: Ada Christengasse 2/B/11, 1100 Vienna; tel (+43 1) 9113552-11; fax (+43 1) 9113552-22; e-mail gerhard.jungert@umweltberatung .at; internet www.umweltberatung.at; contact Gerhard Jungert.

BELGIUM

Espace Environnement: Rue de Montigny 29, 6000 Charleroi; tel (+32) 71-300300; fax (+32) 71-509678; e-mail info@espace-environnement.be; internet www.espace-environnement.be; contact Gilles Meeus.

Provinciaal Instituut voor Milieu Educatie (PIME): Mechelsesteenweg 365, 2500 Lier; tel (+32) 15-319511; fax (+32) 15-315880; e-mail gike.neels@pime .provant.be; internet www.pime.be; contact Gike Neels.

CYPRUS

Strovolos Municipality: Town Clerk, 100 Strovolos Ave, PO Box 28403, 2094 Strovolos; e-mail gtsiakkas@strovolos .org.cy; contact Georgios Tsiakkas.

DENMARK

Aalborg & North of Denmark EU Office: Aalborg Local Authority, Boulevarden 13, 9000 Aalborg; tel (+45) 99-31-15-10; fax (+45) 99-31-31-32; e-mail andersen@aalborg.be; internet www.eu -aalborg.dk; contact Martin Andersen.

ESTONIA

Tallinn Urban Forum: Raekoja Plats 12, 10146 Tallinn; tel (+372) 645-71-78; fax (+372) 645-71-80; e-mail epp.lankots@ tallinnlv.ee; internet www.tallinn.ee; contact Epp Lankots.

FINLAND

City of Espoo: City Planning Department, Forum Espoo, PO Box 43, 02070 Espoo; tel (+358 9) 81657991; fax (+358 9) 81624317; e-mail mervi.romppanen@ espoo.fi; internet http://english.espoo.fi/ forum; contact Mervi Romppanen.

GERMANY

Städtisches Forum für Nachhaltige Entwicklung: C/o Öko-Zentrum Nordrhein-Westfalen, Sachsenweg 8, 59073 Hamm; tel (+49 2381) 3022017; fax (+49 2381) 3022030; e-mail karsten@ oekozentrum-nrw.de; internet www .oekozentrum-nrw.de; contact Tobias Karsten.

GREECE

Volos Municipality – DITEV: Environmental Office, Athinon 25, 38334 Volos; tel (+30) 24210-82364; fax (+30) 24210-82363; e-mail environment@volos-city.gr; internet www.volos-m.gr/indexen.htm; contact Evi Karaiskou.

IRELAND

Urban Institute Ireland – Dublin: University College Dublin – Richview, Clonskeagh Drive, Dublin 14; tel (+353 1) 2697988; fax (+353 1) 2837889; e-mail louise.dunne@ucd.ie; internet www .urbaninstitute.net; contact Louise Dunne.

ITALY

Forum per La Laguna – Venice: Calle Vitturi 2923, San Marco, 30124 Venice; e-mail giosella.difelice@ forumlagunavenezia.org; internet www .forumlagunavenezia.org; contact Giosella Di Felice.

Terni Municipality – Town Planning Department: Corso del Popolo 96, 05100 Terni (Umbria); tel (+39) 0744-549955; fax (+39) 0744-549966; e-mail roberto .meloni@comune.terni.it; contact Roberto Meloni.

LITHUANIA

Vilnius City Municipality: Environmental Protection Division and Urban Development Department, Gedimino Ave 37-408, 2600 Vilnius; tel (+370 524) 97177; fax (+370 524) 97420; e-mail violeta.ivinskiene@vilnius.lt; contact Violeta Ivinskiene.

NETHERLANDS

International Institute for the Urban Environment: Nickersteeg 5, 2611 EK Delft; tel (+31 15) 2623279; fax (+31 15) 2624873; e-mail iiue@urban.nl; internet www.urban.nl; contact Mark Kras.

POLAND

City of Warsaw, Public Consultation and Dialogue Centre: Jazdow 10a, 00-467 Warsaw; tel (+48 22) 626-90-82 ext. 119; fax (+48 22) 626-90-88; e-mail mherbst@warszawa.um.gov.pl; contact Marcin Herbst.

PORTUGAL

Porto Municipality – Environmental Office: Rua 5 Dinis 249, 4250 Porto; tel (+351 22) 8349494; fax (+351 22) 8349498; e-mail claudiacardoso@cm-porto.pt; contact Ana Claudia Cardoso.

SPAIN

Municipality of Donostia-San Sebastián: Department of Economic Development, Employment and Commerce, C/ Ljentea 6 (Palacio Goikoa), 20003 Donostia-San Sebastián; tel (+34) 943-48-15-04; fax (+34) 943-48-16-69; e-mail elisabeth_jorge@donostia.org; internet www.donostia.org; contact Elisabeth Jorge.

SWEDEN

Göteborg & West Sweden Office: Norra Hamngatan 14, 41114 Göteborg; tel (+46 31) 61-25-14; fax (+46 31) 13-18-90; e-mail haleh.lindqvist@westsweden.se; internet www.westsweden.se; contact Haleh Lindqvist.

UNITED KINGDOM

Environ – Leicester: Parkfield, Western Park, Leicester, LE3 6HX; tel (+44 116) 222-0222; fax (+44 116) 255-2343; e-mail kbush@environ.org.uk; internet www.environ.org.uk; contact Kevin Bush.

Envolve – Bath: Green Park Station, Green Park Road, Bath, BA1 1JB; tel (+44 1225) 787910; fax (+44 1225) 460840; e-mail steveb@envolve.co.uk; internet www.envolve.co.uk; contact Steve Bendle.

EUROLIBRARIES

The aim of the Eurolibraries network is to decentralize EU information and to make information on EU policies accessible to the public at the local level. The network is operating presently in Spain, Russia, the United Kingdom, Denmark and Sweden, and is managed by the European Commission Office in that particular Member State.

Each Eurolibrary is equipped both with reference material for the use of its public and with EU documentation for distribution. The libraries receive the following documents free of charge: Treaties, Official Journal Com Documents, Directory of Community Legislation, General Activities Report, basic statistics, SCAD Bulletin, brochures, pamphlets and videos.

List of Eurolibraries

DENMARK

Euro Library: Det Sonderjydske Landsbibliotek, Haderslevvej 3 – Postboks 1037, 6200 Aabenraa; tel (+45) 74 62 25 62; fax (+45) 74 62 14 80; contact Beeck Vita.

Euro Library: Det Nordjyske Landsbibliotek, Nytorv 26 – Postboks 839, 9100 Alborg; tel (+45) 99 31 43 30; fax (+45) 99 31 43 33; e-mail lacsesal@njl.dk; contact Petersen Anette.

Euro Library: Arhus Kommunes Biblioteker, Moellegade 1, 8000 Arhus C; tel (+45) 87 30 45 00; fax (+45) 87 30 45 39; e-mail http:hbinfo@inet.uni-c.dk; contact Kristensen Anette.

Euro Library: Esbjerg Centralbibliotek – Hovedbiblioteket, Noerregade 19 – Postboks 19, 6701 Esbjerg; tel (+45) 75 12 13 77; fax (+45) 75 45 35 09; contact Skov Mogens.

Euro Library: Frederikshaven Bibliotek, Postboks 721, 9900 Frederikshavn; tel (+45) 38 34 48 77; fax (+45) 38 33 36 77; contact Strandgaard Jens.

Euro Library: Gentofte Kommunebibliotek, Ahlmanns Alle 6, 2900 Hellerup; tel (+45) 39 62 75 00; fax (+45) 39 62 75 07; contact Rosenoe Gitte.

Euro Library: Helsingoer Bibliotek Centralbibliotek for Frederiksborg AMT, Marienlyst Allé 4, 3000 Helsingoer; tel (+45) 49 21 73 00; fax (+45) 49 21 00 14; e-mail helserhv@inet.uni-c.dk; contact Meyer Lone.

Euro Library: Herning Centralbibliotek, Braendegaardvej 2, 7400 Herning; tel (+45) 97 12 18 11; fax (+45) 97 12 54 80; contact Halling Grete.

Euro Library: Hjoerring Bibliotek, Postboks 79, 9800 Hjoerring; contact Ilse Vive Larsen.

Euro Library: Holstebro Bibliotek, Kirkestraede 11, 7500 Holstebro; contact Karen Herforth.

Euro Library: Horsens Bibliotek, Tobaksgarden 12, 8700 Horsens; contact Inge Just.

Euro Library: Stadsbiblioteket i Lingby, Lingby Hovedgade 28, 2800 KGS Lingby; contact Eva Nissen.

Euro Library: Hovedbiblioteket, Krystalgade 15, 1172 Kobenhavn K; tel (+45) 33 93 60 60; fax (+45) 33 12 60 80.

Euro Library: Biblioteker, Solbjergvej 21–25, 2000 Koebenhavn F; contact Frederiksberg Kommunes.

Euro Library: Noerre Alslev Kommunes Bibliotek, Helene Strangesvej 1, 4840 Noerre Alslev; contact Hans Moelsted Joergensen.

Euro Library: Nykoebing Centralbibliotek, Box 171, 4800 Nykoebing F; tel (+45) 54 85 05 00; fax (+45) 54 82 27 49; contact Saul Pernille.

Euro Library: Odense Centralbibliotek, Oestre Stationvej 15, 5000 Odense C; tel (+45) 66 14 88 14 lok 4301; fax (+45) 66 12 73 30; contact Tom Meisner Petersen.

Euro Library: Randers Bibliotek, Stemmansgade 2, 8900 Randers; contact Kirsten Toennes Pedersen.

Euro Library: Bornholms Centralbibliotek, Pingels Allé 1, 3700 Roenne; tel (+45) 56 95 07 04; fax (+45) 56 95 45 93; contact Madsen Jon.

Euro Library: Roskilde Bibliotek, Dronning Margrethes Vej 14, Postboks 229, 4000 Roskilde; tel (+45) 46 35 63 00; fax (+45) 46 32 01 70; contact Hove Mette.

Euro Library: Silkeborg Bibliotek, Hostrupsgade 41A, 8600 Silkeborg; contact Inge Lise Ljoerring.

Euro Library: Slagelse Centralbibliotek, Stenstuegade 3, 4200 Slagelse; tel (+45) 53 52 12 45; fax (+45) 58 50 04 20; contact Bjerregaard Hanna.

Euro Library: Svendborg Bibliotek, Viebaeltet 4, 5700 Svendborg; contact Bjoern Lemming Pedersen.

Euro Library: Biblioteket for Vejle By og Amt, Willy Sorensens Plads 1, 7100 Vejle; tel (+45) 75 82 32 00; fax (+45) 75 82 32 13; contact Brunbech Soeren.

Euro Library: Viborg Centralbibliotek, Vesterbrogade 15, 8800 Viborg; tel (+45) 87 25 31 32; fax (+45) 87 25 31 79; contact Hollesen Ulla.

RUSSIA

Euro Library: Info Relay at Kaliningrad, State University, Nevskogo Street 14, 236041 Kaliningradskaya O; contact Arthur Yaganov.

Euro Library: EU Info Relay, Kazan State University, Kremlevskaya 18, 420008 Kazan; contact Andrey Krylov.

Euro Library: Info Relay at Petrozavodsk, State University, Leninsky Prospekt 33, 185640 Petrozavodsk; contact Nikolay Toivinen.

Euro Library: Rostov on Don State University, Sadovaya Street 105, 344006 Rostov on Don; contact Igor Uznarodof.

Euro Library: EU Info Relay, Astrakhanskaya 83, 410071 Saratov; contact Oksana Kolchina.

Euro Library: Tomsk State University, Prospekt Lenina 36, 634050 Tomsk; contact Alexey Timoshenko.

Euro Library: Mari el State University, Pl. Lenina 1, 424001 Yoshkar Ola; contact Andrey Yarigin.

SPAIN

Eurobiblioteca: Biblioteca Publica de Albacete, San José de Calasanz 14, 02002 Albacete; tel (+34 967) 23 80 53; fax (+34 967) 23 82 09; contact Juan Manuel de la Cruz Munoz.

Eurobiblioteca: Biblioteca Publica del Estado "Francisco Villaespesa", Hermanos Machados s/n, 04004 Almeria; tel (+34 950) 23 03 75; fax (+34 950) 25 29 12; contact Eduardo Furtet Cabana.

Eurobiblioteca: Biblioteca Publica del Estado, Tostado 4, 05001 Avila; tel (+34 920) 21 21 32; fax (+34 920) 25 27 02; contact Carmen Prada Velasco.

Eurobiblioteca: Universitat de Barcelona Seccio de Dret – Hemeroteca, Avenida Diagonal 684, 08034 Barcelona.

Eurobiblioteca: Biblioteca de la Diputacion Foral de Vizcaya, Astarloa 10, 48008 Bilbao; tel (+34 94) 420 77 02; fax (+34 94) 415 51 84; contact Clotilde Olaran Mugica.

Eurobiblioteca: Biblioteca Publica del Estado, Plaza de San Juan s/n, 09004 Burgos; tel (+34 947) 20 23 12; fax (+34 947) 27 74 10; contact Carmen Monje Maté.

Eurobiblioteca: Biblioteca Publica, Plaza de Alfonso IX s/n, 10004 Caceres; tel (+34 927) 24 33 00; fax (+34 927) 24 81 18; contact Maria Santiago Fernandez.

Eurobiblioteca: Biblioteca Publica de Cadiz, Av. Ramon de Carranza 16, 11006 Cadiz; contact Maria José Vaquero Vilas.

Eurobiblioteca: Biblioteca Publica, Rafalafena 29, 12003 Castellon La Plana; tel (+34 964) 22 43 09; fax (+34 964) 23 65 57; contact Rosa Maria Diaz Salvador.

Eurobiblioteca: Biblioteca Publica de Ciudad, C/Del Prado 12, 13002 Ciudad Real; tel (+34 926) 22 33 10; fax (+34 926) 23 18 77.

Eurobiblioteca: Biblioteca Publica, Glorieta Gonzalez Palencia 2, 16002 Cuenca; tel (+34 969) 22 23 11; fax (+34 969) 23 12 44; contact Maria B. Marlasca Gutiérrez.

Eurobiblioteca: Biblioteca Publica del Estado, Plaza del Hospital 6, 17001 Girona; tel (+34 972) 20 22 52; fax (+34 972) 22 76 95; contact Maria Teresa Garcia Panadés.

Eurobiblioteca: Biblioteca Publica del Estado, Plaza de los Caidos 11, 19001 Guadalajara; tel (+34 949) 21 17 87; fax (+34 949) 21 45 38; contact Blanca Calvo Alonso-Cortés.

Eurobiblioteca: Biblioteca Publica, Av. Martin Alonzo Pinzon 16, 21003 Huelva; tel (+34 959) 24 72 62; fax (+34 959) 28 35 29; contact Carlos Luna Huertas.

Eurobiblioteca: Biblioteca Publica Provincial, Av. de los Pirineos 2, 22004 Huesca; tel (+34 974) 22 87 61; fax (+34 974) 22 87 61; contact Rosario Collell Beltran.

Eurobiblioteca: Biblioteca Publica Provincial, C/ Santo Reino l, 23008 Jaen; tel (+34 953) 22 39 50; fax (+34 953) 22 39 54; contact Laura Cerezo Navarro.

Eurobiblioteca: Biblioteca Publica del Estado "Miguel Gonzalez Garcés", Rua Miguel Gonzalez Garcés s/n, 15008 La Coruña; tel (+34 981) 17 02 18; fax (+34 981) 17 02 18; contact Laura Gonzalez-Garcés.

Eurobiblioteca: Biblioteca Publica del Estado, Plaza de la Constitucion 3, 35003 Las Palmas de Gran Canaria; tel (+34 928) 36 10 77; fax (+34 928) 38 17 18; contact Ana Maria Martinez Valdivieso.

Eurobiblioteca: Biblioteca Publica del Estado, C/ Santa Nonia 5, 24003 Leon; tel (+34 987) 20 67 10; fax (+34 987) 20 30 25; contact Alfredo Diez Escobar.

Eurobiblioteca: Biblioteca Publica de Lleida, Rambla de Aragon 10, 25002 Lerida; tel (+34 973) 26 75 51; contact Carmen Ariche Axpe.

Eurobiblioteca: Biblioteca Publica del Estado, C / De La Merced 1, 26001 Logroño; tel (+34 941) 21 13 82; fax (+34 941) 21 05 36; contact José Luis Magro Rastrero.

Eurobiblioteca: Biblioteca Publica Provincial, Av. Ramon Ferreiro s/n, 27071 Lugo; tel (+34 982) 22 85 25; contact Blanca M. Pacin Somoza.

Eurobiblioteca: Biblioteca Publica de Salamanca, Azcona 42, 28028 Madrid; tel (+34 91) 726 37 01; fax (+34 91) 726 40 60; contact Maria Antonia Chiveto.

Eurobiblioteca: Punto de Informacion Europa, Ayuntamiento de Malaga, Avenida de Cervantes 4, 29071 Malaga.

Eurobiblioteca: Biblioteca Publica, Concejo 13, 32003 Orense; contact Minia Martul Tobio.

Eurobiblioteca: Biblioteca Publica de Palencia, Eduardo Dato 4, 34005 Palencia; tel (+34 979) 75 11 00; fax (+34 979) 75 11 21; contact José Izquierdo Bertiz.

Eurobiblioteca: Biblioteca General de Navarra, Plaza de San Francisco s/n, 31001 Pamplona; tel (+34 948) 42 77 97; fax (+34 948) 42 77 89; contact Lorenzo Otazu Ripa.

Eurobiblioteca: Biblioteca Publica, Alfonso XIII 3, 36002 Pontevedra; tel (+34 986) 85 08 38; fax (+34 986) 86 21 27; contact Maria A. Vazquez Vamonde.

Eurobiblioteca: Biblioteca Publica de Salamanca, Casa de las Conchas, Compania 2, 37002 Salamanca; tel (+34 923) 26 93 17; fax (+34 923) 26 97 58; contact Ramona Dominguez Sanjurjo.

Eurobiblioteca: Biblioteca Publica del Estado, Gravina 4, 39007 Santander; tel (+34 942) 37 44 14; fax (+34 942) 37 49 55.

Eurobiblioteca: Biblioteca Publica del Estado, Juan Bravo 11, 40001 Segovia; tel (+34 921) 46 35 33; fax (+34 921) 46 35 23; contact Luis Garcia Méndez.

Eurobiblioteca: Biblioteca Publica, Nicolas Rabal 25, 42003 Soria; tel (+34 975) 22 18 00; fax (+34 975) 22 91 70; contact Maria Teresa de la Fuente Leon.

Eurobiblioteca: Biblioteca Publica, Fortuny 30, 43001 Tarragona; tel (+34 977) 24 03 31; fax (+34 977) 24 53 12; contact Rosario Lozano Diaz.

Eurobiblioteca: Biblioteca Publica, Plaza de Perez Prado 3, 44001 Teruel; tel (+34 978) 60 13 59; contact Mercedes Laguia Lacorte.

Eurobiblioteca: Biblioteca Publica del Estado, Paseo del Miradero 4, 45001 Toledo; tel (+34 925) 22 12 24; fax (+34 925) 25 36 42; contact Julia Mendez Aparicio.

Eurobiblioteca: Biblioteca Publica de Valencia, Hospital 13, 46001 Valencia; tel (+34 96) 351 09 39; fax (+34 96) 351 66 61; contact Carolina Sevilla.

Eurobiblioteca: Biblioteca Publica Provincial, Paseo de la Florida 9, 01005 Vitoria-Gasteiz; tel (+34 945) 18 19 44; fax (+34 945) 18 19 45; contact Teresa Castro Legorburu.

Eurobiblioteca: Biblioteca Publica del Estado, Plaza de Claudio Moyano s/n, 49001 Zamora; tel (+34 980) 53 15 51; fax (+34 980) 51 60 32; contact Concepcion Gonzalez Diaz.

Eurobiblioteca: Biblioteca Publica de Aragon, Doctor Cerrada 22, 50005 Zaragoza; tel (+34 976) 23 33 23; fax (+34 976) 21 12 67; contact Javier Villar Pérez.

SWEDEN

Eurobibliotek: Oesteraakers Bibliotek, Box 504, 18425 Aakersberga; contact Margareta Moeller.

Eurobibliotek: Aalmhults Kommun, Box 502, 34323 Aalmhult; contact Ulla Petterson.

Eurobibliotek: Aalvsbyns Kommunbibliotek, 94285 Aalvsbyn; contact Gun Nyberg.

Eurobibliotek: Aange Folkbibliotek, 84181 Aange; contact Karin Jansson.

Eurobibliotek: Aarjaengs Bibliotek, Nertomtvaegen 6, Box 903, 67229 Aarjaeng; contact Lars-Eric Johansson.

Eurobibliotek: Aaseda Bibliotek, Box 50, 36070 Aaseda; contact Ann-Charlotte Thour.

Eurobibliotek: Aastorps Bibliotek, Storgatan 28, Box 17, 26501 Aastorp; contact Jens Nihlen.

Eurobibliotek: Aengelholms Bibliotek, Stortorget, 26280 Aengelholm; contact Bodil Florel.

Eurobibliotek: Alvesta Bibliotek, Folkets Hus, 34280 Alvesta; contact Ann-Katrin Ursberg.

Eurobibliotek: Aneby Folkbibliotek, Box 123, 57823 Aneby; contact Anne-Marie Davidson.

Eurobibliotek: Angereds Bibliotek, Box 83, 42422 Angered.

Eurobibliotek: Vasagymnasiet/ Bibliotek, Box 26, 73221 Arboga; contact Elisabeth Karlsson.

Eurobibliotek: Arboga Bibliotek, Kappelgatan 19B, 73245 Arboga; contact Lotta Von Plomgren.

Eurobibliotek: Arjeplogs Kommunbibliotek, Stroemvaegen 21, 93090 Arjeplog.

Eurobibliotek: Burloevs Sockenbibliotek, Dalbyvaegen 51, 23233 Arloev.

Eurobibliotek: Arvidsjaurs Bibliotek, Box 703, 93327 Arvidsjaurs Bibliotek; contact Gun Hellander.

Eurobibliotek: Arvika Bibliotek, Kyrkogatan 39A, Box 956, 67129 Arvika; contact Eva Naeslund.

Eurobibliotek: Baastads Kommunbibliotek, Vaangavaegen 2, Box 1124, 26922 Baastad; contact Inger Angersjoe.

Eurobibliotek: Bispgaardens Bibliotek, Box 97, 84073 Bispgaarden.

Eurobibliotek: Bjurholms Bibliotek, Box 12, 91621 Bjurholm; contact Karin Gullikson-Hansson.

Eurobibliotek: Bvujs Kommunbibliotek, Box 47, 26721 Bjuv; contact Catharina Guthartz.

Eurobibliotek: Bodens Stadsbibliotek, Box 523, 96128 Boden; contact Jan Olof Frank.

Eurobibliotek: Laensbibliotek Aelvsborg, Box 856, 50115 Boraas; contact Irene Zetterberg.

Eurobibliotek: Borgholms Kommunbibliotek, Box 116, 38722 Borgholm; contact Gunilla Lydmark.

Eurobibliotek: Braecke Kommundelsbibliotek, Box 133, 84060 Braecke.

Eurobibliotek: Oestra Goeinge Bibliotek, Koepmannagatan 1, 28060 Broby; contact Inga Joensson.

Eurobibliotek: Bromoella Folkbibliotek, Hermansens Gata 22, Box 6, 29521 Bromoella; contact Britt Marie Nordstroem.

Eurobibliotek: Torget, Box 56, 673 22 Charlottenberg; contact I. Walander Olsson.

Eurobibliotek: Danderyds Bibliotek, Box 114, 18212 Danderyd; contact Karin Garmer.

Eurobibliotek: Degerfors Bibliotek, Medborgargatan 1, 69330 Degerfors.

Eurobibliotek: Dorotea Kommun, Fol Bibliotek, Byvaegen 3, Box 22, 91781 Dorotea; contact Victoria Soedermark.

Eurobibliotek: Ekeroe Folkbibliotek, Box 206, 17823 Ekeroe; contact Barbro Persson.

Eurobibliotek: Eksjoe Bibliotek, 57580 Eksjoe; contact Ingvor Lindgren.

Eurobibliotek: Emmaboda Kommunbibliotek, Box 67, 36121 Emmaboda; contact Birgit Ekblad.

Eurobibliotek: Eskilstuna Stads- och Laensbibliotek, Kriebsensgatan, 63220 Eskilstuna; contact Ingalill Wihed.

Eurobibliotek: Esloevs Stadsbibliotek, Box 225, 24124 Esloev; contact Birgitta Laurin.

Eurobibliotek: Brinnellskolan Biblioteket, Fridvaegen 5, 73744 Fagersta; contact Birgitta Naesstroem.

Eurobibliotek: Fagersta Bibliotek, Vaestmannavaegen 12, 73740 Fagersta; contact Ulla Bjoerklund.

Eurobibliotek: Falkenbegs Bibliotek, Biblioteksgatan 2, 31135 Falkenberg; contact Jozsef Somi.

Eurobibliotek: Bibliotek Dalarna, Kristinegatan 15, 79183 Falun; contact Rolf Holm.

Eurobibliotek: Filipstads Bibliotek, Stora Torget 3D, 68227 Filipstad; contact Jan Froeding.

Eurobibliotek: Lekebergs Bibliotek, Letstigan 2, 71630 Fjugesta.

Eurobibliotek: Flens Bibliotek, Drottninggatan 3, 64237 Flen; contact Per Hjertzell.

Eurobibliotek: Forshaga Bibliotek, Storgatan 43, Box 23, 66721 Forshaga; contact Kerstin Krona.

Eurobibliotek: Gaelloe Kommundelsbibliotek, Box 44, 84050 Gaelloe.

Eurobibliotek: Bibliotek Gaevleborg, Box 801, 80130 Gaevle; contact Anne-Marie Drougge.

Eurobibliotek: Kommundelsbibliotek, Skolan, 71016 Garphyttan.

Eurobibliotek: Gislaveds Bibliotek, Groena Vaegen 28, 33233 Gislaved; contact Ann-Mari Hellqvist.

Eurobibliotek: Kommundelsbibliotek, Glanshammars Skola, 70385 Glanshammar.

Eurobibliotek: Gnesta Bibliotek, Thulegatan 4, 64680 Gnesta; contact B.I. Ronnqvist.

Eurobibliotek: Gnosjoe Bibliotek, Storgatan 8, 33580 Gnosjoe; contact Mats Johansson.

Eurobibliotek: Majornas Bibliotek, Chapmans Torg 5, 41454 Goeteborg.

Eurobibliotek: Kortedala Regionbibliotek, Box 47066, 40258 Goeteborg.

Eurobibliotek: Hisingens Regionbibliotek, Box 22130, 40072 Goeteborg.

Eurobibliotek: Goeteborg Stadsbibliotek, AVD 4, Huvudbibliotek, Goeteplatsen, Box 5404, 40229 Goeteborg; contact Christina Kristiansson.

Eurobibliotek: Grums Kommunbibliotek, Sveagatan 77–85, Box 23, 66421 Grums; contact Klas Berquist.

Eurobibliotek: Vaermdoe Kommunbibliotek, Box 110, 13400 Gustavsberg; contact Christina Staeldal.

Eurobibliotek: Haellefors Bibliotek, Sikforsvaegen 19–21, 71234 Haellefors.

Eurobibliotek: Haernoesands Bibliotek, Box 1045, 87129 Haernoesand; contact Carin Roennberg.

Eurobibliotek: Laensbiblioteket, Vaesternorrland, Box 1045, 87129 Haernoesand; contact Gunilla Jingborg.

Eurobibliotek: Haesslehoms Bibliotek, Foersta Avenyen 14C, Box 223, 28123 Haessleholm; contact Evy Callmer.

Eurobibliotek: Hagfors Bibliotek, Geijersholmsvaegen 5, 68380 Hagfors; contact Kaethy Andreasson.

Eurobibliotek: Hallsbergs Bibliotek, V Storgatan 10, 69430 Hallsberg.

Eurobibliotek: Hallstahammars Bibliotek, Box 3, 73421 Hallstahammar; contact Airi Emretsson.

Eurobibliotek: Kantzowska Gymnasiet, Box 507, 73427 Hallstahammar; contact Sara Hedman.

Eurobibliotek: Laensbibliotek Halland, Fredsgatan 2, 302 46 Halmstad; contact Benita Hogland.

Eurobibliotek: Halmstads Stadsbibliotek, Fredsgatan 2, 30246 Halmstad; contact Karin Janson.

Eurobibliotek: Ragunda Bibliotek, Centralgatan 55, 84070 Hammarstrand.

Eurobibliotek: Hemse Bibliotek, Storgatan 66, 62012 Hamse; contact Oscar Pettersson.

Eurobibliotek: Haninge Bibliotek, 13681 Haninge; contact Karl-Heinz Mueller.

Eurobibliotek: Haparanda Stadsbibliotek, Packhusgatan 4, 95331 Haparanda; contact Kristina Nystroem.

Eurobibliotek: Heby Bibliotek, 74488 Heby; contact Barbro Gunmar.

Eurobibliotek: Helsingborgs Stadsbibliotek, Bollbrogatan 1, 25225 Helsingborg; contact Ewa Karlsson.

Eurobibliotek: Gotlands Laens Folkhoegskola, Storgatan 11, 62012 Hemse.

Euro Library: Orusts Kommunbibliotek, Bos 84, 47323 Henaan; contact Ruen Niklasson.

Eurobibliotek: Biblioteket I Hoeganaes, Koepmansgatan 10, 26338 Hoeganaes; contact Birgitta Tilly.

Eurobibliotek: Hoegsby Kommunbibliotek, Box 44, 57921 Hoegsby; contact Christina Johansson.

Eurobibliotek: Hoeoers Bibliotek, Friluftsvaegen 13, 24330 Hoeoer; contact Marianne Toernblad Anderberg.

Eurobibliotek: Hoerby Bibliotek, Vallgatan 7, 24231 Hoerby; contact Inga Brattberg.

Eurobibliotek: Huddinge Bibliotek, 14127 Huddinge; contact Maria Perenyi.

Eurobibliotek: Hultsfred Kommunbibliotek, Box 503, 57726 Hultsfred; contact Anna-Maj. Sundstroem.

Eurobibliotek: Hylte Folkbibliotek, Centrumhuset, 31400 Hyltebruk; contact Kerstin Grum.

Eurobibliotek: Biblioteket, 37300 Jaemjoe.

Eurobibliotek: Jaerfaella Bibliotek, Vaepnarstraeket, 17530 Jaerfaella; contact Kajsa Nordberg.

Eurobibliotek: Aarebiblioteken, Box 79, 83005 Jaerpen.

Eurobibliotek: Joenkoepings Stadsbibliotek H.B., Chef, Box 1029, 55111 Joenkoeping.

Eurobibliotek: Jokkmokks Kommunbibliotek, Foereningsgatan 8, 96232 Jokkmokk; contact Ninni Lindberg.

Eurobibliotek: Kaelarne Kommundelsbibliotek, Box 43, 84064 Kaelarne.

Eurobibliotek: Kaevlinge Bibliotek, Kvarngatan 17, 24431 Kaevlinge; contact Bertil Pauli.

Eurobibliotek: Kalix Kommunbibliotek, Box 10070, 95227 Kalix; contact Barbro Mohss.

Eurobibliotek: Kalmar Stadsbibliotek, Box 610, 39126 Kalmar; contact Pia Axeheim.

Eurobibliotek: Stadsbibliotek, Box 40, 37421 Karlshamn.

Eurobibliotek: Vaeggaskolan Bibliotek, Box 71, 37422 Karlshamn.

Eurobibliotek: I Karlshamn Bibliotek, Vaaggaskolan, Raadhusel, 37481 Karlshamn; contact Vaardgymnasiet.

Eurobibliotek: Karlskoga Bibliotek, Karlskoga Kommun, 69183 Karlskoga.

Eurobibliotek: Karlskrona Kommuns Bibliotek, K. Snaar, Box 320, 37125 Karlskrona.

Eurobibliotek: Chapmanskolan Bibliotek, Box 309, 37125 Karlskrona.

Eurobibliotek: Litorina Folkhoegskola Bibliotek, Gullberna Park, 37154 Karlskrona.

Eurobibliotek: Hoegskolan i Karlskrona Bibliotek, 37179 Karlskrona.

Eurobibliotek: Ronneby Biblioteket Grasvik, 371 79 Karlskrona.

Eurobibliotek: Karlstads Stadsbibliotek, Vaestra Torggatan 26, 65184 Karlstad; contact Eva Frederiksson.

Eurobibliotek: Kils Bibliotek, Box 168, 66524 Kil; contact Lisbeth Raaman.

Eurobibliotek: Kiruna Stadsbibliotek, 98185 Kiruna; contact Anne Poromaa.

Eurobibliotek: Klippans Bibliotek, 26480 Klippan; contact Inger Sandell.

Eurobibliotek: Koepings Bibliotek, 73141 Koeping; contact Henry Segerstroem.

Eurobibliotek: Ullviskolan Biblioteket, Box 30, 73121 Koeping; contact Margot Johnsson.

Eurobibliotek: Ljusnarsberg Bibliotek, Box 74, 71422 Kopparberg.

Eurobibliotek: Kramfors Kommunbibliotek, Box 144, 87223 Kramfors; contact Monica Andersson.

Eurobibliotek: Laensbibliotek, Kristiandstadts Laen, Foereningsgatan 4, 29133 Kristianstad; contact Birgitta Aspelin.

Euro Library: Kristianstads Stadsbibliotek, Foereningsgatan 4, 29133 Kristianstad; contact Kajsa Tell.

Eurobibliotek: Krokoms Kommunbibliotek, 83580 Krokom.

Eurobibliotek: Kulma Bibliotek, 69280 Kulma.

Eurobibliotek: Kungaelvs Stadsbibliotek, Gymnasiegatan 3, 44234 Kungaelv; contact Catarina Stake.

Eurobibliotek: Upplands-Bro Bibliotek, Box 34, 19621 Kungsaengen; contact Christine Blom.

Eurobibliotek: Kungsbacka Bibliotek, 43432 Kungsbacka; contact Marie-Louise Frick.

Eurobibliotek: Sotenaas Kommunbibliotek, Box 103, 45622 Kungshamn; contact Aslaug Myhrhberg.

Eurobibliotek: Kungsoers Bibliotek, Drottninggatan 34, 73631 Kungsoer; contact Irene Svensson.

Eurobibliotek: Laholms Bibliotek, Humlegaangen 6, 31280 Laholm; contact Eva Thornell.

Eurobibliotek: Landskrona Stadsbibliotek, Eriksgatan 66, 26133 Landskrona; contact Ingrid Johansson.

Eurobibliotek: Laxaa Bibliotek, 69580 Laxaa.

Eurobibliotek: Lessebo Bibliotek, Box 44, 36050 Lessebo; contact Anders Isaksson.

Eurobibliotek: Lidingoe Stadsbibliotek, Box 1244, 18124 Lidingoe; contact Gunnel De Geer-Tolstoy.

Eurobibliotek: Lindesbergs Bibliotek, Kungsgatan 37A, 71180 Lindesberg.

Eurobibliotek: Laensbibliotek Oestergoetland, Box 3054, 58003 Linkoeping; contact Kerstin Olsson.

Eurobibliotek: Ljungby Bibliotek, S Jaernvaegsgatan 8, 34183 Ljungby; contact Ulla-Margarethe Carlsson.

Eurobibliotek: Lomma Bibliotek, Box 29, 23421 Lomma; contact Ingrid Arwidi.

Eurobibliotek: Luleaa Kulturfoervaltning, 97179 Luleaa; contact Birgit Lindmark.

Eurobibliotek: Luleaa Folkbibliotek, Kyrkogatan 11, 97179 Luleaa; contact Jimmy Gaerdemalm.

Eurobibliotek: Lunds Stadsbibliotek, Box 111, 22100 Lund; contact Helena Holmstroem Berntsson.

Eurobibliotek: Biblioteket Vaester, Oernvaegen 66, 22731 Lund; contact Inger Landen.

Eurobibliotek: Lyckeby Bibliotek, Lyckaavaegen 25, 37162 Lyckeby.

Eurobibliotek: Lycksele Bibliotek, Lycksele Kommun, N. Torgg. 12, 92181 Lycksele; contact Bengt Oestbom.

Eurobibliotek: Lysekils Stadsbibliotek, Kungsgatan 18, 45333 Lysekil; contact Lisen Joensson.

Eurobibliotek: Malaa Bibliotek, Centralskolan, Box 54, 93070 Malaa; contact Gunilla Josefsson.

Eurobibliotek: Gaellivare Kommuns, Folkbibliotek, Box 6, 98321 Malmberget; contact Liselott Lagnestig.

Eurobibliotek: Malmoe Stadsbibliotek, Regementsgat 3, 21142 Malmoe; contact Eva Olson.

Eurobibliotek: Markaryds Bibliotek, Box 133, 28523 Markaryd; contact Torsten Ekelund.

Eurobibliotek: Sigtuna Kommuns Bibliotek, 19585 Marsta; contact Rose Marie Nygren.

Eurobibliotek: Moelndals Stadsbibliotek, Goeteborgsvaegen 19–21, 43130 Moelndal; contact Margareta Ljunge.

Eurobibliotek: Moelnlycke Bibliotek, Biblioteksvaegen 2, 43530 Moelnlycke; contact Lars Malmgren.

Eurobibliotek: Moensteraas Kommunbibliotek, Box 4, 38300 Moensteraas; contact Karin Broman.

Eurobibliotek: Moerbylaanga Kommunbibliotek, Storgatan 2, 38062 Moerbylaanga; contact Dag Johansson.

Eurobibliotek: Munkedals Kommunbibliotek, Forum, 45580 Munkedal; contact Kerstin Wockatz.

Eurobibliotek: Munkfors Bibliotek, Smedsgatan 16, Box 24, 68421 Munkfors; contact Harriet Ljungdhal.

Eurobibliotek: Nacka Stadsbibliotek, Box 4150, 13104 Nacka; contact Sjoelund Boerde.

Eurobibliotek: Naessjoe Kommunbibliotek, Mariagatan 2, 57131 Naessjoe; contact Lena Petersson.

Eurobibliotek: Naettraby Bibliotek, Box 104, 37024 Naettraby.

Eurobibliotek: Nora Bibliotek, Box 123, 71323 Nora.

Eurobibliotek: Norbergs Bibliotek, Box 25, 73821 Norberg; contact Bengt Raattamaa.

Eurobibliotek: Nordmalings Bibliotek, Kungsvaegen 31, Box 47, 91421 Nordmaling.

Eurobibliotek: Norrtaelje Bibliotek, Box 805, 16128 Norrtaelje; contact Kerstin Ericsson.

Eurobibliotek: Norsjoe Bibliotek, Skolgatan 26, 93532 Norsjoe; contact Linnea Dahlberg.

Eurobibliotek: Nybro Stadsbibliotek, Box 113, 38222 Nybro; contact Birgitta Gustafsson.

Eurobibliotek: Nynaeshamns Bibliotek, 14981 Nynaeshamn; contact Kerstin Frederiksson.

Eurobibliotek: Odensbackens, Kommundelsbibliotek, Odenskolan, 71531 Odensbacken.

Eurobibliotek: Oeckeroe Kommunbibliotek, Box 1003, 43090 Oeckeroe; contact Lars Thorsson.

Eurobibliotek: Adolfsbergs Kommundelsbibliotek, Box 31640, 70135 Oerebro.

Eurobibliotek: Brickebackens Kommundelsbibliotek, Box 31800, 70135 Oerebro.

Eurobibliotek: Haga Kommundelsbibliotek, Haga Centrum, Box 31900, 70135 Oerebro.

Eurobibliotek: Hovsta Kommundelsbibliotek, Hovsta Centrum, Box 32600, 70135 Oerebro.

Eurobibliotek: Markbackens Kommundelsbibliotek, Box 32000, 70135 Oerebro.

Eurobibliotek: Mikaels Kommundelsbibliotek, Box 32000, 70135 Oerebro.

Eurobibliotek: Olaus Petri Kommundelsbibliotek, Box 32210, 70135 Oerebro.

Eurobibliotek: Varberga Kommundelsbibliotek, Box 32300, 70135 Oerebro.

Eurobibliotek: Vivalla Kommundelsbibliotek, Box 32500, 70135 Oerebro.

Eurobibliotek: Oerebro Stads- och Laensbibliotek, Naebbtorgsg. 12, Box 31010, 70135 Oerebro; contact Lars Gunnar Krantz.

Eurobibliotek: Oarkelljunga Bibliotek, Storgatan 2, 28637 Oerkelljunga; contact Krister Aronsson.

Eurobibliotek: Oernskoeldsviks Stadsbibliotek, Box 840, 89118 Oernskoeldsvik; contact Ann Ingberg.

Eurobibliotek: Jaemtlands Laens Bibliotek, Raadhusgatan 25–27, 83180 Oestersund; contact Bengt Engdahl.

Eurobibliotek: Oeverkalix Kommunbibliotek, Brogatan 4, 95681 Oeverkalix; contact A. Paganus.

Eurobibliotek: Tornedalens Bibliotek, Box 18, 95721 Oevertorneaa; contact Tommy Larsson.

Eurobibliotek: Olofstroems Bibliotek, Box 301, 29324 Olofstroem.

Eurobibliotek: Nordenbergskolan Bibliotek, Box 304, 29324 Olofstroem.

Eurobibliotek: Osby Bibliotek, Oe Jaernvaegsgatan 14, Box 13, 28100 Osby; contact Gunilla Maartensson.

Eurobibliotek: Oskarshamns Bibliotek, Box 705, 57228 Oskarshamn; contact Kjell Ljones.

Eurobibliotek: Oxeloesunds Bibliotek, Box 133, 61323 Oxeloesund; contact Madeleine Andersson.

Eurobibliotek: Pajala Bibliotek, Box 13, 98421 Pajala; contact Karin Johansson.

Eurobibliotek: Partille Bibliotek, Box 602, 43328 Partille; contact Mats Claesson.

Eurobibliotek: Perstorps Bibliotek, Box 112, 28422 Perstorp; contact Marie Sjoevik.

Eurobibliotek: Piteaa Kultur och Fritid, 94128 Piteaa; contact Klara Persson.

Eurobibliotek: Robertsfors Bibliotek, Skolgatan 6, 91531 Robertsfors; contact Lars G. Andersson.

Eurobibliotek: Roedeby Bibliotek, Box 14, 37030 Roedeby.

Eurobibliotek: Salems Kommuns bibliotek, Box 1054, 14401 Roenninge; contact Yngve Johnsson.

Eurobibliotek: Roma Bibliotek, Vysbyvaegen 33B, 62023 Romakloster; contact Leif Joensson.

Eurobibliotek: Stadsbibliotek, Kungsgatan 35, 37237 Ronneby.

Eurobibliotek: Bibliotek, 37235 Ronneby; contact Knut Hahnskolan.

Eurobibliotek: Saeffle Bibliotek, Kanaltorget 3, 66180 Saeffle; contact Eva Bjoerk.

Eurobibliotek: Saevsjoe Stadsbibliotek, Box 201, 57624 Saevsjoe; contact Haldis Oredsson.

Eurobibliotek: Sala Bibliotek, Norra Esplanaden 5, 73338 Sala; contact Elisabeth Norinder.

Eurobibliotek: Kungsaengsskolan Biblioteket, Box 144, 73322 Sala; contact Kristina Helge.

Eurobibliotek: Simrishamns Bibliotek, Jaernvaegsgatan 2, 27280 Simrishamn; contact Kristina Ross.

Eurobibliotek: Sjoebo Bibliotek, 27580 Sjoebo; contact Carin Joensson.

Eurobibliotek: Tjoerns Kommunbibliotek, Kommunkontoret, 47180 Skaerhamn; contact Asa Hedberg.

Eurobibliotek: Laensbibliotek i Skaraborgs Laen, Traedgaardgatan 2, Box 194, 53223 Skara; contact Elisabeth Erikson.

Eurobibliotek: Skellefteaa Bibliotek, Box 703, 93127 Skellefteaa; contact Birgitta Larsson.

Eurobibliotek: Skinnskattebergs Bibliotek, Box 103, 73922 Skinnskatteberg; contact Karin Nilsson.

Eurobibliotek: Hammaroe Kommunbibliotek, Skogaasvaegen 3, Box 46, 66321 Skoghall; contact Margaretha Rydberg.

Eurobibliotek: Skurups Bibliotek K.G. Leustedt, Box 34, 27421 Skurup.

Eurobibliotek: Slite Bibliotek, Box 75, 62030 Slite; contact Christer Lundin.

Eurobibliotek: Soedertaelje Stadsbibliotek, St. Ragnhildsgatan 2, 15183 Soedertaelje; contact Wera Sundin.

Eurobibliotek: Stadsbibliotek, Rundgatan 4, 29431 Soelvesborg.

Eurobibliotek: Furulundsskolan Bibliotek, Yndevaegen 2, 29433 Soelvesborg; contact Margareta Jadesjoe.

Eurobibliotek: Solefteaa Kommunbibliotek, 88181 Solefteaa; contact Marianne Rietz.

Eurobibliotek: Sollentuna Bibliotek, Box 63, 19121 Sollentuna; contact Kjell Schroeder.

Eurobibliotek: Solna Stadsbibliotek, Box 1049, 17121 Solna; contact Barbro Borg.

Eurobibliotek: Sorsele Bibliotek, Storgatan 11, Box 8, 92070 Sorsele; contact Torgny Henriksson.

Eurobibliotek: Staffanstorps Bibliotek, 24580 Staffanstorp; contact Kerstin Gunnarsson.

Eurobibliotek: Stenungsunds Kolkbibliotek, Box 187, 44423 Stenungsund; contact Inger Thorsen.

Eurobibliotek: Stockholms Stadsbibliotek Laensbibliotek, Box 6533, 11383 Stockholm; contact Roger Ullmark.

Eurobibliotek: Storfors Kommun Bibliotek, Box 1001, 68829 Storfors; contact Goete Andersson.

Eurobibliotek: Storumans Bibliotek, Stationsgatan 1, Box 103, 92322 Storuman; contact Anna-Lena Jonsson.

Eurobibliotek: Biblioteket, 64580 Straengnaes; contact Ragnhild Lundgren.

Eurobibliotek: Stroemstads Stadsbibliotek, Karlsgatan 17, 45282 Stroemstad; contact Per Henrik Askeroed.

Eurobibliotek: Centralbiblioteket, Box 530, 83324 Stroemsund.

Eurobibliotek: Stuguns Bibliotek, Box 80, 83076 Stugun.

Eurobibliotek: Sundbybergs Stadsbibliotek, Box 1526, 172 29 Sunbyberg.

Eurobibliotek: Sundsvalls Stadsbibliotek, Kulturmagasinet, 85196 Sundsvall; contact Karin Westberg.

Eurobibliotek: Sunne Bibliotek, Storgatan 22, Box 79, 68622 Sunne; contact Elli-Britt Sundman.

Eurobibliotek: Surahammars Bibliotek, Box 206, 73523 Surahammar; contact Ingrid Raij.

Eurobibliotek: Svaloevs Bibliotek, Box 73, 26821 Svaloev; contact Per Hedberg.

Eurobibliotek: Svedala Bibliotek, 23380 Svedala; contact Bo Maansson.

Eurobibliotek: Haerjedalens Bibliotek, Medborgarhuset, 84280 Sveg.

Eurobibliotek: Bergs Kommunbibliotek, Skolvaegen 4, 84040 Svenstavik.

Eurobibliotek: Taeby Bibliotek, Box 152, 18322 Taeby; contact Eva Magnusson.

Eurobibliotek: Tanums Bibliotek, Box 4, 45721 Tanumshede; contact Johan Edgren.

Eurobibliotek: Timraa Kommunbibliotek, Box 44, 86122 Timraa; contact Anders Lohman.

Eurobibliotek: Tingsryds Bibliotek, Box 113, 36222 Tingsryd; contact Lisa Haakansson.

Eurobibliotek: Tomelilla Bibliotek, Centralgatan 13, 27330 Tomelilla; contact Torbjoern Nilsson.

Eurobibliotek: Torsaas Bibliotek, Box 503, 38525 Torsaas; contact Lolita Persson.

Eurobibliotek: Torsby Bibliotek, Biografgatan 5, Box 504, 68529 Torsby; contact Karin Lindqvist.

Eurobibliotek: Tranaas Stadsbibliotek, Storgatan 22, 57382 Tranaas; contact Gunvor Aspviken.

Eurobibliotek: Trelleborgs Bibliotek, Box 93, 23122 Trelleborg; contact Johnny Maartensson.

Eurobibliotek: Trosa Bibliotek, Oe Laangatan 28, 61900 Trosa; contact Kerstin Jensen.

Eurobibliotek: Tumba Bibliotek, Box 52, 147 21 Tumba; contact Olof Sparre.

Eurobibliotek: Tyresoe Kommunbibliotek, Box 36, 13521 Tyresoe; contact Sverre Eriksson.

Eurobibliotek: Uddevalla Stadsbibliotek, 45181 Uddevalla; contact Anna-Lena Holm.

Eurobibliotek: Laensbiblioteket I Vaesterbotten, Raadhusesplanaden 8, 90178 Umeaa; contact Anita Lindmark.

Eurobibliotek: Umeaa Stadsbibliotek, Raadhusesplanaden 8, S90178 Umeaa; contact Inger Sikstrom.

Eurobibliotek: Upplands Vaesby Bibliotek, Box 68, 19421 Upplands – Vaesby; contact Margareta Berg.

Eurobibliotek: Uppsala Stads- och Laensbibliotek, Box 643, 75127 Uppsala; contact Inger Alstroem.

Eurobibliotek: Vaennaes Bibliotek, Oe Jaernvaegsgatan 10, 91132 Vaennaes; contact Susanne Ljungstroem.

Euro Library: Vaernamo Kommunbibliotek, Box 414, 33124 Vaernamo; contact Karen Andersson.

Eurobibliotek: Baeckby Bibliotek, Box 20005, 72020 Vaesteraas.

Eurobibliotek: Vaesteraas Stadsbibliotek, Box 717, 72120 Vaesteraas; contact Anders Rystedt.

Eurobibliotek: Vaardgymnasiet Bibliotek, Centrallasarettet, 72189 Vaesteraas; contact Anita Thorell.

Eurobibliotek: Oensta Gryta Bibliotek, Daggrosgatan 2, 72343 Vaesteraas; contact Anna-Kari Gelius.

Eurobibliotek: Rudbeckianska Gymnasiet-Bibliotek, Skolgatan 5, 72215 Vaesteraas; contact Birgitta Fjaellros.

Eurobibliotek: Korsaengsskolan Bibliotek, Runebergsgatan 22, 72335 Vaesteraas; contact Boerje Hellberg.

Eurobibliotek: Skiljebobiblioteket, Skiljeboplatsen 1, 72341 Vaesteraas; contact Maj Eklund.

Eurobibliotek: Wenstroemska Gymnasiet-Bibliotek, Vedbovaegen 1, 72480 Vaesteraas; contact Maria Lundstroem Johnson.

Eurobibliotek: Carlforsska Gymnasiet-Bibliotek, Eriksborgsgatan 13, 72218 Vaesteraas; contact Solveig Hedenstroem.

Eurobibliotek: Vaesterviks Kommunbibliotek, Box 342, 59324 Vaestervik; contact Kajsa Andersson.

Eurobibliotek: Vaggerryds Kommunbibliotek, Box 157, 56723 Vaggeryd; contact Uli Wollrab.

Eurobibliotek: Vallentuna Bibliotek, Box 104, 19600 Vallentuna; contact Ingrid Ullman.

Eurobibliotek: Varbergs Bibliotek, 43280 Varberg; contact Nina Runze.

Eurobibliotek: Vaxholms Stadsbibliotek, Box 104, 18522 Vaxholm; contact Brittmari Thomaeus Allen.

Eurobibliotek: Landsbiblioteket I Vaxjoe, Box 1202, 35112 Vaxjoe.

Eurobibliotek: Vellinge Bibliotek, Malmoevaegen 1, 23536 Vellinge; contact Inga-Lil Berglund.

Eurobibliotek: Vetlanda Bibliotek, Biblioteksgatan 5, 57432 Vetlanda; contact Eva Cederborg.

Eurobibliotek: Vilhelmina Bibliotek, Postgatan 15, Box 59, 91232 Vilhelmina; contact Lars Lagerstroem.

Eurobibliotek: Vimmerby Bibliotek, Stadshuset, 59881 Vimmerby; contact Peter Duering.

Eurobibliotek: Vindelns Bibliotek, Jaernvaegsallen 15, 92232 Vindeln; contact Carl-Axel Gyllenram.

Eurobibliotek: Vingaakers Bibliotek, Box 64, 64321 Vingaaker; contact Lars Furborg.

Eurobibliotek: Vintrosa Kommundelsbibliotek, Vintrosahemmet, 71015 Vintrosa.

Eurobibliotek: Gotlands Laensbibliotek, Huvudbibliotek, Haesgatan 4, 62181 Visby; contact Anna Soederbergh.

Eurobibliotek: Saeveskolan, 62182 Visby; contact Harriette Ehnberg.

Eurobibliotek: Hoegskolan Paa Gotland, Cramergatan 3, 62157 Visby; contact Leif Hagberg.

Eurobibliotek: Ystads Bibliotek, 27180 Ystad; contact Ingvar Gottfridsson.

UNITED KINGDOM

Euro Library: Central Library, Rosemount Viaduct, Aberdeen, AB25 1GW; tel (+44 1224) 652 534; fax (+44 1224) 641 985; contact Bruce Niel.

Euro Library: Ceredidgion County Council, Public Library, Corporation Street, Aberystwyth, SY23 2BU; contact William H. Howells.

Euro Library: Clackmannan District Council, District Library H.Q., 26–28 Drysdale Street, Alloa, FK10 1JL; tel (+44 1259) 722 262; fax (+44 1259) 219 469; e-mail cdl@leapfrog.almac.co.uk; contact Ian Murray.

Euro Library: Altrincham Library, Stamford New Rd 20, Altrincham, WA14 1EJ; tel (+44 161) 912 59 23; fax (+44 161) 912 59 26; e-mail Alt.lib@mcr1 .poptel.org.uk.

Euro Library: North Ayrshire Council Library, 39–41 Princes Street, Ardrossan, KA22 8BT; tel (+44 1294) 469 137; fax (+44 1294) 604 236; contact Sandra E.E. Kerr.

Euro Library: Argyll and Bute Council Library Services, Highland Avenue, Sandbank, Dunoon, Argyll and Bute, PA23 8PB; contact Andrew Ewan.

Euro Library: Tameside Reference Library, Old Street, Ashton under Lyne, OL6 7SG; contact P. Jones.

Euro Library: County Reference Library, County Hall, Walton Street, Aylesbury, HP20 1UU; contact Bob Strong.

Euro Library: South Ayrshire Education Service, Library HQ, 26 Green Street, Ayr, KA8 8AD; tel (+44 1292) 288 820; fax (+44 1292) 619 019; contact Charles Deas.

Euro Library: North-Eastern Education & Library Board, Area Headquarters, 25–31 Demesne Avenue, Ballymena, BT43 7BG; contact Lynn Buick.

Euro Library: London Borough of Barking & Dagenham, Central Library, Barking, Essex, IG11 7NB; tel (+44 20) 8517 8666; fax (+44 20) 8594 1156; e-mail fm019@viscount.org.uk; contact Maria Barnes.

Euro Library: European Business Information Unit Barnsley Metropolitan Borough Council, Central Library, Shambles Street, Barnsley, South Yorkshire, S70 2JF; tel (+44 1226) 773 935; fax (+44 1226) 773 955; contact Sue Hunt.

Euro Library: Vale of Glamorgan Libraries, Barry Library, King Square, Barry, CF63 4RW; tel (+44 1446) 735 722; contact Sandra Wildsmith.

Euro Library: Bath & North East Somerset Council, The Library, 19 The Podium, Northgate Street, Bath, BA1 5AN; contact David Moger.

Euro Library: Principal Library, Information Service, Bedford Central Library, Harpur Street, Bedford, NK40 1PG; tel (+44 1234) 350 931; fax (+44 1234) 342 163; contact Nicola Avery.

Euro Library: Belfast Public Libraries, Central Library, Royal Avenue, Belfast, BT1 1EA; tel (+44 28) 9024 3233; fax (+44 28) 9033 2819; contact Liz Cooke.

Euro Library: Reference Library, Champney Road, Beverley, HU17 9BG; contact Pamela Martin.

Euro Library: Customer Services, Bexley Council, Central Library, Townley Road, Bexleyheath, DA16 7HJ; contact Sharon Burgum.

Euro Library: Birkenhead Central Library – Information Services, Borough Road, Birkenhead, L41 2XB; tel (+44 151) 652 61 06; fax (+44 151) 653 73 20; contact P. Black.

Euro Library: Social Sciences Dept., Chamberlain Square, Birmingham, West Midlands, B3 3HQ; tel (+44 121) 235 4370; fax (+44 121) 235 4372; contact Stephen Wood.

Euro Library: Blackburn with Darwen Borough Council, Backburn Library, Town Hall Street, Blackburn, BB2 1AG; contact Ian Sutton.

Euro Library: Library Headquarters, Connolly House, Hopefield Road, Blackburn, EH47 7HZ; tel (+44 1506) 776 336; fax (+44 1506) 776 345; contact Geraldine Bodey.

Euro Library: Blackpool Central Library, Queen Street, Blackpool, FY1 1PX; contact Tony Sharkey.

Euro Library: Central Area – Central Library, Le Mans Crescent, Bolton, BL1 1SE; tel (+44 1204) 522 311 ext. 2173; fax (+44 1204) 363 224; contact Ken Bell.

Euro Library: Bournemouth Borough Council, Lansdowne Library, Meyrick Road, Bournemouth, BH1 3DJ; contact Katherine Spackman.

Euro Library: Bracknell Forest Borough Council, Bracknell Library, Town Square, Bracknell, RG12 1BH; contact Helen Beckett.

Euro Library: Central Library, Princes Way, Bradford, West Yorkshire, BD1 1NN; tel (+44 1274) 753 657; fax (+44 1274) 753 687; contact Chris Dyson.

Euro Library: Bridgend Library and Information Service, Coed Parc, Park Street, Bridgend, CF31 4BA; tel (+44 1656) 767 451; fax (+44 1656) 645 719; e-mail blis@bridgendlib.gov.uk; contact John Woods.

Euro Library: Brighton & Hove Council, Brighton Library, Advantage Point, New England Street, Brighton, BN1 4GW; tel (+44 1273) 691 195; fax (+44 1273) 695 882; contact Stephanie Coates.

Euro Library: Bristol Central Library, College Green, Bristol, BS1 5TL; tel (+44 117) 929 91 48; fax (+44 117) 922 67 75; contact Robert Harrison.

Euro Library: London Borough of Bromley, Central Reference Library, High Street, Bromley, BR1 1EX; contact Alexandra Marin.

Euro Library: Reference & Info Services, Manchester Road, Bury, BL9 0DG; tel (+44 161) 253 50 54; fax (+44 161) 253 59 15; contact Gary Phillips.

Euro Library: Cambridge Central Library, Senior Library Information, 7 Lion Yard, Cambridge, CB2 3QD; contact Jon Anderson.

Euro Library: Cardiff County Council, Cardiff Central Library, St Davids Link, Frederick Street, Cardiff, CF1 4DT; tel (+44 29) 2038 2116; fax (+44 29) 2064 4427; contact Robert Davies.

Euro Library: Reference & Local Studies, Medway Council, Chatham Library, Riverside, Chatham, ME4 4SN; contact Lyn Rainbow.

Euro Library: Information Services, Chelmsford Library, PO BOX 882, Market Road, Chelmsford, CM1 1LH; contact Joanna Clark.

Euro Library: Cheltenham Reference Library, Clarence Street, Cheltenham, GL50 3JT.

Euro Library: Monmouthshire County Council, Chepstow Library, Manor Way, Chepstow, NP6 5HZ; contact Mary Rooney.

Euro Library: Information Services, Derbyshire County Council, Chesterfield Central Library, New Beetwell Street, Chesterfield, S40 1QN; contact Barbara Jube.

Euro Library: Chichester Public Library, Information Library, Tower Street, Chichester, PO19 1QJ; tel (+44 1243) 777 352; fax (+44 1243) 531 610; contact Douglas Hayler.

Euro Library: West Dunbartonshire Council, Central Library, Dumbarton Road, Clydebank, G81 1XH; tel (+44 141) 952 14 16; fax (+44 141) 952 05 73; contact Pat Malcolm.

Euro Library: South Eastern Education and Library Board, Library HQ, Ballynahinch, Co. Down, BT24 8DH; tel (+44 28) 9756 2639; fax (+44 28) 9756 5072; contact Mr M. Buchanan.

Euro Library: Colwyn Bay Library, Woodland Road West, Conwy, LL29 7DH; tel (+44 1492) 562 048; fax (+44 1492) 592 114; contact Sheila Evans.

Euro Library: County Reference Library, Union Place, Truro, Cornwall, TR1 1EP; contact Sandra Forester.

Euro Library: Senior Team Librarian, Central Library, Smithford Way, Coventry, CV1 1FY; tel (+44 24) 7683 2325; fax (+44 24) 7683 2440; e-mail covinfo@ discover.co.uk; contact Karen Berry.

Euro Library: Reference and Information Services, Central Library, Katharine Street, Croydon, CR9 1ET; contact Esther Greenwood.

Euro Library: Gwent House Public Library, Gwent Square, Cwmbran, NP44 1XQ; contact Robert Price.

Euro Library: Darlington Borough Council, Central Library, Crown Street, Darlington, DL1 1ND; tel (+44 1325) 462 034; fax (+44 1325) 381 556; contact P. White.

Euro Library: Derby Central Library, The Wardwick, Derby, DE1 1HS; tel (+44 1332) 255 398; fax (+44 1332) 359 570; contact Margaret Jay.

Euro Library: Exeter Central Library, Reference Services, Exeter, Devon, EX4 3PQ; tel (+44 1392) 384 281; fax (+44 1392) 384 228; contact Mark Peasley.

Euro Library: Doncaster Central Library (Reference Library), Waterdale, Doncaster, DN1 3JE; tel (+44 1302) 734 320; fax (+44 1302) 369 749; contact Gill Goodman.

Euro Library: Reference Library, Colliton Park, Dorchester, DT1 1XJ; tel (+44 1305) 224 442; fax (+44 1305) 266 120; contact Nick G. Lawrence.

Euro Library: Dudley Library, St James's Road, Dudley, DY1 1HR; tel (+44 1384) 815 554; fax (+44 1384) 815 543; e-mail dudlib@dudley.gov.uk; contact Michael Gay.

Euro Library: Libraries Headquarters, Levenford House, Helenslee Road, Dumbarton, G82 4AH; tel (+44 1389) 738 325; fax (+44 1389) 734 204; contact Michael C. Taylor.

Euro Library: Dumfries & Galloway Libraries, Ewart Library, Catherine Street, Dumfries, DG1 1JB; tel (+44 1387) 253 820; fax (+44 1387) 260 294; e-mail alistair_johnson@dumgal.gov.uk; contact Alistair R. Johnson.

Euro Library: Central Library, The Wellgate, Dundee, DD1 1DB; tel (+44 1382) 434 336; fax (+44 1382) 434 642; e-mail ptullock@taynet.co.uk; contact Pamela Tullock.

Euro Library: Durham County Council, Arts, Libraries and Museums Department, Durham County Council, County Hall, Durham, DH1 5TY; tel (+44 191) 383 42 31; fax (+44 191) 384 13 36; e-mail p.conway@durham.gov.uk; contact P. Conway.

Euro Library: East Kilbride Library, Olympia Centre, East Kilbride, G74 1PG; tel (+44 13552) 20046; fax (+44 13552) 29365; contact Mr D. Moncrieff.

Euro Library: Ebbw Vale Library, 21 Bethcar Street, Ebbw Vale, NP3 6HH; tel (+44 1495) 303 069; fax (+44 1495) 350 547; e-mail ebbw-vale-library@dial.pipex.com; contact Julie Davies.

Euro Library: Central Library, Reference Dept., George IV Bridge, Edinburgh, EH1 1EG; tel (+44 131) 225 55 84; fax (+44 131) 225 87 83; e-mail jh13@dial.pipex.com; contact Richard Slaughter.

Euro Library: Libraries Manager, Victoria Building, Queen Street, Falkirk, FK2 7AF; tel (+44 1324) 506 800; fax (+44 1324) 506 801; contact Susan Allison.

Euro Library: Central Library, Libraries & Arts, Prince Consort Rd, Gateshead, NE8 4LN; tel (+44 191) 477 34 78; fax (+44 191) 477 74 54; e-mail macnaught@gateslib.demon.co.uk; contact Bill MacNaught.

Euro Library: East Renfrewshire Council, Giffnock Community Library, Station Road, Giffnock, G46 6UG; tel (+44 141) 638 6349; fax (+44 141) 621 0842; contact M. Devine.

Euro Library: Glasgow City Libraries, The Mitchell Library, North Street, Glasgow, G3 7DN; tel (+44 141) 287 28 50; fax (+44 141) 287 28 71; contact Janette Blakeway.

Euro Library: Reference Librarian, Grimsby Central Library, Town Hall Square, Grimsby, DN31 1HG; contact Jenny Mooney.

Euro Library: Llyfrgell Caerarfon Library, Ffordd Pafiliwn, Caernarfon, Gwynedd, LL55 1AS; contact James Hywel.

Euro Library: East Lothian Library Service, User & Support Services, Library Services HQ, Dunbar Road, Haddington, EH41 3DX; contact Morag Tocher.

Euro Library: Calderdale Metropolitan Dist. Council, Central Library, Northgate House, Halifax, HX1 1UN; contact Bernard Murphy.

Euro Library: Hamilton Central Library, 98 Cadzow Street, Hamilton, ML3 6HQ; tel (+44 1698) 453 402; fax (+44 1698) 286 334; contact Isabel Walker.

Euro Library: Civic Centre Library, P O Box 4, Station Road, Harrow, Middx, HA1 2UU; tel (+44 20) 8424 1055; fax (+44 20) 8424 1971; contact Helen Shorter.

Euro Library: Hartlepool Central Library, 124 York Road, Hartlepool, TS26 9DE; tel (+44 1429) 272 905; fax (+44 1429) 275 685; e-mail reflib@hartlepool.gov.uk; contact Julie Blaisdale.

Euro Library: Hastings Reference Library, 13 Claremont, Hastings, East Sussex, TN34 1HE; tel (+44 1424) 716 481; fax (+44 1424) 443 289; contact Brian Scott.

Euro Library: Hertfordshire Libraries, Central Resources Library, New Barnfield, Travellers Lane, Hatfield, AL10 8XG; contact Jane Apling.

Euro Library: Pembrokeshire County Council Reference & Local Studies, The County Library, Dew Street, Haverfordwest, SA61 1SU; contact Anita Thomas.

Euro Library: Huddersfield Central Library, Princess Alexandra Walk, Huddersfield, HD1 2SU; tel (+44 1484) 221 975; fax (+44 1484) 226 342; e-mail cultural-hg@geo2.poptel.org.uk; contact Jane Rose.

Euro Library: Central Library, Commercial & Technical Library, Albion Street, Hull, HU1 3TF; contact J.M. Edge.

Euro Library: London Borough of Redbridge, Central Library, Clements Road, Ilford, IG1 1EA; contact Rebecca Naismith.

Euro Library: Central Library Municipal Buildings, Greenock, Inverclyde, PA15 1LY; contact Lynne Lambie.

Euro Library: Highland Libraries, 31A Harbour Road, Inverness, IV1 1UA; tel (+44 1463) 235 713; fax (+44 1463) 236 986; contact Norman Newton.

Euro Library: County Library, Northgate Street, Ipswich, IP1 3DE; contact Janet Bayliss.

Euro Library: The Council Shop & European Information Point, Kidderminster Library, Market Street, Kidderminster, DY10 1AD; tel (+44 1562) 512 900; fax (+44 1562) 512 901; contact Stewart Scott.

Euro Library: The Reference Library, The Dick Institute, 14 Elmbank Avenue, Kilmarnock, KA1 3BU; tel (+44 1563) 526 401; fax (+44 1563) 529 661; contact Dawn Vallance.

Euro Library: Kingston Library, Fairfield Road, Kingston upon Thames, KT1 2PS; contact Margaret Mitchell.

Euro Library: Fife Council Community Service, Central Area Libraries, East Fergus Place, Kirkcaldy, KY1 1XT; contact Janet Klak.

Euro Library: Reference Department, William Patrick Library, 2 West High Street, Kirkintilloch, G66 1AD; tel (+44 141) 776 80 90; fax (+44 141) 776 04 08; contact Myra Woods.

Euro Library: Orkney Islands Council, Laing Street, Kirkwall, Orkney, contact Robert Leslie.

Euro Library: Knowsley Libraries, Reference and Information Service, Westmorland Road, Huyton, Knowsley, L36 9UJ; contact Graham Watson.

Euro Library: Library – Information for Business, Central Library, Leeds, LS1 3AB; tel (+44 113) 247 82 82; fax (+44 113) 247 82 68; contact Tracy Hopkinson.

Euro Library: Leicestershire Librairies, Rothley Crossroads, Loughborough Road, Leicester, LE7 7NH; contact Ian Van Arkadie.

Euro Library: Leicestershire Librairies, Rothley Crossroads, Loughborough Road, Rothley, Leicester, LE7 7NH; contact Ian Van Arkadie.

Euro Library: Leicester City & Information Services, Reference and Information Library, Bishop Street, Leicester, Leicestershire, LE1 6AA; tel (+44 116) 255 66 99; fax (+44 116) 255 54 35; contact Sally Mitchell.

Euro Library: Shetland Islands Council, Lower Hillhead, Lerwick, Shetland, ZE1 0EL; contact John Hunter.

Euro Library: Lincoln Central Library, Free School Lane, Lincoln, Lincs., LN2 1EZ; tel (+44 1522) 549 160; fax (+44 1522) 535 882; contact Eleanor Nannestad.

Euro Library: Business and Information Library, William Brown Street, Liverpool, L3 8EW; tel (+44 151) 225 54 30; fax (+44 151) 207 13 42; e-mail lvpublic.demon.co.uk; contact Tim Parrott.

Euro Library: Carmarthenshire County Council, Lanelli Public Library, Vaughan Street, Llanelli, Dyfed, SA15 3AS; contact R.H. Davies.

Euro Library: Llangefni Library, Swyddfar Sir, Lon y Felin, Llangefni, LL77 7TW; contact David Handel Evans.

Euro Library: Midlothian, District Library H.Q., 2 Clerk Street, Loanhead, EH20 9DR; contact Neil Macvicar.

Euro Library: London Borough of Newham, Stratford Reference Library, Water Lane, Stratford, London, E15 4NJ; tel (+44 20) 85 19 63 46; fax (+44 20) 85 03 15 25; contact Jacky Appleton.

Euro Library: London Borough of Waltham Forest, Central Library, High Street, Walthamstow, London, E17 7NJ; tel (+44 20) 85 20 30 17; fax (+44 20) 85 09 96 54; contact Dave Watkins.

Euro Library: London Borough of Tower Hamlets, Bethnal Green Library, Cambridge Heath Road, London, E2 0HL; contact John Jasinski.

Euro Library: City of London, City Business Library, 1 Brewers' Hall Garden, London, EC2V 5BX; tel (+44 20) 7638 8215; fax (+44 20) 7332 1847; contact Garry P. Humphreys.

Euro Library: London Borough of Hackney, Shoreditch Library, 80 Hoxton Street, London, N1 6LP; tel (+44 20) 77 39 06 10; contact Marah Cyprian.

Euro Library: London Borough of Haringay, Marcus Garvey Library, Tottenham Green Centre, 1 Philip Lane, London, N15 4JA; contact Linda Jean Fullick.

Euro Library: London Borough of Islington, Central Reference Library, 2 Fieldway Crescent, London, N5 1PF; tel (+44 20) 76 09 30 51 ext. 217; fax (+44 20) 76 00 64 09; contact Mark Pickworth.

Euro Library: Edmonton Green Library, 36–44 South Mall, Edmonton, London, N9 6TW.

Euro Library: Marylebone Library, Marylebone Information Service, Marylebone Road, London, NW1 5PS; tel (+44 20) 77 98 10 39; fax (+44 20) 77 98 10 44; contact Frances Maloney.

Euro Library: Swiss Cottage Central Library, 88 Avenue Road, London, NW3 1PF; tel (+44 20) 7413 6531; fax (+44 20) 7413 6532; contact Gulanar Peake.

Euro Library: London Borough of Barnet, Hendon Library, The Burroughs, Barnet, London, NW4 4BQ; tel (+44 20) 83 59 28 83; fax (+44 20) 83 95 22 97; contact Peter Clark.

Euro Library: London Borough of Lewisham, 199–201 Lewisham High St, London, SE13 6LG; tel (+44 20) 82 97 94 30; fax (+44 20) 82 97 11 69; e-mail reference.library@lewisham.gov.uk; contact Carol Evans.

Euro Library: Reference & Information Library, 155–157 Walworth Road, Southwark, London, SE17 1RS; tel (+44 20) 77 08 05 16; fax (+44 20) 72 52 61 15; e-mail fp96@pipex.dial.com; contact Sue Highley.

Euro Library: London Borough of Greenwich, Woolwich Library, Info Services, Calderwood Street, Woolwich, London, SE18 6QZ; tel (+44 20) 83 12 56 74; fax (+44 20) 83 16 16 45; e-mail lesley.ray@greenwichlis.demon.co.uk; contact Arun Sharma.

Euro Library: Wandsworth Borough Council, Battersea Reference Library, Altenburgh Gardens, London, SW11 1JQ; tel (+44 20) 88 71 74 67; fax (+44 20) 89 78 43 76; contact Howard G. Cooke.

Euro Library: London Borough of Merton, Wimbledon Reference Library, Wimbledon Hill Road 35, London, SW19 7NB; contact Elaine Jones.

Euro Library: London Borough of Lambeth, Tate Library (Brixton), Brixton Oval, London, SW2 1JQ; tel (+44 20) 79 26 10 67; fax (+44 20) 79 26 10 70; contact Christine Maynard.

Euro Library: London Borough of Ealing, Reference Library, Central Library, 103 Ealing Broadway Centre, London, W5 5JY; tel (+44 20) 85 67 36 56; contact John Gauss.

Euro Library: London Borough of Hammersmith & Fulham, Hammersmith Library, Reference Department, Shepherds Bush Road, London, W6 7AT; tel (+44 20) 8576 5053; fax (+44 20) 8576 5022; contact Vernon W. Burgess.

Euro Library: Royal Borough of Kensington & Chelsea, Central Reference Library, Phillimore Walk, London, W8 7RX; tel (+44 20) 79 37 25 42; fax (+44 20) 79 37 05 15; contact Sasi Del Bono.

Euro Library: Westminster Libraries, Central Reference Library, St Martin's Street, London, WC2 7HP; tel (+44 20) 77 98 20 34; contact Adrian Cornish.

Euro Library: Luton Borough Council, Luton Central Library, St George's Square, Luton, LU1 1NG; tel (+44 1582) 301 61; fax (+44 1582) 480 325; contact Robert Evans.

Euro Library: Royal Borough of Windsor & Maidenhead Library, St. Ives Road, Maidenhead, SL6 1QU; contact Sally Todd.

Euro Library: County Central Library, Springfield, Maidstone, Kent, ME14 2LH; contact Christel Pobgee.

Euro Library: European Information Unit, Manchester Central Library, St Peter's Square, Manchester, M2 5PD; tel (+44 161) 234 19 96; fax (+44 161) 237 59 74; e-mail euroinfo.mcl@poptel.org.uk; contact Jenny Morris.

Euro Library: Merthyr Tydfil Central Library, High Street, Merthyr Tydfil, CF47 8AF; tel (+44 1685) 723 057; fax (+44 1685) 370 690; contact G.H. James.

Euro Library: Middlesbrough Libraries & Information, Central Library, Victoria Square, Middlesbrough, TS1 2AY; tel (+44 1642) 263 364; fax (+44 1642) 230 690; e-mail gbm3fvjf@1bmmail.com; contact Denise Turner.

Euro Library: Milton Keynes Central Library, Silbury Boulevard 555, Milton Keynes, MK9 3HL; contact A. Marshall.

Euro Library: Flintshire County Council, Mold Library Museum and Gallery, Daniel Owen Centre, Earl Road, Mold, Flintshire, CH7 1AP; tel (+44 1352) 754 791; fax (+44 1352) 753 662; contact Nia Wyn Jones.

Euro Library: Reference Section, Elgin Library, Cooper Park, Elgin, Moray, IV30 1HS; tel (+44 1343) 542 746; fax (+44 1343) 549 050; e-mail MClib@Cityscape.CO.UK; contact Sheila Campbell.

Euro Library: Central Library, The Willows, Morpeth, NE61 1TA; tel (+44 1670) 511 156; fax (+44 1670) 518 012; contact Mike Dimelow.

Euro Library: Neath and Port Talbot County Borough Council, PO European Support, Civic Centre, Neath, Port Talbot, SA11 3QZ; tel (+44 1639) 764 230; fax (+44 1639) 764 400; contact Larsen Ceri.

Euro Library: West Berkshire County Council, Newbury Library, Carnegie Road, Newbury, RG14 5DW; contact Fiona Davis.

Euro Library: City Library, Princess Square, Newcastle upon Tyne, NE99 1DX; tel (+44 191) 261 06 91; fax (+44 191) 261 14 35; e-mail stephen.darby@ newpl.demon.co.uk; contact Stephen Darby.

Euro Library: Lord Louis Library, Orchard Street, Newport, Isle of Wight, PO30 1LL; contact Michelle Hadlow.

Euro Library: Newport County Borough Council, Central Library, John Frost Square, Newport, NP9 1SG; tel (+44 1633) 211 376; fax (+44 1633) 222 615; contact Ian Evans.

Euro Library: Branch Librarian, Newtown Area Library, Park Lane, Newtown, SY16 1EJ; contact Jane Rimmer.

Euro Library: County Library H.Q., 21 Grammar School Lane, Northallerton, DL6 1DF; contact Elisabeth Melrose.

Euro Library: Northants Central Library, Abington Street, Northampton, Northampton, NN1 2BA; tel (+44 1604) 26774; fax (+44 1604) 230 790; contact Clare Cole.

Euro Library: North Tyneside Metropolitan – Borough Council, Central Library, Northumberland Square, Northshields, NE30 1QU; contact Lesley Green.

Euro Library: Norfolk and Norwich Central Reference Library, Gildengate House, Upper Green Lane, Norwich, Norfolk, NR3 1AX; tel (+44 1603) 215 255; fax (+44 1603) 215 258; contact Ellen Barbara Laws.

Euro Library: Nottingham City Library, Angel Row, Nottingham, NG1 6HP; contact Hilary Waring.

Euro Library: Libraries, Archives & Information, Community Services, 4th Floor, County Hall, West Bridgeford, Nottingham, NG2 7QP; contact David Lathrope.

Euro Library: Nuneaton Library, Church Street, Nuneaton, CV11 4DR; contact Sarah Hayball.

Euro Library: Rutland Libraries & Museums, Rutland County Library, Catmose Street, Oakham, Rutland, LE15 6HW; contact John Byrne.

Euro Library: Oldham Library, Union Street, Oldham, OL1 1DN; tel (+44 161) 911 46 43; fax (+44 161) 627 10 25; contact J. Hetherington.

Euro Library: Library Service, Meldrum Meg Way, The Meadows Industrial Estate, Oldmeldrum, AB51 0GN; tel (+44 1651) 872 707; fax (+44 1651) 872 142; contact Gerald Moore.

Euro Library: Western Education & Library Board, Library H.Q., 1 Spillars Place, Omagh, BT78 1HL; contact Leo Crossey.

Euro Library: Oxfordshire County Council, Dept. of Leisure and Arts, Holton, Oxford, Oxfordshire, OX33 1QQ; tel (+44 1865) 810 182; fax (+44 1865) 721 694.

Euro Library: Central Library, High Street, Paisley, PA1 2BB; tel (+44 141) 889 23 60; fax (+44 141) 887 64 68; e-mail renlib4@cqm.co.uk; contact Cathy Gormal.

Euro Library: Perth and Kinross District Libraries, AK Bell Library, York Place, Perth, PH2 8EP; tel (+44 1738) 477 060; fax (+44 1738) 477 020; contact Mr E. Durkin.

Euro Library: Peterborough Central Library & Theatre, Broadway, Peterborough, PE1 1RX; contact Peter Reynolds.

Euro Library: City of Plymouth, Library and Information Services, Central Library, Business and Information, Drake Circus, Plymouth, PL4 8AL; contact Pat Davey.

Euro Library: Caerphilly County Borough Council, Unit 7, Woodfieldside Business Park, Penmaen Road, Pontlanfaith, NP2 2DG; contact Megan Pinnell.

Euro Library: Poole Central Reference Library, Dolphin Centre, Poole, BH15 1QE; contact Jenny Oliver.

Euro Library: Southern Education and Library Board, Government Information Service, 24–26 Church Street, Portadown, BT62 3LQ; tel (+44 1762) 335 247; fax (+44 1762) 391 759; contact Sandra Young.

Euro Library: Portsmouth City Council, Portsmouth Central Library, Guildhall Square, Portsmouth, PO1 2DX; contact Jackie Painting.

Euro Library: Principal Librarian Field Services, Powys County Council, County Hall, Llandrindod Wells, Powys, LD1 5LG; contact Helen Edwards.

Euro Library: Harris Library, Market Square, Preston, PR1 2PP; tel (+44 1772) 264 002; fax (+44 1772) 264 880; e-mail lancs-co-lib-ha@mcr1.poptel.org.uk; contact David Shuttleworth.

Euro Library: Central Library, Abbey Square, Reading, RG1 3BQ; contact Mike Cooper.

Euro Library: Redcar & Cleveland – Borough Council, Redcar Central Library, Coatham Road, Redcar, TS10 1RP; contact Brenda Robinson.

Euro Library: London Borough of Richmond Upon Thames, Reference & Information Services, Old Town Hall, Whittaker Ave, Richmond upon Thames, TW9 1TP; contact David Mccomb.

Euro Library: Central Reference Library, St Edward's Way, Romford, RM1 3AR; contact Adrian Janes.

Euro Library: Rotherham Metropolitan Borough Council, Central Library, Walker Place, Rotherham, SG5 1JH; tel (+44 1709) 823 614; fax (+44 1709) 823 650; e-mail centlib-sgpl@bbcnc.org.uk; contact Margot Drury.

Euro Library: Halton Borough Council, Halton Lea Library, Halton Lea, Runcorn, WA7 2PF; contact Jean Bradburn.

Euro Library: Ruthin Head Cultural Services, Hy Hen Garchar, Clwyd Street, Ruthin, LL15 1HP; contact Williams Gwyn W. Obe.

Euro Library: Broadwalk Library, Broadwalk, Vulcan House, Salford, M6 5JA; contact Brian Graney.

Euro Library: Scunthorpe Central Library, Carlton Street, Scunthorpe, DN16 6TX; contact H. Dean.

Euro Library: Adult Services, Borders Regional Library, St Mary's Mill, Selkirk, TD7 5EW; tel (+44 1750) 20842; fax (+44 1750) 22875; contact Rosamund Brown.

Euro Library: Business, Science & Technology Library, Sheffield Library & Information Services, Surrey Street, Sheffield, S1 1XZ; tel (+44 114) 273 47 36; fax (+44 114) 273 50 09; contact Joyce Gray.

Euro Library: Shropshire Information Services, 1A Castle Gates, Shrewsbury, SY1 2AQ; contact Pamela Turner.

Euro Library: Slough Borough Council, Slough Library, High Street, Slough, SL1 1EA; contact R. Sirr.

Euro Library: Central Library, Information Services, Homer Road, Solihull, B91 3RG; tel (+44 121) 704 69 74; fax (+44 121) 704 62 12; contact Noel Hird.

Euro Library: South Tyneside Library, Reference Services, Prince George Square, South Shields, NE33 2PE; contact Tom Relph.

Euro Library: Central Library, Civic Way, Ellesmere Port, South Wirral, L65 0BG; contact Hilda Faragher.

Euro Library: Central Library, Civic Centre, Southampton, SO14 7LW; contact H.A. Richards.

Euro Library: Librarian Information, Southend on Sea Borough Libraries, Central Library, Victoria Avenue, Southend, SS2 6EX; contact Toby Evans.

Euro Library: Sefton Library, Bibliographic Service, 244 Liverpool Road, Birkdale, Southport, PR8 4PU; tel (+44 1704) 560 090; fax (+44 151) 928 06 92; contact Mary Wall.

Euro Library: St Helens MBC, Central Library, Gamble Institute, Victoria

Square, St Helens, Merseyside, WA10 1DY; tel (+44 1744) 456 951; fax (+44 1744) 20836; contact Stephen Pindard.

Euro Library: Information Staffordshire Libraries, Arts & Archives HQ, Friars Terrace, Stafford, ST17 4AY; tel (+44 1785) 278 351; fax (+44 1785) 278 309; e-mail staffsinfo@dial.pipex.com; contact Heather Jones.

Euro Library: North Lanarkshire Council Leisure Service Department, Buchanan Business Centre, Cumbernauld Road, Stepps, G33 6HR; tel (+44 141) 304 18 00; contact Ann Malloy.

Euro Library: Community Services Libraries, Heritage and Cultural Services, Library Headquarters, Borrowmeadow Road, Stirling, FK7 7TN; tel (+44 1786) 432 381; fax (+44 1786) 432 395; contact Andrew Muirhead.

Euro Library: Stockport Central Library, Wellington Road South, Stockport, SK1 3RS; tel (+44 161) 474 45 22; fax (+44 161) 474 77 50; e-mail stockport.cenlibrary@dial.pipex.com; contact Lynne Ranson.

Euro Library: Stockton Central Library, Gloucester House, Church Road, Stockton on Tees, TS18 1TU; contact Christine Durnion.

Euro Library: Hanley Library, Information Services, Bethesda Street, Hanley, Stoke on Trent, ST1 2RS; tel (+44 1782) 238 431; fax (+44 1782) 238 434; contact Lesley Jones.

Euro Library: Western Isles Libraries, Keith Street, Stornoway, HS1 2QG; contact David Fowler.

Euro Library: City of Sunderland MBC City Library & Arts Centre, 28–30 Fawcett Street, Sunderland, SR1 1RE; tel (+44 191) 514 12 35; fax (+44 191) 514 84 44; contact Elizabeth Tinker.

Euro Library: Sutton Central Library, St Nicholas Way, Sutton, Surrey, SM1 1EA; tel (+44 20) 87 70 47 00; fax (+44 20) 77 70 47 77; contact Patricia Moore.

Euro Library: City & County of Swansea Reference Library, Alexandra Road, Swansea, SA1 5DX; tel (+44 1792) 655 521; fax (+44 1792) 645 751; contact Peter Matthews.

Euro Library: Swindon Reference Library, Regent Circus, Swindon, SN1 1QG; tel (+44 1793) 463 240; fax (+44 1793) 541 319.

Euro Library: Taunton Library, Paul Street, Taunton, TA1 3PF; contact Jane Gill.

Euro Library: Telford Library, Town Centre, St. Quentin Gate, Telford, TF3 4JG; contact Helen Brooks.

Euro Library: Torquay Library Services, Torquay Central Library, Lymington Road, Torquay, TQ1 3DT; contact Anne Howard.

Euro Library: Rhondda Cynon Taf County, Borough Council, Treorchy Library, Station Road, Treorchy, CF42 6NN; contact Gillian Evans.

Euro Library: Wiltshire Library & Museum Service, Bythesea Road, Trowbridge, BA14 8BS; contact Linda Matthews.

Euro Library: London Borough of Hillingdon, Central Library, 14–15 High Street, Uxbridge, UB8 1HD; contact Tanya Britton.

Euro Library: District Council, Library, Information Service, Balne Lane, Wakefield, WF2 0DQ; contact Kathryn Harrison.

Euro Library: Information Services, Walsall Central Library, Lichfield Street, Walsall, WS1 1TR; tel (+44 1922) 653 110; fax (+44 1922) 654 013; e-mail rkennedy@walsinfo.demon.co.uk; contact Rita Kennedy.

Euro Library: Warrington Borough Council, Warrington Library, Museum Street, Warrington, WA1 1JB; contact Jan Rawsthorn.

Euro Library: London Borough of Brent, Town Hall Library, Forty Lane, Wembley, HA9 9HV; contact C.M. Tasker.

Euro Library: Sandwell Metropolitan Borough Council, Information Service, West Bromwich Library, High Street, West Bromwich, B70 8DZ; tel (+44 121) 569 49 11; fax (+44 121) 525 94 65.

Euro Library: North Somerset Council, Weston Library, The Boulevard, Weston super Mare, BS23 1PL; contact Elaine Mellor.

Euro Library: Wigan Library – Information Unit, College Avenue, Wigan, W1N 1DQ; tel (+44 1942) 827 627; fax (+44 1942) 827 640; contact Julie McDonald.

Euro Library: Hampshire County Library, Headquarters, North Walls 81, Winchester, SO23 8BY; contact Jane Weller.

Euro Library: South Gloucestershire Council, Winterbourne Library, Flaxpits Lane, Winterbourne, BS36 1LA; contact Anne Hooper.

Euro Library: Woking Library, Surrey County Council, Gloucester Walk, Woking, GU21 1EP; contact Vernon White.

Euro Library: Wokingham District Council Library, Denmark Street, Wokingham, RG40 2BB; contact Kate Mitchell.

Euro Library: Wolverhampton Metropolitan Borough Council, Central Library, Snow Hill, Wolverhampton, WV1 3AX; tel (+44 1902) 312 026; fax (+44 1902) 714 579; contact Christine West.

Euro Library: Workington Library, Vulcans Lane, Workington, CA14 2ND; tel (+44 1900) 603 744; fax (+44 1900) 65987; contact Trevor Jones.

Euro Library: Wrexham Library, Rhosddu Road, Wrexham, LL11 1AU; tel (+44 1978) 261 932; fax (+44 1978) 361 876; contact H. AP. Emlyn.

Euro Library: City of York Libraries, York Central Library, Museum Street, York, YO1 7DS; contact R.G. Bowling.

ECSA-NET

ECSA-NET is an interactive instrument provided by the Directorate-General for Education and Culture in collaboration with ECSA (European Community Studies Association) specifically aimed at disseminating information among academics dealing with European Integration. The members of ECSA are directly involved in gathering and updating the information available on ECSA-NET. In January 2005 members comprised 52 national associations for the study of the European Community in the EU Member States and non-Member countries, representing more than 9,000 professors and researchers.

A network of national ECSA-NET Correspondents is working closely with the European Commission to ensure the efficient functioning of the system and in particular to control the accuracy of the information for which they are responsible before it is directed to ECSA-NET.

The ECSA-NET main menu offers the following specific sub-headings:

1. European Community Studies Association – ECSA
1.1. National associations, their members, newsletters and publications.
1.2. Information on ECSA General Secretariat activities.

2. Postgraduate Degrees in European Integration
2.1. The list of postgraduate degrees in European integration in the universities of the EU Member States and in some universities in non-member countries.

3. Who's Who in European Integration Studies
3.1. Search by name, country and discipline.

3.2. Search entry comprises name, academic discipline, work address, degrees awarded, publications, courses on European integration issues and research activities (updated by national associations).

4. Calendar / ECSA News
4.1. Calendar of conferences, seminars, workshops etc. updated by the national ECSA associations; search by country, year, month or free text.

The European Commission unit responsible for ECSA-NET can be contacted at: The European Commission, Education and Culture DG, Directorate A – Education, Rue de la Loi 200, 1049 Brussels, Belgium; tel (+32) 2-2960312; fax: (+32) 2-2999205. ECSA-NET is also accessible via the web at www.ecsanet.org.

NETWORK OF NATIONAL ACADEMIC RECOGNITION INFORMATION CENTRES (NARIC)

Created in 1984, on an initiative of the European Commission, the NARIC network aims to improve academic recognition of diplomas and periods of study in the EU Member States, the EEA countries and the associated countries in Eastern Europe. The network forms part of the community's Socrates/Erasmus programme. The NARICs were designated by the ministries of education in their respective countries, and basically offer information and advice on foreign education systems and qualifications. In addition to dealing with academic recognition, many of the EU NARICs have been nominated by their Member States to function as information points in respect of professional recognition.

EU Countries

AUSTRIA

NARIC Austria: Bundesministerium für Bildung Wissenschaft und Kultur, Teinfaltstrasse 8, 1014 Wien; tel (+43 1) 531 20 59 20; fax (+43 1) 531 20 78 90; e-mail naric@bmwf.gv.at; contact Heinz Kasparovsky.

BELGIUM

ENIC / NARIC: Ministère de l'éducation – Communauté Française de Belgique, Direction générale de l'Enseignement supérieur et de la recherche scientifique, Rue Royale 204, 1010 Brussels; tel (+32 2) 210 55 77; fax (+32 2) 210 59 92; e-mail chantal.kaufman@cfwb.be; internet www.cfwb.be/infosup; contact Chantal Kaufmann.

NARIC-Vlanderen: Ministerie van de Vlaamse Gemeenschap, Henri Consciencegebouw Tower A7, Koning Albert II Laan 15, 1210 Brussels; tel (+32 2) 553 98 19; fax (+32 2) 553 98 05; e-mail erwin.malfroy@ond.vlaanderen.be; contact Erwin Malfroy.

CYPRUS

Ministry of Education and Culture, Cyprus Council for the Recognition of Higher Education Qualifications: Kinonos and Thoukididou Street, 1434 Nicosia; tel (+357 2) 80 06 66; fax (+357 2) 30 51 16; e-mail kysats@cytanet.com.cy; contact Ioannis Paraskevopoulos.

CZECH REPUBLIC

Centre for Equivalence of Documents on Education (ENIC/NARIC), CSVS: U Luzického Seminare 13, 11800 Prague 1; tel (+420 2) 57 53 05 00; fax (+420 2) 57 53 16 72; e-mail skuhrova@csvs.cz; contact Stepanka Skuhrova.

DENMARK

The Danish Centre for Assessment of Foreign Credentials: Fiolstraede 44, 1171 Kobenhavn K; tel (+45) 33 95 7000; fax (+45) 33 95 7001; e-mail helle.otte@cvuu.dk; internet www.cvuu.dk; contact Helle Otte.

ESTONIA

The Estonian ENIC / NARIC: Foundation Archimedes, L. Koidula 13A, 10125 Tallinn; tel (+372 6) 962 415; fax (+372 6) 962 419; e-mail liia@archimedes.ee; internet www.socrates.ee; contact Gunnar Vaht.

FINLAND

National Board of Education: PL 380, 00531 Helsinki; tel (+358 9) 77 47 71 28; fax (+358 9) 77 47 72 01; e-mail carita.blomqvist@oph.fi; contact Carita Blomqvist.

FRANCE

Centre International d'Etudes Pedagogiques: 1 avenue Leon Journault, 92318 Sevres Cedex; tel (+33 1) 55 55 73 57; fax (+33 1) 55 55 00 39; e-mail prfit@ciep.fr; internet www.ciep.fr/enic-naricfr/; contact Albert Prevos.

GERMANY

Zentralstelle für ausländisches Bildungswesen im Sekretariat der Kulturministerkonferenz – KMK: Lennéstrasse 6, 53113 Bonn; tel (+49 228) 501 203; fax (+49 228) 501 229; e-mail zab@kmk.org; internet www.kmk.org; contact Holger Conrad.

GREECE

DI KATSA: Mesognion Avenue 223, 11525 Athens; tel (+30 10) 675 63 62; fax (+30 10) 675 67 09; e-mail leonta@cc.uoi.gr; internet www.dikatsa.gr; contact George Leontaris.

ITE – Institute of Technological Education: Sygrou Avenue 56, 11742 Athens; tel (+30 10) 922 10 00; fax (+30 10) 922 77 16; e-mail ikazazis@teiath.gr; contact G. Eliopoulos.

HUNGARY

Hungarian Equivalence and Information Centre of the Ministry of Education: Szalay u 10/14, 1055 Budapest; tel (+36 1) 473 72 09; fax (+36 1) 332 19 32; e-mail julia.juhasz@om.gov.hu; internet www.naric.hu; contact Gabor Meszaros.

IRELAND

The National Qualifications Authority of Ireland: 5th Floor Jervis House, Jervis Street, Dublin 1; tel (+353 1) 887-1588; fax (+353 1) 887-1595; e-mail vbeatty@nqai.ie; internet www.nqai.ie; contact Valerie Beatty.

ITALY

CIMEA – Fondazione Rui: Viale XXI Aprile 36, 00162 Roma; tel (+39 06) 86 32 12 81; fax (+39 06) 86 32 28 45; e-mail cimea@fondazionerui.it; internet www.fondazionerui.it; contact Carlo Finocchietti.

LATVIA

Academic Information Centre, Latvian ENIC/NARIC: Valnu Street 2, 1050 Riga; tel (+371 7) 225 155; fax (+371 7) 221 006; e-mail baiba@aic.lv; internet www.aic.lv; contact Baiba Ramina.

LITHUANIA

Lithuanian Centre for Quality Assessment in Higher Education: Survalku str 1, 2600 Vilnius; tel (+370 2) 232 552; fax (+370 2) 232 553; e-mail darius@skvc.lt; internet www.skvc.lt; contact Darius Tamosiunas.

LUXEMBOURG

Ministère de la Culture, de l'Enseignement superieur et de la Recherche: 18-20, Montee de la Petrusse, 2912 Luxembourg; tel (+352) 478 51 39; fax (+352) 26 29 60 37; e-mail jean.tagliaferri@mcesr.etat.lu; contact Jean Tagliaferri.

MALTA

Malta Qualification Recognition Information Centre (Malta QRIC): Great Siege Road, Room No 328, Floriana; tel (+356-21) 240 419; fax (+356-21) 239 842; e-mail anthony.v.degiovaani@gov.mt; internet www.education.gov.mt; contact Anthony DeGiovanni.

NETHERLANDS

Nuffic: Postbus 29777, Kortenaerkade 11, 2502 LT Den Haag; tel (+31 70) 426 02 70; fax (+31 70) 426 03 95; e-mail divis@nuffic.nl; internet www.nuffic.nl; contact Jindra Divis.

POLAND

Bureau for Academic Recognition and International Exchanges: Ul Smolna 13, 00375 Warsaw; tel (+48 22) 828 81 61; fax (+48 22) 826 28 23; e-mail bwm@buwiwm.edu.pl; internet www.buwiwm.edu.pl; contact Ewa Majdowska.

PORTUGAL

Ministry for Science, Innovation and Higher Education, Direccao-Geral do Ensino Superior: Av. Duque d'Avila 137 – 2., 1069-016 Lisboa; tel (+351 21) 312 60 00; fax (+351 21) 312 60 41; e-mail manuela.paiva@dges.mcies.pt; contact Manuela Paiva.

SLOVAKIA

Institute of Information and Prognoses of Education: Staré Grunty 52, 84244 Bratislava; tel (+421 2) 65 42 65 21; fax (+421 2) 65 42 65 21; e-mail hrabinska@uips.sk; contact Maria Hrabinska.

SLOVENIA

Ministry of Education, Science and Sport, Education Recognition Office, ENIC/NARIC: Trg OF 13, 1000 Ljubljana; tel (+386 1) 4784 203; fax (+386 1) 4784 324; e-mail naric.mszs@gov.si; internet www.mszs.si/eng/education/enic_naric/default.asp; contact Anita Jesenko.

SPAIN

NARIC España, Subdireccion General de Titulos, Convalidaciones y Homologaciones: Paseo del Prado 28, 28014 Madrid; tel (+34 91) 506 55 93; fax (+34 91) 506 57 06; e-mail misabel.barrios@educ.mec.es; contact Maria Isabel Barrios.

SWEDEN

National Agency for Higher Education (Hogskoleverket): Box 7851, 10399 Stockholm; tel (+46 8) 56 30 88 23; fax (+46 8) 56 30 86 50; e-mail lars.petersson@hsv.se; internet www.hsv.se; contact Lars Petersson.

UNITED KINGDOM

ECCTIS Ltd: Oriel House, Oriel Road, Cheltenham, Gloucestershire, GL50 1XP; tel (+44 1242) 260 010; fax (+44 1242) 258 611; e-mail cloudnaric@ecctis.co.uk; internet www.naric.org.uk; contact Cloud Bai-Yun.

EEA

ICELAND

University of Iceland: Sudurgata 101, 101 Reykjavik; tel (+354) 525 43 60fax (+354) 525 43 17; e-mail thordkri@hi.is, gf@hi.is; internet www.hi.is; contact Thordur Kristinsson.

LIECHTENSTEIN

Schulamt, Departement of Education: Ausstrasse 79, 9490 Vaduz; tel (+423) 236 67 58; fax (+423) 236 67 71; e-mail helmut.konrad@sa.llv.li; internet www.firstlink.li/eu/socrates; contact Helmut Konrad.

NORWAY

Norwegian Agency for Quality Assurance in Education: P.O. 1708 Vilca, 0121 Oslo; tel (+47 21) 02 18 25; fax (+47 21) 02 18 02; e-mail postmottak@nokut.no; internet www.nnr.no; contact Anne Marie Heszlein.

Associated Countries

BULGARIA

Ministry of Education and Science, European Integration Division: Kniaz Dondukov bld 2A, 1000 Sofia; tel (+359 2) 988 49 74; fax (+359 2) 988 49 74; e-mail r.velinova@minedu.government.bg; internet www.minedu.government.bg; contact Rossitza Velinova.

ROMANIA

ENIC/NARIC, National Center of Diplomas Recognition: Ministry of Education and Research, Général Berthelot Str. 28–30, Sector 1, 70738 Bucharest; tel (+40 1) 313 26 77; fax (+40 1) 313 26 77; e-mail girbea@men.edu.ro; contact Liliana-Daniela Girbea.

EURODESK

Eurodesk is a European Network for the dissemination of European information and for the provision of telephone enquiry answering services at national or regional level for young people and those who work with them.

The Directorate-General Education and Culture of the European Commission has supported the piloting of Eurodesk and its subsequent development as a European Network within the framework of the Youth for Europe programme.

Eurodesk is concerned with information relevant to the education, training and youth fields, and the involvement of young people in European activities. Eurodesk can provide both European information from the European Commission and other European level agencies, and other relevant information from a national level in the participating countries. Eurodesk processes and summarizes European information to make it more easily understood by the target groups.

Eurodesk operates free, public enquiry answering and information services, throughout the EU, on European funding and opportunities for young people. Using specially developed multi-lingual enquiry answering software, the Eurodesk staff can offer a fast and accurate answer to an enquiry.

The answer to an enquiry can include: funding information (European funding programmes and budgetlines and national funding sources); Contacts (European and national level organizations to help with taking the enquiry further); Resources (a listing of relevant documents, publications, books, training packs, etc.).

The Eurodesk Network now has partners in 23 countries with more than 150 Eurodesk sites providing Eurodesk information services at national and regional levels. By use of a specially developed database, all the Eurodesk partners can share and exchange information electronically and always have access to a wide range of up-to-date information for the answering of enquiries. The Eurodesk Network is supported by the Eurodesk Brussels Link, which undertakes the Network co-ordination and the researching of European information for dissemination to the Eurodesk Network partners.

Enquiries to the Eurodesk Network should be directed to your nearest national Eurodesk unit.

The Eurodesk Network is co-ordinated by: Eurodesk Brussels Link, Scotland House, Rond-Point Schuman 6, 1040 Brussels, Belgium; tel : (+32) 2-2828384; fax (+32) 2-282-83-90; e-mail info@eurodesk.org.

Eurodesk Network Partners

AUSTRIA

jugendinfo.cc / ARGE Osterreichische Jugendinfos: Lilienbrunngasse 18/2/41, 1020 Wien; tel (+43 669) 120 05 183; fax (+43 1) 216 48 44 - 55; e-mail info@jugendinfo.cc.

BELGIUM

BIJ Bureau International Jeunesse: Rue du Commerce 20-22, 1000 Bruxelles; tel (+32 2) 219 09 06; fax (+32 2) 218 81 08; e-mail veronique.balthasart@cfwb.be.

JINT vzw: Grétrystraat 26, 1000 Bruxelles; tel (+32 2) 209 07 20; fax (+32 2) 209 07 49; e-mail jint@jint.be.

JIZ St. Vith – Jugendinformationszentrum: Hauptstrasse 82 / Rue Principale 82, 4780 St Vith; tel (+32 80) 221 567; fax (+32 80) 221 566; e-mail jiz@rdj.be.

BULGARIA

Ministry of Youth and Sports: Bld Vassil Levski 75, 1040 Sofia; tel (+359 2) 981 75 77; fax (+359 2) 981 83 60; e-mail eurodesk@youthdep.bg.

CYPRUS

Eurodesk Youth Board: Themistokli Dervi Str 41, Hawaii Tower Office 106–108, 1066 Nicosia; tel (+357 2) 765 006; fax (+357 2) 761 135; e-mail eurodesk@cytanet.com.cy.

CZECH REPUBLIC

CAN Mladez / IDM MSMT: Senovážné nam. 24, 11647 Praha, 1; tel (+420 2) 34 621 261; fax (+420 2) 34 621 261; e-mail eurodesk@adam.cz.

DENMARK

Eurodesk Cirius | c/o Cirius: Fiolstraede 44, 1171 Kobenhavn K; tel (+45) 33 95 7000; fax (+45) 33 95 70 01; e-mail eurodesk@ciriusmail.dk.

ESTONIA

The European Movement in Estonia: Roosikrantsi 11, 10119 Tallinn; tel (+372 6) 419 678; fax (+372 6) 306 616; e-mail epp@eurodesk.ee.

FINLAND

Eurodesk CIMO – Centre for International Mobility: PO Box 343, Hakaniemenkatu 2, 00531 Helsinki; tel (+358 9) 7747 7664; fax (+358 9) 7747 7064; e-mail eurodesk@cimo.fi.

FRANCE

CIDJ: Quai Branly 101, 75740 Paris Cedex 15; tel (+33 1) 47 83 40 55; fax (+33 1) 40 65 02 61; e-mail eurodesk@cidj.com.

GERMANY

IJAB eV: Heussallee 30, 53113 Bonn; tel (+49 228) 9506 208; fax (+49 228) 9506 199; e-mail eurodesk@eurodesk.org.

GREECE

Hellenic National Agency: Acharnon 417, 11143 Athens; tel (+30 210) 25 99300; fax (+30 210) 25 31879; e-mail eurodesk@athina.neagenia.gr.

HUNGARY

Mobilitas Informacios Szolgalat / Mobilitas Information Service: Zivatar u 1-3, 1024 Budapest; tel (+36 1) 438 1051; fax (+36 1) 438 1055; e-mail eurodesk@mobilitas.hu.

ICELAND

Evrovisir / Hitt Husid Culture & Information Centre for Young People: Posthusstraeti 3-5, 101 Reykjavik; tel (+354) 520 4620; fax (+354) 520 4601; e-mail hitthusid@hitthusid.is.

IRELAND

Eurodesk Leargas: Parnell Street 189-193, Dublin 1; tel (+353 1) 872 23 94; fax (+353 1) 873 13 16; e-mail eurodesk@leargas.ie.

ITALY

Eurodesk Italia, Ufficio di coordinamento nazionale: Via 29 Novembre n. 49, 09123 Cagliari; tel (+39 070) 68 40 64; fax (+39 070) 68 32 83; e-mail informazioni@eurodesk.it.

LATVIA

National Agency of Latvia, Eurodesk Service: Merkela 11-533, 1050 Riga; tel (+371) 7221875; fax (+371) 7222236; e-mail ansis@eurodesk.org.

LITHUANIA

Council of Lithuanian Youth Organisations (LiJOT): Didzioji str. 8-5, 01128 Vilnius; tel (+370) 52791280; fax (+370) 527 91014; e-mail lijot@lijot.lt.

LUXEMBOURG

Centre Information de Jeunes: Galerie Kons, Place de la Gare 26, 1616 Luxembourg; tel (+352) 26 29 3219; fax (+352) 26 29 3215; e-mail lia.kechagia@info.jeunes.lu.

NETHERLANDS

NIZW International Centre / Eurodesk: Zakkendragershof 34–44, PO Box 19152, 3501 DD Utrecht; tel (+31 30) 230 65 50; fax (+31 30) 230 65 40; e-mail eurodesknl@eurodesk.org.

NORWAY

Norwegian Directorate for Children, Youth and Family Affairs: PO Box 8113 Dep., 0032 Oslo; tel (+47 24) 04 40 23; fax (+47 24) 04 40 01; e-mail eurodesk@bufa.no.

POLAND

Narodowa Agencja Programu Mlodziez / Eurodesk: ul. Mokotowska 43; IV p., 00-551 Warszawa; tel +48 22 622 66 700; fax +48 22 622 80 81; e-mail eurodesk@eurodesk.pl.

PORTUGAL

Departamento de Informaçao aos Jovens: Avenida da Liberdade 194 R/c, 1269-051 Lisboa; tel (+351 21) 317 92 35/6; fax (+351 21) 317 92 19; e-mail ipj@ipj.pt.

ROMANIA

Eurodesk Romania: ANSIT (Agentia Nationala pentru Sprijinirea Initiativelor Tinerilor), Str. Dem. I. Dobrescu 4–6, 010026 Bucharest; tel (+40 21) 312 73 29; fax (+40 21) 312 73 29; e-mail eurodeskro@eurodesk.org.

SLOVAKIA

NAFYM IUVENTA: Budkova ulica 2, 81104 Bratislava 1; tel (+421 2) 5929 6301; fax (+421 7) 544 11 421; e-mail eurodesk@iuventa.sk.

SLOVENIA

Eurodesk Slovenia: Trg Mladinskih delovnih brigad 12, 1000 Ljiubljana; tel (+386 1) 4268 561; fax (+386 1) 4268 558; e-mail eurodesk@mladina.movit.sl.

SPAIN

Unidad Coordinacion Espana, Instituto de la Juventud: C/Marqués de Riscal 16, 280010 Madrid; tel (+34 91) 3637837; fax (+34 91) 319 93 38; e-mail eurodesk@mtas.es.

SWEDEN

Centrum for Internationellt Ungdomsutbyte: Ludvigsbergsgatan 22, 11823 Stockholm; tel (+46 8) 440 87 80; fax (+46 8) 20 35 30; e-mail eurodesk@ciu.org.

UNITED KINGDOM

Eurodesk, European Resource Centre, Youthlink Scotland: Rosebery House, 9 Haymarket Terrace, Edinburgh, EH12 5EZ; tel (+44 131) 313 2488; fax (+44 131) 313 6800; e-mail eurodesk@youthlink.co.uk.

Team Europe (formerly Team '92) was set up in 1989 by the European Commission's Directorate-General for Information, Communication, Culture and Audiovisual Media, in order to promote the Internal Market.

Team Europe is a panel of expert speakers, present throughout the EU and several non-member countries.

The speakers are selected by the Team Europe co-ordinator of the Commission's offices in the different Member States according to their in-depth knowledge of European affairs and their ability to convey this knowledge to others. Team Europe speakers include university professors, national or international civil servants, executives, consultants, journalists, etc.

The speakers of Team Europe regularly receive updated information on the development of EU policies, according to their fields of specialization. They also receive the assistance of a special information service providing them with specific help in the preparation of their speeches, which are delivered at conferences, meetings and seminars at the request of the organizers of the event. Fees should be discussed directly with each expert speaker.

Team Europe Info Service Members in EU Member States

AUSTRIA

Philipp Agathonos: 30 avenue Cortenbergh, 1040 Brussels; tel (+32 2) 234-52-93; fax (+32 2) 235-62-93; e-mail philipp.agathonos@bmaa.gv.at; Vice-President of the Union der Europäischen Föderalisten (UEF); *specialities:* economic and financial affairs, enlargement, employment and social affairs, general EU policy, institutional reform, IGC, trade, development and external relations, institutional affairs; *languages:* German, English, Greek.

Prof. Dr Hans Jörg Bauer: 147 Ottensteinstrasse, 2344 Maria Enzersdorf; tel (+43 2236) 24-32-4; fax (+43 2236) 24-32-4; e-mail hansj.bauer@aon.at; academic and journalist; *specialities:* enlargement, trade, development and external relations; *languages:* German.

Elke Beneke: 6a/1/9a Hans Gasser Platz, 9500 Villach; tel (+43 4242) 225-95-4; fax (+43 4242) 225-95-5; e-mail e.beneke@eb-consulting.at; consultant; *specialities:* education and culture, employment and social affairs, regional policy, research and information society; *languages:* German, English.

Prof. Dr Gerhart Bruckmann: 7 Lichtenfelsgasse, 1010 Vienna; tel (+43 1) 401-26-15-1; fax (+43 1) 406-62-66; academic; *specialities:* economic and financial affairs, enlargement, employment and social affairs, general EU policy, institutional reform, IGC, trade, development and external relations; *languages:* German, English, French.

Dr Kurt Cowling: Kärnten AG, 7 Bahnhofstrasse, 9020 Klagenfurt; tel (+43 50909) 21-11; fax (+43 50909) 90-01; e-mail kurt.cowling@ghbkaernten.volksbank.at; Deputy Regional Director of Bank Austria AG, member of board of the Volksbank of Kärnten; *specialities:* education and culture, economic and financial affairs, general EU policy, institutional reform, IGC, internal market affairs; *languages:* German, English.

Anneliese Friedrich-Mulley: 169 Krottendorf, 8564 Krottendorf-Gaisfeld; fax (+43 3143) 20-42-4; e-mail mulley-friedrich@aon.at; translator; *specialities:* education and culture, enlargement, general EU policy, employment and social affairs; *languages:* German, English, Italian.

Gerda Füricht-Fiegl: 14 Feldgasse, 3701 Grossweikersdorf; tel (+43 2955) 71-46-6; e-mail gerda.fuericht@gmx.net; EU official; *specialities:* agriculture and fisheries, general EU policy, regional policy; *languages:* German, English.

Dr Rene Alfons Haiden: 2 Renngasse, 1010 Vienna; tel (+43 1) 711-91-52-34-2; fax (+43 1) 711-91-52-95-6; e-mail greta.leitenbauer@ba-ca.com; President of the Free Economic Association of Austria-Bank Austria AG; *specialities:* enterprise, competition, state aids, economic and financial affairs, enlargement, trade, development and external relations; *languages:* German, English.

Holger Heller: 4 Schwarzenbergplatz, 1031 Vienna; tel (+43 1) 711-35-24-04; fax (+43 1) 711-35-23-16; e-mail h.heller@iv-net.at; project leader, Industrial Association; *specialities:* general EU policy; *languages:* German, English.

Prof. Dr Markus F. Hofreither: 33 Gregor Mendel-Strasse, 1180 Vienna; tel (+43 1) 476-54-34-71; fax (+43 1) 476-54-36-92; e-mail hofreith@edv1.boku.ac.at; academic; *specialities:* agriculture and fisheries; *languages:* German, English.

Dr Stefan Hornung: 11 Heilbrunnerstrasse, 5020 Salzburg; tel (+43 662) 84-16-16-0; fax (+43 662) 84-16-16-17; e-mail stefan.hornung@lawconsult.at; lawyer; *specialities:* enterprise, competition, state aids, economic and financial affairs, employment and social affairs, general EU policy, institutional reform, IGC, health and consumer protection, internal market affairs, justice and home affairs; *languages:* German, English.

Prof. Dr Hubert Isak: Resowi-Zentrum, 15/C1 Universitätsstrasse, 8010 Graz; tel (+43 316) 38-03-62-7; fax (+43 316) 38-09-47-0; e-mail hubert.isak@kfunigraz.ac.at; academic; *specialities:* enlargement, general EU policy, institutional reform, IGC, internal market affairs, justice and home affairs, trade, development and external relations, transport and energy; *languages:* German, English.

Carola Jud: 1 Michael-Gaismair-Strasse, 6020 Innsbruck; (+43 512) 508-36-34; fax (+43 512) 508-36-05; e-mail c.jud@tirol.gv.at; expert attached to Tyrol state government; *specialities:* regional policy, employment and social affairs; *languages:* German, English, French.

Matthias Koch: 63 Wiedner Hauptstrasse, 1045 Vienna; tel (+43 5) 909-00-36-39; fax (+43 5) 909-00-28-6; e-mail matthias.koch@wko.at; Vice-President for International Know-how Transfer, Federal Economic Chamber of Austria; *specialities:* enterprise, competition, state aids, economic and financial affairs, enlargement, internal market affairs, research and information society, trade, development and external relations; *languages:* German, English.

Dr Josef Leidenfrost: 5 Minoritenplatz, 1014 Vienna; tel (+43 1) 531-20-55-33; fax (+43 1) 533-77-97; e-mail josef.leidenfrost@bmbwk.gv.at; lawyer; *specialities:* education and culture, enlargement, research and information society, trade, development and external relations; *languages:* German, English.

Robert Leitner: 20 Mozartstrasse, 4010 Linz; tel (+43 5) 909-09-34-50; fax (+43 5) 909-09-34-59; e-mail robert.leitner@wkooe.at; chief, Euro Info Centre of Economic Chamber of Upper Austria; *specialities:* economic and financial affairs, enlargement, general EU policy, institutional reform, IGC, internal market affairs, trade, development and external relations; *languages:* German, English.

Dr Paul Luif: 20B Operngasse, 1040 Vienna; tel (+43 1) 581-11-06-21; fax (+43 1) 581-11-06-10; e-mail Paul.Luif@

compuserve.com; academic; *specialities:* enlargement, general EU policy, trade, development and external relations; *languages:* German, English.

Christian Mandl: 63 Wiedner Hauptstrasse, 1045 Vienna; tel (+43 1) 501-05-43-16; fax (+43 1) 501-05-14-31-6; e-mail christian.mandl@wko.at; Director of the Department of European Integration, Federal Economic Chamber of Austria; *specialities:* economic and financial affairs, enlargement, employment and social affairs, general EU policy, institutional reform, IGC, internal market affairs, regional policy, trade, development and external relations; *languages:* German.

Dr Brigitte Marcher: Dr Karl Renner Institute, 12 Khleslplatz, 1120 Vienna; tel (+43 1) 804-65-01-28; fax (+43 1) 804-08-74; e-mail marcher@renner -institut.at; chief, European Department of the Dr Karl Renner Institute; *specialities:* enlargement, employment and social affairs, general EU policy, institutional reform, IGC, health and consumer protection; *languages:* German, English.

Dr Wolfger Mayrhofer: 15 Herzog-Friedrich-Strasse, 6020 Innsbruck; tel (+43 512) 588-58-91-7; fax (+43 512) 588-58-92-0; e-mail wolfger.mayhofer@ alpconv.org; lawyer; *specialities:* enterprise, competition, state aids, employment and social affairs, general EU policy, institutional reform, IGC, internal market affairs, regional policy, transport and energy; *languages:* German, English.

Werner Mikulitsch: Postfach 122, 6/11 Oppolzergasse, 1014 Vienna; tel (+43 1) 533-49-99-12; fax (+43 1) 533-49-90; e-mail werner.mikulitsch@euro-info.net; member, Austrian Society for European Policy; *specialities:* general EU policy, internal market affairs, trade, development and external relations; *languages:* German, English.

Karl-Heinz Nachtnebel: 10–12 Hohenstaufengasse, 1010 Vienna; tel (+43 1) 534-44-273/249; fax (+43 1) 534-44-349; e-mail kh.nachtnebel@oegb.or.at; chief, International Relations Section of Austrian Federation of Trade Unions; *specialities:* employment and social affairs; *languages:* German, English, French.

Karl Obernosterer: 1 Sparkassenplatz, 6020 Innsbruck; tel (+43 512) 591-04-20-0; fax (+43 512) 591-04-11-5; e-mail karl.obernosterer@tispa.at; member, Board of Directors, Tyrol Sparkasse Bankaktiengesellschaft, Innsbruck; *specialities:* education and culture, enterprise, competition, state aids, economic and financial affairs, enlargement; *languages:* German, English.

Walter Obwexer: Neue Universität, 52 Innrain, 6020 Innsbruck; tel (+43 512) 507-83-23; fax (+43 512) 507-28-24; e-mail walter.obwexer@uibk.ac.at;

academic, lawyer; *specialities:* enlargement, general EU policy, institutional reform, IGC, internal market affairs, regional policy, research and information society, trade, development and external relations, transport and energy; *languages:* German, English.

Erich Putz: 63 Wiedner Hauptstrasse, 1045 Vienna; tel (+43 1) 501-05-45-58; fax (+43 1) 501-05-24-0; e-mail erich.putz@ wko.at; EU expert in the Office of the President of the Economic Chamber of Austria; *specialities:* enlargement, regional policy; *languages:* German, English.

Ilse Rein: 4 Schwarzenbergplatz, 1031 Vienna; tel (+43 1) 177-35-24-08; fax (+43 1) 711-35-29-14; e-mail ilse.rein@ feinspitz.cc; economist; *specialities:* employment and social affairs, trade, development and external relations, enlargement, internal market affairs; *languages:* German, English, Spanish.

Dr Martina Schernthanner: 63 Wiedner Hauptstrasse, 1045 Vienna; tel (+43 1) 501-05-34-80; fax (+43 1) 501-051-38-40; e-mail martina.schernthanner@ wko.at; chief, Euro Info Centre, Salzburg; *specialities:* economic and financial affairs, enlargement, internal market affairs; *languages:* German.

Prof. Dr Manfred Straube: 30 Dr Karl Dorek Strasse, 3500 Krems; tel (+43 2732) 893-2400; fax (+43 2732) 893-4400; e-mail manfred.straube@unvie .ac.at; academic; *specialities:* education and culture, internal market affairs; *languages:* German, English.

Dr Claudia Weyringer: 111–113 Körblergasse, 8021 Graz; tel (+43 316) 60-16-00; fax (+43 316) 60-17-33; e-mail claudia .weyringer@wkstmk.at; chief, Euro Info Centre, Steiermark; *specialities:* enterprise, competition, state aids, economic and financial affairs, enlargement, general EU policy, institutional reform, IGC, internal market affairs; *languages:* German.

Dr Wolfgang Wolte: 6 Oppolzergasse, 1014 Vienna; tel (+43 1) 533-49-99; fax (+43 1) 533-49-40; e-mail europa@euro -info.net; member, board of the Austrian Society for European Policy; *specialities:* agriculture and fisheries, education and culture, economic and financial affairs, enlargement, environment, employment and social affairs, internal market affairs, regional policy, trade, development and external relations; *languages:* German, English, French.

BELGIUM

Nicholas Allen Blow: 110 avenue Albert, 1190 Brussels; tel (+32 2) 346-56-24; fax (+32 2) 345-04-73; e-mail blow@ epri.org; researcher; *specialities:* employment and social affairs, general EU policy,

institutional reform, IGC; *languages:* English.

Bruno Boissière: 214D chaussée de Wavre, 1050 Brussels; tel (+32 2) 508-30-32; fax (+32 2) 626-95-01; e-mail: bboissiere@skynet.be; Secretary-General of the Union des Fédéralistes Européens (UEF); *specialities:* enlargement, general EU policy, institutional reform, IGC, regional policy; *languages:* French, English.

Rogier Chorus: 18 rue des Colonies, 1000 Brussels; tel (+32 2) 511-30-12; fax (+32 2) 511-51-74; e-mail chorus@ cerameunie.org; Secretary-General of Cérame-Unie; *specialities:* enterprise, competition, state aids, environment, internal market affairs, trade, development and external relations; *languages:* Dutch, English, French.

Jacqueline de Hanscutter: Buke, 158, 9620 Leeuwergem (Zottegem); tel (+32 9) 361-09-89; fax (+32 9) 361-09-89; e-mail jacqueline.dehanscutter@diplobel.fed.be; consultant; *specialities:* enlargement, employment and social affairs, internal market affairs, trade, development and external relations; *languages:* Dutch, French, English.

Jos de la Haye: 2B Van Evenstraat, 3000 Leuven; tel (+32 16) 32-32-42; fax (+32 16) 32-30-88; e-mail jos.delahaye@ soc.kuleuven.ac.be; academic; *specialities:* enlargement, general EU policy, institutional reform, IGC, trade, development and external relations; *languages:* Dutch, English, French.

Hubert de Viron: 214D chaussée de Wavre, 1050 Brussels; tel (+32 2) 508-30-35; fax (+32 2) 512-66-73; e-mail h.deviron@uef.be; Administrator, Advocacy Europe; *specialities:* enterprise, competition, state aids, economic and financial affairs, internal market affairs; *languages:* French, English.

Evelyne de Wolf-Lambert: 60 avenue de l'Arbalète, 1170 Brussels; *languages:* English.

Mark Delmartino: 15 Dianalaan, 2600 Berchem; tel (+32 03) 321-98-27; e-mail mark.delmartino@antwerpen.be; Senior Programme Manager, European Association of Service Providers for Persons with Disabilities (EASPD); *specialities:* enlargement, general EU policy, institutional reform, employment and social affairs; *languages:* Dutch, English, French.

Dr Knut Diekmann: 87 rue de l'Aqueduc, 1000 Brussels; tel (+32 2) 537-56-08; fax (+32 2) 280-46-97; e-mail knutdiekmann@hotmail.com; Liaison Officer, Lace Tap; *specialities:* enlargement, general EU policy, institutional reform, IGC, regional policy; *languages:* German, English.

Maria Victoria Gil Casado: 1–6 C Calle Gran Via, 48910 Sestao; tel (+32 619) 36-75-14; e-mail victoriagil@latinmail.com; lawyer; *specialities:* enterprise, competition, state aids, economic and financial affairs, internal market affairs; *languages:* Spanish, French, English.

Gian Michele Giordano: 30 avenue François Folie, 1180 Brussels; tel (+32 2) 374-31-91; fax (+32 2) 374-31-91; former bank manager in charge of international relations and director for EU affairs, member of Group Euro at the European Commission; *specialities:* education and culture, economic and financial affairs, general EU policy, institutional reform, IGC, trade, development and external relations; *languages:* Italian, French.

Ana-Maria Goncalves: 25 rue des Taxandres, 1040 Brussels; tel (+32 2) 742-04-26; e-mail ana-maria.goncalves@ascii.be; communications consultant; *specialities:* research and information society; *languages:* Portuguese, French.

Giovanni Gordiani: 20 avenue des Gaulois, 1040 Brussels; tel (+32 2) 732-71-24; fax (+32 2) 734-25-82; e-mail GiGCBI@carlbro.dk; *languages:* Italian, English.

Alain Guggenbühl: 11 rue d'Egmont, 1000 Brussels; tel (+32 2) 502-10-06; fax (+32 2) 511-67-70; e-mail alain .guggenbuhl@tiscali.be; lecturer, European Institute of Public Administration; *specialities:* enlargement, employment and social affairs, general EU policy, institutional reform, IGC; *languages:* English, French.

Sören Haar: 19–21 rue du Luxembourg, 1000 Brussels; tel (+32 2) 512-41-16; fax (+32 2) 514-69-32; e-mail s.haar@euro-pa -online.com; consultant and researcher, Euro P. A.; *specialities:* enlargement, general EU policy, institutional reform, IGC internal market affairs; *languages:* German, English, French.

Klaus Hullmann: 17 rue Berthelot, 1190 Brussels; tel (+32 2) 735-01-33; fax (+32 2) 735-01-33; e-mail khul1234@ tiscali.be; lawyer, academic; *specialities:* economic and financial affairs, general EU policy, institutional reform, IGC, justice and home affairs; *languages:* German, English, French.

Ciro Irlando: 242 avenue Franklin Roosevelt, 1050 Brussels; tel (+32 2) 646-72-75; fax (+32 2) 646-72-75; e-mail ciroirlando@hotmail.com; consultant; *specialities:* enterprise, competition, state aids, trade, development and external relations; *languages:* Italian, French.

Richard Kokholm-Erichsen: 49–51 rue de Trèves, 1040 Brussels; tel (+32 2) 235-00-67; fax (+32 2) 286-97-99; e-mail richard.kokholm-erichsen@ascii.be; translator; *specialities:* general EU policy; *languages:* Danish, English, French.

Ruben Lombaert: 78 Dampoortstraat, 8310 St Kruis Brugge; tel (+32 2) 629-18-06; fax (+32 2) 629-18-09; e-mail ruben .lombaert@pandora.be; consultant; *specialities:* enlargement, general EU policy, institutional reform, IGC, research and information society; *languages:* Dutch, English, French.

Albert Maes: 9 avenue des Ajoncs, 1150 Brussels; tel (+32 2) 762-99-14; former civil servant; *specialities:* economic and financial affairs, general EU policy, institutional reform, IGC, trade, development and external relations; *languages:* French.

Michel Maroy: 39 square Vergote, 1030 Brussels; tel (+32 2) 742-94-56; fax (+32 2) 732-22-51; e-mail michel.maroy@skynet .be; consultant; *specialities:* education and culture, general EU policy, institutional reform, IGC, internal market affairs, trade, development and external relations; *languages:* French, English.

Philippe Moulart: bte 9, 57 avenue du Derby, 1050 Brussels; tel (+32 2) 672-25-04; fax (+32 2) 673-25-04; e-mail philippe .moulart@swing.be; member, Association of Senior European Counsellors; *specialities:* agriculture and fisheries, enlargement, regional policy, research and information society, trade, development and external relations; *languages:* French.

Els Muyshondt: 11 Vierhuizen, 9255 Buggenhout; tel (+32 52) 34-13-68; fax (+32 52) 33-13-39; e-mail els.muyshondt@ skynet.be; consultant in human resources; *specialities:* enterprise, competition, state aids, environment, employment and social affairs, internal market affairs; *languages:* Dutch, English, French.

Kris Peeters: 8 Spastraat, 1000 Brussels; tel (+32 2) 23-80-31; fax (+32 2) 230-93-54; e-mail kris.peeters@unizo.be; director, NCMV; *specialities:* agriculture and fisheries, economic and financial affairs; *languages:* Dutch, English.

Eric Pollefliet: 2 Havenlaan, 1080 Brussels; tel (+32 2) 429-78-46; fax (+32 2) 422-81-39; e-mail eric.pollefliet@kbc .be; banker; *specialities:* economic and financial affairs, enlargement, employment and social affairs, general EU policy, institutional reform, IGC; *languages:* Dutch, English, French.

Gérard Poolman: 6 Lenneke Marelaan, 1932 Zaventem; tel (+32 2) 749-27-63; fax (+32 2) 749-27-69; e-mail gpoolman@ ssebe.jnj.com; manager, Johnson & Johnson; *specialities:* general EU policy, institutional reform, IGC, research and information society; *languages:* Dutch, English, French.

Dr E. A. Povel: blvd Léopold III, 1110 Brussels; tel (+32 2) 707-50-21; fax (+32 2) 707-54-57; e-mail natodoc@hq.nato.int; Liaison Officer for the Netherlands at the NATO Office of Information and Press; *specialities:* general EU policy, institutional reform, IGC; *languages:* Dutch, English, German.

Florence Ranson: 17 rue de Bordeaux, 1060 Brussels; tel (+32 2) 779-21-30; fax (+32 2) 772-89-80; e-mail floranson@ hotmail.com; Secretary-General, European Advertising Tripartite; *specialities:* general EU policy, institutional reform, IGC, internal market affairs, research and information society; *languages:* French, English, German.

Prof. Dr Fernand H. F. Rogiers: 115 Patijntjestraat, 9000 Ghent; tel (+32 9) 222-86-91; fax (+32 9) 264-35-92; e-mail rogcol@skynet.be; academic; *specialities:* economic and financial affairs, enlargement, employment and social affairs, internal market affairs, transport and energy; *languages:* Dutch, French, English.

Jürgen Rosenbaum: 2B Armendylaan, 1933 Sterrebeek, tel (+32 2) 731-79-72; e-mail rosenbaum@pandora.be; former research manager in the field of education; *specialities:* research and information society, education and culture, general EU policy; *languages:* German, English, French.

Philip Savelkoul: 18 Wolvengracht, 1000 Brussels; tel (+32 3) 645-83-41; fax (+32 3) 233-27-75; e-mail philip .savelkoul@vkw.be; economist, lecturer; *specialities:* economic and financial affairs, general EU policy, institutional reform, IGC; *languages:* Dutch, English, French.

Irnerio Seminatore: 27/A blvd Charlemagne, 1000 Brussels; tel (+32 2) 280-14-95; fax (+32 2) 280-14-95; e-mail ieri@ belgacom.net; academic, President of the Institut Européen des Relations Internationales (IERI); *specialities:* enlargement, general EU policy, commerce, development and external relations; *languages:* Italian, French.

Lutgart Spaepen: 14 Coppenolstraat, 2000 Antwerp; tel (+32 2) 210-16-35; e-mail lutgart.spaepen@staf.ehsal.be; general co-ordinator of export research and market-monitoring projects at EHSAL-Brussels; *specialities:* education and culture, enterprise, competition, state aids, enlargement, trade, development and external relations; *languages:* Dutch, French, English.

Marc Taquet-Graziani: 95 rue Joseph Coosemans, 1030 Brussels; tel (+32 2) 735-04-50; fax (+32 2) 512-53-44; consultant; *specialities:* general EU policy, institutional reform, IGC, health and consumer protection, internal market affairs, trade, development and external relations; *languages:* French.

Raphaël Van Berwaer: 3 avenue Konrad Adenauer, 1200 Brussels; tel (+32 2) 772-65-75; fax (+32 2) 772-66-21; teacher, lecturer; *specialities:* economic and financial affairs, general EU policy, institutional reform, IGC, internal market affairs, trade, development and external relations; *languages:* French, English.

Jo Vandercappellen: 51/B7 rue des Riches Claires, 1000 Brussels; tel (+32 2) 513-41-66; fax (+32 2) 513-47-40; e-mail vandercappellen.jo@compaqnet .be; speaker on European institutions, economic and monetary policy and several other areas of European policy; *specialities:* economic and financial affairs, general EU policy, institutional reform, IGC, health and consumer protection; *languages:* French, English.

Dr Guy Vanhaeverbeke: 24 avenue Maurice, 1050 Brussels; tel (+32 2) 648-86-49; fax (+32 2) 648-86-49; e-mail tepsa@tepsa.be; Secretary-General of the Trans European Policy Studies Association (TEPSA); *specialities:* agriculture and fisheries, enlargement, general EU policy, institutional reform, IGC, regional policy, trade, development and external relations; *languages:* Dutch, French, English.

Bernard Vanheule: 36 avenue Jean Colin, 1160 Brussels; tel (+32 2) 660-83-03; fax (+32 2) 269-26-36; e-mail vanheule_bernard@hotmail.com; legal adviser on European policy *vis-à-vis* maritime affairs; *specialities:* transport, competition, environment, general EU policy; *languages:* French, Dutch, English.

Vincent Vanwijnsberghe: 6 avenue G. Eekhoud, 1030 Brussels; tel (+32 2) 215-87-47; fax (+32 2) 215-87-47; e-mail vanwijnsberghe_v@hotmail.com; adviser, Fédération des Entreprises de Belgique (FEB); *specialities:* enlargement, general EU policy, institutional reform, IGC, trade, development and external relations; *languages:* French, Dutch, German.

Tom Verbeke: 24 Hoveniersberg, 9000 Ghent; tel (+32 9) 264-34-78; e-mail Tom .Verbeke@rug.ac.be; research assistant, University of Ghent; *specialities:* economic and financial affairs, environment, general EU policy, institutional reform, IGC, trade, development and external relations; *languages:* Dutch, English.

Prof. Dr Jan Vranken: 13 Prinsstraat, 2000 Antwerp; tel (+32 3) 220-43-20; fax (+32 3) 220-43-25; e-mail jan.vranken@ ufsia.ac.be; academic; *specialities:* agriculture and fisheries, education and culture, employment and social affairs; *languages:* Dutch, French, English.

DENMARK

John Aagaard: 26 Islands Brygge, 18542300 Copenhagen S; tel (+45 33) 93-20-00; fax (+45 33) 61-76-32; e-mail john_aagaard@hvr.dk; director of produc-

tion and marketing with the Danish Federation of SMEs; *specialities:* enterprise, competition, state aids, economic and financial affairs, enlargement, internal market affairs, trade, development and external relations; *languages:* Danish, English.

Lars Abel: 1. t. v., 7 Åboulevard, 1635 Kista; tel (+45 35) 39-43-44; fax (+45 35) 35-43-44; e-mail lars.abel@ europeanadvisers.com; consultant; *specialities:* enterprise, competition, state aids, economic and financial affairs, enlargement, environment, employment and social affairs, internal market affairs, research and information society; *languages:* Danish, English.

Lilly Andersen: 48 Blenstrupvej 48, 9520 Skørping; tel (+45 98) 33-90-92; fax (+45 98) 33-90-92; e-mail lilly-and@ dlgnet.dk; farmer, instructor for the Agricultural Council of Denmark; *specialities:* agriculture and fisheries, enlargement, environment, health and consumer protection, regional policy; *languages:* Danish, English.

Rastén Bengt: 1–3 Staunings Plads, 1607 V Copenhagen; tel (+45 33) 70-13-06; fax (+45 33) 70-13-33; e-mail br@ dkk.dk; Senior Policy Officer, the Danish Confederation of Municipal Employees; *specialities:* employment and social affairs; *languages:* Danish, English.

Klaus Berg: Postboks 158, 6330 Padborg; tel (+45 22) 61-09-61; e-mail ksb@ pit-stop.dk; Managing Director, Padborg International Transport Center; *specialities:* enterprise, competition, state aids, regional policy, transport and energy; *languages:* Danish, English, German.

Müzeyyen Boztroprak: 3 t. v., 4 Augustagade, 2300 Copenhagen S; tel (+45 25) 78-45-87; e-mail mbo@ams.dk; Head of Section, Labour Market Authorities, Denmark; *specialities:* enlargement, trade, development and external relations; *languages:* Danish, English, Turkish.

Peter Bugge: 5 Jens Chr. Skous Vej, 8000 Århus C; tel (+45 89) 42-64-75; fax (+45 89) 42-64-65; e-mail slapb@hum.au .dk; academic; *specialities:* enlargement; *languages:* Danish, English, Czech.

Thorkild Dahl: 28 Christiansgave, 2960 Rungsted Kyst; tel (+45 45) 57-15-88; fax (+45 45) 57-12-50; e-mail thda@tvs.dk; diplomatic correspondent, TV2, Denmark; *specialities:* general EU policy, enlargement, economic and monetary affairs, agriculture and fisheries; *languages:* Danish, English, German.

Jorgen Elikofer: POB 308, 1780 Copenhagen V; tel (+45 33) 63-20-00; fax (+45 33) 63-21-50; e-mail elikofer@danskmetal .dk; head of department, Danish Metalworkers Union; *specialities:* enterprise, competition, state aids, environment, employment and social affairs, internal

market affairs, transport and energy; *languages:* Danish, English, German.

Ella Grosman: 113 Østerbrogade, 1 2100 Copenhagen; tel (+45 39) 27-10-10; e-mail ellagrosman@yahoo.dk; linguist; *specialities:* education and culture, trade, development and external relations, general EU policy; *languages:* Danish, English, Polish.

Mare Grønbjerg: 200 Islevdalvej 200, 2610 Rødovre; tel (+45 36) 44-21-85; fax (+45 36) 44-21-85; e-mail info@ estkonsult.com; export consultant; *specialities:* enlargement, trade, development and external relations, enterprise, competition and state aids; *languages:* Danish, English, Estonian.

Hans Henrik Hansen: 15 Dalgas Have, 2000 Frederiksberg; tel (+45 38) 15-29-97; fax (+45 38) 15-20-40; e-mail hhh .byg@cbs.dk; Programme Director-CBS-CELL Copenhagen Business School; *specialities:* internal market affairs, trade, development and external relations; *languages:* Danish, English.

John Horsted: 47 Takovski Str., 1000 Sofia; tel (+359 2) 98-59-40-19; fax (+359 2) 98-59-40-13; e-mail john.horsted@ customs.bg; pre-accession adviser, National Customs Agency; *specialities:* enterprise, competition, state aids, environment, research and information society; *languages:* Danish, English.

Lone Hylander: 50 H. C. Andersen Blvd, 1780 Copenhagen V, tel (45 33) 30-48-69; fax (45 33) 30-48-99; e-mail 44lhy@hk.dk; consultant; *specialities:* economic and financial affairs, employment and social affairs; *languages:* Danish, English.

John Iversen: 22 Hvidtjørnevej, 2720 Vanløse; tel (+45 38) 74-31-18; e-mail sjoiv@ft.dk; *languages:* Danish, English.

Henning Jensen: 5 Skovlœet, 2900 Hellerup; tel (+45 40) 30-15-75; e-mail jumiro@tiscali.dk; consultant; *specialities:* agriculture and fisheries, enlargement; *languages:* Danish, English.

Lotte Jensen: 5 C3 Hermodsvej, 8230 Aabyhøj; tel (+45 86) 15-85-11; fax (+45 86) 15-90-09; e-mail info@upfrontnet.dk; director, Up Front Europe; *specialities:* education and culture, enlargement, employment and social affairs, regional policy; *languages:* Danish, English.

Michael Knie-Andersen: 7 mf, 36 Marselis Blvd, 8000 Århus C; tel (+45 86) 19-83-22; fax (+45 86) 19-83-22; e-mail knie-andersen@econ.au.dk; Ph.D. student, Department of Management, School of Economics and Management, University of Aarhus; *specialities:* economic and financial affairs, internal market affairs; *languages:* Danish, English.

Dorthe Larsen: 2 Toften, 8800 Viborg; tel (+45 86) 67-20-52; e-mail dal@privat .dk; *languages:* Danish, English.

Jan O. F. Laustsen: 3, 1. Axeltorv, 1609 Copenhagen; tel (+45 33) 14-56-72; fax (+45 33) 14-62-75; e-mail JL@landbrug .dk; dead of division, Landbrugsrådet; *specialities:* agriculture and fisheries, enlargement, trade, development and external relations; *languages:* Danish, English.

Hans Jørgen Lorenzen: Ordrup Jagt-vej 100, 2920 Charlottenlund; tel (+45 39) 64-84-94; fax (+45 39) 64-84-54; e-mail hjl@eec.dk; Managing Director-Euro Export Consult A/S; *specialities:* enterprise, competition, state aids, enlargement, internal market affairs; *languages:* Danish, English, German.

Elena Markova: 7 Gamlehave Allee, 2920 Charlottenlund; tel (+45 39) 64-24-84; fax (+45 39) 63-49-23; e-mail markova@mail.tele.dk; diplomat at the Embassy of the Republic of Bulgaria in Denmark; *specialities:* enlargement, education and culture; *languages:* Danish, English, Bulgarian, German.

Sven-Peter Nygaard: 113 V. Voldgade, 1790 Copenhagen V; tel (+45 33) 38-94-04; fax (+45 55) 77-40-20; e-mail Spn@da .dk; industrial relations adviser, Danish Employers' Confederation; *specialities:* enterprise, competition, state aids, economic and financial affairs, employment and social affairs; *languages:* Danish, English, France.

Claus Nyrop-Larsen: 49 Ørbœkvej, 5863 Ferritslev; tel (+45 63) 90-99-09; fax (+45 63) 90-99-10; e-mail cnl@ mariuspedersen.dk; Vice-President of Marius Pedersen/Onyx Holding A/S; *specialities:* enlargement, environment, economic and monetary affairs, transport and energy; *languages:* Danish, English, German.

Tine Tolstrup Petersen: 1 t. v., 4 Asminderødgade, 2200 Copenhagen N; tel (+45 35) 55-98-83; e-mail tine_t_ petersen@yahoo.dk; *specialities:* education and culture, general EU policy, employment and social affairs, enlargement; *languages:* Danish, English.

Keld Winther Rasmussen: 22 Frederiks Alle, 8000 Århus C; tel (+45 87) 31-21-94; fax (+45 87) 31-20-01; e-mail Kwr@ mejeri.dk; head of department, Danish Dairy Board; *specialities:* agriculture and fisheries, enlargement, regional policy, trade, development and external relations; *languages:* Danish, English.

Rasmus Tscherning: 4 t. v., Jagtvej 15, 2200 Copenhagen N; tel (+45 28) 40-46-68; e-mail raratsch@mail.dk; consultant; *specialities:* general EU policy, institutional reform, IGC, enlargement, education and culture; *languages:* Danish, English, French, Sweden.

Jørgen Vesta: 292 Rungsted Strandvej, 2970 Hørsholm; tel (+45 45) 76-45-22; fax (+45 45) 76-45-33; e-mail Jv@vesta.dk; managing director, Vesta Management A/S; *specialities:* enterprise, competition, state aids, employment and social affairs, regional policy, trade; *languages:* Danish, English, German.

Peter Warming: 1 t. v., 4 Dr Abildgaards Allé, 1955 Frederiksberg C; tel (+45 35) 36-88-83; e-mail pw@momentum-eu.com; senior adviser, Momentum; *specialities:* enlargement, general EU policy, internal market affairs; *languages:* Danish, English.

Zoe Winding: 57 Oldrupvej, 8350 Hundslund; tel (+45 86) 55-05-38; fax (+45 86) 55-09-40; e-mail zoe.winding@e-kontor .dk; EU consultant/project manager, Consult & Convention Designs; *specialities:* employment and social affairs, environment, regional policy, general EU policy; *languages:* Danish, English, German.

ESTONIA

Diana Eerma: 4 Narva Rd–A203, Tartu 51009; tel (+372 7) 37-63-43; e-mail Diana@mtk.ut.ee; lecturer, Tartu University; *specialities:* economic and monetary affairs, regional policy.

Helina Eha: 17 Roosikrantsi, 10119 Tallinn; tel (+372 63) 14-71-3; e-mail helina@euroopaliit.ee; director, EU Information Centre; *specialities:* EU law, EU institutions.

Mare Ellen: tel (+372 46) 96-20-1; e-mail mare@tuuru.edu.ee; project manager, NGO Tuuru Training Centre; *specialities:* regional policy.

Kristi Jõesaar: tel (+372 52) 76-13-2; e-mail Kristi.joesaar@hotmail.com; attached to Ministry of Finance; *specialities:* structural funds, youth and educational programmes.

Külli Kask: 1 Lossi plats, 15165 Tallinn; tel (+372 63) 16-48-7; e-mail kylli.kask@ riigikogu.ee; councillor, Estonian Parliament; *specialities:* EU history, EU institutions (Parliament), EU information sources.

Urmas Kiil: tel (+372 45) 24-21-8; e-mail urmas@syg.edu.ee; history teacher, Saaremaa Gymnasium; *specialities:* EU history, EU institutions.

Kaie Kork: e-mail kaie.kork@mfa.ee; attached to Ministry of Foreign Affairs; *specialities:* EU history, regional policy.

Jaan Kurm: 14 Tallinna Rd, Rapla 79513; tel (+372 50) 77-32-0; e-mail jaan@raplamv.ee; head of IT department, Rapla County Government; *specialities:* enlargement, the future of the EU, economic and monetary affairs.

Alice Laas: 17 Roosikrantsi, 10119 Tallinn; tel (+372 64) 55-43-6; e-mail alice@ euroopaliit.ee; project manager, EU Information Centre; *specialities:* youth and educational programmes, EU information sources.

Valli Laas: 1 Keskväljak, 41594 Jõhvi; tel (+372 33) 21-26-1; e-mail valli.laas@ ivmv.ee; councillor, Ida-Viru County Government; *specialities:* EU institutions, enlargement, regional co-operation.

Marje Lillimägi: tel (+372 50) 42-64-6; e-mail mhristjuk@hotmail.ee; *specialities:* EU information sources.

Cadrin Lokotar: tel (+372 51) 53-03-2; lecturer, Estonian Business School; *specialities:* EU law, structural funds.

Kaie Rõõm-Laanet: 1 Lossipargi, Kuressaare 93813; tel (+372 45) 39-00-8; e-mail eurohouse@saarlane.ee; director, NGO Eurohouse; *specialities:* regional policy, structural funds.

Toomas Tippi: Rüütli 25, Paide 72713; tel (+372 38) 59-60-9; e-mail toomas .tippi@jarvamv.ee; head of economic department, Järva County Government; *specialities:* regional policy.

FINLAND

Minna Aila: POB 8, 8B Sinimäentie. Helsinki; tel (+358 10) 413-19-08; fax (+358 10) 413-17-35; e-mail minna.aila@ elcoteq.com; project director, Elcoteq Network Corporation; *specialities:* general EU matters, enlargement, enterprise and SME policy, competition policy and state aids; *languages:* Finnish, English, Swedish.

Turo Bergman: PB 157, 00531 Helsinki; tel (+358 9) 772-11; fax (+358 9) 772-12-23; e-mail turo.bergman@sak.fi; deputy director, the Central Organisation of Finnish Trade Unions (SAK); *specialities:* economic and financial affairs, enlargement, employment and social affairs, internal market affairs; *languages:* Finnish, English.

Peter Ekholm: POB 329, 00121 Helsinki; tel (+358 9) 61-89-92-35; fax (+358 9) 64-50-72; e-mail Peter.Ekholm@ sitra.fi; attached to Finnish National Fund for Research and Development (SITRA); *specialities:* enlargement, general EU policy, institutional reform, IGC, justice and home affairs; *languages:* Finnish, English, Swedish.

Filip Hamro Drotz: PB 30, 00131 Helsinki; fax (+358 9) 68-68-23-63; e-mail filip.hamro-drotz@tt.fi; senior adviser, Confederation of Finnish Industry and Employers; *specialities:* enlargement, employment and social affairs, internal market affairs; *languages:* Finnish, English, Swedish.

Tarja Kantola: 4–6 Paasivuorenkatu, 00530 Helsinki; tel (+358 9) 775-76-13; fax (+358 9) 701-11-99; e-mail tarja

.kantola@pamliitto.fi; international secretary, Service Union United (PAM); *languages:* Finnish, English, Swedish.

Kari Tapio Kylkilahti: Nalkalankatu 12F–PL 97, 33101 Tampere; tel (+358 3) 250-32-37; fax (+358 3) 250-32-31; e-mail Kari.kylkilahti@pp.inet.fi; EU co-ordinator, Rural R & D Network, Carrefour Tampere Region; *languages:* Finnish, English.

Kari Liuhto: 3 Rehtorinpellonkatu, 20500 Turku; tel (+358 2) 481-45-75; fax (+358 2) 481-42-68; e-mail Kari.Liuhto@tukkk.fi; academic, director of the Pan-European Institute, Turku School of Economics and Business Administration; *specialities:* transport and energy, foreign investment in Russia, EU-Russian economic relations, Russian investment in the enlarged EU; *languages:* Finnish, English, Russian.

Kaj-Peter Mattsson: 16–18 Eteläesplanadi, 00023 Helsinki; tel (+358 9) 16-02-85-23; fax (+358 9) 16-02-85-94; e-mail kaj-peter@mattsson@mintc.fi; ministerial adviser in the international unit of the Ministry of Transport and Communications; *specialities:* transport and energy, enlargement, future of Europe, European Convention, CFSP, EU foreign policy; *languages:* Finnish, Swedish, English.

Colonel Erkki Nordberg: POB 919, 00131 Helsinki; tel (+358 9) 224-50; fax (+358 9) 224-59; e-mail erkki.nordberg@milnet.fi; head of training division, defence staff, Finnish Defence Forces; *specialities:* enlargement, general EU policy, institutional reform, IGC, justice and home affairs, regional policy, trade, development and external relations; *languages:* Finnish, English, Swedish.

Johannes Pakaslahti: 11B28 Jaakarink., 00150 Helsinki; tel (+381 3) 821-20-20; e-mail KTA@kolumbus.fi; researcher; *specialities:* economic and financial affairs, enlargement, employment and social affairs, general EU policy, institutional reform, IGC, internal market affairs, trade, development and external relations; *languages:* Finnish, English, German.

Eija Ristimäki: PL 1100, 02015 TKK; tel (+358 9) 451-40-26; fax (+358 9) 451-40-45; e-mail eija.ristimaki@virtualuniversity.fi; senior adviser, information services, SVY Kehittämisyksikkö; *specialities:* education and culture, research and information society; *languages:* Finnish, English.

Keijo Olavi Sahrman: 14 Toinen linja, 00530 Helsinki; tel (+358 09) 771-25-31; fax (+358 9) 771-25-35; e-mail keijo.sahrman@kuntaliitto.fi; director, Association of Finnish Local and Regional Authorities; *specialities:* regional and structural policy, enterprise and SME policy, competition policy and state aids,

future of Europe, European Convention, European Constitution, history and theory of European integration; *languages:* Finnish, Swedish, English.

Juha Talvitie: 2 A 3 Tykistökapteenintie, 00340 Helsinki; tel (+358 9) 48-18-29; fax (+358 9) 88-86-48-29; e-mail juha.talvitie@kolumbus.fi; consultant; *specialities:* enlargement, environment, justice and home affairs, research and information society; *languages:* Finnish, English, Swedish.

Eira Varis: 9 Torikatu, 80100 Joensuu; tel (+358 13) 265-41-56; fax (+358 13) 265-41 30; e-mail eira.varis@pohjois-karjala.fi; regional development manager, Regional Council of Karelia; *specialities:* regional and structural policy, enlargement, CFSP, EU foreign policy, defence; *languages:* Finnish, English.

FRANCE

Franck Arnaud: Bâtiment le Galion, 15 blvd Augustin Cieussa, 13007 Marseilles; tel (+33 4) 95-04-57-42; e-mail Franck.Arnaud@wanadoo.fr; consultant; *specialities:* enlargement, environment, trade, development and external relations, regional policy; *languages:* French, English, Italian.

Jean-Claude Aroumougom: 4 rue de Suez, 13007 Marseilles; tel (+33 6) 14-63-54-78; e-mail jca.aroumougom@laposte.net; academic; *languages:* French, English.

Monique Barthalay-Bouvard: Résidence Opéra, 1 rue du Condé, 78150 Le Chesnay; tel (+33 1) 39-66-04-96; fax (+33 1) 48-36-25-57; e-mail monique.barthalay@laposte.fr; course administrator at the Université de Paris XIII; *specialities:* enterprise, competition, state aids, economic and financial affairs, general EU policy, institutional reform, IGC, trade, development and external relations; *languages:* French.

Méziane Benarab: 26 allée Jean Bart, 77200 Torcy; tel (+33 1) 64-62-21-40; fax (+33 1) 64-62-21-41; e-mail benarab.meziane@wanadoo.fr; consultant; *specialities:* enterprise, competition, state aids, general EU policy, institutional reform, IGC, internal market affairs, trade, development and external relations; *languages:* French.

François Berger de Laguillaumie: 7 rue Guichard, 75016 Paris; tel (+33 1) 40-50-64-03; fax (+33 1) 40-50-78-26; e-mail francois.berger@edfgdf.fr; lawyer; *specialities:* agriculture and fisheries, enlargement, environment, general EU policy, institutional reform, IGC, transport and energy; *languages:* French, English.

Laurent Beurdeley: 21 avenue d'Epernay, 51000 Reims; tel (+33 6) 81-16-

90-28; e-mail laurent.beurdeley@univ-reims.fr; lawyer; *languages:* French.

Dr. Christine Bonnefoi: 405 rue Paradis, 13008 Marseilles; tel (+33 4) 91-23-31-08; fax (+33 4) 91-71-96-20; e-mail maitre.bonnefoi@wanadoo.fr; lawyer; *specialities:* agriculture and fisheries, employment and social affairs, general EU policy, institutional reform, IGC, justice and home affairs, regional policy; *languages:* French.

Jean Pierre Bove: 1 avenue Charles Floquet, 75007 Paris; tel (+33 1) 40-65-10-72; fax (+33 1) 40-65-11-85; e-mail jp.bove@datar.gouv.fr; project leader, DATAR; *specialities:* agriculture and fisheries, enterprise, competition, state aids, general EU policy, institutional reform, IGC, regional policy; *languages:* French.

Jean-Michel Branche: 26 blvd Raspail, 75007 Paris; tel (+33 1) 42-22-10-11; fax (+33 1) 45-44-91-17; e-mail branchelawoffice@online.fr; lawyer; *specialities:* enterprise, competition, state aids, environment, internal market affairs, trade, development and external relations; *languages:* French, English.

Isabelle Cariat: 9–11 rue Charles Lecocq, 75015 Paris; tel (+33 1) 45-30-16-10; fax (+33 1) 45-30-16-10; e-mail isabellecariat@hotmail.com; secretary-general of CEDECE; *specialities:* education and culture, economic and financial affairs, employment and social affairs, general EU policy, institutional reform, IGC, internal market affairs; *languages:* French, English.

André Cavallera: 10 rue du Palais, 83170 Brignoles; tel (+33 4) 94-69-37-03; fax (+33 4) 94-69-06-27; e-mail fedcom.eur@wanadoo.fr; director, Fédération des Communes Européennes du Var; *specialities:* agriculture and fisheries, education and culture, general EU policy, institutional reform, IGC, regional policy; *languages:* French.

Danielle Charles-Le Bihan: 7 bis, rue Jean-Claude Camors, 35700 Rennes; tel (+33 2) 99-38-32-25; fax (+33 2) 99-38-32-25; e-mail danielle.lebihan@uhb.fr; maître de conférences, Université de Rennes II; *specialities:* agriculture and fisheries, environment, general EU policy, institutional reform, IGC, internal market affairs, regional policy; *languages:* French.

Pierre-Yves Chicot: 5 lotissement les Hauts de Rémire, 97354 Rémire-Montjoly; tel (+33 0594) 30-11-17; e-mail juris973@hotmail.com; academic; *specialities:* regional policy, general EU policy, trade, development and external relations; *languages:* French.

Michel Clamen: 119 rue des Pyrénées, 75020 Paris; tel (+33 1) 43-70-27-28; fax (+33 1) 43-70-27-28; academic, author; *specialities:* enterprise, competition, state aids, environment, general EU policy, institutional reform, IGC, internal market affairs; *languages:* French.

Laurence D'Andlau: 22 rue La Fontaine, 75016 Paris; tel (+33 1) 40-50-87-27; fax (+33 1) 40-50-69-13; e-mail ldandlau@noos.fr; consultant, Europe Avenir; *specialities:* economic and financial affairs, enlargement, general EU policy, institutional reform, IGC, regional policy, trade, development and external relations; *languages:* French, English, Spanish.

Lorraine de Bouchony: 42 rue Eugène Carrière, 75018 Paris; tel (+33 1) 42-54-60-64; fax (+33 1) 42-54-70-04; e-mail lbouchony@welcomeurope.com; associate director, Welcomeurope; *specialities:* funding and grants, regional and structural policy; *languages:* French, English, German.

Yves Delafon: 1185 chemin de la Bosque d'Antonelle-Celony, 13090 Aix-en-Provence; tel (+33 4) 42-96-96-99; fax (+33 4) 42-96-97-01; e-mail dfa@dfa-sa.fr; head, DFAsa; *specialities:* general EU policy, economic and financial affairs, trade, development and external relations; *languages:* French, English.

Michel Derdevet: 52 rue Balard, 75015 Paris; tel (+33 1) 41-02-19-73; fax (+33 1) 41-02-17-45; e-mail michel.derdevet@rte-france.com; general delegate, Electricité de France, legal academic; *specialities:* enterprise, competition, state aids, general EU policy, institutional reform, IGC, internal market affairs, transport and energy; *languages:* French.

Jean-Pierre Derisbourg: 2 chemin du Collet, 06650 Opio; tel (+33 4) 93-77-23-49; fax (+33 4) 93-77-23-49; former diplomat; *specialities:* enlargement, general EU policy, institutional reform, IGC, trade, development and external relations; *languages:* French, English.

Prof. François Descheemaekere: 40 rue Fief de Grimoire, 86000 Poitiers; tel (+33 5) 49-60-58-32; fax (+33 5) 49-60-59-19; e-mail fd86@yahoo.com; academic; *specialities:* economic and financial affairs, enlargement, general EU policy, institutional reform, IGC; *languages:* French, English.

Frédéric Dobritz: 27 rue de la Houle, 66000 Perpignan; tel (+33) 68-66-07-54; e-mail dobritz@wanadoo.fr; lawyer, consultant; *specialities:* agriculture and fisheries, employment and social affairs, general EU policy, institutional reform, IGC, regional policy, trade, development and external relations; *languages:* French.

Richard Draperie: 38 blvd Jean Giraud, 06530 Peymeinade; tel (+33 4) 93-66-03-06; fax (+33 4) 93-66-03-06; consultant, economist; *specialities:* economic and financial affairs, employment and

social affairs, general EU policy, institutional reform, IGC; *languages:* French, German, Italian.

Eric Egli: 8 rue de Romagnat, 63000 Clermont-Ferrand; tel (+33 4) 73-25-76-27; fax (+33 4) 73-25-76-27; e-mail e.egli@libertysurf.fr; academic, broadcaster; *specialities:* education and culture, enlargement, general EU policy, institutional reform, IGC, internal market affairs, regional policy; *languages:* French.

Loïc Ernest: 59 rue Pierre Taittinger, BP 30251061 Reims Cedex; tel (+33 3) 26-77-46-26; fax (+33 3) 26-04-69-63; e-mail loic.ernest@reims-ms.fr; Doctor of Community Law, Reims Management School; *specialities:* agriculture and fisheries, enterprise, competition, state aids, enlargement, general EU policy, institutional reform, IGC, internal market affairs; *languages:* French.

Gian Pietro Fontana-Rava: 'La Bigarade', 1112 avenue de Pibonson, 06250 Mougins; tel (+33 4) 93-5-36-18; fax (+33 4) 93-75-15-23; e-mail gpfra2001@yahoo.it; former official of the European Commission; *specialities:* education and culture, environment, general EU policy; *languages:* Italian, French, English.

Martine Frager-Berlet: 159 rue de la Pompe, 75016 Paris; tel (+33 1) 45-05-07-18; fax (+33 1) 45-05-07-18; e-mail mfragerberlet@euralia.com; consultant; *specialities:* enterprise, competition, state aids, employment and social affairs, general EU policy, institutional reform, IGC, justice and home affairs, transport and energy; *languages:* French, English.

André Gilbert: 32 blvd Henri IV, 75004 Paris; tel (+33 1) 42-72-09-18; fax (+33 1) 42-72-09-18; e-mail andrehgilbert@yahoo.fr; civil engineer; *specialities:* agriculture and fisheries, environment, general EU policy, institutional reform, IGC, health and consumer protection, regional policy; *languages:* French.

Elsa Glombard: 2 rue des Boucheries, 93200 Saint-Denis; tel (+33 1) 48-20-25-87; fax (+33 1) 48-09-15-54; e-mail elsa.glombard@laposte.net; doctoral student of political science; *specialities:* education and culture, economic and financial affairs, enlargement, general EU policy, institutional reform, IGC, regional policy; *languages:* French, English, German.

Michel Grelier: 33 rue Richelieu, 59100 Roubaix; tel (+33 3) 20-76-09-02; e-mail michel.grelier@wanadoo.fr; *specialities:* economic and financial affairs, enlargement, general EU policy, institutional reform, IGC, trade, development and external relations; *languages:* French.

Danielle Hays: 2 place Henri Barbusse, 33130 Bègles; tel (+33 5) 56-49-61-53; fax (+33 5) 56-49-61-53; e-mail danielle

.hays@wanadoo.fr; maître de conférences, Université de Bordeaux; *specialities:* agriculture and fisheries, enterprise, competition, state aids, general EU policy, institutional reform, IGC, health and consumer protection, regional policy; *languages:* French.

Nadia Hilal: 15 rue Pierre Loti, 92340 Bourg-La-Reine; tel (+33 1) 40-91-02-63; e-mail nadiahilal@yahoo.fr; student, Institut d'Etudes Politiques, Paris; *specialities:* enlargement, general EU policy, trade, development and external relations, transport and energy; *languages:* French, English.

Pascal Jacques: rue du Bou du Bas, Cedex M7, 14480 Colombiers sur Seulles; tel (+33 2) 31-30-15-84; e-mail pascal.jacques@ac-caen.fr; project leader, structural funds, Rectorat de l'Académie de Caen; *specialities:* regional policy, education and culture, employment and social affairs; *languages:* French.

Prof. Michel Labori: Le Hameau sous la Fôret, 71190 Brion; tel (+33 3) 85-82-20-82; fax (+33 3) 85-82-32-98; e-mail valtms@wanadoo.fr; consultant; *specialities:* regional policy, CAP; *languages:* French.

José-Manuel Lamarque: 12 avenue Pierre Grenier, 78220 Viroflay; fax (+33 1) 56-40-14-44; e-mail jm.la@laposte.net; journalist; *specialities:* education and culture, enlargement, employment and social affairs, general EU policy, institutional reform, IGC, transport and energy; *languages:* French.

Bernard Pierre Lebeau: 60 rue Violet, 75015 Paris; tel (+33 1) 45-75-17-28; fax (+33 1) 30-21-13-38; e-mail bplebeau@wanadoo.fr; consultant; *specialities:* agriculture and fisheries, enlargement, general EU policy, regional policy; *languages:* French, English.

Nathalie Leclere: 1 allée Louis Jouvet, Boîte 27, 92600 Asnières-sur-Seine; tel (+33 1) 01-55-02-10-99; fax (+33 1) 01-55-02-10-99; e-mail nleclere@infonie.fr; consultant; *specialities:* education and culture, economic and financial affairs, general EU policy, institutional reform, IGC, internal market affairs, regional policy; *languages:* French.

Régis Malbois: 52 route de la Sablière, 17920 Breuillet; tel (+33 05) 46-22-62-94; e-mail regismalbois@belgacom.net; adviser, Ligue européenne de coopération économique; *specialities:* general EU policy; *languages:* French.

Annick Mallet: 51 rue Lepic, 75018 Paris; tel (+33 1) 42-64-84-42; fax (+33 1) 42-64-84-42; e-mail mallet-consultants@wanadoo.fr; consultant, European social policy, Mallet Consultants; *specialities:* employment and social affairs, general EU policy, institutional reform, IGC; *languages:* French.

Patrick Martin-Genier: 5 rue Emile Zola, 69002 Lyons; tel (+33 3) 81-82-60-00; fax (+33 4) 72-41-08-22; e-mail martingenier@wanadoo.fr; lawyer, educator; *specialities:* enlargement, environment, general EU policy, institutional reform, IGC, regional policy; *languages:* French.

Pierre Menguy: 30 rue Claude Monet, 76310 Sainte; tel (+33 2) 35-54-25-56; fax (+33 2) 32-74-40-86; e-mail menguypier@wanadoo.fr; teacher, Université du Havre, Faculté des Affaires Internationales; *specialities:* general EU policy, economic and monetary affairs, enlargement, justice and home affairs; *languages:* French, English, German.

Daniel Moulis: 5 rue Guillaume Pellicier, 34430 Saint Jean de Vedas; tel (+33 4) 67-47-99-92; e-mail daniel.moulis@laposte.net; teacher, Université de Perpignan; *specialities:* economic and financial affairs, general EU policy, institutional reform, IGC; *languages:* French.

Béligh Nabli: 120 rue du Chemin Vert, 75011 Paris; tel (+33 1) 47-00-03-97; fax (+33 1) 40-63-93-71; e-mail beligh.nable@iue.it; researcher in law, Institut Universitaire Européen de Florence; *specialities:* general EU policy, justice and home affairs, enterprise, competition and state aids; *languages:* French.

Gérard Nafilyan: 10 rue de la Chaise, 75007 Paris; tel (+33 1) 41-25-12-53; fax (+33 1) 41-25-12-13; e-mail gnafilyan@info-europe.fr; professor of European law, Université Paris I, director of the Centre Universitaire d'Etudes des Communautés européennes; *specialities:* education and culture, economic and financial affairs, general EU policy, institutional reform, IGC, internal market affairs, justice and home affairs; *languages:* French, Italian.

Hédia Nasraoui: Appt 71, 2 blvd de Pont Noyelles, 80090 Amiens; tel (+33 3) 22-91-93-03; fax (+33 3) 22-92-64-47; e-mail h.nasraoui@ipe-amiens.com; lawyer; *languages:* French.

Joseph M. Pacini: 65 avenue du Général de Gaulle, 84510 Caumont-sur-Durance; tel (+33 4) 90-23-09-12; e-mail pacini@free.fr; chargé de mission, Ministère de l'Agriculture; *specialities:* agriculture and fisheries, education and culture, environment, general EU policy, institutional reform, IGC, regional policy; *languages:* French, Italian.

Michel Poirot: 3 allée des Chardonnerets, 78510 Triel sur Seine; tel (+33 1) 34-01-10-40; fax (+33 1) 34-01-10-41; e-mail agro.strategie@laposte.net; *specialities:* agriculture and fisheries, economic and financial affairs, general EU policy, institutional reform, IGC, trade, development and external relations; *languages:* French.

Jean-Pierre Quentin: 33 rue Bir Hakeim, 17340 Châtelaillon-La Rochelle; tel (+33 5) 46-56-77-10; e-mail jpq@algoric.com; director-general, Algoric; *specialities:* enterprise, competition, state aids, general EU policy, institutional reform, IGC, internal market affairs, regional policy, research and information society; *languages:* French, English.

Zoran Radovic: 3 rue de l'Avenir, 44300 Nantes; tel (+33 2) 40-49-20-42; e-mail z.radovic@wanadoo.fr; expert on European affairs for Formation Ingénierie du Développement et Expertise du Système Communautaire (FIDES); *specialities:* enlargement, economic and financial affairs, trade, development and external relations, regional policy; *languages:* French, English.

Bénédicte Rajot: 58 cours de la Liberté, 69003 Lyons; tel (+33 4) 78-95-46-57; fax (+33 4) 78-95-46-57; e-mail benedicterajot@aol.com; teacher, Université Jean Moulin Lyon 3; *specialities:* trade, development and external relations, economic and financial affairs, transport and energy, enterprise, competition, state aids; *languages:* French.

Emile Besson Rasolondraibe: 55 rue du Général Sarrail, 92220 Bagneux; tel (+33 1) 46-65-20-25; fax (+33 1) 46-65-20-25; e-mail emile-besson.rasolondraibe@wanadoo.fr; independent consultant; *specialities:* agriculture and fisheries, enlargement, general EU policy, trade, development and external relations; *languages:* French.

Jean-Claude Soum: 15 avenue Thurel, 39000 Lons-le-Saunier; tel (+33 3) 84-44-63-15; fax (+33 3) 84-44-63-15; e-mail soum.jeanclaude@club-internet.fr; journalist; *specialities:* economic and financial affairs, general EU policy, institutional reform, IGC, internal market affairs, regional policy; *languages:* French.

Joselyne Studer-Laurens: 71 blvd National F, 92255 La Garenne-Colombes Cedex; tel (+33 1) 47-81-94-65; fax (+33 1) 47-85-90-41; e-mail jsl@cti.tm.fr; director-general, CTI-Tour Charlebourg; *specialities:* education and culture, enterprise, competition, state aids, economic and financial affairs, general EU policy, institutional reform, IGC, research and information society, trade, development and external relations; *languages:* French.

Christian Talgorn: 27 rue des Iles, 56880 Ploeren; tel (+33 2) 97-40-04-75; fax (+33 2) 97-46-31-76; e-mail christian.talgorn@iu-vannes.fr; academic; *specialities:* agriculture and fisheries, enterprise, competition, state aids, employment and social affairs, general EU policy, institutional reform, IGC, internal market affairs, regional policy; *languages:* French, English, Spanish.

Florent Vanremortere: 65 rue Winoc-Chocqueel, 59200 Tourcoing; tel (+33 3) 20-27-19-39; e-mail fvanremortere@nordnet.fr; *specialities:* trade, development and external relations, general EU policy, employment and social affairs, regional policy; *languages:* French.

Didier Wolf: 49 rue Ampère, 75017 Paris; tel (+33 1) 47-66-27-00; fax (+33 1) 47-66-27-01; e-mail didierwolf@wanadoo.fr; consultant; *specialities:* employment and social affairs, general EU policy, institutional reform, IGC, health and consumer protection; *languages:* French.

GERMANY

Holger-Michael Arndt: 38 Alt-Eller, 40229 Düsseldorf; tel (+49 211) 233-88-55; fax (+49 211) 233-88-55; e-mail harndt@gwdg.de; self-employed lawyer, solicitor; *specialities:* general EU policy, enlargement, justice and home affairs, internal market affairs; *languages:* German, English.

Ingo Beckedorf: 2 Sievekingplatz, 20355 Hamburg; tel (+49 40) 428-43-29-30; fax (+49 40) 428-43-41-83; e-mail Ingo.Beckedorf@lycosxxl.de; judge, Hanseatesches Oberlandesgericht, Hamburg; *specialities:* enlargement, general EU policy, health and consumer protection, justice and home affairs; *languages:* German, English.

Dr Erich Biedermann: 22 Carl-Weinberger-Strasse, 83607 Holzkirchen; tel (+49 8024) 495-88/5005; fax (+49 8024) 495-88; e-mail 080244588-0001@t-online.de; political economist; *specialities:* agriculture and fisheries, enlargement, general EU policy, institutional reform, IGC, transport and energy; *languages:* German, French, English.

Marica Bodruzic: 86 Rilkestrasse, 53225 Bonn; tel (+49 228) 46-14-37; fax (+49 228) 9-72-02-36; e-mail marica.bodruzic@t-online.de; journalist; *specialities:* education and culture, economic and financial affairs, enlargement, employment and social affairs, general EU policy, institutional reform, IGC, regional policy; *languages:* German, English.

Christfried Boelter: 12 Cumbacherstrasse, D-99880 Schnepfenthal; tel (+49 3622) 90-58-21; fax (+49 3622) 90-58-16; e-mail forum.westthueringen@t-online.de; leader, Kirchlicher Dienst auf dem Lande in der Ev.-Luth. Kirche in Thüringen; *specialities:* agriculture and fisheries, education and culture, enlargement, employment and social affairs, regional policy; *languages:* German.

Jürgen Brand: 7b Kölner Str., 90425 Nürnberg; tel (+49 911) 201-45-60; fax (+49 911) 201-41-17; e-mail juergen.brand@db.com; business executive, MEP; *specialities:* education and culture, enterprise, competition, state aids, economic and financial affairs, enlargement, general EU policy, institutional reform, IGC, internal market affairs, regional policy, trade, development and external relations; *languages:* German, English.

Cornelius Brökelmann: 9 Paul Robeson Str., 10439 Berlin; tel (+49 30) 23-28-61-98; fax (+49 30) 22-49-81-75; e-mail Cornelius.broekelmann@wirtschaft-am-wasserturm.de; political scientist; *specialities:* transport and energy, enlargement, general EU policy; *languages:* German, English, French.

Dr Ulrich Brückner: 4 Apostel-Paulus Str., 10823 Berlin; tel (+49 30) 873-50-96; fax (+49 30) 789-58-74-5; e-mail ulib@zedat.fu-berlin.de; political scientist; *specialities:* education and culture, enterprise, competition, state aids, economic and financial affairs, enlargement, environment, employment and social affairs, general EU policy, institutional reform, IGC, internal market affairs, research and information society; *languages:* German, English.

Kerstin Bungert-Hurek: 63 Gutenbergstrasse/Portal II, 14467 Potsdam; tel (+49) 17-94-99-50-78; fax (+49) 30-22-77-63-13; e-mail kerstin.bunger@web.de; legislative assistant, German Bundestag; *specialities:* general EU policy, enlargement, regional policy, enterprise, competition and state aids; *languages:* German, English.

Armin Czysz: 23 Zionskirchstrasse, 10119 Berlin; tel (+49 30) 44-32-44-0; fax (+49 30) 44-32-44-33; e-mail ac@eu-info.de; journalist; *specialities:* enterprise, competition, state aids, economic and financial affairs, enlargement, general EU policy, institutional reform, IGC, justice and home affairs, research and information society, trade, development and external relations; *languages:* German, English, French.

Anja Dahl: Ludwig Erhqrd Haus, 103c Eisenacher Str., 10781 Berlin; tel (+49 30) 31-51-02-49/21-99-66-21; fax (+49 30) 31-51-03-16/01-53; e-mail A.M.Dahl@gmx.de; diplomatic correspondent; *specialities:* enterprise, competition, state aids, economic and financial affairs, enlargement, general EU policy, institutional reform, IGC, trade, development and external relations; *languages:* German, English.

Carsten J. Diercks: 12 Düsseldorfer Strasse, 10719 Berlin; tel (+49 30) 88-70-49-77; fax (+49 30) 88-70-49-78; e-mail CJD@DiercksConsult.de; lawyer, legal consultant; *specialities:* education and culture, enlargement, general EU policy, institutional reform, IGC, internal market affairs, justice and home affairs; *languages:* German, English.

Robert Ernecker: c/o Dichter, 4–6 Waldmeister Strasse, 14193 Berlin; tel (+49 172) 252-92-13; fax (+49 173) 27-90-130; e-mail robert.ernecker@gmx.de; member, German Bundestag; *specialities:* economic and financial affairs, enlargement, regional policy, trade, development and external relations, transport and energy; *languages:* German, English.

Wolfgang Fischbein: 24 Bertolt Brecht-Allee, 01309 Dresden; tel (+49 351) 31-99-31-10; fax (+49 351) 31-99-31-11; e-mail fischbein.consult@gmx.de; export consultant; *specialities:* internal market affairs, trade, development and external relations; *languages:* German, English.

Thomas Fischer: Brieffach 13 55 K-SR Südamerika/Afrika, 38436 Wolfsburg; tel (+49 5361) 92-52-52; fax (+49 5361) 92-11-71; e-mail th.Fischer@volkswagen.de; lawyer, Volkswagen AG; *specialities:* enterprise, competition, state aids, enlargement, trade, development and external relations; *languages:* German, English.

Doris Friedrich: 22 Bundesallee, 10717 Berlin; tel (+49 30) 89-09-01-20; e-mail do.friedrich@web.de; lecturer in political education, Europäisches Informationszentrum in Jean-Monnet-Haus, Berlin; *specialities:* economic and financial affairs, enlargement, employment and social affairs, general EU policy, institutional reform, IGC, regional policy; *languages:* German, English.

Renate Fries: 14 Gneisenaustr., 50733 Köln; tel (+49 221) 952-10-50; fax (+49 221) 952-10-51; e-mail fries@pid-net.de; sociologist, journalist; *specialities:* regional policy, enlargement, employment and social affairs, general EU policy, institutional reform, IGC; *languages:* German, English.

Hermann Frohn: 57 Heidebergenstr., 53229 Bonn; tel (+49 228) 48-44-87; fax (+49 228) 48-12-24; e-mail Hermann.Frohn@t-online.de; market research consultant; *specialities:* agriculture and fisheries, enlargement, internal market affairs, regional policy, research and information society, trade, development and external relations; *languages:* German, English.

Andrea Gehler-Füssel: 4 Maximilianstrasse, 86150 Augsburg; tel (+49 821) 324-30-04; fax (+49 821) 30-15; e-mail europa@augsburg.de; lawyer, European Affairs Officer, City of Augsburg; *specialities:* general EU policy; *languages:* German, English, French, Spanish.

Angelika Hecker-Iseler: 28 Kolberger Strasse, 50374 Erftstadt; tel (+49 2235) 30-90; fax (+49 2235) 437-85; e-mail AHecker123@aol.com; lecturer in career development and social-political further education; *specialities:* economic and financial affairs, employment and social affairs, general EU policy, institutional reform, IGC; *languages:* German, English.

Ralf Hell: 41 Gereonswall, 50670 Köln; tel (+49 221) 130-05-14; e-mail ralfhell@freenet.de; speaker and head of conferences in the field of European Education; *specialities:* enlargement, economic and monetary affairs, regional policy, internal market affairs; *languages:* German, English.

Ute Hirschburger: 24 Vaihinger Strasse, 71063 Sindelfingen; tel (+49 7031) 61-85-80; fax (+49 7031) 61-86-86; e-mail Ute.Hirschburger@Libertas-Institut.com; managing director, LIBERTAS-Europäisches Institut GmbH; *specialities:* enterprise, competition, state aids, economic and financial affairs, enlargement, environment, employment and social affairs, internal market affairs; *languages:* German, English.

Dr jur. Klaus J. Hoepffner: 8 Am Eselsbach, 97078 Würzburg; tel (+49 931) 249-27; fax (+49 931) 235-25; e-mail hoepffner@t-online.de; university lecturer; *specialities:* agriculture and fisheries, economic and financial affairs, enlargement, general EU policy, institutional reform, IGC, justice and home affairs; *languages:* German, English, French.

Bernd Hüttemann: 22 Bundesallee, 10717 Berlin; tel (+49 30) 88-91-34-41/41-71-74-13; fax (+49 30) 88-91-34-99; e-mail bhuettemann@iep-berlin; research associate, Institut für Europäische Politik; *specialities:* education and culture, enlargement, general EU policy, institutional reform, IGC, regional policy, trade, development and external relations; *languages:* German.

Angela Joosten: 23 Zionskirchstraße, 10119 Berlin; tel (+49 30) 44-32-44-0; fax (+49 30) 44-32-44-33; e-mail aj@eu-info.de; head, Euro Info Centre, Bonn; *specialities:* education and culture, economic and financial affairs, enlargement, general EU policy, institutional reform, IGC, internal market affairs, justice and home affairs, regional policy; *languages:* German.

Michael Jörger: 16 Hirtenstr., 80335 München; tel (+49 89) 54-91-41-0; fax (+49 89) 54-91-41-9; e-mail m.joerger@europaeische-akademie.de; head of Europäische Akademie, Bavaria; *specialities:* enlargement, environment, employment and social affairs, general EU policy, institutional reform, IGC, trade, development and external relations; *languages:* German.

Rolf Jungnickel: 21 Neuer Jungfernstieg, 20347 Hamburg; tel (+49 40) 428-34-411; fax (+49 40) 428-34-451; e-mail Jungnickel@hwwa.de; political economist; *specialities:* enterprise, competition, state aids, economic and financial affairs, enlargement, internal market affairs, regional policy, trade, development and external relations; *languages:* German, English.

Martin Kersting: 14 Bäckerstrasse, 44532 Lünen; tel (+49 2306) 180-57; fax (+49 2306) 257-507; e-mail RA-Martin-Kersting@t-online.de; *specialities:* education and culture, economic and financial affairs, environment, employment and social affairs, general EU policy, institutional reform, IGC, health and consumer protection, internal market affairs, justice and home affairs, research and information society; *languages:* German, English, French.

M. A. Michael Kraupa: 30 Lerchenfeldstr. 30, 80538 München; tel (+49 89) 22-44-30; fax (+49 89) 22-44-30; e-mail mkraupa@yahoo.de; assistant manager; *specialities:* agriculture and fisheries, economic and financial affairs, enlargement, general EU policy, institutional reform, IGC, regional policy, research and information society; *languages:* German, English.

Heribert Krekel: 22 Bundesallee, 10717 Berlin; tel (+49 30) 42-25-68-91; e-mail hep2000@gmx.de; lecturer in political education, Euro Info Centre; *languages:* German, English.

Petra Krull: 3 Heiligengeisthof, 18055 Rostock; tel (+49 381) 375-86-46; fax (+49 381) 375-86-48; e-mail pea24krull@t-online.de; project leader and lecturer, Europe Centre, Rostock; *specialities:* employment and social affairs; *languages:* German.

Margit Kunz: 2 Max-Joseph-Str., 80333 München; tel (+49 89) 511-67-70; e-mail kunz@muenchen.ihk.de; *languages:* German.

Birgit Ladwig-Tils: 160 Estermannstr., 53117 Bonn; tel (+49 228) 63-95-83; fax (+49 228) 967-80-23; e-mail Ladwig-Tils@t-online.de; journalist, historian; *specialities:* education and culture, economic and financial affairs, enlargement, environment, employment and social affairs, general EU policy, institutional reform, IGC, internal market affairs, regional policy; *languages:* German.

Ursula Langendorf: 2 Archivstr., 30169 Hannover; tel (+49 511) 120-35-54; fax (+49 511) 120-99-35-54; e-mail ursula.langendorf@mu.niedersachsen.de; lecturer, Ministry of the Environment, Lower Saxony; *languages:* German, English.

Marlene Lenz: 102 Burgstr., 53177 Bonn; tel (+49 228) 31-38-45; fax (+49 228) 31-82-36; e-mail Marlene.Lenz@t-online.de; former MEP; *languages:* German, English, French.

Jürgen Lippold: 8 Birkenweg, 17039 Glocksin; tel (+49 39608) 210-30; fax (+49 39608) 215-03; e-mail juergen_lippold@yahoo.de; university lecturer;

specialities: education and culture, economic and financial affairs, enlargement, internal market affairs, research and information society; *languages:* German.

Astrid Lübke: 36 Mühsamstr., 10249 Berlin; tel (+49 30) 42-01-95-75; e-mail Astrid.Luebke@gmx.de; consultant/adviser, Federal Ministry of Finance; *specialities:* education and culture, economy and monetary affairs; *languages:* German, English, French.

Dr Leo Melian: 14 Raglovichstrasse, 80637 München; tel (+49 89) 15-78-365; fax (+49 89) 15-78-365; *specialities:* agriculture and fisheries, economic and financial affairs, enlargement, environment, general EU policy, institutional reform, IGC, health and consumer protection, internal market affairs, regional policy, trade, development and external relations; *languages:* German.

Ursula Menhart: 15a Kavalierstr., 10781 Berlin; tel (+49 171) 280-22-97; e-mail ursula.menhart@siemens.com; PR expert, political scientist in the Office of the Federal Chancellor; *specialities:* enterprise, competition, state aids, enlargement, employment and social affairs, general EU policy, institutional reform, IGC, research and information society, trade, development and external relations; *languages:* German.

Oliver Mietzsch: Postfach 613142, 10942 Berlin; tel (+49 30) 377-11-0; fax (+49 30) 69-59-93-95; e-mail Hoffmann_Mietzsch@t-online.de; expert on European affairs at the Deutscher Städtetag (German Association of Cities and Towns); *specialities:* enterprise, competition, state aids, enlargement, general EU policy, institutional reform, IGC, regional policy, transport and energy; *languages:* German, English.

Dr Hans Neubauer: 52 Waisenhausstr., 80637 München; tel (+49 89) 157-61-10; e-mail mw16642@mucweb.de; lawyer; *specialities:* general EU policy, institutional reform, IGC; *languages:* German.

Marc-Oliver Pahl: 13 Seydlitzstr., 40476 Düsseldorf; tel (+49 211) 45-66-0; fax (+49 211) 45-66-388; e-mail marc-oliver.pahl@munlv.nrw.de; member of the bureau, Union of European Federalists (UEF); *specialities:* agriculture, enlargement, environment, general EU policy, institutional reform, IGC, justice and home affairs, regional policy, trade, development and external relations; *languages:* German, English.

Hans Arno Petzold: 1 Adophsplatz, 20457 Hamburg; tel (+49 40) 41-91-91-04; fax (+49 40) 41-91-91-05; e-mail ipe@infopoint-europa.de; lawyer/manager, Info Point Europa, Hamburg; *specialities:* justice and home affairs, transport and energy, health and consumer protection,

general EU policy; *languages:* German, English.

Günter Renner: 2 Eitel-Fritz-Strasse, 14129 Berlin; tel (+49 30) 802-60-94; fax (+49 30) 826-64-10; *specialities:* education and culture, economic and financial affairs, enlargement, general EU policy, institutional reform, IGC, internal market affairs; *languages:* German, English.

Margit Rödder: 5 Schönfeldstr., 76131 Karlsruhe; tel (+49 721) 62-75-940; fax (+49 721) 62-75-940; e-mail mroedder@web.de; *specialities:* research and development, regional and structural policy, history of European integration, enlargement; *languages:* German, English.

Raymond Saller: 15 Herzog-Wilhelm-Str., 80331 München; tel (+49 89) 23-32-13-32; fax (+49 89) 23-32-27-34; e-mail raymond.saller@muenchen.de; expert in labour and economy, state capital of Munich; *specialities:* enterprise, competition, state aids, economic and financial affairs, enlargement, general EU policy, institutional reform, IGC, regional policy, research and information society; *languages:* German, English.

Charlotte Schölgens: 55 Auf dem Hügel, 53347 Alfter; tel (+49 2222) 93-19-03; fax (+49 2222) 93-19-05; e-mail charlotte@schoelgens.de; political scientist, author; *specialities:* education and culture, economic and financial affairs, employment and social affairs, general EU policy, institutional reform, IGC; *languages:* German, French.

Felix Schulz: 89 Mariendorfer Damm, D-12109 Berlin; tel (+49 30) 25-89-99-30; fax (+49 30) 25-89-99-30; e-mail felix.schulz@jef.de; *languages:* German.

Rainer Schwarzer: 18 Sportplatzstrasse, Stoffen, 86932 Pürgen; tel (+49 8196) 99-99-76; fax (+49 8196) 99-96-76; e-mail rainer.schwarzer@t-online.de; chief researcher, Europe section of the State Chancellery of Bavaria; *specialities:* education and culture, economic and financial affairs, enlargement, general EU policy, institutional reform, IGC; *languages:* German, English.

Jan Sicha: 7 Prinzregentenstrasse, 80538 München; tel (+49 89) 21-02-49-32; fax (+49 89) 21-02-49-33; e-mail ccmunich@czech.cz; expert in Czech politics and affairs; *specialities:* trade, development and external relations, education and culture, enlargement, general EU policy, research and information society; *languages:* German.

Dr Jürgen Simons: 80 Oberer Steinberg, 63225 Langen; tel (+49 6103) 87-02-17; fax (+49 6103) 87-02-18; e-mail juesim@communications-consult.de; consultant in political communication; *specialities:* economic and financial affairs, general EU policy, institutional reform, IGC, research and information society, trade, development and external relations; *languages:* German, English.

Jaroslav Sonka: 46–48 Bismarckallee, 14193 Berlin; tel (+49 30) 89-59-51-15; fax (+49 30) 89-59-51-95; e-mail js@eaue .de; *languages:* German.

Thomas Stammen: 29 Breite Strasse, 10178 Berlin; tel (+49 30) 20-28-16-29; fax (+49 30) 20-28-26-29; e-mail t.stammen@bdi-online.de; expert on EU industrial relations; *specialities:* enterprise, competition and state aids, economic and monetary affairs, trade, development and external relations, general EU policy; *languages:* German, English, French.

Dr Burkard Steppacher: 12 Rathausallee, 53757 Sankt Augustin; tel (+49 2241) 24-62-32; fax (+49 2241) 24-65-73; e-mail burkard.steppacher@kas.de; scientific collaborator, Konrad Adenauer Foundation; *specialities:* economic and financial affairs, enlargement, general EU policy, institutional reform, IGC, internal market affairs, regional policy, trade, development and external relations; *languages:* German, English, French.

Eckart Stratenschulte: 46/48 Bismarckallee, 14193 Berlin; tel (+49 30) 895-95-10; fax (+49 30) 826-64-10; head of the Europäische Akademie, Berlin; *specialities:* enlargement, general EU policy, trade, development and external relations, environment; *languages:* German.

Prof. Dr Heiner Timmermann: 10–12 Starenweg, 66620 Nonnweiler; tel (+49 6873) 74-10; fax (+49 6873) 10-67/66-23-50; e-mail Prof.Dr.Dr.HeinerTimmermann@t-online.de; member of management team of the Europäische Akademie, Otzenhausen; *specialities:* enlargement, general EU policy, institutional reform, IGC, trade, development and external relations; *languages:* German, English.

Dr Kathleen Toepel: 89 Wallstr., 10179 Berlin; tel (+49 30) 20-45-30-13; fax (+49 30) 20-45-30-26; e-mail ktoepel@ktoepel .de; *specialities:* enterprise, competition, state aids, enlargement, regional policy; *languages:* German, English.

Prof. Dr Michael Tolksdorf: 56a Kurfürstenstr., 13467 Berlin; tel (+49 30) 40-53-60-07; fax (+49 30) 40-42-72-7; e-mail tolksd@fhw-berlin.de; former civil servant with 'Bundeskartellamt' (German Anti-trust authority), now professor of economics; *specialities:* enterprise, competition, state aids, economic and financial affairs, internal market affairs; *languages:* German.

Ilka Tröger: 213–214 Friedrichstrasse, 10969 Berlin; tel (+49 30) 25-29-49-07; fax (+49 30) 25-29-49-07; e-mail Ilka.Troeger@t_online.de; journalist;

specialities: economic and monetary affairs, enlargement, internal market affairs, general EU policy; *languages:* German, English.

Elke Vosteen: 13 Lamontstr., 81679 München; tel (+49 179) 695-90-67; e-mail elke.vosteen@genion.de; political economist; *specialities:* enterprise, competition, state aids, economic and financial affairs, enlargement, employment and social affairs, general EU policy, institutional reform, IGC, regional policy, research and information society, trade, development and external relations; *languages:* German, English.

Cordula Wandel: 189d Walddörferstrasse, 22047 Hamburg; tel (+49 40) 65-03-38-64; fax (+49 40) 65-03-38-69; e-mail cordula.wandel@yahoo.com; project leader, OTTO; *languages:* German, English, French.

Frieder Otto Wolf: 8 Traunsteiner Str., 10781 Berlin; tel (+49 30) 218-93-06; fax (+49 30) 218-84-61; e-mail fow@snafu.de; lecturer, Freie Universität Berlin; *specialities:* economic and financial affairs, enlargement, employment and social affairs, research and information society; *languages:* German.

Dr Anita Wolf-Niedermaier: 28 C Gutleuthofweg, 69118 Heidelberg; tel (+49 6221) 80-57-96; fax (+49 6221) 80-57-96; e-mail anita-wolf-niedermeier@t-online.de; attached to Centre for Social Sciences, University of Mannheim; *specialities:* education and culture, environment, general EU policy; *languages:* German, English, French.

Hans-Jürgen Zahorka: 24 Vaihinger Strasse, 71063 Sindelfingen; tel (+49 7031) 61-86-85; fax (+49 7031) 61-86-86; e-mail zahorka@libertas-institut.com; lawyer, LIBERTAS-Europäisches Institut GmbH; *specialities:* enterprise, competition, state aids, economic and financial affairs, enlargement, general EU policy, institutional reform, IGC, internal market affairs, justice and home affairs, regional policy, trade, development and external relations; *languages:* German, English, French.

Jutta Zemke-Heyl: 59 Steinstraße, 50354 Hürth; tel (+49 2233) 70-84-91; fax (+49 2233) 70-85-43; e-mail RA .Zemke-Heyl@t-online.de; lawyer, Bundesverband der Deutschen Industrie e.V.; *specialities:* enterprise, competition, state aids, economic and financial affairs, enlargement, general EU policy, institutional reform, IGC, internal market affairs; *languages:* German, English, French.

GREECE

Elsa Adamantidou: POB 14 Kalamaria, 55102 Thessaloniki; tel (+30 31) 47-61-03/47-61-04; fax (+30 31) 47-61-05; e-mail ea

-law@otenet.gr; attorney at law, assistant at the Centre of European Economic law, legal adviser in Centre of International and European Economic Law (CIEEL) Public Procurement Monitoring Unit; *specialities:* enterprise, competition, state aids, environment, health and consumer protection, research and information society; *languages:* Greek, English.

Michalis Angelopoulos: 16 Voukourestiou St, 10671 Athens; tel (+30 1) 364-60-80; fax (+30 1) 360-94-01; e-mail mangel@ath.forthnet.gr; lawyer, President of the Union of European Federalists, Greece; *specialities:* enlargement, environment, general EU policy, institutional reform, IGC; *languages:* Greek, English, French.

Kyriakos Arhontakis: Ioannou Kazouli 15 85 100 Rhodes; tel (+30 241) 753-15/316-84; fax (+30 241) 735-52; e-mail Archo_ky@otenet.gr; legal consultant; *specialities:* enterprise, competition, state aids, economic and financial affairs; *languages:* Greek, English.

Zaharias Demathas: 28–32 Labrou Kotsoni, 114 71 Athens; tel (+30 1) 644-72-75; fax (+30 1) 330-12-85; e-mail demathas@panteion.gr; associate professor; *specialities:* enlargement, general EU policy, institutional reform, IGC, regional policy; *languages:* Greek, English.

Helen Geka: 65 Maizonos, 26221 Patras; tel (+30 61) 99-26-32/27-56-54; fax (+30 61) 22-26-61; e-mail gekahel@otenet.gr; economist, financial analyst, Hellenic Industrial Development Bank S.A.; *specialities:* economic and financial affairs; *languages:* Greek, English, French.

Athanase Ghekas: 3 Kouskoura, 54623 Thessaloniki; tel (+30 210) 729-38-36/809-72-31; fax (+30 210) 809-72-21; e-mail t.gekas@michaniki.gr; lawyer, Gekas & Associates (Law Firm/Euro Consulting); *specialities:* economic and financial affairs, general EU policy, institutional reform, IGC; *languages:* Greek, English.

Angelika Ioannides-Sarantis: 9 Rue Solomou, 154 52 P. Psychico; tel (+30 1) 671-21-58; fax (+30 1) 677-88-60/770-05-02; e-mail agelioan@mou.gr; consultant, communications expert; *specialities:* regional policy; *languages:* Greek, French, English.

Grigoris Kafkalas: University Campus, Admin. Bldg, University Box 491, 54 006 Thessaloniki; tel (+30 31) 99-55-91; fax (+30 31) 99-55-92; e-mail kafkalas@estia.arch.auth.gr; associate professor, Aristotle University of Thessaloniki; *specialities:* environment, regional policy; *languages:* Greek, English.

Dimitrios Karageorgopoulos: 8 Rue Dodekanisou, 166 73 Voula, Athens; tel (+30 210) 899-37-35; fax (+30 210) 994-96-67; economist, civil servant with the department of international relations in the Ministry of Labour; *specialities: employment and social affairs; languages:* Greek, French.

Theodore Kokkoris: 19 Artemidos str., 14572 Drosia, Athens; tel (+30 210) 621-11-93; e-mail Kokoris2@otenet.gr; EU senior expert, professor of marketing, Hellenic Organisation of SMEs (EOM-MEX); *specialities:* enterprise, competition and state aids, trade, development and external relations, regional policy, education and culture; *languages:* Greek.

Cheimariotis Konstantinos: 74 Michael Karaoli Str., 67100 Xanthi; tel (+30 25410) 637-55; fax (+30 25410) 637-56; e-mail devass@otenet.gr; agronomist, economist; *specialities:* agriculture, rural development, environment; *languages:* Greek, English.

Stella Kovlaka: 45 Metropoleos St, 10556 Athens; tel (+30 210) 325-01-71; fax (+30 210) 328-35-32; e-mail kovlaka.s@emporiki.gr; senior adviser on European affairs, Emporiki Bank of Greece; *specialities:* economic and financial affairs, enlargement, general EU policy, institutional reform; *languages:* Greek, English.

Catherine Margellou: 5 Pandanassis Str., 151 25 Athens; tel (+30 1) 682-82-36; fax (+30 1) 618-35-73; e-mail kmar@obi.gr; director of international affairs and legal matters, Industrial Property Organisation (OBI); *specialities:* enlargement, general EU policy, institutional reform, IGC; *languages:* Greek, French.

Dr Evi Megari: 64 Koulouras Str., 25100 Aighio; tel (+30 691) 274-70; fax (+30 691) 31-73-34; e-mail megarie@otenet.gr; Carrefour project manager, consultant in the municipality of Aighio in western Greece; *specialities:* education and culture, enlargement, employment and social affairs, general EU policy, institutional reform, IGC; *languages:* Greek, French, English.

Alexandra Nikiforaki: 100 Othonos Str., 14562 Kifissia, Athens; tel (+30) 801-20-01; fax (+30) 801-58-70/801-20-01; e-mail niva@gnhm.gr; environmental expert, Goulandris Natural History Museum; *specialities:* environment; *languages:* Greek, French.

Anna Orologa: 23 Rodou St, 14562 Kifissia, Athens; tel (+30 1) 801-88-82; fax (+30 1) 228-51-22; e-mail aorologa@paep.org.gr; economist, head of department, National Institute of Labour, Athens; *specialities:* employment and social affairs, regional policy; *languages:* Greek, English, French.

Helen Papaconstantinou: 4 Vas. Sofias, 10674 Athens; tel (+30 1) 729-57-50; fax (+30 1) 729-57-56; e-mail hpaplaw@ath.forthnet.gr; lawyer; *specialities:* enterprise, competition, state aids, enlargement, general EU policy, institutional reform, IGC; *languages:* Greek, English, French.

Anthony Papadimitriou: POB 9330 (Solonos), 10032 Athens; tel (+30 210) 364-28-28; fax (+30 210) 364-63-02; e-mail apaplaw@hol.gr; attorney-at-law; *specialities:* enterprise, competition, state aids, enlargement, general EU policy, institutional reform, IGC; *languages:* Greek, English, French.

Constantine Papadopoulos: 3rd Floor, 8 Othonos St, 10557 Athens; tel (+30 210) 333-71-97; fax (+30 210) 333-72-56; e-mail Cpapadopoulos@eurobank.gr; adviser on European affairs, EFG Eurobank Ergasias; *specialities:* economic and financial affairs, enlargement, general EU policy, institutional reform, IGC; *languages:* Greek, English, French.

Markos Papakonstantis: 35 Rue Feakon, 12133 Peristeri; tel (+30 210) 571-15-49; e-mail papmarkos@yahoo.gr; lawyer; *specialities:* general EU policy, enlargement, trade, development and external relations; *languages:* Greek, French.

Dimitrios Provatas: 29 Rue Acharnon, 10439 Athens; tel (+30 10) 882-14-04-6; fax (+30 10) 825-13-68; e-mail provatas@hol.gr; director, Institute for Agricultural Issues; *specialities:* agriculture and fisheries; *languages:* Greek, English.

Nikolitsa Rapti: 141 Rue Mihail Voda, 10446 Athens; tel (+30 210) 86-53-353; fax (+30 210) 88-14-460; e-mail n.rap@gedd.gr; *languages:* Greek.

Zacharias Roditakis: 5 Kidonias, 71201 Heraklion; tel (+30 897) 252-94; fax (+30 897) 252-94/81-22-25-06; e-mail roditakis@hrs.forthnet.gr; economist; *specialities:* employment and social affairs, general EU policy, institutional reform, IGC, regional policy; *languages:* Greek, French, Italian.

Anastasios Sapounakis: 12 Athinas St, 14121 Heraklion; tel (+30 1) 271-57-76; fax (+30 1) 86-23-26(8)-6; e-mail tassos-sapounakis@otenet.gr; consultant on local authorities, expert on local and regional development in relation to local authorities' activities; *specialities:* employment and social affairs, regional policy, research and information society; *languages:* Greek, English, Italian.

Victoria Sotiriadou: 73 Davaki St, Papagou 15663, Athens; tel (+30 1) 654-97-88/360-17-40; fax (+30 1) 654-97-88; e-mail vsotiriadou@hotmail.com; secretary-general, Ministry of Labour, Employment and Management of the Resources of the European Funds; *specialities:* enlargement, environment, general EU policy, institutional reform, IGC, regional policy, research and information society; *languages:* Greek, French, English.

Ioannis Stavrou: 1 Morihovou Sq., 54625 Thessaloniki; tel (+30 31) 539-682; fax (+30 31) 541-491; e-mail eaiybe@otenet.gr; director, E. I. C. Association of

Industries of Northern Greece; *specialities:* economic and financial affairs, enlargement, general EU policy, institutional reform, IGC, regional policy; *languages:* Greek, French, English.

Dimosthenis Theoharopoulos: 2 Seferi, 30100 Agrinio; tel (+30 2631) 225-36; fax (+30 2631) 553-07; e-mail dtheoh@hotmail.com; lecturer, Department of Environmental and Natural Resources, University of Ioannina; *specialities:* agriculture, fisheries, rural development, regional/structural policy, environment; *languages:* Greek, English.

Antonis Tortopidis: 5 Xenophontos Str., 10557 Athens; tel (+30 1) 323-73-25; fax (+30 1) 322-29-29; e-mail main@fgi.org.gr; managing director, OMIKRON Economic Consultants Ltd., partner-director of Athens Consultancy Centre Ltd., consultant to the Federation of Greek Industries and the Hellenic Industrial Development Bank; *specialities:* economic and financial affairs; *languages:* Greek, English.

Alexandros Tsamis: 26 Vasileos Herakliou St, 54624 Thessaloniki; tel (+30 31) 28-18-37/26-36-65; fax (+30 31) 27-39-87; e-mail tasamis@nomos.gr; attorney-at-law, NOMOS Thessaloniki Law Firm; *specialities:* enlargement, general EU policy, institutional reform, IGC; *languages:* Greek, English.

Margaret Tzaphlidou: Medical Physics Laboratory, 45110 Ioannina; tel (+30 2651) 09-75-95; fax (+30 2651) 09-78-54; e-mail mtzaphli@cc.uoi.gr; professor of medical physics, Medical School, University of Ioannina; *specialities:* research and development, education and culture, general EU matters; *languages:* Greek, English.

Johan van Rens: POB 27 Finikas, 55102 Thessaloniki; tel (+30 31) 49-01-11; fax (+30 31) 49-01-02; e-mail jvr@cedefop.gr; director, CEDEFOP, concentrating on vocational training issues; *specialities:* education and culture, enterprise, competition, state aids, economic and financial affairs, employment and social affairs, internal market affairs, research and information society; *languages:* Dutch, German, English.

Maria Elisa Xenogianakopoulo: 14 Loukianou, 10675 Athens; tel (+30 210) 722-65-90; fax (+30 210) 411-43-10/360-17-40; lawyer; *specialities:* enlargement, general EU policy, institutional reform, IGC; *languages:* Greek, English.

HUNGARY

Alexander Blandl: Nyúl utca 13/a, 1024 Budapest; tel (+1) 428-20-29; e-mail alexander_blandl@mckinsey.com.

Pál Bődy: Honvéd u. 49. B., 8360 Keszthely; tel (+83) 31-74-70; e-mail endre33@axelero.hu.

Norbert Csizmadia: Vértanúk tere 1, 1055 Budapest; e-mail csizmadia@gkm .hu.

Dr Ágnes Czimbalmos: Tárkony utca 50, 1028 Budapest; tel (+1) 275-75-74; e-mail agnes.czimbalmos@axelero.hu.

Dr Emese Fáyné: Szent Donát u. 33, 2097 Pilisborosjenő; tel (+26) 33-69-31; e-mail arpad.fay@axelero.hu.

Gabriella Fésüs: Viola u. 34–36/b. III/ 11, 1094 Budapest; e-mail fesus.gabriella@ eszcsm.hu.

Dr László Fésüs: Viola u. 34–36/b. III/ 10, 1094 Budapest; tel (+1) 327-56-16; e-mail laszlo.fesus@pm.gov.hu.

Dr János Földessy: Görömbölyi u. 16, 3519 Miskolc; tel (+46) 56-51-11 (ext. 2311); e-mail fol4781@helka.iif.hu.

Barnabás Forgács: Tartsay Vilmos u. 9/ b, fszt. 003, 1126 Budapest; tel (+1) 451-70-72; e-mail forgacsb@aik.hu.

Gyorgy Foris: 155 rue de la Loi, 1040 Brussels; e-mail gyforis@burxinfo.hu.

István Hegedűs: Gerlóczy u. 11, 1052 Budapest; tel (+1) 318-04-84; e-mail Ihegedus@axelero.

Dr Zoltán Horváth: Zrínyi u. 25, 2600 Vác; tel (+1) 441-42-35; e-mail zoltan .horvath@parlament.hu.

Dr György Kenéz: Beszterce u. 25, 1034 Budapest; tel (+1) 472-87-70; e-mail kenez@gkm.hu.

Julianna Kovács: Andor u. 16/b., II/9, 1119 Budapest; tel (+1) 208-07-44; e-mail juharszirup01@yahoo.com.

Anita Paulovics: Aradi u. 32, 3519 Miskolc; tel (+46) 42-26-40; e-mail ankjog@ freemail.hu.

József Rotyis: Podmaniczky u. 2/2, 1067 Budapest; e-mail rotyis@gkm.hu.

Dr Gotthilf Sik: Szövőgyár u. 12, 1151 Budapest; tel (+1) 306-32-85; e-mail hilfike1@axelero.hu.

Dr Tamás Szemlér: Adria sétány 1/c., 4/ 33, 1148 Budapest; tel (+1) 251-47-27; e-mail tszemler@vki.hu.

Dr Péter Tóth: Etele út 20, 1119 Budapest; tel (+1) 266-56-22; e-mail ae_agro@ hu.inter.net.

Dr György Urkuti: Szent László u. 37, 2011 Budakalász; tel (+26) 34-03-48; e-mail urkuti@vg.hu.

Dr Lászlóné Vízhányó: Mester u. 22, 1095 Budapest; tel (+1) 488-21-65 (ext. 2179); e-mail zso@bkik.hu.

Dr Attila Zöldréti: Tallér u. 19, 1145 Budapest; tel (+1) 221-73-43; e-mail zoldretia@asz.hu.

Attila Zongor: Bem rkp. 30, 1027 Budapest; e-mail zongor@kulturpont.hu.

IRELAND

Gerard Arthurs: Cork Rd, Waterford; tel (+353 51) 30-22-21; fax (+353 51) 30-26-88; e-mail garthurs@wit.ie; lecturer in European Union Studies, Waterford Institute of Technology; *specialities:* enlargement, justice and home affairs, trade, development and external relations; *languages:* English.

Stephen Blair: Assembly House, O'Connell Street, Waterford; tel (+353 51) 86-07-00; fax (+353 51) 87-98-87; e-mail sblair@seregassembly.ie; director, Southern and Eastern Regional Assembly; *specialities:* regional and structural policy, general EU matters; *languages:* English.

Carol Brady: Galway Chamber of Commerce and Industry, Commerce House, Merchant's Rd, Galway; tel (+353 91) 56-26-24; fax (+353 91) 56-19-63; e-mail cbrady@galwaychamber.com; manager, Euro Info Centre, c/o Galway Chamber of Commerce; *specialities:* general EU matters, funding and grants, enterprise and SME policy, competition policy and state aids; *languages:* English.

Margaret Butterfield: Athy, Co. Kildare; tel (+353 87) 759-04-50; e-mail m.butterfield@kildare.teagasc.ie; *languages:* English.

Laura Caslin: Euro Info Centre, 16 Quai St, Sligo; tel (+353 71) 916-12-74/914-00-17; fax (+353 71) 916-09-12; e-mail sligoeic@eircom.net; manager, Euro Info Centre, Sligo Chamber of Commerce; *specialities:* enterprise, competition, state aids, economic and financial affairs, internal market affairs, regional policy; *languages:* English.

Prof. Neil Collins: National University of Ireland, Cork, Western Rd, Cork; tel (+353 21) 490-29-41; fax (+353 21) 490-31-35; e-mail n.collins@ucc.ie; academic; *specialities:* general EU policy, institutional reform, IGC, research and information society, transport and energy; *languages:* English.

James Doorley: Deanhill, Hayes Navan, Co. Meath; tel (+353 46) 902-42-16; e-mail doorley007@yahoo.com; regional support officer, North East Disability Federation of Ireland, vice-president, European Movement Ireland; *specialities:* education and culture, general EU policy, institutional reform, IGC; *languages:* English.

Stephen Flynn: Clonminch Tullamore, Co. Offaly; tel (+353) 871-21-88-40; fax (+353) 50-62-16-59; e-mail s.flynn@offaly .teagasc.ie; agricultural adviser and safety consultant, TEAGASC; *specialities:* agriculture and fisheries, environment, enlargement; *languages:* English.

Mark Garrett: Parnell House, 14 Parnell Sq., Dublin 2; tel (+353) 866-01-96-55; fax (+353) 18-04-54-06; e-mail mg@ tca.ie; communications manager, Competition Authority; *languages:* English.

Kate Geary: Fitzgerald House, Summerhill North, Cork; tel (+353 21) 450-90-44; fax (+353 21) 450-85-68; e-mail eic@ corkchamber.ie; manager, Euro Info Centre, Chamber of Commerce; *specialities:* enterprise, competition, state aids, economic and financial affairs, internal market affairs, regional policy; *languages:* English.

Janet Heeran: The Old Barracks, Cahersiveen, Co. Kerry; tel (+353 66) 947-36-64; fax (+353 66) 947-27-24; e-mail jheeran@skdp.net; community and Carrefour information officer, South Kerry Development Partnership; *languages:* English.

Páraig Hennessy: Kildare St, Dublin 2; tel (+353 1) 631-24-66; e-mail paraig_ hennessy@entemp.ie; *languages:* English.

Adrian Langan: 40 Eastmorelano Lane, Dublin 4; tel (+353) 879-33-10-14; fax (+353) 16-60-27-45; e-mail adrian .langan@bohgroup.ie; consultant, Bill O'Herlihy Communications; *specialities:* enlargement, regional and structural policy, future of Europe, European convention, European constitution, CFSP, defence, EU foreign policy; *languages:* English.

Philip Lynch: Kildare St, Dublin 2; tel (+353 1) 631-23-29; fax (+353 1) 631-28-01; e-mail philip_lynch@entemp.ie; civil servant, EU Affairs Unit, Department of Enterprise, Trade and Employment; *specialities:* general EU matters, institutional matters, history and theory of European integration, employment and social affairs, enterprise and SME policy, competition policy and state aids; *languages:* English.

Katherine Mary Meenan: 4 Esker Villas, Upper Rathmines Rd, Dublin 6; tel (+353 1) 497-48-60; e-mail katherinemeenan@eircom.net; public affairs consultant; *specialities:* general EU matters, future of Europe, European convention, transport and energy, institutional matters; *languages:* English, French, German.

Ann Neville: 28 Merrion Sq., Dublin 2; tel (+353 1) 661-21-82; fax (+353 1) 661-23-15; e-mail eic@irishexporters.ie; manager, Euro Info Centre, Dublin; *specialities:* enterprise and SME policy, competition policy and state aids, funding and grants; *languages:* English, Spanish.

Nuala O'Carroll: 2 Plassey Avenue, Corbally, Limerick; tel (+353 61) 34-89-02; e-mail nualaocarroll@ireland.com; consultant on EU programmes and their implementation; *specialities:* environment, general EU policy, institutional reform, IGC, health and consumer protection, regional policy; *languages:* English.

Julie O'Donnell: 21 Church St, Dungarvan, Co. Waterford; tel (+353 38) 442-79/546-46; fax (+353 58) 541-26; e-mail juliewlp@eircom.net; manager, South East European Centre-Carrefour; *languages:* English.

Dr Kathryn O'Donoghue: Kilcoe, Aughadown, Skibbereen, Cork; tel (+353 28) 381-38; fax (+353 28) 381-38; e-mail odonoghuekathryn@yahoo.co.uk; project management consultant, International Management Training Consultants; *specialities:* education and culture, employment and social affairs, health and consumer protection, research and information society; *languages:* English.

Fachtna O'Driscoll: Parnell St, Limerick; tel (+353 61) 41-59-22; fax (+353 61) 31-08-35; e-mail f.odriscoll@limerick.teagasc.ie; chief agricultural officer, TEAGASC; *specialities:* agriculture and fisheries, environment, regional policy; *languages:* English.

Bernard O'Farrell: Rural Development Division, Mellows Centre, Athenry, Co. Galway; tel (+353 91) 84-52-00-208; fax (+353 91) 84-42-96; e-mail bofarrell@athenry.teagasc.ie; regional education officer, TEAGASC; *specialities:* agriculture, fisheries, rural development, environment, education and culture; *languages:* English, Swedish.

Larry O'Loughlin: Kenbrook-Meelick, Rosenallis, Co. Laois; tel (+353 45) 87-92-03; fax (+353 45) 87-90-93; e-mail l.oloughlin@kildare.teagasc.ie; manager of the TEAGASC office in Co. Wicklow; *specialities:* agriculture and fisheries, environment, regional policy; *languages:* English.

James Stafford: Ballyhaise, Co. Cavan; tel (+353 49) 433-83-00; fax (+353 49) 433-83-04; e-mail j.stafford@cavan.teagasc.ie; chief AG officer, TEAGASC Agricultural College; *specialities:* agriculture and fisheries, environment, general EU policy, institutional reform, IGC; *languages:* English.

Elaine Wakely: Commerce House, Merchants Rd, Galway; tel (+353 91) 56-26-24; fax (+353 91) 56-19-63; e-mail elaine@galwaychamber.com; manager, Euro Info Centre, Galway Chamber of Commerce and Industry; *specialities:* enterprise, competition, state aids, economic and financial affairs; *languages:* English.

ITALY

Paolo Acunzo: 16 P. le Gregorio VII, 00165 Rome; tel (+39 0338) 316-39-77; e-mail pacunzo@hotmail.com; European affairs adviser; *specialities:* research and development, institutional matters, future of Europe, European convention, European constitution, general EU matters; *languages:* Italian.

Dr Lelio Alfonso: 3 Borgo al Collegio Maria Luigia, Parma; tel (+39 0521) 22-56-03; e-mail lelioalfonso@yahoo.it; journalist; *languages:* Italian, English, French.

Carlo Altomonte: Istituto di Economia Politica, Stanza 419, 5 Via Gobbi, 20136 Milan; tel (+39 02) 58-36-54-05; fax (+39 02) 58-36-54-39; e-mail carlo.altomonte@uni-bocconi.it; assistant professor, Università Commerciale 'L. Bocconi'; *specialities:* economic and monetary affairs, enlargement, trade, development and external relations; *languages:* Italian, English, French.

Prof. Ottorino Ascani: 2 Via Cesare Correnti, 20123 Milan; tel (+39 02) 86-45-32-01; fax (+39 02) 700-51-26-17; e-mail ascani8@iol.it; professor, Faculty of Economics, Università degli Studi di Milano; *specialities:* agriculture and fisheries, enterprise, competition, state aids, economic and financial affairs, internal market affairs, trade, development and external relations; *languages:* Italian, French, English.

Dr Oreste Barletta: 103 Via Elio Vittorini, 00144 Roma; tel (+39 06) 502-05-95; fax (+39 06) 62-27-51-78; e-mail mediaroma@mclink.it; journalist; *specialities:* education and culture, employment and social affairs, regional policy, research and information society; *languages:* Italian, French, English.

Dr Maria Giovanna Beretta: 88 Corso Magenta, 20123 Milan; tel (+39 02) 266-68-17/46-63-58; fax (+39 02) 266-68-17; e-mail giovberetta@hotmail.com; expert in legislation concerning industrial items; *specialities:* enterprise, competition, state aids, environment, health and consumer protection, internal market affairs, transport and energy; *languages:* Italian, English, French.

Dr Giannino Bernabei: 84 Via Dandolo, 00153 Roma; fax (+39 06) 581-77-07; e-mail gs.bernabei@libero.it; co-ordinator of international activities, Confindustria; *specialities:* education and culture, enlargement, general EU policy, institutional reform, IGC, internal market affairs, regional policy, research and information society, transport and energy; *languages:* Italian, French, English.

Concetta Bruno: tel (+39 090) 67-56-80; fax (+39 090) 67-95-38; e-mail concetta_b@virgilio.it; manager, Carrefour Sicilia Orientale; *specialities:* education and culture (including e-learning), enlargement, employment and social affairs; *languages:* Italian, French, English.

Antonella Buja: 20 Via Scudari, 41100 Modena; tel (+39 059) 20-66-43; fax (+39 059) 20-66-87; e-mail abuja@comune.modena.it; consultant in EU policies, funding and project management, City of Modena Progetto Europa (Department for European Affairs and International Relations); *specialities:* funding and grants, regional/structural policy, general EU matters; *languages:* Italian, French, Spanish.

Prof. Raimondo Cagiano de Azevedo: 26 Salita de' Crescenzi, 18600 Rome; tel (+39 06) 689-38-64/68-80-33-81; fax (+39 06) 689-27-15; e-mail cagiano@scec.eco.uniroma1.it; academic; *specialities:* education and culture, economic and financial affairs, enlargement, employment and social affairs, general EU policy, institutional reform, IGC, regional policy; *languages:* Italian, English.

Carmelo Calamia: 31 Via Raffaele Maddalo, 73012 Campi Salentina (LE); tel (+39 0832) 79-19-32/24-85-34/68-33-00; fax (+39 0832) 68-33-33; e-mail carmelocalamia@yahoo.it; director, EU Policy Service of Lecce province; *specialities:* education and culture, enlargement, general EU policy, institutional reform, IGC, regional policy; *languages:* Italian, French.

Vittorio Calaprice: c/o Presidente Greco, 2/I/2 Via Devitofrancesco, 70124 Bari; tel (+39 080) 552-04-78; fax (+39 080) 552-04-78; e-mail vittoriocalaprice@libero.it; consultant, EU Policies Committee of Puglia; *specialities:* future of Europe, European convention, European constitution, history and theory of European integration, education and culture, funding and grants; *languages:* Italian, English.

Prof. Fausto Capelli: 12 Via Silvio Pellico, 20121 Milan; tel (+39 02) 86-78-92/80-41-62; fax (+39 02) 86-46-34-80; e-mail capelli@rigel.it; lawyer; *specialities:* enterprise, competition, state aids, internal market affairs, trade, development and external relations, transport and energy; *languages:* Italian, French, Germany.

Roberto Carpano: 30 Via Marmenia, 00178 Rome; tel (+39 06) 718-52-03; fax (+39 06) 71-28-90-19; e-mail roberto_carpano@fastwebnet.it; *specialities:* general EU policy, institutional reform, IGC, research and information society, trade, development and external relations; *languages:* Italian, English.

Dr Carla Cavallini: 2 Via E. Bolognesi, 42100 Reggio Emilia; tel (+39 0522) 27-80-19; fax (+39 0522) 51-89-56; e-mail c.cavallini@crpa.it; manager, Carrefour Europeo Emilia; *specialities:* agriculture, fisheries, rural development, regional/structural policy, education and culture, funding and grants; *languages:* Italian, English, French.

Dr Sara Cavelli: 51 Piazza Di San Marco, 00186 Rome; tel (+39 06) 692-07-81/46; e-mail cavelli@sioi.org; deputy general director, Società Italiana per l'Organizzazione Internazionale (SIOI); *specialities:* information society; *languages:* Italian, French.

Dr Carmelo Cedrone: 6 Via Lucullo, 00187 Rome; tel (+39 06) 475-32-33; fax (+39 06) 475-32-34; e-mail cedrone@uil.it; professor, head, international relations, Unione Italiana del Lavoro (UIL); *specialities:* education and culture, enlargement, employment and social affairs, general EU policy, institutional reform, IGC, regional policy; *languages:* Italian, French, Spanish.

Dr Franco Chittolina: 69 Via Roma, 12049 Trinità (CN); tel (+39 011) 384-10-37; fax (+39 011) 384-10-31; e-mail franco .chittolina@gruppoabele.org; *languages:* Italian, French.

Ornella Cilona: 25 Corso Italia, 00198 Rome; tel (+39) 33-97-05-32-58; fax (+39 06) 847-64-73; e-mail ocilona@virgilio.it; journalist and economic researcher, CGIL (Italian trade union); *specialities:* regional/structural policy, employment and social affairs, enterprise and SME policy, competition policy and state aids, education and culture (including e-learning); *languages:* Italian, English.

Roberto Ciompi: 14 Piazza Vittorio Emanuele II, 56125 Pisa; tel (+39 050) 92-93-24; fax (+39 050) 92-93-50; e-mail robertociompi@tiscali.it; co-ordinator, Office of Community Policy of Pisa; *specialities:* enlargement, regional policy; *languages:* Italian.

Alberto Colabianchi: 30 Via Oslavia, 00195 Rome; tel (+39 06) 372-09-09; fax (+39 06) 370-16-29; e-mail avv .colabianchi@tiscalinet.it; legal consultant on citizens' rights at the European Commission's Italian Office; *specialities:* agriculture and fisheries, employment and social affairs, general EU policy, institutional reform, IGC, internal market affairs, justice and home affairs; *languages:* Italian, French, English.

Dr Rosario Francesco Condorelli: 18 Via Pasubio, 95100 Catania; tel (+39 095) 742-33-01-03; fax (+39 095) 32-76-74; e-mail rosario.condorelli@tin.it; local government officer; *specialities:* enterprise, competition, state aids, internal market affairs, regional policy; *languages:* Italian, English.

Giulia Costantino: 205 rue Belliard, 1040 Brussels; tel (+39 02) 280-39-93; fax (+39 02) 231-12-62; e-mail g.costantino@etsgroup.net; university professor, consultant; *specialities:* funding and grants, general EU matters, education and culture (including e-learning), regional/structural policy; *languages:* Italian, English.

Prof. Corrado Maria Daclon: Nomentano, Rome; professor of nature conservation at the University of Venice; *specialities:* education and culture, enlargement, environment, health and

consumer protection, research and information society; *languages:* Italian, English.

Claudio De Paola: 21/c Via Trieste, 20010 Santo Stefano Ticino MI; tel (+39 02) 97-25-90-30; fax (+39 02) 97-25-61-02; e-mail c.depaola@tin.it; manager, Carrefour Europeo Lombardia; *specialities:* agriculture and fisheries, environment, regional policy, education and culture, general EU policy; *languages:* Italian, English.

Dr Ruggero del Vecchio: 162 Via Emerico Amari, 90139 Palermo; tel (+39 091) 58-44-32; fax (+39 091) 32-53-44; e-mail caseuropa@caseuropa.org; *specialities:* education and culture, employment and social affairs, general EU policy, institutional reform, IGC, regional policy; *languages:* Italian, French.

Dr Cesare Di Martino: 42 Via Arcivescovado, 66100 Chieti; tel (+39 0871) 329-31; fax (+39 0871) 32-17-29; e-mail dimartino@provincia.chieti.it; manager, Info Point Europe of the Province of Chieti; *specialities:* funding and grants, future of Europe, European convention, European constitution, education and culture (including e-learning), general EU matters; *languages:* Italian, French.

Prof. Giuseppe Di Vita: 24 Via E. l'Emiro, 90135 Palermo; tel (+39 091) 652-08-01; fax (+39 091) 652-08-01; e-mail pidivita@libero.it; lecturer, Istituto Tecnico Commerciale di Stato; *specialities:* education and culture, general EU policy, institutional reform, IGC, research and information society, trade, development and external relations; *languages:* Italian, French.

Sergio Diana: 4 Piazza Repubblica, 09126 Cagliari; tel (+39 070) 48-54-80; fax (+39 070) 45-62-63; e-mail studiodianas@tiscalinet.it; lawyer; *specialities:* enterprise, competition, state aids, employment and social affairs, general EU policy, institutional reform, IGC, regional policy; *languages:* Italian, French.

Dr Giuseppe Eusepi: 9 Via del Castro Laurenziano, 00161 Rome; tel (+39 06) 49-76-69-55; fax (+39 06) 446-19-64/ 446-20-40; e-mail Giuseppe.Eusepi@ uniroma1.it; university professor, University of Rome; *specialities:* enlargement, funding and grants, future of Europe, European convention, European constitution, institutional matters; *languages:* Italian, English.

Dr Elisabetta Fonck: 18 square Ambiorix, 1000 Brussels; tel (+32 47) 364-67-46; e-mail elisabettafonck@ hotmail.com; *specialities:* EU budget, justice and home affairs, regional/structural policy, institutional matters; *languages:* Italian, French.

Dr Giuseppe Forlenza: Piazza Mario Pagano, 85100 Potenza; tel (+39 0971)

41-92-73/4; fax (+39 0971) 41-93-15; e-mail prefettura.potenza@interbusiness .it; manager, Info Point Europe, Potenza; *specialities:* education and culture, enlargement, general EU policy, institutional reform, IGC; *languages:* Italian, English.

Andrea Forti: 24 Via XX Settembre, 20123 Milan; tel (+39 02) 46-76-42-40; fax (+39 02) 46-76-42-27; e-mail aforti@ hsn.it; research co-ordinator, Istituto per la Ricerca Sociale; *specialities:* enterprise, competition, state aids, internal market affairs, regional policy; *languages:* Italian, English, French.

Dr Massimo Fragola: 30 Piazza dei Martiri, 80121 Naples; tel (+39 081) 34-73-31-26-35; e-mail fragola@unical.it; professor of EU law, University of Calabria; *specialities:* institutional matters, development policy, humanitarian aid, future of Europe, European convention, European constitution, transport and energy; *languages:* Italian, French, English.

Dr Luna Fragomeni: 7 Via Scotellaro, 42025 Cavriago (RE); tel (+39 0522) 57-69-11; fax (+39 0522) 57-75-08; e-mail lunafragomeni@iol.it; consultant for training and European projects; *specialities:* education and culture (including e-learning), employment and social affairs, funding and grants, regional and structural policy; *languages:* Italian, English.

Dr Angelo Frascarelli: 74 Borgo XX Giugno, 06121 Perugia; tel (+39 075) 585-71-34; fax (+39 075) 585-71-46; e-mail angelof@unipg.it; professor, University of Perugia; *specialities:* agriculture, fisheries, rural development, regional/structural policy; *languages:* Italian, French.

Riccardo Garosci: 40 Corso Venezia, 20121 Milan; tel (+39 02) 76-00-53-43; fax (+39 02) 78-34-10; e-mail gasosci2001@yahoo.com; entrepreneur, academic; *specialities:* economic and financial affairs, environment, health and consumer protection, trade, development and external relations; *languages:* Italian, French.

Massimo Giacomini: 11 Via Riccardo Grazioli Lante, 00195 Rome; tel (+39 06) 37-35-00-29/33-86-16-55-69; fax (+39 06) 23-31-97-19; e-mail massimogiacomini@ yahoo.it; freelance journalist specializing in political economy; *specialities:* education and culture, economic and financial affairs, enlargement, health and consumer protection, research and information society, transport and energy; *languages:* Italian, French.

Antonino Imbesi: Via Parigi, snc 58100 Potenza; tel (+39 0971) 215-93; fax (+39 0971) 215-93; e-mail imbesi@memex.it; director, EURO-NET; *specialities:* education and culture (including e-learning), enterprise and SME policy, competition policy and state aids, funding and grants; *languages:* Italian, English.

Prof. Emanuele Itta: 71/A Corso Belgio, 10153 Turin; tel (+39 011) 812-60-93/831-84-29-64; fax (+39 011) 812-60-93/831-84-29-64; e-mail e.itta@palazzochigi.it; professor of European economy and European monetary integration, University of Lecce; *specialities:* enterprise, competition, state aids, economic and financial affairs, enlargement, general EU policy, institutional reform, IGC, regional policy, trade, development and external relations; *languages:* Italian, French, English.

Elke Kuehnel: 65 Via Saronno, 00188 Rome; tel (+39 06) 33-67-89-12/372-59-07; fax (+39 06) 370-16-29; e-mail elke.kuehnel@tiscali.it; legal consultant; *specialities:* enterprise, competition, state aids, employment and social affairs, general EU policy, institutional reform, IGC, health and consumer protection, internal market affairs; *languages:* German, English.

Michele Lener: 1 P. E. Mattei, 00144 Rome; tel (+39 06) 59-82-25-14; fax (+39 06) 59-82-21-83; e-mail michele.lener@eni.it; industrial manager (institutional relations), ENI SpA; *specialities:* research and development, transport and energy, environment, health and consumer protection; *languages:* English, Italian.

Clotilde Lombardi Satriani: 44 rue d'Ecosse, 1060 Brussels; tel (+39 02) 644-58-21; fax (+39 02) 644-58-22; e-mail euroceru@skynet.be; responsible for institutional relations, Centro Europeo; *specialities:* education and culture (including e-learning), environment, general EU matters, future of Europe, European convention, European constitution; *languages:* Italian, French, English.

Emma Lorrai: 143 Corso Trieste, 00198 Rome; tel (+39 06) 860-65-51; fax (+39 06) 860-65-51; e-mail emmalorrai@yahoo.com; *specialities:* education and culture, employment and social affairs, research and development, transport and energy, history and theory of European integration, future of Europe, European convention, European constitution; *languages:* Italian, French, English.

Chiara Manicardi: 10 Via Bardi, I-42100 Reggio Emilia; tel (+39 0522) 44-00-88; fax (+39 0522) 44-00-88; e-mail chiara.manicardi@tin.it; consultant; *specialities:* education and culture, enterprise, competition, state aids, employment and social affairs, regional policy; *languages:* Italian, French.

Dr Giulia Marcon: 12 Via M. Vittoria, 10123 Turin; tel (+39 011) 861-24-65; fax (+39 011) 861-27-90; e-mail giulia.marcon@provincia.torino.it; attached to Euro Info Point, Turin; *languages:* Italian, English, French.

Giuseppe Mariani: 2 Via Emilio Lussu, 20038 Seregno; tel (+39 0362) 22-93-21; fax (+39 0362) 33-57-75; e-mail gi.mariani@tiscalinet.it; teacher, author; *specialities:* education and culture, general EU policy, institutional reform, IGC; *languages:* Italian, French.

Tommaso Martinelli: Corso Carducci, 58100 Grosseto; tel (+39 0564) 48-82-81; fax (+39 0564) 48-82-87; e-mail carrmar@comune.grosseto.it; manager, Carrefour Maremma; *specialities:* agriculture, fisheries, rural development, funding and grants, regional/structural policy; *languages:* Italian, English.

Stefania Maurino: 165/A/2 Via Tommaso Arcidiacono, 00143 Rome; tel (+39 06) 503-28-33; fax (+39 06) 503-28-33; e-mail laboratorieuropa@hotmail.com; consultant, Euro Consult Desk; *specialities:* education and culture, enterprise, competition, state aids, employment and social affairs, internal market affairs, regional policy; *languages:* Italian, French, Spanish.

Roberto Mezzaroma: 36 Via Zanardelli, 00186 Rome; tel (+39 06) 68-80-24-14; fax (+39 06) 68-80-66-93; e-mail ios.ios@tin.it; *languages:* Italian, French.

Dr Renzo Michieletto: 14 Via dell' Università, 35020 Legnaro (Pd); tel (+39 049) 829-37-16; fax (+39 049) 829-37-18; e-mail renzo.michieletto@venetoagricoltura.org; co-ordinator of Carrefour Europeo of Veneto; *specialities:* agriculture, fisheries, rural development, enlargement, environment, regional/structural policy; *languages:* Italian, English, French.

Dr Stefano Milia: 58 Via Lattanzio, 00136 Rome; tel (+39 06) 69-99-92-45/34-72-34-58-27; fax (+39 06) 678-61-59; e-mail s.milia@cide.it; researcher; *specialities:* future of Europe, European convention, European constitution, institutional matters, history and theory of European integration, general EU matters; *languages:* Italian, German, English.

Mia Milillo: 639 Via Cassia, 00189 Rome; tel (+39 06) 33-26-98-42; fax (+39 06) 33-26-98-42; e-mail miamilillo@libero.it; tax consultant; *specialities:* future of Europe, European convention, European constitution, justice and home affairs (including immigration, asylum, police and judicial co-operation), economic and monetary affairs, Euro; *languages:* Italian, English.

Franco Mollo: 10 Via Gerolamo De Rada, 87100 Cosenza, tel (+39 0984) 230-58; fax (+39 0984) 230-58; e-mail franco.mollo@tin.it; teacher; *languages:* Italian, English.

Dr Anna Mura: 11 Via Rubicone, 00199 Rome; tel (+39 06) 84-89-22-42; fax (+39 06) 84-89-22-22; e-mail amura@formez.it; director, academic; *specialities:* education

and culture, environment, regional policy, research and information society; *languages:* Italian, French.

Prof. Bruno Nascimbene: 12 Via Vincenzo Bellini, 20122 Milan; tel (+39 02) 77-42-31; fax (+39 02) 77-42-344; e-mail info@nascimbene.com; lecturer in Community law, University of Milan; *specialities:* enterprise, competition, state aids, employment and social affairs, general EU policy, institutional reform, IGC, internal market affairs, justice and home affairs; *languages:* Italian, French, English.

Mario Nicolella: 9 rue du Val de Grace, 75005 Paris; fax (+33 1) 53-10-83-18; e-mail cabinet.nicolella@wanadoo.fr; lawyer; *specialities:* enterprise and SME policy, competition policy and state aids, justice and home affairs (including immigration, asylum, police and judicial co-operation), health and consumer protection, future of Europe, European convention, European constitution; *languages:* Italian, English.

Caterina Nisida: 74 Via La Spezia, 00182 Rome; tel (+39 06) 701-25-90; fax (+39 06) 701-25-90; e-mail caterina.nisida@fastwebnet.it; teacher, sociologist and trainer; *languages:* Italian, English.

Gian Piero Orsello: 267 Via del Corso, 00186 Rome; tel (+39 06) 678-00-04; fax (+39 06) 69-94-13-06; e-mail Gianpierorsello@inwind.it; professor, University of Rome; *specialities:* education and culture, enlargement, general EU policy, institutional reform, IGC, research and information society; *languages:* Italian, French.

Dr Giancarlo Orsingher: 15 Via Aurora, 38050 Telve Valsugana (Tn); tel (+39 0461) 61-52-00/76-63-42; fax (+39 0461) 65-08-72; e-mail carrefour@ismaa.it; attached to Carrefour, Alpi; *languages:* Italian, English.

Giuliano Palagi: 128 Via Nizza, 00198 Rome; tel (+39 06) 85-56-83-35; fax (+39 06) 85-56-83-17; e-mail g.palagi@provincia.pisa.it; sector manager, Institute for Services for the Agricultural and Food Market (ISMEA); *specialities:* agriculture, fisheries, rural development, enlargement, future of Europe, European convention, European constitution, history and theory of European integration; *languages:* Italian, English, French.

Dr Blando Palmieri: 13 Via Guattani, 00161 Rome; tel (+39 06) 44-18-82-44; fax (+39 06) 44-24-95-18; e-mail palmieri@rdn.it; responsible for Community policy, Confederazione Nazionale Dell'Artigianato; *specialities:* enterprise, competition, state aids, economic and financial affairs, enlargement, employment and social affairs, internal market affairs, regional policy; *languages:* Italian, English, French.

Dr Pietro Maria Paolucci: 20 Piazza Nicosia, 00186 Rome; tel (+39 06) 67-79-53-25; e-mail pi.paolucci@palazzochigi.it; manager; *specialities:* enlargement, general EU matters, trade, WTO, common commercial policy, external economic matters, transport and energy; *languages:* Italian, English, French.

Gian Paolo Papa: 67R Via Cernizza, Duino (Trieste); tel (+39 040) 20-85-55; fax (+39 040) 57-20-44; e-mail gianpaolopapa@libero.it; consultant; *specialities:* enlargement, trade, development and external relations; *languages:* Italian, French.

Prof. Gianni Paramithiotti: 65 Corso Strada Nuova, 27100 Pavia; tel (+39 0382) 50-43-55; fax (+39 0382) 50-44-02; e-mail paramith@unipv.it; professor of European economics at the State University of Pavia; *specialities:* enterprise, competition, state aids, enlargement, regional policy, trade, development and external relations; *languages:* Italian, English.

Silvana Paruolo: 25 Corso d'Italia, 00198 Rome; tel (+39 06) 847-63-05; fax (+39 06) 884-56-83; e-mail luna_libera@yahoo.it; journalist; *specialities:* economic and financial affairs, employment and social affairs, internal market affairs, regional policy; *languages:* Italian, French.

Daniela Piana: 20 Via delle Fontanelle, 50016 Fiesole (Firenze); tel (+39) 556-68-58-23; e-mail Daniela.Piana@iue.it; research fellow, European University Institute; *specialities:* enlargement, history and theory of European integration, institutional matters, future of Europe, European convention, European constitution; *languages:* Italian, French, English.

Marcello Pierini: 21 Via Vittorio Veneto, 61029 Petriano; tel (+39 0722) 29-83; fax (+39 0722) 40-06; e-mail carrefourmarche@uniurb.it; director, Carrefour Europeo Marche; *languages:* Italian, French.

Mario Pinzauti: 66 Via Casalina sud-Villaggio Giornalisti, 04010 Borgo Sabotino-Latina; tel (+39 0773) 27-32-95; e-mail marpinza@tiscali.it; journalist and adviser; *specialities:* enlargement, employment and social affairs, future of Europe, European convention, European constitution, history and theory of European integration; *languages:* Italian, English.

Silvia Pomes: 19/e Via Isonzo, 00198 Rome; tel (+39 06) 85-44-91; fax (+39 06) 85-44-92-88; e-mail silvia.pomes@tesoro.it; lawyer in the legal department of Consip S.p.A.; *specialities:* justice and home affairs, enlargement, environment, transport and energy; *languages:* Italian, English.

Dr Paolo Prosperini: tel (+39 0347) 178-21-33; fax (+39 050) 237-62; e-mail p.prosperini@diplomacy.edu; senior expert, Department of Cohesion Policies, Ministry of Economy; *specialities:* regional/structural policy, institutional matters, funding and grants, future of Europe, European convention, European constitution; *languages:* Italian, Spanish, French.

Domenico Ragone: 69 Via Mazzini, 85100 Potenza; tel (+39 0971) 223-96; fax (+39 0971) 44-86-30; e-mail doragone@regione.basilicata.it; civil servant, architect; *specialities:* enterprise, competition, state aids, environment, regional policy; *languages:* Italian, French.

Claudio Ravaglia: 132 Via Molinaccio, 48020 San Pancrazio (RA); tel (+39 0544) 53-41-30; fax (+39 0544) 53-41-30; e-mail cravagl@tin.it; consultant on agriculture and rural development; *specialities:* agriculture and fisheries, enterprise, competition, state aids, enlargement, regional policy; *languages:* Italian, French.

Dr Paola Ravelli: 14 Via de Gasperi, 20023 Cerro Maggiore (mi); tel (+39 0331) 42-20-96; e-mail paola.ravelli@libero.it; attached to Carrefour, Lombardy; *languages:* Italian.

Dr Vittorio Regis: 1 Via Giambologna, 20136 Milan; tel (+39 02) 58-10-20-24; fax (+39 02) 58-10-20-24; e-mail vregis@inwind.it; scientist, manager; *specialities:* enterprise, competition, state aids, enlargement, environment, research and information society, transport and energy; *languages:* Italian, English.

Dr Vito Rizzo: 50 Via G. Leopardi, 95127 Catania; tel (+39 095) 37-19-82; fax (+39 095) 37-19-82; e-mail vito_rizzo@virgilio.it; marketing professor, journalist; *specialities:* education and culture (including e-learning), enterprise and SME policy, competition policy and state aids, enlargement, general EU matters; *languages:* Italian, French.

Giorgio Rossetti: 15 Via Roma, 34132 Trieste; (+39 040) 76-39-69; fax (+39 040) 76-39-69; e-mail dialoghieuropei@virgilio.it; journalist; *specialities:* enlargement, transport and energy, future of Europe, European convention, European constitution; *languages:* Italian, French.

Marco Rossi: Studio M. R., 60 Via San Secondo, 10128 Turin; tel (+39 0349) 592-03-67; fax (+39 0349) 898-02-68; e-mail teameurope.it@marcossi.it; lecturer, Scuola Europea Internazionale di Stato 'A. Spinelli'; *specialities:* enlargement, institutional reform, development and external relations, general EU policy, education and culture, research and information society; *languages:* Italian, French.

Dr Pasquale Satalino: 127/H Via Giulio Petroni, 70124 Bari; tel (+39 080) 501-60-40; fax (+39 080) 501-60-40; e-mail p.satalino@libero.it; head, external relations, Fiera del Levante; *specialities:* agriculture and fisheries, economic and financial affairs, enlargement, environment, employment and social affairs, general EU policy, institutional reform, IGC, regional policy, research and information society, transport and energy; *languages:* Italian, French.

Carlo Secchi: 25 Via Sarfatti, 20136 Milan; tel (+39 02) 58-36-54-15/54-17; fax (+39 02) 58-36-54-39; e-mail carlo.secchi@uni-bocconi.it; professor of European economic policy, Università Bocconi di Milano; *specialities:* enterprise, competition, state aids, economic and financial affairs, enlargement, internal market affairs, trade, development and external relations; *languages:* Italian, English.

Prof. Michela Sironi Mariotti: Via dell'Artigliere, 37129 Verona; tel (+39 045) 809-82-44; fax (+39 045) 809-85-29; e-mail michela.sironi@univr.it; professor of economics; *specialities:* employment and social affairs, internal market affairs, research and information society; *languages:* Italian, French.

Attilio Sorice: 5 Via G. B. della Salle, 82100 Benevento; tel (+39 06) 321-61-62; fax (+39 06) 322-59-56; e-mail attilio.sorice@iims.it; chief executive, I.R.P.S.; *specialities:* education and culture, economic and financial affairs, enlargement, general EU policy, institutional reform, IGC, justice and home affairs, regional policy; *languages:* Italian, English.

Filippo Spallina: 312/G Via San Lorenzo, 90145 Palermo; tel (+39 091) 662-87-55; fax (+39 091) 662-87-56; e-mail ue@provincia.palermo.it; director, Provincia Regionale di Palermo-EU relations; *specialities:* general EU policy, regional policy, education and culture, health and consumer protection; *languages:* Italian, French.

Adalgisa Stabilito: 10 Via Luigi Sturzo, 87029 Scalea (Cosenza); tel (+30 0985) 207-76; fax (+39 0985) 209-88; e-mail adalgisa1@virgilio.it; sociologist, college administrator; *specialities:* education and culture (including e-learning), information society, institutional matters, funding and grants, general EU matters, regional/structural policy; *languages:* Italian, French.

Rocco Tancredi: 92 Viale Trentino, 74100 Taranto; tel (+39 099) 37-54-23; fax (+39 099) 37-54-23; e-mail r.tancredi@corecompuglia.it; journalist, teacher of languages; *specialities:* transport and energy, information society, regional/structural policy, future of Europe, European convention, European constitution; *languages:* Italian, French.

Dr Chiara Tornato: 14 Via Leonardo da Vinci, 15001 Acqui Terme; tel (+39) 034-71-55-56-98; fax (+39) 01-44-35-69-74;

e-mail chiaratornat@yahoo.it; manager, Carrefour Piemonte; *specialities:* institutional matters, enlargement; *languages:* Italian, English.

Francesco Vallebona: 49 bte 8 rue de Trèves, 1040 Brussels; tel (+32 2) 280-63-40; fax (+32 2) 280-63-38; e-mail vallebona@medineurope.com; consultant on European affairs and project manager, Medin Europe; *specialities:* funding and grants, research and development, education and culture (including e-learning); *languages:* Italian, English.

Piercarlo Valtorta: 26 Via Francesco Tosi, 22035 Canzo; tel (+32 02) 644-58-21; fax (+32 02) 644-58-22; e-mail euroceru@skynet.be; professor; *specialities:* education and culture, enterprise, competition, state aids, general EU policy, institutional reform, IGC; *languages:* Italian, French.

Dr Antonio Venece: 106 E/6 Via Vasco de Gama, 00121 Rome; tel (+39 06) 569-83-74; fax (+39 06) 69-51-93-13; e-mail Hulysse@yahoo.com; youth projects manager; *specialities:* agriculture and fisheries, education and culture, economic and financial affairs, enlargement, environment, employment and social affairs, general EU policy, institutional reform, IGC, internal market affairs, justice and home affairs, regional policy; *languages:* Italian, English.

Antonio Villafranca: 5 Via Clerici, 20121 Milan; tel (+39 02) 863-31-32-94; fax (+39 02) 863-31-32-64; e-mail antonio.villafranca@ispionline.it; research leader; *specialities:* general EU policy, trade, development and external relations, economic and social affairs, enlargement; *languages:* Italian, English.

Monica Visentin: tel (+39 0544) 45-03-88; e-mail mvisentin@racine.ra.it; manager, Carrefour Romagna; *specialities:* general EU matters, education and culture (including e-learning), regional/ structural policy, funding and grants; *languages:* Italian, English, French.

LATVIA

Inese Allika: Ministry of Economy, Brīvības iela 55, 1519 Rīga; tel 9122215; e-mail inese.allika@apollo.lv; *specialities:* enlargement, internal market affairs, EMU-Euro.

Esmeralda Balode: Ministry of Justice, Basteja bulv. 14–4. stāvs, 17.kab. Rīga; tel 7503107; e-mail Esmeralda.Balode@ tm.gov.lv; *specialities:* justice and home affairs, enterprise, competition and state aids, institutional issues.

Renārs Danelsons: Ministry of Foreign Affairs, Brīvības 36, Rīga; tel 7016388; e-mail renars.danelsons@mfa.gov.lv; *specialities:* justice and home affairs, institutional issues.

Ainārs Dimants: Vidzeme University College, Brīvības iela 312–14, 1006 Rīga; e-mail dimants@latnet.lv; *specialities:* common foreign and security policy, education and culture, enlargement.

Andris Gobiņš: NGO European Movement Latvia, Basteja bulv. 14, Rīga; tel 9626646; e-mail gobins@web.de; *specialities:* youth and intercultural learning.

Linda Jākobsone: State Chancellery, Brīvības 36, 1520 Rīga; tel 9123348; e-mail linda.jakobsone@mk.gov.lv; *specialities:* enlargement, youth and intercultural learning.

Elita Jermolajeva: Preili City Council, Raiņa bulvāris 19, 5301 Preiļi; tel 9444989; *specialities:* internal market affairs, education and culture, regional policy.

Edīte Kalniņa: Coalition for Gender Equality in Latvia; tel 6468079; Vaļņu iela 32-506, 1050 Rīga; tel 6468079; e-mail edite.kalnina@narvesen.lv; *specialities:* justice and home affairs, employment and social affairs, youth and intercultural learning.

Līga Kalvāne: Ministry of Culture, Valdemāra 11 a, Rīga; tel 7356629; e-mail liga.kalvane@km.gov.lv; *specialities:* education and culture, institutional issues, regional policy.

Žaneta Matijesku: Ministry of Environment, Peldu iela 25, Rīga; tel 7026436; e-mail zaneta.matijesku@vidm.gov.lv; *specialities:* environment, institutional issues.

Ligita Melece: State Institute of Agrarian Economy, Struktoru iela 14, 1039 Rīga; tel 7553546; e-mail ligita@lvaei.lv; *specialities:* agriculture and fisheries, health and consumer policy.

Ainārs Nābels Šneiders: Ministry of Agriculture, Republikas laukums 2, Rīga; tel 7027549; e-mail ainars.nabels@ zm.gov.lv; *specialities:* agriculture and fisheries.

Dace Pastare: Farm 'Pērles', Z/S 'Pērles'; tel 9249246; e-mail pasta@ tvnet.lv; *specialities:* agriculture and fisheries.

Artis Puriņš: EU Information Centre, Basteja bulv. 14, Rīga; tel 7212611; e-mail artis.purins@eiropainfo.lv; *specialities:* enlargement, institutional issues, common foreign and security policy.

Liene Ramane: Vidzeme University College, Zvejnieku iela 13–404, 4200 Valmiera; tel 6588924; e-mail liene_ ramane@va.lv; *specialities:* education and culture, trade, development and external issues.

Inta Rimšāne: Rezekne Region Council, Atbrīvošanas aleja 95, 4601 Rēzekne; tel 4625011; e-mail inta.rimsane@rdc.lv; *specialities:* institutional issues, regional policy.

Ivo Rollis: Biķernieku iela 81–5, 1039 Rīga; tel 9137511; e-mail 9137511; *specialities:* integraton of Latvia into the EU, EU history, central and eastern country integration into the EU.

Evija Rudzīte: Programme YOUTH, Merķeļa 11–531, 1050 Rīga; tel 7356231; e-mail evija.rudzite@latnet.lv; *specialities:* education and culture, youth and intercultural learning.

Sanda Serafinoviča: Programme YOUTH, Merķeļa 11–531, 1050 Rīga; tel 7356231; e-mail sandas@latnet.lv; *specialities:* institutional issues, education and culture.

Inese Smildziņa: SIA 'Veidols', Veidenbauma iela 1–19, 2150 Sigulda; tel 6404379; e-mail inese16@hotmail.com; *specialities:* enterprise, competition and state aids, internal market affairs, EMU-Euro.

Māris Sprindžuks: Hypothec Bank, Consultation Centre, Elizabetes 41/43, 1010 Rīga; tel 9457107; e-mail maris@ hipofkc.lv; *specialities:* agriculture and fisheries, regional policy, enterprise, competition and state aids.

Līga Sondore: Ministry of Finance, Smilšu 1, Rīga; e-mail liga.sondore@fm .gov.lv; *specialities:* institutional issues, internal market affairs, enlargement.

Solvita Štrausa: National Radio and Television Council, Smilšu 1/3 – 6.stāvs, Rīga; tel 9273513; e-mail solvita.strausa@ nrtp.lv; *specialities:* internal market law, EU tax and state aid policy, basic EU law.

Inese Šulce: Kronbergs Law office, 11.novembra krastmala 23, 1050 Rīga; tel 7043838 ; e-mail: Inese.Sulce@lv .eylaw.com; *specialities:* internal market affairs, employment and social affairs, regional policy.

Ivo Velde: Zvejnieku iela 1k-14, Rīga; tel 7607145; e-mail velde@mediastock.lv; *specialities:* education and culture, enterprise, competition and state aids.

Kārlis Vilciņš: Club 'The House', Basteja bulv. 14, Rīga; tel 7221658; e-mail karlis.vilcins@inbox.lv; *specialities:* education and culture, structural funds (culture, human resources, tourism), youth.

Hilmārs Zīle: Elizabetes 87-12, 1050 Rīga; tel 9590046; *specialities:* EMU-Euro, trade, development and external issues.

LUXEMBOURG

Franco Avena: 31 rue Dicks, 6744 Niederanven; tel (+352) 34-80-84; fax (+352) 34-18-84; e-mail avena@pt.lu; former civil servant; *specialities:* enlargement, general EU policy, trade, development and external relations, economic and monetary affairs; *languages:* Italian, French, German.

Jul Christophory: Ferme de Grevels, 8059 Bertrange; tel (+352) 31-04-11; fax (+352) 31-47-01; e-mail jchristophory@ yahoo.fr; adviser, Présidence du Centre Universitaire de Luxembourg-Centre Universitaire de Luxembourg; *languages:* Letzeburgish, French, English.

Prof. Carlo Degli Abbati: 225 Val des Bons Malades, 2121 Luxembourg; tel (+352) 42-07-19; e-mail carlo.degliabbat@ tiscalinet.it; former civil servant; *specialities:* economic and financial affairs, regional policy, trade, development and external relations, transport and energy; *languages:* Italian, French, Spanish.

Christian Glöckner: 20 rue d'Altlinster, 6163 Bourglinster; tel (+352) 78-99-75; fax (+352) 78-86-17; e-mail saarlorlux -consult@pt.lu; journalist; *specialities:* enlargement, general EU policy, institutional reform, IGC, justice and home affairs; *languages:* German, English, French.

Patrick Goergen: BP 381, 17 rue de Louvigny, 2013 Luxembourg; tel (+352) 26-27-25-1; fax (+352) 26-27-25-21; e-mail patrick.goergen@barreau.lu; lawyer; *specialities:* internal market affairs, justice and home affairs, regional policy; *languages:* French.

Martine Hansen: avenue Salentiny, L-9080 Ettelbruck; tel (+352) 81-85-25; e-mail martine.hansen@education.lu; engineer; *specialities:* agriculture and fisheries.

John Preston: 42 rue du Kiem, 8030 Strassen; tel (+352) 26-31-35-94; fax (+352) 26-31-35-94; e-mail j.b.preston@ sl.lu; general manager, Ozier, Peterse and Associates (Luxbg) s.a.r.l.; *specialities:* general EU policy, institutional reform, IGC; *languages:* English.

Klaus Pöhle: 18 rue du Grünwald, L-7293 Blaschette; tel (+352) 33-08-87; fax (+352) 33-53-13; e-mail klaus@poehle .com; former MEP; *specialities:* economic and financial affairs, general EU policy, institutional reform, IGC, regional policy; *languages:* German, French, English.

Georges Weyrich: 40A rue des Aubépines, 1145 Luxembourg; tel (+352) 44-15-43; fax (+352) 44-15-43; former head, personnel division of the European Commission, Luxembourg; *specialities:* economic and financial affairs, general EU policy, institutional reform, IGC, regional policy; *languages:* French, English, German.

Jean-François Zimmer: 393 route de Longwy, 1941 Luxembourg; tel (+352) 26) 45-95-45; fax (+352 26) 45-95-50; e-mail almathea@pt.lu; consultant; *specialities:* enterprise, competition and state aids, economic and monetary affairs, employment and social affairs, enlargement; *languages:* French, English, German.

THE NETHERLANDS

Drs Hans Aben: Postbus 70060, 5201 DZ Den Bosch; tel (+39 73) 680-66-00; fax (+31 73) 612-32-10; e-mail info@ egadvies.nl; general manager, EG-Adviescentrum Zuid-Nederland; *specialities:* enterprise, competition, state aids, internal market affairs, regional policy; *languages:* Dutch.

Drs Jan Bron Dik: POB 20904, 2500 EX Den Haag; tel (+31 70) 351-14-48; fax (+31 70) 351-14-76; e-mail jan-bron .dik@dgg.minvenw.nl; head of division, EU policy affairs, Ministry of Transport, Public Works and Water Management; *specialities:* enterprise, competition, state aids, internal market affairs, trade, development and external relations; *languages:* Dutch, English.

René Glaser: 10 Dr Kuyperstraat, NL-2514 BB Den Haag; tel (+31 70) 363-56-56; fax (+31 70) 363-55-40; e-mail glaser@ glaserpublicaffairs.nl; manager, Glaser Public Affairs agency and European Citizen Desk at the European Commission in The Hague; *specialities:* enterprise, competition, state aids, economic and financial affairs, internal market affairs, transport and energy; *languages:* Dutch, English, French.

Drs Peter Hommes: POB 217, 7500 AE Enschede; tel (+31 53) 489-22-42; fax (+31 53) 435-70-42; e-mail p.m.hommes@ dinkel.utwente.nl; managing director of the European Documentation Centre of Twente University Library; *specialities:* enterprise, competition, state aids, internal market affairs, research and information society; *languages:* Dutch, English, German.

Eppo Jansen: 36 Delistraat, 2585 XB Den Haag; tel (+31 70) 350-49-42; fax (+31 70) 351-29-81; e-mail eppo.jansen@ freeler.nl; former head of Information Office, European Parliament, in the Netherlands; *specialities:* general EU policy, institutional reform, IGC, enlargement, economic and financial affairs; *languages:* Dutch, English, French.

Harrie Jeurissen: 36A Batterijstraat, 6211 SJ Maastricht; tel (+31 43) 325-02-45; fax (+31 43) 321-77-42; e-mail jeurissen@regr.nl; *specialities:* general EU policy, institutional reform, IGC, internal market affairs, regional policy; *languages:* Dutch, English, German.

Drs Nannette Ripmeester: 255 Mathenesserlaan, 3021 HD Rotterdam; tel (+31 10) 477-68-16; fax (+31 10) 477-16-23; e-mail n.ripmeester@labourmobility .com; managing director, expertise in labour mobility; *specialities:* education and culture, employment and social affairs, internal market affairs; *languages:* Dutch, English, German.

Maarten Rooderkerk: POB 23, 2230 AA Rijnsburg; tel (+31 71) 408-15-90; fax (+31 71) 408-15-86; e-mail info@ eurassist.nl; director, Business-Compass/EurAssist; *specialities:* enterprise, competition, state aids, internal market affairs; *languages:* Dutch, English, French.

Gus Scheepers: Postbus 38325, 6503 AH Nijmegen; tel (+31 24) 373-72-41; fax (+31 24) 373-67-89; e-mail info@ europeconsult.nl; adviser, Europe Consult; *specialities:* internal market affairs, regional policy, trade, development and external relations; *languages:* Dutch, English, French.

Prof. Dr Jacques J. M. Tromm: 29 Cornelie van Zantenstraat, 2331 LW Leiden; tel (+31 71) 515-66-22; e-mail jjmtromm@freeler.nl; teacher, research officer, T. M. C. Asser Institute; *specialities:* internal market affairs, trade, development and external relations; *languages:* Dutch, English.

Hans van Borselen: 12 Vogelrijd, 8428 HH Fochteloo; tel (+31 541) 53-99-22; fax (+31 541) 53-99-59; e-mail h.van .borselen@planet.nl; director of welfare, education, social affairs and employment at the municipality of Ooststellingwerf; *specialities:* education and culture, enlargement, general EU policy, employment and social affairs; *languages:* Dutch, English, German.

Gérard Van den Broek: Postbus 70060, 5201 DZ Den Bosch; tel (+31 73) 680-66-00; fax (+31 73) 612-32-10; e-mail gb@ egadvies.nl; information manager, EU Advice Centre, Zuid-Nederland; *specialities:* enterprise, competition, state aids, general EU policy, institutional reform, IGC, health and consumer protection, internal market affairs; *languages:* Dutch, English.

Drs Marion Van Emden: 137–139 Riouwstraat, 2585 HP Den Haag; tel (+31 70) 354-11-44; fax (+31 70) 358-76-06; e-mail mvanemden.ebn@xs4all.nl; director, European Movement in the Netherlands (EBN); *specialities:* enlargement, general EU policy, institutional reform, IGC; *languages:* Dutch, English.

Dr Jean-Paul van Marissing: POB 2720, 1000 CS Amsterdam; tel (+31 20) 551-75-32; fax (+31 20) 626-79-49; e-mail jean-paul.van.marissing@bakernet.com; lawyer; *specialities:* enterprise, competition, state aids, internal market affairs; *languages:* Dutch, English.

Drs Jacob Wiersma: 7 Zevenpelsen, 8651 BT Ylst; tel (+31 51) 553-18-48; fax (+31 51) 212-81-69; e-mail j.h.wiersma@ man.nhl.nl; lecturer in political science and European studies, Thorbecke Academie; *specialities:* economic and financial affairs, enlargement, general EU policy, institutional reform, IGC, internal market affairs, justice and home affairs, regional policy; *languages:* Dutch, English, German.

PORTUGAL

Dr José Maria Calheiros: 38 av. Antonio Augusto de Aguiar, 6°, 1050-016 Lisbon; tel (+351 21) 315-27-95; fax (+351 21) 315-27-97; e-mail advogados@jmclawyers.com; lawyer; *specialities:* enterprise, competition, state aids, economic and financial affairs, internal market affairs; *languages:* Portuguese.

Dr Pedro Chaves de Faria e Castro: 23 Rua Marquês da Praia, 9500 Ponta Delgada, Azores; tel (+351 296) 65-00-06; fax (+351 296) 65-00-05; regional administrator; *specialities:* enlargement, general EU policy, institutional reform, IGC, regional policy; *languages:* Portuguese, French.

Dr João de Paiva Boléo Tomé: 4–7B Rua Teófilo Braga, 2685-243 Portela LRS; tel (+351 21) 943-33-84; fax (+351 21) 471-90-74; e-mail boleo.tome@clix.pt; quality control consultant; *specialities:* enterprise, competition, state aids, internal market affairs, trade, development and external relations; *languages:* Portuguese, Spanish, English.

Dr António Estrela Ribeiro: 4 Rua Nova do Zambujal, 2° Dto, 2735-302 Cacém; tel (+351 21) 914-15-78; fax (+351 21) 914-80-96; e-mail aeribeir@esoterica.pt; lawyer; *specialities:* internal market affairs, justice and home affairs, regional policy; *languages:* Portuguese.

Dr Fernanda Ferreira Dias: 1 Rua Cova da Moura, 1350-115 Lisbon; tel (+351 21) 393-55-20; e-mail smiffd@dgac.mne.gov.pt; desk officer for European Union Affairs, Ministry of Foreign Affairs; *specialities:* internal market affairs, trade, development and external relations, employment and social affairs; *languages:* Portuguese, English.

Dr Ana Rita Gomes de Barros e Pereira: Rua das Maravilhas, Edifício Camões, 5 Andar A/B, 9000-180 Funchal, Madeira; tel (+351 291) 75-75-15; fax (+351 291) 23-10-81; e-mail anaritabarros@clix.pt; economist; *specialities:* education and culture, economic and financial affairs, employment and social affairs; *languages:* Portuguese, English, French.

Dr Manuel Antonio Gomes Martins: Edifício Jardim 3660, S. Pedro do Sul; tel (+351 232) 71-12-40; fax (+351 232) 72-33-65; e-mail martinsadvogado@hotmail.com; lawyer; *specialities:* enterprise, competition, state aids, economic and financial affairs, trade, development and external relations; *languages:* Portuguese, French.

Dr António Alfredo Gonçalves-Crisostomo: 6–3 Rua Professor Celestino da Costa, Esq., 1170 Lisbon; tel (+351 21) 812-37-51; fax (+351 21) 322-69-94; e-mail agcrisos@hotmail.com; university professor; *specialities:* economic and financial affairs, enlargement, trade, development and external relations; *languages:* Portuguese, French, English.

Dr Carlos Alberto Medeiros: Rua Bartolomeu Dias, 1400 Lisbon; tel (+351 21) 365-25-00; fax (+351 21) 365-25-30; e-mail medeiros@cijdelors.pt; expert on regional policy and European integration; *specialities:* education and culture, regional policy, research and information society; *languages:* Portuguese, English.

Dr Isabel Meirelles: 84–2 Av. Alvares Cabral, 1200 Lisbon; tel (+351 21) 388-25-54; fax (+351 21) 388-25-54; e-mail imeirelles@mail.com; lawyer; *specialities:* enlargement, internal market affairs, justice and home affairs; *languages:* Portuguese, French.

Dr Mário Luis Melo Rocha: 1327 Rua Diego Botelho, 4150–268 Porto; tel (+351 22) 619-62-00; fax (+351 22) 619-62-91; e-mail mrocha@porto.ucp.pt; professor of law; *specialities:* education and culture, justice and home affairs, trade, development and external relations; *languages:* Portuguese, French.

Dr Ricardo Monteiro Bexiga: 83 Rua Infante D. Henrique, 2 Fr., 4000 Porto; tel (+351 22) 200-60-70; fax (+351 22) 200-60-71; e-mail ricardobexiga@mail.telepac.pt; lawyer; *specialities:* environment, internal market affairs, trade, development and external relations; *languages:* Portuguese, English.

Dr José Miguel Mora do Vale: 32–1 andar Travessa de Santo Ildefonso, 1200–807 Lisbon; tel (+351 21) 396-81-61; fax (+351 21) 390-91-05; e-mail miguel.m.vale@mail.telepac.pt; lawyer; *specialities:* health and consumer protection, justice and home affairs, transport and energy; *languages:* Portuguese, English, Spanish.

Dr Carlos Nunes: Av. 1° de Maio, 42-2° Esq., 2500 Caldas da Rainha; tel (+351 262) 837-300; fax (+351 262) 837-301; e-mail carlosnunes.adv@ip.pt; lawyer; *specialities:* environment, health and consumer protection, trade, development and external relations; *languages:* Portuguese, English, French.

Dr Henrique Palma Nogueira: 22 Praça D. Filipa de Lencastre, 3° Dto. S/46, 4050 Porto; tel (+351 22) 208-62-71/208-65-09; fax (+351 22) 208-62-69; e-mail palma@mail.cesae.pt; lawyer, university lecturer; *specialities:* enterprise, competition, state aids, economic and financial affairs, justice and home affairs; *languages:* Portuguese, French.

Dr David Pina: 176 Av. 5 de Outubro, 5° Esq., 1050 Lisbon; tel (+351 21) 793-11-43/796-69-34; fax (+351 21) 793-11-44; e-mail dpinalaw@aeiou.pt; lawyer; *specialities:* enterprise, competition, state aids, environment, internal market affairs; *languages:* Portuguese, French, English.

Dr Arnaldo Ribeiro: Apartado 293, 4900 Viana-do-Castelo; tel (+351 258) 82-06-78/82-03-77; fax (+351 258) 82-42-33; e-mail arnaldojoaquim@hotmail.com; head officer, European affairs, Câmara Municipal; *specialities:* employment and social affairs, general EU policy, institutional reform; IGC, regional policy; *languages:* Portuguese, French, English.

Dr José Manuel Rodrigues de Almeida: Rua Pedro Queiróz Pereira, 20-4 Dto, 1750 Lisbon; tel (+351 21) 757-38-18; fax (+351 21) 757-38-18; e-mail jose.almeida@glp.pt; *specialities:* general EU policy, institutional reform, IGC; *languages:* Portuguese, English.

Dr Filomena Santos Antonio: Centro Cultural de Bélem, Rua Bartolomeu Dias 1400, Lisbon; tel (+351 21) 365-25-00; fax (+351 21) 365-25-30; e-mail fantonio@cijdelors.pt; member, Europe Secretariat, Centro de Informação Jacques Delors; *specialities:* education and culture, economic and financial affairs, general EU policy, institutional reform, IGC; *languages:* Portuguese, English.

Dr Ana Leonor Sarmento: Pr. Paiva Couceiro n° 2–3° Esq., 1170 Lisbon; tel (+351 21) 811-60-88; fax (+351 21) 811-60-88; e-mail leonorsarmento.dss@scml.pt; consultant; *specialities:* education and culture, economic and financial affairs, regional policy; *languages:* Portuguese, French, English.

Dr Afonso H. Vilhena: 14 Av. Júlio Dinis, 4°B, 1050 Lisbon; tel (+351 21) 782-68-00; fax (+351 21) 782-68-09; e-mail Vilhena.AH.Law@mail.telepac.pt; lawyer; *specialities:* enterprise, competition, state aids, general EU policy, institutional reform, IGC, justice and home affairs; *languages:* Portuguese, English, French.

SLOVAKIA

Juraj Alner: Panská 19, 81101 Bratislava; tel (+2) 54-43-37-97; e-mail paneuropa@paneuropa.sk; Secretary General, Paneuropa-Union, Slovakia.

Petert Beňuška: Biela 6, 81101 Bratislava; tel (+2) 54-64-22-42; e-mail peter.benuska@nextra.sk; President, House of Europe.

Vlado Bilčík: Panenská 33, 81103 Bratislava; tel (+2) 54-43-02-10; fax (+2) 54-43-31-61; e-mail bilcik@sfpa.sk; senior research fellow, Slovak Foreign Policy Association.

Katarina Cigánová: Prostredná 47, 90021 Svätý Jur; tel (+2) 44-97-04-51; fax (+2) 44-97-04-55; e-mail kata@ainova.sk; attached to Academia Istropolitana Nova.

Marta Daruľová: Prostredná 47, 90021 Svätý Jur; tel (+2) 44-97-04-51; fax (+2) 44-97-04-55; e-mail marta@ainova.sk;

attached to Academia Istropolitana Nova.

Ľubica Gallová: e-mail lgallova@pobox.sk; project manager.

Katarína Kellenbergerová: e-mail kelo@zoznam.sk.

Dagmar Kokavcová: Department of Management and Marketing, Faculty of Economics,

University of Matej Bel, Tajovského 10, 97592 banská Bystrica; tel (+48) 446-28-22; fax (+48) 415-27-93; e-mail dagmar .kokavcova@umb.sk.

Tomáš Kozák: Ministry of Foreign Affairs of the SR, Hlboká 2, 83336 Bratislava; tel (+2) 59-78-31-18; fax (+2) 59-78-31-19; e-mail tomas_kozak@foreign .gov.sk.

Zuzana Mogyorosiová: Department of International Trade, Faculty of Trade, University of Economics, Dolnozemská 1, 85235 Bratislava; tel (+2) 67-29-14-15; e-mail mogyorosiova@pobox.sk.

Dana Plučinská: Partnership for Development of the Region Spiš, Námestie sv. Egídia 11, 05801 Poprad; tel (+52) 772-17-68; e-mail partnership@sinet.sk.

Pavol Rybár: e-mail prybar@hotmail .com.; lecturer, Euroškolitelia.

Beáta Šaková: tel (+2) 67-29-14-89; e-mail sakova@dec.euba.sk; lecturer, Euroškolitelia.

Boris Tonhauser: Bezručova 9, 81109 Bratislava; tel (+2) 52-96-49-14; fax (+2) 52-96-42-56; e-mail tonhauser@zmos.sk; director, Foreign Department, Association of Towns and Municipalities of Slovakia (ZMOS).

Viera Uhlárová: Bratislava–Staré mesto, Vajanského nábrežie 3, 81421 Bratislava; tel (+2) 59-24-63-45; e-mail uhlarova@hotmail.com.

Peter Weiss: Faculty of International Relations, University of Economics, Dolnozemská 1, 85235 Bratislava; tel (+2) 62-41-18-56; fax (+2) 62-24-97-50; e-mail weiss@euba.sk.

Patrick Zoltvány: Amrop Jenewein Group, POB 283 Vysoká 30, 81499 Bratislava; tel (+2) 52-92-01-10; e-mail zoltvany@ajg.sk; head, European Office for Slovakia.

SLOVENIA

Dr Vito Bobek: University of Maribor, Faculty of Economics and Business, 14 Razlagova, 2000 Maribor; tel (+386 22) 902-94; e-mail vito.bobek@uni-mb.si; *specialities:* foreign trade, internal market.

Irena Brinar: Ljubljana University, Faculty of Social Sciences, 5 Kardeljeva ploščad, 1000 Ljubljana; tel (+386 1) 580-51-93; E-mail irena.brinar@uni-lj.si; EU institutions, EU enlargement.

Dr Emil Erjavec: University of Ljubljana, Biotechnical Faculty, Groblje 3, 1230 Domžale; tel (+386 1) 721-78-52/40-75; *specialities:* agriculture and fisheries.

Dr Rado Genorio: 11 Šubičeva, 1000 Ljubljana; tel (+386 1) 478-24-47; e-mail rado.genorio@gov.si; deputy director, Government Office for European Affairs; *specialities:* EU institutions, Slovenia's accession process, Slovenia-EU relations.

Peter Grilc: Ljubljana University, Law Faculty, 2 Poljanski nasip, 1000 Ljubljana; tel (+386 1) 420-31-45; e-mail peter .grilc@pf.uni-lj.si; *specialities:* EU law, EU institutions, justice and home affairs, state aids.

Dr Tomaž Ilešič: Tivolska c. 48, 1000 Ljubljana; tel (+386 1) 230-67-50; e-mail ilesic@colja-rojs-partnerji.si; *specialities:* EU law, institutions, justice and home affairs.

Dr Marko Jaklič: Ljubljana University, Faculty of Economics, 17 Kardeljeva ploščad, 1000 Ljubljana; tel (+386 1) 589-24-01; e-mail marko.jaklic@uni-lj.si; Vice-Dean and professor at the Ljubljana University Faculty of Economics; *specialities:* economic theory and policy, industrial policy, SMEs, competition.

Peter Ješovnik: Slovene Chamber of Commerce and Industry, 13 Dimičeva, 1000 Ljubljana; tel (+386 1) 589-80-00/589-81-27; e-mail peter.jesovnik@gzs.si; *specialities:* EU institutions, internal market, EU enlargement.

Dr Rajko Knez: University of Maribor, Law Faculty, Mladinska ulica 9, 2000 Maribor; tel (+386 250) 42-29; e-mail rajko.knez@uni-mb.si; *specialities:* EU law, environment, social politics, internal market, competition.

Dr Mojmir Mrak: Ljubljana University, Economic Faculty, 17 Kardeljeva ploščad, 1000 Ljubljana; tel (+386 1) 589-25-66; e-mail mojmir.mrak@uni-lj.si; former member of Slovenia's EU negotiations team; *specialities:* EMU.

Vojka Ravbar: 11 Šubičeva, 1000 Ljubljana; tel (+386 1) 478-24-51; fax (+386 1) 478-24-85; e-mail vojka.ravbar@gov.si; former member of Slovenia's EU negotiations team; *specialities:* state aids.

Danijela Voljč: Ljubljana University, Faculty of Economics, 17 Kardeljeva ploščad, 1000 Ljubljana; tel (+386 1) 589-24-86; e-mail danijela.voljc@uni-lj .si; *specialities:* education.

Peter Wostner: Government Office for Structural Policy and Regional Development, 28 Kotnikova, 1000 Ljubljana; tel (+386 31) 86-93-68; e-mail peter .wostner@gov.si; *specialities:* regional policy, structural and regional funds, economic analysis.

Dr Drago Zajc: Ljubljana University, Faculty of Social Sciences, 5 Kardeljeva ploščad, 1000 Ljubljana; tel (+386 1) 580-51-76; e-mail drago.zajc@uni-lj.si; *specialities:* EU institutions, legislative procedures.

SPAIN

Mr Eduard Arruga i Valeri: 4 Passeig de la Bonanova, 08022 Barcelona; tel (+34 93) 480-54-10; fax (+34 93) 473-03-27; e-mail eduard.arruga@es.nestle.com; university professor; *specialities:* enlargement, agriculture and fisheries, economic and financial affairs, internal market affairs, trade, development and external relations; *languages:* Spanish, French, Italian.

Juan José Bellod: C/ Rey Francisco 16, 5°, 28008 Madrid; tel (+34 91) 547-38-48; e-mail juanjosebellod@hotmail.com; lawyer; *specialities:* enterprise, competition, state aids, internal market affairs, research and information society; *languages:* Spanish, French.

José Ramón Blanco Rodriguez: 17 Palencia, La Grichxándana, Colonia La Cabaña, 28223 Pozuelo de Alarcón; tel (34 91) 351-06-79/619-88-74-19; fax (+34 91) 394-21-71; e-mail jrblanco@ccinf.ucm .es; professor of economics, Faculty of Information Sciences, University of Madrid; *specialities:* agriculture and fisheries, economic and monetary affairs, enlargement, environment, regional policy, enterprise, competition and state aids; *languages:* Spanish, French, English.

Javier Blas Guasp: 50 Carrer del Oms, Escalera A, 1–1a, 07003 Palma de Mallorca; tel (+34 71) 72-03-76; fax (+34 71) 72-05-70; e-mail jblas@illeslex.com; professor of law; *specialities:* economic and financial affairs, employment and social affairs, health and consumer protection, internal market affairs; *languages:* Spanish, French, English.

Domingo Carbajo Vasco: 17 C/Sor Angela de la Cruz, 9B, 28020 Madrid; tel (+34 91) 411-20-60; e-mail docavasco@yahoo.es; Undersecretary-General, Ministry of Finance; *specialities:* economic and financial affairs, environment, internal market affairs, trade, development and external relations; *languages:* Spanish, English, French.

Jordi Carbonell i Sebarroja: c/Vall d'Aran, 25196 Lleida; tel (+34 973) 70-08-05; fax (+34 973) 70-08-15; e-mail jcarbonell@actel.es; director-general, ACTEL; *specialities:* agriculture and fisheries, enterprise, competition, state aids, economic and financial affairs, internal market affairs, regional policy; *languages:* Spanish, French.

Dr José-Maria Casado Raigon: Facultad de Derecho, Universidad de Córdoba, 14071 Córdoba; tel (+34 957) 25-49-62; fax (+34 957) 26-11-20; e-mail cde1cord@uco.es; director, Centro de Documentación Europea; *specialities:* enterprise, competition, state aids, enlargement, environment; *languages:* Spanish, French, Portuguese.

Juan Antonio Falcon Blasco: 29–31 Alonso V, 50002 Zaragoza; tel (+34 76) 39-00-22; fax (+34 76) 21-92-95; e-mail Jafalcon@cortesaragon.es; President, Centro de Desarrollo Economico y Empresarial; *specialities:* education and culture, enlargement, trade, development and external relations; *languages:* Spanish, French, German.

José Ramón Funes Toyos: C/León y Castillo 431-2a, 35007 Las Palmas de Gran Canaria; tel (+34 928) 30-71-82; fax (+34 928) 30-71-81; e-mail joseramon.funestoyos@gobiernodecanarias.org; head, Servicio Información Empresarial; *languages:* Spanish, English.

Dr Juan Fuster Lareu: 11–9 Joaquin Botia, 07012 Palma de Mallorca; tel (+34 971) 71-90-00; fax (+34 971) 71-14-36; e-mail juanfusterLareu@terra.es; inspector of finances; *specialities:* enterprise, competition, state aids, internal market affairs; *languages:* Spanish, French, English.

José Ignacio Gafo Fernández: 11–4 Calle Prudencio Morales, 35009 Las Palmas de Gran Canaria; tel (+34 928) 45-45-83; e-mail jigafofernandez@telegonica.net; economist; *specialities:* transport and energy, environment, enterprise, competition and state aids, trade, development and external relations; *languages:* Spanish, English, French.

Lucia Gallar Corral: C/Caliza 4, 1°B, Urb. El Guijo, 28260 Galapagar/Madrid; tel (+34 1) 858-80-84/609-66-70-99; fax (+34 1) 559-23-73; e-mail lgallar@polsoc.uc3m.es; associate professor, Universidad Carlos III de Madrid; *specialities:* education and culture, enterprise, competition, state aids, employment and social affairs, regional policy; *languages:* Spanish, French, English.

Jorge-Enrique Garcia Galceran: Hercegovina, 7 at. 1a, 08021 Barcelona; tel (+34 93) 212-72-04; fax (+34 93) 212-72-04; e-mail jegg@economistes.com; economist; *specialities:* enterprise, competition, state aids, economic and financial affairs, internal market affairs; *languages:* Spanish, French.

Oscar Garcia Senis: 1 Alberto Alcocer, 28036 Madrid; (+34 91) 638-53-31; fax (+34 91) 638-53-31; e-mail ogsenis@yahoo.es; director, ASEFI-EFEC; *specialities:* enterprise, competition, state aids, economic and financial affairs, internal market affairs, research and information

society; *languages:* Spanish, French, English.

Carmen-Luz Gonzalez Benitez: 431 León y Castillo, Edificio Urbis, 2 dcha, 35071 Las Palmas de Gran Canaria; tel (+34 928) 30-71-78; (+34 928) 30-71-59; e-mail cgonben@gobiernodecanarias.org; *specialities:* economic and financial affairs, enlargement, internal market affairs, trade, development and external relations; *languages:* Spanish, French.

Santiago González-Varas Ibáñez: Cátedra de Derecho Administrativo, Facultad de Derecho, 03690 Alicante (San Vicente del Raspeig); tel (+34 965) 90-36-36; fax (+34 965) 90-36-86; e-mail sago_va@yahoo.es; professor of public law, Universidad de Alicante; *specialities:* enterprise, competition and state aids, general EU policy, transport and energy; *languages:* Spanish, English, French, German.

Dr Ignacio Granado Hijelmo: 3 C/Vara de Rey, 26071 Logroño; tel (+34 941) 29-13-65; fax (+34 941) 29-14-22; e-mail igranado@ccrioja.es; President, Consejo Consultivo de La Rioja; *specialities:* agriculture and fisheries, enterprise, competition, state aids, general EU policy, institutional reform, IGC, justice and home affairs; *languages:* Spanish, French.

Enrique Guardiola Sacarrera: 43 Traversera de Gracias, 08021 Barcelona; tel (+34 3) 200-02-88; fax (+34 3) 202-33-72; e-mail bji.guardiola@deinfo.es; lawyer; *specialities:* economic and financial affairs, internal market affairs; *languages:* Spanish, English, French.

Marie-Dominique Haan: 30 Mercedes de la Cardiniere, 28223 Madrid; tel (+34 91) 351-18-50; fax (+34 91) 351-51-82; e-mail europehaan@terra.es; professor of Community law; *specialities:* agriculture and fisheries, economic and financial affairs, employment and social affairs, internal market affairs, trade, development and external relations; *languages:* French, Spanish, English.

Isabel de Haro Arramberri: 9 Plaza Giralda, 41927 Mairena del Aljarafe (Sevilla); tel (+34 955) 60-04-16; fax (+34 955) 60-04-16; e-mail Iharo@cica.es; *specialities:* education and culture, environment, regional policy; *languages:* Spanish, French.

Manuel Hidalgo: 126 Calle Madrid, 28903 Getafe (Madrid); tel (+34 91) 624-58-94; fax (+34 91) 624-95-74; e-mail manuel.hidalgo@uc3m.es; titular profesor; *specialities:* economic and monetary affairs, employment and social affairs, general EU policy, regional policy; *languages:* Spanish, English.

Prof. Rafael Illescas Ortiz: 126 Avenida Madrid, 28903 Getafe (Madrid); tel (+34 1) 624-95-07; fax (+34 1) 624-95-89; e-mail rillesca@der-pr.uc3m.es; lawyer,

consultant; *specialities:* enterprise, competition, state aids, economic and financial affairs, internal market affairs; *languages:* Spanish, English, French.

Valentí Llagostera: Edifici A Campus UAB, 08193 Bellaterra, Barcelona; tel (+34 3) 224-01-50; fax (+34 3) 225-19-81; e-mail valenti.llagostera@uab.es; academic manager, Escuela Superior de Administración de Empresas (ESADE), Universidad Ramón Llull, Barcelona; *specialities:* enterprise, competition, state aids, economic and financial affairs, regional policy, trade, development and external relations; *languages:* Spanish, French.

Roberto Losada Maestre: 126 C/Madrid, Office 9.0.24, 28903 Getafe (Madrid); tel (+34 91) 624-98-68; fax (+34 91) 624-58-48; e-mail losada_maestre@hotmail.com; co-ordinator, Universidad Carlos III; *specialities:* economic and monetary affairs, trade, development and external relations, justice and home affairs, agriculture and fisheries; *languages:* Spanish, French, Portuguese.

Miguel Angel Lucia Asín: 36 Santander, 50010 Zaragoza; tel (+34 976) 76-60-60; fax (+34 976) 53-24-93; e-mail mlucia@cepymearagon.es; director of relations with the EU and international affairs, Confederación de la Pequeña y Mediana Empresa de Aragón (CEPYMEARAGON); *specialities:* trade, development and external relations, enterprise, competition, state aids, research and information society, enlargement; *languages:* Spanish, English, French.

Prof. Dr Nicolas Mariscal: 24 Avenida de las Universidades, Apartado 1, 48080 Bilbao; tel (+34 944) 13-90-12; fax (+34 944) 13-92-84; e-mail mariscal@iee.deusto.es; director, Instituto de Estudios Europeos, Universidad de Deusto; *specialities:* enlargement, employment and social affairs, general EU policy, institutional reform, IGC, internal market affairs, trade, development and external relations; *languages:* Spanish, French, English.

Carlos Francisco Molina del Pozo: Centro de Estudios Europeos, 1 C/Trinidad, 28801 Alcala de Henares (Madrid); tel (+34 1) 885-41-93; fax (+34 1) 885-40-95; e-mail carlosf.molina@alcala.es; director, Centro de Estudios Europeos, Universidad de Alcala de Henares; *specialities:* enterprise, competition, state aids, internal market affairs; *languages:* Spanish, French, English.

Carmen Moline Jorques: 90 Rambla Catalunya, entr., 08008 Barcelona; tel (+34 934) 88-00-40; fax (+34 934) 87-05-10; e-mail camoli@icab.es; lawyer; *specialities:* enterprise, competition, state aids, general EU policy, institutional reform, IGC, regional policy; *languages:* Spanish, French, English.

Javier de la Nava: 81 Paseo de la Castellana, 19th Floor, 28046 Madrid; tel (+34 91) 7-25-99-67/3-74-63-58; fax (+34 91) 374-50-21; e-mail NAMART@ grupobbva.net; economist; *specialities:* international economic analysis; *languages:* Spanish.

Dr David Ordóñez Solis: 4 C/Dr Bellmunt, E-33071 Oviedo; tel (+34 985) 24-59-84/85; fax (+34 985) 23-41-87; e-mail d.ordonez@justicia.mju.es; lawyer; *specialities:* enlargement, general EU policy, institutional reform, IGC, regional policy; *languages:* Spanish, French.

Mr Manuel Osuna Martin: 3 C/ Sandoval, Escalera c, 1 Izq, 31002 Pamplona; tel (+34 48) 17-54-92; fax (+34 48) 823-83-82; e-mail OSUNIZ@terra.es; judge and professor; *specialities:* enlargement, general EU policy, institutional reform, IGC, justice and home affairs, trade, development and external relations; *languages:* Spanish, English, French.

Fernando Otero Alvarado: 1 Plaza de Sagrados Corazones, 28036 Madrid; tel (+34 91) 745-45-20; fax (+34 91) 745-45-21; e-mail madrid@cea.es; economist; *specialities:* regional policy, enterprise, competition and state aids, trade, development and external relations; *languages:* Spanish, English, French.

Jaime Parra Parra: 13 C/Cuesta de Abarqueros, 18010 Granada; tel (+34 58) 29-47-63; fax (+34 58) 29-47-63; e-mail rebccigranada@camaras.org; *specialities:* enterprise, competition, state aids, internal market affairs, research and information society, trade, development and external relations; *languages:* Spanish, French, English.

Carlos Puente: POB 35093, 28080 Madrid; tel (+34 91) 320-21-66; fax (+34 91) 320-21-66; e-mail cpmartin@ telegonica.net; lecturer, consultant for Eastern Europe, Euraco Business Consultants; *specialities:* enlargement, trade, development and external relations, general EU policy, institutional reform, IGC; *languages:* Spanish, English, French.

Dr Jesús M. Rodés i Grácia: Llança, 43, 8°, 1a, 08015 Barcelona; tel (+34 43) 226-47-75; fax (+34 43) 226-47-75; e-mail jesusmaria.rodes@uab.es; professor of political science, Autonomous University of Barcelona; enlargement, employment and social affairs, internal market affairs, justice and home affairs, trade, development and external relations; *languages:* Spanish, French.

Francisco Javier Rodriguez Ruiz: 1 Villar y Macias, 37071 Salamanca; tel (+34 923) 29-60-26; fax (+34 923) 29-60-41; e-mail Francisco-javier.Rodriguez@ sa.jcyl.es; local government officer; *specialities:* agriculture and fisheries, environment, regional policy; *languages:* Spanish, French.

Guillem Rovira Jacquet: Carrer del Bruc, 50 2n, 08010 Barcelona; tel (+34 933) 567-26-08; fax (+34 933) 567-26-28; e-mail guillem.rovira@infoeuropa.org; associate professor; *specialities:* economic and financial affairs, enlargement, internal market affairs, regional policy, trade, development and external relations; *languages:* Spanish, French.

José Maria Ruiz Ruiz: C/Rector Royo Villanova s/n, 28040 Madrid; tel (+34 91) 394-61-62; fax (+34 91) 394-62-56; e-mail jmrruiz@ccedu.ucm.es; titular professor; *languages:* Spanish.

Oriol Sagarra Trias: Carrer Enric Granados, 63 2n 1a, 08008 Barcelona; tel (+34 93) 453-56-30; fax (+34 93) 454-99-53; e-mail sagara@icab.es; lawyer; *specialities:* general EU policy, institutional reform, IGC, internal market affairs, regional policy; *languages:* Spanish, French.

Eduard Sagarra Trias: Aribau, 198 8a pl. 2n 1a, 08036 Barcelona; tel (+34 93) 241-92-00; fax (+34 93) 414-50-30; e-mail mc.gali@rocajunyent.com; lawyer; *specialities:* enlargement, general EU policy, institutional reform, IGC, internal market affairs, justice and home affairs, trade, development and external relations; *languages:* Spanish, French.

Julio Sequeiros Tizón: Campus de La Zapateira, 15071 La Coruña; tel (+34 81) 16-70-00; fax (+34 81) 16-70-70; e-mail julioseg@udc.es; *specialities:* economic and financial affairs, employment and social affairs, general EU policy, institutional reform, IGC, internal market affairs; *languages:* Spanish, French, Portuguese.

Joan Carles Suari Aniorte: 696 Diagonal, 08034 Barcelona; tel (+34 93) 402-44-87; fax (+34 93) 402-45-87; jsuari@ eco.ub.es; professor of foreign trade, University of Barcelona; *specialities:* enlargement, trade, development and external relations, transport and energy; *languages:* Spanish, French, English.

Agustin Ulied Martinez: 60 Av. Pedralbes, 08034 Barcelona; tel (+34 93) 495-21-89/280-61-62; fax (+34 93) 204-81-05; e-mail ulied@esade.edu; director-general, ESADE; *specialities:* education and culture, enterprise, competition, state aids, enlargement, internal market affairs, regional policy, trade, development and external relations; *languages:* Spanish, French.

Inma Valencia Bayón: 58 blvd du Régent, 1000 Bruxelles; tel (+32 2) 501-61-81; fax (+32 2) 512-21-29; e-mail inma .valencia@cantabria.be; lawyer; *specialities:* future of Europe, European convention, European constitution; institutional matters, regional policy; history and theory of European integration; *languages:* Spanish, French.

Ramon Vilaró Giralt: Pintor Fortuny, 33 3r, 08001 Barcelona; tel (+34 93) 318-68-34; fax (+34 93) 318-68-64; e-mail rvilaro@worldonline.es; journalist, television producer; *specialities:* education and culture, general EU policy, institutional reform, IGC; *languages:* Spanish, English.

SWEDEN

Ylva Annerstedt: 194 chemin du Siège, 06140 Vence, France; tel (+33 493) 58-92-07; e-mail ylva.annerstedt@tele2.fr; managing director for LIBRA, consultants for SME development in the EU market; *specialities:* enterprise, competition, state aids, economic and financial affairs, general EU policy, institutional reform, IGC, health and consumer protection, internal market affairs, trade, development and external relations; *languages:* Swedish, English, French.

Hadar Cars: 15 Odengatan, 11424 Stockholm; tel (+46 8) 20-31-03; fax (+46 8) 411-61-62; e-mail cars@swipnet.se; former MEP; *specialities:* enlargement, trade, development and external relations; *languages:* Swedish, English.

Niklas Eklund: Umeå University, 90187 Umeå; tel (+46 90) 786-50-00/61-72; fax (+46 90) 786-66-81; e-mail niklas.eklund@ pol.umu.se; lecturer, Vice-Director of Studies, Department of Political Science, Umeå University; *specialities:* enlargement, general EU policy; *languages:* Swedish, English, German.

Jan Engberg: 9 Fridhemsgatan, 43234 Varberg; tel (+46 340) 884-44; fax (+46 340) 893-59; e-mail engberg@varberg.se; Vice-President of the Swedish Council of the International European Movement; *specialities:* economic and financial affairs, enlargement, trade, development and external relations; *languages:* Swedish, English.

Cristina Hallberg: 10 Arosgatan, 41656 Göteborg; tel (+46 31) 19-55-58; e-mail challberg@hotmail.com; administrator; *specialities:* enlargement, general EU policy, institutional reform, IGC, health and consumer protection, regional policy; *languages:* Swedish, English.

Gunilla Herolf: Box 1253, 11182 Stockholm; tel (+46 8) 696-05-29; fax (+46 8) 20-10-49; e-mail herolf@ui.se; senior research fellow, Swedish Institute of International Affairs; *specialities:* CFSP, EU foreign policy, defence; history and theory of European integration, institutional matters; *languages:* Swedish, English.

Lars Holm: Box 441, 9 Ågatan, 58105 Linköping; tel (+46 13) 25-30-80; fax (+46 13) 25-30-85; e-mail lh@fr.se; international co-ordinator at the Swedish federation of private enterprises; *specialities:* economic and financial affairs, internal market affairs; *languages:* Swedish, English.

Rolf A. Hult: NCC Roads New Markets, 17080 Solna; tel (+46 8) 58-55-23-07; fax (+46 8) 58-55-19-50; e-mail rolf.hult@ncc .se; secretary of foreign affairs, Chamber of Commerce, Central Sweden; *specialities:* enterprise, competition, state aids, enlargement, internal market affairs; *languages:* Swedish, English, German.

Richard Jarlestam: 85 Langebergavägen, 25669 Helsingborg; tel (+46 42) 29-68-10; fax (+46 42) 29-68-10; e-mail info@ albergagard.com; director, Euro Info Centre; *specialities:* enterprise, competition, state aids, internal market affairs; *languages:* English, Danish, Swedish.

Anders Kjellström: 10 Storgatan, 26131 Landskrona; tel (+46 418) 128-92; fax (+46 418) 278-75; e-mail anders .kjellstrom@telia.com; assistant professor of civil law, University of Lund; *specialities:* economic and financial affairs, general EU policy, institutional reform, IGC, internal market affairs; *languages:* Swedish, English.

Manuela Leijerfelt: 12 Hantverkargatan, 11221 Stockholm; tel (+46 8) 652-36-14; fax (+46 8) 652-36-14; e-mail mleijerfelt@yahoo.com; consultant in European affairs; *specialities:* general EU policies, enlargement, economic and monetary affairs, trade, development and external relations; *languages:* Swedish, English.

Leif Magnusson: 42 Torsgatan, 73630 Kungsör; tel (+46 227) 316-58; fax (+46 227) 316-58; e-mail eu-info.lemag@ swipnet.se; teacher, Info LeMag HB; *specialities:* economic and financial affairs, employment and social affairs, internal market affairs, trade, development and external relations; *languages:* Swedish, English.

Birgitta Nyrinder: 58186 Linköping; tel (+46 13) 14-88-54; e-mail birgitta .nyrinder@yahoo.se; project manager; *languages:* Swedish, English.

Alexander Reuter: 46 Nybrogatan, 11440 Stockholm; tel (+46 10) 666-66-69; fax (+46 8) 667-25-03; e-mail swedencalling@hotmail.com; manager, consultant, The Northern Outpost/EU-Skylines SA; *specialities:* information society, research and development, transport and energy, CFSP, EU foreign policy, defence; *languages:* Swedish, English.

Shahid Saleem: 40 Sibeliusgången, 8tr 16472 Kista; tel (+46 8) 50-82-56-16; fax (+46 8) 50-80-13-62; e-mail shahid .saleem@brevet.nu; EU co-ordinator, Kista City District Council; *specialities:* education and culture, enterprise, competition, state aids; *languages:* Swedish, English.

Lars Ströman: 8 Järnvägsgatan, 71181 Lindesberg; tel (+46 581) 844-26; fax (+46 581) 844-41; e-mail stroman@ bergslagsposten.se; journalist at the daily Bergulagsposten, contracted as editor at Europa-Posten, newsletter at the European Commission office in Sweden; *specialities:* enlargement, general EU policy, institutional reform, IGC, trade, development and external relations; *languages:* Swedish, English.

Leif Stålblom: 5 Narvavägen, 11460 Stockholm; tel (+46 8) 661-60-10; e-mail leifstalblom@chello.se; head, administration department, Stålbloms Consult Firma; *specialities:* economic and financial affairs, general EU policy, institutional reform, IGC; *languages:* Swedish, English.

Zofia Tucinska: 11 Västra Henriksborgsv, 13131 Nacka; tel (+46 8) 55-69-55-66; e-mail zofia.tucinska@telia.com; head, International Project Section, Swedish Environmental Protection Agency; *specialities:* enlargement, environment, trade, development and external relations; *languages:* Swedish, English, Polish.

Heli Van der Valk: 3 Annedals Trappor, 41128 Göteborg; tel (+46 31) 41-66-25; fax (+46 31) 41-66-05; e-mail heli@ vandervalk.se; President, European Movement Sweden; *specialities:* economic and financial affairs, enlargement, general EU policy, institutional reform, IGC, justice and home affairs; *languages:* Swedish, English, Finnish.

Calle Waller: 1 Trädgårdsvägen, 43535 Mölnlycke; tel (+46 31) 338-07-43; e-mail calle.waller@partnershipforeurope.se; director, Partnership for Europe; *specialities:* general EU policy, enlargement, regional policy, employment and social affairs; *languages:* Swedish, English.

UNITED KINGDOM

Liz Armour: 1 Desert Martin Rd, Magheraselt, County Derry BT45 5HD; tel (+44 1232) 391156; inspector of education and training, Department of Education; *specialities:* education and culture, enterprise, competition, state aids, employment and social affairs, general EU policy, institutional reform, IGC, justice and home affairs; *languages:* English.

Wahé H. Balekjian: Glasgow G12 8QQ; tel (+44 141) 3398855; fax (+44 141) 3305140; e-mail w.balekjian@law.gla.ac .uk; professor, School of Law, University of Glasgow; *specialities:* economic and financial affairs, enlargement, general EU policy, institutional reform, IGC, internal market affairs, trade, development and external relations; *languages:* English, French, German.

Richard Ernest Barker: 41 Barrack Sq., Martlesham Heath, Ipswich IP5 3RF; tel (+44 1473) 611211; fax (+44 1473) 610560; e-mail richard.barker@ barkergotelee.co.uk; lawyer; *specialities:* agriculture, fisheries, rural development, environment, general EU matters; *languages:* English.

Geoffrey Brown: 1st Floor, 46–48 Mount Pleasant, Liverpool L3 5SD; tel (+44 151) 7092564; fax (+44 151) 7098647; e-mail geoffrey@euclid.info; director, EUCLID International; *specialities:* education and culture, employment and social affairs, general EU policy, institutional reform, IGC, regional policy, research and information society; *languages:* English.

Anthony Connolly: Castle Buildings, Womanby St, Cardiff CF10 9SX; tel (+44 29) 20375400; fax (+44 29) 20343612; e-mail bconnolly@accac.org.uk; Chairman, Qualifications, Curriculum and Assessment Authority for Wales; *specialities:* education and culture, employment and social affairs; *languages:* English.

John Cornbill: Coventry University Technology Park, Puma Way, Coventry CVI 2TT; tel (+44 24) 76236236; fax (+44 24) 76236024; e-mail j.cornbill@coventry .ac.uk; chairman of the West Midlands EU information providers, director, EPI Centre, Midlands Innovation Relay Centre (MIRC); *specialities:* trade, development and external relations; *languages:* English.

Pat Donnelly: 8 Edgewater Office Park, Belfast BT3 9JQ; tel (+44 1232) 371023; fax (+44 1232) 371024; e-mail pat .donnelly@proteus-ni.org; director, PROTEUS; *specialities:* education and culture, employment and social affairs; *languages:* English, French.

Catherine Eva: tel (+44) 7951531931; e-mail evacatherine@hotmail.com; trustee, British Council, head, European Commission Office in Wales; *specialities:* general EU policies, regional policy, enlargement, education and culture, social affairs; *languages:* English.

John Fagan: 'Montpellier', 15 Stirling Close, Clitheroe BB7 2QW; tel (+ 44 1200) 425387; fax (+44 1200) 444121; e-mail JFagan@compuserve.com; consultant, European Education Consultancy; *specialities:* education and culture, research and information society, general EU policy; *languages:* English, French.

Dr Virginia Giannelli: Department of Modern Languages, University of Wales, Bangor LL57 2DG; tel (+44 1248) 382099; fax (+44 1248) 382551; e-mail v.giannelli@ bangor.ac.uk; administrative officer, European Resource Centre for Schools and Colleges and CILT Cymru; *specialities:* education and culture, general EU policy, environment; *languages:* English, Italian.

Peter Hall: Baltic Chambers, 50 Wellington St, Glasgow G2 6HJ; tel (+44 141)

2043183; fax (+44 141) 2212953; e-mail peter.hall@hallaitken.co.uk; director, Hall Aitken Associates Ltd, research and consultancy; *specialities:* education and culture, enterprise, competition, state aids, environment; *languages:* English.

Mark Howdle: Merrill Lynch Financial Centre, 2 King Edward St, London EC1A 1HQ; tel (+44 20) 79962471; fax (+44 20) 79952816; e-mail mark_howdle@ml.com; supervisory analyst, Merrill Lynch Europe PLC; *specialities:* economic and monetary affairs, history and theory of European integration, enterprise and SME policy, future of Europe; *languages:* English.

Roberta Ingman Roberts: Anglesey Business Centre, Bryn Cefni Business Park, Llangefni, Isle of Anglesey LL77 7WA; tel (+44 1248) 752493; fax (+44 1248) 752192; e-mail robertaingmanroberts@anglesey.gov.uk; European information officer with the North Wales Carrefour; *specialities:* general EU policy, enlargement; *languages:* English.

Dr Dennis Kennedy: 3 Mornington, Belfast BT7 3JS; tel (+44 28) 641729; e-mail dennis.kennedy1@ntlworld.com; research fellow, Institute of European Studies; *specialities:* enterprise, competition, state aids, general EU policy, institutional reform, IGC, internal market affairs, justice and home affairs, regional policy; *languages:* English, French.

Penny Krucker: Churchdown Lane, Hucclecote, Gloucester GL3 3QN; tel (+44 1452) 427204/270; fax (+44 1452) 427204; e-mail pkrucker@gloscc.gov.uk; European development officer, Gloucester County Council; *specialities:* education and culture, enlargement, health and consumer protection; *languages:* English.

Prof. Juliet Lodge: University of Leeds, Leeds LS2 9JT; tel (+44 113) 3434443; fax (+44 113) 335056; e-mail j.e.lodge@leeds .ac.uk; professor, Faculty of Law; *specialities:* enterprise, competition, state aids, enlargement, employment and social affairs, justice and home affairs, trade, development and external relations; *languages:* English, French, German.

Catherine Madden: 124 Knockbreda Park, Belfast BT6 0HG; tel (+44 2890) 973449; fax (+44 2890) 683543; e-mail c.madden@qub.ac.uk; resource centre manager, Institute of European Studies; *specialities:* education and culture, employment and social affairs, internal market affairs; *languages:* English, French.

Dr James Magowan: Ards Ballygorman, Loughgilly, Armagh BT60 2DP; tel (+44 28) 37507606; fax (+44 28) 90329839; ards@lineone.net; consultant, Local and Regional Development Planning; *specialities:* agriculture and

fisheries, economic and financial affairs, employment and social affairs, internal market affairs, justice and home affairs, regional policy; *languages:* English, French.

Ian Mayfield: Frewen Library, Cambridge Rd, Portsmouth PO1 2ST; tel (+44 1705) 843239; fax (+44 1705) 843233; e-mail ian.mayfield@port.ac.uk; chairman of the UK EDCs Steering Group, University of Portsmouth; *languages:* English.

Jane Morrice: 18 Bally Holme Esplanade, Bangor, Co. Down BT20 522; tel (+44 28) 90521297/91470739; e-mail jane.morrice@niassembly.gov.uk; journalist, broadcaster; *specialities:* education and culture, trade, development and external relations; *languages:* English.

David Mowat: 37 Orchard Rd South, Edinburgh EH4 3JA; tel (+44 1382) 562111; fax (+44 1382) 562583; e-mail iatrosltd@mailhost.sol.co.uk; managing director, IATROS Ltd; *specialities:* enterprise, competition, state aids, environment, internal market affairs; *languages:* English, French.

Gregg Myles: 16 Coolsara Park, Lisburn BT28 3BG; tel (+44 28) 92603195; fax (+44 28) 92603195; e-mail gregg.myles@ locksleybrief.co.uk; solicitor; *specialities:* agriculture and fisheries, economic and financial affairs, employment and social affairs, general EU policy, institutional reform, IGC, internal market affairs, justice and home affairs; *languages:* English, French.

Joan Noble: 5 Brunswick Gardens, London W8 4AS; tel (+44 20) 77279345; fax (+44 20) 77921992; e-mail joan@ joannobleassociates.com; specialist consultant advising on the technicalities of EC agricultural and food legislation, European economic and monetary affairs, EC enlargement, a wide range of internal and external trade issues and environmental policy; *specialities:* agriculture and fisheries, enlargement, environment, regional policy, trade, development and external relations; *languages:* English, French.

Andrew Robinson: Eldon House, Regent Centre, Newcastle upon Tyne NE3 3PW; tel (+44 191) 2026980; fax (+44 191) 2026918; e-mail ar@ist -consultants.com; assistant director, European Operations, The Open University; *specialities:* education and culture, economic and financial affairs, regional policy, research and information society; *languages:* English.

Peter Sain Ley Berry: LLanquian House, St. Athan Rd, Vale of Glamorgan, Cowbridge CF7 7EQ; tel (+44 1446) 773874; fax (+44 1446) 773874; e-mail pslb@europaworld.org; consultant, EUROFI Ltd; *specialities:* education and

culture, enterprise, competition, state aids; *languages:* English, French.

John Scaife: Town Hall, St Ives Rd, Maidenhead, Berkshire SL6 1RF; tel (+44 1628) 796029; e-mail John.Scaife@ RBWM.gov.uk; Change Programme manager, Royal Borough of Windsor and Maidenhead; *languages:* English.

Mary Sharpe: 8 Tenison Rd, Cambridge CB1 2DW; tel (+44 1223) 740390; fax (+44 1223) 742441; e-mail sharpe@ dia-gnostics.com; change management consultant, DIA-GNOSTICS; *specialities:* general EU matters; history and theory of European integration, environment, justice and home affairs (including immigration, asylum, police and judicial co-operation); *languages:* English, French.

John Simpson: 3 Glenmanchan Drive, Belfast BT4 2RE; tel (+44 1232) 862322; fax (+44 1232) 853773; e-mail johnvsimpson@aol.com; economics and business consultant; *specialities:* agriculture and fisheries, enterprise, competition, state aids, internal market affairs; *languages:* English.

Dr Constantin Stefanou: 17 Russell Sq., London WC1B 5DR; tel (+44 20) 7862-5861; fax (+44) 8700520183; e-mail Constantin.Stefanou@sas.ac.uk; fellow at the Institute of Advanced Legal Studies, University of London; *specialities:* history and theory of European integration, institutional matters, justice and home affairs (including immigration, asylum, police and judicial co-operation), enlargement; *languages:* Greek, English.

Stephen Vaughan Thomas: Temple of Peace, Cathays Park, Cardiff CF10 3AP; tel (+44 29) 20228549; fax (+44 29) 20640333; e-mail stephenthomas@ wcia.org.uk; director, Welsh Centre for International Affairs (WCIA); *specialities:* trade, development and external relations, regional policy, education and culture; *languages:* English, French, Portuguese.

Ian Thomson: Cardiff CF24 4HQ; tel (+44 29) 20874262; fax (+44 29) 20874717; e-mail thomsoni@cardiff.ac .uk; information consultant, editor, ProQuest Information and Learning, editor, European Access, EC information officer at the University of Wales, information consultant to the Wales Euro Info Centre, chairman of the European Information Association and member of the Welsh Consumer Council; *specialities:* enlargement, general EU policy, institutional reform, IGC; *languages:* English.

Alma Williams: Dolphin House, Lime Tree Close, Kirkby Rd, Ripon HG4 2HG; tel (+44 1765) 602382; e-mail alma@ deveray.demon.co.uk; writer and consultant on consumer affairs; *specialities:* health and consumer protection, general EU matters, enlargement; *languages:* English, French.

Dr Colin David Wimpory: 39 Dean Park, Ferry Hill, County Durham, DL17 8HR; tel (+44 1740) 657322; fax (+44 1740) 657322; e-mail ColinWimpory@ aol.com; distance-learning editor, tutor and examiner; *specialities:* education and culture, economic and monetary affairs, funding and grants, trade, WTO, general EU matters, future of Europe; *languages:* English, Spanish.

Dr Helen Xanthaki: 17 Russell Square, London WC1B 5DR; tel (+44 20) 7862-5861; fax (+44 20) 7862-5855; e-mail Helen.Xanthaki@sas.ac.uk; senior fellow, Institute of Advanced Legal Studies, University of London; *specialities:* justice and home affairs (including immigration, asylum, police and judicial co-operation), institutional matters, future of Europe, European convention, European constitution, enlargement; *languages:* Greek, English.

European Documentation Centres (EDCs) receive all documentation published by the European Union (though specialized EDCs receive the documentation related to their specialization). Depository libraries provide the general public with access to all the publications that they receive. European Reference Centres receive EU reference publications and the various sector-based annual reports; the process of converting European Reference Centres into EDCs began in 1999.

European Documentation Centres (EDCs) in Member States

AUSTRIA

Graz: RESOWI-Zentrum, Universitätsstr 15/C.1, 8010 Graz; tel (316) 380-36-30; fax (316) 380-94-70; e-mail elfi.eissner@kfuni-graz.at; internet www.kfunigraz.ac.at/eurwww/edz2.htm; Dir: Dr Christian Calliess; Sec/Documentalist: Elfriede Eissner-Eissenstein; specialized information.

Innsbruck: Leopold-Franzens-Universität Innsbruck, Institut für Völkerrecht und Internationale Beziehungen, Innrain 52, 6020 Innsbruck; tel (512) 507-83-23; fax (512) 507-28-24; e-mail walter.obwexer@uibk.ac.at; internet www2.uibk.ac.at/fakultaeten/c3/c310/edz.html; Dir: Prof Waldemar Hummer; Librarian: Walter Obwexer; specialized information.

Klagenfurt: Univ Klagenfurt, Universitätsbibliothek, Universitätsstr 65–67, 9020 Klagenfurt; tel (463) 2700-95-13; fax (463) 2700-95-99; e-mail evelyn.zmuck@uni-klu.ac.at; internet www.uni-klu.ac.at/groups/ub; Documentalist: Evelyn Zmuck.

Krems: Donau-Univ Krems, Zentrum für Euro Integration, Dr Karl Dorrekstr 30, 3500 Krems; tel (2732) 893-22-35; fax (2732) 893-42-30; e-mail winter@donau-uni.ac.at; internet www.donau-uni.ac.at/euro1/de/edz.html; Librarian: Dr Georg Winter.

Linz-Auhof: Inst für Europarecht, Johannes Kepler Univ Linz, Altenbergerstr 69, 4040 Linz-Auhof; tel (732) 246-84-17; fax (732) 246-83-68; e-mail andreas.auer@jku.at; Scientific Asst: Andreas Auer.

Salzburg: Forschungsinst für Europarecht an der Univ Salzburg, Churfürststr 1, 5020 Salzburg; tel (662) 80-44-35-08; fax (662) 63-89-35-08; e-mail martina.ullrich@sbg.ac.at; internet www.sbg.ac.at/ffe/home.htm; Dir: Prof Thomas Eilmansberger; Sec: Martina Ullrich; specialized information.

Vienna: Europainst, Wirtschaftsuniversität Wien, Althanstr 39–45, 1090 Vienna; tel (1) 313-36-41-45; fax (1) 31-33-67-56; e-mail katharina.gamharter@fgr.wu-wien.ac.at; internet http://fgr.wu-wien.ac.at/institut/ef/ief-home; Head: Prof Stefan Griller; Librarian: Katharina Gamharter; specialized information.

Vienna: Inst für Europarecht an der Univ Wien, Teinfalstr 8, 1010 Vienna; tel (1) 427-71-63-60; fax (1) 427-71-63-66; e-mail susanne.slama@univie.ac.at; Dir: Prof Dr Erich Schweighofer; Librarian: Susanne Slama; specialized information.

Depository Library

Vienna: Zentrale Verwaltungsbibliothek und Dokumentation für Wirtschaft und Technik, Stubenring 1, 1011 Vienna; tel (1) 711-00-56-88; fax (1) 713-79-95; Head: Gerhard Glaser; Asst: Helene Musil.

BELGIUM

Antwerp: Univ Antwerpen (UFSIA), Library, 9 Prinsstraat, 2000 Antwerp; tel (3) 220-49-96; fax (3) 220-44-37; Contact: Marc Wauters; specialized information.

Bruges: College of Europe, Library, 9–11 Dijver, 8000 Bruges; tel (50) 47-72-07; fax (50) 47-72-00; e-mail mlievens@coleurop.be; internet edc.coleurop.be; Contact: Mieke Lievens.

Brussels: Centre for European Policy Studies, Library, 1 place du Congrès, 1000 Brussels; tel (2) 229-39-11; fax (2) 229-39-71; Contact: Stéphane Beublet; specialized information.

Brussels: European Trade Union Inst, blvd du Roi Albert II 5, 1210 Brussels; tel (2) 224-04-83; fax (2) 224-05-13; e-mail lwilcox@etuc.org; internet www.etuc.org/etui/doccentre; Librarian: Lilli Wilcox-Poulsen.

Brussels: Univ Libre de Bruxelles, Inst d'Etudes Européennes, 39 ave F. D. Roosevelt, 1050 Brussels; tel (2) 650-30-73; fax (2) 650-30-68; e-mail asomville@ulb.ac.be; internet www.ulb.ac.be/iee; Contact: Alain Somville.

Brussels: Vrije Univ Brussel, Faculteit der Rechtgeleerd, Heid Seminaire Europees Recht, 2 Pleinlaan, 1050 Brussels; tel (2) 629-26-40; fax (2) 629-36-33; Librarian: Prof Dr Tony Joris; specialized information.

Geel: Centrale Mediatheek–Katholieke Hogeschool Kempen, Kleinhoefstraat 4, 2440 Geel; tel (14) 56-23-25; fax (14) 56-23-26; e-mail edc@khk.be; internet edc.khk.be; Contact: Liesbet Eeckhout; specialized information.

Liège: Univ de Liège, Faculté de Droit, Inst d'Etudes Juridiques Européennes 'Fernand Dehousse', 3 Blvd du Rectorat, 4000 Liège; tel (4) 366-31-30; fax (4) 366-31-55; e-mail mercedes.candelasoriano@ulg.ac.be; Contact: Mercedes Candela Soriano; specialized information.

Louvain-la-Neuve: Univ Catholique de Louvain, Inst d'Etudes Européennes, 1 place des Doyens, 1348 Louvain-la-Neuve; tel (10) 47-84-16; fax (10) 47-85-49; e-mail conrad@euro.ucl.ac.be; internet www.euro.ucl.ac.be/cde4.html; Librarian: Yves Conrad; teaching and research.

Namur: Facultés Universitaires Notre Dame de la Paix, Bibliothèque Universitaire Moretus Plantin, 19 rue Grandgagnage, 5000 Namur; tel (81) 22-90-61; fax (81) 72-46-28; e-mail anne-marie.bogaert@bump.fundp.ac.be; internet www.fundp.ac.be/bump; Conservator: Anne-Marie Bogaert-Damin; specialized information.

Depository Libraries

Ghent: Universiteit Gent, Faculteit van de Rechtsgeleerdheid, 4 Universiteitstraat, 9000 Ghent; tel (9) 264-69-01; fax (9) 264-69-98; e-mail marc.maresceau@rug.ac.be; Contact: W. Pieters; specialized information.

Louvain: Katholieke Univ Leuven, Centrale Bibliotheek, 21 Mgr Ladeuzeplein, 3000 Louvain; tel (16) 28-46-18; fax (16) 32-46-44; e-mail erna.mannaerts@bib.kuleuven.ac.be; internet www.kuleuven.ac.be/bibc/leeszalen/bkop; Head of the Library of Official Publication: Erna Mannaerts; specialized information.

CYPRUS

Nicosia: European Inst of Cyprus, 11–13 Presidential Palace St, 1080 Nicosia; tel (22) 661550; fax (22) 662880; e-mail eicnews@eic.ac.cy; internet www.eic.ac.cy; Librarians: Maria Haili, Anna Prodromou.

CZECH REPUBLIC

Brno: Masaryk Univ, Faculty of Law, Veveri 70, 611 80 Brno; tel (5) 41559304; fax (5) 41559325; Contact: Marie Zejdová.

Český Krumlov: Univ of South Bohemia, Horni 155, 380 01 Český Krumlov; tel and fax (337) 713075; Contact: Viola Schimmerova.

Prague: Charles Univ, Manesova 75, 120 58 Prague 2; tel (2) 22000160; fax (2) 22000164; e-mail milena.mazacova@eis.cuni.cz; internet www.eis.cuni.cz; Contact: Milena Mazacová.

Prague: Prague Univ of Economics, Faculty of National Economics, Centre of Information and Library Services, nám W. Churchill 4, 130 67 Prague 2; tel (2) 24095869; fax (2) 24095869; e-mail daza@vse.cz; internet www.vse.cz/eds/default/asp; Contact: Dana Zabranska.

Depository Libraries

Olomouc: Univ of Palacky, Faculty of Law, 17. Listopadu 8, 771 00 Olomouc; tel. (585) 637683; fax. (585) 223537; e-mail kostrhol@pfnw.upol.cz; Contact: Laura Kostrhonová.

Plzen: Univ of West Bohemia, Faculty of Law, Law Library, Univerzitní 8, 306 14 Plzen; tel (377) 320707; fax (377) 222876; e-mail baslova@uk.zku.cz; Contact: Marie Baslová.

DENMARK

Aalborg: Aalborg Univ Library, International Publs, Langagervej 2, POB 8200, 9220 Aalborg Øst; tel 96-35-94-00; e-mail vibeke@aub.auc.dk; internet www.aub.auc.dk; Librarian: Vibeke Brisson.

Aarhus: Handelshøjskolens I Aarhus V, Biblioteket, Fugelsangalle 4, 8210 Aarhus V; tel 89-48-65-42; fax 86-15-96-27; e-mail kin@asb.dk; internet www.lib.hha.dk; Contact: Kirsten Kruuse.

Aarhus: Statsbiblioteket, Section for International Publications, Universitetsparken, 8000 Aarhus C; tel 89-46-20-54; fax 89-46-20-50; e-mail ast@statsbiblioteketdk; internet www.aub.auc.dk; Librarian: Anette Scheel-Thomsen.

Copenhagen: Univ of Copenhagen, Inst for Int Ret Og Europaret, Studiestræde 6-1, 1455 Copenhagen; tel 35-32-31-30; fax 35-32-32-03; e-mail mette.joenson@jur.ku.dk; Librarian: Mette W. Jønson.

Esbjerg: Syddansk Universitetsbibliotek- Esbjerg, Niels Bohrs Vej 9, 6700 Esbjerg; tel 65-50-41-22; fax 76-10-45-77; e-mail jsa@bib.sdu.dk; Contact: Jørgen Salling; specialized information.

Odense: Syddansk Universitetsbibliotek–Odense Universitetsbibliotek, Campusvej 55, 5230 Odense M; tel 65-50-26-26; fax 63-15-00-95; e-mail samf@bib.sdu.dk; internet www.cu.dk.

Roskilde: Roskilde Univ, Bibliotek, POB 258, 4000 Roskilde; tel 46-74-23-37; fax 46-75-11-80; Contact: Helli Skærbak.

Depository Library

Frederiksberg (Copenhagen): Copenhagen Business School Library, Acquisitions Section, Solbjerg Plads 3, 2000 Frederiksberg; tel 38-15-37-12; fax 38-15-36-63; e-mail kh.lib@cbs.dk; internet www.cbs.dk/library; Contact: Kirsten Högberg.

ESTONIA

Tartu: Tartu Univ Library, Struve St 1, 50091 Tartu; tel (27) 375-780; fax (27) 375-701; e-mail ruth@utlib.ee; internet www.euroinfo.ee; Contact: Ruth Tammeorg.

Depository Library

Tallinn: National Library of Estonia, Tônismägi 2, Tallinn 15189; tel 631-1411; fax 631-1410; e-mail anu.nestor@nlib.ee; internet www.nlib.ee/elik; Head of EU Information: Anu Nestor.

FINLAND

Helsinki: Univ of Helsinki, Inst of Int Economic Law, Library, POB 4, Fabianinkatu 24a, 00014 Helsinki; tel (9) 19123392; fax (9) 19123719; e-mail gunilla.hakli@helsinki.fi; Librarian: Gunilla Häkli; specialized information.

Joensuu: Joensuu Univ Library, POB 107, 80101 Joensuu 10; tel (13) 2514061; fax (13) 2512691; e-mail helena.silvennoinen-kuikka@joensuu.fi; internet www.joensuu.fi/library; Librarian: Helena Silvennoinen-Kuikka; specialized information.

Jyväskylä: Univ of Jyväskylä, Library, Tietopalvelu, POB 35, 40014 Jyväskylä; tel (14) 2603381; fax (14) 2603371; e-mail marita.jokinen@library.jyu.fi; Contact: Marita Jokinen.

Lappeenranta: Lappeenrannan Teknillisen Korkeakoulun Kirjasto, Library, POB 20, 53851 Lappeenranta; tel (5) 62111; fax (5) 6212349; e-mail liisa.levomaki@lut.fi; Contact: Liisa Levomäki.

Oulu: Oulun Yliopiston Kirjasto, Linnammaa, POB 7500, 90014 Oulu; tel (8) 5533594; fax (8) 5569135; e-mail outi.klintrup@oulu.fi; Contact: Outi Klintrup.

Rovaniemi: Lapin Yliopiston Kirjasto, POB 8123, 96101 Rovaniemi; tel (16) 3412934; fax (16) 3412933; e-mail rainer.salosensaari@ulapland.fi; internet www.ulapland.fi/?DeptID=9542; Contact: Seija Kulmala.

Tampere: Tampere University Library, POB 617, 33101 Tampere; tel (3) 2157867; fax (3) 2157498; e-mail kileto@uta.fi; internet www.uta.fi/laitokset/kirjasto/eu/; Contact: Leena Toivonen.

Turku: Univ of Turku, Pan-European Inst, Lemminkäisenkatu 14–18c, 20521 Turku; tel (2) 3383556; fax (2) 3383268; e-mail kari.pohjola@tukkk.fi; internet www.tukkk.fi/pei/; Contact: kari Pohjola; specialized information.

Vaasa: Univ of Vaasa, Library, POB 331, 65101 Vaasa; tel (6) 3248166; fax (6) 3248200; e-mail ake@uwasa.fi; Librarian: Anneli.Ketonen; specialized information.

Depository Library

Helsinki: Library of the Eduskunta (Parliament), Eduskunnan Kirjasto, 00102 Helsinki 10; tel (9) 4321; fax (9) 4323495; Head Librarian: Tuula H. Laaksovirta.

FRANCE

Aix-en-Provence: Univ d'Aix-Marseille III, Faculté de Droit et de Sciences Politiques, 38 ave de l'Europe, 13090 Aix-en-Provence; tel 4-42-52-72-50; fax 4-42-52-72-60; e-mail ceric@aix.pacwan.net; internet perso.wanadoo.fr/ceric.

Amiens: Univ de Picardie Jules Verne, Faculté d'Economie et de Gestion, 15 placette Lafleur, BP 446, 80004 Amiens; tel 3-22-82-71-65; fax 3-22-82-71-66; e-mail cde@u-picardie.fr; internet www.u-picardie.fr; Contact: Olivier Morand; specialized information.

Angers: Univ d'Angers, Library, Section de Droit et des Sciences Economiques, 57 quai Félix Faure, 49100 Angers; tel 2-41-35-21-00; fax 2-41-35-21-05; e-mail bib@univ-angers.fr; internet buweb.univ-angers.fr.

Avignon: Univ d'Avignon et des Pays de Vaucluse, 6 blvd St Michel, 84000 Avignon; tel 4-90-16-35-00; fax 4-90-16-35-01; e-mail maison-europe@europe-avignon.com; internet www.univ-avignon.fr; Documentalists: Nathalie Monragnon, Isabelle Sellier.

Bayonne: Univ de Pau et des Pays de l'Adour, Faculté de Droit de Bayonne, 29–31 cours du Comte de Cabarrus, 64100 Bayonne; tel 5-59-52-50-07; fax 5-59-63-07-77; e-mail elisabeth.lafuste@univ-pau.fr; internet www.univ-pau.fr;

Librarian: Elisabeth Lafuste; specialized information.

Besançon: Univ de Franche-Comté, Service Commun de Documentation, Bibliothèque P. J. Proudhon, 45 ave de l'Observatoire, 25030 Besançon Cedex; tel 3-81-66-61-98; fax 3-81-66-61-94; e-mail jean-claude.roy@univ-fcomte.fr; internet www.univ-fcomte.fr; Contact: Jean-Claude Roy.

Bordeaux: Univ Montesquieu Bordeaux IV, Faculté de Droit et des Sciences Economiques, ave Léon-Duguit, 33608 Pessac; tel 5-56-84-85-48; fax 5-56-84-29-25; e-mail crde@montesquieu.u-bordeaux.fr; internet www.montesquieu.u-bordeaux.fr; specialized information.

Boulogne-sur-Mer: Univ du Littoral, Bibliothèque Universitaire, place Henri Heine, BP 155, 62202 Boulogne-sur-Mer; tel 3-21-99-41-30; fax 3-21-99-41-41; e-mail corinfob@opale.univ-littoral.fr; internet www.univ-littoral.fr.

Brest: Univ de Bretagne Occidentale, Faculté de Droit et des Sciences Economiques, BP 816, 12 rue de Kergoat, 29285 Brest Cedex; tel 2-98-01-60-29; fax 2-98-01-65-90; e-mail marie-odile.massuyeau@univ-brest.fr; internet www.univ-brest.fr; Contact: Marie-Odile Massuyeau; specialized information.

Caen: Univ de Caen, Faculté de Droit et des Sciences Politiques, Esplanade de la Paix, 14032 Caen Cedex; tel 2-31-56-58-79; fax 2-31-56-59-70; e-mail stephane.leclerc@droit.unicaen.fr; internet www.unicaen.fr; Dir: Stéphane Leclerc; specialized information.

Clermont-Ferrand: Univ d'Auvergne, Faculté de Droit et des Sciences Politiques, 41 blvd F. Mitterrand, BP 54, 63002 Clermont-Ferrand Cedex 1; tel 4-73-17-75-65; fax 4-73-17-75-75; e-mail gerard@u-clermont1.fr; internet www-droit.u-clermont1.fr.

Corte: Univ de Corse, 7 ave Jean Nicoli, BP 52, 20250 Corte, Corsica; tel 4-95-45-00-67; fax 4-95-45-00-80; e-mail webmaster@univ-corse.fr; internet www.univ-corse.fr; Librarian: Thierry Garcia; specialized information.

Dijon: Univ de Bourgogne, Faculté de Droit et des Sciences Politiques, 4 blvd Gabriel, 21000 Dijon; tel 3-80-39-53-29; fax 3-80-39-56-48; e-mail danielle.lenoir@u-bourgogne.fr; internet www.u-bourgogne.fr; Librarian: Danielle Lenoir; specialized information.

Grenoble: Univ des Sciences Sociales de Grenoble, Centre Universitaire de Recherche Européenne et Internationale (CUREI), BP 47, 38040 Grenoble Cedex; tel 4-76-82-55-93; fax 4-76-82-58-62; e-mail eliane.muzelier@upmf-grenoble.fr; internet www.upmf-grenoble.fr/espace/europe; Contact: Liliane Bensahel.

Grenoble: Univ des Sciences Sociales de Grenoble, Inst d'Etudes Politiques (IEP), Centre de Documentation Européenne, BP 48, 38040 Grenoble Cedex 9; tel 4-76-82-60-20; fax 4-76-82-60-70; e-mail galland@iep.upmf-grenoble.fr; internet www.sciences-po.upmf-grenoble.fr; Librarian: Hélène Galland; specialized information.

Le Mans: Bibliothèque de l'Univ du Maine, Section Lettres-Droit, ave Olivier Messiaen, BP 535, 72085 Le Mans Cedex 9; tel 2-43-83-26-18; fax 2-43-83-35-37; e-mail serge.tytgat@univ-lemans.fr; internet www.univ-lemans.fr; Contact: Serge Tytgat; specialized information.

Lille: Univ de Lille I (Univ des Sciences et Technologies de Lille), Faculté de Sciences Economiques et Sociales, Bâtiment SH2, Cité Scientifique, BP 36, 59655 Villeneuve d'Ascq Cedex; tel 3-20-43-67-27; fax 3-20-43-66-55; e-mail sandrine.maes@univ-lille1.fr; internet www.univ-lille1.fr; Librarian: Sandrine Maes; specialized information.

Lille: Univ de Lille II, Centre de Recherches et Documentation Européennes (CRDE), Faculté de Droit, 1 pl Deliot, BP 629, 59024 Lille; tel 3-20-90-74-87; fax 3-20-90-74-03; e-mail iried-crde@mailsc.univ-lille2.fr; internet www.univ-lille2.fr.

Limoges: Univ de Limoges, Bibliothèque Universitaire Section Droit, 39c rue Camille Guérin 5, 87031 Limoges Cedex; tel 5-55-43-57-18; fax 5-55-43-57-01; e-mail sabine.pommaret@unilim.fr; internet www.unilim.fr/scd; Dir: Sabine Pommaret; specialized information.

Lyons: Ecole de Management de Lyon, 23 ave Guy de Collongue, BP 174, 69132 Ecully Cedex; tel 4-78-33-78-00; fax 4-78-33-78-60; e-mail chavrier@em-lyon.com; internet www.em-lyon.com; Librarian: Cécile Chavrier; specialized information.

Lyons: Univ Jean Moulin, Lyon III, Centre de Documentation et de Recherche Européenne, 15 quai Claude Bernard, BP 0638, 69239 Lyons Cedex 2; tel 4-78-78-70-61; fax 4-78-78-74-66; e-mail cdre@sunlyon3.univ-lyon3.fr; internet www.univ-lyon3.fr.

Lyons: Univ Lumière de Lyon II, Centre d'Etudes de Science Politique et de Documentation Européennes (CESPEDE), Inst d'Etudes Politiques, 14 ave Berthelot, 69365 Lyons Cedex 07; tel 4-37-28-38-89; fax 4-37-28-38-94; e-mail iep.cde@univ-lyon2.fr; internet www.iep.cde@univ-lyon2.fr; Contact: Marie-Claude Dunand; specialized information.

Marseille: Univ de la Méditerranée Aix-Marseille II, Faculté des Sciences Économiques, rue Puvis de Chavannes, 13001 Marseille; tel 4-91-13-96-38; fax 4-91-90-58-29; e-mail anne.chauveinc@bu2.timone.univ-mrs.fr; internet www.mediterranee.univ-mrs.fr; Contact: Anne Chauveinc.

Montpellier: Univ de Montpellier I, Faculté de Droit, 14 rue du Cardinal de Cabrière, 34016 Montpellier Cedex 2; tel 4-67-61-51-92; fax 4-67-60-42-31; e-mail cdeurope@droit.univ-montp1.fr; internet www.univ-montp1.fr.

Nancy: Univ de Nancy II, Centre Européen Universitaire, Bibliothèque, 15 place Carnot, 54042 Nancy Cedex; tel 3-83-19-27-84; fax 3-83-19-27-87; e-mail martine.clavel@univ-nancy2.fr; internet www.univ-nancy2.fr; Librarian: Martine Clavel.

Nantes: Univ de Nantes, Faculté de Droit et des Sciences Economiques, chemin de la Censive du Tertre, BP 12236, 44322 Nantes Cedex 03; tel 2-40-14-14-70; fax 2-40-14-14-71; e-mail sylvie-lemaire@univ-nantes.fr; internet www.bu.univ-nantes.fr; Contact: Sylvie Lemaire; specialized information.

Nice: Univ de Nice Sophia-Antipolis, Inst du Droit de la Paix et du Développement, 39 ave Emile Henriot, 06050 Nice Cedex 1; tel 4-92-15-71-99; fax 4-92-15-71-97; e-mail rideau@unice.fr; internet www.unice.fr; Dir: Prof Joël Rideau; specialized information.

Orléans: Univ d'Orléans, Bibliothèque Universitaire Section Droit, Economie et de Gestion, 7 rue de Blois, 45072 Orléans Cedex 02; tel 2-38-41-72-56; fax 2-38-49-45-29; e-mail Genevieve.Corgier@univ-orleans.fr; internet www.univ-orleans.fr; Librarian: Geneviève Corgier; specialized information.

Paris: Ecole Nationale d'Administration, Centre de Documentation, 13 rue de l'Université, 75343 Paris Cedex 07; tel 1-49-26-43-65; fax 1-42-60-26-95; e-mail tizon@ena.fr; internet www.ena.fr; Contact: Mme Tizon; specialized information.

Paris: Univ de Paris, Bibliothèque Inter-universitaire Cujas de Droit et des Sciences Economiques, Service Public International, 2 rue Cujas, 75005 Paris; tel 1-44-07-76-22; fax 1-44-07-78-32; e-mail phcolomb@univ-paris1.fr; internet www.cujas.univ-paris1.fr; Contact: Philippe Colomb.

Paris: Univ de Paris I, Centre Universitaire d'Etude et de Recherche Européenne (CERES), 12 place du Panthéon, 75231 Paris Cedex 05; tel 1-44-07-77-55; fax 1-44-07-78-69; e-mail lencot@univ-paris1.fr; internet www.univ-paris1.fr.

Paris: Univ de Paris II, Centre de Droit Européen, 12 place du Panthéon, 75231 Paris Cedex 05; tel 1-44-41-56-68; fax 1-44-41-55-24; e-mail lafon@u-paris2.fr; internet www.u-paris2.fr; Librarian: Bernadette Lafon; specialized information.

Paris: Univ René Descartes, Centre de la Porte de Vanves, Bibliothèque de Droit, 10 ave Pierre Larousse, 92245 Paris

Malakof Cedex; tel 1-41-17-30-65; fax 1-42-53-24-81; e-mail c.gras@droit.univ-paris5.fr; internet www.bu.univ-paris5.fr; Librarian: Colette Gras.

Paris: Univ de Paris X (Nanterre), Inst de Politique Internationale et Européenne (IPIE), 200 ave de la République, 92000 Nanterre Cedex; tel 1-40-97-77-22; fax 1-40-97-47-10; e-mail cedin@u-paris10.fr; internet www.u-paris10.fr.

Paris: Univ de Paris XII (Paris Val de Marne), Centre de Documentation Européenne et Centre de Recherches Communautaires, Faculté de Droit de Saint-Maur, 58 ave Didier, 94214 la Varenne Saint-Hilaire Cedex; tel 1-49-76-81-09; fax 1-48-85-96-23; e-mail moulin@univ-paris12.fr; internet www.univ-paris12.fr.

Paris: Univ de Paris Nord (Paris XIII), Faculté de Droit et des Sciences Politiques, 99 ave J. B. Clément, 93430 Villetaneuse; tel 1-49-40-38-22; fax 1-49-40-33-47; e-mail moutardi@upn.univ-paris13.fr; internet www.univ-paris13.fr; Librarian: Claudine Moutardier; specialized information.

Paris: Univ de Paris Sud, Faculté Jean Monnet, 54 blvd Desgranges, 92331 Sceaux Cedex; tel 1-40-91-18-12; fax 1-40-91-18-14; e-mail younes@jm.u-psud.fr; internet www.u-psud.fr.

Pau: Univ de Pau et des Pays de l'Adour, Faculté de Droit et des Sciences Économiques, ave du Doyen Poplawski, 64000 Pau; tel 5-59-80-75-80; fax 5-59-80-75-90; internet www.univ-pau.fr; Contact: Eliane Duthil; specialized information.

Perpignan: Univ de Perpignan, Faculté des Sciences Humaines et Sociales, Centre de Documentation et de Recherche Européenne, 52 ave Villeneuve-Moulin-à-Vent, BP1062, 66102 Perpignan Cedex; tel 4-68-66-22-99; fax 4-68-50-37-72; e-mail boutin@univ-perp.fr; internet www.univ-perp.fr; specialized information.

Poitiers: Univ de Poitiers, Faculté de Droit et des Sciences Sociales, Centre d'Etudes Européennes, Bibliothèque, 93 ave du Recteur Pineau, 86022 Poitiers; tel 5-49-45-31-10; fax 5-49-45-31-52; e-mail francois-hervouet@uni-poitiers.fr; internet www.univ-poitiers.fr; Librarian: François Hervouet.

Reims: Univ de Reims, Faculté de Droit et des Sciences Economiques, Centre de Documentation et de Recherche Européenne, 57 bis rue Pierre Taittinger, 51100 Reims Cedex; tel 3-26-05-38-18; fax 3-26-05-38-00; internet www.univ-reims.fr.

Rennes: Univ de Rennes I, Faculté de Droit, Centre de Documentation et de Recherches Européennes, 9 rue Jean Macé, 35042 Rennes Cedex; tel 2-99-84-76-71; fax 2-99-84-77-40; e-mail marie-claude.cornee@univ-rennes1.fr; Librarian: Marie-Claude Cornée.

Rouen: Univ de Rouen, Bibliothèque Universitaire, Section Droit, 76186 Rouen Cedex; tel 2-32-76-95-57; fax 2-32-76-95-76; internet www.univ.rouen.fr; specialized information.

Strasbourg: École Nationale d'Administration, 1 rue Sainte Marguerite, 67080 Strasbourg Cedex; tel 3-88-21-44-91; fax 3-88-21-44-29; e-mail simon@ena.fr; internet www.ena.fr; Librarian: Cathy Simon-Bloch.

Strasbourg: Univ Robert Schuman, Centre d'Etudes Internationales et Européennes, Recherches Juridiques, Politiques et Sociales, 11 rue du Maréchal Juin, BP 68, 67046 Strasbourg Cedex; tel 3-88-14-30-04; fax 3-88-14-30-05; e-mail beatrice.debrie@urs.u-strasbg.fr; internet www.u-strasbg.fr; Contact: Beatrice Debrie; specialized information.

Strasbourg: Univ Robert Schuman, Inst des Hautes Etudes Européennes, 10 rue Schiller, 67080 Strasbourg Cedex; tel 3-88-15-05-47; fax 3-88-36-86-11; e-mail laurent-stern@urs.u-strasbg.fr; www.ihee.u-strasbourg.fr; Librarian: Laurent Stern; specialized information.

Toulon: Univ de Toulon, Bibliothèque de la Faculté de Droit, 35 ave Alphonse Daudet, BP 1206, 83070 Toulon Cedex; tel 4-94-46-75-61; fax 4-94-46-75-82; e-mail devilleger@univ-tln.fr; internet www.univ-tln.fr; specialized information.

Toulouse: Univ des Sciences Sociales de Toulouse I, Centre de Documentation et de Recherche Européenne, Bibliothèque de la Manufacture de Tabac, 31015 Toulouse Cedex 16; tel 5-61-12-88-00; fax 5-61-12-87-74; e-mail molus@univ-tlse1.fr; internet www.biu-toulouse.fr/uss/manuf; Librarian: Colette Molus.

Tours: Univ F. Rabelais de Tours, Faculté de Droit, d'Economie et des Sciences Sociales, Centre de Documentation et de Recherche Européenne, 50 ave Portalis, BP 0607, 37206 Tours Cedex 3; tel 2-47-36-84-88; fax 2-47-36-84-87; e-mail iee@droit.univ-tours.fr; internet www.univ-tours.fr; Librarian: Joëlle Tranchant; specialized information.

Depository Library

Paris: Bibliothèque Nationale, Département des Publications Officielles, 2–4 rue Vivienne, 75084 Paris Cedex 2; tel 1-47-03-85-46; Dir: D. Duclos-Faure; Librarian: Mme Brenot.

FRENCH OVERSEAS DEPARTMENTS

Pointe-à-Pitre, Guadeloupe: Univ des Antilles et de la Guyane, UFR des Sciences Juridiques et Economiques de la Guadeloupe, BP 270, 97157 Pointe-à-Pitre, Guadeloupe; tel 5-90-35-23-56; fax 5-90-21-48-36; e-mail charbel.macdissi@univ-ag.fr; internet www.univ.ag.fr.

Saint-Denis, Réunion: Univ de la Réunion, Faculté de Droit et de Sciences Economiques, 24–26 ave de la Victoire, 97489 Saint-Denis, Réunion; tel 21-74-75; fax 41-25-05; Dir: E. Putman.

GERMANY

Aachen: Fachbereichsbibliothek Wirtschaftswissenschaften der RWTH Aachen Zusammenarbeit, 52056 Aachen, Ahornstr 55; tel (241) 8894712; fax (241) 8888284; e-mail biblio2@wiwi.rwth-aachen.de; internet www.informatik.rwth-aachen.de; Librarian: Christel Posenauer.

Augsburg: Europäisches Dokumentationszentrum in der Teilbibliothek Spezialwissenschaften der Universitätsbibliothek, 86159 Augsburg, Universitätsstr 22; tel (821) 5984371; fax (821) 5984369; e-mail sybille.meier@bibliothek.uni-augsburg.de; internet www.bibliothek.uni-augsburg.de/sonder/edz.html; Librarian: Sybille Meier; specialized information.

Bamberg: Europäisches Dokumentationszentrum, Universitätsbibliothek Bamberg, 96018 Bamberg, Feldkirchenstr 21; 96018 Bamberg, Postfach 2705; tel (951) 8631525; fax (951) 8631565; e-mail barbara.wild@unibib.uni-bamberg.de; internet www.uni-bamberg.de/unibib/ben/edz.html; Librarian: Barbara Ziegler; specialized information.

Bayreuth: Universitätsbibliothek Bayreuth, Zentralbibliothek, 95440 Bayreuth, Universitätstr 30; 96018 Bayreuth, Postfach 101251; tel (921) 553420; fax (921) 553442; e-mail detlev.gassong@ub.uni-bayreuth.de; internet www.ub.uni-bayreuth.de/; Librarian: Detlev Gassong; specialized information.

Berlin: Stiftung Wissenschaft und Politik, Bibliothek, 3–4 Ludwigkirchplatz, 10719 Berlin; 10673 Berlin, Postfach 151120; tel (30) 88007326; fax (30) 88007100; e-mail morkel@swp.extern.lrz-muenchen.de; Contact: Nele Morkel.

Berlin: Europäische Akademie Berlin, Bibliothek, 14193 Berlin, 46–48 Bismarckallee; tel (30) 89595123; fax (30) 8266410; e-mail pz@eaue.de; Librarian: Petra Zeschke-Buchrucker.

Berlin: Freie Univ Berlin, Universitätsbibliothek, 14195 Berlin, Garystr 39; tel (30) 83852399; fax (30) 83852067; e-mail uneu-dok@ub.fu-berlin.de; Contact: Christina Plessner.

Berlin: Deutsche Gesellschaft für auswärtige Politik, Bibliothek und Dokumentationsstelle, 10787 Berlin, Rauchstr 17/18; tel (30) 2542310; fax (30)

25423116; e-mail bidok@dgap.org; Contact: Heike Zanzig.

Bielefeld: Univ Bielefeld, Fachbibliothek Rechtswissenschaft, 33615 Bielefeld, Universitätsstr 25; tel (521) 1063806; fax (521) 1064052; e-mail koeper@ub.uni-bielefeld.de; internet www.ub.uni-bielefeld.de/biblio/kontakt/fachbibliotheken/edz.htm; Contact: Reinhold Kolbe; specialized information.

Bochum: Ruhr Univ Bochum, Universitätsbibliothek, 44801 Bochum, Universitätsstr 150; tel (234) 3226461; fax (234) 3214737; e-mail beate.ramisch@ruhr-uni-bochum.de; Contact: Beate Ramisch; specialized information.

Bonn: Univ Bonn, Zentrum für Europäische Integrationsforschung, 53113 Bonn, Walter-Flex-Str 3; tel (228) 731723; fax (228) 735097; e-mail v.merx@uni-bonn.de; internet www.zei.de; Librarian: Volker Merx.

Bremen: Univ Bremen, Zentrum für Europäische Rechtspolitik (ZERP), 28359 Bremen, Universitätsallee GW1; tel (421) 2182247; fax (421) 2183403; e-mail zyirga@zerp.uni-bremen.de; internet www.zerp.uni-bremen.de/deutsch/bibliothek/info.html; Librarian: Zion Yirga.

Cologne: Univ Köln, Inst für das Recht der Europäischen Gemeinschaften, 50923 Cologne, Albertus-Magnus-Platz; tel (221) 4703862; fax (221) 4705036; e-mail eurecht@uni-koeln.de; Librarian: Beate Zimmer; specialized information.

Cologne: Universitäts- und Stadtbibliothek, 50931 Cologne, Universitätsstr 33; tel (221) 4703312; fax (221) 4705166; e-mail edz@ub.uni-koeln.de; internet www.ub.uni-koeln.de; Librarian: Cornelia Linnartz.

Darmstadt: Technische Univ Darmstadt, 64289 Darmstadt, Gebäude S102/38, Hochschulstr 3; tel (6151) 164999; fax (6151) 166078; e-mail edz@pg.tu-darmstadt.de; internet www.tu-darmstadt.de/edz/edz.tud; Librarian: Denise André; specialized information.

Dresden: Sächsische Landesbibliothek, Staats- und Universitätsbibliothek Dresden, Zweigbibliothek Rechtswissenschaft, 01054 Dresden, Bergstr 53; tel (351) 4637424; fax (351) 4637446; e-mail edz@rcs.urz.tu-dresden.de; internet www.tu-dresden.de/slub/edzinter/home/home.htm; Librarian: Kalina Muehlfeld.

Duisburg: Gerhard-Mercator Univ, Universitätsbibliothek, 47048 Duisburg, Lotharstr 65; tel (203) 3792083; fax (203) 3792066; e-mail g-ho@duisburg.uni-duisburg.de; internet www.ub.uni-duisburg.de/test/homeneu-ssi/recherch/fachinfo/duisburg/edz; Librarian: Gabriele Jacobs.

Erlangen: Inst für Europäisches Wirtschaftsrecht, Univ Erlangen-Nürnberg, 91054 Erlangen, Schillerstr 1; tel (9131) 8522817; fax (9131) 8522481; e-mail iewr@jura.uni-erlangen.de; internet www.ewr.jura.uni-erlangen.de/dokzent.htm; Contact: Franziska Scheffler.

Frankfurt/Main: Univ Frankfurt/Main, Inst für Ausländisches und Internationales Wirtschaftsrecht, 60054 Frankfurt/Main, Senckenberganlage 31, Postfach 111932; tel (69) 79823193; fax (69) 79828466; e-mail jeanine.koch@jur.uni-frankfurt.de; internet www.rz.uni-frankfurt.de; Librarian: Jeanine Koch; specialized information.

Frankfurt/Oder: Europa-Univ Viadrina, 15230 Frankurt/Oder, Große Scharrnstr 59; tel (335) 5534330; fax (335) 5534234; e-mail hertz@euv-frankfurt-o.de; Librarian: Hans-Jürgen Hertz-Eichenrode.

Freiburg: Albert-Ludwigs-Univ Freiburg, Inst für Öffentliches Recht, 79085 Freiburg, Platz der Alten Synagoge 1; tel (761) 2032245; fax (761) 2032144; Librarian: Margarete Becker; specialized information.

Fulda: Fachhochschule Fulda, Bibliothek, 36039 Fulda, Marquardstr 35; tel (661) 9640151; fax (661) 9640159; e-mail dietrich.haselbach@bibl.fh-fulda.de; internet www.fh-fulda.de/hlb/edz.htm; Librarian: Dietrich Haselbach.

Gießen: Justus-Liebig-Univ, Fachbibliothek Rechtswissenschaft, Lehrstuhl für Öffentliches Recht IV, 35394 Gießen, Licher Str 76, Haus 2; tel (641) 9921153; fax (641) 9921159; e-mail sebastian.heselhaus@recht.uni-giessen.de; Librarian: Sebastian Heselbans.

Göttingen: Univ Göttingen, Bibliothek der Wirtschafts- und Sozialwissenschaftlichen Seminare und Inst, 37073 Göttingen, Platz der Göttinger Sieben 3; tel (551) 397252; fax (551) 392163; e-mail ulws@gwdg.de; Librarian: Aart Foks Ahlrich; specialized information.

Hagen: Fernuniv, Universitätsbibliothek, 58084 Hagen, Feithstr 140; tel (2331) 9872892; fax (2331) 987331; e-mail annette.frerichs@fernuni-hagen.de; internet www.ub.fernuni-hagen.de/edz; Librarian: Annette Frerichs.

Halle (Saale): Martin-Luther Univ, Universitäts- und Landesbibliothek Halle-Wittenberg, 06108 Halle (Saale), Universitätsring 2, Postfach 06099; tel (345) 5522042; fax (345) 5527068; European Documentation Centre: Dr Dagmar Sachse.

Hamburg: Hamburgisches Welt-Wirtschafts-Archiv, Bibliothek, 20347 Hamburg, Neuer Jungfernstieg 21; tel (40) 42834267; fax (40) 42834550; e-mail weilepp@hwwa.de; internet www.hwwa.de/index.htm; Librarian: Dr Manfred Weilepp.

Hamburg: Univ Hamburg, Abteilung für Europäisches Gemeinschaftsrecht, Seminar für Öffentliches Recht und Staatslehre, 20148 Hamburg, Schlüterstr 28/III; tel (40) 428384108; fax (40) 428386352; e-mail edz@jura.uni-hamburg.de; Contact: Heike Humpert.

Hanover: Niedersächsische Landesbibliothek, Fachbereichsbibliothek Wirtschaftswissenschaften, 30167 Hanover, Königsworther Platz 1b; tel (511) 7625598; fax (511) 7622924; e-mail sigrid.fuest@fbb.nlb-hannover.de; internet www.nlb-hannover.de/edz.htm; Contact: Sigrid Fuest; specialized information.

Heidelberg: Max-Planck-Inst für ausländisches öffentliches Recht und Völkerrecht, 69120 Heidelberg, Im Neuenheimer Feld 535; tel (6221) 482224; fax (6221) 482494; e-mail bmueller@mpiv-hd.mpg.de; internet www.virtual-institute.de/de/bibl/edz.cfm; Librarian: Birgit Müller.

Ingolstadt: Katholische Univ Eichstätt, Wirtschaftswissenschaftliche Fakultät Ingolstadt, 85049 Ingolstadt/Donau, Auf der Schanz 49; tel (841) 9371806; fax (841) 17371; e-mail richard.bonnin@ku-eichstaett.de; Contact: Richard Bonnin.

Jena: Friedrich-Schiller-Univ, Bibliothek der Rechtswissenschaftlichen Fakultät, 07743 Jena, Carl-Zeiss-Str 3; tel (3641) 940426; fax (3641) 940032; e-mail j33rr@thulb10.biblio.uni-jena.de; internet www.uni-jena.de/rewi; Librarian: Regine Rosenkranz.

Kehl: Euro-Inst Kehl, Inst für Regionale Zusammenarbeit und Europäische Verwaltung, 77679 Kehl, Rehfusplatz 11, Postfach 1945; tel (7851) 740729; fax (7851) 740733; e-mail drewello@euroinstitut.fh-kehl.de; Contact: Dr Marie-Louise Hild.

Kiel: Inst für Weltwirtschaft, Zentralbibliothek der Wirtschaftswissenschaften in der Bundesrepublik Deutschland, 24105 Kiel, Düsternbrooker Weg 120; tel (431) 8814436; fax (431) 8814520; e-mail e.seusing@zbw.ifw-kiel.de; internet www.uni-kiel.de/ifw/zbw/econis.htm; Contact: Ekkehart Seusing.

Konstanz: Univ Konstanz, Bibliothek, 78457 Konstanz, Universitätsstr 10; tel (7531) 882845; fax (7531) 883082; e-mail gudrun.schwarz@uni-konstanz.de; internet www.ub.uni-konstanz.de/fi/edz; Librarian: Gudrun Schwarz.

Leipzig: Univ Leipzig, Juristenfakultät, 04109 Leipzig, Otto-Schill-Str 2; tel (341) 9735296; fax (341) 9735298; e-mail haucke@rz.uni-leipzig.de; internet www.uni-leipzig.de/edz; Librarian: Ute Haucke.

The Directory of EU Information Sources

Mainz: Johannes-Gutenberg-Univ, Fachbereich Rechts- und Wirtschaftswissenschaften, 55099 Mainz, Jakob-Welder-Weg 9; tel (6131) 392646; fax (6131) 395489; e-mail edz-pullig@uni-mainz.de; Librarian: Winfried Pullig.

Mannheim: Univ Mannheim, 68131 Mannheim, Postfach 103462, L15, 16; tel (621) 1813215; fax (621) 1813212; e-mail edzma@rumms.uni-mannheim.de; Contact: Angelika Grund; specialized information.

Marburg: Philipps-Univ Marburg, Bibliothek Politikwissenschaft, 35032 Marburg/Lahn, Wilhelm-Röpke-Str 6; tel (6421) 2824396; fax (6421) 2828991; e-mail ponitz@ub.uni-marburg.de; internet www.uni-marburg.de/fb03/neu/biblio/bibedz.html; Contacts: Barbara Ponitz-Ouahioune, Edith Englert, Annette Müller.

Munich: Ludwig-Maximilians-Univ München, Forschungsgruppe Europa, Centrum für angewandte Politikforschung, 81675 Munich, Maria-Theresia-Str 21; tel (89) 21801300; fax (89) 21801329; e-mail uf291aa@mail.lrz-muenchen.de; Contact: Stephanie Rösch.

Munich: Ludwig-Maximilians-Univ München, Inst für Europäisches und Internationales Wirtschaftsrecht, 80539 Munich, Ludwigstr 29/III; tel (89) 21803268; fax (89) 21802904; e-mail eu.dokumentationszentrum@jura.uni-muenchen.de; Contact: Marie-Laure Garaud; specialized information, EU databases.

Münster: Westfälische Wilhelms-Univ, Inst für Politikwissenschaft, 48151 Münster, Scharnhorststr 103; tel (251) 8329358; fax (251) 8329352; e-mail edz@uni-muenster.de; internet www.uni-muenster.de/EuropeanDocCentre; Contacts: Christel Franek, Daniel Dräger.

Osnabrück: Univ Osnabrück, Inst für Europarecht, 49034 Osnabrück, Heger-Tor-Wall 14, Postfach 4469; tel (541) 9696106; fax (541) 9696186; e-mail friederike.dauer@fsub1.ub.uni-osnabrueck.de; internet www.ub.uni-osnabrueck.de; Contacts: Friederike Dauer, Manfred Krohs.

Passau: Univ Passau, Universitätsbibliothek, 94030 Passau, Innstr 25, Postfach 2544; tel (851) 5091605; fax (851) 5092203; e-mail michael.strupp@uni-passau.de; internet www.ub.uni-passau.de; Contact: Michael Strupp.

Regensburg: Univ Regensburg, Universitätsbibliothek, 93053 Regensburg, Universitätsstr 31–33; tel (941) 9432561; fax (941) 9433285; e-mail barbara.leiwesmeyer@bibliothek.uni-regensburg.de; internet www.bibliothek.uni-regensburg.de/edz/edz; Contact: Barbara Leiwesmeyer; specialized information.

Rostock: Univ Rostock, Juristische Fakultät, 18109 Rostock, Möllnerstr 9, Postfach 999; tel (381) 4983842; fax (381) 4983770; e-mail klaus.tonner@jurfak.uni-rostock.de; internet www.uni-rostock.de; Librarian: Dr Hiltrud Bahlo.

Saarbrücken: Univ des Saarlandes, Saarländische Universitäts- und Landesbibliothek, 66041 Saarbrücken, Postfach 151141; tel (681) 3023082; fax (681) 3022796; e-mail p.weber@sulb.uni-saarland.de; internet www.sulb.uni-saarland.de; Librarian: Dr Peter Weber.

Saarbrücken: Univ des Saarlandes, Europa Inst, Rechts- und Wirtschaftswissenschaftliche Fakultät, 66041 Saarbrücken, Am Stadtwald, Postfach 151150; tel (681) 3022543; fax (681) 3026698; e-mail rw72eibb@rz.uni-sb.de; internet www.europainstitut.de/euin/institut/index_biblio.html; Contact: Jutta Lamberty.

Siegen: Univ/Gesamthochschule Siegen, Universitätsbibliothek, 57068 Siegen, Adolf-Reichwein-Str 2; tel (271) 7404253; fax (271) 7404279; e-mail edz@ub.uni-siegen.de; internet: www.ub.uni-siegen.de/ueberub/edz; Contacts: Karin Reese, Ulrike Zink, Uwe Kölsch; specialized information.

Speyer: Deutsche Hochschule für Verwaltungswissenschaften, Lehrstuhl für Öffentliches Recht, insbesondere Völker- und Europarecht, 67324 Speyer, Freiherr-vom-Stein-Str 2; tel (6232) 644388; fax (6232) 654208; e-mail edz@dhv-speyer.de; internet www.dhv-speyer.de/edz; Librarian: Holger Holzwar.

Trier: Univ Trier, Universitätsbibliothek, Fachreferat Rechtswissenschaft, 54286 Trier, Universitätsring 15; tel (651) 2012455; fax (651) 2013977; e-mail straub@ub.uni-trier.de; internet www.uni-trier.de/infos/ew/europa/edz_Trier.htm; Librarian: Carlheinz Rolf Straub.

Trier: Europäische Rechtsakademie, Bibliothek, 54295 Trier, Metzer Allee 4; tel (651) 9373717; fax (651) 9373790; e-mail sprobst@era.int; internet: www.era.int/www/en/index.htm; Contact: Sabine Probst.

Tübingen: Univ Tübingen, Universitätsbibliothek, 72074 Tübingen, Wilhelmstr 32; tel (7071) 2972832; fax (7071) 295816; e-mail ulrich.schapka@ub.uni-tuebingen.de; internet www.ub.uni-tuebingen.de/pro/fach/euro/euro.php; Contact: Ulrich Schapka.

Würzburg: Univ Würzburg, Inst für Völker- und Europarecht und Internationales Wirtschaftsrecht, 97079 Würzburg, Domerschulstr 16; tel (931) 312668; fax (931) 312792; e-mail l-europarecht@jura.uni-wuerzburg.de; Contact: Anne Bick, Christoph Ritzer.

Depository Libraries

Berlin: Staatsbibliothek zu Berlin, Preussischer Kulturbesitz, Abteilung Amtsdruckschriften und Internationales, Amt Schriftentausch, 10772 Berlin; tel (30) 2662471; fax (30) 2662341; Dir: Anita Stauch; Librarian: Irene Herrendoerfer.

Frankfurt/Main: Deutsche Bibliothek, Stiftung des öffentlichen Rechts, 60325 Frankfurt/Main, Zeppelinallee 8; tel (69) 7566204; fax (69) 7566176; Dirs: K. Walter, Barbara Schenk; Librarian: C. Hoos-Wilhelmi.

Leipzig: Deutsche Bibliothek, Deutsche Bücherei, 04103 Leipzig, Deutscher Platz 1; tel (341) 22710; fax (341) 2271444; Dir: Roetzsch; Librarian: Kerstin Podszuweit.

Munich: Bayerische Staatsbibliothek, II G Tausch- und Geschenkstelle, 80328 Munich; tel (89) 28638345; fax (89) 28638309; Dir: Dr Philip Pirler.

GREECE

Athens: Hellenic Centre for European Studies, Library, Prassa 1 & Didotou, 10680 Athens; tel (1) 03636963; fax (1) 03631133; e-mail info@ekem.gr; internet www.ekem.gr; Contacts: Panagiotis Iokamidis, Kostas Maragakis.

Athens: Athens Univ of Economics and Business, Dept of International and European Economic Studies, Odos Patission 76, 10434 Athens; tel (1) 08218856; fax (1) 08221456; e-mail library@aueb.gr; internet www.lib.aueb.gr; Contacts: Georgia Theophanopoulou, Vasiliki Rigakou, Theodore Georgakopoulos.

Komotini: 'Demokritos' Univ of Thrace, 1 Panagi Tsaldari, 69100 Komotini; tel (531) 024143; fax (531) 027265; e-mail papoutsi@lib.duth.gr; internet www.lib.duth.gr; Contacts: Olga Papoutsi, Michael Chryssomalis.

Patras: Univ of Patras, Panepistimioupoli Patron, 26500 Rio Patron; tel (61) 0996227; fax (61) 0995056; e-mail efiliana@lis.upatras.gr; internet www.lis.upatras.gr; Contacts: Catherine Synelli, Efstathia Iliopoulou.

Piraeus: Univ of Piraeus, Dept of Business Administration, Odos Karaoli and Dimitriou 80, 18534 Piraeus; tel (1) 04142033; fax (1) 04142335; e-mail sdzima@uinipi.gr; internet www.lib.unipi.gr; Contacts: Panagiotis Kannelopoulos, Irini Tzima.

Rethimnou: Univ of Crete, Panepistimioupoli Rethymnou, 74100 Rethimnou; tel (31) 077844; fax (31) 077849; e-mail thymiatz@libr.uoc.gr; internet www.libr.uoc.gr; Contacts: Andreas Moshonas, Helen Diamantaki, Irene Thymiatzi.

Thessaloniki: Centre of International and European Economic Law, POB 14, 55102 Kalamaria, Thessaloniki; tel (31)

0486913; fax (31) 076366; e-mail edc@ cieel.gr; internet www.cieel.gr; Contacts: Vasilios Skouris, Diana Bougiouka.

Depository Libraries

Athens: National and Kapodistrian Univ of Athens, Faculty of Law, Dept of Political Science and Public Administration, Library, Eolou 42–44 & Kolokotroni, 10560 Athens; tel (1) 09201601; fax (1) 03245387; e-mail pepistdirnd@lib.uoa.gr; Contacts: Michalis Tsinisizelis, Asimina Perri.

Athens: Panteion Univ of Social and Political Sciences, 136 Syngrou Ave, R.314, 17671 Athens; tel (1) 09201601; fax (1) 09213140; e-mail edc@panteion.gr; internet www.panteion.gr/~edc; Contacts: Konstantinos Stefanou, Nikolaos Limouris.

HUNGARY

Budapest: Budapest Univ of Economic Sciences, European Study Centre, 1093 Budapest, Fövám tér 8; tel (1) 217-66- 52; fax (1) 218-07- 96; e-mail marianna .brincken@eustudce.bke.hu; Contact: Prof. Hajna Istvánffy.

Budapest: ELTE Univ, Faculty of Law, 1053 Budapest, Egyetem tér 1–3; tel (1) 266-59-99; fax (1) 266-59-99; Contacts: Lajos Ficzere, Miklós Király.

Budapest: College of Commerce, Trade and Tourism, Central Library, 1055 Budapest, Alkotmány u. 9–11; tel (1) 374-62-18; fax (1) 374-62-18; e-mail vpoosne@kvif.hu; internet http://web .kvif.bgf.hu; Contact: Lászlóné Poós.

Debrecen: European Documentation Centre, Univ of Debrecen, University and National Library, 4010 Debrecen, PF 39; tel (52) 31-68-35; fax (52) 41-04- 43; e-mail ilevay@libware.lib.klte.hu; Contacts: Botondné Lévay, Judit Csukás.

Gödöllö: Gödöllö Univ, European Study Centre, 2103 Gödöllö, Tessedik Samuel u. 6; tel (28) 52-11-33; fax (28) 52-11-39; e-mail agooz@gtk.gau.hu; Contact: Ágnes Goóz.

Miskolc: European Documentation Centre, Miskolc Univ, Central Library, 3515 Miskolc, Egyetemváros; tel (46) 56-51-11; fax (46) 36-95-54; e-mail kov11039@helka .iif.hu; internet www.uni-miskolc.hu; Contact: Beata Kovacs.

Pécs: Janus Pannonius Univ, Faculty of Law Library, 7622 Pécs, 48-as tér 1; tel (72) 21-14-33; fax (72) 21-51-48; e-mail adamne@ajk.jpte.hu; Contacts: Antalné Ádám, Ildikó Szomor.

Szeged: European Documentation Centre, Univ Jozsef Attila of Szeged, Faculty of Law, 6720 Szeged, 54. Tisza Lajos krt; tel (62) 45-41-93; fax (62) 45-41-84; e-mail

kati@lib.juris.u-szeged.hu; Contact: Katalin Forrásné Török.

Szombathely: Berzsenyi Dániel Teachers' Training College, European Study Centre, 9700 Szombathely, Berzsenyi tér 2; tel (94) 51-26-80; fax (94) 32-99-18; e-mail edc@fsd.bdtf.hu; internet www.bdtf.hu; Contact: Ferenc Miszlivetz.

Veszprém: Veszprém Univ, European Study Centre, 8200 Veszprém, Wartha V. u. 1; tel (88) 42-38-52; fax (88) 42-38-52; e-mail iszilagyi@almos.vein.hu; Contact: Zsuzsanna Gergó.

IRELAND

Cork: Univ Coll Cork, Boole Library, Cork; tel (21) 902363; fax (21) 273428; e-mail v.fletcher@ucc.ie; internet booleweb.ucc.ie; Librarian: Valerie Fletcher.

Dublin: Trinity Coll Library, College St, Dublin 2; tel (1) 6082342; fax (1) 6719003; e-mail john.goodwillie@tcd.ie; Librarian: John Goodwillie.

Dublin: Univ Coll Dublin, Main Library, Belfield, Dublin 4; tel (1) 7167508; fax (1) 7061148; e-mail tony.eklof@ucd.ie; Librarian: Tony Eklof.

Galway: Nat Univ of Ireland, James Hardiman Library, Galway; tel (91) 524411; fax (91) 522394; e-mail hugo .kelly@nuigalway.ie; Contact: Hugo Kelly; specialized information.

Limerick: Univ of Limerick, Library and Information Services Bldg, Plassey Technological Park, Limerick; tel (61) 202185; fax (61) 213090; e-mail pattie.punch@ ul.ie; Librarian: Pattie Punch.

Maynooth: Nat Univ of Ireland, Maynooth, Kildare; tel (1) 7083429; fax (1) 6286008; e-mail sandra.firth@may.ie; Contact: Sandra Firth.

Depository Libraries

Dublin: National Library of Ireland, Kildare St, Dublin 2; tel (1) 6618811; fax (1) 6766690; Dir: Dr Patricia Donlon; Keeper of Collections: Donall O'Luanaigh; Keeper of Systems: Brian McKenna.

Dublin: Oireachtas Library, PE, Leinster House, Dublin 2; tel (1) 789911; fax (1) 785945; Librarian: M. Corcoran.

Shankill: European Foundation for the Improvement of Living and Working Conditions, Library, Information Section, Loughlinstown House, Shankill, Co Dublin; tel (1) 826888; fax (1) 826456.

ITALY

Acireale: Scuola Superiore della Pubblica Amministrazione, Biblioteca Sede di Acireale, Via Collegio Pennisi 13, 95024 Acireale; tel (095) 608732; fax

(095) 604541; e-mail sede_acireale@sspa .iunet.it; Librarian: Antonio La Ferrara.

Ancona: Univ degli Studi di Ancona, Centro Alti Studi Europei (CASE)–Sede di Ancona, Via Palestro, 60121 Ancona; tel (071) 2202344; fax (071) 2203995; e-mail biblio@palanz.unian.it; Contact: Marta Sabatini; specialized information.

Arcavacata di Rende: Univ degli Studi della Calabria, Biblioteca Interdipartimentale delle Scienze Economiche e Sociali, 87036 Arcavacata di Rende; tel (0984) 493293; fax (0984) 837210; e-mail malofe@amministrazione.unical.it; internet www.biblioteche.unical.it/sba/cde .htm; Librarian: Mario Lofeudo.

Bari: Univ degli Studi di Bari, Dipartimento di Diritto Internazionale e dell'Unione Europea, Piazza Cesare Battisti 1, 70121 Bari; tel (080) 5717337; fax (080) 5717276; e-mail doceur@lex.uniba.it; Contact: Caterina Zotti.

Benevento: Univ degli Studi del Sannio, Facoltà di Economia, Centro di Documentazione e Cultura Europea, Piazza Guerrazzi 1, 82100 Guerrazzi; tel (0824) 21599; fax (0824) 25599; e-mail cde@ unisannio.it; Contact: Angelo Forni.

Bergamo: Accademia della Guardia di Finanza, Biblioteca, Via dello Statuto 21, 24128 Bergamo; tel (035) 4324229; fax (035) 400404; e-mail uasgesd@tin.it.

Bologna: Univ degli Studi di Bologna, Istituto Giuridico 'A. Cicu', Via Zamboni 27–29, 40126 Bologna; tel (051) 2099627; fax (051) 2099624; e-mail cde@biblio.cib .unibo.it; Contact: Leonarda Martino.

Cagliari: Univ degli Studi di Cagliari, Facoltà di Giurisprudenza, Via Nicolodi 102, 09123 Cagliari; tel (070) 6753988; fax (070) 6753951; e-mail cdeoeu@unica .it; Librarians: Viviana Caponi, Luisa Murino.

Campobasso: Univ degli Studi del Molise, Biblioteca Dipartimento SEGES, Edif Polifunzionale II, Viale de Sanctis snc, 86100 Campobasso; tel (0874) 404287; fax (0874) 311124; e-mail cde@unimol.it; Contact: Dr Vincenzo Giaccio.

Caserta: Scuola Superiore della Pubblica Amministrazione, Biblioteca, Via Nazionale Appia 2/A, 81100 Caserta; tel (0823) 326622; fax (0823) 327670; e-mail giogiud@tin.it; Contact: Maria Barbato.

Catania: Univ degli Studi di Catania, Facoltà di Giurisprudenza, Istituto di Diritto Internazionale, Biblioteca, Via Gallo 24, 95124 Catania, Sicily; tel (095) 311031; fax (095) 312097; e-mail cde@ lex.unict.it; internet www.lex.unict.it/ cde; Contact: Chiara Cantarella.

Ferrara: Univ di degli Studi di Ferrara, Centro di Documentazione e Studi sulle Comunità Europee, Dipartimento di

Economia Istituzioni Territorio, Corso Ercole I d'Este 44, 44100 Ferrara; tel (0532) 291960; fax (0532) 202102; e-mail cde@economia.unife.it; internet http://cde.economia.unife.it; Contact: Sophia Salmaso; specialized information.

Florence: Archivi Storici delle Comunità Europee, Villa Il Poggiolo, Piazza Edison 11, 50133 Florence; tel (055) 4685662; fax (055) 573728; e-mail montinar@datacomm.iue.it; internet www.iue.it; Librarian: Sigrid Montinari.

Florence: Univ degli Studi di Firenze, Dipartimento di Scienza della Politica e Sociologia, Via Francesco Valori 9, 50132 Florence; tel (055) 5032411; fax (055) 5032426; e-mail cde@ccsp6.scpol.unifi.it; Librarian: Giuliana Camarlinghi Scorolli.

Genova: Univ degli Studi di Genova, C. S. B. di Economia–Facoltà di Economia, Via Vivaldi 2, 16126 Genova; tel (010) 2095211; fax (010) 2095295; e-mail faggiani@economia.unige.it; Contact: Marina Faggiani.

Lecce: Univ degli Studi di Lecce, Dipartimento di Studi Giuridici–ECOTEKNE, Via per Monteroni, 73100 Lecce; tel (0832) 322408; fax (0832) 322153; e-mail cdsue@sesia.unile.it; internet http://siba2.unile.it/cdelecce; Contacts: Anne Van den Troost, Daniela Sansonetti.

Macerata: Univ degli Studi di Macerata, Istituto di Diritto Internazionale, Piaggia dell'Università 2, 62100 Macerata; tel (0733) 258488; fax (0733) 261356; e-mail dirint@netserver.unimc.it; Librarian: Patrizia Sabbatini.

Messina: Univ degli Studi di Messina, Istituto di Studi Internazionali e Comunitari, Facoltà di Scienze Politiche, Via Nino Bixio 9, 98100 Messina, Sicily; tel (090) 2931038; fax (090) 2924448; Librarian: Gaetano Duca.

Milan: Centro Internazionale di Studi e Documentazione sulle Comunità Europee (CISDCE), Corso Magenta 61, 20123 Milan; tel (02) 48009072; fax (02) 48009067; e-mail cisdce@libero.it; internet www.cisdce.com; Contacts: Ester Terragni Friz, Adele Cerizza.

Milan: Univ Commerciale Luigi Bocconi, Biblioteca, Via R. Sarfatti 25, 20136 Milan; tel (02) 58365046; fax (02) 58365101; e-mail marisa.santarsiero@biblio.unibocconi.it; internet www.uni-bocconi.it; Librarian: Marisa Santarsiero.

Milan: Univ degli Studi di Milano, Facoltà di Scienze Politiche, Via Conservatorio 7, 20122 Milan; tel (02) 58321030; fax (02) 58312616; e-mail europa@mailserver.unimi.it; internet http://users.unimi.it/bibliosp/CDE; Contact: Lidia Diella.

Modena: Univ degli Studi di Modena, Centro di Documentazione e Ricerche sulle Comunità Europee, Via Università

4, 41100 Modena; tel (059) 2056633; fax (059) 230443; e-mail palandri.ivana@unimo.it; internet www.giurisprudenza.unimo.it/biblioteca/europe.htm; Librarian: Dr Ivana Palandri; specialized information.

Naples: Società Italiana per l'Organizzazione Internazionale (SIOI), Sezione della Campania, Villa Pignatelli, Riviera di Chiaia 200, 80121 Naples; tel (081) 667862; fax (081) 7614391; e-mail norafr@tin.it; Librarian: Nora Franchomme Ingrosso.

Padova: Univ degli Studi di Padova, Servizio Relazioni Internazionali, Via Roma 40, 35122 Padova; tel (049) 2598976; fax (049) 2598999; e-mail rossella.gilli@unipd.it; internet www.unipd.it/programmi/cde/cde; Librarian: Rossella Gilli.

Parma: Collegio Europeo di Parma, Borgo Lalatta 14, 43100 Parma; tel (0521) 207525; fax (0521) 207554; e-mail ceuropeo@libero.it; Contact: Massimiliano Valcada; specialized information.

Pavia: Univ degli Studi di Pavia, Biblioteca del Centro Studi delle Comunità Europee, Corso Strada Nuova 65, 27100 Pavia; tel and fax (0382) 23300; e-mail cde@ipv36.unipv.it; Contact: Andrea Zatti; specialized information.

Perugia: Univ degli Studi di Perugia, Biblioteca Centrale, Piazza dell'Università 1, 06100 Perugia; tel (075) 5852141; fax (075) 5852027; e-mail cde@unipg.it; Contact: Marcello Pitorri.

Pescara: Univ degli Studi 'Gabriele d'Annunzio', Istituto di Studi Giuridici, Facoltà di Economia, Viale Pindaro 42, 65127 Pescara; tel (085) 4537620; fax (085) 692480; e-mail cdepe@ibmpe.unich.it; internet www.unich.it/cde/cde; Librarian: Felice Gnagnarella; specialized information.

Pisa: Univ degli Studi di Pisa, Dipartimento di Diritto Pubblico, Sezione di Diritto Internazionale 'D. Anzillotti', Via S. Giuseppe 22, 56126 Pisa; tel (050) 562178; fax (050) 551392; e-mail rparrotta@ddpsi.unipi.it; Librarian: Rosetta Parrotta; specialized information.

Portici (Naples): Univ degli Studi di Napoli Federico II, Dipartimento di Economia e Politica Agraria, Via Università 96, 80055 Portici; tel (081) 5972315; fax (081) 7755143; e-mail iannuzzi@cds.unina.it; internet www.depa.unina.it; Contact: Antonella Iannuzzi.

Reggio di Calabria: Istituto Superiore Europeo di Studi Politici, Via Torrione 101f, CP 297, 89125 Reggio di Calabria; tel (0965) 331479; fax (0965) 331479; e-mail isespcde@tin.it; Librarian: Concetta Scoppelliti Postorino; specialized information.

Rome: Società Italiana per l'Organizzazione Internazionale (SIOI), Biblioteca, Palazzetto di Venezia, Piazza di San Marco 51, 00186 Rome; tel (06) 69207826; fax (06) 6789102; e-mail cavelli@sioi.org; internet www.sioi.org; Dir: Sara Cavelli.

Rome: Univ degli Studi 'La Sapienza', Facoltà di Economia, Biblioteca 'E. Barone', Via del Castro Laurenziano 9, 00161 Rome; tel (06) 49766889; fax (06) 491458; e-mail davi@scec.eco.uniroma1.it; internet www.eco.uniroma1.it/strutturedifacolt%E0/Barone/index2_file/centro.htm; Contact: Franco Botta.

San Domenico di Fiesole (Florence): Istituto Universitario Europea, Biblioteca, Via dei Roccettini 9, 50016 San Domenico di Fiesole; tel (055) 4685341; fax (055) 4685283; e-mail lawless@datacomm.iue.it; internet www.iue.it; Contact: Emir Lawless.

Sassari: Univ degli Studi di Sassari, Biblioteca Interfacoltà 'Antonio Pigliaru', Viale Mancini 1, 07100 Sassari; tel (079) 228919; fax (079) 228809; e-mail cde@uniss.it; internet www.uniss.it/sba/cde; Librarian: Elisabetta Pilia.

Siena: Univ degli Studi di Siena, Biblioteca 'Circolo Giuridico', Via Mattioli 10, 53100 Siena; tel (0577) 235354; fax (0577) 235358; e-mail castelliv@unisi.it; internet www.unisi.it/sbs/biblioteche/cde; Contact: Vasco Castelli.

Trento: Centro di Documentazione Europea, Provincia Autonoma di Trento, Via Romagnosi 9, 38100 Trento; tel (0461) 495087; fax (0461) 495095; e-mail cde@provincia.tn.it; internet www.provincia.tn.it/cde; Contact: Marina Marcorin.

Trieste: Univ degli Studi, Dipartimento di Scienze Giuridiche, Sezione di Diritto Internazionale e dell'Unione Europea, Piazzale Europa 1, 34127 Trieste; tel (040) 6763062; fax (040) 351092; e-mail riccio@univ.trieste.it; internet www.units.it/~cdets; Librarian: Lorenza Riccio; specialized information.

Turin: Istituto Universitario di Studi Europei, Biblioteca, Via Maria Vittoria 26, 10123 Turin; tel (011) 8394660; fax (011) 8394664; e-mail iuse@iuse.it; internet www.iuse.it; Librarian: Rosalba Cotta.

Urbino: Univ degli Studi di Urbino, Biblioteca Battiferri, Via A. Saffi 42, 61029 Urbino; tel (0722) 305576; fax (0722) 305575; e-mail s.miccoli@uniurb.it; Contacts: Maria Moranti, Sebastiano Miccoli.

Venice: Univ degli Studi 'Ca' Foscari' di Venezia, Biblioteca Centrale dell'Ateneo, Sala delle Colonne, Ca' Bernardo–Dorsoduro 3199, 30123 Venice; tel (041) 2346159; fax (041) 5229247; e-mail cde@unive.it; internet http://venus.unive.it/cde; Contact: Allesandro Bertoni.

Verona: Univ degli Studi di Verona, Facoltà di Giurisprudenza, Dipartimento di Studi Giuridici, Via Carlo Montanari 8, 37122 Verona; tel (045) 8028847; fax (045) 8028846; e-mail gianfranco .rodano@zitelle.univr.it; internet www .giurisprudenza.univr.it/fol/main; Contact: Gianfranco Rodan; specialized information.

Depository Libraries

Florence: Biblioteca Nazionale Centrale, Piazza dei Cavalleggeri 1a, 50122 Florence.

Naples: Biblioteca Nazionale Vittorio Emanuele III, Palazzo Reale, 80100 Naples.

Rome: Consiglio Nazionale delle Ricerche, Biblioteca Centrale, Direzione, Piazzale Aldo Moro 7, 00185 Rome; tel (06) 49931; fax (06) 49933834.

LATVIA

Rīga: Univ of Latvia, Dept of Political Science, Faculty of Social Science, Str. Lomonosova 1, korp. 1, 1019 Rīga; tel 708-9855; fax 708-9852; e-mail palins@ lanet.lv; Contact: Rolands Palins.

LITHUANIA
Depository Library

Vilnius: Univ of Vilnius, Inst of International Relations and Political Science, Library, Didlaukio 47 – 205, 2057 Vilnius; tel (2) 762672; fax (2) 700779; e-mail tspmi@tspmi.vu.lt; Contact: Sigita Baronaite.

LUXEMBOURG
Depository Libraries

Luxembourg: Bibliothèque du Centre Universitaire de Luxembourg, 162a ave de la Faïencerie, 1511 Luxembourg; tel 46-66-44-520; fax 46-66-44-521; Contact: Gilbert Graff; specialized information.

Luxembourg: Centre d'Etudes et de Recherches Européennes Robert Schuman; 4 rue Jules Wilhelm, 2728 Luxembourg; 478-22-90; fax 42-27-97; e-mail crs@cere.smtp.etat.lu; Contact: Mme Glaesener.

Luxembourg: Bibliothèque Nationale de Luxembourg, Erwerbungsabteilung, 37 blvd F. Roosevelt, 2450 Luxembourg; tel 22-62-55; fax 47-56-72.

MALTA

Msida: Univ of Malta, Tal-Qroqq, Msida MSD 06; tel 32902001; fax 337624; Dir: Roderick Pace.

THE NETHERLANDS

Amsterdam: Univ van Amsterdam, Library of International Law, Turfdraagsterpad 9, Postbus 19123, 1012 XT Amsterdam; tel (20) 5252161; fax (20) 5253561; e-mail bir@jur.uva.nl; internet www.jur.uva.nl/jb; Contacts: Karen Smeding, Henja Korsten.

Amsterdam: Free Univ, Amsterdam, Library of Economics, De Boelelaan 1103, 1083 HV Amsterdam; tel (20) 4445161; fax (20) 4445177; e-mail w.vd .brink@ubvu.vu.nl; internet www.ubvu .vu.nl/afdeling/rechten/edc.htm; Contacts: Wilma van den Brink, Anita Mooseker.

Enschede: Univ Twente, Campus, Gebouw 'De Vrijhof', Postbus 217, 7500 AE Enschede; tel (53) 4892242; fax (53) 4351805; e-mail y.m.h.leusink -eikelboom@ub.utwente.nl; internet www.utwente.nl/ub; Contact: Yvonne M. H. Leusink-Eikelboom.

Groningen: Rijksuniversiteit Groningen, Bibliotheek Faculteit Rechtsgeleerdheid, Harmoniegebouw, Oude Kijk in 't Jatstraat 26, 9712 EK Groningen; tel (50) 3635664; fax (50) 635603; e-mail bibliotheek@rechten.rug.nl; internet www.rug.nl/rechten/bibliotheek; Librarians: Digna J. van Boven; specialized information.

The Hague: T. M. C. Asser-Inst, R. J. Schimmelpennicklaan 20–22, Postbus 30461, 2517 JN The Hague; tel (70) 3420319; fax (70) 3420359; e-mail edc@ asser.nl; internet www.asser.nl/lib&doc/ edc; Contact: E. Gorkovoi.

Leiden: Univ Leiden, POB 9250, Hugo de Grootstraat 27, 2300 RA Leiden; tel (71) 5277534; fax (71) 5277600; e-mail r.deboer@law.leidenuniv.nl; internet www.law.leidenuniv.nl; Contacts: B. J. Bonenkamp, R. de Boer; specialized information.

Maastricht: European Inst of Public Administration (EIPA), Onze Lieve Vrouweplein 22, Postbus 1229 BE, 6211 HE Maastricht; tel (43) 3296222; fax (43) 3296296; e-mail c.monda@eipa-nl.com; internet www.eipa.nl; Contact: C. Monda.

Maastricht: Service Buro Europa, Batterijstraat 36a, 6211 SJ Maastricht; tel (43) 3250245; fax (43) 3217742; e-mail serviceburo@regr.nl; internet www.regr .nl/main.htm; Librarian: André G. E. Houpperichs.

Maastricht: Univ Maastricht, Universiteitsbibliotheek, Postbus 616, 6200 MD Maastricht; tel (43) 3883436; fax (43) 3252884; e-mail A.Bessems@ub.unimaas .nl; internet www.ub.unimaas.nl; Contact: A. Bessems.

Nijmegen: Katholieke Univ, Bibliotheek Faculteit der Rechtsgeleerdheid, Thomas van Aquinostraat 6, Postbus 9049, 6500

KK Nijmegen; tel (24) 3612518; fax (24) 3616145; e-mail edc@ubn.kun.nl; Librarian: J.A. Verbaas; specialized information.

Rotterdam: Erasmus Univ Rotterdam, Centrale Bibliotheek, Burgemeester Oudlaan 50, Postbus 1738, 3062 PA Rotterdam; tel (10) 4081205; fax (10) 4089050; e-mail vandePoll@ubib.eur.nl; internet http://web.eur.nl/ub/english/ library/collection/areas/european; Contact: M. L. van de Poll-den Hartog.

Tilburg: Katholieke Univ Brabant, Documentatiecentrum voor Internationale en Statistieken Collecties; Warandalaan 2, Postbus 90153, 5037 GC Tilburg; tel (13) 4662213; fax (13) 4662996; e-mail edc@uvt.nl; internet www .tilburguniversity.nl/services/library/ collections/europeanunion; Contact: J. M. Y. Tims; specialized information.

Utrecht: Univ Utrecht, Juridische Bibliotheek, Ganzenmarkt 32, 3512 GE Utrecht; tel (30) 2537089; fax (30) 2538409; e-mail h.zonneveld@law.uu.nl; internet www.library.law.uu.nl/edc; Librarian: C. W. G. Gofferjé Van Schaik; specialized information.

Wageningen: Landbouw Univ, Leeuwenborch Bibliotheek, Hollandsweg 1, Postbus 8130, 6706 KN Wageningen; tel (317) 482493; fax (317) 485484; e-mail bert.schuurs@pd.bib.wau.nl; internet www.agralin.nl/leeuw/home.html; Dir: B. T. P. Schuurs; specialized information.

POLAND

Gdańsk: Uniwersytet Gdańsk, Inst Ekonomii Politycznej, Osrodek Badan Integracji Europejskiej, ul Armii Krajowej 119–121, 81-824 Sopot; tel (58) 5510061; fax (58) 5511613; Contact: Iwona Fuchs-Jamroga.

Katowice: Europejska Akademia na Śląsku, Centrum Dokumentacji Europejskiej, pl Rady Europy 1, 40-021 Katowice; tel (32) 2083718; fax (32) 2083720; e-mail cde@bs.katowice.pl; internet www .bs.katowice; Pres: Dr Jacek Pietrucha.

Kraków: Kraków Univ of Economics, European Studies Dept, ul Rakowicka 27, 31-510 Kraków; tel (12) 4210954; fax (12) 2935049; e-mail ekse@ae.krakow.pl; Dir: Dr Zbigniew Rudnicki.

Łódź: Uniwersytet Łódzki, Centre for European Studies, ul Piotrkowska 262– 264, 90-361 Łódź; tel (42) 6730593; fax (42) 6730586; Contact: Radoslaw Kasprzyk.

Lublin: Marie Curie-Sklodowska Univ, Plac Litewski 3, 20-080 Lublin; tel (81) 532-42-78; fax (81) 532-66-10; e-mail cde@hektor.umcs.lublin.pl; Contact: Anna Broda.

Olsztyn: Olsztyn Univ of Agriculture and Technology, Central Library, Oczapowskiego Str 4, 10-719 Olsztyn; tel (89) 5324498; fax (89) 5240005; e-mail cde@uwm.edu.pl; internet jet.uwm.edu.pl; Chief of EDC: Magdalena Malanowicz.

Opole: Univ of Opole, Interfaculty Inst of Law and Administration, Plebiscytowa 5, 45-038 Opole; tel (77) 4566569; fax (77) 4566569; e-mail prawo@uni.opole.pl; internet www.uni.opole.pl; Contact: Tadeusz Cielecki.

Poznań: Economic Academy, ul Powstańców Wielkopolskich 16, 61-895 Poznań; tel (61) 8543320; fax (61) 8543309; Dir: Dr Renata Stawarska.

Szczecin: Szczecin Univ, Central Library, ul Mickiewicza 16, 70-384 Szczecin; tel (91) 4442360; fax (91) 4442362; e-mail info@bg.univ.szczecin.pl; internet bg.univ.szczecin.pl; Dir: Jolanta Goc; Librarian: Ariadna Wronska.

Torun: Nicolaus Copernicus Univ, Jean Monnet Centre for European Studies, ul Gagarina 13, 87-100 Torun; tel (56) 6114401; fax (56) 6542952; e-mail E.Urbanska@bu.uni.torun.pl; Contact: Edyta Urbanska.

Warsaw: Coll of Europe Natolin Library, Nowoursynowska 84, POB 120, 02-797 Warsaw 78; tel (22) 5459440; fax (22) 6491290; e-mail library@natolin.edu.pl; internet www.coleurop.be; Dir: Wiktor T. Pozniak; Contact: Marzenna Salek.

Warsaw: Instytut Koniunktur i Cen Handlu Zagranicznego (Foreign Trade Research Inst), ul Frascati 2, 00-483 Warsaw; tel (2) 8268908; fax (2) 8265562; Contact: Anna Pucek.

Warsaw: Polish Inst of International Affairs, Warecka 1a, POB 1000, 00-950 Warsaw; tel (22) 5239024; fax (22) 5239027; e-mail bibinfo@ikp.pl; Chief Librarian: Dr Malgorzata Lawacz.

Warsaw: Uniwersytet Warszawski, Centre for Europe, Al Niepodległości 22, 02-656 Warsaw; tel (22) 8450980; fax (22) 8451907; Dir: Prof Tadeusz Skoczny.

Warsaw: Warsaw School of Economics, Inst of Foreign Trade Policy and European Studies, Al Niepodległości 162, 02-554 Warsaw; tel (22) 8485061; fax (22) 8489132; Dir: Prof Lucjan Ciamaga.

Wrocław: Uniwersytet Wrocław, Dept of Law and Admin, EC Research and Documentation Centre, ul Uniwersytecka 22–26, 50-145 Wrocław; tel (71) 3402358; fax (71) 3402345; Dir: Prof Jarosław Kundera.

Depository Library

Warsaw: Council of Ministers, Al Ujazdowskie 9, 00-583 Warsaw; tel (2) 6946305; fax (22) 294888; Principal Officer: Dr Jacek Saryusz-Wolski.

PORTUGAL

Aveiro: Univ de Aveiro, Serviços de Documentação, Campus Universitário, 3810-193 Aveiro; tel (234) 370200; fax (234) 381260; e-mail sdua@doc.ua.pt; internet www.doc.ua.pt; Contact: Daniel Oliveira.

Beja: Inst Politécnico de Beja, Gabinete de Relações Exteriores, Rua de Santo António 1a, 7800-957 Beja; tel (96) 622178; fax (284) 311929; e-mail paula.mendex@ipbeja.pt; internet www.ipbeja.pt; Contact: Paula Mendes.

Braga: Univ do Minho, Escola Superior de Economia e Gestão, 1°, Sala 1.24–1.25, 4710-045 Braga; tel (53) 604519; fax (53) 676375; e-mail irene@cint01.ci.uminho.pt; Librarian: Dr Irene Rodrigues.

Castelo Branco: Inst Politécnico de Castelo Branco, Av Pedro Álvares Cabral 12, 6000-084 Castelo Branco; tel (72) 339600; fax (72) 339601; e-mail ipcb@mail.ipcb.pt; internet www.ipcb.pt; Librarian: Dr Maria da Conceição Marques Baptista.

Coímbra: Univ de Coímbra, Centro Interdisciplinar de Estudos Jurídico-Económicos (CIEJE), Rua de Aveiro 11, 11°, (Estúdio A), 3000-065 Coímbra; tel (39) 825954; fax (39) 833929; e-mail cdeuc@ci.uc.pt; internet http://dupond.ci.uc.pt/CDEUC/cdeuc.htm; Librarian: Dr Maria da Saudade Miranda.

Covilhã: Univ da Beira Interior, Edif das Ciências Sociais e Humanas, Estrada do Sineiro, 6200 Covilhã; tel (75) 319630; fax (75) 319601; e-mail cdeubi@alpha.ubi.pt; Contact: Joana Lopes Dias; specialized information, mainly in the fields of economics, regional development and statistics; f 1993.

Évora: Univ de Évora, Gabinete de Informação e Apoio (GIA), Largo dos Colegiais 2, 7002-554 Évora; tel (66) 740825; fax (66) 705831; e-mail cde@uevora.pt; Librarian: Prof Dr José Manuel Caetano; specialized information.

Faro: Univ do Algarve, Biblioteca da UCEE/Edif da Reitoria, Campus de Gambelas, 8000 Faro; tel (89) 800900; fax (89) 819025; e-mail cde@ualg.pt; Librarian: Maria João Barradas.

Funchal: Univ da Madeira, Serviços de Documentação, Polo Universitário da Penteada, 9000-390 Funchal; tel (91) 705071; fax (91) 232390; e-mail cdeuma@uma.pt; internet www.uma.pt/portal/modulos/pgeral/; Librarian: Maria Iolanda Pereira da Silva.

Leiria: Inst Politécnico de Leiria, Rua Gen Norton de Matos, 2411-901 Leiria; tel (44) 830010; fax (44) 813013; e-mail miguel@iplei.pt; internet www.ipleiria.pt/index.php?id=24; Contact: Miguel Jerónimo.

Lisbon: Univ Católica Portuguesa, Centro de Estudos Europeus, Edif João Paulo II, Rua da Palma de Cima, 1600-023

Lisbon; tel (1) 7214016; fax (1) 7266160; e-mail afg@libri.ucp.pt; internet www.libri.ucp.pt; Librarian: Dr Anna Folque de Gouveia.

Lisbon: Univ de Lisboa, Faculdade de Direito, Alameda das Universidades, Cidade Universitária, Campo Grande, 1600-214 Lisbon; tel (1) 7967624; fax (1) 7931566; e-mail maria.leal@reitoria.ul.pt; Librarian: Dr Maria Leal Vieira.

Lisbon: Univ Lusíada de Lisboa, Rua da Junqueira 188–198, 1349-001 Lisbon; tel (1) 3611617; fax (1) 3622955; e-mail cde@lis.ulusiada.pt; Contact: Maria Manuela Cardoso; specialized information.

Lisbon: Univ Nova de Lisboa, Faculdade de Economia—UNL, Travessa Estevão Pinto, Campolide, 1070-032 Lisbon; tel (1) 3801612; fax (1) 3856881; e-mail cdeunl@fe.unl.pt; internet http://portal.fe.unl.pt; Librarian: Dr Lurdes Gouveia; specialized information.

Lisbon: Univ Técnica de Lisboa, Inst Superior de Economia e Gestão, Rua das Francesinhas, 1200-078 Lisbon; tel (1) 3922878; fax (1) 3972684; e-mail cde@iseg.utl.pt; Contact: Duarte Vicente da Silva; specialized information.

Oeiras: Inst Nacional de Administração—INA, Palácio do Marquês de Pombal, 2788-540 Oeiras; tel (1) 4465452; fax (1) 4465347; e-mail cde@ina.pt; internet www.ina.pt/cedo/cde.htm; Librarian: Dr Vera Batalha.

Ponta Delgada: Univ dos Açores, Edif de Ciências Humanas, Rua da Mãe de Deus, Apdo 1422, 9502-321 Ponta Delgada, Azores Codex; tel (96) 650060; fax (96) 653245; e-mail cde@notes.uac.pt; Contact: Ana Taveira.

Porto: Univ Católica Portuguesa, Centro Regional do Porto, Faculdade de Direito/Gestão e Administração de Empresas, Rua Diogo Botelho 1327, 4150-005 Porto; tel (2) 6107290; fax (2) 6196291; e-mail mailto:cde@porto.ucp.pt; internet www.porto.ucp.pt/ucp.htm; Contacts: Dr Baião Pinto, Nuno Henriques.

Porto: Univ Lusíada do Porto, Rua Dr Lopo de Carvalho, 4300-006 Porto; tel (2) 5570811; fax (2) 5487972; e-mail cde@por.ulusiada.pt; Contact: Maria Manuela Santos Tavares de Matos Cardoso.

Porto: Univ do Porto, Faculdade de Direito, Praça Coronel Pacheco 15, 4050-453 Porto; tel (2) 2041651; fax (2) 2041654; e-mail mjp@direito.up.pt; Librarian: Dr Maria José Parreira.

Depository Library

Lisbon: Biblioteca Nacional: Campo Grande 83, 1751 Lisbon Codex; tel (1) 767639; Dir: L. Cabral; Librarian: G. Rafael.

SLOVAKIA

Bratislava: Comenius Univ, Faculty of Law, Library, Šafárikovo nám 6, 81805 Bratislava; tel (2) 5924-4111; fax (2) 5924-4401; e-mail majernikova@flaw.uniba.sk; Dir: Melánia Majerníková.

Košice: Pavel Josef Safárik Univ, Faculty of Law, Garbiarska 14, 042-07 Košice; tel (95) 622-3241; e-mail garlib@kosice.upjs.sk; internet library.upjs.sk; Dir Darina Kozuchova; Head of the Law and Science Library: Iveta Krjakova.

SLOVENIA

Ljubljana: Ekonomska Fakulteta, Univerza v Ljubljani, 1000 Ljubljana, Kardeljeva ploščad 17; tel (61) 5892400; fax (61) 5892695; e-mail efedc@uni-lj.si; Head of EDC: Dir: Prof Andrej Kumar; Documentalist and Information Officer: Katja Mlinar-Gerbec.

Maribor: European House, 2000 Maribor, Gospejna ul 10; tel (62) 215851; fax (62) 227558; e-mail petrovic@uni-mb.si; Dir: Milos Petrovič.

SPAIN

Alicante: Univ de Alicante, Edif Germán Bernácer, Campus Universitario, 03690 Alicante; tel (96) 5909800; fax (96) 5909810; e-mail carmen.arias@ua.es; internet www.cde.ua.es; Librarian: Carmen Arias Valls.

Badajoz: Univ de Extremadura, Avda de Europa 4, 06004 Badajoz; tel (924) 2411301; fax (924) 247753; e-mail cdiex@camerdata.es; internet www.cdiex.org; Librarian: Juan Carlos Salas Olgado.

Barcelona: Escuela Superior de Administración y Dirección de Empresas (ESADE), Biblioteca, Calle Marqués de Mulhacén 40–42, 08034 Barcelona; tel (93) 2806162; fax (93) 2048105; e-mail cde@esade.es; internet www.esade.edu/cde; Librarian: Ivet Castells.

Barcelona: Univ Autónoma de Barcelona, Facultad de Económicas, Edif E, Campus Universitario, 08193 Bellaterra-Barcelona; tel (93) 5811681; fax (93) 5813063; e-mail ce.doc.europea@cc.uab.es; internet http://selene.uab.es/ce-documentacio-europea; Librarian: Concepción Muñoz.

Bilbao: Univ de Deusto, Biblioteca Central, Avda de las Universidades 24, s/n Apdo 1, 48080 Bilbao; tel (94) 4139000; fax (94) 4139284; e-mail bprado@iee.deusto.es; Contact: Begoña Prado.

Bilbao: Univ del País Vasco (UPV-EHU), Facultad de Ciencias Económicas, Avda Lehendakari Agirre 83, 48015 Bilbao; tel (94) 406013651; fax (94) 4473566; e-mail bszcde@bs.ehu.es; Librarian: Rosario Martínez Perez; specialized information.

Castellón: Univ Jaume I, Campus del Riu Sec, 12071 Castellón; tel (964) 728766; fax (964) 728778; e-mail aleixand@sg.uji.es; internet http://sic.uji.es/cd/cde; Librarian: Elvira Aleixandre Baeza.

Córdoba: Univ de Córdoba, Facultad de Derecho, Puerta Nueva s/n, 2°, 14002 Córdoba; tel (957) 254962; fax (957) 261120; e-mail cde1cord@uco.es; internet www.uco.es/webuco/cde; Librarian: Magdalena Reifs López.

La Coruña: Univ de la Coruña, Facultad de Derecho, Campus de Elviña s/n, 15071 La Coruña; tel (981) 167000; fax (981) 290310; e-mail cde@udc.es; internet www.udc.es/iuee/cde; Librarian: Mar Fernández.

Getafe: Univ Carlos III, Biblioteca, Avda de Madrid 126–128, 28903 Getafe, Madrid; tel (91) 6249794; fax (91) 6249783; e-mail cde@db.uc3m.es; Librarian: Maria Teresa García Muñoz.

Girona: Univ de Girona, Biblioteca Montilivi, Campus de Montilivi, 17071 Girona; tel (972) 418218; fax (972) 418321; e-mail cde@bib.udg.es; internet http://biblioteca.udg.es/cde; Librarian: Eva Monge Fernández.

Granada: Univ de Granada, Rector López Argüeta s/n, 18071 Granada; tel (958) 248351; fax (958) 242382; e-mail cde@ugr.es; internet http://cde.ugr.es; Contact: Dolores Jerez González.

Las Palmas: Univ de Las Palmas de Gran Canaria, Biblioteca Universitaria–Biblioteca General, Campus Univ de Tafira, 35017 Las Palmas de Gran Canaria; tel (928) 458687; fax (928) 458684; e-mail cde@ulpgc.es; Librarian: Antonia Morales Comalat.

Lleida: Univ de Lleida, Servei de Biblioteca y Documentació, Avda Alcalde Rovira Roure 177, 25198 Lleida; tel (973) 752517; fax (973) 238264; e-mail cde@sbd.udl.es; internet http://pv2.sbd.es/cde/cde.html; Librarian: Rosa Xandri Canals; specialized information.

Logroño: Univ de la Rioja, Calle San José de Calasanz s/n, 26004 Logroño; tel and fax (941) 299200; e-mail cde@bib.unirioja.es; internet www.biblioteca.unirioja.es/biblio/ser/sercde.html; Librarian: Soledad Martínez.

Madrid: Univ Carlos III, Biblioteca, Avda de Madrid 126–128, 28903 Madrid; tel (91) 6249794; fax (91) 6249783; e-mail cde@db.uc3m.es; internet www.uc3m.es/cde; Contact: Maria Teresa García Muñoz.

Madrid: Univ Complutense de Madrid, Facultad de Ciencias Económicas y Empresariales, Edif Biblioteca, Campus de Somosaguas, 28223 Madrid; tel (91) 3942601; fax (91) 3942369; e-mail BUC_BEU@buc.ucm.es; internet www.ucm.es/BUCM/be; Librarian: Maria Ángeles Lacasa Otín.

Madrid: Univ Francisco de Vitoria, Biblioteca Central, Ctra Pozuelo-Majadahonda km 1.800, 28223 Pozuelo de Alarcón (Madrid); tel (91) 7091448; fax (91) 3511716; e-mail cde@fvitoria.com; internet www.ufvitoria.com; Librarian: Eva Ramón Reyero.

Madrid: Gabinete de Documentación Cientifica, Univ Politécnica de Madrid, Paseo de Juan XXIII 11, 2°, 28040 Madrid; tel (91) 3366240; fax (91) 3366258; e-mail ceyde@vga.upm.es; Dir: Carmen Plaza Ruiz.

Madrid: Univ de Alcalá de Henares, Antiguo Colegio Trinitarios, Calle Trinidad 1, 28801 Alcalá de Henares (Madrid); tel (91) 8854184; fax (91) 8855319; e-mail cdeffl@cdoc.alcala.es; internet www.alcala.es; Librarian: Flor Fernández Lopez.

Madrid: Univ Autónoma de Madrid, Facultad de Ciencias Económicas, Cantoblanco, 28049 Madrid; tel (91) 3974797; fax (91) 3975564; e-mail maria.sintes@uam.es; internet www.uam.es; Dir: Maria Sintes Olivar.

Madrid: Univ Complutense de Madrid, Inst de Estudios Europeos, Facultad de Derecho, planta baja, Avda Complutense s/n, Ciudad Universitaria, 28040 Madrid; tel (91) 3945467; fax (91) 3945513; e-mail jcdominguez@buc.ucm.es; Librarian: Juan Carlos Domínguez.

Madrid: Univ Nacional de Educación a Distancia (UNED), Calle Senda del Rey s/n, 28040 Madrid; tel (91) 3987888; fax (91) 3987889; e-mail cde@sr.uned.es; Librarian: Maria Abiega Picatoste.

Madrid: Univ Politécnica de Madrid (CEYDE), Paseo de Juan XXIII, 11 - 2°, 28040 Madrid; tel (91) 3367987; fax (91) 3366258; e-mail ceyde@vga.upm.es; internet www.upm.es/servicios/ceyde; Librarian: Gema Esteban López

Madrid: Univ San Pablo-CEU, Calle Julián Romea 22, 28003 Madrid; tel (91) 5350534; fax (91) 5350991; e-mail europa@ceu.es; internet www.ceu.es/cde; Librarian: Ascensión Gil Martin.

Murcia: Univ de Murcia, Univ de Murcia, Biblioteca General, Campus de Espinardo, 30100 Murcia; tel (968) 363015; fax (968) 363759; e-mail riera@um.es; internet www.um.es/biblioteca/info_gnral/biblio_uni/cde.html; Librarian: María Jóse Riera Esteban.

Oviedo: Univ de Oviedo, Facultad de Derecho, Dept de Derecho Público, Edif Histórico, Plaza de Riego 4, 33003 Oviedo, Asturias; tel (98) 5104065; fax (98) 5104032; e-mail cde@rectorado.uniovi.es; Librarian: Graciela López López.

Palma de Mallorca: Centre Balears Europa, Edif Conselleria d'Hisenda i Pressuposts, Calle Palau Reial 17, 07001 Palma de Mallorca; tel (971) 718989; fax (971) 714681; e-mail documentacio@ cbe.caib.es; internet www.cbe.es; Librarian: Remedios Zaforteza Fortuny; Contact: Catalina Morro Morey.

Pamplona: Univ de Navarra, Facultad de Derecho y Económicas, Campus Universitario, 31080 Pamplona; tel (948) 425634; fax (948) 425622; e-mail ccueto@ unav.es; internet www.unav.es/cee; Librarian: Carmen Cueto Luz.

Reus: Univ Rovira i Virgili, Facultat de Ciéncies Económiques i Empresarials, Avda Universitat 1, 43205 Reus; tel (977) 759806; fax (977) 759808; e-mail cde@urv.es; internet www.fcee.urv.es/ serveis/cde; Librarian: Blanca Farré Vives.

Salamanca: Univ de Salamanca, Biblioteca Francisco de Vitoria, Campus Miguel de Unamuno, Apdo 726, 37080 Salamanca; tel (923) 294400; fax (923) 294738; e-mail cde@usal.es; internet http://cde.usal.es; Librarian: Paz Llorente.

San Sebastián: Fundacion Centro de Estudios Europeos, Paseo Ramón María Lilí 6, 5°, 20002 San Sebastián; tel (943) 291877; fax (943) 291663; e-mail fundación@euroventanilla.org; internet Librarian: Miguel Ángel Cea.

Santander: Univ de Cantabria, Facultad de Ciencias Económicas y Empresariales, Avda de los Castros s/n, 39005 Santander; tel (942) 201619; fax (942) 201603; e-mail ramascor@ccaix3 .unican.es; Librarian: Rita Ramasco Puente.

Santiago de Compostela: Univ de Santiago, Facultad de Ciencias Económicas y Empresariales, Juan XXIII s/n, Bajada al Burgo, 15705 Santiago de Compostela; tel (981) 563990; fax (981) 547025; e-mail cdesec@usc.es; internet www.usc.es/cde; Librarian: Elena Fátima Pérez Carrillo.

Sevilla: Univ de Sevilla, Rectorado de la Univ, Calle San Fernando 4, 41004 Sevilla; tel (954) 213430; fax (954) 210623; e-mail mprieto@cica.es; internet www.us .es/cde; Librarian: Margarita Prieto del Rio.

Tenerife: Univ de la Laguna, Facultad de Derecho, Campus de Guajara, Camino de La Hornera s/n, 38071 La Laguna, Tenerife; tel and fax (922) 317361; e-mail cdeurop@ull.es; Librarian: Simone Panzanelli Rduch.

Toledo: Univ de Castilla-la-Mancha, Palacio Universitario Cardenal Lorenzana, Cardenal Lorenzana 1, 45002 Toledo; tel (925) 268800; fax (925) 251586; e-mail cde@.uclm.es; Librarian: Eva Moreno Alonso.

Valencia: Univ de Valencia, Biblioteca Ciencias Sociales, Campus de Tarongers, 46022 Valencia; tel (96) 3828747; fax (96) 3828746; e-mail cde@uv.es; internet www.uv.es/cde; Librarian: Alfonso Rodríguez Moreira.

Valladolid: Univ de Valladolid, Facultad de Derecho, Plaza Santa Cruz 5–3, 47002 Valladolid; tel and fax (983) 423009; e-mail cde@cdoce.uva.es; internet www .cdoce.uva.es; Dir: Mercedes Arranz Sombría; Librarian: Pilar Sanz Gil.

Zaragoza: Univ de Zaragoza, Facultad de Derecho, Calle Pedro Cerbuna 12, 50009 Zaragoza; tel (976) 761486; fax (976) 751499; e-mail cdeurop@posta .unizar.es; internet www.unizar.es/ derecho/cde/cde.html; Librarian: Loreto Usero Millán.

Depository Library

Madrid: Biblioteca Nacional, Don Juan Riviriego, Paseo de Recoletos 20, 28071 Madrid; tel (91) 4354053; fax (91) 5807876; Dirs: M. L. López-Vidriero.

SWEDEN

Gothenburg: Univ of Gothenburg, Ekonomiska Biblioteket, Vasagatan 3, POB 670, 40530 Gothenburg; tel (31) 773-48-55; fax (31) 773-43-34; e-mail gunnar .oxelqvist@ub.gu.se; Dir and Librarian: Gunnar Oxelqvist.

Jönköping: Univ of Jönköping, Library, POB 1026, 55111 Jönköping; tel (36) 157700; fax (36) 100359; e-mail bibl@ hj.se; internet www.bibl.hj.se; Contact: Inger Hjelm.

Linköping: Univ of Linköping, Universitetsbibliotek, 581 83 Linköping; tel (13) 28-10-96; fax (13) 28-29-41; e-mail annbl@bibl.liu.se; internet www.bibl .liu.se; Librarian: Anna Bladh.

Lund: Univ of Lunds, Jurisdiska Institutionen, Universiteitsbibliotek, POB 207, 221 00 Lund; tel (46) 222-10-88; fax (46) 222-11-65; e-mail annika .kaikkonen@jur.lu.se; Librarian: Annika Kaikkonen.

Örebro: Univ of Örebro, Biblioteket, 701 82 Örebro; tel (19) 30-36-18; fax (19) 33-12-17; e-mail anders.eklund@bibl.oru.se; Contact: Anders Eklund.

Stockholm: Univ of Stockholm, Universitetsbibliothek, 10 University Rd, 106 91 Stockholm; tel (8) 16-27-52; fax (8) 15-77-76; e-mail jenny.widmark@usb.su.se; Contact: Jenny Widmark; specialized information.

Sundsvall: Mitthögskolan Sundsvall, Biblioteket, Holmg. 10, 851 70 Sundsvall; tel (60) 14-89-93; fax (60) 14-88-40; e-mail patrik.sandberg@mh.se; internet www .bib.mh.se/edc/edc.html; Contact: Patrik Sandberg.

Umeå: Umeå Univ, Universitetsbibliotek, POB 1441, 901 74 Umeå; tel (90) 786-53-16; fax (90) 786-66-77; e-mail riitta.kairakari@ub.umu.se; Librarian: Riitta Kairakari-Joss.

Uppsala: Univ of Uppsala, Law Library, POB 6508, 751 38 Uppsala; tel (18) 471-33-52; fax (18) 69-56-65; e-mail margreta .arlebrand@ub.uu.se; Librarian: Margareta Ärlebrand.

Växjö: Växjö University Library, 351 95 Växjö; tel (470) 70-84-41; fax (470) 845-23; e-mail anita.johnson@bib.vxu.se; internet www.bib.vxu.se/edc; Librarian: Anita Johnson.

Depository Libraries

Stockholm: Riksdagsbiblioteket (Parliamentary Library), Storkyrkobrinken 7, 100 12 Stockholm; tel (8) 786-41-95; fax (8) 786-58-71; Dir: B. Alexanderson.

Stockholm: Statistika Centralbyran, Karlsvägen 100, POB 24300, 10451 Stockholm; tel (8) 783-50-66; fax (8) 783-40-45.

UNITED KINGDOM

Aberdeen: Univ of Aberdeen, Taylor Library, Dunbar St, Aberdeen AB24 3UB; tel (1224) 273334; e-mail e.a .mackie@abdn.ac.uk; European Information Officer: Liz Mackie; specialized information.

Aberystwyth: Univ of Wales, Hugh Owen Library, Aberystwyth SY23 3DZ; tel (1970) 622401; fax (1970) 622404; e-mail lis@aber.ac.uk; Principal Officer: Lillian Stevenson.

Ashford: Wye College, Library, Ashford TN25 5AH; tel (1233) 812401; fax (1233) 813074; e-mail w.sage@ic.ac.uk; Contact: Wendy Sage.

Bath: Univ of Bath, Univ Library, Claverton Down, Bath BA2 7AY; tel (1225) 826826; fax (1225) 826229; e-mail a.holbrook@bath.ac.uk; internet www .bath.ac.uk/library/collections/edc; Librarian: Tony Holbrook.

Belfast: Queen's Univ of Belfast, Main Library, University Rd, Belfast BT7 1LS; tel (1232) 273640; fax (1232) 323340; e-mail j.knowles@qub.ac.uk; Contact: John Knowles; specialized information.

Birmingham: Univ of Central England, Information Services, Kendrick Library, Birmingham B42 2SU; tel (121) 3315299; fax (121) 3562875; e-mail linda.garratt@ uce.ac.uk; Principal Officer: Linda Garratt; specialized information.

Birmingham: Univ of Birmingham, European Research Inst, European Resource Centre, Birmingham B15 2TT; tel (121) 4147574; fax (121) 4144691; e-mail g.a.dix@bham.ac.uk; internet www.is.bham.ac.uk/erc; Contact: Graham Dix; specialized information.

Bradford: Univ of Bradford, J. B. Priestley Library, Richmond Rd, Bradford BD7 1DP; tel (1274) 233402; fax (1274) 233398; e-mail g.l.hudson@bradford.ac.uk; internet www.brad.ac.uk/library/services/edc.php; Librarian: Grace Hudson.

Brighton: Univ of Sussex Library, Documents Section, Falmer, Brighton BN1 9QL; tel (1273) 606755; fax (1273) 678441; e-mail i.d.budden@sussex.ac.uk; Contact: Ian Budden.

Bristol: Univ of Bristol, Information Services, Wills Library, Wills Memorial Bldg, Queen's Rd, Bristol BS8 1RJ; tel (117) 9545399; fax (117) 9251870; e-mail sue.pettit@bristol.ac.uk; internet www.bris.ac.uk/is/subjects/europeanunion; Librarian: Sue Pettit; specialized information.

Cambridge: Cambridge Univ Library, Official Publs Dept, West Rd, Cambridge CB3 9DR; tel (1223) 333138; fax (1223) 333160; e-mail wan@ula.cam.ac.uk; Librarian: William A. Noblett.

Canterbury: Univ of Kent at Canterbury, Templeman Library, Canterbury, Kent CT2 7NU; tel (1227) 823111; fax (1227) 823984; e-mail s.h.carter@ukc.ac.uk; Principal Officer: Sarah Carter.

Cardiff: Univ of Wales Cardiff, Guest Library, POB 430, Colum Dr, Cardiff CF10 3XT; tel (29) 20874262; fax (29) 20874717; e-mail edc@cardiff.ac.uk; internet www.cardiff.ac.uk/schoolsanddivisions/divisions/insrv/libr; Man: Ian Thomson.

Colchester: Univ of Essex, Albert Sloman Library, POB 24, Wivenhoe Park, Colchester CO4 3UA; tel (1206) 873333; fax (1206) 872289; e-mail checkc@essex.ac.uk; internet www.essex.ac.uk/european_union/european_union.htm; Contact: Caroline Checkley; specialized information.

Coleraine: Univ of Ulster, Library, Cromore Rd, Coleraine, Co Londonderry BT52 1SA; tel (2870) 324029; fax (2870) 324928; e-mail j.e.peden@ulst.ac.uk; Contact: Janet Peden.

Coventry: Univ of Coventry, Lanchester Library, Gosford St, Coventry CV1 5DD; tel (2476) 887541; fax (2476) 887525; e-mail g.stratford@coventry.ac.uk; Librarian: Geoffrey Stratford.

Coventry: Univ of Warwick, Periodicals Dept, Library, Gibbet Hill Rd, Coventry CV4 7AL; tel (2476) 522717; fax (2476) 524211; e-mail nicola.harwood@warwick.ac.uk; Contact: Nicola Harwood.

Dundee: Univ of Dundee, Faculty of Law, Library, Perth Rd, Dundee DD1 4HN; tel and fax (1382) 344102; e-mail a.duncan@dundee.ac.uk; internet www.dundee.ac.uk/library/edc; Librarian: Anne Duncan.

Durham: Univ of Durham, Official Publications Collection, Univ Library, Stockton Rd, Durham DH1 3LY; tel (191) 374-3044; fax (191) 374-7481; e-mail mailto:n.p.davies@durham.ac.uk; internet www.dur.ac.uk/library/edc/edc.htm; Contact: Neil Davies; specialized information.

Exeter: Univ of Exeter, Centre for European Legal Studies, Law Library, Amory Bldg, Rennes Drive, Exeter EX4 4RJ; tel (1392) 263263; fax (1392) 263196; e-mail p.c.overy@ex.ac.uk; internet www.ex.ac.uk/~pcovery/lib/edc.html; Librarian: Patrick C. Overy.

Glasgow: Glasgow Univ Library, Hillhead St, Glasgow G12 8QE; tel (141) 330-6735; fax (141) 330-4952; e-mail Tania.Konn-Roberts@lib.gla.ac.uk; internet www.lib.gla.ac.uk/Depts/MOPS/EU/index.shtml; Dir: Tania Konn-Roberts.

Guildford: Univ of Surrey, George Edwards Library, Guildford GU2 5XN; tel (1483) 873363; fax (1483) 259500; e-mail j.portman@surrey.ac.uk; Contact: Shona Catto; specialized information.

Hull: Univ of Hull, Brynmor Jones Library, Cottingham Rd, Hull HU6 7RX; tel (1482) 465441; fax (1482) 466205; e-mail j.m.harrison@acs.hull.ac.uk; Contact: Jenny Harrison.

Keele: Univ of Keele, Library, Keele, Staffordshire ST5 5BG; tel (1782) 583238; fax (1782) 711553; e-mail b.g.finnemore@keele.ac.uk; internet www.keele.ac.uk/depts/li/docs/edc.htm; Librarian: Bernard Finnemore; specialized information.

Lancaster: Univ of Lancaster, Univ Library, Serials Section, Bailrigg, Lancaster LA1 4YH; tel (1524) 592539; fax (1524) 63806; e-mail m.dunne@lancaster.ac.uk; internet http://libweb.lancs.ac.uk/g55.htm; Librarian: Michael Dunne.

Leeds: Leeds Metropolitan Univ, Learning Centre, Leslie Silver Bldg, City Campus, Leeds LS1 3HE; tel (113) 283-3126; fax (113) 283-6779; e-mail ic@lmu.ac.uk; internet www.lmu.ac.uk/lss/edc; Contact: Julie Brett; specialized information.

Leeds: Univ of Leeds, Brotherton Library, 20 Lyddon Terrace, Leeds LS2 9JT; tel (113) 2335517; fax (113) 2335561; e-mail s.d.robinson@leeds.ac.uk; Contact: Simon Robinson; specialized information.

Leicester: Univ of Leicester Library, POB 248, University Rd, Leicester LE1 9QD; tel (116) 2522044; fax (116) 2522066; e-mail hmb11@leicester.ac.uk; internet www.le.ac.uk/li/sources/subject2/edc.html; Contact: Helen Young.

London: London School of Economics, British Library of Political and Economic Science, International Organization Collection, Lionel Robbins Bldg, 10 Portugal St, London WC2A 2HD; tel (20) 7955-7242; fax (20) 7955-7454; e-mail m.bell@lse.ac.uk; Contact: Maria Bell.

London: Queen Mary and Westfield College, Library, Mile End Road, London E1 4NS; tel (20) 7882-3306; fax (20) 8981-0028; e-mail n.d.holloway@qmw.ac.uk; Contact: Nick Holloway.

London: Univ of North London, The Learning Centre, 236–250 Holloway Rd, London N7 6PP; tel (20) 7753-5142; fax (20) 7753-5079; e-mail j.bacchus@unl.ac.uk; Contact: Joan Bacchus.

Loughborough: Loughborough Univ, Pilkington Library, Serials Office, Loughborough LE11 3TU; tel (1509) 222351; fax (1509) 223993; e-mail l.a.mcgarry@lboro.ac.uk; Principal Officer: Laurie McGarry.

Manchester: Univ of Manchester, John Rylands Library, Oxford Rd, Manchester M13 9PP; tel (161) 275-3770; fax (161) 273-7488; e-mail h.i.blackhurst@man.ac.uk; Librarian: Dr Hector I. Blackhurst; specialized information.

Newcastle upon Tyne: University of Northumbria Library, Ellison Place, Newcastle upon Tyne NE1 8ST; tel (191) 227-4136; fax (191) 227-4563; e-mail maimie.balfour@unn.ac.uk; internet: www.unn.ac.uk/central/isd/ec.htm; Principal Officer: Maimie Balfour; specialized information.

Norwich: Univ of East Anglia, Library, University Plain, Norwich NR4 7TJ; tel (1603) 592412; fax (1603) 259490; e-mail j.marsh@uea.ac.uk; Principal Officer: William Marsh.

Nottingham: Nottingham Univ, Hallward Library, Nottingham NG7 2RD; tel (115) 951-4579; fax (115) 951-4558; e-mail susan.heaster@nottingham.ac.uk; internet www.nottingham.ac.uk; Librarian: Susan Heaster.

Oxford: Univ of Oxford, Bodleian Law Library, St Cross Bldg, Manor Rd, Oxford OX1 3UR; tel (1865) 271463; fax (1865) 271475; e-mail edc@bodley.ox.ac.uk; Contacts: Robert Logan, Margaret Watson.

Portsmouth: Univ of Portsmouth, Frewen Library, Cambridge Rd, Portsmouth PO1 2ST; tel (23) 92843239; fax (23) 92843233; e-mail ian.mayfield@port.ac.uk; Librarian: Ian Mayfield.

Reading: Univ of Reading, Main Library, Whiteknights, POB 223, Reading RG6 6AE; tel (118) 9318782; fax (118) 9312335; e-mail library-edc@reading.ac.uk; internet www.reading.ac.uk/libweb; Contact: Christine Milne.

Salford: Univ of Salford, Academic Information Services, Clifford Whitworth Bldg, Salford M5 4WT; tel (161) 2953185; fax (161) 2955888; e-mail m.p .carrier@ais.salford.ac.uk; Contact: Michael Carrier; specialized information.

Sheffield: Sheffield Hallam University, Adsetts Centre, City Campus, Howard St, Sheffield S1 1WB; tel (114) 225-2126; fax (114) 225-2125; e-mail p.f .gledhill@shu.ac.uk; Contact: Peter Gledhill.

Southampton: Southampton Univ, Hartley Library, Highfield, Southampton, Hants SO17 5BJ; tel (23) 80593451; fax (23) 80593007; e-mail whw@soton.ac .uk; internet www.library.soton.ac.uk/ subjects/edc/index.shtml; Contact: Wendy White; specialized information.

Wolverhampton: Univ of Wolverhampton, Harrison Learning Centre, St Peter's Square, Wolverhampton WV1 1RH; tel (1902) 322300; fax (1902) 322194; e-mail m.pope@wlv.ac.uk; Librarian: Marion Pope; specialized information.

Depository Libraries

Edinburgh: Univ of Edinburgh, Law and Europa Library, Old College, South Bridge, Edinburgh EH3 9YL; tel (131) 650-2041; fax (131) 650-6343; e-mail stevensonej@SRV4.lib.ed.ac.uk; internet www.lib.ed.ac.uk/sites/law.shtml; Librarian: Elizabeth J. Stevenson.

Liverpool: Business and Information Library, William Brown St, Liverpool L3 8EW; tel (151) 225-5434; fax (151) 207-1342; e-mail lvpublic@demon.co.uk; Librarian: Ruth Grodner.

London: Westminster Reference Library, 35 St Martin's St, London WC2H 7HP; tel (020) 7798-2034; fax (020) 7798-2040; Librarian: Kathleen Oxenham.

Wetherby: c/o EU Liaison Officer, British Library, Document Supply Centre, Boston Spa, Wetherby, Yorks LS23 7BQ; tel (1937) 546044; fax (1937) 546453; e-mail andrew.smith@bl.uk; Librarian: Andrew Smith.

European Documentation Centres (EDCs) in Non-Member States

ALGERIA

Algiers: Inst National d'Etudes et de Stratégie Globale, route les Vergers, BP 137, Birkhadem, Algiers; tel (2) 54-16-29; Dir: Lounès Bourenane.

ANGOLA

Luanda: Centro de Documentação Europeia, Univ Católica de Angola, Biblioteca, Rua Nossa Senhora da Muxima 29, 2064 Luanda; tel (2) 331973; fax (2) 398759; e-mail info@ucan.edu; internet www .ucan.edu; Contact: José Alves Cachadinha.

ARGENTINA

European Reference Centres

Buenos Aires: Biblioteca del Congreso de la Nación, Calle Adolfo Alsina 1861, 1°, 1090 Buenos Aires; tel (1) 40-7657; fax (1) 49-3854; Dir: I. Segura de Varela.

Buenos Aires: Centro de Investigaciones Europeo-Latinoamericanas (EURAL), Corrientes 2554, 3A 'A', 1046 Buenos Aires; tel (1) 951-4504; fax (1) 953-1539; Dir: A. A. Baron.

Buenos Aires: Inst para la Integración de América Latina y el Caribe, Esmeralda 130, 16°–17°, 1035 Buenos Aires; tel (1) 320-1850; fax (1) 320-1865; e-mail int/ inl@iadb.org; internet www.iadb.org/ intal; Dir: Dr Juan José Taccone.

Buenos Aires: Inst Torcuato di Tella, 11 de Setiembre 2193, 1428 Buenos Aires.

Buenos Aires: Univ Argentina de la Empresa, Biblioteca Central, Azcu Naja 1625, 1028 Buenos Aires; tel (1) 821-9693; Dir: R. Loehe.

Buenos Aires: Univ de Buenos Aires, Facultad de Ciencias Económicas, Biblioteca, CP 1120, Avda Córdoba 2122, Buenos Aires.

Buenos Aires: Univ de Buenos Aires, Facultad de Derecho y Ciencias Sociales, Inst de Derecho Internacional Público, Avda Figeora Alcorta 2263, 1245 Buenos Aires.

Buenos Aires: Univ del Salvador, Inst de Investigación en Ciencias Sociales (IDISCO), Facultad de Ciencias Sociales, Teniente General Juen D. Leron 1818, 1089 Buenos Aires; tel (1) 40-0922; Dir: E. Margiotta.

Córdoba: Univ Católica, Inst de Ciencias de la Administración, CEPADE-CIPEAP-CIPAC, Obispo Trejo 323, 5000 Córdoba; tel (51) 23-5331; fax (51) 23-1937.

La Plata: Univ Nacional de la Plata, Facultad de Ciencias Jurídicas y Sociales, Biblioteca 'Joaquín V. Gonzales', Calle 48 E/6 y 7PB, 1900 La Plata.

Mendoza: Univ Nacional de Cuyo, Biblioteca Central, Casilla de Correo 420, 5500 Mendoza; tel 25-7463; Dir: Juan Guillermo Milia.

Santa Fe: Univ Nacional del Litoral, Facultad de Ciencias Jurídicas y Sociales, Inst de Derecho Internacional, Cándido Pujato 2751, 3000 Sante Fe; tel (42) 41429; Librarian: B. Pallares.

AUSTRALIA

Nedlands: Univ of Western Australia, Business Library, 35 Stirling Highway, Nedlands, WA 6009; tel (8) 9380-7056; fax (8) 9380-1888; e-mail snick@library .uwa.edu.au; Dir: Scott Nicholls.

Sydney: Univ of New South Wales, Law Library, Sydney, NSW 2052; tel (2) 9385-3789; fax (2) 9385-1236; e-mail s.knowles@unsw.edu.au; Contact: Susan Knowles.

Victoria: Monash Univ, Sir Louis Matheson Library, Wellington Rd, Victoria 3800; tel (3) 9905-2654; fax (3) 9905-9142; e-mail susan.little@lib .monash.edu.au; Contact: Sue Little; specialized information

Depository Libraries

Adelaide: Univ of Adelaide, Barr Smith Library, Adelaide, SA 5000; tel (8) 8303-5345; fax (8) 8303-4369; e-mail peter .jacobs@adelaide.edu.au; Dir: Peter Jacobs.

Brisbane: Univ of Queensland, Law Library, St Lucia Campus, Brisbane Qld 4072; tel (7) 3365-1482; fax (7) 3365-1552; e-mail j.rees@library.uq.edu .au; Contact: Jan Rees.

Bundoora: La Trobe Univ, Borchardt Library, Bundoora, Vic 3083; tel (3) 9479-1922; fax (3) 9471-0993; e-mail m.hyslop@latrobe.edu.au; Contact: Margo Hyslop.

Canberra: National Library, Parkes Place, Canberra, ACT 2600; tel (2) 6262-1317; fax (2) 6273-4322; e-mail chulse@ nla.gov.au; Contact: Christine Hulse.

Hobart: Univ of Tasmania, Law Library, GPO Box 252-62, Hobart, Tas 7001; tel (3) 6226-2231; fax (3) 6226-7642; e-mail graeme.rayner@utas.edu.au; Contact: Graeme Rayner.

Melbourne: State Library of Victoria (Base DEP), 328 Swanson St, Melbourne, Vic 3000; tel (3) 8664-7003; fax (3) 9639-2978; e-mail info@expressinfo.com.au; Contact: Lisa Peddey.

Parkville: Univ of Melbourne, Baillieu Library, Parkville, Vic 3052; tel (3) 9344-5377; fax (3) 9348-1142; e-mail s.ward@ lib.unimelb.edu.au; Dir: Shirley Ward.

Sydney: State Library of NSW, Macquarie St, Sydney, NSW 2000; tel (2) 9273-1421; fax (2) 9273-1268; e-mail: lravalico@slnsw.gov.au; Contact: Laura Ravalico.

Sydney: Univ of Sydney, Fisher Library, Sydney, NSW 2006; tel (2) 9351-5679; fax (2) 9351-4328; e-mail r.penn@library .usyd.edu.au; Dir: Ray Penn.

BELARUS

Minsk: Belarusian State Univ, Faculty of Int Relations, 220050 Minsk, pr F. Skaryny 4/112; tel and fax (17) 209-54-46; e-mail tchebotarev@bsu.by; internet www.ced.bsu.by; Contacts: Yuori Tchebotarev, Vorotilina Victoria.

BOSNIA AND HERZEGOVINA

Sarajevo: Ekonomski Institut, Branilaca Sarajeva 47, 71000 Sarajevo; tel (33) 442567; fax (33) 664067; Contact: Senadin Fazlibegovič.

BRAZIL

Rio de Janeiro: Univ Federal do Rio de Janeiro, Instituto de Filosofia e Ciências Sociais, Largo de São Francisco 1, S/325-D, 20051-070 Rio de Janeiro, RJ; tel (21) 221-0341; fax (21) 221-1470; e-mail trein@ifcs.ufrj.br; internet www.ifcs.ufrj.br/cde; Dir: Franklin Trein.

São Paulo, SP: Escola de Administração de Empresa de São Paulo da Fundação Getúlio Vargas, EAESEP/FGV, Av 9 de Julho 2029, 1313 São Paulo, SP; tel (11) 284-2311.

BULGARIA

Plovdiv: Plovdiv Univ 'Paisii Hilendarski', 24 Tsar Assen Str, 4000 Plovdiv; tel (32) 630955; fax (32) 630955; e-mail irinatch@pu.acad.bg; Contact: Irina Chongarova.

Sofia: Bulgarian Acad of Sciences, Inst for European Studies and Information, 1125 Sofia, blvd G. M. Dimitrov 52a; tel (2) 971-24-11; fax (2) 70-74-43; e-mail mira@mail.cesbg.org; internet www.cesbg.org; Contact: Miroslava Pigova.

Varna: Municipal Centre for European Integration, ul Shipka 2, 9000 Varna; tel (52) 60-16-28; fax (52) 60-16-38; e-mail edcvarna@hotmail.com; Dir: Svetla Lefterova.

Veliko Turnovo: Veliko Turnovo Univ, Faculty of Economics and Law, Library (European Division), Sq. Centre 2, POB 345, 5000 Veliko Turnovo; tel (62) 605060; fax (62) 30048; e-mail edc@coe.veliko-turnovo.com; internet www.coe.veliko-turnovo.com; Contact: Gergana Daskalova.

Depository Library

Sofia: St Cyril and St Methodius National Library, Official Publs Section, 1504 Sofia, V. Levski 88; tel 88-28-11; fax 43-54-95; e-mail nbkm@bgcict.acad.bg; Dir: Dr Kiril Topalov.

CANADA

Edmonton: Univ of Alberta, Govt Publications, Humanities and Social Sciences Library, 1-101 Rutherford South, Edmonton, Alberta, T6G 2J8; tel (780) 492-3794; fax (780) 492-5083; e-mail lindsay.johnston@ualberta.ca; Contact: Lindsay Johnston.

Kingston: Queen's Univ, Documents Library, Mackintosh-Corry Hall, Kingston, ON K7L 5C4; tel (613) 545-6313; fax (613) 533-6819; e-mail: johnsons@post.queensu.ca; Contact: Sheila Johnson.

Depository Libraries

Halifax: Dalhousie Univ, Killam Memorial Library, Govt Documents Dept, Halifax, NS B3H 4H8; tel (902) 424-3634; fax (902) 494-2319; e-mail: pbross@dal.ca; contact: Phyllis Ross.

Montréal: McGill Univ, Govt Documents Dept, McLennan Library, 3459 McTavish St, Montréal, PQ H3A 1Y1; tel (514) 398-4737; fax (514) 398-7184; e-mail phyllis.rudin@library.mcgill.ca; Contact: Phyllis Rudin; specialized information.

Montréal: Univ de Montréal, BLSH—Publications Officielles, Pav. Samuel-Bronfman, CP 6128, Succursale A, Montréal, PQ H3C 3J7; tel (514) 343-7972; e-mail Nicole.tremblay.1@umontreal.ca; contact: Nicole Tremblay; specialized information.

Ottawa: Carleton Univ Library, Maps, Data and Govt Information Centre, 1125 Colonel By Drive, Ottawa, ON K1S 5B6; tel (613) 788-2600; fax (613) 520-2572; e-mail: Joanne_Cameron@carleton.ca; Contact: Joanne Cameron.

Ottawa: Bibliothèque Nationale du Canada, Section des Dons et Echanges, Bureau 215, 395 rue Wellington, Ottawa, ON K1A 0N4; tel and fax (819) 997-9545; e-mail celeste.blanco@nlc-bnc.ca; Dirs: Marianne Scott, Celeste A. Blanco.

Sainte Foy: Univ Laval, Bibliothèque, Pav. Jean-Charles-Bonenfant, Division des Acquisitions, Cité Universitaire, Ste Foy, PQ G1K 7P4; tel (418) 656-2131; e-mail Christine.Lachance@bibl.ulaval.ca; contact: Christine Lachance

Saskatoon: Univ of Saskatchewan, Library, Govt Publs Section, Saskatoon, SK S7N 0W0; tel (306) 966-5989; fax (306) 966-6040; e-mail: mary.tastad@usask.ca; Contact: Mary Tastad.

Toronto: Univ of Toronto, John P. Robarts Library, Serials Dept, Toronto, ON M5S 1A5; tel (416) 978-3931; e-mail: s.smugler@utoronto.ca; Contact: Sherry Smugler.

Winnipeg: Univ of Manitoba, Govt Publs Section, Elizabeth Dafoe Library, Winnipeg, MB R3T 2N2; tel (204) 474-6361; fax (204) 275-2597; e-mail: hugh_larimer@umanitoba.ca; Contact: Hugh Larimer.

Wolfville: Acadia Univ, Govt Documents Dept, Vaughan Memorial Library, POB 4, Wolfville, NS B4P 2R6.

CHILE

Santiago: Pontificia Univ Católica de Chile, Inst de Ciencia Política, Centro de Estudios Europeos, Avda Bernardo O'Higgins 340, Santiago; tel and fax (2) 222-4516; Dir: O. Godoy; specialized information.

CHINA, PEOPLE'S REPUBLIC

Beijing: Beijing Univ, Centre for European Studies, Univ Campus, Haidian District, 100871 Beijing; tel (10) 62755367; fax (10) 62751650; e-mail eucenter@pku.edu.cn; Contact: Jingjing Chen.

Shanghai: Fudan Univ, Inst of World Economy, 220 Handan Rd, Shanghai 200433; tel (21) 65642268; fax (21) 65646456; e-mail ces@fudan.edu.cn; internet www.fudan.edu.cn; Dir: Prof Dai Bingran.

Depository Libraries

Beijing: National Library of China, UN Materials Section, 7 Wen Jin St, Beijing; tel (1) 8315566; Dir: Ren Jiyu.

Beijing: Chinese Acad of Social Sciences, Centre for EU Studies, Inst for European Studies, 5 Jian Guo Nei Da Jie, Beijing 100732; tel (10) 55138428; fax (10) 65125818; e-mail iescass@public3.bta.net.cn; Dir: Prof Zhou Rongyao.

Chengdu: Sichuan Union Univ, Economics Dept, Chengdu, Sichuan 610064; tel (28) 5412409; fax (28) 5410473; e-mail cwzhao@scuu.esu.cn; Dir: Prof Shi Jian; Librarian: Wang Shijun.

Tianjin: Nan-Kai Univ, Dept of Int Economics, Economics Bldg, 94 Weijin Rd, Tianjin 300071; tel and fax (22) 23509676; e-mail lliping@public1.tpt.tj.cn; Dir: Prof Chen Zhiqiang.

Wuhan: Wuhan Univ, Inst of the Study of the Economy of Western Europe, Dept of Economics, Wuhan, Hubei 430072; tel (27) 87689377; fax (27) 87654745; e-mail wucentre@public.wh.hb.cn; Dir: Prof Zeng Lingliang; Librarian: Xiao Yucai.

CHINESE SPECIAL ADMINISTRATIVE REGION

Hong Kong: Hong Kong Baptist Univ, Faculty of Social Sciences, Room DLB

803A, David C. Lam Bldg, Shaw Campus, Kowloon Tong, Hong Kong; tel 23395701; fax 23395702; e-mail edc@hkbu.edu.hk; internet www.hkbu.edu.hk/%7Eeurope/edc/edcen/starten.htm; Dir: Terence T. Yeung.

Depository Library

Hong Kong: Univ of Hong Kong, Pokfulam Rd, Hong Kong; tel 8592200; fax 8589420; Dir: Dr L. B. Kan.

CHINA (TAIWAN)

Depository Library

Taipei: Tamkang Univ, Graduate Inst of European Studies, Cheuh-Sheng Memorial Library, Tamshui, 151 Ying-Chuan Rd, Taipei 25137; tel (2) 262-156-56; fax (2) 262-351-40; Research Asst: Shiou-Iuan Hsu.

CROATIA

Zagreb: Univ of Zagreb, Inst for Devt and Int Relations (IRMO), 10000 Zagreb, ul Ljudevita Farkaša Vukotinoviča 2, POB 303; tel (1) 4826522; fax (1) 4828361; e-mail edc@irmo.hr; internet www.imo.hr/edc/index.html; Contact: Visnja Samardzija.

INDIA

Calcutta: Nat Library, Foreign Officials Documentation Div, Belvedere, Calcutta 700 027; tel (33) 455381; fax (33) 4791462.

Mumbai (Bombay): Council of EC Chambers of Commerce, Y. B. Chavan Centre, 3rd Floor, Gen J. Bhosale Marg, Mumbai 400 021; tel (22) 2854563.

New Delhi: Delegation of the European Commission, 65 Golf Links, New Delhi 110 003; tel (11) 46292237.

New Delhi: Indian Council of World Affairs, Sapru House, Barakhamba Rd, New Delhi 110 001; tel (11) 3317246; Librarians: Man Singh Deora, A. Jambhekar.

New Delhi: Jawaharlal Nehru Univ, Central Library, New Campus, New Mehrauli Rd, New Delhi 110 067.

New Delhi: Parliament House, Library, New Delhi 110 001.

Pune: Servants of India Society, Pune 411 004; tel (212) 54287.

ISRAEL

Ramat Gan: Bar-Ilan Univ, Faculty of Law, Law Library, Ramat Gan 52900; tel (3) 5318360; fax (3) 5354552; Dir: E. Snyder.

Tel-Aviv: Tel-Aviv Univ, Brender-Moss Library for Social Sciences and Management, POB 39654, Ramat-Aviv, Tel-Aviv 61396; tel (3) 6407757; fax (3) 6409527; e-mail hmre@taulib.tau.ac.il; internet www.tau.ac.il/soclib; Contact: Hemda Levi.

Depository Library

Jerusalem: Jewish National and Univ Library, European Union Collection, Gen Reading Rm, POB 34165, Jerusalem 91341; tel (2) 6584651; fax (2) 6511771; Dir: Prof Sara Japhet; Librarian: S. Benvenisti; specialized information.

JAPAN

Fukuoka: Seinan Gakuin Univ Library, 6-2-92, Nishijin, Sawara-ku, Fukuoka 814-0002; tel (92) 823-3410; fax (92) 823-3480; e-mail t-furush@staff.seinan-gu.ac.jp; internet www.seinan-gu.ac.jp; Dir: N. Kawashima.

Fukuyama: Fukuyama Univ, Central Library, Sanzo, 1, Gakuencho, Fukuyama-shi, Hiroshima 729-0292; tel (849) 36-2111; fax (849) 36-1589; Dir: H. Ishida.

Kagawa: Kagawa Univ Library, Takamatsu-shi, 1-1 Saiwai-cho, Kagawa-ken 760-8525; tel (878) 32-1249; fax (878) 32-1257; internet www.lib.kagawa-u.ac.jp; Dir: T. Sato.

Kanazawa: Kanazawa Univ, Central Library, Kakuma-machi, Kanazawa City, 920-1192 Ishikawa-ken; tel (762) 64-5211; fax (762) 64-5208; internet www.lib.kanazawa-u.ac.jp; Dir: T. Searashi.

Kobe: Kobe Univ of Commerce, Inst of Economic Research, 8-2-1 Gakuen-nishi-machi, Nishi-ku, Kobe 651-2197; tel (78) 794-6161; fax (78) 794-6166; internet www.kobeuc.ac.jp; Dir: K. Nomura.

Kyoto: Doshisha Univ, Library and Information Technology Centre, Karasuma-Higashi-iru, Imadegawa-dori, Kamigyo-ku, Kyoto 602-8580; tel (75) 251-3980; fax (75) 251-3058; e-mail ji-edc@mail.doshisha.ac.jp; internet www.doshisha.ac.jp/gakujo; Dir: T. Kanamaru.

Nagoya: Nagoya Univ, Library of Faculty of Economics, Furoh-cho, Chikusa-ku, Nagoya 464-8601; tel (52) 789-4922; fax (52) 789-2364; internet www.soec.nagoya-u.ac.jp; Dir: K. Yamazaki.

Okinawa: Univ of Ryukyu Library, 1 Senbaru, Nishihara-cho, Nakagami-gun, Okinawa 903-0126; tel (98) 895-8168; fax (98) 895-2252; e-mail kokusai@lib.u-ryukyu.ac.jp; internet www.lib.u-ryukyu.ac.jp/kokusai/index.html; Dir: S. Yamashiro.

Osaka: Kansai Univ Library, Suita-shi, 3-3-35 Yamate-cho, Osaka 564-8680; tel (6) 368-0267; fax (6) 337-5460; internet www.kansai-u.ac.jp/Library/home.htm; Dir: Y. Takashima.

Osaka: Osaka City Univ, Media Centre, Library, 3-3-138 Sugimoto, Sumiyoshi-ku, Osaka 558-8585; tel (6) 605-3250; fax (6) 605-3252; e-mail lib-ref@media.osaka-cu.ac.jp; internet http://libser.media.osaka-cu.ac.jp/index-e.html; Contact: T. Matsuda.

Sapporo: Hokkaido Univ Library, Kita-8, Nishi-5, Kitaku, Sapporo 060-0808; tel (11) 706-2973; fax (11) 746-4595; internet www.lib.hokudai.ac.jp; Dir: K. Ohno.

Sendai: Tohoku Univ, Central Library, Kawauchi, Aoba-ku, Sendai-shi, Miyagi-ken 980-8554; tel (22) 217-5935; fax (22) 217-5949; internet www.library.tohoku.ac.jp; Dir: H. Ohnishi.

Shizuoka: Nihon Univ, Coll of Int Relations Library, Bunkyo-cho 2-31-145, Mishima-shi, Shizuoka-ken 411-8555; tel (559) 80-0860; fax (559) 88-7875; internet www.ir.nihon-u.ac.jp; Dir: T. Nakazawa.

Tokyo: Chuo Univ, Central Library, Int Documents Rm, 742-1 Higashi Nakano, Hachioji-shi, Tokyo 192-0393; tel (426) 74-2591; fax (426) 74-2514; internet www.chuo-u.ac.jp; Dir: S. Sasahara.

Tokyo: Hitotsubashi Univ Library, 2-1 Naka, Kunitachi-shi, Tokyo 186-8602; tel (425) 80-8239; fax (425) 80-8232; internet www.lib.hit-u.ac.jp/service; Dir: Y. Otani.

Tokyo: Keio Univ—Mita Media Centre, Keio Library, 2-15-45 Mita, Minato-ku, Tokyo 108-8345; tel (3) 5427-1664; fax (3) 5427-1665; internet www.mita.lib.keio.ac.jp; Dir: A. Kaneko.

Tokyo: Sophia Univ, Central Library, 7-1 Kioi-cho, Chiyoda-ku, Tokyo 102-8554; tel (3) 3238-3507; fax (3) 3238-3055; internet www.sophia.ac.jp; Dir: J. Fernandez.

Tokyo: Univ of Tokyo Library, 7-3-1 Hongo, Bunkyo-ku, Tokyo 113-0033; tel (3) 5841-2645; (3) 5841-2658; e-mail kokusai@lib.u-tokyo.ac.jp; internet www.lib.u-tokyo.ac.jp/undepo; Dir: Pierre Del Grande.

Tokyo: Waseda Univ, Inst for Research in Contemporary Political and Economic Affairs, 1-6-1 Nishiwaseda, Shinjuku-ku, Tokyo 169-8050; tel (3) 3204-8960; fax (3) 3204-8961; internet www.wul.waseda.ac.jp/index-j.html; Dir: S. Fukuda.

Depository Library

Tokyo: National Diet Library, Int Co-operation Division, 1-10-1, Nagata-cho, Chiyoda-ku, Tokyo 100-8924; tel (3) 3581-2331; fax (3) 3597-9104; e-mail kokusai@ndl.go.jp; internet www.ndl.go.jp; Head of Int Co-operation Division: Akira Kado.

KAZAKHSTAN

Almaty: Al-Farabi Kazakh State Nat Univ, Int Relations Dept, 480121 Almaty, pr Al-Farabi 71; tel (3272) 42-87-03; fax (3272) 42-53-67.

REPUBLIC OF KOREA

Pusan: Pusan National Univ, Central Library, 30 San Changjong-dong, Kumjeong-gu, Pusan 609-735; tel (51) 510-1800; fax (51) 512-9049; Dir: Prof Heo Mane.

Seoul: Hankuk Univ of Foreign Studies, Inst of Western Europe Studies, 89 Wangsan, Mohyeon, Youngin, Kyungki-do, Seoul 449-791; tel (2) 961-4281; fax (2) 969-7596; Dir: Prof Bung-Ik Zhang.

Seoul: Korea Univ, Central Library, 1, 5-ka, Anam-dong, Sungbuk-ku, Seoul 136-701; tel (2) 3290-1492; fax (2) 922-5820; Dir: Prof Hun-Geun Yeo.

Seoul: Seoul National Univ, Graduate Inst for International and Area Studies, San 56-1, Shillim-dong, Kwanak-gu, Seoul 151-742; tel (2) 880-8717; fax (2) 889-0193; Dir: Prof Won-Tack Hong.

MACAO

Macao: Univ of Macao, Library, POB 3001, Taipa, Macao; tel 3974434; fax 8930888; e-mail libhi@umac.mo; Contact: Helen Hoi Keng Ieong.

FORMER YUGOSLAV REPUBLIC OF MACEDONIA

Skopje: Univ 'Sv Kiril i Metodij' (St Cyril and Methodius Univ of Skopje), Faculty of Economics, 91000 Skopje, POB 550, bul Krste Misirkov bb; tel (91) 223245; fax (91) 118701; e-mail valentina@eccf.ukim .edu.mk; internet www.eccf.ukim.edu .mk; Documentalist and Head of Library: Valentina Ganzovska.

MALAYSIA

Kuala Lumpur: European Business Information Centre, Wisma Hong Leong, 7th Floor, 18 Jalan Park, 50450 Kuala Lumpur; tel (3) 2626298; fax (3) 2626198.

MOROCCO

Casablanca: Univ Hassan II, Faculté des Sciences Juridiques, Économiques et Sociales, Aïn Chock, route d'El Jadida, BP 8110, Oasis, Casablanca; Contact: Kouhlani El Bachir.

NEW ZEALAND

Auckland: Univ of Auckland, Davis Law Library, Private Bag 92019, Auckland; tel (9) 373-7599; fax (9) 373-7467; e-mail ma.russell@auckland.ac.nz; Contact: Mary Rose Russell.

Auckland: Auckland City Library, 44 Lorne St, Auckland 1; tel (9) 307-7787; fax (9) 307-7793; email: cameronn@akcity .govt.nz; Contact: Natalie Cameron.

Christchurch: Univ of Canterbury, Library, Private Bag 4800, Christchurch 1; tel (3) 366-8891; fax (3) 364-2055; e-mail j.nicolle@libr.canterbury.ac.nz; Dir: Janette Nicolle.

Wellington: New Zealand Parliamentary Library, Parliamentary Bldgs, Wellington; tel (644) 471-9611; fax (644) 471-2551; e-mail: intdoc@parliament.govt.nz; Contact: Felicity Rashbrooke.

Depository Libraries

Wellington: Int Documents Collection, Parliamentary Library, Parliament Bldgs, Wellington; tel (4) 471-9623; fax (4) 471-1250; Int Documents Librarian: Katherine Close.

NORWAY

Bergen: Univ of Bergen, Høyteknologi-senteret, Library, Dragefjellet, 5020 Bergen; tel 55-58-95-95; fax 55-58-95-22; e-mail edc@ub.uib.no; internet www.ub .uib.no/avdeling/edc/index.htm; Dir: Liv Glasser.

Kristiansand: Hogskolen I Agder, Tordenskioldsgatan 65, 4604 Kristiansand; tel 38-14-17-86; fax 38-14-16-01; e-mail ragnhild.jensen@hia.no; Dir: Ragnhild Jensen.

Oslo: Univ of Oslo, POB 6713, St Olav's plass, 0130 Oslo; tel 22-85-93-52; fax 22-85-96-10; e-mail ingerha@ulrik.uio.no; internet www.ub.uio.no/ujur/instbibl/ eu/; Dir: Inger Hamre.

Trondheim: Norwegian Univ of Science and Technology, NTNU Library, Collection Development Gunnerus-Exchange/ Gifts, Erling Skakkesgt 47c, 7491 Trondheim; tel 73-59-22-05; fax 73-59-20-41; Dir: Aud Lamvik.

Depository Library

Oslo: Det Norske Nobelinstitutt (Norwegian Nobel Inst), Biblioteket, Drammensveien 19, 0255 Oslo; tel 22-44-20-63; fax 22-43-01-68; e-mail ack@nobel.no; internet www.nobel.no; Head Librarian: Anne C. Kjelling.

PERU

Lima: Univ Católica del Perú, Instituto de Estudios de la Pontificia, Rufino Torrico 1164, Plaza Francia, Lima 1; tel (1) 62-25-40; fax (1) 221-11-94; e-mail cdeurop@pucp.edu.pe; Contact: María Isabel Merino.

PHILIPPINES

Manila: De la Salle Univ, Library, 2401 Taft ave, Malate, Manila City 1004; tel (2) 5265917; fax (2) 5240361; e-mail libjll@ mail.dlsu.edu.ph; Contact: Jocelyn Ladlad.

ROMANIA

Bucharest: Legislative Council, Parliament Bldg, Calea 13 September 1–3, Corp. B1 Sector 5, 76117 Bucharest; tel (1) 6145043; fax (1) 3112935; e-mail clegi@gn.exec.gov.ro; Head of Approximation of Legislation with Community Law: Andrej Popescu.

Bucharest: National School of Political Studies and Public Administration, Library, Bucharest, Str Povernei 6–8, POB 1-792; tel (1) 6596672; fax (1) 3122535; Dir: Lucia Preda.

Depository Libraries

Bucharest: Biblioteca Naţională, Bucharest, Str Ion Ghica 4, Sector 3; tel (1) 3157063; fax (1) 3123381; Dir: Ion Dan Erceanu; f 1955.

Bucharest: Centre for European Information, 70074 Bucharest, Sector 1, Str Georges Enescu 27–29; tel (1) 3134928; fax (1) 3126734; e-mail ana.negulescu@ mailexcite.com; internet www.inid.ro; Gen Man: Ana Eugenia Negulescu; Head of Int Relations: Sanda Popescu.

RUSSIAN FEDERATION

Kaliningrad: Kaliningrad State Univ, 236041 Kaliningrad, A. Nevskogo 14; tel. (112) 33-83-22; e-mail zabotkina@ admin.albertina.ru; Librarian: Artur Viktorovich Yaganov.

Kazan: Kazan State Univ, 420008 Kazan, Kremlevskaya ul 35; tel. (8432) 38-74-18; e-mail office@inter.ksu.ru; Librarian: Larisa Viktorovna Kipenskaya.

Moscow: All-Russian Inst of Market Research (Vniki Mves), 119285 Moscow, Pudovkina ul 4; tel (95) 147-61-01; fax (95) 143-02-71; Contact: Dr Sabelnikov Leonid Vladimirovich; Librarian: Chebotareva Elena Dmitievna.

Moscow: Inst of Europe, Russian Academy of Sciences, 103873 Moscow, Mokhovaja ul 8-3b; tel (95) 201-67-75;

fax (95) 200-42-98; e-mail aes@centro.ru; internet www.aes.org.ru; Dir: Borko Yuri; Librarians: Ludmila Stashilevskaya, Valentina Vasilyevna.

Moscow: State Inst of Int Relations, Inst of European Law, 117454 Moscow, Vernadsky pr 76; tel (95) 433-85-88; fax (95) 434-90-72; e-mail irina-akopova@softhome.net; Contact: Dr Lev Endtin.

Moscow: Univ of Moscow, Faculty of Economic Science, 119899 Moscow, Vorobyevi gory, Kholova, Novi gumanitarni korpus; tel (95) 939-17-54; fax (95) 939-17-54; Dir: Prof Leonid Gloukharev; Library: Andrey Semenov.

Petrozavodsk: Petrozavodsk State Univ, 185640 Petrozavodsk, 33 Lenin ul; e-mail: toivinen@mainpgu.karelia.ru; Librarian: Mikhail Vladimirovich Butorin.

St Petersburg: St Petersburg Univ, Faculty of Int Relations, 199034 St Petersburg, Universitetskaya Naberezhnaya 7–9; tel (812) 276-68-56; fax (812) 276-12-70; e-mail morozov@dip.pu.ru; internet www.edc.spb.ru; Contact: Prof Konstantin Konstantinovich Khudoley; Documentalist: Vjacheslav Morozov.

Saratov: Saratov State Univ, 410071 Saratov, Ul Astrakhanskaya 83; tel. (8452) 51-14-38; fax (8452) 24-04-46; e-mail ied@scnit.saratov.su; Librarian: Oksana Kolchina.

Yekaterinburg: A. M. Gorky Ural State Univ, Dept of Regional and International Relations, Faculty of History, 620083 Yekaterinburg, ul Lenina 51; tel (3432) 55-75-43; fax (3432) 51-90-87; e-mail alexandr.nesterov@usu.ru; Contact: Alexander Nesterov.

SERBIA AND MONTENEGRO

Belgrade: Inst of Int Politics and Economics, 11000 Belgrade, Makedonska 25, POB 750; tel (11) 3221433; fax (11) 3224013; e-mail gocater@yahoo.com; Librarian: Gordana Terzič.

SOUTH AFRICA

Pretoria: Univ of South Africa, Inst of Foreign and Comparative Law, Library, Periodicals Division, POB 392, Pretoria 0003; tel (12) 4293128; fax (12) 4292925.

Stellenbosch: Univ of Stellenbosch, Law Faculty, Private Bag X1, Matieland, Stellenbosch 7602; tel (21) 8084853; fax (21) 8866235; e-mail jsaf@maties.sun.ac.za; Contacts: M. Heese, J. H. Viljoen.

Depository Libraries

Cape Town: South African Library, Queen Victoria St, Cape Town 8001; POB 496, Cape Town 8000; tel (21)

246320; fax (21) 244848; Dir: Pieter E. Westra.

SWITZERLAND

Basel: Univ Basel, Juristische Fakultät, Maiengasse 51, 4056 Basel; tel (61) 2672500; fax (61) 2672509; e-mail nicole.buser@unibas.ch; internet www.unibas.ch/ius/biblio.htm; Contact: Nicole Buser-Kuster.

Berne: Juristische Bibliothek der Univ Bern, Hochschulstr 4, 3012 Berne; tel (31) 6318791; fax (31) 6318588; e-mail good@bibl.unibe.ch; Contact: Martin Good.

Fribourg: Univ Fribourg, Bibliothèque des Sciences Economiques et Sociales, Miséricorde, 1700 Fribourg; tel (26) 3008211; fax (26) 3009788; e-mail gerald.gavillet@unifr.ch; Contact: Gérald Gavillet.

Geneva: Univ de Genève, Centre d'Etudes et de Documentation sur la Démocratie Directe, 102 blvd Carl Vogt, 1211 Geneva; tel (22) 7058533; fax (22) 7058536; e-mail c2d@ibm.unige.ch; Dir: Jean-Daniel Delley.

Geneva: Fondation Archives Européennes, 2 rue Jean-Daniel Colladon, 1204 Geneva; tel (22) 7057851; fax (22) 7057852; Dir: L. Jilek.

Geneva: Inst Européen de l'Univ de Genève (IEUG), Uni-Mail, 40 blvd du Pont d'Arve, 1211 Geneva 4; tel (22) 7058292; fax (22) 7057852; e-mail membrez@uni2a.unige.ch; internet www.unige.ch/ieug; Dir: Jean-Marc Membrez.

Lausanne: Inst suisse de droit comparé, Ferme de Dorigny, 1015 Lausanne; tel (21) 6924911; fax (21) 6924949; e-mail inger.eriksson@isdc-dfjp.unil.ch; internet www.isdc.ch/fr/cde.asp/4-0-1800-5-4-1; Contact: Inger Eriksson Haider.

Neuchâtel: Univ de Neuchâtel, Bibliothèque de Sciences Economiques et Sociales, 7 Pierre-à-Mazel, 2000 Neuchâtel; tel (32) 7181340; fax (32) 7181341; e-mail messagerie.bibliotheque@seco.unine.ch; internet www-seco.unine.ch/bses; Dir: Jacques Savoy; Librarian: D. Amstutz; specialized information.

St Gallen: Univ St Gallen, Bibliothek, Dufourstr 50, 9000 St Gallen; tel (71) 2242293; fax (71) 2242294; e-mail christian.schlumpf@unisg.ch; Contact: Christian Schlumpf.

Zürich: Univ Zürich, Inst für Völkerrecht und ausländisches Verfassungsrecht, Hirschengraben 40, 8001 Zürich; tel (1) 6342051; fax (1) 6344993; e-mail ivrbib@ivr.unizh.ch; internet www.ivr.unizh.ch; Contact: Béatrice Keller.

THAILAND

Bangkok: Chulalongkorn Univ, European Studies Programme, Phyathai Rd, Bangkok 10330; tel (2) 218-3922; fax (2) 251-3580.

Bangkok: European Business Information Centre, Vanissa Bldg, 8th Floor, 29 Soi Chidlom, Ploenchit Rd, Bangkok; tel (2) 655-0672; fax (2) 655-0628.

TUNISIA

Ariana: Univ de Tunis II, Faculté des Sciences Juridiques, Politiques et Sociales de Tunis, 14 rue Hédi Karray, 2049 Ariana; tel (1) 753-892; fax (1) 717-255; Dir: Samia Jami.

Sfax: Univ de Sfax, Service des Bibliothèques, route de l'Aéroport, Km 1, BP 559, 3029 Sfax; tel (4) 248-233; fax (4) 240-913; Dir: Habib Chebbi.

TURKEY

Ankara: A. Ü. Ataum (Avrupa Topluluğu Araştırma ve Uygulama Merkezi), Cemal Güresel Cad, 06590 Cebeci, Ankara; tel (312) 3620762; fax (312) 3205061; e-mail nkurt@education.ankara.edu.tr; Librarian: Neşe Kurt.

Ankara: Middle East Technical Univ (METU), Faculty of Economics and Administrative Science, Univ Library, ODTÜ Külüphanesi, 06531 Ankara; tel (312) 2103629; fax (312) 2101119; e-mail sayata@rorqual.cc.metu.esu.tr; Contacts: Sercan Ayata, Handan Baran-Kiliç.

Ankara: Univ of Bilkent Library, 06533 Ankara; fax (312) 2664391; e-mail library@bilkent.edu.tr; internet www.bilkent.edu.tr; Contact: Hande Baskan Ozer.

Balcali/Adana: Cukurova Univ, Central Library, 01330 Balcali/Adana; tel (322) 3386724; fax (322) 3386724; Contacts: Turhan Yilmaz, Nihat Nacar.

Erzurum: Atatürk Üniv, Avrupa Toplulugu, Ilahiyat Kakültesi, Erzurum; tel (442) 2184120; fax (442) 2331135; Contacts: Erol Cakmak, Nese Öztürk; specialized information.

Eskişehir: Anadolu Üniv, Avrupa Ekonomik, Toplülüğü, Arastirma Merkezi, Yunus Emre Kampüsü, 26470 Eskişehir; tel (222) 3208763; fax (222) 334616; e-mail aetdoc@anadolu.edu.tr; internet www.anadolu.edu.tr; Contact: Mesut Kurulgan; specialized information.

Gazimagusa: Eastern Mediterranean Univ, Library, POB 95, Mersin 10, Gazimagusa; tel (392) 3666588; fax (392) 3661077; Contact: Hasan Arslan.

İstanbul: İstanbul Üniv, Centre for Study and Research in European Law,

Hürriyet Meydani Beyazit, 34452 İstanbul; tel (21) 25280423; fax (21) 25134789; e-mail iahaum@istanbul.edu.tr; Contact: Pervin Dedeler.

İstanbul: Marmara Üniv, Avrupa Toplülüğü Enstitüsü, M. Ü. Göztepe Kampüsü Kadrköy, 81040 İstanbul; tel (216) 3384196; fax (216) 3474543; e-mail acakir@marun.edu.tr; internet www.aef .marun.edu.tr/ecinstitute; Documentalist: Münevver Kolay.

İstanbul: Bilgi Univ, Kurtulus Deresi Cad. 47, Dolapdere, 80370 İstanbul; tel (212) 2381010; fax (212) 2162327; e-mail utuphane@bilgi.edu.tr; internet http:// library.bilgi.edu.tr/screens/edc.html; Contact: Sami Cukadar.

İzmir: Kütüphane Dokümantasyon Daire Baskanligi, Ege Üniv, Bornova, 35100 İzmir; tel (232) 3884000; fax (232) 3881862; e-mail ekonomi@ziraat.ege .edu.tr; Documentalist: Müserref Kinaci; specialized information.

Depository Library

İstanbul: Iktisadi Kalkinma Vakfi, Rumeli Cad 85, Kat 7, Osmanbey, İstanbul; tel (212) 487437; Dir: H. Ceyhan; Librarian: A. Demirel.

UKRAINE

Kiev: Kiev Univ, Inst of International Relations, 254119 Kiev, Melnikova Str 36/1; tel (44) 213-09-90; fax (44) 21-30-76; Librarian: Kopeika Valerii.

Kiev: Academy of Public Administration, Cabinet of Ministers, 252057 Kiev, vul Evgeni Pottier 20; tel (44) 446-42-58; fax (44) 296-13-60; internet www.academy .kiev.ua; Librarian: Inna Godzyk.

USA

Depository Libraries

Albany: State Univ of New York at Albany, Govt Publications, Univ Library, 1400 Washington Ave, Albany, NY 12222; tel. (518) 442-3600; internet http:// library.albany.edu.

Albuquerque: Univ of New Mexico, Zimmerman Library, Gifts and Exchange Section, Albuquerque, NM 87131; tel (505) 277-0111; internet http://elibrary .unm.edu/govinfo/; Dir: D. L. Papstein.

Ann Arbor: Univ of Michigan, Law Library, Serials Dept, Ann Arbor, MI 48109-1210; tel (313) 764-9356; fax (313) 763-5080; internet www.law.umich .edu/library; Dean: Donald E. Riggs; Librarian: R. Maripuu.

Arlington: George Mason Univ, Arlington Campus Library, 3401 North Fairfax Drive, Arlington, VA 22201.

Athens: Univ of Georgia, Law Library, Law School, Herty Drive, Athens, GA30602; tel. (706) 542-5191; internet www.law.uga.edu/library.

Atlanta: Emory Univ, MacMillan Law Library, Govt Documents, Gambrell Hall, Atlanta, GA 30322; tel (404) 727-6797; fax (404) 727-2202; internet www .law.emory.edu/library/index.html; Dir: R. Mills; Librarian: A. Flick.

Austin: Univ of Texas, Tarlton Law Library, School of Law, 727 East Dean Keeton St, Austin, TX 78705; tel. (512) 471-7726; internet http://tarlton.law .utexas.edu.

Berkeley: Univ of California, Govt and Social Science Information Service, Doe Library, 2nd Floor, Berkeley, CA 94720; internet www.lib.berkeley.edu/gssi; Librarian: A. Sevetson.

Bloomington: Indiana Univ, Govt Information, Microforms and Statistical Services, Univ Library, 1320 East 10th St, Bloomington, IN 47405; tel. (812) 855-0100; internet www.libraries.iub.edu.

Boulder: Univ of Colorado at Boulder, Library, Govt Publs Division, POB 184, Boulder, CO 80309-0184; tel (303) 571-2000; internet http://ucblibraries .colorado.edu/govpubs/eu/eu.htm; Librarian: Rick J. Ashton.

Buffalo: State Univ of New York at Buffalo, Serials Dept, European Communities, Central Technical Service, Lockwood Library Bldg, Buffalo, NY 14260; tel (716) 645-2000; internet http://ublib .buffalo.edu; Librarian: F. K. Henrich.

Cambridge: Harvard Univ, Law School Library, Collection Development Dept, Langdell Hall, LW 431, Cambridge, MA 02138; tel (617) 495-3172; fax (617) 495-4449; internet www.law.harvard.edu/ library; Dir: Sidney Verba; Librarian: Nancy Cline.

Champaign: Univ of Illinois, Law Library, 504 East Pennsylvania Ave, Champaign, IL 61820; tel (217) 333-2913; fax (217) 244-8500; e-mail jwilliams@ law.uiuc.edu; internet www.law.uiuc.edu; Dir: Jane Williams (acting).

Charlottesville: Univ of Virginia, Alderman Library, Govt Information Resources, Charlottesville, VA 22903-2498; tel (804) 924-3133; fax (804) 924-1431; e-mail crh5f@virginia.edu; internet www.lib.virginia.edu/govdocs; Librarian: Carol R. Hunter.

Chicago: Illinois Inst of Technology, Downtown Campus Library, 565 West Adams St, Chicago, IL 60661; tel. (312) 906-5600; internet http://library.kentlaw .edu.

Chicago: Univ of Chicago, Joseph Regenstein Library, Documents Dept, 2425 East 57th St, Chicago, IL 60637;

tel (312) 702-8768; internet www.lib .uchicago.edu/e; Librarian: M. L. Walters.

Columbia: Univ of South Carolina, Thomas Cooper Library, Documents/ Microforms Dept, Columbia, SC 29208; tel (803) 777-3142; fax (803) 777-4661; internet www.sc.edu/library; Dir: L. E. Duncan, Jr.

Columbus: Ohio State Univ Library, Continuation Acquisition Division, 1858 Neil Ave Mall, Columbus, OH 43210; tel (614) 292-6151; internet http://library .osu.edu; Dir: William J. Studer; Librarian: B. A. Block.

Durham: Duke Univ, Perkins Library, Public Documents and Maps Dept, POB 90177, Durham, NC 27708; tel (919) 684-2380; fax (919) 684-2855; internet http:// library.duke.edu; Librarian: L. Williams.

East Lansing: Michigan State Univ, Library, Documents Dept, East Lansing, MI 48824; tel. (517) 353-8700; internet www.lib.msu.edu; Dir: Clifford H. Haka; Librarian: D. Brunn.

Eugene: Univ of Oregon, Knight Library, 1501 Kincaid St, Eugene, OR 97403; tel. (541) 346-3070; internet http://libweb .uoregon.edu/govdocs.

Evanston: Northwestern Univ, Univ Library, Govt Publ Dept, Evanston, IL 60208-2300; tel (847) 491-7658; fax (847) 491-8306; internet www.library .northwestern.edu/govpub; Dir: David F. Bishop.

Fort Worth: Texas Christian Univ, Govt Information Dept, Mary Couts Burnett Library, Fort Worth, TX 76129; tel. (817) 257-7117; internet http://libnt1.is .tcu.edu/www.

Gainesville: Univ of Florida, Smathers Libraries, Documents Dept, Library West, Gainesville, FL 32611-7001; tel (352) 392-0366; fax (352) 392-3357; e-mail marygay@mail.uflib.ufl.edu; internet www.docs.uflib.ufl.edu; Librarian: M. G. Anderson.

Iowa City: Univ of Iowa Libraries, Govt Publs Dept, Iowa City, IA 52242; e-mail carolyn-kohler@uiowa.edu; internet www.lib.uiowa.edu/govpubs; Librarian: C. W. Kohler.

Ithaca: Cornell Univ, Documents Section, Olin Library, Ithaca, NY 14853; internet http://campusgw.library.cornell .edu.

La Jolla: Univ of California at San Diego, Serial Acquisitions, Acquisitions Dept, Library 0175A, 9500 Gilman Dr, La Jolla, CA 92093-0175; internet http://libraries.ucsd.edu; Librarians: P. Zarins, J. Coolman.

Lawrence: Univ of Kansas, Govt Documents Library, Anschutz Library, 1301 Hoch Auditoria Drive, Lawrence, KS 66045; internet www.lib.ukans.edu.

Lexington: Univ of Kentucky, Govt Publications, William T. Young Library, 1000 Univ Drive, Lexington, KY 40506; tel. (859) 257-0500, Fax (859) 257-8379; internet www.uky.edu/Libraries.

Lincoln: Univ of Nebraska, Govt Documents, Love Library, Lincoln, NE 68588; tel. (402) 472-2848; internet http://iris .unl.edu.

Little Rock: Univ of Arkansas at Little Rock (UALR), Documents Dept, UALR Library, 2801 South Univ Ave, Little Rock, AR 72204; tel (501) 569-8806; fax (501) 569-3017; internet http://library1 .ualr.edu; Librarian: S. Wold.

Los Angeles: Univ of California, Univ Research Library, Public Affairs Service, 405 Hilgard Ave, Los Angeles, CA 90024; Librarian: B. Silvernail.

Los Angeles: Univ of Southern California, Von Klein Smid Library, Univ Park, Los Angeles, CA 90089-0182; e-mail j.hanks@usc.edu; internet www.usc.edu/ isd/libraries; Librarian: J. Hanks.

Los Angeles: Univ of California, International Documents, Reference and Instructional Services, Young Research Library, Los Angeles, CA 90095; internet www2.library.ucla.edu.

Madison: Univ of Wisconsin, Memorial Library, Documents Dept, 728 State St, Madison, WI 53706; tel (608) 262-9852; (608) 262-4649; e-mail radams@doit.wisc .edu; internet www.library.wisc.edu; Principal Officer: Kenneth Frazier; Librarian: Victoria Hill; Documents Librarian: Ruth Adams.

Miami: Florida International Univ, Govt Documents Dept, Green Library, 11200 SW 8th St, Miami, FL 33199; tel. (305) 348-2454; internet http://weblib.fiu.edu/ index.cfm.

Minneapolis: Univ of Minnesota, Govt Publs Library Dept, 10 Wilson Library, 309 19th Ave S, Minneapolis, MN 55455; tel (612) 624-5073; e-mail govref@tc.umn .edu; internet www.lib.umn.edu/gov; Librarian: J. Wallace.

New Haven: Yale Univ, Govt Documents Center, Seeley G. Mudd Library, 38 Mansfield St, POB 208294, New Haven, CT 06520; tel (203) 432-3209; fax (203) 432-3214; internet www.library .yale.edu/govdocs/euinfo.html; Librarian: M. Sullivan.

New Orleans: Univ of New Orleans, Earl K. Long Library, Serials Dept, Lakefront, New Orleans, LA 70148; tel (504) 286-7276; fax (504) 286-7277; Dir: S. Boudreaux; Librarian: M. Hankel.

New York: Harold Pratt House Council on Foreign Relations, Inc, Library, 58 East 68th St, New York, NY 10021.

New York: New York Public Library, Science, Industry and Business Library, 188 Madison Ave, New York, NY 10016; tel (212) 592-7000; internet www.nypl .org/research/sibl/index.html.

New York: New York Univ, School of Law Library, 40 Washington Sq S, New York, NY 10012; tel (212) 998-2505; fax (212) 995-4070; e-mail libweb@nyu.edu; internet www.law.nyu.edu/library; Librarian: J. J. Marke.

Norman: Univ of Oklahoma, Govt Documents Collection, Bizzell Memorial Library, Rm 440, 401 West Brooks, Norman, OK 73019; tel (405) 325-1832; e-mail jwilhite@ou.edu; internet www -lib.ou.net/depts/govdoc/index.htm; Librarian: Jeffrey M. White.

Notre Dame: Univ of Notre Dame, Notre Dame, IN 46556; tel (574) 631-6258; fax (574) 631-6772; internet www.library .nd.edu.

Oxford: Miami Univ of Ohio, Govt Documents, King Library, Oxford, OH 45056; tel. (513) 529-4141; internet www.lib .muohio.edu.

Philadelphia: Univ of Pennsylvania, Van Pelt Dietrich Library Center, Serials Dept, 3420 Walnut St, Philadelphia, PA 19104-6278; tel (215) 898-7555; fax (215) 898-0559; internet www.library.upenn .edu; Librarian: M. A. Crozer.

Pittsburgh: Univ of Pittsburgh, Hillman Library, 3960 Forbes Ave, Pittsburgh, PA 15260; internet www.library.pitt.edu.

Portland: Univ of Maine, Garbrecht Law Library, 246 Deering Ave, Portland, ME 04102; internet http://mainelaw.maine .edu/library.

Princeton: Princeton Univ, Social Science Reference Center, Firestone Library, One Washington Rd, Princeton, NJ 08544; tel. (609) 258-1470; fax (609) 258-0441; internet http://libweb .princeton.edu.

St Louis: Washington Univ, John M. Olin Library, 1 Brookings Drive, St Louis, MO 63130; internet http://library .wustl.edu/collections/eu/; contact: Barbara Rehkop.

Salt Lake City: Univ of Utah, Marriot Library, Documents Division, Salt Lake City, UT 84112; tel (801) 581-8394; fax (801) 585-4882; internet www.lib.utah .edu; Head of Division: Jill Moriearty; Int Documents Librarian: J. Hinz.

Seattle: Univ of Washington Libraries, Govt Publications Division, POB 352900, Seattle, WA 98195-2900; internet www .washington.edu; Int Govt Publications Librarian: David Maack.

Stanford: Stanford Univ, Hoover Inst on War, Revolution and Peace, Central and Western European Collections, Serials Dept, Stanford, CA 94305-6010; tel (415) 725-5295; fax (415) 723-1687; internet www-sul.stanford.edu/depts/ssrc/ main.htm; Dir: Dr John Raisian; Head Librarian, Western Languages Collection: Judith Fortson.

Tucson: Univ of Arizona, Univ Library, Tucson, AZ 85721; tel (602) 621-2101; fax (602) 621-4619; internet http://dizzy .library.arizona.edu; Dir: J. P. Schaefer; Librarian: Carla J. Stoffle.

University Park: Pennsylvania State Univ, Univ Library, Documents Section, University Park, PA 16802; tel (814) 865-0401; internet www.libraries.psu.edu; Dean: Nancy Eaton; Librarian: S. A. Anthes.

Washington, DC: American Univ, Law Library, 4801 Massachusetts Ave, NW, Washington, DC 20016; internet http:// library.wcl.american.edu; tel. (202) 274-4000.

Washington, DC: Library of Congress, Serial Division, Madison Bldg, 10 First St, SE, Washington, DC 20540; tel (202) 707-5000; internet www.loc.gov.

UNITED STATES COMMONWEALTH TERRITORY

San Juan, Puerto Rico: Univ of Puerto Rico, Law Library, POB 23310, Univ Station, Rio Piedras, San Juan, PR 00931-3310; tel (787) 763-7199; fax (787) 764-2660; internet www.upr.clu .edu; Dir: R. Toro.

LIBRARIES AND DOCUMENTATION CENTRES OF THE EU INSTITUTIONS

Central Library of the European Commission

The European Commission's Central Library in Brussels primarily serves the staff of the European Commission and other EU staff. Non-EU staff may be granted a visitor's card if they can show a special need to research EC documentation, such as for doctoral research. Requests to use the library should be made in advance in writing; at least a month's notice is advised. Requests should be addressed to: European Commission, Central Library, Rue Van Maerlant (VM 18 1/12), 1049 Brussels, Belgium; tel (+32) 2-2999172; fax (+32) 2-2961149; open 10.00–17.00 Monday, Tuesday, Thursday; not open to the public Wednesday and Friday; Head of library services A. Melich.

Libraries and Documentation Centres of the Directorates-General

In principle, use of the libraries and documentation centres is reserved to the staff of the European Commission and other EU staff. However, if the central library is unable to assist in the case of specific information, the DG libraries or documentation centres are ready to help. It is best to make demands for information in writing.

Libraries and Documentation Centres of the Directorates-General

DG Agriculture: *Library and Documentation Centre:* fax (+32) 2-2957540; e-mail agri-library@cec.eu.int.

DG Budget: *Document Administration Unit (U.A.D.):* e-mail budget@cec.eu.int.

DG Competition: *Information Unit:* fax (+32) 2-2955437; e-mail infocomp@cec.eu.int.

DG Development: *Library and Documentation:* fax (+32) 2-2952525; e-mail development@cec.eu.int.

DG Economic and Financial Affairs: *Library and Documentation:* fax (+32) 2-2969428; *Information, Publications and Economic Documentation:* e-mail ecfin-info@cec.eu.int.

DG Education and Culture: *Documentation Centre:* fax (+32) 2-2964259; e-mail eac-info@cec.eu.int.

DG Employment and Social Affairs: *Library and Documentation:* fax (+32) 2-2962393; e-mail empl-info@cec.eu.int.

DG Energy and Transport: *Library:* fax (+32) 2-2960416.

DG Entreprise: *Documentation Centre:* fax (+32) 2-2969930.

DG Environment: *Information Centre:* fax (+32) 2-2966198; e-mail envinfo@cec.eu.int.

DG External Relations: fax (+32) 2-2994989.

DG Fisheries: *Library:* fax (+32) 2-2993040; e-mail fisheries-info@cec.eu.int.

DG Health and Consumer Protection: *Library and Documentation:* fax (+32) 2-2963279; e-mail sanco-helpline@cec.eu.int.

DG Information Society: *Library:* fax (+32) 2-2999499; e-mail library-infso@cec.eu.int.

DG Internal Market: *Information Unit:* fax (+32) 2-2994745; e-mail markt-info@cec.eu.int.

DG Justice and Home Affairs: *Information and Communications:* fax (+32) 2-2998054; e-mail jai-information@cec.eu.int.

DG Personnel and Administration: *Information Officer:* fax (+32) 2-2965962.

DG Press and Communication: *Documentation:* fax (+32) 2-2963000.

DG Regional Policy (Inforegio): *Library and Documentation:* fax (+32) 2-2963000; e-mail dgregio@cec.eu.int.

DG Recherche: *Library:* fax (+32) 2-2969823; e-mail research@cec.eu.int.

DG Taxation and Customs Union: *Library:* fax (+32) 2-2961931; e-mail librarian-information@cec.eu.int.

DG Trade: *Archives:* fax (+32) 2-2990599; e-mail trade-a3@cec.eu.int.

DG Translation: *Reference Libraries (Brussels):* fax (+32) 2-2950700; *Reference Libraries (Luxembourg):* fax (+352) 430134309.

Directorate General for Interpretation: e-mail scic-euroscic@cec.eu.int.

Europeaid Co-operation Office: fax (+32) 2-2996407; e-mail europeaid-info@cec.eu.int.

Eurostat: *Data Shop Brussels:* fax (+32) 2-2346751; e-mail datashop@planistat.be.

Humanitarian Aid Office (ECHO): *Library and Documentation:* fax (+32) 2-2954572; e-mail echo-info@cec.eu.int.

Informatics Directorate: *Technical Library, Brussels:* fax (+32) 2-2959382; *Technical Library, Luxembourg:* fax (+352) 430136348.

Internal Audit Service: *Library:* fax (+32) 2-2998363.

Legal Service: *Library:* fax (+32) 2-2964308.

Protocol and Security Service of the Commission: *Archives:* fax (+32) 2-2960834.

Secretariat-General of the Commission: *Publications Secretariat:* fax (+32) 2-2952080; e-mail sg-info@cec.eu.int.

Other EU Institutions

Euratom Supply Agency: *Archives:* Rond-Point Schuman 3 (RP3), 1040 Brussels; tel (+32) 2-2957237; fax (+32) 2-2950527; Library and Information Officer Mr Monasse.

European Parliament: *Documentation:* Rue Wiertz (LEO), 1047 Brussels, Belgium; Luxembourg Library, Kirchberg (SCH 002), 2929 Luxembourg, Luxembourg; tel (+32) 2-2846205; fax (+32) 2-2306581; Officer Sven Backlund.

European Central Bank: *Official Publications, Archives and Library:* Kaiserstrasse 29, 60311 Frankfurt am Main, Germany; tel (+49 69) 1344-0; fax (+49 69) 1344-6000; e-mail info@ecb.int; Officer Dirk Freytag.

Council of the European Union: *Library:* Square Orban 10, 1040 Brussels; tel (+32) 2-2856541; Officer Mrs Ostry.

Court of Justice: *Library:* Kirchberg, Bld Adenauer, 2926 Luxembourg; ; Officer Jochen Streil; tel (+352) 43032270; fax (+352) 43032424.

J. Delors Centre: Centro Cultural de Belem, Rua Bartolomeu Dias, 1400 Lisbon, Portugal; tel (+351 21) 3652500; fax (+351 21) 3625843; Library Officer Marta Melo Antunes.

Sources d'Europe: Socle de la Grande Arche, 92054 Paris La Défense Cedex 61; tel (+33) 1-41-25-12-12; tel (news room)

(+33 1) 41 25 12 09; tel (médiathèque) (+33 1) 41 25 12 45; fax (+33) 1-41-25-12-13; News Room Officer Stéphanie Lanson; Médiathèque Officer Olga Imbert.

Economic and Social Committee: Rue Ravenstein 2, 1000 Brussels, Belgium; tel (+32) 2-5469488; fax (+32) 2-5134893; Library Officer L. Knudsen.

European Court of Auditors: *Library and Documentation:* Rue Alcide Gasperi 12, 1615 Luxembourg, Luxembourg; tel (+352) 439845559; fax (+352) 439846666; Library Officer Raymond Claudel.

The European Agency for the Evaluation of Medicinal Products (EMEA): 7 Westferry Circus, Canary Wharf, London, E14 4HB; tel (+44 20) 7418-8400; tel (Library Officer) (+44 20) 7418-85-33; fax (+44 20) 7418-8416; fax (Library Officer) (+44 20) 7418-8670; e-mail mail@emea .eudra.org, marja-kingma@emea.eudra .org; internet www.eudra.org/emea.html; Library Officer Marja Kingma.

Office for Harmonization in the Internal Market: Avenida Aguilera 20, 03080 Alicante, Spain; tel (+34) 96-513-91-00; fax (+34) 96-513-91-73; Library and Publications Officer Miguel A. Villaroya Sánchez.

European Centre for the Development of Vocational Training: Marinou Antipa 12, 57001 Thessaloniki, Greece; tel (+30) 31-490111; fax (+30) 31-490102; Library and Documentation Officer Marc Willem.

European Monitoring Centre for Drugs and Drug Addiction: Rua da Cruz de Santa Apolonia 23–25, 1149–045 Lisbon, Portugal; tel (+351 21) 218113000; fax (+351 21) 218131711; internet www.emcdda.org; Information Officer Gianni Contestabile; Documentation Officer María José Louro.

Translation Centre for the Bodies of the Union: Nouvel Hémicycle, Niveau 4, 1 rue du Fort Thüngen, 1499 Luxembourg, Luxembourg; tel (+352) 4217111; fax (+352) 421711220; Executive Director Francisco de Vicente.

European Foundation for the Improvement of Living and Working Conditions: *Information unit:* Wayattville Road, Loughlinstown, Co. Dublin, Ireland; tel (+353 1) 2043100; fax (+353 1) 2826456 ext. 4182; Officer Jan van Damme; Library Officer Fiona Murray; External Relations Officer Brid Nolan; Publications Officer Mattanja de Boer.

European Institute for Public Administration: *Library:* O.L. Vrouweplein 22, 6211 HE Maastricht, Netherlands; tel (+31 43) 3296222; tel (Head of Library) (+31) 433 296280; tel (Librarian) (+31) 433 296331; fax (+31 43) 3296296; Head of Library, Documentation and Publications V. Deckmyn; Librarian L. Mertens.

College of Europe: *Library:* Dyver 11, 8000 Brugge, Belgium; tel (+32) 50-449911; fax (+32) 50-347533; e-mail (Librarian Coens) fcoens@coleurop.be, (Librarian Lievens) mlievens@coleurop .be, (Librarian Truyens) ptruyen@ coleurop.be; Librarians F. Coens; M. Lievens; P. Truyen.

Joint Research Centre (CCR – JRC): *Public relations and publications:* Via Fermi, 21020 Ispra (VA); tel (+39) 0332-789180; fax (+39) 0332-785818; Information Officer Le Det; Database Officer Ulla Engelmann; *General information on the JRC's research programmes:* Square de Meeûs 8 (SDME), Brussels, Belgium; tel (+32) 2-2960847; fax (+32) 2-2950146; Library Officer Ettore Caruso.

Eurolib-Per Centre: Institut Universitaire Européen, Villa il Poggiolo, Piazza Edison 11, 50133 Florence; fax (+39) 055-4685618; Library Officer Mr Giordani; tel (+39) 055-4685393; fax (+39) 055-4685618.

European University Florence Institute: Badia Fiesolana, Via dei Roccetini 5, 50016 San Domenico di Fiesole (FI); tel (+39) 055-4685340; fax (+39) 055-4685283; e-mail alcala@datacom.ine.it; Library Director Mrs Pilar Alcala.

EUROPEAN COMMISSION: ORGANIZATION CHART

Former Presidents of the Commission

1958–67: Walter Hallstein

1967–70: Jean Rey

1970–72: Franco Maria Malfatti

1972–73: Sicco Mansholt

1973–77: François-Xavier Ortoli

1977–81: Roy Jenkins

1981–85: Gaston Thorn

1985–95: Jacques Delors

1995–99: Jacques Santer

1999–2004: Romano Prodi

Members of the Commission

José Manuel Durão Barroso (Portugal): President.

Margot Wallström (Sweden): Vice-President, and Commissioner for Institutional Relations and Communication Strategy.

Günter Verheugen (Germany): Vice-President, and Commissioner for Enterprise and Industry.

Jacques Barrot (France): Vice-President, and Commissioner for Transport.

Siim Kallas (Estonia): Vice-President, and Commissioner for Administrative Affairs, Audit and Anti-Fraud.

Franco Frattini (Italy): Vice-President, and Commissioner for Justice, Freedom and Security.

Viviane Reding (Luxembourg): Commissioner for Information Society and Media.

Stavros Dimas (Greece): Commissioner for Environment.

Joaquín Almunia (Spain): Commissioner for Economic and Monetary Affairs.

Danuta Hübner (Poland): Commissioner for Regional Policy.

Joe Borg (Malta): Commissioner for Fisheries and Maritime Affairs.

Dalia Grybauskaitė (Lithuania): Commissioner for Financial Programming and Budget.

Janez Potočnik (Slovenia): Commissioner for Science and Research.

Ján Figeľ (Slovakia): Commissioner for Education, Training, Culture and Multilingualism.

Markos Kyprianou (Cyprus): Commissioner for Health and Consumer Protection.

Olli Rehn (Finland): Commissioner for Enlargement.

Louis Michel (Belgium): Commissioner for Development and Humanitarian Aid.

László Kovács (Hungary): Commissioner for Taxation and Customs Union.

Neelie Kroes (Netherlands): Commissioner for Competition.

Mariann Fischer Boel (Denmark): Commissioner for Agriculture and Rural Development.

Benita Ferrero-Waldner (Austria): Commissioner for External Relations and European Neighbourhood Policy.

Charlie McCreevy (Ireland): Commissioner for Internal Market and Services.

Vladimír Špidla (Czech Republic): Commissioner for Employment, Social Affairs and Equal Opportunities.

Peter Mandelson (United Kingdom): Commissioner for Trade.

Andris Piebalgs (Latvia): Commissioner for Energy.

Secretariat-General

(Rue de la Loi 200, 1049 Brussels, Belgium; tel (2) 299-11-11; fax (2) 296-05-54; e-mail sg-info@cec.eu.int or forename.surname@cec.eu.int; internet www.europa.eu.int/comm/dgs/secretariat_general/index_en.htm; Bâtiment Jean Monnet, rue Alcide de Gasperi, 2920 Luxembourg; tel 4301-1; fax 4301-35049)

Please note: when the first name and/or the surname are composed of more than one word, the different words are linked by a hyphen. If help is needed, you may send a message to address-information@cec.eu.int requesting the correct address of the correspondent.

Secretary-General: David O'Sullivan; tel (2) 295-09-48; fax (2) 299-32-29.

Deputy Secretaries-General: Eckhart Guth (with special responsibility for Directorates D and E); Enzo Moavero-Milanesi (with special responsibility for Directorates A, B, C and G); tel (2) 295-34-27; fax (2) 299-19-29.

Assistant to the Secretary-General: Cesare Onestini, tel (2) 295-75-71; fax (2) 296-05-54.

Advisers reporting to the Secretary-General: Jérôme Vignon (Chief Adviser), tel (2) 295-46-02, fax (2) 296-55-89; Philip Lowe, tel (2) 296-50-40, fax (2) 295-87-19; Bernhard Zepter, tel (2) 295-80-24, fax (2) 299-19-29; Christian Dewaleyne (Audit Capability), tel (2) 295-95-04, fax (2) 295-05-91.

Advisers reporting to the Deputy Secretary-General in charge of Directorates A, B, C and G: Jacques de Baenst (Protocol Service), tel (2) 295-23-25, fax (2) 296-08-34; Hedwig Ebert (Mediation Service), tel (2) 295-16-29, fax (2) 295-52-75; Dieter Koenig (Delegate to Personal Data Protection), tel 4301-32562, fax 4301-34444.

DIRECTORATE A

(Registry)

Director: Patricia Bugnot; tel (2) 295-07-31; fax (2) 296-96-74.

Units

1 Meetings of the Commission, Groups of Members and Chefs de Cabinet; Oral Procedures; Follow-up of Commission Decisions; Dissemination of Documents.

Head of Unit: Henrik Kersting; tel (2) 295-14-08; fax (2) 295-20-44.

2 Written Procedures and Delegation of Powers; Application of Community Law.

Head of Unit: Karl Von Kempis; tel (2) 295-82-97; fax (2) 296-43-16.

3 Electronic Transmission of Documents.

Head of Unit: Richard Joels; tel (2) 295-91-05; fax (2) 296-66-51.

DIRECTORATE B

(Relations with Civil Society)

Director: Jens Nymand-Christensen; tel (2) 296-64-32; fax (2) 296-84-98.

Adviser: Rainer Lau (Relations with the Agencies); tel (2) 295-97-76; fax (2) 296-84-98.

Units

1 Application of Community Law.

Head of Unit: Jonathon Stoodley; tel (2) 296-93-35; fax (2) 296-66-55.

2 Openness and Professional Ethics.

Head of Unit: Maria Angeles Benitez Salas; tel (2) 299-54-72; fax (2) 296-72-42.

3 Simplification and Modernization of Archiving Systems and Historical Archives.

Head of Unit: Frank Brady; tel (2) 295-20-62; fax (2) 296-10-95.

DIRECTORATE C

(Programme and Policy Co-ordination)

Director: Sylvain Bisarre; tel (2) 295-46-95; fax (2) 296-41-85.

Units

1 Strategic Planning and Programming.

Head of Unit: Michel Servoz; tel (2) 295-68-91; fax (2) 296-41-85.

2 Policy Co-ordination.

Head of Unit: Jordi Ayet Puigarnau; tel (2) 295-15-28; fax (2) 295-76-37.

3 Annual Report and Publications.

Head of Unit: Peter Handley; tel (2) 296-24-30; fax (2) 296-07-40.

DIRECTORATE D

(Relations with the Council of the European Union)

Director: Jorge de Oliveira e Sousa; tel (2) 296-03-93; fax (2) 295-37-07.

Units

1 Relations with the Council of the European Union (I).

Head of Unit: Gustaaf Borchardt; tel (2) 296-65-83; fax (2) 295-37-07.

2 Relations with the Council of the European Union (I).

Head of Unit: Maria-Cristina Russo; tel (2) 295-59-75; fax (2) 295-37-07.

3 Relations with the Council of the European Union (II).

Head of Unit: François Genisson; tel (2) 295-80-36; fax (2) 295-37-07.

4 Co-ordination of Institutional matters and Co-decision Procedure.

Head of Unit: Una O'Dwyer; tel (2) 296-09-56; fax (2) 299-66-15.

DIRECTORATE E

(Relations with the European Parliament, the European Ombudsman, the Economic and Social Committee—ECOSOC and the Committee of the Regions)

Director: Giuseppe Massangioli; tel (2) 295-07-46; fax (2) 296-59-57.

Units

1 Relations with the European Parliament (I): Part Sessions, Horizontal Committees, Follow-up to Opinions and Resolutions, Parliamentary Affairs Group.

Head of Unit: Panayotis Anastopoulos; tel (2) 295-81-41, fax (2) 296-59-57.

2 Relations with the European Parliament (II): Sectoral Committees, Petitions and Transmission of Documents; Relations with the European Ombudsman.

Head of Unit: Mary Preston; tel (2) 295-58-62; fax (2) 296-59-57.

3 Relations with the European Parliament (III): Economic and Social, the Committee of the Regions and the European Ombudsman.

Head of Unit: Andrea Pierucci; tel (2) 296-02-23; fax (2) 299-08-82.

4 Task Force on the Future of the Union and Institutional Matters.

Head of Unit: Paolo Ponzano; tel (2) 295-19-34; fax (2) 296-63-27.

DIRECTORATE G

(Resources and General Matters)

Director: Sarah Evans; tel (2) 295-94-71; fax (2) 295-34-28.

Units

1 Human and Financial Resources.

Head of Unit: Marleen Harford; tel (2) 295-35-18; fax (2) 296-59-66.

2 Commission Mail; President's Mail; Internal Information; Grant Management.

Head of Unit: Arthur Pooley; tel (2) 295-68-06, fax (2) 295-39-13.

3 Implementation of IT Audit Recommendations.

Head of Unit: François Kodeck; tel (2) 295-74-35; fax (2) 295-20-32.

4 Programming and Resources.

Head of Unit: Emanuela Bellan; tel (2) 295-31-34; fax (2) 296-59-66.

Group of Policy Advisers

(45 ave d'Auderghem, 1040 Brussels, Belgium; tel (2) 299-11-11; fax (2) 295-23-05; e-mail forename.surname@cec.eu.int; internet www.europa.eu.int/comm/dgs/policy_advisers/index_en.htm)

President: José Manuel Durão Barroso; tel (2) 211-11-11.

Director: Ricardo Franco Levi; tel (2) 295-64-50.

Assistant: William Floyd; tel (2) 296-03-92.

Advisers: Christiane Bardoux (European Group on Ethics in Science and New Technologies), tel (2) 295-45-47; Hervé Bribosia (Institutions, Inter-Governmental Conference and Future of the EU), tel (2) 285-50-47; Paul Clairet (External Relations), tel (2) 285-85-59; Sylvie Goulard (Political and Institutional Issues, External Issues), tel (2) 299-58-65; Mattias Levin (Economic and Social Issues), tel (2) 296-42-35; Peter Ptassek (External Relations—Neighbourhood Policy), tel (2) 299-11-11; Michael Rogers (Economic and Social Issues), tel (2) 299-11-11; André Sapir (Economic and Social Issues), tel (2) 299-43-68; Elena Saraceno (Economic and Social Issues), tel (2) 295-03-44; Peter Smith (Economic and Social Issues), tel (2) 295-39-94; Alexander Stubb (Political and Institutional Issues—Member of the Task Force on Convention); Michael Weninger (Dialogue with Churches, Religions and Humanism, External Relations), tel (2) 299-85-43.

European Anti-fraud Office

(30 rue Joseph II, 1000 Brussels; tel (2) 299-52-47; fax (2) 296-08-53; e-mail olaf.courrier@cec.eu.int or forename.surname@cec.eu.int; internet www.europa.eu.int/olaf)

Director-General: Franz-Hermann Brüner; tel (2) 296-90-63.

Advisers: B. O'Conner (Internal Audit and Evaluation), tel (2) 299-11-11; L. Smeets (Data Protection Officer), tel (2) 299-11-11.

Assistants to Director-General: Bärbel Heinkelmann (Operations), tel (2) 295-01-88; Harald Spitzer (Policy), tel (2) 299-16-33.

Units

1 Administration, Human Resources and Budget.

Head of Unit: Paolo Millich; tel (2) 295-44-10.

2 Communication, Public Relations, Spokesman.

Head of Unit: Alessandro Buttice; tel (2) 296-54-25.

3 Support for Candidate Countries, Training Co-ordination.

Head of Unit: François Beullens.

4 Magistrates, Judicial Advice and Follow-up.

Head of Unit: Joaquín González González; tel (2) 299-14-66.

DIRECTORATE A: POLICY, LEGISLATION AND LEGAL AFFAIRS

Director: Claude Lecou; tel (2) 295-77-36; fax (2) 296-69-97.

Adviser: Luc Schaerlaekens (acting—General Co-ordination and Enlargement), tel (2) 296-50-59; fax (2) 296-69-97.

Units

1 Legislation, Legal Affairs, Relations with other Institutions, Protection of the Euro.

Head of Unit: Lothar Kuhl; tel (2) 296-39-25; fax (2) 296-69-97.

2 Strategic Programming, Reports, Consultative Committee, External Relations.

Head of Unit: Catherine Luc Schaerlaekens; tel (2) 299-14-66; fax (2) 296-69-97.

3 Customs, Indirect Taxation and Trade Policies, Co-ordination of Anti-fraud Legislation, Administrative and Financial Follow-up.

Head of Unit: Joaquim Geraldes Pinto; tel (2) 295-68-23; fax (2) 296-69-97.

4 Agriculture and Structural Actions, Anti-fraud Legislation, Administrative and Financial Follow-up.

Head of Unit: Eddy Weyns.

5 Direct Expenditure, Anti-fraud Legislation, Administrative and Financial Follow-up Recovery.

Head of Unit: Johan Khouw.

6 Protection of the EURO.

Head of Unit: Yannis Xenakis.

DIRECTORATE B: INVESTIGATIONS AND OPERATIONS

Director: Alberto Perduca; tel (2) 299-11-11; (2) 296-75-25.

Heads of Unit-Investigations: Philippe Ullmann (acting) (International Investigations: Eurostat); Peter Baader (acting) (Internal Investigations); Johan Vlogaert (acting) (External Aid, except PHARE amd TACIS); Thierry Cretin (acting) (Director Expenditure, External PHARE and TACIS Aid); Paul L. Roberts (acting) (Multi-Agency Investigations).

Heads of Unit-Operations: Elisabeth Sperber (Agriculture), tel (2) 299-11-11, fax (2) 296-75-25; Ian Walton-George (Cigarettes), tel (2) 299-52-47, fax (2) 296-75-25; Maria Rosa Sá.

DIRECTORATE C: INTELLIGENCE, OPERATIONAL STRATEGY AND INFORMATION TECHNOLOGY

Director: Nicholas Ilett; tel (2) 298-49-86; fax (2) 296-69-96.

Units

1 Intelligence, Strategic Assessment and Analysis.

Head of Unit: Wolfgang Hetzer (acting); tel (2) 298-49-86; fax (2) 296-69-96.

2 Information Technology.

Head of Unit: Harald Sonnberger; tel (2) 299-11-11; fax (2) 296-69-96.

3 Operational Intelligence: Information and Technical Support.

Head of Unit: Mika Makela; tel (2) 299-11-11; fax (2) 296-69-96.

Legal Service

(85 ave des Nerviens, 10490 Brussels, Belgium; tel (2) 299-11-11; fax (2) 296-30-86; e-mail forename.surname@ cec.eu.int; internet www.europa.eu.int/ comm/dgs/legal_service/index_en.htm)

President: José Manuel Durão Barroso; tel (2) 211-11-11.

Director-General: Michel Petite; tel (2) 296-50-52.

Deputy Director-General: Giuliano Marenco; tel (2) 295-17-75.

Assistant to Director-General: Jürgen Grunwald; tel (2) 295-82-63.

Principal Legal Advisers: Richard Wainwright (Competition and Mergers), tel (2) 295-38-07; Francisco Santaolalla Gadea (State Aids and Dumping), tel (2) 296-19-56; Claire Françoise Durand (Internal Markets), tel (2) 295-11-92; Marie-José Jonczy-Montastruc (Employment and Social Affairs), tel (2) 295-29-74; Pieter Jan Kuiper (External Relations), tel (2) 296-12-73; Frank Benyon (Business Law), tel (2) 295-82-41; José Luís Iglesias Buhigues (Justice, Home Affairs), tel (2) 296-27-76; Thomas Van Rijn (Agriculture and Fisheries), tel (2) 295-18-18; Hans-Peter Hartvig (Institutions), tel (2) 295-10-65.

Head of Legal Revisers Group: Bevis Clarke-Smith; tel (2) 295-28-28.

Directorate-General for Press and Communication

(45 ave d'Auderghem, 1049 Brussels, Belgium; tel (2) 299-11-11; fax (2) 295-01-43; e-mail forename.surname@ cec.eu.int;internet www.europa.eu.int/ comm/dgs/press_communication/ index_en.htm)

Spokesman: Reijo Kemppinen; tel (2) 295-33-58.

Deputy Spokesman: Marco Vignudelli; tel (2) 299-45-60.

Administration and Forward Planning: Gerassimos Thomas, tel (2) 299-34-42; Michael Mann (Forward Planning), tel (2) 299-97-80; Pia Ahrenkilde Hansen (Co-ordination), tel (2) 295-30-70.

Relations with the Media—Press Room

Spokespersons: Jean-Christophe Filori (Enlargement), tel (2) 296-56-60; Emma Udwin (External Relations), tel (2) 295-95-77; J. C. Ellerman-Kingombe (Development and Humanitarian Aid), tel (2) 295-60-53; Pietro Petrucci (Justice and Home Affairs), tel (2) 298-94-92; Arancha Gonzalez (Trade), tel (2) 296-15-53; Eric Mamer (Administrative Reform, Budget, Anti-Fraud), tel (2) 299-40-73; Frédéric Vincent (Education and Culture), tel (2) 298-71-66; Michael Mann (Enterprise and the Information Society), tel (2) 299-97-80; Jonathan Todd (Internal Market, Taxation and Customs), tel (2) 299-41-07; Amelia Torres (Competition), tel (2) 295-46-29; Amador Sanchez Rico (Transport and Energy), tel (2) 299-24-59; Gerassimos Thomas (Economic and Monetary Affairs), tel (2) 299-34-42; Antonia Mochan (Employment and Social Affairs), tel (2) 296-48-96; Gilles Gantelet (Regional Policy), tel (2) 299-48-96; Gregor Kreuzhuber (Agriculture, Rural Development and Fisheries), tel (2)

296-65-65; Beate Gminder (Health and Consumer Protection, especially Food Safety), tel (2) 296-56-94; Thorsten Muench (Health, Consumer Protection and Agriculture), tel (2) 296-10-63; Ewa Hedlund (Environment), tel (2) 299-12-23; Fabbio Fabbi (Research), tel (2) 296-41-74

DIRECTORATE A

(Interinstitutional Relations, Information Policy, Representations)

Director: Panos Carvounis (acting); tel (2) 295-21-73; fax (2) 295-24-69.

Units

1 Relations with the European Parliament and other Institutions, and Information Policy.

Head of Unit: Benoît Woringer; tel (2) 296-34-98.

2 Representations: Information Campaigns, Relays and Networks.

Head of Unit: Fabrizia De Rosa; tel (2) 299-37-39.

3 Representations: Co-ordination and Analysis.

Head of Unit: Linda Corugedo-Steneberg; tel (2) 299-63-83.

DIRECTORATE B

(Communication, Media and Services)

Director: Niels Thøgersen; tel (2) 299-90-99; fax (2) 299-92-07.

Units

1 Opinion Polls, Press Reviews, Europe Direct.

Head of Unit: Antonis Papacostas; tel (2) 295-99-67.

2 Europa, SCAD+ and Publications.

Head of Unit: Lindsey Armstrong; tel (2) 299-90-17.

3 TV/Radio Services and Studios.

Head of Unit: Alain Dumort; tel (2) 295-38-49.

DIRECTORATE C

(Resources)

Director: Jean Pierre Vandersteen; tel (2) 298-61-70.

Units

1 Personnel and Administration.

Head of Unit: Alberto Hasson; tel (2) 295-58-00.

2 Budget and Finances.

Head of Unit: Giuseppe Menchi; tel (2) 296-11-93.

3 Informatics.

Head of Unit: Jose Torcato; tel (2) 296-35-37.

Directorate-General for Interpretation

(24 rue de Mot, 1049 Brussels, Belgium; tel (2) 299-11-11; fax (2) 295-95-84; e-mail euroscic@cec.eu.int or forename.surname@cec.eu.int; internet www.europa.eu.int/comm/dgs/interpretation/index_en.htm)

Head of Service: Marco Benedetti; tel (2) 295-70-58; fax (2) 296-62-63.

Assistant to Head of Service: David Baker; tel (2) 296-33-94; fax (2) 295-22-56.

ADMINISTRATIVE UNITS

1 Audit and Evaluation.

Head of Unit: José Antonio López Sánchez (reporting directly to the Head of Service); tel (2) 299-01-05; fax (2) 295-42-88.

2 Programming and Evaluation, Relations with other Institutions, Information Systems.

Head of Unit: Carlos Alegría.

DIRECTORATE A

(Interpretation and Multi-lingualism)

Director: Jean-Pierre Delava (acting); tel (2) 299-37-70; fax (2) 296-43-06.

Units

1 Multi-lingualism.

Head of Unit: Brian Fox; tel (2) 295-54-16; fax (2) 296-60-23.

2 Danish Interpretation.

Head of Unit: Preben Saugstrup; tel (2) 299-06-50; fax (2) 296-70-83.

3 German Interpretation.

Head of Unit: Ursula Paulini; tel (2) 295-84-65; fax (2) 296-70-83.

4 Greek Interpretation.

Head of Unit: Alexandra Panagakou; tel (2) 295-93-19; fax (2) 296-70-83.

5 English Interpretation.

Head of Unit: Peter Midgley; tel (2) 295-66-31; fax (2) 296-70-83.

6 Spanish Interpretation.

Head of Unit: M. Valdivia Benzal; tel (2) 295-52-22; fax (2) 296-70-83.

7 Finnish Interpretation.

Head of Unit: Veijo Kruth; tel (2) 295-37-86; fax (2) 296-70-83.

8 French Interpretation.

Head of Unit: Irène Jansen; tel (2) 295-84-64; fax (2) 296-70-83.

9 Italian Interpretation.

Head of Unit: Luisa Castellani; tel (2) 299-82-65; fax (2) 296-70-83.

10 Dutch Interpretation.

Head of Unit: Annechiene De Mey; tel (2) 296-71-78; fax (2) 296-70-83.

11 Portuguese Interpretation.

Head of Unit: Luís Machado; tel (2) 296-65-18; fax (2) 296-70-83.

12 Swedish Interpretation.

Head of Unit: Annica Östlund; tel (2) 299-52-12; fax (2) 296-70-83.

DIRECTORATE B

(Meetings and Resources)

Director: David Walker; tel (2) 299-93-00.

Units

1 Meetings.

Head of Unit: Wolter Witteveen; tel (2) 295-30-97; fax (2) 296-96-94.

2 Budget and Finance.

Head of Unit: Christopher Curran; tel (2) 296-24-07.

3 Staff Management and Career Development.

Head of Unit: Elisabeth Egelund; tel (2) 295-90-57.

4 New Technologies relted to Conference Interpretation.

Head of Unit: José Esteban Causo; tel (2) 299-05-62.

5 Conferences.

Head of Unit: Jupp Hamacher; tel (2) 295-28-38; fax (2) 295-30-71.

Eurostat

(Bâtiment Jean Monnet, rue Alcide de Gasperi, 2920 Luxembourg; tel 4301-1; fax 4301-33015; e-mail eurostat-infodesk@cec.eu.int or forename.surname@cec.eu.int; internet www.europa.eu.int/comm/eurostat)

DIRECTORATE G

Director-General: Michel Vanden Abeele.

Assistant to the Director-General: Eduardo Barredo Capelot.

Adviser: Klaus Reeh.

Head of Unit: Véronique Wasbauer (Internal Audit).

DIRECTORATE A

Director: Stephen Kaiser; tel 4301-33073.

Units

1 Administration and Staff.

Head of Unit: Roland Lane (reporting directly to the Director-General); tel 4301-34675.

2 Work Programme; Planning.

Head of Unit: Gilles Decand (reporting directly to the Director-General); tel 4301-33411.

3 Budget Policy and Management.

Head of Unit: Robert Van Der Star (reporting directly to the Director-General); tel 4301-36374.

4 Legal Affairs; Statistical Confidentiality.

Head of Unit: Efstratios Chatzidoukakis (reporting directly to the Director-General); tel 4301-36197.

5 Information and Dissemination.

Head of Unit: Gunter Schaefer (reporting directly to the Director-General); tel 4301-33566.

DIRECTORATE B

(Statistical Methodologies and Tools)

Director: Pedro Diaz Muñoz; tel 4301-32443; fax 4301-34771.

Units

1 Co-ordination of Methods.

Head of Unit: Daniel Defays; tel 4301-32854.

2 IT Management and Information Systems.

Head of Unit: Jean Heller; tel 4301-32803.

3 Statistical Information Technologies.

Head of Unit: John Allen; tel 4301-37291.

4 Reference Databases.

Head of Unit: Wolfgang Knueppel; tel 4301-33221.

5 Research.

Head of Unit: Sylvie Ribaille; tel 4301-32953.

DIRECTORATE C

(Economic Statistics and Economic and Monetary Convergence)

Director: Bart Meganck; tel 4301-33533.

Units

1 National Accounts Methodology; Statistics for Own Resources.

Head of Unit: Brian Newson; tel 4301-32086.

2 Economic Accounts and International Markets; Production and Analyses.

Head of Unit: Joachim Recktenwald; tel 4301-34103.

3 Public Finance and Taxation.

Head of Unit: Luca Ascoli; tel 4301-32707.

4 Balance of Payments.

Head of Unit: Maria Helena Figueira; tel 4301-34730.

5 Prices.

Head of Unit: Jean-Claude Roman; tel 4301-33548.

6 Economic Indicators for the Euro Zone.

Head of Unit: Gian Luigi Mazzi (acting); tel 4301-34351.

DIRECTORATE D

(Single Market – Employment and Social Statistics)

Director: Michel Glaude; tel 4301-36848.

Units

1 Labour Market.

Head of Unit: Antonio Baigorri Matamala; tel 4301-35564.

2 Living Conditions and Social Protection.

Head of Unit: Anne Clemenceau; tel 4301-34880.

3 Business.

Head of Unit: Inger Oehman; tel 4301-37286.

4 Energy and Transport.

Head of Unit: Ovidio Crocicchi; tel 4301-33608.

5 Education and Culture.

Head of Unit: Jean-Louis Mercy; tel 4301-34862.

6 Health and Food Safety.

Head of Unit: Marleen De Smedt; tel 4301-33673.

7 Information Society and Services.

Head of Unit: Bettina Knauth; tel 4301-32969.

DIRECTORATE E

(Agriculture, Fisheries, Structural Funds and Environment Statistics)

Director: Laurs Norlund; tel 4301-36850; fax 4301-37316.

Adviser: Derek Peare; tel 4301-35188.

Units

1 Structural Statistics, Agriculture.

Head of Unit: Hubert Charlier; tel 4301-32974.

2 Agricultural Products Statistics.

Head of Unit: Marcel Ernens; tel 4301-34115.

3 Fisheries, Rural Development and Forestry.

Head of Unit: Peter Tavoularidis; tel 4301-33023.

4 Structural Funds.

Head of Unit: Roger Cubitt; tel 4301-33088.

5 Environment and Sustainable Development.

Head of Unit: Rainer Muthmann; tel 4301-37260.

DIRECTORATE F

(External Relations Statistics)

Director: Pieter Everaers; tel 4301-36847; fax 4301-35199.

Units

1 Demography, Migration.

Head of Unit: Michail Skaliotis; tel 4301-32011.

2 International Trade.

Head of Unit: Christine Coin; tel 4301-33722.

3 Technical Co-operation European Third Countries.

Head of Unit: Nikolaus Wurm; tel 4301-33589.

4 Technical Co-operation Non-European Third Countries.

Head of Unit: Ernesto Azorin Minguez; tel 4301-33536.

5 Co-operation with International Institutions.

Head of Unit: James Whitworth (acting); tel 4301-36857.

Directorate-General for Translation

(1 ave de Cortenbergh, 10490 Brussels, Belgium; tel (2) 299-11-11; fax (2) 295-65-03; e-mail sdt-webmaster@cec.eu.int or forename.surname@cec.eu.int; internet europa.eu.int/comm/dgs/translation/index_en.htm; Bâtiment Jean Monnet, rue Alcide de Gasperi, 2920 Luxembourg; tel 4301-1; fax 4301-33299)

Director-General: Karl-Johan Lönnroth; tel 4301-37825.

Assistant to the Director-General: Carole Ory; tel (2) 295-19-30.

Chief Adviser (Luxembourg Depts): (vacant).

Adviser: F. de Vicente Fernández.

ADMINISTRATIVE UNITS

1 Information and Communications.

Head of Unit: Cornelis van der Horst (reporting directly to the Director-General); tel 4301-32397.

2 Audit (SCIC.01).

Head of Unit: José Antonio López Sánchez; tel (2) 299-01-05.

3 Co-ordination, Planning, Priorities.

Head of Unit: Raymond Waltzing; tel (2) 299-56-83.

DIRECTORATE RL

(Resources and Language Support)

Director: Fernand Thurmes; tel (2) 295-50-02.

Advisers: Paola Iovine-Kraus, tel (2) 295-59-34; Paloma Hoffmann-Vevia Romero (Assessment of Quality of Freelance Translations), tel 4301-32438.

Units

1 Resources.

Head of Unit: Basile Koutsivitis; tel (2) 295-84-78.

Heads of Section: Raffaella Longoni (Competitions, Recruitment and In-service Training), tel (2) 295-62-20; Michael Moscholios (Financial Management), tel (2) 295-44-93

2 Information Technology and Development.

Head of Unit: Jean-Louis Cobbaert; tel 4301-35342.

3 Analysis of Needs and Multi-lingual Tools.

Head of Unit: Alain Reichling; tel 4301-32335.

4 Terminology and Language Support Services.

Head of Unit: Hubert Paesmans; tel 4301-32551.

Heads of Section: Rogert Bennet (Language Help Desk—Luxembourg), tel 4301-32277; Augustin Jimenez (Eurodicautom), tel (2) 295-36-61; Bent Hauschildt (Information and Documentation Centres), tel (2) 295-42-70; (vacant—Language Help Desk—Brussels).

5 Freelance Translation.

Head of Unit: Juan Martinez Guillén; tel (2) 296-27-10.

6 Training.

Head of Unit: Rosanna Cao; tel (2) 295-48-58.

DIRECTORATE TR

(Translation)

Director: George Vlachopoulos; tel (2) 295-86-18.

Advisers: Paul Atkins, tel (2) 296-11-30; (vacant).

Units

1 Planning and Interinstitutional Procedures.

Head of Unit: (vacant).

Head of Section: Germán Merinero (Planning); tel (2) 296-58-48.

2 Language Co-ordination and Quality Assurance.

Head of Unit: Manuel De Oliveira Barata; tel (2) 296-04-76.

Advisers: (vacant); Maria Serrão (Portuguese), tel (2) 296-12-20; Jyrki Lappi-Seppälä (Finnish), tel (2) 295-35-60; Bo Kenneth Larsson (Swedish), tel (2) 295-20-70.

Language Co-ordinators: Peter Aurø (Danish), tel (2) 295-86-56; Reinhard Hoheisel (German), tel (2) 295-66-03; Timothy Martin (English), tel 4301-32572; Amadeo Solà Gardell (Spanish), tel 4301-33585; Andrea Benda (French), tel (2) 295-34-67; Constantinos Sotirchos (Greek), tel 4301-33531; (vacant—Italian); (vacant—Dutch).

SDT-TR/AB

(Legal, Economic and Financial Affairs; Competition and Information)

Head of Department: George Vlachopoulos; tel (2) 295-86-18.

Heads of Unit: Inge Waldstrøm (Danish), tel (2) 295-65-82; Klaus Meyer-Koeken (German), tel (2) 295-22-34; William Bythell (English), tel (2) 295-06-08; Jesús Manuel Martinez Garcia (Spanish), tel (2) 295-44-09; Eliane Jabon (French), tel (2) 295-43-98; Georgios Haniotakis (Greek), tel (2) 296-75-12; Claudio Fischer (acting—Italian), tel (2) 295-75-54; Jean-Pierre Sterck (Dutch), tel (2) 295-81-63; Maria Cristina De Preter (Portuguese), tel (2) 295-93-23; Tiina Lohikko (Finnish), tel (2) 296-52-79; Sune Lennart Lundberg (Swedish), tel (2) 295-69-92.

SDT-TR/C

(Agriculture, Fisheries, Regional Policy and Cohesion)

Head of Department: Svend Bech; tel (2) 295-65-63.

Heads of Unit: Tove Blaabjerg Sørensen (Danish), tel (2) 295-65-76; Raymond Waltzing (German), tel (2) 295-56-83; William Fraser (English), tel (2) 296-10-31; Marta Manté Bartra (Spanish), tel (2) 296-31-26; Christian Scocard (French), tel (2) 295-46-68; Dimitrios Chronopoulos (Greek), tel (2) 296-00-95; Luigi Magi (Italian), tel (2) 295-30-83; Marc De Reu (acting—Dutch), tel (2) 295-65-60; Vítor Sinde (Portuguese), tel (2) 295-07-92; Risto Pitkänen (Finnish), tel (2) 299-36-21; Inga Roth (Swedish), tel (2) 295-92-15.

SDT-TR/D

(External Relations, Customs Union, Development, Enlargement and Humanitarian Aid)

Head of Department: María Elena Fernández-Miranda Parra; tel (2) 295-98-93.

Heads of Unit: Derrick Olesen (Danish), tel (2) 295-84-60; Raymund Berners (German), tel (2) 299-46-26; Gillian Colledge

(English), tel (2) 296-20-69; Paloma Diez Pardo (acting—Spanish), tel (2) 295-06-69; Alain Masschelein (French), tel (2) 295-20-10; Athanassios Antoulas (Greek), tel (2) 295-83-81; Marina Santelli (Italian), tel (2) 295-38-36; Kenneth Boumann (acting—Dutch), tel (2) 295-59-53; Maria Corte Real (Portuguese), tel (2) 295-94-41; Risto Nieminen (Finnish), tel (2) 295-91-35; Anna Wallén (Swedish), tel (2) 296-15-12.

SDT-TR/E

(Research, Telecommunications, Energy, Industry, Environment and Transport)

Head of Department: Luigi Vesentini; tel (2) 295-33-73.

Heads of Unit: Preben Fink-Jensen (Danish), tel (2) 295-65-64; Raymond Regh (German), tel (2) 295-09-13; Charles Lucas (English), tel (2) 295-53-83; Magdalena Guilló Fontanills (Spanish), tel (2) 296-28-50; Bruno Libert (French), tel (2) 295-18-31; Jean Caratzicos (Greek), tel (2) 295-83-77; Adelia Bertetto (acting—Italian), tel (2) 295-48-72; Luc Verdegem (Dutch), tel (2) 295-95-94; Peter Soares-Pinto (Portuguese), tel (2) 296-04-73; Paula Ovasko-Romano (Finnish), tel (2) 295-24-03; Gertrud Ingestad (Swedish), tel (2) 299-05-15.

SDT-TR/F

(Social Affairs, Human Resources and Consumer Policy)

Head of Department: Elizabeth Wagner; tel 4301-32307.

Heads of Unit: Poul Andersen (Danish), tel 4301-34324; Margret Heimbeck (German), tel 4301-32341; David Crowther (English), 4301-32430; Francisco Valeri Cobo (Spanish), tel 4301-34712; Armand Spoden (French), tel 4301-33961; Spyridon Bocolinis (Greek), tel 4301-32328; Marcello Angioni (Italian), tel 4301-32756; Antoine de Brabander (Dutch), tel 4301-32550; Jorge Homem (Portuguese), tel 4301-32546; Marja Kalliopuska (Finnish), tel 4301-32166; Ewa Rossing (Swedish), tel 4301-32772.

SDT-TR/G

(Statistics, Internal Market, Enterprise Policy, Information Market and Innovation)

Head of Department: Ludovicus de Prins; tel 4301-32539.

Heads of Unit: Bodil Franssen (Danish), tel (2) 4301-32303; Elisabeth Constant (German), tel 4301-32471; Douglas Jenks (English), tel 4301-35838; Josep Bonet (Spanish), tel 4301-34759; René Foucart (French), tel 4301-33994; Konstantinos Zacharis (Greek), tel

4301-33460; Cristiano Gambari (acting—Italian), tel 4301-32881; Theo Van Dijk (Dutch), tel 4301-32523; Maria Domingos (Portuguese), tel 4301-33984; Päivi Ollila (Finnish), tel 4301-34334; Bengt Haner (Swedish), tel 4301-35227.

Agriculture and Rural Development Directorate-General

(130 rue de la Loi, 1040 Brussels, Belgium; tel (2) 295-32-40; fax (2) 295-75-0; e-mail agri-library@cec.eu.int or forename.surname@cec.eu.int; internet www.europa.eu.int/comm/dgs/agriculture/index_en.htm)

Director-General: José Manuel Silva Rodríguez; tel (2) 295-19-10; fax (2) 295-13-01.

Deputy Director-General, Directorates B, C and D: Alexander Tilgenkamp; tel (2) 295-33-41.

Deputy Director-General, Directorates E, F and G: Dirk Ahner; tel (2) 295-75-55.

Deputy Director-General, Directorates H, I and J: Jean-Luc Demarty; tel (2) 295-61-26.

Adviser: (vacant) (CAP Analysis).

Assistants to the Director-General: Josefine Loriz-Hoffmann; tel (2) 295-79-77; Nicolas Verlet; tel (2) 296-15-08.

ADMINISTRATIVE UNITS

1 Administration.

Head of Unit: (vacant).

2 Internal Audit.

Head of Unit: Antonio Miceli; tel (2) 296-37-83.

DIRECTORATE A1

(International Affairs (I); Negotiations with the World Trade Organization—WTO)

Director: Mary Minch; tel (2) 296-16-51; fax (2) 295-47-79.

Units

1 WTO, OECD, USA and Canada.

Head of Unit: (vacant).

2 Europe; Newly Independent States; Africa; Asia; Oceania; UN Food and Agriculture Organization—FAO.

Head of Unit: Aldo Longo; tel (2) 295-66-90.

DIRECTORATE A2

(International Affairs (II); Enlargement)

Director: João Pacheco; tel (2) 296-15-28.

Units

1 Latin America, Mediterranean, Middle East, Central and Eastern Europe, Western Balkans.

Head of Unit: Jesus Zorrila Torras; tel (2) 296-74-45.

2 Enlargement.

Head of Unit: (vacant).

DIRECTORATE B

(Relations with other Institutions; Communication and Quality)

Director: José Manuel Sousa Uva; tel (2) 295-93-18.

Units

1 Information Policy on Agriculture and Rural Development.

Head of Unit: Eugène Leguen de Lacroix; tel (2) 295-29-63.

2 Promotion of Agricultural Products.

Head of Unit: Hilkka Summa; tel (2) 299-50-93.

3 Agricultural Product Quality Policy.

Head of Unit: Isabelle Peutz; tel (2) 295-23-31; fax (2) 296-42-85.

4 Relations with other Community Institutions and with Agricultural NGOs.

Head of Unit: Gerard Kiely; tel (2) 298-74-27.

DIRECTORATE C

(Organization of Markets for Crop Products)

Director: Russell Mildon; tel (2) 295-32-24; fax (2) 296-60-08.

Units

1 Cereals, Oilseeds and Protein Plants; Management of Food Aid.

Head of Unit: Rudolf Moegele; tel (2) 296-29-30.

2 Rice; Animal Feed; Non-food Uses; Cereal Substitutes; Dried Fodder.

Head of Unit: Emmanuel Jacquin; tel (2) 295-57-98.

3 Olive Oil; Fibre Plants; Sugar, and Outermost Regions.

Head of Unit: Jean-Marc Gazagnes; tel (2) 295-80-05; fax (2) 296-60-08.

4 Fresh and Processed Fruit and Vegetables.

Head of Unit: Tomás García Azcárate; tel (2) 295-33-17.

DIRECTORATE D

(Organization of Markets for Livestock Products; Specialized Crops and Wine)

Director: Lars Christian Hoelgaard; tel (2) 296-33-14; fax (2) 296-12-27.

Units

1 Milk products.

Head of Unit: Herman Versteijlen; tel (2) 295-95-27; fax (2) 296-12-27.

2 Beef; Veal; Pigmeat; Sheepmeat; Poultry.

Head of Unit: Jean-Jacques Jaffrelot; tel (2) 695-28-36.

3 Bananas; Tobacco; Hops; Potatoes; Other Specialized Crops.

Head of Unit: (vacant).

4 Wine; Alcohol and Derived Products.

Head of Unit: Willy Schoofs; tel (2) 295-70-39.

DIRECTORATE E

(Rural Development Programmes)

Director: (vacant).

Units

1 Spain; Finland; Sweden; United Kingdom.

Head of Unit: Jean-François Hulot; tel (2) 295-29-91.

2 Greece; Italy; Portugal.

Head of Unit: Pedro Tarno Fernández; tel (2) 295-93-64.

3 Belgium; Denmark; France; Austria.

Head of Unit: John Lougheed; tel (2) 295-73-06.

4 Germany; Ireland; Luxembourg; Netherlands.

Head of Unit: Markus Holzer; tel (2) 295-17-95.

DIRECTORATE F

(Horizontal Aspects of Rural Development; Special Accession Programme for Agriculture and Rural Development—SAPARD)

Director: Nikiforos Sivenas; tel (2) 295-96-65.

Units

1 Environment and Forestry.

Head of Unit: Leopold Maier; tel (2) 299-81-95.

2 Financial Co-ordination of Rural Development.

Head of Unit: Joern-Uwe Lerbs; tel (2) 295-12-94.

3 Consistency of Rural Development.

Head of Unit: Robertus Peters; tel (2) 296-26-24.

4 SAPARD Programmes.

Head of Unit: (vacant).

DIRECTORATE G

(Economic Analyses and Evaluation)

Director: John Smith-Bensted; tel (2) 295-74-43.

Adviser: (vacant).

Units

1 Studies and Overall Approach.

Head of Unit: Bruno Buffaria; tel (2) 296-31-44.

2 Quantitative Analyses; Forecasts; Statistics and Studies.

Head of Unit: Pierre Bascou; tel (2) 295-08-46.

3 Analysis of the Situation of Agricultural Holdings.

Head of Unit: Keijo Hyvönen; tel (2) 296-63-35.

4 Evaluation of Measures Applicable to Agriculture.

Head of Unit: Martin Scheele; tel (2) 296-39-70.

DIRECTORATE H

(Agriculture Legislation)

Director: Wolfgang Burtscher; tel (2) 299-68-98.

Units

1 Agricultural Law.

Head of Unit: Klaus-Dieter Borchardt; tel (2) 299-40-11.

2 Competition.

Head of Unit: Michael Erhart; tel (2) 295-96-17.

3 Supervision of the Application of Agricultural Legislation; Infringements and Complaints.

Head of Unit: Fabio Gencarelli; tel (2) 295-62-76.

4 Horizontal Aspects Relating to Trade; Simplification of Agricultural Legislation.

Head of Unit: François Vital; tel (2) 295-11-75.

5 Co-ordination of Procedures and Joint Secretariat of Management Committees.

Head of Unit: Jan Verstraete; tel (2) 295-64-06.

DIRECTORATE I

(Resource Management)

Director: Prosper de Winne; tel (2) 295-63-94.

Units

1 Budget Management.

Head of Unit: Irini Papadimitriou; tel (2) 295-91-27.

2 Assistance and Central Financial Control.

Head of Unit: Franco Biscontin; tel (2) 296-71-22.

3 Information Technology.

Head of Unit: Georgios Vlahopoulos; tel (2) 296-23-52.

4 Financial Management of EAGGF Guarantee Section.

Head of Unit: Susanne Nikolajsen; tel (2) 295-80-79.

5 Personnel and Administration.

Head of Unit: Juan Luis Fernández Martín; tel (2) 296-27-50.

6 Activity-based Management, IRMS and Court of Auditors.

Adviser: Soeren Kissmeyer-Nielson; tel (2) 295-32-95.

DIRECTORATE J

(Audit of Agricultural Expenditure)

Director: Chantal Hebette; tel (2) 296-18-14.

Adviser: Gerrit Verhelst; tel (2) 295-24-40.

Units

1 Co-ordination of Horizontal Questions concerning the Clearance of Accounts; Financial Audit.

Head of Unit: Michele Ottati; tel (2) 295-84-02.

2 Audit of Expenditure on Market Measures.

Head of Unit: Hans-Erwin Barth; tel (2) 295-63-63.

3 Integrated Administration and Control Systems (IACS); Audit of Direct Aid.

Head of Unit: Richard Etievant; tel (2) 299-44-68.

4 Audit of Rural Development Expenditure.

Head of Unit: Paul Webb; tel (2) 295-45-33.

Competition Directorate-General

(70 rue Joseph II, 1000 Brussels, Belgium; tel (2) 299-11-11; fax (2) 296-59-93; e-mail infocomp@cec.eu.int or forename.surname@cec.eu.int; internet europa.eu.int/comm/dgs/competition/index_en.htm)

Director-General: Philip Lowe; tel (2) 295-23-87; fax (2) 296-42-98.

Deputy Director-General, Directorate B (Mergers): Götz Drauz.

Deputy Director-General, Directorates C–F (Anti-Trust Activities, Anti-Trust Reform and Security Issues): Gianfranco Rocca; tel (2) 295-11-52.

Deputy Director-General, Directorates G and H (State Aid): Claude Chêne.

Chief Economist: Lars-Hendrik Röller.

Assistants to the Director-General: Nicola Pesaresi; tel (2) 299-29-06; Linsey McCallum.

DIRECTORATE R

(Strategic Planning and Resources)

Director: Sven Norberg.

Adviser: Juan Riviere y Marti.

Units

1 Strategic Planning, Human and Financial Resources.

Head of Unit: Michel Magnier.

2 Information Technology.

Head of Unit: Javier Juan Puig Saques (reporting directly to the Director-General); tel (2) 296-89-89.

3 Document Management, Information and Communications.

Head of Unit: Corinne Dussart-Lefret.

DIRECTORATE A

(Competition Policy and Strategic Support)

Director: Emil Paulis; tel (2) 2956-50-33.

Adviser: Georgios Rounis; tel (2) 295-34-04; fax (2) 299-63-96.

Units

1 Antitrust Policy and Strategic Support.

Head of Unit: Michael Albers.

2 Merger Policy and Strategic Support.

Head of Unit: (vacant).

3 Enforcement Priorities and Decision Scrutiny.

Head of Unit: Olivier Guersent.

4 European Competition Network.

Head of Unit: Kris Dekeyser.

5 International Relations.

Head of Unit: Blanca Rodriguez Galindo.

DIRECTORATE B

(Energy, Water, Food and Pharmaceuticals)

Director: Götz-Heinrich Drauz; tel (2) 295-86-81; fax (2) 296-95-82.

Units

1 Energy, Water.

Head of Unit: Maria Rehbinder.

2 Food, Pharmaceuticals.

Deputy Head of Unit: Dirk Van Erps.

3 Mergers.

Head of Unit: Paul Malric-Smith; tel (2) 295-96-75.

DIRECTORATE C

(Information, Communication and Multimedia)

Director: Jürgen Mensching; tel (2) 295-22-24.

Units

1 Posts and Telecommunications, and Information Society Co-ordination.

Head of Unit: Eric Van Ginderachter.

2 Media and Music Publishing.

Head of Unit: Herbert Ungerer; tel (2) 296-86-23; fax (2) 296-98-09.

3 Information Industries, Internet and Consumer Electronics.

Head of Unit: Cecilio Madero Villarejo; tel (2) 296-09-49; fax (2) 296-98-09.

4 Mergers.

Head of Unit: Dietrich Kleemann.

DIRECTORATE D

(Services)

Director: Lowri Evans; tel (2) 296-50-29..

Adviser: Finn Lomholt.

Units

1 Financial Services (Banking and Insurance).

Head of Unit: Bernhard Friess.

2 Transport.

Head of Unit: Joos Stragier; tel (2) 295-24-82.

3 Distributive Trades and other Services.

Head of Unit: (vacant).

4 Mergers.

Head of Unit: (vacant).

DIRECTORATE E

(Industry)

Director: Angel Tradacete Cocera; tel (2) 295-24-62; fax (2) 296-95-81.

Units

1 Chemicals, Minerals, Petrochemicals, Non-Ferrous Metals and Steel.

Head of Unit: Georg de Bronett; tel (2) 295-92-68; fax (2) 296-98-06.

2 Construction, Paper, Glass, Mechanical and other Industries.

Head of Unit: Nicola Annencchino; tel (2) 296-18-70.

3 Mergers.

Head of Unit: Dan Sjoblom.

DIRECTORATE F

(Capital and Consumer Goods Industries)

Director: Kirtikumar Mehta.

Units

1 Consumer Goods and Agriculture.

Head of Unit: Yves Devellennes.

2 Motor Vehicles and other Means of Transport.

Head of Unit: Paolo Cesarini.

3 Mergers.

Head of Unit: Claude Rakovsky.

DIRECTORATE G

(State Aids I)

Director: Humbert Drabbe, tel (2) 295-00-60.

Units

1 Regional Aid.

Head of Unit: Robert Hankin.

2 Horizontal Aid.

Head of Unit: Jorma Pihlatie.

3 Fiscal Issues.

Head of Unit: Wouter Pieke.

4 Transparency and Scoreboard.

Head of Unit: Wolfgang Mederer.

DIRECTORATE H

(State Aids II)

Director: Loretta Dormal-Marino.

Units

1 Manufacturing.

Head of Unit: Jean-Louis Colson.

2 Services I: Financial Services, Post, Energy.

Head of Unit: Joaquin Fernandez Martin.

3 Services II: Broadcasting, Telecoms, Health, Sports and Culture.

Head of Unit: Stefaan Depypere.

4 Enforcement.

Head of Unit: Dominique Van Der Wee.

Economic and Financial Affairs Directorate-General

(1 ave de Beaulieu, 1160 Brussels, Belgium; tel (2) 299-11-11; fax (2) 296-94-28; e-mail ecfin-info@cec.eu.int or forename.surname@cec.eu.int; internet www.europa.eu.int/comm/dgs/economy_finance/index_en.htm)

Director-General: Klaus Regling; tel (2) 299-43-66.

Deputy Director-General, Directorates B, C and E: António José Cabral; tel (2) 299-43-88.

Directors: Günther Grosche (Secretary of the Economic and Financial Committee and the Economic Policy Committee); tel (2) 299-43-61; Philippe Petit-Laurent (Relations with the European Bank for Reconstruction and Development).

Chief Adviser: Henry Joly Dixon (Secretary of the Economic and Financial Committee and the Economic Policy Committee); tel (2) 295-85-13.

Adviser: (vacant), Matters relating to Financial Engineering.

Assistant to the Director-General: Stefan Pflüger; tel (2) 299-34-13.

ADMINISTRATIVE UNIT

1 Internal Audit.

Head of Unit: Sylvain Simonetti (reporting directly to the Director-General).

DIRECTORATE A

(Economic Studies and Research)

Director: Juergen Kroeger. tel (2) 299-34-88.

Study Advisers: Heikki Oksanen; tel (2) 295-93-26, fax (2) 299-34-99; Karl Pichelmann; tel (2) 299-33-65, fax (2) 299-34-99; Lars Jonung.

Economic Advisers: Klaus Waelde; tel (2) 295-28-00; Maxwell Watson; tel (2) 298-66-62; R.Veugelers; tel (2) 298-68-33.

Units

1 Econometric Models and Medium-term Studies.

Head of Unit: André Louis Dramais; tel (2) 299-43-77; fax (2) 299-34-99.

2 Economic Databases and Statistical Co-ordination.

Head of Unit: Frank Schönborn; tel (2) 299-33-58; fax (2) 299-34-99.

3 Business Surveys.

Head of Unit: Peter Weiss; tel (2) 295-43-50.

4 Forecasts and Economic Situation.

Head of Unit: Mary McCarthy; tel (2) 299-34-93.

DIRECTORATE B

(Member States' Economies)

Director: Marco Buti, tel (2) 296-22-46.

Adviser: Alain Morisset; tel (2) 299-43-81.

Units

1 Member States I: Germany, Estonia, Austria, Portugal, Finland.

Head of Unit: Georg Busch; (2) 295-43-50; fax (2) 299-43-55.

2 Member States II: Belgium, France, Luxembourg, Hungary, Netherlands.

Head of Unit: Barbara Kauffmann; tel (2) 299-34-89.

3 Member States III: Greece, Spain, Italy, Cyprus, Malta.

Head of Unit: Carlos Martinez Mongay; tel (2) 296-12-28.

4 Member States IV: Denmark, Ireland, Latvia, Sweden, United Kingdom.

Head of Unit: José Luis Robledo Fraga; tel (2) 295-66-64; fax (2) 299-35-64.

5 Member States V: Czech Republic, Lithuania, Poland, Slovenia, Slovakia.

Head of Unit: Filip Keereman; tel (2) 295-66-64; fax (2) 299-34-90.

6 Coherence in the Surveillance of the Economies of the Member States.

Head of Unit: Lucio Pench; tel (2) 299-34-33.

DIRECTORATE C

(Economy of the Euro Zone and the Union)

Director: Servaas Deroose; tel (2) 299-43-75.

Units

1 Monetary Affairs within the Euro Zone and the other Member States; ERM 2.

Head of Unit: Johan Baras; tel (2) 299-19-96.

2 Public Finance, with particular reference to the Euro Zone.

Head of Unit: Elena Flores Gual; tel (2) 299-34-61.

3 Co-ordination of Economic Policies within the Member States and the Euro Zone.

Head of Unit: Joost Kuhlmann; tel (2) 299-33-48.

4 Transition Issues related to EMU.

Head of Unit: Johan Verhaeven; tel (2) 299-34-43; fax (2) 299-35-05.

5 Labour Markets including Wages, Tax and Benefit Systems, Human Capital and Labour Productivity.

Head of Unit: Declan Costello; tel (2) 299-33-75.

DIRECTORATE D

(International Questions)

Director: António José Cabral (acting); tel (2) 299-43-88.

Advisers: Vassili Lelakis (Co-ordinating Financial Aid to Non-member States); tel (2) 299-44-15, fax (2) 295-76-19.

Units

1 Economic Affairs within the Candidate Countries and Western Balkans; Economic Policy Relating to Enlargement.

Head of Unit: Peter Grasmann; tel (2) 299-34-17.

2 Economic Affairs within the G7 Countries and Related Multilateral Issues; Asia and Latin America. Trade Policy; External Aspects of EMU.

Head of Unit: Daniel Daco; tel (2) 299-19-96; fax (2) 299-41-10.

3 Economic Affairs within the Mediterranean Countries, Russia and the New Independent States; Economic Aspects of Neighbourhood Policy.

Head of Unit: Jose Leandro; tel (2) 299-54-30.

4 Horizontal Issues and Co-ordination of Financial Assistance; Development Policy; Links with Multilaterial Banks.

Head of Unit: Vassili Lelakis; tel (2) 299-44-15.

DIRECTORATE E

(Economic Evaluation Service)

Director: Jan Høst Schmidt; tel (2) 295-79-04; fax (2) 299-35-02.

Units

1 Financial Markets and Financial Intermediaries.

Head of Unit: John Berrigan; tel (2) 299-35-80.

2 Internal Market and National Products and Services Markets; Competition Policy; Analysis of Competitiveness.

Head of Unit: Fabienne Ilzkovitz; tel (2) 299-33-79; fax (2) 35-02.

Adviser: Roderick Meiklejohn (Competition Policy); fax (2) 299-35-02.

3 Structural Funds and Common Agricultural Policy.

Head of Unit: Carole Garnier; tel (2) 299-43-58; fax (2) 299-35-02.

4 Environment, Transport and Energy Policies.

Head of Unit: Manfred Bergmann; tel (2) 299-34-79; fax (2) 299-35-02.

5 Financial Integration and Capital Movement.

Head of Unit: Lawrence Kenneth Lennan (acting); tel (2) 299-34-22.

DIRECTORATE L

(Financial Operations; Programme Management; Liaison with the European Investment Bank Group)

Director: David McGlue; tel 4301-34067.

Units

1 New Financial Instruments and Liaison with the EIB Group and the other International Financial Institutions.

Head of Unit: Jean-Marie Magnette; tel 4301-36261.

2 Programme Management (SMEs).

Head of Unit: James McGing; tel 4301-36129.

3 New Borrowing and Lending Operations – Euratom and EU.

Head of Unit: Peter Reichel; tel 4301-33050.

4 Accounting and Risk Management.

Head of Unit: Jan Carlsson; tel 4301-36424.

5 Treasury Management and Market Operations.

Head of Unit: Herbert Barth; tel 4301-36182.

6 Risk Capital and SME Financing.

Head of Unit: Maria Kristiina Raade; tel 92) 295-16-63.

DIRECTORATE R

(Resources)

Director: Alexandra Cas Granje; tel (2) 295-62-69.

Advisers: Antonio Espino (Relations with the European Parliament); tel (2) 299-44-04; Christian Ghymers (Information and Communication of DG ECFIN); tel (2) 295-62-27; Enrique Juaristi Martinez (Horizontal Administrative Issues); tel 4301-36253.

Units

1 Human Resources and Administration.

Head of Unit: Roy Dickinson; tel (2) 296-20-16.

2 Financial Management and Control.

Head of Unit: Jean-Pierre Raes; tel (2) 295-60-56.

3 Strategic Programming, Management and Control.

Head of Unit: Bernard Naudts; tel (2) 296-15-37.

4 Information and Communication.

Head of Unit: John-Claude Schutz; tel (2) 299-56-58.

5 Management of IT Resources.

Head of Unit: Pierre Hirn; tel (2) 299-43-92.

Education and Culture Directorate-General

(2 rue de la Loi 200, 1049 Brussels, Belgium; tel (2) 299-11-11; fax (2) 295-60-85; e-mail eac-info@cec.eu.int or forename.surname@cec.eu.int; internet www.europa.eu.int/comm/dgs/education_culture/index_en.htm)

Director-General: Nikolaus van der Pas; tel (2) 296-83-08; fax (2) 299-66-70.

Assistant to Director-General: Nicolas Gibert-Morin; tel (2) 299-11-20.

ADMINISTRATIVE UNITS

1 Interinstitutional Relations; Co-ordination; Evaluation.

Head of Unit: Sylvia Vlaeminck (reporting directly to the Director-General); tel (2) 295-53-85.

2 Audit.

Head of Unit: Carlo Pettinelli (reporting directly to the Director-General); tel (2) 299-40-37; fax (2) 295-88-74.

DIRECTORATE A

(Education)

Director: David Coyne; tel (2) 295-57-41.

Units

1 Lifelong Learning Policy Development.

Head of Unit: Angélique Verli; tel (2) 295-71-36.

2 Higher Education: Socrates, Erasmus, Jean Monnet.

Head of Unit: Marta Maria Ferreira; tel (2) 296-26-58.

3 School Education: Socrates, Comenius.

Head of Unit: Bertrand Delpeuch; tel (2) 296-87-11.

4 Socrates: Co-ordination and Horizontal Actions.

Head of Unit: Anders Hingel; tel (2) 296-05-55.

5 Tempus Programme: Co-operation with the USA and Canada.

Head of Unit: Augusto Gonzalez-Hernandez; tel (2) 296-63-19.

DIRECTORATE B

(Vocational Training)

Director: Michel Richonnier; tel (2) 295-09-73.

Units

1 Development of Vocational Training Policies.

Head of Unit: Gordon Clark; tel (2) 296-29-29; (2) 295-36-56.

2 Implementation of the Leonardo da Vinci Programme.

Head of Unit: Maria Margarida Gameiro; tel (2) 296-58-62.

3 Application and Dissemination of Innovation.

Head of Unit: Alice Copette; tel (2) 296-56-97; fax (2) 299-58-33.

4 Multimedia: Culture, Education, Training.

Head of Unit: Maruja Gutierrez Diaz; tel (2) 295-63-46.

DIRECTORATE C

(Culture, Audiovisual Policy and Sport)

Director: Gregory Paulger; tel (2) 299-94-34.

Units

1 Audiovisual Policy.

Head of Unit: Jean-Eric de Cockborne; tel (2) 296-86-32; fax (2) 299-60-98.

2 Culture: Policy and Framework Programme.

Head of Unit: Harald Hartung; tel (2) 296-54-50.

3 Audiovisual Support (MEDIA).

Head of Unit: Constantin Daskalakis; tel (2) 296-35-96.

4 Language Policy.

Head of Unit: Jacques Delmoly; tel (2) 295-84-06.

5 Sport.

Head of Unit: Jaime Andreu Romeo; tel (2) 299-92-52; fax (2) 295-03-56.

DIRECTORATE D

(Youth, Civil Society, Communication)

Director: João Vale de Almeida; tel (2) 296-56-64; fax (2) 296-08-55.

Units

1 Youth.

Head of Unit: Pierre Mairesse; tel (2) 296-20-09; fax (2) 295-92-09.

2 Visits, Traineeships, Partnerships with Civil Society.

Head of Unit: Antonios Kosmopoulos; tel (2) 299-93-35.

3 Central Library.

Head of Unit: Ana Melich Juste; tel (2) 299-91-72; fax (2) 295-29-82.

4 Communication.

Head of Unit: Francis Gutmann; tel (2) 295-96-50.

DIRECTORATE E

(Resources)

Director: Gilbert Gascard; tel (2) 295-00-17; fax (2) 295-00-48.

Units

1 Human Resources and Administration.

Head of Unit: Christine Boon-Falleur; tel (2) 295-75-96; fax (2) 295-66-87.

2 Budget Planning and Co-ordination.

Head of Unit: Pascal Lejeune; tel (2) 295-08-83; fax (2) 295-15-61.

3 Finance and On-site Control.

Head of Unit: Armin Bosch; tel (2) 299-12-95.

4 IT Resources.

Head of Unit: Simon Smith; tel (2) 296-82-74.

Employment, Social Affairs and Equal Opportunities Directorate-General

(27 and 37 rue Joseph II, 1000 Brussels, Belgium; tel (2) 299-11-11; fax (2) 295-65-07; e-mail empl-info@cec.eu.int or forename.surname@cec.eu.int; internet www.europa.eu.int/comm/dgs/employment_social/index.en.htm; Bâtiment Jean Monnet, rue Alcide de Gasperi, 2920 Luxembourg; tel 4301-1)

Director-General: Odile Quintin; tel (2) 299-22-77; fax (2) 296-36-60.

Deputy Director-General: (vacant).

Assistant to the Director-General: Erick Stefan Olsson; tel (2) 295-35-69.

Advisers: John Morley (Economic Affairs and Speech Writing); tel (2) 295-10-98; Hermanus van Zonneveld, (Relations with the European Parliament and ECOSOC); tel (2) 295-62-54; Paolo Bacchielli (Social Issues); tel (2) 296-04-95; Richard Nobbs (Information); tel (2) 296-95-35.

ADMINISTRATIVE UNITS

1 SPP and Interinstitutional Relations.

Head of Unit: Jorge Curell Gotor; tel (2) 299-04-78.

2 Internal Audit.

Head of Unit: Emilio Dalmonte; tel (2) 299-40-21.

DIRECTORATE A

(Employment Strategy and European Social Fund (ESF—Policy Development and Co-ordination))

Director: Antonis Kastrissianakis; tel (2) 295-73-80; fax (2) 296-97-69.

Units

1 Employment Analysis.

Head of Unit: Georg Fischer; tel (2) 299-21-18; fax (2) 29697-69.

2 Employment Strategies.

Head of Unit: R. Strauss; tel (2) 296-05-31.

3 Employment Services.

Head of Unit: Johan ten Geuzendam; tel (2) 295-78-29; fax (2) 296-97-69.

4 ESF Policy Co-ordination, Employment and Local Development.

Head of Unit: (vacant).

DIRECTORATE B

(National Employment Monitoring, Social Inclusion Monitoring and ESF Operations I)

Director: P. Stub Jorgensen; tel (2) 298-60-00.

Units

1 Italy, Malta, Romania.

Head of Unit: Michel Laine; tel (2) 295-81-38; fax (2) 296-47-16.

2 Belgium, France, Slovakia.

Head of Unit: (vacant).

3 Sweden, Finland, Estonia.

Head of Unit: Philippe Hatt; tel (2) 295-67-01; fax (2) 296-97-73.

4 Community Initiatives.

Head of Unit: M. Donnelly; tel (2) 296-03-32.

DIRECTORATE C

(National Employment Monitoring and ESF Operations II)

Director: Sven Kjellstrom; tel (2) 295-40-10; fax (2) 296-97-73.

Units

1 Austria, Germany, Slovenia.

Head of Unit: (vacant).

2 Denmark, Poland.

Head of Unit: Georges Kintzelé; tel (2) 295-25-39; fax (2) 296-97-73.

3 Lithuania, Spain.

Head of Unit: A. Schulte-Braucks; tel (2) 295-71-59.

4 Article Six ESF and Re-adaptation.

Head of Unit: B. Sinnott; tel (2) 295-86-88.

DIRECTORATE D

(Adaptability, Social Dialogue, Social Rights)

Director: Berhard Jansen; tel (2) 295-76-04; fax (2) 295-60-73.

Units

1 Interprofessional Social Dialogue; Industrial Relations; Adaptation to Change.

Head of Unit: Jackie Morin; tel (2) 296-11-45; fax (2) 295-60-73.

2 Labour Law, Organization of Work.

Head of Unit: Rosendo González Dorrego; tel (2) 295-30-48; fax (2) 295-60-73.

3 Anti-discrimination and Civil Society (Article 13).

Head of Unit: Barbara Nolan; tel (2) 296-07-55; fax (2) 295-60-73.

5 Health Safety and Hygiene at Work.

Head of Unit: José Ramon Biosca de Sagastuy; tel 4301-34988.

DIRECTORATE E

(Social Protection and Social Integration)

Director: J. Vignon; tel (2) 295-46-02.

Units

1 Social and Demography Analysis.

Head of Unit: Constantinos Fotakis; tel (2) 295-02-06; fax (2) 295-30-77.

2 Social Protection, Social Inclusion Policies.

Head of Unit: Armando Silva; tel (2) 296-02-31; fax (2) 295-30-77.

3 Free Movement of Workers and Co-ordination of Social Security Schemes.

Head of Unit: Rob Cornelissen; tel (2) 295-76-67; fax (2) 295-30-77.

4 Socio-Economic Questions and Speech-Writing Team.

Head of Unit: A. Tyson; tel (2) 296-60-56.

DIRECTORATE F

(Management of Resources)

Director: Raoul Prado; tel (2) 296-96-46; fax (2) 296-47-18.

Adviser: Franz-Peter Veits (Auditor Training Policy, Methodological Refinement, Member States' Requirements); tel (2) 299-54-11; fax (2) 296-47-18.

Units

1 Personnel and Administration.

Head of Unit: S. Beernaerts; tel (2) 296-63-15.

2 Budget, Financial Co-ordination and Accounts.

Head of Unit: T. Galeros; tel (2) 295-75-48.

3 Audits of the ESF.

Head of Unit: L. Battistotti; tel (2) 298-57-99.

4 Information Technology and Workflow.

Head of Unit: Jean-François Lebrun; tel (2) 299-22-74; fax (2) 296-47-18.

5 Ex-Post Control of Expenditure in Direct Management.

Head of Unit: Vincent Widdershoven; tel (2) 295-33-30.

DIRECTORATE G

(Horizontal and International Issues)

Director: Luisella Pavan-Woolfe; tel (2) 295-66-38.

Units

1 Equality for Women.

Head of Unit: F. Devonic; tel (2) 295-61-51.

2 Enlargement and International Co-operation.

Head of Unit: Jean-Paul Tricart; tel (2) 299-05-11.

3 Integration of People with Disabilities.

Head of Unit: W. Goelen; tel (2) 295-18-27.

4 Communication.

Head of Unit: Giorgio Clarotti; tel (2) 296-58-94.

5 Evaluation.

Head of Unit: O. Rouland; tel (2) 296-62-18.

DIRECTORATE H

(National Employment and Social Inclusion, Monitoring and ESF Operations III)

Director: Xavier Prats Monne; tel (2) 296-12-30.

Units

1 Bulgaria, Cyprus, Greece.

Head of Unit: W. Faber; tel (2) 295-03-77.

2 Netherlands and Hungary.

Head of Unit: (vacant).

3 Ireland, Latvia, United Kingdom.

Head of Unit: S. Loranca-Garcia; tel (2) 296-68-00.

4 Luxembourg, Portugal, Czech Republic.

Head of Unit: (vacant).

Energy and Transport Directorate-General

(28 rue de Mot, 1040 Brussels, Belgium; tel (2) 299-11-11; fax (2) 295-01-50; e-mail tren-info@cec.eu.int or forename.surname@cec.eu.int; internet www.europa.eu.int/comm/dgs)

Director-General: François Lamoureux; tel (2) 295-19-92; fax (2) 296-83-55.

Deputy Director-General, Directorates H and I: Fernando de Esteban (with special responsibility for Co-ordination of Nuclear Activities); tel (2) 299-52-29; fax (2) 295-01-50.

Principal Adviser: G. Landresse.

ADMINISTRATIVE UNIT

1 Internal Audit.

Head of Unit: Alessandro D'Atri (reporting directly to the Director-General).

Advisers: J. Henningsen, L. Muschel, R. Mayet (reporting directly to the Director-General); tel (2) 299-47-08.

DIRECTORATE A

(General Affairs)

Director: Dominique Ristori; tel (2) 299-24-60; fax (2) 295-58-43.

Units

1 Financial Resources, Activity-based Management.

Head of Unit: Dirk Beckers; tel (2) 695-42-61.

2 Personnel, Training and Information Technology.

Head of Unit: Gerhard Schumann-Hitzler; tel (2) 296-24-23.

3 Inter-Institutional Relations, Enlargement and International Relations.

Head of Unit: Laurent Muschel; tel (2) 299-47-08.

4 Internal Market and Competition.

Head of Unit: Marie Wolfcarius; tel (2) 295-91-20.

5 Services of General Economic Interest and Users' Rights.

Head of Unit: Peter Faross; tel (2) 295-95-66.

DIRECTORATE B

(Trans-European Networks, Energy and Transport)

Director: Günther Hanreich, tel (2) 296-29-42.

Units

1 Sectoral Economy.

Head of Unit: Pirjo-Liisa Koskimäki; tel (2) 295-16-40.

2 TEN Policy and Technology Development.

Head of Unit: Edgar Thielmann; tel (2) 295-46-15; fax (2) 296-43-37.

3 TEN Project Management.

Head of Unit: Klaus Rudischauser; tel (2) 299-04-21.

4 Project Evaluation and Financial Administration.

Head of Unit: J. C. Merciol.

DIRECTORATE C

(Conventional Energies)

Director: Helmut Schmitt Von Sydow; tel (2) 295-42-56.

Units

1 Promoting Dialogue between Energy Producers and Consumers.

Head of Unit: Nina Commeau-Yannoussis; tel (2) 296-72-49.

2 Electricity and Gas.

Head of Unit: Christopher Jones; tel (2) 296-50-30; fax (2) 296-42-54.

3 Coal and Oil.

Head of Unit: Peter Schwaiger.

DIRECTORATE D

(New Sources Energies and Demand Management)

Director: Alfonso González Finat; tel (2) 296-82-87.

Adviser: Gonzalo Molina Iguarta; tel (2) 295-15-24.

Units

1 Regulatory Policy, Promotion of New Energy Sources and Demand Management.

Head of Unit: Luc Werring; tel (2) 296-84-51; fax (2) 296-45-74.

2 New and Renewable Energy Sources.

Head of Unit: Karl Kellner; tel (2) 295-24-10; fax (2) 296-45-74.

3 Demand Management.

Head of Unit: Patrick Lambert; tel (2) 295-05-31.

4 Clean Urban Transport.

Head of Unit: Eleni Kopanezou; tel (2) 299-67-68.

DIRECTORATE E

(Inland Transport)

Director: Heinz Hilbrecht; tel (2) 296-81-74; fax (2) 299-05-68.

Units

1 Road Transport.

Head of Unit: Isabelle Kardacz.

2 Rail Transport and Interoperability.

Head of Unit: Jean-Arnold Vinois; tel (2) 296-84-75.

3 Road Safety and Technology.

Head of Unit: Dimitrios Theologitis; tel (2) 299-55-82.

4 Galileo Satellite Navigation System; Intelligent Transport.

Head of Unit: Olivier Onidi; tel (2) 295-60-40; fax (2) 299-05-68.

DIRECTORATE F

(Air Transport)

Director: Enrico Grillo Pasquarelli; tel (2) 295-62-03.

Units

1 Economic Regulation.

Head of Unit: Ludolf Van Hasselt; tel (2) 299-48-61.

2 Air Traffic Management.

Head of Unit: Bernard van Houte; tel (2) 295-04-94; fax (2) 296-46-94.

3 Airport Policy and Safety.

Head of Unit: Rodrigo Vila De Benavent; tel (2) 296-88-28.

4 Air Transport Agreements.

Head of Unit: Enrico Grillo Pasquarelli.

DIRECTORATE G

(Maritime Transport)

Director: Fotis Karamitsos; tel (2) 296-34-61; fax (2) 296-46-94.

Units

1 Maritime Policy and Technology.

Head of Unit: Philippe Burghelle-Vernet; tel (2) 295-17-99.

2 Short Sea Shipping and Port Policy.

Head of Unit: Dirk Van Vreckem; tel (2) 296-84-39.

3 Intermodality and Logistics.

Head of Unit: Stefan Tostmann; tel (2) 296-88-33; fax (2) 296-46-94.

DIRECTORATE H

(Nuclear Safety and Safeguards)

Director: Christian Waeterloos; tel (2) 293-43-42.

Units

1 Euratom Co-ordination and Nuclear Safety.

Head of Unit: Ute Blohm-Hieber; tel (2) 295-41-51.

2 Nuclear Compatability.

Head of Unit: Stamatios Tsalas; tel (2) 293-71-47.

3 Safeguards and Non-proliferation.

Head of Unit: Augustin Janssens; tel (2) 293-63-95.

DIRECTORATE I

(Nuclear Inspections)

Director: Christian Cleutinx; tel (2) 293-62-36.

Units

1 Logistics and Information Technology.

Head of Unit: Maurizio Boella; tel (2) 293-71-25.

2 Verification of Reprocessing Plants.

Head of Unit: Paul Meylemans; tel (2) 293-27-11.

3 Verification of Fabrication and Enrichment Plants.

Head of Unit: Herman Nackaerts; tel (2) 293-30-08.

4 Verification of Reactors and of Storage and other Facilities.

Head of Unit: José Santos Bento; tel (2) 293-48-60.

5 Personal Protection.

Head of Unit: Jean Trestour.

EURATOM SUPPLY AGENCY

Director: Christian Waeterloos (acting); tel (2) 293-43-42.

Unit

1 Nuclear Fuels Supply Contracts and Research.

Head of Unit: María Dolores Carrillo Dorado; tel (2) 295-12-19.

Enterprise and Industry Directorate-General

(15 rue de la Science, 1040 Brussels, Belgium; tel (2) 299-11-11; fax (2) 295-97-92; e-mail info-entreprises@cec.eu.int or forename.surname@cec.eu.int; internet www.europa.eu.int/comm/dgs/enterprise/index_en.htm)

Director-General: Horst Reichenbach.

Deputy Director-General: Heinz Zourek; tel (2) 299-16-04.

Assistant to the Director-General: Armand Rauch; tel (2) 296-27-37.

ADMINISTRATIVE UNIT

1 Audit.

Head of Unit: Natacha Legras Marechal (acting, reporting directly to the Director-General); tel (2) 299-51-28.

DIRECTORATE R

(Resources)

Director: Belinda Pyke; tel (2) 296-16-73; fax (2) 299-38-62.

Units

1 Financial Resources.

Head of Unit: Manuela Finetti.

2 Human Resources.

Head of Unit: Michael Coomans.

3 Informatics.

Head of Unit: Stefan Nonneman.

4 Information and Communication.

Head of Unit: Peter Wragg.

5 Strategic Planning and Management.

Head of Unit: Valère Moutarlier.

DIRECTORATE A

(Enterprise Policy)

Director: David White; tel (2) 295-57-24; fax (2) 296-08-51.

Units

1 Development of Enterprise Policy.

Head of Unit: Didier Herbert; tel (2) 299-00-87; fax (2) 296-08-51.

2 External Aspects of Enterprise Policy.

Head of Unit: Philippe Jean; tel (2) 295-05-39; fax (2) 296-08-51.

4 Enterprise Aspects of Competition.

Head of Unit: Geneviève Pons-Deladrière.

5 Competitive Analysis and Benchmarking.

Head of Unit: Tassos Belessiotis; tel (2) 299-34-10; fax (2) 299-08-51.

6 Innovation Policy.

Head of Unit: Reinhard Büscher.

DIRECTORATE B

(Promotion of Entrepreneurship and SMEs)

Director: Timo Summa; tel (2) 299-16-71; fax (2) 296-75-26.

Units

1 Entrepreneurship.

Head of Unit: Christian Weinberger.

2 Business Co-operation and Community Business Support Networks.

Head of Unit: Jean-Luc Abrivard.

3 Crafts and Small Businesses, Co-operatives and Mutuals.

Head of Unit: Albrecht Mulfinger; tel (2) 295-39-42.

4 Access to Finance.

Head of Unit: Jean-Noël Durvy; tel (2) 4301-33610.

5 Innovation Networks.

Head of Unit: Renate Weissenhorn.

DIRECTORATE D

(Services; Commerce; Tourism; E-business)

Director: Pedro Ortún-Silvan; tel (2) 295-20-84; fax (2) 299-39-39.

Units

1 Business Services; Enterprise Aspects of Employment Policy.

Head of Unit: Ole Guldberg; tel (2) 295-60-89; fax (2) 299-39-39.

2 Commerce; Tourism; E-business; Networks between Public Administrations (IDA).

Head of Unit: Bernard Schnittger (acting).

3 Tourism.

Head of Unit: Francesco Ianniello.

4 E-business; ICT Industry and Services.

Head of Unit: Constantin Andropoulos.

5 Textiles, Fashion and Design Industries.

Head of Unit: Luis Filipe Girao.

DIRECTORATE E

(Environmental Aspects of Enterprise Policy; Resource-based and Specific Industries)

Director: Patrick Hennessy; tel (2) 296-33-55; fax (2) 296-75-65.

Units

1 Environmental Aspects of Enterprise Policy.

Head of Unit: Michel Catinat; tel (2) 296-95-29; fax (2) 296-75-65.

2 Steel, Non-ferrous Metals and other Materials.

Head of Unit: Liliana Brykman.

3 Chemicals.

Head of Unit: Vicente Leoz-Argüelles.

4 Forest-based Industries.

Head of Unit: Per-Ove Engelbrecht.

5 Aerospace, Defence, Rail and Maritime Industries.

Head of Unit: Daniel Bunch (acting).

6 REACH.

Head of Unit: Geert Dancet.

DIRECTORATE F

(Single Market: Regulatory Environment; Industries under Vertical Legislation)

Director: Paul Weissenberg; tel (2) 296-33-58; fax (2) 295-21-27.

Units

1 Notifications and Infringements.

Head of Unit: Sabine Lecrenier; tel (2) 295-57-38; fax (2) 295-21-27.

2 Pharmaceuticals: Regulatory Framework and Market Authorisations.

Head of Unit: Philippe Brunet; tel (2) 295-41-28; fax (2) 295-21-27.

3 Biotechnology; Competitiveness in Pharmaceuticals; Cosmetics.

Head of Unit: Abraão Carvalho; tel (2) 295-73-97; fax (2) 295-21-27.

4 Food Industry.

Head of Unit: Andreas Menidiatis; tel (2) 295-53-88.

5 Automotive Industry.

Head of Unit: Reinhard Schulte-Braucks.

DIRECTORATE G

(Single Market: Regulatory Environment, Conformity and Standardization; New Approach)

Director: Michel Ayral.

Units

1 Legal Aspects Linked to Internal Market.

Head of Unit: Jacques McMillan.

2 Standardization.

Head of Unit: Norbert Anselmann.

3 Mechanical and Electrical Equipment Engineering; Radio and Telecom Terminal Equipment Industries.

Head of Unit: Luis Montoya Morón.

4 Pressure Equipment; Medical Devices; Metrology.

Head of Unit: Cornelis Brekelmans; tel (2) 295-66-00; fax (2) 296-28-93.

5 Construction.

Head of Unit: Richard Klein.

6 Impact Assessment and Support to Sectorial Analysis.

Head of Unit: Colette Cotter.

Environment Directorate-General

(5 ave de Beaulieu, 1160 Brussels, Belgium; tel (2) 299-11-11; fax (2) 299-03-07; e-mail envinfo@cec.eu.int or forename.surname@cec.eu.int; internet www.europa.eu.int/comm/dgs/environment/index_en.htm)

Director-General: Catherine Day; tel (2) 295-83-12; fax (2) 299-11-05.

Assistant to Director-General: Malachy Hargadon; tel (2) 296-84-50.

ADMINISTRATIVE UNITS

1 Strategic Planning and Policy Co-ordination.

Head of Unit: Elizabeth Golberg (reporting directly to the Director-General); tel (2) 299-20-21.

2 Internal Audit.

Head of Unit: Jan Julius Groenendaal (reporting directly to the Director-General); tel (2) 299-22-71.

DIRECTORATE A

(Governance, Communication and Civil Protection)

Director: David Grant Lawrence; tel (2) 295-35-37; fax (2) 296-88-26.

Units

1 Communications.

Head of Unit: Ylva Tiveus; tel (2) 296-66-73.

2 Infringements.

Head of Unit: George Kremlis; tel (2) 296-65-26.

3 Legal and Governance.

Head of Unit: Ludwig Krämer; tel (2) 299-22-65; fax (2) 296-88-26.

4 Interinstitutional Relations.

Head of Unit: Paulus Brouwer; tel (2) 295-41-25.

5 Civil Protection.

Head of Unit: Pia Bucella; tel (2) 295-70-99.

DIRECTORATE B

(Protecting the Natural Environment)

Director: Prudencio Perera Manzanedo; tel (2) 296-87-05; fax (2) 296-88-25.

Units

1 Agriculture and Soil.

Head of Unit: (vacant).

2 Nature and Bio-diversity.

Head of Unit: Nicholas Hanley; tel (2) 296-87-03; fax (2) 296-88-25.

3 Forests.

Head of Unit: Robert Flies; tel (2) 296-54-44.

4 Biotechnology and Pesticides.

Head of Unit: Herve Martin; tel (2) 296-54-44.

DIRECTORATE C

(Air and Chemicals)

Director: Jos Delbeke; tel (2) 296-8804.

Units

1 Clean Air and Transport.

Head of Unit: Peter Gammeltoft; tel (2) 296-86-95; fax (2) 296-34-40.

2 Climate Ozone and Energy.

Head of Unit: Artur Runge-Metzger; tel (2) 295-68-98.

3 Chemicals.

Head of Unit: Eva Hellsten; tel (2) 299-67-65; fax (2) 296-34-40.

4 Industrial Emissions.

Head of Unit: (vacant).

DIRECTORATE D

(Water and Environmental Programmes)

Director: Catherine Day; tel (2) 295-83-12.

Units

1 The Life Unit.

Head of Unit: Bruno Julien; tel (2) 295-61-33; fax (2) 296-78-70.

2 Water and Marine.

Head of Unit: Patrick Murphy; tel (2) 299-83-39.

3 Cohesion Policy and Environmental Impact Assessments.

Head of Unit: Claude Rouam; tel (2) 295-79-94.

4 Health and Urban Areas.

Head of Unit: Anastasios Nychas; tel (2) 296-87-16.

DIRECTORATE E

(Global and International Affairs)

Director: Claus Sorensen; tel (2) 298-66-44.

Units

1 Climate Change.

Head of Unit: Jos Delbeke; tel (2) 296-88-04; fax (2) 299-03-06.

Deputy Head of Unit: Marianne Wenning; tel (2) 295-59-43; fax (2) 299-03-06.

2 International Affairs, Trade and Environment.

Head of Unit: Julio García Burgues; tel (2) 296-87-63; fax (2) 299-03-06.

3 Development and the Environment; Mediterranean.

Head of Unit: Christoph Bail; tel (2) 295-40-99; fax (2) 299-03-06.

Deputy Head of Unit: Jill Hanna; tel (2) 295-32-32; fax (2) 299-03-06.

DIRECTORATE F

(Resource Management)

Director: Viola Groebner; tel (2) 299-00-78.

Units

1 Human Resources; Administration.

Head of Unit: Hans de Jong; tel (2) 295-13-47; fax (2) 295-53-71.

2 Budget and Finance.

Head of Unit: Philip Owen; tel (2) 296-55-62.

3 Information Technology.

Head of Unit: Martin Gritsch; tel (2) 295-94-67.

DIRECTORATE G

(Sustainable Development and Integration)

Director: Timo Mäkelä; tel (2) 296-26-34.

Units

1 Sustainable Development and Economic Analysis.

Head of Unit: Robin Miege; tel (2) 295-80-43.

2 Environment and Industry.

Head of Unit: Herbert Aichinger; tel (2) 296-69-54.

3 Research, Science and Innovation.

Head of Unit: Ian Clark; tel (2) 296-90-94.

4 Sustainable Production and Consumption.

Head of Unit: Marianne Klingbeil; tel (2) 296-04-93.

Fisheries Directorate-General

(99 rue de Joseph II, 1000 Brussels, Belgium; tel (2) 299-11-11; fax (2) 295-25-69; e-mail fisheries-info@cec.eu.int or forename.surname@cec.eu.int; internet www.europa.eu.int/comm/dgs/fisheries/index_en.htm)

Director-General: Jörgen Holmquist.

Assistant to Director-General: Emmanouil Papaioannou; tel (2) 296-99-88.

ADMINISTRATIVE UNIT

1 Human Resources, Budget and Informatics, Evaluation.

Head of Unit: John Mallett (reporting directly to the Director-General); tel (2) 295-21-00; fax (2) 296-59-52.

FISH 1

(Budget, Procurement and Control)

Unit

Head of Unit: Monique Pariat.

FISH 2

(Audit and Evaluation)

Unit

Head of Unit: Dominique Discors.

FISH 3

(Human Resources, Informatics and Logistics)

Unit

Head of Unit: Fernando Frutuoso Melo.

FISH A

(Conservation Policy)

Director: John Farnell; tel (2) 295-63-97.

Adviser: Ole Tougaard; tel (2) 295-22-09.

Units

1 Management of Stocks.

Head of Unit: Ernesto Penas Lado.

2 Management of Fleets.

Head of Unit: Jean-Claude Cueff; tel (2) 295-12-92.

3 Environment and Health.

Head of Unit: Armando Astudillo Gonzales; tel (2) 296-11-91.

4 Research and Scientific Analysis.

Head of Unit: Jacques Fuchs (acting).

FISH B

(External Policy and Markets)

Director: Cesar Deben Alfonso.

Adviser: (vacant).

Units

1 General Aspects of External Relations.

Head of Unit: Serge Beslier; tel (2) 295-01-15.

2 International and Regional Arrangements.

Head of Unit: Edward Spencer; tel (2) 295-68-58.

Deputy Head of Unit: (vacant).

3 Bilateral Agreements.

Head of Unit: Harm Koster.

4 Common Organization of Markets and Trade.

Head of Unit: Friedrich Wieland; tel (2) 296-32-05.

FISH C

(Structural Policy)

Director: Lea Verstraete.

Adviser: Jacques Soenens; tel (2) 295-12-67.

Units

1 General Aspects of Structural Policy.

Head of Unit: Stefanos Samaras.

2 Belgium, Denmark, Estonia, Germany, Ireland, Latvia, Lithuania, Finland, Poland, Sweden, the Netherlands, United Kingdom, Outermost Regions.

Head of Unit: Jacques Verborgh (acting).

3 Cyprus, France, Greece, Italy, Malta, Portugal, Spain.

Head of Unit: John Mallett.

4 Aquaculture, Transformation, Marketing; Austria, Czech Republic, Hungary, Luxembourg, Slovakia, Slovenia.

Head of Unit: Constantin Vamvakas.

FISH D

(Horizontal Policy)

Director: Emilio Mastracchio; tel (2) 295-55-68

Units

1 Internal Co-ordination, Relations with other Institutions and Dialogue with Industry and Organizations.

Head of Unit: Baudouin Sury; tel (2) 295-63-35.

2 Communication and Information.

Head of Unit: Chiara Gariazzo; tel (2) 299-92-55.

3 Legal Issues.

Head of Unit: Paul Nemitz; tel (2) 296-91-35.

4 Control and Licences.

Head of Unit: Giorgio Gallizioli; tel (2) 295-50-47.

5 Inspections.

Head of Unit: William Brugge.

Health and Consumer Protection Directorate-General

(232 rue Belliard, 1040 Brussels, Belgium; tel (2) 299-11-11; fax (2) 296-62-98; e-mail sanco-helpline@cec.eu.int or forename.surname@cec.eu.int; internet www.europa.eu.int/comm/dgs/health_consumer/index_en.htm)

Director-General: R.Madelin.

Deputy Director-General: J. Husu-Kallio.

Assistant to Director-General: E. Thevenard.

ADMINISTRATIVE UNITS

1 Audit and Evaluation.

Head of Unit: A. Hellman (reporting directly to the Director-General).

DIRECTORATE A

(General Affairs)

Director: Theodius Lennon; tel (2) 295-99-86; fax (2) 299-63-03.

Units

1 Co-ordination and Institutional Affairs.

Head of Unit: Matthew Hudson; tel (2) 296-46-71.

2 Legal Affairs.

Head of Unit: Paul Remits; tel (2) 299-40-52; fax (2) 295-94-90.

3 Financial, Human and other Resources.

Head of Unit: Daniel Janssens; tel (2) 295-12-20; fax (2) 299-54-29.

4 Information Systems and Publications.

Head of Unit: M. P. Benassi.

DIRECTORATE B

(Consumer Affairs)

Director: Agnes Pantelouri; tel (2) 299-01-31; fax (2) 299-18-57.

Units

1 Policy Analysis and Development; E-economy; International Questions.

Head of Unit: Véronique Arnault; tel (2) 299-00-06; fax (2) 298-49-69.

2 Unfair Commercial Practices, Redress and Administrative Co-operation.

Head of Unit: C. Törnblom.

3 Product and Service Safety.

Head of Unit: Bernard. Delogu; tel (2) 299-03-51; fax (2) 299-18-58.

4 Protection of Legal, Economic and other Consumer Interests.

Head of Unit: D. Staudenmayer.

DIRECTORATE C

(Public Health and Risk Assessment)

Director: Fernand Sauer; tel 4301-32719.

Units

1 Programme Management.

Head of Unit: L. Briol.

2 Health Information.

Head of Unit: John F. Ryan; tel 4301-346658.

3 Health Threats.

Head of Unit: Georgios Gouvras; tel 4301-33465.

4 Health Determinants.

Head of Unit: Matti Rajala; tel 4301-38502.

5 Health Strategy.

Adviser: Bernard. Merkel; tel (2) 4301-38020.

6 Risk Assessment.

Head of Unit: Peter Wagstaffe; tel (2) 295-74-64.

DIRECTORATE D

(Food Safety; Production and Distribution Chain)

Director: Paolo Testori Coggi; tel (2) 295-34-30; fax (2) 295-02-85.

Units

1 Animal Nutrition.

Head of Unit: Willem Penning; tel (2) 295-56-51; fax (2) 295-02-85.

2 Biological Risks.

Head of Unit: Eric Poudelet; tel (2) 295-52-07; fax (2) 295-02-85.

3 Chemical and Physical Risks; Surveillance.

Head of Unit: Patricia Brunko; tel (2) 296-25-87; fax (2) 295-02-85.

4 Food Law and Biotechnology.

Head of Unit: Patrick Deboyser; tel (2) 295-15-29; fax (2) 295-02-85.

5 Relations with the European Food Safety Authority.

Head of Unit: R. Vanhoorde.

DIRECTORATE E

(Food Safety; Plant Health; Animal Health and Welfare; International Questions)

Director: Alejandro Checchi Lang; tel (2) 295-68-38; fax (2) 296-42-86.

Advisor: Sara Reinius (Enlargement); tel (2) 297-07-06.

Units

1 Plant Health.

Head of Unit: Goffredo del Bino; tel (2) 299-22-57; fax (2) 296-42-86.

2 Animal Health and Welfare; Zootechnics.

Head of Unit: Bernard van Goethem; tel (2) 295-31-43; fax (2) 296-42-86.

3 International Food, Veterinary and Phytosanitary Questions.

Head of Unit: M. Scannell.

DIRECTORATE F

(Food and Veterinary Office—FVO)

Director: M. Gaynor.

Units

1 Country Profiles, Co-ordination of Follow-up.

Head of Unit: H. Quigley.

2 Food of Animal Origin: Mammals.

Head of Unit: J. Wilson.

3 Food of Animal Origin: Birds and Fish.

Head of Unit: Jacky Le Gosles; tel (2) 297-07-87; fax (2) 297-08-66.

4 Food of Plant Origin; Plant Health; Processing and Distribution.

Head of Unit: Michael Flüh; tel (2) 297-08-02; fax (2) 297-08-64.

5 Animal Nutrition; Import Controls; Residues.

Head of Unit: M. Alvarez Antolinez; tel (2) 297-07-78; fax (2) 297-07-03.

6 Quality, Planning and Development.

Head of Unit: F. Andriessen.

Information Society Directorate-General

(24 ave Beaulieu, 1060 Brussels, Belgium; tel (2) 296-88-00; fax (2) 299-41-70); e-mail infso-desk@cec.eu.int or forename.surname@cec.eu.int; internet europa.eu.int/comm/dgs/information_society/index_en.htm; Bâtiment Jean Monnet, rue Alcide de Gasperi, 2920 Luxembourg; tel 4301-1)

Director-General: Fabio Colasanti; tel (2) 299-43-74; fax (2) 296-90-46.

Deputy Director-General: Peter Zangl (with special responsibility for Administrative and Financial Management of the RTD-specific Programme and of the other Programmes, and of the Contribution of RTD Activities to the E-Europe Action Plan); tel (2) 295-41-47.

Assistants to the Director-General: Armand Rauch; tel (2) 296-2737; John Watson; tel (2) 296-41-66.

ADMINISTRATIVE UNITS

Advisers: Christopher Wilkinson (with special responsibility for International Aspects of Internet Governance and for the Secretariat, ICANN Governmental Advisory Committee (GAC), tel (2) 296-95-38; Heinrich Otruba (with special responsibility for the Secretariat of the European Regulators Group for Communications Networks and Services), tel (2) 296-88-79.

1 Internal Audit.

Head of Unit: Christian Dubs (reporting directly to the Director-General); tel (2) 295-97-77.

DIRECTORATE R

(Integrated Management of Resources; Horizontal Questions)

Director: Bernard Libertalis; tel (2) 296-89-52.

Units

1 Human Resources.

Head of Unit: Gianmarco Di Vita; tel (2) 296-88-46; fax (2) 295-53-71.

2 Budgetary Resources.

Head of Unit: Walter Schwarzenbrunner; tel (2) 299-22-70; fax (2) 295-53-71.

3 Co-ordination and Planning.

Head of Unit: José Cotta; tel (2) 296-64-07.

4 Information Technology Infrastructure and Services.

Head of Unit: Bas de Bruijn; tel (2) 296-34-21; fax (2) 295-53-71.

5 Information Systems Development and Support.

Head of Unit: Massimo Luciolli; tel (2) 295-26-17.

6 Management Support.

Head of Unit: (vacant).

DIRECTORATE A

(Internet, Network Security and General Affairs)

Director: Pedro De Sampaio Nunes; tel (2) 295-86-45.

Units

1 Internet; Network and Information Security.

Head of Unit: Michael Niebel; tel (2) 296-07-05.

2 International Relations.

Head of Unit: Simon Bensasson; tel (2) 296-8066.

3 Information and Communication.

Head of Unit: Pierrette Pelhate; tel (2) 296-96-33.

4 Inter-institutional Relations.

Head of Unit: Enrico Forti; tel (2) 296-51-72.

DIRECTORATE B

(Communication Services: Policy and Regulatory Framework)

Director: Bernd Langeheine; tel (2) 299-18-55.

Units

1 Policy Development and Regulatory Framework.

Head of Unit: Peter Rodford; tel (2) 299-00-15.

2 Implementation of Regulatory Framework; Relations with Member States (II).

Head of Unit: George Papapavlou; tel (2) 295-49-90.

3 Radio Spectrum Policy.

Head of Unit: Ruprecht Niepold; tel (2) 296-89-55.

4 Procedures related to National Regulatory Measures.

Head of Unit: Paraskevi Michou; tel (2) 295-34-37.

DIRECTORATE C

(Miniaturisation, Embedded Systems, Societal Applications)

Director: Rosalie Zobel; tel (2) 296-81-68; fax (2) 299-28-65.

Adviser: Wolfgang Streitenberger (with special responsibility for Market Analysis and Communication Strategy); tel (2) 298-44-26.

Units

1 Nanoelectronics and Photonics.

Head of Unit: Rainer Zimmermann; tel (2) 296-81-10.

2 Integrated Micro- and Nanosystems.

Head of Unit: Dirk Beernaert; tel (2) 296-80-20.

3 Embedded Systems.

Head of Unit: Konstantinos Glinos; tel (2) 296-95-77.

4 ICT for Health.

Head of Unit: Gérard Comyn; tel (2) 299-43-46.

5 ICT for Transport and the Environment.

Head of Unit: André Vits; tel (2) 296-35-23.

6 eGovernment.

Head of Unit: Paul Timmers; tel (2) 299-02-45.

7 Administration and Finance.

Head of Unit: Ramon Haendler Mas (acting); tel (2) 296-81-24.

DIRECTORATE D

(Communication Networks, Security and Software Applications)

Director: João da Silva (acting); tel (2) 296-34-17.

Adviser: Stephen Pascall (with special responsibility for the Analysis of Potential Implications of Policies and of the Regulation of Technological Convergence); tel (2) 296-81-78.

Units

1 Communication and Network Technologies.

Head of Unit: Augusto de Albuquerque; tel (2) 296-34-76.

2 Networked Audio-Visual Systems, Home Platforms.

Head of Unit: João da Silva; tel (2) 296-34-17.

3 Software Technologies and Distributed Systems.

Head of Unit: Jesus Villasante; tel (2) 296-35-21.

4 ICT for Trust and Security.

Head of Unit: Jacques Bus; tel (2) 296-81-16.

5 ICT for Business.

Head of Unit: Gérald Santucci; tel (2) 296-89-63.

6 eTen.

Head of Unit: David Broster; tel (2) 296-80-21.

7 Administration and Finance.

Head of Unit: Joaquín Perez Echagüe (acting); tel (2) 299-36-85.

DIRECTORATE E

(Interfaces, Knowledge and Content Technologies; Applications; Information Market – Luxembourg)

Director: Horst Forster; tel 4301-32123.

Units

1 Interfaces.

Head of Unit: Giovanni Varile; tel 4301-32867.

2 Knowledge Management and Content Creation.

Head of Unit: Roberto Cencioni; tel 4301-32859.

3 Technology-Enhanced Learning; Cultural Heritage.

Head of Unit: Patricia Manson; tel 4301-33261.

4 Information Market.

Head of Unit: Javier Hernandez-Ros; tel 4301-34533.

5 Cognition.

Head of Unit: Colette Maloney; tel 4301-36972.

6 Exploitation of Research Results; Projects.

Head of Unit: Bernard Smith; tel 4301-34195.

7 Administration and Finance.

Head of Unit: Norbert Brinkhoff; tel 4301-32613.

DIRECTORATE F

(Emerging Technologies and Infrastructures; Applications)

Director: Luis Rodriguez Rosello (acting); tel (2) 296-34-06.

Units

1 Future and Emerging Technologies.

Head of Unit: Thierry Van Der Pyl; tel (2) 296-81-05.

2 Grid Technologies.

Head of Unit: Wolfgang Boch; tel (2) 296-35-91.

3 Research Infrastructure.

Head of Unit: Mario Campolargo; tel (2) 296-34-79.

4 New Working Environments.

Head of Unit: Bror Salmelin, tel (2) 296-95-64.

5 e-Inclusion.

Head of Unit: Per Blixt; tel (2) 296-80-48.

6 Administration and Finance.

Head of Unit: Johannes Machnik; tel (2) 296-85-79.

Internal Market and Services Directorate-General

(107 ave de Cortenbergh, 1000 Brussels, Belgium; tel (2) 299-11-11; fax (2) 295-65-00; e-mail markt-info@cec.eu.int or forename.surname@cec.eu.int; internet www.europa.eu.int/comm/dgs/ internal_market/index_en.htm)

Director-General: Alexander Schaub; tel 4301-52387.

Deputy Director-General, Directorates B and D, Application of Internal Market Law and Parliamentary Affairs: Thierry Stoll; tel 4301-52438.

Assistants to the Director-General: Nathalie de Basaldua; tel (2) 295-61-89, fax (2) 296-39-24; Martin Merlin; tel (2) 295-89-47, fax (2) 296-39-24.

ADMINISTRATIVE UNITS

1 Audit.

Head of Unit: Pascale Van Outryve (reporting directly to the Director-General); tel 4301-62740.

DIRECTORATE A

(Administrative Support and Communication)

Director: Jacqueline Minor; tel 4301-57226.

Units

1 Human and Financial Resources.

Head of Unit: Olivier Salles.

2 Information Technology and Document Handling.

Head of Unit: Fernando Toledano Gasca; tel 4301-68177.

3 Internal and External Communication.

Head of Unit: Anthony Dempsey; tel 4301-57357.

DIRECTORATE B

(Policy Development, Strategic Programming and Co-ordination)

Director: Susan Binns; tel 4301-63285.

Adviser: Dag Sverker Håken Ander; tel 4301-63104.

Units

1 Internal Market Strategy and Competitiveness.

Head of Unit: Gerrit Gerard De Graaf; tel 4301-68466.

2 Programming, Legal Affairs and Inter-institutional Relations.

Head of Unit: Pascal Leardini; tel 4301-61306.

3 Economic Analysis and Evaluation.

Head of Unit: Francisco de Asís Caballero Sanz; tel 4301-51168.

4 Internal Market: External Dimension.

Head of Unit: Johannes Hooijer; tel 4301-55885.

DIRECTORATE C

(Free Movement of Goods, Regulated Professions and Postal Services)

Director: Hendrik Post; tel 4301-66606.

Adviser: Ulf Bruehann; tel 4301-57377.

Units

1 Application of Art 28 to 30, Mutual Recognition and Product Liability.

Head of Unit: Ghyslaine Guisolphe; tel 4301-51860.

2 Application of Art 28–30, Product Safety and Related Legislation.

Head of Unit: Joerg Reinbothe; tel 4301-55323.

3 Regulated Professions.

Head of Unit: Pamela Brumter; tel 4301-59408.

4 Postal Services.

Head of Unit: (vacant).

DIRECTORATE D

(Public Procurement Policy)

Director: Bertrand Carsin; tel 4301-55795.

Units

1 Formulation of Public Procurement Law; Surveillance and Application for Belgium, France, Greece, Ireland, Luxembourg, Portugal, Spain and the United Kingdom.

Head of Unit: Matthias Petschke; tel 4301-66867.

Deputy Head of Unit: Gauthier Pierens; tel 4301-59834.

2 Formulation of Public Procurement Law; Surveillance and Application for Austria, Denmark, Finland, Germany, Italy, the Netherlands and Sweden; Relations with other Community Policies.

Head of Unit: Ugo Bassi; tel 4301-53118.

3 Public Procurement: International Negotiations, Economic Aspects, Electronic Procedures; SIMAP.

Head of Unit: Panayotis Stamatopoulos; tel 4301-61772.

DIRECTORATE E

(Services, Copyright, Industrial Property and Data Protection)

Director: Guido Berardis.

Units

1 Services 1.

Head of Unit: Margot Fröhlinger; tel (2) 295-93-77; fax (2) 296-80-10.

2 Services 2.

Head of Unit: Jean Bergevin; tel 4301-51639.

3 Industrial Property.

Head of Unit: Erik Nooteboom; tel (2) 296-03-48; fax (2) 299-31-04.

4 Copyright and Neighbouring Rights.

Head of Unit: (vacant).

5 Data Protection.

Head of Unit: Philippe Renaudiere; tel 4301-68750.

DIRECTORATE F

(Financial Institutions)

Director: Jean-Claude Thébault; tel 4301-50169.

Units

1 Financial Services Policy.

Head of Unit: Irmfried Schwimann.

2 Banking and Financial Conglomerates.

Head of Unit: Patrick Pearson; tel 4301-55758.

3 Insurance.

Head of Unit: Jose Luis Rosello Lopez (acting).

4 Retail Issues and Payment Systems.

Head of Unit: David Deacon; tel 4301-55905.

DIRECTORATE G

(Financial Markets)

Director: David Wright; tel (2) 295-86-26; fax (2) 299-30-56.

Units

1 Financial Markets Infrastructure.

Head of Unit: Mario Nava; tel 4301-64235.

2 Securities Markets.

Head of Unit: Nathalie De Basaldua Lemarchand; tel 4301-56189.

3 Asset Management.

Head of Unit: Niall Bohan; tel 4301-63007.

4 Financial Markets; Company Law, Corporate Governance and Financial Crime.

Head of Unit: Pierre Delsaux; tel 4301-65472.

5 Accounting and Audit.

Head of Unit: Karel Van Hulle; tel 4301-57954.

Justice, Freedom and Security Directorate-General

(46 rue du Luxembourg, 1050 Brussels, Belgium; tel (2) 299-11-11; fax (2) 296-74-81; e-mail forename.surname@cec.eu.int; internet www.europa.eu.int/comm/dgs/justice_home/index_en.htm)

Director-General: Jonathan Faull.

ADMINISTRATIVE UNITS

1 Policy and Strategic Planning; Legal and Institutional Matters.

Head of Unit: Tung-Laï Margue; tel (2) 295-44-37.

2 Internal Audit.

Head of Unit: Claire Magnant; tel (2) 295-16-30.

DIRECTORATE A

(Free Movement of Persons; Citizenship; Fundamental Rights)

Director: Gustaaf Borchardt; tel (2) 296-65-83.

Adviser: Alain Brun (Charter on Fundamental Rights).

Units

1 Free Movement of Persons, Visa Policy, External Borders, Schengen.

Head of Unit: Giuseppe Callovi; tel (2) 295-17-80.

2 Immigration and Asylum (including European Refugee Fund).

Head of Unit: Jean-Louis de Brouwer; tel (2) 296-19-64.

3 Judicial Co-operation in Civil Matters.

Head of Unit: Mário Paulo Tenreiro; tel (2) 295-13-67.

4 Co-ordination of Drug Abuse Prevention.

Head of Unit: (vacant).

5 Citizenship; Charter on Fundamental Rights; Racism and Xenophobia; DAPHNE Programme.

Head of Unit: Alain Brun; tel (2) 296-53-81.

DIRECTORATE B

(Fight against Crime and Terrorism; Enlargement; External Relations)

Director: Denise Sorasio; tel (2) 299-05-84; fax (2) 295-01-74.

Units

1 Fight against Organized Crime.

Head of Unit: Sönke Schmidt; tel (2) 295-44-37.

2 Judicial Co-operation in Criminal Matters.

Head of Unit: Gisèle Vernimmen; tel (2) 295-39-83.

3 External Relations and Enlargement.

Head of Unit: Lotte Knudsen; tel (2) 295-80-66.

4 Management of the Title VI Programme.

Head of Unit: Jean-Jacques Nuss.

DIRECTORATE C

(Resources Management; Communication; Information Networks)

Director: Carel Edwards (acting); tel (2) 295-95-38.

Units

1 Human and Financial Resources; Information Technology; Security.

Head of Unit: Carel Edwards; tel (2) 295-95-38.

2 Information Networks; Information; Communication.

Head of Unit: Gisela Vanwert; tel (2) 295-14-19.

3 Large-scale Information Systems.

Head of Unit: Frank Paul.

Regional Policy Directorate-General

(23 rue Père de Deken, 1040 Brussels, Belgium; tel (2) 299-11-11; fax (2) 295-01-49; e-mail dgregio@inforegio.cec.eu.int or forename.surname@cec.eu.int; internet www.europa.eu.int/comm/dgs/regional_policy/index_en.htm)

Director-General: Graham Meadows (acting); tel 4301-56181.

Deputy Director-General: Michele Pasca-Raymondo; tel 4301-56447.

Assistant to Director-General: Raphael Goulet; tel (2) 299-24-70; fax (2) 299-67-95.

ADMINISTRATIVE UNITS

1 Information and Relations with the European Parliament, Committee of the Regions and the Economic and Social Committee.

Head of Unit: Thierry Daman (reporting directly to the Director-General); tel (2) 295-47-33; fax (2) 299-60-03.

2 Internal Audit.

Head of Unit: Charles Groutage (reporting directly to the Deputy Director-General); fax (2) 296-60-03.

DIRECTORATE A1

(Resources)

Director: Walter Deffaa; tel 4301-57752.

Adviser: Ricardo García Ayala; tel 4301-61724.

Units

1 Strategy and Relations with the European Parliament, the Committee of the Regions and Economic and Social Committee.

Head of Unit: (vacant).

2 Human Resources and Training.

Head of Unit: Christopher Todd; tel 4301-52776.

3 Financial and Budget Management.

Head of Unit: Jean-Marie Seyler; tel 4301-54681.

4 Information Technology.

Head of Unit: Marc Botman; tel 4301-63895.

5 Legal Matters, Procedures and Relations with the Committees and the Council.

Head of Unit: Vittoria Alliata-Floyd; tel 4301-58386.

DIRECTORATE A

(Conception, Impact, Co-ordination and Evaluation)

Director: Jean-Charles Leygues; tel (2) 295-61-47; fax (2) 296-24-03.

Units

1 Conception and Analysis; Regional Impact; Spatial Planning.

Head of Unit: (vacant).

2 Conception, Impact Co-ordination and Evaluation; Accession Negotiations.

Head of Unit: Anastassios Bougas; tel 4301 61078.

3 Development and Impact.

Head of Unit: Everardus Hartog; tel 4301-90084.

4 Co-ordination of Evaluation, Regional Impact of Community Policies and Additionality.

Head of Unit: (vacant).

5 Co-ordination of Matters concerning the Outermost Regions.

Head of Unit: Pascale Wolfcarius.

DIRECTORATE B

(Community Initiatives and Innovative Action)

Director: Elisabeth Helander; tel (2) 295-03-54; fax (2) 296-24-30.

Units

1 INTERREG.

Head of Unit: Esben Poulsen; tel (2) 295-00-07; fax (2) 296-32-90.

2 URBAN and Urban Actions.

Head of Unit: Rudolf Niessler; tel (2) 299-52-80; fax (2) 296-32-71.

3 Innovative Action.

Head of Unit: (vacant).

DIRECTORATE D

(Operations in Denmark, Germany, Austria, Latvia, Lithuania, Slovakia, Sweden and United Kingdom)

Director: José Palma Andres; tel (2) 295-15-53; fax (2) 296-23-72.

Units

1 Latvia and United Kingdom.

Head of Unit: Manfred Beschel; tel (2) 295-35-29; fax (2) 296-32-77.

2 Denmark, Lithuania and Sweden.

Head of Unit: Germán Granda Alva; tel (2) 299-29-92; fax (2) 296-69-09.

3 Slovakia and Austria.

Head of Unit: Colin Wolfe; tel 4301-90516.

4 Germany.

Head of Unit: Eric Dufeil; tel (2) 296-04-90; fax (2) 296-60-06.

DIRECTORATE E

(Operations in Belgium, Estonia, Finland, Ireland, Luxembourg, Czech Republic and Spain)

Director: Ranieri di Carpegna; tel (2) 296-95-08; fax (2) 296-24-25.

Units

1 Spain.

Head of Unit: Rory McKenna; tel (2) 295-55-10; fax (2) 296-32-82.

2 Czech Republic, Belgium and Luxembourg.

Head of Unit: Georgios Yannoussis; tel 4301-54864.

3 Estonia, Finland and Ireland.

Head of Unit: Alain Roggeri; tel 4301-58368.

DIRECTORATE F

(Operations in Cyprus, Greece, Hungary, Italy and Malta)

Director: Robert Shotton (acting).

Units

1 Greece.

Head of Unit: Robert Shotton; tel (2) 295-69-56; fax (2) 296-32-88.

Deputy Head of Unit: Giorgios Yannoussis.

2 Italy and Malta.

Head of Unit: Jack Engwegen; tel (2) 295-64-49; fax (2) 296-60-05.

Deputy Head of Unit: Cecilia Campogrande.

3 Hungary and Cyprus.

Head of Unit: (vacant).

DIRECTORATE G

(Operations in France, Poland, Portugal and Slovenia; ISPA)

Director: Luis Riera Figueras; tel (2) 296-50-68; fax (2) 296-10-96.

Units

1 Poland.

Head of Unit: Friedemann Allgayer; tel (2) 299-43-89; fax (2) 296-51-84.

2 Portugal and Slovenia.

Head of Unit: Marco Orani; tel 4301-57086.

3 France.

Head of Unit: Bernard Lange; tel 4301-51709.

4 ISPA.

Head of Unit: Erich Unterwurzacher; tel 4301-66721.

DIRECTORATE H

(Audit)

Director: (vacant).

Units

1 Budgetary and Financial Management.

Head of Unit: Alain Roggeri; tel (2) 295-83-68; fax (2) 296-33-01.

2 Audit of ERDF.

Head of Unit: Nicholas Martyn; fax (2) 295-66-47.

7 Audit of the Cohesion Fund and Co-ordination of the Audit and Control of the Structural Funds.

Head of Unit: Lena Andersson Pench; fax (2) 296-25-70.

Joint Research Centre

(8 square de Meeûs, 1000 Brussels, Belgium; tel (2) 299-11-11; fax (2) 295-05-46; e-mail forename.surname@cec.eu.int; internet www.jrc.cec.eu.int)

Director-General: Barry McSweeney; tel (2) 295-40-55.

Deputy Director-General: Roland Schenkel (with special responsibility for Nuclear Activities, the Comprehensive Decommissioning Programme and Interaction between Directorates).

ADMINISTRATIVE UNITS

Management Support

Head of Unit: Marc Becquet; tel (2) 299-31-81.

SECRETARIAT OF THE BOARD OF GOVERNORS

Head of Unit: Piedad García de la Rasilla y Pineda; tel (2) 295-85-35.

CO-ORDINATION OF GMES

Adviser: Pieter van Nes; tel (2) 296-01-91.

PROGRAMMES DIRECTORATE

Director: Alejandro Herrero Molina; tel (2) 295-61-87.

Units

1 Work Programme.

Head of Unit: Jean-Paul Malingreau; tel (2) 296-94-33; fax (2) 295-53-65.

2 ERA, Innovation and Evaluation.

Head of Unit: Robin Miege; tel (2) 295-80-43.

3 Interinstitutional Relations.

Head of Unit: Pierre Frigola; tel (2) 295-90-70.

4 Anticipation of Users' Needs and Enlargement.

Head of Unit: Giancarlo Caratti di Lanzacco; tel (2) 296-15-16.

5 Information and Public Relations.

Head of Unit: Gülperi Vural; tel (2) 295-76-24.

DIRECTORATE FOR RESOURCES (ISPRA)

(21020 Ispra, Varese, Italy; tel (332) 789111; fax (332) 789045)

Director: Jean-Pierre Vandersteen; tel (2) 295-58-76.

Advisers: Kenneth Weaving (Resources); tel (332) 789770; Roberto Cuniberti (Social Activities); tel (332) 789949; Michael Fahy (Reform—Brussels); tel (2) 296-72-16.

Units

1 Human Resources.

Head of Unit: Jean-Pierre Vandersteen (acting); tel (2) 295-58-76.

2 Contracts.

Head of Unit: (vacant).

3 Budgets and Resources Programming (Brussels).

Head of Unit: Eric Fischer; tel (2) 295-86-83.

4 Analytical Accounting and Finances.

Head of Unit: Adriano Endrizzi; tel (332) 789213.

5 Technical Services.

Head of Unit: Dolf Van Hattem; tel (332) 789541.

6 Knowledge Management.

Head of Unit: Richard Ross; tel (332) 786450.

7 Management Support.

Head of Unit: Albert Jerabek; tel (322) 786395.

ISPRA SERVICES ATTACHED TO THE DIRECTOR

Advisers: Ettore Caruso (Denuclearization and Valorization of the Ispra Site); tel (2) 296-08-47; Peter Churchill (ERA Dimension for the Ispra Site); tel (322) 785031.

Units

1 Nuclear Decommissioning and Waste Management.

Head of Unit: Giacinto Tartaglia; tel (332) 789338.

2 Safety, Security and Radiological Protection.

Head of Unit: Celso Osimani; tel (332) 789829.

INSTITUTE FOR REFERENCE MATERIALS AND MEASUREMENTS (GEEL)

(Retieseweg/Steenweg op Retie, 2440 Geel, Belgium; tel (14) 57-12-11; fax (14) 58-42-73)

Director: Dr Alejandro Herrero Molina; tel (14) 57-12-92; e-mail alejandro.herrero@cec.eu.int.

Units

1 Management Support.

Head of Unit: Marc Wellens; tel (14) 57-13-27.

2 Reference Materials.

Head of Unit: Hendrik Emons; tel (14) 57-17-22.

3 Safeguards.

Head of Unit: Roger Wellum; tel (14) 57-16-07.

4 Isotope Measurements.

Head of Unit: Philip Taylor; tel (14) 57-16-05.

5 Radionuclide Metrology.

Head of Unit: Uwe Wätjen; tel (14) 57-18-82.

6 Neutron Physics.

Head of Unit: Peter Rullhusen; tel (14) 57-57-476.

7 Informatics and Electronics.

Head of Unit: Colin Woodward (acting); tel (14) 57-15-85

8 Radiation Protection and Security.

Head of Unit: Luc Peters; tel; (14) 57-12-82.

9 Institute Development and Programme Management.

Head of Unit: Doris Florian; tel (14) 57-12-72.

INSTITUTE FOR TRANSURANIUM ELEMENTS (KARLSRUHE)

(Linkenheim, Postfach 2340, 76125 Karlsruhe, Germany; tel (7247) 9510; fax (7247) 951591; internet http://itu.jrc.cec.eu.int)

Director: Gerard Lander; tel (7247) 951350, fax (7247) 951591.

Units

1 Management Support.

Head of Unit: Jean-Pierre Michel; tel (7247) 951352.

2 Hot Cell Technology.

Head of Unit: Jean-Paul Glatz; tel (7247) 951321.

3 Materials Research.

Head of Unit: Claudio Ronchi; tel (7247) 951402.

4 Nuclear Fuels.

Head of Unit: Didier Haas; tel (7247) 951367.

5 Nuclear Chemistry.

Head of Unit: Klaus Lützenkirchen; tel (7247) 951424.

6 Actinides Research.

Head of Unit: Gérard Lander; tel (7247) 951382.

7 Nuclear Safety and Infrastructure.

Head of Unit: Werner Wagner; tel (7247) 951330.

INSTITUTE FOR ENERGY (PETTEN)

(Westerduinweg 3, Postbus 2, 1755 ZG Petten, Netherlands; tel (224) 565656; fax (224) 563393)

Director: Kari Törrönen; tel (224) 565401; e-mail kari.torronen@cec.eu.int.

Units

1 Management Support.

Head of Unit: Patrice Lemaître; tel (224) 565332; e-mail patrice.lemaitre@cec.eu.int.

2 High-flux Reactor and Reactor Applications.

Head of Unit: Marc Becquet; tel (224) 565290.

3 Nuclear Safety.

Head of Unit: Horst Weisshäup; tel (224) 565199.

4 Clean Energies.

Head of Unit: Juha-Pekka Hirvonen; tel (224) 565208.

5 Technical and Scientific Support to TACIS and PHARE.

Head of Unit: Michel Bieth; tel (224) 565157.

6 Scientific and Technical Support.

Head of Unit: Juha-Pekka Hirvonen; tel (224) 565208.

7 Clean Energies.

Head of Unit: Marc Steen; tel (224) 565271.

8 Quality, Safety and Environment.

Head of Unit: Arto Kuusisto; tel (224) 565391.

INSTITUTE FOR THE PROTECTION AND SECURITY OF THE CITIZEN (ISPRA)

(Joint Research Centre, Via Fermi 1, 21020 Ispra, Varese, Italy; tel (0332) 789111; fax (0332) 789923)

Director: Jean-Marie Cadiou; tel (0332) 789947; fax (0332) 789923; e-mail jean-marie.cadiou@cec.eu.int.

Units

1 Management Support.

Head of Unit: James Gray; tel (0332) 785875.

2 Cybersecurity and New Technologies for Combating Fraud.

Head of Unit: D. Al Khudhairy; tel (0332) 789251; fax (0332) 785154.

3 Monitoring Agriculture with Remote Sensing.

Head of Unit: Jacques Delincé; tel (0332) 785579; fax (0332) 785162; e-mail jacques.delince@cec.eu.int.

4 Technological and Economic Risk Management.

Head of Unit: G. Vollmer; tel (0332) 789155; fax 789156; e-mail alfredo.lucia@jrc.it.

5 European Laboratory for Structural Assessment.

Head of Unit: Michel Geradin; tel (0332) 785740; fax (0332) 789049; e-mail michel.geradin@jrc.it.

6 Humanitarian Security.

Head of Unit: Alois Sieber; tel (0332) 789089; (0332) 785339; e-mail alois.siber@jrc.it.

7 Non-proliferation and Nuclear Safeguards.

Head of Unit: André Poucet; tel (0332) 786232; (0332) 785145; e-mail andre.poucet@cec.eu.int.

INSTITUTE FOR ENVIRONMENT AND SUSTAINABILITY (ISPRA)

(Joint Research Centre, TP 263, Via Fermi, 21020 Ispra, Varese, Italy; tel (0332) 786660; fax (0332) 789222)

Director: Manfred Grasserbauer; tel (0332) 789834; e-mail manfred.grasserbauer@cec.eu.int

Units

1 Management Support.

Head of Unit: (vacant).

2 Climate Change.

Head of Unit: Frank Raes; tel (0332) 789958.

3 Global Vegetation Monitoring.

Head of Unit: Alan Belward; tel (0332) 789298.

4 Emissions and Health.

Head of Unit: Giovanni De Santi; tel (0332) 789482.

5 Inland and Marine Waters.

Head of Unit: Steven Eisenreich; tel (0332) 789037.

6 Soil and Waste.

Head of Unit: Giovanni Bidoglio; tel (0332) 789383.

7 Land Management.

Head of Unit: Guido Schmuck.

8 Renewable Energies.

Head of Unit: Heinz Ossenbrink; tel (0332) 789196.

INSTITUTE FOR HEALTH AND CONSUMER PROTECTION (ISPRA)

(Institute for Health and Consumer Protection, TP 202, 21020 Ispra (VA), Italy; tel.: 0332 786282; fax: 0332 789059)

Director: Kees van Leeuwen, tel (0332) 786249, fax (0332) 789059.

Units

1 Management Support.

Head of Unit: Ray Crandon; tel (0332) 789828, fax (0332) 785730.

2 European Centre for the Validation of Alternative Methods.

Head of Unit: Thomas Hartung; tel (0332) 785996, fax (0332) 785939.

3 Biomedical Materials and Systems.

Head of Unit: Hermann Stamm; tel (0332) 789030, fax (0332) 785388.

4 Physical and Chemical Exposure.

Head of Unit: Dimitrios Kotzias; tel (0332) 785950, fax (0332) 789453.

5 Biotechnology and GMOs.

Head of Unit: G. Van den Eede; tel (0332) 785959, fax (0332) 785483.

INSTITUTE FOR PROSPECTIVE TECHNOLOGICAL STUDIES (SEVILLE)

(Edificio Expo, C/ Inca Garcilaso, s/n, 41092 Seville, Spain; tel (95) 448-8318; fax (95) 448-8300)

Director: Peter Kind; tel (95) 448-8282, fax (95) 448-8274.

Units

1 Management Support.

Head of Unit: María Asunción Rubiralta; tel (95) 448-8389.

2 Technologies for Sustainable Growth.

Head of Unit: Per Sørup; tel (95) 448-8405.

3 Information and Communication Technologies.

Head of Unit: Bernard Clements; tel (95) 448-8449.

4 Support to the European Research Area.

Head of Unit: Pietro Moncada Paternò Castello; tel (95) 448-8388.

5 Life Sciences.

Head of Unit: Emilio Rodríguez; tel (95) 448-8398

6 Environment.

Head of Unit: Luis Delgado; tel (95) 448-8218.

Research Directorate-General

(8 square de Meeûs, 1049 Brussels, Belgium; tel (2)299-11-11; fax (2) 295-01-45; e-mail research@cec.eu.int or forename.surname@cec.eu.int; internet www.europa.eu.int/comm/dgs/research/index_en.htm; Bâtiment Jean Monnet, rue Alcide de Gasperi, 2920 Luxembourg; tel 4301-1; fax 4301-436124)

Director-General: Achilleas Mitsos; tel (2) 295-85-60.

Deputy Director-General: Hugh Richardson (with special responsibility for European Research Area); tel (2) 295-90-96.

Assistant to the Director-General: Stavros Chatzipanagiotou.

Chief Adviser: (vacant).

ADMINISTRATIVE UNITS

1 Audit and Internal Control.

Head of Unit: Liliane de Wolf (reporting directly to the Director-General); tel (2) 296-10-73.

DIRECTORATE A

(Co-ordination of Community Activities)

Director: Richard Escritt; tel (2) 295-07-25; fax (2) 299-16-05.

Units

1 Framework Programme; Institutional Relations.

Head of Unit: Clara De La Torre.

2 Research Programmes.

Head of Unit: Graham Stroud; tel (2) 295-38-25.

3 Regulatory and Cross-cutting Aspects.

Head of Unit: Megan Richards

4 Planning, Programming Evaluation.

Head of Unit: Birgit de Boissezon.

5 Impact Analysis of Community Actions.

Head of Unit: Ugur Muldur.

DIRECTORATE B

(Structural Aspects)

Director: Robert Jan Smits (acting).

Units

1 Anticipation of Scientific and Technological Needs: Fundamental Research.

Head of Unit: William Cannell.

2 Strengthening Co-operation in Research and the European Scientific Base.

Head of Unit: Robert Jan Smits.

3 Development of Scientific and Technological Capabilities: Research Infrastructure.

Head of Unit: Hervé Pero.

4 Administration and Finance.

Head of Unit: Miroslav Bures; tel (2) 295-36-57.

DIRECTORATE C

(Science and Society)

Director: Rainer Gerold; tel (2) 295-27-16.

Units

1 Strategy and Policy.

Head of Unit: Etienne Magnien.

2 Scientific Advice and Governance.

Head of Unit: Nicole Dewandre; tel (2) 299-49-25.

3 Ethical Questions in Research and Science.

Head of Unit: Barbara Rhode; tel (2) 295-98-88.

4 Women and Science.

Head of Unit: Rainer Gerold (acting); tel (2) 295-27-16.

5 Information and Communication.

Head of Unit: Michel Claessens (acting).

6 Education and Science.

Head of Unit: Francine Goffaux.

DIRECTORATE D

(The Human Factor, Mobility and Marie Curie Activities)

Director: Raffaele Liberali; tel (2) 295-86-73; fax (2) 299-08-52.

Units

1 Strategy and Policy.

Head of Unit: Raffaele Liberali (acting).

2 European Fellowships.

Head of Unit: Georges Bingen; tel (2) 296-94-18.

3 Research Training Networks.

Head of Unit: Bruno Schmitz; tel (2) 295-05-14.

4 Promotion of Scientific Excellence.

Head of Unit: Rudolf Meijer; tel (2) 296-89-54.

5 International Fellowships.

Head of Unit: Nicholas Newman; tel (2) 295-59-76.

6 Administration and Finances.

Head of Unit: Ugo Heider.

DIRECTORATE E

(Biotechnology, Agriculture and Food)

Director: Christian Patermann.

Units

1 Strategy and Policy.

Head of Unit: Manuel Hallen.

2 Food Quality.

Head of Unit: Callum Searle (acting).

3 Safety of Food Production Systems.

Head of Unit: Laurent Bochereau.

4 Administration and Finances.

Head of Unit: Manuela Soares de Aires; tel (2) 295-77-78.

DIRECTORATE F

(Health)

Director: Octavio Quintana Trias; tel (2) 298-93-30.

Units

1 Strategy and Policy.

Head of Unit: Timothy Hall; tel (2) 295-28-08.

2 Major Diseases.

Head of Unit: Alain Vanvossel; tel (2) 296-25-78.

3 Poverty-related Diseases.

Head of Unit: Arnd Hoeveler; tel (2) 295-68-01.

4 Fundamental Genomics.

Head of Unit: Bernard Mulligan (acting).

5 Biotechnology and Applied Genomics.

Head of Unit: Alfredo Aguilar.

6 Administration and Finance.

Head of Unit: Mireille Delprat.

DIRECTORATE G

(Industrial Technologies)

Director: Ezio Andreta; tel (2) 295-16-60; fax (2) 299-18-48.

Units

1 Strategy and Policy.

Head of Unit: Nicholas Hartley; tel (2) 296-01-35.

2 Products; Processes; Organization.

Head of Unit: Christos Tokamanis.

3 Materials.

Head of Unit: José-Lorenzo Vallés Brau.

4 Nanosciences and Nanotechnologies.

Head of Unit: Renzo Tomellini.

5 Research Fund for Coal and Steel.

Head of Unit: Philippe Vannson.

6 Administration and Finance.

Head of Unit: Bernd Reichert.

DIRECTORATE H

(Space and Transport)

Director: Jack Metthey; tel (2) 296-88-70.

Units

1 Strategy and Policy for Sustainable Transport.

Head of Unit: Kristiaan Larsen (acting).

2 Surface Transport.

Head of Unit: Luisa Prista.

3 Aeronautics.

Head of Unit: Liam Breslin.

4 Space Policy.

Head of Unit: Luc Tytgat.

5 Space: Research Activities, GMES.

Head of Unit: Marco Malacarne.

6 Preparatory Action for Security.

Head of Unit: Herbert Von Bose.

7 Administration and Finance.

Head of Unit: Michael Sucker.

DIRECTORATE I

(Environment)

Director: Pierre Valette (acting); tel (2) 295-63-56.

Units

1 Strategy and Policy for Sustainable Development.

Head of Unit: Pierre Valette; tel (2) 295-63-56.

2 Biodiversity and Global Change.

Head of Unit: Anver Ghazi; tel (2) 295-84-43.

3 Water Management Quality.

Head of Unit: Andrea Tilche; tel (2) 299-63-42.

4 Biodiversity and Marine Ecosystems.

Head of Unit: Pierre Mathy; tel (2) 295-81-60.

5 Administration and Finances.

Head of Unit: Martin Bohle; tel (2) 295-81-11.

DIRECTORATE J

(Energy)

Director: Pablo Fernández Ruiz; tel (2) 295-34-61.

Units

1 Strategy and Policy.

Head of Unit: Michel Poireau; tel (2) 295-14-11.

2 Energy Production and Distribution Systems.

Head of Unit: Ángel Pérez Sainz; tel (2) 296-15-96.

3 New and Renewable Energy Sources.

Head of Unit: Wiktor Raldow.

4 Nuclear Fission and Radiation Protection.

Head of Unit: Hans Forsstrom; tel (2) 295-41-64.

5 Joint Development of Fusion.

Head of Unit: Jean-Pierre Rager; tel (2) 295-30-85.

6 Fusion Association Agreements.

Head of Unit: David Campbell (acting).

7 Administration and Finances.

Head of Unit: Hans Spoor; tel (2) 295-74-53.

DIRECTORATE K

(Social Sciences and Humanities; Foresight)

Director: Jean-François Marchipont; tel (2) 295-79-65; fax (2) 299-20-76.

Units

1 Strategy and Policy.

Head of Unit: Andrew Sors; tel (2) 295-76-59.

2 Science and Technology Foresight; Links with the IPTS.

Head of Unit: Patraskevas Caracostas; tel (2) 295-08-88.

3 Research in the Social Sciences and Humanities.

Head of Unit: Peter Fisch (acting).

4 Administration and Finances.

Head of Unit: Priscila Fernández-Canadas; tel (2) 295-59-45.

DIRECTORATE M

(Investment in Research and Links with other Policies)

Director: Isa Saragossi (acting).

Units

1 Political Aspects, Private Investment, Links with EIB.

Head of Unit: Isa Saragossi.

2 Open Co-ordination of Research Policies.

Head of Unit: Xabier Goenaga.

3 Competition Aspects, Structural Policies.

Head of Unit: Robert Burmanjer.

4 Research and SMEs.

Head of Unit: Thomas Arnold.

5 Administration and Finance.

Head of Unit: Nicholas Sabatier (acting).

DIRECTORATE N

(International Scientific Co-operation)

Director: Louis Bellemin (acting).

Units

1 International Scientific Co-operation Policy.

Head of Unit: Louis Bellemin.

2 Community Co-operation Activities.

Head of Unit: Anna Karaoglou (acting).

3 Multilateral Co-operation Activities.

Head of Unit: Didier Gambier (acting).

4 Administration and Finance.

Head of Unit: Yves Motteu (acting).

DIRECTORATE R

(Resources)

Director: Maria Manuela Soares; tel (2) 296-21-48.

Units

1 Personnel and Equal Opportunities.

Head of Unit: Georges Papageorgiou; tel (2) 296-80-49.

2 Budget and Financial Services.

Head of Unit: Robert Krengal.

3 Training and In-house Information.

Head of Unit: Michel Stavaux; tel (2) 295-46-99.

4 External Audit.

Head of Unit: Eduard Rille; tel (2) 295-46-83.

5 Informatics.

Head of Unit: David Gould; tel (2) 296-97-39.

6 Working Environment: Infrastructure, Logistics, Office Space.

Head of Unit: Hans Christian Sack (acting).

Taxation and Customs Union Directorate-General

(59 rue Montoyer, 1000 Brussels, Belgium; tel (2) 299-11-11; fax (2) 295-07-56; e-mail librarian-information@cec.eu.int or forename.surname@cec.eu.int; internet www.europa.eu.int/comm/dgs/taxation_customs/index_en.htm)

Director-General: Robert Verrue; tel (2) 295-43-76.

Assistant to Director-General: Lilian Bertin; tel (2) 296-89-29.

ADMINISTRATIVE UNIT

1 Management of Human and Financial Resources.

Head of Unit: René Françon (reporting directly to the Director-General).

DIRECTORATE A

(General Matters)

Director: M. Arnal Monreal; tel (2) 296-33-28.

Units

1 Relations with the Institutions; Internal Co-ordination.

Head of Unit: Jean-Louis Vergnolle; tel (2) 296-33-32; fax (2) 295-07-09.

2 Strategy; Political and Economic Forward Studies; Evaluation.

Head of Unit: Bernard Grand; tel (2) 295-53-47; fax (2) 296-55-11.

3 Legal Affairs and Enforcement of Community Provisions.

Head of Unit: Richard van Raan; tel (2) 296-04-31.

4 International Affairs.

Head of Unit: Pierre Faucherand; tel (2) 295-78-14.

DIRECTORATE B

(Customs Policy)

Director: Alexander Wiedow; tel (2) 295-36-05; fax (2) 296-36-53.

Adviser: (vacant).

Units

1 Customs Legislation.

Head of Unit: Michael Lux; tel (2) 295-42-57; fax (2) 299-23-83.

2 Customs Modernization.

Head of Unit: John Pulford; tel (2) 295-81-83; fax (2) 296-54-04.

3 Economic Aspects of Customs and Transit.

Head of Unit: Maria Cabral; tel (2) 295-42-59.

4 Rules of Origin.

Head of Unit: Rosa Maria López Jorrin; tel (2) 296-59-83; fax (2) 296-98-50.

5 Customs Tariff.

Head of Unit: Luigi Casella; tel (2) 295-36-16; fax (2) 296-33-06.

DIRECTORATE C

(Tax Policy)

Director: Michel Aujean; tel (2) 295-66-56; fax (2) 295-05-51.

Units

1 Co-ordination of Tax Matters (Secretariat of the Tax Policy Group and Code of Conduct Group).

Head of Unit: Matthias Mors; tel (2) 299-33-89; fax (2) 295-63-77.

2 Direct Taxation.

Head of Unit: Philip Kermode; tel (2) 296-13-71; fax (2) 295-63-77.

3 VAT and other Turnover Taxes.

Head of Unit: Stephen Bill; tel (2) 295-78-83; fax (2) 299-36-48.

4 Excise Duties and Transport; Environment and Energy Taxes.

Head of Unit: Donato Raponi; tel (2) 295-63-07; fax (2) 296-19-31.

5 Economic Analysis of Taxation.

Head of Unit: Jean-Pierre De Laet; tel (2) 296-06-05.

DIRECTORATE D

(Programme Management)

Director: Manius de Graaf; tel (2) 295-20-25; fax (2) 296-19-31.

Units

1 Information, Training, Management of Customs and Tax Co-operation Programmes.

Head of Unit: Iosif Dascalu; tel (2) 295-82-67.

2 International Technical Assistance on Customs and Taxation.

Head of Unit: Thomas Carroll; tel (2) 295-58-42; fax (2) 295-56-58.

3 Information Technology.

Head of Unit: Paul-Hervé Theunissen; tel (2) 296-30-95.

Development Directorate-General

(12 rue de Genève, 1140 Brussels, Belgium; tel (2) 299-11-11; fax (2) 299-10-25; e-mail development@cec.eu.int or forename.surname@cec.eu.int; internet www.europa.eu.int/comm/dgs/development/index_en.htm)

Director-General: Athanassios Theodorakis; tel (2) 299-32-38.

Deputy Director-General: (vacant).

ADMINISTRATIVE UNIT

1 Internal Audit and Control.

Head of Unit: Klaas Ehbets; tel (2) 299-26-34.

DIRECTORATE A

(General Matters and Operational Support)

Director: Maria Barreiros; tel (2) 299-32-68.

Units

1 Strategic Planning and Finance.

Head of Unit: J. P. Reymondet-Commoy.

2 Relations with the United Nations' System, the Member States and other OECD Donor Countries.

Head of Unit: Hugo Schally; tel (2) 295-85-69.

3 Relations with the European Institutions and ACP, Civil Society and NGOs.

Head of Unit: Paul Malin; tel (2) 299-30-00.

4 Human Resources and Informatics.

Head of Unit: P. Craig-McQuaide.

5 Information and Communication.

Head of Unit: P. Lindvald-Nielsen.

DIRECTORATE B

(Development Policy and Sectoral Issues)

Director: Bernard Petit; tel (2) 299-32-55.

Adviser: V. Du Marteau.

Units

1 Development Policy, Coherence and Forward Studies.

Head of Unit: Françoise Moreau; tel (2) 299-07-72.

2 Economic Co-operation and PRSP Process.

Head of Unit: Gilles Hervio; tel (2) 296-37-00.

3 Social and Human Development.

Head of Unit: Lieve Fransen; tel (2) 296-36-98.

4 Environment and Rural Development.

Head of Unit: P. Mikos.

5 Transport, Infrastructure and Urban Development.

Head of Unit: Antonio García Fragio; tel (2) 299-32-95.

DIRECTORATE C

(Horn of Africa, East and Southern Africa; Pacific; Indian Ocean)

Director: Roger Moore; tel (2) 299-26-72.

Units

1 Relations with the Countries and Regions of the Pacific.

Head of Unit: Valeriano Diaz; tel (2) 296-27-31.

2 Relations with the Countries and the Regions of the Horn of Africa, East Africa and Indian Ocean.

Head of Unit: Roger Moore; tel (2) 299-26-72.

3 Relations with the Countries and the Region of Southern Africa.

Head of Unit: Philippe Darmuzey; tel (2) 296-55-92.

DIRECTORATE D

(West and Central Africa; Caribbean)

Director: S. Brouwer.

Adviser: M. Forcat.

Units

1 Relations with the Countries and the Region of the Caribbean.

Head of Unit: J. Caloghirou.

2 Relations with the Countries and the Region of West Africa.

Head of Unit: Anna-Silvia Piergrossi-Fraschini; tel (2) 299-32-30.

3 Relations with the Countries and the Regions of Central Africa and the Great Lakes.

Head of Unit: Peter Christiansen; tel (2) 299-27-66.

Enlargement Directorate-General

(170 rue de la Loi, 1040 Brussels, Belgium; tel (2) 299-11-11; fax (2) 296-84-90; e-mail elarg-info@cec.eu.int or forename.surname@cec.eu.int; internet www.europa.eu.int/comm/dgs/enlargement/index_en.htm)

Director-General: Fabrizio Barbaso.

Assistant to Director-General: M. Verger.

ADMINISTRATIVE UNITS

1 Audit.

Head of Unit: Michael Berrisford; tel (2) 296-64-80.

TASK FORCE

(Cyprus Follow-up and TF Programme and Financial Assistance)

Director: P. Mirel.

Units

1 Questions Relating to Cyprus.

Head of Unit: L. Maurer.

2 TF Programme and Phare Financial Assistance Follow-up.

Head of Unit: J. Garcia-Lombardero.

DIRECTORATE B

(Co-ordination of Negotiation and Pre-accession; Bulgaria, Romania, Turkey)

Director: M. Ruete.

Units

1 Co-ordination.

Head of Unit: R. Pascual Bremon.

2 Bulgaria.

Head of Unit: B. Czarnota.

3 Romania.

Head of Unit: D. Lange.

4 Turkey.

Head of Unit: M. Harvey.

DIRECTORATE C

(Secretariat Task Force, Wider Europe)

Director: R. Wissels.

Units

1 Co-ordination and Wider Europe.

Head of Unit: R. Wissels (acting).

2 Sector Analysis.

Head of Unit: A. Herdina.

DIRECTORATE D

(Co-ordination of Financial Instruments)

Director: D. Meganck.

Units

1 TAIEX.

Head of Unit: M. Jung-Olsen.

2 Co-ordination of Financial Instruments.

Head of Unit: Vincent Degert; tel (2) 295-35-03.

4 Implementation, Contracts and Nuclear Task Force.

Head of Unit: Helmuth Lohan; tel (2) 296-58-28.

DIRECTORATE E

(Resources and Finance)

Director: August Bonucci; fax (2) 299-31-97.

Units

1 Resources.

Head of Unit: L. Moretti.

2 Financial Execution.

Head of Unit: Carlos Filipe; tel (2) 296-08-62

3 Evaluation.

Head of Unit: Göran Segerlund; tel (2) 299-20-55.

4 Information and Communication Strategy and Interinstitutional relations.

Head of Unit: W. de Lobkowicz.

EuropeAid
Co-operation Office

(41 rue de la Loi, 1040 Brussels, Belgium; tel (2) 299-11-11; fax (2) 296-94-89; e-mail forename.surname@ cec.eu.int; internet www.europa.eu.int/ comm/europeaid/general)

Director-General: Koos Richelle; tel (2) 296-36-38, fax (2) 296-2039.

Deputy Director-General: Marc Franco; tel (2) 295-14-30.

Assistant to Director-General: Emma Toledano Laredo; tel (2) 296-62-04.

ADMINISTRATIVE UNITS

1 General Programming, Co-ordination; Devolution and Internal Auditing.

Head of Unit: Filiberto Ceriani Sebregondi; tel (2) 296-57-58.

2 Internal Auditing.

Head of Unit: Rony Sabah; tel (2) 299-29-79.

3 Innovation, Thematic Networks, O-QSG, Financing Committees.

Head of Unit: Agnes Lindemans-Maes; tel (2) 296-05-28.

DIRECTORATE A

(Europe, Caucasus, Central Asia)

Director: Guy Doucet; tel (2) 295-48-59.

Units

1 Co-ordination for Europe.

Head of Unit: Barbara Luecke; tel (2) 296-32-23.

2 Centralized Operations for Europe.

Head of Unit: Basile Papadopoulos; tel (2) 299-26-08.

3 Thematic Support – Private Sector and Economic Reform.

Head of Unit: Hélène Bourgade; tel (2) 296-54-39.

4 Multisector Thematic Support.

Head of Unit: Dino Sinigallia; tel (2) 296-23-44.

5 Nuclear Safety.

Head of Unit: Jean-Paul Joulia; tel (2) 295-72-10.

6 Financing, Contracts and Audits.

Head of Unit: Konstantin Konstantinou; tel (2) 296-38-18.

DIRECTORATE B

(Southern Mediterranean, Middle East)

Director: Richard Weber; tel (2) 295-30-55.

Units

1 Co-ordination for the Mediterranean Region.

Head of Unit: Ana Gonzalo Castellanos; tel (2) 299-09-46.

2 Centralized Operations for the Mediterranean.

Head of Unit: Carla Montesi; tel (2) 296-14-53.

3 Thematic Support – Economic and Trade Co-operation.

Head of Unit: Johannes Duynhouwer; tel (2) 299-07-21.

4 Thematic Support – Social and Human Development.

Head of Unit: Elisabeth Feret; tel (2) 296-97-94.

5 Multisector Thematic Support.

Head of Unit: Marco Mazzocchi Alemanni; tel (2) 295-30-44.

6 Financing, Contracts and Audits.

Head of Unit: (vacant).

DIRECTORATE C

(Africa, Caribbean, Pacific)

Director: (vacant).

Units

1 Co-ordination for the ACP Countries.

Head of Unit: Mikael Barpod; tel (2) 295-42-72.

2 Co-ordination for the ACP Countries.

Head of Unit: Androulla Kaminara, tel (2) 296-85-75.

3 Economic and Trade Co-operation.

Head of Unit: Jean-Louis Lacube; tel (2) 296-91-66.

4 Regional Integration; Institutional Support.

Head of Unit: Dominique Dellicour; tel (2) 295-59-37.

5 Social Development, Health and Education.

Head of Unit: Jose Luis Trimino Perez; tel (2) 299-08-23.

6 Sustainable Rural Development, Environment.

Head of Unit: (vacant).

7 Transport; Infrastructure.

Head of Unit: Maurice Haik; tel (2) 299-32-53.

8 Financing, Contracts and Audits.

Head of Unit: Carlo Eich; tel (2) 295-78-64.

DIRECTORATE D

(Asia)

Director: Erich Muller; tel (2) 299-07-75.

Units

1 Co-ordination for Asia.

Head of Unit: Thomas McGovern; tel (2) 296-73-71.

2 Centralized Operations for Asia.

Head of Unit: David Macrae; tel (2) 299-82-17.

3 Thematic Support – Economic and Trade Co-operation.

Head of Unit: Alessandro Mariani; tel (2) 296-95-19.

4 Multisector Thematic Support.

Head of Unit: Marianne Wenning; tel (2) 295-59-43.

5 Financing, Contracts and Audits.

Head of Unit: Carla Osorio; tel tel (2) 295-10-84.

DIRECTORATE E

(Latin America)

Director: Fernando Cardesa Garcia; tel (2) 299-23-29.

Units

1 Co-ordination for Latin America.

Head of Unit: Denis Salord; tel (2) 295-60-47.

2 Centralized Operations for Latin America.

Head of Unit: Riccardo Gambini; tel (2) 299-17-60.

3 Thematic Support – Multisector Economic and Trade Cooperation.

Head of Unit: Jan Ten Bloemendal; tel (2) 295-18-17.

4 Financing, Contracts and Audits.

Head of Unit: Michel De Coninck; tel (2) 296-27-99.

DIRECTORATE F

(Horizontal Operations and Innovation)

Director: Francesco de Angelis; tel (2) 295-84-00.

Units

1 Co-ordination.

Head of Unit: Philippe Loop; tel (2) 299-37-20.

2 Co-financing with NGOs.

Head of Unit: Aristotelis Bouratsis; tel (2) 299-92-44.

3 Democracy, Human Rights and Thematic Support.

Head of Unit: (vacant).

4 Social and Human Development, Environment and Thematic Support.

Head of Unit: Javier Puyol Pinuela; tel (2) 295-14-66.

5 Food Security and Thematic Support.

Head of Unit: Chantal Hebberecht; tel (2) 299-25-77.

6 Financial and Contract Management.

Head of Unit: Fermin J. Melendro Arnaiz; tel (2) 296-25-01.

DIRECTORATE G

(Operational Support)

Director: Constantin Stathopoulos; tel (2) 295-24-63.

Units

1 Budgetary Matters.

Head of Unit: Jose Izarra Aguado; tel (2) 299-28-18.

2 Financial and Contractual Matters.

Head of Unit: Raul Mateus Paula; tel (2) 295-92-78.

3 Legal Affairs, Litigation.

Head of Unit: Ole Scott-Larsen; tel (2) 299-27-22.

4 External Auditing of Operations.

Head of Unit: Michael Kagel; tel (2) 295-92-79.

5 Relations with Donors.

Head of Unit: Franco Nicora; tel (2) 299-32-07.

6 Relations with other Institutions.

Head of Unit: Martyn Pennington; tel (2) 299-25-97.

7 Programming, Internal Controls and Ex-post Controls.

Head of Unit: James Reis Conde; tel (2) 296-68-79.

DIRECTORATE H

(General Affairs)

Director: Thierry de Saint Maurice; tel (2) 295-47-27.

Units

1 Human Resources.

Head of Unit: Martine Leveque; tel (2) 298-63-50.

2 Individual Experts.

Head of Unit: Catherine Theodorou-Kalogirou; tel (2) 295-18-33.

3 Computer Systems, Office Technology.

Head of Unit: Wilfried Beurms; tel (2) 296-73-57.

4 Training.

Head of Unit: Gerard Van Bilzen; tel (2) 296-39-91.

5 Information; Communication.

Head of Unit: Santiago Herrero Villa; tel (2) 299-42-37.

6 Evaluation.

Head of Unit: Jean-Louis Chomel; tel (2) 296-29-39.

Directorate-General for Humanitarian Aid (ECHO)

(1 rue de Genève, 1140 Evere; tel 2-2958836)

Director-General: António Cavaco

Assistant to the Director-General: Andrea Koulaimah

Units

1 Africa, Caribbean and the Pacific

Head of Unit: Steffen Stenberg-Jensen

2 Central and Eastern Europe, NIS, Mediterranean Countries, Middle East

Head of Unit: Cornelis Wittebrood

3 Asia, Central and South America, Iraq

Head of Unit: Ruth Albuquerque

4 General Policy Affairs; Relations with European Institutions, Partners and Other Donors; Planning Co-ordination and Support; General Support for Major Crises

Head of Unit: Michel Arrion

5 Human Resources; Training; Administrative Support; Informatics

Head of Unit: René Guth

6 Finance; Audit

Head of Unit: Vijay Bhardwaj

7 Information and Communication

Head of Unit: Simon Horner (acting)

8 Legal, Regulatory and Procedural Affairs

Head of Unit: (vacant)

Internal Audit Capability

Head of Unit: (unit shared with AIDCO)

External Relations Directorate-General

(170 rue de la Loi, 1040 Brussels, Belgium; tel (2) 299-11-11; fax (2) 299-65-29; e-mail relex-feedback@cec.eu.int or forename.surname@cec.eu.int; internet www.europa.eu.int/comm/dgs/external_relations/index_en.htm)

Director-General: Eneko Landaburu.

Deputy Director-General, Directorates A, B and C: Fernando Valenzuela (with special responsibility for CFSP, Multilateral Affairs, North America, East Asia, Australia, New Zealand, EEA and EFTA); tel (2) 296-01-15; fax (2) 296-86-07.

Deputy Director-General, Directorates D, E and F: Michael Leigh (with special responsibility for Europe, Central Asia, Middle East and South Mediterranean).

Deputy Director-General, Directorates G and H: Hervé Jouanjean (with special responsibility for Asia and Latin America).

Chief Adviser: Graham Avery.

Assistant to Director-General: Petros Mavromichalis.

ADMINISTRATIVE UNITS

1 Inspection of the Delegations.

Head of Unit: Joannes Ter Haar (reporting directly to the Director-General).

2 Audit.

Head of Unit: Apostolos Bletsas (reporting directly to the Director-General); tel (2) 295-86-19.

3 Planning Service for External Relations.

Head of Unit: Helmut Steinel (reporting directly to the Director-General); tel (2) 295-16-92.

4 Economic Analysis.

Head of Unit: Michael Green (reporting directly to the Director-General); tel (2) 299-23-08.

DIRECTORATE A

(Common Foreign and Security Policy)

Director: Lodewijk Briet; tel (2) 296-66-65; fax (2) 295-86-25.

Units

1 European Correspondent.

Head of Unit: David Tirr.

2 Institutional and Legal Matters for External Relations; Sanctions.

Head of Unit: Florika Fink-Hooijer; tel (2) 296-49-68.

3 Security Policy.

Head of Unit: Lars-Erik Lundin; tel (2) 296-50-81.

4 Conflict Prevention, Crisis Management and ACP Countries' Political Issues.

Head of Unit: Maria McLoughlin; tel (2) 296-17-61.

DIRECTORATE B

(Multilateral Relations and Human Rights)

Director: Danièle Smadja; tel (2) 299-89-76.

Adviser: Alain-Pierre Allo (Law of the Sea and External Competencies).

Units

1 Human Rights and Democratization.

Head of Unit: Rolf Timans.

2 United Nations, Law of the Sea, Treaties Office.

Head of Unit: (vacant).

3 OSCE and Council of Europe.

Head of Unit: Gilbert Dubois; fax (2) 295-43-02.

DIRECTORATE C

(North America, East Asia, Australia, New Zealand, EEA, EFTA, San Marino, Andorra, Monaco)

Director: Richard Wright.

Units

1 United States, Canada.

Head of Unit: Gunnar Wiegand.

2 Japan, Korea, Australia, New Zealand.

Head of Unit: Seamus Gillespie; tel (2) 296-17-91.

3 EEA, EFTA, San Marino, Andorra, Monaco.

Head of Unit: Matthais Brinkmann; tel (2) 295-60-36.

DIRECTORATE D

(Western Balkans)

Director: Reinhard Priebe; tel (2) 295-01-61.

Units

1 Horizontal Matters.

Head of Unit: Michel Peretti.

2 Serbia and Montenegro.

Head of Unit: Thérèse Sobieski; tel (2) 299-02-25.

3 Albania, Bosnia and Herzegovina, Croatia, Former Yugoslav Republic of Macedonia.

Head of Unit: David Daly; tel (2) 295-25-26.

DIRECTORATE E

(Eastern Europe, Caucasus, Central Asian Republics)

Director: Hughes Mingarelli.

Units

1 Horizontal Matters.

Head of Unit: Alistair MacDonald; tel (2) 299-08-22.

2 Russia, Ukraine, Moldova, Belarus.

Head of Unit: Gerhard Lohan.

3 Caucasus and Central Asia (including Mongolia).

Head of Unit: Kurt Juul.

DIRECTORATE F

(Middle East, South Mediterranean)

Director: Christian Leffler; tel (2) 295-05-02; fax (2) 295-41-47.

Units

1 Horizontal Matters.

Head of Unit: Laura Baeza; tel (2) 296-13-39.

2 Barcelona Process and Gulf Countries, Iran, Iraq and Yemen.

Head of Unit: Patrick Laurent; tel (2) 295-52-55.

3 Near East.

Head of Unit: Alan Seatter; tel (2) 295-49-98.

4 Maghreb.

Head of Unit: Leonello Gabrici.

DIRECTORATE G

(Latin America)

Director: Tomas Dupla del Moral.

Units

1 Horizontal Matters.

Head of Unit: (vacant).

2 Mexico, Central America.

Head of Unit: Victor Andrès Maldonado; tel (2) 296-74-20.

3 Andean Community.

Head of Unit: Astrid Schomaker; tel (2) 296-96-41.

4 Mercosur, Chile.

Head of Unit: Gustavo Martin Prada.

DIRECTORATE H

(Asia, except Japan and Korea)

Director: Fokion Fotiadis; tel (2) 299-23-02.

Units

1 Horizontal Matters.

Head of Unit: Vincent De Visscher.

2 China, Hong Kong, Macao, Taiwan, Mongolia.

Head of Unit: James Moran; tel (2) 299-22-32.

3 India, Bhutan, Nepal.

Head of Unit: Laurence Argimon-Pistre; tel (2) 296-24-77.

4 Pakistan, Afghanistan, Sri Lanka, Bangladesh, Maldives.

Head of Unit: Julian Wilson.

5 South-East Asia.

Head of Unit: Pierre Amilhat.

DIRECTORATE I

(Headquarters Resources, Information and Interinstitutional Relations)

Director: David Lipman; tel (2) 299-07-55.

Units

1 Human Resources and Administration.

Head of Unit: Carmen Ruiz Serrano.

2 Financial and Budgetary Matters; Relations with Court of Auditors.

Head of Unit: Mark Johnston; tel (2) 296-85-13.

3 Information Technology Resources.

Head of Unit: Michael Keymolen; tel (2) 295-37-88.

4 Interinstitutional Relations.

Head of Unit: Reinhold Hack; tel (2) 295-13-45.

5 Information and Communication.

Head of Unit: Saturnino Muñoz Gomez; tel (2) 299-93-32.

DIRECTORATE K

(External Service)

Director: Christian Falkowski; tel (2) 299-08-75.

Units

1 External Service Staff Movements, Protocol Affairs, Administration.

Head of Unit: Chantal Graykowski-Massangioli; tel (2) 299-26-74.

2 Rights and Obligations.

Head of Unit: Stefan Huber.

3 Infrastructures in Delegation.

Head of Unit: Giuseppe Rosin; tel (2) 295-74-32.

4 Budget.

Head of Unit: Maria Luísa Merla; tel (2) 295-12-81.

5 Local Staff.

Head of Unit: Agnès Demassieux.

6 Career Development, Training, Information Technology.

Head of Unit: Annette Mandler.

7 Protection of Delegations.

Head of Unit: (vacant).

Trade Directorate-General

(170 rue de la Loi, 1040 Brussels, Belgium; tel (2) 299-11-11; fax (2) 299-10-29; e-mail trade-unit3@cec.eu.int or forename.surname@cec.eu.int; internet www.europa.eu.int/comm/dgs/trade/index_en.htm)

Director-General: Mogens Peter Carl; tel (2) 299-22-05; fax (2) 299-05-87.

Deputy Director-General: Pierre Defraigne; tel (2) 299-22-99.

Assistant to Director-General: Luc Devigne.

DIRECTORATE A

(General Affairs: Resources, Bilateral Trade Relations I)

Adviser: Françoise Le Bail; tel (2) 299-22-43.

Units

1 Human, Administrative and Financial Resources, External service, Programming.

Head of Unit: Bruno Pragnell; tel (2) 299-11-00.

2 Interinstitutional Relations and Communication Policy.

Head of Unit: Olivier de Laroussilhe; tel (2) 296-85-02.

3 Information Technology.

Head of Unit: Philippe Ruys; tel (2) 295-70-20.

DIRECTORATE B

(Trade Defence Instruments)

Director: Fritz Harald Wenig; tel (2) 295-86-84.

Units

1 General Policy; Complaints Office.

Head of Unit: Peter Klein; tel (2) 295-74-48.

2 Investigations I; Monitoring of Third-Country Measures.

Head of Unit: Neil MacDonald; tel (2) 295-75-36.

3 Anti-dumping and Anti-subsidy Investigations II—Injury and Community Interest.

Head of Unit: Bruno Adinolfi; tel (2) 299-00-44.

4 Monitoring and Follow-up; Investigations III.

Head of Unit: Dominique Avot; tel (2) 299-51-02.

5 Investigations IV.

Head of Unit: T. Jakob.

DIRECTORATE C

(Free-trade Agreements; Agricultural Trade Questions; Africa, Caribbean, Pacific; Latin America, GCC and Iran; GSP)

Director: Karl-Friedrich Falkenberg; tel (2) 299-22-20.

Units

1 Trade Relations with Africa, Caribbean, Pacific Countries, including South Africa.

Head of Unit: Lars Holger Standertskjöld-Nordenstam; tel (2) 295-73-59.

2 Economic Partnerships Agreements I.

Head of Unit: C. Maerten.

3 Economic Partnership Agreements II.

Head of Unit: (vacant).

DIRECTORATE D

(Development and Management of Trade Relations with the CIS, Balkans, Mediterranean, and South and South-East Asia)

Director: Françoise Le Bail; tel (2) 299-22-43.

Units

1 Trade Aspects of European Neighbourhood Policy; Trade Relations with Candidate Countries and Countries of the CIS and Balkans.

Head of Unit: (vacant).

2 Negotiations and Management of Trade or Free-Trade Agreements.

Head of Unit: P. Meyer.

DIRECTORATE E

(Sectoral Trade Questions; Market Access; Export-Related Trade Policy)

Director: I. Wilkinson.

Adviser: Allan Dalvin (Export Credits); tel (2) 299-22-07.

Units

1 Standards and Certification.

Head of Unit: (vacant).

2 Steel, Coal, Shipbuilding, Automotive, Chemicals and other Industries.

Head of Unit: R. Plijter; tel (2) 296-83-47.

3 Market Access.

Head of Unit: (vacant).

4 Export Credits, Controls; Third Country Practices.

Head of Unit: Fernando Perreau de Pinninck; tel (2) 296-19-32.

DIRECTORATE F

(WTO and OECD; Dispute Settlement and Trade Barriers Regulation)

Director: R. Petriccione.

Adviser: Allan Dalvin (Export Credits); tel (2) 299-22-07.

Units

1 Co-ordination.

Head of Unit: J. Clarke.

2 Dispute Settlement and Trade Barriers Regulation.

Head of Unit: I. Garcia Bercero.

DIRECTORATE G

(Services; Agricultural Trade Questions; Sustainable Development)

Director: J. Aguiar Machado.

Units

1 Trade in Services; GATS; Investment.

Head of Unit: (vacant).

2 Agriculture, Fisheries, Sanitary and Phytosanitary Measures; Biotechnology.

Head of Unit: J. Schaps.

3 Sustainable Development; Dialogue with Civil Society; Trade Relations with China.

Head of Unit: R. Schlegelmilch.

DIRECTORATE H

(Textiles, New Technologies, Intellectual Property, Public Procurement; Trade Analysis)

Director: (vacant).

Units

1 Negotiation and Management of Textiles Agreements; Footwear.

Head of Unit: (vacant).

2 New Technologies, Intellectual Property, Public Procurement. Trade Relations with Japan.

Head of Unit: Paul Vandoren; tel (2) 299-24-36.

3 Trade Analysis.

Head of Unit: G. Frontini Cattivello.

Informatics Directorate-General

Director-General: Francisco García Moran (acting)

DIRECTORATE A: INFRASTRUCTURE AND LOGISTICS

Director: Francisco García Moran (acting)

Units

1 Logistics

Head of Unit: Francis Peltgen (acting)

2 Telecommunications and Networks

Head of Unit: Marcel Jortay

3 Data Centre

Head of Unit: Declan Deasy

4 Technical Solutions and Office Systems

Head of Unit: José Marin Navarro

5 User Support Services

Head of Unit: Jean-Pierre Lambot

DIRECTORATE B: INFORMATION SYSTEMS

Director: Francisco García Moran (acting)

Units

1 Consultation and Co-ordination with Other Services, European Institutions and Other EU Entities

Head of Unit: Jean-Pierre Weidert

2 Interoperability, Architecture and Methods

Head of Unit: Theodoros Vassiliadis

3 Information Systems for Human Resources Management

Head of Unit: Philippe Bierlaire

4 Information Systems for Financial Management, Planning and Document Management

Head of Unit: Karel de Vriendt

DIRECTORATE R: RESOURCES

Director: Francisco García Moran (acting)

Units

1 Planning and Resources

Head of Unit: Marc Feidt

2 Finance and Contracts

Head of Unit: Francis Peltgen

Budget Directorate-General

(19 ave d'Auderghem, 1040 Brussels, Belgium; tel (2) 299-11-11; fax (2) 295-95-85; e-mail budget@cec.eu.int or forename.surname@cec.eu.int; internet www.europa.eu.int/comm/dgs/budget/index_en.htm)

Director-General: Luis Romero; tel (2) 295-16-83; fax (2) 299-18-41.

Deputy Director-General: Brian Gray; tel (2) 299-51-50.

Assistant to Director-General: Antoine Quero-Mussot; tel (2) 296-94-38.

ADMINISTRATIVE UNITS

1 Internal Audit.

Head of Unit: Enrique Lobera Argüelles (reporting directly to the Director-General); tel (2) 296-30-85.

2 Relations with the European Parliament, the Court of Auditors.

Head of Unit: Jacques Vonthron (reporting directly to the Director-General); tel (2) 295-29-83; fax (2) 299-57-37.

3 General Co-ordination; Human and Budgetary Resources.

Head of Unit: Luca Dalpozzo (reporting directly to the Director-General); tel (2) 295-17-71.

4 IT Infrastructure and Financial Information Systems.

Head of Unit: Claude Nahon (reporting directly to the Director-General), tel (2) 299-93-07.

5 Financial Information Systems.

Head of Unit: Jean-Pierre Buisseret; tel (2) 295-48-03.

DIRECTORATE A

(Expenditure)

Director: Fritz Brüchert, tel (2) 295-66-88.

Units

1 Budgetary Procedure and Synthesis; ABB and Relations with the COBU.

Head of Unit: Eric Paradis; tel (2) 295-98-11; fax (2) 296-62-53.

2 Common Agricultural Policy and Structural Policies.

Head of Unit: Marc Vanheukelen; tel (2) 295-30-34; fax (2) 296-57-64.

3 Internal Policies.

Head of Unit: Jacques Sant'Ana Calazans; tel (2) 295-63-00; fax (2) 295-58-18.

4 External Actions.

Head of Unit: René Vandermosten; tel (2) 295-05-36; fax (2) 299-45-97.

5 Administration Appropriations and Allocation of IT Resources.

Head of Unit: Philippe Bertrand; tel (2) 296-18-23; fax (2) 295-15-23.

6 Allocation of Human Resources.

Head of Unit: Philippe Jouret; tel (2) 295-57-68.

7 Monitoring and Reporting on Budget Implementation.

Head of Unit: Peter Laurson; tel (2) 295-55-88; fax (2) 296-57-94.

DIRECTORATE B

(Own Resources, Evaluation and Financial Programming)

Director: Jean-Pierre Bache; tel (2) 295-16-79; fax (2) 299-63-66.

Units

1 Mulitannual Financial Framework; Funding Systems and Forecasts; Budgetary Aspects of Enlargement.

Head of Unit: Silvano Presa; tel (2) 295-22-21.

2 Revenue Management.

Head of Unit: Antti Suortti; tel (2) 296-72-58.

3 Control of Traditional Own Resources.

Head of Unit: Robert Gielisse; tel (2) 295-96-49; fax (2) 299-45-96.

4 Control of VAT and GNP-based Resources and ACOR Secretariat.

Head of Unit: Richard Condon; tel (2) 295-78-15; fax (2) 296-91-45.

5 Evaluation.

Head of Unit: Svend Jakobsen; tel (2) 296-07-74.

DIRECTORATE C

(Budget Execution)

Director: Marc Oostens; tel (2) 295-91-14.

Units

1 Cash Office and Treasury Management.

Head of Unit: Basil Holder; tel (2) 295-59-14; fax (2) 295-01-51.

2 General Accounting.

Head of Unit: Maria Rosa Aldea Busquets; tel (2) 295-08-48.

3 Accounting and Budget Execution.

Head of Unit: Willy Hoebeeck; tel (2) 295-40-75; fax (2) 296-62-54.

4 European Development Fund and Joint Research Centre Accounts.

Head of Unit: Herman Mosselmans; tel (2) 295-67-04.

5 User Management of Financial Information Systems.

Head of Unit: Adrian Window; tel (2) 295-22-71.

Internal Audit Service

(28 rue Belliard, 1040 Brussels, Belgium; tel (2) 299-11-11; fax (2) 295-41-40; e-mail ias-europa@cec.eu.int or forename.surname@cec.eu.int; internet europa.eu.int/comm/dgs/internal_audit/index_en.htm)

Director-General: Walter Deffaa.

Assistant to Director-General: Bernard Magenhann.

Audit Supervisors: Américo Cavalheiro; tel (2) 296-25-12; Arturo Caballero Bassedas; tel (2) 295-39-74; Pascal Hallez; tel (2) 295-29-48; Panayotis Hadzidakis; Christian Muller.

DIRECTORATE A

(Horizontal Affairs)

Director: Antony Wright (Deputy Head, Internal Audit Service); tel (2) 295-32-71.

DIRECTORATE B

(Audit Process)

Director: Francisco Merchán Cantos (Head of Audit Staff Pool).

Personnel and Administration Directorate-General

(11 rue de la Science, 1000 Brussels, Belgium; tel (2) 299-11-11; fax (2) 299-62-76; e-mail forename.surname@ cec.eu.int; internet www.europa.eu.int/ comm/dgs/personnel_administration/ index_en.htm; Bâtiment Jean Monnet, rue Alcide de Gasperi, 2920 Luxembourg; tel 4301-1)

Director-General: Horst Reichenbach; tel (2) 299-43-96; fax (2) 295-12-58.

Adviser Hors Classe: Santiago Gómez Reino; tel (2) 299-38-02.

Permanent Rapporteur: Marina Manfredi; tel (2) 298-49-91.

Chief Adviser: Rocco Tanzilli; tel (2) 296-10-11.

Assistant: Diane Schmitt (reporting directly to the Director-General); tel (2) 296-27-01.

ADMINISTRATIVE UNITS

1 Relations with the Institutions, Programming, Evaluation and Internal Communication.

Head of Unit: Martin Terberger (reporting directly to the Director-General); tel (2) 295-39-86.

2 Audit.

Head of Unit: Marc Bellens (reporting directly to the Director-General); tel (2) 295-09-42.

3 Social Dialogue.

Head of Unit: Stefan Huber; tel (2) 295-20-29.

4 Investigation and Disciplinary Office.

Director: Mercedes De Sola Domingo.

DIRECTORATE A

(Staff Policy)

Director: Irène Souka; tel (2) 295-72-06; fax (2) 295-35-90.

Units

1 General Aspects of Personnel Policy.

Head of Unit: Klaus Rudischhauser; tel (2) 299-04-21.

2 Recruitment Policy.

Head of Unit: Roger Fry; tel (2) 295-45-85.

3 Training Office.

Head of Unit: Guido Vervaet; tel (2) 295-92-24.

4 Organigramme and Management Staff.

Head of Unit: Ann d'Haen-Bertier; tel (2) 295-09-93.

5 Career Structures, Evaluation and Promotions.

Head of Unit: Marc Mouligneau; tel (2) 295-67-31.

6 Career Guidance and Development; Training Office.

Head of Unit: Fernando Garcia Ferreiro (Career Guidance and Development); tel (2) 295-02-83.

DIRECTORATE B

(Staff Regulations: Policy, Management and Advisory Services)

Director: Daniel Jacob; tel (2) 295-98-70.

Advisers: Adrian Barnett (Legal); tel (2) 295-21-90; Luc Latouche (Co-ordination); tel (2) 299-36-90.

Units

1 Legal Issues; Staff Regulations.

Head of Unit: Diane Schmitt; tel (2) 296-07-36.

2 Complaints.

Head of Unit: Stefan Rating; tel (2) 299-68-20.

3 Conditions of Employment, Non-Pecuniary Rights and Obligations.

Head of Unit: Jean-Pierre Grillo; tel (2) 295-13-25.

4 Non-Discrimination and Equal Opportunities.

Head of Unit: Ana Laissy; tel (2) 295-32-58.

5 Social Dialogue, Relations with National Public Services; Enlargement.

Head of Unit: Hans-Georg Gerstenlauer; tel (2) 298-40-58.

DIRECTORATE C

(Social Welfare Policy, Luxembourg Staff, Health and Safety)

Director: Mercedes De Sola Domingo, tel (2) 295-62-72.

Units

1 Social Welfare and Policy.

Head of Unit: Giovanni Fracchia; tel (2) 295-50-06.

2 Staff, Staff Regulations and Social Welfare Policy (Luxembourg).

Head of Unit: Bernard Reynolds; tel (2) 293-39-11.

3 Medical Service (Luxembourg).

Head of Unit: Thierry Jadot; tel (2) 293-25-92.

4 Medical Service (Brussels).

Head of Unit: Gabriel Martineau; tel (2) 299-23-36.

5 Health and Safety.

Head of Unit: Franz Tschismarov; tel (2) 295-72-84.

DIRECTORATE D

(Resources)

Director: Emer Daly; tel (2) 296-05-03.

Adviser: Patrice Marcelli (Data Protection and Computer Security); tel (2) 295-25-56.

Units

1 Budget and Contract Support Unit.

Head of Unit: Hendrik Vantilborgh; tel (2) 295-55-21.

2 Relations with Institutions; ABM and Document Management.

Head of Unit: Daniele Dotto; tel (2) 296-27-01.

3 Management of Human Resources and Internal Reform.

Head of Unit: Alain Scriban; tel (2) 296-33-43.

4 Co-ordination and Relations with Administrative Offices; European Schools.

Head of Unit: Joanna Tachmintzis; tel (2) 299-04-28.

5 Internal Communication and Information.

Head of Unit: Nicholas David Bearfield; tel (2) 295-41-26.

DIRECTORATE DS

(Security)

Director: Frank Asbeck (acting); tel (2) 299-83-11.

Advisers: Frank Asbeck (Chief Adviser); Jonathan Lamb (Security Policy Promotion); tel (2) 296-22-84.

Units

1 Protection and Crisis Management.

Head of Unit: Hannu Hyvärinen; tel (2) 293-32-17.

2 Information and Prevention.

Head of Unit: Eduardo Cano Romera; tel (2) 296-15-02.

3 Inspection and Advisory Services.

Head of Unit: Stephen Hutchins; tel (2) 297-07-86.

4 Technical Security, IT and Telecommunications.

Head of Unit: Michaela Di Bucci (acting).

5 Co-ordination.

Head of Unit: (vacant).

DIRECTORATE IDOC

(Information Technology)

Director: Hendrik Van Lier; tel (2) 295-75-95.

Units

1 Disciplinary Investigation and Finance; Advice and Technical Evaluation.

Head of Unit: (vacant).

2 Non-Financial Investigations.

Head of Unit: (vacant).

Publications Office (OPOCE)

(2 rue Mercier, 2985 Luxembourg; tel 2929-1; fax 2929-44691; e-mail info-opoce@cec.eu.int or forename.surname@cec.eu.int;internet www.eur-op.eu.int/general/en/index.htm)

Director-General: Thomas Cranfield; tel 2929-42222.

Adviser: Albrecht Berger (Secretariat of Interinstitutional Committees); tel (2) 295-75-52.

Assistant to the Director-General: Lucia Ceccarelli; tel 2929-42890.

ADMINISTRATIVE UNITS

1 Resources.

Head of Unit: Jacobus Doggen (reporting directly to the Director-General); tel 2929-42110.

2 Infrastructure.

Head of Unit: Friedrich Döll (reporting directly to the Director-General); tel 2929-42050.

3 Author Services.

Head of Unit: Serge Brack; tel 2929-42568.

DIRECTORATE A

(Production)

Director: Jacques Raybaut; tel 2929-42408; fax 2929-42672.

1 Official Journal.

Head of Unit: Yves Steinitz; tel 2929-42251.

2 Publications.

Head of Unit: Richard Golinvaux; tel 2929-42682.

3 Access to Law.

Head of Unit: Pascale Berteloot; tel 2929-42110.

4 Multimedia.

Head of Unit: Philippe Lebaube; tel 2929-42855.

5 Dissemination.

Head of Unit: Michel Langlais; tel 4301-42905.

6 Support Group.

Head of Unit: (vacant).

Office for Infrastructure and Logistics – Brussels (OIB)

Director: P. Verleysen

Units

1 Implementation of Buildings Policy

Head of Unit: Konstantin Konstantinou

2 Space Management and Maintenance

Head of Unit: Reinier Lanneau

3 Purchasing Policy and Inventory

Head of Unit: Roberto Capogrossi

4 Reproduction Services and Mail

Head of Unit: Daniel Germain (acting)

5 Resources

Head of Unit: Mariana Saúde

6 Social Welfare Infrastructure

Head of Unit: Thierry Vinois

7 Administration and Protection of Buildings

Head of Unit: Franz Tschismarov

8 Property Projects

Head of Unit: Reinier Lanneau (acting)

9 Transport and Mobility

Head of Unit: Daniel Germain (acting)

Office for Infrastructure and Logistics – Luxembourg (OIL)

Director: Martine Reicherts

Adviser: Claude Willeme

Units

1 Implementation and Management of Buildings Policy

Head of Unit: Alberto Kozlik

2 Internal Services – Maintenance

Head of Unit: Robert Steinmetz

3 Social Welfare Infrastructure

Head of Unit: Roman Llanso

4 Financial Resources, Contractual Support and Conferences

Head of Unit: Pol François

Consultative Committees

The Directorates-General and Services of the European Commission are supported in all areas of policy by various consultative committees, including *ad hoc*, advisory, scientific and management committees.

EUROSTAT

As the EU was initially an organization with an economic mission, it had to endow itself with a solid statistical structure. The result was the Statistical Office of the European Communities, more commonly known as Eurostat.

Eurostat is able to provide a considerable range of harmonized statistical sequences for the EU's Member States and, in some cases, statistics on their main partners. On 1 October 2004, all Eurostat databases and electronic publications became available free on the Eurostat website. At the same time, a network of European Statistical Data Support (ESDS) centres was being created to provide assistance within individual countries.

The list of publications which follows is taken from the Eurostat catalogue. Material is classified under 9 themes and miscellaneous.

For further information on Eurostat products, contact:

Eurostat: Bâtiment Jean Monnet, 2920 Luxembourg; *premises at:* Bâtiment Joseph Bech, 5 rue Alphonse Weicker, 2721 Luxembourg; tel (+352) 4301-1; fax (+352) 4301-33015; e-mail eurostat-infodesk@cec.eu.int; internet www.europa.eu.int/comm/eurostat.

Cyprus

European Statistical Data Support Centre: e-mail eustatistics@cystat.mof.gov.cy.

Czech Republic

European Statistical Data Support Centre: e-mail esds@gw.czso.cz.

Denmark

European Statistical Data Support Centre: Sejrøgade 11, 2100 Copenhagen Ø, Denmark; e-mail ktl@dst.dk.

Estonia

European Statistical Data Support Centre: e-mail margit.kotisse@stat.ee.

Finland

European Statistical Data Support Centre: Tilastokirjasto, PL 2B, Työpajakatu 13 B, 2 krs, 00022 Tilastokeskus, Finland; e-mail esds@stat.fi.

France

European Statistical Data Support Centre: 195 rue de Bercy, Tour Gamma A, 75582 Paris Cedex 12, France; e-mail noam.leandri@insee.fr.

Germany

European Statistical Data Support Centre: Statistisches Bundesamt, i-Punkt Berlin, EDS Europäischer Datenservice, Otto-Braun-Str. 70–72, 10178 Berlin, Germany; tel (+49 1888) 6449427; fax (+49 1888) 6449430; e-mail eds@destatis.de; internet www.eds-destatis.de.

Greece

European Statistical Data Support Centre: e-mail salappas@statistics.gr.

Italy

European Statistical Data Support Centre: Istat, Centro Diffusione Dati, Via Cesare Balbo 11/a, 00184 Rome, Italy; tel (+39) 06-46733222; fax (+39) 06-46733101; e-mail tiberi@istat.it.

Latvia

European Statistical Data Support Centre: e-mail es@csb.gov.lv.

Lithuania

European Statistical Data Support Centre: e-mail eurostatgidas@std.lt.

Malta

European Statistical Data Support Centre: National Statistics Office, Valletta, Malta; tel. (+356) 25997219; e-mail library.nso@gov.mt; internet www.nso.gov.mt/esds/esds.htm.

Netherlands

European Statistical Data Support Centre: Postbus 4000, 2270 JM Voorburg, Netherlands; e-mail rvlp@cbs.nl.

Norway

European Statistical Data Support Centre: Kongensgate 6, P.O. Box 8131 Dep., 0033 Oslo, Norway; e-mail biblioteket@ssb.no.

Portugal

European Statistical Data Support Centre: Av. António José de Almeida 2, 1000-043 Lisbon, Portugal; e-mail catarina.cunha@ine.pt.

Slovenia

European Statistical Data Support Centre: e-mail esds.stat@gov.si.

Spain

European Statistical Data Support Centre: Paseo de la Castellana 183, Oficina 009, Entrada por Estébanez Calderón, 28046 Madrid, Spain; e-mail infoeuropea@ine.es.

Sweden

European Statistical Data Support Centre: Karlavägen 100, Box 24300, 104 51 Stockholm, Sweden; tel (+46 8) 506-948-01; fax (+46 8) 506-948-99; e-mail information@scb.se.

Switzerland

European Statistical Data Support Centre: Statistisches Amt des Kantons Zürich, Bleicherweg 5, 8090 Zürich, Switzerland; tel (+41) 12251212; fax (+41) 12251299; e-mail datashop@statistik.zh.ch.

United Kingdom

EU Statistics UK: Room 1.015, Office for National Statistics, Government Buildings, Cardiff Road, Newport, NP10 8XG, United Kingdom; tel (+44 1633) 813369; fax (+44 1633) 652699; e-mail eustatistics@ons.gov.uk; internet www.eustatistics.gov.uk.

Publications

THEME 1 – GENERAL STATISTICS

Eurostat Yearbook 2004 – The Statistical Guide to Europe – Data 1992–2002

Contains comparable data on the European Union's 25 Member States, the euro zone, the European Economic Area and other global key players. Explanatory texts, graphs, a glossary and an abbreviations list are included. The 'In the spotlight' section in this edition concentrates on sustainable development.

Available as a combined paper and CD-ROM publication. The CD-ROM has about 1,000 tables and graphs, and it allows data to be extracted to create customized tables and graphs. An electronic version (PDF format), with the same content as the printed version, can be downloaded free of charge from www.europa.eu.int/comm/eurostat.

Language versions. Multilingual DE, EN, FR: A4 format, 280 pages with CD-ROM; catalogue no. KS-CD-04-001-EN-C; price €50.00.

Eurostatistics – Data for Short-term Economic Analysis

Monthly publication to supply the most recent sets of statistics on the European Union and the euro zone for the Member States and their main partners (the USA and Japan) outside the European Community. An electronic version (PDF format) can be downloaded free of charge from www.europa.eu.int/comm/eurostat.

Language version. EN: A4 format, 180 pages; catalogue no. KS-BJ-04-000-EN-C; price per copy €20.00; subscription code VHI000, annual subscription price €180.00.

Statistical Yearbook on the Candidate Countries – Data 1997–2001

Contains detailed tables on demography, education, research and development, social conditions and the labour force, national accounts and finance, agriculture, energy, industry and construction, retail and tourism, transport, telecommunications and the information society, and external trade and the environment. Includes most of the structural indicators adopted by the European Council to monitor the Lisbon competitiveness strategy. An electronic version (PDF format) can be downloaded free of charge from www.europa.eu.int/comm/eurostat.

Language version. EN: A4 format, 219 pages, catalogue no. KS-AG-03-001-EN-C; price €30.00.

Regions: Statistical Yearbook 2003

Focuses on agriculture, population, regional gross domestic product, the labour force survey, research and development, tourism, transport and unemployment at regional level. An electronic version (PDF format) can be downloaded free of charge from www.europa.eu.int/comm/eurostat.

Language versions. Multilingual DE, EN, FR: A4 format, 169 pages with CD-ROM; catalogue no. KS-AF-03-001-EN-C; price €60.00.

Urban Audit Methodological Handbook

Provides the information required by the data suppliers to achieve coherence and comparability of the urban audit data. Helps users to understand the methods applied in data compilation and to assess the relevance of the data for their own purposes. Contains descriptions of the method for selection of spatial units for the three spatial levels (administrative city, larger urban zone and sub-city district) per country, the list of participating towns/cities, the glossary of variables and indicators (definitions and references) and basic information on the estimation methods applied.

Language version. EN; PDF format (can be downloaded free of charge from www.europa.eu.int/comm/eurostat); catalogue no. KS-BD-04-002-EN-N.

Stat-Lex – 1998–2002 Legislation – Secondary Community Legislation Relating to Statistics

Provides an overview (in 11 languages) of all Community legislation relating to statistics for the years 1998 to 2002 to those people working in the field of statistics at European level. Also serves as an aid to the accession process by acquainting candidate countries with the *acquis communautaire* in statistics.

Language versions. Multilingual in 11 official languages of the European Union: CD-ROM format; catalogue no. KS-CW-02-001-1F-Z; price €100.

50 Years of Figures on Europe

Helps to compare data for a broad range of indicators across individual countries and to evaluate the effects of successive enlargements and interim developments. The figures cover area and population, economy, employment and labour costs, sectors of the economy, transport, tourism and external trade. An electronic version (PDF format) can be downloaded free of charge from www.europa.eu.int/comm/eurostat.

Language versions. Multilingual DE, EN, FR: 10.5 × 21 cm, 151 pages; catalogue number KS-49-02-264-3A-C; price €10.00.

Monographs of Official Statistics – Variance Estimation Methods in the European Union

Provides a summary of the currently available variance estimation methods, and gives general recommendations and guidelines for the estimation of variance for the common sampling procedures used at the European level. It can be used by survey statisticians and methodologists when choosing an appropriate method for estimating the sampling variability of their estimates, as well as other professionals when analysing survey data.

Language version. EN: PDF format (can be downloaded free of charge from www.europa.eu.int/comm/eurostat); catalogue no. KS-CR-02-001.

Regional Gross Domestic Product in the Candidate Countries 2001

Part of the Statistics in Focus collection.

Language version. EN: PDF format (can be downloaded free of charge from www.europa.eu.int/comm/eurostat); catalogue no. KS-DN-04-002.

Regional Gross Domestic Product in the European Union 2001

Part of the Statistics in Focus collection.

Language version. EN: PDF format (can be downloaded free of charge from www.europa.eu.int/comm/eurostat); catalogue no. KS-DN-04-001.

European and National Short-term Indicators

Infra-annual economic statistics for the euro zone and the European Union as a whole will continue to gain ever more operational importance for collective and private decision-making.

The Euro-Indicators section is exclusively dedicated to infra-annual economic statistics such as consumer prices, national accounts, balance of payments, external trade, industry, energy, commerce and services, and the labour market, as well as a selection of monetary and financial indicators of the European Central Bank and business and consumer survey results from the European Commission's Economic and Financial Affairs Directorate-General.

The pages are updated daily and offer free of charge key aggregate indicators for the EU and the euro zone. The database contains mostly harmonized and, above all, uniformly structured and documented national and European series. Data can be extracted online and customized extractions can be obtained on request.

URL: www.europa.eu.int/comm/euroindicators.

Structural Indicators

Presents the database of structural indicators used to underpin the Commission's analysis in the 2004 spring report to the European Council. The indicators cover the five domains of employment, innovation and research, economic reform, social cohesion and environment, as well as the general economic background. Also available is a shortlist of 14 indicators presented in the statistical annexe to the spring report. The database and the shortlist are available free of charge.

URL: www.europa.eu.int/comm/eurostat/structuralindicators.

THEME 2 – ECONOMY AND FINANCE

EC Economic Data Pocketbook

Focusing on the structural aspects of the EU economy, this quarterly publication is a collection of data from different domains, covering the European aggregates, EU Member States and its main economic partners. Most of the data are annual, complemented by selected monthly and quarterly indicators.

Language version. EN: A4 format, 167 pages; catalogue no. KS-CZ-04-001-3A-C; price per copy €12.00; subscription code VBO 000, annual subscription price €40.00.

Economic Portrait of the European Union 2002: Data up to 2001

Brings together a wide range of macro-economic data on the European Union and its Member States and provides a statistical analysis of these data. Also examines the structural differences between the Member States and the way in which they are developing. An electronic version (PDF format) can be downloaded free of charge from www.europa.eu.int/comm/eurostat.

Language versions. Multilingual DE, EN, FR: A4 format, 167 pages; catalogue number KS-AI-02-001-EN-C; price €30.00.

European Union Foreign Direct Investment Yearbook 2001: Data 1992–2000

Provides analytical aspects of the foreign direct investment position, flow and income for the European Union. Aims to provide decision-makers with high-quality statistical information on direct investment by providing internationally comparable figures through close co-operation with Member States and the OECD. An electronic version (PDF format) can be downloaded free of charge from www.europa.eu.int/comm/eurostat.

Language version. EN: A4 format, 132 pages with CD-ROM; catalogue no. KS-BK-02-001-EN-C; price €30.00.

European Union International Transactions – Analytical Aspects – Detailed Tables on CD-ROM – Data 1991–2001

Covers international exchanges (exports and imports) in services (53 items) and other balance of payments items, including goods, income received on capital invested abroad or paid on foreign capital invested on EU territory; salaries earned abroad by EU residents or salaries paid to non-residents on EU territory; and current transfers such as international aid and migrant workers' remittances. Emphasizes the EU's geographical trading partners (50). An annexe provides more detailed statistical tables containing harmonized and internationally comparable current account data. The CD-ROM also includes methodological explanations and a short description of the harmonization work undertaken. An electronic version (PDF format) can be downloaded free of charge from www.europa.eu.int/comm/eurostat.

Language version. EN: A4 format, 99 pages with CD-ROM; catalogue no. KS-AP-03-001-EN-C; price €45.00.

Structures of the Taxation Systems in the European Union – Data 1995–2002

Presents a global overview of the corpus of ESA 95 statistics and lays particular emphasis on tax indicators in national accounts, the classification of taxes, and methodology for calculating harmonized implicit tax rates on labour, capital and consumption. Includes a comparative analysis of recent developments in the taxation systems of EU Member States. An electronic version (PDF format) can be downloaded free of charge from www.europa.eu.int/comm/eurostat.

Language version. EN: A4 format, 361 pages; catalogue no. KS-DU-04-001-EN-C; price €28.00.

Households' Financial Assets and Liabilities in Europe

Part of the Statistics in Focus collection.

Language version. EN: PDF format (can be downloaded free of charge from www.europa.eu.int/comm/eurostat); catalogue no. KS-NJ-04-022-EN-N.

Long-term Interest Rates for Acceding Countries

Part of the Statistics in Focus collection.

Language version. EN: PDF format (can be downloaded free of charge from www.europa.eu.int/comm/eurostat); catalogue no. KS-NJ-04-021-EN-N.

Structure of Government Debt in Europe

Part of the Statistics in Focus collection.

Language version. EN: PDF format (can be downloaded free of charge from www.europa.eu.int/comm/eurostat); catalogue no. KS-NJ-04-019-EN-N.

An Overview of the Economies of the New Member States

Part of the Statistics in Focus collection.

Language version. EN: PDF format (can be downloaded free of charge from www.europa.eu.int/comm/eurostat); catalogue no. KS-NJ-04-017-EN-N.

EU-15 FDI in 2002

Part of the Statistics in Focus collection.

Language version. EN: PDF format (can be downloaded free of charge from www.europa.eu.int/comm/eurostat); catalogue no. KS-NJ-04-016-EN-N.

Compulsory Levies in the EU – Structure and Level: 1995–2002

Part of the Statistics in Focus collection.

Language version. EN: PDF format (can be downloaded free of charge from www.europa.eu.int/comm/eurostat); catalogue no. KS-NJ-04-013-EN-N.

Government Accounts in the EU Member States: Key Indicators 2000–2002

Part of the Statistics in Focus collection.

Language version. EN: PDF format (can be downloaded free of charge from www.europa.eu.int/comm/eurostat); catalogue no. KS-NJ-04-014-EN-N.

European FDI in the Mediterranean Region in 2002 (MED)

Part of the Statistics in Focus collection.

Language version. EN: PDF format (can be downloaded free of charge from www.europa.eu.int/comm/eurostat); catalogue no. KS-NJ-04-012-EN-N.

General Government Expenditure and Revenue of EU Member States in 2002

Part of the Statistics in Focus collection.

Language version. EN: PDF format (can be downloaded free of charge from www.europa.eu.int/comm/eurostat); catalogue no. KS-NJ-04-004-EN-N.

Purchasing Power Parities and Related Economic Indicators for EU, Acceding and Candidate Countries and EFTA

Part of the Statistics in Focus collection.

Language version. EN: PDF format (can be downloaded free of charge from www.europa.eu.int/comm/eurostat); catalogue no. KS-NJ-03-064-EN-N.

Relative Prices for New Passenger Cars in EU, EFTA, Acceding and Candidate Countries for 2002

Part of the Statistics in Focus collection.

Language version. EN: PDF format (can be downloaded free of charge from www.europa.eu.int/comm/eurostat); catalogue no. KS-NJ-03-065-EN-N.

THEME 3 – POPULATION AND SOCIAL CONDITIONS

The Social Situation in the European Union – 2003

Provides a holistic view of the population and its social conditions as a background to social policy development and contributes to the monitoring of developments in the social field across Member States. Provides links with other Commission publications such as *Employment in Europe, Industrial Relations in Europe* and the *Gender Equality Report*. Combines harmonized quantitative information with survey data on public opinion so that the perceptions and attitudes of people living in Europe are added to the overall portrait of the social situation. This edition focuses on analysis and research on the health of people living in the European Union, and contains extensive statistical information at EU level. An electronic version (PDF format) can be downloaded free of charge from www .europa.eu.int/comm/eurostat.

Language versions. Multilingual DE, EN, FR: A4 format, 210 pages; catalogue no. KE-AG-03-001-EN-C; price €25.00.

Work and Health in the European Union – a Statistical Portrait

Describes the general picture of working life including characteristics of the European labour force and the overall importance of ill-health due to work-related factors. Specific chapters describe statistical data on risk factors and outcomes of safety at work, work-related diseases and psychosocial problems linked to health and safety at work. The distribution of risk factors and the frequency of accidents at work, work-related diseases and work-related problems of a psychosocial nature are described by age, gender, sector of economic activity, occupation and other relevant variables. Eurostat's data are complemented by data from other sources, especially by data from the European Foundation for the Improvement of Living and Working Conditions. The data mainly cover the Member States of the EU but some preliminary data are available for trends in the incidence of accidents at work in the candidate countries. An electronic version (PDF format) can be downloaded free of charge from www.europa.eu.int/ comm/eurostat.

Language version. EN: A4 format, 129 pages; catalogue no. KS-57-04-807-EN-C; price €30.00.

How Europeans Spend Their Time – Everyday Life of Women and Men – Data 1998–2002

Provides statistics, drawn from time use surveys, about the division between women and men in gainful and domestic work in ten European countries: Belgium, Germany, Estonia, France, Hungary, Slovenia, Finland, Sweden, the United Kingdom and Norway. An electronic version (PDF format) can be downloaded free of charge from www .europa.eu.int/comm/eurostat.

Language version. EN: 10.5 × 21 cm, 140 pages; catalogue no. KS-58-04-998-EN-C; price €10.00.

Living Conditions in Europe: Statistical Pocketbook

Provides data on the 15 old Member States of the European Union and on the four EFTA countries in which information is available. Data are drawn from harmonized sources available in Eurostat, such as the European labour force survey and the European Community

household panel. Different areas of the social field are described by a selection of indicators presented in tables and charts and accompanied by a short commentary. An electronic version (PDF format) can be downloaded free of charge from www .europa.eu.int/comm/eurostat.

Language version. EN: 10.5 × 21 cm, 113 pages; catalogue no. KS-53-03-831-EN-C; price €10.00.

Consumers in Europe – Facts and Figures

Presents a comprehensive collection of the most important data available from different sources on consumption patterns, including expenditure, and on consumer attitudes and quality indicators in the European Union. Provides information to policy-makers concerned with the impact of European and national policies on consumers, to advertisers and other businesses interested in European-wide markets, and to those interested in Europe's spending patterns and consumption habits. An electronic version (PDF format) can be downloaded free of charge from www.europa.eu.int/comm/eurostat.

Language version. EN: A4 format, 290 pages; catalogue no. KS-39-01-134-EN-C; price €30.00.

Disability and Social Participation in Europe

Contains comparisons on the social situation and participation of three population groups: people with severe disabilities, people with moderate disabilities, and people without disabilities, as defined by a 'global disability question' in the European Community household panel. An electronic version (PDF format) can be downloaded free of charge from www .europa.eu.int/comm/eurostat.

Language version. EN: 10.5 × 21 cm, 81 pages; catalogue no. KS-AW-01-001-EN-C; price €7.00.

The Life of Women and Men in Europe – A Statistical Portrait – Data 1980–2000

Begins by covering children and education and initial training, and possible differences between women and men at the age at which they leave the family home and in their lifestyles. Examines the working life of women and men, and focuses on their differing career paths, the respective positions they occupy and their abilities and strategies for reconciling the pursuit of a working career with family responsibilities. Also reviews women and men beyond retirement age, including the income they receive from pensions and other sources, whether they are still working, their household circumstances, their health and social relations. An electronic version (PDF format) can

be downloaded free of charge from www .europa.eu.int/comm/eurostat.

Language versions. Multilingual DE, EN, FR: A4 format, 197 pages; catalogue no. KS-43-02-680-EN-C; price €30.00.

European Social Statistics – Social Protection: Expenditure and Receipts – Data 1992–2001

The data used on expenditure and receipts of social protection schemes are drawn up according the Esspros manual 1996. Esspros stands for European system of integrated social protection statistics, a harmonized system providing a means of analysing and comparing social protection financial flows. An electronic version (PDF format) can be downloaded free of charge from www .europa.eu.int/comm/eurostat.

Language version. EN: 109 pages with CD-ROM; catalogue no. KS-DC-04-001-EN-C; price €45.00.

European Social Statistics – Income, Poverty and Social Exclusion: Second Report – Data 1994–1997

Includes an executive summary and a detailed explanation of the conceptual and methodological framework. Individual chapters deal with income distribution, income poverty and the dynamics of income poverty. Detailed statistical tables are included. An electronic version (PDF format) can be downloaded free of charge from www.europa.eu.int/comm/ eurostat.

Language versions. Multilingual DE, EN, FR: A4 format, 174 pages; catalogue no. KS-BP-02-008-EN-C; price €28.00.

Population Statistics – Data 1960–2003

Includes information on the EU and the world, fertility, mortality, marriage, migration, and the composition and structure of the population. The data relate to the 25 EU Member States and, to a lesser extent, the European Economic Area, Romania, Bulgaria and some western Balkan countries. Countries such as the USA and Japan are also considered, where possible, to provide a high-level international comparison. An electronic version (PDF format) can be downloaded free of charge from www.europa.eu.int/comm/eurostat.

Language versions. Multilingual DE, EN, FR: A4 format, 188 pages with CD-ROM; catalogue no. KS-BP-04-001-**-C; price €33.00.

European Social Statistics – Labour Market Policy –Expenditure and Participants – Data 2002

Contains data on public expenditure on labour market policy measures and numbers of participants in these measures (stocks, entrants and exits). The database covers measures targeted to people who are unemployed, people in employment but at risk of involuntary job-loss, and inactive people who are currently not part of the labour force but who would like to enter the labour market and are disadvantaged in some way.

Labour market policy measures are classified in two ways: by type of action and by type of expenditure. The type of action refers to the way in which the measure acts to achieve its objectives, such as training measures or employment incentives.

Language version. EN: PDF format (can be downloaded free of charge from www .europa.eu.int/comm/eurostat); catalogue no. KS-DO-04-001-EN-C.

European Social Statistics – Labour Force Survey Results 2002 – Data 2002

Presents the detailed results of the 2002 (second quarter for countries having a quarterly survey or yearly results) labour force survey conducted in the EU Member States in accordance with Council Regulation (EC) No. 577/98 and in the following EFTA countries: Iceland, Norway and Switzerland. Four chapters cover population and households, employment, unemployment, and inactivity. At the end of each chapter a table gives the main indicators at NUTS 2 level. An electronic version (PDF format) can be downloaded free of charge from www.europa.eu.int/comm/eurostat.

Language versions. Multilingual DE, EN, FR: A4 format, 227 pages; catalogue no. KS-BP-03-001-EN-C; price €34.00.

European Social Statistics – Continuing Vocational Training Survey (CVTS2)

Provides comparable statistical results on continuing vocational training in enterprises in the pre-May 2004 Member States of the European Union, Norway and nine accession countries. The source of the data is the second continuing vocational training survey (CVTS2) conducted in 2000/01. The reference year was 1999. The survey covered enterprises with 10 or more employees in the NACE sections C to K and O. Some 76,000 enterprises took part in the survey and provided comparable statistical data on the volume and content of continuing vocational training at work as well as background information on training policy and training management. An electronic version (PDF format) can be downloaded free of charge from www.europa.eu.int/comm/eurostat.

Language versions. Multilingual DE, EN, FR: A4 format, 160 pages; catalogue no. KS-BP-02-007-EN-C; price €25.00.

European Social Statistics – Accidents at Work and Work-related Health Problems – Data 1994–2000

Presents in detail the large statistical information and data series collected by Eurostat. An electronic version (PDF format) can be downloaded free of charge from www.europa.eu.int/comm/eurostat.

Language versions. Multilingual DE, EN, FR: A4 format, 236 pages; catalogue no. KS-BP-02-002-3A-C; price €34.00.

Health Statistics – Atlas on Mortality in the European Union

The 1994–96 data in this atlas come from the national statistical institutes and the competent government agencies in the 15 EU Member States, and are analysed at NUTS 2 level for all the Member States. The factors determining the pattern of mortality lead to specific causes of death and this atlas covers their frequency and distribution in the various Member States and regions of the European Union. The figures are analysed by:

- general mortality broken down by age group and sex, and
- the medical causes of death.

An electronic version (PDF format) can be downloaded free of charge from www .europa.eu.int/comm/eurostat. A short publication in the Statistics in Focus collection, *Mortality in the European Union 1997–1999*, which updates some main results of the atlas for the period 1997–99, accompanies the atlas.

Language versions. Multilingual DE, EN, FR: A4 format, 119 pages; catalogue no. KS-AC-04-000-EN-C; price €30.00.

Mortality in the EU 1997–1999

Part of the Statistics in Focus collection. Has updated figures.

Language version. EN: PDF format (can be downloaded free of charge from www .europa.eu.int/comm/eurostat); catalogue no. KS-NK-004-EN-N.

Health Statistics – Key Data on Health 2002 – Data 1970–2001

Contains information on a wide range of health topics from data sources such as NewCronos from Eurostat, Ecosante from the OECD, Health for All from the WHO, FAO, International Agency for Cancer, Euro HIV and specific epidemiological studies. Covers the main diseases and has a statistical description of healthcare systems. Addresses the issues of lifestyles (nutrition, smoking, drinking, physical activity, drug use), mortality (infant, causes of death) and health risks associated with the environment, work, leisure and traffic. Covers the 15 Member States, Iceland, Norway, Liechtenstein and Switzerland. An electronic

version (PDF format) can be downloaded free of charge from www.europa.eu.int/comm/eurostat.

Language versions. Multilingual DE, EN, FR: A4 format, 457 pages; catalogue no. KS-08-02-002-EN-C; price €45.00.

Key Data on Education in Europe – 2002

Provides an overview of the functioning of education systems and the participation of young people at all levels of education in 30 European countries (the 15 Member States of the European Union, the three EFTA/EEA countries and 12 candidate countries). Contains 145 indicators. Has five chapters structured by level of education and three chapters on the teaching of foreign languages, teaching staff and the financing of education. An electronic version (PDF format) can be downloaded free of charge from www.euridice.org/Documents/cc/2002/en/CC2002_EN_home_page.PDF.

Language versions. Multilingual ES, DE, EN, FR, EL: A4 format, 298 pages; catalogue no. NC-AF-02-001-EN-C; price €18.00.

Education across Europe 2003

Provides comparable statistics and indicators on education for 32 countries: the 15 EU Member States, the 10 acceding countries, the three candidate countries, Iceland, Norway, Albania and the Former Yugoslav Republic of Macedonia. The data derive mainly from the Eurostat education data collections built around the joint UOE (UIS, OECD, Eurostat) tables on pupils and students, teaching staff and finance complemented with special EU tables on enrolment at regional level and foreign language learning in schools. Most data refer to the academic year 2000/01.

The statistics refer to public and private, full-time and part-time education in the regular school and university system as defined by the International Standard Classification of Education, Unesco 1997. Other Eurostat sources are used to describe the context and main outcomes of education.

Indicators on enterprise training are also presented from the second continuing vocational training survey, which is the only source of internationally comparable data in this field. An electronic version (PDF format) can be downloaded free of charge from www.europa.eu.int/comm/eurostat.

Language version. EN: A4 format, 193 pages; catalogue no. KS-58-04-869-EN-C; price €35.00.

Working Times

Part of the Statistics in Focus collection.

Language version. EN: PDF format (can be downloaded free of charge from www .europa.eu.int/comm/eurostat); catalogue no. KS-NK-04-0076-EN-N.

Social Protection in Europe

Part of the Statistics in Focus collection.

Language version. EN: PDF format (can be downloaded free of charge from www.europa.eu.int/comm/eurostat); catalogue no. KS-NK-04-006-EN-N.

Household Formation in the EU – Lone Parents

Part of the Statistics in Focus collection.

Language version. EN: PDF format (can be downloaded free of charge from www .europa.eu.int/comm/eurostat); catalogue no. KS-NK-04-005-EN-N.

Annual Net Earnings in Manufacturing 1996–2002

Part of the Statistics in Focus collection.

Language version. EN: PDF format (can be downloaded free of charge from www .europa.eu.int/comm/eurostat); catalogue no. KS-NK-04-004-EN-N.

Acquisition of Citizenship

Part of the Statistics in Focus collection.

Language version. EN: PDF format (can be downloaded free of charge from www .europa.eu.int/comm/eurostat); catalogue no. KS-NK-04-003-EN-N.

First Results of the Demographic Data Collection for 2003 in Europe

Part of the Statistics in Focus collection.

Language version. EN: PDF format (can be downloaded free of charge from www .europa.eu.int/comm/eurostat); catalogue no. KS-NK-04-001-EN-N.

First Demographic Estimates for 2004

Part of the Statistics in Focus collection.

Language version. EN: PDF format (can be downloaded free of charge from www .europa.eu.int/comm/eurostat); catalogue no. KS-NK-05-001-EN-N.

Monetary Poverty in the New Member States and Candidate Countries

Part of the Statistics in Focus collection.

Language version. EN: PDF format (can be downloaded free of charge from www .europa.eu.int/comm/eurostat); catalogue no. KS-NK-04-012-EN-N.

Common Indicators of Poverty and Social Exclusion in the EU: the Latest Data (for EU-15)

Part of the Statistics in Focus collection.

Language version. EN: PDF format (can be downloaded free of charge from www .europa.eu.int/comm/eurostat); catalogue no. KS-NK-04-009-EN-N.

THEME 4 – INDUSTRY, TRADE AND SERVICES

European Business – Facts and Figures – Data 1998–2002 – with CD-ROM

Includes data for the ten new Member States, which (subject to data availability) have been fully integrated into this edition, and EU-25 totals have been included wherever possible. The data reflect the major developments in output, employment and external trade. The commentaries concentrate largely on the three-digit level of the NACE Rev. 1 classification of economic activities. The chapters are structured largely on the basis of the NACE code, starting with energy and the extractive industries and finishing with business services, the information society and media. An electronic version (PDF format) can be downloaded free of charge from www .europa.eu.int/comm/eurostat.

The accompanying CD-ROM contains the commentaries, tables and figures of the paper version and a database with many additional series, such as longer time-series or breakdowns by Member State. The underlying statistics in the database can be easily accessed using Eurostat's dedicated database browser: Eurostat visual application. Data can be extracted and exported for manipulation in database or spreadsheet applications. The CD-ROM also provides background information on the underlying legislation, sources and classifications that have been used, and a glossary of terms.

Language version. EN: 421 pages with CD-ROM; catalogue no. KS-BW-04-001-EN-C; price €50.00.

Quarterly Panorama of European Business Statistics

Reflects the evolution of the short-term trends of the European economy as a whole and from the perspective of a broad range of individual industrial, construction, trade and other service sectors. The split into sectors follows roughly the two-digit level of detail of the NACE classification. A commentary on the EU and euro zone economy and each sector is accompanied by graphs and tables for a range of economic indicators. In addition, the economy is compared with those of the United States and Japan. An electronic version (PDF format) can be downloaded free of charge from www .europa.eu.int/comm/eurostat.

Language version. EN: 135 pages; catalogue no. KS-DL-04-000-EN-C; price per

copy €30.00; annual subscription price €100.00.

Business Demography in Europe – Results for 10 Member States and Norway – Data 1997–2001

Provides a comprehensive data set on enterprise births, deaths and survival rates, and information on related employment and turnover. Also contains information broken down by employee size-class and by the legal form of the enterprise, and a special focus on the information and communication technologies sector.

Language version. EN: PDF format (can be downloaded free of charge from www .europa.eu.int/comm/eurostat); catalogue no. KS-DV-04-001.

E-commerce and the Internet in European Businesses – Data 2001–2002

Reports on the results of the second enterprise survey, undertaken by all Member States and Norway. The surveys were generally carried out during the first half of 2002. They concentrated on the measurement of e-commerce in terms of sales and purchases by enterprises via the Internet and other computer-mediated networks, and looked at the use of key information and communication technologies. An electronic version (PDF format) can be downloaded free of charge from www.europa.eu.int/comm/eurostat.

Language version. EN: A4 format, 112 pages; catalogue no. KS-54-03-889-EN-C; price €20.00.

Business in Candidate Countries – Facts and Figures – Data 1995–1999

Provides information on the economies, the development patterns and the state of the different economic sectors of Bulgaria, Cyprus, the Czech Republic, Estonia, Hungary, Latvia, Lithuania, Poland, Romania, Slovakia and Slovenia. An electronic version (PDF format) can be downloaded free of charge from www .europa.eu.int/comm/eurostat.

Language versions. Multilingual DE, EN, FR: A4 format, 143 pages; catalogue no. KS-45-02-975-EN-C; price €30.00.

SMEs in Europe – Competitiveness and the Knowledge-driven Society

Deals with the structure, performance and conduct of small and medium-sized enterprises in Europe and explains their needs and opportunities. Contains a wide range of up-to-date information from Eurostat and Commission databases. An electronic version (PDF format) can be downloaded free of charge from www .europa.eu.int/comm/eurostat.

Language version. EN: A4 format, 70 pages; catalogue no. KS-CJ-02-001-EN-C; price €14.50.

SMEs in Europe – Candidate Countries

Compares the structure and performance of activities across the whole of the EU and the former candidate countries. Presents data based on harmonized methodology for the candidate countries and an EU-15 aggregate. Information is taken from Eurostat databases, in particular drawing on structural business statistics (SBS), the continuing vocational training survey (CVTS) and the labour costs survey (LCS). The data are generally presented broken down according to standard SME definitions (in terms of employment size classes for enterprises) and according to the main economic activities of enterprises (in accordance with the NACE classification). In most cases the information relates to the latest available period, which is normally the reference year 2001. An electronic version (PDF format) can be downloaded free of charge from www.europa.eu.int/comm/eurostat.

Language version. EN: A4 format, 70 pages; catalogue no. KS-CJ-04-001-EN-C; price €14.50.

Business in Europe: Statistical Pocketbook – Data 1995–2002

Most data are from official sources and are presented according to sectoral themes covering: the business enterprise population, manufacturing, construction, distributive trades, information and communication society and other services. Also included are topics such as industrial specialization of the EU Member States, slow and fast growth industries within the EU, a breakdown of retail trade by product, who buys what, hotel capacity in the EU and household Internet connection rates. An electronic version (PDF format) can be downloaded free of charge from www.europa.eu.int/comm/eurostat.

Language version. EN: 10.5 × 21 cm, 110 pages; catalogue no. KS-DH-03-001-EN-C; price €10.00.

Employment in the Market Economy in the European Union – an Analysis of the Structural Business Statistics – Data 2000–2001

Presents the division of employment and output between different economic activities, the relative importance of different sized enterprises, their productivity and costs of production, and the amount of investment undertaken. Because the data on employment and business-related variables (such as output and value-added) are compiled and classified on the same basis within the

structural business statistics network, their combined use ensures that analysis carried out is internally consistent.

Language version. EN: PDF format (can be downloaded free of charge from www.europa.eu.int/comm/eurostat); catalogue no. KS-59-04-944-EN-N.

Cinema, TV and Radio in the EU – Statistics on Audiovisual Services – Data 1980–2002

Based on the data collected via the AUVIS questionnaire from EU Member States, candidate countries and EFTA countries. The results of the 2002 enquiry have been taken into consideration. An electronic version (PDF format) can be downloaded free of charge from www.europa.eu.int/comm/eurostat.

Language version. EN: A4 format, 164 pages; catalogue no. KS-BT-03-001-EN-C; price €17.50.

Statistics on the Information Society in Europe – Data 1996–2002

Provides detailed information on the information society in the European Economic Area, Switzerland and the candidate countries. Uses data from the pilot enterprise survey on e-commerce and data from the information society questionnaire, which is a collection of data provided by Member States and candidate countries on a voluntary but less harmonized basis. Also brings together extracts from several general Eurostat data sources in so far as they concern information and communication technologies, notably structural business statistics, external trade and the labour force survey. An electronic version (PDF format) can be downloaded free of charge from www.europa.eu.int/comm/eurostat.

Language version. EN: A4 format, 103 pages; catalogue no. KS-DP-03-001-EN-C; price €17.00.

Information Society Statistics – Data 1997–2002 – Pocketbook

Provides a statistical overview of key data on the information society in the European Union and in candidate countries. Also presents aggregated figures of the extent to which information and communication technologies have impacted on the business sector and individuals. An electronic version (PDF format) can be downloaded free of charge from www.europa.eu.int/comm/eurostat.

Language version. EN: 10.5 × 21 cm, 106 pages; catalogue no. KS-56-03-093-EN-C; price €10.00.

Tourism Statistics – Yearbook – Data 1990, 1995, 1998–2002

Data have been collected by the national authorities under Directive 95/97/EC and mainly concern: capacity of collective

accommodation, occupancy in collective accommodation establishments and tourism demand – domestic and outbound tourism.

Language versions. Multilingual DE, EN, FR: CD-ROM format; catalogue no. KS-DS-03-001-3A-Z; price €120.00.

Tourism – Europe, Central European Countries, Mediterranean Countries – Key Figures 2001–2002

Gives an overview of recent trends and key figures in the EU Member States, the EFTA countries, the candidate countries and the MED partner countries. An electronic version (PDF format) can be downloaded free of charge from www.europa.eu.int/comm/eurostat.

Language version. EN: A4 format, 48 pages; catalogue no. KS-55-03-318-EN-C; price €20.00.

Communication in the Candidate Countries – Data 1995–2001

Describes recent developments in the telecommunications and postal sectors in the ten acceding and three other candidate countries. Comparison with the EU-15 is made when possible. Detailed data are presented in tables for downloading and further processing. Aspects such as the economy, employment, traffic, infrastructure and quality of service are covered on an aggregate level.

Language versions. Trilingual DE/EN/FR: CD-ROM format; catalogue no. KS-53-03-871-3A-Z; price €30.00.

Iron and Steel – Yearly Statistics – Concluding Edition – Data 1993–2002

Contains detailed tables presenting annual statistics on the structure and economic situation of this industry at EU level and in each Member State. Collates the latest available data on such topics as production of iron ore, pig iron, finished steel products, the size of enterprises and plants, employment, indirect foreign trade and others. An electronic version (PDF format) can be downloaded free of charge from www.europa.eu.int/comm/eurostat.

Language versions. Trilingual DE/EN/FR: A4 format, 73 pages; catalogue no. KS-BL-03-001-3A-C; price €17.50.

Weights Used in Short-term Statistics Following Enlargement

Part of the Statistics in Focus collection.

Language version. EN: PDF format (can be downloaded free of charge from www.europa.eu.int/comm/eurostat); catalogue no. KS-NP-04-020-EN-N.

Internet Usage by Individuals and Enterprises

Part of the Statistics in Focus collection.

Language version. EN: PDF format (can be downloaded free of charge from www.europa.eu.int/comm/eurostat); catalogue no. KS-NP-04-016-EN-N.

Tourism in the European Union in 2003

Part of the Statistics in Focus collection.

Language version. EN: PDF format (can be downloaded free of charge from www.europa.eu.int/comm/eurostat); catalogue no. KS-NP-04-012-EN-N.

Retail Trade: Volume of Sales

Part of the Statistics in Focus collection.

Language version. EN: PDF format (can be downloaded free of charge from www.europa.eu.int/comm/eurostat); catalogue no. KS-NP-04-008-EN-N.

Market Research and Public Opinion Polling and Advertising Services

Part of the Statistics in Focus collection.

Language version. EN: PDF format (can be downloaded free of charge from www.europa.eu.int/comm/eurostat); catalogue no. KS-NP-04-006-EN-N.

SMEs in the Candidate Countries

Part of the Statistics in Focus collection.

Language version. EN: PDF format (can be downloaded free of charge from www.europa.eu.int/comm/eurostat); catalogue no. KS-NP-04-005-EN-N.

Developments for Short-term Statistics in the Candidate Countries

Part of the Statistics in Focus collection.

Language version. EN: PDF format (can be downloaded free of charge from www.europa.eu.int/comm/eurostat); catalogue no. KS-NP-04-001-EN-N.

THEME 5 – AGRICULTURE AND FISHERIES

Agriculture – Statistical yearbook 2003–2004 – Data 1993–2002

Sets up a synthetic view based on the main figures from Eurostat's special publications on agriculture, forestry and fisheries. The AGRIS database on the CD-ROM covers the prices, quantities and values of agricultural output. An electronic version (PDF format) can be downloaded free of charge from www.europa.eu.int/comm/eurostat.

Language versions. Trilingual DE/EN/FR: A4 format, 210 pages with CD-ROM; catalogue no. KS-AQ-04-001-3A-C; price €40.00.

Agricultural Statistics – Quarterly Bulletin

Contains monthly data on crop production, animal production and agricultural prices with commentary. The first issue also includes forestry statistics, which cover the data on roundwood, other forest products and trade in the EU-25, candidate countries, EFTA countries, Canada, the USA and Russia. The CD-ROM contains AGRIS data. An electronic version (PDF format, but without the content of the CD-ROM) can be downloaded free of charge from www.europa.eu.int/comm/eurostat.

Language versions. Trilingual DE/EN/FR: A4 format with CD-ROM; catalogue no. KS-NT-04-000-3A-C; price per copy €40.00; subscription code VXAS00, annual subscription price €140.00.

Agricultural Statistics – Pocketbook – Data 1999–2003

Includes chapters on general statistics, crop and animal production, farm structure, and agricultural prices and accounts. Most data are presented for the 25 Member States of the European Union. An electronic version (PDF format) can be downloaded free of charge from www.europa.eu.int/comm/eurostat.

Language version. EN: 10 × 21 cm, 100 pages; catalogue no. KS-58-04-675-EN-C; price €10.00.

Farm Structure – 1999/2000 Survey (Paper + CD-ROM)

Data are included by Member State and for the EU as a whole, and cover land use, livestock farming and the agricultural labour force. The results are discussed in comparison with those of previous surveys. The accompanying CD-ROM (in English only) explains the methodology used in each Member State and contains the data in Excel format. An electronic version (PDF format, but without the content of the CD-ROM) can be downloaded free of charge from www.europa.eu.int/comm/eurostat.

Language versions. Trilingual DE/EN/FR: A4 format, 238 pages with CD-ROM; catalogue no. KS-52-03-756-3A-C; price €40.00.

Area under Vines – Third basic Community Survey – Analysis of the Results – Data 1989–1999

The most relevant data collected by Member States have been selected from the VITIS database and have been used to draw up a series of summary tables, graphics and maps. Whenever possible, a comparison between the results of the 1989 and 1999 EU basic surveys has also been made. An electronic version (PDF format) can be downloaded free of charge from www.europa.eu.int/comm/eurostat.

Language versions. Trilingual DE/EN/FR: A4 format, 82 pages; catalogue no. KS-49-02-191-3A-C; price €17.00.

Fisheries – Yearbook 2003 – Data 1993–2002

Presents fishery statistics for the Member States of the European Union, the candidate countries and for other important countries in this economic sector. Contains sections on catches by fishing region, catches of principal species, the fishing fleet and foreign trade in fishery products. The accompanying CD-ROM contains the NewCronos domain FISH and data for the period 1950–2002.

Language versions. Trilingual DE/EN/FR: A4 format, 67 pages with CD-ROM; catalogue no. KS-AX-03-001-3A-C; price €40.00.

Forestry Statistics – Data 1990–2002 – Pocketbook

Covering the forestry sector in the EU, EFTA and the candidate countries, the content is divided into two parts. The first gives a general description of forest resources, forest ownership, forest condition, employment in the forestry sector, the contribution of this sector to national GDP formation and the share of energy produced using woody material. The second part concerns the production and trade of wood and wood products and is based on data from the joint forestry sector questionnaire, which is the result of co-operation by Eurostat, UNECE, FAO and ITTO. There are also supply balance sheets concerning the production and trade of wood, wood-based panels, paper and paperboard. An electronic version (PDF format) can be downloaded free of charge from www.europa.eu.int/comm/eurostat.

Language version. EN: 10 × 21 cm, 75 pages; catalogue no. KS-59-04-306-EN-C; price €10.00.

THEME 6 – EXTERNAL TRADE

Panorama of European Union Trade – Data 1988–2001

Emphasizes the place of the European Union in the world market and analyses its trade flows with its main trading partners as well as the goods exchanged. Also considers the trade between the Member States and of the euro zone. The impact of enlargement is discussed in a separate chapter. An electronic version (PDF format in DE, EN and FR language versions) can be downloaded free of charge from www.europa.eu.int/comm/ eurostat.

Language version. EN: A4 format, 50 pages; catalogue no. KS-DJ-03-001-EN-C; price €30.00.

Intra- and Extra-EU Trade Data – Combined Nomenclature (DVD) - Comext

Published monthly. Contains detailed statistics on trade based on the EU Member States classification of countries and products, methodological notes, notes on the state of data availability and the user manual. It now includes data on the new Member States and the database Prodcom.

Language versions. Trilingual DE/EN/FR: DVD format; catalogue no. KS-CK-04-000-3A-Z; price per copy €700.00; subscription code OCDR00, annual subscription price €4,020.00.

External and Intra-European Union Trade – Statistical Yearbook – Data 1958–2003

Contains data on the trade flows, broken down by major product group, of the EU with its main trading partners on the one hand and between the Member States on the other. Also includes extra chapters on the trade of candidate countries and the EFTA members.

Language version. EN: PDF format (can be downloaded free of charge from www.europa.eu.int/comm/eurostat); catalogue no. KS-CV-04-001.

External and Intra-European Union Trade – Monthly Statistics

Provides data on short-term trends in the trade of the European Union and its Member States. Contains statistics on the trade flows of the EU with its main trading partners on the one hand and between the Member States on the other. These statistics are broken down by major product groups.

Language version. EN: PDF format (can be downloaded free of charge from www.europa.eu.int/comm/eurostat); catalogue no. KS-AR-04-000 EN-N.

Euro-Mediterranean Trade in Agricultural Products (MED)

Part of the Statistics in Focus collection.

Language version. EN: PDF format (can be downloaded free of charge from www.europa.eu.int/comm/eurostat); catalogue no. KS-NO-04-001-EN-N.

Intra- and Extra-EU Trade by Sea

Part of the Statistics in Focus collection.

Language version. EN: PDF format (can be downloaded free of charge from www.europa.eu.int/comm/eurostat); catalogue no. KS-NZ-04-004-EN-N.

Extra-EU Trade of Member States by Mode of Transport

Part of the Statistics in Focus collection.

Language version. EN: PDF format (can be downloaded free of charge from www.europa.eu.int/comm/eurostat); catalogue no. KS-NZ-04-003-EN-N.

Trade in Goods with Candidate Countries by Mode of Transport

Part of the Statistics in Focus collection.

Language version. EN: PDF format (can be downloaded free of charge from www.europa.eu.int/comm/eurostat); catalogue no. KS-NZ-04-002-EN-N.

Trade in a 25-member European Union

Part of the Statistics in Focus collection.

Language version. EN: PDF format (can be downloaded free of charge from www.europa.eu.int/comm/eurostat); catalogue no. KS-NO-03-004-EN-N.

THEME 7 – TRANSPORT

Panorama of Transport – Statistical Overview of Transport in the European Union – Data 1970–2001

Describes transport not only in terms of the quantities of freight and passengers moved and the vehicles and infrastructure used but also as part of the economy, the environment and as a factor in our quality of life. This edition puts special emphasis on the latest road freight transport statistics collected under the recent EU legislation and gives an overview of available data on the ten acceding countries and the remaining candidate countries. Some chapters give information on the EFTA States. An electronic version (PDF format in DE, EN and FR language versions) can be downloaded free of charge from www.europa.eu.int/comm/eurostat.

Language version. EN: A4 format, 139 pages; catalogue no. KS-DA-04-001-EN-C; price €25.00.

Everything on Transport Statistics – Data 1970–2001

Contains about 20 million statistical data and more than 850 documents, mostly produced by Eurostat's transport unit. The data concern transport in the European Union Member States, Norway, Switzerland, candidate and Mediterranean countries. Gives access to many new data, publications and legal acts related to transport statistics, in particular in the fields of aviation, maritime and road transport.

Language versions. Trilingual DE/EN/FR: DVD format; catalogue no. KS-53-03-944-3A-Z; price €700.00.

Transport by Air – National and International Intra- and Extra-EU – Data 1993–2001

Presents air passenger and freight figures, in most cases annual, from the Member States of the European Union, Norway and Switzerland. Includes historical publications, legal acts, glossaries and the Energy and Transport Directorate-General's White Paper. Contains about five million statistical data and hundreds of documents or publications mainly available in German, English and French.

Language versions. Trilingual DE/EN/FR: CD-ROM format; catalogue no. KS-DG-03-001-3A-Z; price €60.00.

Transport by Sea – National and International Intra- and Extra-EU – Data 1997–2001

Contains more than 14 million records of statistical data. Includes data on gross weight of goods, passenger movements, types of cargo, nationality of registration of vessel, number of vessels and gross tonnage of vessels calling at ports. The data are disseminated either at port to maritime coastal area or port to country level. There are three levels of information: dynamic maps interface for each country separately, HTML files with methodological notes, graphs and tables, and access to the whole of the NewCronos maritime data.

Language versions. Trilingual DE/EN/FR: CD-ROM format; catalogue no. KS-CF-03-001-3A-Z; price €500.00.

Transport in the Euro-Mediterranean Region – Data 1990–2001

Provides a statistical overview of transport for Algeria, Cyprus, Egypt, Israel, Jordan, Lebanon, Malta, Morocco, the Palestinian Authority, Syria, Tunisia and Turkey. An electronic version (PDF format, with summary available in Arabic) can be downloaded free of charge from www.europa.eu.int/comm/eurostat.

Language versions. EN, FR: A4 format, 93 pages; catalogue no. KS-CY-02-001-EN-C; price €15.00.

Reference Manual for the Implementation of Council Regulation No. 1172/98/EC on Statistics on the Carriage of Goods by Road – 2003 Edition

The regulation provides a legal basis for the collection of a wide range of data on road freight transport. This manual contains detailed guidance for Member

States and candidate countries engaged in the implementation of this regulation.

Language version. EN: PDF format (can be downloaded free of charge from www.europa.eu.int/comm/eurostat); catalogue no. KS-BI-03-001-EN-N.

Glossary for Transport Statistics – Third Edition

Published to assist member counties during the collection of data on transport made by the UNECE, ECMT and Eurostat through the common questionnaire. Now contains 533 definitions.

Language version. EN: PDF format (can be downloaded free of charge from www.europa.eu.int/comm/eurostat); catalogue no. KS-BI-03-002-EN-N.

Trends in Road Freight Transport 1990–2002

Part of the Statistics in Focus collection.

Language version. EN: PDF format (can be downloaded free of charge from www.europa.eu.int/comm/eurostat); catalogue no. KS-NZ-04-007-EN-N.

Road Freight Transport by Group of Goods 1990–2002

Part of the Statistics in Focus collection.

Language version. EN: PDF format (can be downloaded free of charge from www.europa.eu.int/comm/eurostat); catalogue no. KS-NZ-04-009-EN-N.

Impact of September 11th on Air Passenger Transport

Part of the Statistics in Focus collection.

Language version. EN: PDF format (can be downloaded free of charge from www.europa.eu.int/comm/eurostat); catalogue no. KS-NZ-04-005-EN-N.

Passenger Air Transport 2000–2

Part of the Statistics in Focus collection.

Language version. EN: PDF format (can be downloaded free of charge from www.europa.eu.int/comm/eurostat); catalogue no. KS-NZ-04-011.

Maritime Transport of Goods and Passengers in New Member States and Candidate Countries in 2001

Part of the Statistics in Focus collection.

Language version. EN: PDF format (can be downloaded free of charge from www.europa.eu.int/comm/eurostat); catalogue no. KS-NZ-04-006-EN-N.

Maritime Transport of Goods and Passengers 1997–2002

Part of the Statistics in Focus collection.

Language version. EN: PDF format (can be downloaded free of charge from www

.europa.eu.int/comm/eurostat); catalogue no. KS-NZ-04-008-EN-N.

THEME 8 – ENVIRONMENT AND ENERGY

Energy, Transport and Environment Indicators – Data 1991–2001

Comprises a broad set of data collected by Eurostat and the European Environment Agency. Provides an overview of the most relevant indicators on energy, transport and environment, particularly on sustainable development. Presents data for the EU-25 Member States, EFTA countries, Bulgaria, Romania and Turkey. An electronic version (PDF format) can be downloaded free of charge from www.europa.eu.int/comm/eurostat.

Language version. EN: 10.5 × 21 cm, 169 pages; catalogue no. KS-DK-04-001-EN-C; price €13.00.

Energy Efficiency Indicators

Contains the priority energy efficiency indicators by sector – macro, household, services, industry, transport and transformation – for the EU-15, the Member States and Norway. It is a response to the Commission's communication COM/2000/247 (action plan to improve energy efficiency in the European Community), which invites Eurostat and the Member States to work closely together on the development of energy efficiency indicators. An electronic version (PDF format) can be downloaded free of charge from www.europa.eu.int/comm/eurostat.

Language version. EN: A4 format, 60 pages; catalogue no. KS-49-02-789-EN-C; price €20.00.

Renewable Energy Sources Statistics in the EU, Iceland and Norway – Data 1989–2000

Gives an overview of the evolution of the contribution of renewable energy sources in the European Union for this period, during which surveys and studies were carried out in the Member States on behalf of Eurostat. An electronic version (PDF format) can be downloaded free of charge from www.europa.eu.int/comm/eurostat.

Language version. EN: 10.5 × 21 cm, 80 pages; catalogue no. KS-46-02-080-EN-C; price €10.00.

Energy Prices – Data 1990–2002

Summarizes the recent price information for all the principal energy sources. More recent prices for particular sources can be found in the specialist press and notably in the Commission's weekly Oil Bulletin. An electronic version (PDF format) can be downloaded free of charge from www.europa.eu.int/comm/eurostat.

Language versions. Trilingual DE/EN/FR: A4 format, 163 pages; catalogue no. KS-AB-03-001-3A-C; price €26.50.

Energy: Yearly Statistics – Data 2001

Groups an extensive volume of statistical information relating to the energy economy of the Community and the Member States. Chapters cover: the characteristic data of energy economics in recent years; an overall view of the trends for the principal aggregates, taken from the 'energy supplied' balance sheets of the Community in tonnes of oil equivalent; and historical series for each energy source for the principal aggregates characterizing the structure of energy economics. An electronic version (PDF format) can be downloaded free of charge from www.europa.eu.int/comm/eurostat.

Language versions. Trilingual DE/EN/FR: A4 format, 231 pages; catalogue no. KS-CN-03-001-3A-C; price €20.00.

Electricity Prices – Data 1990–2003

Gives electricity prices in national currencies/100 kWh with updating for January 2003 for five domestic and nine industrial consumers in over 30 locations within the European Union. Also contains comparative tables expressed in ecu or euro/100 kWh and PPS/100 kWh and the 'marker prices'. The years 1990, 1995, and 1999 to 2003 are shown. An electronic version (PDF format) can be downloaded free of charge from www.europa.eu.int/comm/eurostat.

Language versions. Trilingual DE/EN/FR: A4 format, 220 pages; catalogue no. KS-CO-03-001-3A-C; price €37.00.

Electricity Prices – Price Systems 2001

Summarizes every two years the information about the price systems in force in the European Union, according to the directive on the transparency of gas and electricity prices charged to the end-user. An electronic version (PDF format) can be downloaded free of charge from www.europa.eu.int/comm/eurostat.

Language versions. Trilingual DE/EN/FR: A4 format, 104 pages; catalogue no. KS-46-02-056-3A-C; price €17.50.

Gas Prices – Data 1990–2003

Provides gas prices in national currencies/GJ for a wide range of both domestic and industrial consumers in over 30 locations within the EU. Also contains comparative tables expressed in ecu or euro/GJ and PP/GJ. The years 1990, 1995, and 1999 to 2003 are shown. An electronic version (PDF format) can be downloaded free of charge from www.europa.eu.int/comm/eurostat.

Language versions. Trilingual DE/EN/ FR: A4 format, 221 pages; catalogue no. KS-CP-03-001-3A-C; price €37.00.

Gas Prices – Price Systems 2001

Summarizes every two years the information about the price systems in force in the European Union, according to the directive on the transparency of gas and electricity prices charged to the end-user. An electronic version (PDF format) can be downloaded free of charge from www .europa.eu.int/comm/eurostat.

Language versions. Trilingual DE/EN/ FR: A4 format, 80 pages; catalogue no. KS-46-02-064-3A-C; price €14.50.

Competition Indicators in the Electricity Market: EU, Norway and Candidate Countries – Data 1999–2001

Gives the results of a questionnaire-based data collection to monitor competition in the electricity market as a result of the ongoing liberalization process. An electronic version (PDF format) can be downloaded free of charge from www .europa.eu.int/comm/eurostat.

Language version. EN: A4 format, 122 pages; catalogue no. KS-53-03-403-EN-C; price €17.00.

A Selection of Environmental Pressure Indicators for the EU and Candidate Countries

In 1990 and 2001 Eurostat published a set of environmental pressure indicators for the EU, addressing the most important anthropogenic pressures on the environment in eight to ten major policy fields. In 2003 Eurostat updated and extended these data to cover the acceding countries and the indicators in four of these policy fields, namely air pollution, climate change, resource depletion and waste.

Language version. EN: PDF format (can be downloaded free of charge from www .europa.eu.int/comm/eurostat); catalogue no. KS-59-04-249-EN-N.

Environmental Statistics in the Mediterranean Countries – Compendium 2002

Presents the data and metadata collected within the 12 Mediterranean countries in the framework of the Medstat-Environment project. Contains a whole set of general indicators and more specific indicators concerning soils, forests, water, biodiversity, atmospheric pollution, and production and treatment of solid wastes.

Some of the tables are presented to help comparison at a regional level and others illustrate a historical evolution at a national level. Data from 1960 to 2000 appear in the tables.

Language versions. EN, FR: A4 format, 136 pages; catalogue no. KS-49-02-628-EN-C; price €14.50.

The Use of Plant Protection Products in the European Union – Data 1992–1999

Provides statistical information on plant protection products, broken down by Member State, treated crops and chemical classes and, when confidentiality rules allow, on the level of active ingredients. An electronic version (PDF format) can be downloaded free of charge from www.europa.eu.int/comm/eurostat.

Language version. EN: A4 format, 130 pages; catalogue no. KS-49-02-830-EN-C; price €25.00.

Environmental Protection Expenditure in Europe – 2001

Contains statistics on the money spent to protect the environment, any associated revenues or cost savings, and information about the financing of environmental protection activities. The data are the basis for analysis of the 'polluter pays' principle and the effects on enterprise competitiveness, for cost-effective analysis of proposed new regulations and policies, and for estimates of the size of the environmental goods and services industry. An electronic version (PDF format) can be downloaded free of charge from www .europa.eu.int/comm/eurostat.

Language version. EN: A4 format, 238 pages; catalogue no. KS-39-01-320-EN-C; price €35.50.

Environmental Protection Expenditure in Accession Countries

As part of the process of accession to the European Union, applicant countries need to adopt stricter environmental rules and standards. The Environment Directorate-General estimates that the total cost of compliance for the ten accession countries is around 100 billion euros and that they need to spend around 2–3% of GDP on environmental protection in the coming years. This book presents the volume and structure of the spending on environmental protection from 1996 to 2000. An electronic version (PDF format) can be downloaded free of charge from www.europa.eu.int/comm/eurostat.

Language version. EN: A4 format, 238 pages; catalogue no. KS-CM-02-001-EN-C; price €35.50.

Waste Generated and Treated in Europe – Data 1990–2001

Presents a set of official statistics using as a principal source the 2002 joint Eurostat/OECD questionnaire. For some countries additional data have been taken from the national publications of Member States. The six main sections are: Introduction, Total waste generated, Industrial waste, Municipal waste, Hazardous waste, and Recycling/packaging waste. An electronic version (PDF format) can be downloaded free of charge from www.europa.eu.int/comm/eurostat.

Language version. EN: A4 format, 140 pages; catalogue no. KS-55-03-471-EN-C; price €20.00.

THEME 9 – SCIENCE AND TECHNOLOGY

Statistics on Science and Technology in Europe – Data 1991–2002

Presents key data and indicators describing science and technology developments in Europe and compared to other areas of the world. Contains chapters on government appropriations or outlays on R & D (GBAORD), R & D expenditure and personnel, patents, high-tech trade, human resources in science and technology and on other indicators related to high-tech and knowledge-intensive sectors. An electronic version (PDF format) can be downloaded free of charge from www .europa.eu.int/comm/eurostat.

Language version. EN: A4 format, 173 pages; catalogue no. KS-57-03-104-EN-C; price €35.00.

Innovation in Europe – Results for the EU, Iceland and Norway – Data 1998–2001

Presents the results of the third Community innovation survey. Contains a general description of innovation performance in Europe, innovation across enterprise size-classes, innovation in the various economic sectors and employment and market characteristics of innovators. An electronic version (PDF format) can be downloaded free of charge from www.europa.eu.int/comm/eurostat.

Language version. EN: A4 format, 295 pages; catalogue no. KS-59-04-257-EN-C; price €30.00.

Statistics on Science and Technology – Data 1991–2001

Part I presents an analysis of the recent trends in research and development and patenting. In Part II the accompanying methodological information is provided in some detail for more specialist users. Part III presents tables containing both original data and derived indicators, providing users with the opportunity to conduct their own analyses on the research and development situation in Europe and beyond. An electronic version (PDF format) can be downloaded free of charge from www.europa.eu.int/comm/eurostat.

Language versions. Multilingual DE, EN, FR: A4 format, 180 pages; catalogue no. KS-CT-02-001-EN-C; price €29.50.

Statistics on Science and Technology – Data 1980–2002

Contains the most up-to-date data at Eurostat in the fields of government budget appropriations or outlays for R & D (GBAORD), R & D expenditure and personnel, human resources in science and technology (HRST) and employment in high technology (EHT). Data are available for the Member States of the EU, Iceland, Norway and other countries, such as Japan or the USA at national level. HRST and EHT data are also available for the candidate countries. These data are compiled from official national sources and the Community labour force survey, and in general they use internationally agreed concepts and definitions as recommended in the 'Frascati family' of manuals and Eurostat's 'Regional manual'.

Language versions. Trilingual DE/EN/FR: CD-ROM format; catalogue no. KS-CG-03-001-3A-Z; price €140.00.

Science and Technology in Europe – Statistical Pocketbook – Data 1991–2001

Presents the key indicators describing science and technology in Europe and its main competitors. Contains a selection of tables and figures in the fields of government budget appropriations or outlays on R & D (GBAORD), R & D expenditure and personnel, patents, innovation, high-tech trade, human resources in science and technology, and employment in high-technology and knowledge-intensive sectors. The data focus on the 15 EU Member States. However, so as to allow for international comparisons, data for Iceland, Japan, Norway and the USA are also considered when available. An electronic version (PDF format) can be downloaded free of charge from www.europa.eu.int/comm/eurostat.

Language version. EN: 10.5 × 21 cm, 84 pages; catalogue no. KS-43-03-500-EN-C; price €10.00.

Women, Science and Technology: Measuring Recent Progress towards Gender Equality

Part of the Statistics in Focus collection.

Language version. EN: PDF format (can be downloaded free of charge from www.europa.eu.int/comm/eurostat); catalogue no. KS-NS-04-006-EN-N.

Sources and Resources for EU Innovation

Part of the Statistics in Focus collection.

Language version. EN: PDF format (can be downloaded free of charge from www.europa.eu.int/comm/eurostat); catalogue no. KS-NS-04-005-EN-N.

R & D Expenditure in the European Regions

Part of the Statistics in Focus collection.

Language version. EN: PDF format (can be downloaded free of charge from www.europa.eu.int/comm/eurostat); catalogue no. KS-NS-04-003-EN-N.

R & D Personnel in European Regions

Part of the Statistics in Focus collection.

Language version. EN: PDF format (can be downloaded free of charge from www.europa.eu.int/comm/eurostat); catalogue no. KS-NS-04-004-EN-N.

High-tech Trade, Employment and Value Added in High-tech Industries and Knowledge-intensive Services

Part of the Statistics in Focus collection.

Language version. EN: PDF format (can be downloaded free of charge from www.europa.eu.int/comm/eurostat); catalogue no. KS-NS-04-002-EN-N.

Innovation Output and Barriers to Innovation

Part of the Statistics in Focus collection.

Language version. EN: PDF format (can be downloaded free of charge from www.europa.eu.int/comm/eurostat); catalogue no. KS-NS-04-001-EN-N.

Catching up with the EU? Comparing Highly Qualified Human Resources in the EU and the Acceding Countries

Part of the Statistics in Focus collection.

Language version. EN: PDF format (can be downloaded free of charge from www.europa.eu.int/comm/eurostat); catalogue no. KS-NS-03-009-EN-N.

THE EUROPEAN
PARLIAMENT

EUROPEAN PARLIAMENT: OVERVIEW

The European Parliament represents the interests of EU citizens through 732 Members of the European Parliament (MEPs), who are elected for five years. (The last elections took place in 2004.) The Parliament exercises an important influence on the EU legislative procedure, especially since the Single Act and the Maastricht and Amsterdam Treaties. It adopts the budget, supervises the activities of the Commission and the Council, adopts or repeals international agreements and enjoys powers of legislative co-decision. The following ratio of MEPs is attributed to the different Member States: Germany 99; France, Italy and the United Kingdom 78; Poland and Spain 54; Netherlands 27; Belgium, Czech Republic, Greece, Hungary and Portugal 24; Sweden 19; Austria 18; Denmark, Finland and Slovakia 14; Ireland and Lithuania 13; Latvia 9; Slovenia 7; Cyprus, Estonia and Luxembourg 6; and Malta 5.

The Political Groups

MEPs are not grouped in national delegations but according to the political group to which they belong. The groups are of central importance in both the political and the organizational work of the Parliament. Eight groups are currently represented :

- PPE/DE – Group of the European People's Party (Christian Democrats) and European Democrats (268 members)
- PSE – Socialist Group in the European Parliament (202 members)
- ALDE – Group of the Alliance of Liberals and Democrats for Europe (88 members)
- Verts/ALE – Group of the Greens / European Free Alliance (42 members)
- GUE/NGL – Confederal Group of the European United Left / Nordic Green Left (41 members)
- IND/DEM – Independence / Democracy Group (36 members)
- UEN – Union for Europe of the Nations Group (27 members)
- NI – Non-attached members (28 members)

The different political groups are serviced by their own secretariats, based in Brussels, and the level of resources available to each secretariat depends on the number of members belonging to that group.

The Committees

The Parliament's work is prepared by 17 specialist committees. In addition to standing committees, the European Parliament may also set up temporary committees or committees of inquiry to examine specific problems. The committees draw up responses to legislative proposals from the Commission, and may formulate reports on their own initiative (though these do not form part of the legislative process). Committees may also organize public hearings at which experts give advice on the technical aspects of particular problems. Joint parliamentary committees maintain relations with the parliaments of states linked to the European Union by association agreements, while interparliamentary delegations maintain relations with the parliaments of many other countries and with international organizations. The Parliament's work is organized by a secretariat headed by a Secretary-General with a permanent staff of about 3,500, in addition to which there are political group staff and Members' assistants.

The European Parliament's Secretariat

The secretariat is divided into eight Directorates General (DGs). Two of these DGs (DG III and DG IV) are concerned with the provision of information materials.

DG III (Information and Public Relations) co-ordinates a network of external offices in the Member States. These offices, which represent the European Parliament in the Member States, are the first point of contact between EU citizens and the European Parliament. They are well equipped to respond to requests for both information and documentation and are responsible for passing on the centralized information provided by Brussels and Strasbourg, tailored to each Member State's specific requirements. In addition, DG III co-ordinates relations with the press (Directorate B).

DG IV (Research) is responsible for research and documentation: research and documentation papers, the European Parliament library and archives, documentary databases, follow-up to the Parliament's opinions and resolutions, scientific and technological option assessment, etc.

The Brussels Office, the Central Press and Audiovisual Division (DG III) play the leading role in producing European Parliament information. Almost all of their personnel descend on Strasbourg in order to cover the sessions. They may therefore be considered as the Parliament's central information body. The European Parliament's information is basically oriented towards the press and media, as well as towards social and professional organizations and lobbies but there is some information for the general public.

The Plenary Session

For ease of contact with the other institutions, the parliamentary committees generally meet in Brussels for two weeks a month. The third week is set aside for political group meetings and the fourth for the plenary session, which is held in Strasbourg.

Day-to-day operations of the Parliament and its bodies are the responsibility of the Bureau, though the plenary session remains the final authority. The Bureau consists of the President of the Parliament and the 14 Vice-Presidents. There are five Quaestors who are responsible for internal administrative and financial matters.

When the Bureau and the Chairpersons of the political groups meet, they form the Enlarged Bureau. One of their main tasks is to draw up the draft agendas for Parliament's plenary sessions, which are then approved or amended by the Plenary session.

INFORMATION AVAILABLE FROM THE EUROPEAN PARLIAMENT

Directorate-General (DG) III is responsible for the European Parliament's information and public relations and the DG's press service produces general information on the European Parliament's activities intended both for the general public and the press.

Periodicals

The Briefing: summarizes reports and other items on the agenda for the forthcoming part-session; it is published in all EU official languages in the week before the part-session; *addressees:* in practice, the information is available to anyone who requires information on the European Parliament via Internet; *frequency:* the week before the part-session

The Week: reviews, in all EU official languages, the plenary debates and votes after the part-session has ended; *frequency:* published the week after the part-session has ended.

Daily Notebook: provides, in all EU official languages, a summary record of plenary debates and votes on the day they took place.

News Report: previously entitled INFO-MEMO; news bulletin, in English and French, on Parliamentary Committees' activities, hearings etc.; *addressees:* all interested persons; *frequency:* generally daily during committee weeks.

News Alert: news sheet listing the following week's parliamentary activities, in English and French; *frequency:* published every Friday.

Background Notes (in French, 'Dossier'): an occasional publication, in English and French, giving detailed information on a topic of special interest.

Focus on Europe: a newsletter, published in all EU official languages, providing a broad view of European Parliament news; *addressees:* the general public.

EP News: monthly four-page newspaper presenting what happened at the preceding plenary sessions, various subjects and editorials, its content being tailored to the Member State in which it is being disseminated; can appear in all of the Community's official working languages but the paper's title differs according to the country for which a version is produced (the title for the United Kingdom and Ireland is 'EP News'); *addressees:* general public; frequency: monthly (except August); *to obtain a copy,* contact the editorial staff of the various editions; the UK version, EP News, is inserted into 'The European' and the Irish version (with the same title) in 'The Irish Times'; the paper edition is not available through the mail; EP News may also be consulted on Europarl, the European Parliament's web server.

ACP-EU Joint Assembly Report: reviews the debates of the EU-ACP Joint Assembly in French and English and summarizes the reports and resolutions adopted; *addressees:* all interested persons; *frequency:* twice a year; these publications may be accessed via the Internet on the Europa host http://europa.eu.int.

Documents Produced by DG III

The Publications and Public Relations Service (DG III) publishes brochures and leaflets which are aimed particularly at the general public. The purpose of these publications is to inform citizens about the powers and make-up of the European Parliament and how it works as an institution, or about the position of the European Parliament in a priority policy field. They are usually published in the various EU languages and can be obtained from the European Parliament Information Offices in the Members States.

Brochures

The European Parliament: basic brochure.

The Single Currency and the EP.

A Strong Union Needed for a Successful Enlargement.

European Union Charter of Fundamental Rights.

Leaflets

The European Parliament at a Glance: the essentials on the working of the European Parliament.

The World is a Village: solidarity with the developing countries and with the least-developing countries.

The Right of Petition at the EP.

Map

The EU: a map of the entire EU.

Documents Produced by DG IV – Directorate-General for Research

DG IV provides information back-up to the MEPs and to the various Committees to assist them in their work. The information may also be of interest to other external users. Publications include:

Fact Sheets on the European Union: available online at www.europarl.eu.int/factsheets/default_en.htm; the fact sheets offer concise and updated information on the following subjects: How the European Community Works; Citizens' Europe; The Single Market; Common Policies; Economic and Monetary Union; The Union's External Relations.

D4 Working Papers Online (E Studies): are available online at www.europarl.eu.int/factsheets/default_en.htm.

Documents Published during the Session

The European Parliament's sessional services (DG I) are responsible for documents published during the session.

Debates of the European Parliament: during the sittings a verbatim report of proceedings is published each day in the languages used by the speakers; it includes everything which was said during that day's sitting; the 'Debates of the European Parliament' was published as an annex to the Official Journal of the European Communities until July 1999; it is now available only on Europarl, or on CD-Rom from the Office for Official Publications; *addressees:* anyone interested; *frequency:* for Strasbourg part-sessions, the morning after the sitting in pdf, one working day later in html; for Brussels part-sessions, early in the week following the part-session;

translations are published a few weeks later; *to obtain a copy* of the CD-ROM version, order from the Office for Official Publications in 2985 Luxembourg, or from its sales offices in the Member States.

Other European Parliament Information Initiatives

Visits to the European Parliament in Strasbourg, Brussels and Luxembourg can be aranged according to availability and solely by appointment. Contact: European Parliament – Visits Service, Rue Wiertz, 1047 Brussels, Belgium; tel (+32) 2-2843457; fax (+32) 2-284-35-30; e-mail visserm@europarl.eu.int.

It is also possible to borrow promotional material for public events, depending on availability and the size of the event. Contact one of the Parliament's information offices.

Documentation Produced by the Political Groups

All of the groups represented in the Parliament generate internal documentation in the course of their work, such as agendas for group meetings, minutes and reports from delegations. Most of the documents are not confidential, and can be made available to researchers.

In addition, the group secretariats produce publications aimed at the general public. The EPP Group produces an annual Report of Activities and a series of research papers. In addition, the EPP group press service produces a range of information leaflets explaining the group's policy. All the group secretariats provide special documentation services. The Group of the European People's Party manages a documentation centre in Brussels which can be accessed via the Internet at www.europarl.eu.int/PPE. The Party of European Socialists maintains a documentation centre and reference library, which contains, among other items, a collection of periodicals with a socialist perspective. Researchers wishing to use the Centre should notify the group secretariat (documentation centre) in advance.

For more information concerning these documentation services, contact the group secretariats directly at: European

Parliament, Rue Wiertz, 1047 Brussels, Belgium. The fax and telephone numbers and e-mail addresses of the Secretary-General of each group can be found in this book in the section 'Transnational Party Groups within the European Parliament'.

EUROPARL – European Parliament Multilingual Web Server

The European Parliament World Wide Web information service, launched in November 1996, is designed to disseminate information on Parliament's work not only to MEPs, officials of the EU institutions and journalists, but also to information professionals, researchers and the general public. Information is updated daily and is available in all 20 official languages of the EU.

A wide range of vital and timely information about the European Parliament and its work is available. The main areas covered include:

- full calendar of European Parliament part-sessions and of meetings of its committees and delegations, draft agendas, minutes, verbatim reports of proceedings;
- legislative observatory (OEIL), motions for resolutions tabled for adoption in plenary sittings, texts adopted by the European Parliament;
- press releases and session news, News Alert and News Report, background briefings, European Parliament magazine;
- Who's who of Members, updates on Members' activities;
- political group Web information services, national parliaments on the Web, links to other EU Web sites;
- European Parliament information offices in Member States, correspondence with the public, forthcoming staff recruitment competitions;
- European Parliament studies and documentation, STOA;
- state and development of the Union: the euro, enlargement, key background information, the Convention.

All European Parliament directorates and departments concerned with disseminating information within and beyond the European Parliament are involved in this venture, as well as the political groups, most of which now have their own Web sites linked to Europarl.

The service is available to all, free of charge, via the internet address http://www.europarl.eu.int.

The service is maintained by the European Parliament, Data Processing and Telecommunications Directorate, Publishing Division, Information Directorate. The contact for Press and Information is Erik Peeters (tel (+32) 2-284-29-31; fax (+32) 2-284-69-76; e-mail epeeters@europarl.eu.int). The contact for Publishing is Frédéric Tonhofer (tel (+352) 430022475; fax (+352) 435578; e-mail ftonhofer@europarl.eu.int).

European Parliament Information Offices and their Information

AUSTRIA

European Parliament Information Office: Kärntner-Ring 5–7, 1010 Vienna, Austria; tel (+43 1) 51617-0; fax (+43 1) 5132515; e-mail epwien@europarl.eu.int; internet www.europarl.at; the Information Office's aim is to focus on the work of the European Parliament. High priority is given to schools and other educational institutions. The documentation service offers database research; *library opening hours:* 9.00–18.00; Director Michael Reinprecht; Deputy Head of Office Monika Strasser; Librarian Judith Lackner.

Publications (all free of charge):

- Europa neu gestalten: brochure.
- *Commander Europa:* youth paperback.
- *Die 21 österreichischen Mitglieder des Europäischen Parlaments*: folder.
- *Europarl.at – Informationsbüro des Europäischen Parlaments:* card.
- *Europäisches Parlament:* brochure, folder and video.
- *Die Erweiterung der Europäischen Union:* brochure.
- *Leihfaden:* Fact Sheets on CD-ROM.
- *Eurotour:* CD-ROM game for children.
- *Sacharov Preis:* brochure.
- *Petitionsrecht:* folder.
- *Charta:* brochure.
- *EU-Ombudsman:* brochure, folder and flyer.
- *Blickpunkt Europa:* quarterly magazine.

BELGIUM

European Parliament Information Office: Rue Wiertz 60, 1047 Brussels, Belgium; tel (+32) 2-2842005; fax (+32) 2-2307555; e-mail epbrussels@europarl.eu.int; internet www.europarl.eu.int/brussels; the Belgian office is involved in the production of the Belgian edition of the European Parliament periodical

(French version: 'Débats sur l'Europe', Dutch version: 'Kijk op Europa') and the EC-periodical (French version: 'Eurinfo', Dutch version: 'Europa-Bericht', German version: 'Euro-Info'); it also produces general information brochures as well as radio reports and magazines; dossiers and wall charts are available for use in schools and an exhibition pack can be ordered from the office; the Information Office organizes debates and seminars; Infopoint open to general public Monday to Friday 9.00–17.30 (tel (+32) 2-2842679); Infodoc, for assistance in document research, open Monday to Thursday 10.00–16.00 (tel (+32) 2-2842005); Director Peter Thomas (tel (+32) 2-2842006);

CYPRUS

European Parliament Information Office: 5A Demophontos Street, P.O. Box 23440, 1683 Nicosia, Cyprus; tel (+357) 22460694; fax (+357) 22767733; e-mail epnicosia@europarl.eu.int; internet www.europarl.eu.int/nicosia.

CZECH REPUBLIC

European Parliament Information Office: Jungmannova 24, 110 00 Prague 1, Czech Republic; tel (+420 2) 55708208; fax (+420 2) 55708200; e-mail eppraha@europarl.eu.int; internet www.evropsky-parlament.cz.

DENMARK

European Parliament Information Office: Christian IX's Gade 2,2, 1111 Copenhagen K, Denmark; tel (+45) 33-14-33-77; fax (+45) 33-15-08-05; e-mail epkobenhavn@europarl.eu.int; internet www.europarl.dk; the Copenhagen office produces a document catalogue every two to three months giving details of all European Parliament reports, listed according to committee; the documentation produced by the office is aimed at specific groups, particularly libraries and municipalities; although the Danish office has no documentation centre, European Parliament session documents are available as far back as 1979 in paper form and earlier on microfiche; searches are carried out on Epoque and other Community databases; opening hours: Monday to Thursday 09.00–16.30 and Friday 09.00–15.00; Head of Information Office Søren Søndergaard.

ESTONIA

European Parliament Information Office: Swiss House, Roosikrantsi 11, 10119 Tallinn, Estonia; tel (+372 6) 67-63-20; fax (+372 6) 67-63-22; e-mail eptallinn@europarl.eu.int.

FINLAND

European Parliament Information Office: PO Box 26, 00131 Helsinki, Finland; *premises at:* Pohjoisesplanadi 31, 3rd floor, 00100 Helsinki, Finland; tel (+358 9) 6220450; fax (+358 9) 6222610; e-mail ephelsinki@europarl.eu.int; internet www.europarl.fi; the European Parliament's office in Finland provides information to the public, the media, government agencies and other target groups about the role and activities of the Parliament and the European Union; the office arranges briefings and seminars, participates in exhibitions, responds to enquiries and produces and distributes publications and other material free of charge; *opening hours:* Monday to Thursday 08.30–17.30 and Friday 08.30–16.00; *Infopoint opening hours:* Monday to Friday 10.00–16.30; Head of Office Renny Jokelin; Information Officer and Deputy Head of Office Satu Raisamo.

FRANCE

European Parliament Information Office in Paris: 288 Boulevard Saint Germain, 75341 Paris Cedex 07; tel (+33) 1-40-63-40-00; fax (+33) 1-45-51-52-53; e-mail epparis@europarl.eu.int; internet: www.europarl.eu.int/paris; the Paris office, in conjunction with the Commission's Information Office, has produced the videotex system, Minitel – 3615/EUROPE, which contains information about the EU institutions; there is a documentation centre in the Paris office and session documents, dating back to 1979, are kept in stock; Head of Division Jean-Guy Giraud.

European Parliament Information Office in Marseilles: 2 rue Henri Barbusse, 13241 Marseille, France; tel (+33) 4-91-91-46-00; fax (+33) 4-91-90-95-03; e-mail epmarseille@europarl.eu.int; internet www.europarl.eu.int/marseille; Head Isabelle Coustet.

European Parliament Information Office in Strasbourg: Bâtiment Louise Weiss, Allée du Printemps, B.P. 1024/F, 67070 Strasbourg Cedex, France; tel (+33) 3-88-17-40-01; fax (+33) 3-88-17-51-84; e-mail epstrasbourg@europarl.eu.int; Head of Division Jean-Jacques Fritz.

GERMANY

European Parliament Information Office in Berlin: Europäisches Parlament Informationsbüro für Deutschland, Unter den Linden 78, 10117 Berlin, Germany; tel (+49 30) 2280-1000; fax (+49 30) 2280-1111; e-mail: epberlin@europarl.eu.int; internet: www.europarl.de; the Berlin office has a documentation centre and an Information and Service Point; searches can be carried out on the European Parliament Intranet and internal European databases; copies of reports are usually available in the documentation centre; reports on special topics are available in electronic form on the server www.europarl.de; the Minutes of the Session are also available for consultation and date back to 1952; those wishing to use the centre should notify the office in advance; dossiers are produced concerning issues of particular interest to the German public; regular information in German includes EP-Medienservice, Europa (annual publication) and information for the press; *opening hours:* Monday to Wednesday 10.00–17.15, Thursday 10.00–18.00 and Friday 10.00–15.30; Head of Office Klaus Löffler; Deputy Head of Office Bernd Kunzmann; Documentation Kerstin Schlüter; Press Ingo Beckedorf; Publications Anja Fuchs-König.

European Parliament Information Office in Munich: Europäisches Parlament Informationsbüro, Erhardstr. 27, 80331 Munich, Germany; tel (+49 89) 2020879-0; fax (+49 89) 2020879-73; e-mail epmuenchen@europarl.eu.int.

GREECE

European Parliament Information Office: Amalias Ave 8, 10557 Athens, Greece; tel (+30) 210-3278900; fax (+30) 210-3311540; e-mail epathinai@europarl.eu.int; internet www.europarl.gr; the Athens office has a documentation centre, where session documents and minutes of proceedings (Arc en Ciel and Minutes of the Session) are available; searches in Community databases are carried out on request; there is also a press centre in the office; dossiers are supplied to journalists on a regular basis, as well as information on specific subjects; *library opening hours:* 09.30–13.30 (except Fridays); Director Georgios Papadopoulos; Documentalists Eleni Kyranaki, Argyro Liakou.

HUNGARY

European Parliament Information Office: Országház, Kossuth Lajos tr 1–3, 1357 Budapest, Hungary; tel (+36 1) 441-660-02; fax (+36 1) 441-66-03; e-mail epbudapest@europarl.eu.int.

IRELAND

European Parliament Information Office: European Union House, 43 Molesworth Street, Dublin 2, Ireland;

tel (+353 1) 6057900; fax (+353 1) 6057999; e-mail epdublin@europarl.eu .int; internet www.europarl.ie; the European Parliament Office in Ireland provides information for Irish citizens, the media and non-governmental organizations, and liaises with the Irish government and parliament; the Office produces a range of teaching materials for schools, including worksheets, wall charts and videos, and holds European Parliament session documents, questions, debates and minutes dating back to 1973; the Office is online to European Parliament databases and to the European Parliament network; Head of Office James O'Brien.

ITALY

European Parliament Information Office in Rome: Via IV Novembre 149, 00187 Rome, Italy; tel (+39) 06-699501; fax (+39) 06-69950200; e-mail eproma@ europarl.eu.int; internet www.europarl .it; the main tasks of the Italian information office are to represent the European Parliament before national institutions, to prepare the visit of the European Parliament's President and to collaborate in the work of the European Parliament's committees and delegations during their frequent visits and meetings in Italy; Rome's information office is a genuine reference point for citizens and replies to a wide range of questions on the work of the European Parliament and MEPs; it also meets requests for documentation; the office acts as a press agency, drafting articles and press releases and organizing press conferences; it has a teletext page (n° 368) on RAI – the Italian television service – which provides institutional information on the European Parliament's activities and initiatives and on other themes relating to Europe; the teletext also mentions the competitions published in the Official Journal of the European Communities; it manages the broadcasting of the programme 'Welcome to Europe' on a network of more than 100 local radio stations with an audience of some 5 million; in addition, the office promotes the staging of colloquia entitled 'European Parliament Casefiles', which deal with themes of national or community interest and are held in different towns throughout Italy with the object of familiarizing a broader public with the work of the European Parliament; the colloquia are attended by national and european Parliamentary members, government representatives, journalists and experts; the office also organizes and promotes large-scale public events, like the 'Festival of Europe', which is held on 9 May each year in Rome or in another Italian town, and publishes brochures on the European Parliament, maintains a stand at major national fairs and exhibitions and has produced two

diskettes intended primarily for young people – 'The diskette of Europe' and 'The diskette special euro'; *library opening hours:* 09.30–12.30 and 14.30–17.00; Director Giovanni Salimbeni; Documentalist A. Ruggiero.

European Parliament Information Office in Milan: Corso Magenta 59, 20123 Milan, Italy; tel (+39) 02-4344171; fax (+39) 02-434417500; e-mail epmilano@europarl.eu.int.

LATVIA

European Parliament Information Office: Basteja Blvd 14, 1050 Riga, Latvia; tel (+371 7) 22-51-77; fax (+371 7) 22-30-63; e-mail epriga@europarl.eu .int; internet www.europarl.lv.

LITHUANIA

European Parliament Information Office: Naugarduko 10, 2001 Vilnius, Lithuania; tel (+370) 52-61-92-20; fax (+370) 52-61-98-28; e-mail epvilnius@ europarl.eu.int.

LUXEMBOURG

European Parliament Information Office: Parlement Européen, Bâtiment Robert Schuman, Place de l'Europe, 2929 Luxembourg, Luxembourg; tel (+352) 430022597; fax (+352) 430022457; e-mail epluxembourg@europarl.eu.int; the European Parliament's Information Office in Luxembourg seeks primarily to inform EU citizens living in the Grand Duchy about the role and activities of the European Parliament; to this end, it produces press releases as well as information on the work of the European Parliament and its Committees both before and during the sessions; the Office responds to requests for documentation from residents of Luxembourg and neighbouring areas; it also organizes, in collaboration with the European Commission's representation, priority information actions on actual topics such as enlargement and different international fairs in Luxembourg; Director Monique Schumacher.

MALTA

European Parliament Information Office: 280 Republic Street, VLT 04 Valletta, Malta; tel (+356) 21235075; fax (+356) 21227580; e-mail epvalletta@ europarl.eu.int; internet www.europarl .eu.int/valletta.

NETHERLANDS

European Parliament Information Office: Korte Vijverberg 6, 2513 AB Den Haag, Netherlands; tel (+31 70) 3624941; fax (+31 70) 3647001; e-mail epdenhaag@europarl.eu.int; internet www.europeesparlement.nl; the Netherlands office has a documentation centre staffed by a documentalist, while a stock of European Parliament session documents is maintained; the office produces a free quarterly newsletter in Dutch entitled 'Kijk op Europa'; searches are carried out in Epoque and Europarl on request, while the office also distributes DG III and DG IV publications; *library opening hours:* 09.00–17.30; Director Jan Verlaan; Librarian Ans de Klerk.

POLAND

European Parliament Information Office: Biuro informacyjne Parlamentu Europejskiego, Warszawskie Centrum Finansowe, ul. Emilii Plater 53, 19 pitro, 00-113 Warsaw, Poland; tel (+48 22) 520-66-55; fax (+48 22) 520-66-59; e-mail epwarszawa@europarl.eu.int.

PORTUGAL

European Parliament Information Office: Centro Europeu Jean Monnet, Largo Jean Monnet 1-6°, 1269-070 Lisbon, Portugal; tel (+351 21) 3504900; fax (+351 21) 3540004; e-mail eplisboa@ europarl.eu.int; internet www.parleurop .pt; the Lisbon office has a documentation centre, where European Parliament session documents are kept in stock and copies of the Official Journal are available on microfiche; the office maintains a computerized list of European Parliament reports, resolutions and studies; requests for information regarding subjects in progress are answered using Epoque; otherwise the 'Directory of Legislation' is available on microfiche; *library opening hours:* Monday to Thursday 10.00–17.00; Director Nuno Antas de Campos; Librarian José Antonio Martins.

Publications of the Lisbon Office, all in Portuguese

- *Temas Europeus* which appears three or four times a year and is aimed at a specialist readership, such as journalists and EDCs.
- *Tribuna da Europa*, a monthly newspaper about the sessions of the European Parliament.
- *Directório*, a basic information guide.

SLOVAKIA

European Parliament Information Office: Informacná kancelária Európskeho parlamentu, Palisády 29, 811 06

Bratislava, Slovakia; tel (+421 2) 59203297; fax (+421 2) 54648013; e-mail epbratislava@europarl.eu.int.

SLOVENIA

European Parliament Information Office: Trg republike 3, 1000 Ljubljana, Slovenia; tel (+386 1) 426-98-87; fax (+386 1) 426-99-06; e-mail epljubljana@ europarl.eu.int; internet www.europarl .si.

SPAIN

European Parliament Information Office in Madrid: Paseo de la Castellana 46, 28046 Madrid, Spain; tel (+34) 91-436-47-47; fax (+34) 91-577-13-65; documentation fax (+34) 91-578-31-71; e-mail epmadrid@europarl.eu.int; internet www.europarl.es; a Documentation Centre houses the series of the OJEC since 1951, European Parliament documents since 1981, a library containing 1,500 monographs and 50 titles of external series, while a photothèque and a videothèque complete the range of stored material; documentation search is based on the use of databases, databanks and other electronic information resources available on the internet; the Office has access to all EC hosts, especially to the European Parliament databases like EPOQUE and SIMBAD which are the most often used. Some others like CELEX, ABEL, SCAD and RAPID are complementary tools in this information research; the Office is responsible for representing the EPOQUE database for Spanish users; a large stock of DG III, DG IV and European Commission publications is maintained; a seminar on 'European Information Resources', addressed to the professionals of the Documentation Centres involved in European matters, is organized by the Office twice a year in co-operation with the Spanish Representation of the Commission; the Documentation Centre maintains a close relationship with approximately 350 Spanish libraries and documentation centres which usually receive some of the official EC documents; these collections are complemented by certain European Parliament documents shipped directly by the Office once a month; from the outset, the Spanish European Parliament Office has prac-

tised a decentralized documentation policy, based on the EC networks of 'relays' (European Documentation Centres, 'Euro-guichets', Euro-libraries, Euro-bookshops, etc.); for young people, the Office maintains a complete collection of documents relating to European studies and scholarships. In co-operation with Madrid's universities, students of journalism may accomplish with the Office a practical training period of three months as a complement to their studies; a website (www.europarl.es) has been developed to provide a large variety of information about the European Parliament; the Office also supplies a service to Internet users named 'Correo del Ciudadano' (Citizen's mailbox) where users may send their specific requests for information through electronic mail facilities; a database called EUROJOVEN provides information about seminars, courses, grants, awards, etc., for young people; *documentation service opening hours:* Monday to Thursday 9.30–14.00 and 15.30–17.30 and Friday 9.30–13.30; officers Fernando Carbajo, Juan Rodriguez, Isabel Mateo.

Publications of the Information Office

- *Tribuna del Parlamento Europeo,* a periodical covering the most important activities and subjects carried out by the European Parliament, is published and mailed free of charge to more than 40,000 suscribers.
- *Guía de la Sesión* and *Ecos de la Sesión* are sent to journalists and specialists in European Community matters and are available on the internet web page www.europarl.eu.int.
- *La Unión Europea ... y ...* is a series of documents covering different subjects such as culture, Latin-America and youth.
- *Guía del Parlamento Europeo* is a Who's Who of Spanish MEPs.

European Parliament Information Office in Barcelona: Passeig de Gràcia 90, planta 1, 08008 Barcelona, Spain; tel (+34) 93-272-20-44; fax (+34) 93-272-20-45; e-mail epbarcelona@europarl.eu.int; officer Josep M° Ribot.

SWEDEN

European Parliament Information Office: Nybrogatan 11, 3 tr., 114 39

Stockholm, Sweden; tel (+46 8) 56-24-44-55; fax (+46 8) 56-24-44-99; e-mail info@europarl.se; internet www.europarl .se; the Swedish information office has a documentation centre containing most of the European Parliament's publications and provides the quarterly publication 'Europadebatt', which is free; the Office also produces the newsletter 'Nästa Vecka i Europaparlamentet' (Next week in the European Parliament), which is sent by fax or e-mail to subscribers; it also keeps an updated brochure with information on the Swedish members of the European Parliament; research may be conducted on Epoque (on request); *library opening hours:* 10.00–12.00; Head of Office Christian Andersson; Deputy Head of Office Klas Jansson; Documentalist Cecilia Möller.

UNITED KINGDOM

European Parliament Information Office in London: 2 Queen Anne's Gate, London, SW1H 9AA, United Kingdom; tel (+44 20) 7227-4300; fax (+44 20) 7227-4302; library fax (+44 20) 7227-4301; media fax (+44 20) 7227-4327; e-mail eplondon@europarl.eu.int; internet www.europarl.org.uk; the European Parliament office in London produces and distributes a wide range of free publications, maps and audiovisual aids, much of which is sent to educational outlets; in addition, a monthly briefing is prepared for the press; copies of the Official Journal dating back 12–18 months are available for consultation, as are European Parliament session documents dating back to 1979, minutes and debates dating back to 1973 and dossiers on certain specific subject areas; database searches can be carried out on request; reports, agendas, press releases, etc., are available from the European Parliament's website; *documentation centre opening hours:* Tuesday to Thursday 10.00–13.00 and 14.00–17.00, Monday and Friday by appointment only; Director Chris Piening; Media Officer Edward McVeigh; Public Affairs Officer Lynne Charles.

European Parliament Information Office in Edinburgh: The Tun, 4 Jackson's Entry, Holyrood Road, Edinburgh, EH8 8PJ, United Kingdom; tel (+44 131) 557-7866; fax (+44 131) 557-4977; e-mail epedinburgh@europarl.eu.int.

EUROPEAN PARLIAMENT

Bureau*

President: Josep Borrell Fontelles (PSE).

OFFICE OF THE PRESIDENT

(rue Wiertz, 1047 Brussels; tel (2) 284-53-63; fax (2) 284-93-63; e-mail pcox@europarl.eu.int; internet www.europarl.eu.int; Palais de l'Europe, 67006 Strasbourg Cedex; tel 3-88-17-40-01; fax 3-88-17-48-60; Plateau du Kirchberg, L-2929 Luxembourg; tel 4300-1; fax 4300-4842)

Vice-Presidents

Alejo Vidal-Quadras Roca (PPE/DE), Antonios Trakatellis (PPE/DE), Dagmar Roth-Behrendt (PSE), Edward H. C. McMillan-Scott (PPE/DE), Ingo Friedrich (PPE/DE), Mario Mauro (PPE/DE), António Costa (PSE), Luigi Cocilovo (ALDE), Jacek Emile Saryusz-Wolski (PPE/DE), Pierre Moscovici (PSE), Miroslav Ouzký (PPE/DE), Janusz Onyszkiewicz (ALDE), Gérard Onesta (VERTS)ALE), Sylvia-Yvonne Kaufmann (GUE/NGL).

Quaestors

James Nicholson (PPE/DE), Genowefa Grabowska (PSE), Mia De Vits (PSE), Godelieve Quisthoudt-Rowohl (PPE/DE), Astrid Lulling (PPE/DE).

FORMER PRESIDENTS

1958–60: Robert Schuman.

1960–62: Hans Furler.

1962–64: Gaetano Martino.

1964–65: Jean Duvieusart.

1965–66: Victor Leemans.

1966–69: Alain Poher.

1969–71: Mario Scelba.

1971–73: Walter Behrendt.

1973–75: Cornelis Berkhouwer.

1975–77: Georges Spenale.

1977–79: Emilio Colombo.

1979–82: Simone Veil.

1982–84: Piet Dankert.

1984–87: Pierre Pflimlin.

1987–89: Lord Henry Plumb.

1989–92: Enrique Barón Crespo.

1992–94: Egon Klepsch.

1994–97: Dr Klaus Hänsch.

1997–99: José Maria Gil-Robles Gil-Delgado.

1999–2002: Nicole Fontaine.

2002–2004: Pat Cox.

Alphabetical List of Members by Member State and Political Affiliation*

(After 2004 elections)

(Palais de l'Europe, 67070 Strasbourg Cedex, France; tel 3-88-17-40-01; fax 3-88-25-65-01; internet www.europarl.eu.int)

Name	Member State	Telephone	E-mail	Party	Political Group
Adamou, K. Adamos	Cyprus	3-88-17-95-57	adamosad@spidernet.com.cy	ND	GUE/NGL
Adwent, Filip	Poland		f.adwent@filip.adwent.pl	LPR	IND/DEM
Agnoletto, Vittorio Emanuele . .	Italy	3-88-17-94-44		PRC-Se	GUE/NGL
Albertini, Gabriele	Italy	3-88-17-93-66	galbertini@europarl.eu.int	FI	PPE/DE
Allister, James Hugh	UK	3-88-17-92-75		DUP	NI
Alvaro, Alexander Nuno	Germany	3-88-17-93-28	apickartalvaro@europarl.eu.int	PdDS	ALDE
Andersson, Jan	Sweden		jandersson@europarl.eu.int	SAP	PSE
Andrejevs, Georgs	Latvia			LC	
Andria, Alfonso	Italy	3-88-17-91-09		Uniti nell'Ulivo	ALDE
Andrikienė, Laima Liucija	Lithuania	3-88-17-98-58	laandr@lrs.lt	TS	PPE/DE
Angelilli, Roberta	Italy	3-88-17-59-02	rangelille@europarl.eu.int	AN	UEN
Antoniozzi, Alfredo	Italy	3-88-17-95-16		FI	PPE/DE
Arif, Kader	France	3-88-17-91-70		PS	PSE
Arnaoutakis, Stavros	Greece			PASOK	PSE
Ashworth, Richard James	UK	3-88-17-93-09	rashworth@europarl.eu.int	Cons	PPE/DE
Assis, Francisco	Portugal			PS	PSE
Atkins, Sir Robert	UK	3-88-17-53-73	ratkins@europarl.eu.int	Cons	PPE/DE
Attard-Montalto, John	Malta	3-88-17-91-16	jattard@europarl.eu.int	MLP	PSE
Attwooll, Elspeth	UK	3-88-17-57-95	eattwooll@europarl.eu.int	LD	ALDE
Aubert, Marie-Hélène	France	3-88-17-94-75	aubert.marie_helene@wanadoo.fr	VEE	V/ALE
Auken, Margrete	Denmark	3-88-17-93-27	mauken @europarl.eu.int	F	V/ALE
Ayala Sender, Inés	Spain	3-88-17-95-08		PSOE	PSE
Aylward, Liam	Ireland	3-88-17-97-82		FF	UENP
Ayuso González, María del Pilar	Spain	3-88-17-53-98	mayuso@europarl.eu.int	PP	PPE/DE
Bachelot-Narquin, Roselyne . . .	France	3-88-17-96-30	roselyne.bachelot@wanadoo.fr	UMP	PPE/DE
Baco, Peter	Slovakia		peterbaco@slovanet.sk	HZDS	NI
Badía Cutchet, Maria	Spain	3-88-17-96-82	mbadia@psc.es	PSOE	PSE
Barón Crespo, Enrique	Spain	3-88-17-54-90	ebaroncrespo@europarl.eu.int	PSOE	PSE
Barsi Pataky, Etelka	Hungary	3-88-17-95-82		FIDESZ-MPSZ	PPE/DE
Batten, Gerard Joseph	UK	3-88-17-99-20		UKIP	IND/DEM

* A list of abbreviations used for affiliations to European Parliament political groups and to national political parties follows the Alphabetical List of Members.

Name—*continued*	Member State	Telephone	E-mail	Party	Political Group
Battilocchio, Alessandro	Italy	3-88-17-94-96		NPSI	NI
Batzeli, Katerîna.	Greece		kbatz@otenet.gr	PASOK	PSE
Bauer, Edit	Slovakia	3-88-17-96-73		SMK-MPK	PPE/DE
Beaupuy, Jean Marie	France	3-88-17-93-54		UDF	ALDE
Beazley, Christopher.	UK	3-88-17-52-26	cbeazley@europarl.eu.int	Cons	PPE/DE
Becsey, Zsolt László	Hungary	3-88-17-98-88	becsey.zsolt@axelero.hu	FIDESZ-MPSZ	PPE/DE
Beer, Angelika.	Germany	3-88-17-91-35	lberenguer@europarl.eu.int	Grüne	V/ALE
Beglitis, Panagiotis.	Greece		beglitis@politicalforum.gr	PASOK	PSE
Belder, Bastiaan	Netherlands	3-88-17-92-70	bbelder@europarl.eu.int	CU-SGP	IND/DEM
Belet, Ivo	Belgium	3-88-17-96-23	ibelet@europarl.eu.int	CD&V-N.VA	PPE/DE
Belohorská, Irena	Slovakia			HZDS	NI
Bennahmias, Jean-Luc	France	3-88-17-95-74		VEE	V/ALE
Beňová, Monika	Slovakia	3-88-17-91-60	asistent.benova@strana-smer.sk	SMER	PSE
Berend, Rolf	Germany	3-88-17-94-13		CDU	PPE/DE
Berès, Pervenche.	France	3-88-17-97-77	pberes@europarl.eu.int	PS	PSE
van den Berg, Margrietus J.. . . .	Netherlands	3-88-17-96-69	mvandenberg@europarl.eu.int	PvdA	PSE
Berger, Maria	Austria	3-88-17-97-21	maria.berger@europerq.co.at	SPÖ	PSE
Berlato, Sergio	Italy	3-88-17-92-13	info@sergioberlato.it	AN	UEN
Berlinguer, Giovanni	Italy	3-88-17-91-70	g.berlinguer@aprileperlasinistra.it	Uniti nell'Ulivo	PSE
Berman, Thijs	Netherlands	3-88-17-94-79	tberman@europarl.eu.int	PvdA	PSE
Bersani, Pier Luigi	Italy	3-88-17-98-81	plbersani@europarl.eu.int	Uniti nell'Ulivo	PSE
Bertinotti, Fausto	Italy	3-88-17-91-19		PRC-SE	GUE/NGL
Bielan, Adam Jerzy.	Poland	3-88-17-99-25	adam.bielan@sejm.pl	PiS	UEN
Birutis, Šarūnas	Lithuania	3-88-17-96-71	sabiru@lrs.lt	DP	ALDE
Blokland, Johannes.	Netherlands	3-88-17-98-20	jblokland@europarl.eu.int	CU-SGP	IND/DEM
Bloom, Godfrey William	UK	3-88-17-94-69		UKIP	IND/DEM
Bobosíková, Paní Jana	Czech Republic	3-88-17-92-84	vozabova@sahm.cz	Non-party	NI
Böge, Reimer.	Germany	3-88-17-93-26	info@reimerboege.de	CDU	PPE/DE
Bösch, Herbert	Austria	3-88-17-96-77	hboesch@europarl.eu.int	SPÖ	PSE
Bonde, Jens-Peter.	Denmark	3-88-17-91-67		J	IND/DEM
Bonino, Emma	Italy	3-88-17-92-88	ebonino@europarl.eu.int	LEB	IND/DEM
Bono, Guy	France	3-88-17-94-24	sdegioanni@hdr.cr-paca.fr	PS	PSE
Bonsignore, Vito	Italy	3-88-17-93-82		CCD	PPE/DE
Booth, Graham H..	UK	3-88-17-97-63	mrgrahamboot@aol.com	UKIP	IND/DEM
Borghezio, Mario.	Italy	3-88-17-97-04		LN	IND/DEM
Borrell Fontelles, Josep	Spain	3-88-17-93-41		PSOE	PSE
Bossi, Umberto	Italy	3-88-17-97-35		LN	IND/DEM
Bourlanges, Jean-Louis	France	3-88-17-98-76		UDF	IND/DEM
Bourzai, Bernadette	France	3-88-17-94-32	bernadette.bourzai@ mairie-egletons.fr	PS	PSE
Bowis, John.	UK	3-88-17-97-80		Cons	PPE/DE
Bozkurt, Emine.	Netherlands	3-88-17-99-40		PvdA	PSE
Bradbourn, Philip Charles	UK	3-88-17-94-07	pbradbourn@europarl.eu.int	Cons	PPE/DE
Brejc, Mihael.	Slovenia	3-88-17-96-36	miha.brejc@dz-rs.si	SDS	PPE/DE
Brepoels, Frederika M. M.	Belgium	3-88-17-98-62	fbrepoels@skynet.be	CD&V-N.VA	PPE/DE
Bresso, Mercedes	Italy	3-88-17-95-24	mbresso@europarl.eu.int	Uniti nell'Ulivo	PSE
Breyer, Hiltrud	Germany	3-88-17-92-87	hbreyer@europarl.eu.int	Grüne	V/ALE
Březina, Jan	Czech Republic	3-88-17-94-84		KDU-ČSL	PPE/DE
Brie, André	Germany	3-88-17-94-03	abrie@europarl.eu.int	PDS	V/ALE
Brok, Elmar . . . . , . .	Germany	3-88-17-93-23	ebrok@t-online.de	CDU	PPE/DE
Brunetta, Renato	Italy	3-88-17-93-93	rbrunetta@@europarl.eu.int	FI	PPE/DE
Budreikaitė, Danutė.	Lithuania	3-88-17-96-35		DP	ALDE
van Buitenen, Paul K. T. J. . . .	Netherlands	3-88-17-99-72		ET	V/ALE
Buitenweg, Kathalijne Maria . .	Netherlands	3-88-17-92-66	k.buitenweg@chello.nl	GL	V/ALE
Bullmann, Udo	Germany	3-88-17-93-42	ubullmann@europarl.eu.int	SPD	PSE
van den Burg, Ieke	Netherlands	3-88-17-93-94	ivandenburg@europarl.eu.int	PvdA	PSE
Bushill-Matthews, Philip	UK	3-88-17-91-14		Cons	PPE/DE
Busk, Niels	Denmark	3-88-17-93-65	nbusk@europarl.eu.int	V	ALDE
Busquin, Philippe	Belgium				
Busuttil, Simon.	Malta	3-88-17-96-86		PN	PPE/DE
Buzek, Jerzy	Poland		jbuzek@ap.edu.pl	PO	PPE/DE
Cabrnoch, Milan	Czech Republic	3-88-17-93-78		ODS	PPE/DE
Calabuig Rull, Joan	Spain	3-88-17-98-93		PSOE	PSE
Callanan, Martin	UK	3-88-17-97-01		Cons	PPE/DE
Camre, Mogens N. J.	Denmark	3-88-17-92-05	mcamre@europarl.eu.int	O	UEN
Capoulas Santos, Luis Manuel .	Portugal			PS	PSE
Carlotti, Marie-Arlette	France	3-88-17-97-89		PS	PSE
Carlshamre, Maria	Sweden			FP	ALDE
Carnero González, Carlos	Spain	3-88-17-99-69		PSOE	PSE
Carollo, Giorgio.	Italy	3-88-17-91-78		FI	PPE/DE
Casa, David.	Malta	3-88-17-94-45		PN	PPE/DE
Casaca, Paulo	Portugal	3-88-17-93-36	pcasaca@europarl.eu.int	PS	PSE
Cashman, Michael	UK	3-88-17-97-59		Lab	PSE
Caspary, Daniel	Germany	3-88-17-99-78	daniel@caspary.de	CDU	PPE/DE
Castex, François	France	3-88-17-91-29	frcastex@wanadoo.fr	PS	PSE
Castiglione, Giuseppe	Italy	3-88-17-98-66		FI	PPE/DE
del Castillo Vera, Pilar	Spain	3-88-17-99-82		PP	PPE/DE
Catania, Giusto.	Italy	3-88-17-98-74		PRC-SE	V/ALE

Name—*continued*	Member State	Telephone	E-mail	Party	Political Group
Cavada, Jean-Marie	France	3-88-17-93-67		UDF	ALDE
Cederschiöld, Charlotte	Sweden	3-88-17-98-23		M	PPE/DE
Cercas, Alejandro	Spain	3-88-17-94-55	acercas@europarl.eu.int	PSOE	PSE
Cesa, Lorenzo	Italy	3-88-17-94-18		UDC	PPE/DE
Chatzimarkakis, Jorgo	Germany	3-88-17-91-49	chatzi@chatzi.de	FDP	PPE/DE
Chichester, Giles Bryan	UK	3-88-17-92-96	GilesChichesterMEP@ecliPSE.co.uk	Cons	PPE/DE
Chiesa, Giulietto	Italy	3-88-17-96-02	g.chiesa@megachip.info	IdV	ALDE
Chmielewski, Zdzisław Kazimierz	Poland			PO	PPE/DE
Christensen, Ole	Denmark	3-88-17-94-64	ochristensen@europarl.eu.int	A	PSE
Chruszcz, Sylwester	Poland		chruszcz@lpr.pl	LPR	IND/DEM
Cirino Pomicino, Paolo	Italy	3-88-17-93-02		UDE	PPE/DE
Claeys, Philip	Belgium	3-88-17-92-81		Vl Blok	NI
Clark, Derek Roland........	UK	3-88-17-95-52		UKIP	IND/DEM
Cocilovo, Luigi.............	Italy	3-88-17-98-54		Uniti nell'Ulivo	ALDE
Coelho, Carlos.............	Portugal	3-88-17-95-51		CFP	PPE/DE
Cohn-Bendit, Daniel Marc ...	Germany	3-88-17-94-98		Grüne	V/ALE
Corbett, Richard	UK	3-88-17-95-04		Lab	PSE
Corbey, Dorette...........	Netherlands	3-88-17-92-36		PvdA	PSE
Cornillet, Thierry	France	3-88-17-95-79		UDF	PPE/DE
Correia, Fausto............	Portugal		pwb@netcabo.pt	PS	PSE
Costa, António.............	Portugal			PS	PSE
Costa, Paolo	Italy	3-88-17-95-37	demcosta@tin.it	Uniti nell'Ulivo	ALDE
Cottigny, Jean Louis........	France	3-88-17-97-03		PS	PSE
Coûteaux, Paul Marie.......	France	3-88-17-92-06	pcouteaux@europarl.eu.int	MPF	IND/DEM
Coveney, Simon............	Ireland	3-88-17-94-17		FG	PPE/DE
Cramer, Michael...........	Germany	3-88-17-97-79		Grüne	V/ALE
Crowley, Brian	Ireland	3-88-17-97-51		FF	UEN
Czarnecki, Marek Aleksander	Poland	3-88-17-91-94	czarnecki@medianet.pl	SO	NI
Czarnecki, Ryszard.........	Poland	3-88-17-94-41	kontakt@RyszardCzarnecki.pl	SO	NI
D'Alema, Massimo	Italy	3-88-17-92-49	dmassimo@dol.it	Uniti nell'Ulivo	PSE
Daul, Joseph	France	3-88-17-95-25	jdaul@europarl.eu.int	UMP	PPE/DE
Davies, Chris.............	UK	3-88-17-93-53		LD	ALDE
De Poli, Antonio	Italy	3-88-17-94-89	adepoli@europarl.eu.int	UDC	PPE/DE
de Brún, Bairbre...........	UK	3-88-17-92-22	ndeva@europarl.eu.int	SF	GUE/NGL
Degutis, Arūnas	Lithuania	32-56-22-96-04		DP	ALDE
Dehaene, Jean-Luc	Belgium	3-88-17-98-67	jeanluc@dehaene.be	CD&V-N.VA	PPE/DE
De Keyser, Véronique	Belgium	3-88-17-97-74	vdekeyser@europarl.eu.int	PS	PSE
Del Turco, Ottaviano........	Italy	3-88-17-91-62	odelturco@europarl.eu.int	Uniti nell'Ulivo	PSE
Demetriou, Panayiotis	Cyprus	3-88-17-98-52	p.demetriou@avacom.net	DI.SY	PPE/DE
De Michelis, Gianni	Italy	3-88-17-94-54		NPSI	NI
Demszky, Gábor	Hungary	3-88-17-96-28	demszkyg@budapest.hu	SZDSZ	ALDE
Deprez, Gérard	Belgium	3-88-17-92-23	gdeprez@europarl.eu.int	MR	ALDE
De Rossa, Proinsias	Ireland	3-88-17-96-81	pderossa@europarl.eu.int	Lab	PSE
De Sarnez, Marielle	France	3-88-17-92-97		UDF	ALDE
Descamps, Marie-Hélène	France	3-88-17-97-30	mhdescamps@europarl.eu.int	UMP	PPE/DE
Désir, Harlem	France	3-88-17-98-53	harlem.desir@free.fr	PS	PSE
Dess, Albert...............	Germany	3-88-17-92-31		CSU	PPE/DE
Deva, Nirj	UK	3-88-17-92-45		Cons	PPE/DE
De Veyrac, Christine........	France	3-88-17-97-39		UMP	PPE/DE
De Vits, Mia	Belgium	3-88-17-97-15	mdevits@europarl.eu.int	SP	PSE
Díaz De Mera García, Agustín	Spain	3-88-17-96-24		PP	PPE/DE
Dičkutê, Jolanta	Lithuania	3-88-17-96-32		DP	ALDE
Didžiokas, Gintaras	Lithuania	23-88-17-95-46	gdidziokas@europarl.eu.int	VNDPS	UEN
Díez González, Rosa M.	Spain	3-88-17-98-64	rdiez@europarl.eu.int	PSOE	PSE
Dillen, Koenraad...........	Belgium	3-88-17-92-82	koen.dillen@skynet.be	Vl Blok	NI
Dimitrakopoulos, Giorgos	Greece	3-88-17-99-41		ND	PPE/DE
Dionisi, Armando	Italy	3-88-17-93-30	info@armandodionisi.it	UDC	PPE/DE
Di Pietro, Antonio..........	Italy	3-88-17-98-56	adipietro@europarl.eu.int	IdV	ALDE
Dobolyi, Alexandra	Hungary	3-88-17-93-70	adobolyi@europarl.eu.int	MSZP	PSE
Dombrovskis, Valdis.........	Latvia	3-88-17-93-35	vdombrovskis@europarl.eu.int	JL	PPE/DE
Doorn, Bert	Netherlands	3-88-17-95-43	ldoorn@europarl.eu.int	CDA	PPE/DE
Douay, Brigitte	France	3-88-17-97-86	Brigitte.douay@wanadoo.fr	PS	PSE
Dover, Den	UK	3-88-17-97-87	ddover@europarl.eu.int	Cons	PPE/DE
Doyle, Avril...............	Ireland	3-88-17-97-84	adoyle@europarl.eu.int	FG	PPE/DE
Drčar Murko, Mojca	Slovenia		d.murko@siol.net	LDS	ALDE
Duchoň, Petr..............	Czech Republic	3-88-17-93-75		ODS	PPE/DE
Dührkop Dührkop, Bárbara ..	Spain	3-88-17-94-78		PSOE	PSE
Duff, Andrew Nicholas	UK	3-88-17-99-98	aduff@europarl.eu.int	LD	ALDE
Duin, Garrelt. , , ...	Germany	3-88-17-94-31	gduin@europarl.eu.int	SPD	PSE
Duka-Zólyomi, Árpád	Slovakia		dzarpad@yahoo.com	SMK-MKP	PPE/DE
Duquesne, Antoine	Belgium	3-88-17-92-16		MR	ALDE
Ebner, Michl	Italy	3-88-17-94-60	mebner@europarl.eu.int	Uniti nell'Ulivo-SVP	PPE/DE
Ehler, Jan Christian........	Germany	3-88-17-93-25	wahlkreisbuero@christian-ehler.de	CDU	PPE/DE

Name—*continued*	Member State	Telephone	E-mail	Party	Political Group
Ek, Lena	Sweden			C	ALDE
El Khadraoui, Saïd	Belgium	3-88-17-95-64	said.elkhadraoui@skynet.be	SP.A-SPIRIT	PSE
Elles, James E. L.	UK	3-88-17-99-51		Cons	PPE/DE
Esteves, María da Assunção	Portugal	3-88-17-95-66	assumpta@clix.pt	CFP	PPE/DE
Estrela, Edite	Portugal	3-88-17-95-15		PS	PSE
Ettl, Harald	Austria	3-88-17-97-26	hettl@europarl.eu.int	SPÖ	PSE
Eurlings, Camiel	Netherlands	3-88-17-95-09	ceurlings@europarl.eu.int	CDA	PPE/DE
Evans, Jillian	UK	3-88-17-91-03		PC	V/ALE
Evans, Jonathan	UK	3-88-17-9528		Cons	PPE/DE
Evans, Robert J. E.	UK	3-88-17-92-98	robertevansmep@btclick.com	Lab	PSE
Fajmon, Hynek	Czech Republic	3-88-17-98-06	hynekfajmon@seznam.cz	ODS	PPE/DE
Falbr, Richard	Czech Republic	3-88-17-94-70	asistent@falbr.cz	ČSSD	PSE
Farage, Nigel Paul	UK	3-88-17-98-55		UKIP	IND/DEM
Fatuzzo, Carlo	Italy	3-88-17-92-19	cfatuzzo@europarl.eu.int	PPen	PPE/DE
Fava, Giovanni Claudio	Italy	3-88-17-92-03		Uniti nell'Ulivo	V/ALE
Fazakas, Szabolcs	Hungary	3-88-17-98-18	szabolcs.fazakas@parlament.hu	MSZP	PSE
Ferber, Markus	Germany	3-88-17-92-30	mferber@europarl.eu.int	CSU	PPE/DE
Fernandes, Emmanuel Vasconcelos Jardim	Portugal			PS	PSE
Fernández Martín, Fernando	Spain	3-88-17-96-05		PP	PPE/DE
Ferreira, Anne	France	3-88-17-91-93	anferreira@europarl.eu.int	PS	PSE
Ferreira, Elisa	Portugal		eferreira@europarl.eu.int	PS	PSE
Figueiredo, Ilda	Portugal	3-88-17-94-65	jfigueiredo@europarl.eu.int	CDU	GUE/NGL
Fjellner, Christofer	Sweden	3-88-17-55-36	christofer@muf.se	M	PPE/DE
Flasarová, Věra	Czech Republic	3-88-17-99-13		KSČM	GUE/NGL
Flautre, Hélène	France	3-88-17-93-64		VEE	V/ALE
Florenz, Karl-Heinz	Germany	3-88-17-93-20	Europabuero.Niederrhein@t-online.de	CDU	PPE/DE
Foglietta, Alessandro	Italy	3-88-17-91-81	afoglietta@europarl.eu.int	AN	UEN
Fontaine, Nicole	France	3-88-17-92-25		UMP	PPE/DE
Ford, Glyn	UK	3-88-17-95-18	penny_Richardson@new.labour.org.uk	Lab	PSE
Fotyga, Anna Elżbieta	Poland	3-88-17-95-33		PiS	UEN
Fourtou, Janelly	France	3-88-17-91-50		UDF	ALDE
Fraga Estévez, Carmen	Spain	3-88-17-92-39		PP	PPE/DE
Frassoni, Monica	Italy	3-88-17-99-32		Fed Verdi	V/ALE
Freitas, Duarte	Portugal	3-88-17-97-90		CFP	PPE/DE
Friedrich, Ingo	Germany	3-88-17-93-24		CSU	PPE/DE
Fruteau, Jean-Claude	France	3-88-17-97-45		PS	PSE
Gahler, Michael	Germany	3-88-17-99-77	mgahler@europarl.eu.int	CDU	PPE/DE
Gál, Kinga	Hungary	3-88-17-95-99		FIDESZ-MPSZ	PPE/DE
Gaľa, Milan	Slovakia			SDKÚ	PPE/DE
Galeote Quecedo, Gerardo	Spain	3-88-17-98-92		PP	PPE/DE
García-Margallo y Marfil, José Manuel	Spain	3-88-17-99-04		PP	PPE/DE
García Pérez, Iratxe	Spain	3-88-17-96-46		PSOE	PSE
Gargani, Giuseppe	Italy	3-88-17-91-68		FI	PPE/DE
Garriga Polledo, Salvador	Spain	3-88-17-93-03		PP	PPE/DE
Gaubert, Patrick	France	3-88-17-91-56		UMP	PPE/DE
Gauzès, Jean-Paul	France	3-88-17-97-00		UMP	PPE/DE
Gawronski, Jas	Italy	3-88-17-92-92	jgawronski@europarl.eu.int	FI	PPE/DE
Gebhardt, Evelyne	Germany	3-88-17-94-66	egebhardt@europarl.eu.int	SPD	PSE
Gentvilas, Eugenijus	Lithuania	3-88-17-94-63		LCS	ALDE
Geremek, Bronisław	Poland	3-88-17-98-41	biuro@unia-wolnosci.pl	UW	ALDE
Geringer de Oedenberg, Lidia Joanna	Poland	3-88-17-98-09	lgeringer@europrl.eu.int	SLD-UP	PSE
Gibault, Claire	France	3-88-17-96-13	claire.gibault@wanadoo.fr	UDF	ALDE
Gierek, Adam	Poland	3-88-17-97-81		SLD-UP	PSE
Giertych, Maciej Marian	Poland	3-88-17-92-37	mgiertych@europarl.eu.int	LPR	IND/DEM
Gill, Neena	UK	3-88-17-91-25		Lab	PSE
Gklavakis, Ioannis	Greece	3-88-17-94-09		N. D.	PPE/DE
Glante, Norbert	Germany	3-88-17-93-56	info@glante.de	SPD	PSE
Glattfelder, Béla	Hungary	3-88-17-98-89		FIDESZ-MPSZ	PPE/DE
Goebbels, Robert	Luxembourg	3-88-17-96-48	rgoebbels@europarl.eu.int	POSL	PSE
Goepel, Lutz	Germany	3-88-17-97-60		CDU	PPE/DE
Golik, Bogdan	Poland	3-88-17-91-97	bgolik@wp.pl	SO	NI
Gollnisch, Bruno	France	3-88-17-92-65		FN	NI
Gomes, Ana Maria R. M.	Portugal			PS	PSE
Gomolka, Alfred	Germany	3-88-17-93-07		CDU	PPE/DE
Goudin, Hélène	Sweden		helene.goudin@telia.com	Junilistan	IND/DEM
Grabowska, Genowefa	Poland	3-88-17-92-60		SDPL	PSE
Grabowski, Dariusz Maciej	Poland	3-88-17-92-35		LPR	EDDPSE
Graefe zu Baringdorf, Friedrich-Wilhelm	German	3-88-17-91-54	fgraefe@europarl.eu.int	Grüne	V/ALE
Grässle, Ingeborg	Germany	3-88-17-98-68		CDU	PPE/DE
de Grandes Pascual, Luis	Spain	3-88-17-95-12		PP	PPE/DE
Graça Moura, Vasco	Portugal	3-88-17-93-69	vgraca@europarl.eu.int	CFP	PPE/DE
Grech, Louis	Malta	3-88-17-92-35		MLP	PSE

Name—*continued*	Member State	Telephone	E-mail	Party	Political Group
Griesbeck, Nathalie	France	3-88-17-93-91	ng1@mairie.metz.fr	UDF	ALDE
de Groen-Kouwenhoven, Elly . .	Netherlands	3-88-17-94-80		ET	V/ALE
Grosch, Mathieu	Belgium	3-88-17-92-29	mgrosch@europarl.eu.int	CSP	PPE/DE
Grossetête, François	France	3-88-17-99-52		UMP	PPE/DE
Gruber, Dietlinde	Italy	3-88-17-91-74		Uniti nell'Ulivo	PSE
Guardans Cambó, Ignasi	Spain	3-88-17-96-08	iguardans@europarl.eu.int	G-PE	ALDE
Guellec, Ambroise	France	3-88-17-95-20		UMP	PPE/DE
Guidoni, Umberto	Italy	3-88-17-97-22		PdCI	GUE/NGL
Gurmai, Zita	Hungary	23-88-17-98-19	zgurmai@europarl.eu.int	MSZP	PSE
Gutiérrez-Cortines, Cristina. . .	Spain	3-88-17-95-94	cguterrez@europarl.eu.int	PP	PPE/DE
Guy-Quint, Catherine	France	3-88-17-99-31	c.guyquint@wanadoo.fr	PS	PSE
Gyürk, András	Hungary	3-88-17-97-27	agyurk@europarl.eu.int	FIDESZ-MPSZ	PPE/DE
Hänsch, Klaus.	Germany	3-88-17-94-67	Klaus.haensch@spd.de	SPD	PSE
Hall, Fiona Jane	UK	3-88-17-95-61	fiona_jane_hall@btopenworld.com	LD	ALDE
Hammerstein Mintz, David . . .	Spain	3-88-17-97-54		PSOE	V/ALE
Hamon, Benoît	France	3-88-17-94-76	bhamon@europarl.eu.int	PS	PSE
Handzlik, Małgorzata Maria . .	Poland	3-88-17-93-19		PO	PPE/DE
Hannan, Daniel J.	UK	3-88-17-91-37	dhannan@europarl.eu.int	Cons	PPE/DE
Harangozó, Gábor	Hungary	3-88-17-98-73	gabor.harangozo@mszp.hu	MSZP	PSE
Harbour, Malcolm.	UK	3-88-17-91-32	manor.cottage@compuserve.com	Cons	PPE/DE
Harkin, Marian.	Ireland	3-88-17-97-97			ALDE
Harms, Rebecca	Germany	3-88-17-96-95		Grüne	V/ALE
Hassi, Maijastiina.	Finland	3-88-17-94-37		VIHR	V/ALE
Hatzidakis, Konstantinos	Greece	3-88-17-91-92	khatzidakis@ath.forthnet.gr	N.D.	PPE/DE
Haug, Jutta D.	Germany	3-88-17-95-95		SPD	PSE
Hazan, Adeline	France	3-88-17-91-58	ahazan@europarl.eu.int	PS	PSE
Heaton-Harris, Christopher . . .	UK	3-88-17-95-23		Cons	PPE/DE
Hedh, Anna.	Sweden	3-88-17-95-27	anna.hedh@telia.com	SAP	PSE
Hedkvist Petersen, Ewa	Sweden	3-88-17-92-62	ehedkvist@europarl.eu.int	SAP	PSE
Hegyi, Gyula	Hungary	3-88-17-98-29	gyula.hegyi@parlament.hu	MSZP	PSE
Helmer, Roger.	UK	3-88-17-97-64	rhelmer@europarl.eu.int	Cons	PPE/DE
Henin, Jacky.	France	3-88-17-91-80		PCF	GUE/NGL
Hennicot-Schoepges, Erna	Luxembourg	3-88-17-98-36		PCS	PPE/DE
Hennis-Plasschaert, Jeanine . .	Netherlands	3-88-17-98-17		VVD	ALDE
Herczog, Edit.	Hungary	3-88-17-95-96	edit.herczog@axelero.hu	MSZP	PSE
Herranz García, María Esther .	Spain	3-88-17-92-74	eherranz@europarl.eu.int	PP	PPE/DE
Herrero-Tejedor, Luis Francisco	Spain	3-88-17-96-44		PP	PPE/DE
Hieronymi, Ruth	Germany	3-88-17-98-59	rhieryonymi@europarl.eu.int	CDU	PPE/DE
Higgins, Jim	Ireland	3-88-17-98-43		FG	PPE/DE
Hökmark, Gunnar.	Sweden	3-88-17-98-22	gunnar@moderat.se	M	PPE/DE
Honeyball, Mary	UK	3-88-17-92-09	mhoneyball@europarl.eu.int	Lab	PSE
Hoppenstedt, Karsten Friedrich	Germany	3-88-17-96-60	hoppenstedt@epri.org	CDU	PPE/DE
Horáček, Milan	Germany	3-88-17-91-96		Grüne	V/ALE
Hortefeux, Brice	France	3-88-17-81-26	bhortefeux@europarl.eu.int	UMP	PPE/DE
Howitt, Richard.	UK	3-88-17-94-77	rhowitt@europarl.eu.int	Lab	PSE
Hudacký, Ján	Slovakia	3-88-17-92-86		KDH	PPE/DE
Hudghton, Ian Stewart.	UK	3-88-17-94-99	jhudghton@europarl.eu.int	SNP	V/ALE
Hughes, Stephen.	UK	3-88-17-94-08	sthughes@europarl.eu.int	Lab	PSE
Huhne, Christopher	UK	3-88-17-92-21	chuhne@europarl.eu.int	LD	ALDE
Hutchinson, Alain.	Belgium	3-88-17-94-51	ahutchinson@europarl.eu.int	PS	PSE
Hybášková, Jana.	Czech Republic	3-88-17-95-19	jana@hybaskova.cz	SNK	PPE/DE
Ibrisagic, Anna	Sweden	3-88-17-97-75	aibrisagic@europarl.eu.int	M	PPE/DE
Ilves, Toomas Hendrik	Estonia	3-88-17-91-48	thilves@mac.com	SDE	PSE
in't Veld, Sophia Helena	Netherlands	3-88-17-97-96		D66	ALDE
Isler Béguin, Marie Anne	France	3-88-17-95-72	maisler@europarl.eu.int	Les Verts	V/ALE
Itälä, Ville.	Finland	3-88-17-96-47	ville.itala@ssi-law.fi	KOK	PPE/DE
Iturgaiz Angulo, Carlos José . .	Spain	3-88-17-99-65	regional2.pv@pp.es	PP	PPE/DE
Jackson, Caroline F.	UK	3-88-17-92-55	cjackson@europarl.eu.int	Cons	PPE/DE
Jäätteenmäki, Anneli	Finland	3-88-17-96-14	ajaateenmaki@europarl.eu.int	KESK	ALDE
Jałowiecki, Stanisław	Poland	3-88-17-99-73		PO	PPE/DE
Janowski, Mieczysław Edmund	Poland	3-88-17-92-63	senator@janowski.rzeszow.pl	PO	UEN
Járóka, Lívia.	Hungary	3-88-17-92-18		FIDESZ-MPSZ	PPE/DE
Jarzembowski, Georg	Germany	3-88-17-93-06	gjarzembowski@compuserve.com	CDU	PPE/DE
Jeggle, Elisabeth.	Germany	3-88-17-93-51	ejeggle@europarl.eu.int	CDU	PPE/DE
Jensen, Anne Elisabet	Denmark	3-88-17-97-98	ajensen@europarl.eu.int	V	ALDE
Joan i Marí, Bernat	Spain	3-88-17-92-99	bjoan@europarl.eu.int	Europa de los Pueblos	V/ALE
Jöns, Karin	Germany	3-88-17-95-35	kjoens@europarl.eu.int	SPD	PSE
Jørgensen, Dan	Denmark	3-88-17-97-71	danj@danj.dk	A	PSE
Jonckheer, Pierre	Belgium	3-88-17-58-96		ECOLO	V/ALE
Jordan Cizelj, Romana	Slovenia	3-88-17-92-80		SDS	PPE/DE
Juknevičienė, Ona.	Lithuania	3-88-17-98-30		DP	ALDE
Kacin, Jelko.	Slovenia	3-88-17-97-48	jelko.kacin@dz-rs.si	LDS	ALDEPSE
Kaczmarek, Filip Andrzej	Poland	3-88-17-93-17		PO	PPE/DE
Kallenbach, Gisela	Germany	3-88-17-93-39	Gisela.kallenbach@ grUENe-leipzig.de	Grüne	V/ALE

Name—*continued*	Member State	Telephone	E-mail	Party	Political Group
Kamiński, Michał Tomasz	Poland	3-88-17-99-27	michal.Kaminski@sejm.pl	PiS	UEN
Karas, Othmar	Austria	3-88-17-96-27	okaras@europarl.eu.int	ÖVP	PPE/DE
Karatzaferis, Georgios	Greece		gkaratzaferis@europarl.eu.int	LA. O.S.	IND/DEM
Karim, Sajjad Haider	UK	3-88-17-96-40		LD	ALDE
Kasoulides, Ioannis..........	Cyprus	3-88-17-93-02	ykasoulides@ddkstrategy.com	DI. SY	PPE/DE
Kaufmann, Sylvia-Yvonne	Germany	3-88-17-97-56	europabuero.pds@bundestag.de	PDS	GUE/NGL
Kauppi, Piia-Noora	Finland	3-88-17-98-94	pkauppi@europarl.eu.int	KOK	PPE/DE
Kelam, Tunne	Estonia	3-88-17-92-79	tkelam@europarl.eu.int	IL	PPE/DE
Kilroy-Silk, Robert	UK	3-88-17-91-95		UKIP	IND/DEM
Kindermann, Heinz	Germany	3-88-17-90-60	hkindermann@europarl.eu.int	SPD	PSE
Kinnock, Glenys	UK	3-88-17-94-02	gkinnock@europarl.eu.int	Lab	PSE
Kirkhope, Timothy	UK	3-88-17-93-21	tkirkhope@europarl.eu.int	Cons	PPE/DE
Klamt, Ewa................	Germany	3-88-17-99-71		CDU	PPE/DE
Klass, Christa	Germany	3-88-17-93-13	cklass@europarl.eu.int	CDU	PPE/DE
Klich, Bogdan Adam	Poland	3-88-17-97-33	bklich@europarl.eu.int	PO	PPE/DE
Klinz, Wolf	Germany	3-88-17-96-41	wolf@klinz.com	FDP	ALDE
Knapman, Roger Maurice.....	UK	3-88-17-95-59		UKIP	IND/DEM
Koch, Dieter-Lebrecht........	Germany	3-88-17-97-61	dkoch@europarl.eu.int	CDU	PPE/DE
Koch-Mehrin, Silvana........	Germany	3-88-17-91-12		FDP	ALDE
Kohlíček, Jaromír	Czech Republic	3-88-17-94-97		KSČM	GUE/NGL
Konrad, Christoph Werner	Germany	3-88-17-93-33	ckonrad@europarl.eu.int	CDU	PPE/DE
Korhola, Eiji-Riita Anneli.....	Finland	3-88-17-94-72	ekorhola@europearl.eu.int	KOK	PPE/DE
Kósáne Kovács, Magda.......	Hungary	351-291-76-98-31	gyorgyne.mezofi@parlament.hu	MSZP	PSE
Koterec, Miloš	Slovakia	3-88-17-91-75	mkoterec@europarl.eu.int	Smer	PSE
Kozlík, Sergej	Slovakia	3-88-17-92-57	sergej.kozlik@nrsr.sk	HZDS	NI
Krahmer, Holger............	Germany	3-88-17-93-44	fdp@holger-krahmer.de	FDP	ALDE
Krarup, Ole................	Denmark	3-88-17-91-52	Ole.Krarup@jur.ku.dk	N	GUE/NGL
Krasts, Guntars	Latvia	3-88-17-99-09	guntars.krasts@saeima.lv	TB/LNNK	UEN
Kratsa-Tsagaropoulou, Rodi ...	Greece	3-88-17-93-08		ND	PPE/DE
Krehl, Constanze Angela	Germany	3-88-17-91-34	krehl.europabuero@t-online.de	SPD	PSE
Kreissl-Dörfler, Wolfgang	Germany	3-88-17-91-10	europa@kreissl-doerfler.de	SPD	PSE
Kristensen, Henrik Dam.....	Denmark	3-88-17-94-91	shekr@ft.dk	S	PSE
Kristovskis, Ģirts Valdis......	Latvia	3-88-17-97-44		TB/LNNK	UEN
Krupa, Urszula	Poland	3-88-17-95-83		LPR	IND/DEM
Kuc, Wiesław Stefan	Poland	3-88-17-91-98	wisla.c@wp.pl	SO	NI
Kudrycka, Barbara	Poland	3-88-17-97-29	barbara@kudrycka.pl	PO	PPE/DE
Kuhne, Helmut	Germany	3-88-17-94-28	hkuhne@europarl.eu.int	SPD	PSE
Kułakowski, Jan Jerzy	Poland	3-88-17-98-48	magdanetzel@hotmail.com	UW	ALDE
Kušķis, Aldis...............	Latvia	3-88-17-94-10	akuskis@europarl.eu.int	JL	PPE/DE
Kusstatscher, Sepp	Italy	3-88-17-91-43	skusstatscher@europarl.eu.int	Fed Verdi	V/ALE
Kuźmiuk, Zbigniew Krzysztof........	Poland	3-88-17-92-54		PSL	PPE/DE
Lagendijk, Joost	Netherlands	3-88-17-91-76		Groenlinks	V/ALE
Laignel, André	France	3-88-17-99-35		PS	PSE
Lamassoure, Alain	France	3-88-17-97-06		UMP	PPE/DE
Lambert, Jean Denise........	UK	3-88-17-95-07	jelambert@europarl.eu.int	GP	V/ALE
Lambrinidis, Stavros	Greece		stala@politicalforum.gr	PASOK	PSE
Lambsdorff Graf, Alexander ...	Germany	3-88-17-91-18		FDP	ALDE
Landsbergis, Vytautas	Lithuania	3-88-17-95-70		TS	PPE/DE
Lang, Carl.................	France	3-88-17-92-61		FN	NI
Langen, Werner	Germany	3-88-17-93-85	wlangen@europarl.eu.int	CDU	PPE/DE
Langendries, Raymond.......	Belgium	3-88-17-96-15	raymondlangendries@tubize.be	cdH	PPE/DE
Laperrouze, Anne	France	3-88-17-94-50	laperrouzeanne@aol.com	UDF	ALDE
La Russa, Romano Maria	Italy	3-88-17-99-14		AN	UEN
Laschet, Armin	Germany	3-88-17-95-678	alaschet@europrl.eu.int	CDU	PPE/DE
Lauk, Kurt Joachim	Germany	3-88-17-97-72	info@prof.lauk.de	CDU	PPE/DE
Lax, Henrik................	Finland	3-88-17-98-28	henrik.lax@eduskunta.fi	SFP	ALDE
Lechner, Kurt	Germany	3-88-17-98-26	klechner@europarl.eu.int	CDU	PPE/DE
Le Foll, Stéphane	France	3-88-17-94-95		PS	PSE
Lehideux, Bernard	France	3-88-17-95-47		UDF	ALDE
Lehne, Klaus-Heiner	Germany	3-88-17-90-47		CDU	PPE/DE
Lehtinen, Lasse Antero.......	Finland	3-88-17-91-89	riita.aarrevuo@brutto.inet.fi	SDP	PSE
Leichtfried, Jörg	Austria	3-88-17-94-36		SPÖ	PSE
Leinen, Jo	Germany	3-88-17-98-42	jleinen@europarl.eu.int	SPD	PSE
Le Pen, Jean-Marie..........	France	3-88-17-97-20	montretoutv80@wanadoo.fr	FN	NI
Le Pen, Marine	France			FN	NI
Letta, Enrico..............	Italy			Uniti nell'Ulivo	PSE
Lévai, Katalin	Hungary			MSZP	PSE
Lewandowski, Janusz........	Poland		jlewandowski@europarl.eu.int	PO	PPE/DE
Liberadzki, Bogusław Marian..	Poland	3-88-17-94-23	biuro@liberadzki.pl	SLD-UP	PSE
Libicki, Marcin	Poland	3-88-17-99-34	mlibicki@europarl.eu.int	PiS	UEN
Lichtenberger, Evelin	Austria	3-88-17-91-39		Grüne	V/ALE
Lienemann, Marie-Noëlle	France	3-88-17-91-02	mn.lienemann@wanadoo.fr	PS	PSE
Liese, Peter...............	Germany	3-88-17-99-81		CDU	PPE/DE
Liotard, Kartika Tamara	Netherlands	3-88-17-97-78		SP	GUE/NGL
Lipietz, Alain	France	3-88-17-92-07		Les Verts	V/ALE
Locatelli, Pia Elda...........	Italy	2-284-94-43		Uniti nell'Ulivo	PSE
Lombardo, Raffaele..........	Italy	3-88-17-94-33		UDE	PPE/DE

Name—*continued*	Member State	Telephone	E-mail	Party	Political Group
López-Istúriz White, Antonio	Spain	3-88-17-97-13	alopez@evppe.be	PP	PPE/DE
Louis, Patrick	France	3-88-17-99-61	Patrick-louis@wanadoo.fr	MPF	IND/DEM
Lucas, Caroline.	UK	3-88-17-91-53	clucas@europarl.eu.int	GP	V/ALE
Ludford, Baroness Sarah . . .	UK	3-88-17-91-04	sludford@europarl.eu.int	LDP	ALDE
Lulling, Astrid.	Luxembourg	3-88-17-93-86	alulling@europarl.eu.int	PCS	PPE/DE
Lundgren, Nils	Sweden	3-88-17-97_25	lundgren@veraoiter.se	Junilistan	IND/DEM
Lynne, Elizabeth.	UK	3-88-17-95-21	elynne@europarl.eu.int	LDP	ALDE
Maat, Albert Jan.	Netherlands	3-88-17-99-54	amaat@europrl.eu.int	CDA	PPE/DE
Maaten, Jules	Netherlands	3-88-17-96-06	europa@maaten.net	VVD	ALDE
McAvan, Linda	UK	3-88-17-94-38	lmcavan@europarl.eu.int	Lab	PSE
McCarthy, Arlene	UK	3-88-17-52-95-01	arlene.mccarthy@easynet.co.uk	Lab	PSE
McDonald, Mary Lou	Ireland	3-88-17-99-45		SF	GUE/NGL
McGuinness, Mairead.	Ireland	3-88-17-92-14	info@mcguinness4europe.ie	FG	PPE/DE
McMillan-Scott, Edward H. C.	UK	3-88-17-99-59		Cons	PPE/DE
Madeira, Jamila	Portugal	3-88-17-98-98		PS	PSE
Malmström, Cecilia.	Sweden	3-88-17-95-41	cmalstrom@europarl.eu.int	FP	ALDE
Manders, Toine.	Netherlands	3-88-17-96-29	tmanders@europarl.eu.int	VVD	ALDE
Maňka, Vladimír.	Slovakia	3-88-17-94-49	vmanka@europarl.eu.int		PSE
Mann, Erika	Germany	3-88-17-91-91		SPD	PSE
Mann, Thomas	Germany	3-88-17-93-18	tmann@europarl.eu.int	CDU	PPE/DE
Manolakou, Diamanto	Greece	3-88-17-91-63	dmanolakou@europarl.eu.int	KKE	GUE/NGL
Mantovani, Mario	Italy	3-88-17-94-22		FI	PPE/DE
Markov, Helmuth	Germany	3-88-17-99-80		PDS	GUE/NGL
Marques, Sérgio	Portugal	3-88-17-94-04		CFP	PPE/DE
Martens, Maria.	Netherlands	3-88-17-98-57	mmartens@europarl.eu.int	CDA	PPE/DE
Martin, David W.	UK	3-88-17-95-39	martin@martinmep.com	Lab	PSE
Martin, Hans-Peter.	Austria	3-88-17-91-57	hpmartin@kke.gr		NI
Martinez, Jean-Claude	France	3-88-17-99-68		FN	NI
Martínez Martínez, Miguel Angel.	Spain	3-88-17-92-69	mimartinez@europarl.eu.int	PSOE	PSE
Masiel, Jan Tadeusz	Poland	3-88-17-92-11	masiel.jan@skynet.be	SO	NI
Masip Hidalgo, Antonio	Spain	3-88-17-94-74	amasipeuropa@yahoo.es	PSOE	PSE
Maštálka, Jiří	Czech Republic	3-88-17-99-05	mastalka@mastalka.cz	KSČM	GUE/NGL
Mastenbroek, Edith	Netherlands	3-88-17-99-92		PvdA	PSE
Mathieu, Véronique.	France	3-88-17-92-20		UMP	PPE/DE
Mato Adrover, Ana	Spain	3-88-17-94-27		PP	PPE/DEPSE
Matsakis, Marios	Cyprus	3-88-17-98-16	mmatsakis@parliament.cy	DI.KO	ALDE
Matsis, Yiannakis.	Cyprus	3-88-17-91-28		Gia tin Evropi	PPE/DE
Matsouka, Maria.	Greece			PASOK	PSE
Mauro, Mario	Italy	3-88-17-93-87		FI	PPE/DE
Mavrommatis, Manolis.	Greece	3-88-17-93-34		ND	PPE/DE
Mayer, Hans-Peter	Germany	3-88-17-99-94	europa-mayer@t-online.de	CDU	PPE/DE
Mayor Oreja, Jaime	Spain	3-88-17-96-01	mirenaguirre@pp.es	PP	PPE/DE
Medina Ortega, Manuel	Spain	3-88-17-98-82	mmedina@europarl.eu.int	PSOE	PSE
Meijer, Erik.	Netherlands	3-88-17-94-92	emeijer@sp.nl	SP	GUE/NGL
Méndez De Vigo, Íñigo	Spain	3-88-17-97-55	imendezdevigo@europarl.eu.int	PP	PPE/DE
Menéndez del Valle, Emilio .	Spain	3-88-17-97-52		PSOE	PSE
Meyer Pleite, Willy	Spain	3-88-17-99-64		IU-IPCV-EUA	GUE/NGL
Miguélez Ramos, Rosa	Spain	3-88-17-95-32		PSOE	PSE
Mikko, Marianne	Estonia	3-88-17-91-22	mariannemikko@hot.ee	SDE	PSE
Mikolášik Miroslav	Slovakia	3-88-17-92-89		KDH	PPE/DE
Millán, Francisco José	Spain	3-88-17-94-30		PP	PPE/DE
Mitchell, Gay.	Ireland	3-88-17-92-28		FG	PPE/DE
Mölzer, Andreas	Austria	3-88-17-91-41	a.moelzer@aon.at	FPÖ	NI
Montoro Romero, Cristóbal Ricardo	Spain	3-88-17-99-49		PP	PPE/DE
Moraes, Claude.	UK	3-88-17-95-53	cmoraes@europarl.eu.int	Lab	PSE
Moreno Sánchez, Javier	Spain	3-88-17-91-65		PSOE	PSE
Morgan, Eluned	UK	3-88-17-94-57	emorgan@europarl.eu.int	Lab	PSE
Morgantini, Luisa	Italy	3-88-17-91-51	lmorgantini@europarl.eu.int	PRC-SE	GUE/NGL
Morillon, Philippe.	France	3-88-17-95-06		UDF	ALDE
Moscovici, Pierre.	France	3-88-17-99-93	pierre.moscovici@parti-socialiste.fr	PS	PSE
Mote, Ashley	UK	3-88-17-97-47	amote@europarl.eu.int	UKIP	NI
Mulder, Jan.	Netherlands	3-88-17-96-07	jmulder@europarl.eu.int	VVD	ALDE
Musacchio, Roberto.	Italy	3-88-17-96-64		PRC-SE	GUE/NGL
Muscardini, Cristiana.	Italy	3-88-17-92-77	cmuscardini@tin.it	AN	UEN
Muscat, Joseph	Malta	3-88-17-93-76	joseph@josephmuscat.com	MLP	PSE
Musotto, Francesco.	Italy	3-88-17-95-97		FI	PPE/DE
Mussolini, Alessandra.	Italy	3-88-17-95-17		Lista Mussolini	NI
Musumeci, Sebastiano	Italy	3-88-17-97-65	musumeci@csanet.it	AN	UEN
Myller, Riitta.	Finland	3-88-17-97-38	rmyller@europarl.eu.int	SDP	PSE
Napoletano, Pasqualina	Italy	3-88-17-91-30	pnapoletano@europarl.eu.int	Uniti nell'Ulivo	PSE
Nassauer, Hartmut	Germany	3-88-17-93-61	hnassauer@europarl.eu.int	CDU	PPE/DE
Nattrass Michael	UK	3-88-17-91-33		UKIP	IND/DEM
Navarro, Robert	France	3-88-17-94-21		PS	PSE
Newton Dunn, Bill	UK	3-88-17-97-12	wnewton@europarl.eu.int	LD	ALDE
Neyts-Uyttebroeck, Annemie	Belgium	3-88-17-96-61		VLD-Vivant	ALDE

Name—*continued*	Member State	Telephone	E-mail	Party	Political Group
Nicholson, James	UK	3-88-17-99-33		UUP	PPE/DE
Nicholson of Winterbourne, Baroness	UK	3-88-17-96-25	enicholson@europarl.eu.int	LD	ALDE
Niebler, Angelika	Germany	3-88-17-93-90		CSU	PPE/DE
Nistelrooij, Lambert van.	Netherlands	3-88-17-94-34	lnist@home.nl	CDA	PPE/DE
Novak, Ljudmila	Slovenia	3-88-17-93-95	ljudmila.novak@quest.arnes.si	NSi	PPE/DE
Obiols i Germà, Raimon	Spain	3-88-17-95-92	robiols@psc.es	PSOE	PSE
Öger, Vural	Germany	3-88-17-94-11	voeger@europarl.eu.int	SPD	PSE
Özdemir, Cem	Germany	3-88-17-94-46		Grüne	V/ALE
Olajos, Péter	Hungary	3-88-17-93-15		MDF	PPE/DE
Olbrycht, Jan Marian	Poland	3-88-17-95-11	jolbrycht@onet.pl	PO	PPE/DE
Ó Neachtain, Seán	Ireland	3-88-17-96-11	seanoneachtain@eircom.net	FF	UE
Onesta, Gérard	France	3-88-17-95-05		Les Verts	V/ALE
Onyszkiewicz, Janusz	Poland	3-88-17-98-72	biuro@unio-wolnosci.pl	UW	ALDE
Oomen-Ruijten, Ria G. H. C. .	Netherlands	3-88-17-98-63	roomen@europarl.eu.int	CDA	PPE/DE
Ortuondo Larrea, Josu	Spain	3-88-17-92-67	jortuondo@europarl.eu.int	G-PE	ALDE
Öry, Csaba	Hungary	3-88-17-98-33	csaba.ory@parlament.hu	FIDESZ-MPSZ	PPE/DE
Ouzký, Miroslav	Czech Republic	3-88-17-98-10	miroslav@ouzky.cz	ODS	PPE/DE
Oviir, Siiri	Estonia	3 88-17-98-15		K	ALDE
Paasilinna, Reino	Finland	3-88-17-97-34	rpaasilinna@europarl.eu.int	SDP	PSE
Pack, Doris	Germany	3-88-17-93-10	dorispack@aol.com	CDU	PPE/DE
Pafilis, Athanasios	Greece	3-88-17-99-11		KKE	GUE/NGL
Pahor, Borut	Slovenia	3-88-17-92-40	borut.pahor@zlsd.si	ZLSD	PSE
Paleckis, Justas Vincas.	Lithuania	3-88-17-99-21	jpaleckis@hotmail.com	LSDP	PSE
Pálfi, István.	Hungary	3-88-17-97-02		FIDESZ-MPSZ	PPE/DE
Panayotopoulos-Cassiotou, Marie.	Greece		mpanayotopoulos@europarl.eu.int	ND	PPE/DE
Pannella, Marco	Italy	3-88-17-91-20	mpannella@europarl.eu.int	Lista Bonino	ALDE
Panzeri, Pier Antonio	Italy	3-88-17-93-49		Uniti nell'Ulivo	PSE
Papadimoulis, Dimitrios	Greece	3-88-17-97-19	papadimoulis@syn.gr	SYN	GUE/NGL
Papastamkos, Georgios	Greece	3-88-17-94-48	gpapastamkos@europarl.eu.int	ND	ALDE
Parish, Neil	UK	3-88-17-93-92		Cons	PPE/DE
Patrie, Béatrice	France	3-88-17-98-83	aquitaine@beatrice-patrie.org	PS	PSE
Pavilionis, Rolandas	Lithuania	3-88-17-95-75	rolandas.pavilionis@lrs.lt	LDP	UEN
Peillon, Vincent Benoît Camille	France	3-88-17-93-12	peillon.v@wanadoo.fr	PS	PSE
Pęk, Bogdan Marek	Poland	3-88-17-95-84		LPR	IND/DEM
Peterle, Alojz.	Slovenia	3-88-17-96-38	apeterle@europarl.eu.int	NSi	PPE/DE
Pflüger, Tobias	Germany	3-88-17-95-55	tpflueger@europarl.eu.int	PDS	GUE/NGL
Piecyk, Willi	Germany	3-88-17-95-02	willi.piecyk-lv-schleswig-holstein@ spd.de	SPD	PSE
Pieper, Markus	Germany	3-88-17-93-05		CDU	PPE/DE
Pīks, Rihard	Latvia	3-88-17-92-93	rpiks@saeima.lv	TP	PPE/DE
Pinheiro, João de Deus	Portugal	3-88-17-93-74		CFP	PPE/DE
Pinior, Józef	Poland	3-88-17-98-75	pinior@credit.ae.wroc.pl	SDPL	PSE
Piotrowski, Mirosław Mariusz	Poland	3-88-17-95-88		LPR	IND/DEM
Pirilli, Umberto	Italy	3-88-17-99-79	upirilli@europarl.eu.int	AN	UEN
Piskorski, Pawel Bartłomiej . .	Poland	3-88-17-95-31		PO	PPE/DE
Pistelli, Lapo	Italy	3-88-17-98-87		Uniti nell'Ulivo	ALDE
Pittella, Giovanni	Italy	3-88-17-91-59	gpittella@europarl.eu.int	Uniti nell'Ulivo	PSE
Pleguezuelos Aguilar, Francisca.	Spain	3-88-17-98-97	gpsocialista@psoe-granada.com	PSOE	PSE
Pleštinská, Zita	Slovakia	3-88-17-92-04	plestinska@stonline.sk	SDKÚ	PPE/DE
Podestà, Guido	Italy	3-88-17-93-40	gpodesta@europarl.eu.int	FI	PPE/DE
Podkański, Zdzisław Zbigniew	Poland	3-88-17-92-48		PSL	PPE/DE
Poettering, Hans-Gert.	Germany	3-88-17-97-69	hpoettering@europarl.eu.int	CDU	PPE/DE
Poignant, Bernard.	France	3-88-17-94-05	bernard.poignant@wanadoo.fr	PS	PSE
Polfer, Lydie	Luxembourg	3-88-17-96-21		DP	ALDE
Poli Bortone, Adriana	Italy	3-88-17-97-07		AN	UEN
Pomés Ruiz, José Javier	Spain	3-88-17-98-99		PP	PPE/DE
Portas, Miguel.	Portugal	3-88-17-91-23		BE	GUE/NGL
Posselt, Bernd	Germany	3-88-17-92-32	mail@bernd-posselt.de	CSU	PPE/DE
Prets, Christa	Austria	3-88-17-95-91	cprets@europarl.eu.int	SPÖ	PSE
Prodi, Vittorio	Italy	3-88-17-95-81	vprodi@europarl.eu.int	Uniti nell'Ulivo	ALDE
Protasiewicz, Jacek.	Poland	3-88-17-97-43	jprotasiewicz@europarl.eu.int	PO	PPE/DE
Purvis, John	UK	3-88-17-96-84	jpurvis@europarl.eu.int	Cons	PPE.DE
Queiró, Luís	Portugal	3-88-17-92-27	queiro@netcabo.pt	CFP	PPE/DE
Quisthoudt-Rowohl, Godelieve.	Germany	3-88-17-93-38		CDU	PPE/DE
Rack, Reinhard	Austria	3-88-17-97-73	rrack@europarl.eu.int	ÖVP	PPE/DE
Radwan, Alexander.	Germany	3-88-17-95-38	aradwan@europarl.eu.int	CSU	PPE.DE
Ransdorf, Miloslav	Czech Republic	3-88-17-99-07	ransdorf@ksem.cz	KSČM	GUE/NGL
Rapkay, Bernhard.	Germany	3-88-17-95-93	brapkay@europarl.eu.int	SPD	PSE
Rasmussen, Poul Nyrup	Denmark	3-88-17-94-63		A	PSE
Remek, Vladimír.	Czech Republic	3-88-17-91-31		KSČM	GUE/NGL
Resetarits, Karin.	Austria	3-88-17-913	resetarits@marx.at	MARTIN	NI
Reul, Herbert Otto	Germany	3-88-17-92-44		CDU	PPE/DE
Reynaud, Marie-Line	France	3-88-17-93-60		PS	PSE

Name—*continued*	Member State	Telephone	E-mail	Party	Political Group
Ribeiro, Sérgio.	Portugal	3-88-17-99-63	Sergio.j.ribeiro@mail.telepac.pt	CDU	GUE/NGL
Ribeiro e Castro, José.	Portugal	3-88-17-97-83	jcastro@europarl.eu.int	CFP	PPE/DE
Riera Madurell, Teresa.	Spain	3-88-17-94-15	trieramadurell@europarl.eu.int	PSOE	PSE
Ries, Frédérique	Belgium	3-88-17-95-49	fries@europarl.eu.int	MR	ALDE
Riis-Jørgensen, Karin	Denmark	3-88-17-97-94		V	ALDE
Rizzo, Marco	Italy	3-88-17-92-52		PdCI	GUE/NGL
Rocard, Michel	France	3-88-17-97-85	mrocard@europarl.eu.int	PS	PSE
Rogalski, Bogusław.	Poland	3-88-17-96-16	LPR	LPR	IND/DEM
Roithová, Zuzana	Czech Republic	3-88-17-94-85		KDU-ČSL	PPE/DE
Romagnoli, Luca	Italy	3-88-17-95-30	lucaromagnoli@libero.it	MSFT	NI
Romeva i Rueda, Raúl	Spain	3-88-17-96-45		IU-IPCV-EUA	V/ALE
Rosati, Dariusz Kajetan	Poland	3-88-17-91-82		SDPL	PSE
Roszkowski, Wojciech	Poland	3-88-17-95-73	wojciech@roszkowski.pl	PiS	UEN
Roth-Behrendt, Dagmar	Germany	3-88-17-94-53	drothbehrendt@europarl.eu.int	SPD	PSE
Rothe, Mechtild.	Germany	3-88-17-94-14		SPD	PSE
Rouček, Libor	Czech Republic	3-88-17-92-59	lroucek@europarl.eu.int	ČSSD	PSE
Roure, Martine	France	3-88-17-91-38		PS	PSE
Rudi Ubeda, Luisa Fernanda	Spain	3-88-17-92-68		PP	PPE/DE
Rübig, Paul	Austria	3-88-17-97-49	pruebig@europarl.eu.int	ÖVP	PPE/DE
Rühle, Heide	Germany	3-88-17-96-09	hruehle@europarl.eu.int	Grüne	V/ALE
Rutowicz, Leopold Józef	Poland	3-88-17-92-17	amackowk@op.pl	SO	NI
Ryan, Eoin.	Ireland	3-88-17-96-12		FF	UEN
Sacconi, Guido.	Italy	3-88-17-97-76	gsaconi@europarl.eu.int	Uniti nell'Ulivo	PSE
Saïfi, Tokia	France	3-88-17-95-62		UMP	PPE/DE
Sakalas, Aloyzas	Lithuania	3-88-17-95-42		LSDP	PSE
Salafranca Sánchez-Neyra, José Ignacio	Spain	3-88-17-96-03		PP	PPE/DE
Salinas García, María Isabel .	Spain	3-88-17-93-48		PSOE	PSE
Salvini, Matteo	Italy	3-88-17-91-21		LN	IND/DEM
Samaras, Antonis	Greece	3-88-17-92-42		ND	PPE/DE
Samuelsen, Anders	Denmark	3-88-17-99-16	rvansa@ft.dk	B	ALDE
Sánchez Presedo, Antolín	Spain	3-88-17-94-71	antolinsp@hotmail.com	PSOE	PSE
Santoro, Michele	Italy	3-88-17-95-65		Uniti nell'Ulivo	PSE
Santos, Manuel António dos . .	Portugal	3-88-17-98-69	mdossantos@europarl.eu.int	PS	PSE
Sartori, Amalia	Italy	3-88-17-95-56	asartori@europarl.eu.int	FI	PPE/DE
Saryusz-Wolski, Jacek Emil . .	Poland	3-88-17-93-71	gvanorden@europarl.eu.int	PO	PPE/DE
Savary, Gilles	France	3-88-17-94-20	gsavary@europarl.eu.int	PS	PSE
Savi, Toomas.	Estonia	3-88-17-98-14	tsavi@europarl.eu.int	ER	ALDE
Sbarbati, Luciana	Italy	3-88-17-99-10	lsbarbati@europarl.eu.int	Uniti nell'Ulivo	ALDE
Schapira, Pierre Lionel Georges	France	3-88-17-97-91	pierre-schapira@mairie-paris.fr	PS	PSE
Scheele, Karin.	Austria	3-88-17-93-97	kscheele@europarl.eu.int	SPÖ	PSE
Schenardi, Lydia	France	3-88-17-92-56		FN	NI
Schierhuber, Agnes.	Austria	3-88-17-97-41	aschierhuber@europarl.eu.int	ÖVP	PPE/DE
Schlyter, Carl	Sweden	3-88-17-92-73	carl.schlyter@mp.se	MP	V/ALE
Schmidt, Frithjof.	Germany	3-88-17-92-15	fsschmidt@grUENe.nrw.de	Grüne	V/ALE
Schmitt, Ingo.	Germany	3-88-17-94-42	raesp@t-online.de	CDU	PPE/DE
Schmitt, Pál	Hungary	3-88-17-95-44		FIDESZ-MPSZ	PPE/DE
Schnellhardt, Horst.	Germany	3-88-17-96-18		CDU	PPE/DE
Schöpflin, György	Hungary	3-88-17-98-84	schopflingy@hotmail.com	FIDESZ-MPSZ	PPE/DE
Schröder, Jürgen.	Germany	3-88-17-95-60	jschroeder@europarl.eu.int	CDU	PSE
Schroedter, Elisabeth	Germany	3-88-17-92-34	info@elisabeth-schroedter.de	Grüne	V/ALE
Schulz, Martin	Germany	3-88-17-95-03		SPD	PSE
Schuth, Willem	Germany	3-88-17-92-91	pederwachtmeister@nyköping.se	FDP	ALDE
Schwab, Andreas.	Germany	3-88-17-99-38		CDU	PPE/DE
Seeber, Richard.	Austria	3-88-17-94-68		ÖVP	PPE/DE
Seeberg, Gitte	Denmark	3-88-17-92-43	gitte.seeberg@ft.dk	C	PPE/DE
Segelström, Inger	Sweden	3-88-17-91-99		SAPLab	PSE
Seppänen, Esko Olavi.	Finland	3-88-17-92-71	eseppanen@europarl.eu.int	VAS	GUE/NGL
Siekierski, Czesław Adam . . .	Poland	3-88 17-97-93	csiekierski@interia.pl	PSL	PPE/DE
Sifunakis, Nikolaos.	Greece		ni.si@mail.gr	PASOK	PSE
Silva Peneda, José Albino. . . .	Portugal	3-88-17-93-81		CFP	PPE/DE
Sinnott, Kathy.	Ireland	3-88-17-96-92			IND/DEM
Siwiec, Marek Maciej	Poland	3-88-17-96-53		SLD-UP	PSE
Sjöstedt, Jonas	Sweden	3-88-17-95-63		V	GUE/NGL
Skinner, Peter William	UK	3-88-17-94-58	pskinner@europarl.eu.int	Lab	PSE
Škottová, Nina	Czech Republic	3-88-17-93-58	ris.olonz.ods@volny.cz	ODS	PPE/DE
Smith, Alyn Edward	UK	3-88-17-91-87		SNP	V/ALE
Sommer, Renate	Germany	3-88-17-93-83	rsommer@europarl.eu.int	CDU	PPE/DE
Sonik, Bogusław Andrzej	Poland	3-88-17-96-90		PO	PPE/DE
Sornosa Martínez, María	Spain	3-88-17-99-74		POND	PSE
Sousa Pinto, Sérgio.	Portugal	3-88-17-94-86	ssousa@europarl.eu.int	PS	PSE
Spautz, Jean	Luxembourg	3-88-17-97-93		PCS	PPE/DE
Speroni, Francesco Enrico . . .	Italy	3-88-17-97-05	fsperoni@europarl.eu.int	LN	IND/DEM
Staes, Bart	Belgium	3-88-17-96-42	bstaes@europarl.eu.int	GROEN	V/ALE
Staniszewska, Grażyna	Poland	3-88-17-98-49	agata.bialas@pro.onet.pl	UW	ALDE
Starkevičiūtė, Margarita	Lithuania	3-88-17-96-10		LCS	ALDE

Name—*continued*	Member State	Telephone	E-mail	Party	Political Group
Šťastný, Peter	Slovakia	3-88-17-96-83		SDKÚ	PPE/DE
Stenzel, Ursula	Austria	3-88-17-97-66	ustenzel@europarl.eu.int	ÖVP	PPE/DE
Sterckx, Dirk De Heer	Belgium		dsterckx@europarl.eu.int	VLD-Vivant	ALDE
Stevenson, Struan.	UK	3-88-17-97-10	struanmep@aol.com	Cons	PPE/DE
Stihler, Catherine	UK	3-88-17-94-62	cstihler@cstihlermep.freeserve.co.uk	Lab	PSE
Stockmann, Ulrich	Germany	3-88-17-96-87	ustockmann@europarl.eu.int	SPD	PSE
Strejček, Ivo	Czech Republic	3-88-17-96-67		ODS	PPE/DE
Stroz, Daniel	Czech Republic	3-88-17-94-56		KSČM	GUE/NGL
Stubb, Alexander	Finland	3-88-17-92-64	astubb@europarl.eu.int	KOK	PPE/DE
Sturdy, Robert William.	UK	3-88-17-92-94		Cons	PPE/DE
Sudre, Margie	France	3-88-17-94-73		UMP	PPE/DE
Sumberg, David	UK	3-88-17-93-72		Cons	PPE/DE
Surján, László	Hungary	3-88-17-98-35	lsurjan@europarl.eu.int	FIDESZ-MPSZ	PPE/DE
Svensson, Eva-Britt	Sweden	3-88-17-91-05	e-b.svensson@bredband.net	V	GUE/NGL
Swoboda, Johannes.	Austria			SPÖ	PSE
Szájer, József.	Hungary	3-88-17-98-71	jszajer@europarl.eu.int	FIDESZ-MPSZ	PPE/DE
Szejna, Andrzej Jan	Poland	3-88-17-96-52	aszejna@europarl.eu.int	SLD-UP	PSE
Szent-Iványi, István	Hungary	3-88-17-95-78	istvan.szent-ivanyi@parlament.hu	SZDSZ	ALDE
Szymański, Konrad Krzysztof	Poland	3-88-17-91-36	redakcja@mpp.org.pl	PiS	UEN
Tabajdi, Csaba Sándor	Hungary	3-88-17-98-21	csaba.tabajdi@parlament.hu	MSZP	PSE
Tajani, Antonio	Italy	3-88-17-93-96	atajani@europarl.eu.int	FI	PPE/DE
Takkula, Hannu	Finland	3-88-17-98-51	htakkula@europarl.eu.int	KESK	ALDE
Tannock, Charles	UK	3-88-17-98-70		Cons	PPE/DE
Tarabella, Marc.	Belgium		mtarabella@europarl.eu.int	PS	PSE
Tarand, Andres	Estonia	3-88-17-94-29	andres.tarand@riigikogu.ee	SDE	PSE
Tatarella, Salvatore	Italy	3-88-17-92-76		AN	UEN
Thomsen, Britta	Denmark	3-88-17-94-52		A	PSE
Thyssen, Marianne	Belgium	3-88-17-99-18	mthyssen@europarl.eu.int	CD&V-N.VA	PPE/DE
Titford, Jeffrey William	UK	3-88-17-97-58	eastern@ukip.org	UKIP	IND/DEM
Titley, Gary.	UK	3-88-17-92-12	gtitley@europarl.eu.int	Lab	PSE
Toia, Patrizia	Italy	3-88-17-91-27	ptoia@europarl.eu.int	Uniti nell'Ulivo	PPE/DE
Tomczak, Witold	Poland	3-88-17-92-41		LPR	IND/DEM
Toubon, Jacques	France	3-88-17-91-66		UMP	PPE/DE
Toussas, Georgios	Greece	3-88-17-92-78		KKE	GUE/NGL
Trakatellis, Antonios	Greece	3-88-17-97-62	atrakatellis@europarl.eu.int	ND	PPE/DE
Trautmann, Catherine	France	3-88-17-94-25		PS	PSE
Triantaphyllides, Kyriacos . .	Cyprus	3-88-17-99-58		AKEL-ARISTERA-ND	GUE/NGL
Trüpel, Helga	Germany		helga.truepel@t-online.de	Grüne	V/ALE
Turmes, Claude.	Luxembourg	3-88-17-92-46	cturmes@europarl.eu.int	Déi Gréng	V/ALE
Tzampazi, Evangelia.	Greece	3-88-17-93-45	etzampazi@europarl.eu.int	PASOK	PSE
Uca, Feleknas	Germany	3-88-17-94-19	fuca@europarl.eu.int	PDS	GUE/NGL
Ulmer, Thomas	Germany	3-88-17-93-14	doculmer@aol.com	CDU	PPE/DE
Väyrynen, Paavo	Finland	3-88-17-98-50	pvayrynen@europarl.eu.int	KESK	ALDE
Vaidere, Inese	Latvia	3-88-17-96-39	inese@leaf.lv	TB/LNNK	UEN
Vakalis, Nikolaos	Greece	3-88-17-99-37		ND	PPE/DE
Valenciano Martínez-Orozco, María Elena	Spain	3-88-17-94-40	evalenciano@ukip.org	PSOE	PSE
Vanhecke, Frank.	Belgium	3-88-17-91-08		Vl Blok	NI
Van Hecke, Johan	Belgium	3-88-17-91-90	jvanhecke@europarl.eu.int	VLD	ALDE
Van Lancker, Anne	Belgium	3-88-17-94-94	avanlancker@europarl.eu.int	SP.A-SPIRIT	PSE
Van Orden, Geoffrey	UK	3-88-17-93-32		Cons	PPE/DE
Varela Suanzes-Carpegna, Daniel	Spain	3-88-17-99-50	dvarela@europparl.eu.int	PP	PPE/DE
Varvitsiotis, Ioannis	Greece	3-88-17-96-80		ND	PPE/DE
Vatanen, Ari	France	3-88-17-99-95	avatanen@europarl.eu.int	UMP	PPE/DE
Vaugrenard, Yannick	France	3-88-17-91-13		PS	PSE
Ventre, Riccardo	Italy	3-88-17-94-61	info@riccardoventre.org	FI	PPE/DE
Verges, Paul	France	3-88-17-91-24		PCF	GUE/NGL
Vergnaud, Bernadette.	France	3-88-17-92-10		PS	PSE
Vernola, Marcello	Italy	3-88-17-93-04	marcellovernola@tiscalinet.it	FI	PPE/DE
Vidal-Quadras Roca, Alejo . .	Spain	3-88-17-93-22	avidal@europarl.eu.int	PP	PPE/DE
Villiers, Philippe de	France	3-88-17-98-95		MPF	IND/DEM
Villiers, Theresa	UK	3-88-17-97-58	tvilliers@europarl.eu.int	Cons	PPE/DE
Vincenzi, Marta.	Italy	3-88-17-93-31	mvincenzi@europarl.eu.int	Uniti nell'Ulivo	PSE
Virrankoski, Kyösti Tapio. . .	Finland	3-88-17-98-47	kvirrankoski@europarl.eu.int	KESK	ALDE
Vlasák, Oldřich	Czech Republic	3-88-17-93-57	oldrich.vlasak@mmhk.cz	ODS	PPE/DE
Vlasto, Dominique.	France	3-88-17-91-61		UMP	PPE/DE
Voggenhuber, Johannes	Austria	3-88-17-92-72	jvoggenhuber@europarl.eu.int	Grüne	V/ALE
Wagenknecht, Sahra.	Germany	3-88-17-96-19	swagenknecht@europarl.eu.int	PDS	GUE/NGL
Wallis, Diana	UK	3-88-17-92-01	diana@dianawallismep.org.uk	LD	ALDE
Walter, Ralf.	Germany	3-88-17-94-26	ralf.walter.mdep@t-online.de	SPD	PSE
Watson, Graham R.	UK	3-88-17-96-26	gwatson@europarl.eu.int	LD	ALDE
Weber, Henri.	France	3-88-17-97-88	hweber@europarl.eu.int	PS	PSE
Weber, Manfred	Germany	3-88-17-98-90	info@weber-manfred.de	CSU	PPE/DE
Weiler, Barbara.	Germany	3-88-17-94-39	b.weiler.mdep@t-online.de	SPD	PSE

Name—*continued*	Member State	Telephone	E-mail	Party	Political Group
Weisgerber, Anja	Germany	3-88-17-93-37		CSU	PPE/DE
Westlund, Åsa	Sweden	3-88-17-95-86		SAP	PSE
Whitehead, Phillip	UK	3-88-17-94-59	pwhitehead@europarl.eu.int	Lab	PSE
Whittaker, John	UK	3-88-17-91-69		UKIP	IND/DEM
Wieland, Rainer	Germany	3-88-17-95-45	rwieland@europarl.eu.int	CDU	PPE/DE
Wiersma, Jan Marinus	Netherlands	3-88-17-94-35	jwiersma@europarl.eu.int	PvdA	PSE
Wierzejski, Wojciech	Poland	3-88-17-96-59		LPR	IND/DEM
Wijkman, Anders	Sweden	3-88-17-94-01		KD	PPE/DE
Wise, Thomas Harold	UK	3-88-17-95-98	tomwise@ukip.org	UKIP	IND/DEM
Wogau, Karl von	Germany	3-88-17-93-01	info@wogau.de	CDU	PPE/DE
Wohlin, Lars	Sweden	3-88-17-96-79	lars-wohlin@telia.com	Junilistan	IND/DEM
Wojciechowski, Janusz Czesław	Poland	3-88-17-98-02	biuronkw@nkw.psl.org.pl	PSL	PPE/DE
Wortmann-Kool, Corien M.	Netherlands	3-88-17-95-70	cwortmann@europarl.eu.int	CDA	PPE/DE
Wuermeling, Joachim	Germany	3-88-17-97-11	jwuermeling@europarl.eu.int	CSU	PPE/DE
Wurtz, Francis	France	3-88-17-91-06		PCF	GUE/NGL
Wynn, Terence	UK	3-88-17-95-10	twynn@europarl.eu.int	Lab	PSE
Xenogiannakopoulou, Marilisa	Greece	3-88-17-93-43		PASOK	PSE
Yañez-Barnuevo García, Luis	Spain	3-88-17-97-18		PSOE	PPE/DE
Záborská, Anna	Slovakia	3-88-17-99-23	azaborska@europarl.eu.int	KDH	IND/DEM
Zahradil, Jan	Czech Republic	3-88-17-96-66	jzahradil@europarl.eu.int	ODS	PPE/DE
Zaleski, Zbigniew	Poland	3-88-17-94-81	zal@kul.lublin.pl	PO	PPE/DE
Zani, Secondo	Italy	3-88-17-95-26		Uniti nell'Ulivo	PSE
Zappala, Stefano	Italy	3-88-17-92-08	szappala@europarl.eu.int	FI	PPE/DE
Zatloukal, Tomáš	Czech Republic	3-88-17-95-34		SNK	PPE/DE
Ždanoka, Tatjana	Latvia	3-88-17-99-12	tat-zhdanok@yandex.ru	PCTVL	V/ALE
Železný, Vladimír	Czech Republic	3-88-17-92-95	Vladimir.zelezny@centrum.cz	Non-party	IND/DEM
Zieleniec, Josef	Czech Republic	3-88-17-95-40		SNK	PPE/DE
Zīle, Roberts	Latvia	3-88-17-92-24		TB/LNNK	UEN
Zimmer, Gabriele	Germany	3-88-17-91-01		PDS	GUE/NGL
Zingaretti, Nicola	Italy	3-88-17-93-88		Uniti nell'Ulivo	PSE
Zvěřina, Jaroslav	Czech Republic	3-88-17-94-83	zverina@mbox.vol.cz	ODS	PPE/DE
Zwiefka, Tadeusz Antoni	Poland	3-88-17-92-58		PO	PPE/DE

TRANSNATIONAL PARTY GROUPS—ACRONYMS

IND/DEM	Independence/Democracy Group
ALDE	Alliance of Liberals and Democrats for Europe
GUE/NGL	Confederal Group of the European United Left/Nordic Green Left
NI	Non-attached
PPE/DE	Group of the European People's Party (Christian Democrats) and European Democrats
PSE	Group of the Party of European Socialists
UEN	Union for Europe of the Nations Group
V/ALE	Group of the Greens/European Free Alliance

NATIONAL PARTIES AND LISTS—ACRONYMS

Agalev	Anders Gaan Leven (Belgium)
AKEL-ARISTERA-ND	Anorthotiko Komma Ergazomenou Laou-Aristera-Nees Dynameis (Cyprus)
AN	Alleanza Nazionale (Italy)
B	Det Radikale Venstre (Denmark)
BNG	Bloque Nacionalista Galego (Spain)
BS	België Spirit (Belgium)
C	Det Konservative Folkeparti (Denmark)
CCD	Centro Cristiano Democratico (Italy)
CDA	Christen-Democratisch Appel (Netherlands)
CDC	Convergència Democràtica de Catalunya (Spain)
CDU	Christlich-Demokratische Union Deutschlands (Germany)
CDU	Cristiani Democratici Uniti (Italy)
CDV	Christen-Democratisch and Vlaams (Belgium)
Cons	Conservative and Unionist Party (United Kingdom)
CP	Centerpartiet (Sweden)
CPNT	Chasse, Pêche, Nature, Traditions (France)
CSP-EVP	Christliche Soziale Partei—Europäische Volkspartei (Belgium)
ČSSD	Česká strana sociálně demokratická (Czech Republic)
CSU	Christlich-Soziale Union in Bayern eV (Germany)
CU–SGP	ChristenUnie–Staatkundig Gereformeerde Parti (Netherlands)
CVP	Christelijke Volkspartij (Belgium)
D66	Democraten 66 (Netherlands)
DF	Dansk Folkeparti (Denmark)
DFS	Den Frie Socialdemokratiet (Denmark)
DI.KO	Dimokratiko Komma (Cyprus)
DI.SY	Dimokratikos Synagermos (Cyprus)

DKK	Dimokratiko Kinoniko Kinima (Greece)
DL	Démocratie Libérale (France)
DP	Darbo partija (Lithuania)
DP	Demokratesch Partei (Luxembourg)
DRV	Det Radikale Venstre (Denmark)
DS	Democratici di Sinistra (Italy)
DUP	Democratic Unionist Party (United Kingdom)
ECOLO	Ecolo (Belgium)
EH	Euskal Herritarrok (Spain)
ER	Eesti Reformierakond (Estonia)
ERC	Esquerra Republicana de Catalunya (Spain)
F	Socialistisk Folkeparti (Denmark)
Fed Verdi	Federazione dei Verdi (Italy)
FF	Fianna Fáil (Ireland)
FG	Fine Gael (Ireland)
FIDESZ-MPSZ	Fidesz-Magyar Polgári Szövetség (Hungary)
FI	Forza Italia (Italy)
FmEU	Folkebevægelsen mod EU (Denmark)
FN	Front National (Belgium and France)
FP	Folkpartiet liberalerna (Sweden)
FPÖ	Freiheitliche Partei Österreichs (Austria)
GL	GroenLinks (Netherlands)
GP	Green Party (Ireland and United Kingdom)
G-PE	Galeuska – Pueblos de Europa (Spain)
Grüne	Bündnis 90/Die Grünen (Germany)
Grüne	Die Grünen–Die Grüne Alternative (Austria)
HZDS	L'udová strana-Hnutie za demokratické Slovensko (Slovakia)
ID	I Democratici (Italy)
IdV–LDP	Italia dei Valori–Lista Di Pietro (Italy)
IL	Erakond Isamaaliit (Estonia)
IU-IPCV-EUA	Izquierda Unida – Iniciativa per Catalunya Verds – Esquerra Unida i Alternativa (Spain)
J	JuniBevægelsen (Denmark)
JL	Jaunais laiks (Latvia)
K	Eesti Keskerakond (Estonia)
Kd	Kristdemokraterna (Sweden)
KDU-ČSL	Křest'anskà a demokratická unie – Československá strana lidová (Czech Republic)
Kesk	Suomen Keskusta (Finland)
KF	Det Konservative Folkeparti (Denmark)
KKE	Kommunistiko Komma Ellados (Greece)
Kok	Kansallinen Kokoomus (Finland)
KSČM	Komunistická strana Čech a Moravy (Czech Republic)
Lab	Labour Party (Ireland and United Kingdom)
LC	Latvijas Cels (Latvia)
LCR	Ligue Communiste Révolutionnaire (France)
LCS	Liberalu ir Centro Sajunga (Lithuania)
LD	Liberal Democrats (United Kingdom)

LDP	Liberalu demokratu partija (Lithuania)
LDS	Liberalna Demokracija Slovenije (Slovenia)
LEB	Lista Emma Bonino (Italy)
LIF	Liberales Forum (Austria)
LN	Lega Nord per l'Independenza della Padania (Italy)
LO	Lutte Ouvrière (France)
LPR	Liga Polskich Rodzin (Poland)
MCC	Mouvement des Citoyens pour le Changement (Belgium)
MdC	Mouvement des Citoyens (France)
MDF	Magyar Demokrata Fórum (Hungary)
MLP	Partit Laburista (Malta)
MP	Miljöpartiet (Sweden)
MPF	Mouvement pour la France (France)
MS	Moderata Samlingspartiet (Sweden)
MSZP	Magyar Szocialista Párt (Hungary)
ND	Nea Dimokratia (Greece)
Non-party	Not belonging to any national party
NSi	Nova Slovenija (Slovenia)
NUDF	Nouvelle Union pour la Démocratie Française (France)
NUDF Rad	Nouvelle Union pour la Démocratie Française—Parti Radical
ODS	Občanská demokratická strana (Czech Republic)
ÖVP	Österreichische Volkspartei (Austria)
PA	Partido Andalucista (Spain)
PaS	Patto Segni Liberaldemocratici (Italy)
PASOK	Panellinion Socialistikon Kinema (Greece)
PC	Plaid Cymru (United Kingdom)
PCF	Parti Communiste Français (France)
PCP	Partido Comunista Português (Portugal)
PCS	Parti Chrétien Social (Luxembourg)
PCTVL	Par cilvēka tiesībām vienotā Latvijā (Latvia)
PdCI	Partito dei Comunisti Italiani (Italy)
PdDS	Partei des Demokratischen Sozialismus (Germany)
PDL	Parti Démocratique Luxembourgeois (Luxembourg)
PiS	Prawo i Sprawiedliwość (Poland)
PN	Partit Nazzjonalista (Malta)
PNV	Partido Nacionalista Vasco (Spain)
PO	Platforma Obywatelska (Poland)
POSL	Parti Ouvrier Socialiste Luxembourgeois (Luxembourg)
PP	Partido Popular (Spain)
PP	Partido Popular (formerly Partido do Centro Democrático Social, Portugal)
PPen	Partito Pensionati (Italy)
PPI	Partito Popolare Italiano (Italy)
PPInd	Partido Popular (Independiente) (Spain)
PRep	Pôle Républicain (France)

PRG	Parti Radical de Gauche (France)
PRI	Partito Repubblicano Italiano (Italy)
PRL	Parti Réformateur Libéral (Belgium)
PRL/FDF	Parti Réformateur Libéral/ Front Démocratique des Francophones (Belgium)
PS	Parti Socialiste (Belgium and France)
PS	Partido Socialista (Portugal)
PSC	Parti Social-Chrétien (Belgium)
PSC	Partit dels Socialistes de Catalunya (Spain)
PSD	Partido Social-Democrata (Portugal)
PSI	Partito Socialista Italiano (Italy)
PSL	Polskie Stronnictwo Ludowe (Poland)
PSOE	Partido Socialista Obrero Español (Spain)
PSOEInd	Partido Socialista Obrero Español (Independiente) (Spain)
PvdA	Partij van de Arbeid (Netherlands)
RC	Partito della Rifondazione Comunista (Italy)
RI	Rinnovamento Italiano (Italy)
RPF	Rassemblement pour la France (France)
RPR	Rassemblement pour la République (France)
RV	Det Radikale Venstre (Denmark)
S	Socialdemokratiet (Denmark)
SAP	Sveriges Socialdemokratiska Arbetareparti (Sweden)
SDE	Sotsiaaldemokraatlik Erakond (Estonia)
SDI	Socialisti Democratici Italiani (Italy)
SDLP	Social Democratic and Labour Party (United Kingdom)
SDP	Suomen Sosialidemokraattinen Puolue (Finland)
SDPL	Socjaldemocracja Polska (Poland)
SDS	Socialdemokratska stranka Slovenije (Slovenia)
SF	Socialistisk Folkeparti (Denmark)
SFP	Svenska Folkpartiet (Finland)
SGP/GPV/ RPF	Staatkundig Gereformeerde Partij/Gereformeerd Politiek Verbond/ Reformatorische Politieke Federatie (Netherlands)
SKD	Suomen Kristillisdemokraatit (Finland)
SKDÚ	Slovenská Demokratická a Kresťanská Únia (Slovakia)
SLD-UP	Sojusz Lewicy Demokratycznej – Unia Pracy (Poland)
SMER	Smer (Slovakia)
SMK-MKP	Strana maďarskej koalície-Magyar Koalíció Pártja (Slovakia)
SNK	Sdružení nezávislých a Evropští demokraté (Czech Republic)
SNP	Scottish National Party (United Kingdom)
SO	Samoobrona RP (Poland)
SP	Socialistische Partij (Belgium and Netherlands)

SPD	Sozialdemokratische Partei Deutschlands (Germany)
SPÖ	Sozialdemokratische Partei Österreichs (Austria)
SVP	Südtiroler Volkspartei (Italy)
Synaspismos	Synaspismos tis Aristeras kai tis Proodou (Greece)
SZDSZ	Szabad Demokraták Szövetsége (Hungary)
TB/LNNK	Tēvzemei un Brīvībai/LNNK (Latvia)
TP	Tautas partija (Latvia)
TS	Tēvynės sąjunga (Lithuania)
UDC	Unió Democràtica de Catalunya (Spain)
UDE	Unione Democratici per L'Europa (Italy)
UKIP	UK Independence Party (United Kingdom)
UMP	Union pour un Mouvement Populaire (France)
UUP	Ulster Unionist Party (United Kingdom)
UV	Unione Valdôtaine (Italy)
UV	Unió Valenciana (Spain)
UW	Unia Wolnisci (Poland)
V	Venstre (Denmark)
VEE	Verts-Europe-Ecologie (France)
Vihr	Vihreä Liitto (Finland)
Vl Blok	Vlaams Blok (Belgium)
VLD	Vlaamse Liberalen en Demokraten (Belgium)
VNDPS	Valstiečių ir Naujosios demokratijos partijų sąjunga (Lithuania)
VP	Vänsterpartiet (Sweden)
VU	Volksunie (Belgium)
VV	Vasemmistoliitto Vänsterförbundet (Finland)
VVD	Volkspartij voor Vrijheid en Democratie (Netherlands)
ZLSD	Združena lista socialnih demokratov (Slovenia)

Committees and Interparliamentary Delegations

(April 2004)

COMMITTEES

C1 Committee on Budgets

Chairman: Janusz Lewandowski (PPE/ DE).

Vice-Chairmen: Ralf Walter (PSE), Jan de Heer Mulder (ALDE), Reimer Böge (PPE/DE).

C2 Committee on Budgetary Control

Chairman: Szabolcs Fazakas (PSE).

Vice-Chairmen: Nils Lundgren (EDD), Herbert Bösch (PSE), Petr Duchon (PPE/ DE).

C3 Committee on Economic and Monetary Affairs

Chairman: Christa Randzio-Plath (PSE).

Vice-Chairmen: José García-Margallo y Marfil (PPE/DE), Philippe Herzog (GUE/ NGL), John Purvis (PPE/DE).

C4 Committee on Employment and Social Affairs

Chairman: Ottaviano Del Turco (PSE).

Vice-Chairmen: Ilda Figueiredo (GUE/ NGL), Jan Andersson (PSE), Thomas Mann (PPE/DE).

C5 Committee on Environment, Public Health and Food Safety

Chairman: Karl-Heinz Florenz (PPE/ DE).

Vice-Chairmen: Johannes Blokland (EDD), Hassi Maijastiina (V/ALE), Andrejevs Georgs (ALDE).

C6 Committee on Industry, Research and Energy

Chairman: Giles Bryan Chichester (PPE/DE).

Vice-Chairmen: Miroslav Ransdorf (GUE/NGL), Britta Thomsen (PSE), Renato Brunetta (PPE/DE).

C7 Committee on the Internal Market and Consumer Protection

Chairman: Phillip Whitehead (PSE).

Vice-Chairmen: Zuzana Roithová (PPE/ DE), Marco Rizzo (GUE/NGL).

C8 Committee on Transport and Tourism

Chairman: Paolo Costa (ALDE).

Vice-Chairmen: Luís Queiró (PPE/DE), Sylwester Chruszcz (EDD), Gilles Savary (PSE).

C9 Committee on Regional Development

Chairman: Gerardo Galeote Quecedo (PPE/DE).

Vice-Chairmen: Giovanni Claudio Fava (PSE), Jan Marian Olbrycht (PPE/DE), Elspeth Attwooll (ALDE).

C10 Committee on Agriculture

Chairman: Joseph Daul (PPE/DE).

Vice-Chairmen: Friedrich-Wilhelm Graefe zu Baringdorf (V/ALE), Jean-Claude Fruteau (PSE), Janusz Czesław Wojciechowski (PPE/DE).

C11 Committee on Fisheries

Chairman: Philippe Morillon (ALDE).

Vice-Chairmen: Antonio De Poli (PPE/DE), Philippe de Villiers (EDD), Rosa Miguélez Ramos (PSE).

C12 Committee on Culture and Education

Chairman: Nikolaos Sifunakis (PSE).

Vice-Chairmen: Pál Schmitt (PPE/DE), Helga Trüpel (V/ALE), Manolis Mavrommatis (PPE/DE).

C13 Committee on Legal Affairs

Chairman: Guiseppe Gargani (PPE/DE).

Vice-Chairmen: Andrzej Jan Szejna (PSE), Rainer Wieland (PPE/DE), Katalin Lévai (PSE).

C14 Committee on Civil Liberties, Justice and Home Affairs

Chairman: Jean-Louis Bourlanges (ALDE).

Vice-Chairmen: Stefano Zappala (PPE/DE), Stavros Lambrinidis (PSE), Patrick Gaubert (PPE/DE).

C15 Committee on Constitutional Affairs

Chairman: Jo Leinen (PSE).

Vice-Chairmen: Johannes Voggenhuber (V/ALE), Riccardo Ventre (PPE/DE), Ignasi Guardans Cambó (ALDE).

C16 Committee on Women's Rights and Equal Opportunities

Chairman: Anna Karamanou (PSE).

Vice-Chairmen: Edite Estrela (PSE), Eva-Britt Svensson (GUE/NGL), Zita Gurmai (PSE).

C17 Committee on Petitions

Chairman: Marcin Libicki (UEN).

Vice-Chairmen: Michael Cashman (PSE), Marie Panayotopoulos-Cassiotou (PPE/DE), Maria Matsouka (PSE).

ACP–EU JOINT ASSEMBLY

Seventy-seven members from the European Parliament participate in the Joint Assembly of the Agreement between the African, Caribbean and Pacific (ACP) States and the European Union (EU) (ACP–EU). The ACP States are listed in the ACP–EU Institutions section of the Council of the European Union.

Co-Presidents: Glenys Kinnock (PSE), Ramdien Sardjoe.

Vice-Presidents: Giuseppe Brienza (PPE/DE), Niels Busk (ALDE), Marie-Arlette Carlotti (PSE), Thierry Cornillet (PPE/DE), John Corrie (PPE/DE), Concepció Ferrer i Casals (PPE/DE), Karin Junker (PSE), Miguel Martínez Martínez (PSE), Konrad Schwaiger (PPE/DE), Fodé Sylla (GUE/NGL), Maj Britt Theorin (PSE), Didier Rod (V/ALE).

INTERPARLIAMENTARY DELEGATIONS

Europe

Delegation to the EU–Bulgaria Joint Parliamentary Committee

Delegation for relations with Switzerland, Iceland and Norway and to the European Economic Area (EEA) Joint Parliamentary Committee

Delegation to the EU–Former Yugoslav Republic of Macedonia Joint Parliamentary Committee

Delegation to the EU–Romania Joint Parliamentary Committee

Delegation to the EU–Turkey Joint Parliamentary Committee

Delegation to the EU–Armenia, EU–Azerbaijan and EU–Georgia Parliamentary Co-operation Committees

Delegation to the EU–Moldova Parliamentary Co-operation Committee

Delegation to the EU–Russia Parliamentary Co-operation Committee

Delegation to the EU–Ukraine Parliamentary Co-operation Committee

Delegation for relations with Albania, Bosnia and Herzegovina, and Serbia and Montenegro (including Kosovo)

Delegation for relations with Belarus

Outside Europe

Delegation to the EU–Chile Joint Parliamentary Committee

Delegation to the EU–Mexico Joint Parliamentary Committee

Delegation to the EU–Kazakhstan, EU–Kyrgyzstan and EU–Uzbekistan Parliamentary Co-operation Committees and Delegation for relations with Tajikistan, Turkmenistan and Mongolia

Delegation for relations with Israel

Delegation for relations with the Palestinian Legislative Council

Delegation for relations with the Maghreb countries and the Arab Maghreb Union (including Libya)

Delegation for relations with the Mashreq countries

Delegation for relations with the Gulf States, including Yemen

Delegation for relations with Iran

Delegation for relations with the United States

Delegation for relations with Canada

Delegation for relations with the countries of Central America

Delegation for relations with the countries of the Andean Community

Delegation for relations with MERCOSUR

Delegation for relations with Japan

Delegation for relations with the People's Republic of China

Delegation for relations with the countries of South Asia and the South Asia Association for Regional Co-operation (SAARC)

Delegation for relations with the countries of Southeast Asia and the Association of Southeast Asian Nations (ASEAN)

Delegation for relations with the Korean Peninsula

Delegation for relations with Australia and New Zealand

Delegation for relations with South Africa

Other Interparliamentary Delegations

Delegations for relations with the NATO Parliamentary Assembly

Transnational Party Groups within the European Parliament

GROUP OF THE PARTY OF EUROPEAN SOCIALISTS (PSE)

(200 members)

Secretariat

rue Wiertz, 1047 Brussels, Belgium; tel (2) 284-21-11; fax (2) 230-66-64; e-mail webmaster@socialistgroup.org; internet www.socialistgroup.org.

Secretary-General: David Harley.

Deputy Secretaries-General: Jesper Schunck, Anna Colombo.

GROUP OF THE EUROPEAN PEOPLE'S PARTY AND EUROPEAN DEMOCRATS (PPE/DE)

(268 members)

Secretariat

rue Wiertz, 1047 Brussels, Belgium; tel (2) 284-22-34; fax (2) 230-62-08; Luxembourg; tel (2) 4300-1; e-mail epp-ed@europarl.eu.int; internet www.epp-ed.org.

Secretary-General: Niels Pederson.

Chef de Cabinet and Deputy Secretary-General: John Biesmans.

Deputy Secretaries-General: Johann Friedrich Colsman, Anthony Teasdale, Paolo Licandro.

Chairman of Group: Hans-Gert Pöttering.

Vice-Chairmen: João de Deus Pinheiro, Ville Itälä, Marianne Thyssen, József Szájer, Lorenzo Cesa, Jaime Mayor Oreja, Françoise Grossetête, Timothy Kirkhope.

Treasurer: Othmar Karas.

UNION FOR A EUROPE OF NATIONS GROUP (UEN)

(27 members)

Secretariat

rue Wiertz, 1047 Brussels, Belgium; tel (2) 284-29-44; fax (2) 284-49-88; e-mail fbarrett@europarl.eu.int; internet www.europarl.en.int/uen.

Secretary-General: Frank Barrett.

Deputy Secretary-General: Eugenio Preta.

Chairman of Group: Charles Pasqua.

Vice-Chairmen: Mogens Camre, Gerard Collins, Cristiana Muscardini, Luís Queiró, Michal Tomasz Kaminski, Guntars Krasts, Janno Reiljan, Rudolf Ziak.

Treasurer: Mauro Nobilia.

ALLIANCE OF LIBERALS AND DEMOCRATS FOR EUROPE (ALDE)

(88 members)

Secretariat

rue Wiertz, 1047 Brussels, Belgium; tel (2) 284-21-11; fax (2) 230-24-85; e-mail aldegroup@europarl.eu.int; internet www.eurolib.org.

Secretary-General: Alexander Beels.

Deputy Secretary-General: Niccolò Rinaldi.

Chairman of Group: Graham Watson.

Vice-Chairmen: Silvana Koch-Mehrin, Karin Riis-Jørgensen, Marielle de Sarnez, Eugenijus Gentvilas, Lapo Pistelli.

CONFEDERAL GROUP OF THE EUROPEAN UNITED LEFT/NORDIC GREEN LEFT (GUE/NGL)

(41 members)

Secretariat

rue Wiertz, 1047 Brussels, Belgium; tel (2) 284-26-85; fax (2) 284-17-74; e-mail guengl@europarl.eu.int; internet www.europarl.eu.int/gue.

Secretary-General: Maria D'Alimonte.

Deputy Secretaries-General: Stellan Hermansson, Stefano Squarcina.

Chairman of Group: Francis Wurtz.

Vice-Chairman: Sylvia-Yvonne Kaufmann.

Treasurer: Helmuth Markov.

GREENS/EUROPEAN FREE ALLIANCE GROUP (V/ALE)

(42 members)

Secretariat

Bâtiment Leopold 2c, rue Wiertz, 1047 Brussels, Belgium; tel (2) 284-30-45; fax (2) 230-78-37; internet www.greens-efa.org.

Secretaries-General: Juan Behrend, Vula Tsetsi.

Deputy Secretary-General: Neil Fergusson.

Co-chairmen of Group: Daniel Cohn-Bendit, Monica Frassoni.

Vice-Chairmen: Pierre Jonckheer, Jean Lambert, Heide Rühle, Claude Turmes.

GROUP OF INDEPENDENTS (NI)

(28 members)

Secretariat

rue Wiertz, 1047 Brussels, Belgium; tel (2) 284-25-79; fax (2) 284-69-49.

Chairman of Group: Francesco Speroni.

Co-ordinator: Germano Vecchio Verderame.

INDEPENDENCE/ DEMOCRACY GROUP (IND/DEM)

(37 members)

Secretariat

rue Wiertz, 1047 Brussels, Belgium; tel (2) 284-51-67; fax (2) 284-91-67.

Co-Presidents: Jens-Peter Bonde, Nigel Farage.

Chairman of Bureau: Maciej Marian Giertych.

Treasurer: Hans Blokland.

National Parties and Lists Represented in the European Parliament

AUSTRIA

Freiheitliche Partei Österreichs (FPÖ/Die Freiheitlichen) (Freedom Party): Esslingasse 14–16, 1010 Vienna; tel (1) 512-35-35; fax (1) 513-35-35-9; internet www.fpoe.at; Chair: Dr Susanne Riess-Passer; Gen Secs: Peter Sichrovsky, Theresia Zierler; f 1955, partially succeeding the Verband der Unabhängigen (League of Independents, f 1949); popularly known as Die Freiheitlichen; populist right-wing party advocating the participation of workers in management, stricter immigration controls and deregulation in the business sector; opposes Austria's membership of the European Union.

Die Grünen–Die Grüne Alternative (Greens–Green Alternative): Lindengasse 40, 1070 Vienna; tel (1) 521-25-0; fax (1) 526-91-10; e-mail bundesbuero@gruene.at; internet www.gruene.at; Chair: Prof Dr Alexander Van der Bellen; campaigns for environmental protection, peace and social justice.

Liste Dr Hans-Peter Martin: e-mail office@hpmartin.net; internet www.hpmartin.net/htmlStatic; f. 2004.

Österreichische Volkspartei (ÖVP) (Austrian People's Party): Lichtenfelsgasse 7, 1010 Vienna; tel (1) 401-26; fax (1) 401-26-329; Office for European Union Affairs: tel (1) 401-26-312; e-mail email@oevp.or.at; internet www.oevp.at; Chair: Dr Wolfgang Schüssel; Sec-Gen: Reinhold Lopatka; f 1945; Christian-Democratic party; advocates an ecologically orientated social market economy.

Sozialdemokratische Partei Österreichs (SPÖ) (Social-Democratic Party of Austria): Löwelstr 18, 1014 Vienna; tel (1) 534-27-0; fax (1) 535-96-83; e-mail spoe@spoe.at; internet www.spoe.or.at; Chair: Dr Alfred Gusenbauer; Secs: Norbert Darabos, Doris Bures; f 1889 as the Social-Democratic Party, subsequently renamed the Socialist Party, reverted to its original name in June 1991; advocates democratic socialism and Austria's permanent neutrality.

BELGIUM

Centre Démocrate Humaniste (CDH): 41 rue des Deux-Eglises, 1000 Brussels; tel (2) 238-01-11; fax (2) 238-01-29; e-mail info@lecdh.be; internet www.lecdh.be; Pres: Joelle Milquet; Vice-Pres: Ingrid Eloy; f 1945 as the Parti Social Chretien/Christelijke Volkspartij (PSC/CVP), the PSC separated from the CVP by 1972, name changed as above in May 2002.

Christen-Democratisch en Vlaams Partij (CD&V): 89 Wetstraat, 1040 Brussels; tel (2) 238-38-11; fax (2) 238-01-29; e-mail inform@cdenv.be; internet www.cdenv.be; Pres: Yves Leterme; f 1945; formerly known as Christelijke Volkspartij; Christian Social Party's Dutch-speaking wing.

Christliche Soziale Partei–Europäische Volkspartei (CSP–EVP): c/o European Parliament, rue Wiertz, 1047 Brussels; tel (2) 284-21-11; fax (2) 230-69-33; Pres: Hubert Chantraine; Christian Social Party's German-speaking wing.

Ecologistes Confédérés pour l'Organisation de Luttes Originales (ECOLO): 12 rue Charles VI, 1200 Brussels; tel (2) 218-30-35; fax (2) 217-52-90; e-mail service.presse@ecolo.be; internet www.ecolo.be; Fed Secs: Jacques Bauduin, Philippe Defeyt, Brigitte Ernst; Ecologist Party; French-speaking.

Groen!: Sergeant De Bruynestraat 78–82, 1070 Anderlecht; tel. (2) 219-19-19; fax (2) 223-10-90; e-mail info@groen.be; internet www.groen.be; Chair: Vera Dua; f 1982; formerly known as Anders Gaan Leven (Agalev), name changed 2003.

Mouvement des Citoyens pour le Changement (MCC): 50 rue de la Vallée, 1000 Brussels; tel (2) 642-29-99; fax (2) 642-29-90; e-mail info@lemcc.be; internet www.lemcc.be; Pres: Nathalie De T'Serclaes; forms part of Mouvement Réformateur alliance.

Mouvement Réformateur (MR): 39 rue de Naples, 1050 Brussels; tel. (2) 500-35-43; fax (2) 500-35-42; e-mail mr@mr.be; internet www.mr.be; f 2002; Pres: Antoine Duquesne; formed through alliance of the Front Démocratique des Francophones (FDF), Mouvement des Citoyens pour le Changement (MCC) and Parti Réformateur Libéral (PRL).

Parti Réformateur Libéral (PRL): 41 rue de Naples, 1050 Brussels; tel (2) 500-35-11; fax (2) 500-35-00; e-mail prl@prl.be; Pres: Daniel Ducarme; f 1846 as Parti Libéral; Liberal Party's French-speaking wing; forms part of Mouvement Réformateur alliance.

Parti Socialiste (PS): Maison du PS, 13 blvd de l'Empereur, 1000 Brussels; tel (2) 548-32-11; fax (2) 548-33-80; e-mail secretariat@ps.be; internet www.ps.be; Pres: Elio di Rupo; Sec: Jean-Pol Baras; f 1885 as Parti Ouvrier Belge; split from Flemish wing in 1979; Socialist Party's French-speaking wing.

Nieuw-Vlaamse Alliantie (NVA): 12 Barrikadenplein, 1000 Brussels; tel (2) 219-49-30; fax (2) 217-35-10; e-mail info@n-va.be; internet www.n-va.be; f 2001 as breakaway group from Volksunie; Flemish nationalist party advocating a federal structure for Belgium and a European federation of nations and regions.

Sociaal Progressief Alternatief (SPA): 105/37 Grasmarkt, 1000 Brussels; tel (2) 552-02-00; fax (2) 552-02-55; e-mail info@s-p-a.be; internet www.s-p-a.be; Pres: Patrick Janssens; Sec: Alain André; f 1885 as Parti Ouvrier Belge, known as Socialistische Partij until 2001; split from French-speaking wing in 1979; Socialist Party's Flemish wing; forms an alliance in the European Parliament with Spirit.

Spirit–Sociaal, Progressief, Internationaal, Regionalistisch, Integraaldemocratisch en Toekomstgericht: Woeringenstraat 19, 1000 Brussels; tel (2) 513-20-63; fax (2) 512-85-75; e-mail info@meerspirit.be; internet www.meerspirit.be; Chair: Geerd Lambert; f 2001 as breakaway group from Volksunie; forms an alliance in the European Parliament with SPA.

Vlaams Blok (Vl Blok): 8 Madouplein, bus 9, 1210 Brussels; tel (2) 219-60-09; fax (2) 219-72-74; e-mail vlblok@vlaams-blok.be; Chair: Frank Vanhecke; Chief Officer: Luk Van Nieuwenhuysen; f 1979 as a breakaway party from the Volksunie; Flemish Bloc; advocates Flemish separatism and is anti-immigration.

Vlaamse Liberalen en Demokraten—Partij van de Burger (VLD): 34 Melsensstraat, 1000 Brussels; tel (2) 549-00-20; fax (2) 512-60-25; e-mail vld@vld.be; internet www.vld.be; Pres: Karel De Gendt; Sec-Gen: Clair Ysebaert; f 1961 as Partij voor Vrijheid en Vooruitgang, name changed, as above, 1992; Flemish Liberals and Democrats—Citizens' Party; Liberal Party's Flemish-speaking wing.

CYPRUS

Anorthotiko Komma Ergazomenou Laou-Aristera-Nees Dynameis (AKEL-ARISTERA-ND) (Progressive Party of Working People): 4 Ezekias Papaioannou Street, 1075 Nicosia; tel 22761121; fax 22761574; internet www.akel.org.cy; Sec-Gen: Demetris Christofias; f 1926; socialist; supports an independent, demilitarized and non-aligned Cyprus.

Dimokratiko Komma (DI.KO) (Democratic Party): 50 Grivas Dighenis Avenue, 1687 Nicosia; tel 22873800; fax 22873801; e-mail diko@diko.org.cy; internet www.diko.org.cy; Leader: Tassos Papadopoulos; f 1976; centre-right party.

Dimokratikos Synagermos (DI.SY) (Democratic Rally): 25 Pindarou Street, PO Box 25305, 1308 Nicosia; tel 22883000; fax 22753821; e-mail epikinonia@disy.org.cy; internet www.disy.org.cy; Pres: Nicos Anastasiades; Dir-Gen: George Liveras; f 1976; 35,000 mems.

Gia tin Evropi (For Europe): Salaminos 14, 2406 Egomi; Leader: Ionnis Matsis; f 2004 to contest the European election.

CZECH REPUBLIC

Česká strana sociálně demokratická (ČSSD) (Czech Social Democratic Party): Lidovy dum, Hybernska 7, 110 00 Prague; tel. (2) 96522111; e-mail info@socdem.cz; internet www.socdem.cz; Chair: Stanislav Gross; f 1878; prohibited 1948; re-established 1989; fmrly the Czechoslovak Social Democratic Party.

Komunistická strana Čech a Moravy (KSČM) (Communist Party of Bohemia and Moravia): Politických vìzù 9, 111 21 Prague; tel (2) 22897111; fax (2) 22897207; e-mail news@kscm.cz; internet www.kscm.cz; Leader: Miroslav Grebenicek; f 1991 as a result of the reorganization of the fmr Communist Party of Czechoslovakia; 108,000 mems.

Křesťanská a demokratická unie – Československá strana lidová (KDU – ČSL) (Christian Democratic Union – Czechoslovak People's Party): Palác Charitas Karlovo nám. 5, 128 01 Prague 2; tel (2) 24914793; fax (2) 24917630; e-mail info@kdu.cz; internet www.kdu.cz; Chair: Miroslav Kalousek; f 1992.

Občanská demokratická strana (ODS) (Civic Democratic Party): Jansky Vrsek 13, 118 00 Prague 1; tel (2) 34707111; fax (2) 34707101; e-mail hk@ods.cz; internet www.ods.cz; Leader: Mirek Topolanek; f 1991; moderate right-wing.

Sdružení nezávislých a Evropští demokraté (SNK-ED) (Union of Independents–European Democrats): Prague; tel (5) 67308907; e-mail kancelar@snk.cz; internet www.snk.cz; Leader Igor Petrov; f 2002.

DENMARK

Dansk Folkeparti: Christiansborg, 1240 Copenhagen K; tel 33-37-51-99; fax 33-37-51-91; e-mail df@ft.dk; internet www.danskfolkeparti.dk; Leader: Pia Kjaersgaard; f 1995 by defectors from the Progress Party; right-wing.

Folkebevægelsen mod EU: 39a Sigurdsgade, 2200 Copenhagen N; tel 35-82-18-00; fax 35-82-18-06; e-mail folkebevaegelsen@folkebevaegelsen.dk; internet www.folkebevaegelsen.dk; Danish People's Movement Against the European Union; opposes membership of the EU, in favour of self-determination for Denmark and all European countries; 21-mem collective leadership.

JuniBevægelsen (J): Skindergade 29, 1159 Copenhagen K; tel 33-93-00-46; fax 33-93-30-67; e-mail jb@junibevaegelsen.dk; internet www.junibevaegelsen.dk; Leaders: Jens-Peter Bonde, Drude Dahlerup; f 1992; June Movement; opposes the European Union.

Det Konservative Folkeparti (KF): Nyhavn 4, POB 1515, 1020 Copenhagen K; tel 33-13-41-40; fax 33-93-37-73; e-mail info@konservative.dk; internet www.konservative.dk; Leader: Bendt Bendtsen; Sec-Gen: Jan Høgskilde; f 1916; Conservative People's Party.

Det Radikale Venstre (RV): Christiansborg, 1240 Copenhagen K; tel 33-37-47-47; fax 33-13-72-51; e-mail radikale@radikale.dk; internet www.radikale.dk; Chair: Søren Bald; Leader: Marianne Jelved; Gen Sec: Anders Kloppenborg; f 1905; Social Liberal Party.

Socialdemokratiet (SD): Thorvaldsenvej 2, 1780 Copenhagen V; tel 35-39-15-22; fax 35-39-40-30; e-mail socialdemokratiet@net.dialog.dk; internet www.socialdemokratiet.dk; Leader: Mogens Lykketoft; f 1871; Social Democratic Party.

Socialistisk Folkeparti: Christiansborg, 1240 Copenhagen K; tel 33-12-70-11; fax 33-32-72-48; e-mail sf@sf.dk; internet www.sf.dk; Chair: Holger K. Nielsen; Parliamentary Leader: Aage Frandsen; Sec: Ole Hvas Kristiansen; f 1959; Socialist People's Party.

Venstre (V): Søllerødvej 30, 2840 Holte; tel 45-80-22-33; fax 45-80-38-30; e-mail venstre@venstre.dk; internet www.venstre.dk; Chair: Anders Fogh Rasmussen; Sec-Gen: Claus Hjort Frederiksen; f 1870; Liberal Party.

ESTONIA

Eesti Keskerakond (K) (Estonian Centre Party): Toom-Rüütli 3/5, 10130 Tallinn; POB 3737, Tallinn; tel 627-3460; fax 627-3461; e-mail keskerakond@keskerakond.ee; internet www.keskerakond.ee; Chair: Edgar Savisaar; Gen. Sec: Kadri Must; f 1991; absorbed the Estonian Green Party in mid-1998; 5,000 mems.

Eesti Reformierakond (ER) (Estonian Reform Party): Onismagi 3a, 15 Tallinn; tel 640-8740; fax 640-8741; e-mail info@reform.ee; internet www.reform.ee; Gen Sec: Heiki Kranich; Chair: Siim Kallas; f 1994; liberal.

Erakond Isamaaliit (IL) (Fatherland Union): Wismari 11, 10136 Tallinn; fax 669-1071; e-mail info@isamaaliit.ee; internet www.isamaaliit.ee; Leader Tunne Kelam; f 1995 by merger of several former parties; conservative nationalist party.

Sotsiaaldemokraatlik Erakond (SDE) (Social Democratic Party): Pärnu mnt. 41a, Tallinn; tel 641-4071; e-mail kantselei@sotsdem.ee; internet www.sotsdem.ee; Chair: Ivari Padar; Sec-Gen: Tonu Koiv; f 1999 as the People's Party Moderates, by merger of the People's Party and the Moderates' Party; name changed in 2004.

FINLAND

Kansallinen Kokoomus (Kok): Pohjoinen Rautatiekatu 21b, 00100 Helsinki; tel and fax (9) 1603004; e-mail jori.arvonen@kokoomus.fi; internet www.kokoomus.fi; Chair: Ville Itälä; Sec-Gen: Matti Kankare; Chair, Parliamentary Group: Ben Zyskowicz; Chair, European Parliamentary Group: Marjo Matikainen-Kallström; f 1918; National Coalition Party; moderate conservative political ideology.

Suomen Keskusta (Kesk): Apollonkatu 11a, 00100 Helsinki; tel (9) 75144200; fax (9) 75144240; e-mail puoluetoimisto@keskusta.fi; internet www.keskusta.fi; Chair: Esko Aho; Sec-Gen: Eero Lankia; Chair, Parliamentary Group: Mauri Pekkarinen; f 1906; Centre Party of Finland; a radical centre party founded to promote the interests of the rural population, now a reformist 'green' movement favouring individual enterprise, equality and decentralization.

Suomen Sosialidemokraattinen Puolue (SDP): Saariniemenkatu 6, 00530 Helsinki; tel (9) 478988; fax (9) 712752; e-mail palaute@sdp.fi; internet www.sdp.fi; Chair: Paavo Lipponen; Gen-Sec: Kari Laitinen; Chair, Parliamentary Group: Antti Kalliomäki; f 1899; Finnish Social Democratic Party; constitutional socialist programme

Svenska Folkpartiet (SFP): Simonsgatan 8a, 00100 Helsinki; tel (9) 693070; fax (9) 6931968; internet www.sfp.fi; Chair: Jan-Erik Enestam; Sec: Berth Sundström; Chair, Parliamentary Group: Ulla-Maj Wideroos; f 1906; Swedish People's Party; a liberal party representing the interests of the Swedish-speaking minority.

Vasemmistoliitto Vänsterförbundet (VV): Viherniemenkatu 5a 2, 00530 Helsinki; tel (9) 774741; fax (9) 77474200; e-mail vas@vasemmistoliitto.fi; internet www.vasemmistoliitto.fi; Chair: Suvi-Anne Siimes; Sec-Gen: Aulis Ruuth; Chair, Parliamentary Group: Outi Ojala; f 1990 as a merger of the Finnish People's Democratic League (f 1944), the Communist Party of Finland (f 1918), the Democratic League of Finnish Women, and other left-wing groups; Left Alliance.

Vihreä Liitto (Vihr): Runeberginkatu 5b, 00100 Helsinki; tel (9) 58604160; fax (09) 58604161; e-mail vihreat@vihrealitto.fi; internet www.vihrealiitto.fi; Chair: Osmo Soininvaara; Sec: Ari Heikkinen; f 1988; Green League of Finland.

FRANCE

Front National (FN): 4 rue Vauguyon, 92210 Saint-Cloud; tel 1-41-12-10-00; fax 1-41-12-10-86; Pres: Jean-Marie Le Pen; Sec-Gen: Carl Lang; f 1972; extreme right-wing nationalist party.

Mouvement pour la France (MPF): 35 ave de la Motte-Piquet, 75007 Paris; Chair: Philippe de Villiers; f 1994; opposes terms of the Treaty on European Union (the Maastricht treaty).

Parti Communiste Français (PCF): 2 place du Colonel Fabien, 75940 Paris Cédex 19; tel 1-40-40-12-12; fax 1-40-40-13-56; e-mail pcf@pcf.fr; internet www.pcf.fr; Pres: Robert Hue; Nat Sec: Marie-George Buffet; advocates independent foreign policy.

Parti Socialiste (PS): 10 rue de Solférino, 75333 Paris Cédex 07; tel 1-45-56-77-00; fax 1-47-05-15-78; e-mail infops@parti-socialiste.fr; internet www.parti-socialiste.fr; First Sec: François Hollande; f 1971; subscribed to common programme of United Left (with PCF) until 1977; advocates solidarity, full employment and the eventual attainment of socialism through a mixed economy.

Union pour la Démocratie Française (UDF): 133 bis rue de l'Université, 75007 Paris; tel 1-53-59-20-00; fax 1-53-59-20-59; e-mail communication@udf.org; internet www.udf.org; Chair: François Bayrou; Sec-Gen: Anne-Marie Idrac; f 1978 to unite for electoral purposes non-Gaullist 'majority' candidates.

Union pour un Mouvement Populaire (UMP): 55, rue La Boétie, 75384 Paris Cedex 08; tel 1-40-76-60-00; internet www.u-m-p.org; Sec. Gen. Philippe Douste-Blazy; f. 2002 as Union pour la Majorité Présidentielle by mems of the former Rassemblement pour la République and Démocratie Liberale parties, in conjunction with elements of the UDF (q.v.); centre-right grouping formed to ensure that President Jacques Chirac had a majority grouping in the Assemblée nationale.

Les Verts-Europe-Ecologie: 25 rue Mélingue, 75019 Paris; tel 1-53-19-53-19; fax 1-53-19-03-93; e-mail verts@les-verts.org; internet www.les-verts.org; Spokespersons: Marie-Hélène Aubert, Yves Contassot, Mireille Ferri, Yann Wehrling; Nat. Sec: Gilles Lemaire; f 1984; ecologist party.

GERMANY

Bündnis 90/Die Grünen (Grüne): Pl. vor dem Neuen Tor 1, 10115 Berlin; tel (30) 284420; fax (30) 28442210; e-mail bgst@gruene.de; internet www.gruene.de; Chair: Fritz Kuhn, Claudia Roth; Parliamentary Leaders: Rezzo Schlauch, Kerstin Müller; Sec-Gen: Reinhard Bütikofer; f 1993 by merger of Bündnis 90 (f 1990, as an electoral political asscn of citizens' movements of the former GDR) and Die Grünen (f 1980); Alliance 90/The Greens; essentially left-wing programme includes ecological issues, democratization of society, social justice, comprehensive disarmament.

Christlich-Demokratische Union Deutschlands (CDU): Konrad-Adenauer-Haus, Klingelhöferstr. 8, 10785 Berlin; tel (30) 220700; fax (30) 22070111; e-mail post@cdu.de; internet www.cdu.de; Chair: Dr Angela Merkel; Sec-Gen: Laurenz Meyer; Parliamentary Leader: Friedrich Merz; f 1945; Christian Democratic Union; Christian-Democratic party became a federal party in 1950; incorporated the CDU of the former German Democratic Republic in Oct 1990.

Christlich-Soziale Union Deutschlands (CSU): Nymphenburgerstr. 64, 80335 Munich; tel (89) 12430; fax (89) 1243220; Chair: Dr Edmund Stoiber; Sec-Gen: Dr Thomas Goppel; f 1946; Christian Social party; combines national consciousness with support for a united Europe.

Freie Demokratische Partei (FDP): Reinhardtstr. 14, 10117 Berlin; tel (30) 2849580; fax (30) 28495822; e-mail tdh@fdp.de; internet www.fdp.de; Chair: Dr Guido Westerwelle; Sec-Gen: Cornelia Pieper; f 1948; represents democratic and social liberalism and makes the individual the focal point of the State and its laws and economy; 65,192 mems (Dec. 2003).

Partei des Demokratischen Sozialismus (PDS): Kleine Alexanderstr. 28, 10178 Berlin; tel (30) 240090; fax (30) 24009425; e-mail redaktion@pds-online.de; internet www.pds-online.de; Chair: Prof Gabrielle Zimmer; Chair, Parliamentary Party: Roland Claus; successsor to the Sozialistische Einheitspartei Deutschlands (SED—Socialist Unity Party, f 1946 as a result of the unification of the Social Democratic Party and the Communist Party in Eastern Germany), which had been the dominant political force in the GDR until late 1989; adopted present name Feb. 1990; Party of Democratic Socialism; has renounced Stalinism, opposes fascism, right-wing extremism and xenophobia, advocates a socially- and ecologically-orientated market economy with public, collective and private ownership of the means of production, supports international disarmament and peaceful solutions to international conflicts.

Sozialdemokratische Partei Deutschlands (SPD): Wilhelmstr. 141, 10963 Berlin; tel (30) 259910; fax (30) 410; e-mail parteivorstand@spd.de; internet www.spd.de; Chair: Gerhard Schröder; Gen Sec: Franz Müntefering; f 1863; Social Democratic Party; incorporated the SPD of the former German Democratic Republic in Sept 1990; maintains that a vital democracy can be built only on the basis of social justice; advocates for the economy as much competition as possible, as much planning as necessary to protect the individual from uncontrolled economic interests; favours a positive attitude to national defence, while supporting controlled disarmament; rejects any political ties with Communism.

GREECE

Kommunistiko Komma Ellados (KKE): Leoforos Irakliou 145, Perissos, 142 31 Athens; tel (1) 02592111; fax (1) 02592286; e-mail cpg@kke.gr; internet www.kke.gr; Gen Sec: Aleka Papariga; f 1918; banned 1947, reappeared 1974; Communist Party of Greece.

Laikos Orthodoxos Synagermos (LAOS): Athens; Leader Giorgos Karatzaferis; f. 2004; nationalist, anti-immigration.

Nea Dimokratia (ND): Odos Rigillis 18, 106 74 Athens; tel (1) 07290071; fax (1) 7214327; Leader: Dr Konstantinos Al. Karamanlis; Dir-Gen: Ioannis Vartholomeos; f 1974 by Konstantinos Karamanlis; New Democracy Party; centre-right party advocating social reform in the framework of a liberal economy; led and completed Greece's accession to the European Union.

Panellinion Socialistikon Kinema (PASOK): Odos Charilaou Trikoupi 50, Athens; tel (1) 03232049; Leader: Konstantinos (Costas) Simitis; Sec-Gen: Konstantinos Skandalides; f 1974; Panhellenic Socialist Movement; incorporates Democratic Defence and Panhellenic Liberation Movement resistance organizations; supports social welfare, decentralization and self-management, aims at a Mediterranean socialist development through international co-operation.

Synaspismos tis Aristeras kai tis Proodou (Synaspismos): Pl. Elefthrias 1, 105 53 Athens; tel (1) 03378400; fax (1) 03217003; e-mail intrelations@syn.gr; internet www.syn.gr; Pres: Nikos Konstantopoulos; f 1989 as an alliance between the Greek Left Party and the Communist Party of Greece ('of the Exterior'); in 1991 the conservative faction of the Communist Party withdrew from the alliance; however, the Coalition continued to command considerable support from the large reformist faction of the KKE; transformed into a single party in 1992; Coalition of the Left and Progress.

HUNGARY

Fidesz – Magyar Polgári Szövetség (FIDESZ-MPSZ) (Hungarian Citizens' Party): 1062 Budapest, Lendvay u. 28; tel. (1) 269-5353; fax (1) 269-5343; e-mail fidesz@fidesz.hu; internet www.fidesz.hu; Chair: Viktor Orban; f 1988 as the Federation of Young Democrats; renamed April 1995; re-formed as an alliance in 2003, with a new charter; conservative; 10,000 mems.

Magyar Demokrata Fórum (MDF) (Hungarian Democratic Forum): 1026 Budapest, Szilagyi Erszebet fasor 73; 1539 Budapest, POB 579; tel. (1) 212-2828; fax (1) 225-2290; internet www.mdf.hu; Chair: Dr Ibolya David; f 1987; centre-right; 25,000 mems (2001).

Magyar Szocialista Párt (MSZP) (Hungarian Socialist Party): 1081 Budapest, Köztarsasag ter 26; tel. (1) 210-0046; fax (1) 210-0081; internet www.mszp.hu; Chair: Laszlo Kovacs; f 1989 to replace the Hungarian Socialist Workers' Party; 40,000 mems (Dec. 1999).

Szabad Demokraták Szövetsége (SZDSZ) (Alliance of Free Democrats): 1143 Budapest, Gizella u. 36; tel. (1) 223-2045; e-mail: dora.veress@szdsz.hu; internet www.szdsz.hu; Chair: Gabor Kuncze; f 1988; liberal; 19,000 mems (2000).

IRELAND

Fianna Fáil (FF): 65–66 Lower Mount St, Dublin 2; tel (1) 6761551; fax (1) 6785690; e-mail info@fiannafail.ie; internet www.fiannafail.ie; Pres and Leader: Bertie Ahern; Gen Sec: Martin Macken; f 1926; Republican Party; literally 'Soldiers of Destiny'; centrist.

Fine Gael (FG): 51 Upper Mount St, Dublin 2; tel (1) 6198444; fax (1) 6625046; e-mail finegael@finegael.com; internet www.finegael.ie; Pres and Leader: Enda Kenny; Gen Sec: Tom Curran; f 1933; United Ireland Party; centrist.

Green Party—Comhaontas Glas (GP): 5a Upper Fownes St, Temple Bar, Dublin 2; tel (1) 6790012; fax (1) 6797168; e-mail info@greenparty.ie; internet www.greenparty.ie; Pres: Michael McDowell; Leader: Trevor Sargent; f 1982; fmrly The Ecology Party; aims include political decentralization.

Labour Party (Lab): 17 Ely Place, Dublin 2; tel (1) 6612615; fax (1) 6612640; e-mail head_office@labour.ie; internet www.labour.ie; Chair: Ruairí Quinn; Gen Sec: Mike Allen.

Sinn Féin (Ourselves Alone): 44 Parnell Sq., Dublin 1; tel. (1) 8726100; fax (1) 8783595; e-mail sfadmin@eircom.net; internet www.sinnfein.ie; Pres: Gerry Adams; Chair: Mitchel McLaughlin; f 1905; advocates the termination of British rule in Northern Ireland; seeks the establishment of a democratic socialist republic in a reunified Ireland.

ITALY

Alleanza Nazionale (AN): Via della Scrofa 39, 00186 Rome; tel (06) 688171; fax (06) 688172; internet www.alleanza-nazionale.it; Sec-Gen: Gianfranco Fini; f 1994; in early 1995 absorbed the neo-fascist Movimento Sociale Italiano—Destra Nazionale (MSI—DN); National Alliance.

Alleanza Popolare – Unione Democratici per l'Europa (UDEUR): Largo Arenula 34, 00186 Rome; tel (06) 684241; fax (06) 68210615; e-mail info@alleanza -popolare.it; internet www.alleanza -popolare.it.org; Pres: Mino Martinazzoli; Sec: Clemente Mastella; f 1999.

Centro Cristiano Democratico (CCD): Via dei Due Macelli 66, Rome; tel (06) 69791001; fax (06) 6795940; e-mail amministrazione@ccd.it; internet www.ccd.it; Pres: Marco Follini; f 1994; Christian-Democratic Centre; advocates centre-right policies.

Cristiani Democratici Uniti (CDU): Piazza del Gesù 46, 00186 Rome; tel (06) 6775204; fax (06) 6785956; e-mail cdu@wmail.axnet.it; internet www.cdu.it; Gen Sec: Rocco Buttiglione; f 1995 after split with Partito Popolare Italiano; advocates centre-right policies; United Christian Democrats.

Democratici di Sinistra (DS): Via delle Botteghe Oscure 4, 00186 Rome; tel (06) 67111; fax (06) 6711596; e-mail ufficio .stampa@democraticidisinistra.it; internet www.dsonline.it; Pres: Massimo D'Alema; Gen Sec: Piero Fassino; f 1921 as Partito Comunista Italiano (PCI—Italian Communist Party); name changed to Partito Democratico della Sinistra in 1991; name changed as above 1998; Democrats of the Left; advocates a democratic and libertarian society.

Federazione dei Verdi (Fed Verdi): Via Antonio Salandra 6, 00187 Rome; tel (06) 4203061; fax (06) 42004600; e-mail federazione@verdi.it; internet www .verdi.it; Leader: Grazia Francescato; f 1986; branch of the European Green movement; advocates environmentalist and anti-nuclear policies.

Forza Italia: Via dell'Umiltà 36, 00187 Rome; tel (06) 67311; fax (06) 6788255; e-mail lettere@forza-italia.it; internet www.forza-italia.it; Leader: Silvio Berlusconi; f 1993; literally 'Come on, Italy'; advocates principles of market economy.

Italia dei Valori – Lista Di Pietro: Via dei Prefetti 17, 00186 Rome; tel (06) 6840721; fax (06) 68132711; e-mail italiadeivalori@antoniodipietro.it; internet www.antoniodipietro.it; Pres: Antonio Di Pietro.

Lega Nord per l'Indipendenza della Padania (LN): Via C. Bellerio 41, 20161 Milan; tel (02) 662341; fax (02) 66234266; e-mail webmaster@leganord.org; internet www.leganord.org; Pres: Stefano Stefani; Sec: Umberto Bossi; f 1991; Northern League for the Independence of Padania; advocates federalism in Italy and transfer of control of resources to regional govts; in 1996 declared the 'Independent Republic of Padania'; opposes immigration.

Movimento Sociale – Fiamma Tricolore (MSFT): Via Simon de Saint Bon 89, 00195 Rome; tel (06) 3701756; fax (06) 3720376; e-mail fiamma@msifiammatric .it; internet www.msifiammatric.it; Nat Sec: Pino Rauti; f 1996; electoral alliance incorporating former mems of neo-fascist Movimento Sociale Italiano-Destra

Nazionale; Social Movement of the Tricolour Flame.

Partito dei Comunisti Italiani (PdCI): Corso Vittorio Emanuele II 209, 00186 Rome; tel (06) 6862721; fax (06) 68627230; e-mail direzionenazionale@ comunisti-italiani.it; internet www .comunisti-italiani.it; Chair: Armando Cossutta; f 1998.

Partito Pensionati: Via Boezio 17, 00193 Rome; tel. (06) 6878628; fax (06) 6878697; Pres: Giuseppe Polini; Sec: Balilla Tata.

Partito Popolare Italiano (PPI): Piazza del Gesù 46, 00186 Rome; tel (06) 699591; fax (06) 6790449; e-mail ufficiostampa@pronet.it; internet www.popolari.it; Sec-Gen: Pierluigi Castagnetti; f 1994 as the successor to the Partito della Democrazia Cristiana (DC); Italian Popular Party; centrist.

Partito Repubblicano Italiano (PRI): Corso Vittorio Emanuele 326, 00186 Rome; tel (06) 6865044; fax (06) 6893002; internet www.pri.it; Pres: Guglielmo Negri; Gen Sec: Giorgio La Malfa; f 1897; Italian Republican Party; followers of modern liberalism.

Partito della Rifondazione Comunista (PRC): Viale del Policlinico 131, 00161 Rome; tel (06) 441821; fax (06) 44239490; e-mail direzione .prc@rifondazione.it; internet www .rifondazione.it; Sec-Gen: Fausto Bertinotti; f 1991 by former mems of the Partito Comunista Italiano (PCI—Italian Communist Party); Reconstructed Communist Party.

Patto Segni Liberaldemocratici: Via Belsiana 100, 00187 Rome; tel (06) 6780840; fax (06) 6789890; e-mail edpatto@tin.it; Leader: Mario Segni; f 1993; Segni's Pact—Liberal Democrats; liberal party, advocating institutional reform.

Rinnovamento Italiano: Via di Ripetta 142, 00186 Rome; tel (06) 68808380; fax (06) 68808380; e-mail informa@ rinnovamento.it; internet www .rinnovamento.it; Leader: Prof Lamberto Dini; f 1996; centrist; Italian Renewal.

Socialisti Democratici Italiani (SDI): Piazza S. Lorenzo in Lucina 26, 00186 Rome; tel (06) 68307666; fax (06) 68307659; e-mail socialisti@nexus.it; internet www.socialisti.org; Pres: Enrico Bosselli; f 1892 as Partito Socialista Italiano (PSI); name changed to Socialisti Italiani in 1994; in 1998 re-merged with Social Democratic Party, name changed as above; Italian Democratic Socialists; centre-left party; adheres to Socialist International and believes that socialism is inseparable from democracy and individual freedom.

Südtiroler Volkspartei (SVP): Brennerstr. 7a, 39100 Bozen/Bolzano; tel (0471) 304000; fax (0471) 981473; e-mail info@svpartei.org; internet www.svpartei.org; Pres: Siegfried Brugger; Gen Sec: Thomas Widmann; South Tyrol People's Party; regional party of the German- and Ladin-speaking people in the South Tyrol.

Union Valdôtaine: Ave. des Maquisards 27/29, 11100 Aosta; tel (0165) 235181; fax (0165) 364289; internet www.unionvaldotaine.org; Pres: Auguste Rollandin.

Uniti nell'Ulivo: Piazza SS. Apostoli 55, 00187 Rome; tel (06) 696881; fax (06) 69380442; e-mail info@ulivo.it; internet www.ulivo.it; Leader: Francesco Rutelli; centre-left alliance comprising the Democratici di Sinistra, the Partito Popolare Italiano, the Südtiroler Volkspartei, the Unione Democratica, the Lista Romano Prodi, the Rinnovamento Italiano, the Margherita coalition, the Federazione dei Verdi and the Movimento Repubblicani Europe.

LATVIA

Jaunais Laiks (JL) (New Era): Jekaba Kazarmas, Torca iela 4, Rīga 1050; tel. 720-5472; fax 720-5473; e-mail birojs@jaunaislaiks.lv; internet www.jaunaislaiks.lv; Chair. Einars Repse; Sec-Gen: Uldi Gravu; f 2002; right-wing.

Latvijas Celš (LC) (Latvian Way): Jaunu iela 25/29, Rīga 1050; tel. 728-5539782-1121; e-mail lc@lc.lv; internet www.lc.lv; Chair: Janis Naglis; f 1993; 900 mems.

Par cilvēka tiesībām vienotā Latvijā (PCTVL) (For Human Rights in United Latvia): Elizabetes iela, 23a-15, Rīga; tel 750-8552; fax 750-8553; e-mail tsp@latnet.lv; internet www.pctvl.lv; alliance of several parties; supports stronger ties with Russia; opposes NATO membership.

Tautas Partija (TP) (People's Party): Dzirnavu iela 68, Rīga 1050; tel. 728-6441; fax 728-6405; e-mail arno@tautas.lv; internet www.tautaspartija.lv; Chair. Atis Slakteris; f 1998; conservative.

Tēvzemei un Brīvībai/LNNK (TB/LNNK) (Conservative Union for Fatherland and Freedom): Kaleju iela 10, Rīga 1050; tel. 708-7273; fax 708-7268; e-mail tb@tb.lv; internet www.tb.lv; Chair: Janis Straume; f 1997 by merger of the Union for Fatherland and Freedom and the Latvian National Independence Conservative Movement.

LITHUANIA

Darbo Partija (DP) (Labour Party): Lukiškių g. 5 (penktas aukštas, 523 kab.), Vilnius; tel (5) 210-7152; fax (5) 210-7153; e-mail info@darbopartija.lt; internet www.darbopartija.lt; f 2003; Leader Viktor Uspaskich.

Liberalų ir Centro Sąjunga (LCS) (Liberal and Central Union): Centro Sojunga Vilniaus g. 22/1, Vilnius 1119; tel (5) 231-3264; fax (5) 261-9363; e-mail info@lics.lt; internet www.lics.lt; Chair: Arturas Zuokas; f 2003 by merger of the Lithuanian Centre Union, the Lithuanian Liberal Union and the Modern Christian-Democratic Union; over 5,000 mems.

Liberalų demokratų partija (LDP) (Liberal Democratic Party): Pylimo 27/14, Vilnius 2000; tel (5) 262-3493; e-mail sekretoriatas@ldp.lt; internet www.ldp.lt; Chair: Valentinas Mazuronis; f 2002; right-wing; 1,500 mems.

Lietuvos Socialdemokratų Partija (LSDP) (Lithuanian Social Democratic Party): Barboros Radvilaites 1, Vilnius 2600; tel (5) 261-3907; fax (5) 261-5420; e-mail info@lsdp.lt; internet www.lsdp.lt; Chair: Algirdas Brazauskas; absorbed the Lithuanian Democratic Labour Party in 2001; 11,000 mems.

Tėvynės sąjunga (TS) (Homeland Union): Gedimino pr. 15, Vilnius 1103; tel (5) 2615703; e-mail sekretoriatas@tsajunga.lt; internet www.tslk.lt; Leader Andrius Kubilius; f 1993; right-wing.

Valstiečių ir Naujosios demokratijos partijų sąjunga (VNDPS) (Peasants and New Democratic Union Party): Šv. Stepono g. 7 b. 6, Vilnius 1139; Leader Kazimiera Prunskiene; conservative.

LUXEMBOURG

Déi Gréng: BP 454, 2014 Luxembourg; tel 46-37-40-1; fax 46-37-43; e-mail adr@greng.lu; internet www.greng.lu; Secs: Abbes Jacoby, Nadine Entringer; f 1983 as Gréng Alternativ Partei, joined with Gréng Lëscht Ekologesch Initiativ in 1994 to form Déi Gréng; Green Party; advocates 'grass-roots' democracy, environmental protection, social concern and increased aid to developing countries.

Parti Chrétien Social (PCS): 4 rue de l'Eau, BP 826, 2018 Luxembourg; tel 22-57-31-1; fax 47-27-16; e-mail csv@csv.lu; internet www.csv.lu; Pres: Erna Hennicot-Schoepges; Sec-Gen: Jean-Louis Schiltz; f 1914; Christian Social Party; advocates political stability, sustained economic expansion, ecological and social progress.

Parti Démocratique Luxembourgeois (PDL): 46 Grand'rue, BP 794, 2017 Luxembourg; tel 22-10-21; fax 22-10-13; e-mail groupdp@dp.lu; internet www.dp.lu; Leader: Lydie Polfer; Sec-Gen: Henri Grethen; Democratic Party; liberal.

Parti Ouvrier Socialiste Luxembourgeois (POSL): 16 rue de Crécy, 1364 Luxembourg; tel 45-59-91; fax 45-65-75; e-mail info@lsap.lu; internet www.lsap.lu; Pres: Jean Asselborn; Sec-Gen: Paul Bach; f 1902; social-democrat; Socialist Workers' Party.

MALTA

Partit Laburista (Malta Labour Party, MLP): Labour Centre, Mile End Rd, Hamrun HMR; tel 21249900; fax 21244204; e-mail mlp@mlp.org.mt; internet www.mlp.org.mt; Leader: Dr Alfred Sant; Pres: Stefan Zrinzo Azzopardi; Gen Sec: Jason Micallef; f 1921; democratic socialist; 39,000 mems.

Partit Nazzjonalista (PN): (Nationalist Party): Herbert Ganado St, HMR; tel 21243641; fax 21243640; e-mail pn@pn.org.mt; internet www.pn.org.mt; Leader: Dr Lawrence Gonzi; Sec-Gen: Joe Saliba; f 1880; Christian democratic; advocates full membership of the EU; 33,000 mems.

THE NETHERLANDS

Christen Unie (CU): POB 439, 3800 AK Amersfoort; tel. (33) 4226969; e-mail bureau@christenunie.nl; internet www.christenunie.nl; Chair: M. van Daalen; Parliamentary Leader: K. Veling; f 2000 by merger of two evangelical parties, the Gereformeerd Politiek Verbond and the Reformatische Politieke Federatie; interdenominational, based on biblical precepts; represented in the European Parliament jointly with the SGP.

Christen-Democratisch Appèl (CDA): Dr Kuyperstraat 5, POB 30453, 2500 GL The Hague; tel (70) 3424888; fax (70) 3643417; e-mail bureau@cda.nl; internet www.cda.nl; Chair: M. L. A. Van Rij; Parliamentary Leader: Jan Peter Balkenende; f 1980 by merger of three 'confessional' parties; Christian Democratic Appeal.

Democraten 66 (D66): Noordwal 10, 2513 EA The Hague; tel (70) 3566066; fax (70) 3641917; e-mail landelijk.secretariaat@D66.nl; internet www.D66.nl; Chair: Gerard Schouw; Parliamentary Leader: Thom de Graaf; f 1966; Democrats '66.

GroenLinks: POB 8008, 3503 RA Utrecht; tel (30) 2399900; fax (30) 2300342; e-mail partijbureau@groenlinks.nl; internet www.groenlinks.nl; Chair: Mirjam De Rijk; Parliamentary Leader: Paul Rosenmöller; f 1990 by merger of the Communistische Partij van Nederland, Evangelische Volkspartij, Pacifistisch Socialistische Partij and Politieke Partij Radikalen; The Green Left.

Partij van de Arbeid (PvdA): Herengracht 54, POB 1310, 1000 BH Amsterdam; tel (20) 5512155; fax (20) 5512330; e-mail pvda@pvda.nl; internet www.pvda.nl; Chair: Ruud Koole; Parliamentary Leader: Jeltje van Nieuwenhoven; f 1946 by merger of progressive and liberal organizations; Labour Party; democratic socialist.

Socialistische Partij (SP): Vijverhofstraat 65, 3032 SC Rotterdam; (10) 2435555; fax (10) 2435566; e-mail sp@sp.nl; internet www.sp.nl; Leader: Jan Marijnissen; Socialist Party.

Staatkundig Gereformeerde Partij (SGP): Laan van Meerdervoort 165, 2517 AZ The Hague; tel (70) 3456226; fax (70) 3655959; e-mail voorlichting@sgp.nl; internet www.sgp.nl; Chair: Rev D. J. Budding; Parliamentary Leader: Bas J. van der Vlies; Sec: A. de Boer; f 1918; Political Reformed Party; Calvinist; female membership banned in 1993; represented in the European Parliament jointly with the CU.

Volkspartij voor Vrijheid en Democratie (VVD): POB 30836, 2500 GV The Hague; tel (70) 3613061; fax (70) 3608276; e-mail alg.sec@vvd.nl; internet www.vvd.nl; Chair: Bas Eenhoorn; Parliamentary Leader: Gerrit Zalm; f 1948; advocates free enterprise, individual freedom and responsibility, but its programme also supports social security and recommends the participation of workers in profits and management; People's Party for Freedom and Democracy—Netherlands Liberal Party.

POLAND

Liga Polskich Rodzin (LPR) (League of Polish Families): 00-528 Warsaw, ul. Hoza 9; tel (22) 6223648; fax (22) 6223138; e-mail biuro@lpr.pl; internet www.lpr.pl; f 2001 as alliance comprising the National Party, All-Poland Youth, the Polish Accord Party, the Catholic National movement and the Peasant National Bloc; Leader: Roman Giertych; Chief of Staff: Zygmunt Wrzodak; Christian, nationalist, anti-EU.

Platforma Obywatelska (PO) (Civic Platform): 00-548 Warsaw, al. Ujazdowskie 18; tel (22) 6227548; fax (22) 6225386; internet www.platforma.org.pl; Leader: Donald Tusk; f 2001 by a popular independent presidential candidate and factions of the UW and the AWS; also known as the Citizens' Platform.

Polskie Stronnictwo Ludowe (PSL) (Polish People's Party): 00-131 Warsaw, ul. Grzybowska 4; tel (22) 6206020; fax (22) 6206026; e-mail psl@psl.org.pl; internet www.psl.org.pl; Chair: Janusz Wojciechowski; f 1990 to replace United Peasant Party (Zjednoczone Stronnictwo Ludowe; f 1949) and Polish Peasant Party – Rebirth (Polskie Stronnictwo Ludowe – Odrodzenie; f 1989); centrist, stresses development of agriculture and social-market economy; 120,000 mems.

Prawo i Sprawiedliwość (PiS) (Law and Justice Party): 02-018 Warsaw, ul. Nowogrodzka 84/86; tel. (22) 6215035; fax (22) 6216767; e-mail biuro.organizacyjne@pis.org.pl; internet www.pis.org.pl; Leader: Lech Kaczynski; f 2001; conservative.

Samoobrona RP (SRP) (Self Defence Party): 00-024 Warsaw, Al. Jerozolimskie 30; tel. (22) 6250472; fax (22) 6250477; e-mail samoobrona@samoobrona.org.pl; internet www.samoobrona.org.pl; Leader: Andrzej Lepper; f 2000 by trade union leaders opposed to the Government's social and economic policies; conservative, anti-EU.

Socjaldemocracja Polska (SDPL) (Polish Social Democracy): 00-660 Warsaw, ul. Lwowskiej 5 lok. 3a; tel (22) 8255394; e-mail sdpl.wybory@onet.pl; internet www.sdpl.pl; Leader: Marek Borowski; f 2004; leftist.

Sojusz Lewicy Demokratycznej-Unia Pracy (SLD-UP) (Union of Labour): 00-513 Warsaw, ul. Nowogrodzka 4; tel (22) 6256776; e-mail biuro@uniapracy.org.pl; internet www.uniapracy.org.pl; Chair: Izabela Jaruga; f 1993.

Unia Wolnisci (UW) (Freedom Union): 00-683 Warsaw, ul. Marszalkowska 77/79; tel. (22) 8275047; fax (22) 8277851; e-mail uw@uw.org.pl; internet www.uw.org.pl; Leader: Wladyslaw Frasyniuk; f 1994 by merger of Democratic Union (Unia Demokratyczna-UD) and the Liberal Democratic Congress (Kongres Liberalno-Demokratyczny – KLD); 12,500 mems.

PORTUGAL

Bloco de Esquerdo: Av. Almirante Reis, n.° 131, 2° andar, Lisbon; tel (21) 3510510; fax (21) 3510519; internet www.bloco.org; f 1999; left-wing

Partido Comunista Português (PCP): Rua Soeiro Pereira Gomes 3, 1600-196 Lisbon; tel (21) 7813800; fax (21) 7969126; e-mail pcp@pcp.pt; internet www.pcp.pt; Sec-Gen: Carlos Carvalhas; f 1921, legalized 1974; Portuguese Communist Party; theoretical foundation is Marxism-Leninism; aims are the defence and consolidation of the democratic regime and the revolutionary achievements, and ultimately the building of a socialist society in Portugal.

Partido Popular (PP): Largo Adelino Amaro da Costa 5, 1149-063 Lisbon; tel (21) 8869735; fax (21) 8860454; e-mail cds-pp@esoterica.pt; internet www.partido-popular.pt; Pres: Paulo Portas; f 1974; Popular Party; formerly Centro Democrático Social; centre-right; mem of International Democratic Union; supports social market economy and reduction of public-sector intervention in the economy.

Partido Social Democrata (PSD): Rua de São Caetano 9, 1249-087 Lisbon; tel (21) 3952140; fax (21) 3976967; Leader: José Manuel Durão Barroso; Sec-Gen: Artur Torres Pereira; f 1974; Social Democratic Party; formerly Partido Popular Democrático (PPD); supports European Union membership.

Partido Socialista (PS): Largo do Rato 2, 1269-143 Lisbon; tel (21) 3822000; fax (21) 3822016; e-mail info@ps.pt; internet www.ps.pt; Sec-Gen: Eduardo Ferro Rodrigues; Pres: António Almeida Santos; Socialist Party; f 1973 from former Acção Socialista Portuguesa (Portuguese Socialist Action); advocates a society of greater social justice and co-operation between public, private and co-operative sectors, while respecting public liberties and the will of the majority attained through free elections.

SLOVAKIA

Hnutie za Demokraticke Slovensko (HZDS) (Movement for a Democratic Slovakia): MDS Tomasikova 32a, 830 00 Bratislava; tel (2) 4329-3800; fax (2) 4341-0225; e-mail webmast@hzds.sk; internet www.hzds.sk; Chair: Vladimír Mečiar; f 1991.

Krestansko-demokratické Hnutie (KDH) (Christian Democratic Alliance): Zabotova 2, 811 04 Bratislava; tel. (2) 396-308; fax (2) 396-313; e-mail kdh@kdh.sk; internet www.kdh.sk; Chair: Pavol Hruščovsky; f 1990.

Slovenska Demokraticka a Krestanska Unia (SDKU) (Slovak Democratic and Christian Union): Ruzinovska 28, 821 03 Bratislava; tel (2) 4341-4102; fax (2) 4341-4106; e-mail sdku@sdkuonline.sk; internet www.sdkuonline.sk; Leader: Mikuláš Dzurinda; Gen Sec: Ivan Harman; f 2000.

SMER (Direction): Súmračná 27, 821 02 Bratislava; tel and fax (2) 4342-6297; e-mail kancelaria@asistent.sk; internet www.strana-smer.sk; Chair: Robert Fico; f 1999; absorbed the Party of Civic Understanding in 2003; centre-right, pro-EU, pro-NATO.

Strana mad'arskej koalície – Magyar Koalíció Pártja (SMK-MKP) (Party of the Hungarian Coalition): Partja Cajakova 8, 811 05 Bratislava; tel (2) 5249-5164; fax (2) 5249-5264; e-mail smk@smk.sk; internet www.mkp.sk; Chair: Bela Bugar; f 1998 by merger of Coexistence, the Hungarian Christian Democratic Movement and the Hungarian Civic Party.

SLOVENIA

Liberalna Demokracija Slovenije (LDS) (Liberal Democracy of Slovenia): 1000 Ljubljana, Republike trg 3; tel (1) 2000310; fax (1) 1256150; e-mail lds@lds.si; internet www.lds.si; Pres: Dr Janez Drnovsek; Gen Sec: Gregor Golobic; f 1994 by merger of the Liberal Democratic Party, the Greens of Slovenia-Eco-Social Party, the Democratic Party and the Socialist Party of Slovenia; 18,000 mems.

Nova Slovenija (NSi) (New Slovenia – Christian People's Party): 1000 Ljubljana, Cankarjeva 11; tel (1) 5004180; fax (1) 5004190; e-mail tajnistvo@nsi.si; internet www.nsi.si; Pres: Dr Andrej Bajuk; f 2000 by disaffected mems of the Slovenian People's Party; right-wing.

Slovenska demokratska stranka (SDS) (Slovenian Democratic Party): 1000 Ljubljana, Linhartova 13; tel (1) 1261073; fax (1) 1255077; Leader: Janez Jansa; f 1994 by mems of Democratic Party who opted not to join the LDS; 2,200 mems.

Zdruena lista socialnih demokratov (ZLSD) (United List of Social Democrats): 1000 Ljubljana, Levstikova 15; tel (1) 2515897; fax (1) 4261170; e-mail info@zlsd.si; internet www.zlsd.si; Pres: Borut Pahor; Gen Sec: Dusan Kumer; f 1992 as the United List, an electoral alliance of the Democratic Party of Pensioners, the Party of Democratic Reform of Slovenia, the Social Democratic Union and the Workers' Party of Slovenia; became a single party in 1993 under current name; 23,000 mems.

SPAIN

Convergència Democràtica de Catalunya (CDC): Córcega 331–333, 08037 Barcelona; tel (93) 2363100; fax (93) 2363120; e-mail cdc@convergencia.org; internet www.convergencia.org; Pres: Jordi Pujol i Soley; Sec-Gen: Artur Mas i Gavorró; f 1974; allied with Unió Democràtica de Catalunya (UDC) under the name Convergència i Unió (CiU) for the purposes of national elections; Catalan nationalist; centre.

Euzko Alderdi Jeltzalea/Partido Nacionalista Vasco (EAJ/PNV): Ibáñez de Bilbao 16 (Sabin Etxea), 48001 Bilbao; tel (94) 4039400; fax (94) 4039412; e-mail prensa@eaj-pnv.com; internet www.eaj-pnv.com; Pres: Josu Jon Imaz; Sec: Josune Ariztondo; f 1895; Basque nationalist; seeks to achieve autonomous region through peaceful means.

Izquierda Unida (IU): Olimpo 35, 28043 Madrid; tel (91) 7227500; fax (91) 3880405; e-mail gabinete.prensa@izquierda-unida.es; internet www.izquierda-unida.es; Co-ordinator-Gen:

Gaspar Llamazares Trigo; f 1989 by left-wing parties to contest elections; includes **Candidatura Unitaria de Trabajadores (CUT)**, **Izquierda Republicana (IR)**, **Partido de Acción Socialista (PASOC)**, **Partido Comunista de España (PCE)**.

Partido Popular (PP): Génova 13, 28004 Madrid; tel (91) 5577300; fax (91) 3085587; e-mail atencion@pp.es; internet www.pp.es; Pres: Mariano Rajoy; Sec-Gen: Javier Arenas Bocanegra; f 1976; fmrly Alianza Popular, name changed 1989; absorbed Democracia Cristiana (fmrly Partido Demócrata Popular) and Partido Liberal in 1989; Popular Party; centre-right, Christian Democrat.

Partido Socialista Obrero Español (PSOE): Ferraz 68 y 70, 28008 Madrid; tel (91) 5820444; fax (91) 5820422; internet www.psoe.es; Sec-Gen: José Luis Rodríguez Zapatero; f 1879; merged with Partido Socialista Popular in 1978; joined by Partido de los Trabajadores de España—Unidad Comunista (PTE—UC) in 1991 and Partido de Nueva Izquierda (PDNI) in 2001; socialist workers' party; affiliated to Socialist International.

Unió Democràtica de Catalunya (UDC): Travessera de Gràcia 17–21, àtic, 08021 Barcelona; tel (93) 2402200; fax (93) 2402201; e-mail info@uniodemocratica.org; internet www.uniodemocratica.org; Pres of Nat Council: Núria Gispert i Català; Pres of Exec Cttee: Josep Antoni Duran i Lleida; f 1931; allied with Convergència Democràtica de Catalunya (CDC) under the name Convergència i Unió (CiU) for the purposes of national elections.

SWEDEN

Centerpartiet (Centern—CP): Bergsgt 7b, POB 22107, 104 22 Stockholm; tel (8) 617-38-00; fax (8) 652-64-40; e-mail centerpartiet@centerpartiet.se; internet www.centerpartiet.se; Chair: Lennart Dalléus; Sec-Gen: Åke Pettersson; f 1910 as an agrarian party; previously known as Centerpartiets Riksorganisation; Centre Party; advocates social, environmental and progressive development and decentralization.

Folkpartiet Liberalerna (FP): POB 6508, 113 83 Stockholm; tel (8) 509-11-600; fax (8) 509-11-660; Chair: Lars Leijonborg; Sec-Gen: Johan Pehrson; f 1902; Liberal Party; advocates market-oriented economy and social welfare system.

Junilistan: POB 16 280, 103 25 Stockholm; tel. (8) 23-01-11; e-mail info@junilistan.nu; internet www.junilistan.nu; Leaders: Nils Lundgren, Lars Wohlin; f. 2004 to contest elections to the European Parliament; opposed to further powers for EU.

Kristdemokraterna (Kd): Målargt. 7, POB 3337, 103 67 Stockholm; tel (8) 723-25-00; fax (8) 723-25-10; e-mail brev.till@kristdemokrat.se; internet www.kristdemokrat.se; Chair: Gorän Hägglund; f 1964, as Kristdemokratiska Samhällspartiet (KdS), to promote emphasis on Christian values in political life; Christian Democratic Party.

Miljöpartiet de Gröna (MpG): International Secretary, Swedish Parliament, 100 12 Stockholm; tel (8) 786-57-44; fax (8) 786-53-75; e-mail info@mp.se; internet www.mp.se; Co-Leaders: Peter Eriksson, Maria Wetterstrand; f 1981; Green Party.

Moderata Samlingspartiet (MS): POB 1243, 111 82 Stockholm; tel (8) 676-80-00; fax (8) 21-61-23; e-mail info@moderat.se; Chair: Bo Lundgren; Sec: Gunnar Hökmark; f 1904; Moderate Party; advocates liberal-conservative market-orientated economy.

Sveriges Socialdemokratiska Arbetareparti (SAP): Sveavägen 68, 105 60 Stockholm; tel (8) 700-26-00; fax (8) 21-93-31; e-mail sap.international@sap.se; internet www.sap.se; Chair: Göran Persson; Sec-Gen: Lars Stjernkvist; f 1889; Swedish Social Democratic Labour Party; egalitarian.

Vänsterpartiet (VP): Kungsgt 84, POB 12660, 112 93 Stockholm; tel (8) 654-08-20; fax (8) 653-23-85; e-mail orjan.svedberg@vansterpartiet.se; Chair: Gudrun Schyman; Sec: Lars Ohly; f 1917 as Left Social Democratic Party of Sweden; affiliated to the Communist International 1919; renamed the Communist Party in 1921; renamed Left Party—Communists in 1967; renamed Left Party in 1990; policies based on the principles of Marxism, feminism and other theories.

UNITED KINGDOM

Conservative and Unionist Party (Cons): Conservative Central Office, 25 Victoria St, London SW1H 0DL; tel (20) 7222-9000; fax (20) 7222-1135; internet www.conservatives.com; Leader: Michael Howard; Co-Chairs: Lord Maurice Saatchi, Dr Liam Fox; f 1870 as Conservative Central Office; aims include increasing the United Kingdom's influence abroad, not least through commitment to the European Union.

Democratic Unionist Party (DUP): 91 Dundela Ave, Belfast BT4 3BU; tel (28) 9047-1155; fax (28) 9047-1797; e-mail info@dup.org.uk; internet www.dup.org.uk; Leader: Dr Ian R. K. Paisley; Party Sec: Nigel Dodds; f 1971; Protestant pro British-Union party.

Green Party: 1a Waterlow Rd, London N19 5NJ; tel (20) 7272-4474; fax (20) 7272-6653; e-mail office@greenparty.org.uk;

internet www.greenparty.org.uk; Exec Chair: Penny Kemp; Principal Speaker: Darren Johnson; f 1973 as the Ecology Party; present name adopted in 1985; campaigns for the protection of the environment and the promotion of social justice.

Labour Party (Lab): Millbank Tower, Millbank, London SW1P 4GT; tel (8705) 900200; fax (20) 7802-1234; e-mail join@labour.org.uk; internet www.labour.org.uk; Leader: Anthony (Tony) Blair; Chair: Charles Clarke; Gen Sec: Matt Carter; f 1900; a democratic socialist party affiliated to the Socialist International and the Party of European Socialists; supports European economic and political union.

Liberal Democrats (LD): 4 Cowley St, London SW1P 3NB; tel (20) 7222-7999; fax (20) 7799-2170; e-mail libdems@cix.co.uk; internet www.libdems.org.uk; Leader: Charles Kennedy; Pres: Lord (Navnit) Dholakia; f 1988 following the merger of the Liberal Party and the Social Democratic Party.

Plaid Cymru—The Party of Wales: 18 Park Grove, Cardiff CF10 3BN; tel (29) 2064-6000; fax (20) 2064-6001; e-mail post@plaidcymru.org; internet www.plaidcymru.org; Leader: Ieuan Wyn Jones; Chair: Elin Jones; Gen Sec: Karl Davies; f 1925; promotes Welsh interests and seeks national status for Wales.

Scottish National Party (SNP): 107 McDonald Rd, Edinburgh EH7 4NW; tel (131) 525-8900; fax (131) 525-8901; e-mail snp.hq@snp.org; internet www.snp.org.uk; National Convener (Leader): John Swinney; Pres: Winifred M. Ewing; Nat Sec: Stewart Hosie; f 1934; advocates independence for Scotland as a mem of the European Union, and Scottish control of national resources.

Sinn Féin: 51–55 Falls Rd, Belfast, BT12 4PD; tel (28) 9032-3214; fax (28) 9023-1723; e-mail sinnfein@iol.ie; internet www.sinnfein.ie; Chair: Mitchel McLaughlin; Pres: Gerry Adams; f 1905; political wing of the Provisional IRA; seeks the reunification of Ireland and the establishment of a 32-county democratic socialist state.

Social Democratic and Labour Party (SDLP): 121 Ormeau Rd, Belfast BT7 1SH; tel (28) 9024-7700; fax (28) 9023-6699; e-mail sdlp@indigo.ie; internet www.sdlp.ie; Leader: Mark Durkan; f 1970; radical left-of-centre principles with a view to eventual reunification of Ireland by popular consent; mem of Socialist International.

Ulster Unionist Party (UUP): 3 Glengall St, Belfast BT12 5AE; tel (28) 9032-4601; fax (28) 9024-6738; e-mail uup@uup.org; internet www.uup.org; Leader: David Trimble; Pres: Rev Martin Smith; f 1905; supports parity and equality for Northern Ireland within the United Kingdom.

United Kingdom Independence Party (UKIP): 123 New John St, Birmingham, B6 4LD; tel; (121) 333-7737; fax (121) 333-1520; e-mail webmail@ukip.org; internet www.ukip.org; National Leader: Roger Knapman; Chair. Petrina Holdsworth; f 1993; opposes United Kingdom's membership of the European Union.

European Federations of Political Parties

EUROPEAN PEOPLE'S PARTY (PPE)

Secretariat

67 rue d'Arlon, 1047 Brussels, Belgium; tel (2) 285-41-40; fax (2) 285-41-41; e-mail secgen@evppe.be; internet www.eppe.org; f 1976.

President: Wilfried A. E. Martens.

Vice-Presidents: Antonio Tajani, John Bruton, Alberto João Jardim, Peter Hintze, Kostas Karamanlis, Nadezhda Mihailova, Viktor Orban, Wim van Velzen, Pierre Lequiller, Bo Lundgren.

Treasurer: Sauli Niinisto.

Secretary-General: Antonio Lopez Isturiz.

Deputy Secretaries-General: Luc Vandeputte, Christian Kremer.

Press Spokesman: Beatriz Toribio.

Members

Centro Cristiano Democratico (CCD—Italy)

Christelijke Volkspartij (CVP—Belgium)

Christen-Democratisch Appel (CDA—Netherlands)

Christlich-Demokratische Union Deutschlands (CDU—Germany)

Christlich-Soziale Union in Bayern eV (CSU—Germany)

Cristiani Democratici Uniti (CDU—Italy)

Erakond Isamaaliit (IL—Estonia)

Fidesz—Magyar Polgári Szövetség (FIDESZ—MPSZ—Hungary)

Fine Gael (FG—Ireland)

Forza Italia (FI—Italy)

Kansallinen Kokoomus (Kok—Finland)

Det Konservative Folkeparti (KF—Denmark)

Dimokratikos Synagermos (DI.SY—Cyprus)

Křestanská a demokratická uniei—Československá strana lidová (KDU—CSL—Czech Republic)

Krest'ansko-demokratické hnutie (KDH—Slovakia)

Kristdemokraterna (Kd—Sweden)

Kristeligt Folkeparti (KrF—Denmark)

Magyar Demokrata Fórum (MDF—Hungary)

Moderata Samlingspartiet (MS—Sweden)

Nea Dimokratia (ND—Greece)

Nova Slovenija—Krščanska Ljudska Stranka (NSi—Slovenia)

Nouvelle Union pour la Démocratie Française (UDF—France)

Österreichische Volkspartei (ÖVP—Austria)

Parti Chrétien Social (PCS—Luxembourg)

Partido Popular (PP—Spain)

Partido Social Democrata (PSD—Portugal)

Partit Nazzjonalista (PN—Malta)

Partito Popolare Italiano (PPI—Italy)

Platforma Obywatelska (PO—Poland)

Socialdemokratska stranka Slovenija (SDS—Slovenia)

Stranka Madarskej Koalicie—Magyar Koalicio Partja (SMK—MKP—Slovakia)

Tautas partija (TP—Latvia)

Tėvynės Sajunga (TS—Lithuania)

Unió Democràtica de Catalunya (UDC—Spain)

Unione Democratici per l'Europa (UDEUR—Italy)

Union pour la majorité présidentielle (UMP—France)

Members not represented in the European Parliament

Független Kisgazda-, Földmunkás- és Polgári Párt (FkGP—Hungary)

Kristdemokraterna (Kd—Sweden)

Lietuvos Kirkscionys demokratai (LKd—Lithuania)

Ruch Społeczny (RS—Poland)

Unie svobody (US—Czech Republic)

Associate Members

Christlichdemokratische Volkspartei der Schweiz (CVP—Switzerland)

Conservative Peasant Party—Ruch Nowej Polski (SKL—RNP—Poland)

Evangelische Volkspartei (CVP—Switzerland)

Høyre (H—Norway)

Partidul Naţional Ţărănesc Creştin-Democrat din Romania (PNŢCD—Romania)

People's Union (PU—Bulgaria)

Romániai Magyar Demokrata Szövetség (RMDSZ—Romania)

Observers

Demokratski Centar (DC—Croatia)

Hrvastska Demokratska Zajednica (HDZ—Croatia)

Hrvastska Seljačka Stranka (HSS—Croatia)

Kristelig Folkeparti (KrF—Norway)

Partia Demokrate (PD—Albania)

Partito Democratico Cristiano Sammarinese (PDCS—San Marino)

Slovenska ljudska stranka (SLS—Slovenia)

Südtiroler Volkspartei (SVP—Italy)

Suomen Kristillisdemokraatit (KD—Finland)

GROUP OF THE ALLIANCE OF LIBERALS AND DEMOCRATS FOR EUROPE (ALDE)

Secretariat

rue Wiertz, 1047 Brussels, Belgium; tel (2) 284-25-61; fax (2) 230-95-34; e-mail aldeparty@europarl.eu.int; internet www.eurolib.org; f 2004.

President: Graham Watson.

Vice-Presidents: Silvana Koch-Mehrin, Karin Riis Jørgensen, Marielle de Sarnez, Eugenijus Gentvilas, Lapo Pistelli.

Secretary-General: Alexander Beels, e-mail abeels@europarl.eu.int.

Members

Centerpartiet (Sweden)

Democraten 66 (D66—Netherlands)

I Democratici (D—Italy)

Democratic Party (DI.KO—Cyprus)

Demokratesch Partei (DP—Luxembourg)

Estonian Reform Party (ER—Estonia)

Folkpartiet Liberalerna (FP—Sweden)

Italia dei Valori—Lista Di Pietro (IdV—LdP—Italy)

KEP (Greece)

Liberal Democrats (United Kingdom)

Liberales Forum (LF—Austria)

Liberal Democracy of Slovenia (LDS—Slovenia)

Parti Réformateur Libéral (PRL—Belgium)

Partito Repubblicano Italiano (PRI—Italy)

Det Radikale Venstre (RV—Denmark)

Rinnovamento Italiano (RI—Italy)

Suomen Keskusta (Kesk—Finland)

Svenska Folkpartiet (SFP—Finland)

Venstre (V—Denmark)

Vlaamse Liberalen en Democraten (VLD—Belgium)

Volkspartij voor Vrijheid en Democratie (VVD—Netherlands)

Members not represented in the European Parliament

Alliance Party of Northern Ireland (APNI—United Kingdom)

Alliance of Free Democrats (SzDSz—Hungary)

ANO (Slovakia)

Freie Demokratische Partei (FDP—Germany)

Gibraltar Liberal Party (GLP—United Kingdom)

Latvian Way (Latvia)

Lithuanian Liberal Union (Lithuania)

New Union (NU—Lithuania)

Obcanská democratická aliance (ODA—Czech Republic)

Progressive Democrats (PD—Ireland)

United Democrats Movement (Cyprus)

Members and Affiliates from non-European Union Countries

Croatian Social-Liberal Party (HSLS—Croatia)

Democratic Alliance Party (DAP—Albania)

Dvizhenie za Prava i Svobodi (DPS—Bulgaria)

Freisinnig-Demokratische Partei der Schweiz (FDP—Switzerland)

Hrvatska Narodna Stranka (HNS—Croatia)

Liberal Democratic Party (LDP—Macedonia)

Liberal Democratic Union (LDU—Bulgaria)

Liberal Party (Andorra)

Liberal Party of Kosovo (Serbia)

Liberalna Demokratska Stranka (LDS—Bosnia-Herzegovina)

Liberalna Stranka (LS—Croatia)

LPM (Macedonia)

National Liberal Party (PNL—Romania)

New Democracy (ND—Serbia)

Venstre (V—Norway)

PARTY OF EUROPEAN SOCIALISTS (PSE)

Secretariat

13 Boulevard de L'Empereur, 1000 Brussels, Belgium; tel (2) 548-9080; e-mail pes@pes.org; internet www.pes.org; f 1992, formerly Confederation of Socialist Parties of the EC (f 1974).

President: Poul Nyrup Rasmussen.

Senior Vice-President: Giuliano Amato.

General Secretary: Philip Cordery, e-mail cordery@pes.org.

Members

Ceská strana sociálne demokratická (CSSD—Czech Republic)

Democratici di Sinistra (DS—Italy)

Labour Party (Ireland)

Labour Party (United Kingdom)

Lietuvos Socialdemokratu Partija (LSDP—Lithuania)

Magyar Szocialista Párt (MSP—Hungary)

Panellinion Socialistikon Kinema (PASOK—Greece)

Parti Ouvrier Socialiste Luxembourgeois (POSL—Luxembourg)

Parti Socialiste (PS—Belgium)

Parti Socialiste (PS—France)

Partido Socialista (PS—Portugal)

Partido Socialista Obrero Español (PSOE—Spain)

Partij van de Arbeid (PvdA—Netherlands)

Social Democratic and Labour Party (SDLP—United Kingdom)

Socialdemokratiet (S—Denmark)

Socialisti Democratici Italiani (SDI—Italy)

Socialistische Partij (SP—Belgium)

Sojusz Lewicy Demokratycznej (SLD—Poland)

Sozialdemokratische Partei Deutschlands (SPD—Germany)

Sozialdemokratische Partei Österreichs (SPÖ—Austria)

Suomen Sosiaalidemokraattinen Puolue (SDP—Finland)

Sveriges Socialdemokratiska Arbetareparti (SAP—Sweden)

Members not represented in the European Parliament

Det norske Arbeiderparti (DnA—Norway)

Kinima Sosialdimokraton (KISOS—Cyprus)

Latvijas Socialdemokratiska stradnieku partija (LSDSP—Latvia)

Moodukad (Estonia)

Sociaal Progressief Alternatief (SPa—Belgium)

Strana demokratickej l'avice (SDL—Slovakia)

Unia Pracy (UP—Poland)

Zdruzena lista socialnih demokratov (ZLSD—Slovenia)

Associate Members

Cumhuriyet Halk Partisi (CHP—Turkey)

Partidul Democrat (PD—Romania)

Partidul Social Democrat (PSD—Romania)

Sozialdemokratische Partei der Schweiz—Parti Socialiste Suisse (Switzerland)

Observers

Althýduflokkurinn (Iceland)

Israel Labour Party (Israel)

Malta Labour Party (MLP—Malta)

Meretz (Israel)

Partit Socialdemocràta (PS—Andorra)

Partito Socialista Sammarinese (PSS—San Marino)

Secretariat-General

(Plateau du Kirchberg, 2929 Luxembourg; tel 4300-1; fax 4300-29494; rue Wiertz, 1047 Brussels, Belgium; tel (2) 284-21-11; fax (2) 284-69-33; internet www.europarl.eu.int.

Note: Telephone and fax numbers, unless otherwise stated, are in Luxembourg)

Secretary-General: Julian Priestley; tel 4300-22483.

Legal Adviser: Gregorio Garzon Clariana; tel 4301-22626.

Director: Constantin Startigakis; tel 4300-22874.

Heads of Division: Ricardo Passos, tel 4301-22720; Christian Pennera, tel 4301-22272; Hannu von Hertzen, tel 4301-22330; Hans Krueck, tel 4301-24294; Harry Duintjer Tebbens, tel 4301-43737; Timothy Millett; Fernando Hervás Dempster, tel 4301-22272; Didier Petersheim, tel 4301-23608.

Legal Service

Jurisconsult: Gregorio Garzón Clariana; tel 4300-22626.

Director: Johann Schoo; tel 4300-22439.

DIRECTORATE-GENERAL I: PRESIDENCY

Director-General: Harald Rømer; tel 4300-22553.

Central Secretariat

Head of Division: Joseph Lannon; tel 4300-22654.

Directorate A

(Presidency Services)

Director: Francesca Ratti; tel (Brussels) (2) 284-39-21.

Divisions

1 Bureau, Conference of Presidents and Quaestors' Secretariat.

Head of Division: Hans Peder Kyst; tel (Brussels) (2) 284-22-81.

2 Protocol Service.

Head of Division: Wilfried Baur; tel (Brussels) (2) 284-46-43.

3 Security.

Head of Division: Jonas Condomines Beraud; tel (Brussels) (2) 284-60-33.

4 Office Mail Service.

Principal Administrator: Svend Leon Clausen, tel (2) 284-45-45.

Directorate B

(Plenary Sittings)

Director: Birgitte Stensballe; tel (Brussels) (2) 284-40-65.

Administrator: Emilia Gallego Perona (Organization and Conducts of Part-Sessions); tel (Brussels) (2) 284-40-61.

Division

1 Plenary Acts.

Head of Division: Eva Dudzinska; tel (Brussels) (2) 284-40-20.

Directorate C

(Parliamentary Planning)

Director: Vittorio Porta Frigeri; tel (Brussels) (2) 284-36-61.

Divisions

1 Parliamentary Planning and Co-ordination.

Head of Division: Angel Luis Guillén Zanón; tel (Brussels) (2) 284-40-80.

2 Members' Activities.

Head of Division: João Correa; tel 4301-22289.

Directorate D

(Information Technology)

Director: Pierre Lora-Tonet; tel (Brussels) (2) 284-36-92.

Divisions

1 Budget and Finance.

Head of Division: Franco Piodi; tel 4300-24457.

2 Engineering and Project Support.

Head of Division: Patrick Facchin; tel 4301-24500.

3 Information Resources Management.

Head of Division: Peter Pappamikail; tel 4300-20221.

4 Information Technology Infrastructure Management.

Head of Division: Pierre Jegu; tel 4300-22255.

5 Information Technology User Support

Head of Division: Pietro Bianchessi; tel 4301-22185.

6 Information Systems Development and Management.

Head of Division: Rainer Klotzbücher; tel 4301-222145.

DIRECTORATE-GENERAL II: COMMITTEES AND INTERPARLIAMENTARY DELEGATIONS

Director General: Dietmar Nickel; tel (Brussels) (2) 284-27-59.

Directorate A

(External Relations)

Director: José Manuel Nuñes Liberato; tel (Brussels) (2) 284-44-37.

Adviser: Mignon Houben (Election Observation); tel (Brussels) (2) 284-35-53.

Divisions

1 Committee on Foreign Affairs, Human Rights, Common Security and Defence Policy.

Head of Division: Christian Huber; tel (Brussels) (2) 284-17-56.

Principal Administrator: Francesco Perroni (Euro-Mediterranean Parliamentary Forum Secretariat); tel (Brussels) 2-284-24-73.

2 Committee on Development and Co-operation.

Head of Division: Gero Friedel; tel (Brussels) (2) 284-60-60.

3 Interparliamentary Delegations (Non-European Countries).

Head of Division: Daniel Quemener; tel (Brussels) (2) 284-21-86.

4 Joint Parliamentary Committees, Parliamentary Co-operation Committees and *ad hoc* Committees.

Head of Division: Geoffrey Harris; tel (Brussels) (2) 284-36-08.

5 Human Rights.

Head of Division: Jan Kurlemann; tel (Brussels) (2) 284-38-45.

Directorate B

(Legislative Co-ordination, Relations between Institutions and between Parliaments)

Director: Ezio Perillo; tel (Brussels) (2) 284-63-36.

Adviser: Alison Davies (Legislative Co-ordination); tel (Brussels) (2) 284-39-67.

Principal Administrator: Nicolas Foscolos (Monitoring of Parliamentary Acts); tel (Brussels) (2) 284-26-61.

Divisions

1 Conciliation and Concertation Procedures.

Head of Division: Michael Shackleton; tel (Brussels) (2) 284-27-32.

2 Relations with National Parliaments and International Parliamentary Assemblies.

Head of Division: (vacant).

Adviser: Gorm Kornrup (ESC and COR Activities, Legislative Field); tel 45300-22038.

Directorate C

(Internal Affairs and Quality of Life)

Director: Thérèse Lepoutre-Dumoulin; tel (Brussels) (2) 284-43-74.

Administrator: Juho Eskelinen (Office Systems and IT); tel (Brussels) (2) 284-22-67.

Divisions

1 Freedoms and Rights.

Head of Division: Emilio de Capitani; tel (Brussels) (2) 284-35-08.

2 Committee on Legal Affairs and the Internal Market.

Head of Division: Hans-Peter Schiffauer; tel (Brussels) (2) 284-31-92.

3 Committee on the Environment, Public Health and Consumer Policy.

Head of Division: Francis Jacobs; tel (Brussels) (2) 284-26-95.

4 Committee on Industry, External Trade, Research and Energy.

Head of Division: Luis Martin Oar; tel (Brussels) (2) 284-36-29.

Directorate D

(Economic, Monetary and Budgetary Affairs)

Director: Gérard Laprat; tel (Brussels) (2) 284-37-57.

Principal Administrator: Clara Albani-Liberali (Secretariat of the Convention on the Future of Europe); tel (Brussels) (2) 284-36-64.

Divisions

1 Committee on Economic and Monetary Affairs.

Head of Division: Jean-Louis Berton; tel (Brussels) (2) 284-24-42.

2 Committee on Budgets.

Head of Division: Alfredo de Feo; tel (Brussels) (2) 284-36-32.

Principal Administrator: Martine Charriot-Schneider (Committee on Budgetary Control); tel (Brussels) (2) 284-20-96.

3 Committee on Constitutional Affairs.

Head of Division: Charles Reich; tel (Brussels) (2) 284-22-17.

4 Committee on Petitions.

Head of Division: Enrico Boaretto; tel 4300-22522.

5 Committee on Women's Rights and Equal Opportunities.

Head of Division: Elvy Svennerstal; tel (Brussels) (2) 284-62-23.

Directorate E

(Common Policies)

Director: Ismael Olivares Martínez; tel (Brussels) (2) 284-32-97.

Divisions

1 Committee on Agriculture and Rural Development.

Head of Division: Armand Franjulien; tel (Brussels) (2) 284-25-11.

2 Committee on Fisheries.

Head of Division: Alberto Rodas; tel (Brussels) (2) 284-35-14.

3 Committee on Employment and Social Affairs.

Head of Division: (vacant).

4 Committee on Regional Policy, Transport and Tourism.

Head of Division: Frank Wiehler; tel 4300-23109.

5 Committee on Culture, Youth, Education, the Media and Sport.

Head of Division: Ignacio Samper; tel (Brussels) (2) 284-48-95.

Principal Administrator: Josephus Coolegem (Temporary Committee on Foot and Mouth Disease); tel (Brussels) (2) 284-28-48.

DIRECTORATE-GENERAL III: INFORMATION AND PUBLIC RELATIONS

Director-General: Heinrich Rolvering; tel 4300-22188.

Directorate: A

(Information and Public Relations)

Director: David Harley; tel (Brussels) (2) 284-39-09.

Principal Administrators: Jaime Duch Guillot (Planning and Press Room), tel (Brussels) (2) 284-30-00; Dominique Robert-Besse (Media Monitoring and Analysis), tel (Brussels) (2) 284-14-80.

Divisions

Press

Head of Division: Ute Kassnitz; tel (Brussels) (2) 284-42-69.

Principal Administrator: Jorn Hansen; tel (Brussels) (2) 284-25-30.

Audiovisual

Head of Division: Jean-Charles Pierron; tel 4300-22582.

Directorate B

(Communications and Co-ordination of External Offices, Publications and Public Events)

Director: Juana Lahousse; tel (Brussels) (2) 284-34-79.

Divisions

1 Publications and Events.

Head of Division: François Brunagel; tel (Brussels) (2) 284-28-86.

2 Visits and Seminars.

Head of Division: Helen McAvoy.

3 Citizens' Mail.

Head of Division: Jean-Louis Cougnon; tel 4300-23940.

Information Offices

Athens Information Office.

Leof. Amalias 8, 10557 Athens, Greece; tel (1) 331-15-41; fax (1) 331-15-40; e-mail epathinai@europarl.eu.int; internet www .ana.gr/ee/main.htm.

Principal Administrators: Ioannis Coccalas, Nikolaos Kostitsis.

Barcelona Information Office.

Passeig de Gracia 90, 08008 Barcelona, Spain; tel (93) 2722044; fax (93) 2722045; e-mail epbarcelona@europarl.eu.int.

Administrator: José María Ribot Igualada.

Berlin Information Office.

10117 Berlin, Unter den Linden 78, Germany; tel (30) 22801000; fax (30) 22801111; e-mail epberlin@europarl .eu.int; internet www.europarl.de.

Representatives: Klaus Loffler, Bernd Kunkmann.

Brussels Information Office.

rue Wiertz 60, 1047 Brussels, Belgium; tel (2) 284-20-05; fax (2) 230-75-55; e-mail epbrussels@europarl.eu.int; internet www.europarl.eu.int/brussels.

Head of Division: Peter Thomas.

Administrator: André de Munter.

Copenhagen Information Office.

Christian IX's Gade 22, 1111 Copenhagen, Denmark; tel 33-14-33-77; fax 33-15-08-05; e-mail epkobenhavn@europarl .eu.int; internet www.europarl.dk.

Representative: Soren Sondegard.

Principal Administrator: Henrik Gerner Hansen.

Dublin Information Office.

European Union House, 43 Molesworth St, Dublin 2, Ireland; tel (1) 6057900; fax (1) 6057999; e-mail epdublin@europarl .eu.int; internet www.europarl.ie.

Head of Division: James O'Brien.

Representative: Sarah Sheil.

Edinburgh Information Office.

9 Alva St, Edinburgh EH2 4PH, United Kingdom; tel (131) 225-2058; fax (131) 226-4105; e-mail epedinburgh@europarl .eu.int.

Principal Administrator: William Dermot Scott.

The Hague Information Office.

Korte Vijverberg 6, 2513 AB The Hague, Netherlands; tel (70) 362-49-41; fax (70) 364-70-01; e-mail epdenhaag@europarl .eu.int; internet www.europarl.eu.int/ denhaag.

Administrator: Johannes Verlaan.

Helsinki Information Office.

Pohjoisesplanadi 31, PL 26, 00131 Helsinki, Finland; tel (9) 6220450; fax (9) 6222610; e-mail ephelsinki@europarl .eu.int; internet www.europarl.fi.

Head of Office: Renny Jokelin.

Deputy Head of Office: Satu Raisano.

Lisbon Information Office.

Centro Europeu Jean Monnet, 6°, Largo Jean Monnet 1–6, 1269-070 Lisbon, Portugal; tel (21) 3504900; fax (21) 3540004; e-mail eplisboa@europarl.eu .int; internet www.parleurop.pt.

Head of Division: Nuno Antas de Campos.

Principal Administrator: José António Sobrinho.

London Information Office.

2 Queen Anne's Gate, London SW1H 9AA, United Kingdom; tel (20) 7227-4300; fax (20) 7227-4302; e-mail eplondon@europarl.eu.int; internet www .europarl.org.int.

Representative: William Dermot Scott.

Luxembourg Information Office.

Bâtiment Schuman, place de l'Europe, 2929 Luxembourg; tel 4300-22597; fax 4300-22457; e-mail epluxembourg@ europarl.eu.int.

Head of Division: Monique Schumacher.

Madrid Information Office.

Paseo de la Castellana 46, 28046 Madrid, Spain; tel (91) 4364747; fax (91) 5783171; e-mail epmadrid@europarl.eu.int; internet www.europarl.es.

Head of Division: Fernando Cabajo.

Marseilles Information Office.

2 rue Henri Barbusse, 13241 Marseille, France; tel 4-91-91-46-00; fax 4-91-90-95-03; e-mail icouset@europarl.eu.int; internet www.europarl.eu.int/marseille.

Administrator: Isabelle Coustet.

Milan Information Office

Corso Magenta 59, 20123 Milan, Italy; tel (02) 4818645; fax (02) 4814619; e-mail mcavenaghi@europarl.eu.int.

Principal Administrator: Maria-Grazia Cavenaghi-Smith.

Munich Information Office.

Erhardtstr 27, 80331 Munich; tel (89) 202-08-790; fax (89) 202-08-7973; e-mail epmuenchen@europarl.eu.int.

Administrator: Frank Piplat.

Paris Information Office.

288 blvd St Germain, 75341 Paris Cedex 07, France; tel 1-40-63-40-00; fax 1-45-51-52-53; e-mail epparis@europarl.eu.int; internet www.europarl.eu.int/paris.

Head of Division: Jean-Guy Giraud.

Principal Administrator: Christian Garrigues.

Rome Information Office.

Via IV Novembre 149, 00187 Rome, Italy; tel (06) 699501; fax (06) 69950200; e-mail eproma@europarl.eu.int.

Head of Division: Giovanni Salimbeni.

Principal Administrator: Roberto Pistacchi.

Stockholm Information Office.

Nybrogatan 11, 3°, 11439 Stockholm, Sweden; tel (8) 562-444-55; fax (8) 562-444-99; e-mail info@europarl.se; internet www.europarl.se.

Head of Division: Christian Andersson.

Deputy Head of Division: Klaus Jansson.

Strasbourg Information Office.

allée du Printemps, Louise Weiss Bldg, BP 1024/F, 67070 Strasbourg Cedex, France; tel 3-88-17-40-01; fax 3-88-17-51-84; e-mail epstrasbourg@europarl .eu.int.

Head of Division: Jean-Jacques Fritz.

Principal Administrator: Otmar Philippe.

Vienna Information Office.

Kärntner Ring 5–7, 1010 Vienna, Austria; tel (1) 51-61-70; fax (1) 513-25-15; e-mail epwien@europarl.eu.int; internet www.europarl.eu.int.

Head of Division: Michael Reinprecht.

Deputy Head of Division: Monika Strasser.

DIRECTORATE-GENERAL IV: RESEARCH

Director-General: Enrico Cioffi; tel (Brussels) (2) 284-36-90.

Directorate A

(Medium and Long-term Research)

Director: Massimo Silvestro (Co-ordination of Publications); tel (Brussels) (2) 284-29-79.

Divisions

1 Publications.

Head of Division: Rodolfo Raspanti; tel 4300-23361.

2 International and Constitutional Affairs.

Head of Division: Saverio Baviera; tel 4300-22538.

3 Monetary and Budgetary Affairs.

Head of Division: Mairéad Cranfield; tel 4300-22657.

4 Industry, Research, Energy and the Environment; STOA.

Head of Division: Paul Engstfeld; tel 4300-22627.

5 Social and Legal Affairs.

Head of Division: Philippe Ventujol; tel 4300-22520.

6 Agriculture, Regional Policy, Transport and Development.

Head of Division: John Bryan Rose; tel 4300-22091.

Directorate B

(Parliamentary Documentation and International Co-operation)

Director: Dick Toornstra; tel (Brussels) (2) 284-21-38.

Division

1 Parliamentary Documentation and International Co-operation.

Head of Division: Sven Backlund; tel (Brussels) (2) 284-62-05.

DIRECTORATE-GENERAL V: PERSONNEL

Director-General: Barry Wilson; tel 4300-22068.

Personnel Directorate

Director: Manfred Peter; tel 4300-22593.

Divisions

1 Personnel.

Head of Division: Brigitte Nouaille-Degorce; tel 4300-22519.

---

2 Social Affairs.

Head of Division: Hélène Puech; tel 4300-24516.

3 Pay and Allowances.

Head of Division: Wolfdieter Hell; tel 4300-22570.

4 Relations with Staff.

Head of Division: Barry Waters; tel (Brussels) (2) 284-36-76.

Units

1 Appropriations Management Unit.

Head of Unit: Michael Gordon; tel 4300-23285.

2 IT Unit.

Head of Unit: Pierre Poulet; tel 4300-24839.

3 Legal Affairs Unit.

Head of Unit: Poul Runge Nilsen; tel 4300-24414.

4 Personal Data Protection.

Head of Unit: Jonathan Steele; tel 4300-24864.

5 Medical Office.

Head of Unit: Sandro Colantonio; tel 4300-22592.

Divisions

1 Internal Organization and Human Resources Planning.

Head of Division: Yves Quitin; tel 4300-20116.

2 Professional Training.

Head of Division: Laura Viqueira; tel 4300-23270.

DIRECTORATE-GENERAL VI: ADMINISTRATION

Director-General: Nicolas Pierre Rieffel; tel 4300-22734.

Division

1 External Offices Management.

Head of Division: Roger Glass; tel 4300-23500.

Administrator: Daniel Ratcliffe (Central Secretariat); tel 4300-23423.

Directorate A

(Infrastructure and In-house Services)

Director: Stavros Gavril; tel 4300-22278.

Divisions

1 Buildings.

Head of Division: Francis Schaff; tel 4300-24881.

2 Logistics.

Head of Division: Tove Fihl; tel 4300-22059.

3 Purchasing and Catering.

Head of Division: Lambert Kraewinkels; tel 4300-24429.

Directorate B

(Interpretation and Conferences Interinstitutional Service)

Director: Olga Cosmidou; tel 4300-22892.

DIRECTORATE-GENERAL VII: TRANSLATION AND GENERAL SERVICES

Director-General: Gérard Bokanowski; tel 4300-27799.

Division

1 Planning.

Head of Division: Philippe Graas; tel 4300-23399.

Directorate A

(Publishing and Distribution)

Director: (vacant).

Division

1 Publishing.

Head of Division: Frédéric Tonhofer; tel 4300-22475.

Unit

1 Distribution.

Head of Unit: Franky Depuydt; tel 4300-24044.

Directorate B

(Translation)

Director: Helmut Spindler; tel 4300-23145.

DIRECTORATE-GENERAL VIII: FINANCE

Director-General: Roger Vanhaeren; tel (Brussels) (2) 284-25-51.

Directorate A

(Finance)

Director: Karl Colling; tel (Brussels) (2) 284-26-02.

Division

1 Budget.

Head of Division: Bernard Hellot; tel 4300-22115.

Units

1 Treasury and Accounts.

Head of Unit: David Young; tel 4300-22629.

2 Inventory and Management of Assets.

Head of Unit: Francis Wattiau; tel 4300-22392.

3 Financial Affairs.

Head of Unit: Renée Hentges-Neins; tel 4300-22616.

Directorate B

(Financial Management and Control)

Director: Clare Wells-Shaddad; tel (Brussels) (2) 284-26-10.

INDEX OF MEPs BY COUNTRY

Austria

Berger, Maria
Bösch, Herbert
Ettl, Harald
Karas, Othmar
Leichtfried, Jörg
Lichtenberger, Evelin
Martin, Hans-Peter
Mölzer, Andreas
Prets, Christa
Rack, Reinhard
Resetarits, Karin
Rübig, Paul
Scheele, Karin
Schierhuber, Agnes
Seeber, Richard
Stenzel, Ursula
Swoboda, Johannes
Voggenhuber, Johannes

Belgium

Belet, Ivo
Brepoels, Frederika M. M.
Busquin, Philippe
Claeys, Philip
De Keyser, Véronique
De Vits, Mia
Dehaene, Jean-Luc
Deprez, Gérard
Dillen, Koenraad
Duquesne, Antoine
El Khadraoui, Saïd
Grosch, Mathieu
Hutchinson, Alain
Jonckheer, Pierre
Langendries, Raymond
Neyts-Uyttebroeck, Annemie
Ries, Frédérique
Staes, Bart
Sterckx, Dirk De Heer
Tarabella, Marc
Thyssen, Marianne
Van Hecke, Johan
Van Lancker, Anne
Vanhecke, Frank

Cyprus

Adamou, K.Adamos
Demetriou, Panayiotis
Kasoulides, Ioannis
Matsakis, Marios
Matsis, Yiannakis
Triantaphyllides, Kyriacos

Czech Republic

Bobosíková, Paní Jana
Březina, Jan
Cabrnoch, Milan
Duchoň, Petr
Fajmon, Hynek
Falbr, Richard
Flasarová, Věra
Hybášková, Jana
Kohlíček, Jaromír
Maštálka, Jiří

Ouzký, Miroslav
Ransdorf, Miloslav
Remek, Vladimír
Roithová, Zuzana
Rouček, Libor
Škottová, Nina
Strejček, Ivo
Stroz, Daniel
Vlasák, Oldřich
Zahradil, Jan
Zatloukal, Tomáš
Železný, Vladimír
Zieleniec, Josef
Zvěřina, Jaroslav

Denmark

Auken, Margrete
Bonde, Jens-Peter
Busk, Niels
Camre, Mogens N. J.
Christensen, Ole
Jensen, Anne Elisabet
Jørgensen, Dan
Krarup, Ole
Kristensen, Henrik Dam
Rasmussen, Poul Nyrup
Riis-Jørgensen, Karin
Samuelsen, Anders
Seeberg, Gitte
Thomsen, Britta

Estonia

Ilves, Toomas Hendrik
Kelam, Tunne
Mikko, Marianne
Oviir, Siiri
Savi, Toomas
Tarand, Andres

Finland

Hassi, Maijastiina
Itälä, Ville
Jäätteenmäki, Anneli
Kauppi, Piia-Noora
Korhola, Eiji-Riita Anneli
Lax, Henrik
Lehtinen, Lasse Antero
Myller, Riitta
Paasilinna, Reino
Seppänen, Esko Olavi
Stubb, Alexander
Takkula, Hannu
Väyrynen, Paavo
Virrankoski, Kyösti Tapio

France

Arif, Kader
Aubert, Marie-Hélène
Bachelot-Narquin, Roselyne
Beaupuy, Jean Marie
Bennahmias, Jean-Luc
Berès, Pervenche
Bono, Guy
Bourlanges, Jean-Louis
Bourzai, Bernadette

Carlotti, Marie-Arlette
Castex, François
Cavada, Jean-Marie
Cornillet, Thierry
Cottigny, Jean Louis
Coûteaux, Paul Marie
Daul, Joseph
De Sarnez, Marielle
De Veyrac, Christine
Descamps, Marie-Hélène
Désir, Harlem
Douay, Brigitte
Ferreira, Anne
Flautre, Hélène
Fontaine, Nicole
Fourtou, Janelly
Fruteau, Jean-Claude
Gaubert, Patrick
Gauzès, Jean-Paul
Gibault, Claire
Gollnisch, Bruno
Griesbeck, Nathalie
Grossetête, François
Guellec, Ambroise
Guy-Quint, Catherine
Hamon, Benoît
Hazan, Adeline
Henin, Jacky
Hortefeux, Brice
Isler Béguin, Marie Anne
Laignel, André
Lamassoure, Alain
Lang, Carl
Laperrouze, Anne
Le Foll, Stéphane
Le Pen, Jean-Marie
Le Pen, Marine
Lehideux, Bernard
Lienemann, Marie-Noëlle
Lipietz, Alain
Louis, Patrick
Martinez, Jean-Claude
Mathieu, Véronique
Morillon, Philippe
Moscovici, Pierre
Navarro, Robert
Onesta, Gérard
Patrie, Béatrice
Peillon, Vincent Benoît Camille
Poignant, Bernard
Reynaud, Marie-Line
Rocard, Michel
Roure, Martine
Saïfi, Tokia
Savary, Gilles
Schapira, Pierre Lionel Georges
Schenardi, Lydia
Sudre, Margie
Toubon, Jacques
Trautmann, Catherine
Vatanen, Ari
Vaugrenard, Yannick
Verges, Paul
Vergnaud, Bernadette
Villiers, Philippe de
Vlasto, Dominique

Weber, Henri
Wurtz, Francis

Germany

Graefe zu Baringdorf, Friedrich-Wilhelm
Alvaro, Alexander Nuno
Beer, Angelika
Berend, Rolf
Böge, Reimer
Breyer, Hiltrud
Brie, André
Brok, Elmar
Bullmann, Udo
Caspary, Daniel
Chatzimarkakis, Jorgo
Cohn-Bendit, Daniel Marc
Cramer, Michael
Dess, Albert
Duin, Garrelt
Ehler, Jan Christian
Ferber, Markus
Florenz, Karl-Heinz
Friedrich, Ingo
Gahler, Michael
Gebhardt, Evelyne
Glante, Norbert
Goepel, Lutz
Gomolka, Alfred
Grässle, Ingeborg
Gröner, Lissy
Hänsch, Klaus
Harms, Rebecca
Haug, Jutta D.
Hieronymi, Ruth
Hoppenstedt, Karsten Friedrich
Horáček, Milan
Jarzembowski, Georg
Jeggle, Elisabeth
Jöns, Karin
Kallenbach, Gisela
Kaufmann, Sylvia-Yvonne
Kindermann, Heinz
Klamt, Ewa
Klass, Christa
Klinz, Wolf
Koch, Dieter-Lebrecht
Koch-Mehrin, Silvana
Konrad, Christoph Werner
Krahmer, Holger
Krehl, Constanze Angela
Kreissl-Dörfler, Wolfgang
Kuhne, Helmut
Lambsdorff Graf, Alexander
Langen, Werner
Laschet, Armin
Lauk, Kurt Joachim
Lechner, Kurt
Lehne, Klaus-Heiner
Leinen, Jo
Liese, Peter
Mann, Erika
Mann, Thomas
Markov, Helmuth
Mayer, Hans-Peter
Nassauer, Hartmut
Niebler, Angelika
Öger, Vural
Özdemir, Cem
Pack, Doris
Pflüger, Tobias
Piecyk, Willi
Pieper, Markus

Poettering, Hans-Gert
Posselt, Bernd
Quisthoudt-Rowohl, Godelieve
Radwan, Alexander
Rapkay, Bernhard
Reul, Herbert Otto
Roth-Behrendt, Dagmar
Rothe, Mechtild
Rühle, Heide
Schmidt, Frithjof
Schmitt, Ingo
Schnellhardt, Horst
Schröder, Jürgen
Schroedter, Elisabeth
Schulz, Martin
Schuth, Willem
Schwab, Andreas
Sommer, Renate
Stockmann, Ulrich
Trüpel, Helga
Uca, Feleknas
Ulmer, Thomas
Wagenknecht, Sahra
Walter, Ralf
Weber, Manfred
Weiler, Barbara
Weisgerber, Anja
Wieland, Rainer
Wogau, Karl von
Wuermeling, Joachim
Zimmer, Gabriele

Greece

Arnaoutakis, Stavros
Batzeli, Katerîna
Beglitis, Panagiotis
Dimitrakopoulos, Giorgos
Gklavakis, Ioannis
Hatzidakis, Konstantinos
Karatzaferis, Georgios
Kratsa-Tsagaropoulou, Rodi
Lambrinidis, Stavros
Manolakou, Diamanto
Matsouka, Maria
Mavrommatis, Manolis
Pafilis, Athanasios
Panayotopoulos-Cassiotou, Marie
Papadimoulis, Dimitrios
Papastamkos, Georgios
Samaras, Antonis
Sifunakis, Nikolaos
Toussas, Georgios
Trakatellis, Antonios
Tzampazi, Evangelia
Vakalis, Nikolaos
Varvitsiotis, Ioannis
Xenogiannakopoulou, Marilisa

Hungary

Barsi Pataky, Etelka
Becsey, Zsolt László
Demszky, Gábor
Dobolyi, Alexandra
Fazakas, Szabolcs
Gál, Kinga
Glattfelder, Béla
Gurmai, Zita
Gyürk, András
Harangozó, Gábor
Hegyi, Gyula
Herczog, Edit

Járóka, Lívia
Kósáne Kovács, Magda
Lévai, Katalin
Olajos, Péter
Öry, Csaba
Pálfi, István
Schmitt, Pál
Schöpflin, György
Surján, László
Szájer, József
Szent-Iványi, István
Tabajdi, Csaba Sándor

Ireland

Aylward, Liam
Coveney, Simon
Crowley, Brian
De Rossa, Proinsias
Doyle, Avril
Harkin, Marian
Higgins, Jim
McDonald, Mary Lou
McGuinness, Mairead
Mitchell, Gay
Ó Neachtain, Seán
Ryan, Eoin
Sinnott, Kathy

Italy

Agnoletto, Vittorio Emanuele
Albertini, Gabriele
Andria, Alfonso
Angelilli, Roberta
Antoniozzi, Alfredo
Battilocchio, Alessandro
Berlato, Sergio
Berlinguer, Giovanni
Bersani, Pier Luigi
Bertinotti, Fausto
Bonino, Emma
Bonsignore, Vito
Borghezio, Mario
Bossi, Umberto
Bresso, Mercedes
Brunetta, Renato
Carollo, Giorgio
Castiglione, Giuseppe
Catania, Giusto
Cesa, Lorenzo
Chiesa, Giulietto
Cirino Pomicino, Paolo
Cocilovo, Luigi
Costa, Paolo
D'Alema, Massimo
De Michelis, Gianni
De Poli, Antonio
Del Turco, Ottaviano
Di Pietro, Antonio
Dionisi, Armando
Ebner, Michl
Fatuzzo, Carlo
Fava, Giovanni Claudio
Foglietta, Alessandro
Frassoni, Monica
Gargani, Giuseppe
Gawronski, Jas
Gruber, Dietlinde
Guidoni, Umberto
Kusstatscher, Sepp
La Russa, Romano Maria
Letta, Enrico

Locatelli, Pia Elda
Lombardo, Raffaele
Mantovani, Mario
Mauro, Mario
Morgantini, Luisa
Musacchio, Roberto
Muscardini, Cristiana
Musotto, Francesco
Mussolini, Alessandra
Musumeci, Sebastiano
Napoletano, Pasqualina
Pannella, Marco
Panzeri, Pier Antonio
Pirilli, Umberto
Pistelli, Lapo
Pittella, Giovanni
Podestà, Guido
Poli Bortone, Adriana
Prodi, Vittorio
Rizzo, Marco
Romagnoli, Luca
Sacconi, Guido
Salvini, Matteo
Santoro, Michele
Sartori, Amalia
Sbarbati, Luciana
Speroni, Francesco Enrico
Tajani, Antonio
Tatarella, Salvatore
Toia, Patrizia
Ventre, Riccardo
Vernola, Marcello
Vincenzi, Marta
Zani, Secondo
Zappala, Stefano
Zingaretti, Nicola

Latvia

Andrejevs, Georgs
Dombrovskis, Valdis
Krasts, Guntars
Kristovskis, Ģirts Valdis
Kuškis, Aldis
Pīks, Rihard
Vaidere, Inese
Ždanoka, Tatjana
Zīle, Roberts

Lithuania

Andrikienė, Laima Liucija
Birutis, Šarūnas
Budreikaitė, Danutė
Degutis, Arūnas
Dičkutê, Jolanta
Didžiokas, Gintaras
Gentvilas, Eugenijus
Juknevičienė, Ona
Landsbergis, Vytautas
Paleckis, Justas Vincas
Pavilionis, Rolandas
Sakalas, Aloyzas
Starkevičiūtė, Margarita

Luxembourg

Goebbels, Robert
Hennicot-Schoepges, Erna
Lulling, Astrid
Polfer, Lydie
Spautz, Jean
Turmes, Claude

Malta

Attard-Montalto, John
Busuttil, Simon
Casa, David
Grech, Louis
Muscat, Joseph

Netherlands

Belder, Bastiaan
van den Berg, Margrietus J.
Berman, Thijs
Blokland, Johannes
Bozkurt, Emine
van Buitenen, Paul K. T. J.
Buitenweg, Kathalijne Maria
van den Burg, Ieke
Corbey, Dorette
Doorn, Bert
Eurlings, Camiel
de Groen-Kouwenhoven, Elly
Hennis-Plasschaert, Jeanine
in't Veld, Sophia Helena
Lagendijk, Joost
Liotard, Kartika Tamara
Maat, Albert Jan
Maaten, Jules
Manders, Toine
Martens, Maria
Mastenbroek, Edith
Meijer, Erik
Mulder, Jan
Nistelrooij, Lambert van
Oomen-Ruijten, Ria G. H. C.
Wiersma, Jan Marinus
Wortmann-Kool, Corien M.

Poland

Adwent, Filip
Bielan, Adam Jerzy
Buzek, Jerzy
Chmielewski, Zdzisław Kazimierz
Chruszcz, Sylwester
Czarnecki, Marek Aleksander
Czarnecki, Ryszard
Fotyga, Anna Elżbieta
Geremek, Bronisław
Geringer de Oedenberg, Lidia Joanna
Gierek, Adam
Giertych, Maciej Marian
Golik, Bogdan
Grabowska, Genowefa
Grabowski, Dariusz Maciej
Handzlik, Małgorzata Maria
Jałowiecki, Stanisław
Janowski, Mieczysław Edmund
Kaczmarek, Filip Andrzej
Kamiński, Michał Tomasz
Klich, Bogdan Adam
Krupa, Urszula
Kuc, Wiesław Stefan
Kudrycka, Barbara
Kułakowski, Jan Jerzy
Kuźmiuk, Zbigniew Krzysztof
Lewandowski, Janusz
Liberadzki, Bogusław Marian
Libicki, Marcin
Masiel, Jan Tadeusz
Olbrycht, Jan Marian
Onyszkiewicz, Janusz
Pęk, Bogdan Marek
Pinior, Józef

Piotrowski, Mirosław Mariusz
Piskorski, Pawel Bartłomiej
Podkański, Zdzisław Zbigniew
Protasiewicz, Jacek
Rogalski, Bogusław
Rosati, Dariusz Kajetan
Roszkowski, Wojciech
Rutowicz, Leopold Józef
Saryusz-Wolski, Jacek Emil
Siekierski, Czesław Adam
Siwiec, Marek Maciej
Sonik, Bogusław Andrzej
Staniszewska, Grażyna
Szejna, Andrzej Jan
Szymański, Konrad Krzysztof
Tomczak, Witold
Wierzejski, Wojciech
Wojciechowski, Janusz Czesław
Zaleski, Zbigniew
Zwiefka, Tadeusz Antoni

Portugal

Assis, Francisco
Capoulas Santos, Luis Manuel
Casaca, Paulo
Coelho, Carlos
Correia, Fausto
Costa, António
Esteves, María da Assunção
Estrela, Edite
Fernandes, Emmanuel Vasconcelos Jardim
Ferreira, Elisa
Figueiredo, Ilda
Freitas, Duarte
Gomes, Ana Maria R. M.
Graça Moura, Vasco
Madeira, Jamila
Marques, Sérgio
Pinheiro, João de Deus
Portas, Miguel
Queiró, Luís
Ribeiro e Castro, José
Ribeiro, Sérgio
Santos, Manuel António dos
Silva Peneda, José Albino
Sousa Pinto, Sérgio

Slovakia

Baco', Peter
Bauer, Edit
Belohorská, Irena
Beňová, Monika
Duka-Zólyomi, Árpád
Gaľa, Milan
Hudacký, Ján
Koterec, Miloš
Kozlík, Sergej
Maňka, Vladimír
Mikolášik Miroslav
Pleštinská, Zita
Šťastný, Peter
Záborská, Anna

Slovenia

Brejc, Mihael
Drčar Murko, Mojca
Jordan Cizelj, Romana
Kacin, Jelko
Novak, Ljudmila
Pahor, Borut
Peterle, Alojz

Spain

Ayala Sender, Inés
Ayuso González, María del Pilar
Badía Cutchet, Maria
Barón Crespo, Enrique
Borrell Fontelles, Josep
Calabuig Rull, Joan
Carnero González, Carlos
del Castillo Vera, Pilar
Cercas, Alejandro
Díaz De Mera García, Agustín
Díez González, Rosa M.
Dührkop Dührkop, Bárbara
Fernández Martín, Fernando
Fraga Estévez, Carmen
Galeote Quecedo, Gerardo
García-Margallo y Marfil, José Manuel
García Pérez, Iratxe
Garriga Polledo, Salvador
de Grandes Pascual, Luis
Guardans Cambó, Ignasi
Gutiérrez-Cortines, Cristina
Hammerstein Mintz, David
Herranz García, María Esther
Herrero-Tejedor, Luis Francisco
Iturgaiz Angulo, Carlos José
Joan i Marí, Bernat
López-Istúriz White, Antonio
Martínez Martínez, Miguel Angel
Masip Hidalgo, Antonio
Mato Adrover, Ana
Mayor Oreja, Jaime
Medina Ortega, Manuel
Méndez De Vigo, Íñigo
Menéndez del Valle, Emilio
Meyer Pleite, Willy
Miguélez Ramos, Rosa
Millán, Francisco José
Montoro Romero, Cristóbal Ricardo
Moreno Sánchez, Javier
Obiols i Germà, Raimon
Ortuondo Larrea, Josu
Pleguezuelos Aguilar, Francisca
Pomés Ruiz, José Javier
Riera Madurell, Teresa
Romeva i Rueda, Raúl
Rudi Ubeda, Luisa Fernanda
Salafranca Sánchez-Neyra, José Ignacio
Salinas García, María Isabel
Sánchez Presedo, Antolín
Sornosa Martínez, María
Valenciano Martínez-Orozco, María Elena
Varela Suanzes-Carpegna, Daniel
Vidal-Quadras Roca, Alejo
Yañez-Barnuevo García, Luis

Sweden

Andersson, Jan
Carlshamre, Maria
Cederschiöld, Charlotte
Ek, Lena
Fjellner, Christofer
Goudin, Hélène
Hedh, Anna
Hedkvist Petersen, Ewa
Hökmark, Gunnar
Ibrisagic, Anna
Lundgren, Nils
Malmström, Cecilia
Schlyter, Carl
Segelström, Inger
Sjöstedt, Jonas
Svensson, Eva-Britt
Westlund, Åsa
Wijkman, Anders
Wohlin, Lars

United Kingdom

Allister, James Hugh
Ashworth, Richard James
Atkins, Sir Robert
Attwooll, Elspeth
Batten, Gerard Joseph
Beazley, Christopher
Bloom, Godfrey William
Booth, Graham H.
Bowis, John
Bradbourn, Philip Charles
Bushill-Matthews, Philip
Callanan, Martin
Cashman, Michael
Chichester, Giles Bryan
Clark, Derek Roland
Corbett, Richard
Davies, Chris
de Brún, Bairbre
Deva, Nirj
Dover, Den
Duff, Andrew Nicholas
Elles, James E. L.
Evans, Jillian
Evans, Jonathan
Evans, Robert J. E.
Farage, Nigel Paul
Ford, Glyn
Gill, Neena
Hall, Fiona Jane
Hannan, Daniel J.
Harbour, Malcolm
Heaton-Harris, Christopher
Helmer, Roger
Honeyball, Mary
Howitt, Richard
Hudghton, Ian Stewart
Hughes, Stephen
Huhne, Christopher
Jackson, Caroline F.
Karim, Sajjad Haider
Kilroy-Silk, Robert
Kinnock, Glenys
Kirkhope, Timothy
Knapman, Roger Maurice
Lambert, Jean Denise
Lucas, Caroline
Ludford, Baroness Sarah
Lynne, Elizabeth
Martin, David W.
McAvan, Linda
McCarthy, Arlene
McMillan-Scott, Edward H. C.
Moraes, Claude
Morgan, Eluned
Mote, Ashley
Nattrass Michael
Newton Dunn, Bill
Nicholson of Winterbourne, Baroness
Nicholson, James
Parish, Neil
Purvis, John
Skinner, Peter William
Smith, Alyn Edward
Stevenson, Struan
Stihler, Catherine
Sturdy, Robert William
Sumberg, David
Tannock, Charles
Titford, Jeffrey William
Titley, Gary
Van Orden, Geoffrey
Villiers, Theresa
Wallis, Diana
Watson, Graham R.
Whitehead, Phillip
Whittaker, John
Wise, Thomas Harold
Wynn, Terence

THE EU's OTHER INSTITUTIONS

COUNCIL OF THE EUROPEAN UNION

The Council of the European Union is composed of one Ministerial-level representative of each Member State. The Presidency is held for a term of six months by each Member State in turn.

The Council meets in different formations, depending on the subject matter, the most common being: General Affairs, Agriculture, Budget, Consumers, Culture, Development, Economic and Financial Questions (ECOFIN), Education, Energy, Environment, Industry, Justice and Home Affairs, Internal Market, Fisheries, Research, Health, Telecommunications, Transport and Labour and Social Affairs.

The General Affairs, Economic and Financial Affairs (ECOFIN) and Agriculture Councils meet once a month. The others meet two to four times a year depending on the urgency of the topics discussed.

The Member States have Permanent Representations to the European Union in Brussels. Permanent Representatives usually meet each week in a committee known as the Permanent Representatives Committee (COREPER). That Committee, which is divided into two parts – one being composed of the Permanent Representatives, the other of their Deputies – is responsible for preparing the Council's proceedings. Preparation for the Agriculture Council is the responsibility of the Special Committee on Agriculture (SCA).

The numerous working parties, composed of national delegates and experts, submit their reports, following thorough examination of proposals, to COREPER and the SCA.

The Treaties stipulate those cases in which the Council acts by a simple majority, qualified majority or unanimously.

The structure of the Treaty on European Union (TEU) divides the Union's activities into three fields ('pillars'), on the basis of which the Council's proceedings are arranged.

The first pillar covers activities deriving from the Treaty establishing the European Community (TEC), involving 'Community' policies such as agriculture, environmental protection or economic and commercial questions. The second and third pillars cover the Common Foreign and Security Policy (CFSP) and co-operation in the fields of Justice and Home Affairs (JHA) respectively. With the Treaty of Amsterdam some third-pillar subjects such as visas, immigration, asylum and other policies connected with the free movement of persons have been transferred to the first pillar.

Council acts may take the form of Regulations, Directives, Decisions, Recommendations or Opinions. The Council may also adopt conclusions of a political nature or other types of act such as Declarations or Resolutions. As regards Common Foreign and Security Policy and Justice and Home Affairs, the main instruments provided for by the Treaty are joint actions and common positions, common strategies, joint positions and conventions (Justice and Home Affairs only).

Information on the Council's activities may be derived from several sources: the Presidency, the Press Office of the General Secretariat, the delegations and the Commission, which has representatives at every Council meeting.

Explanations about decisions and the work of the Council are provided at the end of each session by the President at a Press conference. A detailed press release is published by the Press Office, on the General Secretariat's responsibility, after each meeting. This information is supplemented by the Member States – Ministers and their spokesmen – with details of their respective positions in the deliberations.

All correspondence for the Presidency of the Council should be addressed to: Council of the European Union, 175 rue de la Loi, 1048 Brussels, Belgium; tel (2) 285-61-11; fax (2) 285-73-97; e-mails to the pattern firstname.surname@ consilium.eu.int; internet http://ue.eu .int.

PRESS OFFICE

Information available includes:

- European Union declarations in the field of Common Foreign and Security Policy.
- *Latest News* contains all recently published texts, usually in English or French. Since 1995 these, and the relevant translations, have been archived in the Press Release Library.
- Press releases, which are drafted under the Secretariat General's own responsibility and are issued after Council meetings, provide summaries of the outcome of proceedings and contain conclusions, statements, resolutions, etc. agreed by the Council; the press releases also give the results of votes and voting explanations.
- Press releases concerning meetings of the Parliament–Council Conciliation Committee and press releases relating to meetings and agreements with third countries. Declarations by the Presidency on behalf of the European Union in the framework of the Common Foreign and Security Policy have their own heading: 'CFSP Statements'.
- Agendas prior to Council meetings, basically setting the agenda, which are published in the form of a press release.
- Background notes commenting on the key issues of forthcoming Council agendas and on other Council activities (available generally at the same time as pre-Council Presidency briefings take place).

Information is also available on the Internet site of the Press Office: http:// ue.eu.int-Newsroom.

The Press Service contributes also to day-to-day information through direct media contacts and mainly informal briefings before, during and after Council meetings. In addition, it provides any available documentation relating to the work of the Council. Furthermore, it is responsible for the management of the Council Press Centres in Brussels and Luxembourg. It provides technical assistance to Member States' delegations for their press activities and in particular assists each Presidency in organizing briefings and press conferences.

The Press office can be contacted at: 175 rue de la Loi, 1048 Brussels, Belgium; tel (2) 285-81-11; fax (2) 285-80-26 e-mail press.office@consilium.eu.int; internet http://ue.eu.int/Newsroom.

PUBLICATIONS

The Council has a publications service and some of the publications are disseminated by the Office for Official Publications.

The basic publications are annual reports on association agreements, co-operation agreements and the Cotonou Agreement, as well as an annual report providing a synopsis of the Council's activities.

The Council is also involved in the compilation of the inter-institutional directory which provides details of officials working in the different EU institutions. The publication is distributed online and is updated annually.

LIBRARY

The Council has a library of about 57,000 volumes, open to persons doing work relating to the Council of Ministers. Its reception capacities are limited, however.

Librarian: Anne Ostry, 8 square de Meeûs, 1048 Brussels, Belgium; tel (2) 285-65-41; fax (2) 285-81-74.

General Secretariat

(175 rue de la Loi, 1048 Brussels, Belgium; tel (2) 285-61-11; fax (2) 285-73-97; e-mail public.relations@consilium.eu.int; internet ue.eu.int)

Secretary-General and High Representative for Common Foreign and Security Policy: Javier Solana; tel (2) 285-56-60.

Deputy Secretary-General: Pierre de Boissieu; tel (2) 285-62-15.

PRIVATE OFFICE OF THE SECRETARY-GENERAL

Head of Cabinet, High Representative and Director: Alberto Navarro González; tel (2) 285-55-72.

Deputy Head of Cabinet, High Representative (CFSP, liaison with the PPEWU) and Head of Division: Leonardo Schiavo; tel (2) 285-55-75.

Head of Cabinet of the Deputy Secretary-General: David Galloway; tel (2) 285-61-94.

Advisers: Ralph Kaessner, tel (2) 285-94-22; Veronica Cody, tel (2) 285-85-43; Paul Reiderman, tel (2) 285-87-04.

1 Departments attached to the Secretary-General/High Representative

PPEWU—Policy Planning and Early Warning Unit

Director: Christoph Heusgen; tel (2) 285-54-30.

TASK FORCE: EUROPEAN SECURITY AND DEFENCE POLICY (ESDP)

Head of Division: Marc Otte; tel (2) 285-53-20.

Administrator: Hans-Bernhard Weisserth; tel (2) 285-58-48.

TASK FORCE: WESTERN BALKANS/ CENTRAL EUROPE

Administrators: Giorgio Aliberti, tel (2) 285-80-37; Stephan Müller, tel (2) 285-80-36; Carl Hallergard, tel (2) 285-54-37; Patrice Bergamini, tel (2) 285-55-71; Torbjörn Sohlström, tel (2) 285-58-44.

TASK FORCE: PREVENTION OF CONFLICTS AND SITUATION CENTRE

Administrators: Niall Burgess, tel (2) 285-58-42; Andreas Papconstantinou, tel (2) 285-58-40; Andreas Wiedenhoof, tel (2) 285-54-82.

TASK FORCE: HORIZONTAL QUESTIONS—LATIN AMERICA

Head of Division: José Gómez-Llera; tel (2) 285-53-22.

Administrators: Jette Nordam, tel (2) 285-58-22; Leonor Costa Rosa, tel (2) 285-58-41.

TASK FORCE: RUSSIA/UKRAINE— TRANSATLANTIC BALTICS/ASIA

Head of Division: Cornelis Van Rij; tel (2) 285-53-28.

Administrators: Carl Hartzell, tel (2) 285-58-45; Antti Turunen, tel (2) 285-58-46; Christopher Holtby, tel (2) 285-58-50.

TASK FORCE: MEDITERRANEAN/ BARCELONA—MIDDLE EAST/AFRICA

Head of Division: Pascal Charlat; tel (2) 285-53-24.

Administrators: Wolfgang Barwinkel, tel (2) 285-82-41; Björn Larsson, tel (2) 285-94-15; Irene Simantoni Empl, tel (2) 285-77-02.

TASK FORCE: PU ADMINISTRATION/ SECURITY

Administrator: François Van Hövell; tel (2) 285-72-68.

2 Departments attached to the Secretary-General/High Representative and to the Deputy Secretary-General

Directorate for General Political Questions

Director: Max J. Keller-Noëllet; tel (2) 285-74-17.

Heads of Division: Georges Zbyszewski (Meetings, ANTICI Group), tel (2) 285-76-59; Jurgen Neisse (Coreper I Group and QL; Mertens and QR Group), tel (2) 285-70-97; André Gillissen (Coreper II Group and QL; Antici and QR); François Van Hövell (Financial Control), tel (2) 285-72-68; Dominique Anglaret (Internal Audit), tel (2) 285-80-13.

Adviser, General Political Questions: Guy Milton; tel (2) 285-85-19.

Military Staff: Rainer Schuwirth (General Director-General), tel (2) 285-59-90; Jean-Pierre Herreweghe (General Deputy Director-General), tel (2) 285-58-88.

Director-General, Administrative Reform: Marc Lepoivre; tel (2) 285-82-67.

Administrators: Emile Ceuppens (Internal Audit), tel (2) 285-60-86; Paulo Branco (Internal Audit), tel (2) 285-54-84; Pierre Vernhes (Data Protection), tel (2) 285-90-09; Bartolomeo Manenti (Information Systems Security), tel (2) 285-76-45; Ulrich van Essen (Information Systems Security), tel 285-98-40; Eric Bleyaert (Dept for Prevention), tel (2) 285-82-43; Nessa Delaney (Dept for Administrative Reform), tel (2) 285-73-44; Helio Gómez De Mayor Rojas (Dept for Administrative Reform), tel (2) 285-69-46.

LEGAL SERVICE

Director-General—Legal Adviser: Jean-Claude Piris; tel (2) 285-62-27; fax (2) 285-73-94.

Deputy Director-General: (vacant).

Assistant to the Director-General: Thérèse Blanchet; tel (2) 285-87-75.

Team I

(Internal Market; Industry; Telecommunications; Tourism; Energy; Civil Protection; Research; Trans-European Networks; Transport; Social Affairs; Culture; Education; Youth; Regional Policy; Environment; Harmonization of Food Legislation; Consumer Protection; Health; Competition Rules and Public Procurement)

Directors: Jean-Paul Jacqué, tel (2) 285-62-26; Jürgen Huber, tel (2) 285-73-48.

Heads of Division: Amadeu Lopes-Sabino, tel (2) 285-71-09; Bjarne Hoff-Nielsen, tel (2) 285-62-65.

Legal Advisers: Maria-Cristina Giorgi, tel (2) 285-64-59; Anna Lo Monaco, tel (2) 285-83-42; Eva Karlsson, tel (2) 285-79-83.

Team II

(Agriculture and Fisheries; Policy on Economic and Monetary Union—EMU; Taxation; Free Movement of Capital; Structural Funds; all matters prepared by Coreper II for the attention of the Economic and Financial Council of Ministers—ECOFIN)

Director: Giorgio Maganza; tel (2) 285-79-50.

Head of Division: John Carberry; tel (2) 285-64-61.

Legal Advisers: Jorge Monteiro, tel (2) 285-85-33; Maria Balta, tel (2) 285-49-69; Anna-Maria Colaert, tel (2) 285-83-65;

Francesco Ruggeri Laderchi, tel (2) 285-54-85; Fernando Florindo Gijón, tel (2) 285-61-96.

Team III

(External Relations, including Common Foreign and Security Policy—CFSP; Development Co-operation; African, Caribbean and Pacific—ACP States; all matters relating to International Agreements and Relations with International Organizations)

Director: Ricardo Gosalbo Bono; tel (2) 285-62-59.

Heads of Division: Gilles Marhic, tel (2) 285-50-23; Eric Chaboureau, tel (2) 285-50-24.

Legal Advisers: Micail Vitsentzatos, tel (2) 285-76-62; Sofia Kyriakopoulou, tel (2) 285-82-21; Michael Bishop, tel (2) 285-83-03; Stephan Marquardt, tel (2) 285-84-70; Gert-Jan Van Helgelssom, tel (2) 285-57-47; Gilles Marhic, tel (2) 285-50-23; Eric Chaboureau, tel (2) 285-50-24.

Team IV

(Institutional Budgetary Affairs)

Director: Jill Aussant; tel (2) 285-79-19.

Head of Division: Felix van Craeyenest, tel (2) 285-74-27; Marta Arpio Santacruz (Convention on the Future of the European Union), tel (2) 285-61-83.

Legal Advisers: Moyra Sims, tel (2) 285-78-49; Ignacio Díez Parra, tel (2) 285-83-13; Martin Bauer, tel (2) 285-83-41; Frédéric Anton, tel (2) 285-87-80; Alain Pilette, tel (2) 285-89-89; Bart Driessen, tel (2) 285-73-98.

Team V

(Justice and Home Affairs—JHA)

Director: Julian Schutte; tel (2) 285-62-29.

Head of Division: Ole Petersen; tel (2) 285-71-69.

Legal Advisers: Martin Bauer, tel (2) 285-83-41; Jan Peter Hix, tel (2) 285-78-11; Emer Finnegan, tel (2) 285-52-83; Kristien Michoel, tel (2) 285-57-02; Marion Simm, tel (2) 285-51-23.

Team VI

(Interinstitutional Relations)

Director: Frank Wall; tel (2) 285-80-55.

Head of Division: Ettore Mosca (Parliamentary Affairs: Council of Europe, COSAC); tel (2) 285-65-62.

Advisers: François Nemoz-Hervens (Institutional Affairs), tel (2) 285-60-41; Elena Pozzani (Institutional Affairs), tel (2) 285-64-40; Ingeborg Lippe (Consulta-tions), tel (2) 285-82-79; Micheline Janssen (Consultations), tel (2) 285-63-16; Nathalie Creste (Parliamentary Questions), tel (2) 285-83-17; Stella Theodossiadis (Parliamentary Questions), tel (2) 285-83-27; Hartmut Berger (Economic and Social Cttee and Cttee of the Regions), tel (2) 285-73-05; Leo Schulte Nordholt (Parliamentary Affairs), tel (2) 285-84-83.

Research and Documentation Unit

Legal Adviser: Christos Mavrakos; tel (2) 285-71-90.

Counsellor (Legal/Linguistic Experts): Klaus Borchers; tel (2) 285-76-31.

DIRECTORATE-GENERAL A

(Administration and Protocol)

Director-General: Vittorio Griffo; tel (2) 285-65-40; fax (2) 285-72-49.

Deputy Director-General: Dirk Hellwig; tel (2) 285-69-58.

Directorate I

(Personnel and Administration)

Director: Leopold Radauer; tel (2) 285-89-15.

Deputy to the Director: Godelieve van den Bossche; tel (2) 285-65-59.

Welfare Office: Privileges and Immunities

Principal Officer: Godelieve van den Bossche.

Studies, Disputes, Staff Regulations and other Administrative Questions

Head of Division: Jean-Frédéric Fauré; tel (2) 285-66-54.

Administrators: Philippe Demonceau (Data processing), tel (2) 285-73-36; Daniel Dulbecco (Sickness insurance, accident insurance, interinstitutional relations), tel (2) 285-74-28.

Medical Service

Medical Officer: Manuel García Pérez; tel (2) 285-69-70.

Medical Assistant: Irene Ounifi-Höller.

Personnel

Head of Division: Yves Crétien; tel (2) 285-65-85.

Principal Administrator: Benjamín Moya Murcia; tel (2) 285-60-75.

Salaries, Pensions and Missions

Principal Officer: Maarten Bogaardt; tel (2) 285-73-46.

Staff Training

Principal Officer: Serenella Morelli; tel (2) 285-75-68.

Directorate II

(Conferences, Organization, Infrastructures, Information Technology)

Director: Stephen Ellis; tel (2) 285-76-24.

Conferences and Protocol

Head of Division: Walpurga Speckbacher; tel (2) 285-64-21.

Assistant Head of Division: Silvia Bianchi; tel (2) 285-77-37.

Administrators: Michael Waldron, tel (2) 285-71-84; Tobias Pabsch, tel (2) 285-62-35.

Information Technology

Head of Division: Hans-Werner Grenzhäuser; tel (2) 285-64-62.

Administrators: (Management control, administration) Antonio Rubio, tel (2) 285-65-74; Lluis Jaume Pujol, tel (2) 285-69-23; Thierry Daloze, tel (2) 285-91-86; (Administration solutions) Bernhard Müller, tel (2) 285-77-67; Jean-Marie Vandeputte, tel (2) 285-72-00; Susanne Corti-Goebel, tel (2) 285-75-19; Franco Ghedina, tel (2) 285-66-60; Maria-Elisa Ganzini, tel (2) 285-78-73; Mieke Libbrecht, tel (2) 285-82-88; Jean-Claude Dethier, tel (2) 285-72-89; Luc Suetens, tel (2) 285-87-56; Gerd Holzhauer, tel (2) 285-72-00; Pascal Dermience, tel (2) 285-87-25; (Production solutions) Philippe Vleminckx, tel (2) 285-71-38; Achilleas Karras, tel (2) 285-53-17; Laura Di Rosa, tel (2) 285-73-67; Nicola Kubiceck, tel (2) 285-85-36; Nikos Giannopoulos, tel (2) 285-48-99; Guido Feyaerts, tel (2) 285-92-81; Johan Lammers, tel (2) 285-86-09; Benedikt Luyckx, tel (2) 285-79-58; (Macintosh solutions) Erik Schultz-Nielsen, tel (2) 285-73-72; (Networks and telecommunications) Daniel Sprengers, tel (2) 285-73-99; Kalenga D'Almeida, tel (2) 285-54-60; Marc van den Brande, tel (2) 285-60-62; Curioni Donato, tel (2) 285-95-81; Dietmar Wichert, tel (2) 285-79-68; Mauricio Schettin Perez, tel (2) 285-95-81; (Help desk) Chris Merckx, tel (2) 285-81-68; Luciano Gissi, tel (2) 285-81-10; Didier Van Elderen, tel (2) 285-61-78; Henrique Coelho, tel (2) 285-81-67; Bénédicte Lamalle, tel (2) 285-82-04; Toni Sörensen, tel (2) 285-63-38.

Logistics services

Administrators: (Purchasing) Monique Kopp, (2) tel 285-73-40; (Inventory Control and Removals) Frans Gijsenberg, tel (2) 285-81-39; (Drivers) Jean-Claude Huaux, tel (2) 285-78-83; (Office machinery) Edgard Jespers, tel (2) 285-66-43; (Restaurant) Graziella Scebba, tel (2) 285-66-69; (Buildings, Head of Division) Johan Burgers, tel (2) 285-71-74; (Administrative Management) (vacant); (Technical Equipment and Premises) Heinrich Müller, tel (2) 285-66-47.

Directorate III
(Translation and Production of Documents)

Director: Margarida Lacerda; tel (2) 285-72-05.

Working Methods and Tools

Head of Division: Brendan O'Brien; tel (2) 285-77-17.

Translation Department

Head of Division: Hendrik Baes; tel (2) 285-77-89.

Heads of Section: (Vacant) (Secretarial Department), Eddie Bonesire (Terminology Department), tel (2) 285-71-95; Grethe Sørensen (Danish), tel (2) 285-68-35; Christine Heiting (Dutch), tel (2) 285-67-85; Joyce Gilabert (English), tel (2) 285-99-32; Risto Helle (Finnish), tel (2) 285-86-91; Geneviève Valente (French), tel (2) 285-68-48; Sonja Koller (German), tel (2) 285-68-56; (Vacant) (Greek), tel (2) 285-64-33; Silvia Khamal (Italian), tel (2) 285-68-28; Ana Fernandes (Portuguese), tel (2) 285-80-28; Charo Marín Villar (Spanish), tel (2) 285-82-89; Marianne Winoy (Swedish), tel (2) 285-77-65.

Technical Departments; Reproduction; Circulation; Registry; Telex; Imaging

Head of Division, Central Co-ordination: (vacant).

Principal Administrators: Jennifer Wadley, tel (2) 285-74-77; Armondo Gonçalves, tel (2) 285-63-89.

Administrators: Dino Cividin (Reproduction, circulation, special reprography), tel (2) 285-68-76; Michel Beeckman (Imaging), tel (2) 285-71-25; (vacant) (Telex); Jean-Marie Hollman (Central co-ordination), tel (2) 285-76-37; Andrew Unwin (Language co-ordination), tel (2) 285-61-53; Philip Evans (Agreements office), tel (2) 285-73-50; Gabriel Olivier (Bureau for classified information), tel (2) 285-62-80.

Directorate IV
(Finances of the Secretariat)

Director: José Antonio Mariguesa; tel (2) 285-60-58.

Deputy to the Director: Alan M. Piotrowski; tel (2) 285-62-40.

Budget Management

Principal Administrators: Johannes Gilbers, tel (2) 285-98-91; Hélène Lillgäls, tel (2) 285-95-62; Thierry Boucher, tel (2) 285-65-69.

Accounting

Principal Administrator: Ingrid Rullkoetter; tel (2) 285-64-30.

Horizontal Matters

Principal Administrator: Michel Koltz; tel (2) 285-56-59.

Procurement Co-ordination Unit

Principal Administrators: Sergio Zangaglia, tel (2) 285-80-62; Göran Welin, tel (2) 285-66-64.

DIRECTORATE-GENERAL B
(Agriculture and Fisheries)

Director-General: Angel Boixareu Carrera; tel (2) 285-62-34; fax (2) 285-82-22.

Directorate I
(Agricultural Policy, including International Aspects; Organization of the Markets in Agricultural Products and Harmonization of Veterinary and Zootechnical Legislation)

Director: Luigi Mazzaschi; tel (2) 285-75-71.

Co-ordination of International Aspects of Agricultural Policy, Enlargement, Fruit and Vegetables, Wine, Spirits, Vinegar, Olive Oil and Table Olives

Heads of Division: Paul Culley, tel (2) 285-61-97; Catherine Tyliacos, tel (2) 285-49-40; Antonio Ataz, tel (2) 285-49-64.

Food Safety: Veterinary and Zootechnical Harmonization, Animal Welfare, Meat and Dairy Products

Head of Division: Georges Adelbrecht; tel (2) 285-66-23.

Principal Administrators: Daniel Renaers, tel (2) 285-62-63; Simon Coates, tel (2) 285-57-68.

Horizontal Problems of Agricultural Policy, Arable Crops, Sugar, Cotton, Other Textile Fibres, Silkworms, Tobacco and Other Products

Head of Division: Johannes Ten Have; tel (2) 285-66-25.

Principal Administrator: Hans Joachim Holstein; tel (2) 285-85-18.

Directorate II
(Agricultural Structures Policy, Agri-monetary and Agri-financial Questions, Harmonization of Legislation on the Safety of Plants, Organic Products)

Director: Francisco Javier Matut Archanco; tel (2) 285-66-26.

Agricultural Structures and Statistics, Rural Development, Agri-monetary and Agri-financial Affairs, Forestry

Head of Division: Claudio d'Aloya; tel (2) 285-64-46.

Principal Administrators: Christina Strömholm, tel (2) 285-74-09; Joan Mier, tel (2) 285-74-09; Robert Dautzenberg, tel (2) 285-70-89.

Harmonization of Legislation on Plant Safety, Organic Products and Codex Alimentarius

Head of Division: Marc Schober; tel (2) 285-64-50.

Principal Administrators: Andreas Lernhart, tel (2) 285-62-41; Philip Lernhart, tel (2) 285-49-66; Kari Töllikkö, tel (2) 285-78-41.

Directorate III
(Fisheries Policy, including External Relations)

Director: Svend Kristensen; tel (2) 285-75-61.

Structural Policy; Market Organization; the Mediterranean; Relations with Africa, the Indian Ocean and South and Central America; Antarctica

Head of Division: Aldo Siragusa; tel (2) 285-65-43.

Principal Administrators: Klaus Skovsholm, tel (2) 285-83-79; Leni Rikkonen, tel (2) 285-87-23; Aldo Siragusa, tel (2) 285-65-43.

Resource Management and Conservation Policy; Monitoring of Fishing Activities; Relations with Northern and Eastern Europe and North America; International Organizations in the North Atlantic and Baltic Sea Areas; Research

Administrators: Luís Teixeira Da Costa, tel (2) 285-98-08; Christian Frøik, tel (2) 285-63-81.

DIRECTORATE-GENERAL C

(Internal Market; Customs Union; Industrial Policy; Telecommunications; Information Society; Research; Energy; Transport)

Director-General: Klaus Gretschmann; tel (2) 285-55-50; fax (2) 285-57-00.

Directorate I

(Internal Market, Competition, Customs)

Director: Anders Olander, tel (2) 285-63-92.

Internal Market, Intellectual Property, Technical Barriers (including Motor Vehicles), Chemical Products

Head of Division: Keith Mellor; tel (2) 285-66-79.

Principal Administrators: Massimo Mauro, tel (2) 285-6162; Leonidas Karamountzos, tel (2) 285-85-46; Filipa Melo Antunes, tel (2) 285-85-70; Pia Sellerup, tel (2) 285-52-98; Gérard Taquin, tel (2) 285-98-65.

Post and Telecommunications; Information Society; Multi-media; HDTV; Data Protection

Head of Division: Emilio González-Sancho; tel (2) 285-62-36.

Principal Administrator: Nicholas Platten; tel (2) 285-74-31.

Directorate II

(Internal Market; Intellectual Property; Customs Union; Right of Establishment and Freedom to Provide Services, including Insurance; Company Law; Free Movement of Persons; Public Contracts; Chemical and Pharmaceutical Products)

Director: Anders Olander; tel (2) 285-63-92.

Internal Market Policy; Technical Barriers; Intellectual Property

Principal Administrators: Keith Mellor, tel (2) 285-66-79; Mauro Massimo, tel (2) 285-61-62; Leonidas Karamountzos, tel (2) 285-85-46; Danielle Laveau, tel (2) 285-64-03; Gérard Taquin, tel (2) 285-98-65.

Free Movement of Persons; Technical Barriers; Chemical and Pharmaceutical Products

Principal Administrator: Pia Sellerup; tel (2) 285-52-98.

Customs Union

Principal Administrator: Danielle Laveau; tel (2) 285-64-03.

Right of Establishment and Freedom to provide Services; Insurance; Public Contracts; Company Law

Principal Administrators: Gérard Taquin, tel (2) 285-98-65; Andreas Weida, tel (2) 285-86-05.

Directorate III

(Research; Energy)

Director: Barbara Humphreys-Zwart; tel (2) 285-72-15.

Research Policy: European Co-operation on Scientific and Technical Research (COST); Scientific and Technical Research Committee (CREST)

Principal Administrators: Erwin van Rij, tel (2) 285-69-43; Donald Ellis, tel (2) 285-73-62; Thomas Brandtner, tel (2) 285-70-72; Kimmo Peippo, tel (2) 285-73-63; Frits Smulders, tel (2) 285-55-86.

Energy Policy: Coal; Hydrocarbons; Nuclear Energy; New Forms of Energy; Electricity; Rational Use of Energy; Crisis Measures; External Relations in the field of Energy; European Energy Charter

Principal Administrators: Jean-Paul Decaestecker, tel (2) 285-68-07; Ulrike Rackow, tel (2) 285-75-04; Lutz Goebbel, tel (2) 285-65-23.

Directorate IV

(Transport)

Director: Gaetano Testa; tel (2) 285-65-33.

Surface Transport—Roads, Railways, Inland Waterways; Relations with the European Conference of Ministers for Transport

Head of Division: Luc Lapere; tel (2) 285-66-40.

Principal Administrators: Aris Tekelenburg, tel (2) 285-55-11; (Sea Transport) Carine Claeys, tel (2) 285-84-43; Jesper Tvevad, tel (2) 285-59-30; (Air Transport) Stieg Holmgren, tel (2) 285-99-38; Steven Crass, tel (2) 285-54-83.

(Directorate-General D no longer exists)

DIRECTORATE-GENERAL E

(External Economic Relations and Common Foreign and Security Policy (CFSP))

Directors-General: Robert Cooper; tel (2) 285-85-52; (vacant) (with responsibility for Enlargement, Development and Multilateral Economic Affairs), tel (2) 285-62-72.

Deputy Directors-General: Anastassios Vikas (with responsibility for CFSP and Regional Affairs), tel (2) 285-62-85; Pieter Cornelis Feith (with responsibility for European Security and Defence Policy), tel (2) 285-52-20; Elda Stifani (New York: Liaison office with the UN), tel (1 212) 292-8608.

Directorate I

(Enlargement)

Director: (vacant); tel (2) 285-89-15.

Enlargement

Principal Administrators: Christos Katharios, tel (2) 285-75-67; David Johns, tel (2) 285-86-00; Constantinos Tsoutsoplides, tel (2) 285-63-58; Inés Hempel, tel (2) 285-56-88; Elisabeth Willocks, tel (2) 285-62-16; Manfred Lavicka, tel (2) 285-55-36.

Europe Agreements

Principal Administrators: Gabrielle Scaramucci, tel (2) 285-64-47; Rainer Ruge, tel (2) 285-93-01; Caroline Speck, tel (2) 285-54-91; Pia Luomakortes, tel (2) 285-95-95.

Directorate II

(Development)

Director: Jacques Bel; tel (2) 285-66-61.

Development Co-operation; Centre for Development of Industry (Lomé Convention); Staple Foods; Food Aid; UN Conferences on Development, including UNCTAD

Principal Administrators: Charles Murdock, tel (2) 285-77-85; Jeremy Rand, tel (2) 285-56-06

ACP/OCT; Post-Lomé Negotiations

Principal Administrators: Andrés Tobias y Rubio, tel (2) 285-70-06; Gianluigi Faure, tel (2) 285-64-68; María Mercedes García Pérez, tel (2) 285-64-86; Catherine MacDonald, tel (2) 285-95-59.

Directorate III

(Multilateral Economic Affairs)

Head of Division: André Donnadou; tel (2) 285-74-29.

World Trade Organization; Commercial Policy

Principal Administrators: Olli Mattila, tel (2) 285-83-57; Mauritz Enqvist, tel (2) 285-83-01; Bert Hofmann, tel (2) 285-80-98.

Instruments of Commercial Policy; Co-operation Agreements; ECSC Treaty; Ship-building; Reports by Commercial Counsellors

Administrator: Josef Breuls; tel (2) 285-73-58; Helga Berger, tel (2) 285-73-58.

EEA/EFTA; Switzerland; Faroe Islands; Andorra; San Marino; OECD; Instruments of Commercial Policy (Textiles); Fairs and Exhibitions

Administrator: Georgios Kritikos, tel (2) 285-51-59.

Textile Agreements

Administrator: Bert Hofmann; tel (2) 285-80-98.

Directorate IV
(Transatlantic Relations; United Nations; Human Rights)

Director: Jim Cloos; tel (2) 285-93-30.

Transatlantic Relations

Principal Administrators: Noel Purcell O'Byrne, tel (2) 285-73-85; Ulf Karlsson, tel (2) 285-99-84; Massimo Parnisari, tel (2) 285-83-16.

United Nations; Human Rights; Public International Law; Drugs

Principal Administrators: Hadewych Hazelzet, tel (2) 285-68-25; Francesca Riddy, tel (2) 285-65-15; Ulf Karlsson, tel (2) 285-99-84; Francesco Presutti, tel (2) 285-79-84.

Latin America

Principal Administrators: Karl Buck, tel (2) 285-75-74; Paolo Oliveira, tel (2) 285-66-19.

Directorate V
(Mediterranean Basin; Middle East, Africa; Asia)

Director: Franz Eichinger; tel (2) 285-55-22.

Barcelona Process; Common Strategy on the Mediterranean Region; Turkey; Malta; Cyprus; Mashreq/Maghreb; Persian (Arabian) Gulf; Iraq; Iran; Yemen

Head of Division: Dominique Sarat; tel (2) 285-65-60.

Principal Administrators: Alexander Zafiriou, tel (2) 285-91-21; Lene Hove, tel (2) 285-84-72; Rainer Uher, tel (2) 285-69-87; Ruth Kaufman-Buhler, tel (2) 285-62-19.

Middle East Peace Process; Palestine Liberation Organization

Principal Administrator: Andreas Strub; tel (2) 285-83-21.

Asia/Oceania

Head of Division: James Baneham; tel (2) 285-72-39.

Principal Administrators: Ana Ramírez Fueyo, tel (2) 285-70-04; Roland Zinzius, tel (2) 285-83-31.

Africa

Principal Administrators: Peter Clausen, tel (2) 285-73-56; Maria-Luise Lindorfer, tel (2) 28592-80.

Directorate VI
(Western Balkans Region; Eastern Europe and Central Asia)

Director: Stefan Lehne; tel (2) 285-53-27.

Western Balkans

Principal Administrators: Jean-Claude Meyer, tel (2) 285-82-32; Patrice Bergamini, tel (2) 285-55-71; Yannis Alexandros, tel (2) 285-58-13.

Eastern Europe and Central Asia

Head of Division: Jukka Leskelä; tel (2) 285-85-28.

Principal Administrators: Christian Brunmayr, tel (2) 285-68-36; Antonio De Castro Carpeno, tel (2) 285-83-34; Marie-France Drubigny, tel (2) 285-66-51; Michael Swann, tel (2) 285-58-23; Sofia Moreira De Sousa, tel (2) 285-54-75.

Directorate VII
(European Security and Defence Policy)

Director: Annalisa Gianella; tel (2) 285-80-44.

Principal Administrators: Alda Silveira Reis, tel (2) 285-60-93; Frédéric Doré, tel (2) 285-73-32; Mika-Markus Leinonen, tel (2) 285-54-86; Antonio Tanca, tel (2) 285-86-01; Clara Gans-landt, tel (2) 285-80-38; Laure Frier, tel (2) 285-62-49; Kaija Vanonen, tel (2) 285-81-50; Rosemary Chabanski, tel (2) 285-68-93.

Directorate VIII
(Defence Aspects)

Director: Claude-France Arnould; tel (2) 285-61-85.

Head of Division: Patrick Namer; tel (2) 285-57-12.

Internal Co-ordination and General Support

Principal Administrator: Marie-Pierre Devroedt; tel (2) 285-67-46.

ESDP Registry

Principal Administrator: Rosemary Chabanski; tel (2) 285-68-93.

Capabilities

Principal Administrators: Jan Alha-deff, tel (2) 285-57-99; Didier Lenoir, tel (2) 285-56-75; Alda Silveira Reis, tel (2) 285-60-93.

EU–NATO Relations

Principal Administrator: Antonio Tanca; tel (2) 285-86-01.

Politico-military Co-ordination

Principal Administrators: Antonio Tanca; Laure Frier.

Co-ordination concerning the Military Committee and the Military Committee Working Group

Principal Administrator: Matthew Reece; tel (2) 285-59-94.

Armaments Policy

Principal Administrator: Laure Frier.

Satellite Centre

Principal Administrator: Sarah Mattocks; tel (2) 285-60-08.

Institute for Security Studies

Principal Administrator: Antonio Tanca.

Exercises

Principal Administrators: Marina Vraila, tel (2) 285-60-10; Fritz Radema-cher, tel (2) 285-52-56.

Planning and Operations

Principal Administrators: Birgit Löser, tel (2) 285-60-00; Matthew Reece; Didier Lenoir.

Crisis Management Procedures

Principal Administrator: Matthew Reece.

Conventional Arms Exports (COARM); Disarmament (CODUN); Non-proliferation (CONOP); Terrorism (COTER); Dual-use Goods

Principal Administrators: Antonio Tanca; Kaija Vanonen; Rosemary Chabanski; Laure Frier; Marie-Pieree Devroedt; Juan De Luis.

Defence Policy Co-operation; Relations with Third Countries and International Organizations

Principal Administrators: Didier Lenoir; Antonio Tanca.

Directorate IX

(Civilian Crisis Management and Co-ordination)

Director: Michael Matthiessen; tel (2) 285-53-21.

Principal Administrator: Frédéric Doré; tel (2) 285-73-32.

Police Unit

Head of Division: Vincenzo Coppola; tel (2) 285-54-62.

Principal Administrators: Francesco Bruzzese De Pozzo, tel (2) 285-56-35; Michael Coat, tel (2) 285-56-38; Michael Coleman, tel (2) 285-56-36; Francisco Díaz Alcantud, tel (2) 285-56-33; John Henriksen, tel (2) 285-56-31; Alexius Schubert, tel (2) 285-56-32; Jan Timmermans, tel (2) 285-54-67.

Civilian Crisis Management and Conflict Prevention

Principal Administrators: Frédérick Doré, tel (2) 285-73-32; Mika-Markus Leinonen, tel (2) 285-80-38; Renate Dwan, tel (2) 285-55-58; Clara Ganslandt, tel (2) 285-80-38; Kim Freidberg, tel (2) 285-51-06; Michael Jorsback, tel (2) 285-76-09.

Crisis Management Relations with International Organizations

Principal Administrators: Frédérick Doré, Mika-Markus Leinonen; Kim Freidberg; Clara Glanslandt.

OSCE and Council of Europe; Planning and Analysis

Principal Administrator: Stefan Schulz.

Institutional and Horizontal CFSP Matters; External Relations

Counsellors: Margarita Comamala Lana, tel (2) 285-70-39; Jacob Vries, tel (2) 285-56-19.

Administrative Affairs and CFSP Protocol Matters; Communications; Consular Affairs; Law of the Sea

Head of Division: Giorgio Porzio; tel (2) 285-61-02.

Communications Centre

Principal Administrator: Michel Sdougas; tel (2) 285-80-40.

GENEVA OFFICE FOR LIAISON WITH THE EUROPEAN OFFICE OF THE UNITED NATIONS

(Attached to Directorate-General E)

Director, Head of the Liaison Office: Jacques Brodin; tel (22) 919-74-08.

Deputy Director: Guus Houttuin; tel (22) 919-74-10.

Principal Administrators: Luigi Cisnetti, tel (22) 919-74-03; Servatius van Thiel, tel (22) 734-27-20; André Gillissen, tel (22) 919-74-42; Oliver Allen, tel (22) 919-74-03.

NEW YORK–UNITED NATIONS LIAISON OFFICE

(Attached to Directorate-General E)

Director: Elda Stifani; tel (212) 292-86-08.

Principal Administrators: David Hollister, tel (212) 292-86-03; Joëlle Hivonnet, tel (212) 292-86-04.

DIRECTORATE-GENERAL F

(Press; Communications; Protocol)

Deputy Director-General, Head of Protocol: Hans Brunmayr; tel (2) 285-91-97.

General Affairs, Foreign Policy, Security and Defence, Development

Administrators: Nicolas Kerleroux, tel (2) 285-82-39; François Head, tel (2) 285-60-83.

Ecofin, Budget, Justice, Home Affairs and Civil Protection

Principal Administrator: Jesús Carmona Núñez; tel (2) 285-95-48.

Internal Market, Consumers and Tourism, Industry and Energy, Research, Transport and Communications, Health

Principal Administrator: (vacant).

Environment, Employment and Social Policy, Education, Youth and Culture

Principal Administrator: Luis Amorim, tel (2) 285-84-15.

Agriculture, Food Legislation and Fisheries

Principal Administrator: Laurent Benhamou; tel (2) 285-95-89.

Internal Market, Consumers and Tourism, Transport and Telecommunications

Principal Administrator: Georg Biekötter; tel (2) 285-67-00.

Press and Audiovisual Centre

Principal Administrators: Margarete Gilot-Köhler, tel (2) 285-62-31; Christina Gallach (Head of Division), tel (2) 285-64-67, fax (2) 285-56-94.

Communication, Information Policy, Interinstitutional Relations

Principal Administrator: Ramón Jiménez Fraile; tel (2) 285-61-76; fax (2) 285-53-33.

The Internet, Media, Monitoring

Principal Administrator: Johan Slotboom; tel (2) 285-55-05; fax (2) 285-53-35.

Transparency, Access to Documents, Public Information

Principal Administrator: Jacob Visscher; tel (2) 285-71-83; fax (2) 285-63-61.

Publications, Documentation, Relations with the Publications Office

Principal Administrator: Jorge Tavares Da Silva; tel (2) 285-81-80; fax (2) 285-53-34.

Visits, Public Events

Principal Administrator: Charis Xirouchakis; tel (2) 285-71-92; fax (2) 285-66-09.

Libraries

Principal Administrator: Anne Ostry; tel (2) 285-65-41; fax (2) 285-81-74.

Budget

Principal Administrator: Gerda Daidone; tel (2) 285-71-68.

Protocol

Principal Administrator: Maria Cristina Bertacca; tel (2) 285-64-38.

Archives

Principal Administrator: Willem Stols; tel (2) 285-72-92; fax (2) 285-81-24.

DIRECTORATE-GENERAL G

(Economic and Social Affairs)

Director-General: Sixten Korkman; tel (2) 285-62-13.

Directorate I

(Economic Affairs)

Economic Policies, European Investment Bank—EIB, Own Resources

Head of Division: Arthur Brautigam; tel (2) 285-72-34.

Principal Administrators: Pedro San José, tel (2) 285-82-66; Kyle Galler, tel (2) 285-72-98.

Tax Policy

Head of Division: Michel Graf; tel (2) 285-66-17.

Principal Administrators: Glykeria Markopouliotou, tel (2) 285-68-99; Mariano Abad Menéndez, tel (2) 285-50-93.

Export Credits

Principal Administrators: Liam O'Luanaigh, tel (2) 285-73-57; Monique Derelou, tel (2) 285-65-57.

Financial Legislation

Principal Administrators: Bodil S. Nielsen, tel (2) 285-61-95; Tomas Brännström, tel (2) 285-94-16

Directorate II

(Social and Regional Affairs)

Employment and Social Policy

Head of Division: Andrew George; tel (2) 285-73-54.

Principal Administrators: Sally Bliss, tel (2) 285-85-09; Mauritz Enqvist, tel (2) 285-83-01; Maria Paula Marques, tel (2) 285-87-16; Uwe Harms, tel (2) 285-50-12; Muriel De Puifferrat, tel (2) 285-85-09; Rafael De Bustamante Tello, tel (2) 285-51-90.

Directorate III

(Budget and Financial Regulations)

Director: Merrick Bryan-Kinns; tel (2) 285-65-83.

Principal Administrators (Budget and Finance): José Luis Gómez Lasaga, tel (2) 285-60-90; Jean-Paul Grossir, tel (2) 285-81-18; Marjatta Makinen, tel (2) 285-86-58; Ilkka Saarilahti, tel (2) 285-55-24; Luisa Balsells Traver, tel (2) 285-49-43; Piera Chignone, tel (2) 285-58-86.

DIRECTORATE-GENERAL H

(Justice and Home Affairs)

Director-General: Charles Elsen; tel (2) 285-85-05; fax (2) 285-84-88.

Directorate I

Head of Division: Enrique González Sánchez; tel (2) 285-65-46.

Section I (Asylum, Immigration, CIREA, CIREFI, Eurodac)

Principal Administrators: Guillermo Troncoso González, tel (2) 285-82-17; Erwin Buyssens, tel (2) 285-53-97; Paolo Martino Cossui, tel (2) 285-81-13; Danielle Laveau, tel (2) 285-64-03; Gavriil Kampouroglou, tel (2) 285-49-48; Anne Marie Sørensen, tel (2) 285-56-50.

Directorate II

Director: Gilles de Kerchove d'Oussel-ghem; tel (2) 285-79-33.

Section II (Police and Customs Co-operation)

Principal Administrators: Wilhelm Fahr, tel (2) 285-78-17; Johannes Vos, tel (2) 285-78-19; Niels Bracke, tel (2) 285-77-91.

Section III (Judicial Co-operation)

Head of Division: Hans Nilsson; tel (2) 285-79-15.

Principal Administrators: Fernando Rui Paulino Pereira, tel (2) 285-66-21; Bent Mejborn, tel (2) 285-67-22; Bernard Philippart, tel (2) 285-53-93; Nathalie Pensaert, tel (2) 285-54-25; Guy Stessens, tel (2) 285-67-11.

Section IV—SIS

Head of Division: Luc Vandamme; tel (2) 285-53-99.

Principal Administrators: Gerrit Huybreghts, tel (2) 285-67-12; Nathalie Pensaert; Ioannis Karadimitropoulos, tel (3) 88-40-78-21; Frank Hoogervorst, tel (3) 88-40-78-23.

Horizontal Questions (Relations with the European Parliament; Title VI Financing; Commission on Racism and Xenophobia)

Principal Administrators: Fernando Rui Paulino Pereira, tel (2) 285-66-21; Johannes Vos; Laetitia Bot, tel (2) 285-89-81; Niels Bracke, tel (2) 285-77-91; Bernard Philippart, tel (2) 285-53-93.

DIRECTORATE-GENERAL I

(Environmental and Consumer Protection; Civil Protection; Health; Food Legislation; Drug Addiction; AIDS; Education and Youth; Culture; Audiovisual Media)

Director-General: Kerstin Niblaeus; tel (2) 285-74-21; fax (2) 285-76-81.

Director: Sabine Ehmke Gendron; tel (2) 285-85-69.

Environment; Consumer Affairs; Civil Protection

Principal Administrators: Wolfgang Ploch, tel (2) 285-77-71; Joaquim Marinho de Bastos, tel (2) 285-60-72; Lieven Vermote, tel (2) 285-64-36; Chiara Mantegazzini, tel (2) 285-49-49; Joanna Goodburn, tel (2) 285-71-70; Anders Kjellgren, tel (2) 285-58-01; Maria Marotta, tel (2) 285-62-25; Maurizio Di Lullo, tel (2) 285-65-79; Jürgen Förster, tel (2) 285-77-49; Yves-Marie Leonet, tel (2) 285-60-87; Terkel Petersen, tel (2) 285-82-56.

Health; Food Legislation

Head of Division: Adèle Airoldi; tel (2) 285-78-75.

Principal Administrators: Laurent Labouré, tel (2) 285-74-00; Jonathan Cavanagh, tel (2) 285-58-00; Vassilios Kanaras, tel (2) 285-51-70.

Education and Youth; Culture; Audiovisual Arts

Head of Division: Carlo Frediani; tel (2) 285-64-39.

Principal Administrators: John Whitton, tel (2) 285-73-13; Mervi Hietanan, tel (2) 285-81-97.

Administrative Reform

Director-General: Marc Lepoivre; tel (2) 285-62-87; fax (2) 285-91-96.

Committees

COMMITTEE OF PERMANENT REPRESENTATIVES (COREPER I)

Peter Witt: Ambassador, Deputy Permanent Representative of Germany, 19–21 rue Jacques de Lalaing, 1040 Brussels, Belgium; tel (2) 238-18-11; fax (2) 238-19-78; e-mail eurogerma.eu@bruessel.auswaertiges-amt.de.

Kare Halonen: Minister Plenipotentiary, Deputy Permanent Representative of Finland, 100 rue de Trèves, 1040 Brussels, Belgium; tel (2) 287-84-25; fax (2) 287-84-00; e-mail kare.halonen@formin.fi; internet www.uunet.be/finland.

Domingo Fezas Vital: Minister Plenipotentiary, Deputy Permanent Representative of Portugal, 12–22 ave de Cortenbergh, 1040 Brussels, Belgium; tel (2) 286-42-11; fax (2) 231-00-26; e-mail reper@reper-portugal.be; internet www.reper-portugal.be.

Christian Masset: Minister Plenipotentiary, Deputy Permanent Representative of France, 14 place de Louvain, 1000 Brussels, Belgium; tel (2) 229-82-11; fax (2) 229-82-82; internet www.rpfrance.org.

Ingrid Hjelt af Trolle: Minister Plenipotentiary, Deputy Permanent Representative of Sweden, 30 square de Meeûs, 1000 Brussels, Belgium; tel (2) 289-56-11; fax (2) 289-56-00; e-mail representationen.bryssel@foreign.ministry.se; internet www.utrikes.regeringen.se/eu/startsidan.htm.

François Roux: Minister Counsellor, Deputy Permanent Representative of Belgium, Rondpoint Schuman 6, 1040 Brussels, Belgium; tel (2) 233-21-11; fax (2) 231-10-75; e-mail belrep@belgoeurop.diplobel.fgov.be.

Miguel Ángel Navarro Portera: Minister Plenipotentiary, Deputy Permanent Representative of Spain, 52–54 blvd du Régent, 1000 Brussels, Belgium; tel (2) 509-86-06; fax (2) 511-39-62.

Claus Grube: Envoy Extraordinary and Ambassador, Deputy Permanent Representative of Denmark, 73 rue d'Arlon, 1040 Brussels, Belgium; tel (2) 233-08-66; fax (2) 230-93-84; e-mail brurep@um.dk.

Dimitrios Rallis: Minister Plenipotentiary, Deputy Permanent Representative of Greece, 25 rue Montoyer, 1000 Brussels, Belgium; tel (2) 551-56-01; fax (2) 551-56-02; e-mail mea.bruxelles@rp-grece.be.

Alessandro Pignatti Morano Di Custoza: Minister Plenipotentiary, Deputy Permanent Representative of Italy, 9 rue du Marteau, 1000 Brussels, Belgium; tel (2) 220-04-11; fax (2) 219-34-49; e-mail rpue@rpue.it; internet www.rpue.it.

Peter Gunning: Minister Plenipotentiary, Deputy Permanent Representative of Ireland, 89–93 rue Froissart, 1040 Brussels, Belgium; tel (2) 282-32-20; fax (2) 230-31-88; e-mail reppermirl@belgium.online.be.

H. J. J. Schuwer: Minister Plenipotentiary, Deputy Permanent Representative of the Netherlands, 48 ave Hermann Debroux, 1160 Brussels, Belgium; tel (2) 679-15-06; fax (2) 679-17-74.

Christian Braun: Deputy Permanent Representative of Luxembourg, 75 ave de Cortenbergh, 1000 Brussels, Belgium; tel (2) 737-56-14; fax (2) 736-14-29; e-mail secretariat@rpue.etat.lu.

Anne Lambert: Deputy Permanent Representative of the United Kingdom, 10 ave d'Auderghem, 1040 Brussels, Belgium; tel (2) 287-82-11; fax (2) 287-83-98; e-mail anne.lambert@fco.gov.uk; internet ukrep.fco.gov.uk.

Judith Gebetsroithner: Envoy Extraordinary and Minister Plenipotentiary, Deputy Permanent Representative of Austria, 30 ave de Cortenbergh, 1040 Brussels, Belgium; tel (2) 234-51-22; fax (2) 234-61-22; e-mail austria.press@pophost.eunet.be; internet www.bmaa.gv.at.

COMMITTEE OF PERMANENT REPRESENTATIVES (COREPER II)

Wilhelm Schönfelder: Permanent Representative, and Ambassador Extraordinary and Plenipotentiary of Germany, 19–21 rue Jacques de Lalaing, 1040 Brussels, Belgium; tel (2) 238-18-11; fax (2) 238-19-78; e-mail eurogerma.eu@bruessel.auswaertiges-amt.de.

Eikka Kosonen: Permanent Representative, and Ambassador Extraordinary and Plenipotentiary of Finland, 100 rue de Trèves, 1040 Brussels, Belgium; tel (2) 287-84-22; fax (11) 287-84-00; e-mail eikka.kosonen@formin.fi; internet www.uunet.be/finland;

Álvaro Mendonça e Moura: Permanent Representative, and Ambassador Extraordinary and Plenipotentiary of Portugal, 12–22 ave de Cortenbergh, 1040 Brussels, Belgium; tel (2) 286-43-20; fax (2) 230-90-95; e-mail reper@reper-portugal.be; internet www.reper-portugal.be.

Pierre Sellal: Permanent Representative, and Ambassador Extraordinary and Plenipotentiary of France, 14 place de Louvain, 1000 Brussels, Belgium; tel (2) 229-82-09; fax (2) 229-82-82; internet www.rpfrance.org.

Sven-Olof Petersson: Permanent Representative, and Ambassador Extraordinary and Plenipotentiary of Sweden, 30 square de Meeûs, 1000 Brussels, Belgium; tel (2) 289-56-11; fax (2) 289-56-00; e-mail representationen.bryssel@foreign.ministry.se; internet www.utrikes.regeringen.se/eu/startsidan.htm.

Jan De Bock: Permanent Representative, and Ambassador Extraordinary and Plenipotentiary of Belgium, Rond-point Schuman 6, 1040 Brussels, Belgium; tel (2) 233-21-11; fax (2) 231-10-75; e-mail belrep@belgoeurop.diplobel.fgov.be.

Carlos Bastarreche Sagües: Permanent Representative, and Ambassador Extraordinary and Plenipotentiary of Spain, 52–54 blvd du Régent, 1000 Brussels, Belgium; tel (2) 509-86-11; fax (2) 511-19-40.

Poul Skytte Christoffersen: Permanent Representative, and Ambassador Extraordinary and Plenipotentiary of Denmark, 73 rue d'Arlon, 1040 Brussels, Belgium; tel (2) 233-08-65; fax (2) 230-93-84; e-mail brurep.um.dk.

Aristides Agathocles: Permanent Representative, and Ambassador Extraordinary and Plenipotentiary of Greece, 25 rue Moutoyer, 1000 Brussels, Belgium; tel (2) 551-56-37; fax (2) 512-69-50; e-mail mea.bruxelles@rp-grece.be.

Umberto Vattani: Permanent Representative, and Ambassador Extraordinary and Plenipotentiary of Italy, 9 rue du Marteau, 1000 Brussels, Belgium; tel (2) 220-04-11; fax (2) 219-34-49; e-mail rpue@rpue.it; internet www.rpue.it.

Anne Anderson: Permanent Representative, and Ambassador Extraordinary and Plenipotentiary of Ireland, 89–93 rue Froissart, 1040 Brussels, Belgium; tel (2) 282-32-10; fax (2) 230-30-18; e-mail reppermirl@belgium.online.be.

T. J. A. M. De Bruijn: Permanent Representative, and Ambassador Extraordinary and Plenipotentiary of the Netherlands, 48 ave Hermann Debroux, 1160 Brussels, Belgium; tel (2) 679-15-11; fax (2) 679-17-75.

Nicolas Schmit: Permanent Representative, and Ambassador Extraordinary and Plenipotentiary of Luxembourg, 75 ave de Cortenbergh, 1000 Brussels, Belgium; tel (2) 737-56-01; fax (2) 737-14-29; e-mail secretariat@rpue.etat.lu.

Sir Nigel Sheinwald: Permanent Representative, and Ambassador Extraordinary and Plenipotentiary of the United Kingdom, 10 ave d'Auderghem, 1040 Brussels, Belgium; tel (2) 287-82-71; fax (2) 287-83-83; e-mail nigel.sheinwald@fco.gov.uk; internet ukrep.fco.gov.uk.

Gregor Woschnagg: Permanent Representative, and Ambassador Extraordinary and Plenipotentiary of Austria, 30 ave de Cortenbergh, 1040 Brussels, Belgium; tel (2) 234-51-30; fax (2) 235-61-30; e-mail austria.press@pophost.eunet.be; internet www.bmaa.gv.at.

Permanent Representations of Member States

AUSTRIA

(130 ave de Cortenbergh, 1040 Brussels, Belgium; tel (2) 234-51-00; fax (2) 234-63-00); e-mail austria.press@pophost.eunet.be; internet www.bmaa.gv.at)

Permanent Representative, and Ambassador Extraordinary and Plenipotentiary: Gregor Woschnagg; tel (2) 234-51-30; fax (2) 234-53-18.

The Directory of EU Information Sources

First Deputy Permanent Representative, Minister Plenipotentiary: Judith Gebetsroithner; tel (2) 234-51-22; fax (2) 235-61-22.

Permanent Representation to the Political and Security Committee: Ambassador and Representative: Franz-Josef Kuglitsch; tel (2) 234-52-02; fax (2) 235-62-02; First Sec: Michael Doczy.

Permanent Representation to the Military Committee of the EU: Representative: Wolfgang Jilke; Advisers: Col Manfred Hohenwarter, Lt-Col Johann Trummer.

Federal Chancellery: Willi Kempel; tel (2) 234-53-70; fax (2) 235-63-70; Bernadette Klösch; First Secs: Gerhard Mayer, Marie-Therese Hermges, Klaus Kögeler; Second Sec: Thomas Schnöll; Attachés: Nicole Bayer, tel (2) 234-53-64, fax (2) 235-63-64; Heidi Meissnitzer, Martin Hermges; Counsellors: Thomas Pappenscheller, Sigrid Klein.

Ministry of Economic Affairs and Labour: Minister: Herbert Preglau; tel (2) 234-51-50; fax (2) 235-61-50; First Sec: Michael Stern; Second Sec: Robert Prochazka; Counsellors: Wolfgang Igler, Johannes Krenn, Susanne Achberger; Attaché: Peter Hofer.

Ministry of Social Security, Generations and Consumer Protection: Minister: Franz Urlesberger; Counsellor: Charlotte Sachse, tel (2) 234-52-16, fax (2) 235-62-16.

Ministry of Financial Affairs: Minister: Gerhard Lerchbaumer; tel (2) 234-51-57; fax (2) 235-61-57; Counsellor: Andrea Binder; Attachés: Rudolf Paul, Helmut Schamp.

Ministry of Health and Women: Counsellor: Gertraud Fischinger; tel (2) 234-52-12; fax (2) 235-62-21; Attaché: Aziza Haas.

Ministry of the Interior: Minister: Gerhard Ziegler; tel (2) 234-51-38; fax (2) 235-61-38; Attaché: Andreas Fellner.

Ministry of Justice: Counsellor: Birgit Tschütscher; tel (2) 234-52-22; fax (2) 235-62-62; Attaché: Gertraud Eppich.

Ministry of Agriculture, Forestry, the Environment and Water Management: Attachés: Verena Maria Hagg, tel (2) 234-51-68, fax (2) 235-61-68; Günther Walkner, Maria Fladl, Christoph Müller, Michael Sebanz.

Ministry of Education, Science and Culture: Minister: Franz Pichler; tel (2) 234-51-44; fax (2) 235-61-44; Attaché: Mirjam Rinderer.

Ministry of Transport, Innovation and Technology: Attachés: Thomas Glöckel, Thomas Egermaier.

Liaison Office of the Länder: Minister Counsellor: Klemens H. Fischer; tel (2) 234-52-34; fax (2) 230-25-44.

Association of Austrian Cities and Towns: Attaché: Simona Wohlesa; tel (2) 234-52-88; fax (2) 282-06-82.

Confederation of Austrian Local Authorities: Dept Head: Michaela Petz; tel (2) 234-52-54; fax (2) 282-06-88.

Austrian National Bank: Attachés: Reinhard Petschnigg, tel (2) 285-48-41, fax (2) 285-48-48; Romana Lehner.

Federal Economic Chamber: Minister Counsellor: Stefan Pistauer; tel (2) 234-51-80; fax (2) 286-58-99; Attachés: Barbara Schennach, Victoria Oeser, Edda Knittel, Alexander Foidl, Markus Stock.

Federal Chamber of Labour: Counsellor: Elisabeth Aufheimer; tel (2) 234-51-98; fax (2) 230-29-73; Attachés: Franz Greil, Susanne Brenner.

Chambers of Agriculture: Counsellor: Nikolaus Morawitz; tel (2) 285-46-70; fax (2) 285-46-71.

Austrian Federation of Trade Unions: Unit Head: Olivier Röpke; tel (2) 230-74-63; fax (2) 231-17-10; Attaché: Evelyn Regner.

Austrian Federation of Industry: Counsellor: Berthold Berger-Henoch; tel (2) 235-04-31; fax (2) 230-95-91; Attachés: Dominik Lamezan-Salins, Marion Poglitsch.

BELGIUM

(Rond-point Schuman 6, 1040 Brussels, Belgium; tel (2) 233-21-11; fax (2) 231-10-75; e-mail belrep@belgoeurop.diplobel.fgov.be)

Permanent Representative, and Ambassador Extraordinary and Plenipotentiary: Jan De Bock.

Deputy Permanent Representative: Geneviève Tuts.

Permanent Representation to the Political and Security Committee: Ambassador and Representative: Alexis Brouhns; Dep Representative: Bruno Angelet; Military Representative: Maj-Gen Jo Coelmont; Dep Military Representative: Col Jacques Van de Veken; Attaché: Pierre Gillon; Assistants: Lt-Col Patrick Geysen, Ingrid Snoeck, Georges Roman.

Ministry of Foreign Affairs (also responsible for External Trade and Development Co-operation): Dir-Gen: Paul Rietjens; Minister-Counsellors: Renilde Loeckx, Brigitte Minart; Counsellors: Jean-Joël Schittecatte, Geert Muylle; Dep Counsellors: Dominique Laurent, Kristina Eyskens; First Secs: Jan Bayart, Bruno Georges, Peter

Lescouhier, Marc Calcoen, Marc Reyntjens; Attachés: Natacha Defeche, Myriam Bacquelaine.

Ministry of the Economy, Small and Medium-sized Enterprises, the Liberal Professions, Self-Employed and Energy: Counsellor: Eric Van Den Abeele; Assistant Counsellor: Françoise De Vleeschouwer.

Ministry of Finance: Insps-Gen: Yves Van Honacker, Paul Annicaert; General Auditor: Jacques Delbeke; Counsellor: Pierre Verly; Attaché: Jean-Marc Willems.

Ministry of Mobility and Transport: Counsellor: Philippe Colpaert.

Ministry of Social Security: Counsellor: Muriel Rabau.

Ministry of Employment, Labour and Social Affairs: Counsellors: Annemie Pernot; Advisor: Thérèse Boutsen.

Ministry of Public Health, Food Security and Environment: Dep Counsellors: Anne Deltour, Frédéric Chemay.

Post and Telecommunications Institute: Counsellor: Fabienne Marcelle.

National Bank of Belgium: Insp-Gen: Philippe Vigneron.

Wallonia and the French-speaking Community: Delegates-Gen: Yves De Greef, Thierry Delaval; Delegate: Christiane Bourgoignie; Counsellors: Fabienne Thirion, Daniel Soil; Attachés: Joël Bastin, Véronique Patte, David Royaux.

Flemish-speaking Community: Representative: Filip D'Have; Attachés: Jan Hostens, Inge Moors, Jan Van Hellemont, Lore Van Eylen, Ellen Valkenborgs, Olav Luyckx.

Brussels Capital Region: Representative: Pascal Goergen; Dep Representative: Geert De Proost; Economic Counsellor: Bernd Schneider.

CYPRUS

(Square Ambiorix 2, 1000 Brussels, Belgium; tel (2) 735-35-10; fax (2) 735-45-52); e-mail be.cydelegation.eu@mfa.gov.cy)

Permanent Representative, and Ambassador Extraordinary and Plenipotentiary: Nicholas Emiliou; tel (2) 741-67-37; e-mail nemiliou@mfa.gov.cy.

First Deputy Permanent Representative, Minister Plenipotentiary: Kornelios Korneliou; tel (2) 741-67-33; e-mail kkorneliou@mfa.gov.cy.

Permanent Representation to the Political and Security Committee: Representative: Pantelakis Eliades; tel

(2) 741-67-47; e-mail peliades@mfa.gov.cy.

Ministry of Foreign Affairs: First Counsellor: Panayotis Kyriacou; tel (2) 741-67-35; First Secs: Pericles D. Stivaros, Louis Telemachou, Theodora Constantinidou; Second Secs: Yannis Michaelides, Christina Rafti, Alkis Ieromonachou, Koula Sophianou.

Ministry of Defence: Counsellor: Angelos Christodoulou; tel (2) 650-06-26.

Ministry of Commerce, Industry and Tourism: Counsellor: Xenios Xenopoulos; tel (2) 735-35-10; Attaché: Konstantinos Karageorgis.

Ministry of Finance: Counsellor: Yiannakis Asimakis; tel (2) 735-35-10; Attachés: Lina Papamichalopoulou, Georgiana Georgiou.

Ministry of Communications and Public Transport: Attaché: Neophytos Neophytou; tel (2) 735-35-10.

Ministry of Social Security: Attaché: Annita Tsiappari-Kyriacou; tel (2) 741-67-36.

Ministry of Justice and Public Order: Attaché: Soterios Prodromou; tel (2) 741-67-51.

Ministry of Education and Culture: Attaché: Christina Valanidou; tel (2) 741-67-44.

CZECH REPUBLIC

(Rue Caroly 15, 1050 Brussels, Belgium; tel (2) 213-01-10; fax (2) 513-71-54; e-mail eu.brussels@embassy.mzv.cz)

Permanent Representative, and Ambassador Extraordinary and Plenipotentiary: Jan Kohout.

Deputy Permanent Representative, Counsellor Plenipotentiary: Stavinoha Luděk.

Permanent Representation to the Political and Security Committee: Representative: Petr Mooz.

Ministry of External Affairs: First Counsellor: Petra Gombalová; First Secretary: Blanka Fajkusová; Second Sec: Václav Kolaja.

Ministry of Defence: Counsellors: Col. Jaroslav Urik, Lt. Col. Zdeněk Petráš

Ministry of Economics and Finance: First Secs. Šárka Zeizingerová, Stanislav Trakal; Second Sec: Petr Jeník; Third Secs: Radek Pilař, Tomá Nejdl.

Ministry of Home Affairs and Justice: Second Secs: Tomá Buřil, Petr Solský.

Ministry of Agriculture and the Environment: Counsellor: Milan Kuna; First Secs: Zdeněk Hájek, Václav Dvořák.

Ministry of Industry, Energy, Information, Internal Markets and Transport: Counsellor: Václava Horáková; Second Sec: Petr Dolejší.

Ministry of Employment, Social Affairs, Health, Education, Research, Culture and Youth: Counsellor: Miroslav Fuchs; Second Secs: Anna Vosečková, Hana Bošková.

Ministry of Security: Counsellors: Jarmila Madejová, Pavel Černý.

DENMARK

(73 rue d'Arlon, 1040 Brussels, Belgium; tel (2) 233-08-11; fax (2) 230-93-84; e-mail brurep@um.dk)

Permanent Representative, and Ambassador Extraordinary and Plenipotentiary: Claus Grube; tel (2) 233-08-65; fax (2) 230-93-84.

Deputy Permanent Representative, Envoy Extraordinary and Ambassador: Jeppe Tranholm-Mikkelsen; tel (2) 233-08-66; fax (2) 230-93-84.

Permanent Representation to the Political and Security Committee: Reimer Reinholdt Nielsen; tel (2) 233-09-70.

Permanent Representation to the Military Committee of the EU: Vice-Adml Kristen Winther; tel (2) 707-61-50; fax (2) 230-93-84.

Ministry of Foreign Affairs: Counsellors: Ann Sophie Kisling, tel (2) 233-08-57; Vibeke Roosen Bell, tel (2) 233-08-60; Steffen Ryom, tel (2) 233-08-81; Per Fabricus Andersen, tel (2) 233-08-68; Jørgen Gammelgård, tel (2) 233-09-79; Peter Brun, tel (2) 233-08-54; Lars Bredal, tel (2) 233-08-26; First Sec: Merete Bilde, tel (2) 233-08-07.

Ministry of Finance: Adviser: Jacob Buhl Vestergaard, tel (2) 233-09-05.

Ministry of Trade and Industry: Minister-Counsellor: Preben Pettersson, tel (2) 233-09-02; fax (2) 233-93-84; Counsellors: Henrik Lindegaard Christensen, tel (2) 233-08-94; Frisdahl René, tel (2) 233-08-89.

Ministry of Transport: Minister-Counsellor: Michael Klinker Hansen; tel (2) 233-09-35; fax (2) 233-93-84.

Ministry of the Environment: Attachés: Henrik Steen Laursen, tel (2) 233-08-02; Henrik Hedemann Olsen, tel (2) 233-08-01.

Ministry of Justice: Attachés: Tomas Frydenberg, tel (2 233-08-05; Mads Christian Christensen, tel (2) 233-08-98.

Ministry of Health: Counsellor: Hanne Charlotte Findsen; tel (2) 233-08-15.

Ministry of Food, Agriculture and Fisheries: Minister-Counsellor: Anders Buch Kristensen; tel (2) 233-08-64; fax (2) 233-93-84; Attachés: Lene Breum Larsen, Tania Buch-Weeke, Birgitte Riber Rasmussen, Lene Haagensen.

Ministry of Cultural Affairs: Counsellor: Martin Vive Ivø; tel (2) 233-09-29; fax (2) 233-93-84.

Ministry of Labour: Attaché: Cecilie Kisling, tel (2) 233-08-12.

Ministry of the Interior: Attaché: Nanna Fischer, tel (2) 233-08-53.

Ministry of Taxation: Attachés: Lotte Langhoff-Roos, tel (2) 233-09-08; Susse Meulengracht, tel (2) 233-09-49.

Ministry of Science, Technology and Innovation: Counsellor: Thorkil Kjems, tel (2) 233-08-25; Attaché: Ulrich Pinstrup, tel (2) 233-08-58.

Ministry of Defence: Deputy Counsellor: Jens Oddershede, tel (2) 233-09-74.

Ministry of Education: Attaché: Sebastian Volkers, tel (2) 233-08-04.

Ministry of Social Affairs and Equal Opportunities: Minister-Counsellor: Poul Vorre, tel (2) 233-08-38.

ESTONIA

(Rue Guimard 11/13, 1040 Brussels, Belgium; tel (2) 227-39-10; fax (2) 227-39-25; e-mail mission@estemb.be)

Permanent Representative, and Ambassador Extraordinary and Plenipotentiary: Väino Reinart, tel (2) 227-43-12.

Deputy Permanent Representative and Minister Plenipotentiary: Margus Rahuoja, tel (2) 227-43-03.

Political and Security Committee: Ambassador: Tõnis Idarand, tel (2) 227-43-18.

Foreign Affairs: Counsellor: Kristina Meius, tel (2) 227-43-18.

Political Affairs: Adviser: Mariin Ratnik; First Sec. Tiit Aleksejev, tel (2) 227-39-10.

Economic Affairs: Counsellors: Maria Koidu, tel (2) 227-43-42; Annelie Andresson, tel (2) 227-39-10; First Secs: Jana Vanaveski, tel (2) 227-43-50; Allan Luik, tel (2) 227-43-50.

Internal Affairs and Justice: Attachés: Klen Jäärats, tel (2) 227-43-50; Tõnu Pihegas, tel (2) 227-43-50; Kristo Põllu.

Economic and Financial Affairs: Attachés: Andres Kuningas, tel (2) 227-39-19; Leelo Liive, tel (2) 227-43-35; Ingrid Toming (Banque d'Estonie), tel (2) 227-43-35.

Agriculture and Fisheries: Adviser: Peeter Seestrand, tel (2) 227-43-40; Attachés: Signe Aaskivi, tel (2) 227-43-40; Kaido Kroon, tel (2) 227-43-40; Tauno Lukas, tel (2) 227-43-40.

Environment: Attachés: Signe Ohakas, tel (2) 227-43-40; Aare Sirendi, tel (2) 227-43-40.

Transport: Attaché: Olev-Erik Leino, tel (2) 227-43-42.

Social Affairs and Employment: Attaché: Leili Matsar, tel (2) 227-43-37.

Health: Attaché: Edda-Helen Link, tel (2) 227-39-26.

Education and Science: Attachés: Kalmar Kurs, tel (2) 227-43-37; Toivo Räim, tel (2) 227-43-42.

Cultural Affairs: Attaché: Tamara Luuk, tel (2) 227-43-37.

Administrative Affairs: Counsellor: Heiti Mäemees, tel (2) 227-39-10.

FINLAND

(100 rue de Trèves, 1040 Brussels, Belgium; tel (2) 287-84-11; fax (2) 287-84-00; e-mail firstname.surname@formin.fi; internet www.uunet.be/finland)

Permanent Representative, and Ambassador Extraordinary and Plenipotentiary: Eikka Kosonen; tel (2) 287-84-22; fax (2) 287-84-00.

Deputy Permanent Representative and Minister Plenipotentiary: Kare Halonen; tel (2) 287-84-25; fax (2) 287-84-00.

Interim Political and Security Committee: Ambassador: Teemu Tanner; tel (2) 287-84-85; Counsellors: Hilkka Nenonen, tel (2) 287-84-65; Mari Eteläpää, tel (2) 287-84-79.

Interim Military Body: Capt Henrik Nystén, tel (2) 287-84-35; Vice-Adml Esko Illi, tel (2) 287-84-75; Lt-Col Ossi Sivén, tel (2) 287-84-92.

Enlargement, Central Europe and Western Europe: Counsellor: Marjatta Hiekka; tel (2) 287-84-66.

External Relations: Counsellors: Leena-Kaisa Mikkola, tel (2) 287-85-51; Hilkka Nenonen, tel (2) 287-84-65; First Secs: Hannu Räisänen, tel (2) 287-84-34; Juha Ottman, tel (2) 287-84-12; Pekka Kosonen, tel (2) 287-84-48; Petteri Vuorimäki, tel (2) 287-84-71; Second Sec: Teemu Sepponen; tel (2) 287-85-95.

Co-ordination and Information: Counsellor: Liisa Talonpolka, tel (2) 287-84-40; First Sec: Outi Hyvärinen, tel (2) 287-85-71.

Legal and Institutional Affairs: Counsellor: Alexander Stubb, tel (2) 287-85-14; First Sec: Pekka Kosonen, tel (2) 287-84-48.

Parliamentary Affairs: Counsellor: Pekka Shemeikka; tel (2) 287-84-44.

Regional Policy: Counsellor: Paavo Pirttimäki; tel (2) 287-85-80.

Justice and Home Affairs: Counsellors: Kalle Kekomäki, tel (2) 287-85-04; Lauri Hollmén, tel (2) 287-84-20; Maarit Loimsukoski, tel (2) 287-85-94; Mari Aalto, tel (2) 287-84-31.

Economic and Financial Affairs: Counsellors: Turo Hentilä, tel (2) 287-85-26; Ilkka Mytty, tel (2) 287-85-24; Marti Anttinen, tel (2) 287-85-28.

Taxation and Customs: Counsellors: Tiina Maisala, tel (2) 287-84-51; Merja Mallivuori, tel (2) 287-84-38.

Industrial Policy, Energy, Internal Markets and Research: Counsellors: Riku Huttunen, tel (2) 287-84-49; Kirsti Vilen, tel (2) 287-84-33; Eeva-Liisa Kortekallio, tel (2) 287-84-52; Marjut Leskinen, tel (2) 287-84-50.

Culture and Education: Counsellor: Jori Jokinen, tel (2) 287-85-25.

Agriculture, Forestry and Fisheries: Counsellors: Jaarmo Vilhunen, tel (2) 287-84-64; Outi Tyni, tel (2) 287-84-68; Risto Artjöki, tel (2) 287-84-32.

Environment: Counsellors: Camilla Lommi-Kippola, tel (2) 287-84-46; Tuija Talsi, tel (2) 287-84-77.

Social Policy: Counsellor: Mari Korhonen, tel (2) 287-84-45.

Employment and the Labour Market: Counsellor: Stina Modeen, tel (2) 287-85-83.

Public Health: Counsellor: Arto Koho, tel (2) 287-84-67.

Transport: Counsellors: Minna Kivimäki, tel (2) 287-84-63; Jussi Myllärniemi, tel (2) 287-85-38.

Telecommunications: Counsellor: Olli-Pekka Rantala, tel (2) 287-85-50.

Åland Islands: Counsellor: Yngve Mörn; tel (2) 287-84-59.

Administration: Counsellor: Anja Vilo; tel (2) 287-84-03.

FRANCE

(14 place de Louvain, 1000 Brussels, Belgium; tel (2) 229-82-11; fax (2) 229-82-82; internet www.rpfrance.org)

Permanent Representative, and Ambassador Extraordinary and Plenipotentiary: Pierre Sellal; tel (2) 229-82-09; fax (2) 229-82-82.

Deputy Permanent Representative and Minister Plenipotentiary: Christian Masset; tel (2) 229-82-10; fax (2) 229-82-82.

External Relations: Counsellors: Philippe Setton, tel (2) 229-82-90; Fabien Pénone, tel (2) 229-82-36; Anne-Marie Descôtes, tel (2) 229-82-51; Florence Jeanblanc Risler, tel (2) 229-84-44; Cyrille Pierre, tel (2) 229-84-37; Hugues de Chavagnac; Christophe Leonzi; Gaël Veyssiere; Aurelie Lapidus; Raphaël Bello; Attaché: Françoise Breysse, tel (2) 229-84-36.

Home Affairs and Justice: Head of Service: Daniel Lecrubier; tel (2) 229-82-24; Counsellors: Philippe Conduché, tel (2) 229-83-32; Patrick Debaere, tel (2) 229-83-31; Gérard Schoen, tel (2) 229-83-90; Jean Alegre; Gilbert Elkaim; Olivier Bardin; Patrick Debaere; François-Xavier Bourges.

Press and Information: Spokesperson/Counsellor: Etienne De Poncins, tel (2) 229-82-78; Deputy Counsellors: Aurélie Royet-Gounin; Valérie Rampi.

Economic, Financial and Monetary Affairs: Counsellor: Alban Aucoin, tel (2) 229-83-53; Deputy Counsellor: Christophe Strassel; Attachés: Bruno-Philippe Jeudi, tel (2) 229-83-32; Jean-Paul Lemée, tel (2) 229-8341; Marie-Hélène Pradines, tel (2) 229-83-45; Martin Le Coeur; Emmanuel Lacresse.

Commercial Section: Minister-Counsellor: Florence Jeanblanc-Risler, tel (2) 229-84-44; Counsellors: Cyrille Pierre, tel (2) 229-84-37; Françoise Breysse, tel (2) 229-84-36; Yvan Vassart; Raphaël Bello.

EURATOM and Nuclear Questions: Counsellor: Cyril Pinel; tel (2) 229-84-05.

Agriculture and Fisheries: Counsellors: Alexis Dutertre, Eric Zunino; Delegate: Jean-Marc Bournigal.

Social Policy and Employment: Counsellors: Bernard Krynen, tel (2) 229-86-31; Mireille Jarry, tel (2) 229-86-29; Laure de la Breteche.

Environment: Counsellors: Lilas Bernheim, tel (2) 229-82-33; Ghislaine de Hartingh-Boca, tel (2) 229-82-98.

Regional Policy: Counsellor: Gilles Pelurson; tel (2) 229-84-73; Attaché: Patricia Pedelabat; tel (2) 229-84-76; Hugues de Chavagnac; Alexis Dutertre.

Internal Market: Counsellors: Gérard Schoen, tel (2) 229-83-90; Laurent Pic; Deputy Counsellor: Anne Verron.

Health: Counsellor: Nicole Pruniaux; tel (2) 229-84-27.

Education, Culture, Youth and Sport: Adviser: Dominique Besser.

Legal Affairs: Counsellor: Fabien Raynaud; tel (2) 229-82-35.

Enterprises and Co-operation: Counsellors: Pierre Vernhes; Gaël Veyssière, tel (2) 229-84-63.

Transport: Adviser: Alexandra Subremon.

Political and Security: Ambassador: Sylvie Bermann; Counsellors: Fabien Pénone; Hélène Le Gal; Philippe Sutter; Jacques Bayet.

GERMANY

(19–21 rue Jacques de Lalaing, 1040 Brussels, Belgium; tel (2) 238-18-11; fax (2) 238-19-78; e-mail eurogerma.eu@ bruessel.auswaertiges-amt.de)

Permanent Representative, and Ambassador Extraordinary and Plenipotentiary: Wilhelm Schönfelder; tel (2) 238-18-11; fax (2) 238-19-78.

Deputy Permanent Representative, and Minister Plenipotentiary: Peter Witt; tel (2) 238-18-11; fax (2) 238-19-78.

Ministry of Political Affairs: Ambassador: Reinhard Schäfers; Minister: Klaus Knoop; Minister-Counsellor: Peter Roell; First Counsellor: Ernst Schwall; Press section (Counsellors): Peter Schoof, Hardy Boeckle, Thomas Schieb, Gabriele Boner, Gabrielle Bischoff, Hans-Ulrich Südbeck, Tania von Uslar-Gleichen; First Secs: Corinna Fricke, Karsten Geier, Tilman Hochmüller, Jens Lorentz, Henning Simon.

Ministry of the Interior: Minister-Counsellor: Friedrich Löper; First Counsellor: Dorothea Knackstedt; Counsellors: Andrea Schumacher, Andreas Beckmann; First Secs: Andreas Hoeger, Thomas Pohl; Second Secs: Peter Simoncelli, Thomas Michel.

Ministry of Justice: First Counsellor: Thomas Blöink; Counsellors: Klaus-Jörg Meyer, Martin Kraus-Vonjahr.

Ministry of Economic Affairs and Technology: Minister-Counsellor: Heinz Hetmeier; Counsellors: Eberhard Schollmeyer, Frank Wetzel; First Secs: Michael Schultz, Wolfdieter Böhler; Second Secs: Frank-Michael Radde, Jürgen Rohm, Ulrike Engels.

Ministry of the Environment: First Sec: Christine Wistuba.

Ministry of Economic Co-operation and Development: First Counsellor: Friedrich Kitschelt; First Sec: Frank Schmiedchen.

Ministry of Financial Services: Minister Counsellor: Wolfgang Glomb; First Counsellor: Adelheid Sailer-Schuster; Counsellors: Gabriele Arnoldi, Werner Kerkloh.

Ministry of Finance: Minister Counsellor: Wilhelm Rissmann; Counsellors: Ulrike Ten Eicken, Kristina Haverkamp, Clemens Wetz; Second Secs: Michael Meyer, Hans-Günther Steinhauer; Attaché: Andrea Romeis.

Federal Bank of Germany: Counsellor: Günter Heuser.

Ministry of Consumer Protection, Food and Agriculture: Minister Counsellor: German Jeub; First Counsellor: Wolfgang Trunk; First Sec: Wolfgang Löhe.

Ministry of Education and Research: Minister-Counsellor: Walter Mönig; Counsellor: Rüdiger Von Preuschen; First Sec: Susanne Madders; Second Sec: Manfred Faas.

Ministry of Transport: First Counsellor: Stefan Schimming; Second Sec: Katja Bürkholz.

Ministry of Labour and Social Affairs: Minister-Counsellor: Eckehard Hagen; Counsellor: Bruno Barth; Third Sec: Werner Heidrich.

Ministry of Health: Counsellor: Frank Niggemeier; Second Sec: Roland Hein.

Administration: Counsellor: Bernd Stadtmüller; Second Sec: Heinrich Golz; Third Secs: Werner Langer, Jürgen Kauffeld.

Military Policy: Minister-Counsellor: Wolfgang Meyer; Counsellors: Axel-Georg Binder, Ulrich Pfeiffer, Helmut von Schroeter.

GREECE

(25 rue Montoyer, 1000 Brussels, Belgium; tel (2) 551-56-11; fax (2) 551-56-51; e-mail mea.bruxelles@rp-grece.be)

Permanent Representative, and Ambassador Extraordinary and Plenipotentiary: Vassilis Kaskarelis; tel (2) 551-56-37; fax (2) 512-69-50.

Deputy Permanent Representative, Minister Plenipotentiary: Dimitrios Rallis; tel (2) 551-56-01; fax (2) 551-56-02.

Ministry of Foreign Affairs: First Counsellors: Theimistoklis Demiris, tel (2) 551-56-49; Constantin Chalastanis, tel (2) 551-56-04; Vassilios Moutsoglou, tel (2) 551-57-71; Constantinos Moatsos, tel (2) 551-56-97.

Ministry of Economic and Financial Policy: Counsellors: Maria Assimakopoulou, tel (2) 551-56-95; Constantin Nihoritis, tel (2) 551-56-86; Eleni Chytopoulou, tel (2) 551-56-82; Markos Karmiris, tel (2) 551-57-65; Maria Oikonomou, tel (2) 551-56-92; Helene-Pulcherie Psarros, tel (2) 551-56-76; Secs: Stiliani Ntasiou, tel (2) 551-56-67;

Christina Papakonstantinou, tel (2) 551-56-54; Athina Kaliva, tel (2) 551-56-33.

Ministry of Defence: Secretary: Panagiotis Gavathas, tel (2) 551-56-18.

Ministry of Justice and Home Affairs: First Counsellor: Nikolaos Argyros, tel (2) 551-56-03; Counsellors: Maria Micheloyiannaki, tel (2) 551-56-89; Panayotis Zarifis, tel (2) 551-57-79; Evangelos Kassalias, tel (2) 551-57-37; Styliani Kouroutou-Maniopoulou, tel (2) 551-57-01; Thomas Zarvalis, tel (2) 551-57-38.

Ministry of Agriculture: Counsellors: Sofia Kondylaky, tel (2) 551-57-67; Spiros Doudounakis, tel (2) 551-56-26; Georgia Bazoti-Mitsoni, tel (2) 551-57-72; Olga Agiovlassiti, tel (2) 551-57-23; Ioannis Karyofillis, tel (2) 551-56-20.

Ministry of Transport and Telecommunications: Counsellors: Grigorios Nanidis, tel (2) 551-57-00; Triantafyllos Papatriantafyllou, tel (2) 551-57-62; Serafeim-Ionnis Petrou, tel (2) 551-57-00; Kanstantinos Voudouris, tel (2) 551-56-40. Sec: Irirni Pavli, tel (2) 551-56-72.

Ministry of Employment and Social Security: Counsellor: Nelly Koureta; tel (2) 551-57-44.

Ministry of Health: Sec: Georgios Georgakopoulos; tel (2) 551-57-02.

Ministry of Education: Counsellor: Konstantinos Siakaris, tel (2) 551-56-41.

Ministry of Maritime Transport: Counsellor: Ionnais Karageorgopoulos, tel (2) 551-56-23.

Ministry of the Environment: Second Sec: Lazaros Stathakis, tel (2) 551-56-09.

Ministry of Industry, Energy, Research, Internal Markets and Consumer Affairs: Counsellors: Alexandros Akritopoulos, tel (2) 551-56-61; Georgios Asonitis, tel (2) 551-57-08; Charalambos Pippos, tel (2) 551-56-88; Georgios Frysalakis, tel (2) 551-57-89.

Ministry of the Press and the Media: Advisor: Vassilis Kapetanyannis, tel (2) 235-03-70.

Ministry of Culture: First Sec: Sophia Gialama, tel (2) 551-57-86.

Press Office: Attachés: Angelos Avgoustidis, tel (2) 230-62-37; Pavlos Pantsios, tel (2) 230-62-37; Constantinos Mavroidis, Sofia Tsantzalou-Patakia.

HUNGARY

(Rue de Treves 92–98, 1040 Brussels, Belgium; tel (2) 234-12-00; fax (2) 372-04-84; e-mail sec@hunrep.be; internet www.hunrep.be)

Permanent Representative, and Ambassador Extraordinary and Plenipotentiary: Tibor Kiss, tel (2) 234-12-05; e-mail amb@hunrep.be.

Deputy Permanent Representative, and Minister Plenipotentiary: Egon Dienes-Oehm, tel (2) 234-13-39; e-mail deputy@hunrep.be.

Permanent Representative: Ambassador to the PSC: Banai Károly, tel (2) 234-12013.

Ministry of Economics and Finance: Counsellor: Mikolt Csap, tel (2) 234-12-28; Attachés: Eszter Kroll, tel (2) 234-12-86; Katalin Koós-Hutás, tel (2) 234-12-67; Peter Tárnoki, tel (2) 234-12-88.

Ministry of Justice and Home Affairs: Counsellors: Gyula Rádi, tel (2) 234-12-14; György Gátos, tel (2) 234-12-24; János Zsigmond Kendernay, tel (2) 234-12-92; Second Sec: Gizella Vaz, tel (2) 234-12-24.

Ministry of Trade: Counsellors: Iván Kali, tel (2) 234-12-43; Péter Kertész, tel (2) 234-12-09; Sándor Szelekovszky, tel (2) 234-13-22; Attaché: Edina Varkoly, tel (2) 234-12-69; Third Sec: Szabolcs Orosz, tel (2) 234-13-24.

Ministry of Agriculture: Counsellors: Anlikó Kormos, tel (2) 234-12-54; Nándor Pete, tel (2) 234-12-84; First Secs: Ágnes Horváth, tel (2) 234-12-42; Zoltán Somogyi, tel (2) 234-12-85.

Ministry of Infrastructure and Environment: First Secs: László Bajan, tel (2) 234-12-19; Katalin Garáné, tel (2) 234-12-68; Andrej Sík, tel (2) 234-12-21; Péter Lengyel, tel (2) 234-13-34; Second Sec: Péter Bartha, tel (2) 234-12-20; Third Sec: Zsuzsanna Erdélyi, tel (2) 234-13-32.

Ministry of International Affairs: Counsellor: Sándor Molnár, tel (2) 234-14-19; Attaché: Dóra Loydl, tel (2) 234-14-07; First Sec: Károly Sárdi, tel (2) 234-14-15.

Ministry of Defence: Third Secs: Zoltán Varga, tel (2) 234-14-10; Andrea Puskás, tel (2) 234-13-09.

Ministry of Administration: First Sec: István Strehó, tel (2) 234-12-90; Attaché: Zoltán Bundik, tel (2) 234-12-89.

IRELAND

(89–93 rue Froissart, 1040 Brussels, Belgium; tel (2) 230-85-80; fax (2) 230-32-03; e-mail reppermirl@belgium.online.be)

Permanent Representative, and Ambassador Extraordinary and Plenipotentiary: Anne Anderson; tel (2) 282-32-10; fax (2) 230-30-18.

Deputy Permanent Representative, and Minister Plenipotentiary: Peter Gunning; tel (2) 282-32-20; fax (2) 230-31-88.

Administration: Counsellor: Noel White; tel (2) 282-32-27; Third Sec: Margaret Carton; tel (2) 282-32-55.

Ministry of Foreign Affairs: Counsellors: Michael Forbes, tel (2) 282-32-17; Noel White, tel (2) 282-32-27; Angela O'Farrell, tel (2) 282-33-30; Noel Purcell-O'Byrne; James McIntyre; First Secs: Feilim McLaughlin, tel (2) 282-32-15; Sinead Ryan, Kyle O'Sullivan, Jim Kelly, Fiona Hunt, Ciara Delaney, Seamus Hempenstall, Brian Glynn, Tom Kelly, Lorraine Christian.

Department of Justice, Equality and Law Reform: Counsellors: Vera Kelly; tel (2) 282-33-46; Fergus O'Callaghan, William Byrne; First Secs: Martin McDonald, tel (2) 282-32-69; John O'Dwyer, tel (2) 282-33-40; Catherine Territt, Geraldine Moore.

Department of Finance: Counsellors: Patrick Barry, tel (2) 282-32-54; John Norris, tel (2) 282-33-71; First Secs: John Palmer, tel (2) 282-32-53; Jimmy McMeel, tel (2) 282-32-50, Evelyn O'Connor, Michael Perkins, Orla O'Brien.

Department of Agriculture and Food: Counsellor: John Muldowney; tel (2) 282-32-57; First Sec: Dermot Murphy; tel (2) 282-32-58.

Department of Transport: Counsellor: Fintan Towey; Third Sec: Ide de Burca.

Department of Enterprise, Trade and Employment: Counsellors: Maurice Kennedy, tel (2) 282-32-39; Eugene Forde, tel (2) 282-32-39; Maurice Kennedy; First Secs: Geraldine Hurley, tel (2) 282-32-38; Anne Marie O'Connor, tel (2) 282-32-42.

Department of the Environment and Local Government: Counsellor: Mark Griffin; tel (2) 282-32-64; First Sec: Tom Sheridan; tel (2) 282-33-37.

Department of Education and Science: First Sec: John Quinlan; tel (2) 282-33-02.

Ministry of Communications, Marine and Natural Resources: First Secs: Michael O'Dwyer, Niall Curran, Majella O'Dea.

Department of Arts, Sport and Tourism: First Sec: Cian ó Lionáin; tel (2) 282-33-34.

Department of Health and Children: Counsellor: John O'Toole; tel (2) 282-32-72; First Sec: Greg Canning.

Department of Social, Community and Family Affairs: First Sec: Eamonn Moran, tel (2) 282-32-12; Third Sec: Darragh Doherty.

Revenue and Customs Tariff: First Sec: Gerard Moran; tel (2) 282-33-21; Third Sec: Karen Lane; tel (2) 282-32-82.

Department of Marine and Natural Resources: First Sec: Michael O'Dwyer; tel (2) 282-32-24.

Press: First Sec: Sinead Ryan; tel (2) 282-32-33.

ITALY

(9 rue du Marteau, 1000 Brussels, Belgium; tel (2) 220-04-11 (from 1pm to 4pm (2) 220-04-10); fax (2) 219-34-49; e-mail rpue@rpue.it; internet www.rpue.it)

Permanent Representative, and Ambassador Extraordinary and Plenipotentiary: Rocco Antonio Cangelosi; tel (2) 220-04-11; fax (2) 219-34-49.

Deputy Permanent Representative and Minister Plenipotentiary: Alessandro Merola; tel (2) 220-04-69; fax (2) 220-04-16.

Deputy Permanent Representative and Minister Plenipotentiary: Alessandro Pignatti Morano di Custoza.

Political and Security Committee: Ambassador: Maurizio Melani.

Ministry of Foreign Affairs: First Counsellors: Luca Giansanti, Pietro G. Donnici, Vittorio Rocco Di Torre Padula, Gianfranco Incarnato, Federico Failla, Michele Esposito, Giorgio Marrapodi, Amedeo Trambajolo, Giovanni Pugliese, Counsellor: Caterina Bertolini; First Secs: Nicola Verola, Luca Gori, Fabrizio Saggio, Lorenzo Fanara, Serena Lippi, Tiziana D'Angelo, Marie Sol Fulci.

Ministry of the Interior: Attaché: Pier Luigi Faloni.

Ministry of Justice: Attaché: Giovanni Giacalone.

Ministry of the Economy and Finance: Attachés: Antonio Ionta, Claudio Casini, Guiseppe Cipollone, Alfredo di Tommaso, Fulvio Bello, Antonio Leone, Maurizio Pulcianese, Francesco Sganga.

Ministry of Agriculture and Forestry: Attachés: Mario Catania, Luigi Polizzi, Roberto Laudato, Georgia Sanchez Laudato, Cesare Tabacchini.

Ministry of Infrastructure and Transport: Attachés: Stanislao Ritacco, Manuela Tomassini.

Ministry of Health: Attaché: Marco Castellina.

Ministry of Industry: Attachés: Franco de Giglio, Antonio Oreste Donatelli, Elvira Gaeta, Francesco Piccarreta, Guiseppe Pronto.

Ministry of Education and Research: Attachés: Roberto Adam, Marcello Limina.

Ministry of Employment and Social Affairs: Attachés: Clara Mughini, Clara Antonucci.

Centre for New Technologies, Energy and the Environment: Attaché: Vittorio de Crescenzo.

Bank of Italy: Attaché: Daniele Ciani.

Regional Experts: Attachés: Clelia Boesi, Gabriella Guacci.

LATVIA

(rue d'Arlon 39–41, 1000 Brussels, Belgium; tel (2) 282-03-60; fax (2) 282-03-69; e-mail missioneu@mfa.gov.lv)

Permanent Representative, and Ambassador Extraordinary and Plenipotentiary: Andris Kesteris.

Deputy Permanent Representative: Eduards Stiprais.

Ministry of Foreign Affairs: Counsellors: Ingrida Levrence, Lelde Lice-Licite; First Secs: Liene Drozdova, Benita Sirone.

Ministry of Finance: Counsellors: Mihails Kozlovs, Imants Tiesnieks; First Secs: Edite Dzalbe, Juris Stinka.

Ministry of Justice: Counsellors: Inese Birzniece, Sandris Laganovskis.

Ministry of the Interior: Counsellors: Liene Indriksone, Ilze Juhansone, Arijs Jansons.

Ministry of Economic Affairs: Counsellor: Aivars Berners; First Secs: Gints Zadraks, Gatis Abele.

Ministry of Employment and Social Affairs: Counsellor: Ruta Zilvere; First Sec: Renata Orlova.

Ministry of Agriculture: Counsellors: Dace Ozola, Gundega Micule; First Sec: Maris Berzins.

Ministry of the Environment: Second Sec: Ugis Zanders.

Ministry of Education: Third Sec: Inese Podgaiska.

Ministry of Transport: Attaché: Kristine Caunite.

Ministry of Public Health: First Sec: Signe Velina.

Ministry of Cultural Affairs: First Sec: Jolanta Mikelsone.

Ministry of Defence: First Sec: Dilarde Teilane.

LITHUANIA

(rue Belliard 6, 1040 Brussels, Belgium; tel (2) 771-01-40; fax (2) 771-45-97)

Permanent Representative, and Ambassador Extraordinary and Plenipotentiary: Oskaras Jusys, tel (2) 775-90-82; fax (2) 771-45-97.

Deputy Permanent Representative, Minister Plenipotentiary: Romas Švedas, tel (2) 788-18-70, fax (2) 788-18-78.

Ministry of Foreign Affairs: Minister-Counsellor: Kęstutis Sadauskas, tel (2) 775-90-80, fax (2) 771-45-97; Counsellors: Jurgita Virbickaitė, tel (2) 775-90-97, fax (2) 788-18-78; Arūnas Ribokas, tel (2) 775-90-85, fax (2) 771-45-97; Lina Terra, tel (2) 788-18-66, fax (2) 513-46-51; First Sec: Aodra Plepyte, tel (2) 775-90-96, fax (2) 771-45-97.

Ministry of Justice: Attaché: Darius Žilys, tel (2) 788-18-64, fax (2) 771-45-97.

Ministry of Internal Affairs: Attachés: Kristina Barakauskienė, tel (2) 763-04-34, fax (2) 771-45-97; Audronė Perkauskienė, tel (2) 503-18-78, fax (2) 771-45-97.

Ministry of Finance: Attachés: Miglė Tuskienė, tel (2) 770-41-49, fax (2) 770-46-91; Giedrė Švedienė, tel (2) 788-18-75; Audronė Misiūnaitė, tel (2) 502-58-54; Valdas Verbus, tel (2) 502-04-66.

Ministry of Social Security and Work: Attaché: Rita Žemaitytė, tel (2) 788-18-98, fax (2) 788-18-78.

Ministry of Health: Attaché: Rūta Liaudanskienė, tel (2) 788-18-63, fax (2) 788-18-78.

Ministry of the Economy: Attachés: Martynas Barysas, tel (2) 763-08-65, fax (2) 788-18-90; Asta Žalnieriūtė, tel (2) 513-01-52, fax (2) 788-18-90.

Ministry of Transport and Communications: Attachés: Raimonda Liutkevičienė, tel (2) 779-82-72, fax (2) 513-54-82; Valentinas Kvietkus, tel (2) 513-78-54, fax (2) 788-18-78; Virgilijus Danilevičius, tel (2) 788-18-92, fax (2) 788-18-78.

Ministry of Agriculture: Attachés: Vaidotas Ašmonas, tel (2) 775-90-88, fax (2) 762-02-64; Jolanťa Žutautienė, tel (2) 503-54-07, fax (2) 762-02-64; Tadas Briedis, tel (2) 503-16-07, fax (2) 788-18-78.

Ministry of the Environment: Attaché: Ligita Vaičiūnienė, tel (2) 502-81-70, fax (2) 788-18-78.

Ministry of Education and Science: Attaché: Neringa Kranauskienė, tel (2) 788-18-74, fax (2) 771-45-97.

Ministry of Culture: Attaché: Eglė Saudargaitė, tel (2) 513-20-96, fax (2) 503-40-61.

LUXEMBOURG

(75 ave de Cortenbergh, 1000 Brussels, Belgium; tel (2) 737-56-00; fax (2) 737-56-10; e-mail secretariat@rpue.etat.lu)

Permanent Representative, and Ambassador Extraordinary and Plenipotentiary: Nicolas Schmit; tel (2) 737-56-01; fax (2) 736-14-29.

Deputy Permanent Representative: Christian Braun; tel (2) 737-56-14; fax (2) 736-14-29.

Ministry of Finance: Counsellor: Jean-Pierre Lahire.

Ministry of Justice and Internal Affairs: Counsellor: Roland Genson.

Ministry of Foreign Affairs: Counsellors: Marcel Reimen, Camille Weis, Jean-Claude Meyer, Ronald Döfing; Attaché: Carlo Mullesch (Informatics).

Ministry of Economic Affairs: Attaché: Anne van Goethem.

Ministry of Defence: Lt. Col Jean-Louis Nurenberg.

Ministry of Agriculture: Counsellor: Pierre Treinen; Attaché: Sarah Blau.

Ministry of the Environment: Attachés: Georges Gehl, Jup Weber.

Ministry of Health: Attachés: Sarah Blau, Stéphane Tock.

Ministry of Transport: Attachés: William Helminger, Sam Weissen.

Ministry of Labour: Counsellor: Luc Wies.

MALTA

(rue Belliard 65–67, 1040 Brussels, Belgium; tel (2) 343-01-95; fax (2) 343-01-06; e-mail maltarep@gov.mt)

Permanent Representative, and Ambassador Extraordinary and Plenipotentiary: Richard Cachia Caruana, tel (2) 234-50-89; fax (2) 343-01-06.

Deputy Permanent Representative: Chris Grima, tel (2) 349-58-53; fax (2) 343-01-06.

Department of Political Affairs: First Sec: Rachel Sapiano, tel (2) 349-58-57, fax (2) 343-01-06.

Ministry of Economics and Financial Affairs: Attaché: Josanne Bonnici, tel (2) 343-01-95.

Ministry of Justice and Home Affairs: Attaché: Antoine Casha, tel (2) 234-50-77.

Ministry of Transport, Telecommunications and Energy: Attaché: Nicolette Camilleri, tel (2) 234-50-76.

Ministry of Agriculture and Fisheries: Attaché: Martin Bugelli, tel (2) 343-01-95.

Ministry of the Environment: Attaché: Anne Marie Sciberras, tel (2) 234-50-74.

Ministry of Employment, Social Affairs and Health: Attaché: Charles Sultana, tel (2) 349-58-54.

Ministry of Education, Youth and Health: Attaché: Rebecca Vella, tel (2) 343-01-95.

Ministry of Enterprise: Attaché: Jacqueline Aquilina, tel (2) 349-58-56.

Ministry of Administration: Second Sec: Walter Mallia, tel (2) 349-58-46.

THE NETHERLANDS

(48 ave Hermann Debroux, 1160 Brussels, Belgium; tel (2) 679-15-11; fax (2) 679-17-75)

Permanent Representative, and Ambassador Extraordinary and Plenipotentiary: T .J. A .M. de Bruijn ; tel (2) 679-15-00; fax (2) 679-17-95.

Deputy Permanent Representative, and Minister Plenipotentiary: H. J. J. Schuwer; tel (2) 679-15-08; fax (2) 679-17-74.

Ministry of Foreign Affairs: Counsellors: M. J. Th. Jorna, tel (2) 679-15-10, fax (2) 679-17-74; S. J. H. Smits, tel (2) 679-15-19, fax (2) 679-15-91; R. H. Cohen, tel (2) 679-15-23, fax (2) 679-17-79; P. J. Langenberg, tel (2) 679-15-18, fax (2) 679-17-91; F. F. M. Kemperman, tel (2) 679-15-09, fax (2) 679-17-74; J. L. Westhoff, tel (2) 679-15-35, fax (2) 679-17-77; J. Kraak, tel (2) 679-16-07, fax (2) 679-17-18; P. J. Ijmkers, tel (2) 679-15-03; fax (2) 679-17-78; P. H. Sastrowijoto, tel (2) 679-16-06, fax (2) 679-17-79; First Secs: S. Van Veldhoven-Van Der Meer, tel (2) 679-16-65, fax (2) 679-15-91; H. M. Van Der Plas, tel (2) 679-16-64; fax (2) 679-15-91; D. M. J. Kopmels, tel (2) 679-15-01, fax (2) 679-17-95; M. Halma, tel (2) 679-16-61, fax (2) 679-17-95; J. S. Van Den Oosterkamo, tel (2) 679-16-20, fax (2) 679-17-74; F. W. Steenks, tel (2) 679-15-07, fax (2) 679-17-74; M. W. Verheijden, tel (2) 679-16-59, fax (2) 679-17-74; J. J. P. Nijssen, tel (2) 679-16-60, fax (2) 679-17-74; N. J. Schermers, tel (2) 679-16-58, fax (2) 679-17-95; J. Faber, tel (2) 679-15-24; fax (2) 679-17-79; S. K. Walkate, tel (2) 679-15-36, fax (2) 679-17-77; F. Duijn, tel (2) 679-15-38, fax (2) 679-17-78; W. Libon-Van Der Wal, tel (2) 679-15-33, fax (2) 679-17-78; R. De Jong, tel (2) 679-17-05, fax (2) 679-17-71.

Ministry of Economic Affairs: Minister Plenipotentiary: S. K. Schuur; tel (2) 679-15-12; fax (2) 679-17-92; Counsellor: L. A. van Duyvendijk; tel (2) 679-15-13; fax (2) 679-17-92; K. Fraterman, tel (2) 679-15-15; First Secs: M. A. Haijer, tel (2) 679-15-16, fax (2) 679-17-92; T. C. Opmeer, tel (2) 679-15-61, fax (2) 679-17-92; Economic Attaché: R. Luttikhuizen; tel (2) 679-16-08; fax (2) 679-17-92.

Ministry of Defence: Defence Counsellor: D. H. Zandee; tel (2) 679-17-20; fax (2) 726-32-99; Mems of the EU Military Cttee: Rear Adml M. T. Tegelberg, tel

(2) 679-17-20, fax (2) 726-32-99; Col A. J. T. A. M. Verbeeten, tel (2) 707-66-92, fax (2) 726-47-48; Lt-Col E. A. de Landmeter, tel (2) 679-15-66, fax (2) 726-32-99; Col G. H. Besselink tel (2) 679-16-09, fax (2) 726-47-48.

Ministry of the Interior: Counsellor: G. Bronkhorst; tel (2) 679-15-25; fax (2) 679-17-93; Attaché: S. W. F. H. Bruinsma; tel (2) 679-15-26; fax (2) 679-17-93.

Ministry of Justice: Counsellor: Wouter Sturms; tel (2) 679-15-30; fax (2) 679-17-93.

Ministry of Finance: Financial Counsellors: L. Groenendal, tel (2) 679-15-55, fax (2) 679-17-90; L. A. de Blieck, tel (2) 679-15-59, fax (2) 679-17-90; Attachés: R. D. Boogert, tel (2) 679-15-56, fax (2) 679 17-90; W. Poesiat, tel (2) 679-15-67, fax (2) 679-17-90; R. Tjalkens, tel (2) 679-15-63, fax (2) 679-17-90; J. W. M. Gerritsen, tel (2) 679-16-69, fax (2) 679-17-90; R. A. De Boer, tel (2) 679-16-33, fax (2) 679-17-90.

Ministry of Transport, Public Works and Water Management: Counsellor: Jan M. van Heest; tel (2) 679-15-39; fax (2) 679-17-78; Attaché: L. J. Bal, tel (2) 679-15-40, fax (2) 679-17-78.

Ministry of Housing, Planning and the Environment: First Sec: E. J. Dame; tel (2) 679-15-20; fax (2) 679-17-91; Second Sec: I. E. A. Pauwels, tel (2) 679-15-41; fax (2) 679-17-91.

Ministry of Agriculture, Nature Conservation and Fisheries: Counsellors: A. J. Vaes, tel (2) 679-15-43, fax (2) 679-17-76; C. C. J. M. van der Meijs, tel (2) 679-15-49, fax (2) 679-17-76; A. M. Akkerman, tel (2) 679-15-49, fax (2) 679-17-76; Attachés: Oscar Meuffels, tel (2) 679-15-47, fax (2) 679-17-76; Frans Vroegop, tel (2) 679-15-44, fax (2) 679-15-44, fax (2) 679-17-76; S. J. C. W. Bont-van Tilburg, tel (2) 679-16-28, fax (2) 679-17-76.

Ministry of Employment and Social Affairs: Counsellor: Frank Schumacher; tel (2) 679-15-51; fax (2) 679-17-91; Attachés: G. A. Ten Dolle, tel (2) 679-17-32, fax (2) 679-17-91; R. Kuggeleijn, tel (2) 679-15-48, fax (2) 679-17-91.

Ministry of Health, Welfare and Sport: Counsellor: E. L. Engelsman; tel (2) 679-15-28; fax (2) 679-17-91; First Sec: H. Floor; tel (2) 679-15-29; fax (2) 679-17-91.

Ministry of Education, Culture and Science: Counsellor: J. C. Mebes; tel (2) 679-16-15; fax (2) 679-17-78.

Netherlands Antilles Affairs: Counsellor: C. M. C. Monti; tel (2) 679-17-52; fax (2) 679-17-78.

POLAND

(Avenue de Tervueren 282–284, 1150 Brussels, Belgium; tel (2) 777-72-20; fax (2) 777-72-97; e-mail mail@pol-mission-eu.be; internet www.polrepeu.be)

Permanent Representative, and Ambassador Extraordinary and Plenipotentiary: Marek Grela.

Deputy Permanent Representative, and Minister Plenipotentiary: Ewa Synowiec.

Representative to the Political and Security Committee, Minister Plenipotentiary: Maciej Popowski.

Political and Foreign Affairs: Counsellors: Jaroslaw Starzyk, Anna Raduchowska-Brochwicz; First Sec: Jaroslaw Timofiejuk; Attaché: Ireneusz Fidos.

Agriculture and Fisheries: Minister-Counsellor: Wladyslaw Piskorz; Counsellors: Andrzej Krawczyk, Jan Prandota.

Legislation: First Counsellor: Marta Cygan; Counsellor: Artur Harazim.

Culture, Information and Press: Counsellor: Malgorzata Alterman.

Justice and Home Affairs: First Counsellor: Janusz Gaciarz; Counsellor: Wojciech Kalamarz, Maciej Lewandowski.

Financial Affairs: Minister-Counsellors: Jacek Dominik, Tomasz Michalak; Counsellors: Damian Jaworski, Aleksander Wolowiec; First Sec: Marek Beldzikowski.

Commercial and Economic Affairs: First Counsellor: Malgorzata Mika-Bryska; Counsellors: Arkadiusz Michonski, Adam Orzechowski.

Infrastructure: Counsellor: Jan Lisiecki; Second Sec: Lukasz Wojtas.

Social Affairs and Employment: First Counsellors: Janusz Galeziak, Ewa Borowczyk.

Education and Research: Counsellor: Bogdan Rokosz.

Environment: Counsellor: Izabela Kakol.

Information and Telecommunications: First Counsellor: Wlodzimierz Marcinski.

Promotion: First Counsellor: Andrzej Rudka.

Administration: First Sec: Witold Rudas.

PORTUGAL

(12–22 ave de Cortenbergh, 1040
Brussels, Belgium; tel (2) 286-42-11;
fax (2) 231-00-26;
e-mail reper@reper-portugal.be;
internet www.reper-portugal.be)

Permanent Representative, and Ambassador Extraordinary and Plenipotentiary: Álvaro Mendonça e Moura; tel (2) 286-43-20; fax (2) 230-90-95.

Deputy Permanent Representative, and Minister Plenipotentiary: Domingos Fezas Vital, tel (2) 286-43-17; fax (2) 231-00-26.

Representative to the Political and Security Committee, Minister Plenipotentiary: José Júlio Pereira Gomes.

Co-ordination with COREPER and Institutional Affairs: Counsellor: José Rui Caroço; Secs: Pedro Lourtie, Paulo Simões.

Political and Foreign Affairs: Counsellors: Manuel De Jesus; Carolina Quina, tel (2) 286-43-06; Orlando Veiga; Secs: Jorge César Das Neves, tel (2) 286-42-93; Rui Correia, tel (2) 286-42-94; João Neves da Costa, Manuela Paula Teixeira Pinto, João Pedro Antunes; Attaché: Elsa Botas.

Agricultural Affairs: Counsellors: Edite Azenha, Antonio Cerca Miguel, Ana Isabel Batalha.

Fisheries: Counsellor: Antonio Pinho.

Health: Counsellor: Jorge Menezes.

Home Affairs and Justice: Counsellors: Gabriela Ventura, tel (2) 286-42-31; José Luis Lopes da Moto, tel (2) 286-42-28.

Industrial Policy, Energy and Internal Market: Counsellors: António Pinheiro, Jorge Mendoça e Costa, Paulo Silva, João Sena.

Economic and Financial Affairs: Counsellors: Rui Mourato, tel (2) 286-42-71; Luís Laço, tel (2) 286-42-74; Mario Alexandre; António Carlos Dos Santos, José Brito Antunes.

Social Affairs: Counsellor: Carlos Duarte; tel (2) 286-42-47.

Regional Policy: Counsellor: Virgílio José Rapaz.

Environment: Counsellors: Antonio Marques Carvalho, tel (2) 286-42-77; Mário Fernandes.

Research, Education and Culture: Counsellor: Ana Cristina Das Neves; tel (2) 286-42-48.

Transport and Communications: Counsellors: Ilídio Lemos Vieira, tel (2) 286-42-63; Jorge Leonardo, tel (2) 286-42-62.

Legal Affairs: Counsellors: Miguel Serpa Soares, tel (2) 286-42-30; Ana Oliveira e Silva; Maria José Salazar Leite.

Commercial Affairs: Counsellors: Jorge Castelbranco Soares, Rosário Prata.

Press and Information: Counsellor: Jaime Van Zeller Leitão; tel (2) 286-42-32.

Personnel and Administration: Attaché: Hernâni Mesquita.

Informatics: Attaché: Pedro Pereira; tel (2) 286-42-18.

Protocol: Attaché: Reinaldo Barreiros; tel (2) 286-43-28.

SLOVAKIA

(Avenue de Cortenbergh 79, 1000
Brussels, Belgium; tel (2) 743-68-11, fax
(2) 743-68-88; e-mail
slovakmission@pmsreu.be;
internet www.eubrussels.mfa.sk)

Permanent Representative, Ambassador Extraordinary and Plenipotentiary: Miroslav Adamiš, tel (2) 743-68-00.

Deputy Permanent Representative: Juraj Nociar; tel (2) 743-68-02.

Representative to the Political and Security Committee: Ambassador: Jaroslav Auxt; tel (2) 743-68-60.

Coordination: First Sec: Dušan Chrenek; tel (2) 743-68-40; Third Sec: Miriam Topčanská.

Administration and Protocol: First Sec: Mária Klampáriková; tel (2) 743-68-25.

Press and Information: Third Sec: Marta Dömöková; tel (2) 743-68-07.

Foreign Affairs: Second Sec: Beata Urbanová; tel (2) 743-68-03.

Justice and Home Affairs: Counsellor: Ľubomír Hanus; tel (2) 743-68-38.

Economy and Finance: Counsellors: Anna Šťavinová, tel (2) 743-68-30; Jaroslav Náhlik, tel (2) 743-68-39; Viliam Harvan, tel (2) 743-68-29.

Agricultural and Fisheries: Counsellor: Ľubomír Miček; tel (2) 743-68-23.

Commerce, Energy, and Internal Markets: Counsellors: Stanislaw Kubinec, tel (2) 743-68-93; Ľubomír Kuchta, tel (2) 743-68-96.

Telecommunications: Counsellor: Viliam Podhorský; tel (2) 743-68-48.

Transport: Second Sec: Ján Krak; tel (2) 743-68-26.

Employment, Social Security and Health: Counsellor: Mária Nádadyová; tel (2) 743-68-37.

Regional Policy: Counsellor: László Flórián; tel (2) 743-68-35.

Education and Research: First Sec: Jozef Pitel; tel (2) 743-68-08.

Environment: First Sec: Andrea Hlavatá; tel (2) 743-68-33.

SLOVENIA

(Avenue Marnix 30, 1000 Brussels,
Belgium; tel (2) 512-44-66,
fax (2) 512-09-97)

Permanent Representative, Ambassador Extraordinary and Plenipotentiary: Ciril Štokelj.

Deputy Permanent Representative: Marjeta Jager.

Representative to the Political and Security Committee: Igor Senčar.

Ministry of Foreign Affairs: Counsellors: Metka Ipavic, Mateja Norčič, Uroš Mahkovec.

Ministry of Defence: Counsellors: Alojz Jehart, Cvetoko Zorko.

Ministry of Finance: Counsellors: Alenka Jerkič, Maja Markovič.

Education: Counsellor: Peter Volasko.

Agriculture: Counsellor: Zoran Kovač.

Environment: Counsellor: Zoran Kus.

Economic Affairs: Counsellors: Minika Jakše, Vinka Soljačič.

Social Affairs and Health: Second Secs: Maja Rupnik-Potokar, Bozica Matič.

Information Technology and Telecommunications: Counsellor: Ljudmila Tozon.

Regional Development: First Sec: Dimitrij Pur.

Parliament: Counsellor: Jerica Zupan.

SPAIN

(52–54 blvd du Régent, 1000 Brussels,
Belgium; tel (2) 509-86-11;
fax (2) 511-19-40)

Permanent Representative, and Ambassador Extraordinary and Plenipotentiary: Carlos Basterreche Sagües; tel (2) 509-86-01; fax (2) 511-26-30.

Deputy Permanent Representative, and Minister Plenipotentiary: Cristóbal González-Aller; tel (2) 509-86-06; fax (2) 511-39-62.

Representative to the Political and Security Committee: Alonso Lucini Mateo.

Foreign Affairs: Counsellors: Antonio Bullón Camarasa, Javier Hernández Peña, Ignacio Ybañez Rubio, Juan Gonzalez-Barba Pera, Raul Fuentes Milani, Cándido Creis Estrada, Elena Gómez Castro.

Justice: Counsellors: Fernando Irurzun Montoro, Luis Aguilera Ruiz, Rafael Gil Nievas.

Legal Service: Counsellors: Eva Chamizo Llatas, Rafael León Cavero.

Economic Affairs: Counsellors: Erno Palla Sagües, María Isabel Colina Sánchez.

Finance and Customs: Counsellors: Antonio Rodríguez Laso, Rafael Arana Mendiguren, Miguel Ferre Navarrete, Ana de la Fuente Santorcuato, José María Vellejo Chamorro.

Trade: Counsellors: Cecilio Oviedo, Angel Viñas Martín, Carlos Paños Collado; Attachés: Emilia Pérez de Castro, Carmen Senz Castrillo, María Dolores Fernandez Gómez.

Home Affairs: Counsellors: Luis Luengo Alfonso, Eugenio Burgos, Camilo Vázquez Ballo, Francisco Alvarez Santamaría.

Public Works, Transport and Communications: Counsellors: Jesús P. Izarzugaza, Carlos Ortiz Bru.

Education and Culture: Counsellors: Pilar Barrero García.

Research and Development: Counsellor: Miguel Royo Macía.

Labour and Social Security: Counsellor: Vicente Pérez Menayo, Francisco Alonso Soto.

Industrial Affairs and Energy: Counsellors: Timoteo de la Fuente, José Luis Guzmán, Luis-Antonio Rico Urios, Ignacio Atorrasagasti.

Agriculture, Fisheries and Food: Counsellors: José Manuel Rodríguez Molina, Antonio Bardon Artacho, Alfredo Delgado Saenz, Carlos Cabanas Godino, Valentín Almansa de Lara.

Press and Information: Counsellors: Agustín Galán Macho. Deputy Counsellor: Eva Arbizu Duralde.

Health and Consumer Questions: Counsellor: Carlos Crespo Sabaris.

Environment: Counsellors: Hilario Domínguez Hernández, Miguel Castroviejo Bolívar, Antonio Troya Panduro.

Economic and Administrative Affairs: Counsellor: Domingo Soriano Gómez; Chancellor and Attaché: César Pla Barniol; Attaché: Carmina Navarro.

SWEDEN

(30 square de Meeûs, 1000 Brussels, Belgium; tel (2) 289-56-11; fax (2) 289-56-00; e-mail firstname.surname@ foreign.ministry.se; internet www.utrikes.regeringen.se/eu/ startsidan.htm)

Permanent Representative, and Ambassador Extraordinary and Plenipotentiary: Sven-Olof Petersson; tel (2) 289-56-45; fax (2) 289-56-00.

Deputy Permanent Representative, Minister Plenipotentiary: Ingrid Hjelt af Trolle; tel (2) 289-56-42; fax (2) 289-56-00.

Foreign Affairs: (Common Foreign and Security Policy) Ambassador: Staffan Tillander; tel (2) 289-57-63; Minister: Ulf Hammarström; tel (2) 289-58-28; Counsellors: Jonas Lovén, tel (2) 289-58-42; (Defence) Counseller: Peter Göthe; tel (2) 289-58-70; First Sec: Johan Frisell; tel (2) 289-56-46.

Foreign Relations: Ministers: Gunnar Klinga, tel (2) 289-56-32; Björn Lyrvall, tel (2) 289-56-57; Jan Söderberg, tel (2) 289-56-64; Counsellors: Charlotta Sparre, tel (2) 289-56-22; Paula Wennerblom, tel (2) 289-57-42; Veronika Wand-Danielsson, tel (2) 289-56-54; Malena Mård, tel (2) 289-56-67; Lars Schmidt, tel (2) 289-56-37; First Secs: Mattias Frumierie, tel (2) 289-57-57; Lars Johan Lönnback, tel (2) 289-56-79; Maria Sargren, tel (2) 289-56-06; Second Sec: Jörgen Karlsson; tel (2) 289-56-97.

Co-ordination: Counsellors: Katarina Areskoug, tel (2) 289-56-21; Eva Lindholm, tel (2) 289-56-38.

Legal Affairs, Justice and Home Affairs, Internal Market: Counsellors: Louise Bonbeck, tel (2) 289-56-33; Helena Garme, tel (2) 289-56-15; Kristina Holmgren, tel (2) 289-58-54.

Health: Counsellor: Anna-Eva Amplélas; tel (2) 289-57-19.

Transport and Communications: Counsellors: Maria Gelin, tel (2) 289-58-30; Erik Kiesow, tel (2) 289-56-18; Anders Åhlund, tel (2) 289-57-23.

Economic and Financial Affairs: Åsa Johansson; tel (2) 289-57-11; Counsellors: Mats Walberg, tel (2) 289-56-93; Anna Wallin, tel (2) 289-57-14; Carl Asplund, tel (2) 289-57-04; Kristina Åkesson, tel (2) 289-57-48; Attaché: Patrik Heinesson, tel (2) 289-56-74.

Education and Research: Counsellors: Peter Johansson, tel (2) 289-57-01; Bjarne Kirsebom, tel (2) 289-57-03.

Agriculture and Fisheries: Ministers: Stefan de Maré, Pernilla Ivarsson; Attaché: Carl-Johan Lindén, tel (2) 289-56-89.

Employment and Social Affairs: Counsellors: Johanna Möllerberg, tel (2) 289-57-25; Frederik Sjögren, tel (2) 289-57-45.

Cultural Affairs: Counsellor: Pia Erson; tel (2) 289-56-35.

Industry, Energy and Regional Affairs: Counsellor:s Anna Carlsson, tel (2) 289-58-47; Sara Emanuelsson, tel (2) 289-56-25.

Environment: Counsellors: Ann-Louise Månsson, tel (2) 289-57-29; Ulf Björnholm Ottosson, tel (2) 289-56-31.

Administrative Affairs: Minister: Karl Skybrant; tel (2) 289-56-91.

Press and Information: Press Counsellor: Anders J. Ericson; tel (2) 289-56-55.

UNITED KINGDOM

(10 ave d'Auderghem, 1040 Brussels, Belgium; tel (2) 287-82-11; fax (2) 287-83-98; e-mail firstname.lastname@fco.gov.uk; internet ukrep.fco.gov.uk)

Permanent Representative, and Ambassador Extraordinary and Plenipotentiary: John Grant; tel (2) 287-82-71; fax (2) 287-83-83.

Deputy Permanent Representative: Anne Lambert; tel (2) 287-82-62; fax (2) 287-83-92.

Commercial: First Sec: Joyce Martin; tel (2) 287-83-46; fax (2) 287-83-49.

Political and Institutional Affairs, Press: Counsellor: Michael Aron; tel (2) 287-82-45; First Secs: Caroline Wilson, tel (2) 287-82-82; Matthew Taylor, tel (2) 287-89-37; David Chitty, tel (2) 287-83-91; Corin Robertson, tel (2) 287-82-92; Jonathan Allen, tel (2) 287-82-06; Joyce Martin, tel (2) 287-82-46; Second Sec: Hilary McFarland; tel (2) 287-82-07; Commercial Attaché: Linda Geller.

Legal Affairs: Adviser: Paul Berman, tel (2) 287-83-37; First Secs: Hazel Cameron, tel (2) 287-89-32; Michael Addison, tel (2) 287-83-64.

Agriculture: Counsellor: David Barnes; tel (2) 287-82-54; fax (2) 287-83-94; First Secs: Katherine Riggs, tel (2) 287-82-49; Roy Norton, tel (2) 287-82-14; Gareth Baynham-Hugues, tel (2) 287-83-89; Second Secs: Keith Morrison, tel (2) 287-83-36; Simon Stannard, tel (2) 287-82-86; Caoimhe Treanor, tel (2) 287-82-55.

Industrial Affairs, Energy, Internal Market and Transport: Counsellor: Antony Vinall; tel (2) 287-82-40; fax (2) 287-83-96; First Secs: Chris Barton, tel (2) 287-82-36; Andrew Van der Lem, tel (2) 287-82-95; Ian Holt, tel (2) 287-82-53; Ben Turner, tel (2) 287-82-18; Michael Rossell, tel (2) 287-83-02; Second Secs:

Nick Thompson, tel (2) 287-82-78; 03; Johanna Keech, tel (2) 287-82-03.

Social Affairs, Environment and Regional Policy: Counsellor: Shan Morgan; tel (2) 287-82-66; fax (2) 287-83-97; First Secs: Tim Figures, tel (2) 287-83-58; Lindsay Appleby, tel (2) 287-83-01; Marc Holland, tel (2) 287-82-13; Andrew Dalgleish, tel (2) 287-82-01; Second Secs: Kevin Dench, tel (2) 287-82-21; Philip McMurray, tel (2) 287-83-51.

Economic Affairs, Finance and Taxation: Counsellor: Peter Curwen; tel (2) 287-82-58; fax (2) 287-83-33; First Secs: (Budget) Fabia Jones, tel (2) 287-82-83; (Economic and financial affairs) Gary Roberts, tel (2) 287-82-93; (Economic and financial affairs) Edward Smith, tel (2) 287-82-23; (Taxation) James Robertson, tel (2) 287-82-04; Second Secs: Hannah Robinson, Rebecca Jones, Karen Parkes.

External Relations: Minister: Peter Gooderham; tel (2) 287-83-19; Advisers: Dr Carolyn Browne, tel (2) 287-82-48, fax (2) 287-82-99; Peter Landymore, tel (2) 287-82-35; Counsellor: Giles Portman, tel (2) 287-82-22; First Secs: Ken O'Flaherty, tel (2) 287-82-52; Jan Vollbracht, tel (2) 287-82-32; Anna Clunes, tel (2) 287-82-55; Sandy Johnston, tel (2) 287-82.56; Karne Betts, tel (2) 287-83-22; Hamish Cowell, tel (2) 287-83-50; Duncan Sparkes, tel (2) 287-83-77; Damian Thwaites, tel (2) 287-82-19; Second Secs: Stephen Hickey, tel (2) 287-83-50; Serra Teziler, tel (2) 287-89-36; Harriet Rodger, tel (2) 287-82-05; Maryam Teschke, tel (2) 287-83-47; Sarah Cullum, tel (2) 287-82-91.

Justice and Home Affairs: Counsellor: Jonathan Sweet; tel (2) 287-82-81; First Secs: Jane Ferrier, tel (2) 287-82-57; Neil Bradley, tel (2) 287-82-59; Paul McKell, tel (2) 287-83-84; Second Secs: Ben Llewellyn-Jones, tel (2) 287-82-41; Rod McLean, tel (2) 287-89-16.

Administrative Affairs: First Sec: Phil May, tel (2) 287-83-38; Ian Wright, tel (2) 287-82-27.

COURT OF JUSTICE

Court of Justice of the European Communities, Palais de la Cour de Justice, Blvd Konrad Adenauer, Kirchberg, 2925 Luxembourg.
Tel 4303-1
Fax 4303-2500 (Press and Information Division)
Fax 4303 2650 (Publications Section)
E-mail info@curia.eu.int
Internet www.curia.eu.int

Cases brought by Member States, the EU institutions, private individuals or companies may be referred to the Court of Justice. The Court of Justice operated alone until 1989. The Court of First Instance was then added in order to improve the legal protection of the EU's citizens and to enable the Court of Justice to concentrate its efforts on its primary task of ensuring that Community law is interpreted uniformly, working closely with national judges through the preliminary ruling procedure.

The Court of First Instance is empowered to deal with all actions brought by individuals and companies against EU institutions and bodies. The judgments of the Court of First Instance may go to further appeal to the Court of Justice, but the appeal is limited to points of law.

Having no political message to convey, the Court of Justice's basic information role is to bring to the public's knowledge the case law created through its judgments. It also informs EU citizens about its organization, powers and procedures. The Court is made up of judges, who are assisted by advocates-general. The members of these bodies are appointed for a six-year term of office by common agreement of the Member States' governments. The judges select one of their number to be President of the Court for a renewable term of three years. The President directs the work of the Court and presides at hearings and deliberations. The advocates-general assist the Court in its task. They deliver, in open court and with complete impartiality and independence, opinions on the cases brought before the Court.

The Court of First Instance is composed of judges appointed by the governments of the Member States to hold office for a renewable term of six years. The Members of the Court of First Instance select one of their number as President. There are no permanent advocates-general in the Court of First Instance. The duties of advocate-general are performed, in a limited number of cases, by one of the judges.

The Court of Justice may sit in plenary session or in chambers of three or five judges. It sits in plenary session when a Member State or a Community institution that is a party to the proceedings so requests, or in particularly complex or important cases. Other cases are heard by a chamber.

The Court of First Instance sits in chambers of three or five judges. It too may sit in plenary session in certain particularly important cases.

The Court of Justice does not have any external information offices and all of its activities take place at the Court's seat in Luxembourg. Information about the Court may possibly be obtained via Commission offices in the Member States. Some documents may also be ordered from the Office for Official Publications of the European Communities or from its sales offices.

The Court provides, on request, a small catalogue of its publications entitled *Publications of the Court of Justice*.

Additional information, including a weekly bulletin, press releases and the complete text of judgments, is available on the Court's internet site: www.curia .eu.int.

INFORMATION AVAILABLE

Information is basically intended for legal specialists and the press.

Offset Copies of the Judgments of the Court of Justice and the Court of First Instance and Opinions of the Advocates-General

Information content. The Court publishes a report on its case-law. In order to enable interested parties to have the judgments and opinions of the advocates-general rapidly, it publishes an offset edition, which is available immediately in French, and in the procedural language of the case.
Addressees. All interested persons.
Frequency. Irregular. Documents are sent in batches every ten or fifteen days so as to keep down mailing costs.
Languages. French and the procedural language available immediately. The other languages are available within approximately 6 months.
How to obtain. Orders for offset copies, subject to availability, may be made in writing, stating the language desired, to the Internal Services Division of the Court of Justice of the European Communities, 2925 Luxembourg, on payment of a fixed charge for each document. Orders are no longer accepted once the issue of the Reports of Cases before the Court containing the required Judgment or Opinion has been published.

Subscribers to the Reports may pay a subscription to receive offset copies in one or more of the official Community languages of the texts contained in the Reports of Cases before the Court of Justice and the Court of First Instance, with the exception of the texts appearing only in the Reports of European Community Staff Cases. All the recent judgments of the Court of Justice and the Court of First Instance are accessible quickly and free of charge on the Court's internet site (www.curia.eu.int). Judgments are available on the site, in all official languages, from approximately 3 p.m. on the day they are delivered. The Advocate-General's Opinions are also available, in the language of the Advocate-General as well as, initially, in the language of the case.

Proceedings of the Court of Justice and of the Court of First Instance of the European Communities

Information content. Short summary of all the Courts' judgments; brief notes on opinions delivered by the Advocates-General; new cases brought during the previous week.

A special annual issue provides an analytical table of the Court's judgments and indicates the week in which they appear. The publication is now available on the Commission's Rapid database, while the judgments are also included in the CELEX databank and the CELEX CD-ROM. The proceedings are also published every week on the Court's internet site.
Addressees. All interested persons.
Frequency. Weekly, during the Court's judicial terms. About 35 issues a year.
Languages. The French version is available about 2 or 3 weeks after the Court's judgment. The other languages are available shortly afterwards.
How to obtain. Free from the Press & Information Division, Court of Justice of the European Communities, 2925 Luxembourg; fax (+352) 4303 2500. The Court's internet site can be visited at www.curia.eu.int.

Calendrier de la Semaine

Information content. List of sittings of the Court. The week's timetable: summary of all the cases which are to be heard with an indication of the day and the time. Following week's timetable: list and date of the cases, without any particular details. The list may be altered and is therefore for information only.
Addressees. Press agencies.
Frequency. Weekly.
Languages. French, but German version also distributed.
How to obtain. Available only on the internet, free of charge, at www.curia .eu.int.

Press Summaries

Press summaries are published by the Court's Press and Information Division. The releases are intended for the press and may be obtained, on request, from the Court's Press and Information Division. They are also available on the internet at www.curia.eu.int.

Current Bibliography

Information content. Bi-monthly bibliography comprising a complete list of all the works received or catalogued by the library of the Court during the reference period. It consists of two separate parts: Part A, legal publications concerning European integration; Part B, jurisprudence, international law, comparative law, and national legal systems.
How to obtain. Enquiries should be sent to the Library Division of the Court of Justice, Blvd K. Adenauer, 2525 Luxembourg.

Legal Bibliography of European Integration

Information content. Annual publication based on books acquired and periodicals analysed during the year in question in the area of Community law. Since the 1990 edition this Bibliography has become an official European Communities publication. It contains approximately several thousand bibliographical references with a systematic index of subject-matter and an index of authors.

Reports of Cases before the Court of Justice and the Court of First Instance

Information content. With respect to each case heard: reports for the Hearing; opinions of the Advocates-General; judgments of the Court.
Frequency. Since 1994, the Reports of Cases before all the Courts have been published simultaneously in Union languages, and the time lag between the pronouncement of the judgments and their publication has been reduced to around six months instead of about 24 between the French version and the others. They are the sole authentic source for citations of decisions of the European Courts. The reports are annual. The final volume of the year's Reports contains a chronological table of the cases published, a table of cases classified in numerical order, an alphabetical index of parties, a table of the Community legislation cited, an alphabetical index of subject-matter and a systematic table containing all of the summaries with their corresponding chains of head-words for the cases reported.
Languages. The languages of the EU.
How to obtain. From the Office for Official Publications or sales points in the Member States.

Diary

A multilingual weekly list of the Courts' judicial activity, announcing the hearings, readings of opinions and delivery of judgments taking place in the week in question. There is also an overview of the subsequent week. Each case is described in brief and the subject matter is indicated. The weekly calendar is published every Thursday and is available on the Court's internet site.

Reports of European Community Staff Cases

Information content. Since 1994 the Reports of European Community Staff Cases (ECR-SC) has contained all the judgments of the Court of First Instance in staff cases in the language of the case together with an abstract in one of the official languages, of the subscriber's choice. It also contains summaries of the judgments delivered by the Court of Justice on appeals in this area, the full text of which continues to be published in the general Reports. The Index is also available in all the languages.
Frequency. Annual.
Languages. Languages of the case plus an abstract in the official language of the subscriber's choice.
How to obtain. From the Office for Official Publications or sales points in the Member States.

Digest of Case-Law Relating to the European Communities

Information content. The Court of Justice publishes the Digest of Case-law relating to the European Communities, which systematically presents not only its case-law but also selected judgments of courts in the Member States.
The Digest comprises two series, which may be obtained separately, covering the following fields:
A Series. Case-law of the Court of Justice and the Court of First Instance of the European Communities and cases relating to the Convention of 27 September 1968 on Jurisdiction and the Enforcement of Judgments in Civil and Commercial Matters (3 volumes). The A Series covers the case-law of the Court of Justice of the European Communities from 1977. A consolidated version covering the period 1977 to 1990 replaces the various looseleaf issues which have been published since 1983. The French version is already available and will be followed by German, English, Danish, Italian and Dutch versions. Publication in the other official Community languages is being considered. The A series is to be published every five years in all the official Community languages, the first covering 1991 to 1995. Annual updates will be available, although initially only in French.
D Series. Case-law of the Court of Justice of the European Communities and of

the courts of the Member States relating to the Convention of 27 September 1968 on Jurisdiction and the Enforcement of Judgments in Civil and Commercial matters (3 volumes).
Frequency. Irregular.
How to obtain. From the Office for Official Publications or sales points in the Member States.

Annual Report

Information content. A publication giving a synopsis of the work of the Court of Justice and the Court of First Instance, both in their judicial capacity and in terms of their other activities (meetings and study courses for members of the judiciary, visits, seminars, etc.). This publication contains much statistical information.
Addressees. Practitioners, teachers and students of Community law.
Frequency. In principle, every year.
Languages. English or French.
How to obtain. Although this free book appears in the catalogue of the Office for Official Publications, it may be obtained only from the Court of Justice, 2925 Luxembourg.

Selected Instruments Relating to the Organisation, Jurisdiction and Procedure of the Court

Information content. This work contains the main provisions concerning the Court of Justice and the Court of First Instance to be found in the Treaties, in secondary law and in a number of conventions. An index is provided.
Addressees. Practitioners of EC law, students, professors.
Frequency. Irregular.
Languages. All the Community's languages.
How to obtain. From the Office for Official Publications or sales offices in the Member States.

Internal Documents

Bulletin périodique de jurisprudence. This document assembles, for each quarterly, half-yearly and yearly period, all the summaries of the judgments of the Court of Justice and of the Court of First Instance which will appear in due course in the *Reports of Cases before the Court*. It is set out in a systematic form identical to that of the Digest, so that it forms a precursor, for any given period, to the Digest and can provide a similar service to the user. It is available in French.

Index A–Z. Computer-generated publication containing a numerical list of all the cases brought before the Court of Justice and the Court of First Instance since 1954, an alphabetical list of names of parties, and a list of national courts or tribunals which have referred cases to the Court for a preliminary ruling. The Index A–Z gives details of the publication of the Court's judgments in the *Reports of Cases before the Court*. This publication is available in French and English and is updated annually. It may also be consulted on the Court's internet site (www.curia.eu.int).

Jurisprudence en matière de fonction publique communautaire. A publication in French containing abstracts of the decisions of the Court of Justice and of the Court of First Instance in cases brought by officials and other servants of the European Communities, set out in systematic form.

Jurisprudence nationale en matière de droit communautaire. The Court has established databases covering the case-law of the courts of the Member States concerning Community law and also the Brussels, Rome and Lugano Conventions.

Brussels and Lugano Conventions. A collection of the texts of the Brussels Convention of 1968 and the Lugano Convention of 1988 on Jurisdiction and the Enforcement of Judgments in Civil and Commercial Matters, together with the acts of accession, protocols and declarations relating thereto, in all the original languages.

For further information on the above internal publications contact the Research and Documentation Division of the Court of Justice, Blvd K. Adenauer, 2925 Luxembourg; fax (+352) 43032500.

Internet Site of the Court of Justice

Information content. The Court's website, located at www.curia.eu.int, offers access to a wide range of information and documents concerning the institution. Most of the documents are available in the official languages. The index page gives an indication of the contents of the site at present. 'Case-Law' has provided, since June 1977, rapid access free of charge to all the recent judgments delivered by the Court of Justice and the Court of First Instance. The judgments are available at the site, in the official languages, from 3 p.m. of the day of delivery. The Opinions of the Advocates-General are also available under this heading in both the language of the Advocate-General and the language of the case. The site offers the following major headings:

- Introduction to the institutions;
- Press and information;
- Recent case-law;
- Research and documentation;
- Library;
- Texts relating to the institution.

Members

(Order of Precedence from 13 May 2004)

President: Judge Vassilios Skouris (Greece).

Judge: Peter Jann (Austria).

Judge: Christiaan Timmermans (Netherlands—President of the Second Chamber).

Judge: Allan Rosas (Finland—President of the Third Chamber).

Judge: Claus Christian Gulmann (Denmark—President of the Fifth Chamber).

Judge: Jean-Pierre Puissochet (France—President of the Sixth Chamber).

First Advocate General: Antonio Tizzano (Italy).

Judge: José Narciso da Cunha Rodrigues (Portugal—President of the Fourth Chamber).

Advocate General: Francis G. Jacobs (United Kingdom).

Judge: Antonio La Pergola (Italy).

Advocate General: Philippe Léger (France).

Advocate General: Dámaso Ruiz-Jarabo Colomer (Spain).

Judge: Romain Schintgen (Luxembourg).

Judge: Fidelma Macken (Ireland).

Judge: Ninon Colneric (Germany).

Judge: Stig von Bahr (Sweden).

Advocate General: Leendert A. Geelhoed (Netherlands).

Advocate General: Christine Stix-Hackl (Austria).

Judge: Rosario Silva de Lapuerta (Spain).

Judge: Koen Lenaerts (Belgium).

Advocate General: Juliane Kokott (Germany).

Advocate General: Luís Miguel Poiares Pessoa Maduro (Portugal).

Judge: Konrad Hermann Theodor Schiemann (United Kingdom).

Judge: Jerzy Makarczyk (Poland).

Judge: Pranas Kūris (Lithuania).

Judge: Endre Juhász (Hungary).

Judge: George Arestis (Greece).

Judge: Anthony Borg Barthet U.O.M. (Malta).

Judge: Marko Ilešič (Slovenia).

Judge: Jirí Malenovský (Czech Republic).

Judge: Ján Klučka (Slovakia).

Judge: Uno Lõhmus (Estonia).

Judge: Egils Levits (Latvia).

Registrar: Roger Grass (France).

Composition of the Chambers

First Chamber

President: Peter Jann.

Judges: J. N. Cunha Rodrigues, N. Colneric, K. Lenaerts, K. Schiemann, E Juhász, M. Elešič, E. Levits.

Second Chamber

President: C. W. A. Timmermanns.

Judges: C. Gulmann, R. Schintgen, R. Silva de Lapuerta, J. Makarczyk, P. Kūris, G. Arestis, J. Klučka.

Third Chamber

President: Allan Rosas.

Judges: J. P. Puissochet, A. M. La Pergola, F. Macken, S. von Bahr, A. Borg Barthet, J. Malenovský, U. Lõhmus.

Fourth Chamber

President: J. N. Cunha Rodrigues.

Judges: N. Colneric, K. Lenaerts, K. Schiemann, E. Juhász, M. Elešič, E. Levits.

Fifth Chamber

President: C. Gulmann.

Judges: R. Schintgen, R. Silva de Lapuerta, J. Makarczyk, P. Kūris, G. Arestis, J. Klučka.

Sixth Chamber

President: Jean-Pierre Puissochet.

Judges: A. M. La Pergola, F. Macken, S. von Bahr, A. Borg Barthet, J. Malenovský, U. Lõhmus.

Court of First Instance

MEMBERS

(Order of Precedence—from 7 October 2004)

President: Judge Bo Vesterdorf (Denmark—President of the First Chamber and of the First Extended Chamber).

Judge: Pernilla Lindh (Sweden—President of Chamber).

Judge: Josef Azizi (Austria—President of Chamber).

Judge: Jörg Pirrung (Germany—President of Chamber).

Judge: Hubert Legal (France—President of Chamber).

Judge: Rafael García-Valdecasas y Fernández (Spain—President of the Fifth Chamber and of the Fifth Extended Chamber).

Judge: Virpi Tiili (Finland—President of the Fourth Chamber and of the Fourth Extended Chamber).

Judge: John Cooke (Ireland).

Judge: Marc Jaeger (Luxembourg).

Judge: Paolo Mengozzi (Italy).

Judge: Arjen W. H. Meij (Netherlands).

Judge: Mihalis Vilaras (Greece).

Judge: Nicholas Forwood (United Kingdom—President of the Second Chamber and of the Second Extended Chamber).

Judge: Maria Eugénia Martins de Nazaré Ribeiro (Portugal).

Judge: Franklin Dehousse (Belgium).

Judge: Ena Cremona (Malta).

Judge: Ottó Czúcz (Hungary).

Judge: Irena Wiszniewska-Bialecka (Poland).

Judge: Irena Pelikánová (Czech Republic).

Judge: Daniel Šváby (Slovakia).

Judge: Vilenas Vadapalas (Lithuania).

Judge: Küllike Jürimäe (Estonia).

Judge: Ingrida Labucka (Latvia).

Judge: Savvas S. Papasavvas (Greece).

Judge: Verica Trstenjak (Ljubljana).

Registrar: Hans Jung (Germany).

Composition of the Chambers
First Chamber
President: Bo Vesterdorf.

Judges: P. Mengozzi, M. E. Martins Ribeiro, I. Labucka, V. Trstenjak.

Members for Extended Chamber: B. Vesterdorf, P. Mengozzi, M. E. Martins Ribeiro, I. Labucka, V. Trstenjak.

Second Chamber
President: Jörg Pirrung.

Judges: A. W. H. Meij, N. J. Forwood, I. Pelikánová, S. S. Papasavvas.

Members for Extended Chamber: Jörg Pirrung, A. W. H. Meij, N. J. Forwood, I. Pelikánová, S. S. Papasavvas.

Third Chamber
President: Josef Azizi.

Judges: M. Jaeger, F. Dehousse, E. Cremona, O. Czúcz.

Members for Extended Chamber: Josef Azizi, M. Jaeger, F. Dehousse, E. Cremona, O. Czúcz.

Fourth Chamber
President: Hubert Legal.

Judges: V. Tilli, M. Vilaras, I. Wiszniewska-Bialecka, V. Vadapalas.

Members for Extended Chamber: Hubert Legal, V. Tilli, M. Vilaras, I. Wiszniewska-Bialecka, V. Vadapalas.

Fifth Chamber
President: Pernilla Lindh.

Judges: R. García-Valdecasas, J. Cooke, D. Šváby, K. Jürimäe.

Members for Extended Chamber: Pernilla Lindh, R. García-Valdecasas, J. Cooke, D. Šváby, K. Jürimäe.

Administration
Registry
Registrar: Roger Grass; e-mail ECJ .Registry@curia.eu.int.

Registry of the Court of First Instance
Registrar: Hans Jung; e-mail CFI .Registry@curia.eu.int.

Divisions
Press and Information: e-mail info@ curia.eu.int.

Interpreting: fax 4303-3697; e-mail interpret@curia.eu.int.

Interior: fax (general) 4303-2650, (publications) 4303-2577; e-mail div.int@ curia.eu.int.

Personnel: e-mail pers@curia.eu.int.

Computer Division: e-mail dint@curia .eu.int.

Library: tel 4303-2681; fax 4303-2424; e-mail HDB@curia.eu.int.

EUROPEAN ECONOMIC AND SOCIAL COMMITTEE

European Economic and Social Committee, 2 rue Ravenstein, 1000 Brussels, Belgium
Tel (+32) 2-5469011
Fax (+32) 2-5134893
E-mail info@esc.eu.int
Internet www.esc.eu.int

Made up of representatives of the EU's socio-professional groups, the European Economic and Social Committee (EESC) acts in an advisory capacity in the EU decision-making process. The representatives are divided into three groups – employers (I), workers (II) and various interests (III) – and are drawn as follows from the respective Member States: 24 members each from France, Germany, Italy and the United Kingdom; 21 members each from Poland and Spain; 12 members each from Austria, Belgium, Czech Republic, Greece, Hungary, Netherlands, Portugal and Sweden; 9 members each from Denmark, Finland, Ireland, Lithuania and Slovakia; 7 members each from Estonia, Latvia and Slovenia; 6 members each from Cyprus and Luxembourg; 5 members from Malta. Members are proposed by national governments and appointed by the Council of Ministers for a renewable four-year term.

Employers' Group (Group I). The Employers' Group (Group I) has members from private and public sectors of industry, chambers of commerce, wholesale and retail trade, banking and insurance, transport and agriculture. Group I policy in general reflects the opinion of European industrial federations in supporting the development of a European Union of free market economies with freedom of trade and movement within the internal market, in the belief that this is the best road to growth, competitiveness and employment.

Workers' Group (Group II). The vast majority of the workers' group at the European Economic and Social Committee belong to the European Trade Union Confederation. Others are members of the Organization of Managerial and Executive Staff. The group has its own secretariat. The concerns of the group are: the fight against unemployment (the new Treaty has a chapter on employment); the improvement of living and working conditions (worker information and consultation, inter alia); the protection of fundamental freedoms, relations with third countries and world peace; the repercussions of economic globalization and the jeopardizing of the EU's social achievements.

Various Interests Group (Group III). The unique feature which forges Group III's identity is the wide range of categories represented therein. Its members are drawn from farmers' organizations, small businesses, the crafts sector, the professions, co-operatives and non-profit associations, consumer organizations, environmental organizations, associations representing the family, women, persons with disabilities, and the scientific and academic community.

The EESC elects from amongst its number, for a two-year period, a bureau of 37 members, including a President and two Vice-Presidents chosen alternately from each of the three groups. The Presidency, assisted by the Secretary-General, is responsible for relations with the EU's institutions and the EESC's external representation. The basic function of the bureau is to organize the Committee's work.

The EESC is divided into six sections:

- ECO – Economic and Monetary Union and Economic and Social Cohesion
- INT – Single Market Production and Consumption
- TEN – Transport, Energy, Infrastructure and the Information Society
- SOC – Employment, Social Affairs and Citizenship
- NAT – Agriculture, Rural Development and the Environment
- REX – External Relations

The sections' opinions are prepared by study groups, including a rapporteur, assisted by several experts.

The EESC's plenary assembly adopts opinions by simple majority on the basis of the sections' opinions. These opinions are then forwarded to the institutions and published in the Official Journal of the EU.

THE EUROPEAN ECONOMIC AND SOCIAL COMMITTEE'S INFORMATION STRUCTURES

The EESC has a website (www.esc.eu.int) giving access to all opinions and a calendar of activities. The Committee also produces a wide range of information for the press, including a newsletter tailored to each Member State. A specialized department welcomes groups of visitors, while the library, which contains more than 15,000 volumes, is accessible free of charge by appointment.

INFORMATION AVAILABLE
Summary of Plenary Sessions

These documents outline the opinions adopted during plenary sessions. The opinions are presented by section and the summary includes a description of the opinion, referred to by the key points made by the Committee. A contact for further information is also provided.

Publications

Publications of the European Economic and Social Committee (EESC) are available upon request from the Publications Unit; tel (+32 2) 546-96-04; e-mail publications@esc.eu.int.

- The common fisheries policy – the road travelled and the challenges ahead
- Immigration, asylum and social integration
- Rules of procedures
- The EESC and the Northern dimension – taking the initiative
- Ways forward for sustainable agriculture
- Europe's single market with the Euro in circulation
- The Euro and the European Economic and Social Committee
- Solidarnosc
- Sustainable development
- EU India round table
- A bridge between Europe and civil society
- Towards a sixth environment action programme of the European Community: views of the European Economic and Social Committee
- New knowledge, new jobs
- A general vision of the information society
- PRISM (Progress Report on Initiatives in the Single Market)
- Jobs, learning and social inclusion: the work of the European Economic and Social Committee

How to obtain. Contact the Publications Unit, European Economic and Social Committee, 2 rue Ravenstein, 1000 Brussels, Belgium; tel (+32 2) 546-92-13; fax (+32 2) 546-98-22; e-mail publications@esc.eu.int.

INFORMATION FOR THE PRESS

The Press and Media Division is responsible for supplying the following information:

Press Releases

Information content. All EESC activities. Ministers' or Commissioners' speeches at plenary sessions or section meetings; the most important opinions to emerge from each plenary session; trips (official visits, working parties, etc.); events organized by the EESC between plenary sessions (colloquia, seminars, etc.); the programme for the plenary sessions.
Addressees. Journalists, as well as some specialists, e.g. transport, consumer, farming representatives (targeted lists).
Frequency. Irregular. About two hundred a year.
Languages. The majority are published in all the EU languages.
How to obtain. Contact the Press and Media Division, European Economic and Social Committee, 2 rue Ravenstein, 1000 Brussels, Belgium.

CESE Info

Information content. CESE Info is a monthly newsletter that highlights all the major issues that the EESC has to examine and spotlights the opinions adopted during the plenary sessions.
Addressees. The following groups, in order of priority: Press, radio and television; The EU's press offices; Governmental and political institutions (including Embassies, Ministries, administrations and chambers, Regional institutions, Political parties); National economic and social advisers; EC trade organizations; National trade organizations; Academies, libraries, institutes, universities; International organizations; Consultants; Experts; Miscellaneous.
Languages. All the EU's languages.
How to obtain. Contact the Press and Media Division, European Economic and Social Committee, 2 rue Ravenstein, 1000 Brussels, Belgium.

Bureau

Chairman: Roger Briesch.

Vice-Chairmen: Göke Daniel Frerichs, Leif E. Nielsen.

Members of the Bureau

Paulo Jorge Andrade, Grace Attard, Wilfried Beirnaert, Peter Boldt, Marjolijn Bulk, Liina Carr, Henriks Danusēvics, Ann Davison, Dimitrios Dimitriadis, Ernst Erik Ehnmark, José María Espuny Moyano, Alexander-Michael Graf von Schwerin, Bernardo Hernandez Bataller, Derek Hunter, Paul Junck, Seppo Ilmari Kallio, Demetris Kittenis, Henri Malosse, Jan Erik Anders Olsson, Peter Mihók, Gintaras Morkis, Jaroslaw Mulewicz, Giacomo Regaldo, Lutz Ribbe, Mario Sepi, Metka Roksandic, Victor Hugo Sequeira, Anne-Marie Sigmund, Dana Stechova, Janos Tóth, Jillian van Turnhout.

Members of the European Economic and Social Committee

The EESC consists of 317 representatives of the Member States. National delegations consist of representatives from three interest groups, and each delegate (with the exception of the Chairman) belongs to one or more of the six specialized sections. The delegations of France, Germany, Italy and the United Kingdom have 24 members each, those of Spain and Poland have 21 members, those of Austria, Belgium, Greece, the Netherlands, Portugal, Sweden, Czech Republic and Hungary 12 members, those of Denmark, Finland, Ireland, Lithuania and Slovakia 9, those of Estonia, Latvia and Slovenia 7, those of Luxembourg and Cyprus 6, and that of Malta 5.

The three interest groups are:

Employers (Group I)

President: Giacomo Regaldo.

Workers (Group II)

President: Mario Sepi.

Various Interests (Group III)

President: Anne-Marie Sigmund.

The six specialized sections for the principal fields covered by the Treaties of Rome (EC and Euratom) are:

Economic and Monetary Union and Economic and Social Cohesion (Section 1)

President: Henri Malosse.

Vice-Presidents: John Simpson, Susanna Florio.

Single Market, Production and Consumption (Section 2)

President: Victor Hugo Sequeira.

Vice-Presidents: Jean François Hoffelt, Göran Lagerholm.

Transport, Energy, Infrastructure and the Information Society (Section 3)

President: Alexander-Michael Graf von Schwerin.

Vice-Presidents: Hubert Ghigonis, Ulla Birgitta Sirkeinen.

Employment, Social Affairs and Citizenship (Section 4)

President: Jan Erik Anders Olsson.

Vice-Presidents: Wilfried Beirnaert, Ursula Engelen-Kefer.

Agriculture, Rural Development and the Environment (Section 5)

President: José María Espuny Moyano.

Vice-Presidents: Gilbert Bros, Hans Joachim Wilms.

External Relations (Section 6)

President: Ann Davison.

Vice-Presidents: Christoforos Koryfidis, Filip Hamro-Drotz.

Secretariat-General

Secretary-General: Patrick Venturini; tel (2) 546-93-52.

Administrator: Birgit Fular; tel (2) 546-90-44.

Head of Communication Division: Martin Westlake; tel (2) 546-92-26.

PRESIDENT'S OFFICE

Head of Private Office: Thomas Jansen; tel (2) 546-97-41.

Assistant: Jeanne Kindermann; tel (2) 546-94-86.

Group Secretariats
Group I

Principal Administrator: Marco Thyssen; tel (2) 546-95-67.

Group II

Principal Administrator: Leo Straetemans; tel (2) 546-95-66.

Group III

Administrator: Marc Beffort; tel (2) 546-95-47.

DIRECTORATE FOR CONSULTATIVE WORK A

Director: Robert Hull; tel (2) 546-93-16.

Assistant: Rita Van Mieghem; tel (2) 546-93-64.

Single Market, Production and Consumption Division.

Head of Unit: João Pereira dos Santos; tel (2) 546-92-45.

Principal Administrators: Nemesio Martinez, tel (2) 546-95-01; Jean-Pierre Faure, tel (2) 546-96-15; Aleksandra Klenke, tel (2) 546-98-99.

Transport, Energy, Infrastructure and the Information Society Division.

Head of Unit: Luigi del Bino; tel (2) 546-93-53.

Principal Administrator: Luis Lobo; tel (2) 546-97-17.

Administrators: Raffaele del Fiore, tel (2) 546-97-94; Siegfried Jantscher, tel (2) 546-92-87.

Agriculture, Rural Development and the Environment Division.

Head of Unit: Silvia Calamandrei; tel (2) 546-96-57.

Administrators: Robert Wright, tel (2) 546-91-09; Johannes Kind, tel (2) 546-91-11; Eleonora Di Nicolantonio, tel (2) 546-94-54; Katalin Gönczy, tel (2) 546-96-29.

Industrial Change.

Head of Unit: Jakob Andersen; tel (2) 546-92-58.

Administrator: José Miguel Colera Rodriguez; tel (2) 546-96-29.

DIRECTORATE FOR CONSULTATIVE WORK B

Director: Wolfgang Jungk; tel (2) 546-96-23.

Assistant: Waltraud Oechsner; tel (2) 546-93-76.

Economic and Monetary Union and Economic and Social Cohesion Division.

Head of Unit: Alberto Allende; tel (2) 546-96-79.

Principal Administrator: Roberto Pietrasanta; tel (2) 546-93-13.

Administrator: Borbala Szij, tel (2) 546-92-54; Gilbert Marchlewitz, tel (2) 546-93-58.

Employment, Social Affairs and Citizenship Division.

Head of Unit: Alan Hick; tel (2) 546-93-02.

Principal Administrator: Stefania Barbesta; tel (2) 546-95-10.

Administrators: Susanne Johansson, tel (2) 546-96-19; Pierluigi Brombo, tel (2) 546-97-18.

External Relations Division.

Head of Unit: Jean-François Bence; tel (2) 546-93-99.

Administrators: Michael Wells, tel (2) 546-82-83; Susanna Baizou, tel (2) 546-98-45.

DIRECTORATE FOR GENERAL AFFAIRS

Director: Nicolas Alexopoulos; tel (2) 546-93-70.

Assistant: Luisa Cabral; tel (2) 546-93-11.

Registry.

Head of Unit: Georgine Willems; tel (2) 546-94-71.

Administrators: Olivier Hanrion, tel (2) 546-90-96; Judite Berkemeier, tel (2) 546-98-97.

Relations with the institutions and the national ESCs.

Head of Unit: Fritz Rath; tel (2) 546-92-50.

Administrator: Veronica Tomei; tel (2) 546-99-29.

Relations with civil society organisations, Future of Europe.

Head of Unit: Patrick Feve; tel (2) 546-96-16.

Administrator: Helmi Juuti; tel (2) 546-98-21.

Conferences, Information and visits.

Principal Administrator: Vera Parr; tel (2) 546-92-57.

Administrator: Laila Wold; tel (2) 546-91-58.

Legal Affairs.

Legal Adviser: Moisés Bermejo; tel (2) 546-98-14.

DIRECTORATE FOR HUMAN AND FINANCIAL RESOURCES

Director: Cornélis Bentvelsen; tel (2) 546-98-13.

Assistant: Ingeborg von Beschwitz; tel (2) 546-93-36.

Recruitment, reception, mobility and enlargement.

Head of Unit: Erik Madsen; tel (2) 546-90-39.

Administrator: Marie-Hélène Burhin; tel (2) 546-95-39.

Vocational training, archives, internal communication.

Administrator: Päivi Seppänen; tel (2) 546-98-11.

Staff regulations and social action.

Head of Unit: Dominique-François Bareth; tel (2) 546-90-89.

Finance.

Head of Unit: Pol Liemans; tel (2) 546-82-15.

Accounting.

Administrator: Päivi Ohman; tel (2) 546-98-72.

DIRECTORATE FOR LOGISTICS AND TRANSLATION (SERVICES SHARED WITH THE COMMITTEE OF THE REGIONS)

Director: Geremia Scianca; tel (2) 546-90-01.

Principal Administrator: Steven Phillips; tel (2) 546-94-61.

Audit.

Principal Administrator: Carlos Martins Ferreira; tel (2) 546-92-51.

Programming and management.

Principal Administrator: Steven Phillips; tel (2) 546-94-61.

Planning.

Head of Service: Satu Kankala; tel (2) 546-91-35.

Co-ordination of Logistics.

Deputy Director: Noëlle Mattei; tel (2) 546-98-68.

Infrastructure and New Buildings.

Head of Unit: Sybren Singelsma; tel (2) 546-93-62.

Administrators: Vibeke Hansen, tel (2) 546-93-24; Amir Dhanani, tel (2) 546-9483; Fabio Pandolfi, tel (2) 546-90-90; Giuseppe Macaione, tel (2) 546-92-61.

Meetings and internal services.

Administrator: Claudine Kesteloot; tel (2) 546-93-62.

IT and telecommunications.

Head of Unit: Niall O'Higgins; tel (2) 546-96-68.

Administrators: Jean-Marc Debrue (Telecommunications), tel (2) 546-95-15; Jan De Sutter (Information systems), tel (2) 546-96-39.

CO-ORDINATION OF THE PRODUCTION CHAIN

Head of Division: Gurli Hauschildt; tel (2) 546-92-51.

Translation and typing.

Danish translation and typing.

Head of Division: Steen Fink-Jensen; tel (2) 235-93-79.

Dutch translation and typing.

Head of Division: Jacques Vandewaetere; tel (2) 235-93-12.

English translation and typing.

Head of Division: Francis Patterson; tel (2) 235-95-22.

Finnish translation and typing.

Head of Division: Erja Uusitalo; tel (2) 235-90-51.

French translation and typing.

Head of Division: Catherine Hess; tel (2) 235-93-59.

German translation and typing.

Head of Division: Erwin Neumaier; tel (2) 235-9361.

Greek translation and typing.

Head of Division: Nicolas Tsarnavas; tel (2) 235-95-94.

Italian translation and typing.

Head of Division: Eugenia Ponzoni-Paganuzzi; tel (2) 235-92-44.

Portuguese translation and typing.

Head of Division: Luis Filipe Sabino; tel (2) 235-97-87.

Spanish translation and typing.

Head of Division: Miguel Paredes; tel (2) 235-95-91.

Swedish translation and typing.

Head of Division: Hans Kellerman; tel (2) 235-99-14.

Printing/distribution.

Principal Administrator: Jan Baumgartl; tel (2) 546-98-51.

COMMITTEE OF THE REGIONS

Established by the Treaty on European Union, the Committee of the Regions (COR) provides a voice for the regional and local authorities of the European Union, enabling them to take part, in an advisory capacity, in the Community decision-making process.

Under the terms of the Treaties, the COR must be consulted on the following areas of Union policy: economic and social cohesion; trans-European infrastructure networks; health; education; culture; employment; social issues; environment; training; transport.

The Council or the Commission may also consult the COR on other matters where they consider it appropriate to do so, especially in the field of cross-border co-operation. The European Parliament may also consult the COR on matters of mutual interest. The COR is informed when the European Economic and Social Committee is consulted, and may issue an opinion on the matter if it considers specific regional interests are concerned. Finally, the COR may issue an opinion on its own initiative if it judges such action appropriate.

There are 317 members of the Committee of the Regions and an equal number of alternate members broken down as follows: 24 each from Germany, France, Italy and the United Kingdom; 21 from Poland and Spain; 12 each from Austria, Belgium, Czech Republic, Greece, Hungary, the Netherlands, Portugal and Sweden; 9 each from Denmark, Finland, Ireland, Lithuania and Slovakia; 7 each from Estonia, Latvia and Slovenia; 6 each from Cyprus and Luxembourg; 5 from Malta.

The Committee holds five plenary sessions in Brussels every year.

Members and alternate members are appointed for four years, this term of office being renewable. The COR elects a President and a Bureau from among its members for a two-year term.

The Committee of the Regions publishes a regular newsletter, *Regions and Cities of Europe*. This is issued six times a year and is available in all Community languages. To obtain a copy, contact: Press and Communication Unit, Committee of the Regions, 101 rue Belliard, 1040 Brussels, Belgium; tel (+32 2) 282-22-11; fax (+32 2) 282-23-25; internet www.cor.eu.int.

GENERAL CONTACT DETAILS

Committee of the Regions, 101 rue Belliard, 1040 Brussels, Belgium; tel (+32 2) 282-22-11; fax (+32 2) 282-23-25; e-mail info@cor.eu.int or to pattern forename .surname@cor.eu.int; internet www .cor.eu.int.

Bureau

President: Peter Straub.

First Vice-President: Albert Bore.

Alternate: (vacant).

MEMBERS OF THE BUREAU

Austria: Herwig van Staa, Walter Zimper.

Belgium: Jean-Claude Van Cauwenborghe (Vice-Pres), Paul Van Grembergen.

Cyprus: Christos Mesis.

Czech Republic: Pavel Bem, Josef Pavel.

Denmark: Knud Andersen (Vice-Pres), Henning Jensen.

Estonia: Teet Kallasvee.

Finland: Risto Koivisto.

France: Jean-Louis Joseph (Vice-Pres), Michel Delebarre, Jean Puech.

Germany: Ernst Walter Görisch, Hans Kaiser (Vice-Pres), Karl Heinz Klär.

Greece: Theodora Bakogianni (Vice-Pres), Fofi Gennimata.

Hungary: Istvan Serto-Radics, Gyula Szabo.

Ireland: Constance Hanniffy, Seamus Murray (Vice-Pres).

Italy: Gianfranco Lamberti (Vice-Pres), Mercedes Bresso, Roberto Formigoni, Isidoro Gottardo.

Latvia: Andris Jaunsleinis.

Lithuania: Darius Gudelis, Gediminas Adolfas Pavirzis.

Luxembourg: Simone Beissel (Vice-Pres).

Malta: Ian Micallef.

Netherlands: Geert Jansen, B. Verkerk (Vice-Pres).

Poland: Michal Czarski, Rafal Dutkiewicz, Karol Karski.

Portugal: Alberto Jardim, Francisco Mesquita Machado.

Slovakia: Rudolf Bauer, Alexander Slafkovsky.

Slovenia: Boris Sovic.

Spain: Vicente Alvarez Areces, Marcelino Iglesias Ricou, Pedro Sanz Alonso.

Sweden: Roger Kaliff (Vice-Pres), Anders Gustâv, Kent Johansson.

United Kingdom: Kenneth Bodfish (Vice-Pres), Keith Brown, Rosemary Butler, Lord Hanningfield of Chelmsford.

COMMISSIONS

1 COTER: Commission for Territorial Cohesion Policy

President: J. C. Van Cauwenberghe; tel (81) 331365.

First Vice-President: Rafaele Fitto; tel 556-5253.

Co-ordinators: Serafino Nardi, tel (2) 282-25-08; Damian Lluna Taberner, tel (2) 282-21-69.

2 ECOS: Commission for Economic and Social Policy

President: Anders Gustâv; tel (8) 734-2191.

First Vice-President: F. Mesquita Machado; tel (253) 613380.

Co-ordinators: Paulo Rocha Trindade, Kaido Sirel.

3 DEVE: Commission for Sustainable Development

President: Olivier Bertrand; tel (5) 55676247.

First Vice-President: Wim Van Gelder; tel (118) 631313.

Co-ordinators: Robert Kaukewitsch, Chantal Fontaine.

4 EDUC: Commission for Culture and Education

President: Annette McNamara.

First Vice-President: Henning Jensen; tel (2) 732-8520.

Co-ordinators: Marie-Claire Neill-Cowper; tel (2) 282-21-93; Silke Toenshoff, Bogna Rodziewicz.

5 CONST: Commission for Constitutional Affairs and European Governance

President: Franz Schausberger; tel (80) 422209.

First Vice-President: Graham Tope; tel (20) 8770-7269.

Co-ordinators: Béatrice Taulegne; tel (2) 282-21-71; Luisa Domenichelli, Miriam Burajova.

6 RELEX: Commission for External Relations

President: Ramón Luis Valcárcel Siso; tel (9) 68366015.

First Vice-President: Christos Paleológos; tel (26) 180987.

Co-ordinator: Elita Georgana; tel (2) 282-21-41.

Secretariat-General

Secretary-General: Gerhard Stahl; tel (2) 282-20-05.

Head of Cabinet: Michael Collins; tel (2) 282-21-05.

PRESIDENT'S CABINET

Head: Jean-Pierre Berg; tel (2) 282-23-12.

Administrator: Paul Willems; tel (2) 282-23-08.

SECRETARIAT OF POLITICAL GROUPS

1 European People's Party (PPE).

Administrators: Heinz-Peter Knapp, tel (2) 282-22-50; Filippo Terruso, tel (2) 282-22-91.

2 European Socialist Party (PSE).

Administrators: Jordi Harrison, tel (2) 282-22-24; Chiara Malagodi, tel (2) 282-22-43; Mathieu Hornung, tel (2) 282-22-43.

3 Alliance of Liberals and Democrats for Europe (ALDE).

Administrator: Sophie In't Veld, tel (2) 282-22-26.

4 European Alliance (AE).

Administrator: Michael O'Conchuir, tel (2) 282-22-38.

DIRECTORATE FOR ADMINISTRATION

Director: Gonzalo Bescos Ferraz; tel (2) 282-21-56.

Units

1 Budget/Finance.

Administrators: Eric Leurquin (Budget), tel (2) 282-22-86; Pedro Assunção (Accounting), tel (2) 282-22-72.

2 Personnel.

Head of Unit: Kyriakos Tsirimiagos; tel (2) 282-21-22.

Administrators: Thierry Firmin, tel (2) 282-20-76; Tom Haenebalcke, tel (2) 282-22-28.

DIRECTORATE FOR CONSULTATIVE WORK

Director: (Vacant).

Commissions Work Unit

Head of Unit: Thierry Castillon; tel (2) 282-20-83.

COTER, ECOS and EDUC Commissions Service

Commission for Territorial Cohesion Policy (COTER)

Administrators: Serafino Nardi, tel (2) 282-25-08; Damian Lluna, tel (2) 282-21-69.

Commission for Economic and Social Policy

Administrators: Paulo Rocha Trindade, tel (2) 282-22-42; Kaido Sirel, tel (2) 282-21-92.

Commission for Culture and Education

Administrators: Marie-Claire Neill-Cowper, tel (2) 282-21-93; Silke Toenshoff, tel (2) 282-24-55; Bogna Rodziewicz, tel (2) 282-20-28.

RELEX, CONST and DEVE Commissions Service

Principal Administrator: Robert Kaukewitsch; tel (2) 282-23-66.

Commission for Sustainable Development (DEVE)

Administrators: Robert Rönström; tel (2) 282-22-83.

Commission for Constitutional Affairs and European Governance (CONST)

Administrators: Béatrice Taulegne, tel (2) 282-21-75; Luisa Domenichelli, tel (2) 282-2025; Miriam Burajova, tel (2) 282-23-65.

Commission for External Relations (RELEX)

Administrator: Elita Georgana; tel (2) 282-21-51.

Legislative Programme, Interinstitutional Relations and External Relations Unit

Head of Unit: Elisa Garosi, tel (2) 282-22-46.

Administrators: Christiane Charles-Pieck (Legislative Planning and Studies Service), tel (2) 282-20-08; Sophie Bachotet (Legislative Planning and Studies Service), tel (2) 282-21-81; Christian Gsodam (Interinstitutional and External Relations Service), tel (2) 282-21-21; Tom Ashwanden (Interinstitutional and External Relations Service), tel (2) 282-21-85; Liina Munari Warsell (Interinstitutional and External Relations Service), tel (2) 282-24-59.

REGISTRY AND PRESS

Head of Division: Steen Illeborg; tel (2) 282-21-84.

Units

1 Registry, Protocol (National Delegations, Archives–Mail).

Head of Unit: Stergios Baniotopoulos; tel (2) 282-21-86.

Administrator, Registry Service: Pierre-Alexis Feral; tel (2) 282-22-05.

Principal Administrator, National Delegations Service: (vacant).

Administrator: Saskia Verhoeven; tel (2) 282-23-15.

2 Press and Communication.

Head of Unit: Laurent Thieule; tel (2) 282-21-99.

Administrators: Estelle Poidevin (Press Officer), tel (2) 282-22-70; Dennis Abbott (Press Officer), tel (2) 282-20-85.

FINANCIAL CONTROL

Financial Controller: Robert McCoy; tel (2) 282-23-05.

LEGAL SERVICE

Head of Unit: Pedro Cervilla; tel (2) 282-21-89.

Administrator: Petra Karlsson; tel (2) 282-21-96.

Note: The Committee of the Regions shares certain administrative services, including those responsible for translation and typing, with the Economic and Social Committee.

EUROPEAN INVESTMENT BANK

The European Investment Bank (EIB) was established in 1958 as part of the decision to create a European Economic Community. Its aims are to contribute to the steady and balanced development of the European Union by providing loans for capital investment projects furthering Union policy objectives, and in particular: the economic development of the Union's less developed regions; the improvement of European transport and telecommunications infrastructure; the protection of the environment and the quality of life; the attainment of the Union's energy policy objectives; strengthening the international competitiveness of industry and promoting its integration at Union level; and supporting the activities of small and medium-sized enterprises.

Outside the European Union, the EIB participates in the implementation of the Union's development policy in countries in the Mediterranean region, in the African, Caribbean and Pacific countries which are signatories to the Cotonou Agreement, in South Africa, in the countries of Central and Eastern Europe and in 30 countries in Latin America and Asia.

EIB Information Structures

The information and communications department is responsible for external information and press contacts. It may be contacted for all queries and documentation as well as for taking out a subscription to EIB publications. Contact: Information and Communications Department, Information Desk, 100 blvd Konrad Adenauer, 2950 Luxembourg; tel (+352) 43793122; fax (+352) 43793191; e-mail info@eib.org; internet www.eib.org.

Contacts for Information related to EIB Activities within the European Union:

Austria: Dusan Ondrejicka; tel (+352) 4379 3150; e-mail d.ondrejicka@eib.org.
Belgium, France, Luxembourg: Sabine Parisse; tel (+352) 43793138; e-mail s.parisse@eib.org.
Denmark, Finland, Sweden: Pé Verhoeven; tel (+352) 43793118; e-mail p.verhoeven@eib.org.
Germany: Paul Gerd Löser; tel (+352) 43793139; e-mail p.loeser@eib.org.

Greece: Helen Kavvadia; tel (+352) 43796756; e-mail h.kavvadia@eib.org.
Ireland, United Kingdom: Adam McDonaugh; tel (+352) 43793147; e-mail a.mcdonaugh@eib.org.
Italy: Daniela Sacchi; tel (+352) 43793130; e-mail d.sacchi@eib.org.
Netherlands: Yvonne Berghorst; tel (+352) 43793154; e-mail y.berghorst@eib.org.
Portugal, Spain: Juan Manuel Sterlin Balenciaga; tel (+352) 43793126; e-mail j.sterlin@eib.org.
(For Member States which joined the EU in May 2004, see Accession Countries below.)

Contacts for Information related to EIB Activities outside the European Union:

Accession countries (AC): Dusan Ondrejicka; tel (+352) 43793150; e-mail d.ondrejicka@eib.org.
Mediterranean countries (MED) and Balkan countries (BLK): Helen Kavvadia; tel (+352) 43796756; e-mail h.kavvadia@eib.org.
African, Caribbean and Pacific countries (ACP) and South Africa (SA): Bram Schim van der Loeff; tel (+352) 43793134; e-mail a.schimvanderloeff@eib.org.
Asian and Latin America countries (ALA) and non EU-OECD countries: Orlando Arango; tel (+32 2) 235-00-84; e-mail o.arango@eib.org.
EFTA countries: Pé Verhoeven; tel (+352) 43793118; e-mail p.verhoeven@eib.org.

Contact for Information related to the EIB's Electronic Media

Marc Bello; tel (+352) 43793119; e-mail m.bello@eib.org.

Information Available

Any party interested in the building of Europe in general and the EIB's activities in particular can obtain EIB publications, which are intended mainly for project promoters, Member-State administrations, economic and financial circles, universities, and opinion 'multipliers'. If need be (for teaching purposes, conferences etc.), several copies may be requested at a time.

Annual Report

The EIB's statutory and reference publication. It provides details of activities during the previous financial year, both within and outside the European Union, and includes statistical analyses covering the preceding five years. It is available in all EU official languages.

Statute

The EIB's Statute sets out the legal, financial and administrative framework for the Bank's activities, having been established by a Protocol annexed to the Treaty of Rome creating the European Economic Community, of which it forms an integral part. It is available in all EU official languages.

Annual Brochure

An annually updated brochure which provides an illustrated summary of the Bank's major objectives and fields of activity, both within and outside the European Union. It is available in all EU official languages.

Videotapes and Video Library

Corporate films are available explaining how the EIB works, and a film library supplies 'rough' film to TV journalists.

Press Releases

The EIB regularly issues press releases covering its activities in different sectors in all countries. They are distributed to the media as well as to public administrations and companies.

Bulletin

EIB Information, a quarterly bulletin featuring topical articles on EIB activities, is available in all EU official languages.

Country Fact Sheets

These publications describe the EIB financing facilities available in different countries and geographical areas (Member States, Central and Eastern Europe, the Mediterranean region, the African, Caribbean and Pacific States, South Africa, Asia and Latin America).

Ex-Post Evaluations

The Operations Evaluation department carries out ex-post evaluations and coordinates the evaluation process in the Bank. It carries out thematic, sectoral and regional/country evaluations of projects financed by the Bank, once they have been completed.

Hard copies of the reports are available upon request. Contact evaluations@eib.org.

Economic Reports

Economic and Financial Studies (EFS) produces and distributes two external research publications in economics and finance:

- The six-monthly EIB Papers present the results of research carried out by EIB staff together with contributions from external scholars and specialists.
- The Economic and Financial Reports, the EFS working papers series, contain economic research on topics related to the operations of the EIB.

For more information concerning Economic and Financial Studies (EFS), please visit www.eib.org/efs.

GENERAL CONTACT DETAILS

European Investment Bank, 100 blvd Konrad Adenauer, 2950 Luxembourg; tel (+352) 43791; fax (+352) 43793191; e-mail info@eib.org; internet www.eib.org.

Other Offices

Department for Interinstitutional Affairs, Brussels Office: 227 rue de la Loi, 1040 Brussels, Belgium; tel (2) 235-00-70; fax (2) 230-58-27.

Department for Lending Operations in Italy, Greece, Cyprus and Malta: Via Sardegna 38, 00187 Rome, Italy; tel (06) 47191; fax (06) 4873438.

Athens Office: 364 Kifissias Ave and 1 Delfon, 15233 Halandri, Athens, Greece; tel (1) 6824517/9; fax (1) 6824520.

Berlin Office: Lennéstraße 11, 10785 Berlin, Germany; tel (30) 59-00-47-90 fax: (30) 59-00-47-99; email: berlinoffice@eib.org

Cairo Office: 6 Boulos Hannah Street, Dokki, Giza (Cairo), Egypt; tel (2) 7620077.

Lisbon Office: Regus Business Centre, Avda da Liberdade 144-156, 8°, 1269-146 Lisbon, Portugal; tel (1) 3428989; fax (1) 3470487.

Madrid Office: Calle José Ortega y Gasset 29, 28006 Madrid, Spain; tel (91) 4311340; fax (91) 4311383.

London Office: Royal Exchange Buildings, London EC3V 3LF, United Kingdom, tel (20) 7375960; fax (20) 73759699.

BOARD OF GOVERNORS

Chairman: Pedro Solbes Mira (Second Deputy Prime Minister and Minister of Economic Affairs and Finance, Spain)

Members: Didier Reynders (Minister of Finance, Belgium), Bohuslav Sobotka (Deputy Prime Minister and Minister of Finance, Czech Republic), Bendt Bendtsen (Deputy Prime Minister and Minister of Economic Affairs, Trade and Industry, Denmark), Hans Eichel (Minister of Finance, Germany), Taavi Veskimägi (Minister of Finance, Estonia), Giorgos Alogoskoufis (Minister of Economic Affairs and Finance, Greece), Nicolas Sarkozy (Minister of Economic Affairs, Finance and Industry, France), Charles McCreevy (Minister of Finance, Ireland), Domenico Siniscalco (Italy), Makis Keravnos (Minister of Finance, Cyprus), Oskars Spurdzinš (Minister of Finance, Latvia), Algirdas Butkevicius (Minister of Finance, Lithuania), Jean-Claude Juncker (Prime Minister and Minister of State and Finance, Luxembourg), Lawrence Gonzi (Prime Minister and Minister of Finance, Malta), Tibor Draskovics (Minister of Finance, Hungary), Gerrit Zalm (Deputy Prime Minister and Minister of Finance, The Netherlands), Karl-Heinz Grasser (Minister of Finance, Austria), Miroslaw Gronicki (Poland), António José Bagão Félix (Portugal), Dusan Mramor (Slovenia), Ivan Miklos (Deputy Prime Minister and Minister of Finance, Slovakia), Ulla-Maj Wideroos (Second Minister of Finance, Finland), Bosse Ringholm (Minister of Finance, Sweden), Gordon Brown (Chancellor of the Exchequer, United Kingdom).

Audit Committee: Chairman: Michael P. Haralabidis; Members: Caj Nackstad, Marc Colas, Observer: Alicia Díaz Zurro.

BOARD OF DIRECTORS

Directors: Philippe Maystadt (Chairman), Wolfgang Roth (Vice Chairman, Germany), Peter Sedgwick (Vice Chairman, United Kingdom), Isabel Martín Castellá (Vice Chairman, Spain), Gerlando Genuardi (Vice Chairman, Italy), Philippe de Fontaine Vive Curtaz (Vice Chairman, France), Sauli Niinistö (Vice Chairman, Finland), Ivan Pilip (Vice Chairman, Czech Republic), Torsten Gersfelt (Vice Chairman, Denmark), Jean-Pierre Arnoldi (Belgium), Lorenzo Bini Smaghi (Italy), Alexandra da Costa Gomes (Portugal), János Eros (Hungary), Vincent Grech (Malta), Kurt Hall (Sweden), Zdenek Hrubý (Czech Republic), Aare Järvan (Estonia), Kyriacos Kakouris (Cyprus), John Kingman (United Kingdom), Irena Krumane (Latvia), Vilma Macerauskiene (Lithuania), Tytti Noras (Finland), Herrn Klaus Oehler (Austria), Noel Thomas O'Gorman (Ireland), Ioannis Papadakis (Greece), María Pérez Ribes (Spain), Per Bremer Rasmussen (Denmark), Klaus Regling (Belgium), Gaston Reinesch (Luxembourg), Odile Renaud-Basso (France), Sibil Svilan (Slovenia), Sigrid Selz (Germany), Jacek Tomorowicz (Poland), Valdimír Tvaroška (Slovakia), Jan Willem van der Kaaj (Netherlands).

Alternates: Stefania Bazzoni (Italy), Gianpaolo Bologna (Italy), Karl-Ernst Brauner (Germany), Kevin Cardiff (Ireland), Anne-Laure de Coincy (France), Stewart James (United Kingdom), Graham Meadows (United Kingdom), Rudolf de Korte (Netherlands), Ralph Müller (Germany), Wolfgang Nitsche (Austria), Mário de Pinto Lobo (Portugal), Juraj Rencko (Slovakia), Jean-Michel Severino (France), Frixos Sokoros (Cyprus), Rachel Turner (United Kingdom).

MANAGEMENT COMMITTEE

President: Philippe Maystadt.

Vice-Presidents: Peter Sedgwick, Isabel Martín Castellá, Sauli Niinistö, Wolfgang Roth, Gerlando Genuardi, Philippe de Fontaine Vive Curtaz, Ivan Pilip, Torsten Gersfelt.

Secretariat-General

Secretary-General: Eberhard Uhlmann.

GENERAL ADMINISTRATION

Deputy Secretary-General: Rémy Jacob.

Divisions

1 Governing Bodies, Secretariat, Protocol.

Head of Division: Hugo Woestmann.

2 Planning, Budget and Control.

Head of Division: Theoharry Grammatikos.

3 Translation.

Head of Division: Georg Aigner.

4 Purchasing and Administrative Service.

Head of Division: Manfredo Paulucci de Calboli.

5 Facilities Management.

Head of Division: Agustin Auría.

Institutions

Director: Rémy Jacob.

1 Interinstitutional Affairs and Brussels Office.

Director: Dominique de Crayencour.

2 External Co-ordination.

Associate Director: Jack Reversade.

Press Office and Communications

Director: Gabrielle Lauermann.

1 Corporate Promotion.

Director: Adam McDonaugh.

2 Press Office.

Director: Paul Gerd Löser.

3 Records and Information Management.

Associate Director: Duncan Lever.

4 Audit Enactment, EIB Group Development.

Director: Helmut Kuhrt.

5 Resource Management and Enlargement.

Principal Adviser: Ferdinand Sassen.

DIRECTORATE FOR LENDING OPERATIONS— EUROPE

Director-General: Terence Brown.

Operational Support and Administration

Chief Operational Co-ordinator: Jürgen Moehrke.

Divisions

1 Co-ordination.

Head of Division: Dominique Courbin.

2 IT and Management Information.

Head of Division: Thomas Fahrtmann.

3 Business Support.

Head of Division: Ralph Bast.

Operations in the United Kingdom, Ireland and Nordic Countries

Director: Thomas Barrett.

Divisions

1 Banking, industry and securitization.

Head of Division: Bruno Denis.

2 Infrastructure.

Head of Division: Tilman Seibert.

3 Structured finance and PPPs.

Head of Division: Cheryl Fisher.

4 Nordic countries.

Head of Division: Michael O'Halloran.

Operations in Spain and Portugal

Director: Alfonso Querejeta.

Divisions

1 Spain—PPPs, infrastructure, social and urban sectors.

Head of Division: Carlos Guille.

2 Spain—banks, industry, energy and telecoms.

Head of Division: Fernando de la Fuente.

3 Madrid office.

Head of Division: Andrea Tinagli.

4 Portugal.

Head of Division: Rui Artur Martins.

5 Lisbon office.

Head of Division: Pedro Eiras Antunes.

Operations in France and Benelux

Director: Laurent de Mautort.

Divisions

1 France—infrastructure.

Head of Division: Jacques Diot.

2 France—enterprises.

Head of Division: Jean-Christophe Chaline.

3 Belgium, Luxembourg, Netherlands.

Head of Division: Henk Delsing.

Operations in Germany, Czech Republic and Slovakia

Director: Joachim Link.

Divisions

1 Germany (Northern Länder).

Head of Division: Peggy Nylund Green.

2 Germany (Southern Länder).

Head of Division: Kim Kreilgaard.

3 Czech Republic, Slovakia.

Head of Division: Jean Vrla.

Operations in Italy and Malta

Director: Antonio Pugliese.

Divisions

1 Infrastucture.

Head of Division: Bruno Lago.

2 Energy, Environment and Telecoms.

Head of Division: Paolo Munini.

3 Industry and Banks.

Head of Division: Alexander Andò.

Operations in Central Europe

Director: Emanuel Maravic.

Divisions

1 Austria and Croatia.

Head of Division: Franz-Josef Vetter.

2 Hungary and Slovenia.

Head of Division: Cormac Murphy.

3 Bulgaria and Romania.

Head of Division: Rainer Saerbeck.

Operations in South East Europe

Director: Grammatiki Tsingou-Papadopetrou.

Divisions

1 Greece.

Head of Division: Themistoklis Kouvarakis.

2 Athens Office.

Head of Division: Christos Kontogeorgos.

3 Balkans and Cyprus.

Head of Division: Romualdo Massa Bernucci.

4 Turkey.

Head of Division: Patrick Walsh.

Operations in Baltic Sea

Deputy Director General: Thomas Hackett.

Divisions

1 Poland, Euratom.

Head of Division: Heinz Olbers.

2 Baltic States, Russia.

Head of Division: Constantin Synadino.

3 Finland and Sweden.

Head of Division: Michael O'Halloran.

DIRECTORATE FOR LENDING OPERATIONS— OTHER COUNTRIES

Director-General: Jean-Louis Biancarelli.

Development Economics Advisory Service

Chief Development Economist: Daniel Ottolenghi.

Mediterranean (FEMIP)
Director: Claudio Cortese.

Divisions

1 Maghreb.

Head of Division: Bernard Gordon.

2 Mashreq, Middle East.

Head of Division: Jane MacPherson.

3 Cairo Office.

Head of Division: Luigi Marcon

4 Private Sector Support.

Head of Division: Alain Sève.

Africa, Caribbean, Pacific (Cotonou Investment Facility)
Director: Martin Curwen.

Divisions

1 West Africa and Sahel.

Head of Division: Gustaaf Heim.

2 Central and East Africa.

Head of Division: Tassulo Hendus.

3 Southern Africa and Indian Ocean.

Head of Division: Justin Loasby.

4 Caribbean and Pacific.

Head of Division: David Crush.

Asia and Latin America
Director: Francisco de Paula Coelho.

Divisions

1 Asia.

Head of Division: Matthias Zöllner.

2 Latin America.

Head of Division: Alberto Barragán.

FINANCE DIRECTORATE
Director-General: René Karsenti.

Capital markets (funding)
Director: Barbara Bargagli-Petrucci.

Divisions

1 Euro.

Head of Division: Carlos Ferreira da Silva.

2 Europe (excluding euro), Africa.

Head of Division: David Clark.

3 America, Asia, Pacific.

Head of Division: Eila Kreivi.

4 Investor Relations and Marketing.

Head of Division: Peter Munro.

Treasury
Director: Anneli Peshkoff.

Divisions

1 Liquidity management.

Head of Division: Francis Zeghers.

2 Asset/liability management.

Head of Division: Jean-Dominique Potocki.

3 Portfolio management.

Head of Division: James Ranaivoson.

Planning and Settlement of Operations
Director: Gianmaria Musella.

Divisions

1 Back Office (Loans).

Head of Division: (Vacant)

2 Back Office (Treasury).

Head of Division: Yves Kirpach.

3 Back Office (Borrowing).

Head of Division: Erling Cronqvist.

4 Systems and loans databases.

Head of Division: Charles Anizet.

5 Co-ordination and Financial policies.

Head of Division: Marie Luce Sampietro.

PROJECTS DIRECTORATE

Director-General: Michel Deleau.

TransEuropean Networks and PPPs

Associate Director: Mateo Turró Calvet.

Economic and Financial Studies

Director: Eric Perée.

Infrastructure
Director: Christopher Hurst.

Divisions

1 General Infrastructure and Resource Management.

Head of Division: Andrew Allen

2 Co-ordinator for the Balkans.

Head of Division: Axel Hörhager.

3 Rail and road.

Head of Division: José Luis Alfaro.

4 Air, maritime and urban transport.

Head of Division: Philippe Ostenc.

5 Water and wastewater.

Head of Division: José Frade.

Energy, telecommunications, waste management
Director: Günter Westermann.

Divisions

1 Electricity, renewable energies and waste management.

Head of Division: René van Zonneveld.

2 Oil and gas.

Head of Division: Angus Nicolson.

4 Telecommunications and information technology.

Head of Division: Carillo Rovere.

Industry and services
Director: Constantin Christofidis.

Division

1 Primary resources and life sciences.

Head of Division: Jean-Jacques Mertens.

2 Manufacturing industry and services.

Head of Division: Hans-Harald Jahn.

3 Human capital.

Head of Division: Stephen Wright.

Policy support department
Director: Patrice Géraud.

Division

1 Operational lending policies.

Head of Division: Guy Clausse.

2 Project quality and monitoring.

Head of Division: Angelo Boioli.

3 Resources management.

Head of Division: Daphne Venturas.

4 Environmental unit.

Head of Division: Peter Carter.

LEGAL AFFAIRS DIRECTORATE

General Counsel: Eberhard Uhlmann.

Co-director (Institutional Matters): Evelyne Pourteau.

Heads of Division: Carlos Gomez de la Cruz (Legal Aspects of Institutional and

Staff Issues), Nicola Barr (Legal Aspects of Financial issues).

Operations

Director: Alfonso Querejeta.

Divisions

1 Operational Policy and Balkans and Croatia.

Head of Division: Roderick Dunnett (Associate Director).

2 Germany, Austria, Poland, Czech Republic, Hungary, Slovakia, Slovenia, Lithuania, Latvia, Estonia, Bulgaria, Romania, Russia.

Head of Division: Gerhard Hütz.

3 Spain, Portugal.

Head of Division: Ignacio Lacorzana.

4 United Kingdom, Sweden, Denmark, Finland, Ireland, EFTA countries.

Head of Division: Patrick Hugh Chamberlain.

5 Belgium, France, Luxembourg, Netherlands.

Head of Division: Pierre Albouze.

6 Greece, Italy, Cyprus, Malta.

Head of Division: Manfredi Tonci Ottieri.

7 Mediterranean (FEMIP), Africa, Caribbean, Pacific (Cotonou Investment Facility), Asia and Latin America.

Head of Division: Regan Wylie-Otte.

DIRECTORATE FOR ECONOMICS AND INFORMATION

Chief Economist: Alfred Steinherr.

Divisions

1 Economic and Financial Studies.

Heads of Division: Christopher Hurst, Eric Perée.

2 Documentation and Library.

Head of Division: Marie-Odile Kleiber.

Information technology

Chief Information Officer: Patrick Klaedtke.

Divisions

1 Planning, support and compliance.

Head of Division: Joseph Foy.

2 Business Applications.

Head of Division: Simon Norcross.

3 Technology and Infrastructure.

Head of Division: José Grincho.

Risk management

Director-General: Pier Luigi Gilbert.

Divisions

1 Credit Risk.

Head of Division: Per Jedefors (Director).

2 Corporates, Public, Infrastructure

Head of Division: Stuart Rowlands.

3 Project Finance (EIF).

Head of Division: Klaus Trömel.

4 Financial and Operational Risks.

Head of Division: Alain Godard (Director).

5 ALM and Market Risk Management.

Head of Division: Giancarlo Sardelli.

6 Derivatives.

Head of Division: Luis Gonzalez-Pacheco.

7 Operational Risks.

Head of Division: Antonio Roca Iglesias.

8 Co-ordination and Support.

Head of Division: Elisabeth Matiz.

Human Resources

Director: Andreas Verykios.

Divisions

1 Management Systems.

Head of Division: Zacharias Zachariadis.

2 Staffing.

Head of Division: Jörg-Alexander Uebbing.

3 Development.

Head of Division: Luis Garrido.

4 Administration.

Head of Division: Michel Grilli.

Operations Evaluation

Director: Horst Feuerstein.

Heads of Division: Juan Alario Gasulla, Guy Berman.

Internal Audit

Head of Division: Peter Maertens.

EUROPEAN COURT OF AUDITORS

The European Court of Auditors examines "the accounts of all the revenue and expenditure of the Community". It audits not only the general budget of the European Union but also Community loans and borrowings, the revenue and expenditure entered in the European Coal and Steel Community Budget, and the operations of the European Development Fund, which are financed outside the budget by contributions from the Member States. It also provides a Statement of Assurance as to the reliability of the accounts and the legality and regularity of the underlying transactions.

The Court of Auditors, which is composed of one member from each EU Member State, appointed unanimously by the Council after consultation with the Parliament, also examines the accounts of all revenue and expenditure of all bodies set up by the Community in so far as the relevant constituent instrument does not preclude such examination. Amongst those organizations under its supervision are:

- Euratom Supply Agency
- European Centre for the Development of Vocational Training
- European Foundation for the Improvement of Living and Working Conditions
- European Schools
- Joint European Torus (JET)
- European Central Bank
- European Monitoring Centre on Racism and Xenophobia
- European Environment Agency
- European Agency for Reconstruction
- European Agency for Safety and Health at Work
- Translation Centre
- European Agency for the Evaluation of Medicinal Products
- Community Plant Variety Office
- European Monitoring Centre for Drugs and Drug Addiction
- Office for Harmonisation in the Internal Market

In addition, the Court has a consultative role. It is involved in the Community's legislative process in the fields of finance and budgeting. As far as financial regulations are concerned, the Court of Auditors is required to deliver an opinion which is published in the Official Journal. Furthermore, it may also, at any time, submit observations on specific questions and deliver opinions at the request of one of the Institutions of the Community.

Information Available

Annual Reports

- Annual report on the management of the general budget and the European Development Fund (published in about mid-November in the Official Journal of the European Communities – OJ).
- Statement of Assurance (SoA) report as to the reliability of the accounts and the legality and regularity of the underlying transactions, which is published in mid-November in the Official Journal of the European Communities.
- Report on the financial state of the European Coal and Steel Community (published in July–August in the OJ).
- Report by the external auditor on the accounts of the Court of Auditors.
- Specific annual reports relating to the European Centre for Development of Professional Training in Thessalonica and the European Foundation for the Improvement of Living and Working Conditions in Dublin.
- Report (annex to the ECSC annual report) relating to the accounting and financial management of the European Coal and Steel Community (not published in the OJ).
- Specific annual reports concerning the accounts of external Community organizations (Euratom Supply Agency, European Schools, JET (Joint European Torus)) (not published in the OJ).
- Specific annual reports concerning the accounts of the new satellite agencies of the European Union which are published in the OJ.

Special Reports

- Special reports on specific subjects prepared by the Court either on its own initiative or at the request of an institution (usually published in the OJ).

Opinions of the Court of Auditors

- Compulsory opinions relating to all draft financial rulings (published in the OJ).
- Optional opinions given at the request of one of the Community's institutions (not published in the OJ).

WHERE TO OBTAIN THE DOCUMENTS PREPARED BY THE COURT

Documents Published in the Official Journal of the European Communities

- Annual report.
- Statement of Assurance (SoA).
- Annual report relating to the financial state of the ECSC.
- Report by the external auditor on the accounts of the Court of Auditors.
- Specific annual report relating to the European Centre for Development of Professional Training, the European Foundation for the Improvement of Living and Working Conditions and all the other satellite agencies.
- Special reports.
- Opinions.

Addressees: any interested party.
Languages: all languages of the EU.
Prices: prices vary depending on the Official Journal in which the document appears.
How to obtain: from the Office for Official Publications at 2985 Luxembourg, or from its sales offices in the Member States.

Documents not Published in the Official Journal of the European Communities

- Report relating to the accounting and financial management of the ECSC.
- Reports relating to the accounting and financial management of the European Schools, Euratom and the Joint European Torus (JET).

How to obtain: for special reports, studies and opinions, contact the External Relations Department, European Court of Auditors, 12 rue Alcide de Gasperi, 1615 Luxembourg; tel (+352) 439845518; fax (+352) 439846430; e-mail euraud@eca.eu.int.

Specific annual reports relating to outside organizations are not made public by the European Court of Auditors. However, interested parties can contact the relevant organizations directly (Euratom Supply Agency, 200 rue de la Loi, 1040 Brussels, Belgium; Representative of the Upper Council of the European Schools, Route d'Arlon 80, 1040 Brussels, Belgium; JET (Joint European Torus), Abingdon, OX14 3EA, United Kingdom).

Press Releases

Notification of the Court's main publications is given in press releases intended for accredited journalists. These press releases can be obtained on request from the External Relations Department, European Court of Auditors, 12 rue Alcide de Gasperi, 1615 Luxembourg; tel (+352) 439845518; fax (+352) 439846430; e-mail euraud@eca.eu.int.

GENERAL CONTACT DETAILS

European Court of Auditors, 12 rue Alcide de Gasperi, 1615 Luxembourg; tel (+352) 439845410; fax (+352) 439846430; e-mail to pattern firstname .surname@eca.eu.int; internet www .eca.eu.int.

   European Court of Auditors, Bâtiment Eastman, 135 rue Belliard, 1040 Brussels, Belgium; tel (+32 2) 230-50-90; fax (+32 2) 230-64-83.

PRESIDENCY

President: Juan Manuel Fabra Vallés; tel 4398-44592; fax 4398-46818.

Head of Cabinet: Sabine Hiernaux-Fritsch; tel 4398-45454; fax 4398-46818.

Attaché: Alvaro Garrido-Lestache, tel 4398-45225, fax 4398-46818.

Secretariat of the Court, Personnel and Administration, Translation Service, IT and Telecommunications Department, Buildings, Budget and Library

Secretary-General: Michael Hervé; tel 4398-45522; fax 4398-46666.

AUDIT GROUP I— AGRICULTURAL POLICIES

Animal and plant products, rural development, fisheries and the sea, arable crops, milk products and beef and veal markets, statement of assurance – agricultural policies, clearance of accounts, export refunds.

Senior Member of the Court: Jean-François Bernicot; tel 4398-45203; fax 4398-46817.

Members of the Court: Hedda von Wedel, David Bostock, Gejza Halász, Július Molnár.

AUDIT GROUP II— STRUCTURAL AND INTERNAL POLICIES

Regional policy and cohesion policy, internal policies, including research, social and employment policies.

Senior Member of the Court: Giorgio Clemente; tel 4398-45374; fax 4398-46815.

Members of the Court: François Colling, Lars Tobisson, Josef Bonnici, Vojko Anton Antončič, Kersti Kaljulaid.

AUDIT GROUP III— EXTERNAL ACTIONS

Co-operation with developing countries (general budget of the EU), expenditure relating to Central and East European Countries and the Commonwealth of Independent States, European Development Funds (African, Caribbean and Pacific States).

Senior Member of the Court: Hubert Weber; tel 4398-45951; fax 4398-46957.

Members of the Court: Maarten B. Engwirda, Robert Reynders, Jan Kinšt, Jacek Uczkiewicz.

AUDIT GROUP IV—OWN RESOURCES, BANKING ACTIVITIES, ADMINISTRATIVE EXPENDITURE, COMMUNITY INSTITUTIONS AND BODIES

Traditional own resources, own resources (VAT/GNP), administrative expenditure of the institutions of the EU, borrowing and lending activities, banking activities, community agencies and other decentralized bodies.

Senior Member of the Court: Aunus Salmi; tel 4398-45965271; fax 4398-46971.

Head of Cabinet: Elizabeth Franco, tel 4398-45484, fax 4398-46971.

Attaché: Laura Viita, tel 4398-45467, fax 4398-46971.

Members of the Court: Morten Louis Levysohn, Ioannis Sarmas, Igors Ludbors, Irena Petruškevičienė.

CEAD GROUP— CO-ORDINATION, EVALUATION, ASSURANCE, DEVELOPMENT

Members of the Court: Máire Geoghegan-Quinn; tel 4398-45370; fax 4398-46493; Vitor Manuel da Silva Caldeira; tel 4398-45586, fax 4398-46813; Juan Manuel Fabra Vallés, tel 4398-45592, fax 4398-46818; David Bostock, Maarten B. Engwirda, tel 4398-45236, fax 4398-46202; Morten Louis Levysohn, tel 4398-45264, fax 4398-46811.

ADAR Sector: Audit and training methodology, quality assurance, co-ordination of the procedure for drawing up reports; other professional assistance services; relations with OLAF (European Anti-fraud Office).

Senior Member of the Court: Máire Geoghegan-Quinn; tel 4398-45370; fax 4398-46493.

Head of Cabinet: Gilbert Johnston; tel 4398-45307; fax 4398-46493.

Attaché: Gerard Madden; tel 4398-45516; fax 4398-46493.

DAS Sector: co-ordination of work on the Statement of Assurance.

Member of the Court: Vitor Manuel da Silva Caldeira; tel 4398-45586; fax 4398-46813.

Head of Cabinet: Manuel Lorenço de Oliveira; tel 4398-45160; fax 4398-46813.

Attaché: Paula Betencourt; tel 4398-45059; fax 4398-46813.

ORGANIZATION

Presidency

Director-Adviser: Terrence James; tel 4398-45433; fax 4398-46433.

1 Legal service, institutional external relations and public relations.

Director: Chris Kok; tel 4398-45812; fax 4398-46430.

Principal Administrators: Raymond Claudel, tel 4398-45559, fax 4398-46559; Geoffey Simpson, tel 4398-45347, fax 4398-46347.

Administrator: Dieter Böckem; tel 4398-45350; fax 4398-46350.

Press Officer: Helen Piron-Mäki-Korvela; tel 4398-45314; fax 4398-46430.

2 Financial control.

Financial Controller: Marceliano Cuesta de la Fuente; tel 4398-45245; fax 4398-46245.

3 Translation.

Unit Heads: Agnete Dickmeiss (Danish and Czech), tel 4398-45219, fax 4398-46685; Maurice Loos (Dutch and Lithuanian), tel 4398-45573, fax 4398-46685; Stephen Harrison (English), tel 4398-45532, fax 4398-46685; Seija Gråsten (Finnish and Estonian), tel 4398-45702, fax 4398-46685; Alain Verkaeren (French), tel 4398-45512, fax 4398-46685; Renata Fackler (German), tel 4398-45544, fax 4398-46685; Zisis Klapanaris (Greek and Slovak), tel 4398-45457, fax 4398-46685; Elisabetta Palla (Italian and Slovenian), tel 4398-45509, fax 4398-46685; António Callixto (Portuguese and Polish), tel 4398-45527, fax 4398-46685; Pilar Cano de Gardoqui (Spanish and Latvian), tel 4398-45670, fax 4398-46685; Carolina Ask (Swedish and Maltese), tel 4398-45939, fax 4398-46685.

AUDIT GROUP I

Director: Walter Hubl; tel 4398-45226; fax 4398-46235.

Divisions

1 EAGGF Guarantee: Animal and Plant Products, other EAGGF Expenditure and Agricultural Measures.

Head of Division: Meletios Stavrakis; tel 4398-45261; fax 4398-45235.

2 Rural Development, Fisheries and the Sea.

Head of Division: David Ramsay; tel 4398-45500; fax 4398-46686.

3 EAGGF Guarantee: Arable Crops, Milk and Milk Products, Beef and Veal.

Head of Division: Léon Kirsch; tel 4398-45298; fax 4398-46351.

4 EAGGF Guarantee: Financial Audit; Direct Expenditure; General Matters; Risk Analysis.

Heads of Division: Philippe Blocman, tel 4398-45427, fax 4398-46356; Klaus Werner, tel and fax 4398-46356; David Richardson, tel 4398-45445, fax 4398-46356.

AUDIT GROUP II

Director: Gabriele Cipriani; tel 4398-45556; fax 4398-46686.

Divisions

1 Regional Sector, Cohesion Fund.

Head of Division: Jacques Timmermans; tel 4398-45241; fax 4398-46686.

2 Internal Policies and Research (including the Joint Research Centre).

Head of Division: Hendrik Fehr; tel 4398-45503; fax 4398-46800.

3 Employment and Social Affairs.

Head of Division: Willem van der Hooft; tel 4398-45211; fax 4398-46686.

AUDIT GROUP III

Director: Colin Maynard; tel 4398-45415; fax 4398-46686.

Divisions

1 Co-operation with Development and Third Countries (general budget).

Head of Division: Harm Rozema; tel 4398-45537; fax 4398-46353.

2 Central and East European countries, the newly-independent states and Mongolia.

Head of Division: Ossi Louko; tel 4398-45546; fax 4398-46353.

3 European Development Fund.

Head of Division: Emmanuel Gabolde; tel 4398-45213, fax 4398-46686.

AUDIT GROUP IV

Director: Jean-Michel Gavanier; tel 4398-45428, fax 4398-46235.

Divisions

1 Traditional Own Resources.

Head of Division: Bernard Loesel; tel 4398-45282; fax 4398-46356.

2 Own Resource (VAT/GNP).

Head of Division: Cornelius Groeneveld; tel 4398-45343; fax 4398-46356.

3 Community Agencies and other Decentralized Bodies.

Head of Division: Pierre Hugé; tel 4398-45560; fax 4398-46351.

4 Banking Activities.

Head of Division: Klaus Werner; tel 4398-45257; fax 4398-46235.

5 Administrative Expenditure of the Institutions of the EU.

Head of Division: David Lingua; tel 4398-45555; fax 4398-46351.

CEAD GROUP

Director: Jesús Lázaro Cuenca; tel 4398-45978; fax 4398-46767.

EUROPEAN CENTRAL BANK

On 25 May 1998, the governments of the eleven Member States participating in the third stage of Economic and Monetary Union (EMU) appointed the President, the Vice-President and four other members of the Executive Board of the European Central Bank, the successor to the European Monetary Institute. Their appointment took effect from 1 June 1998 and marked the establishment of the European Central Bank (ECB). The ECB and the national central banks form the European System of Central Banks (ESCB), whose basic tasks are:

- to define and implement the monetary policy of the Community;
- to conduct foreign exchange operations;
- to hold and manage the official foreign reserves of the participating Member States;
- to promote the smooth operation of payment systems;
- to contribute to the smooth conduct of policies pursued by the competent authorities relating to the prudential supervision of credit institutions
- and the stability of the financial system.

The ESCB is governed by the decision-making bodies of the European Central Bank: the Governing Council, the Executive Board and the General Council.

The Governing Council of the European Central Bank (ECB) comprises the members of the Executive Board of the ECB and the governors of the National Central Banks of those Member States which have adopted the Euro.

The Executive Board comprises the President, the Vice-President and four other members, all chosen from among persons with professional experience in monetary or banking matters, and appointed by common accord of the governments of the Member States.

The General Council is composed of the President and the Vice-President and the governors of all National Central Banks, and performs the tasks which the ECB took over from the European Monetary Institute (EMI).

GENERAL CONTACT DETAILS

European Central Bank, Kaiserstr. 29, 60311 Frankfurt am Main, Germany; Postfach 160319, 60066 Frankfurt am Main, Germany; tel (+49 69) 1344-0; fax (+49 69) 1344-6000; e-mail info@ecb.int; internet www.ecb.int.

Governing Council

President: Jean-Claude Trichet.

Vice-President: Lucas D. Papademos.

Members of the Executive Board: José Manuel González-Páramo, Gertrude Tumpel-Gugerell, Otmar Issing, Tommaso Padoa-Schioppa.

National Representatives: Guy Quaden (Governor, Nationale Bank van België/Banque Nationale de Belgique), Axel A. Weber (President, Deutsche Bundesbank), Nicholas C. Garganas (Governor, Bank of Greece), Jaime Caruana (Governor, Banco de España), Christian Noyer (Governor, Banque de France), John Hurley (Governor, Central Bank of Ireland), Antonio Fazio (Governor, Banca d'Italia), Yves Mersch (Governor, Banque Centrale du Luxembourg), Nout Wellink (President, De Nederlandsche Bank), Klaus Liebscher (Governor, Oesterreichische Nationalbank), Vítor Manuel Ribeiro Constâncio (Governor, Banco de Portugal), Erkki Liikanen (Governor, Suomen Pankki–Finlands Bank).

Executive Board

(Comprising the President, the Vice-President and four other members)

Members: Jean-Claude Trichet; Lucas D. Papademos; José Manuel González-Páramo; Gertrude Tumpel-Gugerell; Otmar Issing; Tommaso Padoa-Schioppa.

General Council

Members: Jean-Claude Trichet (President of the ECB), Lucas D. Papademos (Vice-President of the ECB), Guy Quaden (Governor, Nationale Bank van België/Banque Nationale de Belgique), Zdeněk Tůma (Governor, Česká národní banka), Bodil Nyboe Andersen (Governor, Danmarks Nationalbank), Alex A. Weber (President, Deutsche Bundesbank), Vahur Kraft (Governor, Eesti Pank), Nicholas C. Garganas (Governor, Bank of Greece), Jaime Caruana (Governor, Banco de España), Christian Noyer (Governor, Banque de France), John Hurley (Governor, Central Bank and Financial Services Authority of Ireland), Antonio Fazio (Governor, Banca d'Italia), Christodoulos Christodoulou (Governor, Central Bank of Cyprus), Ilmārs Rimšēvičs (Governor, Latvijas Banka), Reinoldijus

Šarkinas (Chairman of the Board, Lietuvos Bankas), Yves Mersch (Director-General, Banque Centrale du Luxembourg), Zsigmond Járai (President, Magyar Nemzeti Bank), Michael C. Bonello (Governor, Central Bank of Malta), Nout Wellink (President, De Nederlandsche Bank), Klaus Liebscher (Governor, Oesterreichische Nationalbank), Leszek Balcerowicz (President, Narodowy Bank Polski), Vítor Manuel Ribeiro Constâncio (Governor, Banco de Portugal), Mitja Gaspari (Governor, Banka Slovenije), Marián Jusko (Governor, Národná banka Slovenska), Erkki Liikanen (Governor, Suomen Pankki–Finlands Bank), Lars Heikensten (Governor, Sveriges Riksbank), Mervyn King (Governor, Bank of England).

DIRECTORATE-GENERAL: ADMINISTRATION

Director-General: Hans-Peter K. Scheller.

Directorates

1 Internal Finance.

Director: Ian Ingram.

Heads of Division: Manfred Striegl (Accounting), Niall Merriman (Financial Reporting and Policy).

2 Personnel.

Director: Berend van Baak.

Heads of Division: Klaus Riemke (Personnel and Development), Martin Carroll (Personnel Policy Division).

3 Banknotes.

Director: Antti Heinonen.

Heads of Division: Brian Dennis (Banknote Printing), Thomas Schweikart (Banknote Issue).

4 External Relations.

Director: Manfred J. Körber.

Heads of Division: Dirk Freytag (Official Publications, Archives and Library), Regina Schüller (Press and Information), Helga Meister (Protocol and Conferences).

DIRECTORATE-GENERAL: LEGAL SERVICES

Director-General: Antonio Sáinz de Vicuña.

Heads of Division: Erwin Nierop (Financial Law), Chiara Zilioli (Institutional Law).

DIRECTORATE-GENERAL: INFORMATION SYSTEMS

Director-General: Jim Etherington.

Deputy Director-General: Christian Boersch.

Directors: Christian Boersch (IS Security), Matthew Lapper (Dedicated IT Application Support).

Heads of Division: François Laurent (IT Business Devt), Jean-Luc Gérardy (IT Operations and Customer Service), Pär Dickman (IT Infrastructure and Systems Support), Corinne Garaud (IT Planning and Major Projects).

DIRECTORATE-GENERAL: OPERATIONS

Director-General: Francesco Papadia.

Deputy Directors-General: Paul Mercier, Werner Studener.

Heads of Division: Roberto Schiava (Front Office), Denis Blenck (Operations Analysis), Eric Vermeir (Back Office), Magnus Fried (Portfolio Management Systems), Torsti Silvonen (Own Funds Management).

DIRECTORATE-GENERAL: ECONOMICS

Director-General: Gert Jan Hogeweg.

Deputy Directors-General: Philippe Moutot, Wolfgang Schill.

Directorates

1 Monetary Policy.

Director: Hans-Joachim Klöckers.

Heads of Division: Klaus Masuch (Monetary Policy Strategy), José Luis Escriva (Monetary Policy Stance), Jesper Berg (Capital Markets and Financial Structure).

2 Economic Developments.

Director: Wolfgang Schill.

Heads of Division: Gerard Korteweg (Euro Area Macroeconomic Developments), Ad van Riet (EU Countries), Filippo di Mauro (External Developments), José Marin Arcas (Fiscal Policies).

DIRECTORATE-GENERAL: RESEARCH

Director-General: Vitor Gaspar.

Deputy Director-General: Ignazio Angeloni.

Heads of Division: Gabriel Fagan (Econometric Modelling), Ignazio Angeloni (General Economic Research).

DIRECTORATE-GENERAL: INTERNATIONAL AND EUROPEAN RELATIONS

Director-General: Pierre van der Haegen.

Deputy Director-General: Georges Pineau.

Director: Christian Thimann (Bilateral Relations).

Heads of Division: Georges Pineau (International Relations), Julio Durán (European Relations).

DIRECTORATE-GENERAL: PAYMENT SYSTEMS

Director-General: Jean-Michel Godeffroy.

Deputy Director-General: (vacant).

Heads of Division: Koenraad De Geest (Payment Systems Policy), Hans-Dieter Becker (TARGET—Trans-European Automated Real-time Gross Settlement Express Transfer System, and Payment Processing), Daniela Russo (Securities Settlement Systems Policy).

DIRECTORATE-GENERAL: STATISTICS

Director-General: Peter Bull.

Heads of Division: Jean-Marc Israel (Balance of Payments Statistics and External Reserves), Werner Bier (General Economic and Financial Statistics), Michel Stubbe (Monetary Banking Statistics), Mike Clements (Statistical Information Systems).

DIRECTORATE-GENERAL: SECRETARIAT AND LANGUAGE SERVICES

Director: Frank Moss.

Heads of Division: Clive Stone (Secretariat), Sarah Johns (Language Services).

DIRECTORATE: INTERNAL AUDIT

Director: Michèle Caparello.

Heads of Division: Dominique Dubois (ECB Audit), Harm Metselaar (ESCB Audit).

DIRECTORATE: FINANCIAL STABILITY AND SUPERVISION

Director: Mauro Grande.

DIRECTORATE: PLANNING AND CONTROLLING

Director: Klaus Gressenbauer.

Heads of Division: Angioli Rolli (Budgets and Projects), Francis Gross (Organizational Planning).

Permanent Representation in Washington, D.C.

Representative: Gerald Grisse.

EUROPEAN OMBUDSMAN

The proposal of an ombudsman for the European Union was launched by the European Parliament in 1979. The right of appeal to the European Ombudsman was finally included in the chapter of the Maastricht Treaty introducing EU citizenship. In 1995, the European Parliament elected Jacob Söderman as the EU's first ombudsman.

To deal with complaints from EU citizens, the ombudsman has a team of thirty, including twelve lawyers. The offices are located in the European Parliament's buildings in Strasbourg.

The Ombudsman's basic task is to check and report on poor administration within the EU's institutions and agencies. Only the Court of Justice and the Court of First Instance, in the exercise of their legal functions, fall outside its remit.

The Ombudsman usually conducts his enquiries in response to a complaint. Any EU citizen or any legal or natural person residing in or having their registered office in an EU Member State may contact the Ombudsman. The Ombudsman also has the right to conduct checks on his own initiative.

GENERAL CONTACT DETAILS

European Ombudsman, 1 ave du Président Robert Schuman, BP 403, 67001 Strasbourg, France; tel (+33) 3-88-17-23-13; fax (+33) 3-88-17-90-62; e-mail euro-ombudsman@europarl.eu.int; internet www.euro-ombudsman.eu.int.

97–113 rue Belliard, 1040 Brussels, Belgium; tel (+32 2) 284-21-11.

Ombudsman

European Ombudsman: P. Nikiforos Diamandouros; tel 3-88-17-23-23.

Secretariat

Head of Legal Dept: Ian Harden; tel 3-88-17-23-84.

Head of Administration and Finance Dept: João Sant'Anna; tel 3-8817-53-46.

Assistant to the European Ombudsman: Nicholas Catephores; tel 3-88-17-23-83.

Principal Legal Advisers: José Martínez Aragon, tel 3-88-17-24-01; Marta Hirsch-Ziembinska, tel 3-88-17-27-46; Gerhard Grill, tel 3-88-17-24-23; Andrea Janosi, tel 3-88-17-24-29.

Internet Communication Officer: Ben Hagard; tel 3-88-17-24-24.

Principal Legal Adviser; Head, Brussels Office: Benita Broms; tel (2) 284-25-43.

Legal Officer: Tina Nilsson; tel (2) 284-14-17.

Administrative and Financial Affairs Officer: Véronique Vandaele; tel (2) 284-23-00.

Legal Assistant, Brussels Office: Elodie Belfy; tel (2) 284-39-01.

EUROPEAN FOUNDATION FOR THE IMPROVEMENT OF LIVING AND WORKING CONDITIONS

(Wyattville Rd, Loughlinstown, Co Dublin, Ireland; tel (1) 204-3100; fax (1) 282-6456; e-mail postmaster@eurofound.ie; internet www.eurofound.eu.int)

Administrative Board

Bureau

Chairman: Marjaana Valkonen (Trade Unions' Group).

Vice-Chairmen: Marc Boisnel (Governments' Group), Jan Willem van den Braak (Employers' Group), Bernhard Jansen (European Commission).

Co-ordinators

Natascha Waltke (Union of Industrial and Employers' Confederations of Europe—UNICE), Walter Cerfeda (European Trade Union Confederation—ETUC).

Representatives of the European Commission

Members: Bernhard Jansen, Ylva Tiveus, Andres Sors.

Alternates: Jackie Morin, Klaus Schnuer, Ronan O'Brien.

Members of the Administrative Board

(Group I: Representatives of Employers' Organizations; Group II: Representatives of Trade Unions; Group III: Representatives of National Governments)

Name	Group
Austria	
Brauner, Dr Heinrich	I
Czeskleba, Frau Mag. Renate	II
Schaller, Mag. Andreas	III
Belgium	
de Gols, Michel	III
Fonck, Herman	II
Waeyaert, Dr Roland	I
Cyprus	
Samuel, Lenia	III
Antoniou, Michael	I
Kittenis, Demetris	II
Czech Republic	
Váňa, Vlastimil	III
Drbalová, Vladimira	I
Málková, Hana	II

Name—*continued*	Group
Denmark	
Bendixen, Annette	II
Bennicke, Henriette	I
Nedergaard, Peter	III
Estonia	
Kaadu, Tiit	III
Päärendson, Eve	I
Parkel, Vaike	II
Finland	
Salmenperä, Matti	III
Saukkonen, Tapani	I
Valkonen, Marjaana	II
France	
Boisnel, Marc	III
Cordier, Florence	I
Vanoye, Jean	II
Germany	
Horst, Andreas	III
Pougin, Dieter	II
Schmidt-Rudloff, Rainer	I
Greece	
Kalyvis, Alexandros	II
Tangas, Dimitrios	III
Tsoumani-Spentza, Eugenia	I
Hungary	
Ladó, Maria	III
Csuport, Antal	I
Hanti, Erzsebet	II
Ireland	
Callender, Rosheen	II
Ward, Sean	III
Killen, Dermot	I
Italy	
Barbucci, Giulia	II
Terraneo, Dr Carlo	I
Reboani, Paolo	III
Latvia	
Tāre, Ineta	III
Egle, Elina	I
Ozola, Iveta	II
Lithuania	
Kazlaiskiene, Rita	III
Sirvydiene, Laura	I
Matuiziene, Janina	II
Luxembourg	
Pizzaferri, René	II
Welsch, Nicolas	I
Welter, Nadine	III

Name—*continued*	Group
Malta	
Camilleri, John P.	III
Scicluna, John B.	I
Parnis, Michael	II
Netherlands	
van den Braak, Dr Jan Willem	I
Pentenga, Erik	II
Vos, Dr Kees J.	III
Poland	
Chlon-Dominczak, Agnieszka	III
Boni, Michał	I
Olszewski, Bogdan	II
Portugal	
Costa Artur, Dr Alexandra	I
de Deus Gomes Pires, João	II
Santos Leitão, Dr José Afonso dos	III
Slovakia	
Michaldová, Elena	III
Kromerová, Viola	I
Meštanová, Eva	II
Slovenia	
Komel, Vladka	III
Ravnik, Marjan	I
Vrhovec, Pavle	II
Spain	
Morillo, Rosario	II
Gonzalez Bayo, Pilar	III
Asenjo Dorado, Maria Angeles	I
Sweden	
Essemyr, Mats	II
Ohlsson, Inger	III
Thorsén Lind, Marie-Louise	I
United Kingdom	
Clark, George	III
Exell, Richard	II
Groucutt, Kate	I
EEA/EFTA (Observers)	
Blöndal, E.	III
Kallevig, Anthony	II
Skjølaas K.	I

Administration

Directorate

Director: Willy Buschak (acting).

Heads of Secretariat to Director: Annick Menzies, Cécile Deneys.

Advisers: Eberhard Köhler, Barry O'Shea.

Brussels Liaison Officer: Sylvie Jacquet.

Deputy Director: (vacant).

Head of Secretariat to Deputy Director: Catherine Cerf.

Research Teams

European Monitoring Centre on Change

Co-ordinator: Jacques Terrenoire.

Research Managers: Barbara Gerstenberger, Janet Smith.

Industrial Relations.

Co-ordinator: Stavroula Demetriades.

Research Managers: Isabella Biletta, David Foden, Timo Kauppinen, Christian Welz.

Living Conditions

Co-ordinator: Robert Anderson.

Research Managers: Philippe Bronchain, Hubert Krieger, Henrik Litske.

Working Conditions

Co-ordinator: Agnès Parent-Thirion.

Research Managers: Michel Miller, Sabrina Tesoka, Juhani Pekkola.

Information and Communication

Head of Information and Communication: Elisabeth Lagerlöf.

Secretariat: Antonella Pirami.

Programme Manager: Michael Wimmer.

Content Management and Dissemination Unit

Programme Manager: Mattanja de Boer.

Language Services

Programme Manager: Cristina Sequeira Frawley.

Translation (French and Greek): Evanghelos Psaroudakis.

Public Affairs Unit

Programme Manager: Brid Nolan.

Secretariat: Sophie Flynn.

Administration and Technical Services

Head of Administration: Terry Sheehan.

Head of General Secretariat: Dolores McCarthy.

Head of Human Resources: Ray Comerford.

Head of Operations: Eberhard Köhler.

Head of Information and Communication Technologies Section: Barry O'Shea.

EUROPEAN TRAINING FOUNDATION (ETF)

(Villa Gualino, Viale Settimio Severo 65, 10133 Turin, Italy; tel (011) 6302222; fax (011) 6302200; e-mail info@etf.eu.int; internet www.etf.eu.int)

Directorate

Director: Dr Muriel Dunbar.

Deputy Director: Ulrich Hillenkamp.

Senior Adviser: Jean-Raymond Masson.

Expertise Development Co-ordinator: Peter Grootings.

Units

1 External Communication

Head of External Communication: Sørensen Bent.

2 Planning, Monitoring and Evaluation

Head of Planning, Monitoring and Evaluation: Peter Greenwood.

EUROPEAN AGENCY FOR THE EVALUATION OF MEDICINAL PRODUCTS (EMEA)

(7 Westferry Circus, Canary Wharf, London E14 4HB, United Kingdom; tel (20) 7418-8400; fax (20) 7418-8416; e-mail mail@emea.eudra.org; internet www.emea.eu.int)

Directorate

Executive Director: Thomas Lönngren; tel. (20) 7418-8406; fax (20) 7418-8409.

Executive Support: Martin Harvey Allchurch; tel (20) 7418-8427; fax (20) 7418-8409.

Management Board

Chairman: Prof Hannes Wahlroos (Finland).

Representatives: Dr Christian Kalcher (Austria), Prof. Dr Robert Schlögel (Austria), Johan van Calster (Belgium), André Pauwels (Belgium), Panayiota Kokkinou (Cyprus), Louis Panayi (Cyprus), Dr Milan Šmíd (Czech Republic), Prof. Alfred Hera (Czech Republic), Jytte Lyngvig (Denmark), Paul Schüder (Denmark), Dr Kristin Raudsepp (Estonia), Dr Alar Irs (Estonia), Pekka Järvinen (Finland), Dr Philippe Duneton (France), Jean Marimbert (France), Dr Walter Schwerdtfeger (Germany), Dr Ilse-Dore Schütt (Germany), Prof. Dimitrios Vagionas (Greece), Vassilis Kontozamanis (Greece), Prof. Tamás L Paál (Hungary), Beatrix Horváth (Hungary), Inguna Adovica (Iceland), Rannveig Gunnarsdóttir (Iceland), Pat O'Mahony (Ireland), Dr Joan Gilvarry (Ireland), Dr Nello Martini (Italy), Dr Jānis Ozoliņš (Latvia), Inguna Adovica (Latvia), Dr Vytautas Basys (Lithuania), Dr Juozas Jokimas (Lithuania), Brigitte Batliner (Liechtenstein), Dr Peter Malin (Liechtenstein), Mariette Backes-Lies (Luxembourg), Claude A. Hemmer (Luxembourg), Dr Patricia Vella Bonanno (Malta), Kenneth Mifsud (Malta), Dr Aginus A.W Kalis (Netherlands), Pim Kapitein (Netherlands), Dr Gro Ramsten Wesenberg (Norway), Hans Halse (Norway), Dr Piotr Blaszczyk (Poland), Dr Piotr Blaszczyk (Poland), Dr Rui dos Santos Ivo (Portugal), Prof. Ludevit Martinec (Slovakia), Stanislava Gajdosova (Slovakia), Prof Dr Stanislav Primoic (Slovenia), Dr Vesna Koblar (Slovenia), Dr Maria del Val Diez Rodrigálvarez (Spain), José Martínez Olmos (Spain), Prof. Gunnar Alván (Sweden), Dr Anders Broström (Sweden), Prof. Kent Woods (United Kingdom), Steve Dean (United Kingdom), Jean-Paul Mingasson (European Commission), Fernand Sauer (European Commission), Prof. Gianmartino Benzi (appointed by European Parliament), Prof. José Luis Valverde (appointed by European Parliament).

Scientific Committees

Committee for Medicinal Products for Human Use (CHMP)

Chairman: Dr Daniel Brasseur (Belgium).

Members: Prof. Heribert Pittner (Austria), Prof. Bruno Flamion (Austria), Prof. Bruno Flamion (Belgium), Dr Pieter Neels (Belgium), Arthur Isseyegh (Cyprus), Panayiota Kokkinou (Cyprus), Dr Milan Šmíd (Czech Republic), Dr Steffen Thirstrup (Denmark), Dr Jens Ersbøll (Denmark), Dr Raul Kiivet (Estonia), Dr Alar Irs (Estonia), Dr Pekka Kurki (Finland), Dr Markku Toivonen (Finland), Dr Eric Abadie (France), Prof. Jean-Hugues Trouvin (France), Prof. Gottfried Kreutz (Germany), Dr Manfred Haase (Germany), Prof. János Borvendég (Hungary), Prof. János Borvendég (Hungary), Prof. Magnus Jóhannsson (Iceland), Dr Sif Ormarsdóttir (Iceland), Dr David Lyons (Ireland), Dr Patrick Salmon (Ireland), Prof. Giuseppe Nisticò (Italy), Dr Pasqualino Rossi (Italy), Prof. Juris Pokratnieks (Latvia), Jacqueline Genoux-Hamer (Luxembourg), Dr Jean-Louis Robert (Luxembourg), Helen Vella (Malta), Dr Patricia Vella Bonanno (Malta), Dr Frits Lekkerkerker (Netherlands), Dr Barbara van Zwieten-Boot (Netherlands), Dr Liv Mathiesen (Norway), Prof. Eva Skovlund (Norway), Prof. Michal Pirozynski (Poland), Dr. Piotr Siedlecki (Poland), Prof. Cristina Sampaio (Portugal), Prof. Beatriz Silva Lima (Portugal), Dr Piotr Siedlecki (Slovakia), Metoda Lipnik-Stangelj (Slovenia), Barbara Razinger (Slovenia), Prof. Fernando de Andrés-Trelles (Spain), Dr Gonzalo Calvo Rojas (Spain), Dr Per Nilsson (Sweden), Dr Tomas Salmonson (Sweden), Dr Julia Dunne (United Kingdom), Dr Ian Hudson (United Kingdom).

Committee for Veterinary Medicinal Products (CVMP)

Chairman: Dr Gérard Moulin (France).

Members: Dr Johannes Dichtl (Austria), Dr Jean-Pierre Binder (Austria), Dr Bruno Urbain (Belgium), Dr Lionel Laurier (Belgium), Kleitos Andreou (Cyprus), Kleitos Andreou (Cyprus), Prof. Alfred Hera (Czech Republic), Dr Jiri Bures (Czech Republic), Dr Anja Holm (Denmark), Prof. Christian Friis (Denmark), Dr Birgit Aasmäe (Estonia), Dr Helen Mahla (Estonia), Dr Liisa Kaartinen (Finland), Dr Kristina Lehmann (Finland), Jean-Claude Rouby (France), Dr Michael Holzhauser-Alberti (France), Prof. Dr Reinhard Kroker (Germany), Dr Manfred Moos (Germany), Ioannis Malemis (Greece), Dr Orestis Papadopoulos (Greece), Dr Tibor Soós (Hungary), Gábor Kulcsár (Hungary), Dr Sigurdur Örn Hansson (Iceland), Dr Halldór Runólfsson (Iceland), Dr J. Gabriel Beechinor (Ireland), Rory Breathnach (Ireland), Dr Maria Tollis (Italy), Dr Virgiliuo Donini (Italy), Liga Villa (Latvia), Laimis Jodkonis (Lithuania), Dr Juozas Jokimas (Lithuania), Marc Wirtor (Luxembourg), Maurice Holper (Luxembourg), Kenneth Mifsud (Malta), Joseph Vella (Malta), Dr Ivo J. T. M. Claassen (Netherlands), Dr Johannes Hoogland (Netherlands), Hanne Bergendahl (Norway), Dr Tonje Høy (Norway), Dr. Katarzyna Krzyanska (Poland), Prof. Józef Debowy (Poland), Prof. Roman Lechowski (Poland), Dr Maria Leonor Meisel (Portugal), Dr Eduardo Marques-Fontes (Portugal), Judita Hederová (Slovakia), Prof. Stane Srcic (Slovenia), Blanka Emersic (Slovenia), Prof. Margarita Arboix (Spain), Prof. Ricardo de la Fuente López (Spain), Dr Eva Johnsson (Sweden), Peter Ekström (Sweden), John O'Brien (United Kingdom), Dr Martin Ilott (United Kingdom).

Committee for Orphan Medicinal Products (COMP)

Chairperson: Prof. Josep Torrent-Farnell (Spain).

Members: Prof. Bernd Jilma (Austria), Dr André Lhoir (Belgium), Ioannis Kkolos (Cyprus), Dr Katerina Kubáčková (Czech Republic), Dr Heidrun Bosch Traberg (Denmark), Dr Vallo Tillmann (Estonia), Dr Veijo Saano (Finland), Dr Emmanuel Héron (France), Dr Rembert Elbers (Germany), Dr George Stathopoulos (Greece**)**, Dr Judit Eggenhofer (Hungary), Prof George Shorten (Ireland), Dr Domenica Taruscio (Italy), Kristina Pavlovska (Latvia), Dr Algirdas Utkus (Lithuania), Prof. Henri Metz (Luxembourg), Dr Joseph Giglio (Malta), Dr Harrie J. J. Seeverens (Netherlands), Dr Jolanta Wieckowska (Poland), Prof. José Manuel Toscano Rico (Portugal), Prof. Magdaléna Kuelová (Slovakia), Dr Martin Moina (Slovenia), Dr José Félix Olalla Marañón (Spain), Dr Kerstin Westermark (Sweden),

Dr Rashmi Shah (United Kingdom), Dr Eric Abadie (CPMP representative), Dr David Lyons (CPMP representative), Prof. Gianmartini Benzi (Management Board representative), Birthe Byskov Holm (European Organisation for Rare Disorders representative), Yann Le Cam (European Organisation for Rare Disorders representative), Alastair Kent (European Alliance of Genetic Support Groups representative).

Observers: Dr Annie Lorence (France), Dr Chantal Belorgey (France), Fabrizia Bignami (France), Dr Panagiota Bouka (Greece).

Administration Unit

Head of Unit: Andreas Pott; tel. (20) 7418-8405; fax (20) 7418-8660.

Sections

1 Personnel and Budget.

Head of Section: Frances Nuttall; tel. (20) 7418-8475; fax (20) 7418-8660.

2 Infrastructure services.

Head of Section: Sara Mendosa; tel. (20) 7418-8403; fax (20) 7418-8660.

3 Accounting.

Head of Section: Gerard O'Malley; tel. (20) 7418-8466; fax (20) 7418-8690.

Evaluation of Medicines for Human Use

Units

1 Pre-Authorization Evaluation.

Head of Unit: Patrick Le Courtois; tel. (20) 7418-8649; fax (20) 7523-7050.

Sections

Scientific Advice and Orphan Drugs

Head of Section: Agnès Saint Raymond; tel. (20) 7523-7017; fax (20) 7523-7040.

Quality of Medicines

Head of Section: John Purves; tel. (20) 7418-8436; fax (20) 8545.

Safety and Efficacy of Medicines

Head of Section: Isabelle Moulon; tel. (20) 7418-8443; fax (20) 7418-8613.

2 Post-Authorization Evaluation.

Head of Unit: Noël Wathion; tel. (20) 7418-8592; fax (20) 7418-8420.

Sections

Regulatory Affairs and Organizational Support

Head of Section: Anthony Humphreys; tel. (20) 7418-8583; fax (20) 7523-7051.

Pharmacovigilance and Post-Authorization Safety and Efficacy of Medicines

Head of Section: Panos Tsintis; tel. (20) 7523-7108; fax (20) 7418-8668.

Veterinary Medicines and Inspections

Head of Unit: Peter Jones; tel. (20) 7418-8413.

Sections

1 Veterinary Marketing Authorization Procedures.

Head of Section: Jill Ashley-Smith; tel. (20) 7418-8646; fax (20) 7418-8447.

2 Safety of Veterinary Medicines.

Head of Section: Kornelia Grein; tel. (20) 7418-8432; fax (20) 7418-8447.

3 Inspections.

Head of Section: Emer Cooke; tel. (20) 7523-7075; fax (20) 7418-8595.

Communications and Networking

Head of Unit: Hans-Georg Wagner; tel (20) 7523-7119; fax (20) 7418-8670.

Sections

1 Document Management and Publishing.

Head of Section: Beatrice Fayl; tel. (20) 7418-8426.

2 Meeting Management and Conferences.

Head of Section: Sylvie Bénéfice; tel. (20) 7418-8651; fax (20) 7418-8501.

3 Project Management.

Head of Section: Timothy Buxton; tel. (20) 7418-8631; fax (20) 7418-8670.

4 Information Technology.

Head of Section: David Drakeford; tel. (20) 7418-8599; fax (20) 7418-8669.

EUROPEAN MONITORING CENTRE FOR DRUGS AND DRUG ADDICTION (EMCDDA)

(Palacete Mascarenhas, Rua da Cruz de Santa Apolónia 23–25, 1149-045 Lisbon, Portugal; tel (21) 8113000; fax (21) 8131711; e-mail info@emcdda.org; internet www.emcdda.eu.int)

Management Board

Chairman: Marcel Reimen (Luxembourg).

Vice-Chairman: Dr Panagiota Bouka (Sweden).

Members: Franz Pietsch (Austria), Dr Willy Brunson (Belgium), Kyriakos Veresies (Cyprus), Josef Radimecký (Czech Republic), Mogens Jørgensen (Denmark), Eda Leesalu (Estonia), Tapani Sarvanti (Finland), Didier Jayle (France), Marion Caspers-Merk (Germany), Christos Giannakis (Greece), Edina Gábor (Hungary), David Moloney (Ireland), Mariano Martone (Italy), Audroné Astrauskiené (Lithuania), Richard Muscat (Malta), Fons Vloemans (Netherlands), Piotr Jablonski (Poland), Fernando Negrão (Portugal), Milan Krek (Slovenia), Blaej Slabý (Slovakia), Elena Garzón Otamendi (Spain), Nick Lawrence (United Kingdom), Luis Romero Requena (European Commission), Carel Edwards (European Commission), Sir Jack Stewart-Clark (appointed by European Parliament), Santiago De Torres Sanahuja (appointed by European Parliament); Non-voting Members: Salme Ahiström (EMCDDA Scientific Committee), Nasra Hassa (United Nations International Drug Control Programme), Klaus Fuchs (Pompidou Group of the Council of Europe), Haik Nikogosian (World Health Organisation); Observer: Inger Gran (Norway).

Administration

Director: Georges Estievenart.

Secretaries: Cristina Paisana, Ann Van Mello.

Assistant to the Director: Kathleen Hernalsteen.

Quality Manager: Arne Tvedt.

Internal Communication Manager: Rita Steyaert.

Inter-institutional Liaison: Alain Wallon.

Management Board Support: Monika Blum.

Scientific Committee Support: Roumen Sedefov.

Liaison Office (Brussels): (Vacant).

Internal Management Co-ordination Committee

Co-ordination Manager: Jaume Bardolet.

Secretary: Catarina Reymão.

Situation Analysis

Programme Co-ordinator: Paul Griffiths.

Responses Analysis

Programme Co-ordinator: Margareta Nilson.

New Synthetic Drugs

Programme Co-ordinator: Alain Wallon.

Strategies and Impact

Programme Co-ordinator: Henri Bergeron.

Reitox and Enlargement

Programme Co-ordinator: Wolfgang Götz.

Information Technologies

Co-ordinator: Pedro Ribeiro.

Communication and Dissemination

Co-ordinator: Jaume Bardolet (acting).

Support Services

Co-ordinator: Arne Tvedt (acting).

Sections

1 Human and Material Resources.

Head of Section: Kathleen Hernalsteen.

2 Finance.

Head of Section: Fátima Carvalho.

3 Planning, Evaluation and Legal Matters.

Head of Section: Dante Storti.

4 Documentation.

Head of Section: Adelaide Seita Duarte.

EUROPEAN ENVIRONMENT AGENCY (EEA)

(Kongens Nytorv 6, 1050 Copenhagen, Denmark; tel 33-36-71-00; fax 33-36-71-99; e-mail eea@eea.eu.int; internet www.eea.eu.int; individual e-mails, unless otherwise indicated, forename.surname@eea.eu.int)

Management Board

Chairman: Lars-Erik Liljelund (Sweden).

Vice-Chairmen: Corrado Clini (Italy), Marko Slokar, Hendrik Vygen (Germany).

Members: Georg Rebernig (Austria); Philippe D'Hondt (Belgium); Dimitar Vergiev (Bulgaria); Michael Constantinides (Cyprus); Tomáš Novotný (Czech Republic); Ole Christiansen (Denmark); Allan Gromov (Estonia); Markku Nurmi (Finland); Dominique Bureau (France); John Vournas (Greece); Óttar Freyr Gislason (Iceland); Geraldine Tallon (Ireland); Einars Cilinskis (Latvia); Felix Näscher (Liechtenstein); Aleksandras Spruogis (Lithuania); Jean-Paul Feltgen (Luxembourg); Godwin Cassar (Malta); Yvo De Boer (Netherlands); Harald Rensvik (Norway); Krzysztof Zareba (Poland); João Nobre Gonçalves (Portugal); Ioan Jelev (Romania); Miroslav Toncik (Slovakia); Domingo Jiménez-Beltrán (Spain); Dr Hasan Zuhuri Sarikaya (Turkey); John Custance (United Kingdom); Nigel Haigh (designated by European Parliament, United Kingdom); Prof. Michael Scoullos (designated by European Parliament, Greece); Prof. Bedrich Moldan (EEA Scientific Committee, Czech Republic); Catherine Day (European Commission).

Scientific Committee

Chairman: Prof. Bedrich Moldan (Czech Republic).

Vice-Chairman: Prof. Katherine Richardson (Denmark).

Members: Helmut Haberl (Austria); Prof. André Berger (Belgium); Dr Pierre Laconte (Belgium); Prof. Bernd Bilitewski (Germany); Dr Constantinos Cartalis (Greece); Prof. László Somlyódy (Hungary); Dr Margaret O'Mahony (Ireland); Theo Vermeire (Netherlands); Dr Tomasz Zylicz (Poland); Prof. Teresa Andresen (Portugal); Dr Július Oszlányi (Slovakia); Prof. Franc Lobnik (Slovenia); Prof. Juan Martinez-Alier (Spain); Prof. Bo Jansson (Sweden); Prof. David Briggs (United Kingdom).

Directorate

Executive Director: Jacqueline McGlade.

OTHER MAJOR EUROPEAN UNION INSTITUTIONS

European Centre for the Development of Vocational Training (CEDEFOP)

(Evropis 123, POB 22427, 57001
Thessaloniki (Pylea), Greece; tel (310)
490111; fax (310) 490102; e-mail
info@cedefop.eu.int; internet
www.cedefop.eu.int)

Chairman of the Management Board:
Peter Thiele.

Director: Johann van Rens; e-mail
jvr@cedefop.gr.

Deputy Director: Stavros Stavrou;
e-mail sts@cedefop.gr.

Senior Adviser to the Director: Werner P. Herrmann.

Adviser for Administrative Reform:
Georges Paraskevaïdis.

Assistant to the Director: Colin
McCullogh; e-mail cmc@cedefop.gr.

Office for Harmonization in the Internal Market (Trade Marks and Designs)

(Avda de Europa 4, 03008 Alicante,
Spain; tel (96) 5138800; fax (96)
5139173; internet http://oami.eu.int)

Administrative Board

Chairman: Carl-Anders Ifvarsson
(Sweden).

Deputy Chairwoman: Adamantia
Nikolakopoulou (Greece).

Members: Helmut Czuba (Austria),
Jérôme Debrulle (Belgium), Karel Ćada
(Czech Republic), Stalo Papaioannou
(Cyprus), Henrik Dahl Sorensen (Denmark), Matti Päts (Estonia), Martti
Enäjärvi (Finland), Benoît Battistelli
(France), Elmar Hucko (Germany),
Adamantia Nikolakopoulou (Greece),
Mihály Ficsor (Hungary), Michael
English (Ireland), Carlo Presenti (Italy),
Zigrīds Aumeisters (Latvia), Lex
Kaufhold (Luxembourg), Godwin Warr
(Malta), Harry Geijzers (Netherlands),

Andrzej Pyrza (Poland), Jaime Serrão
Andrez (Portugal), Darina Kylianova
(Slovakia), Teresa Mogin Barquin
(Spain), Carl-Anders Ifvarsson (Sweden),
Robin Webb (United Kingdom), Guido
Berardis (European Commission).

Budget Committee

Chairman: Peter Lawrence (United
Kingdom).

Deputy Chairman: José Maria
Mauricio (Portugal).

Members: Robert Ullrich (Austria),
Régis Massant (Belgium), Josef Dvronák
(Czech Republic), Soteroula Tsokou
(Cyprus), Henrik Dahl Sorensen
(Denmark), Aasa Süld (Estonia), Eija
Nuorlahti-Solarmo (Finland), Denis
Plantamp (France), Raimund Lutz
(Germany), Adamantia Nikolakopoulou
(Greece), Mihály Ficsor (Hungary),
Michael English (Ireland), Renzo
Antonini (Italy), Zigrīds Aumeisters
(Latvia), Jean-Pierre Lahire (Luxembourg), A. J. M. Kerkvliet (Netherlands),
Andrzej Pyrza (Poland), José Maria
Mauricio (Portugal), Ján Poljovka (Slovakia), Eugenia Bellver Moreira (Spain),
Rolf Swärd (Sweden), Peter Lawrence
(United Kingdom), Guido Berardis (European Commission).

ADMINISTRATION

President: Wubbo de Boer.

Vice-Presidents: Alberto Casado Cerviño (Administrative and Technical
Affairs), Alexander von Mühlendahl
(Legal Affairs).

Administration of Trade Marks and
Designs Department

Director: Vincent O'Reilly.

Deputy Director: Fernando Martínez
Tejedor

Heads of Service: Jean Rousseaux
(Data Reception, Capture and Distribution), Gordon Humphreys (Register and
Related Databases), Michael Dickas
(Formalities Examination).

Designs Department

Director: Paul Maier.

Finance Department

Director: Peter Rodinger.

General Affairs and External Relations
Department

Director: João Miranda de Sousa.

Deputy Directors: Virginia Melgar,
Javier Rujas Mora-Rey.

Human Resources Department

Director: Juan Ramón Rubio Muñoz.

Information Technologies and Facilities
Management Department

Director: Marc Vanaeken.

Heads of Service: Günther Marten
(Asset and Performance Management),
Miguel Angel Villarroya Sanchez (Facilities Management), Rainer Tretter (IT
Development), Talma de Castro e Costa
Rodrigues (IT Production and Telecommunications), Francisco García Valero
(User Support and IT Security).

Quality Management Department

Director: William Copine.

Trade Marks Department

Director: Hans Jakobsen.

Deputy Director: Panayotis Geroulakos.

Heads of Service: Detlef Schennen
(Industrial Property Matters), Bernhard
Müller (Service 1), Hendrik Dijkema
(Service 2), Ilse Mayer (Service 3), Dimitris Botis (Service 4), Jörg Weberndorfer
(Service 5), Benoît Lory (Production).

Industrial Property Litigation Unit

Director: Oreste Montalto.

Financial Controller: Mariano
Ramirez Battistig.

Boards of Appeal

President: Bruno Machado.

First Board of Appeal

Chairperson: Sylvie Mandel.

Members: Kathleen Lee, Theophilos
Margellos, Carlo Rusconi, José Luis
Soares Curado.

Second Board of Appeal

Chairperson: Kerstin Sundström.

Members: Achim Bender, Peter Dyrberg,
David Keeling, Tomás De Las Heras
Lorenzo.

Third Board of Appeal

Chairperson: Sylvie Mandel.

Members: David Keeling, Walter
Peeters, Carlo Rusconi.

Fourth Board of Appeal

Chairperson: Christiane Hoffrichter-Daunicht.

Members: Maria Bra, Fernando López de Rego, Walter Peeters.

Registry

Head of Service: Eric Gastinel.

Scientific Service

Head of Service: Karin Klüpfel.

Translation Centre for Bodies in the European Union

(Bâtiment Nouvel Hémicycle, 1 rue du Fort Thüngen, L-1499 Luxembourg Kirchberg; tel 4217-11-1; fax 4217-11-220; e-mail cdt@cdt.eu.int)

Director: Francisco de Vicente.

Chairman of the Management Board: M. Vanden Abeele.

Departments

1 Translation.

Head of Department: Marie-Anne Fernández.

Advisers: Rebecca West (Freelance), Alastair Macphail (Standardization).

2 General Administration, Finance and Personnel.

Head of Department: Isidoro Rodríguez.

3 Computers.

Head of Department: Bernard Hawes.

European Agency for Safety and Health at Work

(Gran Vía 33, 48009 Bilbao, Spain; tel (94) 4794360; fax (94) 4794383; e-mail information@osha.eu.int; internet http://agency.osha.eu.int)

Director: Hans-Hörst Konkolewsky.

Units

1 Network Secretariat.

Network Manager: Finn Sheye.

2 Information and Communication.

Head of Unit: Andrew Smith.

3 Working Environment.

Head of Unit: Pascal Paoli.

4 Task Force Campaigns and Programmes.

Head of Task Force: Françoise Murillo.

5 Administration.

Head of Unit: Aisling O'Neill.

Community Plant Variety Office

(3 blvd Maréchal Foch, BP 2141, 49021 Angers Cedex 02, France; tel 2-41-25-64-00; fax 2-41-25-64-10; e-mail cpvo@cpvo.eu.int; internet www.cpvo.eu.int)

President: Bart Kiewiet.

Vice-President: José Elena.

Secretary to the President: Marleen Van de Meulebroeke.

Secretary to the Vice-President: Cyrille Antoine.

Units

1 Administrative and Financial.

Head of the Administrative and Financial Unit: Thomas Wollersen.

2 Technical.

Head of Unit: Dirk Theobald.

Experts: Ton Kwakkenbos (Ornamentals), Anne Weitz (Agricultural Crops), Sergio Semon (Fruits and Vegetables), Jean Maison (Ornamentals and Variety Denominations).

3 Legal.

Head of Unit: Martin Ekvad.

4 Information Technology.

Computer Scientists: Patrick Lecoq, Jean-Louis Curnier.

5 Personnel.

Head of Unit: Anna Isgren.

European Investment Fund (EIF)

(43 ave J. F. Kennedy, 2968 Luxembourg; tel 4266-88-1; fax 4266-88-200; e-mail info@eif.org; internet www.eif.org)

Chief Executive: Francis Carpenter.

Chairman of the Board of Directors: Giovanni Ravasio.

Chairman of the Audit Board: Sylvain Simonetti.

Secretary-General: Robert Wagener.

Director of Operations: John A. Holloway.

Responsible for Human Resources and Facility Management: Petra de Bruxelles.

Responsible for Accounting and Treasury: Frédérique Schepens.

Divisions

1 Risk Management and Monitoring.

Head of Division: Thomas Meyer.

2 Policy and Institutional Co-ordination/Advisory Services.

Head of Division: Marc Schublin.

3 Legal Service.

Head of Division: Maria Leander.

4 Venture Capital 1 (Belgium, France, Greece, Italy, Luxembourg, Netherlands, Spain, United Kingdom).

Head of Division: Jean-Philippe Burcklen.

4 Venture Capital 2 (Austria, Denmark, Finland, Germany, Ireland, Portugal, Sweden and Candidate Countries).

Head of Division: Ulrich Grabenwarter.

5 Guarantees, MAP and Securitisation.

Head of Division: Alessandro Tappi.

6 Product Development and Operations Research.

Head of Division: Frank Tassone.

Europol

(Raamweg 47, 2596 HN The Hague, Netherlands; POB 90850, 2509 LW The Hague, Netherlands; tel (70) 3025000; fax (70) 3455896; e-mail info@europol.eu.int; internet www.europol.eu.int)

Management Team

Director: Mariano Simancasm (acting).

Deputy Directors: Gilles Leclair (Serious Crime); Willy Bruggeman (Development and Research); Caspar van den Wall Blake (Technological Services); Leo van Kampen (Assistance to Management).

Management Board: Søren Beier (Secretary), Aat van der Meer (Financial Controller), Klaus Kalk (Chairman, Joint Supervisory Body).

FOREIGN, REGIONAL AND INSTITUTIONAL REPRESENTATION IN BRUSSELS

DIPLOMATIC CORPS ACCREDITED TO THE EUROPEAN UNION

Afghanistan: 61 ave de Wolvendael, 1180 Brussels, Belgium; tel (2) 761-31-66; fax (2) 761-31-67; e-mail ambassade.afghanistan@brutele.be; internet www.ambafghane.web.com; Ambassador: Humayun Tandar; First Sec: Chekeba Hachemi.

Albania: 30 rue Tenbosch, 1000 Brussels, Belgium; tel (2) 644-33-29; fax (2) 640-31-77; e-mail albanian.ec1@skynet.be; Ambassador: Artur Kuko; Minister-Counsellor: Mimoza Kondo; First Sec: Arian Turhani.

Algeria: 209 ave Molière, 1050 Brussels, Belgium; tel (2) 343-50-78; fax (2) 343-51-68; Ambassador: Halim Benattallah.

Andorra: 10 rue de la Montagne, 1000 Brussels, Belgium; tel (2) 502-12-11; fax (2) 513-07-41; e-mail ambassade@andorra.be; internet www.andorra.be; Ambassador: Meritxell Mateu.

Angola: 182 rue Franz Merjay, 1050 Brussels, Belgium; tel (2) 346-18-72; fax (2) 344-08-94; e-mail angola.embassy.brussels@skynet.be; Chargé d'affaires a.i.: Maria Eugénia Feijo de Almeida Ferreira dos Santos.

Antigua and Barbuda: 42 rue de Livourne, 1000 Brussels, Belgium; tel (2) 534-26-11; fax (2) 539-40-09; e-mail ecs.embassie@skynet.be; internet www.caribisles.org; Ambassador: (vacant); Minister-Counsellor: Dr Arnold Thomas.

Argentina: 225 ave Louise, BP 2, 1050 Brussels, Belgium; tel (2) 648-93-71; fax (2) 648-08-04; e-mail info@eceur.org; internet www.eceur.org; Ambassador: Jorge Remes Lenicov; Minister Plenipotentiary: Horacio Salvador.

Armenia: 157 rue Franz Merjay, 1050 Brussels, Belgium; tel (2) 348-44-00; fax (2) 348-44-01; e-mail armembel@wanadoo.be; internet www.armenian-embassy.be; Ambassador: Viguen Tchitetchian; Minister Plenipotentiary: Edouard Panoian.

Australia: Guimard Centre, 6–8 rue Guimard, 1040 Brussels, Belgium; tel (2) 286-05-00; fax (2) 230-68-02; e-mail austemb.brussels@dfat.gov.au; internet www.austemb.be; Ambassador: Peter Grey; Minister: Michael Mugliston.

Azerbaijan: 78 ave Général Lartigue, 1200 Brussels, Belgium; tel (2) 735-98-80; fax (2) 735-92-70; e-mail az.missioneu@chello.be; Ambassador: Arif Mamedov; First Sec: Emin Eyyubov.

Bahamas: 10 Chesterfield St, London W1X 8AH, United Kingdom; tel (20) 7408-4488; fax (20) 7499-9937; e-mail info@bahamashclondon.net; Ambassador: Basil O'Brien; Minister-Counsellor: Marilyn T. Zonicle.

Bahrain: 3 *bis* place des Etats-Unis, 75016 Paris, France; tel 1-47-23-48-68; Ambassador: Shaikha Haya bint Rashid al-Khalifa.

Bangladesh: 29–31 rue Jacques Jordaens, 1000 Brussels, Belgium; tel (2) 640-55-00; fax (2) 646-59-98; e-mail bdootbrussels@freegate.be; Ambassador: Syed Maudud Ali.

Barbados: 100 ave F. D. Roosevelt, 1050 Brussels, Belgium; tel (2) 732-17-37; fax (2) 732-32-66; e-mail brussels@foreign.gov.bb; Ambassador: Errol L. Humphrey.

Belarus: 192 ave Molière, 1050 Brussels, Belgium; tel (2) 340-02-70; fax (2) 340-02-87; e-mail embbel@skynet.be; Ambassador: (vacant); Minister-Counsellor, Dep Head of Mission: Aleksandr Baichorov.

Belize: 136 blvd Brand Whitlock, 1200 Brussels, Belgium; tel (2) 732-62-04; fax (2) 732-62-46; e-mail embel.bru@pophost.eunet.be; internet www.belize.gov.bz; Ambassador: Yvonne Hyde; First Sec: Keisha Diego.

Benin: 5 ave de l'Observatoire, 1180 Brussels, Belgium; tel (2) 375-06-74; fax (2) 375-83-26; e-mail ambassade.de.benin@skynet.be; Ambassador: Euloge Hinvi; Minister-Counsellor: Désiré Auguste Adjahi.

Bhutan: 17–19 chemin du Champ d'Anier, 1209 Geneva, Switzerland; tel (22) 799-08-90; fax (22) 799-08-99; e-mail mission.bhutan@ties.itu.int; Ambassador: Bap Kesang; First Sec: Kinga Singye.

Bolivia: 176 ave Louise, BP 6, 1050 Brussels, Belgium; tel (2) 627-00-10; fax (2) 647-47-82; e-mail embajada.bolivia@embolbrus.be; Ambassador: Fernando Laredo Aguayo; Minister-Counsellor: Arturo Suarez Vargas.

Bosnia and Herzegovina: 34 rue Tenbosch, 1000 Brussels; tel (2) 644-20-08; fax (2) 644-16-98; e-mail mis-eu-nato-bru@skynet.be; Ambassador: Zdenko Martinovic; Minister-Counsellors: Nazif Kadric, Jugoslav Jovicic.

Botswana: 169 ave de Tervuren, 1150 Brussels, Belgium; tel (2) 735-20-70; fax (2) 735-63-18; e-mail embasofbotswana@yahoo.co.uk; internet www.gov.bw; Ambassador: Sasara Chasala George; Minister-Counsellor: Edith Basadi Tamplin.

Brazil: 30 ave F. D. Roosevelt, 1050 Brussels, Belgium; tel (2) 640-20-40; fax (2) 648-80-40; e-mail missao@braseuropa.be; Ambassador: José Alfredo Graça Lima; Minister-Counsellor: Leda Lúcia Martins Camargo.

Brunei: 238 ave F. D. Roosevelt, 1050 Brussels, Belgium; tel (2) 675-08-78; fax (2) 672-93-58; e-mail kedutaan-brunei.brussels@skynet.be; Ambassador: (vacant); Chargé d'affaires a.i.: Amalina Murad.

Bulgaria: 108 rue d'Arlon, 1040 Brussels, Belgium; tel (2) 374-84-68; fax (2) 374-91-88; e-mail info@missionbg.be; Ambassador: Stanislav Daskalov; Minister Plenipotentiary, Dep Head of Mission: Roussi Ivanov.

Burkina Faso: 16 place d'Arezzo, 1180 Brussels, Belgium; tel (2) 345-99-12; fax (2) 345-06-12; e-mail ambassade.burkina@skynet.be; Ambassador: Kadré Désiré Ouedraogo.

Burundi: 46 square Marie-Louise, 1000 Brussels, Belgium; tel (2) 230-45-35; fax (2) 230-78-83; e-mail ambassade.burundi@skynet.be; Ambassador: Ferdinand Nyabenda; First Counsellors: Salvator Kaburundi, Philippe Ntahonkuriye.

Cambodia: 4 rue Adolphe Yvon, 75116 Paris, France; tel 1-45-03-47-20; fax 1-45-03-47-40; e-mail ambcambodgeparis@mangoosta.fr; Ambassador: (vacant); Minister Plenipotentiary: Chant Rith Yao.

Cameroon: 131–133 ave Brugmann, 1190 Brussels, Belgium; tel (2) 345-18-70; fax (2) 344-57-35; Ambassador: Isabelle Bassong; Minister-Counsellor: Iya Tidjani; First Sec: Michel Guy Tsala Belibi.

Canada: 2 ave de Tervuren, 1040 Brussels, Belgium; tel (2) 741-06-60; fax (2) 741-06-29; internet www.dfait-maeci.gc.ca/eu-mission/index.htm; Ambassador: Jeremy Kinsman; Minister-Counsellor, Dep. Head of Mission: Laurette Glasgow.

Cape Verde: 29 ave Jeanne, 1050 Brussels, Belgium; tel (2) 643-62-70; fax (2) 646-33-85; e-mail emb.caboverde@skynet.be; Ambassador: Fernando Wahnon Ferreira.

Central African Republic: 416 blvd Lambermont, 1030 Brussels, Belgium; tel (2) 242-28-80; fax (2) 215-13-11; e-mail ambassade.centreafrique@skynet.be; Ambassador: Armand-Guy Zounguere-Sokambi.

The Directory of EU Information Sources

Chad: 52 blvd Lambermont, 1030 Brussels, Belgium; tel (2) 215-19-75; fax (2) 216-35-26; e-mail ambassade.tchad@ skynet.be; Ambassador: Abderahim Yacoub Ndiaye; First Counsellor: Idriss Adjideye.

Chile: 106 ave des Aduatiques, 1040 Brussels, Belgium; tel (2) 743-36-60; fax (2) 736-49-94; e-mail misue@ misionchile-ue.org; Ambassador: Alberto van Klaveren; Minister-Counsellor: José Manuel Silva; First Sec: Francisco Berguño.

China, People's Republic: 443–445 ave de Tervuren, 1150 Brussels, Belgium; tel (2) 775-30-82; fax (2) 775-30-94; Ambassador: Chengyuan Guan; Minister- Counsellor: Zhiming Liu.

Colombia: 96a ave F. D. Roosevelt, 1050 Brussels, Belgium; tel (2) 649-56-79; fax (2) 646-54-91; e-mail colombia@emcolbru .org; internet www.emcolbru.org; Ambassador: Nicolas Echavarría Mesa; Minister Plenipotentiary: Victoria Eugenia Senior.

Comoros: 128 ave Paul Hymans, 1200 Brussels, Belgium; tel and fax (2) 779-58-38; e-mail ambacom.bxl@skynet.be; Ambassador: Sultan Chouzour.

Congo, Democratic Republic: 6 ave de Foestraat, 1180 Brussels, Belgium; tel (2) 375-47-96; fax (2) 372-23-48; Ambassador: Jean-Pierre Mavungu-di-Ngoma.

Congo, Republic: 16–18 ave F. D. Roosevelt, 1050 Brussels, Belgium; tel (2) 648-38-56; fax (2) 648-42-13; Ambassador: Jacques Obia; Minister-Counsellor: Jean-Paul Engaye.

Cook Islands: 10 rue Berckmans, 1060 Brussels, Belgium; tel (2) 543-10-00; fax (2) 543-10-01; e-mail cookislands@ prmltd.com; Ambassador: Todd McClay.

Costa Rica: 489 ave Louise, 1050 Brussels, Belgium; tel (2) 640-55-41; fax (2) 648-31-92; e-mail ambcrbel@coditel.net; Ambassador: Maria Salvadora Ortiz Ortiz; Minister-Counsellor: Michel Chartier.

Côte d'Ivoire: 234 ave F. D. Roosevelt, 1050 Brussels, Belgium; tel (2) 672-23-57; fax (2) 672-04-91; Ambassador: Marie Gosset; First Counsellor: Konan Narcisse Kouadio.

Croatia: 50 ave des Arts, 1000 Brussels, Belgium; tel (2) 500-09-30; fax (2) 646-56-64; e-mail cromissioneu@skynet.be; Ambassador: Mirjana Mladineo; Minister-Counsellor, Dep Head of Mission: Andrej Plenković.

Cuba: 77 rue Robert Jones, 1180 Brussels, Belgium; tel (2) 343-00-20; fax (2) 344-96-91; e-mail consejero@embacuba .be; Ambassador: Rodrigo Malmierca Diaz.

Djibouti: 204 ave F. D. Roosevelt, 1050 Brussels, Belgium; tel (2) 347-69-67; fax (2) 347-69-63; e-mail amb_djib@yahoo.fr; Ambassador: Mohamed Moussa Chehem; First Counsellor: Moussa Ali Meigague.

Dominica: 42 rue de Livourne, 1000 Brussels, Belgium; tel (2) 534-26-11; fax (2) 539-40-09; e-mail ecs.embassies@ skynet.be; internet www.caribisles.org; Ambassador: George Randolph Earle Bullen.

Dominican Republic: 12 ave Bel Air, 1180 Brussels, Belgium; tel (2) 346-49-35; fax (2) 346-51-52; e-mail embajada@ dominicana.be; Ambassador: Clara Quiñones de Longo; Minister-Counsellor: Rafael Molina Pulgar.

Ecuador: 363 ave Louise, BP 1, 1050 Brussels, Belgium; tel (2) 644-30-50; fax (2) 644-28-13; e-mail amb.equateur@ skynet.be; Ambassador: Méntor Villagomez Merino; Minister: Andrés Teran Parral.

Egypt: 19 ave de l'Uruguay, 1000 Brussels, Belgium; tel (2) 663-58-00; fax (2) 675-58-88; e-mail embassy.egypt@skynet .be; Ambassador: Soliman Awaad; Minister Plenipotentiary, Dep Head of Mission: Osama El Magdoub.

El Salvador: 171 ave de Tervuren, 1150 Brussels, Belgium; tel (2) 733-04-85; fax (2) 735-02-11; e-mail amb.elsalvador@ brutele.be; Ambassador: Héctor Gonzalez Urrutia; Minister-Counsellor: Anabella Machuca Machuca.

Equatorial Guinea: 17 ave Jupiter, 1190 Brussels, Belgium; tel (2) 346-25-09; fax (2) 346-33-09; e-mail guineaecuatorial.brux@skynet.be; Ambassador: Victorino Nka Obiang Maye.

Eritrea: 15–17 ave Wolvendael, 1180 Brussels, Belgium; tel (2) 374-44-34; fax (2) 372-07-30; e-mail eri_emba_brus@ hotmail.com; Ambassador: Andebrhan Woldegiorgis.

Ethiopia: 231 ave de Tervuren, 1150 Brussels, Belgium; tel (2) 771-32-94; fax (2) 711-49-14; e-mail etebru@brutele.be; Ambassador: Berhane Gebre Christos; Minister-Counsellor: Teruneh Zenna.

Fiji: 92–94 square Plasky, 1030 Brussels, Belgium; tel (2) 736-90-50; fax (2) 736-14-58; e-mail info@fijiembassy.be; Ambassador: Isikeli Uluinairai Mataitoga.

Gabon: 112 ave Winston Churchill, 1180 Brussels, Belgium; tel (2) 340-62-10; fax (2) 346-46-69; e-mail be.175335@skynet .be; Ambassador: René Makongo; First Counsellors: François Ebibi Mba, Louis Mouloungui Mbadinga.

The Gambia: 126 ave F. D. Roosevelt, 1050 Brussels, Belgium; tel (2) 640-10-49; fax (2) 646-32-77; Ambassador: Yusuoha Alieu Kah.

Georgia: 58 ave Orban, 1150 Brussels, Belgium; tel (2) 761-11-93; fax (2) 761-11-99; e-mail mdgadc@skynet.be; Ambassador: Konstantin Zaldastanishvili; First Counsellor: Ioseb Kujiashvili.

Ghana: 7 blvd Général Wahis, 1030 Brussels, Belgium; tel (2) 705-82-20; fax (2) 705-66-53; e-mail head@ghembassy .arc.be; internet www.ghanabru.net; Ambassador: Kobina Wudu.

Grenada: 123 rue de Laeken, 1000 Brussels, Belgium; tel (2) 223-73-03; fax (2) 223-73-07; internet www.caribisles.org; Ambassador: Joan Marie Coutain.

Guatemala: 185 ave Winston Churchill, 1180 Brussels, Belgium; tel (2) 345-90-58; fax (2) 344-64-99; e-mail obguab@ infoboard.be; Ambassador: Edmond Mulet Lesieur; Minister-Counsellor: Jorge Ricardo Putzeys Uriguen.

Guinea: 108 blvd Auguste Reyers, 1030 Brussels, Belgium; tel (2) 771-01-26; fax (2) 762-60-36; e-mail ambassadeguinee .bel@skynet.be; Ambassador: Kazaliou Balde; Minister Plenipotentiary: Ousmane Tolo Thiam.

Guinea-Bissau: 70 ave F. D. Roosevelt, 1050 Brussels, Belgium; tel (2) 647-08-90; fax (2) 640-43-12; Chargé d'affaires a.i.: Serafim Ianga.

Guyana: 12 ave du Brésil, 1000 Brussels, Belgium; tel (2) 675-62-16; fax (2) 675-63-31; e-mail embassy.guyana@skynet.be; Ambassador: Dr Kenneth F. S. King.

Haiti: 139 chaussée de Charleroi, 1060 Brussels, Belgium; tel (2) 649-73-81; fax (2) 640-60-80; e-mail amb.haiti.bel@ skynet.be; Ambassador: Yolette Azor-Charles; Minister-Counsellor: Jacques Nixon Myrthil.

Holy See: 289 ave Brugmann, 1180 Brussels, Belgium; tel (2) 340-77-00; fax (2) 340-77-04; e-mail nuntius.eu@village .uunet.be; Apostolic Nuncio: Monsignor Faustino Sainz Muñoz; Counsellor: Monsignor Martin Krebs.

Honduras: 3 ave des Gaulois, 1040 Brussels, Belgium; tel (2) 734-00-00; fax (2) 735-26-26; e-mail ambassade.honduras@ chello.be; Ambassador: Teodolinda Banegas de Makris.

Iceland: 74 rue de Trèves, 1040 Brussels, Belgium; tel (2) 286-17-00; fax (2) 286-17-70; e-mail icemb.brussel@utn.stjr .is; internet www.iceland.org/be; Ambassador: Kjartan Jóhannsson; Minister-Counsellor, Dep Head of Mission: Thórir Ibsen.

India: 217 chaussée de Vleurgat, 1050 Brussels, Belgium; tel (2) 640-91-40; fax (2) 648-96-38; e-mail infogen@ missionindia-belgium.org; internet www.missionindia-belgium.org; Ambassador: Pradeep Kumar Singh; Minister, Dep Head of Mission: Rameshwar Pal Agrawal.

Indonesia: 38 blvd de la Woluwe, 1200 Brussels, Belgium; tel (2) 779-09-15; fax (2) 772-82-10; e-mail primebxl@skynet.be; Ambassador: Abdurachman Mattalitti.

Iran: 415 ave de Tervuren, 1150 Brussels, Belgium; tel (2) 762-37-45; fax (2) 762-39-15; e-mail eiri.bxl@skynet.be; Ambassador: Abolghasem Delfi; First Counsellor, Dep Head of Mission: Gholamreza Ebrahim Pour.

Iraq: 23 ave des Aubépines, 1180 Brussels, Belgium; tel (2) 374-59-92; fax (2) 374-76-15; e-mail ambassade.irak@skynet.be; Ambassador: (vacant).

Israel: 40 ave de l'Observatoire, 1180 Brussels, Belgium; tel (2) 373-55-00; fax (2) 373-56-17; e-mail isr.mis.eu@online.be; Ambassador: Oded Eran; Minister-Counsellor, Dep Head of Mission: Alon Snir.

Jamaica: 2 ave Palmerston, 1000 Brussels, Belgium; tel (2) 230-11-70; fax (2) 230-37-09; e-mail emb.jam.brussels@skynet.be; Ambassador: Evadne Coye.

Japan: 5–6 square de Meeûs, 1000 Brussels, Belgium; tel (2) 500-77-11; fax (2) 513-32-41; e-mail inf@jmission-eu.be; internet www.jmission-eu.be; Ambassador: Kazuo Asakai; Minister, Dep Head of Mission: Yoshihisa Kuroda.

Jordan: 104 ave F. D. Roosevelt, 1050 Brussels, Belgium; tel (2) 640-77-55; fax (2) 640-27-96; e-mail jordan.embassy@skynet.be; Chargé d'affaires a.i.: Malek E. Twal.

Kazakhstan: 30 ave Van Bever, 1180 Brussels, Belgium; tel (2) 374-95-62; fax (2) 374-50-91; e-mail kazakstan.embassy@linkline.be; Ambassador: Konstantin V. Zhigalov.

Kenya: 208 ave Winston Churchill, 1180 Brussels, Belgium; tel (2) 340-10-40; fax (2) 340-10-50; e-mail kenbrussels@hotmail.com; Ambassador: Peter Nkuraiya.

Korea, Democratic People's Republic: Glinkastr. 5/7, 1017 Berlin, Germany; tel (30) 2293189; fax (30) 2293191.

Korea, Republic: 173–175 chaussée de La Hulpe, 1170 Brussels, Belgium; tel (2) 675-57-77; fax (2) 675-52-21; e-mail eukorea@skynet.be; Ambassador: Haeng-Kyeom Oh; Ministers: Choong-Joo Choi, Dong-Hee Chang.

Kuwait: 43 ave F. D. Roosevelt, 1050 Brussels, Belgium; tel (2) 647-79-50; fax (2) 646-12-98; e-mail embassy.kwt@skynet.be; Ambassador: Abdulazeez A. ash-Sharikh.

Kyrgyzstan: 47 rue de l'Abbaye, 1050 Brussels, Belgium; tel (2) 640-18-68; fax (2) 640-01-31; Ambassador: Chingiz Torekulovitch Aitmatov.

Laos: 19–21 ave de la Brabançonne, 1000 Brussels, Belgium; tel (2) 740-09-50; fax (2) 734-16-66; e-mail secretaire@yucom.be; Ambassador: Thongphachanh Sonnasinh.

Lebanon: 2 rue Guillaume Stocq, 1050 Brussels, Belgium; tel (2) 645-77-65; fax (2) 645-77-69; e-mail ambassade.liban@brutele.be; Ambassador: Fawzi Fawaz.

Lesotho: 44 blvd Général Wahis, 1030 Brussels, Belgium; tel (2) 705-39-76; fax (2) 705-67-79; e-mail lesothobrussels@hotmail.com; Ambassador: Moliehi Mathato Adel Matlanyane

Liberia: 50 ave du Château, 1081 Brussels, Belgium; tel (2) 411-01-12; fax (2) 411-09-12; Chargé d'affaires a.i.: Youngor Telewoda.

Libya: 28 ave Victoria, 1000 Brussels, Belgium; tel (2) 649-37-37; fax (2) 644-01-55; Ambassador: Hamed Ahmad el Houderi.

Liechtenstein: 1 Place du Congrès, 1000 Brussels, Belgium; tel (2) 229-39-00; fax (2) 219-35-45; e-mail ambassade.liechtenstein@bbru.llv.be; Ambassador: Prince Nikolas de Liechtenstein; First Sec: Günther Ettl.

Macedonia, Former Yugoslav Republic: 209a ave Louise, 1050 Brussels, Belgium; tel (2) 732-91-08; fax (2) 732-91-11; e-mail mk.mission@brutele.be; Ambassador: Sasko Stefkov; Minister-Counsellor: Dimitar Beltsev.

Madagascar: 276 ave de Tervuren, 1150 Brussels, Belgium; tel (2) 770-17-26; fax (2) 772-37-31; e-mail info@ambassademadagascar.be; www.ambassademadagascar.be; Ambassador: Jean Omer Beriziky.

Malawi: 15 rue de la Loi, 1040 Brussels, Belgium; tel (2) 231-09-80; fax (2) 231-10-66; e-mail malawi.embassy@pi.be; Ambassador: Dr Jerry A. A. Jana.

Malaysia: 414a ave de Tervuren, 1150 Brussels, Belgium; tel (2) 776-03-40; fax (2) 762-50-49; e-mail mwbrusel@euronet.be; Ambassador: Dato' Deva Mohd Ridzam bin Abdullah; Dep Head of Mission, Minister-Counsellor: Zainal Abidin Bakar.

Maldives: East 47th St, Apt 15B, New York, NY 10017, USA; tel (212) 688-0776.

Mali: 487 ave Molière, 1050 Brussels, Belgium; tel (2) 345-74-32; fax (2) 344-57-00; e-mail ambassademali@skynet.be; Ambassador: Ibrahim B. Ba.

Marshall Islands: 800 2nd Ave, 18th Floor, New York, NY 10017, USA; tel (212) 983-30-40; fax (212) 983-32-02; e-mail rmiun@aol.com.

Mauritania: 6 ave de la Colombie, 1000 Brussels, Belgium; tel (2) 672-18-02; fax (2) 672-20-51; e-mail amb.bxl.mauritanie@skynet.be; internet www.mauritania.com; Ambassador: Aliou Ibra Ba.

Mauritius: 68 rue des Bollandistes, 1040 Brussels, Belgium; tel (2) 733-99-88; fax (2) 734-40-21; e-mail ambmaur@skynet.be; Ambassador: Sutiawan Gunessee.

Mexico: 94 ave F. D. Roosevelt, 1050 Brussels, Belgium; tel (2) 629-07-11; fax (2) 644-08-19; e-mail embamexbel@pophost.eunet.be; Ambassador: Porfirio Alejandro Muñños Ledo y Lazo de la Vega; Minister, Dep Head of Mission: Jorge Chen Charpentier.

Moldova: 54 rue Tenbosch, 1050 Brussels, Belgium; tel (2) 732-96-59; fax (2) 732-96-60; e-mail moldovamission@brutele.be; Ambassador: Mihai Popov; Dep Head of Mission, Counsellor: Veaceslav Pituscan.

Monaco: 17 place Guy d'Arezzo, 1180 Brussels, Belgium; tel (2) 347-49-87; fax (2) 343-49-20; Ambassador: Jean Pastorelli.

Mongolia: 18 ave Besme, 1190 Brussels, Belgium; tel (2) 344-69-74; fax (2) 344-32-15; e-mail sonon@chello.be; internet users.skynet.be/mongolia; Ambassador: Onon Sodoviin.

Morocco: 275 ave Louise, 1050 Brussels, Belgium; tel (2) 626-34-10; fax (2) 626-34-34; e-mail mission.maroc@skynet.be; Ambassador: Fath'allah Sijilmassi; Dep Head of Mission, First Counsellor: Nabil Adghoghi.

Mozambique: 97 blvd Saint-Michel, 1040 Brussels, Belgium; tel (2) 736-25-64; fax (2) 735-62-07; e-mail embamoc.bru@skynet.be; Ambassador: Maria Manuela dos Santos Lucas.

Myanmar: 60 rue de Courcelles, 75008 Paris, France; tel 1-42-25-56-95; fax 1-42-56-49-41; e-mail me-paris@wanadoo.fr; internet www.myanmarembassyparis.com; Ambassador: U Wunna Maung Lwin; Minister-Counsellor: Myint Soe.

Namibia: 454 ave de Tervuren, 1150 Brussels, Belgium; tel (2) 771-14-10; fax (2) 771-96-89; e-mail nam.emb@brutele.be; Ambassador: Peter Hitjitevi Katjavivi.

Nepal: 210 ave Brugman, 1050 Brussels, Belgium; tel (2) 346-26-58; fax (2) 344-13-61; e-mail rne.bru@skynet.be; Ambassador: Narayan Shumshere Thapa; Dep Head of Mission, Counsellor: Shanker Bairagi.

New Zealand: 1 square de Meeûs, 1000 Brussels, Belgium; tel (2) 512-10-40; fax (2) 513-48-56; e-mail nzemb.bru@skynet.be; Ambassador: Wade Armstrong; Dep Head of Mission, Counsellor: Stephen Payton.

Nicaragua: 55 ave de Wolvendael, 1180 Brussels, Belgium; tel (2) 375-65-00; fax

(2) 375-71-88; e-mail sky77706@skynet.be; Chargé d'affaires a.i.: Ricardo Paúl Lira.

Niger: 78 ave F. D. Roosevelt, 1050 Brussels, Belgium; tel (2) 648-59-60; fax (2) 648-27-84; e-mail ambnigerbxl@advalvas.be; Ambassador: Abdou Agbarry.

Nigeria: 288 ave de Tervuren, 1150 Brussels, Belgium; tel (2) 762-52-00; fax (2) 762-37-63; e-mail nigeriaembassy@belgacom.net; www.nigeriabru.net; Chargé d'affaires a.i.: V. A. Okoedion.

Niue: 10 rue Berckmans, 1060 Brussels, Belgium; tel (2) 543-10-00; fax (2) 543-10-01; e-mail cookislands@prmltd.com; Ambassador: Todd McClay.

Norway: 17 rue Archimède, 1000 Brussels, Belgium; tel (2) 234-11-11; fax (2) 234-11-50; e-mail eu.brussels@mfa.no; internet www.eu-norway.org; Ambassador: Bjorn T. Grydeland; Minister, Dep Head of Mission: Elisabeth Walaas.

Oman: 27 Koninginnegracht, 2514 AB The Hague, Netherlands; tel (70) 361-58-00; fax (70) 360-53-64; e-mail embassyoman@wanadoo.nl; Ambassador: Khadija bint Hassan Salman al-Lawati.

Pakistan: 57 ave Delleur, 1170 Brussels, Belgium; tel (2) 673-80-07; fax (2) 675-83-94; e-mail parepbrussels@skynet.be; Ambassador: Tariq Fatemi; Counsellor, Dep Head of Mission: Nasrullah Khan.

Panama: 390–392 ave Louise, BP 2, 1050 Brussels, Belgium; tel (2) 649-07-29; fax (2) 648-92-16; e-mail embajada.panama@skynet.be; Ambassador: Rolando Guevara Alvarado; Minister-Counsellor: Elena Barletta de Nottebohm.

Papua New Guinea: 430 ave de Tervuren, 1150 Brussels, Belgium; tel (2) 779-06-09; fax (2) 772-70-88; e-mail kundu.brussels@skynet.be; Chargé d'affaires a.i.: Kapi Maro.

Paraguay: 475 ave Louise, 1050 Brussels, Belgium; tel (2) 649-90-55; fax (2) 647-42-48; e-mail embapar@skynet.be; Ambassador: Emilio Gimenez Franco.

Peru: 179 ave de Tervuren, 1150 Brussels, Belgium; tel (2) 733-33-19; fax (2) 733-48-19; e-mail comunicaciones@embassy-of-peru.be; Ambassador: José Urrutia; Minister: Juan Carlos Gamarra.

Philippines: 297 ave Molière, 1050 Brussels, Belgium; tel (2) 340-33-77; fax (2) 345-64-25; e-mail brussels.pe/pm-eu@skynet.be; internet www.philembassy.be; Ambassador: Clemencio F. Montesa; First Sec: Alex V. Lamadrid.

Qatar: 57 quai d'Orsay, 75007 Paris, France; tel 1-45-51-90-71; fax 1-45-51-77-07; Chargé d'affaires a.i.: Khamis B. as-Sahoti.

Romania: 12 rue Montoyer, 1000 Brussels, Belgium; tel (2) 700-06-40; fax (2) 700-06-41; e-mail bru@roumisue.org; internet www.roumisue.org; Ambassador: Lazar Comanescu; Dep Head of Mission, Minister-Counsellor: Viorel Ardeleanu.

Russia: 31–33 blvd du Régent, 1000 Brussels, Belgium; tel (2) 502-17-91; fax (2) 513-76-49; e-mail misrusce@mail.interpac.be; Minister (Political Affairs), Dep Head of Mission: Andrei Avetisyan; Minister (Economic Affairs), Dep Head of Mission: Evgeny Manakin; Dep Head of Mission: Konstantin Trofimov; First Counsellor (Political Affairs), Dep Head of Mission: Mikhail Petrakov.

Rwanda: 1 ave des Fleurs, 1150 Brussels, Belgium; tel (2) 763-07-21; fax (2) 763-07-53; e-mail ambarwanda@skynet.be; internet ambarwanda.net; Ambassador: Emmanuel Kayitana Imanzi; First Counsellor: Augustin Habimana.

Saint Christopher and Nevis: 42 rue de Livourne, 1000 Brussels, Belgium; tel (2) 534-26-11; fax (2) 539-40-09; e-mail ecs.embassies@skynet.be; internet www.caribisles.org; Ambassador: Georges Bullen; Minister-Counsellor: Dr Arnold Thomas.

Saint Lucia: 42 rue de Livourne, 1000 Brussels, Belgium; tel (2) 534-26-11; fax (2) 539-40-09; e-mail ecs.embassies@skynet.be; internet www.caribisles.org; Ambassador: Georges Bullen; Minister-Counsellor: Dr Arnold Thomas.

Saint Vincent and the Grenadines: 42 rue de Livourne, 1000 Brussels, Belgium; tel (2) 534-26-11; fax (2) 539-40-09; e-mail ecs.embassies@skynet.be; internet www.caribisles.org; Ambassador: Georges Bullen; Minister-Counsellor: Dr Arnold Thomas.

Samoa: 123 ave F. D. Roosevelt, BP 14, 1050 Brussels, Belgium; tel (2) 660-84-54; fax (2) 675-03-36; e-mail samoa.emb.bxl@skynet.be; Ambassador: Tau'ili'ili Uili Meredith.

San Marino: 62 ave F. D. Roosevelt, 1050 Brussels, Belgium; tel (2) 644-22-24; fax (2) 644-20-57; e-mail ambrsm.bxl@coditel.net; Ambassador: Savina Zafferani.

São Tomé e Príncipe: 175 ave de Tervuren, 1150 Brussels, Belgium; tel (2) 734-89-66; fax (2) 734-88-15; e-mail ambassade.sao.tome@skynet.be; Chargé d'affaires a.i.: António de Lima Viegas.

Saudi Arabia: 45 ave F. D. Roosevelt, 1050 Brussels, Belgium; tel (2) 649-20-44; fax (2) 647-24-92; Ambassador: Nassir A. H. al-Assaf.

Senegal: 196 ave F. D. Roosevelt, 1050 Brussels, Belgium; tel (2) 673-00-97; fax (2) 675-04-60; e-mail senegal.ambassade@coditel.net; Ambassador: Saliou Cisse.

Serbia and Montenegro: 11 ave Emile de Mot, 1000 Brussels, Belgium; tel (2) 649-83-65; fax (2) 649-08-78; e-mail mission.rfy@skynet.be; Ambassador: Pavle Jevremović.

Seychelles: 51 ave Mozart, 75016 Paris, France; tel 1-42-30-57-47; fax 1-42-30-57-40; e-mail ambsey@aol.com; Ambassador: Callixte François-Xavier d'Offay.

Sierra Leone: 410 ave de Tervuren, 1150 Brussels, Belgium; tel (2) 771-00-53; fax (2) 771-82-30; Ambassador: Fode Maclean Dabor.

Singapore: 198 ave F. D. Roosevelt, 1050 Brussels, Belgium; tel (2) 660-29-79; fax (2) 660-86-85; e-mail amb.eu@singembbru.be; Ambassador: Walter Woon; First Sec: Siew Fei Chin.

Solomon Islands: 17 ave Edouard Lacomblé, 1040 Brussels, Belgium; tel (2) 732-70-85; fax (2) 732-68-85; e-mail siembassy@compuserve.com; internet www.commerce.gov.sb; Ambassador: Robert Sisilo.

South Africa: 26 rue de la Loi, BP 14–15, 1040 Brussels, Belgium; tel (2) 285-44-60; fax (2) 285-44-87; e-mail saembassy.belgium@swing.be; internet www.ambassade.net/southafrica/index.html; Ambassador: Jeremy Matthews Matjila; Minister: Albert Manley.

Sri Lanka: 27 rue Jules Lejeune, 1050 Brussels, Belgium; tel (2) 344-53-94; fax (2) 344-67-37; e-mail sri.lanka@euronet.be; Ambassador: Chrysantha R. Jayasinghe; Minister (Economic and Commercial Affairs): A. A. K. Perera.

Sudan: 124 ave F. D. Roosevelt, 1050 Brussels, Belgium; tel (2) 647-51-59; fax (2) 648-34-99; e-mail sudanbxl@yahoo.com; Ambassador: Dr Ali Yousif Ahmed.

Suriname: 379 ave Louise, BP 20, 1050 Brussels, Belgium; tel (2) 640-11-72; fax (2) 646-39-62; e-mail sur.amb.bru@online.be; Ambassador: Gerhard Hiwat.

Swaziland: 188 ave Winston Churchill, 1180 Brussels, Belgium; tel (2) 347-47-71; fax (2) 347-46-23; Ambassador: Dr Thembayena Annastasia Dlamini.

Switzerland: 1 place du Luxembourg, 1000 Brussels, Belgium; tel (2) 286-13-11; fax (2) 230-45-09; e-mail vertretung@brm.rep.admin.ch; internet www.eda.admin.ch/brussels_miss/f/home.html; Ambassador: Dante Martinelli; Minister, Dep Head of Mission: Philippe Guex.

Syria: 3 ave F. D. Roosevelt, 1050 Brussels, Belgium; tel (2) 648-01-35; fax (2) 646-40-18; Ambassador: Toufic Salloum.

Tajikistan: 363–365 ave Louise, BP 14, 1050 Brussels, Belgium; tel (2) 640-69-33; fax (2) 649-01-95; e-mail tajemb-belgium@skynet.be; Ambassador: Sharif Rakhimov.

Tanzania: 363 ave Louise, 1050 Brussels, Belgium; tel (2) 640-65-00; fax (2) 646-80-26; e-mail tanzania@skynet.be; Ambassador: Ali Abeid Aman Karume.

Thailand: 2 square du Val de la Cambre, 1050 Brussels, Belgium; tel (2) 640-68-10; fax (2) 648-30-66; e-mail thaibxl@pophost .eunet.be; internet www.waw.be/rte-be; Ambassador: (vacant); Minister: Sonchai Ninnad.

Timor-Leste: 12 ave Cortenbergh, 1000 Brussels, Belgium; tel (2) 280-00-96; fax (2) 280-02-77; Ambassador: José Antonio Amorim Dias.

Togo: 264 ave de Tervuren, 1150 Brussels, Belgium; tel (2) 770-17-91; fax (2) 771-50-75; Ambassador: Ohara Kati Korga; Minister-Counsellor: Anani Kokou Nyawouame.

Tonga: 36 Molyneux St, London, W1H 6AB, United Kingdom; tel (20) 7724-5828; fax (20) 7723-9074; e-mail fetu@ btinternet.com; Ambassador: Fetu'utolu Tupou.

Trinidad and Tobago: 14 ave de la Faisanderie, 1150 Brussels, Belgium; tel (2) 762-94-00; fax (2) 772-27-83; e-mail information@ttm.eunet.be; Ambassador: Learie Edgar Rousseau; Minister-Counsellor: Susan Nancy Gordan.

Tunisia: 278 ave de Tervuren, 1150 Brussels, Belgium; tel (2) 771-73-95; fax (2) 771-94-33; e-mail amb.detunisie@ brutele.be; Ambassador: Tahar Sioud.

Turkey: 4 rue Montoyer, 1000 Brussels, Belgium; tel (2) 513-28-36; fax (2) 511-04-50; e-mail info@turkdeleg.org; Ambassador: Mustafa Oguz Demiralp.

Turkmenistan: 106 ave F. D. Roosevelt, 1050 Brussels, Belgium; tel (2) 648-18-74; fax (2) 648-19-06; Ambassador: Niyazklych Nurklychev.

Uganda: 317 ave de Tervuren, 1150 Brussels, Belgium; tel (2) 762-58-25; fax (2) 763-04-38; e-mail ugembrus@brutele .be; Chargé d'affaires a.i.: Lewis D. Balinda.

Ukraine: 99–101 ave Louis Lepoutre, 1180 Brussels, Belgium; tel (2) 340-98-72; fax (2) 340-98-79; e-mail pr_es@mfa .gov.ua; internet www.ukraine-eu.mfa .gov.eu; Ambassador: Roman Vasyliovych Shpek; Dep Head of Mission, Minister-Counsellor (Political Affairs): Kostiantyn Yeliseyev.

United Arab Emirates: 73 ave F. D. Roosevelt, 1050 Brussels, Belgium; tel (2) 640-60-00; fax (2) 646-24-73; e-mail uae_embassy@skynet.be; Ambassador: Abdel Hadi Abdel Wahid al-Khajah; Minister-Counsellor: Abdulla Sulaiman al-Hammadi.

USA: 13 rue Zinner, 1000 Brussels, Belgium; tel (2) 508-22-22; fax (2) 514-43-39; e-mail vvvbrus@pd.state.gov; internet www.useu.be; Ambassador: Rockwell A. Schnabel; Minister-Counsellor, Dep Head of Mission: Dr James J. Foster.

Uruguay: 22 ave F. D. Roosevelt, 1050 Brussels, Belgium; tel (2) 640-11-69; fax (2) 648-29-09; e-mail uruemb@skynet.be; Ambassador: Elbio Oscar Rosselli Frieri; Minister-Counsellor: Julio Tealdi.

Uzbekistan: 99 ave F. D. Roosevelt, 1050 Brussels, Belgium; tel (2) 672-88-44; fax (2) 672-39-46; e-mail ambassador@ uzbekistan.be; internet www.eu .uzbekembassy.com; Ambassador: Alisher Shaykhov.

Vanuatu: 125 ave Paul Hymans, BP 3, 1200 Brussels, Belgium; tel (2) 736-90-93.

Venezuela: 10 ave F. D. Roosevelt, 1050 Brussels, Belgium; tel (2) 639-03-40; fax (2) 647-88-20; e-mail embajada@ venezuela-eu.org; internet www .venezuela-eu.org; Ambassador: Luisa Romero Bermudez.

Viet Nam: 1 blvd Général Jacques, 1050 Brussels, Belgium; tel (2) 379-27-37; fax (2) 374-93-76; e-mail vnemb.brussels@ skynet.be; internet vietnamfestival.com; Ambassador: Phan Thuy Thanh; Minister-Counsellor: Dinh Kha Ngo.

Yemen: 114 ave F. D. Roosevelt, 1050 Brussels, Belgium; tel (2) 646-52-90; fax (2) 646-29-11; e-mail gazem@skynet.be; Ambassador: Dr Jaffer Mohamed Jaffer.

Zambia: 469 ave Molière, 1060 Brussels, Belgium; tel (2) 343-56-49; fax (2) 347-43-33; e-mail zambiansbrussels@skynet.be; Ambassador: Irene Mumba Kamanga.

Zimbabwe: 11 square Joséphine-Charlotte, 1200 Brussels, Belgium; tel (2) 762-58-08; fax (2) 762-96-05; e-mail zimbrussels@skynet.be; Ambassador: Gift Punungwe; Dep Head of Mission, Minister-Counsellor: Dr Godfrey Chipare; Minister-Counsellor (Political Affairs): Ignatius Graham Mudzimba.

LIAISON OFFICES OF INTERNATIONAL ORGANIZATIONS IN THE EUROPEAN UNION

Council of Europe: Résidence Palace, 155 rue de la Loi, BP 3, 1040 Brussels, Belgium; tel (2) 230-41-70; fax (2) 230-94-62; e-mail bureau.bruxelles@coe.int; internet www.coe.int; Dir: Thomas Ouchterlony.

European Free Trade Association (EFTA): 74 rue de Trèves, 1040 Brussels, Belgium; tel (2) 286-17-11; fax (2) 286-17-50; e-mail efta-mailbox@efta.int; Dir P. Mannes.

International Labour Organization (ILO): 40 rue Aimé Smekens, 1030 Brussels, Belgium; tel (2) 736-59-42; fax (2) 735-48-25; e-mail brussels@ilo.org; internet www.ilo.org/europe; Dir: Eddy Laurijssen.

United Nations (UN): 14 rue Montoyer, 1000 Brussels, Belgium; tel (2) 289-28-90; fax (2) 502-40-61; e-mail unicbel@mbox .unicc.org; Dir: H. Fodha.

UN High Commissioner for Refugees (UNHCR): 11b rue Van Eyck, 1050 Brussels, Belgium; tel (2) 649-0151; fax (2) 627-17-32; e-mail belbr@unhcr.ch; internet www.unhcr.ch; Senior Liaison Officer: Johannes van der Klaauw.

REGIONAL AUTHORITIES WITH REPRESENTATIONS IN BRUSSELS

ASSOCIATIONS WITH LOCAL AND REGIONAL POWERS

Alliance des Intérêts Maritimes Régionaux en Europe – AMRIE: Rue du Commerce 20-22, 1000 Brussels; tel (2) 736 17 55; fax (2) 735 22 98; e-mail imazieres@amrie.org, info@amrie.org; contacts Jacques Mazières (Managing Director), Michael Lloyd (Deputy Director).

Assemblée des Régions D – Are'Europe: Place Sainctelette 2, 1080 Brussels; tel (2) 421 85 12; fax (2) 421 84 81; e-mail s.cools@mrw.wallonie.be, secretariat@are-regions-europe.org; contact Stéphane Cools (Director).

Association Européenne des Elus de Montagne – AEM: Avenue des Arts 1 Bte 9, 1210 Brussels; tel (2) 221 04 39; fax (2) 217 69 87; e-mail aem@promote-aem .org; contacts Luciano Caveri (President), Carlos Pinto (Secretary).

Communauté de Travail des Régions Alpines – Arge Alp: Avenue de Cortenbergh 52/4, 1000 Brussels; tel (2) 743 27 00; fax (2) 742 09 80; e-mail info@argealp .org; contact Fritz Staudigl (Secretary).

Conférence des Régions Périphériques Maritimes (CRPM): Square Marie-Louise 77, 1000 Brussels; tel (2) 230 74 99; fax (2) 280 27 65; e-mail crpm .bruxelles@skynet.be; contact Pascal Gruselle (Delegate).

Conseil des Communes et Régions d'Europe – CCRE: Rue d'Arlon 22-24, 1050 Brussels; tel (2) 511 74 77; fax (2) 511 09 49; e-mail cemr@ccre.org, jeremy .smith@bxl-ccre.org; contacts Jeremy Smith (Secretary General), Walter Wenzel (Director).

Coopération Subrégionale des Etats de la Mer Baltique – CSREMB: Avenue Palmerston 20, 1000 Brussels; tel (2) 285 46 20; fax (2) 285 46 57; e-mail guenther.schulz@hobru.landsh.de; contact Guenther Schultz.

Eurocities: Square de Meeûs 18, 1050 Brussels; tel (2) 552 08 88, (2) 552 08 86; fax (2) 552 08 89; e-mail c.parmentier@ eurocities.be, info@eurocities.be; contacts Eva Ritta (President), Catherine Parmentier (Chief Executive Officer).

European Industrial Regions Association – EIRA: Rue Joseph II 36-38, 1000 Brussels; tel (2) 230 91 07; fax (2) 230 27 12; e-mail secretariat@eira.org;

contacts Roger Stone (President), Maria Domzal (Policy Officer).

Union des Capitales de l'Union Européenne: Hôtel de Ville, Grand-Place, 1000 Brussels; tel (2) 279 49 52; fax (2) 279 23 91; e-mail francis.deleau@brucity .be; contact Francis Deleau.

AUSTRIA

Bureau de Liaison de la Haute-Autriche: Rue Joseph II 36, 1000 Brussels; tel (2) 223 14 04; fax (2) 219 20 87; e-mail eub.post@ooe.gv.at; contact Dr Gérald Lonauer (Director).

Bureau de Liaison de Salzbourg: Rue Frédéric Pelletier 107, 1030 Brussels; tel (2) 743 07 60; fax (2) 743 07 61; e-mail bruessel@salzburg.gv.at, gritlind.kettl@ salzbourg.gv.at; contact Gritlind Kettl (Manager).

Land Kärnten – Bureau de Liaison: Avenue d'Auderghem 67, 1040 Brussels; tel (2) 282 49 10; fax (2) 280 43 80; e-mail sekretariat@vbb-karnten.com; contacts Martina Rattinger (Director), Elisabeth Pirstinger.

Land Tirol / Tirol Buro: Avenue de Cortenbergh 52, 1000 Brussels; tel (2) 743 27 00; fax (2) 742 09 80; e-mail info@ alpeuregio.org, r.seeber@alpeuregio.org; contacts Dr Richard Seeber (Head of Office), Dagmar Hoebarth (Assistant).

Liaison Office of the City of Vienna: Avenue de Tervueren 58, 1040 Brussels; tel (2) 743 85 00; fax (2) 733 70 58; e-mail post@be.magwien.gv.at; contacts Eva Pretscher (Director), Martin Schimek (Deputy Director).

Niederösterreich: Rue Montoyer 14, 1000 Brussels; tel (2) 549 06 67-68; fax (2) 502 60 09; e-mail post.noevbb@noel.gv .at; internet www.noel.gv.at; contacts Roland Langthaler (Rep./COR), Benedikt Madl (Deputy Director).

Österreichischer Gemeindebund: Avenue de Cortenbergh 30, 1040 Brussels; tel (2) 282 06 80; fax (2) 282 06 88; e-mail 106162.3302@compuserve.com; contact Michaela Petz.

Österreichischer Stadtebund: Avenue de Cortenbergh 30, 1040 Brussels; tel (2) 282 06 80; fax (2) 282 06 82; e-mail stb-bxl@wanadoo.be; contact Simone Wolesa.

Représentation Permanente de l'Autriche – Représentation des Lander: Avenue de Cortenbergh 30, 1040

Brussels; tel (2) 230 54 43; fax (2) 230 25 44; e-mail post@bruessel.vst.gv.at, klemens.fischer@bruessel.vst.gv.at; contact Dr Klemens Fischer (Minister Counsellor).

Steiermark Büro: Place des Gueux 8, 1000 Brussels; tel (2) 732 03 61; fax (2) 732 12 63; e-mail ta3b-bxl@stmk.gv.at; contacts Erich Korzinek, Claudia Suppan.

Verbindungsbüro des Landes Burgenland zur Europaischen Union: Rue Montoyer 39, 1000 Brussels; tel (2) 514 30 11; fax (2) 514 23 91; e-mail andrea .krainer@bgld.gv.at, post.bruessel@bgld .gv.at; contact Andrea Krainer.

Vienna Business Agency (Wiener WirtschaftSförderungsfonds): Avenue de Tervueren 58, 1040 Brussels; tel (2) 743 85 16; fax (2) 733 70 58; e-mail dos@be.magwien.gv.at; contact Suzanne Strohm (Director).

BELGIUM

Administration Régionale pour les Affaires Européennes en Belgique pour la Communauté Germanophone: Klötzerbahn 32, 4700 Eupen; contact Carl Hellebrandt (Secretary General).

Administration Régionale pour les Affaires Européennes en Belgique pour la Communauté Germanophone – Commissariat Général aux Relations Internationales: Saincteletteplein 2, 1000 Brussels; contact Francine Nagels (Contact Person).

Bureau de la Communauté Germanophone à Bruxelles: Rue des Minimes 21, 1000 Brussels; tel (2) 502 30 80; fax (2) 502 76 46; e-mail xavier.kalbusch@dgov .be; contact Xavier Kalbusch (Director).

Bureau de Liaison Bruxelles-Europe: Avenue d'Auderghem 63, 1040 Bruxelles; tel (2) 280 00 80; fax (2) 280 03 86; e-mail blbe@irisnet.be; contacts Carlo Luyckx (Director), Annemarie Renard.

Délégation Générale de la Communauté Française Auprès de l'Union Européenne: Rond-Point Schuman 6, 1040 Brussels; tel (2) 233 21 86-87; fax (2) 280 34 38; e-mail yves.degreef@ belgoeurop.diplobel.fgov.be; contact Yves De Greef (General Delegate).

Direction des Relations Extérieures, Ministère de la Région de Bruxelles-Capitale: Boulevard du Botanique 20,

1035 Bruxelles; tel (2) 204 21 11; e-mail cmancel@mbhg.irisnet.be; contacts Nobert de Cooman (Direction Relations Extérieures), Caroline Mancel (Attachée).

Espace International Wallonie-Bruxelles CGRI: Place Sainctelette 2, 1080 Brussels; tel (2) 421 82 11, (2) 421 82 77; fax (2) 421 84 81, (2) 421 87 64; e-mail hindey@cgri.cfwb.be; contacts Philippe Suinen (General Manager – General Commissioner), Jean Beelen (Responsible for relations with the Committee of the Regions).

Ministère de la Région Wallonne Direction Générale des Pouvoirs Locaux: Rue Van Opre 95, 5100 Jambes; tel (81) 32 37 24-29; fax (81) 30 90 93; e-mail b.fontaine@mrw.wallonie.be, py.bolen@mrw.wallonie.be; contacts B. Fontaine (1er attaché), Pierre-Yves Bolen (attaché).

Ministère de l'Administration de la Communauté Flamande, Section Europe: Boudewijnlaan 30, 1000 Brussels; tel (2) 553 60 32; fax (2) 553 60 37; e-mail isabelle.dirkx@coo.vlaanderen.be; contacts Diane Verstraeten (Managing Director), Isabelle Dirkx (EU Affairs).

Représentation Permanente de la Région Bruxelles Capitale auprès de l'Union Européenne: Rond Point Schuman 6, 1040 Brussels; tel (2) 233 03 02; fax (2) 280 40 04; e-mail pgoergen@europ.irisnet.be; contacts Pascal Goergen (Représentant), Geert De Proost (Représentant Adjoint).

Représentation Permanente de la Région Flamande auprès des Communautés Européennes: Rond Point Schuman 6, 1040 Brussels; tel (2) 233 03 12; fax (2) 233 03 12; e-mail vlaamse@belgoeurop.diplobel.fgov.be; contact Filip D'Have (Director).

Union des Villes et Communes Belges: Rue d'Arlon 53 Bte 4, 1040 Bruxelles; tel (2) 233 20 01; fax (2) 231 15 23; e-mail vbsg@pop.kpn.be; contact Thérèse Renier (Responsible for the COR).

Union des Villes et Communes de Wallonie – Cellule Europe: Rue d'Arlon 53 Bte 4, 1040 Bruxelles; tel (2) 233 20 83; fax (2) 233 31 13; e-mail isabelle.compagnie@uvcw.be; contact Isabelle Compagnie.

CANADA

Délégation Générale du Québec (Quebec Government Office): Avenue des Arts 46, 1000 Brussels; tel (2) 512 00 36; fax (2) 514 26 41; e-mail qc.bruxelles@mri.gouv.qc.ca; contacts Véronique Guevremont (Adviser – EU Affairs), Nicole Stafford (Gen Del).

DENMARK

Aarhus E.C. Office: Av. de Tervuren 35, 1040 Brussels; tel (2) 230 87 32; fax (2) 230 89 52; e-mail info@bxl.aarhus.dk; internet www.aarhus.dk/bruxelles; contact Jacob Haarup Jorgensen (Director).

Association of County Councils in Denmark: Rue de la Science 4-6, 1000 Brussels; tel (2) 550 12 80; fax (2) 550 12 75; e-mail arf@arf.be; contact Asger Andreasen.

Copenhagen City Office: Avenue Palmerston 26, 1000 Brussels; tel (2) 285 43 20; fax (2) 285 43 29; e-mail adm@copenhagencity.be, marc.joergensen@copenhagencity.be; internet www.copenhagencity.dk; contacts Esther Bulow Davidsen (Head of Office), Marc Jorgensen (Deputy Head of Office).

Eura EU Office: Avenue de Tervuren 35, 1040 Brussels; tel (2) 230 72 02; fax (2) 280 17 59; e-mail eurabxl@eurabxl.com; contacts Ingrida Seduikyte, Hans Kurt Rasmussen, Agnes Uhereczky.

EU-Vest: Rue du Cornet 22, 1040 Brussels; tel (2) 280 32 54; fax (2) 280 33 29; e-mail jkp@euvest.com; internet www.euvest.com; contact Johnny Killerup Pedersen (Director).

Local Government Denmark (LGDK): Rue de la Science 4-6, 1000 Brussels; tel (2) 550 12 60; fax (2) 550 12 72; e-mail tha@kl.dk; internet www.kl.dk; contact Thomas Alstrup (Responsible for relations with the COR).

North of Denmark EU Office: Avenue de Tervuren 35, 1040 Brussels; tel (2) 282 03 73; fax (2) 230 90 15; e-mail aalborgeu@aalborg.be; internet www.aalborgeu.be; contacts Charlotte Pedersen, Anne Britt Larsson.

Odense Denmark EU Office: Avenue Palmerston 3, 1000 Brussels; tel (2) 503 09 04; fax (2) 503 15 70; e-mail odense@odense.be; internet www.odense.be; contact Peter T. Saugman (Director).

South Denmark – European Office: Avenue Palmerston 3, 1000 Brussels; tel (2) 280 40 95; fax (2) 285 40 99; e-mail jakob.bork@southdenmark.be; contacts Jakob Bork (County of Fyn), Henrik Esmann (County of South Jutland).

Storstrom Region EU Office: South Denmark House, Avenue de Palmerston 3, 1000 Brussels; tel (2) 235 66 53; fax (2) 280 38 28; e-mail Kaas@oek.stam.dk; contact Katrine Aadal Andersen (Head of Office).

West Zealand EU Office: Avenue de Palmerston 3, 1000 Brussels; tel (2) 235 66 50; fax (2) 280 38 28; e-mail info@westzealand.be; contact Katarina Borgh-Rahm.

EU FORMER APPLICANT COUNTRIES

AACC – Association of Agricultural Co-operatives and Cities of the Czech Republic: Ch. d'Alsemberg 876, 1180 Brussels; tel (2) 376 10 81; fax (2) 376 10 81; e-mail km.agri@compaqnet.be; contact Karl Matousek.

Association of Lower Silesia in the EU (Poland): Avenue de Cortenbergh 75, 1000 Brussels; tel (2) 740 27 26; fax (2) 740 27 20; e-mail alsieu@sn.com.pl; contact Bogna Rodziewicz.

Association of Rural Communities of Pomerania – EU Affairs Office (Poland): Square de Meeûs 18, 1050 Brussels; tel (2) 505 34 47; fax (2) 505 34 41; e-mail pomerania@brutele.be; contact Alicja Galeziak.

Bureau de Liaison de la Région Autonome de Bratislava (Slovakia): Avenue Michel-Ange 75, 1200 Brussels; tel (2) 742 07 77; fax (2) 742 07 77; e-mail bratislava.region@skynet.be; contact Andrea Oelbrettschneider (Director – Rel./COR).

Czech European Center: Rond Point Schuman 6, 1040 Brussels; tel (2) 282 84 30; fax (2) 282 84 31; contact M. Milan (Director).

Delegation of Prague to the EU (Czech Republic): Avenue Palmerston 16, 1000 Brussels; tel (2) 230 94 91; fax (2) 230 94 91; e-mail zdenek.werner@mag.mepnet.cz; contact Werner Zdenek (Director).

Eastern Poland Euro-Office Lubelskie-Podlaskie (Poland): Rue de Trèves 49 bat. 7, 1040 Brussels; tel (2) 285 06 15; fax (2) 230 70 35; e-mail obara@taseuro.com; contact Anata Obara (Director).

Information Office of the Opole Voivodeship (Poland): Square de Meeûs 18, 1050 Brussels; tel (2) 550 10 30-31; fax (2) 505 34 41; e-mail opole@brutele.be; contact Marta Chudzikaewicz.

Kaunas Regional Representation: Rue Zinner 1, 1000 Brussels; tel (2) 289 60 04; fax (2) 289 60 01; e-mail gaile@bce-network.be; contact Gaile Kasmaciauskiene (Assistant Attaché for Regional Policy of the Lithuanian Mission to the EC).

Representation of Regions of Hungary: Square Vergote 5, 1200 Brussels; tel (2) 737 14 00; fax (2) 735 65 99; e-mail rep.hongrie@skynet.be; contacts Hans Beck (Director), Magdolna Baranyl (Rel./COR).

Representation of the Malopolskie Voivodeship (Poland): Rue de Trèves 49-51, 1040 Brussels; tel (2) 280 14 92; fax (2) 280 60 71; e-mail andrzej.pawlica@skynet.be; contact Andrzej Pawlica.

Representation Office of Budapest (Hungary): Avenue d'Auderghem 63, 1040 Brussels; tel (2) 230 78 57; fax (2) 230 90 04; e-mail bpoffic@skynet.be; contact Gizella Matyas (Director).

Representation Office of the Mazovia Region (Poland): Avenue Auderghem 63, 1040 Brussels; tel (2) 230 96 62; fax (2) 230 70 83; e-mail anna.burylo@skynet.be; contact Anna Burylo (Director).

Tallin (Estonia) EU Office: Rue du Luxembourg 3, 1000 Brussels; tel (2) 501 08 37; fax (2) 501 08 42; e-mail kaido .sirel@tallinnlv.ee, bruxelles@hot.ee; contact Kaido Sirel (Manager).

FINLAND

Association of Finnish Local and Regional Authorities: Rue de la Science 4, 1000 Brussels; tel (2) 502 87 38, GSM: (2) 478 33 83 22; fax (2) 502 72 27; e-mail jorma.palola@aflra.fi; contact J. Palola (Permanent representative).

City of Turku – Southwest Finland European Office: Rue du Luxembourg 14 A, 1000 Brussels; tel (2) 287 12 95; fax (2) 287 12 09; e-mail european.office@turku.fi; contact Krista Taipale-Salminen (Head of Office).

East Finland EU Office: Scotland House, Rond Point Schuman 6, 1040 Brussels; tel (2) 282 83 70-71, GSM: (2) 474 90 60 21; fax (2) 282 83 73; e-mail jani .taivalantti@pophost.eunet.be, lisbeth .mattsson@eastfinland.org; internet www.eastfinland.fi; contacts Jani Taivalantti (Director), Lisbeth Mattsson (Adviser).

European North – Lapland Oulu (Finland): Rond-Point Schuman 6 Bte 5, 1040 Brussels; tel (2) 234 63 70, (2) 234 63 74; fax (2) 234 79 11; e-mail seppo .heikkila@lapland-oulu.fi, satu.huuha@lapland-oulu.fi; contacts Seppo Heikkila (Director), Satu Huuha (Special Adviser).

Helsinki EU Office: Rue du Luxembourg 14a, 1000 Brussels; tel (2) 287 12 50, GSM: (+358 50) 307 18 82; fax (2) 287 12 57; e-mail helsinki.euoffice@hel.fi, eija.nylund@euhel.be; internet www .uudenmanliitto.fi; contact Eija Nylund (Head of Office).

Rovaniemi-Lapland Office: Rue d'Arlon 38, 1000 Brussels; tel (2) 233 37 31; fax (2) 230 23 91; e-mail henri .hirvenoja@laplandoffice.be; internet www.rovaniemi.fi; contacts Henri Hirvenoja (Director), Kim Kuivelainen (Rel./COR).

South Finland EU Office: Av de Tervuren 35, 1040 Brussels; tel (2) 282 03 78; fax (2) 230 90 15; e-mail loikkanen@euronet.be; contact Tuula Loikkanen (Director).

Tampere EU Office: Avenue Palmerston 3, 1000 Brussels; tel (2) 503 14 89; fax (2) 503 15 70; e-mail markku .valtonen@odense.be, tampere@odense .be; contact Markku Valtonen (General Delegate).

West Finland European Office: rue Joseph II 36-38, 1000 Brussels; tel (2) 286 90 80-81; fax (2) 286 90 89; e-mail european.office@westfinland.be, kari .hietala@westfinland.be, elina.humala@westfinland.be; contacts Kari Hietala (Director), Elina Humula (Assistant).

FRANCE

Antenne Basse-Normandie Europe: Avenue des Gaulois 3, 1040 Brussels; tel (2) 732 46 83; fax (2) 732 47 67; e-mail info@abne.be; contact Adeline Jacob (Chargée de mission).

Antenne de Bruxelles de la Région de Picardie: Avenue de la Joyeuse Entrée 1-5, 1040 Brussels; tel (2) 234 66 40; fax (2) 234 66 41; e-mail pierre.emmanuel .thomann@skynet.be; contact Pierre Emmanuel Thomann (Chargé de mission).

Antenne de la Collectivité Territoriale de Corse: Avenue des Arts 1-2 Bte 9, 1210 Brussels; tel (2) 221 04 35; fax (2) 217 66 12; e-mail ctc.dunyach@pophost.eunet.be, sbaron@acfci.cci.fr; contact Emmanuelle Thévignot Dunyach (Director).

Association des Maires de France: Avenue des Arts 39, 1040 Brussels; e-mail mkeller@amf.asso.fr; contacts François Leonelli (Director), Michael Keller (Responsible for COR).

Association des Régions Françaises du Grand Est: Rue d'Arlon 55, 1040 Brussels; tel (2) 231 10 50; fax (2) 230 38 48; e-mail grand.est@skynet.be; contacts Christophe Goult (Director), Florence Bonollo (Assistant).

Association Europe//Bretagne/Pays de la Loire: Avenue de Tervueren 12, 1040 Brussels; tel (2) 735 40 36; fax (2) 735 24 11; e-mail bretloire@bretloire.org; internet www.bretloire.org; contact Martine Allais (Director).

Association Poitou-Charentes Europe (APCE): Square Marie-Louise 77, 1000 Brussels; tel (2) 230 55 51; fax (2) 230 68 72; e-mail speyhorgue@apce.org; contact Stéphane Peyhorgue (Chargé de mission).

Association pour le Développement Européen de l'Ile-de-France – ADEIF: Rue Guimard 15, 1040 Brussels; tel (2) 289 25 10; fax (2) 513 63 74; e-mail adeif@adeif.be, f.chotard@adeif.be; internet www.adeif.be; contact Françoise Chotard (Director).

Bureau Alsace (Association for the Promotion of Alsace): Avenue des Arts 1-2 Bte 11, 1210 Brussels; tel (2) 221 04 30; fax (2) 217 66 12; e-mail b.alsace@easynet.be; contact Valérie Bour (Administrator).

Bureau Aquitaine Europe (Aquitaine Europe Office): Avenue de l'Yser 19, 1040 Brussels; tel (2) 738 04 74; fax (2) 738 04 75; e-mail info@bureau-aquitaine.be; contacts Marie-Pierre Mesplède (Representative for Aquitaine), Mathieu Grisel (Chargé de mission).

Bureau de Représentation de Provence-Alpes-Côte d'Azur à Bruxelles: Avenue des Celtes 20, 1040 Brussels; tel (02) 735 18 70; fax (02) 733 25 36; e-mail Representation.paca@wanadoo.be; contacts Cyrille Perez (Director), Lila Bettin (Regional Delegate), Stéphanie Vincent (Regional Delegate).

Chambres de Commerce Ile-de-France: Avenue des Arts 36, 1040 Brussels; tel (2) 223 18 40; fax (2) 223 18 56; e-mail europe@ccipif.be; contact Sandra Penning (Directrice).

Delegation à l'Aménagement du Territoire et à l'Action Régionale – Datar Europe: Place de Louvain 14, 1000 Brussels; tel (2) 229 84 71; fax (2) 229 84 75; e-mail patricia.pedelabat@diplomatie .gov.fr; contact Gilles Pelurson (CP).

Délégation de la Lorraine: Rue des Drapiers 40, 1050 Brussels; tel (2) 502 88 40; fax (2) 502 88 42; e-mail patrickcourtin@brutele.be, delegationlorraine@brutele.be; contact Patrick Courtin (Regional Representative).

Délégation de la Polynésie Française: Square Marie-Louise 2, 1000 Brussels; tel (2) 230 16 16; fax (2) 230 14 00; contact Bruno Peaucellier.

Délégation de la Région Limousin: Avenue de Tervuren 12, 1040 Brussels; tel (2) 733 35 17; fax (2) 734 25 82; e-mail limousin@compaqnet.be; contacts Colette Gadioux (Permanent Delegate), Anna Giglio (Assistant).

Délégation des Côtes d'Armor: Avenue Victor Gisoul 76, 1200 Brussels; tel (2) 771 58 71; fax (2) 771 58 71; contact Bernard Le Marchand.

Délégation du Conseil Régional de Haute-Normandie: Rue Montoyer 61, 1000 Brussels; tel (2) 235 08 23; fax (2) 230 13 20; e-mail haute-normandie@skynet.be, barbara.lehembre@cr-haute -normandie.fr; contacts Barbara Lehembre (Chargée de mission), Anouk Hattab (Rel./CdR).

Délégation du Nord-Pas-de-Calais: Rue de l'Industrie 11, 1000 Brussels; tel (2) 230 30 36; fax (2) 230 16 49; e-mail bureau.nordpasdecalais@skynet.be; contact Stéphane Gerbaud (Director).

Délégation Régionale de la Région Rhône-Alpes: Rue de Trèves 49-51 – Bte 2, 1040 Brussels; tel (2) 282 00 20; fax (2) 280 60 71; e-mail deleg.rhone -alpes@skynet.be; contact Frédérique Barellon (General Delegate).

Espace Moselle: Rue des Drapiers 40, 1050 Brussels; tel (2) 502 65 45; fax (2) 502 66 26; e-mail sales@espace-moselle .be; internet www.espace-moselle.be; contact Alain Swinnen.

Représentation Midi-Pyrénées: Rue d'Arlon 55, 1040 Brussels; tel (2) 280 09 19; fax (2) 230 67 83; e-mail elie.spiroux@ midipyreneeseurope.be; contact Elie Spiroux (Regional Delegate).

GERMANY

Beobachter der Lander: Rue de Trèves 45, 1040 Brussels; tel (2) 235 02 70; fax (2) 230 35 55; e-mail laenderbeobachter@ bruessel.eu-lb.de; contact Martin Bohle.

Büro des Landes Berlin: Avenue Michel-Ange 71, 1000 Brussels; tel (2) 738 00 70; fax (2) 732 47 46; e-mail renate .voelpel@lvbe.verwalt-berlin.de; contacts Gert Hammer (Director), Renate Volpel (Assistant Director (Responsible for the COR)).

Europabüro der Baden-Württember-gischen Kommunen: Rue Guimard 7, 1040 Brussels; tel (2) 513 65 46 – 513 64 08; fax (2) 513 88 20; e-mail c.glietsch@ europabuero-bw.de; contact Carsten Glietsch (Director).

Europabüro der Bayerischen Kom-munen: Rue Guimard 7, 1040 Brussels; tel (2) 549 07 00; fax (2) 512 24 51; e-mail info@ebbk.de; contact A. Poth-Mogele.

Europabüro der Deutschen Kom-munalen Selbstverwaltung (German Local Government European Office – Eurocommunale): Avenue de la Renaissance 1, 1000 Brussels; tel (2) 732 35 96; fax (2) 732 40 91; e-mail eurocommunale@arcadis.be; contacts Dr Ralf von Ameln (Director), Dr Klaus Nutzenberg (Deputy Director).

Europabüro der Sachsischen Kom-munen: Rue Guimard 7, 1040 Brussels; tel (2) 513 64 08; fax (2) 513 88 20; e-mail info@europabuero-sn.de.

Europabüro des Deutschen Land-kreistages & Baghkv: Avenue de la Renaissance 1, 1000 Brussels; tel (2) 740 16 30; fax (2) 740 16 31; e-mail sekretariat.dlt@eurocommunale.org; contact Régine Brunsl (Director).

Europabüro des Deutschen Städte und Gemeindebundes: Avenue de la Renaissance 1, 1000 Brussels; tel (2) 740 16 30; fax (2) 740 16 31; e-mail dstgb@ eurocommunale.org; contact Klaus Nutzenberg (Director).

Europabüro des Deutschen Städte-tages: Avenue de la Renaissance 1, 1000 Brussels; tel (2) 740 16 20; fax (2) 740 16 21; e-mail dst@eurocommunale .org; contact Walter Leitermann (Director).

Frankfurt Rhein-Main EU Office: Rue de l'Amazone 2, 1050 Brussels; tel (2) 535 72 40; fax (2) 534 96 96; e-mail repraesentanz-europa@frankfurt.de; contact Jorn Kronenwerth.

Hanse Office (Hambourg et Schles-wig-Holstein): Avenue Palmerston 20, 1000 Brussels; tel (2) 285 46 40; fax (2) 285 46 57; e-mail gunter.schulz@hobru .landsh.de; contacts Dr Franz Froschma-ier (Director), Günter Schulz (Deputy Director (Schleswig-Holstein – Responsi-ble for the COR)), Peter Scheck (Deputy Director (Hamburg)).

Informationsbüro des Landes Meck-lenburg-Vorpommern bei der Euro-päischen Union: Boulevard Louis Schmidt 87, 1040 Brussels; tel (2) 741 60 04; fax (2) 741 60 09; e-mail r.boest@ mv.bei-der-eu.de, k.schwander@mv.bei -der-eu.de; internet www.mv.bei-der-eu .de; contacts Reinhard Boest (Director), Kirsten Schwander.

Stuttgart Region European Office Stuttgart in Brussels: Square Vergote 39, 1030 Brussels; tel (2) 737 04 05; fax (2) 737 04 06; e-mail europa@region -stuttgart.de; contact Heike Thumm.

Thüringer Büro: Rue Frédéric Pelletier 111, 1030 Brussels; tel (2) 736 20 60; fax (2) 736 53 79; e-mail postbox@TSKBxl .thueringen.de; internet www.thuringer .de/de/tsk/tskbxl; contacts Paul Brock-hausen (Director), Holeshovsky (Responsible for COR).

Verbindung des Landes Branden-burg bei der Europäischen Union: Rue Père Eudore Devroye 47, 1040 Brussels; tel (2) 737 74 51-52; fax (2) 737 74 69; e-mail poststelle@mdjebrx .brandenburg.de; contact Marcus Wenig (Director).

Verbindungsbüro der Freien Han-sestadt Bremen bei der Euro-päischen Union: Avenue Palmerston 22, 1000 Brussels; tel (2) 230 27 65; fax (2) 230 36 58; e-mail vertretung@bremen .be, ripke@bremen.be; contacts Christian Bruns (Director), Constance Ripke (Responsible for the COR).

Verbindungsbüro des Landes Sachsen-Anhalt bei der Euro-päischen Union: Boulevard Saint-Michel 78-80, 1040 Brussels; tel (2) 741 09 33; fax (2) 741 09 39; e-mail schlemme@vb-bruessel.stk.lsa-net.de; contact Juergen Schlemme (Director).

Verbindungsbüro des Saarlands bei der Europäischen Gemeinschaften: Avenue de la Renaissance 46, 1000 Brus-sels; tel (2) 743 07 90; fax (2) 732 73 70;

e-mail office@saarlandbuero.be; contact Herta Adam (Director).

Vertretung des Freistaates Bayern bei der Europäischen Union: Boule-vard Clovis 18, 1000 Brussels; tel (2) 743 04 40; fax (2) 743 04 42; e-mail Friedrich .vonheusinger@stk.bayern.de; internet www.bayern.de; contacts Edeltraud Boehm-Amtmann (Director), Friedrich von Heusinger (Deputy Director (Respon-sible for the COR)).

Vertretung des Landes Baden-Würtemberg bei der Europäischen Union: Square Vergote 9, 1200 Brussels; tel (2) 741 77 11; fax (2) 741 77 99; e-mail poststelle@bruessel.bwl.de, richard .arnold@bruessel.bwl.de; contact Richard Arnold (Director).

Vertretung des Landes Hessen bei der Europäischen Union: Avenue de l'Yser 19, 1040 Brussels; tel (2) 732 42 20; fax (2) 732 48 13; e-mail hessen.eu@lv -bruessel.hessen.de; contact Dr. Hans-Martin Bachmann (Director).

Vertretung des Landes Niedersach-sen bei der Europäischen Union: Rue Montoyer 61, 1000 Brussels; tel (2) 230 00 17; fax (2) 230 13 20; e-mail eu .vertretung@niedersachsen.be, wolfgang .pelull@niedersachsen.be; contacts Michael Bertram (Director), Dr Wolfgang Pelull.

Vertretung des Landes Nordrhein-Westfalen bei der Europäischen Union: Avenue Michel-Ange 10, 1000 Brussels; tel (2) 739 17 10-75; fax (2) 739 17 07; e-mail poststelle@lv-eu.nrw .de; contacts Folker Schreiber (Director), Norbert Spinrath (Relations with COR).

Vertretung des Landes Rheinland-Pfalz bei der Europäischen Union: Avenue de Tervueren 60, 1040 Brussels; tel (2) 736 97 29, (2) 737 13 22; fax (2) 737 13 33; e-mail vertretungbruessel@ lv-rlp.de, gdoepgen@lv.rlp.de, srichter@ lv.rlp.de; contacts Hans-Joachim Gunther (Director), Gabrielle Doepgen.

GREECE

Agence de Développement de Hera-clion: Square de Meeûs 18, 1050 Brus-sels; tel (2) 505 34 43; fax (2) 505 34 41; e-mail da.heraklion@brutele.be, info@ anher.gr; contact Eleni Iniotaki.

Bureau de la Région de l'Epire: Lan-cashire House, Rue d'Arlon 38, 1000 Brussels; tel (2) 282 96 67; fax (2) 282 96 17; e-mail regioeuropa@skynet.be; contact Athanassios Goumas (Director).

Central Union of Municipalities and Communes of Greece: Avenue d'Auder-ghem 59, 1040 Brussels; tel (2) 230 13 76; fax (2) 230 27 50; e-mail eetaa@arcadis .be; contact Katerina Karavolabouyer.

IRELAND

Irish Regions Office: Rond-Point Schuman 6, 1040 Brussels; tel (2) 282 84 74; fax (2) 282 84 75; e-mail robert.collins@pophost.eunet.be; contact Robert Collins.

Nasc, West Ireland EC Liaison: Rond-Point Schuman 6, 1040 Brussels; tel (2) 282 84 03; fax (2) 282 84 06; e-mail eolas@nasc.be, bennett@nasc.be; contact John Bennett (Director).

ITALY

Anci-Ideali – Identità Europea per le Autonomie Locali Italiane: Avenue des Arts 39, 1040 Bruxelles; tel (2) 213 30 80; fax (2) 513 52 27; e-mail secretariat@ideali.be; contact Maria Baroni.

Conferenza dei Rettori delle Universite Italiane (Crui): Rond Point Schuman 6, 1040 Bruxelles; tel (2) 235 73 42; fax (2) 235 73 48; e-mail cascone@crui.it, bruno@crui.it; contacts Laura Cascone, Giordana Bruno.

CRCI Ligurie / Unioncamere Liguri: Rue du Luxembourg 15, 1000 Brussels; tel (2) 289 13 91; fax (2) 289 13 90; e-mail raffaella.bruzzone@casaliguria.org, ucliguria@casaliguria.org; contact Drssa Raffaella Bruzzone.

Desk Basilicata: Rue de l'Industrie 22, 1040 Bruxelles; tel (2) 502 31 31; fax (2) 502 58 98; e-mail basilicata@easynet.be; internet www.regione.basilicata.it; contact Flavio Burlizzi (Director).

Europaregion Tirol-Sudtirol-Trentino: Avenue de Cortenbergh 52, 1000 Brussels; tel (2) 743 27 00; fax (2) 742 09 80; e-mail info@alpeuregio.org, v.rodaro@alpeuregio.org; contact Vittorino Rodaro (Director).

Europaregion Tirol-Sudtirol-Trentino (Tirol Buro) (Provincia Autonoma di Bolzano): Avenue de Cortenbergh 52, 1000 Bruxelles; tel (2) 743 27 00; fax (2) 742 09 80; e-mail c.quaranta@alpeuregio.org, info@alpeuregio.org; contact Claudio Quaranta (Director).

Regione Abruzzo: Rond Point Schuman 6, 1040 Bruxelles; tel (2) 286 85 21; fax (2) 286 85 28; e-mail i.napolione@regionicentroitalia.org; internet www.abruzzoeuropa.com; contact Isabella Napolione (Head of Office).

Regione Autonoma della Sardegna: Avenue des Arts 3-5 10e étage, 1210 Bruxelles; tel (2) 219 40 58; fax (2) 219 41 05; e-mail sardegna@sardaigne.org; internet www.regionesardegna.it; contacts Dott. Mario Leoni (Director), Bianca Maria Bianco (Head of Office).

Regione Calabria: Rue d'Arlon 55, 1040 Bruxelles; tel (2) 280 19 91; fax (2) 280 20 86; e-mail regione.calabria@cercaeuropa.net; internet www.biccal.it, www.cercaeuropa.net; contacts Giuseppe Amoruso (Director), Giuseppe Mazzotta.

Regione Campania: Av. de Cortenberg 60, 1040 Bruxelles; tel (2) 737 91 80; fax (2) 737 91 99; e-mail dario.gargiulo@regionecampania.be, claudio.daroma@regionecampania.be; contacts Dario Gargiulo (Responsible), Claudio D'Aroma.

Regione del Veneto: Rue de l'Industrie 22, 1040 Bruxelles; tel (2) 551 00 10; fax (2) 551 00 19; e-mail BRUXELLS@regione.veneto.it; contact Gianlorenzo Martini (Director).

Regione Emilia Romagna: Avenue de l'Ysère 19, 1040 Bruxelles; tel (2) 732 30 90; fax (2) 736 31 90; e-mail emilia-romagna@optinet.be; internet www.regione.emilia-romagna.it; contact Lorenza Badiello (Head of Office).

Regione Friuli Venezia Giulia: Rue Wiertz 50-28, 1050 Brussels; tel (2) 401 61 30; fax (2) 401 68 68; e-mail ines.rubino@regione.fvg.it; contacts Ines Rubino (Director), Luisa Poclen (Rel./COR).

Regione Lazio: Rond Point Schuman 6, 1040 Bruxelles; tel (2) 286 85 31; fax (2) 286 85 38; e-mail lazio@regionicentroitalia.org, f.deleonardis@regionicentroitalia.org; contacts Franco Oliva (Director), Fabiano de Leonardis (Rel./COR).

Regione Liguria: Rue de Luxembourg 15, 1000 Bruxelles; tel (2) 289 13 89; fax (2) 289 13 99; e-mail info@casaliguria.org, bruxelles@regione.liguria.it; internet www.regione.liguria.it; contacts Antonio Parodi (Director), Simona Costa (Vice-Director).

Regione Lombardia: Rue du Luxembourg 3, 1000 Bruxelles; tel (2) 518 76 00; fax (2) 518 76 26; e-mail lombard.regio.brus@arcadis.be, delegazione_bruxelles@regione.lombardia.it; internet www.regione.lombardia.it; contacts Prof. Claude Scheiber (Director), Domenico Beber.

Regione Marche: Rue Point Schuman 6, 1040 Bruxelles; tel (2) 286 85 44; fax (2) 286 85 48; e-mail marche@regionicentroitalia.org, v.cimino@regionicentroitalia.org; internet www.regionicentroitalia.it; contacts Vincenzo Cimino (Head of Office), Antonella Passarani.

Regione Molise: Rue Point Schuman 6 boîte 6, 1000 Bruxelles; tel (2) 234 63 05; fax (2) 234 79 11; e-mail carlo63marinelli@yahoo.it; contact Carlo Marinelli (Head of Office).

Regione Puglia: Rue du Luxembourg 3, 1000 Bruxelles; tel (2) 501 08 75; fax (2) 501 08 77; e-mail regione.puglia@skynet.be; contact Carla Capriati (Responsible for the COR).

Regione Siciliana: Place du Champ de Mars 5, 1050 Bruxelles; tel (2) 550 38 00/55; fax (2) 550 38 50; e-mail presidenza.bruxelles@regionesiciliana.be; contacts Francesco Attaguile (Office representative), Guido Lo Porto.

Regione Toscana: Rond Point Schuman 6, 1040 Bruxelles; tel (2) 286 85 61-64; fax (2) 286 85 68; e-mail toscana@regionicentroitalia.org, m.badii@regionicentroitalia.org; contact Mario Badii (Head of Office).

Regione Umbria: Rond Point Schuman 6, 1040 Bruxelles; tel (2) 286 85 71; fax (2) 286 85 78; e-mail umbria@regionicentroitalia.org, m.benelli@regionicentroitalia.org; contacts Dott. Massimiliano Benelli (Head of Office), Paola Simone (Rel./COR).

Regione Valle d'Aosta: Rue de Trèves 49-51, 1040 Bruxelles; tel (2) 282 18 50; fax (2) 282 18 58; e-mail vda_bruxelles@valleeurope.net; contact Gian Garancini (Adviser to the Government's President).

Union Camere Piemonte: Rue de l'Industrie 22, 1040 Bruxelles; tel (2) 550 02 50; fax (2) 550 02 59; e-mail ufficio.bruxelles@regione.piemonte.it; contact Rosa Corradin.

Unioncamere Veneto: Rue de l'Industrie 22, 1040 Bruxelles; tel (2) 551 04 90; fax (2) 551 04 99; e-mail ucv.bxl@ntah.net; contact Tania Wolski.

NETHERLANDS

Amsterdam Eurolink Brussel: Rue des Aduatiques 71-75, 1040 Brussels; tel (2) 732 23 99; fax (2) 732 04 42; e-mail amsterdam@nl-prov.be; contact Lo Breemer (Coordinator).

Association of Netherlands Municipalities (VNG): Rue de la Science 4, 1000 Brussels; tel (2) 550 11 70; fax (2) 550 12 72; e-mail frank.hilterman@vng.nl; contact Frank Hilterman.

Association of the Provinces of the Netherlands (IPO): Rue des Aduatiques 71-75, 1040 Brussels; tel (2) 737 99 58; fax (2) 736 70 89; e-mail leeuwen@ipo.nl; contact Henk Van Leeuwen (Adviser).

Caster Conference and Association of Steel Territories: Avenue de Cortenbergh 118 Bte 13, 1040 Brussels; tel (2) 742 25 80; fax (2) 742 25 81; e-mail t.bakker@econcepteurope.com; contact Tamara Bakker.

East Netherlands Provinces (Overijssel/Gelderland): Rue des Aduatiques 71-75, 1040 Brussels; tel (2) 737 99 62-63; fax (2) 737 99 61; e-mail oost.nl@nl-prov.be; contacts Hein Cannegieter (Coordinator), Rob Van Eijkeren.

Huis van de Nederlandse Provincies: Rue des Aduatiques 71-75, 1040 Brussels; tel (2) 737 99 60; fax (2) 737 99 61; e-mail cannegieter@nl-prov.be, schilder@nl-prov.be, bairy@nl-prov.be, burger@nl-prov.be; contacts Fein Cannegieter (Coordinator), Karin Schilder (Information Officer).

North Netherlands Provinces (Friesland/Groningen/Dente): Rue des Aduatiques 71-75, 1040 Brussels; tel (2) 737 99 40; fax (2) 737 99 61; e-mail dick .michel@worldonline.nl, roona@nl-prov .be; contacts Dick Michel, Bert Roona (EU-Contact Officer).

Province of Flevoland: Rue des Aduatiques 71-75, 1040 Brussels; tel (2) 737 99 53; fax (2) 737 70 89; e-mail venema@ flevoland.nl; contact Sidony Venema.

Province of Noord-Holland: Rue des Aduatiques 71-75, 1040 Brussels; tel (2) 737 99 52; fax (2) 737 70 89; e-mail keulenh@noord-holland.nl; contact Marion Van Kampen.

Province of South-Holland: Rue des Aduatiques 71-75, 1040 Brussels; tel (2) 737 99 51; fax (2) 736 70 89; e-mail schim@nl-prov.be; contact Regina Schim van der Loeff.

Province of Utrecht: Rue des Aduatiques 71-75, 1040 Brussels; tel (2) 737 99 53; fax (2) 736 70 89; e-mail barg@nl -prov.be; contact Bas van den Barg.

Regio Randstad (Randstad Region): Rue des Aduatiques 71-75 Bte 2, 1040 Brussels; tel (2) 737 99 55; fax (2) 736 70 89; e-mail pluckel@nl-prov.be; contact Hans Pluckel (Director).

Southern Netherlands Provinces Zeeland-Noord Brabant-Limburg: Rue des Aduatiques 71-75, 1040 Brussels; tel (2) 737 99 71, (2) 737 99 72; fax (2) 737 99 61; e-mail degroot@nl-prov.be; contact Jacqueline De Groot.

NORWAY

Kommunenes Sentralforbund (Norwegian Association of Local and Regional Authorities): Rue de la Science 4, 1000 Brussels; e-mail erdal@epri.org; contact Aase Erdal (Manager).

Stavanger-Regionens Europakontor: Rue de la Tourelle 37, 1040 Brussels; tel (2) 231 18 84; fax (2) 280 06 90; e-mail one.market@pop.kpn.be; contact Pal Jacobsen (Director).

PORTUGAL

Représentation Permanente du Portugal auprès de l'Union Européenne: Avenue de Cortenbergh 12, 1040 Brussels; tel (2) 286 42 00; fax (2) 231 00 26; e-mail acs@reper-portugal.be; contact Antonio Santos (Managing Director).

SPAIN

Cabildo Insular de Gran Canaria: Rue A. Fauchille 7, 1150 Brussels; tel (2) 732 65 85; fax (2) 733 02 00; e-mail bruselas@eurovias.com.

Centre des Baleares Europe: Avenue des Arts 3-5, 7ème étage, 1210 Brussels; tel (2) 223 14 10; fax (2) 223 25 24; e-mail centre.balears.europa@skynet.be; internet www.ebe.es/nova.htm; contacts Antoni Costa (Regional delegate), Margalida Amoros (Responsible for the COR).

Delegación de la Comunidad Valenciana en Bruselas: Rue de la Loi 227 – Bte 6, 1040 Brussels; tel (2) 230 28 20; fax (2) 230 90 19; e-mail info@ delcomval.be, ycolorado@delcomval.be; contact Yolanda Colorado (Responsible for the COR).

Delegación de la Diputación de Barcelona: Avenue des Arts 3-5, 1210 Brussels; tel (2) 223 35 21; fax (32 2) 223 35 27; e-mail diba.bxl@skynet.be; contact Blanca Soler-Tobella (Director).

Delegación del Gobierno de Canarias: Avenue de la Toison d'Or 55, 4ème étage, 1060 Brussels; tel (2) 534 97 33; fax (2) 534 97 34; e-mail jluebar@ gobiernodecanarias.org, jzafdia@ gobiernodecanarias.org; internet www.gobiernodecanarias.org; contacts José Miguel Luengo Barreto (Director), Julián Zafra (Rel./COR).

Delegación del Gobierno de Navarra: Avenue des Arts 3-4, 1210 Brussels; tel (2) 223 75 39; fax (2) 223 75 42; e-mail europa@navarra.be, maria.lozano@ skynet.be; contact María Lozano Ruiz (Director).

Délégation du Pays Basque à Bruxelles (Euskadi): Rue des Deux Eglises 27, 1000 Brussels; tel (2) 285 45 10; fax (2) 285 45 11; e-mail bruselas@ej-gv.es; contact Imanol Bolinaga (Delegate).

Fundación Galicia-Europa: Avenue Milcamps 105, 1030 Brussels; tel (2) 735 54 40; fax (2) 735 46 78; e-mail bruselas@ fundationgalaciaeuropa.org; contacts Ana Ramos Barbosa (Director), Sonia Fentanes Fortes (Rel./COR).

Gobierno de Aragón: Square de Meeûs 18, 1050 Brussels; tel (2) 502 43 44, (2) 504 79 84; fax (2) 502 76 61; e-mail dga3@brutele.be; contacts Mateo Sierra Bardaji (Director), Pedro García (Rel./ COR).

Instituto de Fomento de la Región de Murcia: Avenue des Arts 3-5, 1210 Brussels; tel (2) 223 33 48; fax (2) 219 14 58; e-mail of.murcia@skynet.be, lucia .huertas@skynet.be; internet www .carm.es; contact Lucia Huertas Suanzes (Director).

Junta de Andalucía: Avenue des Arts 3-5, 1210 Brussels; tel (2) 209 03 30; fax (2) 209 03 31; e-mail delegacion.bruselas@

junta-andalucia.org, esaintgerons@ junta-andalucia.org; contacts Miguel Lucena (Director), Elvira Saint-Gerons Herrera.

Junta de Comunidades de Castilla La Mancha: Rue de la Loi 83-85, 1040 Brussels; tel (2) 231 14 77; fax (2) 231 03 13; e-mail castilla-lamancha@jccm.skynet .be; contacts Juan Francisco Fernández (Director), Abencio Cutanda (Rel./COR).

Oficina de Asuntos Europeos Principado de Asturias: Avenue des Arts 3-5, 1210 Brussels; tel (2) 223 02 14; fax (2) 223 04 94; e-mail pasbrus@euronet.be, pasbrus4@euronet.be; contacts Javier Fernández López (Director), Santiago Martínez Iglesias (Rel./COR).

Oficina de Extremadura: Square Ambiorix 17, 1000 Brussels; tel (2) 736 59 50; fax (2) 736 60 10; e-mail poses@ prejuntex.org; contacts Teresa Rainha (Director), Paula Oses Arregui (Assistant).

Oficina de la Comunidad de Madrid en Bruselas: Avenue de la Toison d'Or 55 Bte 3, 1060 Brussels; tel (2) 534 74 39; fax (2) 534 74 31; e-mail comunidad .madrid.oficina@skynet.be; contacts Alfredo Sánchez Jimino (Director), Pilar García de la Cuadra (Responsible for the COR).

Oficina de la Junta de Castilla y León: Avenue des Arts 3-5, 1210 Brussels; tel (2) 223 02 55; fax (2) 223 00 57; e-mail oficina.cyl@skynet.be; internet www.jcyl.es; contacts Maria José de No Sánchez de León (Director), José Juan Rosado Sánchez (Responsible for the COR).

Oficina de La Rioja: Avenue des Arts 3-5, 9ème étage, 1040 Brussels; tel (2) 219 03 57; fax (2) 219 35 38; e-mail ofirioja1@ euronet.be, ofirioja@euronet.be; contact Marta Romo (Director).

Oficina del Gobierno de Cantabria: Boulevard du Régent 58, 1000 Brussels; tel (2) 512 81 01; fax (2) 512 21 29; e-mail ue@cantabria.be; contacts Inmaculada Valencia Bayón (Director), Raquel Rodríguez (Rel./COR).

Patronat Catala pro Europa: Rue de la Loi 227 – 2ème étage, 1040 Brussels; tel (02) 231 03 30; fax (02) 230 21 10; e-mail sd@infoeuropa.org; internet www .gencat.es/pcpe; contact Immaculada Buldufreixa (Delegate).

SWEDEN

Baltic Sea Islands EU Office: Scotland House, Rond Point Schuman 6, 1040 Brussels; tel (2) 282 84 50; fax (2) 282 84 49; e-mail b7@eurodesk.org; contacts Juergen Samuelson (Director), Jacob Hensen (Rel./COR).

Central Sweden Brussels Representative Office: Rue du Luxembourg 3, 1000 Brussels; tel (2) 501 08 83; fax (2) 501 07 49; e-mail maria-fogelstrom -kylberg@centralsweden.be; contacts Per Widell, Maria Fogelstrom-Kylberg.

City of Malmö EU Office: The Baltic House, Avenue de Palmerston 26, 1000 Brussels; tel (2) 285 43 23; fax (2) 285 43 29; e-mail ola.nord@malmo.be; contact Ola Nord (Head of Office).

East Sweden: Avenue Palmerston 26, 1000 Brussels; tel (2) 235 00 11; fax (2) 230 90 87; e-mail annelie.nylander@ eastsweden.be, maria.mollergren@ eastsweden.be; contacts Annelie Nylander (Director), Maria Mollergren (Rel./COR).

Federation of Swedish County Councils: Rue de la Science 4, 1000 Brussels; tel (2) 549 08 63; fax (2) 502 72 27; e-mail eag@lf.se; contacts Elmire Af Geijerstam (CP), www.landstingforbundet.se.

Mid Scandinavia European Office (Mid Sweden Office): Rue Guillaume Tell 59b, 1060 Brussels; tel (2) 542 63 11; fax (2) 543 10 45; e-mail mseo@wanadoo .be; contact Lisa Jonsson (Director and Rel./CdR).

North Sweden European Office: Avenue Palmerston 26, 1000 Brussels; tel (2) 282 18 20; fax (2) 282 18 21; e-mail contact@northsweden.org, anna .olofsson@northsweden.org; contact Anna Olofsson (Head of Office).

South Sweden European Office: Avenue Palmerston 26, Ground Floor, 1000 Brussels; tel (2) 235 26 60-61; fax (2) 235 26 69; e-mail sophie.gardestedt@ sydsam.be, per.hilmersson@sydsam.be; contacts Sophie Gardestedt (Director), Per Hilmersson.

Stockholm Region Brussels Office: Avenue de Cortenbergh 52, 1000 Brussels; tel (2) 740 06 04; fax (2) 740 06 16; e-mail thomas.friis.konst@srbo.org; contact Thomas Friis Konst (Director).

Swedish Association of Local Authorities and Regions: Rue de la Science 4, 1000 Brussels; tel (2) 549 08 60; fax (2) 502 72 27; e-mail eag@lf.se; internet www.svekom.se; contact Elmire Af Geijerstam (Director).

West Sweden EU & Representation Office: Sweden House, Rue du Luxembourg 3, 1000 Brussels; tel (2) 501 08 40; fax (2) 501 08 42; e-mail kp@westsweden .se, kajsa.sundstrom@westsweden.se; contacts Kjell Peterson (Director), Kajsa Sundstrom Van Zeveren (Rel./CdR).

SWITZERLAND

Representation of Swiss Cantons: c/o Oppenheimer Wolff and Donnelly, Avenue Louise 240 Bte 5, 1050 Brussels; tel (2) 626 05 00; fax (2) 626 05 10; e-mail jrussotto@oppenheimer.com; contact Mr. Roche (Managing Partner).

UNITED KINGDOM

Association of London Government European Service: London House, Rue du Trône 108, 1050 Brussels; tel (2) 650 08 19; fax (2) 650 08 26; e-mail amanda .b@gle.co.uk, alg-brussels@gle.co.uk; contact Amanda Brandellero (Head of Office).

Cheshire Brussels Office: Rue du Marteau 21, 1000 Brussels; tel (2) 229 53 76; fax (2) 229 53 83; e-mail johnstonn@ cheshire-brussels.com; contact Nicola Johnston.

COSLA/ Scottish Local Government Office: Scotland House, Rond Point Schuman 6, 1040 Brussels; tel (2) 282 83 95, (2) 282 84 25; fax (2) 282 84 29; e-mail cosla@pophost.eunet.be; internet cosla.gov.co.uk; contact Silke Isbrand.

East Midlands Regional European Office: Avenue de Tervueren 78, 1040 Brussels; tel (2) 735 99 38, (2) 736 57 53; fax (2) 735 27 58; e-mail info@ eastmidlandseurope.org; contact Carol Thomas-Hirsbrunner (Director).

East of England European Partnership: Square de Meeûs 18 Bte 7, 1000 Brussels; tel (2) 289 12 00; fax (2) 289 12 09; e-mail brusselsoffice@eastofengland .be; contacts Jenny De Rykman (Head of Office), Helen Jackson.

East of Scotland European Consortium (ESEC): Scotland House, Rond Point Schuman 6, 1040 Brussels; tel (2) 282 84 28; fax (2) 282 84 29; e-mail esec@ dundeecity.gov.uk; contact Andrea Schwedler.

Essex International: Square de Meeûs 18, 1050 Brussels; tel (2) 505 34 40; fax (2) 505 34 41; e-mail essex@brutele.be; internet www.essexcc.gov.uk; contact Mark West (Head of Office).

Greater Manchester Brussels Office: Rue du Marteau 21, 1000 Brussels; tel (2) 229 53 74; fax (2) 229 53 83; e-mail catherine.feore@agma-brussels.org, assistant@agma-brussels.org; contact Catherine Feore (Director).

Hampshire – Isle of Wight Office – West Sussex Office: South East England House, Square de Meeûs 35, 1000 Brussels; tel (2) 504 07 20; fax (2) 504 07 22; e-mail info@hwws .southeastenglandhouse.net, d.terruso@ hwws.southeastenglandhouse.net; contact Daniela Pace (Director).

Highlands & Islands of Scotland European Partnership: Scotland House, Rond Point Schuman 6, 1040 Brussels; tel (2) 282 83 60; fax (2) 282 83 63; e-mail marie.orban@pophost .eunet.be; contact Marie-Yvonne Orban (Head of Office).

Kent Partnership Office: South East England House, Square de Meeûs 35, 1000 Brussels; tel (2) 504 07 50; fax (2) 504 07 55; e-mail brussels.office@kent .gov.uk; contacts Marie Dancourt (Head of European Affairs), Stacy Watts.

Lancashire Brussels Office North-West of England House: Rue du Marteau 21, 1000 Brussels; tel (2) 229 53 71, (2) 229 53 78, (2) 229 53 72; fax (2) 229 53 83; e-mail alona.bruce.lancashire -brussels.org, james.sharples@ lancashire-brussels.org, carla.schmitz@ lancashire-brussels.org; contacts Alona Bruce (Head of Office), James Sharples (European Policy Officer).

Local Government International Bureau and Local Government Association – Joint Brussels Office: Rue d'Arlon 22-24, 1050 Brussels; tel (2) 502 36 80; fax (2) 502 40 35; e-mail brussels .office@lgib.org, richardk@lgib.org, anna@lgib.org; contacts Richard Kitt (Head of Office), Anna Daniel (Policy and Coordination Officer).

Locate in Scotland: Rond point Schuman 6, 1040 Brussels; tel (2) 282 84 00; fax (2) 282 84 14; e-mail maryse .marcherta@cotent.co.uk; contact Maryse Marcherat (European Manager).

London's European Office, Greater London Authority: London House, Leopold Plaza, Rue du Trône 108, 1050 Brussels; tel (2) 650 08 00; fax (2) 650 08 24; e-mail european.office@london.gov.uk; contact Anna Harradine (Head of Office).

Merseyside: Rue du Marteau 21, 1000 Brussels; tel (2) 229 53 77; fax (2) 229 53 83; e-mail mbo@merseyside-europe.org, alex.weston@merseyside-europe.org; contact Alex Weston.

North of England Office: Avenue de Tervueren 78, 1040 Brussels; tel (2) 735 35 47; fax (2) 735 40 74; e-mail euro@ neobxl.be; internet www.neobxl.be; contacts Stephen Howell (Head of Office), Nadege Bon-Betemps (Assistant EU Liaison Officer).

North West House – Regional Assembly/Development Agency: Rue du Marteau 21, 1000 Brussels; tel (2) 229 53 73; fax (2) 229 53 83; e-mail abigail .howarth@northwesthouse-brussels.org; contact Abigail Howarth (Office Coordinator).

Northern Ireland Centre in Europe: Rue Wiertz 50, 1050 Brussels; tel (2) 290 13 34; fax (2) 290 13 32; e-mail William .Dukelow@ofmdfmni.gov.uk; contact William Dukelow (Deputy Director).

Scotland Europa: Scotland House, Rond-Point Robert Schuman 6, 1040 Brussels; tel (2) 282 83 02-15; fax (2) 282 83 00; e-mail information.desk@ scotent.co.uk, craig.french@scottish

.parliament.uk; contacts Donald Mac Innes, Anna-Marie de Pillecyn (Secretary).

Scottish Executive – Scottish Office: Scotland House, Rond-Point Schuman 6, 1040 Brussels; tel (2) 282 83 30; fax (2) 282 84 29; e-mail ewan.f.cameron@ scotland.gsi.gov.uk; internet www .scotland.gov.uk/eurooffice; contact George Calder.

Scottish Parliament: Scotland House, Rond Point Schuman 6, 1040 Brussels; tel (2) 282 83 77; e-mail terry.shevlin@ scottish.parliament.uk; contact Terry Shevlin.

South and North-East Scotland: Rue Franklin 113, 1000 Brussels; tel (2) 735 58 73; fax (2) 735 57 66; e-mail dunsmore@compuserve.com; contact Richard Dunsmore (European Manager).

South East Partners: South East England House, Square de Meeûs 35, 1000 Brussels; tel (2) 504 07 30; fax (2) 504 07 22; e-mail info@southeastpartners .southeastenglandhouse.net; contacts Korrina Stewart (Head of Office), Banbee Fee.

South West UK Brussels Office: Avenue Michel-Ange 86, 1000 Brussels; tel (2) 734 41 10; fax (2) 734 44 34; e-mail info@southwestuk.be; internet www .westofenglandineurope.org.uk; contact Eleni Marianou (Head of Office).

Thames Valley Brussels Office: South East England House, Square de Meeûs 35, 1000 Brussels; tel (2) 504 07 36; fax (2) 504 07 22-38; e-mail paola.ottonello@ thamesvalley.southeastenglandhouse .net; contact Paola Ottonello (Head of Office).

Welsh Local Government Association: Rue Joseph II 20, 1000 Brussels; tel (2) 506 44 77, (2) 506 44 78; fax (2) 502 83 60; e-mail reception@ewrop.com; contacts Simon Pascoe (Policy Officer), Nia Lewis.

West Midlands in Europe: Avenue de Cortenbergh 75, 1000 Brussels; tel (2) 740 27 10-20; fax (2) 740 27 20; e-mail info@westmidlandsineurope.org; contacts Glynis Whiting (Head of Office), Gail Harris (Rel./COR).

West of Scotland European Consortium: Scotland House, Rond Point Schuman 6, 1040 Brussels; tel (2) 282 84 25; fax (2) 282 84 29; e-mail cosla@pophost .eunet.be; contact Malcolm Leitch.

Yorkshire & Humberside European Office: Avenue de Cortenbergh 118 Bte 13, 1000 Brussels; tel (2) 735 34 08; fax (2) 735 62 14; e-mail european.office@ yorkshire.be; contact Paul Wardle (Director).

CHAMBERS OF COMMERCE AND INDUSTRY AND TRADE CHAMBERS WITH REPRESENTATIONAL OFFICES IN BRUSSELS

AUSTRIA

Austrian Economic Chamber: Avenue de Cortenberg 30, 1040 Brussels; tel (+32 2) 286 58 80; fax (+32 2) 286 58 99; e-mail eu@eu.austria.be; contact Stefan Pistauer (Representative).

HandelsdelegationÖsterreichs (Austrian Commercial Delegation): Avenue Louise 479 Bte 52, 1050 Brussels; tel (+32 2) 645 16 50; fax (+32 2) 645 16 69; e-mail bruessel@austriantrade.org; internet www.austria.be; contact Dr. Gustav Gressel (Commercial Counsellor).

Vereinigung der Österreichischen Industrie (Federation of Austrian Industry): Avenue de Cortenbergh 30, 1040 Brussels; tel (+32 2) 231 18 47; fax (+32 2) 230 95 91; e-mail iv.brussels@iv-net.at; internet www.iv-net.at; contact Berthold Berger-Henoch.

BELGIUM

Agence pour le Commerce Extérieur – ACE (Agency for Foreign Trade): WTC 1, Blvd du Roi Albert II 30 bte 6, 1000 Brussels; tel (+32 2) 206 35 11; fax (+32 2) 203 18 12; e-mail info@abh-ace.org.

FEB – Fédération des Entreprises de Belgique (Federation of Belgian Businesses): Rue Ravenstein 4, 1000 Brussels; tel (+32 2) 515 08 11; fax (+32 2) 515 09 99; e-mail red@vbo-feb.be; internet www.vbo-feb.be; contact Diane Struyven (Permanent Delegate).

DENMARK

Confederation of Danish Industries (DI): Rue Joseph II 40 Bte 5, 1000 Brussels; tel (+32 2) 285 05 50; fax (+32 2) 285 05 55; e-mail bruxafd@di.dk; internet www.di.dk; contact Harritz Fallesen (Director).

Handvaerksradet: Rue Jacques de Lalaing 4, 1040 Brussels; tel (+32 2) 230 75 99; fax (+32 2) 230 78 61; e-mail ueapme@euronet.be; internet www.ueapme.com; contact Christina Lindeholm.

FINLAND

Confederation of Finnish Industry and Employers: Rue de la Charité 17, 1210 Brussels; tel (+32 2) 209 43 11; fax (+32 2) 223 08 05; e-mail jukka.ahtela@tt.fi; contact Jukka Ahtela (Permanent Delegate).

FRANCE

Assemblée des Chambres Françaises de Commerce et d'Industrie (ACFCI) (Assembly of French Chambers of Commerce and Industry): Avenue des Arts 1-2 Bte 9, 1210 Brussels; tel (+32 2) 221 04 11/19; fax (+32 2) 217 69 87/66 12; e-mail o.lemerle@acfci.cci.fr; internet acfci.cci.fr; contacts Henry Malosse (Director), Olivier Lemerle.

Chambre Française de Commerce et d'Industrie de Belgique – CFCIB (French Chamber of Commerce and Industry in Belgium): Avenue des Arts 8, Square Antonis, 1210 Brussels; tel (+32 2) 506 88 11; fax (+32 2) 506 88 93, (+32 2) 506 88 17; e-mail cfcib@cfci.be; internet www.cfci.be; contact Mr. Van Cauwenbergh (Director).

Mouvement des Entreprises de France – MEDEF (French Businesses Association): Rue de Trèves 45, 1040 Brussels; tel (+32 2) 231 07 30; fax (+32 2) 231 08 38; e-mail medef.brux@skynet.be; internet www.medef.fr; contact Marie-Christine Vaccarezza (Responsible).

Représentation des Chambres de Commerce et d'Industrie Paris/Ile-de-France (Representation of the Paris/Ile de France Chambers of Commerce): Avenue des Arts 36, 1040 Brussels; tel (+32 2) 223 18 40; fax (+32 2) 223 18 56; e-mail sandra.penning@ccipif.be, europe@ccipif.be (central); contact Sandra Penning (Director).

Représentations Provence Alpes Côte d'Azur (Representation of Provence, Alpes and Côte d'Azur Chambers of Commerce): Avenue des Celtes 20, 1040 Brussels; tel (+32 2) 735 13 70; fax (+32 2) 733 25 36; e-mail vincent.paca@wanadoo.be; contact Stéphanie Vincent (Responsible).

GERMANY

Bundesverband der Deutschen Industrie (BDI) e.V. (Federal Association of German Industry): Rue du Commerce 31, 1000 Brussels; tel (+32 2) 548 90 20; fax (+32 2) 548 90 29; e-mail s.grikschat@bdi-online.de, b.dittmann@bdi-online.de; internet www.bdi-online.de; contact Bernd Dittmann (Director).

Debelux: Manhattancenter, Avenue du Boulevard 21, 1210 Brussels; tel (+32 2) 204 01 72; fax (+32 2) 203 22 71; e-mail ahk@debelux.org; internet www.debelux.org; contact Dr. Hans-Joachim Maurer.

Deutscher Industrie und Handelskammertag (German Industry and Chamber of Commerce): Boulevard Clovis 49a, 1000 Brussels; tel (+32 2) 286 16 11; fax (+32 2) 286 16 05; e-mail dihk@bruessel.dihk.de; internet www.dihk.de; contact Peter Korn (Director).

Handelskammer Hamburg (Hamburg Chamber of Commerce): Boulevard Clovis 49A, 1000 Brussels; tel (+32 2) 286 16 80; fax (+32 2) 286 16 84; e-mail papaschinopoulou.mary@bruessel.dihk.de; contact Mrs. Papaschinopoulou.

Zentralverband des Deutschen Handwerks (German Trades Association): Rue Jacques de Lalaing 4, 1040 Brussels; tel (+32 2) 230 85 39; fax (+32 2) 230 21 66; e-mail info@zdh-brussels.com; internet www.zdh.de; contact Karin Rögge (Office Manager).

GREECE

Federation of Greek Industries: Avenue de Cortenbergh 168, 1000 Brussels; tel (+32 2) 231 00 53; fax (+32 2) 280 08 91; e-mail fgi.bxl@skynet.be; internet www.fgi.org.gr; contact Ireni Pari (Permanent Delegate).

ICELAND

Federation of Icelandic Industries: Rue de la Charité 17, 1210 Brussels; tel (+32 2) 209 43 04; fax (+32 2) 223 08 05; e-mail kristofer.kristinsson@skynet.be; contact Kristofer Kristinsson (Permanent Delegate).

IRELAND

Enterprise Ireland: Rue Wiertz 50, 1050 Brussels; tel (+32 2) 673 98 66; fax (+32 2) 672 10 66; e-mail charlotte.field@enterprise-ireland.com; internet www.enterprise-ireland.com; contact Charlotte Field (Manager).

Irish Business and Employers Confederation: Rue Montoyer 17-19 Bte 3, 1000 Brussels; tel (+32 2) 512 33 33; fax (+32 2) 512 13 53; e-mail brussels.ibb@ibec.be; internet www.ibec.ibb.ie; contact Arthur Forbes.

ITALY

Confederazione Nazionale Artigianato e Piccole Imprese (National Confederation of Trades and Small Businesses): Rue du Commerce 124, 1000 Brussels; tel (+32 2) 230 74 42; fax (+32 2) 230 72 19; e-mail bruxelles@cna.ipi; internet www.cna.it; contact Patrizia Di Mauro.

Confindustria – SII – General Confederation of Italian Industry: Avenue de la Joyeuse Entrée 1 Bte 11, 1040 Brussels; tel (+32 2) 286 12 11; fax (+32 2) 230 63 36; e-mail p.pesci@confindustria.be; contact Patrizio Pesci (Permanent Delegate).

Cong. Gen. It. Commercio (Confcommercio): Avenue Marnix 30, 1000 Brussels; tel (+32 2) 289 62 30; fax (+32 2) 289 62 35; e-mail confcomtur@skypro.be; contact Giacomo Regaldo (Director).

Institut Italien pour le Commerce Extérieur (IICE) (Italian Institute for Foreign Trade): Place de la Liberté 12, 1000 Brussels; tel (+32 2) 229 14 30; fax (+32 2) 223 15 96; e-mail bruxelles@bruxelles.ice.it; internet www.ice.it; contact Mr. Del Monte.

Unioncamere: Rue de l'Industrie 22, 1040 Brussels; tel (+32 2) 512 22 40; fax (+32 2) 512 49 11; e-mail marco.lopriore@unioncamere.be; contact Marco Lopriore (Director).

JAPAN

Belgium-Japan Association & Chamber of Commerce: Avenue Louise 287 Bte 7, 1050 Brussels; tel (+32 2) 644 13 33; fax (+32 2) 644 23 60; e-mail info@bja.be; internet www.bja.be; contact Anja Kellens (Executive Director).

Japan External Trade Organization – JETRO: Rue d'Arlon 69-71 Bte 2, 1040 Brussels; tel (+32 2) 282 05 00; fax (+32 2) 280 25 30; internet www.jetro.be; contact Mr. Tanaka.

MALTA

Malta Federation of Industry: Rue Montoyer 17-19 bte 3, 1000 Brussels; tel (+32 2) 512 13 13; fax (+32 2) 512 13 53; e-mail leonard.mizzi@ibec.ie; internet www.mbb-org.mt; contact Leonard Mizzi (Permanent Delegate).

NETHERLANDS

Middel en Klein Bedrijf Nederlandse – MKB – Nederland (Dutch Small and Medium-Sized Enterprises): Rue Jacques de Lalaing 4, 1040 Brussels; tel (+32 2) 230 78 03; fax (+32 2) 230 18 07; e-mail gert.eggermont@kmonet.be, ulrichschroder@mkb.nl; internet www.mkb.nl; contact Gert Eggermont.

Netherlands Chamber of Commerce for Belgium and Luxembourg: Rue du Congrès 18, 1000 Brussels; tel (+32 2) 219 11 74; fax (+32 2) 218 78 21; e-mail info@nkvk.be; internet www.nkvk.be; contact Mr. Charles.

Verbond van Nederlandse Ondernemingen – VNO – NCW (Confederation of Netherlands Industry and Employers): Kunstlaan 41 Bte 4, 1040 Brussels; tel (+32 2) 510 08 80; fax (+32 2) 510 08 85; e-mail bou@vno-ncw.nl; internet www.vno-ncw.nl; contact Jan Karelbout (Permanent Delegate).

NORWAY

NHO – Confederation of Norwegian Business and Industry: Avenue de Cortenbergh 168, 1000 Brussels; tel (+32 2) 285 05 60; fax (+32 2) 285 05 70; e-mail nho.brussel@nho.no; contact Kjersti Methi (Director).

Norwegian Trade Council: Rue Archimède 17, 2ème étage, 1000 Brussels; tel (+32 2) 646 50 70; fax (+32 2) 646 07 44; e-mail brussels@ntc.no; internet www.nortrade.no; contact Lutgard Gielen (Director).

PORTUGAL

Associação Industrial Portuguesa – AIP (Portuguese Industrial Association): Avenue de Cortenbergh 168, 1000 Brussels; tel (+32 2) 513 19 94; fax (+32 2) 513 63 62; e-mail eipaip@skynet.be; internet www.aip.pt; contact Fernando Almeida (Permanent Delegate).

Associação Nacional dos Jovens Empresarios (National Association of Young Entrepreneurs): Rue de la Montagne 37 Bte C3, 1000 Brussels; tel (+32 2) 511 34 47; fax (+32 2) 511 51 45; e-mail angebro@unicall.be; internet www.ange.pt; contact Gonçalo Leitão (Relations Director).

Comércio de Portugal (Portuguese Chamber of Commerce): Rue Blanche 15 bte 5, 1050 Brussels; tel (+32 2) 230 83 23; fax (+32 2) 230 68 66; e-mail ccportugal@skynet.be; contact Mrs. Thomas (Delegate).

Confederação da Industria Portuguesa – CIP (Confederation of Portuguese Industry): Avenue de Cortenbergh 168, 1000 Brussels; tel (+32 2) 230 92 70; fax (+32 2) 230 08 37; e-mail cipbxl@skynet.be.

Investimentos Comercio e Turismo de Portugal – ICEP (Portuguese Trade and Tourism Office): Rue Blanche 15, 1050 Brussels; tel (+32 2) 230 96 25; fax (+32 2) 231 04 47; e-mail icep.bruxelas@icep.pt; internet www.icep.pt, www.portugalinsite.pt; contact Elia Rodrigues (Director).

SPAIN

Chambre Officielle de Commerce d'Espagne en Belgique et au Luxembourg (Official Spanish Chamber of Commerce in Belgium and Luxembourg): Rue Belliard 20, 1040 Brussels; tel (+32 2) 517 17 40; fax (+32 2) 513 88 05; e-mail info@cocebyl.be; internet www.cocebyl.be; contact Miguel-Angel Arrimadas (Director).

Representation of the Spanish Chambers of Commerce and Industry at the EC: Rue de Luxembourg 19-21, 1000 Brussels; tel (+32 2) 705 67 50; fax (+32 2) 705 66 40; e-mail del.bruselas@cscamaras.es; contact Fernando Llanos (Director).

SWEDEN

Confederation of Swedish Enterprise: Rue du Luxembourg 3, 1000 Brussels; tel (+32 2) 501 53 00; fax (+32 2) 501 53 20; e-mail bryssel@swedishenterprise.se; internet swedishenterprise.se; contact Jan Herin (Permanent Delegate).

Swedish Trade Council: Rue du Luxembourg 3, 1000 Brussels; tel (+32 2) 501 53 55; fax (+32 2) 501 53 56; e-mail belgium@swedishtrade.se; internet www.swedishtrade.com, www.swedishtrade.com/belgium; contact Stefan Eld (Trade Commission).

SWITZERLAND

Chambre de Commerce Suisse pour la Belgique et le Grand-Duché de Luxembourg (Swiss Chamber of Commerce for Belgium and the Grand Duchy of Luxembourg): Square des Nations 24, 1000 Brussels; tel (+32 2) 649 87 87; fax (+32 2) 649 80 19; contact Philippe Kenel (Administrator).

Représentation Suisse du Commerce et de l'Industrie (Swiss Representation for Commerce and Industry): Avenue de Cortenbergh 168, 1000 Brussels; tel (+32 2) 280 08 44; fax (+32 2) 280 06 99; e-mail economiesuisse@skynet.be; internet www.economiesuisse.ch/be; contact Mr. Zeilenbos (Permanent Delegate).

TURKEY

Turkish Industrialists and Businessmen Association – TUSIAD: Avenue des Gaulois 13, 1040 Brussels; tel (+32 2) 736 40 47; fax (+32 2) 736 39 93; e-mail kaleagasi@tusiad.org; internet tusiad.org; contact Bahadir Kaleagasi (Permanent Delegate).

Turkish Research & Business Organizations – TuR&Bo – PPP: Rue du Luxembourg 14 A, 1000 Brussels; tel (+32 2) 285 40 23; fax (+32 2) 285 40 25; e-mail oaydogmus@turboppp.org.

Union des Chambres de Commerce, d'Industrie, de Commerce Maritime et des Bourses de Turquie (TOBB) (Union of Chambers of Commerce, Industry, Maritime Trade and Stock Exchanges in Turkey): c/o Fondation pour le Développement Economique (IKV), Avenue F. Roosevelt 148A, 1050 Brussels; tel (+32 2) 646 40 40; fax (+32 2) 646 95 38; e-mail ikvnet@skynet.be; contact Haluk Nuray (Permanent Delegate).

Young Businessmen Association of Turkey – TUGIAD: Landhuizenlaan 27, 1850 Grimbergen; tel (+32 2) 261 18 08; fax (+32 2) 261 18 08; e-mail atthakanhanli@skynet.be; contact Hakan Hanli.

UNITED KINGDOM

British Business Bureau – BBB: Rue Wiertz 50, 1050 Brussels; tel (+32 2) 280 06 12; fax (+32 2) 230 26 36; e-mail jacqueline.philips@cbi.org.uk; internet www.cbi.org.uk; contact Jacqueline Philips.

British Chamber of Commerce in Belgium: Rue d'Egmont 15, 1000 Brussels; tel (+32 2) 540 90 30; fax (+32 2) 512 83 63; e-mail britcham@britcham.be; internet www.britcham.be; contact Edward Cutting (President).

Confederation of British Industry – CBI: Rue Wiertz 50, 1050 Brussels; tel (+32 2) 231 04 65; fax (+32 2) 230 98 32; e-mail andrew.moore@cbi.org.uk; internet www.cbi.org.uk; contact Andrew Moore (Director).

AGRICULTURAL ORGANIZATIONS

AUSTRIA

Präsidentenkonferenz der Landwirtschaftskammern Österreichs (Austrian Chambers of Agriculture): Avenue de Cortenberg 30, 1040 Brussels; tel (+32 2) 285 46 70; fax (+32 2) 285 46 71; e-mail pkbrux@pklwk.at; internet www.pklwk.at; contact Martin Laengauer (Director).

DENMARK

Danish Bacon & Meat Council: Rue du Luxembourg 47-51, 1040 Brussels; tel (+32 2) 230 27 05; fax (+32 2) 230 00 98; e-mail ds@agridan.be; internet www.doenskeslagterier.dk; contact Knud Buhl (Director).

Danish Council of Agriculture: Rue de la Science 23-25 bte 12, 1040 Brussels; tel (+32 2) 230 27 05; fax (+32 2) 230 01 43; e-mail dca@agridan.be; contact Jacob Bagge Hanson.

Danish Dairy Board Brussels: Rue de la Science 23-25, 1040 Brussels; tel (+32 2) 230 27 05; fax (+32 2) 230 46 43; e-mail ddb@agridan.be; contacts Paul Andersen (Administrator), Hans Bender (Director).

FRANCE

AEIDL: Chaussée Saint-Pierre 260, 1040 Brussels; tel (+32 2) 736 49 60; fax (+32 2) 736 04 34; e-mail info@aeidl.be; internet www.aeidl.be; contact William Van Dingenen.

Assemblée Permanente des Chambres d'Agriculture – APCA: Rue de la Science 23-25 Bte 17, 1040 Brussels; tel (+32 2) 285 43 82; fax (+32 2) 285 43 81; e-mail sylvain-lhermitte@skynet.be; internet www.apca.chambagri.fr; contact Sylvain Lhermitte.

Association de la Transformation Laitière Française – ATLA: Avenue des Arts 53, 1000 Brussels; tel (+32 2) 502 09 89; fax (+32 2) 514 23 37; e-mail jean-pierre.carlier@atla.asso.fr; contact Jean-Pierre Carlier.

Association Nationale Interprofessionnelle des Fruits et Légumes Transformes – ANIFELT: Avenue Palmerston 9, 1000 Brussels; tel (+32 2) 230 71 10; fax (+32 2) 230 87 67; e-mail anifelt@skynet.be; internet www.anifelt.com; contact Marie-Claude Amphoux.

Centre National du Machinisme Agricole, des Eaux et Forêts – DICOVA – CEMAGREF: Avenue des Arts 8, 1040 Brussels; tel (+32 2) 506 88 66; fax (+32 2) 506 88 45, (+32 2) 506 88 73; e-mail cemagref@clora.net, secretaria@clora.net; internet www.clora.net; contact Daro Sarr (Secretary).

Confédération Française de la Coopération Agricole – CFCA: Rue de la Science 23-25 Bte 17, 1040 Brussels; tel (+32 2) 231 19 52; fax (+32 2) 230 65 98; e-mail cfca.bxl@pophost.eunet.be; contact Véronique Guerin.

Fédération Française des Commerçants en Bestiaux: Rue de la Loi 81A Bte 9, 1040 Bruxelles; tel (+32 2) 230 46 03; fax (+32 2) 230 94 00; e-mail uecbv@pophost.eunet.be; contact Jean-Luc Meriaux.

Gie-Bureau Européen de l'Agriculture Française: Rue de la Science 23-25 Bte 17, 1040 Brussels; tel (+32 2) 285 43 80; fax (+32 2) 285 43 81; e-mail brigitte.daffargues@skynet.be; contact Mlle. Daffargues (Secretary).

Inter Professionnelle Fruits et Légumes – INTERFEL: Avenue Palmerston 9, 1000 Brussels; tel (+32 2) 230 73 48; fax (+32 2) 230 87 67; e-mail eurodialog@skynet.be; internet www.interfel.com; contact Jean Ruiz.

Union Française des Commerçants en Bestiaux – FFCB / FNICGV: Rue de la Loi 81A Bte 9, 1040 Brussels; tel (+32 2) 230 46 03; fax (+32 2) 230 94 00; e-mail uecbv@pophost.eunet.be; internet www.uecbv.eunet.be; contact J.-L. Meriaux.

GERMANY

Centrale Marketinggesellschaft der Deutschen Agrarwirtschaft – CMA: Rue du Luxembourg 47-51, 1050 Brussels; tel (+32 2) 505 34 80; fax (+32 2) 505 34 81; e-mail cma-benelux@skynet.be; contact Werner Friedrich (Director).

Deutscher Fleischer-Verband: Rue Jacques de Lalaing 4, 1040 Brussels; tel (+32 2) 230 66 90; fax (+32 2) 230 34 51; e-mail info@cibc.be; contacts Kirsten Diessner (Director), Mme. Hansen (Assistant to the Director).

Milchindustrie-Verband e.V.: Rue de l'Industrie 13, 1000 Brussels; fax (+32 2) 28 50 173; e-mail anton@milchindustrie.de; contact Alexander Anton.

GREECE

Confédération Panhellénique des Unions de Coopératives Agricoles – PASEGES (Panhellenic Confederation of Unions of Agricultural Co-operatives): Rue de la Science 23-25, 1040 Brussels; tel (+32 2) 230 66 85; fax (+32 2) 230 59 15; e-mail paseges@infonie.be; contact Giannis Kolybas (Director).

IRELAND

Irish Cooperative Organisation Society – ICOS: Rue de la Science 23-25 Bte 2, 1040 Brussels; tel (+32 2) 231 06 85; fax (+32 2) 231 06 98; e-mail mail@icosbrussels.be; contact Michael Quigley (Director).

Irish Dairy Board Benelux SA – IDB: Radiatorenstraat 1, 1800 Vilvoorde; tel (+32 89) 36 33 88; fax (+32 89) 36 27 74; e-mail james.oregan@idb.be; internet www.idb.be; contact Jim O'Regan (General Manager).

Irish Farmers Associations – IFA: Rue de la Science 23-25 bte 2, 1040 Brussels; tel (+32 2) 230 31 37; fax (+32 2) 231 06 98; e-mail mail@ifabrussels.be; contact Michael Treacy (Director).

ITALY

Assolatte (Private Milk Industry & Co-operative): Place de la Liberté 12, 1000 Brussels; tel (+32 2) 223 11 05; fax (+32 2) 219 40 21; e-mail assolatte.bxl@skynet.be; contact Rosanna Pecere (Director).

Coldiretti (Agricultural Union): Avenue de Tervuren 27, 1040 Brussels; tel (+32 2) 230 98 93; fax (+32 2) 231 14 78; e-mail maurizio.reale@euronet.be; internet www.coldiretti.it; contact Dr. Maurizio Reale (Director).

Confederazione Generale Agricoltura Italiano – Confagricoltura: Rue de la Science 23-25 bte 4, 1040 Brussels; tel (+32 2) 230 67 32; fax (+32 2) 230 92 87; e-mail confagricoltura@euronet.be; contact Dr. Sandro Mascia (Director).

Confederazione Italiana Agricoltori: Rue Philippe Le Bon 46, 1000 Brussels; tel (+32 2) 230 30 12; fax (+32 2) 280 03 33; e-mail cia.bxl@skynet.be; internet www.cia.it; contact Dr. Claudio Di Rollo.

JAPAN

Alic Europe: Avenue des Arts 10-11 10e étage, 1040 Brussels; tel (+32 2) 513 90 93; fax (+32 2) 513 76 25; e-mail alicbxl@skynet.be; contact Masa Miroseki (Manager).

NETHERLANDS

LTO-Nederland: Wetenschapsstraat 23-25 Bus 21, 1040 Brussels; tel (+32 2) 230 75 00, (+32 2) 230 75 00; fax (+32 2) 230 67 49; e-mail pvebrus3@skynet.be; internet www.lto.nl; contacts Martin Van Drial, Mr. Lobis.

Produktschap Vee en Vlees – PVV (Cattle and Meat): Rue de la Science 23-25 Bte 21, 1040 Brussels; tel (+32 2) 230 75 00; fax (+32 2) 230 67 49; e-mail pvebrus3@skynet.be; contact Frans Van Dongen (Representative).

Vereniging van Bloemenveilingen in Nederland – VBN (Flower Auctions): Rue de la Science 23-25 Bte 21, 1040 Brussels; tel (+32 2) 231 50 02, (+32 2) 231 50 03; fax (+32 2) 230 67 49; e-mail pvebrus3@skynet.be; contact Tom Blom (Responsible EU Affairs).

PORTUGAL

Associação dos Jovens Agricultores de Portugal – AJAP (Young Farmers Association): Rue de la Science 23-25 Bte 28, 1040 Brussels; tel (+32 2) 230 57 08; fax (+32 2) 230 84 17; e-mail ajap@skynet.be; contact Paulo Padrol.

Confederação dos Agricultores de Portugal (Confederation of Portuguese Farmers): Rue Ste Gertrude 15, 1040 Brussels; tel (+32 2) 736 85 28; fax (+32 2) 732 30 54; e-mail cap.bxl@skynet.be; internet www.cap.pt; contact Jose Diégo Santiago (Delegate).

Confederação Nacional da Agricultura – CNA (National Confederation of Agriculture): Blvd Jamar 53, 1060 Brussels; tel (+32 2) 527 37 89; fax (+32 2) 527 37 90; contact Carla Semeador (Delegate).

SWEDEN

Federation of Swedish Farmers – LRF: Rue d'Arlon 82, 1040 Brussels; tel (+32 2) 280 06 64; fax (+32 2) 280 06 08; e-mail Rolf.Eriksson@lrf.be; contact Rolf Eriksson (Director).

UNITED KINGDOM

British Agriculture Bureau: Rue de la Science 25 Bte 5, 1040 Brussels; tel (+32 2) 285 05 80; fax (+32 2) 230 39 28; e-mail Betty.lee@nfu.org.uk; contact Betty Lee (Director).

Dairy Trade Federation – DTF: Rue Montoyer 14, 1000 Brussels; tel (+32 2) 503 56 10; fax (+32 2) 736 20 71; contact J. Begg.

Meat and Livestock Commission – MLC: Rue de la Science 23-25 Bte 18, 1040 Brussels; tel (+32 2) 230 86 68; fax (+32 2) 230 86 20; e-mail Peter.Hardwick@skynet.be; contact P. Hardwick (International Manager).

EMPLOYER ORGANIZATIONS AND TRADES UNION ORGANIZATIONS

AUSTRIA

Bundesarbeitkammer (National Chamber of Labour): Avenue de Cortenberg 30, 1040 Brussels; tel (+32 2) 230 62 54; fax (+32 2) 230 29 73; e-mail office@aken.at; internet www.aken.at; contact Dr Elisabeth Aufheimer (Head of Office).

Österreichischer Gewekschaftsbund (Austrian Federation of Trade Unions): Avenue de Cortenbergh 30, 1040 Brussels; tel (+32 2) 230 74 63; fax (+32 2) 231 17 10; e-mail europabuero@oigb-eu.at; internet www.oigb.at; contact Evelyne Rigner (Head of bureau).

CZECH REPUBLIC

Svaz Prumyslu a Dopravy Ceske Republiky: Square Vergote 39, 1030 Brussels; tel (+32 2) 737 04 02; fax (+32 2) 737 04 00; e-mail cez.lukas@skynet.be; contact Karel Lukas.

DENMARK

Danish Employers' Confederation – DA: Avenue de Cortenbergh 168, 1000 Brussels; tel (+32 2) 285 05 40; fax (+32 2) 285 05 45; e-mail da-bxl@da.dk; internet www.da.dk; contacts Jorgen Roennest (Head of Office), Thomas Roennow.

Danish Teacher Trade Unions: Boulevard du Roi Albert II 5, 1210 Brussels; tel (+32 2) 224 06 70; fax (+32 2) 224 06 71; e-mail dli@dlint.org; internet www.dlint.org; contact Martin Romer (Head of Office).

Landorganisationen: Bd du roi Albert II 5/24, 1210 Brussels; tel (+32 2) 204 06 90; fax (+32 2) 203 56 57; e-mail lo@lo.dk; contacts Prijben Karlsen (Adviser), Peder Monchansen.

FINLAND

Finnish Industries' and Finnish Employers' Confederation: Rue de la Charité 17, 1210 Brussels; tel (+32 2) 209 43 11; fax (+32 2) 223 08 05; e-mail jukka.ahtela@tt.fi; internet www.tt.fi; contact Jukka Ahtela (Permanent Delegate).

FRANCE

Chambre Syndicale des Constructeurs de Navires – CSCN (Federated Union of Shipbuilders): c/o AMRIE, Rue du Commerce 20-22, 1000 Brussels; tel (+32 2) 736 17 55; fax (+32 2) 735 22 98; e-mail info@amrie.org; internet www.amrie.org; contact Jacques Mazières (Director).

Syndicat Français de l'Industrie Cimentière (French Federation of the Cement Industry): Rue de Trèves 45, 1040 Brussels; tel (+32 2) 231 07 30; fax (+32 2) 231 08 38; e-mail r.lambert@sfic.net; contact Renaud Lambert.

GERMANY

Arbeitsgemeinschaft Berufsstandischer VersorgungseinrichTungen (ABV): Avenue des Gaulois 3, 1040 Brussels; tel (+32 2) 736 38 34; fax (+32 2) 735 25 45; e-mail abv.ev@skynet.be; contacts Michael Prossliner (Geschäftsführer), Madeleine Schavoir (Ansprechpartnerin).

Arbeitsgemeinschaft Selbständiger Unternehmer Bundesverband Junger Unternehmer: Avenue Milcomps 21, 1030 Brussels; tel (+32 02) 734 11 02; fax (+32 02) 735 80 09; contact Klaus P. Rohardt.

BundesarbeitsgemeinSchaft der Senioren – Organisationen e.V.: Rue de la Pacification 65-67, 1000 Brussels; tel (+32 2) 286 90 21; fax (+32 2) 230 94 51; e-mail bagso@easynet.be; contact Elke Tippelmann (Leiterin).

Bundesverband der Freien Berufe: Avenue de Cortenbergh 52, 1000 Brussels; tel (+32 2) 743 05 99; fax (+32 2) 734 57 74; e-mail bfbbruessel@compuserve.com; contacts Arno Metzier (Hauptgeschäftsführer RA), Florian Lemor (Ansprechpartner EU-Referent).

Bundesvereinigung Bauwirtschaft: Rue Jacques de Lalaing 4 Bte 7, 1040 Brussels; tel (+32 2) 230 18 52; fax (+32 2) 230 34 51; e-mail a.jung@bv-bauwirtschaft.de; internet www.bv-bauwirtschaft.de; contact Axel Klaus Jung (Director).

Bundesvereinigung der Deutschen Arbeitgeberverbande: Rue du Commerce 31, 1000 Brussels; tel (+32 2) 290 03 00; fax (+32 2) 290 03 19; e-mail buero-bruessel@bda-online.de; contact A. F. Von Schoenaich-Carolath.

Bundesvereinigung Deutscher Handelsverbande e.V. (BDH): Avenue des Nerviens 9-31, 1040 Brussels; tel (+32 2) 231 09 98; fax (+32 2) 230 84 97; e-mail hkrueger.bdhbru@wanadoo.be; contact Horst Kruger (Leiter Dipl.-Volksw.).

VATM – Verband der Anbieter von Telekommunikation und Mediendienste: Avenue Livingstone 33, 1000 Brussels; tel (+32 2) 235 09 80; fax (+32 2) 286 51 79; contact Andrea Weibenfels (Leiterin).

GREECE

General Labour Confederation – GSEE: Av. Général Eisenhower 104, 1030 Brussels; tel (+32 2) 216 78 82; fax (+32 2) 216 46 13; e-mail gdassis@belgacom.net; contact Georgios Dassis (Political Affairs Adviser).

HUNGARY

Confederation of Hungarian Employers' Organization for International Co-operation – CEHIC: Rue du Commerce 31, 1000 Brussels; tel (+32 2) 548 90 10; fax (+32 2) 548 90 19; e-mail vonosvath@eu-select.com; contact Gyorgy von O'Svath.

ICELAND

Industries and Employers Icelandic Federations: Rue de Cortenbergh 168, 1000 Brussels; tel (+32 2) 280 08 52; fax (+32 2) 223 08 05; e-mail kristofer@sa.is; contact K. Kristinsson (Permanent Delegate).

ITALY

Unione Italiana del Lavoro (UIL EUROPA) (Italian Labour Union): Rue du Gouvernement Provisoire 34, 1000 Brussels; tel (+32 2) 219 97 34; fax (+32 2) 219 98 34; e-mail inf.europa@uil.be; contact Giorgio Liverani.

NORWAY

LO – Brussels Office of the Norwegian Confederation of Trade Unions: Boulevard Roi Albert II 5/23, 1210 Brussels; tel (+32 2) 201 18 10; fax (+32 2) 201 18 12; e-mail lo.bru@lono.be; contact Knut Arne Sanden (Director).

SLOVAKIA

Federation of Employers' Associations of the Slovak Republic: Rue Wiertz 50, 1050 Brussels; tel (+32 2) 401 68 99; fax (+32 2) 401 68 68; e-mail nanias@nci.be.

SPAIN

CEOE – Confederation of Spanish Employers: Avenue de Tervuren 52, 1040 Brussels; tel (+32 2) 736 60 80; fax (+32 2) 736 80 90; e-mail jirdriguez@ceoe.es; internet www.ceoe.es; contact José Isaias Rodríguez (Director).

SWEDEN

LO – TCO – SACO: Avenue de Tervueren 15, 1040 Brussels; tel (+32 2) 732 18 00; fax (+32 2) 732 21 15; e-mail sven.svensson@bryssel.lo.se, info@bryssel.lo.se; internet www.brysselkontor.com; contact Sven Svensson (Director).

TURKEY

Turkish Confederation of Employer Associations: Avenue des Gaulois 13, 1040 Brussels; tel (+32 2) 736 40 47; fax (+32 2) 736 39 93; e-mail kaleagasi@tusiad.org; contact Bahadir Kaleagasi.

NATIONAL ASSOCIATIONS WITH REPRESENTATION IN BRUSSELS

AUSTRIA

Österreichische Fremdenverkehrs-Werbung (Austrian National Tourism Office): BP 700, 1050 Brussels; tel (+32 2) 646 06 10; fax (+32 2) 640 46 93; e-mail info@oewbru.be; internet www.austria-tourism.at; contact Mr. Janauschek (Director).

Österreichische Notariatskammer (The Austrian Chamber of Notaries): Rue Newton 1, 1000 Brussels; tel (+32 2) 737 90 00; fax (+32 2) 737 90 09; e-mail notar@arcadis.be; internet www.notar.at; contact Stefan Matyk.

Österreichischer Raiffeisenverband (Austrian Raiffeisen Verband): Rue du Commerce 20-22, 1000 Brussels; tel (+32 2) 549 06 78; fax (+32 2) 502 64 07; e-mail raiffbxl@raiffeisenbrussels.be; internet www.raiffeisenverband.at; contact Helga Steinberger (Office Manager).

DENMARK

Danmarks Rederiforening: Rue du Cornet 83, 1040 Brussels; tel (+32 2) 230 81 41; fax (+32 2) 230 88 29; e-mail brx@hipowners.dk; contact Michael Lund (General Manager).

DL International (Danish Teacher Trade Unions): Bd du Roi Albert II 5, 1210 Brussels; tel (+32 2) 224 06 70; fax (+32 2) 224 06 71; e-mail dli@dlint.org; internet www.dlint.org.

ETUC / CES (European Trade Union Confederation): Boulevard du Roi Albert II 5, 1210 Brussels; tel (+32 2) 224 04 11; fax (+32 2) 224 04 54; e-mail etuc@etuc.org; internet www.etuc.org; contacts F. Verzetnisch (President), J. Monks (SG).

Landsorganisationen: Boulevard du Roi Albert II 5/24, 1210 Brussels; tel (+32 2) 204 06 90; fax (+32 2) 203 56 57; e-mail lo@lo.dk; internet www.lo.dk; contact Preben Karlsen (President and SG).

FRANCE

Agence de l'Environnement et de la Maîtrise de l'Energie – ADEME (Agency for the Environment and Energy Management): Avenue des Arts 53, 1000 Brussels; tel (+32 2) 545 11 41; fax (+32 2) 513 91 70; e-mail ademe.brux@euronet.be; contact Gérard Saunier (Responsible-Energy).

ANVAR – Agence Nationale de Valorisation de la Recherche (National Agency for the Development of Research): Rue de Luxembourg 3, 1000 Brussels; tel (+32 2) 501 07 32; fax (+32 2) 501 07 33; e-mail bruxe@anvar.fr; contact Jean-Claude Porée.

Association des Ecoles des Mines – ARMINES (Association of Schools of Mining): c/o CLORA, Avenue des Arts 8, 1210 Brussels; tel (+32 2) 506 88 64; fax (+32 2) 506 88 45; e-mail organisme@clora.net.

Association Française des Entreprises Privées – Section Commerce (French Association of Private Companies Business Section): Rue Royale 35, 1000 Brussels; tel (+32 2) 219 90 20; fax (+32 2) 219 95 06; e-mail afep@skynet.be; contact Armand Maheas (Project Manager).

Association Nationale des Elus de la Montagne – ANEM (National Association of Representatives of Mountain Regions): c/o ACFCI, Avenue des Arts 1-2 bte 9, 1210 Brussels; tel (+32 2) 221 04 11; fax (+32 2) 217 69 87; e-mail aem@promonte-aem.org; contacts Enrico Kirschen (Consultant), Nicolas Evrard.

BEAF – Bureau Européen de l'Artisanat Français – Section Commerce (European Office of French Craftsmanship Business Section): Rue Jacques de Lalaing 4, 1040 Brussels; tel (+32 2) 280 14 43; fax (+32 2) 230 78 61; e-mail r.sioldea@ueapme.com; contact Hubert Delorme.

Breiz Europe (Brittany in Europe): Rue Froissart 141, 1040 Brussels; tel (+32 2) 230 44 26; fax (+32 2) 230 51 83; e-mail breiz.europe@skynet.be; contact Christophe Hamon (Director).

CEMAGREF-La Recherche pour l'Ingénierie de l'Agriculture et de l'Environnement (Research into Agricultural and Environmental Engineering): c/o CLORA, Rue Montoyer 47, 1000 Brussels; tel (+32 02) 506 66; fax (+32 02) 506 88 45; e-mail vidal@clora.net; contact Alain Vidal (General Secretary).

Centre National de la Recherche Scientifique – CNRS (National Centre for Scientific Research): c/o CLORA, Rue Montoyer 47, 1000 Brussels; tel (+32 2) 506 88 42/44/49; fax (+32 2) 506 88 45; e-mail cnrs@clora.net; internet www.cnrs.fr; contact Monika Dietl (CP).

Club des Organismes de Recherche Associés – CLORA (Associated Research Bodies Club): Rue Montoyer 47, 1000 Brussels; tel (+32 2) 506 88 64; fax (+32 2) 506 88 45; e-mail secretariat@clora.net; internet www.clora.net; contact Mme de Hennin (SG).

CNES-Centre National d'Etudes Spatiales (National Centre for Space Studies): c/o CLORA, Rue Montoyer 47, 1000 Brussels; tel (+32 02) 506 02; fax (+32 02) 506 88 45; e-mail marbach@clora.net; contact André Marbach (General Secretary).

Commissariat à l'Energie Atomique CEA (Commissariat for Atomic Energy): c/o CLORA, Rue Montoyer 47, 1000 Brussels; tel (+32 2) 506 88 46; fax (+32 2) 506 88 45; e-mail cea@clora.net; contact Guillaume Gillet.

Conférence des Présidents d'Université (University Presidents' Conference): c/o CLORA, Rue Montoyer 47, 1000 Brussels; tel (+32 2) 506 88 59; fax (+32 2) 506 88 45; e-mail dalle@clora.net; contacts Geneviève Dalle, Patrick Navatte.

Délégation des Barreaux de France auprès de l'UE (French Bar Association in the EU): Avenue de la Joyeuse Entrée 1, 1040 Brussels; tel (+32 2) 230 83 31; fax (+32 2) 230 62 77; e-mail dbf@skynet.be; internet www.dbfbruxelles.com; contact Laurent Petitjean (Director).

Entreprise Rhône-Alpes International – ERAI – Section Commerce (Rhône-Alpes International Undertaking Business Section): Rue de Trèves 49-51 bte 1, 1040 Brussels; tel (+32 2) 282 00 30; fax (+32 2) 280 60 72; e-mail erai.bru@skynet.be, benelux@erai.org; contact Lionel Dupré.

Entreprises Equipement France – EEF (French Equipment Firms): c/o ACFCI, Avenue Boileau 16, 1040 Brussels; tel (+32 2) 739 15 39; fax (+32 2) 217 66 12; e-mail eef@arcadis.be; contact Alain Jaffre.

Fédération des Industries des Equipements pour Véhicules – FIEV (Federation of Vehicle Components Industries): c/o MEDEF, Rue de Trèves 45, 1040 Brussels; tel (+32 2) 231 07 30; fax (+32 2) 231 08 38; e-mail medef.brux@skynet.be; contact Marie-Christine Vaccarezza.

Fédération Nationale des Transports Routiers – FNTR Bureau de Représentation (National Road Transport Federation): Avenue Louis Gribeaumont 1Bte 2, 1150 Brussels; tel (+32 2)

772 65 56; fax (+32 2) 772 11 26; contact Isabelle Maître (Perm Rep).

I.R.D.- Institut de Recherche pour le Développement (Institute of Development Research): c/o CLORA, Rue Montoyer 47, 1000 Brussels; tel (+32 2) 506 88 48; fax (+32 2) 506 88 45; e-mail brugaillere@clora.net; contact Marie-Christine Brugaillère (CP).

Institut Français de Recherche pour l'Exploitation de la Mer – IFREMER (French Institute for Research into Harvesting the Sea): c/o CLORA, Rue Montoyer 47, 1000 Brussels; tel (+32 2) 506 88 60; fax (+32 2) 506 88 45; e-mail carbonniere@clora.net, ifremer@clora.net; contact Aurélien Carbonnière (CP).

Institut National de la Recherche Agronomique – INRA (National Institute for Agricultural Research): c/o CLORA, Rue Montoyer 47, 1000 Brussels; tel (+32 2) 506 88 54; fax (+32 2) 506 88 45; e-mail inra@clora.cfcib.be, lamarque@clora.net; contact Claudine Lamarque (CP).

Institut National de la Santé et la Recherche Médicale – INSERM (National Institute of Health and Medical Research): c/o CLORA, Rue Montoyer 47, 1000 Brussels; tel (+32 02) 506 88 50; fax (+32 02) 506 88 45; e-mail bennigsen@clora.net; contact Elisabeth Bennigsen.

La Poste (Postal Service): Rue du Luxembourg 3, 1000 Brussels; tel (+32 2) 501 07 46; fax (+32 2) 501 07 44; e-mail f.mary@laposte.skynet.be; internet www.laposte.fr; contact F. Mary (Director).

Medef: Rue de Trèves 45, 1040 Brussels; tel (+32 2) 231 07 30; fax (+32 2) 231 08 38; e-mail medef.brux@skynet.be; contact Marie-Christine Vaccarezza (Permanent Delegate).

ONERA – Office National d' Etudes et de Recherches Aérospatiales (National Office for Aerospace Studies and Research): c/o CLORA, Rue Montoyer 47, 1000 Brussels; tel (+32 02) 506 41; fax (+32 02) 506 88 45; e-mail mainguy@clora.net; contact Anne-Marie Mainguy (General Secretary).

Président des Conseillers du Commerce Extérieur de la France (President of Advisers on French Foreign Trade): c/o CCIF, Avenue des Arts 8, 1210 Brussels; tel (+32 2) 506 88 06; fax (+32 2) 506 88 17; contact Andrée Dufau (Responsible).

RST – Réseau Scientifique et Technique du Ministère de l'Equipement, des Transports et du Logement (Scientific and Technical Network of the Ministry of Infrastructure, Transport and Housing): c/o CLORA, Rue Montoyer 47, 1000 Brussels; tel (+32 02) 506 74 ou 75; fax (+32 02) 506 88 45; e-mail binotte@clora.net; contact Michel Binotte (General Secretary).

Sopexa: Rue du Luxembourg 47-51, 1050 Brussels; tel (+32 2) 512 79 69; fax (+32 2) 512 19 52; e-mail françois .pommereau@sopexa.com; internet www.frenchfoods.com, www.sopexa.be; contact François Pommereau (Director).

Syndicat Français de l'Industrie Cimentière – SFIC (French Federation of the Cement Industry): c/o MEDEF, Rue de Trèves 45, 1040 Brussels; tel (+32 2) 231 07 30; fax (+32 2) 231 08 38; e-mail medef.brux@skynet.be; contacts Marie-Christine Vaccarezza-Silvestre, Renaud Lambert.

Syndicat National de la Restauration Collective – SNRC (National Federation for Collective Restoration): c/o MEDEF, Rue de Trèves 45, 1040 Brussels; tel (+32 2) 231 07 30; fax (+32 2) 231 08 38; e-mail medef.brux@skynet.be; contacts Marie Audrin, Emmanuelle Butaud.

Union des Industries Textiles – UIT (Textile Industries Union): c/o MEDEF, Rue de Trèves 45, 1040 Brussels; tel (+32 2) 231 07 30; fax (+32 2) 231 08 38; e-mail medef.brux@skynet.be; contact Marie Audrin (Director).

Union Nationale des Industries Carrières et Matériels de Construction (National Union of the Quarrying and Construction Materials Industries): c/o MEDEF, Rue de Trèves 45, 1040 Brussels; contact Mme Vaccarella.

GERMANY

Arbeitsgemeinschaft Berufsständischer VersorgungseinrichTungen (ABV): Avenue des Gaulois 3, 1040 Brussels; tel (+32 2) 736 38 34; fax (+32 2) 735 25 45; e-mail abv.ev@skynet.be; contacts Michael Prossliner (President), Madeleine Schavoir (General secretary).

Arbeitsgemeinschaft Deutscher Tierzüchter e. V.: Rue du Luxembourg 47-51, 1050 Brussels; tel (+32 2) 286 59 54; fax (+32 2) 285 40 59; e-mail hp .schons@adt.de; contact Dr. Hans-Peter Schons (President).

Arbeitsgemeinschaft Deutscher Verkehrsflughafen Verbindungsburo Brussel: Avenue Louise 350 Bte 6, 1050 Brussels; tel (+32 2) 647 79 54; fax (+32 2) 647 26 34; contact Birgit Schoenrock.

Ausstellungs- und Messe-Ausschuss der Deutschen Wirtschaft e.V. – AUMA: Rue Grovelines 56, 1000 Brussels; fax (+32 2) 280 12 90; e-mail a.heidenreich@auma.de; internet www .auma.messen.de; contact Anna Maria Heidenreich (SG).

AWM – Aktionsgemeinschaft Wirtschaftlicher Mittelstand: Place du Luxembourg 11, 1050 Brussels; tel (+32 2) 230 94 99; fax (+32 2) 231 06 01; e-mail koch-mehrin@awm-online.de; contact Silvana Koch Mehrin (SG).

Bagso- Kontaktstelle Brüssel BundesarbeitsgemeinSchaft der Senioren-Organisationen e.V.: Rue de la Pacification 65-67, 1000 Brussels; tel (+32 2) 286 90 21; fax (+32 2) 230 94 51; e-mail bagso@easynet.be; contact Elke Tippelmann (Director).

Brüsseler Büro der Deutschen Arzteschaft: Rue Belliard 197, 1040 Brussels; tel (+32 2) 280 18 17; fax (+32 2) 230 81 10; e-mail deutschen .arzteschaft@skynet.be; internet www .bundesaerztekammer.de, www.kbv.de; contacts Stefan Graf (Director), Susanne Döring.

Bund für Lebensmittelrecht und Lebensmittelkunde e.V.: Avenue des Arts 43, 1040 Brussels; tel (+32 2) 508 10 23; fax (+32 2) 508 10 21; e-mail Ploosen@bll-online.be; contact Rechtsanwalt Peter Loosen (Director).

Bundesagentur für Aussenwirtschaft-BFAI: Avenue du Boulevard 21, 1210 Brussels; tel (+32 2) 204 01 73; fax (+32 2) 206 67 60; e-mail hungermann@ bfai.de; contact Kirsten Hungermann (Director).

BundesarbeitgeberverBand Chemie: Rue du Commerce 31, 1000 Brussels; tel (+32 2) 290 89 80; fax (+32 2) 290 89 74; e-mail Bruessel@bavc.de; contact Markus Handke (Director).

BundesarbeitsgemeinSchaft der Mittel- und Grossbetriebe des Einzelhandels e. V. – BAG: Avenue des Vaillants 5 Bte 7, 1200 Brussels; tel (+32 2) 734 32 89; e-mail femged@pi.be; internet www.bag.de; contact Mr. Droulans.

BundesarchitektenKammer: Avenue des Arts 12 bte 15, 1210 Brussels; tel (+32 2) 219 77 30; fax (+32 2) 219 24 94; e-mail lottes@bak.de; internet www .bak.de; contact Anton Dauch (Director).

Bundesingenieurkammer, EU-Verbindungsburo Brussel: Avenue des Arts 12 Bte 15, 1210 Brussels; tel (+32 2) 219 77 30; fax (+32 2) 219 24 94; e-mail ralf.lottes@wanadoo.be; internet http://blingk.de; contact RA Ralf Lottes (Director).

Bundesnotarkammer: Rue Newton 1, 1000 Brussels; tel (+32 2) 737 90 00; fax (+32 2) 737 90 09; e-mail t.schleifenbaum@bnotk.de; internet www.bnotk.de; contact Till Schemman.

BundesrechtsanwaltsKammer (Association of Federal Bars): Avenue de Tervuren 142-144, 1150 Brussels; tel (+32 2) 743 86 46; fax (+32 2) 743 86 56; e-mail brak.bxl@brak.be; internet www.brak.be; contact Dr. Heike Lorcher.

BundessteuerberaterKammer-Büro Brüssel: Avenue de Cortenbergh 52,

1000 Brussels; tel (+32 2) 743 05 96; fax (+32 2) 734 91 17; e-mail bruessel@bstbk.be; contact Karin Sauerteig (EU referent).

Bundesverband der Deutschen EntsorgungswirtSchaft e.V. (BDE): Rue du Commerce 31, 1000 Brussels; tel (+32 2) 500 57 80; fax (+32 2) 500 57 03;

Bundesverband der Deutschen Gas- und Wasserwirtschaft (BGW): Rond-Point Schuman, 1040 Brussels; tel (+32 2) 234 78 08; fax (+32 2) 234 79 11; e-mail aertker@bgw.de; contact Dr. Peter Aertker.

Bundesverband der Deutschen Volks- und Raiffeisenbanken-BVR: Rue de l'Industrie 26-38, 1040 Brussels; tel (+32 2) 286 98 48; fax (+32 2) 230 06 49; e-mail v.heegemann@bvr.de; contact Dr. Volker Heegemann (EU Relations Manager).

Bundesverband der Freien Berufe: Avenue de Cortenbergh 52, 1000 Brussels; tel (+32 2) 743 05 99; fax (+32 2) 734 57 74; e-mail bfbbruessel@compuserve.com; contacts Arno Metzler (Director), Florian Lemor (EU referent).

Bundesverband der Mittelstandischen Wirtschaft: Avenue de la Renaissance 1, 1000 Brussels; tel (+32 2) 739 63 59; fax (+32 2) 736 05 71; e-mail grupp.walter@skynet.be; internet www.bvmonline.be; contact Walter Grupp.

Bundesverband des Deutschen GetränkefachgrossHandels e.V., c/o APRI: Avenue du Boulevard 21, 1210 Brussels; tel (+32 2) 204 01 88; fax (+32 2) 203 47 58; e-mail info@apri.web.org; internet www.apri-web.org; contact Matthias Popp (Project Manager).

Bundesverband Guterkraftverkehr und Logistik – BGL: Rue d'Arlon 55, 1040 Brussels; tel (+32 2) 230 10 82; fax (+32 2) 230 78 56; e-mail brussels@BGL-EV.de; internet www.bgl-ev.de; contact Dirk Saile (Director).

Bundesverband Junger Unternehmer: Avenue Milcamps 21, 1030 Brussels; tel (+32 2) 734 11 02; fax (+32 2) 735 80 09; contact Klaus P. Rohardt (Representative).

Bundesverband Öffentlicher Banken Deutschland: Avenue de la Joyeuse Entrée 1, 1040 Brussels; tel (+32 2) 286 90 61; fax (+32 2) 231 02 19; e-mail henning.schoppmann@voeb.de; internet http://voeb.de; contact Henning Schoppman (Director).

Bundesvereinigung Deutscher Apothekenverbande – Abda Buro Brussel: Rue Newton 1, 1000 Brussels; tel (+32 2) 735 30 57; fax (+32 2) 735 02 68; e-mail abda-buero.bruessel@aponet.de; internet www.abda.de; contact Dr. Susanne Hof (Head of European Affairs).

Bundesvereinigung Deutscher Handelsverbände e.V. (BDH): 9-31 Avenue des Nerviens, 1040 Brussels; tel (+32 2) 735 43 79; fax (+32 2) 230 84 97; e-mail bgallus.bdhbru@wanadoo.be; contact Britta Gallus (Director).

Bundeszahnärztekammer (Association of Medical Practitioners): Avenue de la Renaissance 1, 1000 Brussels; tel (+32 2) 732 84 15; fax (+32 2) 735 56 79; e-mail bzakbxl@arcadis.be; contact Mary Van Driel (Director).

Büro Brüssel Jugend und Arbeit: Rue de la Pacification 65, 1000 Brussels; tel (+32 2) 230 41 45; fax (+32 2) 230 94 51; e-mail central@bbj.be; internet www.bbj.be; contact Ulrike Wisser (Director).

Büro der Evangelischen Kirche Deutschlands in Brüssel: Rue Joseph II 166, 1000 Brussels; tel (+32 2) 230 16 39; fax (+32 2) 280 01 08; e-mail ekd.bruessel@ekd.be; contact Sabine Von Zanthier (Director).

CMA – Zentrale Marketinggesellschaft der Deutschen Agrarwirtschaft: Rue du Luxembourg 47-51, 1050 Brussels; tel (+32 2) 505 34 81; fax (+32 2) 505 34 80; e-mail cma-benelux@skynet.be; contact Onno Christians (Director).

COMECE – Kommission der Bischofskonferenzen der Europäischen Gemeinschaft: Rue Stévin 42, 1000 Brussels; tel (+32 2) 235 05 17; fax (+32 2) 230 33 34; e-mail stefan.lunte@comece.org; internet www.comece.org; contact Stefan Lunte (Director).

Dekra e.V.: Avenue de Cortenbergh 52, 1000 Brussels; tel (+32 2) 740 24 90; fax (+32 2) 672 96 06; e-mail oliver.deiters.dekra@skynet.be; contact Oliver Deiters.

Deutsche Postgewerkschaft: Avenue de Tervuren 273/7, 1150 Brussels; tel (+32 2) 775 02 21; fax (+32 2) 775 02 22; e-mail k.vonbonin@deutschepost.de; internet www.deutschepost.de; contact K. von Bonin (Office Manager).

Deutsche Sozialversicherung Europavertretung: Rue d'Arlon 50, 1000 Brussels; tel (+32 2) 230 75 22; fax (+32 2) 230 77 73; e-mail dsv@esip.org; contact Franz Terwey (Director).

Deutsche Zentrale für Tourismus: Rue Gulledelle 92, 1200 Brussels; tel (+32 2) 245 97 00; fax (+32 2) 245 39 80; e-mail gntobru@d-z-t.com; contact Rijkert Kettelhake.

Deutscher Anwaltverein: Avenue de la Joyeuse Entrée 1, 1040 Brussels; tel (+32 2) 280 28 12; fax (+32 2) 280 28 13; e-mail bruessel@anwaltverein.de; internet www.anwaltverein.de; contact Alexander Gemberg-Wiesike (Director).

Deutscher Bauernverband e.V.: Rue du Luxembourg 47-51, 1050 Brussels; tel (+32 2) 285 40 50; fax (+32 2) 285 40 59; e-mail w.kampmann@bauernverband.net; internet www.bauernverband.net; contact Willi Kampmann (Director).

Deutscher Beamtenbund – DBB (Federation of German Civil Servants): Avenue de la Joyeuse Entrée 1-5, 1040 Brussels; tel (+32 2) 282 18 70; fax (+32 2) 282 17 71; contact Bernd Rupp (Director).

Deutscher Bundeswehr-Verband: Avenue Général de Gaulle 33, 1050 Brussels; tel (+32 2) 626 06 80; fax (+32 2) 626 06 99; e-mail euromil@euromil.org; internet www.dbwv.de; contact Dr. Ulrich A. Hundt (SG).

Deutscher Fleischerverband Vertretung bei der Europäischen Union: Rue Jacques de Lalaing, 1040 Brussels; tel (+32 2) 230 66 90; fax (+32 2) 230 34 51; e-mail info@cibc.be; internet www.fleischerhandwerk.de; contact Kirsten Diessner (Director).

Deutscher Gewerkschaftsbund Verbindungsbüro Brüssel: Boulevard de l'Empereur 24, 1000 Brussels; tel (+32 2) 548 36 90; fax (+32 2) 548 36 99; e-mail dgb.brux@pophost.eunet.be; contact Gloria Müller (Director of office).

Deutscher Kohlebergbau: Avenue de Tervuren 168 Bte 5, 1150 Brussels; tel (+32 2) 772 46 30; fax (+32 2) 771 41 04; e-mail prior@eurocoal.org; contact Leopold Janssens.

Deutscher Paritatischer Wohlfahrtsverband Gesamtverband e.V.: Rue Prince Royale 83, 1050 Brussels; tel (+32 2) 502 14 32; fax (+32 2) 502 13 91; e-mail eu.bruessel@paritaet.org; contact Dr. Özgür Öner (Director).

Deutscher Raiffeisenverband e.V.: Rue du Luxembourg 47/51, 1050 Brussels; tel (+32 2) 285 40 50; fax (+32 2) 285 40 59; e-mail drv.bxl@raiffeisen.be; contact Thomas Memmert (Director).

Deutscher Sparkassen- und Giroverband: Avenue de la Joyeuse Entrée 1-5 bte 6, 1040 Brussels; tel (+32 2) 230 74 90; fax (+32 2) 230 82 45; e-mail brussels.office@dsgv.de; internet www.dsgv.de; contact Christian Konig (CP).

Deutscher Verkehrssicherheitsrat: Avenue des Arts 44, 1040 Brussels; tel (+32 2) 213 40 43; fax (+32 2) 213 40 49; e-mail MR-Consult@t-online.de; contact Dr. Manfred Raisch (Representative).

Deutsches Aktieninstitut – Représentation auprès de l'Union Européenne: Rue du Commerce 31, 1000 Brussels; tel (+32 2) 290 89 90; fax (+32 2) 290 89 91; e-mail europa@dai.de; contact Ralf Fischer zu Cramburg (Director).

EU-Büro des Deutschen Sports: Avenue de Cortenbergh 89, 1000 Brussels; tel (+32 2) 738 03 20; fax (+32 2) 738 03 27;

e-mail info@eu-sports-office.org; contact Tilo Friedmann (EU Representative).

Europavertretung der Deutsche Sozial Versicherung: Rue d'Arlon 50, 1040 Brussels; tel (+32 2) 230 75 22; fax (+32 2) 230 77 73; contact Dr. Franz Terwey (Director).

EU-Vertretung BAGFW: Rue de Pascale 4-6, 1040 Brussels; tel (+32 2) 230 45 00; fax (+32 2) 230 57 04; e-mail euvertretung@bay-wohlfahrt.de; internet www.caritas.de; contact Bernd-Otto Kuper (Director).

Friedrich Ebert Stiftung: Rue Archimède 5, 1000 Brussels; tel (+32 2) 231 04 89; fax (+32 2) 230 76 51; e-mail fes@fesbrussels.org; internet www.fes.de; contact Dr. Ernst Stetter (Director).

Friedrich Naumann Stiftung: Rue Froissart 109, 1040 Brussels; tel (+32 2) 282 09 30; fax (+32 2) 282 09 31; e-mail ipd@brussels.fnst.org; internet www.fnst.org; contact Dr Jurgen Wickert (Director).

Gemeinschaft zur Forderung der Privaten Deutschen Pflanzenzuchtung e.V.: Rue du Luxembourg 47-51, 1050 Brussels; tel (+32 02) 282 08 40; fax (+32 02) 282 08 41; e-mail GFP-FEI@euronet.be; contact Dr. Hilke Riemer.

Gesamtverband der Deutschen VersicherungswirtSchaft e.V.: Avenue de Cortenbergh 60, 1000 Brussels; tel (+32 2) 282 47 30/31; fax (+32 2) 282 47 39; e-mail bruessel@gdv.org; internet www.gdv.org; contact Ulf Lemor (Director of European Affairs).

Gesamtverband der Textilindustrie in der Bundesrepublik Deutschland – Gesamttextil e.V.: Rue de l'Amazone 2, 1050 Brussels; tel (+32 2) 534 95 95; fax (+32 2) 534 96 96; e-mail joern.kronenwerth@belgium.messefrankfurt.com; internet www.gesamttextil.de; contact J. Kronenwerth (Director).

GTZ-Verbindungsburo Brussel: Avenue d'Auderghem 67, 1040 Brussels; tel (+32 2) 230 91 23; fax (+32 2) 230 87 50; e-mail gtz.brussels@skynet.be; internet www.gtz.de; contact Dr. Jurgen Koch (Director).

Hanns Seidel Stiftung: Rue de Pascal 45-47, 1040 Brussels; tel (+32 2) 230 50 81; fax (+32 2) 230 70 27; internet www.hss.de; contact Markus Russ (Director).

Hauptverband der Deutschen Bauindustrie (German Construction Industry): Rue du Commerce 31 – 4e étage, 1000 Brussels; tel (+32 2) 512 95 97; fax (+32 2) 512 50 66; e-mail marleen.heyndrickx@bauindustrie.de; internet www.bauindustrie.de; contact Sébastien Richter (Director).

Hauptverband der Deutschen Holz und Kunststoffe Verarbeitenden

Industrie und Verwandter Industriezweige – HDH: Rue du Commerce 31, 1000 Brussels; tel (+32 2) 503 07 05; fax (+32 2) 503 07 07; e-mail j.kurth@hdh-ev.de; contact Jan Kurth.

Hauptverband des Deutschen Einzelhandels: Rue Foissart 123-133, 1040 Brussels; tel (+32 2) 231 09 98; fax (+32 2) 230 84 97; e-mail Horst.Krueger@euronet.be; contact Horst Krueger (Dir).

Heinrich Böll Stiftung: Rue d'Arlon 15, 1050 Brussels; tel (+32 2) 743 41 00; fax (+32 2) 743 41 09; e-mail brussels@boell.de; internet www.boell.de; contact Claude Weinberg (Head of Office).

Institut der Deutschen Wirtschaft Köln: Rue des Sols 8, 1000 Brussels; tel (+32 2) 515 09 75; fax (+32 02) 515 09 76; e-mail bush@iwkoeln.de; contact Berthold Bush.

Institut der Wirtschaftsprufer In Deutschland e.D.-IDW: Rue de Spa 15, 1000 Brussels; tel (+32 2) 230 42 90; fax (+32 2) 280 14 29; e-mail klaas@idw.de; internet www.idw.de; contact Dr. Klaas (Head of Office).

Inwent (Association of Medical Practitioners): Rue du Commerce 31, 1000 Brussels; tel (+32 2) 500 89 61; fax (+32 2) 500 89 68; e-mail harbuschf@cdg.de, franck.harbusch@inwent.org; internet www.cdg.de; contact Franck Harbusch.

Kassenärztliche Bundesvereinigung: Rue d'Arlon 50, 1000 Brussels; tel (+49) 2225 704-705 (tel); fax (+49) 2225 704-704 (fax); e-mail Wilke-Holtheide@t-online.de; contact Petra Wilke-Holtheide (Director).

Konrad-Adenauer-Stiftung: Avenue de l'Yser 11, 1040 Brussels; tel (+32 2) 743 07 43; fax (+32 2) 743 07 49; e-mail sekretariat@eukas.be; internet www.kas.de; contact Peter Weilemann (Director).

Ostasiatischer Verein e.V.: Boulevard Clovis 49A, 1000 Brussels; tel (+32 2) 286 16 80; fax (+32 2) 286 16 84; e-mail papaschinopoulou.mary@bruessel.dink.de; contact Dr. Mary Papaschinopoulou.

Represantanz der Berliner Wirtschaft: Avenue Livingstone 33, 1000 Brussels; tel (+32 2) 286 51 70; fax (+32 2) 286 51 79; e-mail berlin.business@skynet.be; internet www.beoberlin.de; contacts Jorn Exner (CP), Christine Wild (CP).

VATM – Verband der Anbieter von Telekommunikations und Mehrwertdiensten e.V.: 33 Avenue Livingstone, 1000 Brussels; tel (+32 2) 235 09 80; fax (+32 2) 286 51 79; e-mail brussels@vatm.de; contact Dirk Grewe (Director).

VDMA European Office: Boulevard A. Reyers 80, 1030 Brussels; tel (+32 2) 706 82 20; fax (+32 2) 706 82 10; e-mail burkhart.vonrauch@mcm.be; internet

www.vdma.org/europa; contact Burkhart Von Rauch (Director).

Verband Beratender Ingenieure (VBI) (Consulting Engineer's Liaison-Office Brussels): Avenue de la Renaissance 1, 1000 Brussels; tel (+32 2) 732 07 88; fax (+32 2) 732 07 95; e-mail Honert@Liaison-Office.org; contact Reinhard Honert (Director).

Verband der Automobilindustrie e.V. (VDA) Büro Brüssel: Rue du commerce 31, 1000 Brussels; tel (+32 2) 548 90 23; fax (+32 2) 548 90 29; e-mail niedenthal@vda.de; contact Dr. Michael Niedenthal (Director).

Verband der Chemischen Industrie – VCI: Rue du Commerce 31, 1000 Brussels; tel (+32 2) 548 06 90; fax (+32 2) 548 06 99; e-mail quick@bruessel.vci.de; contact Dr. Reinhard Quick (Director).

Verband der Deutschen Essenzenindustrie e.V.: Boulevard Charlemagne 96, 1000 Brussels; tel (+32 2) 234 37 37; fax (+32 2) 234 37 39; e-mail vddei-vdrh@aktuell.be; contact Bettina Muermann (Director).

Verband der Elektrizitätswerk-Schaft (German Producers and Distributors of Electricity): Avenue de Tervuren 148 Bte 17, 1150 Brussels; tel (+32 2) 771 96 42; fax (+32 2) 763 08 17; e-mail michael.wunnerlich@vdew.net; internet www.vdewNet; contact Michael Wunnerlich (Director).

Verband der Technischen Uberwachungsvereine e.V.: Rue Jacques de Lalaing 4, 1040 Brussels; tel (+32 2) 534 82 77; fax (+32 2) 534 31 10; e-mail vdtuev.bruessel@t-online.de; contact Daniel Pflumm (SG).

Verband Deutscher Hypothekenbanken: Avenue Michel Ange 13, 1000 Brussels; tel (+32 2) 732 46 38; fax (+32 2) 732 48 02; e-mail vdh@hypverband.be; internet www.hypverband.de; contact Wolfgang Kalberer.

Verband Deutscher Maschinen und Anlagenbau – VDMA (Federation of German Mechanical Industry): Boulevard A. Reyers 80, 1030 Brussels; tel (+32 2) 706 82 05; fax (+32 2) 706 82 10; e-mail european.office@vdma.org; internet www.vdma.org.

Verband Deutscher Verkehrsunternehmen: c/o UITP-EURO TEAM, Rue Sainte-Marie 6, 1080 Brussels; tel (+32 2) 663 66 26; fax (+32 2) 663 66 36; e-mail klaus.meyer@uitp.com; internet www.uitp.com; contact Klaus J. Meyer (Director of the UITP euroteam).

Verband Kommunaler Unternehmen e.V. (VKU): Rue de la Charité bte 12, 1210 Brussels; tel (+32 2) 229 21 48; fax (+32 2) 218 12 13; e-mail widmer@vku.de; contact Beatrix Widmer (Director).

Verein Deutscher Eisenhuttenleute Büro Brussel: Square Marie Louise 18 Bte 3, 1000 Brussels; tel (+32 2) 230 18 55; fax (+32 2) 230 50 63; e-mail alexander.heck@skynet.be; contact Alexander Heck (Director).

Verein Deutscher Ingenieure – VDI: Rue du Commerce 31, 1000 Brussels; tel (+32 2) 500 89 65; fax (+32 2) 511 33 67; e-mail bruxelles@vdi.de; internet www.vdi.de; contact Jorg Niehoff (Head of Department).

Wirtschaftsvereinigung Bergbau: Rue du Commerce 31, 1000 Brussels; tel (+32 2) 290 89 85; fax (+32 2) 290 89 74; e-mail manfred.steinhage@freebel.net; internet www.wv-bergbau.de; contact Manfred Steinhage.

Wirtschaftsvereinigung Stahl (German Steel Industry): Square Marie-Louise 18 Bte 3, 1000 Brussels; tel (+32 2) 230 18 55; fax (+32 2) 230 50 63; e-mail alexander.heck@skynet.be; internet www.stahl-online.de; contact Alexander Heck (Director).

Zentral Verband des Deutschen Handwerks: Rue Jacques de Lalaing 4, 1040 Brussels; tel (+32 2) 230 85 39; fax (+32 2) 230 21 66; e-mail info.brussels@ zdh.de; internet www.zdh.de; contact Karin Rogge.

Zentralverband Elektrotechnik- und Elektronikindustrie – ZVEI: Rue du Commerce 31, 1000 Brussels; tel (+32 2) 548 90 28; fax (+32 2) 548 90 29; e-mail b.john@bdi-online.de; contact Dr Beatrix John.

ITALY

Consiglio Nazionale delle Ricerche: Rue de la Loi 26, 1040 Brussels; tel (+32 02) 219 41 46; fax (+32 02) 217 74 15; e-mail cnr-brux@euronet.be; contact Giuseppe Roffi (Director).

Federacciai (Italian Steel Industry): Rue Belliard 205 box 7, 1040 Brussels; tel (+32 2) 231 02 85; fax (+32 2) 231 19 74; e-mail bruxelles@federacciai.it; contact Salvadore Salerno (Director).

Federlegno – Arredo (Timber): Avenue de la Joyeuse Entrée 1 Bte 11, 1040 Brussels; tel (+32 2) 286 12 11; fax (+32 2) 230 69 08; contact Filippo Perrone Donnorso (Director).

Istituto Italiano di Cultura (Italian Cultural Institute): Rue de Livourne 38, 1000 Brussels; tel (+32 2) 533 27 20; fax (+32 2) 534 62 92; e-mail italculture

.bruxelles@euronet.be, info@iicbruxelles .be; contact Sira Miori (Cultural Attaché).

JAPAN

Japan Automobile Manufacturers' Association – JAMA: Avenue Louise 287, 1050 Brussels; tel (+32 2) 639 14 30; fax (+32 2) 647 57 54; e-mail ga@ jama-e.be, sas@jama-e.be; internet www .japanauto.com; contact Shinji Kanno (Managing Director).

Japan Machinery Centre for Trade Investment: Rue d'Arlon 69-71 Bte 1, 1040 Brussels; tel (+32 2) 230 69 92; fax (+32 2) 230 54 85; e-mail imai@jmceu.org; contact T. Imai (Director).

NORWAY

Avholdsfolkets Landsrad – Eurocare: Rue des Confédérés 96-98, 1000 Brussels; tel (+32 2) 736 05 72; fax (+32 2) 736 73 51; e-mail eurocare@village.be; contact Florence Berteletti-Kemp (Communication Officer).

SWITZERLAND

Swiss Contact Office for Research & Higher Education – Swisscore: Rue du Trône 98, 1050 Brussels; tel (+32 02) 549 09 80; fax (+32 02) 549 09 89; e-mail infodesk@swisscore.be; contact Martine Weiss (Director).

TAIWAN

National Science Council Taipei: Bd du Régent 40, 1040 Brussels; tel (+32 2) 517 17 31; fax (+32 2) 218 76 58; internet www.belgium.nsc.gov.tw; contact Joseph Ehsu (Managing Director).

Taipei Representative Office: Boulevard du Régent 40, 1000 Brussels; tel (+32 02) 511 06 87; fax (+32 02) 511 17 89; e-mail mofa-brussels@taipei-officer .be; contact Mr Lee (Director).

TURKEY

Foundation for Professional Training and Small Industry in Turkey – MEKSA: Rue du Luxembourg 14 A, 1000 Brussels; tel (+32 02) 285 40 20; fax (+32 02) 230 40 25; e-mail eyor@euronet.be; contact A. Ecmel Yorganci (Director).

Organisation for the Development of Small and Medium-Sized Enterprises – KOSGEB: Rue du Luxembourg 14 A, 1000 Brussels; tel (+32 02) 285 40 20; fax (+32 02) 285 40 25; e-mail eyor@ euronet.be; contact A. Ecmel Yorganci (Director).

UNITED KINGDOM

Electricity Association: Scotland House, Rond point n°6, 1040 Brussels; tel (+32 2) 282 84 56; fax (+32 2) 282 84 55; e-mail shercock@csi.com; contact Stuart Hercock (Representative).

Freight Transport Association – FTA: Rue Wiertz 50, 3rd floor, 1050 Brussels; tel (+32 2) 231 03 21; fax (+32 2) 230 41 40; e-mail esc@pophost.eunet.be; internet www.fta.co.uk; contact Damian Viccars (Head of EU Affairs).

Institute of Chartered Accountants in England and Wales: Rue de la Loi 227, 1040 Brussels; tel (+32 2) 230 32 72; fax (+32 2) 230 28 51; e-mail european .office@icaew.co.uk; internet www .icaew.co.uk; contact M. Manuzi (Head Director).

UK Research and Higher Education European Office – UKRHEEO: Rue de la Loi 83 Bte 10, 1040 Brussels; tel (+32 2) 230 52 75 – 230 15 35; fax (+32 2) 230 48 03; e-mail ukro@bbsrc.ac.uk; internet www.ukro.ac.uk; contact Martin Penny (Director).

UNITED STATES

American Electronics Association Europe – AEA Europe: Rue des Drapiers 40, 1050 Brussels; tel (+32 2) 502 70 15; fax (+32 2) 502 67 34; e-mail james_ lovegrove@aeanet.org; internet www.aeanet.org; contact James Lovegrove (Director).

Motion Picture Association – MPA: Rue du Trône 108, 1050 Brussels; tel (+32 2) 778 27 11; fax (+32 2) 778 27 00; e-mail firstname-name @mpaa.org; internet www.mpaa.org; contacts Christopher Marcich (Managing Director), Nikolas Lagergrum (Director of EU Affairs).

Society of Plastics Engineers European Office – SPE: Bistkapellei 44, 2180 Anvers; tel (+32 3) 541 77 55; fax (+32 3) 541 84 25; e-mail ypauwels@4spe .be; internet www.4spe.org; contact Yetty Pauwels (Director).

PRESS AGENCIES, CONFERENCE ORGANIZERS AND THINK TANKS SPECIALIZING IN EU AFFAIRS

PRESS AGENCIES SPECIALIZING IN EU AFFAIRS

These agencies play an essential role in the European Union information network as they are, in the final analysis, the only specialist information sources totally free from any political affiliations or sectoral interests. The information bodies are not by nature identical: a press agency which supplies daily information does not obey the same rules as an information agency which looks at certain sensitive European Union issues on a more irregular basis. All seek to be objective, however, and to supply quality information. The agencies are presented in alphabetical order.

Agence Europe S.A.

Head Office: Agence Europe S.A., Rue Philippe II 34B, BP 428, 2014 Luxembourg, Luxembourg
Tel (+352) 220032
Fax (+352) 462277
Management and Editorial Office: Agence Europe S.A., Rue de la Gare 36, 1040 Brussels, Belgium
Tel (+32) 2-7379494
Fax (+32) 2-7363700
E-mail info@agenceurope.com
Internet www.agenceurope.com
The news agency produces a wide range of titles on EU and international affairs.

- **"Europe Daily Bulletin"** is published five days a week.

Subscribers to the "Europe Daily Bulletin" also receive the following supplements (at no extra cost):

- **"Weekly Selected Statistics"** – weekly (French or English).
- **"Europe/Documents"** – about 50 issues per year (French, English, German or Italian).
- **"European Library"** – weekly (French, English, German or Italian).
- **"Economic Interpenetration in Europe and the rest of the world"** – Daily (French, English, German or Italian).

The bulletin may also be received now by internet. "Dantenet" enables subscribers to download the day's bulletin in the same language as the printed version.

- **"Atlantic News"** – twice-weekly bulletin (French and English).
- **"Uniting Europe"** – English, weekly (except in August), every Monday; "Uniting Europe" analyses and explains the European Union's enlargement process.
- **"CD-ROM Agence Europe"** contains all daily bulletins (supplements included) since 1 January 1995.

Agence France-Presse

Place de la Bourse 11–15, 75002 Paris, France
Tel (+33) 1-40-41-46-46
Fax (+33) 1-40-41-45-50
Agence France-Presse, Rue Archimède 17, Bte 3, 1000 Brussels, Belgium
Tel (+32) 2-2308394
Fax (+32) 2-2302304
E-mail afp.bru@euronet.be
For an overview of AFP's products and services, contact: www.afp.com.

Agra Europe (London) Ltd

80 Calverley Road, Tunbridge Wells, Kent, TN2 5JT, United Kingdom
Tel (+44 1892) 533813
Fax (+44 1892) 544895
E-mail marketing@agra-europe.com
Internet www.agra-food-news.com

Brussels Agency, 262 Rue du Noyer, 1030 Brussels, Belgium
Tel (+32) 2-7366313
Fax (+32) 2-7344681
E-mail brussels@agra-europe.com

Agra Europe (London) Ltd is a leading publisher and conference company specializing in food, agriculture and fisheries in the European Union.

Butterworths European Information Services

35 Chancery Lane, London WC2A 1EL, United Kingdom
Tel (+44 20) 7400-2556
Fax (+44 20) 7400-2559
E-mail sandra.dutczak@butterworths.co.uk
E-mail www.butterworths.co.uk

Encyclopedic and major works:
- **"Vaughan: Law of the European Communities Looseleaf"**.
- **"European Court Practice"**.

Research aids:
- **"European Communities Legislation"**.
- **"EC Case Citator and Service"**.
- **"EC Legislation Implementation Service"**.

Information services:
- **"Annual European Review"**.
- **"EC Legal Developments"** series.

Basic textbooks:
- **"Guide to the European Communities"** – includes distance-learning PC disk-based package.
- **"EC Legal Systems: An Introductory Guide"**.

- **"EFTA Legal Systems: An Introductory Guide"**.
- **"Glossary of EC Terms"** – in English, German, French, Italian and Spanish.

Electronic products:
- **"EU Direct"** – online service offering daily coverage of all European legal developments plus access to the full text of legislation via a seamless interface to Europa; the product also includes a monthly journal containing articles on topical issues, a glossary of key EU terms and a daily news update section highlighting the most important legal developments; e-mail alert service also included.
- **"Gold Service"**.
- **"Platinum Service"** .

Chadwyck-Healey Ltd

The Quorum, Barnwell Road, Cambridge CB5 5SW, United Kingdom
Tel (+44 1223) 215512
Fax (+44 1223) 215513
E-mail knoweurope@chadwyck.co.uk
Internet www.knoweurope.net
Internet www.chadwyck.co.uk

Founded in 1973, Chadwyck-Healey specializes in the publication of reference and research materials for libraries and academic institutions in the fields of current affairs and reference, literature, British and European history, the history of art and architecture, official information and bibliography, in print, microform and on CD-ROM and the World Wide Web; publishes not only in English but also in French, German, Italian and Latin; since October 1999, the company has been part of Bell & Howell Information and Learning.

Online services:
- **"KnowEurope"** – Web-based subscription information service providing integrated access to a broad range of information about the European Union and the wider Europe.
- **"ABI/Inform"** – provides in-depth coverage of business conditions, trends, corporate strategies and tactics, management techniques, competitive product information, and a wide variety of other business topics.
- **"European Access and European Access Plus"** – European Access catalogues all the latest EU publications and documents plus information sources from commercial publishers, UK Government, European and other international organizations, pressure groups, trade

unions and professional and trade organizations of relevance to the EU and the wider Europe.

Editions Delta

Rue Scailquin, 55, 1210 Brussels, Belgium
Tel (+32) 2-2175555
Fax (+32) 2-2179393
E-mail editions.delta@skynet.be

Recent directories include:

- **"Euro Guide"** – yearbook of the institutions of the European Union.
- **"Euro-Who is Who"** – who's who in the institutions of the European Union and in other European organizations.
- **"Euro Lobbying 2003"** – directory of European Union trade and professional associations.

Euractiv.com

Place du Congrès 1, 1000 Brussels, Belgium
Tel (+32) 2-226580
Fax (+32) 2-2265820
E-mail info@euractiv.com
Internet www.euractiv.com

EurActiv's services:

Online information services on EU affairs available free of charge, and complementing the existing institutional websites.

- **"Update e-mail"** – weekly electronic newsletters.
- **"News"** – daily key EU stories, press clippings, "EU Actors" positions.
- **"LinksDossiers"** – summary and selection of web links on a specific topic.
- **"Guide"** – online directory of EU affairs (10,000 organizations).
- **"Policy section"** – policy analysis of selected topics, including positions of associations and institutions, before Commission proposals. Also includes "NegoMonitor" (visual policy overview) and "Forces at Work" (comparing positions).

Europe Information Service

Avenue Adolphe Lacomblé 66, 1030 Brussels, Belgium
Tel (+32) 2-7377700
Fax (+32) 2-7326608
E-mail eis@eis.be
Internet www.eis.be

Europe Information Service specializes in reporting on European affairs and also offers its expertise in training for working with the European Union (through the European Centre for Public Affairs Brussels) and in organizing topical EU-related events.

Publications:

Every subscription automatically includes:

- **"Bulletin"** – traditional hard-copy bulletin.

Bulletins:

- **"European Report Daily"** – daily (+/- 250 issues per year); all political and legislative activities and initiatives of the EU institutions and of the other major European organizations (published electronically on www.eis.be).
- **"European Report"** – twice-weekly (94 issues per year); provides a regular update on EU affairs and activities, and political and legislative initiatives.
- **"European Insight"** – weekly (48 issues per year); brief information package on EU-related events of the week.
- **"European Intelligence"** – monthly (11 issues per year; an update on the completion of the Single Market.
- **"Monthly Report on Europe"** – monthly (11 issues per year); comprehensive coverage of one month of EU affairs and events.
- **"Europe Environment"** – fortnightly (22 issues per year).
- **"Europe Agri"** – fortnightly (22 issues per year); reviews the common agricultural and common fisheries policies, along with the latest Community developments affecting the agri-foods sector, biotechnology, and pharmaceutical and non-food applications for farm products.
- **"Europe Energy"** – fortnightly (22 issues per year).
- **"Tech Europe"** – fortnightly (22 issues per year); covers European policies supporting the 'Information Society'.
- **"Transport Europe"** – monthly (11 issues per year).
- **"European Social Policy"** – monthly (11 issues per year).
- **"EU Enlargement Watch"** – fortnightly (22 issues per year).

European Study Service

Avenue Paola 43, 1330 Rixensart, Belgium
Tel (+32) 2-6521184
Fax (+32) 2-6530180
E-mail nigel.hunt@skynet.be

European Study Service has been editing and marketing EU-related handbooks and reports since 1984.

- **"Access to European Union"** – reference book on the evolution of EU policies and legislation, updated on an annual basis.

- **"Guide to European Policies"** – previously entitled "Handbook of European Union"; key EU political and legislative developments in each major industrial and commercial sector.
- **"Access to Social Europe"** – examines all the major aspects of EU social policy.

Groupe Agra

Bd de Sébastopol 84, 75003 Paris, France
Tel (+33) 1-42-74-28-16
Fax (+33) 1-42-74-29-35
Brussels Office, Rue de la Loi, 235, Bte 11, 1040 Brussels, Belgium

Agra Europe (France)

The AGRA group is responsible for the following publications:

- **"Agra Europe"** – weekly bulletin in French from Brussels covering EU and world developments in the farming and agri-food sector.
- **"Agra Presse"** – weekly publication in French from Paris concentrating more specifically on developments and news in the French agriculture and agri-food sectors.
- **"Agra Fil"** – daily fax service (1-page) in French.

Agra Facts / Agra Focus

- **"Agra Facts"** – 100–120 issues a year; Brussels-based rapid response fax service.
- **"Agra Focus"** – 12 issues a year; Brussels-based monthly newsletter in English provides a reference or digest of developments in EU agriculture policy.

Reuters

Rue de Trèves 61, 1040 Brussels, Belgium
Tel (+32) 2-2876611
Fax (+32) 2-2305540
Fax (press) (+32) 2-2307710
E-mail brussels.newsroom@reuters.com
Internet www.bizinfo.reuters.com

Reuters supplies electronic information on the European Union through its specialized Reuters EU Briefing service.

VWD – Vereinigte Wirtschaftsdienste GmbH

Niederurseler Allee 8–10, 65760 Eschborn, Germany
Tel (+49 6196) 405-0
Fax (+49 6196) 405-240
E-mail euro@vwd.de
Internet www.vwd.de

Brussels Office: VWD – Vereinigte Wirtschaftsdienste GmbH, I.P.C., Bd. Charlemagne 1, bte 78, 1041 Brussels, Belgium
Tel (+32) 2-2307250
Fax (+32) 2-2307381
E-mail europa@vwd.de

Publications:
- **"vwd Europa aktuell"** – a bulletin concentrating on EU news.
- **"Nachrichten für Aussenhandel"** – a daily newspaper which focuses on foreign trade.

There are some 30 other bulletins covering: the building sector, chemicals, electronics, energy, EU affairs, financial and economic affairs, the drinks industry, cereals, fodder and oils, leather, commodities (coffee/cocoa/tea/sugar), food and agriculture, machinery, metals, steel, textiles, meat.

CONFERENCE ORGANIZERS AND THINK TANKS

Centre for European Policy Studies (CEPS)

Place du Congrès 1, 1000 Brussels, Belgium
Tel (+32) 2-2293911
Fax (+32) 2-2194151
E-mail info@ceps.be
Internet www.ceps.be
Founded 1982
Chief Executive: Karel Lannoo, Director and Head of Research: Daniel Gros, Deputy Director and Director of Corporate Relations: Staffan Jerneck, Director of Finance: Willem Roekens
CEPS undertakes research and analysis in public affairs in Europe. It is a non-profit organization which provides its members with information resources and opportunities for networking with key decision-makers in the realm of European public affairs. CEPS maintains strong relations with the EU Commission, the Council of Ministers and the Parliament, as well as with politicians and decision-makers in the member countries.

The Centre's researchers provide detailed analysis for interpreting key issues and provide recommendations for change. CEPS can boast a strong track record in being an influence for change with studies such as the blueprint for the stability pact for the Balkans, the groundwork for the Financial Services Action Plan and its annual macroeconomic policy report. CEPS research is subdivided into two broad areas: Economic Policy and Politics, and Institutions and Security. Within these two broad areas, CEPS runs different programmes, and internally these programmes comprise many different projects.

In conjunction with the research programmes, CEPS also organizes a wide range of lunchtime meetings, working groups and conferences in Brussels and elsewhere throughout the year. These bring together officials, business representatives and experts to discuss topical issues in European affairs. More information can be found by visiting the CEPS website, which is continuously updated.

CIDEC – Research Centre for the Economy, Employment and Vocational Qualification Issues

Avenida de la Libertad 17–19, 20004 San Sebastian, Spain
Tel (+34) 943-42-52-57
Fax (+34) 943-42-93-31
E-mail cidec@sarenet.es
Founded 1990
Chairman: Juan José de Andres Gils, General Co-ordinator: Teresa Hernando

Sectors of activity:
- Development and evaluation of strategies, programmes and European incentives in the fields of employment, training and vocational qualifications.
- Identification of needs, elaboration of vocational profiles, restructuring of the training offer, and certification.
- Design and implementation of tools for monitoring and evaluating the employment market, jobs and competence trends.
- Development of projects related to changes in training and modernization of training systems: initial, occupational and vocational training.
- Didactic innovation and production of different training materials, application of new technologies, creation of simulation games, teletraining and vocational competency management systems.
- Design of local development strategies and actions. Studies exploring new employment initiatives, feasibility and setting up of projects.
- Laboratory for innovation and change in organizations and management in SMEs.
- Management and development of co-operation programmes and international transfers concerning Latin America, the World Bank, IDB, Mexico, Argentina, Colombia, Honduras, Venezuela and Cuba.
- Organization of conferences and workshops.
- Publications.
- Information and documentation services.

EMRC International Association

Avenue Louise 283, Bte 22, 1050 Brussels, Belgium
Tel (+32) 2-6261515
Fax (+32) 2-6261516
E-mail info@emrc.be
Internet www.emrc.be
Founded 1992
Contact: I. Miller
EMRC (European Marketing Research Center) is an autonomous international association duly incorporated by Belgian Royal Decree. It is composed of a vast network of business leaders, manufacturers, marketing experts, academic personalities and governmental institutions, and enjoys the professional support of European, international and national organizations. Therefore, EMRC sees itself as a catalyst for the promotion of trade between business leaders from around the world and, more specifically,

between EU and non-EU companies and countries.

EMRC offers its expertise and services in four main areas:
- The EuroMarket Forum, which is a biannual international event held in Brussels, attracting senior executives from a wide spectrum of industries world-wide. It includes a comprehensive seminar on the practical problems of the business community and provides participants with interactive lectures and workshops, professional meetings with financial institutions, government ministers, and legal, financial and marketing experts, as well as business leaders.
- The EMRC Business Forums, which are multilateral business co-operation symposia, organized at the request of EMRC members and aimed at further strengthening the direct dialogue between business leaders and regional policy makers. The Business Forums are held in various places depending on specific needs (for instance, in Moscow, Tel-Aviv, Kiev and New York).
- International Business Club EMRC. Through participation at the Euro-Market Forums, the company becomes automatically a member of the EMRC International Association. The participants receive several advantages and privileges for one year.
- 'Dialogues', the EMRC Newsletter, offers a highly targeted communications vehicle highlighting developments, projects and desired co-operation from EMRC international network members. The newsletter is distributed to all EMRC members, business leaders, international financial institutions, embassies, government ministries and EU officials in more than 60 countries in Africa, Europe, America and Asia.

Euro Institute

Rue Président Carnot 8, 69002 Lyon, France
Tel (+33) 4-72-56-42-32
Fax (+33) 4-72-41-84-91
E-mail euroinstitut@asi.fr
Internet www.euro.institut.org
Founded 1982
Chairman: Frans Andriessen, Director: Alain Malegarie, Secretary: Odette Lopez
Sectors of activity:
- The aim of the EURO Institute is to study and analyse the development of the legal, financial and economic issues raised by the adoption of a

single currency. The Institute brings together public and private national and European institutions and is supported by an international network of experts.
- The documentation centre of the Euro Institute is accessible to the public on demand.

European Policy Centre

Résidence Palace, Rue de la Loi 155, 1040 Brussels, Belgium
Tel (+32) 2-2310340
Fax (+32) 2-2310704
E-mail info@TheEPC.be
Internet www.TheEPC.be
Chairman: Stanley Crossick, President: Max Kohnstamm, Director: John Palmer
The EPC's mission is to help the European Union meet the challenges of the 21st century by encouraging debate and channelling the results into policy-making.

The Centre provides:
- Input into EU policy-making.
- Open debate and briefings on strategic policy issues.
- Active contacts among all parties involved in European development.

The Centre works on three main tracks:
- Business, including companies, associations and trades unions.
- Government, including the EU institutions, Member States and other countries.
- Civil society, including NGOs, academic groups, policy institutions, policy networks and independent foundations.

The Centre puts special emphasis on strengthening the interface of government with business, to help the business community understand where EU policies are leading it, and to help EU leaders understand what policies are needed to build a more prosperous Europe. The Centre has strong media links and expertise.

Services to business:
- Information and insight about strategic developments in Europe.
- Contact and exchange of experience with other business groups.
- External contacts with Commissioners, Directors-General, MEPs, Permanent Representatives, other politicians and officials, journalists and NGOs.
- An opportunity to influence policy-making on issues important to business.

Services to government and EU institutions:
- Studies.
- Input in public policy issues from business and the other constituents of the civil society.
- Informal contacts with the business community and NGOs.

Services to civil society:
- Information and insight about strategic developments in Europe.
- Informal contacts with the business community.

Activities:
- Financial Services Action Plan Forum.
- Tax Policy Forum.
- E Business Forum.
- Forum on Risk.
- State of the Union Business Briefings.
- State of the Union Diplomatic Briefings.
- State of the Union NGO and Regional Briefings.
- Breakfast Policy Briefings.
- Policy Dialogues.
- The Europe We Need Initiative.
- State of the Union conference.
- Occasional papers.
- Regular briefings for members.
- Website Policy Papers.
- Commentaries for the media.
- Public policy advice.
- Challenge Europe online interactive public policy journal.

European Round Table of Industrialists

Avenue Henri Jaspar 113, 1060 Brussels, Belgium
Tel (+32) 2-5343100
Fax (+32) 2-5347348
E-mail contact@ert.be
Internet www.ert.be
Founded 1983
Contact: W. Philippa
The ERT aims to strengthen Europe's economy and improve its global competitiveness.

Themes of working groups:
- Accounting standards.
- Competitiveness.
- Corporate governance.
- Employment and SMEs.
- Enlargement.
- Taxation.
- Environment.
- Governance of Europe.
- Pension reform.
- Foreign economic relations.
- Competition policy.

Themes of experts:
- Environment.
- Export controls.
- Industrial relations and social policy.
- Corporate governance.

Forum Europe SA

La Maison de l'Europe à la Bibliothèque Solvay, Rue Belliard 137, 1040 Brussels, Belgium
Tel (+32) 2-7361430
Fax (+32) 2-7363216
E-mail info@forum-europe.com
Internet www.forum-europe.com

Forum Europe specializes in A–Z high-level conference organization, including programme design and content, press relations and publications. Headed by Giles Merritt, a former 'Financial Times' correspondent and a columnist on EU affairs in the 'International Herald Tribune' since 1984, Forum Europe goes beyond logistics in its conference planning and organization. Through its pre-conference research on the programme, speakers and participants, Forum Europe aims to create a neutral platform for debate on the issues shaping the European economy and the EU's political agenda.

Conference topics range from Europe's defence industry, healthcare issues, and investment opportunities in Southeast Asia to enlargement, financial markets, telecoms, energy, transport, and globalization, and from Europe's competitiveness drive to the links between cultural and economic development.

Forum Europe events take place throughout Europe, and regularly feature high-level speakers such as EU Commissioners, senior government ministers, CEOs, and company Chairmen, and are also regularly attended by the international press.

Philip Morris Institute for Public Policy Research (PMI)

Rue Joseph II 168, 1000 Brussels, Belgium
Tel (+32) 2-2801662
Fax (+32) 2-2304487
E-mail admin@pmi-inst.org
Founded 1993
Contact: Pauline Rozen
Mission:
- Since 2000, the Institute's mission has been to research and address issues of societal concern and to make a meaningful contribution to critical and emerging social issues. Since its creation in 1993, the Institute has addressed major European public policy issues through a series of conferences and publications.

Activities:
- The Institute undertakes original research and stimulates discussion among key players to promote innovative solutions. It also supports, in co-operation with NGOs and public authorities, projects to tackle social needs. The Institute's discussion papers, conferences and seminars are designed to provide a forum for ideas and to promote innovative thinking that will shape the Europe of tomorrow. The Philip Morris Institute's conferences, seminars and debates bring together policy makers, business leaders, NGOs, prominent academics, commentators and the media to discuss and promote actions that address societal issues.

Trans European Policy Studies Association (TEPSA)

Rue d'Egmont 11, 1000 Brussels, Belgium
Tel (+32) 2-5113470
Fax (+32) 2-5116770
E-mail tepsa.gepe@skynet.be
Internet www.tepsa.be
Founded 1974
Contact: W. Wessels, Contact: G. Vanhaeverbeke

TEPSA is an independent organization which seeks to promote international research on European integration in order to stimulate discussion on policies and political options for Europe. The Association links affiliated national institutes in several EU Member States. Through a common framework for the exchange of information and the co-ordination of activities, the participating institutes are able to give their research projects a truly European dimension and can make the results easily known using transnational working methods which involve the co-operation of experts from different countries.

Twice a year TEPSA organizes a conference, in co-operation with the government of the Member State which is scheduled to assume the next presidency of the EC.

In the course of its activities over the years, TEPSA has acquired collective know-how relating to institutional affairs and to the creation of a European Union and organizes conferences on specific topics, such as Economic and Monetary Union, the Intergovernmental Conferences, external relations, political co-operation, and social and economic cohesion.

CONSULTANTS SPECIALIZING IN EU QUESTIONS

CONSULTANTS SPECIALIZING IN EU QUESTIONS

At the end of this list is an index of areas of specialization.

BELGIUM

2M Public Affairs Consultants S.C.: Square Vergote 39, 1030 Brussels; tel (+32 2) 742-94-56; fax (+32 2) 732 22 51; e-mail michel.maroy@skynet.be; founded 1987; political affairs consultancy; contact M. Maroy.

Areas of specialization:
- Lobbying
- Advocacy
- Monitoring
- Funding opportunities

Anna Macdougald: Avenue des Arts 5, Bte 20, 1000 Brussels; tel (+32 2) 733-87-85; fax (+32 2) 733-92-55; e-mail anna@macdougald-eu.com; founded 1987; political affairs consultancy; contact A. Macdougald.

Areas of specialization:
- Environment
- Consumer affairs
- Transport
- Research and development policy
- Enterprise policy
- Structural funds
- Agriculture
- Tourism
- Health
- Lobbying
- Early warning service for clients regarding Commission proposals
- Forestry
- Food

APCO Europe S.A.: Rue du Trône 130, 1050 Brussels; tel (+32 2) 645-98-11; fax (+32 2) 645-98-12; e-mail mail@apco-europe.com; internet www.apco-europe.com; founded 1995; political affairs and public relations consultancy; contact L. Chokouale Datou.

Areas of specialization:
- Audiovisual
- Aviation and transport
- Coalition-building
- Community relations
- Competition policy (mergers and acquisitions)
- Consumer goods, food and beverages
- Corporate events management
- Corporate positioning
- Crisis communication
- Digital Communication
- Energy
- Enlargement
- Environment
- Financial services
- Government relations
- Healthcare and pharmaceuticals
- Information society
- Intellectual property
- Internal communication
- Issues management
- Litigation support
- Media relations
- Mergers and acquisitions
- Postal services
- Research and intelligence
- Sport
- Trade

Archimede Consulting Services: Rue Joseph II 36, 1000 Brussels; tel (+32 2) 217-39-39; fax (+32 2) 219-18-42; e-mail richard.steel@wanadoo.be; founded 1989; political affairs consultancy; contact R. Steel.

Areas of specialization:
- European Parliament's committees and plenary sessions

ARPES: Square Ambiorix 32, bte 22, 1000 Brussels; tel (+32 2) 230-56-09; fax (+32 2) 230-28-98; e-mail etoile@village.unnet.be; founded 1997; management consultancy; contact Mr. Zanarelli.

Areas of specialization:
- Agro-industry

Arthur D. Little: Bd de la Woluwe 2, 1150 Brussels; tel (+32 2) 7617200; fax (+32 2) 7620758; e-mail adlittle.brussels@adlittle.com; internet www.adlittle.com; founded 1966; management consultancy; contact F. Wirtz.

Areas of specialization:
- Strategy and organization
- Change management
- Technology management
- Informatics
- Operations
- Industrial, financial and commercial sectors

AT Kearney: Avenue des Arts 46, 1000 Brussels; tel (+32 2) 504-48-11; fax (+32 2) 511-01-03; e-mail recruitment.benelux@atkearney.com; internet www.atkearney.com; founded 1926.

Areas of specialization:
- Aerospace and defence
- Automotive industry
- Chemicals sector, oil and gas
- Consumer and retail sectors
- Forest products
- Healthcare and pharmaceuticals
- Public sector
- Telecommunications and electronics
- Transport
- Utilities
- Finance and economics
- Manufacturing and supply chain
- Strategy and restructuring
- Strategic information technology
- Strategic sourcing
- Change management
- Transforming the enterprise
- Executive search

B & S – Business & Show – Syntagmes: Avenue de la Couronne 340, 1050 Brussels; tel (+32 2) 647-24-00; fax (+32 2) 640-55-01; e-mail info@bs.be; internet www.bs.be; founded 1985; public relations consultancy; contact P. Lefebvre.

Areas of specialization:
- Public relations
- Press
- Events (organization)

Babel P.R.: Rue Royale 326, 1030 Brussels; tel (+32 2) 219-30-88; fax (+32 2) 219-00-16; e-mail babel.c@yvcom.be; founded 1986; public relations consultants; contact L.M. Colot.

Areas of specialization:
- Consumer goods
- Culture
- Leisure

Barabino & Partners Europe SA: Rue Thérésienne 7, 1000 Brussels; tel (+32 2) 502-15-58; fax (+32 2) 502-48-69; e-mail info@barabino.be; internet www.barabinoeurope.com; founded 1991; political affairs consultancy; contacts F. Steiner (Chairman), Mr Pirina (Consultant).

Areas of specialization:
- Public affairs
- Press
- Corporate communication
- Crisis management

Berkley Associates Sprl: Rue de la Presse 11, 1000 Brussels; tel (+32 2) 219-05-32; fax (+32 2) 219-04-98; e-mail berkleyassociates@skynet.be; founded 1987; management and public relations consultancy; contact J. Stringer.

Areas of specialization:
- SMEs
- Education and training
- Environment
- Research
- Enterprise policy
- Project management
- Training project managers
- Fraud prevention training for grant-funded projects

Bureau Européen de Recherches S.A.: Avenue Eugène Plasky 22, 1030 Brussels; tel (+32 2) 738-05-11; fax (+32 2) 732-13-61; e-mail conrad.caspari@ceas.com; internet www.promar-ceas.be; founded 1973; political affairs consultancy; contacts C. Caspari, M. Christodoulou.

Areas of specialization:
- Common Agricultural Policy
- International trade policy
- Farm supply industries
- Food processing
- Fisheries

The Directory of EU Information Sources

- Environment
- Consumer protection
- Regional affairs
- Agriculture
- Food
- Rural environment
- EU policy

Bureau Van Dijk – Management Consultants: Avenue Louise 250, 1050 Brussels; tel (+32 2) 639-06-06; fax (+32 2) 648-82-30; e-mail vg@bvdep.com; internet www.bvdep.it; founded 1970; management consultancy; contact V. Goossens.

Areas of specialization:
- Telecommunications
- Statistics
- Finance
- Electronic publishing
- Information and documentation systems
- Energy
- Strategy
- Research and development
- Computer applications

Burson-Marsteller Sprl: Avenue de Cortenbergh 118, 1000 Brussels; tel (+32 2) 743-66-11; fax (+32 2) 733-66-11; e-mail info@bmbrussels.be; internet www.bmbrussels.be; founded 1961; political affairs and public relations consultancy; contact J. Galbraith.

Areas of specialization:
- Public relations
- Public affairs
- Communication
- Government relations

Business Environment Europe S.A. – BEE: Rue de l'Industrie 42, 1000 Brussels; tel (+32 2) 230-83-60; fax (+32 2) 230-83-70; e-mail info@bee.be; internet www.bee.be; founded 1988; management and political affairs consultancy; contact B. Liebhaberg.

Areas of specialization:
- Public affairs (EU)
- Competition
- Environment
- Trade
- Scenario planning
- Strategy
- Food and drink
- Agriculture
- Automobile industry
- Energy
- Chemicals
- Telecommunications
- Packaging
- Pulp and paper

BW & Partners: Rue Hector Denis 55, 1050 Brussels; tel (+32 2) 219-18-98; fax (+32 2) 219-32-15; e-mail bwp@ubique .org; founded 1991; EU public affairs management consultancy; contact P. Wacker.

Areas of specialization:
- Information society
- Enterprise policy
- Internal market

Cabinet Stewart: Rue d'Arlon 40, 1000 Brussels; tel (+32 2) 230-70-20; fax (+32 2) 230-50-43; e-mail cabinetstewart@ cabinetstewart.com; internet www .cabinetstewart.com; founded 1990; public relations consultancy; contact C. Stewart.

Areas of specialization:
- Tailored monitoring
- European policy and law
- Lobbying strategy
- Secretariat services

CEASC Consultants (Wye) Ltd: Rue du Commerce 20–22, 1030 Brussels; tel (+32 2) 736-00-88; fax (+32 2) 732-13-61; e-mail info@ceasc.com; founded 1986; economic consultancy.

Areas of specialization:
- Agricultural economics policy
- Environmental policy
- Marketing
- EU accession
- Food
- Drink

Centre For European Not-for-Profit Organisations – CENPO: Rue de la Concorde 57, 1050 Brussels; tel (+32 2) 740-00-00; fax (+32 2) 740-00-09; e-mail info@cenpo.org; founded 1994; political affairs consultancy; contact D. Wedgwood.

Areas of specialization:
- Third Sector
- Not-for-Profit Sector
- Aid
- Charities
- Voluntary work
- Arts
- Culture
- Heritage
- Education
- Training
- Central Europe
- Eastern Europe
- Social affairs
- Health
- Development
- Research

Citigate Public Affairs: Avenue de Cortenbergh 66, 1000 Brussels; tel (+32 2) 736-81-35; fax (+32 2) 736-88-47; e-mail johnny.pring@citigopo.com; internet www.citigatepa.com; founded 1987; political affairs consultancy; contact T. Lebeaux.

Areas of specialization:
- Energy
- Transport
- Financial services

CLAN Public Affairs: Rue Froissart 57, 1040 Brussels; tel (+32 2) 736-58-00; fax (+32 2) 738-71-20; e-mail clanpa@clan -public-affairs.be; internet www.clan -public-affairs.be; founded 1996; management and political affairs consultancy; contact Mrs Catalozzi.

Areas of specialization:
- Agriculture
- Food products
- Health
- Automotive industry
- Transport
- Financial services
- Trade

Clerens Consulting: Avenue de l'Opale 80, 1030 Brussels; tel (+32 2) 743-29-80; fax (+32 2) 743-29-90; e-mail marc@ clerens.com; founded 1991; management and public relations consultancy.

Areas of specialization:
- Transport
- Energy
- Environment
- Research and development

Communication Partners: Rue Konkel 105–107, 1150 Brussels; tel (+32 2) 772-40-70; fax (+32 2) 772-30-65; e-mail comm .partners@skynet.be; founded 1986; management and public relations consultancy; contact Jean-Luc Pleunes.

Areas of specialization:
- Crisis management
- Internal and external communication (audits and strategies)
- Copywriting
- Public affairs
- Press
- Evaluation

Communications Group S.A.: Avenue Louise 497, bte 1, 1050 Brussels; tel (+32 2) 640-92-07; fax (+32 2) 640-92-24; e-mail terry@eurocom.be; founded 1981; public relations consultancy; contact T. Davidson.

Areas of specialization:
- Technology
- Finance
- Industry
- EU (relations with)

COPCA – Coopération Internationale: Rue Belliard 199, 1040 Brussels; tel (+32 2) 230-97-46; fax (+32 2) 230-26-12; e-mail cooperacio.internacional@ euronet.be; internet www.copca.com; founded 1987; management consultancy; contact Ana Coelho.

Areas of specialization:
- Development Co-operation
- Export promotion

Crehan, Kusano & Associates Sprl: Rue Arenberg 2, 1000 Brussels; tel (+32 2) 742-18-65; fax (+32 2) 742-37-63; e-mail patrick.crehan@cka.be; founded 1999; management consultancy; contact P. Crehan.

Areas of specialization:
- Hi tech new business development
- RTD innovation
- Technology transfer
- Economic and social development
- Industrial co-operation policy
- Actions (design and implementation)

DECITIME: Chaussée de Charleroi 96, 1060 Brussels; tel (+32 2) 534-66-86; fax (+32 2) 534-66-98; e-mail decitime@ decitime.be; internet www.decitime.be; founded 1982; Corporate and financial communications; contact E. Gessler.

Areas of specialization:
- Institutional communication
- Financial communication
- Crisis communication
- Internal and external communication
- Lobbying

Deloitte & Touche: Rue Archimède 17, 1000 Brussels; tel (+32 2) 282-03-33; fax (+32 2) 282-03-10; e-mail dgjini@deloitte .com; internet www.deloitte.be; founded 1986; management and political affairs consultancy.

Areas of specialization:
- Public affairs (Europe)
- Grants (EU)
- Inward investment
- Projects (EU)
- Evaluation
- Economic development

Deloitte & Touche – Tax & Legal: Brussels Airport Business Park, Berkenlaan 7, 1831 Diegem; tel (+32 2) 600-60-00; fax (+32 2) 600-60-01; e-mail dbrinckmansalzedo@deloitte.com; e-mail arainer@deloitte.com; founded 1988; management and political affairs consultancy; contact S. Degruytere.

Areas of specialization:
- Competition law (European)
- State aids
- Taxation law
- European Single Market (entry into)
- Eastern Europe (business with)
- Grants and subsidies
- Trade law and customs procedures (EU)
- Anti-dumping procedures
- Influencing EU law
- Competition issues (awareness training programmes)
- Public procurement law (EU) and its interpretation
- Legislative reviews and monitoring services (EU)

Dialogic: Avenue du Colvert 5, 1070 Brussels; tel (+32 2) 426-64-66; fax (+32 2) 426-53-78; e-mail dialogic@dialogic -agency.com; founded 1986; public relations consultancy; contact P. Housiaux.

Areas of specialization:
- Corporate communication
- Sports communication
- Institutional communication

Eamonn Bates Europe Public Affairs SA: Avenue d'Auderghem 67, 1040 Brussels; tel (+32 2) 286-94-94; fax (+32 2) 286-94-95; e-mail info@eamonnbates .com; internet www.eamonnbates.com; founded 1991; public affairs consultancy; contact E. Bates.

Areas of specialization:
- Environment
- Consumer affairs
- Health and safety
- Food policy
- Public health
- Structural funds
- Third country representation

Ecotec Research and Consulting Ltd: Avenue de Tervuren 13 B, 1040 Brussels; tel (+32 2) 743-89-49; fax (+32 2) 732-71-11; e-mail ecotec@ecotec.com; internet www.ecotec.com; founded 1983; contact R. Hains.

Areas of specialization:
- Economic affairs
- Business advice services
- Employment
- Labour market
- Vocational training studies
- Regional policy
- Feasibility and impact evaluation studies
- Town and country planning strategy
- Enterprise policy
- Tourism
- Environmental management and policy
- Pollution control technology
- Waste management and disposal (research)

Edelman Public Relations Worldwide – Brussels: Rue des Deux Eglises 20, 1000 Brussels; tel (+32 2) 227-61-70; fax (+32 2) 227-61-89; e-mail request@ edelman.com; internet www.edelman .com; founded 1954; political affairs and public relations consultancy; contact Mme Pester.

Edelman Public Relations Worldwide: 1500 Broadway, New York NY 10036, USA; tel (+1 212) 768-0550; fax (+1 212) 704-0128.

ENHESA SA: Rue du Mail 15, 1050 Brussels; tel (+32 2) 775-97-97; fax (+32 2) 775-97-99; e-mail enhesa@enhesa.com; internet www.enhesa.com; founded 1992; management consultancy; contact Man Hung Lee.

Areas of specialization:
- Environmental health and safety law and policy
- Occupational health and safety law and policy

Environmental Resources Management – ERM: Visverkopersstraat 13, 1000 Brussels; tel (+32 2) 550-02-93; fax (+32 2) 550-02-99; e-mail kathleen .goossens@erm.com; internet www.erm .com; founded 1971; environmental management consultancy; contact W. van Breusegem.

Areas of specialization:
- Waste policy
- Environmental management
- Soil investigation remediation
- Environmental audits
- Sustainable development

- Environmental strategy
- Environmental economy and policy

EPPA: Place de Luxembourg 2, 1050 Brussels; tel (+32 2) 735-82-30; fax (+32 2) 735-44-12; e-mail pascal.michaux@ eppa.com; internet www.eppa.com; founded 1987; political affairs consultancy; contact P. Michaux.

Areas of specialization:
- Agriculture
- Competition
- Employment
- Food
- Pharmaceuticals
- Media
- Telecommunications
- Trade
- Transport
- Business
- Law
- Economics
- Politics
- Public administration
- Journalism

EPRO – European Project: Avenue Marnix 19A, 1000 Brussels; tel (+32 2) 512-79-80; fax (+32 2) 514-21-19; e-mail info@eu-project.org; founded 1987; political affairs consultancy; contact G. Ripa Di Meana.

Areas of specialization:
- Common Agricultural Policy
- External relations
- Trade policies with third countries
- Internal industrial and trade policies
- Customs
- Public procurement
- EU funded programmes in favour of EU enterprises
- EU programmes in favour of third countries
- Economic co-operation

Ernst & Young: Avenue Marcel Thiry 204, 1200 Brussels; tel (+32 2) 774-91-11; fax (+32 2) 774-90-90; internet www .ey.be; founded 1989; management consultancy; contact G. Herrewijn.

Areas of specialization:
- Services to the EU institutions
- Evaluation
- Public sector
- SMEs
- ETM (interim, management)
- Taxation
- Audit

ESL & Network Europe: Rue de la Loi 81A, 1040 Brussels; tel (+32 2) 230-56-29; fax (+32 2) 230-53-19; e-mail annabellet@ eslnetwork.com; internet www .eslnetwork.com; founded 1989; political affairs consultancy; contact C. Calvez.

Areas of specialization:
- Finance
- Energy
- Post, media and telecommunications
- Telecommunications
- Industry
- EU affairs

EU Business Care – Brandenburg Group – EU Liaison Office: Square Vergote 39, 1030 Brussels; tel (+32 2) 737-04-04; fax (+32 2) 737-04-00; e-mail tgrusemann@compuserve.com; internet www.tuev-rheinland.de; founded 1872; management consultancy.

Areas of specialization:
- Environment
- Energy
- Transport
- Certification
- Training
- Occupational safety and health

Euralia – Guerin Sprl – Euralia Group: Rue du Luxembourg 19–21, 1000 Brussels; tel (+32 2) 506-88-20; fax (+32 2) 506-88-25; e-mail info@euralia .com; internet www.euralia.com; founded 1992; contacts F. Gras, B. Dupont.

Areas of specialization:
- Banking and finance
- Information technology
- Communications technology
- Agro-food industry
- External relations
- Development aid
- SMEs
- Professional organizations and associations
- European Parliament (relations with)
- Market access/WTO

Euralia France: 38 avenue Hoche, 75008 Paris, France; tel (+33) 1-45-63-65-00; fax (+33) 1-45-63-65-05; e-mail info@euralia.com; internet www.euralia.com; contact B. Dupont.

Euro Keys: Avenue de Broqueville 40, 1200 Brussels; tel (+32 2) 777-99-77; fax (+32 2) 770-36-01; e-mail euro.keys@ euro-keys.com; internet www.euro-keys .com/; founded 1995; management and political affairs consultancy; contact M. Derecque-Pois.

Areas of specialization:
- Quality control
- Energy
- Transport
- Plastics
- Chemicals
- Environment
- Textiles
- Pharmaceuticals
- Food.

Euro P.A. Consulting: Rue de la Buanderie 24, 1000 Brussels; tel (+32 2) 512-41-16; fax (+32 2) 514-69-32; e-mail info@euro-pa-online.com; internet www .euro-pa-online.com; founded 1998; political affairs consultancy; contact S. Haar.

Areas of specialization:
- Internal market
- Health care
- SMEs
- External aid
- Research
- Environment

Euro RSCG Corporate: Rue du Doyenné 58, 1180 Brussels; tel (+32 2) 348-38-00; fax (+32 2) 347-59-11; e-mail christian.d@eurorscg.be; internet www .eurorscg.be; founded 2000; political affairs and public relations consultancy; contact Mrs Ligne.

Areas of specialization:
- European public affairs
- Corporate communication

Euro RSCG Corporate: 84 rue de Villiers, 92300 Levallois Perret Cédex, France; tel (+33) 1-41-34-42-08; fax (+33) 1-41-34-34-34; e-mail bernard .sananes@eurorscg.fr.

Euro Tec – Trading, Engineering, Consulting: Rond Point Schuman 9, Bte 15, 1040 Brussels; tel (+32 2) 282-00-80; fax (+32 2) 230-31-68; e-mail info@ eurotec.be; founded 1996; management, political affairs and public relations consultancy; contacts A. D'Alessandro, M. D'Alessandro.

Areas of specialization:
- EU law
- Customs and taxation
- Funding and investment programmes (EU)
- Structural funds.
- Investment
- Venture capital

Eurocity – European Consultants Information Technology: Rue d'Arlon 39–41, 1000 Brussels; tel (+32 2) 285-40-10; fax (+32 2) 285-40-19; e-mail consult@ eurocity.be; internet www.eurocity.be; founded 1992; contact S. Dowsett.

Areas of specialization:
- Information technology
- Project management
- Programme management

Eurocontact SRL: Rue Montoyer 18, 1040 Brussels; tel (+32 2) 280-00-62; fax (+32 2) 280-16-55; e-mail eurocontact@ tin.it; internet www.eurocontact.it; founded 1989; public relations consultancy; contact S. Diana.

Areas of specialization:
- SMEs
- Tourism
- Local authorities
- Local development
- Culture
- Information
- Training

Europa SA: Rue du Luxembourg 19, 1000 Brussels; tel (+32 2) 280-11-95; fax (+32 2) 280-12-45; e-mail europa@europa .be; internet www.europa.be; founded 1989; management consultancy; contact Phil Pickard.

Areas of specialization:
- Procurement
- Goods (supply)

Europabüro für Projektbegleitung GmbH (EFP): Rue le Titien 28, 1000 Brussels; founded 1989; contact Dr S. Honnef.

Areas of specialization:
- Social policy
- Labour policy
- Employment Community Initiative (national support structure)
- EQUAL Community Initiative (national support structure)
- XENOS (national support structure)
- Local Social Capital programme (national support structure)

Europabüro für Projektbegleitung GmbH (EFP): Ellerstrasse 48, 53119 Bonn, Germany; tel (+49 228) 98599-11; fax (+49 228) 98599-80; e-mail info@efp-bonn.de; internet www.efp -bonn.de; contact Dr S. Honnef.

Europe Analytica: Avenue Livingstone 26, 1000 Brussels; tel (+32 2) 231-12-99; fax (+32 2) 230-76-58; e-mail info@europe -analytica.com; internet www.europe -analytica.com; founded 1999; political affairs consultancy; contact D. Herbison.

Areas of specialization:
- Political affairs
- European Union and Member States
- Finance
- Information technology
- Food policy
- Industrial policy
- Agriculture

Europe Contact Service (ECOS): Avenue Adolphe Lacomblé 66, 1030 Brussels; tel (+32 2) 737-77-42; fax (+32 2) 732-75-25; e-mail ecos@eis.be; internet www.eis .be; founded 1990; management and political affairs consultancy (EU information monitoring); contact L. Gutman-Grauer.

Europe Télématique Information Conseil (ETIC): Rue Archimède 50, 1000 Brussels; tel (+32 2) 230-67-56; fax (+32 2) 230-23-06; e-mail etic@skynet.be; internet www.foureuro.com/etic; founded 1988; political affairs consultancy; contact J. Echkenazi.

Areas of specialization:
- Monitoring of European law
- European Parliament

European Advisory Services: Rue de l'Association 50, 1000 Brussels; tel (+32 2) 218-14-70; fax (+32 2) 219-73-42; e-mail info@eas.be; internet www.eas.be; founded 1992; political affairs consultancy; contact Mr. Pettman.

Areas of specialization:
- Food
- Health
- Food supplements
- Functional foods
- Herbal products

European Consulting Company (ECCO): Avenue des Gaulois 9, 1040 Brussels; tel (+32 2) 736-53-54; fax (+32 2) 732-34-27; e-mail euroconsult@ecco-eu .com; internet www.ecco.be; founded 1975; association management; contact A. Galaski.

Areas of specialization:
- Agricultural policy
- Food law

European Development Projects: Avenue des Nerviens 67, bte 12, 1040 Brussels; tel (+32 2) 734-87-91; fax (+32 2) 734-15-88; e-mail macarena.ybarra@euronet.be; founded 1993; management consultancy; contact M. Ybarra.

Areas of specialization:
- Regional policy
- Development aid
- Agriculture
- Fisheries
- Audiovisual
- Publishing
- Media
- Competition policy
- Energy
- Utilities
- Environment
- Food
- Drink industry
- Industrial and intellectual property
- SMEs
- Telecoms
- Transport

European Multimedia Forum: Rue du Moniteur 9, 1000 Brussels; tel (+32 2) 219-03-05; fax (+32 2) 219-32-15; e-mail secretariat@emf-multimedia.org; internet www.emf.be; founded 1994; public relations consultancy.

Areas of specialization:
- Internet
- Multimedia
- Information technology
- Communications technology

European Policy Centre: Résidence Palace, Rue de la Loi 155, 1040 Brussels; tel (+32 2) 231-03-40; fax (+32 2) 231-07-04; e-mail info@theepc.be; internet www.theepc.be; founded 1997; contact E. Bisland.

Areas of specialization:
- European Union
- Political affairs

European Research Associates (ERA): Avenue des Nerviens 79, bte 1, 1040 Brussels; tel (+32 2) 735-72-60; fax (+32 2) 735-91-41; e-mail rtaylor@erabrussels.be; internet www.erabrussels.be; founded 1979; management and political affairs consultancy; contact R. Taylor.

Areas of specialization:
- Economic developments (Europe)
- Political developments (Europe)
- Industrial policy
- European Single Market
- Enlargement
- Business regulation (EC)
- Technology transfer
- Trade
- Trade law
- Environmental policy and regulation in Europe
- European industrial co-operation in advanced technology sectors

- Economic Co-operation with EFTA and Eastern European countries
- Urban and regional development
- Multinational corporate management issues
- Telecommunications
- Information technology
- Motor industry
- Consumer electronics
- Pharmaceuticals
- Biotechnology
- Aerospace
- Defence
- Financial services
- Environmental protection
- Energy

European Service Network: Rue du Collège 27, 1050 Brussels; tel (+32 2) 646-40-20; fax (+32 2) 646-53-57; e-mail esn@esn.be; internet www.esn.be; founded 1986; communications, information and public relations consultancy; conference organizer; contact P. Gosseries.

Areas of specialization:
- European affairs
- Science and technology
- Innovation
- Information society
- SMEs
- Industry
- Environment
- Trade
- Education
- Training
- Development co-operation
- Social issues
- Human rights
- Regional policy

Europool SA: Rue de l'Industrie 11, 1000 Brussels; tel (+32 2) 231-14-05; fax (+32 2) 230-33-00; e-mail europool@tiscalinet.be; founded 1976; management and public relations consultancy; contact R. Lastenouse.

Areas of specialization:
- Access to EU markets
- Business regulation
- PHARE
- TACIS
- EDF

Europublic SA/NV: Avenue Winston Churchill 118, bte 3, 1180 Brussels; tel (+32 2) 343-77-26; fax (+32 2) 343-93-30; e-mail kminke@europublic.com; internet www.europublic.com; founded 1988; public affairs consultancy; contacts K. Minke, R. Hill.

Areas of specialization:
- Communication strategy
- Media relations

Eurostrategies Sprl: Avenue des Nerviens 79, 1040 Brussels; tel (+32 2) 735-72-60; fax (+32 2) 735-91-41; internet es@erabrussels.be; founded 1987; management consultancy; contact R. Taylor.

Areas of specialization:
- Economic consultancy and studies
- Telecommunications
- Information technology

EURO-TOP Cooperation Partners: Avenue Louise 490, 1050 Brussels; tel (+32 2) 649-59-94; fax (+32 2) 640-37-59; e-mail secretariat@eurotop.be; internet www.eurotop.be; founded 1990; management, political affairs and public relations consultancy; contact Dr J. Viseur.

Areas of specialization:
- Technology transfer (energy-environment-bioindustry).
- Project management
- Feasibility studies
- Grants and loans
- RTD
- Web design
- Internet management tools

Eurowin Communications SA: Avenue de la Fontaine 31, 1435 Hévillers; tel (+32 10) 65-89-03; fax (+32 10) 65-84-48; e-mail marc.callemien@euronet.be; founded 1986; political affairs and public relations consultancy.

Areas of specialization:
- European affairs

Excoser S.A.: Rue M. Lietart 14, 1150 Brussels; tel (+32 2) 772-27-37; fax (+32 2) 771-44-39; e-mail excoser.j.agie@skynet.be; internet www.excoser.com; founded 1983; management consultancy; contact J. Agie de Selsaten.

Areas of specialization:
- Environment
- Agri-business
- Wood processing and forestry

Gerling Consulting Group Europe NV: Av. de Tervuren 273, 1150 Anvers; tel (+32 3) 773-08-11; fax (+32 3) 773-09-50; e-mail patrick.thiels@gerling.be; founded 1989; management consultancy; contact Patrick Thiels.

Areas of specialization:
- Environmental and safety management
- Risk analysis
- Risk management
- Environmental and safety auditing
- Quality management

Gerling Consulting Gruppe België – Risk Consulting Plus Security Management: Institut Für Risiko-Consulting Plus Sicherheits-Management GmbH, Frankfurter Strasse 720–726, 51145 Köln, Germany; tel (+49 221) 1442962; fax (+49 221) 1445324; contact Dr Annighöfer.

Global Europe – Consulting Group: Avenue Louise 106, 1050 Brussels; tel (+32 2) 6401259; fax (+32 2) 6477328; e-mail global.europe@global-eu.com; internet www.global-eu.com; founded 1997; management consultancy; contact D. Villanueva, J. Papi.

Areas of specialization:
- Infrastructure
- Telecommunications
- Environment
- Transport

The Directory of EU Information Sources

- RTD
- Marketing

GPC International: Rue d'Arlon 50, 1000 Brussels; tel (+32 2) 230-05-45; fax (+32 2) 230-57-06; internet www .gpcinternational.com; founded 1988; public affairs and strategic communications consultancy; contact Sam Rowe.

Areas of specialization:
- Food
- Pharmaceuticals
- Financial services
- Retailing
- Telecommunications
- Tourism
- Trade
- Transport
- Mergers and acquisitions
- Taxation
- Excise
- Health care
- Company law
- Funding (EU)
- State aids
- Environment
- European Union
- North America
- Eastern Europe

Gracious: Rue du Trône 216, 1050 Brussels; tel (+32 2) 346-60-59; fax (+32 2) 346-48-17; e-mail gracious@village.uunet.be; founded 1993; public relations consultancy; contact I. Peemans.

Areas of specialization:
- Lifestyle consumer
- Pharmaceuticals
- Goods (fast-moving)
- Computers
- Food

Grayling Political Strategy: Avenue des Arts 58, 1000 Brussels; tel (+32 2) 732-70-40; fax (+32 2) 732-71-76; e-mail info@grayling.be; internet www .grayling.be; founded 1985; political affairs consultancy; contact M. Bruggink.

Areas of specialization:
- Monitoring and analysis
- Strategy
- Lobbying
- Media relations
- Crisis management
- Issues and policy monitoring
- Issues analysis and evaluation
- Association management

Heidi Lambert Communications Sprl: Rue Stévin 212, 1000 Brussels; tel (+32 2) 732-55-46; fax (+32 2) 735-36-03; e-mail hlc@skynet.be; founded 1993; public relations consultancy; contact H. Lambert.

Areas of specialization:
- Media
- Brussels-based press corps of EU correspondents (relations with)
- Conferences

Hill and Knowlton International Belgium: Avenue de Cortenbergh 118, 1000 Brussels; tel (+32 2) 737-95-00; fax (+32 2) 737-95-01; e-mail ecruiksh@ hillandknowlton.com; internet www .hillandknowlton.be; founded 1967; political affairs and public relations consultancy; contact E. Cruikshanks.

Areas of specialization:
- Lobbying strategy
- Contact building
- Crisis management
- Media training
- Media relations
- Legislation (EU)

Houston Consulting Europe: Avenue de la Joyeuse Entrée 1–5, 1040 Brussels; tel (+32 2) 504-80-40; fax (+32 2) 504-80-50; e-mail info@houston-consulting.com; internet www.houston-consulting.com; founded 1997; political affairs consultancy; contact N. Rheinhardt.

Areas of specialization:
- Financial services
- Electronic commerce
- Consumer protection
- Competition
- EU–US relations.
- Economic and social policy in EMU context.
- Enterprise policy
- European Single Market
- Telecommunications

IDOM: Rue de Trèves 49, Bte 7, 1040 Brussels; tel (+32 2) 230-59-50; fax (+32 2) 230-70-35; e-mail idom@taseuro.com; internet www.idom.com; founded 1957; management consultancy.

Areas of specialization:
- Environment
- Energy
- Telecommunications
- Industrial engineering
- Civil engineering
- Architecture
- Project management
- Territorial management

IDOM: Lehendakari Aguirre 3, 48014 Bilbao, Spain; tel (+34) 94-479-76-00; fax (+34) 94-476-18-04.

Impact: Rue J.S. Bach 33, 1190 Brussels; tel (+32 2) 776-78-30; fax (+32 2) 776-78-39; e-mail info@impactcommunications .be; internet www@gcibrussels.com; founded 1983; public relations consultancy; contact C. Decroix.

Areas of specialization:
- Automotive industry
- Health care
- Telecommunications
- Consumer affairs
- Information technology
- Banking
- Finance
- Biotechnology
- Tourism
- Leisure

Interel European Public Affairs: Avenue de Tervueren 402, 1150 Brussels; tel (+32 2) 761-66-11; fax (+32 2) 761-66-00; e-mail iepa@interel.be; internet www .interel.be/iepa; founded 1983; public affairs consultancy; contact F. Lofthagen.

Areas of specialization:
- Environment
- Social affairs
- Food
- Taxation
- Sport
- Air transport
- Enlargement
- Telecommunications
- Pharmaceuticals
- Health

International Cooperation Europe Ltd: Bd du Régent 47–48, 5th floor, 1000 Brussels; tel (+32 2) 503-04-19; fax (+32 2) 514-13-42; e-mail icel@pophost .eunet.be; founded 1993; management consultancy; contact T. Bourke.

Areas of specialization:
- Industrial development
- Economic development
- Banking
- Environment

International Relations Consulting Company – IRELCO: Avenue Emile de Mot 19, 1000 Brussels; tel (+32 2) 640-18-69; fax (+32 2) 648-21-61; e-mail general@irelco.com; internet www.irelco .com; founded 1975; management, political affairs and public relations consultancy; contact P. Bähr.

Areas of specialization:
- Information management systems
- Lobbying
- Funding

International Technology and Trade Associates Inc (ITTA) Europe: Rue Washington 50, 1050 Brussels; tel (+32 2) 640-86-61; fax (+32 2) 646-09-15; e-mail baker.mre@skynet.be; internet www.itta.com; founded 1989; management consultancy; contact R. E. Baker.

Areas of specialization:
- Trade
- Technology
- Investment
- EBRD
- Public affairs
- International market research
- International marketing
- Defence industry
- NATO

Ipstrategies: Chaussée de Louvain 490, 1380 Lasne; tel (+32 2) 351-00-11; fax (+32 2) 351-01-14; e-mail info@ ipstrategies.be; founded 1984; management consultancy; contacts J.L. Mentior, A. Pierre.

Areas of specialization:
- SMEs
- Company development
- European studies
- Technological innovation
- Strategy and alliance
- European aid
- Mergers and acquisitions
- VAT

J.M. Didier & Associates S.A.: Avenue Marquis de Villalobar 6, 1050 Brussels; tel (+32 2) 736-99-10; fax (+32 2) 736-89-94; e-mail jmdidier@wanadoo.be; founded 1970; European affairs consultancy; contact J.M. Didier.

Areas of specialization:
- Industrial relations
- Labour law
- Worker information, consultation and participation
- Health and safety
- Social dialogue

KPMG: Avenue du Bourget 40, 1130 Brussels; tel (+32 2) 708-43-00; fax (+32 2) 708-43-99; e-mail info@kpmg.be; internet www.kpmg.be; contact T. Erauw.

Areas of specialization:
- Business compliance with EU law.
- Business risk
- Business opportunities
- Mergers and acquisitions
- External trade
- Taxation
- Grants and loans (EU)
- Competition rules
- Audit
- Assurance advice
- Financial advice
- Legal advice
- Management
- Banking
- Insurance
- Consumer markets
- Communication
- Entertainment
- Industrial markets

KPMG European Headquarters: Avenue Louise 54, 1050 Brussels; tel (+32 2) 548-09-11; fax (+32 2) 548-09-09; e-mail marie-claire.snocks@kpmg.be; internet www.eu.kpmg.net; founded 1870; management consultancy; contact M.-C. Snocks.

Areas of specialization:
- Management
- Accounting
- Audit
- Taxation

KPMG International Headquarters: PO Box 74111, 1070 BC Amsterdam, Netherlands.

Kreab Europe: Avenue de Tervueren 13A, 1040 Brussels; tel (+32 2) 737-69-00; fax (+32 2) 737-69-40; e-mail kreab@kreab.com; internet www.kreab.com; founded 1992; political affairs and public relations consultancy; contact G. Danell.

Areas of specialization:
- European affairs
- Public affairs
- Internal relations
- Public relations
- Investor relations
- Market communication
- Crisis management
- Events
- Exhibitions
- Campaigns

Longin & Associés: Avenue des Nerviens 67, 1040 Brussels; tel (+32 2) 230-72-73; fax (+32 2) 230-81-65; e-mail pierre.longin@swing.be; founded 1990; public affairs consultancy; contact P.E. Longin.

Areas of specialization:
- Strategic monitoring
- Public affairs plans
- Lobbying
- PHARE
- TACIS

Lucy Rozenbaum Sprl: Rue Fernand Neuray 8, 1050 Brussels; tel (+32 2) 344-21-12; fax (+32 2) 344-08-56; e-mail lucy@rozenbaum-associates.net; founded 1978; political affairs and public relations consultancy; contact L. Rozenbaum.

Areas of specialization:
- Audiovisual
- Communication
- Aeronautics

M. P. G. Research Sprl: Avenue H. Hoover 163, 1030 Brussels; tel (+32 2) 230-95-68; fax (+32 2) 230-95-68; e-mail michael.gaum@skynet.be; founded 1989; management consultancy; contact M. Gaum.

Areas of specialization:
- International market
- Economic research
- Automotive industry
- Retail trade
- Wholesale trade
- Distribution
- Food and drink
- Textiles
- Clothing
- Construction
- Country monitoring
- Agriculture

Maxess Sprl: Rue du Coq 87, 1180 Brussels; tel (+32 2) 332-35-45; fax (+32 2) 332-35-75; e-mail maxess@skynet.be; founded 1993; management, telecommunications and marketing consultancy; contact C. Henny.

Areas of specialization:
- Telecommunications
- Technology
- Marketing

MEA Etudes et Services Sprl: Fontaine Fonteny 8, 1332 Genval; tel (+32 2) 633-60-30; fax (+32 2) 633-60-29; e-mail clodong@skynet.be; founded 1986; political affairs consultancy; contact André Clodong.

Areas of specialization:
- Transport
- Energy
- Trade

Metzdorff & Associates: Avenue de la Ferme Rose 9A, bte 21, 1180 Brussels; tel (+32 2) 346-16-99; fax (+32 2) 346-16-99; e-mail c.metzdorff@aces.be; internet www.metzdorff.com; founded 1989; political affairs consultancy; contact C. Metzdorff.

Areas of specialization:
- Pharmaceuticals

MONDIMPRESA: Rue de l'Industrie 22, 1040 Brussels; tel (+32 2) 502-31-31; fax (+32 2) 502-58-98; e-mail mondimpresa@easynet.be; founded 1988; political affairs and public relations consultancy; contact F. Burlizzi.

Areas of specialization:
- European projects
- Regional desks
- Seminars
- Conferences
- Lobbying

Moores Rowland Europe S.C. / C.V. MRI European Coordination Office: Avenue Louise 109, 1050 Brussels; tel (+32 2) 541-07-50; fax (+32 2) 541-07-54; e-mail jerome.adam@euronet.be; founded 1989; contact J. Adam.

Areas of specialization:
- European Union
- Central Europe
- Eastern Europe
- CIS

MRI Moores Rowland: Sceptre House, 169–173 Regent Street, London W1R 7FB, United Kingdom; tel (+44 20) 7470-0000; fax (+44 20) 7287-3896.

National Economic Research Associates – NERA: Rue de la Loi 23, 1040 Brussels; tel (+32 2) 282-43-40; fax (+32 2) 282-43-60; internet www.nera.com; founded 1961; economic consultancy; contact Alison Oldale.

Areas of specialization:
- Application of micro-economics to regulatory and competition issues, policy evaluation, and business strategy.
- Competition
- Privatization
- Market regulation
- Law
- Economic affairs
- Third-party access
- International trade
- Energy
- Transport
- Water and sewerage
- Telecommunications
- Broadcasting
- Media
- Health
- Pharmaceuticals
- Environment
- Regional policy

National Economic Research Associates (NERA): 15 Stratford Place, London W1N 9AF, United Kingdom; tel (+44 20) 7659-8500; fax (+44 20) 7659-8501.

Newton 21: Rue des Anciens Etangs 55, 1190 Brussels; tel (+32 2) 340-95-03; fax (+32 2) 374-86-58; e-mail erwin.deweerdt@newton21.com; internet www.newton21.com; founded 2000; management, corporate affairs and public relations consultancy firms; contact E. De Weerdt.

Areas of specialization:
- Automotive industry
- Finance
- Fashion
- Food
- Environment
- Telecommunications
- Information technology
- Transport
- Media
- Audiovisual
- Television
- Events
- Sport
- Agriculture
- Chemicals
- Biochemicals
- Health

Nicholas Phillips Associates SA: Rue Joseph II 36, Bte 9, 1000 Brussels; tel (+32 2) 218-13-70; fax (+32 2) 219-18-42; e-mail nicholas.phillips@wanadoo.be; founded 1989; political affairs consultancy; contact K. Muylaert.

Areas of specialization:
- European Parliament

Nordic Transport Development: NTU Bruxelles Sprl, Rue de Trèves 49–51, 1040 Brussels; tel (+32 2) 280-19-46; fax (+32 2) 280-01-40; e-mail ntu-bruxelles@ntu.dk; internet www.ntu.dk; contact L. Bentzen.

Office Kirkpatrick SA: Avenue Wolfers 32, 1310 La Hulpe; tel (+32 2) 652-16-00; fax (+32 2) 652-19-00; e-mail info@office-kirkpatrick.com; founded 1852; intellectual property consultancy; contact D. Hubart.

Areas of specialization:
- Industrial property
- Patents
- Trademarks
- Designs

Ogilvy Public Relations Worldwide: Bd de l'Impératrice 13, 1000 Brussels; tel (+32 2) 545-66-00; fax (+32 2) 545-66-10; e-mail ogilvypr@ogilvy.be; internet www.ogilvypr.com; founded 1956; political affairs and public relations consultancy; contact E. Mulders.

Areas of specialization:
- Health
- Medicine
- Banking
- Pharmaceuticals
- Payment systems
- Public awareness campaigns
- Media training
- Crisis communication
- Business to business
- Public affairs
- Public relations co-ordination (Pan-European)
- Environmental communication
- Product launches
- Internal communication

One Market Sprl: Rue de la Tourelle 37, 1040 Brussels; tel (+32 2) 231-18-84; fax (+32 2) 280-06-90; e-mail one.market@pop.kpn.be; founded 1991; management, political affairs and public relations consultancy; contact P.J. Jacobsen.

Areas of specialization:
- EU–Scandinavia relations
- Training
- Marketing
- European Union

Orbyte bvba: St-Hubertuslaan 4A, 3080 Tervuren; tel (+32 2) 305-04-36; fax (+32 2) 767-02-74; e-mail orbyte@pandora.be; internet www.bioresco.ch; founded 1986; food and feedstuffs law consultancy; contact Ir Dr R. Verbruggen.

Areas of specialization:
- Food
- Animal feedstuffs
- Food science
- Food regulations

PA Consulting Group: Rue des Colonies 11, 1000 Brussels; tel (+32 2) 761-79-00; fax (+32 2) 517-65-00; e-mail nathalie.jevdjenijevitch@pa-consulting.com; internet www.paconsulting.com; founded 1943; management consultancy; contact M. Hunter.

Areas of specialization:
- Economic affairs
- Training
- Information technology
- Customer relations
- Business solutions
- Technology

PA Consulting Group: 123 Buckingham Palace Road, London SW1W 9SR, United Kingdom; tel (+44 20) 7730-9000; fax (+44 20) 7333-5050; e-mail info@paconsulting.com.

Porter Novelli Brussels: Bd L. Mettewielaan 272/5, 1080 Brussels; tel (+32 2) 413-03-40; fax (+32 2) 413-03-49; e-mail info@pnbrussels.com; internet www.pnbrussels.com; founded 1994; public relations consultancy; contact L. Missinne.

Areas of specialization:
- European affairs
- Community relations
- Media relations

PricewaterhouseCoopers: Avenue de Cortenbergh 75, 1000 Brussels; tel (+32 2) 741-08-11; fax (+32 2) 741-08-92; fax (+32 2) 741-08-99; e-mail davies.mike@be.pwcglobal.com; internet www.pwc.com; founded 1990; European public affairs consultancy; contact M. Davies.

Areas of specialization:
- Public affairs
- Accounting
- Audit
- Taxation

Public Relations Partners: Vandendriesschelaan 5, 1150 Brussels; tel (+32 2) 762-04-85; fax (+32 2) 771-19-59;

e-mail eeckman@prp.be; e-mail info@prp.be; founded 1963; public relations consultancy; contact E. Eeckman.

Areas of specialization:
- Communication
- Environment
- Marketing
- Media relations
- Change management

RP Conseils: Chemin des Moines 1, 1640 Rhode Saint-Genèse; tel (+32 2) 358-11-89; fax (+32 2) 358-45-66; e-mail c.leclercq@euronet.be; founded 1970; public relations and political affairs consultancy; contact C. Le Clercq.

Areas of specialization:
- Public relations
- Press relations
- Publications
- Seminars
- Events
- Crisis management
- Public affairs

Schuman Associates: Rue Archimède 5, 1000 Brussels; tel (+32 2) 230-74-39; fax (+32 2) 230-74-26; e-mail gerard@schumanassociates.com; internet www.schumanassociates.com; founded 1989; management consultancy; contact G. McNamara.

Areas of specialization:
- Energy
- Transport
- Environment
- Agriculture
- External relations
- Employment
- Training
- Health
- Funding (EU)
- Technical assistance
- Consortia creation
- Partnerships

Single Market Ventures Sprl: Rue Faider 87, 1050 Brussels; tel (+32 2) 537-26-03; fax (+32 2) 537-10-78; e-mail info@SMV-online.com; internet www.smv-online.com; founded 1988; management consultancy; contact R.M. Schonfeld.

Areas of specialization:
- Packaging
- Quality control
- Technical Barriers to Trade (TBT)

Skan Europe: Avenue de la Pinède 3, 1380 Lasne; tel (+32 2) 653-21-64; fax (+32 2) 653-93-89; e-mail skaneurope@compuserve.com; founded 1991; public relations consultancy; contact Mrs Strauss.

Areas of specialization:
- EC (relations with)
- Telecommunications
- Environment

Stern Malkinson & Partners: Rue de Stassart 84, 1050 Brussels; tel (+32 2) 552-09-00; fax (+32 2) 552-09-11; e-mail info@stern.be; founded 1990; political affairs and public relations consultancy.

Areas of specialization:
- EU institutions
- EU procedures
- EU law
- Lobbying
- Central Europe
- Asia
- Public relations
- Press

Strat. & Com. SA: Avenue des Phalènes 25, 1000 Brussels; tel (+32 2) 649-62-82; fax (+32 2) 649-18-85; e-mail info@stratcom.be; internet www.stratcom.be; founded 1986; public relations consultancy.

Areas of specialization:
- Information strategy
- Communication
- Editorial management
- Publications

TESEO – Technical Support for European Organisations: Avenue de Tervueren 32, 1040 Brussels; tel (+32 2) 230-10-90; fax (+32 2) 230-13-77; e-mail bianchi@teseo.be; founded 1991; management consultancy; contact M. Bianchi.

Areas of specialization:
- Industrial materials
- Environment
- Life sciences
- Human resources
- Worker mobility
- Telecommunications
- Telematics
- Training
- Exploitation of technological research
- Information industry
- SMEs
- Conferences
- Seminars
- Multimedia
- Electronic publishing

Touchstone Europe: Rue Wiertz 11, 1050 Brussels; tel (+32 2) 644-06-98; fax (+32 2) 640-10-84; e-mail annetouchstone@skynet.be; internet www.energychoicesforeurope.com; founded 1994; political affairs and public relations consultancy; contact A. Erlam.

Areas of specialization:
- EU institutions (relations with)
- Funding applications
- Public affairs

Value Added Europe: Avenue de Tervueren 233, 1150 Brussels; tel (+32 2) 772-25-25; fax (+32 2) 772-55-55; e-mail vae@vae.be; founded 1990; management consultancy; contact J. Rassart.

Weber Shandwick / Adamson: Park Leopold, Rue Wiertz 50, 1050 Brussels; tel (+32 2) 230-07-75; fax (+32 2) 230-14-96; e-mail info@webershandwick.com; internet www.webershandwick.com; founded 1980; political affairs and public relations consultancy.

Areas of specialization:
- Pharmaceuticals
- Environment
- Media
- Audiovisual
- Telecommunications
- Transport
- Health care
- Energy
- Mergers and acquisitions
- Anti-trust law
- Strategic communication

Weber Shandwick Belgium: Bd Lambermont 436, 1030 Brussels; tel (+32 2) 240-97-60; fax (+32 2) 216-91-65; e-mail pr@webershandwick.com; internet www.webershandwick.com; founded 1970; public relations consultancy; contact L. Goethals.

Areas of specialization:
- Strategy analysis
- Monitoring EU and national institutions
- Lobbying

Weber Shandwick UK: Fox Court, 14 Gray's Inn Road, London WC1X 8WS, United Kingdom; tel (+44 20) 7067-0000; internet www.webershandwick.com.

Westminster Europe – Citigate Public Affairs: Avenue de Cortenbergh 66, 1000 Brussels; tel (+32 2) 736-81-35; fax (+32 2) 736-88-47; e-mail johnny.pring@citigopa.com; internet www.citigopa.com; founded 1994; political affairs consultancy; contact Th. Lebeaux.

Areas of specialization:
- Financial services
- Energy
- Environment
- Aviation
- Regulatory impact assessments
- Pharmaceuticals
- Electronic commerce
- Mergers and acquisitions
- Sport
- Mail transport
- Automotive industry

Westminster Europe – Citigate Public Affairs: Cowlery House, Little College St., London SW1P 3XS, United Kingdom; tel (+44 20) 7222-0666; fax (+44 20) 7233-0335.

Yellow Window Management Consultants NV: Minderbroedersstraat 14, 2000 Antwerp; tel (+32 3) 241-00-24; fax (+32 3) 203-53-03; e-mail mail@yellowwindow.com; internet www.yellowwindow.com; founded 1989; management consultancy; contact A. Denis.

Areas of specialization:
- EU regulations
- Markets
- Industry
- Companies
- Lobbying (technical)

Zenab: Avenue Beau Séjour 46, 1180 Brussels; tel (+32 2) 374-59-11; fax (+32 2) 375-52-58; e-mail zenab@skynet.be; founded 1989; political affairs and management consultancy; contact N. La Bouverie.

Areas of specialization:
- Audiovisual
- Telecommunications
- Multimedia
- Intellectual property

CZECH REPUBLIC

Baloun, J.C. a Rosehill: Nekrasova 2, 160 00 Prague 6; tel (+420 2) 312-23-13; fax (+420 2) 312-23-13; e-mail boyden_baloun@mbox.vol.cz; founded 1990; management, public affairs and public relations consultancy.

Areas of specialization:
- Lobbying
- Executive search

DENMARK

Kreab AS: Vester Sogade 10 – 2, 1601 Kobenhavn V; tel (+45) 88-33-11-00; fax (+45) 88-33-11-11; e-mail info.sund@kreab.com; founded 1981; management, political affairs and public relations consultancy; contact K. Steen.

Areas of specialization:
- Environment
- Construction
- Finance
- Lobbying
- Health care
- Medicine
- Electronics
- Internet
- Intranet
- Mergers and acquisitions
- Publications
- Corporate communication
- Financial communication
- Marketing communication
- Competition

FINLAND

Eurofacts OY: Brahenkatu 1 B 4, 20100 Turku; tel (+358 2) 4693030; fax (+358 2) 4693031; e-mail eurofacts@eurofacts.fi; internet www.eurofacts.fi; founded 1989; management, political affairs and public relations consultancy; contact A. Blom.

Areas of specialization:
- European affairs
- Telecommunications
- Political risks
- Family business
- Finance
- Industrial policy
- Trade and competition
- Information society
- Taxation
- Graphical industry

FRANCE

Aromates SA: Rue d'Aguesseau 169, 92100 Boulogne Billancourt; tel (+33) 1-46-99-10-80; fax (+33) 1-46-04-70-98; e-mail j.marceau@aromates.fr; internet www.aromates.com; founded 1987; public relations consultancy; contact J. Marceau.

Areas of specialization:
- Telecommunications and informatics
- Internet
- Logistics and transport
- Business centre

Droit et Pharmacie: Rue de Lorraine 12, 92309 Levallois-Perret Cédex; tel (+33) 1-55-46-91-00; fax (+33) 1-55-46-91 01; e-mail info@droit-et-pharmacie.fr; e-mail jerome.conquet@parexel.com; founded 1952; management consultancy; contacts J. Conquet, M. C. Belleville.

Areas of specialization:
- Pharmaceutical industry
- Legal affairs
- Regulatory affairs
- Economic affairs
- Marketing authorization dossiers

ESL Network Paris: 123 avenue des Champs Elysées, 75008 Paris; tel (+33) 1-40-73-14-00; fax (+33) 1-40-73-14-01; e-mail simonwh@eslnetwork.com; contact P. Allain-Dupré.

Essor Europe: 25 avenue de l'Europe, 92310 Sèvres; tel (+33) 1-49-66-22-35; fax (+33) 1-45-34-96-95; e-mail mailbox@essoreurope.fr; internet www.essoreurope.fr; founded 1989; management and political affairs consultancy; contact Ph. de Montgolfier.

Areas of specialization:
- Research and development
- Technology
- EU programmes
- EUREKA
- EU projects (establishment of)
- SMEs
- Technology transfer
- Industrial property
- Biotechnology
- Environment
- Transport

Euromission: 6 Bd St Michel, 84000 Avignon; tel (+33) 4-90-16-35-00; fax (+33) 4-90-16-35-01; founded 1994; contact G. Crest.

FINECO Eurofinancements: Le Florentin, 71 chemin du Moulin Carron, 69570 Dardilly; tel (+33) 4-78-33-81-79; fax (+33) 4-78-33-80-63; e-mail contacts@fineco.fr; founded 1994; management consultancy; contact M.-A. Pamokdjian.

Areas of specialization:
- European programmes engineering (RTD)
- CIS countries (co-operation with)
- Companies partnership
- Technology transfer
- Innovation financing

Maison de l'Europe d'Avignon – Méditerranée: 6 Bd St Michel, 84000 Avignon; tel (+33) 4-90-16-35-00; fax (+33) 4-90-16-35-01; e-mail maison .europe@europe-avignon.com; internet www.europe-avignon.com; founded 1994; political affairs and public relations consultancy; contact C. Perez.

Areas of specialization:
- Europe
- Euro

RSM Salustro Reydel: 8 Avenue Delcassé, 75378 Paris Cedex 08; tel (+33) 1-53-77-38-00; fax (+33) 1-53-77-39-38; founded 1989; auditing firm.

Areas of specialization:
- Mergers and acquisitions
- Accounting

GERMANY

Rödl & Partner GmbH: Aussene-Sulztbacker-Str. 100, 90491 Nuremberg; tel (+49 911) 9193601; fax (+49 911) 9193660; internet www.rödl.de; founded 1973; management consultancy; contacts M. Kastl, M. Tröger.

Areas of specialization:
- European Union
- Structural funds
- PHARE
- TACIS
- Central Europe
- Eastern Europe
- Baltic countries
- CIS
- Accounting
- Audit
- Public management
- Vocational training

GREECE

Synergon S.A. – International Consulting Group: Minoos Str. 10–16, Eleftherotypia Building, 11743 Athens; tel (+30) 210-9270000; fax (+30) 210-9270003; e-mail synergon@innet.gr; founded 1994; management consultancy; contact K. Valleras.

IRELAND

International Development Ireland Ltd: Wilton Park House, Wilton Place, Dublin 2; tel (+353 1) 6687555; fax (+353 1) 6601733; e-mail idi@dublin.idi .ie; contact R. Deignan.

ITALY

ARPES: Viale G. Mazzini 55, 00195 Rome; tel (+39) 06-3217786; fax (+39) 06-3217783; e-mail info@arpes.it; e-mail arpesco@tin.it; contact F. Lupi.

Mondimpresa – Roma S.C.P.A.: Viale Pasteur 10, 00142 Rome; tel (+39) 06-549541; fax (+39) 06-54954409; e-mail servizi@mondimpresa.it; internet www .mondimpresa.it.

NETHERLANDS

Bennis Porter Novelli: Amsterdamseweg 204, 1182 HL Amstelveen; tel (+31 20) 5437600; fax (+31 20) 5437676; e-mail bennispn.av@bennispn.nl; founded 1985; political affairs and public relations consultancy; contact S. van den Ende.

Areas of specialization:
- Health
- Food
- Consumer goods (fast-moving)
- Industry
- Government communication
- Information technology
- Communications technology

Ellis Publications BV: Wilhelminasingel 105, 6201 Maastricht; tel (+31 43) 3215313; fax (+31 43) 3253959; e-mail sales@ellispub.com; internet www .ellispub.com; founded 1986; contact D. Fairweather.

Areas of specialization:
- Legal information (EU)

Euroscope: Expertise in the EU and World Economy: Lg Kanaakdijk 62, 6212 AH Maastricht; tel (+31 43) 3639189; fax (+31 43) 3256780; e-mail euroscope@hetnet.nl; founded 1989; contact J. Pelkmans.

Areas of specialization:
- Internal market strategy
- Standards
- Telecoms
- Textiles
- EU–East Asia relations

Expertise in Labour Mobility: Elandsgracht 17, 1016 TM Amsterdam; tel (+31 20) 6836964; fax (+31 20) 4125295; e-mail info@labourmobility.com; internet www .labourmobility.com; founded 1993; management consultancy; contact N. Ripmeester.

Areas of specialization:
- Labour mobility

Hobéon Management Consult BV: Scheveningseweg 46, 2517 KV The Hague; tel (+31 70) 3066800; fax (+31 70) 3066870; e-mail stoltenborg@hobeon .xs4all.nl; internet www.hobeon.nl; founded 1992; management consultancy; contact H. Stoltenborg.

Areas of specialization:
- Higher education

Twijnstra Gudde: PO Box 907, 3800 AX Amersfoort; tel (+31 33) 4677478; fax (+31 33) 4677479; founded 1964; management consultancy; contacts H. Stoop, J. Viling.

Areas of specialization:
- Banking
- Insurance
- Eastern Europe
- Environmental control
- Health care
- Human resources
- Information
- Logistical management
- Project management
- Public sector
- Privatization management
- Strategic management
- Quality control

SPAIN

C. B. Europa: Las Huertas 50, 28220 Majadahonda (Madrid); tel (+34) 91-634-64-66; fax (+34) 91-634-65-86; e-mail mail@cbeuropa.com; founded 1993; political affairs consultancy; contact I. Corrochano.

Areas of specialization:
- Telecommunications
- Energy
- Environment
- Media
- Latin America
- Funding

Euro-Consejeros S.L.: C/ Cortes de Aragon 35, Entlo Dcha, 50005 Zaragoza; tel (+34) 976-35-68-12; fax (+34) 976-56-12-94; e-mail euro-consejeros@red3i.es; internet www.red3i.es/euro; founded 1992; management consultancy; contact N. Morte de Rego.

Areas of specialization:
- EU Law
- International commercial law

GADESO S.L.: Ter, n°14, 1° – B, Poligono Son Suster, 07009 Palma de Mallorca; tel (+34) 971-47-94-74; fax (+34) 971-47-00-42; e-mail gadeso_1@infonegocio.com; founded 1970; management consultancy; contacts A. Tarabini-Castellani Cabot, R. Oro Gaillart.

Areas of specialization:
- Tourism
- SMEs
- Trade
- Training

Infyde – Informacion y Desarrollo S.L.: Av. Zugazarte n° 8, Edificio Abra 4, 3rd floor, 48930 Las Arenas; tel (+34) 94-480-40-95; fax (+34) 94-481-16-39; e-mail infyde@sarenet.es; founded 1987; political affairs consultancy; contact J. del Castillo.

Areas of specialization:
- Regional policy
- Technology policy
- Training policy
- Local development
- Evaluation of policies
- European networks (design)
- Innovation
- SMEs

- RITTS/RIS

Intersalus: Tarragona 107–115, 9th floor, 08014 Barcelona; tel (+34) 93-292-42-40; fax (+34) 93-292-42-38; e-mail internacional@intersalus.com; founded 1972; management consultancy in hospitals; contact M. Burgell.

Areas of specialization:
- Architecture
- Engineering
- Hospitals

Seconde S.L.: Castello 50, 28001 Madrid; tel (+34) 91-435-85-56; fax (+34) 91-577-83-60; e-mail erseconde@retemail.es; founded 1992; management consultancy; contact E. Ruiz.

Areas of specialization:
- Private sector development
- Customs
- Project management
- Institutional development

SWEDEN

Gullers Group Information Counsellors: Box 7004, 10386 Stockholm; tel (+46 8) 679-09-40; fax (+46 8) 611-07-80; e-mail post@gullers.se; internet www.gullers.se; founded 1989; political affairs and public relations consultancy; contact M. Gullers.

Areas of specialization:
- Lobbying
- Community issues
- Media relations
- Crisis management
- Strategic planning and analysis
- Communication strategy

SWITZERLAND

Burson-Marsteller AG: Grubenstrasse 40, 8045 Zurich; tel (+41) 14558400; fax (+41) 14558401; e-mail info_bm@ch.bm.com; internet www.b-m.ch; founded 1971; political affairs and public relations consultancy; contact P. Eberhard.

Areas of specialization:
- Marketing communication
- Public relations
- Advertising

Orbyte bvba: Bundesstrasse 29, 4054 Basel; tel (+41) 612737700; fax (+41) 612737703; e-mail contact@bioresco.ch; internet www.bioresco.ch; contact Dr A. Bär.

UNITED KINGDOM

Association for Information Management – ASLIB: Temple Chambers, 3–7 Temple Ave, London EC4Y 0HP; tel (+44 20) 7583-8900; fax (+44 20) 7583-8401; e-mail aslib@aslib.com; management consultancy.

Areas of specialization:
- Information management

CEASC Consultants (Wye) Ltd: Imperial College, Wye, Ashford, Kent TN25 5AH; tel (+44 1233) 812181; fax (+44 1233) 813309; e-mail info@promar-ceas.be; internet www.predure-studies.com/CEAS; contact C. Caspari.

Charlemagne Group: Charlemagne House, 2 Enys Road, Eastbourne BN21 2DE; tel (+44 1323) 434710; fax (+44 1323) 434720; e-mail p.barron@charlemagne.co.uk; internet www.charlemagne.co.uk; founded 1991; political affairs consultancy; contact P. Barron.

Areas of specialization:
- European Union
- Information networking and delivery

Citigate Public Affairs: Rochester Row 50, London SW1P 1JU; tel (+44 20) 7838-4800; contact D. Forest.

CSM European Consultants: Rochester Row 72A, London SW1P 1JU; tel (+44 20) 7233-9090; fax (+44 20) 7233-9595; e-mail info@csm.prestel.co.uk; founded 1978; political affairs consultancy; contact Ch. Stewart Munro.

Areas of specialization:
- Internal market
- Financial services
- Environment
- Consumer affairs
- Social policy
- Industrial policy
- Energy
- Health policy

Ecotec Research and Consulting Ltd: 28–34 Albert Street, Birmingham B4 7UD; tel (+44 121) 616-1010; fax (+44 121) 616-1099; contact H. Williams.

Entec UK Ltd: Northumbria House, Regent Centre, Gosforth, Newcastle upon Tyne NE3 3PX; tel (+44 191) 272-6100; fax (+44 191) 272-6592; e-mail marketing@entecuk.co.uk; founded 1946; management consultancy; contact Mr. Corsil.

Areas of specialization:
- Ground and water management
- Contaminated land investigation and remediation
- Water and wastewater engineering
- Urban and regional planning and development
- Tourism
- Corporate and technical risk management
- Rural and economic development
- Fisheries development

Environmental Policy Consultants: 71 Greencroft Gardens, London NW6 3LJ; tel (+44 20) 7328-0050; fax (+44 20) 7328-0050; e-mail adrian.wilkes@eic-uk.co.uk; founded 1990; political affairs and public relations consultancy; contact A. Wilkes.

Areas of specialization:
- Environment

EPRC: 40 George Street, Glasgow G1 1QE; tel (+44 141) 548-3672; fax (+44 141) 548-4898; e-mail eprc@strath.ac.uk; internet www.eprc.strath.ac.uk; founded 1979; regional policy research institute; contact J.A. Vance.

Areas of specialization:
- Economic policy
- Industrial policy
- Regional policy (Western and Eastern Europe)
- Structural funds
- Economic development policy

Eric Deakins – International Public Affairs: 36 Murray Mews, London NW1 9RJ; tel (+44 20) 7267-6196; fax (+44 20) 7267-3151; e-mail epdeakins@netscapeonline.co.uk; founded 1989; political affairs consultancy; contact E. Deakins.

Areas of specialization:
- International trade
- EU–US relations
- UK government and labour party contacts
- UK taxation

Eurofi Ltd: Eurofi House, 37 London Road, Newbury RG14 1JL; tel (+44 1635) 31900; fax (+44 1635) 37370; e-mail eurofi@headoffice.freeserve.co.uk; internet www.eurofi.co.uk; founded 1980; management consultancy; contact B.G.T. Harris.

Areas of specialization:
- Funding (EU)
- Grants (UK government)

Europe Economics: Chancery House, 53–64 Chancery Lane, London WC2A 1QU; tel (+44 20) 7831-4717; fax (+44 20) 7831-4515; e-mail enquiries@europe-economics.com; founded 1998; economics and management consultancy; contacts D. Glynn, S. McCarron.

Areas of specialization:
- Economic regulation
- Competition policy
- Public policy
- Telecommunications
- Electricity
- Gas
- Water
- Transport
- Pharmaceuticals
- Lotteries and gaming.

Europe for Business and Europe for Health: 41 Portland Avenue, Hove, East Sussex BN3 5NF; tel (+44 1273) 421485; fax (+44 1273) 383033; e-mail info@europe-business.co.uk; internet www.europe-for-business.co.uk; founded 1991; management and political affairs consultancy; contact L. Wittenberg.

Areas of specialization:
- Research and development

- Funding (EU)
- Food
- Consumer policy
- Social policy
- Environment
- Information Technology
- SMEs
- Health
- Information society
- Electronic commerce
- Euro

Finance for Business Ltd – Grantfinder Ltd: Enterprise House, Carlton Road, Worksop, Nottinghamshire; S81 7QF; tel (+44 1909) 501200; fax (+44 1909) 501225; e-mail enquiries@grantfinder.co.uk; internet www.grantfinder.co.uk; founded 1985; management consultancy; contact J. Dilworth.

Areas of specialization:
- Grants
- Financial opportunities

Henley Centre: 33 St John Street, London EC1M 4PG; tel (+44 20) 7955-1800; fax (+44 20) 7559-1900; e-mail future@henleycentre.com; internet www.henleycentre.com; founded 1974; management consultancy; contact C. Christie.

Areas of specialization:
- Retailing
- Food and drink
- Transport
- Telecommunications
- Tourism
- Goods (fast-moving)
- Media
- Financial services

Hurlstons Corporate Consultancy Ltd: 2 Ridgmount Street, London WC1E 7AA; tel (+44 20) 7636-5214; fax (+44 20) 7580-0016; e-mail ishepard@hurlstons.com; founded 1980; political affairs consultancy; contact M. Hurlston.

Areas of specialization:
- Competition
- Pharmaceuticals
- Employee participation
- Agriculture
- Social affairs
- Trade associations
- Packaging
- Sunday trading
- Beverages

IMC Associates: PO Box 25, Lymington, Hants. SO41 3WU; tel (+44 1590) 673689; fax (+44 1590) 670525; e-mail maritime@tcp.co.uk; internet www.homepages.tcp.co.uk/~maritime; founded 1983; management consultancy; contact G. J. Clarke.

Areas of specialization:
- Industry
- Marine industry
- Defence industry
- International marketing
- Business strategy
- Business systems

J & A B Associates: 3 The Butts, Warwick, Warwickshire CV34 4SS; tel (+44 1926) 403040; fax (+44 1926) 403048; e-mail alan.badger@jandab.co.uk; founded 1984; management consultancy; contact A. Badger.

Areas of specialization:
- European Social Fund
- Grants for research (EU)
- Leonardo

Joan Noble Associates Ltd: Braywick House, Gregory Place, London W8 4NG; tel (+44 20) 7376-1401; fax (+44 20) 7376-1402; e-mail joan@joannobleassociates.com; internet www.joannobleassociates.com; founded 1989; political affairs consultancy; contact J. Noble.

Areas of specialization:
- Food and drinks law
- Environmental policy
- Trade law
- Economic affairs
- Agriculture

Keene Public Affairs Consultants Ltd: 1st floor, Victory House, 99–101 Regent Street, London W1B 4EZ; tel (+44 20) 7287-0652; fax (+44 20) 7494-0493; e-mail kpac@keenepa.co.uk; internet www.keenepa.co.uk; founded 1986; political affairs and public relations consultancy; contact A. G. Richards.

Areas of specialization:
- Aviation
- Travel
- Tourism
- Pharmaceuticals
- Health care
- Energy
- Utilities
- Chemicals
- Trade associations
- Information technology
- Transport
- Metals
- Minerals

Parliamentary & EU News Service: 19 Douglas Street, Westminster, London SW1P 4PA; tel (+44 20) 7233-8283; fax (+44 20) 7821-9352; e-mail lionel.zetter@parliamentary-monitoring.co.uk; internet www.parliamentary-monitoring.co.uk; founded 1935; management, political affairs and public relations consultancy; contact L. Zetter.

Areas of specialization:
- Publishing and news distribution on EU affairs

Perchards: Drover House, 16 Adelaide Street, St Albans AL3 5BH; tel (+44 1727) 843227; fax (+44 1727) 843193; e-mail info@perchards.com; internet www.perchards.com; founded 1987; political affairs consultancy; contact D. Perchard.

Areas of specialization:
- Producer responsibility
- Waste management
- Environment
- Consumer affairs

PMS – Parliamentary Monitoring Services: 19 Douglas Street, London SWIP 4PA; tel (+44 20) 7233-8283; fax (+44 20) 7821-9352; e-mail lionel.zetter@parliamentary-monitoring.co.uk; internet www.parliamentary-monitoring.co.uk; founded 1979; political affairs consultancy; contact L. Zetter.

Profile Corporate Communications: 31 Great Peter Street, London SW1P 3LR; tel (+44 20) 7222-2121; fax (+44 20) 7222-2030; e-mail eastoes@profilecc.com; internet www.profilecc.com; founded 1981; political affairs and public relations consultancy; contact S. Eastoe.

Areas of specialization:
- Political contact building
- Lobbying
- Competition
- Media
- Trade relations

Project Development and Support Ltd: 30 Gritstone Road, Matlock, Derbyshire DE4 3GD; tel (+44 1629) 57501; fax (+44 1629) 584972; e-mail pdsl@dial.pipex.com; internet www.esf.uk.com; founded 1990; management consultancy; contact J. Roberts.

Areas of specialization:
- Education
- Training

- SMEs
- Travel
- Tourism
- Business development
- ESF/ERDF/LEADER II
- Learning disability
- Project monitoring software

Project Monitor Ltd: 30 Gritstone Road, Matlock, Derbyshire DE4 3GD; tel (+44 1629) 583916; fax (+44 1629) 584972; e-mail pdsl@dial.pipex.com; internet www.projectverify.co.uk; founded 2002; management consultancy specializing in project verification and audit services for projects funded by European Community funders such as ESF and ERDF and a wide range of government funding; contact J. Roberts.

UK Johnson & Jones: Little Buckland Farm, Hollywood Lane, Lymington, Hants. SO41 9HD; tel (+44 1590) 688899; fax (+44 1590) 688950; e-mail johnsonandjones@compuserve.com; internet www.johnsonandjones.co.uk.

UNITED STATES OF AMERICA

APCO Associates: 1615 L Street NW, Suite 900, Washington DC 20036; tel (+1 202) 778-1000; fax (+1 202) 466-6002; e-mail info@apcoassoc.com; contact M. Kraus.

Arthur D. Little Inc.: Acorn Park, Cambridge MA 02140-2390; tel (+1 617) 498-5000; fax (+1 617) 498-7200; e-mail adlittle.cambridge; internet www.adlittle.com.

European Document Research: 1100 17th Street NW (Suite 301), Washington DC 20036; tel (+1 202) 785-85-94; fax (+1 202) 785-85-89; e-mail info@europeandocuments.com; founded 1992; public relations consultancy; contact G. Lesser.

Areas of specialization:
- EU documentation
- EU law

Hill and Knowlton Inc: 466 Lexington Avenue (3rd Floor), New York NY 10017; tel (+1 212) 885-0300; fax (+1 212) 885-0570; contact H. Paster.

ITTA Inc: 1330 Connecticut Ave NW, Suite 210, Washington DC 20036-1704; tel (+1 202) 828-2614; fax (+1 202) 828-2617; e-mail cdyke@itta.com; internet www.itta.com; contact C.W. Dyke.

INDEX OF CONSULTANTS' SPECIALITIES

Business strategy
IMC Associates, 370

Business systems
IMC Associates, 370

Business to business
Ogilvy Public Relations Worldwide, 366

Campaigns
Kreab Europe, 365

Central Europe
Centre For European Not-for-Profit
　　Organisations – CENPO, 360
Moores Rowland Europe S.C. / C.V. MRI
　　European Coordination Office, 365
Rödl & Partner GmbH, 368
Stern Malkinson & Partners, 367

Certification
EU Business Care – Brandenburg Group
　　– EU Liaison Office, 362

Change management
Arthur D. Little, 359
AT Kearney, 359
Public Relations Partners, 366

Charities
Centre For European Not-for-Profit
　　Organisations – CENPO, 360

Chemicals
Business Environment Europe S.A. –
　　BEE, 360
Euro Keys, 362
Keene Public Affairs Consultants
　　Ltd, 370
Newton 21, 366

Chemicals sector, oil and gas
AT Kearney, 359

CIS
Moores Rowland Europe S.C. / C.V. MRI
　　European Coordination Office, 365
Rödl & Partner GmbH, 368

CIS countries (co-operation with)
FINECO Eurofinancements, 368

Civil engineering
IDOM, 364

Clothing
M. P. G. Research Sprl, 365

Coalition-building
APCO Europe S.A., 359

Common Agricultural Policy
Bureau Européen de Recherches
　　S.A., 359
EPRO – European Project, 361

Communication
Burson-Marsteller Sprl, 360
KPMG, 365
Lucy Rozenbaum Sprl, 365
Public Relations Partners, 366
Strat. & Com. SA, 367

Communication strategy
Europublic SA/NV, 363

Gullers Group Information
　　Counsellors, 369

Communications technology
Bennis Porter Novelli, 368
Euralia – Guerin Sprl – Euralia
　　Group, 362
European Multimedia Forum, 363

Community issues
Gullers Group Information
　　Counsellors, 369

Community relations
APCO Europe S.A., 359
Porter Novelli Brussels, 366

Companies
Yellow Window Management
　　Consultants NV, 367

Companies partnership
FINECO Eurofinancements, 368

Company development
Ipstrategies, 364

Company law
GPC International, 364

Competition
Business Environment Europe S.A. –
　　BEE, 360
EPPA, 361
Houston Consulting Europe, 364
Hurlstons Corporate Consultancy
　　Ltd, 370
Kreab AS, 367
National Economic Research Associates –
　　NERA, 365
Profile Corporate Communications, 371

**Competition issues (awareness
training programmes)**
Deloitte & Touche – Tax & Legal, 361

Competition law (European)
Deloitte & Touche – Tax & Legal, 361

Competition policy
Europe Economics, 370
European Development Projects, 363

**Competition policy (mergers and
acquisitions)**
APCO Europe S.A., 359

Competition rules
KPMG, 365

Computer applications
Bureau Van Dijk – Management
　　Consultants, 360

Computers
Gracious, 364

Conferences
Heidi Lambert Communications Sprl, 364
MONDIMPRESA, 365
TESEO – Technical Support for
　　European Organisations, 367

Consortia creation
Schuman Associates, 366

Construction
Kreab AS, 367
M. P. G. Research Sprl, 365

Consumer affairs
Anna Macdougald, 359
CSM European Consultants, 369
Eamonn Bates Europe Public Affairs
　　SA, 361
Impact, 364
Perchards, 370

Consumer and retail sectors
AT Kearney, 359

Consumer electronics
European Research Associates
　　(ERA), 363

Consumer goods
Babel P.R., 359

Consumer goods (fast-moving)
Bennis Porter Novelli, 368

Consumer goods, food and beverages
APCO Europe S.A., 359

Consumer markets
KPMG, 365

Consumer policy
Europe for Business and Europe for
　　Health, 370

Consumer protection
Bureau Européen de Recherches
　　S.A., 360
Houston Consulting Europe, 364

Contact building
Hill and Knowlton International
　　Belgium, 364

**Contaminated land investigation
and remediation**
Entec UK Ltd, 369

Copywriting
Communication Partners, 360

**Corporate and technical risk
management**
Entec UK Ltd, 369

Corporate communication
Barabino & Partners Europe SA, 359
Dialogic, 361
Euro RSCG Corporate, 362
Kreab AS, 367

Corporate events management
APCO Europe S.A., 359

Corporate positioning
APCO Europe S.A., 359

Country monitoring
M. P. G. Research Sprl, 365

Crisis communication
APCO Europe S.A., 359
DECITIME, 361
Ogilvy Public Relations Worldwide, 366

The Directory of EU Information Sources

Waste policy

Environmental Resources Management – ERM, 361

Water

Europe Economics, 370

Water and sewerage

National Economic Research Associates – NERA, 365

Water and wastewater engineering

Entec UK Ltd, 369

Web design

EURO-TOP Cooperation Partners, 363

Wholesale trade

M. P. G. Research Sprl, 365

Wood processing and forestry

Excoser S.A., 363

Worker information, consultation and participation

J.M. Didier & Associates S.A., 365

Worker mobility

TESEO – Technical Support for European Organisations, 367

XENOS (national support structure)

Europabüro für Projektbegleitung GmbH (EFP), 362

LAWYERS AND LEGAL ADVISERS SPECIALIZING IN EU LAW

LAW FIRMS SPECIALIZING IN THE LAW OF THE EUROPEAN UNION

The reference "Head Office" indicates the country in which the head office of the law firm is located (when outside Belgium). At the end of this list is an index of areas of specialization.

LAW ASSOCIATIONS

Bundesrechtsanwaltskammer – Brak: Littenstrasse 9, 10179 Berlin; tel (+49 30) 2849390; fax (+49 30) 284939-11; e-mail zentrale@brak.de; the Bundesrechtsanwaltskammer (The German Federal Bar) is the representative body of the whole German legal profession, which consists of some 120,000 lawyers and represents the interests of the 28 Rechtsanwaltskammern (regional Bars).

Delegación del Consejo General de la Abogacia Española: Paseo 2 Recoletos 13, 28001 Madrid; tel (+34 91) 523 25 93; fax (+34 91) 532 78 36; internet www .cga.es.

Delegation of the "Barreaux de France": 1 Avenue de la Joyeuse Entrée, 1040 Brussels; tel (+32 2) 230 83 31; fax (+32 2) 230 62 77; e-mail dbf@dbfbruxelles .com; internet www.dbfbruxelles.com; the Delegation of the French Bars, representing French lawyers before the European Union, is placed under the authority of a commission composed of members of the Paris Bar and the Conférence des Batonniers; the delegation has as tasks: to offer assistance in EC Law to French lawyers dealing with their clients' dossiers; to offer a regular information brochure to French lawyers by means of a bi-monthly publication summarizing EC judicial news, "L'Observateur de Bruxelles", and a weekly publication "L'Europe en Bref"; to organize meetings to promote relations between lawyers and the EC institutions and to help lawyers improve their knowledge of EC Law; to monitor EC draft proposals that may have an effect on lawyers or the interests which they defend and to indicate to the relevant institutions the position of the French Bars in this respect.

International Bar Association: 271 Regent Street, London W1R 7PA; tel (+44 207) 629 12 06; fax (+44 207) 409 04 56; e-mail member@int-bar.org; internet www.ibanet.org; the International Bar Association comprises some 18,000 individual members as well as 190 bar associations and law societies; the Association produces 4 magazines entitled "International Bar News" (quarterly), "International Business Lawyer" (11 pa, £195), "International Legal Practitioner" (quarterly, £95), and "Journal of Energy & Natural Resources" (quarterly, £192) to keep members up to date with latest developments; it also publishes a directory of members, containing details of its 18,000 lawyer members worldwide; the IBA publishes numerous books and papers every year.

Law Society of England, Wales and the Law Society of Scotland and The Law Society of Northern Ireland: 142–144 Avenue de Tervuren, 1150 Brussels; tel (+32 2) 743 85 85; fax (+32 2) 743 85 86; e-mail june.o'keeffe@lawsociety .org.uk; the "Law Societies" represent the 85,000 solicitors of England, Wales and Scotland; the tasks of the Brussels office are, inter alia: to represent its members' interests to the European Institutions; to provide working and conferencing facilities for lawyers and others, and to give information and guidance to its members; the Law Societies welcome visitors from all of the other Member States and are keen to be associated with linking solicitors of England and Wales with their fellow lawyers throughout the European Union; the Law Societies also provide notes for guidance on a whole range of overseas practice issues, keep details of international legal organizations and codes of conduct, and prepare notes on such issues as multi-national partnerships and the mutual recognition of higher education diplomas; in addition, the Law Society's library offers a European Community Information Service, operating as an information relay centre for the European Commission and having privileged access to many information sources; for further details, contact: The Information Office, The Law Society, 50 Chancery Lane, London, WC2A 1SX, United Kingdom; tel (+44 20) 7320-5673; fax: (+44 20) 7405-9522; the Library, The Law Society's Hall, 113 Chancery Lane, London, WC2A 1PL, United Kingdom; tel (+44 20) 7320-5946; fax (+44 20) 7831-1687.

TELFA – Trans European Law Firms Alliance: 208 Avenue Louise, 1050 Brussels; tel (+32 2) 642 27 59; fax (+32 2) 642 27 93; e-mail info@telfa.be; internet www.telfa.org; established in 1990, in the belief that the efficient practice of law now requires the consideration of transnational and cross-border issues, TELFA is an association of independent law firms located in the principal European jurisdictions including Cyprus, Liechtenstein, Norway, Switzerland and Turkey; TELFA members are: Eiselberg Natlacen Walderdorff Cancola (Austria), Afschrift (Belgium), Flagstad Lund Elmer (Denmark), Wedlake Bell (England), Campbell Philippart & Associés (France), Scholz Probandt v Dassel (Germany), A Metaxopoulos (Greece), Bihary Balassa & Partners (Hungary), O'Donnell Sweney (Ireland) Franzosi Dal Negro & Associati (Italy), Advokaturbüro Dr Markus Wanger (Liechtenstein), Tabery & Associés (Luxembourg), Lyng & Co (Norway), Dirkzwager Advocaten en Notarissen (The Netherlands), Lebre, Sa & Carvalho (Portugal), Mariana Anghel Law Office (Romania), Ledingham Chalmers (Scotland), Brugueras Garcia-Bragado Molinero & Asociados (Spain-Barcelona), Fylgia (Sweden), Lachenal Brechbuhl Cottier & Roguet (Switzerland), Mehmet Gün & Co (Turkey); TELFA also has an associate member in Egypt; TELFA has created a framework for co-operation between its members and provides a forum of facilities enabling the members to enhance the quality and scope of their professional services across Europe; the association has a central office in Brussels, which allows direct and immediate access to the institutions of the European Union, and provides a full range of information and consultancy services on all aspects of EC legislation and its implementation.

AUSTRIA

Law Offices Dr F Schwank: Stock Exchange Building, Wipplingerstrasse 34, 1010 Vienna; tel (+43 1) 533 57 04; fax (+43 1) 533 57 06.

BELGIUM

Addelsaw Goddard: 118 Avenue de Cortenberg, 1000 Brussels; tel (+32 2) 732 27 00; fax (+32 2) 735 23 52; e-mail tgbrussels@theodoregoddard.co.uk; *head office in:* United Kingdom.

Areas of specialization:
- Competition law
- State aids
- Financial services
- Transport law
- Anti-dumping
- Telecommunications
- Informatics
- Litigation
- WTO

Advokatfirmaet Hjort DA: 130 A Avenue Louise, 1050 Brussels; tel (+32 2) 280 06 70; tel (+32 2) 280 05 52; fax (+32 2) 230

72 78; e-mail lawoffice.hjort@skynet.be; *head office in:* Norway.

Areas of specialization:
- Competition law
- Procurement law
- Energy law
- Free movement of goods
- Financial services
- Telecommunications
- Industrial property rights
- Norwegian law
- Shipping

Advokatfirman Vinge: 3 Rue du Luxembourg, 1000 Brussels; tel (+32 2) 501 07 00; fax (+32 2) 501 07 07; e-mail O.rislund@vinge.se; internet www.vinge .se; *head office in:* Sweden.

Areas of specialization:
- Competition law
- Distribution
- Franchising agreements
- Agency agreements
- Licensing
- Joint ventures
- EU law
- Deregulation

AKD Prinsen van Wijmen: 240 Avenue Louise, 1050 Brussels; tel (+32 2) 534 53 76; fax (+32 2) 534 55 35; e-mail pkuypers@akd.be; internet www.akd.be; *head office in:* The Netherlands.

Allen & Overy: 268 A Avenue de Tervuren, 1150 Brussels; tel (+32 2) 780 29 22; tel (+32 2) 739 50 31; fax (+32 2) 780 22 44; fax (+32 2) 739 50 99; e-mail michael .reynolds@allenovery.com; internet www .allenovery.com; *head office in:* United Kingdom.

Association d'Avocats Humblet Marchal Orban Louis & Vanraes: 149 Avenue W. Churchill, 1180 Brussels; tel (+32 2) 349 11 10; fax (+32 2) 343 75 80; e-mail jean.noel.louis@churchim.be.

Baker & McKenzie: 149 Avenue Louise, 1050 Brussels; tel (+32 2) 639 36 11; fax (+32 2) 639 36 99; e-mail koen .vanhaerents@bakernet.com; internet www.bakernet.com; *head office in:* United States.

Bappert Witz & Selbherr: 9 Rond Point Schuman, 1040 Brussels; tel (+32 2) 541 03 30; fax (+32 2) 538 49 80; e-mail Brussels@westphalen-law.com; internet www.westphalen-law.com; *head office in:* Germany.

Barents & Krans: 187 Chaussée de la Hulpe, 1170 Brussels; tel (+32 2) 661 32 50; fax (+32 2) 675 38 70; e-mail Holant@barentskrans.be; internet www .barentskrans.nl.

Beachcroft Wansbroughs: 116 Avenue de Broqueville, 1200 Brussels; tel (+32 2) 776 78 18; fax (+32 2) 770 43 78; e-mail mbroadhurst@bwlaw.co.uk; internet www.bwlaw.co.uk; *head office in:* United Kingdom.

Areas of specialization:
- Competition law
- Anti-dumping
- Internal market
- Agricultural law
- Company law
- Consumer law
- Education
- Employment law
- Environmental law
- Pharmaceutical law
- Insurance
- Public procurement
- EU structural funds
- Telecommunications
- Intellectual property law
- Commercial contracts
- Mergers
- Acquisitions
- Joint ventures
- Commercial law
- Water
- Lobbying the EU's institutions

Berlioz & Co: 113 Avenue Louise, 1050 Brussels; tel (+32 2) 538 22 34; fax (+32 2) 538 22 46; e-mail berlioz@europlaw.com; internet www.berlioz.com; *head office in:* France.

Areas of specialization:
- Anti-dumping
- Audiovisual and telecommunications
- Banking regulation
- Competition law
- Consumer law
- Corporate law
- EU litigation
- Environmental law
- Financial law
- Intellectual property law
- Labour law
- Mergers
- Acquisitions
- State enterprises
- Trade regulation
- Transport law
- Telecommunications
- Distribution law
- Energy law
- Tax law

Berwin Leighton Paisner: 150 Chaussée de la Hulpe, 1170 Brussels; tel (+32 2) 741 86 30; fax (+32 2) 741 86 47; e-mail Monique.Jacques@blplaw.com; internet www.berwinleighton.com; *head office in:* United Kingdom.

Bircham Dyson Bell: 6 Rond-Point Schuman, Bte 5, 1040 Brussels; tel (+32 2) 234 63 06; fax (+32 2) 234 79 11; e-mail reception@bdb.law.co.uk; *head office in:* United Kingdom.

Areas of specialization:
- Public affairs

Bird & Bird: 15 Rue de la Loi, 1040 Brussels; tel (+32 2) 282 6000; fax (+32 2) 282 6011; e-mail simon.topping@ twobirds.com; internet www.twobirds .com; *head office in:* United Kingdom.

Brick Court Chambers: 36 Avenue d'Auderghem, 1040 Brussels; tel (+32 2) 230 31 61; fax (+32 2) 230 33 47; e-mail (surname)@brickcourt.be; internet www .brickcourt.co.uk; *head office in:* United Kingdom.

Cabinet Fontaneau: 45 Boulevard Saint Michel, 1040 Brussels; tel (+32 2) 736 59 44; fax (+32 2) 736 58 68; e-mail avocat@fontaneau.com; internet www .fontaneau.com; *head office in:* France.

Areas of specialization:
- Administrative law
- Immigration law
- Agricultural law
- Labour law
- Anti-trust law
- Insurance law
- Banking law
- International contracts
- Competition law
- International private law
- Construction law
- Maritime law
- Admiralty law
- Consumer protection
- Property
- Real estate law
- Corporate law
- Rent
- Leasing
- Customs and excise
- Social security
- Employer's liability
- Transport law
- Entertainment
- Foreign investments
- Distributorship law
- Agency law
- Franchise law
- Environmental law
- Family law
- Health, hospitals and malpractice
- Intellectual property practice
- Tax law

Cabinet Storrer: 154 Avenue F. Roosevelt, 1050 Brussels; tel (+32 2) 647 30 21; fax (+32 2) 646 07 73; e-mail jl .bosteels@storre-law.net; internet www .storrer-law.no.

Areas of specialization:
- Arbitration
- Commercial law
- Foreign law
- Civil law
- Company law
- Intellectual property law
- Family law
- Insurance
- Labour law

Cleary, Gottlieb, Steen & Hamilton: 57 Rue de la Loi, 1040 Brussels; tel (+32 2) 287 20 00; fax (+32 2) 231 16 61; internet www.cgsh.com; *head office in:* United States.

Areas of specialization:
- Anti-dumping
- Financial law
- Insurance law
- Mergers

- Acquisitions
- Environmental law

Clifford Chance Pünder: 65 Avenue Louise – Bte 2, 1050 Brussels; tel (+32 2) 533 59 11; fax (+32 2) 533 59 59; e-mail Yves.Herinckx@cliffordchance.com; internet www.cliffordchance.com; *head office in:* United Kingdom.

Areas of specialization:
- Anti-trust law
- International trade
- Single market
- Agricultural law
- Coal and steel
- Environment policy
- Company law
- Social and employment policy
- Product liability
- Enforcement of judgments
- Tax law
- Public procurement
- EU funding
- Transport policy
- Telecommunications
- Media policy
- Computer policy
- Intellectual property law
- Consumer policy
- Appeals from national courts to the Court of Justice of the European Communities
- Appeals from national courts to the Court of First Instance of the European Communities

CMS Bureau Francis Lefebvre: 200 Avenue Louise, 1050 Brussels; tel (+32 2) 650 04 30; fax (+32 2) 626 22 51; e-mail bflbxl@cms-bfl-avocats.be; *head office in:* France.

Areas of specialization:
- Competition law
- Tax law
- Free movement of goods
- Free movement of persons
- Litigation
- Product liability
- Commercial law
- Environmental law
- Transport law

CMS Cameron McKenna: 200 Avenue Louise, 1050 Brussels; tel (+32 2) 627 50 20; fax (+32 2) 627 50 21; fax (+32 2) 627 50 22; e-mail robert.maclean@cmck.com; internet www.cmck.com; *head office in:* United Kingdom.

Areas of specialization:
- Competition law
- Commercial law
- Internal market
- WTO
- Litigation

CMS Derks Star Busmann: 200 Avenue Louise, 1050 Brussels; tel (+32 2) 626 23 00; fax (+32 2) 626 23 09; e-mail general@cmsderks.be; internet www.cms.derks.nl; *head office in:* The Netherlands.

Areas of specialization:
- Competition law
- Anti-dumping

- Customs law
- Commercial law
- EEA
- Free movement of persons
- Free movement of services
- Free movement of goods
- Free movement of capital
- Pharmaceutical law
- Public procurement

CMS Hasche Sigle: 200 Avenue Louise, 1050 Brussels; tel (+32 2) 6500 420; fax (+32 2) 6500 422; e-mail bruessel@cmslegal.de; *head office in:* Germany.

Areas of specialization:
- Corporate law
- Competition law
- Subsidies
- Procurement law
- Banking law
- Capital market law
- Tax law
- Distribution law
- Franchise law
- Intellectual property law
- Maritime law
- Transport law
- Employment law
- Energy law
- Environmental law
- Insolvency
- Insurance law
- Information technology
- Telecommunications
- Media law
- Product liability
- Real estate law
- Construction law
- Sale of goods
- Provision of services
- Transactions
- Mergers and acquisitions
- Utilities

Coudert Brothers Coppens Van Ommeslaghe & Faures: 81 Avenue Louise Bte 1, 1050 Brussels; tel (+32 2) 542 88 88; fax (+32 2) 542 89 89; e-mail pvanderschueren@belgium.coudert.com; internet www.coudert.com; *head office in:* United States.

Coutrelis & Associés: 235 Rue de la Loi bte 12, 1040 Brussels; tel (+32 2) 230 48 45; fax (+32 2) 230 82 06; e-mail n.coutrelis@coutrelis.com; *head office in:* France.

Covington & Burling: 44 Av des Arts bte 8, 1040 Brussels; tel (+32 2) 549 52 30; fax (+32 2) 502 15 98; e-mail dharfst@cov.com; internet www.cov.com; *head office in:* United States.

Areas of specialization:
- Commercial law
- Competition law
- Media law
- Telecommunications
- Product liability
- Food regulations
- Pharmaceuticals regulations
- Cosmetics regulations
- Intellectual property law

- Litigation
- Arbitration
- International trade
- E-commerce
- Internet

Crowell & Moring: 71 Rue Royale, 1040 Brussels; tel (+32 2) 231 17 99; fax (+32 2) 230 63 99; e-mail jashetaylot@crowell.com; internet www.crowell.com; *head office in:* United States.

Areas of specialization:
- Competition law
- Mergers and acquisitions
- Banking law
- Payment systems
- Tax law
- Intellectual property law
- Information technology
- Shipping investment and regulation
- Aerospace industries' investment and regulation
- Environmental law

Cuatrecasas Abogados: 50 Avenue Cortenberg, 5ème étage, 1000 Brussels; tel (+32 2) 743 3900; fax (+32 2) 743 3901; e-mail Brussels@cuatrecasas.com; internet www.cuatrecasas.com; *head office in:* Spain.

De Backer & Partners: 30 Bd Brand Whitlock, 1200 Brussels; tel (+32 2) 742 12 12; fax (+32 2) 734 14 39; internet www.debacker.com.

De Schrijver – Van De Gehuchte & Partners: Baarledorpsstraat 93, 9031 Gent; tel +32 9/224 44 28; fax +32 9/224 18 70; e-mail office@vacaten.be; internet www.vacaten.be.

Areas of specialization:
- EU Law in general

De Smedt Philippe Law Offices: 391 Avenue Louise, Bte 5, 1050 Brussels; tel (+32 2) 640 90 75; fax (+32 2) 640 93 12; e-mail phil.etk@skynet.be.

Areas of specialization:
- Single market
- Free movement of goods
- Free movement of services
- Free movement of persons
- Free movement of capital
- Financial law
- Tax law
- EC banking law
- EC investment services law
- EC insurance law
- Trade with Eastern Bloc countries
- Investment in Eastern Bloc countries
- EC commercial law
- Telecommunications
- Media law
- Transport law
- Public contracts
- Environmental law
- Agricultural policy
- Intellectual property law
- EC litigation
- Transactional law

Dechert: 65 Avenue Louise, 1050 Brussels; tel (+32 2) 535 54 11; fax (+32 2) 535 54 00; e-mail sylvia.deruyver@dechert .com; internet www.dechert.com; *head office in:* United States.

Areas of specialization:
- Competition law
- Telecommunications
- Broadcasting
- Environmental law
- Food law
- Pharmaceutical law
- Tax law
- Banking services
- Financial services
- Aviation
- Public procurement
- Intellectual property law

Demolin & Brulard – Société d'Avocats, Lawrope: 46 Avenue des Arts, 1000 Brussels; tel (+32 2) 2131450; fax (+32 2) 2131460; e-mail info@ demolinbrulard.be; internet www .demolinbrulard.com.

Denton Wilde Sapte: 140 Avenue Louise, 1050 Brussels; tel (+32 2) 646 20 00; fax (+32 2) 646 20 40; e-mail brussels@dentonwildesapte.be; internet www.dentonwildesapte.com; *head office in:* United Kingdom.

Didier Pierre: 163 Avenue de Tervueren, 1150 Brussels; tel (+32 2) 735 01 82; fax (+32 2) 736 52 53; e-mail didlex@ skynet.be; internet http://users.skynet .be/PierreDidier.

DLA: 106 Avenue Louise, 1050 Brussels; tel (+32 2)500 15 00; fax (+32 2)500 16 00; e-mail steven.deKeyser@dla.com; internet www.dla.com; *head office in:* United Kingdom.

Feltgen & Mahaux: 19 Rue du Tabellion, 1050 Brussels; tel (+32 02) 538 60 80; fax (+32 02) 538 61 01; e-mail jeanpierremahaux@compuserve.com.

Areas of specialization:
- Competition law
- Equal opportunities between women and men
- Non-contractual liability of institutions

Fidal: 40 Avenue du Bourget, 1130 Brussels; tel (+32 2) 708 46 46; fax (+32 2) 708 46 45; e-mail frederic.puel@fidal.fr; internet www.fidal.fr; internet www .klegal.com.

Areas of specialization:
- Competition law
- Distribution law
- Social law
- Tax law
- Litigation
- Lobbying
- Environmental law
- Intellectual property law
- E-commerce
- Customs

Field Fisher Waterhouse: 65 Avenue Louise, Box 11, 1050 Brussels; tel (+32 2) 535 78 46; fax (+32 2) 535 77 00; *head office in:* United Kingdom.

Foley & Lardner: 6 Avenue Lloyd Georges, Box 3, 1000 Brussels; tel (+32 2) 639 27 10; fax (+32 2) 646 03 11; e-mail foley.law.brussels@euronet.be; *head office in:* United States.

Freshfields Bruckhaus Deringer: Bastion Tower, 5 Place du champ de Mars, 1050 Brussels; tel (+32 2) 504 7000; fax (+32 2) 504 7200; e-mail brussels@freshfields.com; internet www.freshfields.com; internet www .deringer.de; *head office in:* United Kingdom.

Areas of specialization:
- Competition law
- State aids
- International trade
- Public procurement
- Environmental law
- Liaison with EC institutions in relation to proposed legislation
- Telecommunications and media
- Transport law
- Pharmaceutical law
- Financial services
- Insurance
- Energy law
- Litigation (EU law at member state level)
- Litigation (EU law at EU level)
- Litigation (before European Court of Justice)
- Litigation (before Court of First Instance)
- Litigation (before EFTA Court)
- EU law implications of transactions taking place outside the Community
- International corporate matters
- International commercial matters

Garrigues: 245 Rue Père Eudore Devroye, 1150 Brussels; tel (+32 2) 545 37 00; fax (+32 2) 545 37 99; e-mail Stephen .pickard@garriguesabogados.com; internet www.garrigues.com; *head office in:* Spain.

Areas of specialization:
- Anti-dumping
- Financial services
- Internal market
- Intellectual property law
- Competition law
- Technical assistance

Geater & Co: 152 Boulevard Brand Whitlock, 1200 Brussels; tel (+32 2) 735 82 72; fax (+32 2) 732 01 43; e-mail A.Geater@geater-and-co.be.

Areas of specialization:
- Company law
- Competition law
- Environmental law
- Intellectual property law
- Financial services
- Tax law
- Fisheries law
- Commercial law
- EU law relating to various specific sectors of industry

- Free movement of goods
- Free movement of persons
- Free movement of services
- Free movement of capital
- Energy law
- Social law
- Transport law

Gide Loyrette Nouel: 26-28 Rue de l'Industrie, 1040 Brussels; tel (+32 2) 231 11 40; fax (+32 2) 231 11 77; internet www.gide.fr; *head office in:* France.

Areas of specialization:
- Competition law
- Agricultural law
- Corporate law
- Transport law
- Free movement and freedom of establishment
- Environmental law
- Customs law
- Tax law
- Dumping
- Social law

Gleiss Lutz: 7 Rue Guimard, 1040 Brussels; tel (+32 2) 551 10 20; fax (+32 2) 512 15 68; e-mail info@gleisslutz.com; internet www.gleisslutz.com; *head office in:* Germany.

Areas of specialization:
- EU law
- Competition law
- Anti-trust law
- Mergers and acquisitions
- Anti dumping and subsidies
- State aids
- EC litigation
- International trade

Gomez – Acebo & Pombo: 267 Avenue Louise, 1050 Brussels; tel (+32 2) 231 12 20; fax (+32 2) 230 80 35; e-mail abogados .brx@gomezacebo-pombo.com; internet www.gomezacebo-pombo.com; *head office in:* Spain.

Grupp W.G.: 1 Av de la Renaissance, 1000 Brussels; tel (+32 2) 736 67 35; fax (+32 2) 735 76 96; fax (+32 2) 736 05 71.

Hammonds: 250 Avenue Louise, Box 65, 1050 Brussels; tel (+32 2) 627 76 76; fax (+32 2) 627 76 86; e-mail konstantinos .adamantopoulos@hammonds.com; *head office in:* United Kingdom.

Haver & Mailänder: 221 Avenue Louise, 1050 Brussels; tel (+32 2) 639 47 15; fax (+32 2) 639 47 28; e-mail bo@ haver-mailaender.de; *head office in:* Germany.

Areas of specialization:
- Economic law
- Competition law
- Company law
- Arbitration

Heiermann, Franke, Knipp Rechtsanwälte: 37 Rue de la Tourelle, 1040 Brussels; tel (+32 2) 230 09 24; fax (+32 2) 230 09 01; *head office in:* Germany.

Hengeler Mueller: 118 Avenue de Cortenbergh, bte 2, 1000 Brussels; tel (+32 2) 788 55 99; fax (+32 2) 737 15 31; e-mail hmwwbrx@hengeler.com; internet www.hengeler.com; *head office in:* Germany.

Herbert Smith: 15 Rue Guimard, 1040 Brussels; tel (+32 2) 511 74 50; fax (+32 2) 511 77 72; e-mail nicola.hanly@herbertsmith.com; internet www.herbertsmith.com; *head office in:* United Kingdom.

Areas of specialization:
- Competition law
- Public procurement
- Trade/WTO issues
- Media/sport
- Regulations
- Commercial law
- Environmental law
- State aids
- Mergers

Heuking, Kühn, Lüer, Wojtek: 140 Avenue Louise, 1050 Brussels; tel (+32 2) 646 20 00; fax (+32 2) 646 20 40; e-mail brussels@heuking.de; *head office in:* Germany.

Areas of specialization:
- EU law
- Anti-trust law
- International trade
- International customs law
- EU trade law
- EU customs law
- Environmental regulations
- Health regulations
- Safety regulations
- Telecommunications
- Media law
- Intellectual property rights
- Transport law
- Information technology law
- Computer law
- Employment law
- Mergers and acquisitions
- Tax law
- Arbitration

Hoffmann & Associés: 385 Avenue Louise, Bte 1, 1050 Brussels; tel (+32 02) 648 09 70; fax (+32 02) 640 27 79; e-mail secretar@hoffmann-partners.com; internet www.hoffman-partners.com.

Areas of specialization:
- Competition law
- Lobbying

Hogan & Hartson: View Building, 26 Rue de l'industrie, 7th floor, 1040 Brussels; tel (+32 2) 505 09 11; fax (+32 2) 505 09 96; e-mail ncueto@hhlaw.com; internet www.hhlaw.com; *head office in:* United States.

Areas of specialization:
- Food law
- Cosmetics
- Agricultural law
- Commercial law
- Telecommunications and satellites
- Pharmaceutical products
- Competition regulation
- Trade regulation

- Environmental law
- Safety law
- Aviation
- Industrial standards
- Technical standards
- Public procurement
- State aids
- Labour law
- Free movement of persons
- Free movement of goods
- Free movement of services
- Litigation (before European Court of Justice)
- Litigation (before Court of First Instance)
- Mergers and acquisitions
- International trade
- International investment
- Data protection

International Law Chambers: ILC House, 91-93 Avenue Emile Max, 1030 Brussels; tel (+32 2) 732 56 63; fax (+32 2) 732 55 70; e-mail ILCUK@aol.com; *head office in:* United Kingdom.

International Legal Counsel Sprl: 23 Av Ernest Cambier, 1030 Brussels; tel (+32 2) 216 36 55; fax (+32 2) 216 42 78.

Areas of specialization:
- Intellectual property law
- Energy law
- Environmental law
- Tax law

J. P. Karsenty et Associés: 85 Rue du Prince Royal, 1050 Brussels; tel (+32 2) 511 91 26; fax (+32 2) 511 95 25; e-mail jnazerali@bwlaw.co.uk; internet www.bwlaw.co.uk; *head office in:* France.

Areas of specialization:
- Competition law
- Anti-dumping
- Internal market
- Agricultural law
- Company law
- Consumer law
- Education
- Employment law
- Environmental law
- Pharmaceutical law
- Insurance
- Public procurement
- Funding under EU Structural Funds
- Telecommunications
- Intellectual property law
- Commercial contracts
- Mergers and acquisitions
- Joint ventures
- Commercial law
- Water

Jalles Advogados: 23 Rue J A Demot, 1040 Brussels; tel (+32 2) 230 13 18; fax (+32 2) 230 79 07; e-mail 106043.1322@compuserve.com; *head office in:* Portugal.

Areas of specialization:
- Competition law
- Trade barriers
- Dumping
- Information technology
- Freedom of establishment
- Food law

- Pharmaceutical law
- International trade
- EC public function
- Free movement of services
- Relations with ACP countries
- Social law
- Environmental law
- Transport law
- Customs
- Banking law
- Insurance
- Telecommunications
- Industrial property law
- Intellectual property law
- Contract law
- Company law
- Agricultural law
- State aids

Jean Van Riel: 2/24 Rue de l'Aurore, 1000 Brussels; tel (+32 2) 626 07 35; fax (+32 2) 646 11 36; e-mail vanriel@skynet.be.

Jones, Day, Reavis & Pogue: 480 Avenue Louise, ITT Tower, 1050 Brussels; tel (+32 2) 645 14 11; fax (+32 2) 645 14 45; e-mail bruoffmail@jonesday.com; internet www.jonesday.com; *head office in:* United States.

Keller & Heckman: 25 Rue Blanche, 1060 Brussels; tel (+32 2) 541 05 70; fax (+32 2) 541 05 80; e-mail savigny@khlaw.be; internet www.khlaw.com; *head office in:* United States.

Kelley Drye & Warren: 106 Avenue Louise, 1050 Brussels; tel (+32 2) 646 11 10; fax (+32 2) 640 05 89; e-mail avanlanduyt@kelleydrye.com; internet www.kelleydrye.com; *head office in:* United States.

Areas of specialization:
- Financial law
- Commercial law
- EU law

Kemmler Rapp Böhlke: 9 Rond Point Schuman Bte 9, 1040 Brussels; tel (+32 2) 230 90 75; fax (+32 2) 230 14 16; e-mail krb&c@eurojura.be; internet www.eurojura.be.

Areas of specialization:
- Competition law
- Free movement of goods
- Free movement of services
- Free movement of persons
- Indirect taxation
- State aids
- Telecommunications
- Air transport
- Energy law
- External trade

Kiethe Rechtsanwälte: 179 Avenue Louise, 1050 Brussels; tel (+32 02) 646 70 72; fax (+32 02) 646 33 47; *head office in:* Germany.

Areas of specialization:
- EU law
- Commercial law
- Banking law
- Financial law

- Mergers and acquisitions
- Public law
- Competition law
- Anti-trust law

Kromann Reumert: 3 Rue du Luxembourg, 1000 Brussels; tel (+32 2) 501 07 00; fax (+32 2) 501 07 01; e-mail bru@kromannreumert.com; internet www.kromannreumert.com; *head office in:* Denmark.

Areas of specialization:
- Competition law
- Telecommunications
- Free movement of goods
- Public procurement

Lafili, Van Crombrugghe & Partners: 6 Drève des Renards Bte 1, 1180 Brussels; tel (+32 2) 373 09 10; fax (+32 2) 375 45 25; e-mail office.bru@lafili-law.be; internet www.lafili-law.be.

Areas of specialization:
- Notification procedure (Art 81)
- Distributorship agreements
- Franchise agreements
- Agency
- Know-how licensing (Reg 556/89)
- Patent licensing (Reg 2349/84)
- Mergers and acquisitions (Reg 4064/89)
- Product liability (Dir 25071985)
- Aviation, ground handling (Dir 98/67)
- CRS
- Dominant position (Art 82)

Lallemand Et Legros: 19 Avenue E. De Mot, 1000 Brussels; tel (+32 2) 648 75 30; fax (+32 2) 648 78 41.

Lambert & Associés: 19 Avenue Defré, 1180 Brussels; tel (+32 2) 375 59 73; fax (+32 2) 375 59 80; e-mail desk@lambert.be.

Areas of specialization:
- Public law
- Construction law
- Pharmaceutical law
- International law
- European law
- Press
- Audiovisual communication
- Social law

Law Offices Dr F Schwank: 198/2 Avenue Coghen, 1180 Brussels; tel (+32 2) 345 79 34; fax (+32 2) 345 79 34; e-mail offices@schwank.com; internet www.schwank.com; *head office in:* Austria.

Le Boeuf, Lamb, Greene & Macrae: 14a Rue du Luxembourg, 1000 Brussels; tel (+32 2) 227 09 00; fax (+32 2) 227 09 09; e-mail vnuyts@llgm.sprint.com; internet www.llgm.com; *head office in:* United States.

Areas of specialization:
- Competition law
- Commercial law
- Customs
- Environmental law
- Telecommunications
- Insurance

- Financial services
- Public procurement
- EEA and Eastern Europe
- Energy law
- Free movement of goods
- Free movement of persons
- Free movement of services
- Free movement of capital
- Audiovisual communication

Liedekerke Siméon Wessing Houthoff-LSWH: 3 Boulevard de l'Empereur, 1000 Brussels; tel (+32 2) 551 16 16; fax (+32 2) 551 14 14; e-mail info@lswh.be; internet www.liedekerke-law.be.

Areas of specialization:
- All areas of EU law with a special focus on: litigation before EU courts, competition, state aid, regulated industries (telecoms, energy)

Linklaters De Bandt: 13 Rue Brederode, 1000 Brussels; tel (+32 2) 501 94 11; fax (+32 2) 501 94 94; e-mail europe.infor@linklaters.com; internet www.linklaters.com.

Areas of specialization:
- Financial law
- Banking law
- Corporate law
- Environmental law
- Intellectual property law
- Investment management
- Labour law
- Litigation
- Arbitration
- Real estate law

Lovells: 523 Avenue Louise – Bte 24, 1050 Brussels; tel (+32 2) 647 06 60; fax (+32 2) 647 11 24; e-mail nick.bromfield@lovells.com; internet www.lovells.com; *head office in:* United Kingdom.

Loyens Advokaten: Woluwe Atrium, Neerveldstraat 101-103, 1200 Brussels; tel (+32 2) 743 43 53; fax (+32 2) 743 43 40; e-mail information@loyens.com; internet www.loyens.be.

Areas of specialization:
- Competition law
- Merger control
- State aids
- Energy law
- Telecommunications
- Transport law
- Environmental law
- Public procurement
- Free movement

Macfarlanes: 104 Avenue Louise, 1050 Brussels; tel (+32 2) 647 06 50; fax (+32 2) 646 47 29; internet www.macfarlanes.com; *head office in:* United Kingdom.

Areas of specialization:
- Competition law
- Commercial law
- Free movement of goods
- Free movement of financial services
- Transport law
- Entertainment
- Telecommunications
- Environmental law

Mannheimer Swartling: 13 Avenue de Tervuren, 1040 Brussels; tel (+32 2) 732 22 22; fax (+32 2) 736 96 52; e-mail jc@msa.se; internet www.msa.se; *head office in:* Sweden.

Marissens: 183 Avenue Molière, 1190 Brussels; tel (+32 2) 343 95 32; fax (+32 2) 343 68 11; e-mail secretariatmarissens@pophost.eunet.be.

Areas of specialization:
- Trade regulation
- Anti-trust law
- Air transport
- Telecommunications
- Media law
- Pharmaceutical law
- European law

McCann Fitzgerald: 89 Avenue de Cortenbergh bte 7, 1000 Brussels; tel (+32 2) 740 0370; fax (+32 2) 740 03 71; e-mail damian.collins@mccann-fitzgerald.ie; internet www.mccann-fitzgerald.ie; *head office in:* Ireland.

Areas of specialization:
- Anti-trust law
- State aids
- Public undertakings
- Mergers and acquisitions
- Intellectual property law
- Exclusive distribution
- Joint ventures
- Commercial law
- Internal market
- Agricultural law
- Fisheries law
- Banking law
- Financial services
- Telecommunications
- Environmental law
- Air transport
- Public procurement
- Regional issues
- Structural funds

Miller, Bolle and Partners: 283 Avenue Louise Bte 19, 1050 Brussels; tel (+32 2) 640 44 00; fax (+32 2) 648 99 95; e-mail office@millerlaw.be.

Areas of specialization:
- Commercial law
- Company law
- Corporate law
- Financial law
- Tax law
- Mergers and acquisitions

Misson Bureau d'Avocats SPRL: 41 Rue de Pitteurs, 4020 Liège; tel (+32 4) 341 43 44; fax (+32 4) 343 79 72; e-mail info@misson.be; internet www.misson.be.

Areas of specialization:
- Free movement of goods
- Free movement of persons
- Competition law
- Sports law

Moons: 158 Boulevard Brand Whitlock Bte 6, 1200 Brussels; tel (+32 2) 736 71 77; fax (+32 2) 736 65 91; e-mail moons.@advocaten.de; internet www.advocaten.de/moons.htm.

Areas of specialization:
- Contract law
- Commercial law
- Company law
- Corporate law
- Labour law
- EU law
- Arbitration

Morgan, Lewis & Bockius: 7 Rue Guimard, 1040 Brussels; tel (+32 2) 507 7500; fax (+32 2) 507 7555; e-mail isinan@ morganlewis.com; internet www .morganlewis.com; *head office in:* United States.

Areas of specialization:
- Anti-trust law
- Competition law
- Commercial law
- Customs
- IPR
- Consumer protection
- Public procurement
- Environmental law

Morrison & Foerster LLP: 262 Avenue Molière, 1180 Brussels; tel (+32 2) 347 04 00; fax (+32 2) 347 18 24; e-mail Tvinje@ mofo.com; internet www.mofo.com; *head office in:* United States.

Nabarro Nathanson: 209A Avenue Louise, 1050 Brussels; tel (+32 2) 626 07 40; fax (+32 2) 626 07 49; e-mail rbickler@nabarro.com; internet www .nabarro.com; *head office in:* United Kingdom.

Areas of specialization:
- Competition law
- Commercial law
- Information technology
- Telecommunications
- Anti-dumping
- Public procurement
- Customs and origin legislation
- Energy law
- Single market
- Financial services

Nauta Dutilh: 177/6 Chaussée de La Hulpe, 1170 Brussels; tel (+32 2) 566 80 00; fax (+32 2) 566 80 01; e-mail ndbru@ nautadutilh.com; internet www .nautadutilh.com; *head office in:* The Netherlands.

Areas of specialization:
- EU law

Norton Rose: 489 Avenue Louise, 1050 Brussels; tel (+32 2) 237 61 11; fax (+32 2) 237 61 36; internet www.nortonrose.com; *head office in:* United Kingdom.

Areas of specialization:
- EU law

Oppenheimer Wolff & Donnelly: 240 Avenue Louise Bte 5, 1050 Brussels; tel (+32 2) 626 05 00; fax (+32 2) 626 05 10; e-mail jrussotto@owdlaw.com; internet www.owdlaw.com/; *head office in:* United States.

Areas of specialization:
- Competition law
- Commercial law
- Free movement of goods
- Free movement of services
- Free movement of capital
- Customs
- Environmental law
- Consumer protection
- Company law
- Tax law
- Internal market
- Harmonization of technical standards
- Banking sector
- Information technology
- Chemicals sector
- Motor vehicles sector
- Pharmaceutical law
- Telecommunications
- Food sector
- Biotechnology sector
- Financial services
- Consumer products sector
- Medical devices sector
- Sports law

Rechtsanwältin Katrin Markus: 1/8 Avenue de la Renaissance, 1000 Brussels; tel (+32 2) 735 99 39; fax (+32 2) 735 10 76; e-mail KatrinMarkus@belgacom.net.

Areas of specialization:
- Family law

Richards Butler: 149 Av Louise, Bte 24, 1050 Brussels; tel (+32 2) 535 74 74; fax (+32 2) 535 75 75; *head office in:* United Kingdom.

S J Berwin & Co: 19 Square de Meeûs – Box 3, 1050 Brussels; tel (+32 2) 511 53 40; fax (+32 2) 511 59 17; e-mail brussels@ sjberwin.com; internet www.sjberwin .com; *head office in:* United Kingdom.

Areas of specialization:
- Competition law
- Anti-trust law
- Anti-dumping regulations
- Customs regulations
- Free movement of goods
- Intellectual property law
- Common agricultural policy
- State aids
- Grants
- Financial services
- Banking sector
- Securities sector
- Finance sector
- Telecommunications
- Information technology law
- Tax law
- Environmental law
- Civil liability for waste
- Mergers and acquisitions
- Commercial policy
- Regulations
- EC-based litigation before domestic courts
- EC-based litigation before the European Court of Justice
- Competition law
- Fisheries sector

S.C. Grollet et Associés: 6 Rue Hydraulique, 1210 Brussels; tel (+32 2) 217 39 90; fax (+32 2) 218 06 72; e-mail rygaert@ grollet-partners.be; internet www.grollet -partners.be.

Simmons & Simmons: 149 Avenue Louise, B16, 1050 Brussels; tel (+32 2) 542 09 60; fax (+32 2) 542 09 61; e-mail anthony.orr@simmons-simmons.com; internet www.simmons-simmons.com; *head office in:* United Kingdom.

Areas of specialization:
- EU law
- Competition law
- Public procurement
- Transport law
- State aids
- Free movement of goods
- Agricultural law
- Anti-dumping
- Representation of clients in dealings and proceedings involving the European Commission
- Representation of clients in dealings and proceedings involving the European Court of Justice
- Representation of clients in dealings and national proceedings involving questions of EU law

Skadden, Arps, Slate, Meagher & Flom LLP: 523 Avenue Louise, 1050 Brussels; tel (+32 2) 639 03 00; fax (+32 2) 639 03 39; e-mail bhawk@skadden .com; internet www.skadden.com; *head office in:* United States.

Slaughter and May: 118 Avenue de Cortenbergh, 1000 Brussels; tel (+32 2) 737 94 00; fax (+32 2) 737 94 01; e-mail John.boyce@slaughterandmay.com; internet www.slaughterandmay.com; *head office in:* United Kingdom.

Areas of specialization:
- Competition law
- State aids
- Public procurement
- Commercial law
- Air transport

Spandre et Associés: 9 Rond Point Schuman Bte 3, 1040 Brussels; tel (+32 2) 230 91 80; fax (+32 2) 230 21 24; e-mail mario.spandre@infoboard.be.

Squire Sanders & Dempsey LLP: 165 Avenue Louise – Bte 13-14, 1050 Brussels; tel (+32 2) 627 11 11; fax (+32 2) 627 11 00; e-mail bhartnett@ssd.com; internet www.ssd.com; *head office in:* United States.

Areas of specialization:
- Competition law
- Telecommunications regulations
- Information technology
- Environmental law
- Pharmaceutical law
- Energy law
- Mergers

Stanbrook & Hooper: 245 Rue Père Eudore Devroye, 1150 Brussels; tel (+32 2) 230 50 59; fax (+32 2) 230 57 13; e-mail stanbrook.hooper@stanbrook.com; internet www.stanbrook.com.

Areas of specialization:
- International trade
- Competition law
- 1992 programme for the completion of the single market
- Customs
- Transport law
- Intellectual property law
- Free movement of goods
- Free movement of persons
- Free movement of services
- Environmental law
- Public procurement
- Financial services
- Food law
- Energy law
- Telecommunications
- Public utilities

Stewart and Stewart: 13 Bd Dewandre, 6000 Charleroi; tel (+32 071) 32 51 31; fax (+32 071) 32 35 26; e-mail spinoit.wese@brutélé.be; *head office in:* United States.

Areas of specialization:
- Anti-dumping
- Anti-subsidies
- Customs
- Competition law
- International trade

Stibbe Simont Monahan Duhot: 47-51 Rue H. Wafelaerts, 1060 Brussels; tel (+32 2) 533 52 11; fax (+32 2) 533 52 12; e-mail info@stibbe.be; internet www.stibbe.com; *head office in:* The Netherlands.

Areas of specialization:
- Competition law
- State aids
- Media law
- Telecommunications
- Pharmaceutical law
- Cosmetics
- Environmental law
- Agricultural law
- Energy law
- Tax law
- Anti-dumping
- Trade protection laws
- Pension law
- Banking law
- Transport law
- Free movement of goods
- Free movement of capital
- Free movement of persons
- Intellectual property
- Industrial property
- Food sector

Studio Legale Bonelli Erede Pappalardo: 8 Rue Montoyer, 1000 Brussels; tel (+32 2) 552 00 70; fax (+32 2) 552 00 71; e-mail bep.bxl@beplex.com.

Studio Legale Sergio Diana: 18 Rue Montoyer, 1080 Brussels; tel (+32 2) 280 00 62; fax (+32 2) 280 16 55; e-mail eurocontact@coditel.net; internet www.eurocontact.it; *head office in:* Italy.

Taylor Wessing: Trône House, Rue du Trône 4, 1000 Brussels; tel (+32 2) 289 60 60; fax (+32 2) 289 60 70; e-mail peter.willis@taylorwessing.com; internet www.taylorwessing.com; *head office in:* United Kingdom.

Areas of specialization:
- Competition law
- Commercial law
- Free movement of goods
- Public procurement
- EC energy
- Environmental law
- Telecommunications
- Intellectual property law
- Biotechnology
- Employment law

Terry R. Broderick, Esq.: 51 Avenue Pierre Curie, 1050 Brussels; tel (+32 2) 646 00 19; fax (+32 2) 646 01 52; e-mail terry.broderick@pop.kpn.be; internet www.terry-broderick.com.

Areas of specialization:
- Company law
- Competition law and procedure
- Distribution
- Franchising
- Internal market developments
- Intellectual property
- Licensing
- Joint ventures
- Mergers and acquisitions
- Commercial law and procedure

Thommessen Krefting Greve Lund A/S – Advokatfirma: 3 Rue du Luxembourg, 1000 Brussels; tel (+32 2) 501 07 00; fax (+32 2) 501 07 01; e-mail brussels@thommessen.no; internet www.tkgl.no; *head office in:* Norway.

Areas of specialization:
- Competition law
- Merger control
- Distribution systems
- Cartel cases
- Public procurement
- Internal market
- Information technology
- Media law
- Maritime law

Uettwiller Grelon Gout Canat & Associés: 46 Avenue Albert-Elisabeth, 1200 Brussels; tel (+32 2) 736 66 14; fax (+32 2) 736 68 18; e-mail pvandoorn@uggc-law.be; internet www.uggc-law.be.

Areas of specialization:
- European business law
- Tax law
- VAT

Van Bael & Bellis: 165 Avenue Louise, 1050 Brussels; tel (+32 2) 647 73 50; tel (+32 2) 643 46 10; fax (+32 2) 640 64 99; e-mail brussels@vanbaelbellis.com; internet www.vanbaelbellis.com.

Areas of specialization:
- Anti-trust law
- Anti-dumping
- Customs
- Commercial law

- EU law
- Competition law
- Deregulation
- Free movement of goods

Van Cutsem Wittamer Marnef et Associés: 137 Avenue Louise Bte 1, 1050 Brussels; tel (+32 2)543 02 00; fax (+32 2)538 13 78; e-mail legal@vancutsem.be.

Weil, Gotshal & Manges LLP: 81 Avenue Louise Btes 9-10, 1050 Brussels; tel (+32 2) 543 74 60; fax (+32 2) 543 74 89; e-mail Shay.ben-shaool@weil.com; internet www.weil.com; *head office in:* United States.

Areas of specialization:
- Competition law
- State aids
- Telecommunications
- EU law

Weser & Partners: 22 Avenue Armand Huysmans, 1050 Brussels; tel (+32 2) 640 12 49; fax (+32 2) 640 12 49.

Areas of specialization:
- Competition law
- Contractual obligations
- Arbitration before national courts
- Arbitration before international courts
- Litigation before national courts
- Litigation before international courts
- EU grants
- EU loans
- Banking law
- Financial law
- Intellectual property law
- Audiovisual communication
- Telecommunications
- Free movement of persons
- Free movement of services
- Free movement of capital
- Dumping
- Abuse of dominant position
- Subsidiaries
- Investments in EU countries
- Investments in eastern European countries
- Free movement of judgments
- Comparative social law
- Mergers
- Holdings
- Joint ventures
- Appeal to the Court of Justice of the EC
- Litigation (before Court of First Instance)
- Product liability
- Foreign companies
- Tax law
- International conventions between EU countries
- International Conventions between EU countries and other countries
- Consumer protection
- Environmental law
- Lobbying
- Goods and finance

White & Case: 62 Rue de la Loi, 1040 Brussels; tel (+32 2) 219 16 20; fax (+32

2)219 16 26; e-mail PLindfelt@whitecase .com; internet www.whitecase.com; *head office in:* United States.

Wilmer Cutler & Pickering: 15 Rue de la Loi, 1040 Brussels; tel (+32 2) 285 49 00; fax (+32 2) 285 49 49; e-mail Marco .bronckers@wilmer.com; internet www .wilmer.com; *head office in:* United States.

Areas of specialization:
- Telecommunications regulations
- Media regulations
- Intellectual property law
- Competition law
- EU trade law
- Aviation regulations
- European transactional work

DENMARK

Advokaterne Amaliegade N° 42: Amaliegade 42, 1256 Copenhagen K; tel (+45) 33 11 33 99; fax (+45) 33 32 46 25; e-mail adv42@amalex.com.

Areas of specialization:
- Company law
- VAT

Bernhard Gomard: Law Department, Copenhagen Business School, Julius Thomsens Plads 10,5, 1925 Copenhagen Frederiksberg; tel (+45) 38 15 26 26; fax (+45) 38 15 26 10.

Gorrissen Federspiel Kierkegaard: H.C. Andersens Bd 12, 1553 Copenhagen V; tel (+45) 33 41 41 41; fax (+45) 33 41 41 33; e-mail gfk@gfklaw.dk; internet www .gfklaw.uk.

Areas of specialization:
- Competition law
- Company law
- Banking law
- Public procurement
- State aids
- Employment law
- Intellectual property law

Jonas Bruun Advokatfirma: Bredgade 38, 1260 Copenhagen K; tel (+45) 33 47 88 00; fax (+45) 33 47 88 88; e-mail jb@ jonasbruun.dk.

Areas of specialization:
- EU law
- Competition law
- Free movement of goods
- Free movement of services
- Free movement of capital
- Establishment
- Procurement of public supply contracts
- Procurement of public works contracts
- Telecommunications
- Trade mark law

Juridisk Institut Copenhagen Business School: Jullus Thomsens Plads 10, 5, 1925 Frederiksberg C.; tel (+45) 38 15 26 26; fax (+45) 38 15 26 10; e-mail fejoe .jur@cbs.dk.

Kromann Reumert: Sundkrogisgade 5, 2100 Copenhagen 0; tel (+45) 70 12 12 11; fax (+45) 70 12 12 11; e-mail jmp@ kromannreumert.com; internet www .kromannreumert.com.

Lett & Co: Radhuspladsen 4, 1550 Copenhagen K; tel (+45) 33 77 00 00; fax (+45) 33 77 00 01; e-mail lettco@ lettco.dk; internet www.lettco.dk.

Areas of specialization:
- Company law
- Competition law
- Mergers
- Insurance
- Banking law
- Litigation (before European Court of Justice)
- Litigation (before Court of First Instance)
- Food law
- Public procurement
- Labour law

Magnusson Wahlin Qvist Stanbrook: 58-4 Pilestraede, 1112 Copenhagen; tel (+45) 33 12 45 22; fax (+45) 33 93 60 23; e-mail copenhagen@dk.maqs.com; e-mail michael.svendsen@dk.maqs.com; internet www.maqs.com.

Moltke-Leth Lawyers: Amaliegade 12, 1256 Copenhagen K; tel (+45) 33 11 65 11; fax (+45) 33 11 49 11; e-mail Law@ moltke-leth.dk.

Areas of specialization:
- Competition law
- Purchase of businesses
- Sale of businesses

Nebelong & Partnere: Ostergade 16, Postboks 1051, 1007 Copenhagen K; tel (+45) 33 11 75 22; fax (+45) 33 32 47 75; e-mail nebelong@nebelong.dk; internet www.nebelong.dk.

Olav Willadsen: Tunnelvej 7, 2600 Glostrup; tel (+45) 43 63 26 54.

Areas of specialization:
- Counselling clients
- Assisting clients
- Court proceedings
- EU law
- Public procurement

FINLAND

Hannes Snellman Attorneys at Law Ltd: PO Box 333, Eteläranta 8, 00131 Helsinki; tel (+358 9) 228 841; fax (+358 9) 177 228; e-mail forename.surname@ hannessnellman.fi; internet www .hannessnellman.fi.

FRANCE

Andersen Legal: 41 Rue Ybry, 92576 Neuilly-sur-Seine Cedex; tel (+33 1) 55 61 10 10; fax (+33 1) 55 61 15 15; e-mail olivier.chaduteau@fr.ey.com; internet www.ey.com.

Areas of specialization:
- Tax law
- Labour law
- Commercial law
- Free movement of goods
- Competition law
- Free movement of services
- Distribution law
- Transfer pricing
- Intellectual property law
- New technologies law
- Expatriate policy developments
- Immigration services

Berlioz & Co: 68 Boulevard de Courcelles, 75017 Paris; tel (+33 1) 44 01 44 01; fax (+33 1) 44 15 94 15.

Bureau Francis Lefebvre Lawyers: 3 Villa Emile Bergerat, 92522 Neuilly sur Seine Cedex; tel (+33 1) 47 38 55 00; fax (+33 1) 47 38 55 55; e-mail central@bfl -avocats.com.

Cabinet Fontaneau: 28 Rue de Franqueville, 75116 Paris; tel (+33 1) 45 03 03 40; fax (+33 1) 45 03 08 14; e-mail avocats@fontaneau.com; internet www .Fontaneau.com.

Coutrelis & Associés: 55 Avenue Marceau, 75116 Paris; tel (+33 1) 53 57 47 95; fax (+33 1) 53 57 47 97; e-mail acoutrelis@ coutrelis.com.

Dahan, Dahan-Bitton & Dahan: 6 Pl Saint Germain des Prés, 75006 Paris; tel (+33 1) 45 49 16 16; fax (+33 1) 42 22 68 61; e-mail avocats@ddbd.com; internet www.ddbd.com.

Gide Loyrette Nouel: 26 Cours Albert Ier, 75008 Paris; tel (+33 1) 40 75 60 00; fax (+33 1) 43 59 37 79.

J. P. Karsenty et Associés: 70 Bd de Courcelles, 75017 Paris; tel (+33 1) 47 63 74 75; fax (+33 1) 46 22 33 27.

Juriscope: Teleport 2 Avenue René Cassin, BP194, 86960 Futuroscope Cedex; tel (+33 5) 49 49 41 41; fax (+33 5) 49 49 00 66; e-mail contact@juriscope.org; internet www.juriscope.org.

Lafarge – Flecheux – Campana – Le Blevennec: 24 Rue de Prony, 75809 Paris Cedex 17; tel (+33 1) 44 29 32 32; fax (+33 1) 44 29 31 00; e-mail lfc@ 24rueprony.fr.

Lamy, Ribeyre & Associés: 40 Rue de Bonnel, 69484 Lyon Cedex 03; tel (+33 4) 78 62 14 00; fax (+33 4) 78 62 14 49; e-mail info@lamy-ribeyre.com; internet www .lamy-ribeyre.com.

SCP Granrut: 12 Rue d'Astorg, 75008 Paris; tel (+33 1) 53 43 15 15; fax (+33 1) 53 43 15 79; e-mail gvb@gvb-avocats.com.

Société d'Avocats Charrière – Champetier – Spitzer: 5 Rue de Logelbach, 75017 Paris; tel (+33 1) 42 67 57 50; fax (+33 1) 47 63 32 65; e-mail jpspctzeraccs -scp.avocat.fr.

GERMANY

Bappert Witz & Selbherr: Kaiser Joseph Strasse 284, 79098 Freiburg; tel (+49 761) 21 80 80; fax (+49 761) 21 80 500; e-mail freiburg@bappert.bws.com; internet www.bappert-bws.com.

CMS Hasche Sigle: Friedrich-Ebert-Anlage 44, 60325 Frankfurt; tel (+49 69) 71 70 10; fax (+49 69) 71 70 1-110; e-mail frankfur@cmslegal.de.

Ehle & Schiller: Mehlemer Strasse 13, 50968 Cologne; tel (+49 221) 937017-0; fax (+49 221) 937017-15; e-mail drehle@ehle-schiller.de.

Areas of specialization:
- Anti-dumping
- Countervailing duty
- Tax law
- Customs duty
- Agricultural law
- Anti-trust law
- Food law
- State aids

Haver & Mailänder: Lenzhalds 83-85, 70192 Stuttgart; tel (+49 711) 22 74 40; fax (+49 711) 29 919 35; e-mail mailaender.partner@counsel.com.

Heiermann, Franke, Knipp Rechtsanwälte: Kettenhofweg 126, 60325 Frankfurt/M; tel (+49 69) 975 822 0; fax (+49 69) 74 70 83; fax (+49 69) 74 68 68.

Hengeler Mueller Weitzel Wirtz: Bockenheimer Landstr 51, 60325 Frankfurt am Main; tel (+49 69) 17 09 50; fax (+49 69) 72 57 73; fax (+49 69) 72 39 83.

Heuking, Kühn, Lüer, Wojtek: Cecilienallee 5, 40474 Duesseldorf; tel (+49 211) 600 55 00; fax (+49 211) 600 55 050; e-mail duesseldorf@heuking.de.

Kiethe Rechtsanwälte: Vollmannstrasse 59, 81925 Munich; tel (+49 89) 92001-0; fax (+49 89) 92 00 11 11.

GREECE

Christophoridis & Associates: 89-91 Avenue Kifissias, 115 23 Athens; tel (+30 10) 6984 734; fax (+30 10) 6984 733; e-mail angchris@otenet.gr.

Areas of specialization:
- Commercial law
- Labour law
- Banking law
- Financial law
- Tax law
- Industrial property law
- Intellectual property law
- Public procurement
- Transport law
- Telecommunications
- Insurance law
- EU law
- International trade

Ioanna Vosiki, Maria Vosiki, Photis Papachristou & Collaborators: Venizelou Street 43, 546 24 Thessaloniki; tel (+32 31) 235 716; tel (+32 31) 241 216; tel (+32 31) 286 416; fax (+32 31) 220 216; e-mail vosiki@the.forthnet.gr.

Areas of specialization:
- Labour law
- Corporate law
- Administrative law
- Family law
- Tax law

Kokkinos & Associates, European Legal Consultancy: Hippocratous Str 4, 10679 Athens; tel (+30 210) 36 13 379; fax (+30 210) 36 12 084; e-mail eurolegal@attglobal.net; internet www.euro-legal.com.

Law Offices Papaconstantinou: Queen Sophia Avenue 4, 106 74 Athens; tel (+30 210) 729 57 50; tel (+30 210) 729 57 54; fax (+30 210) 729 57 56; e-mail hpaplaw@ath.forthnet.gr.

Souriadakis, Frangakis and Associates: Rue Kriezotou 6, 106 71 Athens; tel (+30 210) 362 68 88; tel (+30 210) 361 32 37; fax (+30 210) 363 16 31; e-mail sofralaw@otenet.gr.

Areas of specialization:
- Competition law
- State aids
- Institutional affairs
- External relations
- Free movement of capital
- Company law
- Energy law
- Litigation (before European Court of Justice)
- Public contracts
- Free movement of goods
- Free movement of workers and social policy
- Freedom of establishment
- Freedom to provide services
- Industrial policy and the internal market
- Transport law

Zepos & Zepos: Vas Sophias Avenue 120, 115 26 Athens; tel (+30 210) 775 45 71; tel (+30 210) 775 33 41; fax (+30 210) 770 28 25; fax (+30 210) 771 12 50; e-mail info@zeya.com; internet www.zeya.com.

IRELAND

A & L Goodbody: International Financial Services Centre, North Wall Quay, Dublin 1; tel (+353 1) 649 20 00; fax (+353 1) 649 26 49; e-mail law@algoodbody.securemail.ie.

Areas of specialization:
- Competition law
- Restrictive practices
- Anti-trust law
- Transport law
- Commercial law
- Product liability
- Non-tariff barriers
- Free movement of goods
- Free movement of persons
- Free movement of services
- Free movement of capital
- Internal market
- EC law in Ireland
- Public procurement
- Telecommunications
- EU law

Arthur Cox: Earlsfort Centre, Earlsfort Terrace, Dublin 2; tel (+353 1) 618 00 00; fax (+353 1) 618 06 18; e-mail mail@arthurcox.com; internet www.arthurcox.com.

Areas of specialization:
- Competition law
- Commercial law
- Inward investment
- Banking services
- Financial services
- Company law
- Telecommunications
- Public procurement
- Environmental law
- Agricultural law
- Intellectual property rights
- Labour law
- Pharmaceutical law
- Food law

Eugene F. Collins: Temple Chambers, 3 Burlington Road, Dublin 4; tel (+353 1) 202 6400; fax (+353 1) 667 52 00; e-mail lawyer@efc.ie; internet www.efc.ie.

Areas of specialization:
- Corporate law
- Banking law

McCann Fitzgerald: 2 Harbourmaster Place, International Financial Services Centre, Dublin 1; tel (+353 1) 829 0000; fax (+353 1) 829 0010; e-mail postmaster@mccann.fitzgerald.ie; internet www.mccann-fitzgerald.ie.

ITALY

Avv. Giovanna Andreoni Prof. Avv. Bruno Nascimbene: Via V. Bellini 12, 20122 Milan; tel (+39 02) 774 231; fax (+39 02) 774 2344; e-mail info@nascimbene.com.

Areas of specialization:
- Free movement of persons
- Transport law
- Institutional affairs
- Public procurement

Avv. Cesare Trebeschi: Via Battaglie 50, 25122 Brescia; tel (+39 030) 291 599; fax (+39 030) 37 54 058; e-mail studio.trebeschi@iol.it.

Areas of specialization:
- Administrative law
- Civil law
- Penal law
- Agriculture

Cappelli e De Caterini Avvocati Associati: Via Nicolo Tartaglia 5, 00197 Rome; tel (+39 06) 808 15 56; tel (+39

06) 808 37 46; fax (+39 06) 808 07 31; e-mail cappelliedecaterini@tiscalinet.it.

Areas of specialization:
- Environmental law
- Agricultural law
- Anti-trust law
- Freedom of establishment and services
- Public procurement

Cabinet Morera: Corso Venezia 10, 20121 Milan; tel (+39 02) 760 22 553; fax (+39 02) 784 677; e-mail morera@digibank.it.

Prof. Avv CorapI Diego: Via Flaminia 318, 00196 Rome; tel (+39 06) 321 8563; tel (+39 06) 321 8539; tel (+39 06) 325 00861; fax (+39 06) 320 0992; e-mail info@studiolegalecorapi.it; internet www.studiolegalecorapi.it.

Areas of specialization:
- Arbitration
- Corporate law
- Financial markets
- Banking sector
- Insurance
- Construction contracts

Studio Legale Sabelli: Via Parigi 11, 00185 Rome; tel (+39 06) 481 71 41; fax (+39 06)488 45 66; e-mail sabelli@tin.it; internet www.sabellilawfirm.it.

Studio Legale Sergio Diana: Piazza Repubblica 4, 09125 Cagliari; tel (+39 070) 48 54 80; fax (+39 070) 45 62 63; e-mail eurocontact@coditel.net; internet www.eurocontact.it.

Studio Legale Tonucci: Via Principessa Clotilde 7, 00196 Rome; tel (+39 06) 36 22 71; fax (+39 06) 323 51 61; e-mail SGrisolia@tonucci.it; internet www.tonucci.it.

Areas of specialization:
- Telecommunications
- Energy law
- Environmental law
- Company law
- Commercial property law
- Industrial property law
- Free movement of persons
- Free movement of goods
- Free movement of services
- EU public procurement
- Competition law
- Anti-trust law
- Multimedia law
- Computer law
- Data protection

Studio Steccanella Maurizio: Via Aurelio Saffi 23, 20123 Milan; tel (+39 02) 469 28 38; tel (+39 2) 48 01 07 96; tel (+39 2) 48 51 46 37; fax (+39 02) 469 28 38; e-mail stecca.maur@id.it.

NETHERLANDS

AKD Prinsen van Wijmen: Claudius Prinsenlaan 126, 4818 CP Breda; tel (+31 76) 522 31 00; fax (+31 76) 514 25 75.

CMS Derks Star Busmann: Pythagoraslaan 2, 3584 BB Utrecht; tel (+31 30) 21 21 111; fax (+31 30) 21 21 333.

Nauta Dutilh: Weena 750, 3014 DA Rotterdam; tel (+31 10) 224 00 00; fax (+31 10) 414 84 44.

Stibbe Simont Monahan Duhot: Stibbe Toren, Strawinskylaan 2001, 1077 ZZ Amsterdam; tel (+31 20) 546 06 06; fax (+31 20) 546 01 23; e-mail ssmdinfo@stibbe.nl; internet www.stibbe.com.

NORWAY

Hjort Law Office DA: Akersgt. 2, Postboks 471 Sentrum, 0105 Oslo; tel (+47) 22 47 18 00; fax (+47) 22 47 18 18; e-mail advokatfirma@hjort.no.

Thommessen, Krefting & Greve Lund A/S – Advokatfirma: PO Box 1484 Vika, 0116 Oslo; tel (+47) 23 11 11 11; fax (+47) 23 11 10 10; e-mail siri.teigum@tkgl.no; internet www.tkgl.no.

PORTUGAL

Dr Luis Brito Correia: Av Alvares Cabral 84 2° dto, 1250 Lisbon; tel (+351 21) 387 08 56; fax (+351 21) 388 25 54; e-mail lbricor@mail.telepac.pt.

Jalles Advogados: Av. Alvares Cabral 34-6, 1250 Lisbon; tel (+351 21) 388 40 95; fax (+351 21) 388 19 55; e-mail 106115,20@compuserve.com.

P L M J: Edificio Eurolex, Av. da Liberdade 224, 1250-148 Lisbon; tel (+351 21) 319 73 21; fax (+351 21) 319 73 19; e-mail jcv@plmj.pt.

Rui Peixoto Duarte & Associados – Advogados: Rua Antonio Patricio 203/205, 4150-100 Porto; tel (+351 22) 606 79 08; fax (+351 22) 600 18 16; e-mail info@rpda-law.com; internet www.rpda-law.com.

SPAIN

Bufete Dexeus: Tuset 8 – 8°, 08006 Barcelona; tel (+34) 93 292 22 66; fax (+34) 93 237 37 20; e-mail bufetedexeus@icab.es; internet www.bufetedexeus.com.

Cuatrecasas Abogados: Paseo de Gracia 111, 4°, 08008 Barcelona; tel (+34 93) 290 55 00; fax (+34 93) 290 55 67; e-mail Barcelona@cuatrecasas.com.

Echecopar Abogados: Calle del Doctor Fleming 3 – 6°, 28036 Madrid; tel (+34) 914 589 940; fax (+34) 914 589 949; e-mail madrid@echecopar.es.

Areas of specialization:
- Competition law
- Customs law

Garrigues: José Abascal 45, 28003 Madrid; tel (+34 91) 514 52 00; fax (+34 91) 399 24 08.

Gomez – Acebo & Pombo: Castellana 164, 28046 Madrid; tel (+34 91) 582 91 00; fax (+34 91) 345 36 79; fax (+34 91) 582 91 14; e-mail abogados@gomezacebo-pombo.es.

Martinez Lage & Asociados: Claudio Coello 37, 28001 Madrid; tel (+34 91) 426 44 70; fax (+34 91) 577 37 74; e-mail abogados@m-lage.es.

Areas of specialization:
- EC institutions
- Litigation
- Competition law
- State aids
- Intellectual property law
- EC freedoms
- Public contracts
- Concentration of companies
- Dumping
- Transport law
- EU aids and subsidies

Roca Junyent: c/ Aribau, 198, 8a, 08036 Barcelona; tel +34 93 241 92 06; fax +34 93 240 50 48; e-mail r.rafols@rocajunyent.com.

Areas of specialization:
- Anti-trust law
- Agency agreements
- Distribution agreements
- Intellectual property law
- Directives
- Regulations
- Free movement of goods
- EU proceedings
- Mergers and acquisitions

SWEDEN

Advokatfirman Lindahl: Box 14240, 10440 Stockholm; tel (+46 8) 670 58 00; fax (+46 8) 667 73 80; e-mail reception.stockholm@lindahl.se; internet www.lindahl.se.

Areas of specialization:
- Competition law
- Public procurement

Mannheimer Swartling: Norrmalmstorg 4, Box 1711, 111 87 Stockholm; tel (+46 8) 505 76500; fax (+46 8) 505 76501; e-mail lexner@msa.se.

Advokatfirman Vinge: Smålandsgatan 20, Box 1703, 111 87 Stockholm; tel (+46 8) 614 30 00; fax (+46 8) 614 31 90; e-mail michael.wigge@vinge.se.

UNITED KINGDOM

20 Essex Street: 20 Essex Street, London WC2R 3AL; tel (+44 20) 78421200; fax (+44 20) 78421270; e-mail clerks@20essexst.com; internet www.20essexst.com.

Areas of specialization:
- Competition law
- Free movement of goods
- Private international law (Brussels and Rome Conventions)
- Environmental law
- Social law
- Institutions

Addelsaw Goddard: 150 Aldersgate Street, London EC1A 4EJ; tel (+44 20) 7606 88 55; fax (+44 20) 7606 43 90; e-mail tg@theodoregoddard.co.uk.

Allen & Overy: One New Change, London EC4M 9QQ; tel (+44 20) 7330 30 00; fax (+44 20) 7330 99 99.

Barlow Lyde & Gilbert: Beaufort House, 15 St Botolph Street, London EC3A 7NJ; tel (+44 20) 7071 9000; fax (+44 20) 7643 8500; internet www.blg.co.uk.

Areas of specialization:
- Commercial litigation
- Arbitration
- EU law in the UK
- Insurance
- Free movement of goods
- Free movement of persons
- Free movement of services
- Free movement of capital
- Reinsurance
- Competition law
- Professional indemnity
- Mergers
- Acquisitions
- Joint ventures
- Company law
- Commercial law
- Insolvency
- Marine regulation
- Air transport regulation
- Personal injury
- Product liability
- Customs
- Tax law
- Environmental law
- Employment law
- Construction law
- Intellectual property law
- Information technology
- E-commerce

Beachcroft Wansbroughs: 100 Fetter Lane, London EC4A 1BN; tel (+44 20) 7242 10 11; fax (+44 20) 7831 66 30; e-mail rheslett@bwlaw.co.uk@bwlaw.co.uk.

Berwin Leighton: Adelaide House, London Bridge, London EC4R 9HA; tel (+44 20) 7760 1000; fax (+44 20) 7760 1111.

Bird & Bird: 90 Fetter Lane, London EC4A 1JP; tel (+44 20) 7415 60 00; fax (+44 20) 7415 61 11; e-mail morag.macdonald@twobirds.com.

Brick Court Chambers: 7/8 Essex Street, London WC2R 3LD; tel (+44 20) 7379 3550; fax (+44 20) 7379 3558; e-mail surname@brickcourt.be.

Bristows: 3 Lincoln's Inn Fields, London WC2A 3AA; tel (+44 20) 7400 8000; fax (+44 20) 7400 8050; e-mail info@bristows.co.uk; internet www.bristows.com.

Cleaver Fulton Rankin: 50 Bedford Street, Belfast BT2 7FW; tel (+44 28) 9024 31 41; fax (+44 28) 9024 90 96; e-mail cfr@cfrlawonline.com; internet www.cfrlawonline.com.

Areas of specialization:
- Agricultural law
- Fisheries law
- Civil jurisdictional judgments
- Competition law
- Consumer protection
- Employment law
- Environmental law
- Intellectual property law
- Social policy
- State aids

Clifford Chance Pünder: 200 Aldersgate Street, London EC1A 4JJ; tel (+44 20) 7600 10 00; fax (+44 20) 7600 55 55; e-mail John.Osborne@CliffordChance.com; internet www.CliffordChance.com.

CMS Cameron McKenna: Mitre House, 160 Aldersgate Street, London EC1A 4DD; tel (+44 20) 7367 30 00; fax (+44 20) 7367 20 00; e-mail info@cmck.com; internet www.cmck.com.

CWG – Chambers of Mark Watson-Gandy: Delacourt House, 3 Delacourt Road, Blackheath, London SE3 8XA; tel (+44 20) 8305 29 67; fax (+44 20) 8305 29 68; e-mail eg@cwglaw.com.

Areas of specialization:
- Arbitration
- Commercial law
- Copyright law
- Industrial contracts
- Mergers and acquisitions
- Accountancy law
- Start-ups
- Takeovers

Dechert: 2 Serjeants' Inn, London EC4Y 1LT; tel (+44 20) 7583 53 53; fax (+44 20) 7353 36 83; e-mail advice@dechertEU.com; internet www.dechert.com.

Areas of specialization:
- International trade
- International taxation
- Customs and excise
- Environmental law
- Competition law
- Commercial law
- Finance leasing
- International arbitration

Denton Wilde Sapte: 5 Chancery Lane, Clifford's Inn, London EC4A 2BU; tel (+44 20) 7242 12 12; fax (+44 20) 7404 00 87; e-mail info@dentonhall.com; internet www.dentonhall.com.

DLA: 3 Noble Street, London EC2V 7EE; tel (+44 20) 8700 111111; fax (+44 20) 7796 6666.

Dyson Bell Martin: 1 Dean Farrar Street, London SW1H 0DY; tel (+44 20) 7222 9458; fax (+44 20) 7222 0650; e-mail dbm@dysonbell.co.uk.

Fasken Martineau: 10 Arthur Street, 5th floor, London EC4R 9AY; tel (+44 20) 7929 28 94; fax (+44 20) 7929 36 34; e-mail info@lon.fasken.martineau.com; internet www.fasken.com.

Areas of specialization:
- EU law and Canadian corporations
- EU research and development programmes
- Competition law
- Environmental law
- Telecommunications
- Financial issues
- Economic issues
- Financial institutions
- Corporate law

Field Fisher Waterhouse: 41 Vine Street, London EC3N 2AA; tel (+44 20) 7481 4841; fax (+44 20) 7488 0084.

Fox Williams: Ten Dominion Street, London EC2M 2EE; tel (+44 20) 7628 20 00; fax (+44 20) 7628 21 00; e-mail mail@foxwilliams.co.uk; internet www.foxwilliams.co.uk.

Freshfields Bruckhaus Deringer: 65 Fleet Street, London EC4Y 1HS; tel (+44 20) 7936 40 00; fax (+44 20) 7936 70 01; e-mail email@freshfields.com; internet www.freshfields.com.

Hammonds: 2 Park Lane, Leeds LS3 1ES; tel (+44 113) 284 70 00; fax (+44 113) 284 70 01.

Herbert Smith: Exchange House, Primrose Street, London EC2A 2HS; tel (+44 20) 7374 80 00; fax (+44 20) 7496 0043; e-mail enquiries@herbertsmith.com; internet www.herbertsmith.com.

Holman Fenwick & Willan: Marlow House, Lloyd's Avenue, London EC3N 3AL; tel (+44 20) 7488 23 00; fax (+44 20) 7481 03 16; e-mail holmans@hfw.co.uk; internet www.hfw.com.

International Law Chambers: ILC House, 77 Chepstow Road, London W2 5QR; tel (+44 20) 7221 56 84; tel (+44 20) 7221 48 40; fax (+44 20) 7221 56 85; fax (+44 20) 7221 01 93; e-mail ilcuk@aol.com.

Linnells: Greyfriars Court – Paradise Square, Oxford OX1 1BB; tel (+44 1865) 24 86 07; fax (+44 1865) 72 84 45; e-mail law@linnells.co.uk; internet www.linnells.co.uk.

Lovells: Atlantic House, 65 Holborn Viaduct, London EC1A 2FG; tel (+44 20) 7236 00 66; fax (+44 20) 7248 42 12.

Macfarlanes: 10 Norwich Street, London EC4A 1BD; tel (+44 20) 7831 92 22; fax (+44 20) 7831 96 07.

Macroberts: 152 Bath Street, Glasgow, Scotland G2 4TB; tel (+44 141) 332 99 88; fax (+44 141) 332 88 86; e-mail maildesk@ macroberts.co.uk; internet www .macroberts.co.uk.

Areas of specialization:
- Corporate law
- Commercial law
- Competition law

Nabarro Nathanson: Lacon House, 2 Theobald's Court, Theobald's Road, London WC1X 8RW; tel (+44 20) 7524 6000.

Norton Rose: Kempson House, 35-37 Camomile Street, London EC3A 7AN; tel (+44 20) 7283 60 00; fax (+44 20) 7283 65 00.

Pritchard Englefield: 14 New Street, London EC2M 4HE; tel (+44 20) 7972 97 20; fax (+44 20) 7972 97 22; e-mail po@ pritchardenglefield.EU.com; internet www.pritchardenglefield.co.uk.

RadcliffesLeBrasseur: 5 Great College Street, Westminster, London SW1P 3SJ; tel (+44 20) 7222 70 40; fax (+44 20) 7222 62 08; e-mail info@rlb-law.com.

Areas of specialization:
- Intellectual property
- Consumer agency
- Competition law
- Environmental law
- Public procurement
- Employment
- Equal opportunities
- Company law
- Establishment of businesses
- Monitoring of forthcoming EU legislation
- Lobbying

Richards Butler: Beaufort House, 15 St Botolph Street, London EC3A 7EE; tel (+44 20) 7247 65 55; fax (+44 20) 7247 50 91.

S J Berwin & Co: 222 Grays Inn Road, London WC1X 8HB; tel (+44 20) 7533 22 22; fax (+44 20) 7533 20 00.

Simmons & Simmons: City Point, One Ropemaker Street, London EC2Y 9SS; tel (+44 20) 7628 20 20; fax (+44 20) 7528 20 70.

Slaughter and May: One Bunhill Row, London EC1Y 8YY; tel (+44 20) 7600 1200; fax (+44 20) 7090 5000; e-mail mail@slaughterandmay.com.

Taylor Wessing: Carmelite, 50 Victoria Embankment, Blackfriars, London; EC4Y 0DX; tel (+44 20) 7300 7000; fax (+44 20) 7300 7100; e-mail london@ taylorwessing.com.

Travers Smith Braithwaite: 10 Snow Hill, London EC1A 2AL; tel (+44 20) 7248 91 33; fax (+44 20) 7236 37 28.

Wedlake Bell: 16 Bedford St, Covent Garden, London WC2E 9HF; tel (+44 20) 7395 30 00; fax (+44 20) 7836 99 66; e-mail legal@wedlakebell.com; internet www.wedlakebell.com.

UNITED STATES OF AMERICA

Baker & McKenzie: Prudential Plaza One, 30 East Randolph Drive, Chicago IL 60601; tel (+1 312) 861 8000; fax (+1 312) 861 2899.

Cleary, Gottlieb, Steen & Hamilton: One Liberty Plaza, New York NY 10006-1470; tel (+1 212) 225 20 00; fax (+1 212) 225 39 99.

Coudert Brothers Coppens Van Ommeslaghe & Faures: 1114 Avenue of the Americas, New York NY 10036-7703; tel (+1 212) 626 44 00; fax (+1 212) 626 41 20; e-mail info@nyo.coudert .com; internet www.coudert.com.

Covington & Burling: PO Box 7566, 1201 Pennsylvania Avenue, Washington DC 20004-2401; tel (+1 202) 662 60 00; fax (+1 202) 662 62 91; fax (+1 202) 737 05 28.

Crowell & Moring: 1001 Pennsylvania Avenue N. W., Washington DC 20004-2595; tel (+1 202) 624 2500; fax (+1 202) 628 5116.

Dechert: 4000 Bell Atlantic Tower, 1717 Arch Street, Philadelphia, PA 19103-2793; tel (+1 215) 994 4000; fax (+1 215) 994 2222.

Foley & Lardner: 777 East Wisconsin Avenue, Milwaukee WI 53202-5367; tel (+1 414) 271 24 00; fax (+1 414) 297 49 00; e-mail Rboër@Foleylaw.com.

Hogan & Hartson: Thirteenth Street 555 NW, Washington DC 20004 1109; tel (+1 202) 637 56 00; fax (+1 202) 637 59 10.

Jones, Day, Reavis & Pogue: North Point, 901 Lakeside Avenue, Cleveland OH 44114; tel (+1 216) 586 3939; fax (+1 216) 579 0212.

Keller & Heckman: 1001 G Street NW, Suite 500 West, Washington DC 20001; tel (+1 202) 434 4100; fax (+1 202) 434 4646.

Kelley Drye & Warren: 101 Park Avenue, New York NY 10178-0002; tel (+1 212) 808 78 00; fax (+1 212) 808 78 97.

Le Boeuf, Lamb, Greene & Macrae: 125 West 55th Street, New York NY 10019-5389; tel (+1 212) 424 80 00; fax (+1 212) 424 85 00.

Morgan Lewis & Bockius: 1701 Market Street, Philadelphia PA 19103-2921; tel (+1 215) 963 50 00; fax (+1 215) 963 52 99.

Oppenheimer, Wolff & Donnelly: 1700 First Bank Building, 332 Minnesota Street, Saint-Paul MN 55101-1313; tel (+1 612) 605 20 00; fax (+1 612) 605 21 00.

Pillsbury Winthrop LLP: One Battery Park Plaza, New York NY 10004-1490; tel (+1 212) 858 10 00; fax (+1 212) 858 15 00; internet www.pillsburywinthrop.com.

Skadden, Arps, Slate, Meagher & Flom LLP: 919 Third Avenue, New York NY 10022; tel (+1 212) 735 30 00; fax (+1 212) 735 20 00.

Stewart and Stewart: 2100 M Street, NW Suite 200, Washington DC 20037; tel 202 785 4185; fax 202 466 1286; e-mail general@stewartlaw.com; internet www .stewartlaw.com.

Weil, Gotshal & Manges LLP: 767 Fifth Avenue, New York NY 10153; tel (+1 212) 310 8000; fax (+1 212) 310 8007; e-mail john.neary@weil.com.

White & Case: 1155 Avenue of the Americas, New York NY 10036-2787; tel (+1 212) 819 82 00; fax (+1 212) 354 81 13.

Wilmer Cutler & Pickering: 2445 M Street NW, Washington, DC 20037-1420; tel (+1 202) 663 60 00; fax (+1 202) 663 63 63.

INDEX OF LAW FIRMS' SPECIALITIES

TRADE AND PROFESSIONAL ASSOCIATIONS, INTEREST GROUPS, NGOs AND CHURCH ASSOCIATIONS

TRADE AND PROFESSIONAL ASSOCIATIONS

Socio-professional organizations play an important role in the European Union. They defend the interests of the categories that they represent by trying to influence the guidelines or decisions of the EU's institutions. In this respect, some associations readily acknowledge their role as a lobby. However, except in a few specific cases, it is fair to say that all of the organizations might be considered to fulfil the role of a lobby to some extent.

As they have a thorough knowledge of their sector, they are valuable information sources, although the range of information available to non-members differs from one organization to another. Where information is available, the letters M and NM signal whether the information is supplied to members (M) or non-members (NM).

The following abbreviations are used in the item 'Working languages': D = German, Dan = Danish, E = English, Esp = Spanish, F = French, Gr = Greek, It = Italian, Jap = Japanese, Nl = Dutch, Port = Portuguese, Turk = Turkish.

An index indicating the sectors of activity of the professional organizations is provided at the end of this section.

Associations

(Listed alphabetically by acronym or abbreviation)

AAC

Association of the European Starch Industries of the EU

Association des Amidonneries de Céréales de l'UE

Avenue des Arts, 43, 1040 Bruxelles, Belgium
Tel: +32 2/289 67 60
Fax: +32 2/513 55 92
E-mail: aac@aac-eu.org

Pres.: Mrs. KLAEIJEN
Sec.-Gen.: Mrs. I. AXIOTIADES

Founded: 1988
Working languages: E
Secretariat: 5 members of staff

Information available:
- List of members available to the general public.

ACE / CAE

Architects' Council of Europe
Conseil des Architectes d'Europe
Rat der Architekten Europa's

Rue Paul Emile Janson 29, 1050 Bruxelles, Belgium

Tel: +32 2/543 11 40
Fax: +32 2/543 11 41
E-mail: info@ace-cae.org
Internet: http://www.ace-cae.org

Pres.: Mr. L. FREYRIE
Sec.-Gen.: A. SAGNE
Contact: A. JOYCE

Founded: 1990
General meeting: Twice a year : Spring, Autumn
Working languages: F/E
Secretariat: 4 members of staff

Information available:
- ACE info, twice a month, free, E/F, MN.
- Annual report, free, E/F.
- Database: List of architectural journals, centres, etc. in member countries, M.
- List of members available to the general public, free.

ACE

The Alliance for Beverage Cartons and the Environment

Rue Belliard 15-17 bte 6, 1040 Bruxelles, Belgium
Tel: +32 2/504 07 10
Fax: +32 2/504 07 19
E-mail: information@ace.be
Internet: www.ace.be

Pres.: Mr. Erik AKRE
Contact: K. BRADLEY (Dir. Gen.)

Founded: 1990
General meeting: December
Working languages: E
Secretariat: 4 members of staff

Information available:
- "Alliance Newsletter", M-NM, 5/year, E, free.
- "Info leaflets" – all subjects, E/F, free.
- Brochure, E/F, free.
- ACE Photo Library CD-Rom, free, E.
- The members' list is available free of charge.

ACEA

Association of European Automobile Manufacturers

Association des Constructeurs Européens d'Automobiles

Rue du Noyer 211, 1000 Bruxelles, Belgium
Tel: +32 2/732 55 50
Fax: +32 2/738 73 10
E-mail: ih@acea.be

Contact: I. HODAC
Working languages: E/F
Secretariat: 26 members of staff

Information available:
- List of members, free.

ACEM

Association des Constructeurs Européens de Motocycles

Avenue de la Joyeuse Entrée 1, 1040 Bruxelles, Belgium
Tel: +32 2/230 97 32
Fax: +32 2/230 16 83
E-mail: j.compagne@acembike.org
E-mail: r.sterckx@acembike.org
Internet: www.acembike.org

Pres.: Herbert DIESS
Sec.-Gen.: Jacques COMPAGNE

Founded: 1994
General meeting: March
Working languages: E
Secretariat: 3 members of staff

Historical note:
- ACEM is the professional association of the Motorcycle Industry in Europe and was founded in 1994 as a merger of 2 previous associations, namely COLIMO and ACEM. ACEM members are responsible for 85% of the total production and up to 90% of the total market in Europe.

Information available:
- "PTW Statistics".
- "Motorcycle Safety: a decade of progress".
- "Solving the Urban Transport Dilemma: Powered Two-Wheelers – a practical alternative".
- "Motorcycle Noise: the Curious Silence".
- List of members available to the general public, free.
- All publications and members' list free of charge can be downloaded from the ACEM website on www.acembike.org

ACI EUROPE

Airports Council International – European Region

Square de Meeûs 6, 1000 Bruxelles, Belgium
Tel: +32 2/552 09 82
Fax: +32 2/513 32 42
E-mail: roman.anderson@aci-europe.org
Internet: http://www.aci-europe.org

Pres.: Dr. BURKE
Contact: Pr. P. KLEES

Founded: 1991
Working languages: E/F
Secretariat: 13 members of staff

Information available:
- "Communiqué", monthly, F/E, M
- "Communiqué Airport Business Magazine", M
- "Committee Yearbook", M
- "Winter Services Yearbook", E, M
- "Policy Handbook", F/E, M
- "European Airports Traffic Report", E, M
- "Environmental Handbook", E, M
- "Airports – Partners in Vital Economies", F/E, M
- "Economic Impact Study Kit", F/E, M
- "Sources of Finance for Airport Development", E, M
- "Airports Contribute to the Social Fabric of Europe", F/E, M
- "The Development of the Trans-european Transport Networks", F/E, M
- "Commercial Marketing – Best Practices Handbook", E, M
- "Corporate Brochure", F/E, M
- "How to Create a Corporate Image", E, M
- Databases: members and airports, M
- List of members on request only, free, M
- "Membership Directory", E, M

ACME

Association of European Cooperative and Mutual Insurers

Association des Assureurs Coopératifs et Mutualistes Européens

Europäischer Genosserschaftlicher und Wechselseitiger Versicherungsverband

Rue d'Arlon 50, 1000 Bruxelles, Belgium
Tel: +32 2/231 08 28
Fax: +32 2/280 03 99
E-mail: acme@skynet.be
Internet: http://www.acme.eu.org

Contacts: Mr. DE BOISSIEU (Dél. Gén), Ms. C. HOCK

Founded: 1978
Working languages: F/E
Secretariat: 4 members of staff

Sectors of activity:
- ACME is the European regional association of the International Cooperative and Mutual Insurance Federation (ICMIF), which groups together over 150 insurance companies in 62 countries world wide.
- ACME has 32 full members comprising 43 insurers in 20 European countries.
- ACME has three standing working parties:
  – legislation (monitoring EU legislation and preparing ACME opinions on EU insurance directives);
  – human resources and social affairs (monitoring social legislation and preparing ACME opinions);
  – development.

Information available:
- "Together", M, quarterly, E/F
- Activity report, M.
- List of members available free of charge.

ACT

Association of Commercial Television in Europe

Association des Télévisions Commerciales Européennes

Rue Joseph II 9/13, 1000 Bruxelles, Belgium
Tel: +32 2/736 00 52
Fax: +32 2/735 41 72
E-mail: info@acte.be
Internet: www.acte.be

Pres.: Nicolas DE TAVERNOST
Sec.-Gen.: Ross BIGGAM
Contact: Mrs. C. HUSNOT (Office Man.)

Founded: 1989
General meeting: April or May
Working languages: E/F
Secretariat: 6 members of staff

Historical note:
- Founded in 1989 with five members, now nineteen members, operating in 14 European States, we represent the commercial broadcasting business to EU legislators. Covering the whole industry: pay-TV and free to air, large and small markets, pan-European and nationally focused, we are preparing to expand as the EU takes on new Member States.

Sectors of activity:
- The ACT is member of the EASA (European Advertising Standards Alliance), which is the single authoritative voice defending and promoting advertising self-regulation.
- As an Observer at the Council of Europe, the ACT has actively contributed to the work on the Convention on Transfrontier Television and other policy initiatives.
- The ACT also collaborates (as an Observer) in the work carried out by the World Intellectual Property Organisation (WIPO), on issues such as the protection of broadcasters and neighbouring rights. ACT is currently involved with the drafting a new treaty on the protection of broadcasters' rights.
- The ACT is also an Observer at the DVB Project (Digital Video Broadcasting).

Information available:
- "ACT Monographs", E/F.
- The members' list is available, free of charge.

ACTIP

Animal Cell Technology Industrial Platform

PO Box 9143, 3007 AC Rotterdam, Netherlands
Tel: +31 10/482 83 06
Fax: +31 10 482 77 50
E-mail: actip@actip.org
Internet: http://www.actip.org

Pres.: Drs. H. VAN DEN BERG
Contact: Mrs. Dr. HERMANS

Founded: 1990
General meeting: May + November – different cities
Working languages: E
Secretariat: 2 members of staff

Sectors of activity:
- Following research projects funded by the EU in the fields of animal cell technology, gene therapy and vaccinology.
- Advising the European Commission on fields of research most likely to benefit from EU support.

Information available:
- List of members available to the general public, names only.

ACTUARIES / ACTUAIRES

European Actuarial Consultative Group

Groupe Consultatif Actuariel Européen

Napier House, 4 Worcester Street, Oxford OX1 2AW, United Kingdom
Tel: +44 1865/268 218
Fax: +44 1865/268 233
E-mail: mlucas@gcactuaries.org.uk
Internet: www.gcactuaries.org

Pres.: A. GULDBERG
Contact: M. LUCAS (Secr)

Founded: 1978
General meeting: 06/09/2002
Working languages: E/F
Secretariat: 2 members of staff

Sectors of activity:
- Insurance.
- Pensions.
- Finance.
- Education.
- The group organizes colloquia and summer schools.
- The consultative group does not defend member interests. It gives advice and opinions to the EU organisations on actuarial issues and acts as a forum for discussion amongst its members.

Information available:
- Database: list of members.

ADDE

Association of Dental Dealers in Europe

Association des Dépôts Dentaires en Europe

Moosstrasse 29, 3073 Gümligen-Berne, Switzerland
Tel: +41 31/952 78 92
Fax: +41 31/952 76 83
E-mail: uwanner@swissonline.ch

Pres.: F. BRUGGEMAN
Sec.-Gen.: Dr. U. WANNER

Founded: 1950
General meeting: May 2004, Lucerne
Working languages: E/F/D

Sectors of activity:
- Comparative studies on legal matters, regulations.
Conference:
- "Economic Survey" – every year.

Information available:
- "Economic survey", E, M-NM.
- "Hygiene" – study, E, M.
- "MDD", study, E, M.
- "Trade customs", E, M.
- List of members available to the general public, CHF 1000.

AEA

Association of European Airlines

Avenue Louise 350, 1050 Bruxelles, Belgium
Tel: +32 2/639 89 89
Fax: +32 2/639 89 99
E-mail: aea.secretariat@aea.be
Internet: http://www.aea.be

Pres.: J.-C. SPINETTA (Air France)

Founded: 1954
Working languages: E
Secretariat: 23 members of staff

Sectors of activity:
- Research.
- Statistical compilation.
- Organisation of meetings for European Airlines.

Information available:
- "Yearbook – plus statistical appendices" – yearly.
- "Traffic and Punctuality Update" – monthly.
- "ATC in Europe".
- "Towards a Single System for Air Traffic Control in Europe".
- "White Paper on Air Transport and the Internal Market".
- The members' list is available, free of charge.

AECMA

European Association of Aerospace Industries

Association Européenne de Constructeurs de Matériel Aérospatial

Europäischer Verband der Luftfahrt-, Raumfahrt- und Ausrüstungsindustrie

Gulledelle 94 – B5, 1200 Bruxelles, Belgium
Tel: +32 2/775 81 10
Fax: +32 2/775 81 11
E-mail: info@aecma.org
Internet: www.aecma.org

Contact: M. HAESE

Founded: 1950
Working languages: E
Secretariat: 16 members of staff

Historical note:
- 2004: Merger planned between AECMA, EDIG and EUROSPACE. Please refer to www.asd-europe.org for further information of the new association ASD

Sectors of activity:
- AECMA represents the European aerospace industry in all matters of common interest. International initiatives are carried out mainly via ICCAIA (the International Coordination Committee for Industrial Aerospace Associations), at the level of the ICAO (International Civil Aviation Organisation). AECMA has a continuing dialogue with the EU and makes a strong contribution to the creation of a common European aerospace operations framework.

Information available:
- Specifications.
- Standards (M-NM), E/F/D.
- "Pr EN Green Papers and EN White Paper".
- "2000 M – Internat. Spec. for Material Management Integrated Data", M: £181, NM: £362, E.
- "1000 D – Int. Spec. for Tech. Data Publications", M: £175, NM: £350, E.
- AECMA Simplified English.
- Position papers on several subjects (M, NM).

AEDE

European Association of Teachers

Association Européenne des Enseignants

Europäische Erzieherbund

Rue du Faubourg National 68, 67000 Strasbourg, France
Tel: +33 3/88 32 63 67
Fax: +33 3/88 22 48 34
E-mail: aede.sgeurope@wanadoo.fr
Internet: www.aede.org

Pres.: P. FARNARARO
Sec.-Gen.: J.C. GONON

AEDT

European Association of National Organizations of Textiles Retailers

Association Européenne des Organisations Nationales de Détaillants en Textiles

Europäische Vereinigung der Spitzenverbande des Textileinzelhandels

Avenue des Nerviens 9-31, 4è étage, 1040 Bruxelles, Belgium
Tel: +32 2/230 52 96
Fax: +32 2/230 25 69
E-mail: info@aedt.org
Internet: www.aedt.org

Pres.: S. UETZ
Sec.-Gen.: R. SOENENS

Founded: 1958
General meeting: June
Working languages: E
Secretariat: 2 members of staff

Sectors of activity:
Conference:
- "Power of social accountability", 07.06.2002, The Netherlands.

Information available:
- General information, M – NM.
- Databank fashion brand names, M.
- Travel service, M.
- Access databank, €30.

AEEBC

Association of European Building Surveyors

Association d'Experts Européens du Bâtiment et de la Construction

Vereinigung der Europäischen Bauingenieure

c/o Mr. M. Russell-Croucher, 12 Great George Street, London SW1P 3AD, United Kingdom
Tel: +44 20/72 22 70 00
Fax: +44 20/73 34 38 44
E-mail: aeebc@rics.org.uk
Internet: www.aeebc.org

Pres.: Pr. Tr. MOLE (U.K.)
Sec.-Gen.: F. WARGNIES (Belgium)

Founded: 1991
General meeting: date and place are variable – in one of the member countries – usually Spring and Autumn
Working languages: E
Secretariat: 1 member of staff

Sectors of activity:
- Special working parties on education and building pathology.

Information available:
- The association's expertise includes a knowledge of the economic and legal framework within which building projects are conceived, funded and constructed.

- Database: records of meetings.
- List of member organisations and delegates available free of charge.

AEGPL

European LPG Association

Association Européenne des Gaz de Pétrole Liquéfiés

Europäischer Flüssiggasverband

Rue Galilée 6, 75782 Paris Cedex 16, France
Tel: +33 1/47 23 52 74
Fax: +33 1/47 23 52 79
E-mail: aegpl@aol.com
Internet: http://www.aegpl.com

Pres.: W. LINDENHOVIUS
Contact: H. CHAPOTOT (Dir Gen)

Founded: 1968
General meeting: June
Working languages: F/E/Esp/D/It
Secretariat: 6 members of staff

Sectors of activity:
- Cooperation with several DGs of the EU.
Conference:
- "Annual Congress".

Information available:
- "AEGPL COMMUNICATION" – quarterly – F/E.
- Convention communications, once a year, NM.

AEGRAFLEX

European Association of Engravers and Flexographers

Association Européenne des Graveurs et des Flexographes

Europäische Vereinigung der Graveure und Flexografen

Postfach 1869, 65008 Wiesbaden, Germany
Tel: +49 611/80 31 15
Fax: +49 611/80 31 17
E-mail: so@bvdm-online.de
Internet: www.aegraflex.org

Pres.: L. WAAGE
Contact: Torben THORN

Founded: 1966
General meeting: 24/05/2003
Working languages: D

Information available:
- "GRAFLEX" professional newsletter, providing technical information. Published three times a year in F/E/D/Norw, €10 per copy.

AEJ / AJE

Association of European Journalists

Association des Journalistes Européens

Vereinigung Europäischer Journalisten

Calle Cedaceros 11, 3° F, 28014 Madrid, Spain
Tel: +34 91/429 68 69
Fax: +34 91/429 27 54
E-mail: info@apeuropeos.org
Internet: www.apeuropeos.org

Pres.: C.L. ALVAREZ
Sec.-Gen.: M.A. AGUILAR

Founded: 1962
General meeting: October
Working languages: E/F
Secretariat: 1 member of staff

Sectors of activity:
- European journalists exchange – PHARE programme for journalists in Eastern Europe.
- Objectives:
  – participate in creation of European consciousness,
  – deepen knowledge of European affairs,
  – promote knowledge and understanding of each country,
  – enhance the moral and practical status of journalism.
- Promote European integration on a democratic basis and maintain freedom of the press and of information.

Information available:
- "The European Union in the Media", yearly, E/Esp.
- Newsletter, bimonthly, E.
- List of members, 1 000 ESP/6 EUR, E.

AEMUM

Association of European Municipal Equipment Manufacturers

Lyoner Strasse 18, 60528 Frankfurt am Main, Germany
Tel: +49 69/6603-13 01
Fax: +49 69/6603-23 01
E-mail: carmen.simon@vdma.org
Internet: www.vdma.org/vdma_root/ www_muneq_vdma_com

Contacts: Dr Bernd SCHERER, Carmen SIMON

Founded: 2002

Sectors of activity:
- Focuses on international standardisation of interfaces, participation in shaping European safety standards, provision of information on markets and the economic climate and influencing organisation of relevant trade fairs in Europe

Information available:
- Bimonthly Newsletter, M

AEPOC

Association Européenne pour la Protection des Oeuvres et Services Cryptés

Avenue Louise 165, 1050 Bruxelles, Belgium
Tel: +32 2/706 55 85
Fax: +32 2/706 55 85
E-mail: info@aepoc.org
Internet: www.aepoc.org

Pres.: J. GRENIER

Founded: 1997
General meeting: April
Working languages: E/F

Sectors of activity:
- Encouraging the adoption of European legislation caused by illicit decoding devices (hacked decoders and smart cards).
- Promotion of enforcement of such legislation including thorough training of enforcement authorities.

Information available:
- List of members available to the general public, free.

AER

Association of European Radios

Association Européenne des Radios

Vereinigung des Europäischen Rundfunks

Av. d'Auderghem 76, 1040 Bruxelles, Belgium
Tel: +32 2/736 91 31
Fax: +32 2/732 89 90
E-mail: aer@aereurope.org
Internet: www.aereurope.org

Pres.: Sergio NATUCCI
Sec.-Gen.: Frederik STUCKI
Contact: Christina SLESZYNSKA (Manager)

Founded: 1992
General meeting: February
Working languages: E/F
Secretariat: 1 member of staff

Sectors of activity:
- Representation of commercial radio broadcasters' interests in Europe and in international bodies, and technical assistance on questions related to the commercial radio broadcasting sector: copyright, restrictions on advertising, implementation of competition rules, taxation and technical aspects.

Information available:
- AER Newsletter, bimonthly, M.
- Database: European Radio Data, M.
- List of members, free, NM, on the website.

AEROBAL

European Association of Aluminium Aerosol Container Manufacturers

Association Européenne des Fabricants de Boîtes en Aluminium pour Aérosol

Europäische Vereinigung der Hersteller von Aluminium-Aerosoldosen

Am Bonneshof 5, 40474 Düsseldorf, Germany
Tel: +49 211/47 96 144
Fax: +49 211/47 96 408
E-mail: aerobal@aluinfo.de

Contact: G. SPENGLER

Founded: 1976
General meeting: May–June every year
Working languages: E

Information available:
- Brochure: Aerosol Cans in Aluminium.
- List of members available to the general public.

AERTEL

European Association for Tapes, Braids, Elastic Materials

Association Européenne Rubans, Tresses, Tissus Elastiques

Europäische Vereinigung der Bandweber- und Flechterindustrie

Poortakkerstraat 98, 9051 Gent/St. Denijs-Westrem, Belgium
Tel: +32 9/242 98 20
Fax: +32 9/242 98 29
E-mail: info@gent.febeltex.be

Pres.: P. GLEICH
Sec.-Gen.: P. VAN MOL

Founded: 1959
Working languages: F/E
Secretariat: 1 member of staff

Information available:
- "Newsletter" – F/D/E/Esp/It – 3 editions yearly.
- "AERTEL Directory".

AESAD

Association Européenne de Soins et d'Aides à Domicile

Avenue Ad. Lacomblé 69, 1030 Bruxelles, Belgium
Tel: +32 2/736 79 72
Fax: +32 2/736 74 98
E-mail: EACHH@skynet.be
Internet: http://www.aeosad.org

Pres.: R. SEUTIN

AESGP

Association of the European Self-Medication Industry

Association Européenne des Spécialités Pharmaceutiques Grand Public

Europäischer Fachverband der Arzneimittel-Hersteller

Avenue de Tervuren 7, 1040 Bruxelles, Belgium
Tel: +32 2/735 51 30
Fax: +32 2/735 52 22
E-mail: info@aesgp.be
Internet: http://www.aesgp.be

Pres.: A. ESTEVE
Contact: H. CRANZ (Dir Gen)

Founded: 1964
General meeting: June
Working languages: E
Secretariat: 7 members of staff

Sectors of activity:
- Promotion of self-medication in Europe.
- 28-29 September 2004, Brussels – "Changing the rules for food supplements and herbal products in Europe"

Information available:
Publications:
- "OTC in Europe – Facts and Figures", May 2000, only available on-line.
- "Economic and Legal Framework for non-prescription medicines", May 2000, 100 EURO, E.
- "Deregulation 2001 – The Future of Medecines Regulation in Europe", January 1999.
- "AESGP Euro OTC News", M, every 6 weeks, E.
- List of members available to the general public, free.

AEXEA

Association of European Recognized Experts

Association des Experts Européens Agréés

Arbeitsgemeinschaft der Europäischen Anerkannten Savchverständigen

Rue du Colonel Moll 3, 75017 Paris, France
Tel: +33 1/53 81 77 00
Tel: +33 4/67 64 37 10
Fax: +33 1/53 81 77 03
Fax: +33 4/67 64 37 10
E-mail: alinea.sa@wanadoo.fr
Internet: www.aexea.org

Pres.: B. ROBERT
Sec.-Gen.: L. NEGRIER-DORMONT

Founded: 1990
Working languages: F/D/E
Secretariat: 5 members of staff

Sectors of activity:
- AEXEA seeks to bring together recognised experts from the EU Member States capable of conducting expert missions for the private sector, public services and the EU's institutions.
- AEXEA is pursuing its efforts with regard to the mutual recognition of its members in the different Member States, based on the principle of subsidiarity laid down in the Maastricht Treaty, and the three bases of the profession of expert: competence, independence and impartiality.
- Building public works and allied activities.
- Trade, industry and informatics.
- Accounting, finances and diagnosis – corporate management.
- Estimates and surveyors.
- Health professions.
- Translators.
- A group entitled "miscellaneous" incorporating disciplines with a small number of persons.

Information available:
- European Expert Certification Handbook, being drafted in collaboration with the European Union.

AFCASOLE

Association of Soluble Coffee Manufacturers of the European Community

Association des Fabricants de Café Soluble des Pays de la Communauté Européenne

Vereinigung der Hersteller von Löslichem Kaffee der Europäischen Gemeinschaft

Tourniairestraat 3, 1065 KK Amsterdam, Netherlands
Tel: +31 20/71 30 702
Fax: +33 51 13891
E-mail: afcasole@coffee-associations.org

Pres.: G. LEMOREHEDEC

Founded: 1960
Working languages: E
Secretariat: 2 members of staff

Information available:
- List of members available to the general public.

AFECOR

European Control Manufacturers' Association

Association des Fabricants Européens d'Appareils de Contrôle et de Régulation

Verband Europäischer Kontrollgerätehersteller

c/o Honeywell, Phileas Foggstraat 7, 7821 AJ Emmen, Netherlands
Tel: +31 591/695 323
Fax: +31 591/695 203
E-mail: gerhard.vedder@honeywell.com
Internet: www.afecor.org

Sec.-Gen.: G.J. VEDDER

Founded: 1963
General meeting: Spring/Fall – usually once in Brussels
Working languages: E/F/D
Secretariat: 3 members of staff

Historical note:
- The association was founded in 1963 as EGCMA (European Gas Control Manufacturers' Association). Expansion of activities caused a change of the name in 1968 to AFECOGAS (European Gas and Oil Control Manufacturers' Association) becoming AFECOR in 1988.

AFEMS

Association of European Manufacturers of Sporting Ammunition

Association des Fabricants Européens de Munitions de Sport

Vereinigung der Europäischen Sportmunitionshersteller

c/o CEFIC, Avenue E. Van Nieuwenhuyse 4, 1160 Bruxelles, Belgium
Tel: +32 2/676 72 11
Fax: +32 2/676 73 03
E-mail: afems@afems.org
Internet: http://www.afems.org

Pres.: K. IRVING
Contact: B. JENSEN
Working languages: F/E

Sectors of activity:
- Study of all problems of interest to the sporting ammunition industry in particular those of a scientific, technical, regulatory and institutional nature or work safety related.

Information available:
- List of members available to the general public.

AFERA

European Adhesive Tapes Manufacturers Association

Association des Fabricants Européens de Rubans Auto-Adhésifs

Verband des Europäischen Klebebandhersteller

Laan Copes van Cattenburch 79, PO Box 85612, 2508 CH Den Haag, Netherlands

Tel: +31 70/312 39 16
Fax: +31 70/363 63 48
E-mail: mail@afera.com
Internet: www.afera.com

Sec.-Gen.: Mrs. A. LEJEUNE

Founded: 1999
General meeting: 18–20/09/2002
Working languages: E

AFG

Association of the Glucose Producers in the EU

Association des Fabricants de Glucose de l'UE

Avenue des Arts, 43, 1040 Bruxelles, Belgium
Tel: +32 2/289 67 60
Fax: +32 2/513 55 92
E-mail: aac@aac-eu.org

Contact: Mrs. SQARCE
Working languages: E
Secretariat: 5 members of staff

AFTA

Association for Fair Trade in Alcohol

J.B. Denayerstraat 25, 1560 Hoeilaart, Belgium
Tel: +32 2/657 66 79
Fax: +32 2/657 35 69
E-mail: afta@pandora.be
Internet: www.afta.be

Contact: R. VIERHOUT

Founded: 1990
Working languages: E
Secretariat: 1 member of staff

AGE

Automotive Glazing Europe UEMV

PO Box 416, 1800 AK Alkmaar, Netherlands
Tel: +31 72/511 41 61
Fax: +31 72/511 37 83
E-mail: auto@uemv.com

Pres.: M. BERRESFORD DUTTON
Contact: P.H.K. DE RIDDER

Founded: 1993
Working languages: D/E/F
Secretariat: 2 members of staff

AICV

Association of the Cider and Fruit Wine Industry of the EU

Association des Industries des Cidres et Vins de Fruits de l'UE

Vereinigung der Obst- und Fruchtweinindustrie der EG

Rue de la Loi 221 box 5, 1040 Bruxelles, Belgium
Tel: +32 2/235 06 20
Fax: +32 2/282 94 20
E-mail: aicv@skynet.be
Internet: www.aicv.org

Pres.: K. DEMUTH
Sec.-Gen.: J. HERMANS
Working languages: E
Secretariat: 2 members of staff

AIDA

International Association for the Distributive Trade

Association Internationale de la Distribution

Internationale Vereinigung des Handels

Rue Marianne 34, 1180 Bruxelles, Belgium
Tel: +32 2/345 99 23
Fax: +32 2/346 02 04
E-mail: info@cbd_bcd.be
Internet: www.infocbd.bcd

Pres.: G. CAMPBELL
Contact: L.F. WEGNEZ

Founded: 1950
Working languages: F/E/D

Information available:
- AIDA International Bulletin, quarterly, multilingual.
- Database for members only.

AIE

European Association of Electrical Contractors

Association Européenne des Entreprises d'Equipement Electrique

Europäische Vereinigung der Unternehmungen für Elektrische Anlagen

J. Chantraineplantsoen 1, 3070 Kortenberg, Belgium
Tel: +32 2/253 42 22
Fax: +32 2/253 67 63
E-mail: info@aie-elec.org
Internet: www.aie-elec.org

Pres.: B. E. PETTERSEN
Sec.-Gen.: Mrs. E. SCHELLEKENS

Founded: 1954
General meeting: September
Working languages: E
Secretariat: 2 members of staff

Information available:
- "Technical Directory", M.
- International Vocabulary.
- List of members available to the public

AIECE

Association of European Conjuncture Institutes

Association d'Instituts Européens de Conjoncture Economique

Vereinigung der Europäischen Wirtschaftsprognoseinstitute

Place Montesquieu 3, 1348 Louvain-La-Neuve, Belgium
Tel: +32 10/47 41 43
Fax: +32 10/47 39 45
E-mail: olbrechts@aiece.org
Internet: www.aiece.org

Pres.: P. VARTIA
Sec.-Gen.: Paul OLBRECHTS

Founded: 1957
General meeting: October
Working languages: F/E

Sectors of activity:
- Analysis of Europe's economy.
- Conferences: October 2004, Kiel; May 2005, Geneva; October 2005, Brussels.

Information available:
- Information on the association.
- List of members available to the general public, free.

AIJN

Association of the Industry of Juices and Nectars from Fruits and Vegetables of the EU

Association de l'Industrie des Jus et Nectars de Fruits et de Légumes de l'UE

Vereinigung der Fruchtsaftindustrie der EG

Rue de la Loi 221 box 5, 1040 Bruxelles, Belgium
Tel: +32 2/235 06 20
Fax: +32 2/282 94 20
E-mail: aijn@ajin.org
Internet: www.aijn.org

Pres.: R. RYAN
Sec.-Gen.: J. HERMANS
Working languages: E
Secretariat: 2 members of staff

Information available:
- List of members – free.

AIM

European Brands Association

Association des Industries de Marque

Europäischer Markenverband

Avenue des Gaulois 9, 1040 Bruxelles, Belgium
Tel: +32 2/736 03 05
Fax: +32 2/734 67 02

E-mail: brand@aim.be
Internet: www.aim.be

Pres.: Lars OLOFSSON
Contact: A. GALASKI (Dir Gen)

Founded: 1967
Working languages: E
Secretariat: 8 members of staff

Information available:
- Database: membership details.

AIMA

The Alternative Investment Management Association Limited

Lower Ground Floor, 10 Stanhope Gate, Mayfair, London W1K 1AL, United Kingdom
Tel: +44 20/76 59 99 20
Fax: +44 20/76 59 99 21
E-mail: info@aima.org
Internet: http://www.aima.org

Pres.: Christopher FAWCETT
Contacts: Mrs. F. LOMBARD (Exec. Dir.), Miss E. MUGRIDGE (Dir.), Mary RICHARDSON (Regulatory and Legal Associate)

Founded: 1990
General meeting: December
Working languages: E/F
Secretariat: 6 members of staff

Sectors of activity:
- Education.
- Research.
- Lobbying.
- Hedge funds, managed futures funds, managed currency funds, alternative investments.

Information available:
- Special Report on Regulations governing the distribution of Hedge Funds in France, Germany, Switzerland and the UK, 1999, free.
- Benefits of Managed Futures, 2002 (summary, free) M-NM.
- Alternative Investments in the Institutional Portfolio, 1999 (summary: free; full research: £20). M-NM
- AIMA Journal, published 5/ann. (free to members, institutional investors, regulators; £250 per year to subscribers). M-some NM
- "Market Neutral and Hedged Strategies", 2000, £15 per copy. M-some NM
- List of members is not available to the public

AIPCE

EU Fish Processors Association

Association des Industries du Poisson de l'UE

Avenue de Roodebeek 30, 1030 Bruxelles, Belgium

Tel: +32 2/743 87 30
Fax: +32 2/736 81 75
E-mail: aipcee@sia-dvi.be

Pres.: Peder HYLDTOFT
Sec.-Gen.: Michel COENEN
Contacts: Mr. P. COMMERE (1st Vice-Pr.), Mr. M. KELLER (2nd Vice-Pr.)

Founded: 1973
Working languages: E/F
Secretariat: 2 members of staff

Information available:
- White fish, free.
- List of members available to the general public, free.

AISE

International Association of the Soap, Detergent and Maintenance Products Industry

Association Internationale de la Savonnerie, de la Détergence et des Produits d'Entretien

Internationaler Verband der Seifen-, Wasch- , Putz- und Pflegemittelindustrie

Square Marie-Louise 49, 1000 Bruxelles, Belgium
Tel: +32 2/230 83 71
Fax: +32 2/230 82 88
E-mail: aise.main@aise-net.org
Internet: www.aise-net.org

Contact: M. LABBERTON (Dir.)

Founded: 1952
General meeting: June
Working languages: E/F/D
Secretariat: 12 members of staff

Information available:
- Web site: www.washright.com
- List of members, free.

AIUFFASS

International Association of Users of Artificial and Synthetic Filament Yarns and of Natural Silk

Association Internationale des Utilisateurs de Fils de Filaments Artificiels et Synthétiques et de Soie Naturelle

Internationaler Verband der Verarbeiter von Chemiefaser Filament- und Naturseidengamen

Poortakkerstraat 98, 9051 Gent/St. Denijs-Westrem, Belgium
Tel: +32 9/242 98 20
Fax: +32 9/242 98 29
E-mail: pvm@gent.febeltex.be

Sec.-Gen.: P. VAN MOL

Founded: 1954
Working languages: F/E
Secretariat: 1 member of staff

Information available:
- Statistics, M.
- Information letters, M.
- The association works in collaboration with EURATEX.

AMAFE

Association of Manufacturers of Animal-derived Food Enzymes

Association des Fabricants d'Enzymes Alimentaires Dérivés d'Animaux

Vereinigung der Tierischen Nahrungsenzymhersteller

CSK Food Enrichment, PO Box 225, 8901
  BA Leeuwarden, Netherlands
Tel: +31 58/288 52 55
Fax: +31 58/288 06 73
E-mail: vanboven@cskfood.nl

Pres.: P. VISSCHEDIJK
Contact: A. VAN BOVEN

Founded: 1979
General meeting: May 2003
Working languages: E
Secretariat: 1 member of staff

Sectors of activity:
- AMAFE's objectives are to promote contacts between its members and national and international authorities and organisations, and to provide explanations to the public and consumers on health-political and health-legal aspects of the use of natural animal-derived food enzymes.

Information available:
- Circular Letters, M.
- List of members available to the general public, free.

AMFEP

Association of Manufacturers and Formulators of Enzyme Products

Avenue de Roodebeek 30, 1030 Bruxelles,
  Belgium
Tel: +32 2/743 87 30
Fax: +32 2/736 81 75
E-mail: amfep@sia-dvi.be
Internet: http://www.amfep.org

Pres.: H. SCHERES
Sec.-Gen.: M. COENEN
Contact: Karolien DE NEVE (Advisor)

Founded: 1977
General meeting: September
Working languages: E
Secretariat: 3 members of staff

Information available:
- List of members available to the general public, free.

ANAC

European Community Seamen's Associations

Association des Navigants de la Communauté Européenne

Rue Keriagu, 22500 Paimpol Cedex,
  France
Tel: +33 2/96 22 00 95
Fax: +33 2/96 20 72 48
E-mail: anac.france@fnac.net

Pres.: R. COURLAND

Founded: 1987
Working languages: F
Secretariat: 2 members of staff

Sectors of activity:
- Job searching for seamen.
- Maritime and International Documentation Centre.

ANEC

European Association for the Coordination of Consumer Representation in Standardization

Association Européenne pour la Coordination de la Standardisation des Consommateurs

Avenue de Tervuren 36 (4), 1040
  Bruxelles, Belgium
Tel: +32 2/743 24 70
Fax: +32 2/706 54 30
E-mail: g.fabisch@anec.org
Internet: www.anec.org

Pres.: Mrs. FEDERSPIEL
Sec.-Gen.: Mrs. FABISCH

Founded: 1995
General meeting: Spring
Working languages: E
Secretariat: 7 members of staff

Sectors of activity:
Representing consumer interests in standardisation at European level according to priorities:
  - child safety;
  - domestic appliances;
  - traffic safety;
  - environment;
  - design for all;
  - information society.

Information available:
- Documentation including monthly newsletter on webpage, www.anec.org, NM.
- Annual report, NM.
- Comments on policy items, NM.
- Databases: comments, reports, etc.
- List of members available to the general public, free.

AOCFI-Europe

Association of Career Management Consulting Firms International-Europe

Jansweg 40, 2011 KN Haaren,
  Netherlands
Tel: +31 23/553 59 85
Fax: +31 23/553 59 88
E-mail: secretariat@aocfi-europe.com
Internet: http://www.aocfi-europe.com

Pres.: H. MUHLENHOFF
Sec.-Gen.: Ms. A. LEFEVRE

Founded: 1994
General meeting: November
Working languages: E

Information available:
- Database: members' addresses.

APAG

The European Oleochemicals & Allied Products Group

Groupement Européen des Produits Oléochimiques & Associés

Avenue E. Van Nieuwenhuyse 4 Bte 1,
  1160 Bruxelles, Belgium
Tel: +32 2/676 72 55
Fax: +32 2/676 73 01
E-mail: cdc@cefic.be

Pres.: Mrs. C. DE COOMAN
Working languages: E/F

APEAL

Association of European Producers of Steel for Packaging

Association Professionnelle des Producteurs Européens d'Acier pour Emballage

Vereinigung der Europäischen Hersteller von Stahl für Verpackung

Avenue Louise 89, 1050 Bruxelles,
  Belgium
Tel: +32 2/537 91 51
Fax: +32 2/537 86 49
E-mail: info@apeal.be
Internet: http://www.apeal.org
Internet: http://www.steelforpackaging

Pres.: Klaus-Neuhaus WEVER
Contacts: Philippe WOLPER (General
  Manager), R. BATIER (Public Affairs
  Manager)

Founded: 1986
Working languages: E/F/Esp/D
Secretariat: 7 members of staff

Sectors of activity:
- Steel for packaging (cans).
Conference:
- International Congress, Dusseldorf, 2002.

Information available:
- "APEAL News", 3-4 times/year, free, D/E/F/Esp, M-NM.
- Database: contact database based on profession/sector.
- List of members, free.

APFE

European Glass Fibre Producers Association

Association des Producteurs de Fibres de Verre Européens

Europäischer Verband der Glasfaserhersteller

Avenue Louise 89 Box 2, 1050 Bruxelles, Belgium
Tel: +32 2/538 44 46
Tel: +32 477/69 96 74 (GSM)
Fax: +32 2/537 84 69
E-mail: v.favry@cpivglass.be

Pres.: J.H. GAARENSTROOM
Sec.-Gen.: G. MAEYAERT

Founded: 1987
Working languages: E/F
Secretariat: 2 members of staff

Information available:
- List of members available to the general public, free.

API

Association of the Producers of Isoglucose of the EU

Association des Producteurs d'Isoglucose de l'UE

Avenue des Arts, 43, 1000 Bruxelles, Belgium
Tel: +32 2/289 67 60
Fax: +32 2/513 55 92
E-mail: aac@aac-eu.org

Sec.-Gen.: Ms. I. AXIOTIADES
Working languages: E
Secretariat: 5 members of staff

Information available:
- List of members available to the general public.

APME

Association of Plastics Manufacturers in Europe

Avenue Van Nieuwenhuyse 4/3, 1160 Bruxelles, Belgium
Tel: +32 2/676 17 32
Fax: +32 2/675 39 35
E-mail: info.apme@apme.org
Internet: www.apme.org

Pres.: W. PRATORIUS
Contact: Mrs. N. RUSSOTTO (Director General)

Founded: 1976
General meeting: May, December
Working languages: E
Secretariat: 22 members of staff

Sectors of activity:
- IDENTIPLAST: 18-19 April 2005 (International Conference on the automatic identification, sorting and separation of plastics)

Information available:
- For details of APME publications, see APME's web site on www.apme.org.
- Annual report – free – E – M-NM.
- Newsletter: free – E – 3/year – M-NM.
- Database: addresses of members + contacts available on the website.
- List of members, free.
- General information on plastics – M-NM – free.
- For details of APME publications, see APME's web site on http://www.apme.org/literature

APPE

Association of Petrochemical Producers in Europe

Association des Producteurs de Produits Pétroléochimiques en Europe

Verband der Hersteller von Petrochemikalien in Europa

Avenue E. Van Nieuwenhuyse 4, 1160 Bruxelles, Belgium
Tel: +32 2/676 72 11
Fax: +32 2/676 73 00
E-mail: pfe@cefic.be
Internet: www.petrochemistry.net/templates/shwArticles.asp?TID=5&NID=20&AID

Sec.-Gen.: J. AUTIN

AQUA

European Association of Water Meter Manufacturers

Association Européenne des Fabricants de Compteurs d'Eau

Europäische Vereinigung der Hersteller von Wasserzählern

c/o Syndicat de la Mesure, Maison de la Mécanique, Rue Louis Blanc 39-41, 92038 Paris La Défense, France
Tel: +33 1/43 34 76 80/81
Fax: +33 1/43 34 76 82/83
E-mail: aqua@syndicat-mesure.fr
Internet: http://www.syndicat-mesure.fr

Pres.: P. BONNARD
Sec.-Gen.: M. VALITCHEK

Founded: 1959
General meeting: May
Working languages: E

AQUA EUROPA

European Water Conditioning Association

Fédération Européenne du Traitement de l'Eau

Europäische Vereinigung für Wasseraufbereitung

Rue de Louvranges 58, 1325 Dion-Valmont, Belgium
Tel: +32 43/79 26 33
Fax: +32 10/22 56 59
E-mail: henderyckx.aqua@skynet.be

Pres.: L. CHANTRAINE
Sec.-Gen.: Y. HENDERYCKX
Working languages: E

Information available:
- The members' list is available, free of charge.

AREA

Air Conditioning & Refrigeration European Association

Beau Site Première Avenue 88, 1330 Rixensart, Belgium
Tel: +32 2/653 88 35
Fax: +32 2/652 38 72
E-mail: info@area-eur.be
Internet: http://www.area-eur.be

Pres.: N. MITCHELL
Sec.-Gen.: R. BERCKMANS
Contact: R. BERCKMANS (Gen. Del.)

ARGE

The European Federation of Associations of Lock and Builders Hardware Manufacturers

Fédération Européenne des Associations de Fabricants de Serrures et de Ferrures

Arbeitsgemeinschaft der Verbände der Europäischen Schloss- und Beschlagindustrie

PO Box, 4502 Solothurn, Switzerland
Tel: +41 32/621 91 76
Fax: +41 32/621 91 77
E-mail: arge.europe@bluewin.ch
Internet: www.arge.nu

Pres.: Henri MOORE
Sec.-Gen.: Alfred SCHEURER

Founded: 1956
General meeting: September or October
Working languages: F/E/D
Secretariat: 2 members of staff

Information available:
- ARGE Brochure.
- List of manufacturers affiliated to ARGE.
- List of members.

ARTGLACE

Confederation of Associations of Ice-field's Craftsmen of the EC

Confédération des Associations des Artisans Glaciers de la CE

Konföderation der Eishersteller der EG

Via del Parco 3, 32013 Longarone (Belluno), Italy
Tel: +39 0437/577 577
Fax: +39 0437/770 340
E-mail: fiera@longaonefiere.itinfo@artglace.org
Internet: www.artglace.org

Pres.: Mr. G. DE LORENZI
Sec.-Gen.: J.L. GISBERT VALLS

Founded: 1989
General meeting: October/November
Working languages: Esp/It/F
Secretariat: 2 members of staff

Sectors of activity:
• Ice cream.

Information available:
• List of members.

ASERCOM

Association of European Refrigeration Compressor and Controls Manufacturers

Motzstrasse 91, 10779 Berlin, Germany
Tel: +49 30/214 79 872
Fax: +49 30/214 79 871
E-mail: asercomjaw@t-online.de
Internet: www.asercom.org

Pres.: J.A. WINKLER
Contact: H.P. MEURER (Chairman)

Founded: 1992
General meeting: October 2003
Working languages: E
Secretariat: 1 member of staff

Information available:
• Papers of symposia on request.
• Statements on use of various refrigerants on request.
• List of members available via internet: www.asercom.org.

ASPEC

Association of Sorbitol Producers within the EEC

c/o ECCO, Avenue des Gaulois 9, 1040 Bruxelles, Belgium
Tel: +32 2/736 53 54
Fax: +32 2/732 34 27
E-mail: wirkler@asercom.com

Contact: Mr. Michael BELLINGHAM

Founded: 1977
Working languages: E
Secretariat: 2 members of staff

Sectors of activity:
• Production of Sorbitol.

Information available:
• The members' list is available upon written request.

ASSIFONTE

Association de l'Industrie de la Fonte de Fromage de l'UE

Godesberger Allee 157, 53175 Bonn, Germany
Tel: +49 228/959 690
Fax: +49 228/37 15 35
E-mail: hetzner@milchindustrie.de
Internet: www.milchindustrie.de

Sec.-Gen.: E. HETZNER

Founded: 1964
General meeting: July
Working languages: D/E/F

Information available:
• Annual report, D/E/F.

ASSUC

Association of Professional Organizations for the Sugar Trade in EU Countries

Association des Organisations Professionnelles du Commerce des Sucres pour les Pays de l'UE

Vereinigung der Beruflichen Organisationen des Zuckerhandels für die EU Länder

Suare Ambiorix F4/bte 24, 1000 Bruxelles, Belgium
Tel: +32 2/736 79 97
Fax: +32 2/732 67 66
E-mail: sacar@linkline.be
Internet: http://www.sugartraders.co.uk

Pres.: M. LOOMANS
Sec.-Gen.: Mrs. MOMIAS

Founded: 1959
General meeting: May
Working languages: E
Secretariat: 2 members of staff

ASSURRE

Association for the Sustainable Use and Recovery of Resources in Europe

Rue du Luxembourg 19-21, 1200 Bruxelles, Belgium
Tel: +32 2/772 52 52
Fax: +32 2/772 54 19
E-mail: management@assurre.org
Internet: http://www.assurre.org

Contact: W. DUCAN (Man. Dir.)

Founded: 2000
Working languages: E
Secretariat: 3 members of staff

AVEC

Association of Poultry Processors and Poultry Import and Export Trade in the EU

Association des Centres d'Abattage de Volailles et du Commerce d'Importation et d'Exportation de Volailles des Pays de l'UE

Trommesalen 5, 1614 Copenhagen V, Denmark
Tel: +45/33 25 41 00
Fax: +45/33 25 35 52
E-mail: avec@poultry.dk
Internet: http://www.avec.dk

Pres.: J. RISSE
Sec.-Gen.: T. LYSGAARD

Founded: 1966
General meeting: September
Working languages: F/E
Secretariat: 4 members of staff

Information available:
• EU Documents, M.
• Reports, M.
• Statistics, M.
• List of members available to the general public, free.
• Annual report may be obtained through the secretariat

BCME

Beverage Can Makers Europe

Fabricants de Boîtes pour Boissons en Europe

Hersteller von Getränkdosen in Europa

Rue T. Decuyper 284, 1200 Bruxelles, Belgium
Tel: +32 2/761 23 71
Fax: +32 2/761 23 73
E-mail: bobschmitz@compuserve.com
Internet: http://www.bcme.org

Pres.: L. EMILSON
Contact: B. SCHMITZ

Founded: 1990
Working languages: E
Secretariat: 1 member of staff

Sectors of activity:
• To monitor and cooperate on EU and national regulatory issues.
• To establish and maintain databases.
• To promote beverage cans.

Information available:
• List of members available to the general public, free.

BEDA

The Bureau of European Designers' Associations

Bureau des Associations de Designers Européens

Büro der Europäischen Designer-Verbanden

Diagonal 452, 5°, 08006 Barcelona, Spain
Tel: +34 934/15 36 55
Fax: +34 934/15 54 19
E-mail: office@beda.org
Internet: http://www.beda.org

Pres.: F. CARRERA
Contact: Ms. E. VERA-NOBLE

Founded: 1969
Working languages: E
Secretariat: 1 member of staff

Information available:
- Newsletter "BEDA Affairs", every 2-3 months, E, M/NM.
- Database: Register of European designers in the E.U.
- The list of member organisations is available to the public.

BIBM

International Bureau for Precast Concrete

Bureau International du Béton Manufacturé

Internationale Büro der Beton- und Fertigteilindustrie

Voltastraat 12, 1050 Bruxelles, Belgium
Tel: +32 2/738 74 42
Fax: +32 2/734 77 95
E-mail: ar@bibm.org
Internet: http://www.bibm.org

Pres.: W. ZANDBERGEN
Sec.-Gen.: E. DANO
Contact: A. RIMOLDI (Consulting Engineer)

Founded: 1954
General meeting: June–July
Working languages: E/F/D
Secretariat: 2 members of staff

Sectors of activity:
- "18th International Congress of the Precast Concrete Industry", Amsterdam, The Netherlands (May 11th – 14th 2005

Information available:
- "BIBM News", 4-5/year, M, free, E/F/D.
- BIBM report to the annual EU publication "Panorama of EU Industry", (available at: Office des Publications Officielles des Communautés Européennes, L-2985 Luxembourg).
- BIBM Brochure, M-NM, E/F/D.
- Congress Proceedings, M-NM, E/F/D.
- List of members available to the general public, free, see web site.

BIPAR

International Federation of Insurance Intermediaries

Bureau International des Producteurs d'Assurances et de Réassurances

Internationaler Dachverband der Versicherungs- und Ruckversicherungsvermittler

Av. Albert-Elisabeth 40, 1200 Bruxelles, Belgium
Tel: +32 2/735 60 48
Fax: +32 2/732 14 18
E-mail: BIPAR@skynet.be
Internet: www.biparweb.org

Pres.: K. SEDLER
Contact: H. KRAUSS (Dir)

Founded: 1937
Working languages: F/E
Secretariat: 6 members of staff

Sectors of activity:
- Insurance.
- Distribution.
- Europe.

Information available:
- BIPAR Intern (4/year) – E/F, M.
- BIPAR Press, monthly, F/E, M.
- All other documentation available on request, NM.
- Database: General information on the market.

BLIC

European Association of the Rubber Industry

Bureau de Liaison des Industries du Caoutchouc de l'UE

Avenue des Arts 2 Bte 12, 1210 Bruxelles, Belgium
Tel: +32 2/218 49 40
Fax: +32 2/218 61 62
E-mail: info@blic.be
Internet: www.blic.be

Sec.-Gen.: Mrs. F. CINARALP

Founded: 1959
Working languages: E
Secretariat: 4 members of staff

Information available:
- List of members, free of charge.

CAEF

The European Foundry Association

Sohnstrasse 70, Postfach 10 19 61, 40237 Düsseldorf, Germany
Tel: +49 211/68 71 215
Fax: +49 211/68 71 205
E-mail: info@caef-eurofoundry.org
Internet: http://www.caef-eurofoundry.org

Pres.: Theo LAMMERS
Sec.-Gen.: K. URBAT

Founded: 1953
General meeting: May–June
Working languages: E

Historical note:
- CAEF represents 20 national associations, thereof Czech Republic as associated.

Sectors of activity:
- Vocational training.
- Environment.
- Quality, Warranty and Liability.
- Business Administration.
- Statistics.
Conference:
- International Foundry Forum (IFF), 17-18/06/2004 Stresa, Italy.

Information available:
- Annual statistical document giving production in Member States and EFTA Countries – F/E/D – M-NM.
- Glossary – Technical Terms – M-NM. For list of members see website.

CAFIM

Federation of the Musical Instruments Manufacturers Associations in the European Community

Confédération des Associations des Facteurs d'Instruments de Musique de la CEE

Vereinigung der Musikinstrumenten-Herstellerverbande in der EG

Tennelbachstrasse 25, 65193 Wiesbaden, Germany
Tel: +49 611/95 45 886
Fax: +49 611/95 45 885
E-mail: info@cafim.org

Pres.: G. A. MEINL

CAMME

Committee of Apparel Machinery Manufacturers in Europe

c/o VDMA, Richard Strauss Strasse 56/III, 81677 München, Germany
Tel: +49 89/27 82 87-50
Fax: +49 89/27 82 87-22
E-mail: bul@vdma.org

Sec.-Gen.: E. STRAUB
Working languages: D/E

CANDLES / BOUGIES ET CIERGES

Association of European Candle Manufacturers

Association Européenne des Syndicats de Fabricants de Bougies et de Cierges

Europäische Vereinigung der Verbände der Kerzenhersteller

Avenue Achille Peretti 118, 92200 Neuilly sur Seine, France
Tel: +33 1/46 37 23 01
Fax: +33 1/46 37 15 60
E-mail: bougies@fncg.fr
Internet: http://www.europecandles.com

Pres.: M. O'CARROLL
Sec.-Gen.: J.C. BARSACQ
Working languages: E/F

Information available:
- The members' list is available, free of charge.
- "Annual Report", free.

CAOBISCO

Association of the Chocolate-, Biscuit- and Confectionery Industries of the UE

Association des Industries de la Chocolaterie, Biscuiterie-Biscotterie et Confiserie de l'UE

Rue Defacqz 1, 1000 Bruxelles, Belgium
Tel: +32 2/539 18 00
Fax: +32 2/539 15 75
E-mail: caobisco@caobisco.be

Pres.: H. RYSGAARD

Founded: 1959
General meeting: June
Working languages: F/E
Secretariat: 8 members of staff

Information available:
- Statistical monography – annual – M-NM.

CAPIEL

Coordinating Committee for the Associations of Manufacturers of Industrial Electrical Switchgear and Controlgear in the European Union

Comité de Coordination des Associations de Constructeurs d'Appareillage Industriel Electrique de l'Union Européenne

Koordinierendes Komitee der Fachverbände der Schaltgerätehersteller in der Europäischen Union

Sercobe, Principe de Vergara 74, 28006 Madrid, Spain
Tel: +34 94/11 51 15
Fax: +34 95/62 19 22
E-mail: g_eisenberg@terra.es

Sec.-Gen.: N. ASSAF

Founded: 1959
Working languages: D/F/E

CARTOON

European Association of Animation Film

Association Européenne du Film d'Animation

Europäische Vereinigung des Zeichentrickfilms

Bd Lambermont 314, 1030 Bruxelles, Belgium
Tel: +32 2/245 12 00
Fax: +32 2/245 46 89
E-mail: info@cartoon.skynet.be
Internet: http://www.cartoon-media.be

Pres.: B. BALSER
Contacts: Mrs. C. JENART, M. VANDEWEYER

Founded: 1988
General meeting: June
Working languages: F/E
Secretariat: 9 members of staff

Sectors of activity:
- Cartoon Forum, September.
- Cartoon Movie, March.
- Cartoon Masters, November, April, June.

Information available:
- Databases, M-NM.
- Technical Bible, 100 EUR, M-NM.
- "Lay Out", 30 EUR, M-NM.
- "Story-Board", 30 EUR, M-NM.
- Information on the web site: www.cartoon-media.be
- Databases: details of companies and professionals working in the field of European animation.

CBMC

The Brewers of Europe
Les Brasseurs Européens
Die Europäischen Brauer

Rue Caroly 23-25, 1050 Bruxelles, Belgium
Tel: +32 2/672 23 92
Fax: +32 2/660 94 02
E-mail: info@brewersofeurope.org
Internet: http://www.cbmc.org

Pres.: P. PERRON
Sec.-Gen.: R. de LOOZ-CORSWAREM

Founded: 1958
Working languages: E/F/D
Secretariat: 7 members of staff

Information available:
- Statistical brochure on production, consumption, import, export, excises.
- CBMC Statistics, annual, F/E/D.
- List of members available to the general public, free.

CCACE

Coordination Committee of European Cooperative Associations

Comité de Coordination des Associations Coopératives Européennes

Koordinierung der Europäischen Genossenschaftsverbande

Rue Guillaume Tell 59, 1060 Bruxelles, Belgium

Tel: +32 2/543 10 43
Fax: +32 2/543 10 45
E-mail: cecop@cecop.org
Internet: http://www.ccace.org

Pres.: M. CAMPLI
Contact: R. SCHLUTER (Exec. Dir)

CCA-EUROPE

Calcium Carbonate Association – Europe

Bd S. Dupuis 233 bt124, 1070 Bruxelles, Belgium
Tel: +32 2/524 55 00
Fax: +32 2/524 45 75
E-mail: secretariat@ima-eu.org
Internet: http://www.ima-eu.org/cca.html

Sec.-Gen.: M. WYART-REMY

Founded: 1995
Working languages: F/E
Secretariat: 5 members of staff

Sectors of activity:
- Health and safety.
- Environment.

CCBE

Council of the Bars and Law Societies of the European Union

Conseil des Barreaux de l'Union Européenne

Rat der Anwaltschaften der Europäischen Union

1, Avenue de la Joyeuse entrée, 1040 Bruxelles, Belgium
Tel: +32 2/234 65 10
Fax: +32 2/234 65 11
E-mail: ccbe@ccbe.org
Internet: www.ccbe.org

Pres.: H-J HELLWIG
Sec.-Gen.: J. GOLDSMITH

Founded: 1960
General meeting: Twice a year (November and May).
Working languages: F/E
Secretariat: 10 members of staff

Sectors of activity:
- The CCBE's principal object is to study all questions affecting the legal profession in the Member States and to formulate solutions designed to coordinate and harmonise professional practice.

Information available:
- "Newsletter", E/F, M-NM.
- List of information offices available on request, M-NM.
- Leaflet "What is the CCBE", F/E, M-NM.
- Code of Conduct, M-NM.
- Practical guide for the application of Community law, F.

- Guide to Legal Aid and Advice in the European Economic Area, E, M-NM

CEA

Comité Européen des Assurances

Rue de la Chaussée d'Antin 3 bis, 75009 Paris, France
Tel: +33 1/44 83 11 74
Fax: +33 1/47 70 03 75
E-mail: caudet@cea.assur.org
Internet: http://www.cea.assur.org

Delegation in Brussels:
Square de Meeûs 29
B-1000 Bruxelles
Tel: +32 2/547 58 11
Fax: +32 2/547 58 19

Pres.: G. SWALEF
Sec.-Gen.: D. SCHANTE

Founded: 1953
Working languages: F/E/D
Secretariat: 28 members of staff

Sectors of activity:
- To represent European insurers:
  – promoting, defending and illustrating views within international bodies;
  – giving qualified opinions to public or private European and international organisations involved in insurance or reinsurance.

Information available:
- "CEA INFO – Special Issues", F/E/D, M-NM.
- "CEA ECO", F/E/D, M-NM.
- "Annual Report", F/E/D.
- Documentation service, free, M-NM.
- Databases: CEA circulars and documentation, studies, etc., for members only.
- List of members available to the general public, free.

CEAB

European Confederation of Property Managers
Confédération Européenne des Administrateurs de Biens
Europäische Konföderation der Immobilienmakler

Avenue de Tervuren 36 bte 2, 1040 Bruxelles, Belgium
Tel: +32 2/735 49 90
Fax: +32 2/735 99 88
E-mail: cepi@cepi.be
Internet: www.cepi.be

Pres.: F. BURGERING
Sec.-Gen.: M. AUNOLA
Contact: Mrs. M. VAN ADORP

Founded: 1989
General meeting: February and October.
Working languages: E/F
Secretariat: 1 member of staff

Sectors of activity:
- Monitoring of existing or upcoming legislation or regulations likely to have a direct or indirect influence on matters relating to property, property management, administration, valuation and negotiation. Information as well as training for members.

Information available:
- "CEPI Info", 6 times/year, via internet.
- List of members.

CEBP

European Confederation of National Bakery and Confectionery Organizations
Confédération Européenne des Organisations Nationales de la Boulangerie et de la Pâtisserie

Bd Louis Mettewie 83 bte 42, 1080 Bruxelles, Belgium
Tel: +32 2/469 20 00
Fax: +32 2/469 21 40
E-mail: admin@cebp.be
Internet: http://www.bakeruib.org

Contact: Mr. CLAES

Founded: 1992
Working languages: F/E
Secretariat: 1 member of staff

Information available:
- List of members.
- Notes – Newsletters, M.

CEC

Confédération Européenne des Cadres

Rue de la Loi 81A, 1040 Bruxelles, Belgium
Tel: +32 2/420 10 51
Fax: +32 2/420 12 92
E-mail: info@cec-managers.org
Internet: www.cec-managers.org

Pres.: M. ANGELO
Sec.-Gen.: C. CAMBUS

Founded: 1989
Working languages: F/E
Secretariat: 3 members of staff

Information available:
- Newsletter, 4/year, E/F, free of charge.
- CEC Brochure, free of charge.
- List of members, free of charge.

CEC

European Confederation of the Footwear Industry
Confédération Européenne de l'Industrie de la Chaussure

Europäische Konföderation der Schuhindustrie

Rue F. Bossaerts 53, 1030 Bruxelles, Belgium
Tel: +32 2/736 58 10
Fax: +32 2/736 12 76
E-mail: cec@vidac.be
Internet: http://www.cecshoe.be

Pres.: A. BROTINI
Contact: R. SMETS

Founded: 1981
General meeting: May – October
Working languages: E/F
Secretariat: 5 members of staff

Sectors of activity:
- World Footwear Congress – Brussels – 3/4/5 April 2005: www.worldfootwearcongress.com

Information available:
- Statistics, M-NM.
- List of members on website.
- CD-ROM Efnet Congress €30

CECA

Committee of European Coffee Associations

Tourniairestraat 3, PO Box 90 445, 1065 BK Amsterdam, Netherlands
Tel: +31 20 511 38 58
Fax: +31 20 511 38 10
E-mail: ceca@coffee-associations.org

Pres.: P. INSTALLE
Sec.-Gen.: Mrs. C.G. KRIETEMEIJER

CECAPI

European Committee of Electrical Installation Equipment Manufacturers
Comité Européen des Constructeurs d'Appareillage Electrique d'Installation

Avenue de la Joyeuse Entrée 1, 1040 Bruxelles, Belgium
Tel: +32 2/286 12 34
Fax: +32 2/230 69 08
E-mail: cecapi@skynet.be

Sec.-Gen.: R. SCHILLING

CECCM

Confederation of European Community Cigarette Manufacturers
Confédération des Fabricants de Cigarettes de la Communauté Européenne

Avenue Louise 125, 1050 Bruxelles, Belgium
Tel: +32 2/541 00 41
Fax: +32 2/541 00 45
E-mail: ceccm@ceccm.be

CECE

Committee for European Construction Equipment

Comité Européen des Matériels de Génie Civil

Europäisches Baumaschinen Komitee

Boulevard Reyers 80, 1030 Bruxelles, Belgium
Tel: +32 2/706 82 25
Fax: +32 2/706 82 29
E-mail: cece@skynet.be
Internet: http://www.cece-eu.org

Pres.: Mr. ARGHIMENTI
Contact: R. WEZEL

Founded: 1959
General meeting: October
Working languages: E
Secretariat: 2 members of staff

Sectors of activity:
- Main activities:
- Harmonisation of national regulations to remove technical barriers to trade in collaboration with the EC.
- Promotion of international standards and safety regulations in co-operation with ISO and CEN (European Standardisation).
- Development of test procedures and nomenclatures.
- Product liability.
- Organisation of market trend seminars, press conferences.
- Analysing international competition.
- CECE gives patronage to the following European construction equipment exhibitions: INTERMAT (F), BAUMA (D), SAMOTER (It), and SMOPYC (E).

Information available:
- Leaflet:
  – information on members – every 2 years – free – E – M-NM.
  – statistics – yearly – free – E – M.
- European standards for construction equipment – M-NM – £5.
- Illustrated terminologies for different construction equipment – E.
- List of members, free.

CECED

Federation of European Manufacturers of Domestic Appliances

Conseil Européen des Constructeurs d'Appareils Ménagers

Bd. Auguste Reyers 80, 1030 Bruxelles, Belgium
Tel: +32 2/706 82 90
Fax: +32 2/706 82 89
E-mail: secretariat@ceced.be
Internet: http://www.ceced.org

Sec.-Gen.: L. MELI

Founded: 1959
General meeting: June
Working languages: E
Secretariat: 2 members of staff

Information available:
- List of members – free.

CECIMO

European Committee for Co-operation of the Machine Tools Industries

Comité Européen de Coopération des Industries de la Machine-Outil

Europäisches Komitee für die Zusammenarbeit der Werkzeugmaschinenindustrien

Avenue Louise 66, 1050 Bruxelles, Belgium
Tel: +32 2/502 70 90
Fax: +32 2/502 60 82
E-mail: info@cecimo.be
Internet: http://www.cecimo.be

Pres.: K. BAILEY
Sec.-Gen.: R. GROOTHEDDE

Founded: 1950
Working languages: F/E/D/It/Esp/Nl
Secretariat: 5 members of staff

Sectors of activity:
- Patronage of European machine-tool exhibitions, drawing participants from throughout the world.

Information available:
- "Directory of European Machine Tools", NM, E.
- "International Statistics", E, NM.
- List of members available to the general public, free.

CECIP

European Committee of Scale and Weighing Machines Manufacturers

Comité Européen des Constructeurs d'Instruments de Pesage

Europäisches Komitee der Hersteller von Waagenapparaturen

Domaine d'Armainvilliers, Impasse François Coli 4, 77330 Ozoir la Ferrière, France
Tel: +33 1/60 02 89 58
Fax: +33 1/60 02 89 58
E-mail: turpain.cecip@wanadoo.fr
Internet: www.cecip.de

Pres.: David CASTLE
Contact: Michel TURPAIN

Founded: 1959
General meeting: May
Working languages: F/E
Secretariat: 1 member of staff

Information available:
- List of members available to the public – free.

CECOD

Committee of European Manufacturers of Petroleum Measuring and Distributing Equipment

Comité des Fabricants Européens d'Installation et de Distribution de Pétrole

Komitee der Europäischen Hersteller von Einrichtungen zur Messung und Verteilung von Flüssigen Brennstoffen

Maison de la Mécanique, 39-41 Rue Louis Blanc, 92038 Paris La Défense Cedex, France
Tel: +33 1/43 34 76 80
Tel: +33 1/43 34 76 81
Fax: +33 1/43 34 76 82
Fax: +33 1/43 34 76 83
E-mail: cecod@syndicat-mesure.fr
Internet: http://www.syndicat-mesure.fr/acceuil.htm

Pres.: M. DELL OMO
Sec.-Gen.: M. VALITCHEK

Founded: 1969
General meeting: May
Working languages: E

CECODE

European Retail Trade Centre

Centre Européen du Commerce de Détail

Zentrum des Europäischen Einzelhandels

Gothaer Allée 2, 50969 Köln, Germany
Tel: +49 221/93655 – 770/771
Fax: +49 221/93655 – 779
E-mail: nzilat.hde@einzelhandel.de
Internet: www.bbeberatung.com
Internet: www.einzelhandel.de

Pres.: J. DEMESMACRE
Contact: H. KRÜGER
Working languages: F/D
Secretariat: 2 members of staff

Information available:
- Newsletters, M.

CECOF

European Committee of Industrial Furnace and Heating Equipment Manufacturers

Comité Européen des Constructeurs de Fours et d'Equipements Thermiques Industriels

Europäisches Komitee der Hersteller von Industrieöfen und Industrie-Wärmeanlagen

Lyoner Strasse 18, 60528 Frankfurt am
  Main, Germany
Tel: +49 69/66 03 12 78
Fax: +49 69/66 03 16 92
E-mail: cecof@vdma.org
Internet: http://www.cecof.org

Pres.: M. DEBIER
Sec.-Gen.: Dr. G. HABIG

Founded: 1972
Working languages: F/E/D

Information available:
- The members' list is available free of
  charge.

CECOMAF

**European Committee of
  Manufacturers of Refrigeration
  Equipment**

**Comité Européen des Constructeurs
  de Matériel Frigorifique**

Boulevard Reyers 80, 1030 Bruxelles,
  Belgium
Tel: +32 2/706 79 85
Fax: +32 2/706 79 66
E-mail: info@eurovent-cecomaf.org
Internet: http://www.eurovent
  -cecomaf.org

Contact: M. VAN DER HORST

Founded: 1956

CECOP

**European Confederation of Workers'
  Co-operatives, Social Co-
  operatives and Participative
  Enterprises**

**Confédération Européenne des
  Coopératives de Production et de
  Travail Associé, des Coopératives
  Sociales et des Entreprises
  Participatives**

Rue Guillaume Tell 59 B, 1060 Bruxelles,
  Belgium
Tel: +32 2/543 10 33
Fax: +32 2/543 10 37
E-mail: cecop@cecop.org
Internet: www.cecop.org

Pres.: F. SCALVINI
Contact: R. SCHLUTER

Founded: 1979
Working languages: F/E/It
Secretariat: 3 members of staff

Sectors of activity:
- Organisation of training and
  information seminars.
- Promotion of workers' co-operative
  systems.
- Management of members'
  transnational projects.

Information available:
- Brochure presenting CECOP's
  activities, F/E/It, free, M-NM.

- Press releases.
- Database: ARIES, EIC.
- List of members, free.

CECRA

**European Council for Motor Trades
  and Repairs**

**Conseil Européen du Commerce et
  de la Réparation Automobiles**

**Europäischer Verband des
  Kraftfahrzeuggewerbes**

Boulevard de la Woluwe 46 Bte 17, 1200
  Bruxelles, Belgium
Tel: +32 2/771 96 56
Fax: +32 2/772 65 67
E-mail: mail@cecra.org
Internet: http://www.cecra.org

Pres.: J. CREUTZIG
Sec.-Gen.: Ms. R. SOETAERT

Founded: 1983
General meeting: January/September
Working languages: E/F
Secretariat: 2 members of staff

Information available:
- List of members.

CECT

**European Committee of Boiler,
  Vessel and Pipework
  Manufacturers**

**Comité Européen de la
  Chaudronnerie et de la Tuyauterie**

**Europäisches Komitee für
  Dampfkessel- Behälter- und
  Rohrleitungsbau**

c/o SNCT, Maison de la Mécanique, Rue
  Louis Blanc 39-41, 92038 Courbevoie,
  France
Tel: +33 1/47 17 62 71
Fax: +33 1/47 17 62 77

Pres.: J.L. TISSOT
Sec.-Gen.: Mrs. BARON
General meeting: October
Working languages: E

Information available:
- "CECT Directory", F/E.
- List of member associations, F/E.
- Composition of the different
  departments of the CECT, F/E.

CED

**European Hardware Trade
  Confederation**

**Confédération Européenne de la
  Droguerie**

**Konföderation der Europäischen
  Drogistenverbänd**

Vogelsanger Strasse 165, PO Box 301413,
  50784 Köln, Germany

Tel: +49 221/95 29 17-0
Fax: +49 221/95 29 17-20
E-mail: bsv-vdd@einzelhandel.de
Internet: http://
  www.drogistenverband.de

Pres.: G. FISCHLER
Sec.-Gen.: C. KNOBLICH
Working languages: F/D/E/Nl

Information available:
- CED-information (Info-Service), M.
- Working party reports for the CED
  and by the CED for Member States, M.

CEDEC

**European Confederation of Local
  Public Energy Distribution
  Companies**

**Confédération Européenne des
  Distributeurs d'Energie Publics
  Communaux**

**Europäischer Dachverband der
  Öffentlichen Kommunalen
  Energieversorgungsunternehmen**

Rue Royale 55b – 10, 1000 Bruxelles,
  Belgium
Tel: +32 2/217 81 17
Tel: +32 2/218 86 40
Fax: +32 2/219 20 56
E-mail: melanie.zylverberg@cedec.com
Internet: http://www.cedec.com

Pres.: A. DIEGENANT
Contact: G. DE BLOCK (Secr.)

Founded: 1992
Working languages: F/E/D

CEDI

**European Confederation of
  Independents**

**Confédération Européenne des
  Indépendants**

**Europaverband der Selbständigen-
  CEDI**

Hüttenbergstrasse 38-40, 66538
  Neunkirchen, Germany
Tel: +49 6821/30 62 40
Fax: +49 6821/30 62 41
E-mail: info@bvd-cedi.de
Internet: http://www.bvd-cedi.de

Pres.: Pedro FERNANDES
Sec.-Gen.: H.D. SCHAEFER

Founded: 1973
Working languages: F/D/It
Secretariat: 15 members of staff

Information available:
- "Gewerbe Report", D, monthly.
- "De Zelfstandige – L'indépendant",
  fortnightly, F/Nl.
- "La Tribune des Indépendants", F.
- "Il Mercurio", It.
- "CEDI-Info", quarterly, F.

- Database: addresses, information, …
- Database: members' addresses – contacts.

CEDIP

European Committee of Professional Diving Instructors

Syndicat Européen des Moniteurs de Plongée Professionnels

Europäischer Verband der Berufstauchlehrer

Avenue des Pins du Cap 62, 06160 Antibes – Juan les Pins, France
Tel: +33 4/93 61 45 45
Fax: +33 4/93 67 34 93
E-mail: cedip.antibes@wanadoo.fr
Internet: www.cedip.org

Pres.: D. MERCIER
Sec.-Gen.: Valérie HOUCHARD

Founded: 1993
General meeting: March
Working languages: F/E
Secretariat: 1 member of staff

Sectors of activity:
- Underwater diving

Information available:
- Information brochures, M-NM.
- Participation at numerous fairs (Antibes, Paris, Düsseldorf, Rome, Belgrade, Moscow, Kiev, Montenegro, …).
Database:
- List of members available to the general public, free, available on website.
- List of certified divers. For private archives only.
- Database cannot be purchased.

CEDT

Confédération Européenne des Détaillants en Tabac

Rue Montoyer 31, 1000 Brussels, Belgium
Tel: +32 2/772 13 05
Fax: +32 2/772 44 01
E-mail: cedt@skynet.be

Pres.: M. J. Fernandez VICARIO
Sec.-Gen.: G. RISSO
Contact: M. SPERANZA

Founded: 1970
General meeting: March
Working languages: F/E
Secretariat: 3 members of staff

Information available:
- List of members available to the general public, free.

CEEC

The European Committee of Construction Economists

Comité Européen des Economistes de la Construction

Europäischer Ausschuss der Bauwirtschaftler

Avenue Percier 8, 75008 Paris, France
Tel: +44 20/7334 3877
Fax: +44 20/7334 3844
E-mail: john.frewen-lord@pgcn.net
Internet: http://www.ceec.org

Pres.: M. WEBB (Ireland)
Sec.-Gen.: C. DEPREZ (Belgique)
Contact: Ms. L. MARCOULY (England)

Founded: 1979
General meeting: 2 general meetings per year
Working languages: E/F
Secretariat: 1 member of staff

Sectors of activity:
- Involved in a project of European Training/Network of Construction Economists with European Funding (Leonardo).

Information available:
- Database: records of meetings.
- List of members available to the general public, free.

CEEP

European Centre for Enterprises with Public Participation and of Enterprises of General Economic Interest

Centre Européen des Entreprises à Participation Publique et des Entreprises d'Intérêt Economique Général

Rue de la Charité 15 Bte 12, 1210 Bruxelles, Belgium
Tel: +32 2/219 27 98
Fax: +32 2/218 12 13
E-mail: ceep@ceep.org
Internet: www.ceep.org

Pres.: J. CRAVINHO
Sec.-Gen.: R. PLASSMANN
Contact: Inge REICHERT (Director)

Founded: 1961
General meeting: 4 meetings a year
Working languages: F/E/D
Secretariat: 7 members of staff

Sectors of activity:
Social European partner with ETUC and UNICE.
The aim of the Centre is:
- to study the to study the situation and problems of public undertakings as such faced with the development of European organisations;
- to organise congresses, in principle every three years. Participation is open to interested scientists and

personnel from government and Community administrations.

Information available:
- "Actes du Congrès", every 3 years, F.
- "Annales du CEEP", every 3 years.
- List of members on web site.

CEEREAL

European Breakfast Cereal Association

Rond Point Schuman 9 Bte 11, 1040 Bruxelles, Belgium
Tel: +32 2/230 43 54
Fax: +32 2/230 94 93
E-mail: v.hees@verbaende-hees.de

Contact: W. HEES

Founded: 1992
Working languages: E
Secretariat: 2 members of staff

Sectors of activity:
- EU matters.
- CAP.
- Food law.
- External trade.

Information available:
- The members' list is available, free of charge.

CEETB

European Technical Contractors Committee for the Construction Industry

Comité Européen des Equipements Techniques du Bâtiment

Europäischer Verband der Technischen Gebäudeausrüstung

Rue Jacques de Lalaing 4, 1040 Bruxelles, Belgium
Tel: +32 2/285 07 27
Fax: +32 2/230 78 61
Internet: www.ceetb.org

Pres.: John R. HARROWER
Sec.-Gen.: O. LOEBEL

Founded: 1976
General meeting: November
Working languages: F/E
Secretariat: 1 member of staff

Sectors of activity:
- Construction.
- Technical building equipment.
- Energy efficiency.

Information available:
- "Recommendations on sub-contracting" – F/E/Nl/D/It/Esp/Dan – free – M-NM.
- Annual report, free, M-NM.
- "Regular Inspection and Maintenance of Technical Building Equipment", free, M-NM, E.
- List of members, free.

CEETTAR

European Confederation of Technical Agricultural and Rural Contractors

Confédération Européenne des Entrepreneurs de Travaux Techniques Agricoles et Ruraux

Europäische Konföderation der Technischen, Landwirtschaftlichen und Ländlichen Unternehmen

Centre d'entreprise DANSAERT, Rue d'Alost 7, 1000 Bruxelles, Belgium
Tel: +32 2/213 38 74
Fax: +32 2/213 36 37
E-mail: ceettar.europe@skynet.be

Pres.: R. SABATHIE
Sec.-Gen.: J. MARIS

Founded: 1963
General meeting: February
Working languages: E/F
Secretariat: 1 member of staff

Sectors of activity:
- Rural and agricultural contracting activities.

Information available:
- The members' list is available, free of charge.

CEEV

Comité Européen des Entreprises Vins

Avenue des Arts 43, 1040 Bruxelles, Belgium
Tel: +32 2/230 99 70
Fax: +32 2/513 02 18
E-mail: ceev@ceev.be

Pres.: G. SANDEMAN
Contact: Mrs. M. WOLFERS

Founded: 1959
Working languages: F
Secretariat: 3 members of staff

CEFACD

European Committee of Manufacturers of Domestic Heating and Cooking Appliances

Comité Européen des Fabricants d'Appareils de Chauffage et de Cuisine Domestique

Europäischer Auschuss der Heiz- und Kochgeräte Industrie

c/o Agoria, Boulevard Reyers 80, 1030 Bruxelles, Belgium
Tel: +32 2/706 79 61
Fax: +32 2/706 79 66
E-mail: françois-xavier.belpaire@agoria.be

Internet: http://www.agoria.be

Pres.: C. BERLAIMONT
Contact: F.X. BELPAIRE

Founded: 1952
Working languages: F/E/D

CEFIC

European Chemical Industry Council

Conseil Européen de l'Industrie Chimique

Europäischer Rat der Chemischen Industrie

Av. E. Van Nieuwenhuyse 4 Bte 1, 1160 Bruxelles, Belgium
Tel: +32 2/676 72 11
Fax: +32 2/676 73 00
E-mail: mail@cefic.be
Internet: http://www.cefic.org

Pres.: E. VOSCHERAU

Founded: 1972
General meeting: June
Working languages: E
Secretariat: 100 members of staff

Sectors of activity:
- CEFIC is the representative organization of the Western European Chemical Industry – an industry which employs over two million people and produces 30% of the world's chemicals.
- Located in Brussels, CEFIC is the forum in which the European Chemical Industry coordinates its positions and prepares its approaches to the international bodies and authorities which influence its business environment.
- Issues tackled by CEFIC on its members' behalf cover international trade, environmental matters, health, safety, transport and distribution of chemicals, energy and raw material supplies, information and statistical surveys and many other fields of interest to the European Chemical Industry.
- Through the importance of the industry it represents, its work and the standing it has achieved, CEFIC is now an integral part of the consultative machinery of many international organizations

Information available:
- "CEFIC Annual Report".
- "Facts and Figures", annual.
- List of publications upon request (position papers, brochures, etc.).
- The members' list is available, free of charge.

CEFS

European Committee for Sugar Manufacturers

Comité Européen des Fabricants de Sucre

Avenue de Tervueren 182, 1150 Bruxelles, Belgium
Tel: +32 2/762 07 60
Fax: +32 2/771 00 26
E-mail: info@cefs.org
Internet: http://www.cefs.org

Pres.: J. MARIHART
Contact: J.-L. BARJOL

Founded: 1954
General meeting: June
Working languages: F/E/D
Secretariat: 9 members of staff

Information available:
- Statistical directory, annual, free.
- Database: scientific and institutional.
- All official texts.

CEHP / UEHP

European Committee of Private Hospitals and European Union of Independent Hospitals

Comité Européen de l'Hospitalisation Privée et Union Européenne de l'Hospitalisation Privée

Office: Avenue A. Solvay 5 Bte 3, 1179 Brussels, Belgium
Tel: +32 2/660 35 50
Fax: +32 2/672 90 62
E-mail: genevieve.robin@skynet.be
Internet: http://www.uehp.org

Pres.: Mrs. SCIACHI
Contact: H. ANRYS (Del. Gen.)

Headquarters:
Via Lucrezio Caro 67
I-00192 Roma
Tel: +39 06/321 56 53
Fax: +39 06/321 57 03
Mrs. SCIACCHI (SG)
Mrs. ALBERTA

Founded: 1991
General meeting: February
Working languages: F/E/It/D
Secretariat: 1 member of staff

Sectors of activity:
- Studying and defending the best conditions for independent hospitals' management.
- Collaborating in the preparation of the free establishment of health-care institutions in Europe and the EU.

Information available:
- "Annual report".
- Database on hospital statistics in preparation.
- List of members available to the general public, free.

CEI

European Confederation of Estate Agents

Confédération Européenne de l'Immobilier

Sainctelettesquare 11/12, 1000
Bruxelles, Belgium
Tel: +32 2/219 40 08
Fax: +32 2/217 88 41
E-mail: cei@web-cei.com
Internet: http://www.web-cei.com

Pres.: André GROOT
Sec.-Gen.: I. TONGE
Contact: Ph. RUELENS

Founded: 1988
General meeting: January–February
Working languages: E/F

Historical note:
- 14 leading estate agent associations working together to protect members' interests in Europe.

Sectors of activity:
- Harmonisation of estate agency in Europe. Conference: Congress, 3rd February 2005, Brussels

Information available:
- Database: list of members, M, €300

CEI-BOIS

European Confederation of Woodworking Industries

Confédération Européenne des Industries du Bois

Zentralverband der Europäischen Holzindustrie

Hof-Ter-Vleestdreef 5, boîte 4, 1070
Bruxelles, Belgium
Tel: +32 2/556 25 85
Fax: +32 2/556 25 95
E-mail: info@cei-bois.org
Internet: www.cei-bois.org

Pres.: B. BORGSTRÖM
Sec.-Gen.: Filip DE JAEGER

Founded: 1952
General meeting: March and November
Working languages: F/E/D
Secretariat: 3 members of staff

Sectors of activity:
- Representation of the European woodworking industries before supranational authorities.

Information available:
- "Technical documents", M.
- The members' list is available, free of charge.
- List of members available, free, see also the website.
- CD-ROM: "Roadmap 2010", free, see also the website

CEIR

European Committee for the Valve Industry

Comité Européen de l'Industrie de la Robinetterie

Europäisches Komitee der Armaturenindustrie

c/o Orgalime, Boulevard Reyers 80, 1030
Bruxelles, Belgium
Tel: +32 2/706 82 35
Fax: +32 2/706 82 50
E-mail: l.platteur@marketseurope.eu.-com
Internet: http://www.ceir-online.org

Contact: G. Van DOORSLAER

Founded: 1959
Working languages: E

Information available:
- Status of CEIR, F/E/D.
- "Valves from Europe", bi-annual.
- List of member associations, F/E/D.

CEJA

European Council of Young Farmers

Conseil Européen des Jeunes Agriculteurs

Europäischer Rat der Junglandwirte

Rue de la Science 23-25 Bte 11, 1040
Bruxelles, Belgium
Tel: +32 2/230 42 10
Fax: +32 2/280 18 05
E-mail: ceja@ceja.be
Internet: www.ceja.org

Pres.: H.-B. WICHERT
Sec.-Gen.: Mrs. H. CHRISTENSEN

Founded: 1958
General meeting: January or February
Working languages: D/E/Esp/F/It

Sectors of activity:
- Promoting the development of agriculture and of rural areas in the EU.
- Promoting the vocational training of young farmers.
- Education of children of young farmers.
- To develop relations between young farmers of EU and CEEC countries: seminars, training, youth exchange, agriculture.

Information available:
- The members' list is available, free of charge.
- Activity Report.
- Press Release.
- Information brochure for young farmers.
- Directory of organisations which offer services to women in the rural environment, available on internet.
- Study of the prices of agricultural inputs in the EU.

CEJH

European Community of Young Horticulturists

Communauté Européenne des Jeunes de l'Horticulture

Europäische Gemeinschaft der Jungen Gartenbauer

Giessener Strasse 47, 35305 Grünberg,
Germany
Tel: +49 6401/910 150
Fax: +49 6401/910 176
E-mail: info@cejh.org
Internet: http://www.cejh.org

Pres.: K. SCHNAIDT
Contact: Mrs. N. BECKER

Founded: 1965
General meeting: July
Working languages: E
Secretariat: 1 member of staff

Sectors of activity:
- CEJH helps young gardeners to find jobs in other countries.
Conferences:
- The CEJH organises congresses, meetings, study days and seminars for young horticulturists.

Information available:
- Minutes of the CEJH General Meeting, yearly, free, E.
- "Grow Young", twice a year, E, free.
- List of members.

CELCAA

Comité Européen de Liaison des Commerces Agro-alimentaires

Rond Point Schuman 9 – Bte 4, 1040
Bruxelles, Belgium
Tel: +32 2/230 99 70
Fax: +32 2/230 43 23
E-mail: celcaa@schuman9.com

Pres.: M. ROUGE
Contact: Mme WOLFERS

Founded: 1979
Working languages: E/F
Secretariat: 3 members of staff

Sectors of activity:
- Promotes scientific research and technical progress in this professional sector, notably through the exchange of ideas and experiences as well as of all documentation on horizontal agri-foodstuffs issues of interest to the trade;
- defend and to promote (horizontally) the commercial function of agri-foodstuffs and to coordinate the action of the member organisations and represent its members vis-a-vis the bodies of the European Community, without however undermining the specific competence of the member organisations.

The Liaison Committee shall examine all issues likely to be of interest to its members, notably problems arising in relation to horizontal Community matters.

CEMA

European Committee of Associations of Manufacturers of Agricultural Machinery

Comité Européen des Groupements de Constructeurs du Machinisme Agricole

Europäisches Komitee der Verbände der Landmaschinenhersteller

Rue Jacques Bingen 19, 75017 Paris, France
Tel: +33 1/43 66 72
Fax: +33 1/40 54 95 60
E-mail: cema@sygma.org
Internet: http://www.cema-agri.org

Sec.-Gen.: J. DEHOLLAIN

Founded: 1959
General meeting: June
Working languages: F/E/D
Secretariat: 1 member of staff

Information available:
- List of members, free.

CEMAFON

European Committee for Materials and Products for Foundries

Comité Européen des Matériels et Produits pour la Fonderie

Europäisches Komitee der Hersteller von Giessereimaschinen und Giessereiausrüstungen

Lyoner Strasse 18, 60528 Frankfurt am Main, Germany
Tel: +49 69/66 03 12 78
Fax: +49 69/66 03 16 92
E-mail: cemafon@vdma.org
Internet: http://www.cemafon.org

Pres.: G. GALANTE
Contact: Dr. G. HABIG (Man. Dir.)

Founded: 1972
General meeting: Twice a year
Working languages: D/E/F

Sectors of activity:
- "GIFA/METEC/Thermprocess", 16-21/06/2003, Dusseldorf.

Information available:
- Members' list – free of charge.

CEMATEX

European Committee of Textile Machinery Manufacturers

Comité Européen des Constructeurs de Machines Textiles

Europäisches Komitee der Textilmaschinenhersteller

c/o UCMTF, 92038 Paris La Défense Cedex, France
Tel: +33 1/47 17 63 45
Fax: +33 1/47 17 63 48
E-mail: ucmt@worlnet.fr

Sec.-Gen.: Mrs. E. CHOLET

Founded: 1953
Working languages: E
Secretariat: 1 member of staff

Sectors of activity:
- "ITMA' 2003, Birmingham .

CEMBUREAU

The European Cement Association

Association Européenne du Ciment

Rue d'Arlon 55, 1040 Bruxelles, Belgium
Tel: +32 2/234 10 11
Fax: +32 2/230 47 20
E-mail: secretariat@cembureau.be
Internet: http://www.cembureau.be

Pres.: M. LODGE
Sec.-Gen.: A. VAN DER VAET
Contact: J.-M. CHANDELLE (Chief Executive)

Founded: 1947
General meeting: June
Working languages: F/E
Secretariat: 21 members of staff

Information available:
- "Inflation Accounting for the Cement Industry", E, M-NM.
- "World Cement Directory", E, M-NM.
- "World Statistical Review", E, M-NM.

CEMEP

European Committee of Manufacturers of Electrical Machines and Power Electronics

Comité Européen de Constructeurs de Machines Electriques et d'Electronique de Puissance

Europäisches Komitee der Hersteller von Elektrischen und Kraftelektronischen Maschinen

Rue Evariste Galois, Site de Chalembert bp31, 86130 Jaunay Clan, France
Tel: +33 5/49 62 86 16
Fax: +33 5/49 62 86 19
E-mail: jmolina@gimelec.fr
Internet: http://www.cemep.org

Founded: 1990
Working languages: E/F
Secretariat: 1 member of staff

Information available:
- Minutes of meetings between members every 6 months, M.
- Statistical data only for members.
- List of members available to the general public.
- List of members free.
- UPS European Guide (E/Sp and Italian shortly)
- Brochure on EU marking.

CEN

European Committee for Standardization

Comité Européen de Normalisation

Europäisches Komitee für Normung

Rue de Stassart 36, 1050 Bruxelles, Belgium
Tel: +32 2/550 08 11
Fax: +32 2/550 08 19
E-mail: infodesk@cenorm.be
Internet: http://www.cenorm.be

Pres.: C. BECKERVORDERSAND-FORTH
Sec.-Gen.: G. HONGLER

Founded: 1961
General meeting: October
Working languages: E/F/D
Secretariat: 95 members of staff

Historical note:
- CEN was founded in 1961 in Paris but moved to Brussels and was legally registered in 1975.

Sectors of activity:
- The CEN prepares, often in collaboration with the European Commission and EFTA, European standards so as to remove technical trade barriers and to encourage a free market for goods and services within Europe. CEN carries out this task by coordinating the work of the committees established by the national standardisation organisations.

Information available:
- "CEN Work Programme", twice annually, E, CD-Rom only, €101.
- Annual Report, also on web.
- Newsletter, every second month, E.
- Booklet: "Directives and related standards", 2002, €9,95
- "The Bulletin of the European Standards Organisations"E.
- "CEN Catalogue of European Standards and their National Implementation, twice annually,E,F,D, on CD-Rom only, €79.
- Members' list: free on web.

CENELEC

European Committee for Electrotechnical Standardization

Comité Européen de Normalisation Electrotechnique

Europäisches Komitee für Elektrotechnische Normung

Rue de Stassart 35, 1050 Bruxelles, Belgium
Tel: +32 2/519 68 71
Fax: +32 2/519 69 19
E-mail: info@cenelec.org
Internet: http://www.cenelec.org

Pres.: Y. SAULNIER
Sec.-Gen.: P. PARLEVLIET

Founded: 1973
Working languages: F/E/D
Secretariat: 32 members of staff

Historical note:
- CENELEC has been since 1973 the official standards organisation in Europe for the electrotechnical field.

Sectors of activity:
- One of CENELEC's objectives is to prepare (in collaboration with the European Commission and with the help of EFTA's Secretariat) electrotechnical standards for Europe, so that goods and services are able to move freely within the EU and abroad.

Information available:
- "Report on current activities", twice a year, E, M-NM.
- "Catalogue of European Standards", three times a year, E, M-NM.
- "Information on the Links between Products, Directives and Standards in the Electrotechnical Field", once a year, E, M-NM.
- "Directory", twice a year, E, M-NM.
- "CECC 00 200, Register of Approvals", three times a year, E/F, M-NM.
- "The Bulletin of the European Standards Organisations", published with CEN and ETSI, eleven times a year, E, M-NM.
- The members' list is available, free of charge.
- List of publications on request.
- Most of CENELEC publications are published on CD-Rom.
- Databases: standards references, titles, scopes, status, related Directives, ...

CEOAH

European Committee for Agricultural and Horticultural Tools and Implements

Comité Européen de l'Outillage Agricole et Horticole

Europäisches Komitee der Gerätehersteller für

Landwirtschaft und Garten",4>Europäisches Komitee der Gerätehersteller für Landwirtschaft und Garten

Light Trades House, Melbourne Avenue 3, Sheffield S10 2QJ, United Kingdom
Tel: +44 114/266 3084
Fax: +44 114/267 0910
E-mail: light.trades@virgin.net
Internet: www.britishtools.co.uk

Pres.: D. MACDOMHNAILL
Contact: J.G. TILL
Working languages: E
Secretariat: 9 members of staff

CEOC

European Confederation of Control, Inspection, Certification and Prevention Organisations

Confédération Européenne des Organismes de Contrôle, d'Inspection, de Certification et de Prévention

Europäische Vereinigung der Überwachungs-, Prüf-, Zertifizierung- und Präventivorganisationen

Rue du Commerce 20-22, 1000 Bruxelles, Belgium
Tel: +32 2/511 50 65
Fax: +32 2/502 50 47
E-mail: voelzow@ceoc.com
Internet: http://www.ceoc.com

Pres.: Dr. H. EBERHARDT
Sec.-Gen.: Michael VÖLZOW

Founded: 1961
General meeting: May
Working languages: F/E/D
Secretariat: 2 members of staff

Sectors of activity:
- to eliminate technical barriers to trade;
- to define practical requirements for the inspection of installations and equipment with regard to safety;
- to coordinate the activities of its members;
- to present a united opinion to national, European and internat.

Information available:
A publications brochure may be obtained free of charge from the CEOC General Secretariat or through the web site. The brochure is published in F/E/D and contains, inter alia:
1) Technical recommendations:
- 110 recommendations on "pressure vessels";
  – "machines, lifts and cranes";
  – "major hazards, environmental protection".
2) List of the 30 CEOC member organisations, freely available to the public.

- Database of Recommendations (1005) available on CD, regularly updated, price €150

CEP

E.U. Federation of National Organisations of Importers and Exporters of Fish

Comité des Organisations Nationales des Importateurs et Exportateurs de Poisson de l'U.E.

Avenue de Roodebeek 30, 1030 Bruxelles, Belgium
Tel: +32 2/743 87 30
Fax: +32 2/736 81 75
E-mail: aipcee@sia-dvi.be

Pres.: Gus PASTOOR
Sec.-Gen.: Michel COENEN
Contacts: Mr. J. A. MAZOS (1st Vice-Pr.), Mr. M. KELLER (2nd Vice-Pr.)

Founded: 1973
Working languages: E/F
Secretariat: 2 members of staff

Information available:
- White fish, free.
- List of members available to the general public, free.

CEPA

Confederation of European Pest Control Associations

Confédération Européenne des Associations de Pesticides Appliqués

Rue de l'Association 27, 1000 Bruxelles, Belgium
Tel: +32 2/225 83 30
Fax: +32 2/225 83 39
E-mail: info@cepa-europe.org
Internet: www.cepa-europe.org

Pres.: Mrs. M. FERNANDEZ
Contact: O. RICHARD

Founded: 1974
General meeting: September
Working languages: E/F
Secretariat: 1 member of staff

Information available:
- "Professional Pest Controller BPCA", 3 times a year, E.
- "Belgian Pest Control Magazine", 2 times a year, F/Nl.
- "Der praktische Schädlingsbekämpfer", monthly, D.
- "Bulletin d'information 3D", annually, F.
- The members' list is available, free of charge.

CEPE

European Council of Paint, Printing Ink and Artists' Colours Industry

Conseil Européen de l'Industrie des Peintures, des Encres d'Imprimerie et des Couleurs d'Art

Europäische Vereinigung der Lack-, Druckfarben und Künstlerfarbenindustrie

Av E. Van Nieuwenhuyse 4, 1160 Bruxelles, Belgium
Tel: +32 2/676 74 80
Fax: +32 2/676 74 90
E-mail: secretariat@cepe.org
Internet: www.cepe.org

Pres.: N. PETERSEN
Sec.-Gen.: J. SCHODER
Contact: P. KEYMOLEN

Founded: 1951
General meeting: June
Working languages: F/E/D
Secretariat: 6 members of staff

Information available:
- Statistics, E, M.
- "European Scale of Degree of Rusting for Anticorrosive Paints", E/F/D.
- List of members available to the general public, free.

CEPEC

Confédération Européenne des Professionnels de l'Esthétique Cosmétique

Rue de la Briquetterie 64, 17000 La Rochelle Cedex 1, France
Tel: +33 5/46 41 69 79
Fax: +33 5/46 42 25 96
E-mail: info@fngae.fr
Internet: www.fngae.fr

Pres.: Mrs. LAMOUREUX-STERN
Sec.-Gen.: E. FORTE

CEPI

Confederation of European Paper Industries

Confédération des Industries Papetières Européennes

Europäische Konföderation der Papierindustrien

Avenue Louise 250 Bte 80, 1050 Bruxelles, Belgium
Tel: +32 2/627 49 11
Fax: +32 2/646 81 37
E-mail: c.carlisle@cepi.org
Internet: www.cepi.org

Contacts: Carl BJÖRNBERG (Chairman), Teresa PRESAS (Managing Director)

Founded: 1992
General meeting: December
Working languages: E
Secretariat: 22 members of staff

Information available:
- See publications on website.All publications on website are available to non-members.
- Database of environmental and general statistical data on the paper industry.
- List of members available on website free of charge.
- "GHG emissions calculation tools", free, English, August 2002.
- "Report on the SAVE study" (European Commission project, free, English, November 2002.
- "CEPI 10 years statistics", free, English, November 2002.

CEPI

European Council for Real Estate Professions

Conseil Européen des Professions Immobilières

Europäischer Immobilien Rat

Avenue de Tervueren 36 bte 2, 1040 Bruxelles, Belgium
Tel: +32 2/735 49 90
Fax: +32 2/735 99 88
E-mail: cepi@cepi.be
Internet: http://www.cepi.be

Pres.: Andrea MERELLO
Sec.-Gen.: A. BENEDETTI
Contact: Martine VAN ADORP (Off. Man.)

Founded: 1990
General meeting: Twice a year March and November
Working languages: F/E
Secretariat: 1 member of staff

Historical note:
- CEPI is a non profit making international association which has its headquarters in Brussels.Its members are the most important professional organisations or institutes for Property Managers and Property Agents in the EU Member States.
  It has two branches:
  – CEAB Confédération européenne des administrateurs de biens
  – EPAG European Property Agents Group
- Today CEPI represents 120,000 European real estate professionals (30 professional associations in 20 countries).

Sectors of activity:
- 1. To inform real estate professionals on the various European regulations concerning real estate matters.
- 2. To harmonise (not to standardize) as much as possible the various regulations on real estate matters in force in the EU Member States: education, studies, access to the profession, rules of the profession, code of conduct, quality care, liability insurance, financial guarantee and consumer's protection.
- 3. To initiate and coordinate among the European Authorities matters regarding real estate professionals' and consumers' interests.
- 4. Upon the request of the European authorities, to give an advice on draft proposals on real estate matters.
- 5. To collect information on real estate legislation, regulations, local customs and practices in force in the various Member States
- 6. To inform the professionals, public and private organisations and the public on real estate legislation, regulations, local customs and practices in force in the various Member States by publishing the results of thematic questionnaires and surveys sent to the national member associations.
- 7. To facilitate the exchange of trainees among the EU Member States (CEPI Eurotraining programme) and to set up a basic common European study programme (CEPI Eureduc programme) in collaboration with the most important universities, high-vocational and professional schools.
- 8. To facilitate cross-border real estate transactions by informing professionals on the legislation and regulations on real estate transactions access to property in force in the EU Member States (CEPI Transeuropa programme) supported by the European Commission and the Leonardo da Vinci programme.
- 9. To create a European awareness among the real estate professionals of the EU Member States in order to facilitate mutual understanding between them and to establish a solid and dynamic European real estate sector.
- 10. To get to a real European status for Real Estate Professionals (studies, education, continuing education, access to the profession, code of conduct, liability insurance, financial guarantee, code of measuring practice, website), taking, nevertheless, into account that every country has its own specificities.

Information available:
- "CEPI Info": available on the website of CEPI.
- "Annual Report": avaible as hard copy, CD-ROM or on the web (free of charge).
- List of members, free.

CEPIS

Council of European Professional Informatics Societies

c/o VDE-Haus, Stresemannallee 15,
  60596 Frankfurt am Main, Germany
Tel: +49 69/6308 392
Fax: +49 69/9631 5233
Internet: http://www.cepis.org

Pres.: J. RUISSAFO

Founded: 1998
General meeting: April & November
Working languages: E

Sectors of activity:
- Voice of IT professionals.
- IT certification.

Information available:
- "Journal for IT-professionals", http://www.upgrade-cepis.org, free of charge.
- List of members available to the general public, http://www.cepis.org.

CEPLIS

European Council of the Liberal Professions

Conseil Européen des Professions Libérales

Coudenberg 70, 1000 Bruxelles, Belgium
Tel: +32 2/511 44 39
Fax: +32 2/511 01 24
E-mail: ceplis@pi.be
Internet: http://www.chez.com/photomaton/ceplis

Pres.: B. BOUR
Sec.-Gen.: E. MANGOLD

Founded: 1974
General meeting: Twice a year (Spring and Winter)
Working languages: F/E
Secretariat: 2 members of staff

Information available:
- "CEPLIS Telegram", E/F, weekly, M.
- Internal papers, M.
- Leaflets.
- Occasional publications in numerous news bulletins belonging to member associations.
- Database: addresses.

CEPMC

Council of European Producers of Materials for Construction

Conseil Européen des Producteurs de Matériaux de Construction

Vereinigung Europäischer Baustoffhersteller

Gulledelle 98 – box 7, 1200 Bruxelles, Belgium
Tel: +32 2/775 84 91
Fax: +32 2/771 30 56

E-mail: info@cepmc.org
Internet: www.cepmc.org

Pres.: J. O'BRIEN
Sec.-Gen.: P. BENNETT

Founded: 1988
Working languages: E
Secretariat: 2 members of staff

Sectors of activity:
- CEPMC is a fairly new organisation (1988) and its expanding membership includes 3 EFTA countries. The following EU country is currently without representation, because no appropriate national body exists: Greece.

Information available:
- Database: List of members.
- List of members, free.

CEPS

European Confederation of Spirits Producers

Confédération Européenne des Producteurs de Spiritueux

Avenue de Tervueren 192 Bte 3, 1150 Bruxelles, Belgium
Tel: +32 2/779 24 23
Fax: +32 2/772 98 20
E-mail: ceps1@skynet.be
Internet: www.europeanspirits.org

Pres.: J.P. BOUYAT
Contact: Anthony ARKE (Director General)

Founded: 1993
General meeting: June
Working languages: E/F
Secretariat: 6 members of staff

Information available:
- "Info-Flash", 1/month, M, F/E, free.
- List of members available to the general public.

CEPT

European Conference of Postal and Telecommunications Administrations

Conférence Européenne des Administrations des Postes et des Télécommunications

Europäische Konferenz der Verwaltungen für Post und Telekommunikation

Avenue de l'astronomie 14 bt21, 1210 Bruxelles, Belgium
Tel: +32 2/226 88 96
Fax: +32 2/226 88 77
E-mail: cerp.secretariat@ibpt.be
Internet: http://www.cept.org

Pres.: M. DUTORDOIT

Founded: 1959
Working languages: F/E/D

Information available:
- List of publications (20 pages), F/E, free.
- General information brochure, free.
- List of members available to the general public, free.
- "CEPT Information Desk": Holsteinsgade 63, DK-2100 Copenhague, Denmark.

CER / CCFE / GEB

Community of European Railways

Communauté des Chemins de Fer Européens

Gemeinschaft der Europäischen Bahnen

Avenue des Arts 53, 1000 Bruxelles, Belgium
Tel: +32 2/213 08 70
Fax: +32 2/512 52 31
E-mail: contact@cer.be
Internet: http://www.cer.be

Pres.: G. CIMOLI

Founded: 1988
Working languages: F/E/D
Secretariat: 15 members of staff

Sectors of activity:
- Assisting, in collaboration with the EU institutions, in formulating a common transport policy and other EU policies of interest to European railways.
- Promoting a genuine synergy between railway networks in Europe.
The members of the secretariat focus on:
- common transport policy;
- competition and state aid;
- trans-European networks;
- environment;
- research and technical issues;
- industrial policies;
- social policy;
- taxation.

Information available:
- Press releases.
- A series of written statements on: environment, transport, research, public services, trans-European networks, rail freight freeways, energy, single market, noise reduction, railway news.

CERAME-UNIE

Liaison Office of the European Ceramic Industries

Bureau de Liaison des Industries Céramiques Européennes

Verbindungsbüro der europäischen Keramikindustrie

Rue des Colonies 18-24, 1000 Bruxelles, Belgium
Tel: +32 2/511 30 12

Tel: +32 2/511 70 25
Fax: +32 2/511 51 74
E-mail: sec@cerameunie.net
Internet: http://www.cerameunie.net

Pres.: L.G. VON BOCH
Sec.-Gen.: R. CHORUS

Founded: 1962
Working languages: F/E/D
Secretariat: 5 members of staff

Information available:
- "Courier", bimonthly, F/E/D (M).
- "Brochure Cerame-Unie".
- Database: addresses, M.

CERP

European Public Relations Confederation

Confédération Européenne des Relations Publiques

Europäische Konföderation der Public Relations Gesellschaften

Chaussée de Gand 443 bte 4, 1030 Bruxelles, Belgium
Tel: +32 2/414 04 32
Fax: +32 2/414 96 05
E-mail: secretariat@bprc.be
Internet: http://www.cerp.org

Pres.: J-J STRIJP

Founded: 1959
General meeting: Every Spring
Working languages: F/E
Secretariat: 3 members of staff

Information available:
- List of members.

CESA

Committee of European Union Shipbuilders Associations

Rue Marie de Bourgogne 52-54 3ét, 1000 Bruxelles, Belgium
Tel: +32 2/230 27 91
Fax: +32 2/230 43 32
E-mail: info@cesa-shipbuilding.org
Internet: http://www.cesa-shipbuilding.org

Pres.: Dr. LUKEN

Founded: 1937
General meeting: May–June
Working languages: E
Secretariat: 2 members of staff

Information available:
- Annual Report, free, E.
- List of members available to the general public, free.

CESCE

European Committee for Business Support Services

Comité Européen des Services de Soutien aux entreprises

Kanselarijstraat 19, 1000 Brugge, Belgium
Tel: +32 2/227 49 40
Tel: +32 (0)2/41 25 45 50
Fax: +32 2/227 63 91
E-mail: fabienne.sorba@ffcgea.fr
E-mail: ben.bruyndonckx@vizo.be
Internet: http://www.cesce.org

Pres.: Jean-Claude BACHELOT
Contacts: Fabienne SORBA (Co-ordinator), Ben BRUYNDONCKX (Co-ordinator)

Founded: 1969
General meeting: November
Working languages: F/E
Secretariat: 1 member of staff

Sectors of activity:
- SME: Business support services
- Objectives: Organises a yearly seminar for Business Supporting Experts (EBS-programme);
  – promotes joint actions for the implementation of projects and activities at an European level;
  – composes and issues newsflashes for the affiliated organisations;
  – functions as an information centre providing members with publications of fellow members that might be of interest.
- The Cesce Support Team represents the network at different meetings, seminars and conferences at an the European level, including the DG Enterprise meetings with Business Organisations.
- Seminars: yearly "Programme for Exchange Seminars for European Experts in Business Support (EBS)"
- "Evaluation of Business Supporting Activities", Slovenia, 24-26 November 2004

Information available:
- Website (N.NM)
- Mail flashes (M)
- Report of annual forum, (N.NM)
- List of members: available to the public through the website

CESI

European Confederation of Independent Trade Unions

Confédération Européenne des Syndicats Indépendants

Europäische Union der Unabhängigen Gewerkschaften

Avenue de la Joyeuse Entrée 1-5, 1040 Bruxelles, Belgium
Tel: +32 2/282 18 70
Fax: +32 2/282 18 71

E-mail: info@cesi.org
Internet: www.cesi.org

Pres.: Valerio SALVATORE
Sec.-Gen.: Helmut MÜLLERS

Founded: 1990
General meeting: Congress every 4th year
Working languages: E/F/D
Secretariat: 9 members of staff

Sectors of activity:
- Defending the professional interests of European public and private sector workers.
- Specific training in various sectors.

Information available:
- General information on the CESI, press releases and position papers.
- List of members available to the general public, free.

CET

European Taxi Confederation

Confédération Européenne des Taxis

Europäische Konföderation der Taxis

Rue des Carburants 54-56, 1190 Bruxelles, Belgium
Tel: +32 2/349 43 43
Tel: +32 2/349 49 49
Fax: +32 2/349 41 42
E-mail: m.petre@taxis.be
Internet: www.taxis.be

Pres.: Mr. PETRE
Contact: A. VAN LAUWE (Secretary)
Working languages: F/E/Nl
Secretariat: 44 members of staff

CET

European Ceramic Tile Manufacturers' Federation

Fédération Européenne des Producteurs de Carreaux

Europäischer Industrieverband der Keramikfliesen

Rue des Colonies 18-24, 1000 Bruxelles, Belgium
Tel: +32 2/511 30 12
Fax: +32 2/511 51 74
E-mail: sec@cerameunie.net
Internet: http://www.cerameunie.net

Sec.-Gen.: R. CHORUS

Founded: 1959
Working languages: F/E/D
Secretariat: 5 members of staff

Information available:
- "Courier", bimonthly, F/E/D, M.

CETOP

European Oil Hydraulic and Pneumatic Committee

Comité Européen des Transmissions Oléohydrauliques et Pneumatiques

Europäisches Komitee Ölhydraulik und Pneumatik

Lyoner Strasse 18, 60528 Frankfurt am Main, Germany
Tel: +49 69/6603-1319
Tel: +49 69/6603-1658
Fax: +49 69/6603-1459
E-mail: info@cetop.org
Internet: www.cetop.org

Sec.-Gen.: Mrs. S. GROHMANN-MUNDSCHENK

Founded: 1962
General meeting: June
Working languages: F/E/D

Information available:
- "CETOP Directory", every 2 years, E/F/D, free, M/NM.
- "CETOP Reporter", newsletter, irregular, E/F/D, free, M.
- "CETOP Technical Recommendations", wide price range, E/F/D, M-NM.
- The members' list is available, free of charge, M/N.

CETS / SITS

Comité Européen des Traitements de Surfaces

Rue Louis Blanc 39-41, 92038 Paris La Défense Cedex, France
Tel: +33 1/47 17 63 73
Fax: +33 1/47 17 63 74
E-mail: info@sits.fr
Internet: http://www.sits.fr

Pres.: D. ODILLE
Sec.-Gen.: Mrs. F. LECLERC

Founded: 1980
Working languages: E/F/D/It
Secretariat: 2 members of staff

Information available:
- The members' list is available at the price of €200.

CFE

Confédération Fiscale Européenne

General secretariat: Neue Promenade 4, 10178 Berlin-Mitte, Germany
Tel: +49 30/2400 87 22
Fax: +49 30/2400 8799
E-mail: generalsecretary@cfe-eutax.org
Internet: http://www.cfe-eufax.org

Pres.: Mario BOIDI
Sec.-Gen.: Dr. H. WEILER
Contact: Ms. C. KELLER

Brussels office:
Avenue de Cortenbergh 52
B-1000 Bruxelles
Tel: +32 2/743 05 94
Fax: +32 2/732 36 39
E-mail: brusselsoffice@cfe-eutax.org

Founded: 1959
General meeting: September
Working languages: D/E/F
Secretariat: 5 members of staff

Information available:
- Journal: "European Taxation", monthly.
- The members' list is available, free of charge.

CIAA

Confederation of the Food and Drink Industries of the EU

Confédération des Industries Agro-Alimentaires de l'UE

Avenue des Arts 43, 1040 Bruxelles, Belgium
Tel: +32 2/514 11 11
Fax: +32 2/511 29 05
E-mail: ciaa@ciaa.be
Internet: http://www.ciaa.be

Contact: R. DESTIN (Dir Gen)

Founded: 1982
General meeting: Variable, minimum once a year
Working languages: F/E
Secretariat: 14 members of staff

Information available:
- "Status Report on food legislation in the EU", quarterly, M/NM.
- "Brochure on the CIAA, its structure, functioning and scope of activity", free, M/NM.
- Various position papers, M/NM.
- The members' list is available on the website.

CIBE

International Confederation of European Beet Growers

Confédération Internationale des Betteraviers Européens

Internationale Vereinigung Europaeischer Rübenanbauer

Rue du Général Foy 29, 75008 Paris, France
Tel: +33 1/44 69 39 00
Fax: +33 1/42 93 28 93

Pres.: O. VON ARNOLD
Sec.-Gen.: H. CHAVANES

Founded: 1925
General meeting: April
Working languages: D/E/F/Esp/It
Secretariat: 8 members of staff

Sectors of activity:
- 39th Congress, for members.

Information available:
- "European Beet growers", every 2 years, free, F/E/D/Esp/It, M-NM.

CIDE

European Dehydrators Association

Commission Intersyndicale des Déshydrateurs Européens

Arbeitsgemeinschaft Europäischer Trocknungsbetriebe

Rue Richelieu 45, 75001 Paris, France
Tel: +33 1/42 61 72 94
Fax: +33 1/49 27 02 73
E-mail: cide@wanadoo.fr
Internet: http://www.luzerne.org

Pres.: L. NAGLIA
Sec.-Gen.: E. GUILLEMOT

Founded: 1959
General meeting: May
Working languages: F/E
Secretariat: 2 members of staff

Sectors of activity:
- Artificial drying of fodder.

Information available:
- Annual Report, M-NM, F/E, free.
- Statistics, 3-4/year, M-NM, free.
- Report of General Assembly, yearly, F/E.

CIELFFA

International Research Committee for Cold-Rolled Strips

Comité International d'Etude du Laminage à Froid du Feuillard d'Acier

Kaiserswerther Strasse 137, Postfach 300333, 40474 Düsseldorf, Germany
Tel: +49 211/47 806-0
Fax: +49 211/47 806-22
E-mail: info@cielffa.org
Internet: http://www.cielffa.org

Pres.: H. WESTERBARKEY
Sec.-Gen.: F. NEUHAUS

Founded: 1953
Working languages: D/E/F
Secretariat: 5 members of staff

Sectors of activity:
- Steel industry, 1st transformation.

CIMO

European Fresh Produce Importers Association

Av. de Broqueville 272 – Bte 4, 1200 Bruxelles, Belgium
Tel: +32 2/777 15 80
Fax: +32 2/777 15 81
E-mail: info@freshfel.org
Internet: www.cimo.be

Contact: Mr. Ph. BINARD (Del Gen)
Working languages: F/E/Esp
Secretariat: 3 members of staff

CIPF

International Confederation for Trade in Straw, Fodders and Derivatives

Confédération Internationale du Commerce et de l'Industrie des Pailles, Fourrages, Tourbes et Dérivés

Bureau 273, Bourse de Commerce, Rue de Viarmes 2, 75040 Paris Cedex 02, France
Tel: +33 1/42 36 84 35
Fax: +33 1/42 36 44 93
E-mail: ucipf@mageos.com

Pres.: B. CREUWELS
Contact: G. COUDERT

Founded: 1968
General meeting: April
Working languages: F/D/It/Esp/Nl

Information available:
- Specific information available on written request.

CIPF

International Committee for Cold-Rolled Sections

Comité International du Profilage à Froid

c/o Confederation of British Metal Forming, National Metal Forming Center, Birmingham Road 47, West Bromwich B70 6TW, United Kingdom

Pres.: M. BERTRAMS
Contact: J. FIELD

Founded: 1960

CIRCCE

International Confederation of the Commercial Representation of the European Community

Confédération Internationale de la Représentation Commerciale de la Communauté Européenne

Internationale Vereinigung der Handelsvertretung der Europäischen Gemeinschaft

Rue d'Hauteville 2, 75010 Paris, France
Tel: +33 1/48 24 97 59
Fax: +33 1/45 23 19 48
E-mail: csm.secretariat@libertysurf.fr
Internet: www.csm.fr

Pres.: J. P. BROGGI
Sec.-Gen.: S. JAMES

Founded: 1906
General meeting: May
Working languages: F
Secretariat: 22 members of staff

Information available:
- "La Tribune Libre", 10/year, F, M-NM.

CIRFS

International Rayon and Synthetic Fibres Committee

Comité International de la Rayonne et des Fibres Synthétiques

Internationale Chemiefaservereinigung

Av. E. Van Nieuwenhuyse 4, 1160 Bruxelles, Belgium
Tel: +32 2/676 74 55
Fax: +32 2/676 74 54
E-mail: info@cirfs.org
Internet: www.cirfs.org

Contact: C.M. PURVIS

Founded: 1950
General meeting: May of each year.
Working languages: E
Secretariat: 11 members of staff

Information available:
- "Statistical yearbook", F/E/D, yearly, €250.
- Database: external trade.

CITPA

International Confederation of Paper and Board Converters in Europe

Confédération Internationale des Transformateurs de Papier et Carton en Europe

Internationale Konföderation der Verarbeiter von Papier und Pappe in Europa

Chaussée de waterloo 715 bte25, 1180 Bruxelles, Belgium
Tel: +32 2/340 66 30
Fax: +32 2/344 86 61
E-mail: info@citpa-europe.org
Internet: http://www.citpa-europe.org

Pres.: S. SANGUINAZZI
Sec.-Gen.: T. PFEIFFER

Founded: 1961
Working languages: E
Secretariat: 2 members of staff

Historical note:
- Enlargement: 1972: members from England, Denmark. 1983/1985: members from Spain, Portugal and Greece. 1990: members from Sweden, Finland, Austria and associated Norway.

Sectors of activity:
- Opening the federation to Baltic States and Central and Eastern European countries.

Information available:
- Circular information letters, free, E, M.
- List of members.

CLCCR

Liaison Committee of the Body and Trailer Building Industry

Comité de Liaison de la Construction de Carrosseries et de Remorques

Verbindungsausschuss der Aufbauen- und Anhängerindustrie

c/o Verband der Automobilindustrie e.V. (VDA), Westendstrasse 61, 60325 Frankfurt am Main, Germany
Tel: +49 69/975 07 308
Fax: +49 69/975 07 261
E-mail: heibach@vda.de
Internet: http://www.vda.be

Pres.: H. NOOTEBOOM
Sec.-Gen.: M. HEIBACH

Founded: 1961
Working languages: E
Secretariat: 1 member of staff

Information available:
- Database: registrations, production, export of trailers and semi-trailers.

CLECAT

European Association for Forwarding, Transport, Logistic and Customs Services

Rue Montoyer 33 Bte 10, 1000 Bruxelles, Belgium
Tel: +32 2/503 47 05
Fax: +32 2/503 47 52
E-mail: info@clecat.org
Internet: www.clecat.org

Pres.: Manfred BOES
Sec.-Gen.: Han VANOS
Contact: Marco L. SORGETTI (Director General)

Founded: 1958
General meeting: December
Working languages: E
Secretariat: 4 members of staff

Historical note:
- CLECAT has represented the interests of the logistic service providers in Brussels for almost 50 years

Sectors of activity:
- Freight Forwarding Day, 2nd Dec. 2004.
- Freight Transport Security Conference, autumn, 2004

Information available:
- Information is available to members.
- List of members available on the website

CLEDIPA

European Liaison Committee of the Independent Distribution of Spare Parts and Equipment for Motor Cars

Comité de Liaison Européen de la Distribution Indépendante de Pièces de Rechange et Equipement pour Automobiles

Europäischer Verbindungsausschuss der Selbsständigen Verteilung von Ersatzteilen & Ausrüstungen für Kraftwagen

Bd de la Woluwe 46 bte 12, 1200 Bruxelles, Belgium
Tel: +32 2/778 62 00
Fax: +32 2/762 12 55
E-mail: figiefa@federauto.be
Internet: www.figiefa.org

Pres.: F. VAN HECK
Sec.-Gen.: Mrs. S. GOTZEN

Founded: 1982
General meeting: May
Working languages: F/E

Sectors of activity:
- Maintenance of competition for the automotive aftermarket.
Conferences:
- Consult the website: www.figiefa.org

Information available:
- List of members, free.

CLEO

European Liaison Committee of Osteopaths

Comité de Liaison Européen des Ostéopathes

Europäisches Verbindungskomitee der Osteopathen

Avenue des Champs Elysées, 116, 75008 Paris, France
Tel: +33 1/44 21 80 75
Fax: +33 1/44 21 82 99

Pres.: J. BARKWORTH
Sec.-Gen.: F.P. BERTHENET
Working languages: E/F

Sectors of activity:
- Liberalisation of diplomas within the EU and regulation of the profession.

CLEPA

European Association of Automotive Suppliers

Association Européenne des Equipementiers Automobiles

Verband der Europäischen Autozulieferer

Bvd Brand Whitlock 87 bte 1, 1200 Bruxelles, Belgium
Tel: +32 2/743 91 30
Fax: +32 2/732 00 55
E-mail: info@clepa.be
Internet: http://www.clepa.be

Pres.: J. HARNISCH
Contact: Mrs. M. CREPLET
Working languages: E/F

Information available:
- "Newsletter", monthly, E, free.
- List of members available to the general public, free.

CLGE

Council of European Geodetic Surveyors

Comité de Liaison des Géomètres Européens

c/o BEV c/o VA Innsbruck, Bürgerstrasse 34, 6010 Innsbruck, Austria
Tel: +43 512/588 411 60
Fax: +43 512/588 41 161
E-mail: gerda.schennach@bev.gv.at
Internet: www.clge.org

Pres.: K. RÜRUP
Sec.-Gen.: G. SCHENNACH

Founded: 1972
General meeting: March–May + October–December
Working languages: E
Secretariat: 10 members of staff

Historical note:
- CLGE was created in 1972 by the Surveyors' International Federation and became an independant liaison committee in 1986.

Sectors of activity:
- To facilitate the exchange of experience and information among qualified surveyors in Europe.
- To facilitate training and mutual recognition of qualification by supporting the European Institutions in their undertakings and to contribute within the European jurisdiction on professional matters.
- To promote the work of the surveying profession.

Information available:
- "The Assurance of Quality in the Geodetic Surveying Profession".
- "Market Analysis Report on the Geodetic Surveying Profession in the EU".
- "Geodetic Surveying and Property in the EU".
- "Enhancing professional competence of surveyors in Europe". List of associations and delegates available, free of charge.
- Website: membership register.

CLITRAVI

Liaison Centre for the Meat Processing Industries in the EU

Centre de Liaison des Industries Transformatrices de Viandes de l'UE

Boulevard Baudouin 18 Bte 4, 1000 Bruxelles, Belgium
Tel: +32 2/203 51 41

Fax: +32 2/203 32 44
E-mail: devries@skypro.be

Sec.-Gen.: D. DOBBELAERE

Founded: 1958
General meeting: May
Working languages: F/E
Secretariat: 3 members of staff

Information available:
- List of members.

CLPEU / CLPUE / VKPEU

Liaison Committee of Podiatrists of the EU

Comité de Liaison des Podologues de l'UE

Verbindungskomitee für Podologen der EU

c/o Mrs. Roofthooft, St. Bernardse Steenweg 98, 2620 Hemiksen, Belgium
Tel: +32 3/877 39 38
Fax: +32 3/877 59 02
E-mail: fip.roofthooft.jose@pi.be

Pres.: C. JACOBS

Founded: 1969
Working languages: E/F
Secretariat: 1 member of staff

CNUE

Conférence des Notariats de l'Union Européenne

Avenue de Cortenbergh, 52, 1000 Bruxelles, Belgium
Tel: +32 2/513 95 29
Fax: +32 2/513 93 82
E-mail: info@cnue.be
Internet: http://www.cnue.be

Contact: Mrs. C. MARTIN

Founded: 1976: CPNCE – 1993: CNUE
General meeting: March – October
Working languages: F
Secretariat: 3 members of staff

Information available:
- The members' list is available.

COCERAL

Committee of Cereals, Oilseeds, Animal Feed, Olive Oil, Oils and Fats and Agrosupply Trade in the EU

Comité du Commerce des Céréales, Aliments du Bétail, Oléagineux, Huile d'Olive, Huiles et Graisses et Agrofournitures de l'UE

Komitee des Getreide-, Futtermittel-, Ölsaaten, Olivenöl, Ölen und Fetten und landwirtschaftliche Betriebsmittelhandels in der EG

Square de Meeûs 18 Bte 1, 1050
  Bruxelles, Belgium
Tel: +32 2/502 08 08
Fax: +32 2/502 60 30
E-mail: secretariat@coceral.com
Internet: http://www.coceral.com

Sec.-Gen.: Mrs. C. FAUTH
Contact: M.K. SCHUMACHER (Vice-Pr)

Founded: 1958
Working languages: F/E/D
Secretariat: 5 members of staff

Information available:
- Fax – E-mail on the daily problems of
  the cereals' market, M.
- Reports of the Cereals and Cattle
  Feed Consultative Committees. Price:
  postage costs for NM – free for M.
- Database: list of members.

COCIR

**European Coordination Committee
of the Radiological and
Electromedical Industries**

**Comité Européen de Coordination
des Industries Radiologiques et
Electromédicales**

c/o ZVEI Fachveband,
  Electromedizinische Technik,
  Stresemannallee 19, 60596 Frankfurt
  am Main, Germany
Tel: +49 69/6302 206
Fax: +49 69/6302 390
E-mail: office@cocir.org
Internet: www.cocir.org

Pres.: T. EGELUND
Contact: Mr. BURSIG

Founded: 1959
Working languages: E
Secretariat: 3 members of staff

Information available:
- The members' list is available, free of
  charge.

COFAG

**Glutamic Acid Manufacturers
Association of the EU**

**Comité des Fabricants d'Acide
Glutamique de l'UE**

**Glutaminsaüre Herstellers Komitee
bei der EG**

c/o EUROLYSINE, Rue de Courcelles,
  153, 75817 Paris Cedex 17, France
Tel: +33 1/44 40 12 29
Fax: +33 1/44 40 12 15
E-mail: guion-philippe@eli.ajunomoto.-
  com
Internet: www.glutamat.com

Contact: P. GUION

Founded: 1964
Working languages: E/F

Sectors of activity:
- Promotion of glutamates.
- Public relations.
- Regulation.
- Scientific studies.

Information available:
- "What is MSG", E.
- "Food Industry Guide: all about
  Glutamate", E.
- "Glutamate: facts", E.
- List of members, free

COFALEC

**Committee of Bakers Yeast
Manufacturers of the EU**

**Comité des Fabricants de Levure
Panification de l'UE**

Komitee der Hefeindustrie in der EG

Rue de Turbigo 14, 75001 Paris, France
Tel: +33 1/45 08 54 82
Fax: +33 1/42 21 02 14
E-mail: info@cofalec.com
Internet: www.cofalec.com

Pres.: A. DE SCHEPPER
Contact: J.P. LOUP
Working languages: F
Secretariat: 2 members of staff

COGECA

**General Committee for Agricultural
Cooperation in the EU**

**Comité Général de la Coopération
Agricole de l'UE**

**Allgemeiner Ausschuss des
Ländlichen
Genossenschaftswesens der
Europäischen Union**

Rue de la Science 23-25, BP 3, 1040
  Bruxelles, Belgium
Tel: +32 2/287 27 11
Fax: +32 2/287 27 00
E-mail: mail@copa-cogeca.be
Internet: www.copa-cogeca.be

Pres.: Eduardo BAAMONDE
Sec.-Gen.: Franz-Josef FEITER
Contacts: Dominique SOUCHON
  (Director, Co-ordination and Strategy),
  Joel CASTANY (1sr Vice-Pr.), Donal
  CASHMAN (2nd Vice-Pr.), Christer
  ELIASSON (3rd Vice-Pr.), Zoltan
  SZABO (4th Vice-Pr.)

Founded: 1959
Working languages: E/F/D/Esp/It
Secretariat: 47 members of staff

Information available:
- COGECA's brochure, M-NM.
- Database: "AGRI-INFO Service", M.
- List of members, free.
- The development of agricultural
  cooperatives in the EU (languages: E,
  F, D, I, Esp.).

COGEN EUROPE

**European Association for the
Promotion of Cogeneration**

Gulledelle 98, 1200 Bruxelles, Belgium
Tel: +32 2/772 82 90
Fax: +32 2/772 50 44
E-mail: info@cogen.org
Internet: http://www.cogen.org

Pres.: G. VAN INGEN
Contact: S. MINETT (Managing
  Director)

Founded: 1993
General meeting: March
Working languages: E, (I, F, D, S)
Secretariat: 7 members of staff

Sectors of activity:
- COGEN Europe works to promote
  energy efficiency through the wider
  use of cogeneration (Combined Heat
  and Power) with its many
  environmental and economic benefits.

Information available:
- "COGEN Europe Yearbook", E.
- "COGEN Europe Brochure", 1 per
  year, E.
- Various briefings.
- Various studies – free to members,
  priced to non-members, E.
- "COGEN Update", e-mail newsletter,
  E, M.
- Database: 6500 contacts related to
  cogeneration.
- List of members available to the
  general public.

COLIBI

**Liaison Committee of European
Bicycle Manufacturers**

**Comité de Liaison des Fabricants de
Bicyclettes de la Communauté
Européenne**

**Verbindungskomitee der
Fahrradhersteller in der
Europäischen Gemeinschaft**

Boulevard de la Woluwe 46 bte 16, 1200
  Bruxelles, Belgium
Tel: +32 2/778 64 58
Fax: +32 2/762 81 71
E-mail: contact@colibi.com
Internet: www.colibi.com

Pres.: R. J. TAKENS
Sec.-Gen.: Ms. G. ENGELEN
Contact: R. ANTICHI (Vice-Pr)

Founded: 1973
Working languages: E
Secretariat: 1 member of staff

Information available:
- List of members available to the
  general public, free.
- All available information at:
  www.colibi.com

COLIPA

European Cosmetic, Toiletry and Perfumery Association

Avenue Hermann Debroux 15A, 1060 Bruxelles, Belgium
Tel: +32 2/227 66 10
Fax: +32 2/227 66 27
E-mail: colipa@colipa.be
Internet: http://www.colipa.com

Pres.: M. PUIG E.
Sec.-Gen.: Bertil HEERINK
Contact: Sebastian MARX (Communications Manager)

Founded: 1962
General meeting: June
Working languages: E/F
Secretariat: 16 members of staff

Sectors of activity:
- COLIPA's mission is to help maintain and develop a sustainable, competitive and respected industry in Europe:
  – by demonstrating the inherent value of our industry (as stated in our vision);
  – by striving to create the most favourable economic and regulatory environment in which to operate;
  – and by advocating best practices, thereby ensuring that consumers benefit from continuously innovative and safe products.

Information available:
- "Advisory Notes to Manufacturers of Cosmetics and Toiletries".
- "CICI, Colipa Database EU Inventory of Cosmetics Ingredients", 2000.
- "Colipa Sun Protection Factor Test Method".
- "Cosmetic Good Manufacturing Practices, Guidelines for the Manufacturer of Cosmetic Products".
- "EU Cosmetics Directive, legal text and brochure on 6th Amendment".
- "The European Union Cosmetics Directive – explanatory brochure", January 2004.
- "Guidelines for Assessment of Skin Tolerance of Potentially Irritant Cosmetic Ingredients".
- "Guidelines for the Evaluation of the Efficacy of Cosmetic Products".
- "Guidelines for Percutaneous Absorption/Penetration".
- "Guidelines for the Safety Assessment of a Cosmetic Product".
- "Guidelines on Ingredient Labelling in the EU".
- "Guidelines on Microbial Quality Management (MQM)".
- "Guidelines on the Exchange of Information between Fragrance Suppliers and Cosmetic Manufacturers".
- "Product Information: Guidelines based on the 6th Amendment to the EU Cosmetics Directive".

- "Product Test Guidelines for the Assessment of Human Skin Compatibility".
- "EAPCCT/Colipa Cosmetic Frame Formulations", March 2000, free, M-NM.

COLIPED

Association of The European Two-Wheeler Parts' And Accessories' Industry

Bd de la Woluwe 46 Bte 16, 1200 Bruxelles, Belgium
Tel: +32 2/778 64 58
Fax: +32 2/762 81 71
E-mail: greet.engelen@coliped.com
Internet: www.coliped.com

Sec.-Gen.: Mr. BLOME
Contact: Mr P. MARCHAND (Vice-President)

Founded: 1960
Working languages: E
Secretariat: 1 member of staff

Information available:
- List of members available to the general public, free.
- All other available information at: www.coliped.com

CONCAWE

The Oil Companies' European Organization for Environment, Health and Safety

Organisation Européenne des Compagnies Pétrolières pour l'Environnement, la Santé et Sécurité

Europäische Organisation der Ölgesellschaften für Umwelt, Gesundheit und Sicherheit

Boulevard du Souverain 165, 1160 Bruxelles, Belgium
Tel: +32 2/566 91 60
Fax: +32 2/566 91 81
E-mail: info@concawe.org
Internet: http://www.concawe.org

Pres.: W. BONSE-GEUKING
Sec.-Gen.: J. CASTELEIN

Founded: 1963
General meeting: November
Working languages: E
Secretariat: 13 members of staff

Sectors of activity:
- Study of scientific and technical issues on environmental, health and safety aspects concerning the European oil refining industry and petroleum products.

Information available:
- "CONCAWE Review", biannual, E, free.

- Catalogue of "CONCAWE" reports, E.
- "CONCAWE" general interest (yellow) and special interest (white) reports provide technical and economic analyses of topical issues and are published regularly, E.
- Some reports are available on the CONCAWE website and can be downloaded free of charge. There is a small charge for paper copies.

COPA

Committee of Agricultural Organizations in the EU

Comité des Organisations Professionnelles Agricoles de l'UE

Rue de la Science 23-25 Box 3, 1040 Bruxelles, Belgium
Tel: +32 2/287 27 11
Fax: +32 2/287 27 00
E-mail: mail@copa-cogeca.be

Pres.: Peter GAEMELKE
Sec.-Gen.: Franz-Josef FEITER

Founded: 1959
Working languages: F/E/D/It/Esp
Secretariat: 47 members of staff

Sectors of activity:
- One of COPA's objectives is to ensure that increases in the income of farmers and their families is comparable to that of their socio-professional categories.

Information available:
- Database: "AGRI-INFO Service", M.
- COPA Brochure, M.
- List of members, free.
- "The development of agricultural cooperatives in the EU", (E,F,D,I,Esp.)

COTANCE

Confederation of National Associations of Tanners and Dressers of the EC

Confédération des Associations Nationales de Tanneurs et Mégissiers de la CE

Vereinigung der Nationalen Verbanden der Lederindustrie

Rue Belliard 3, 1040 Bruxelles, Belgium
Tel: +32 2/512 77 03
Fax: +32 2/512 91 57
E-mail: info@euroleather.com
Internet: http://www.euroleather.com

Pres.: Josep COSTA
Sec.-Gen.: Gustavo GONZALEZ-QUIJANO
Contact: Gustavo GONZALEZ-QUIJANO

Founded: 1981
General meeting: June

Working languages: F/E
Secretariat: 4 members of staff

Information available:
- Database: list of European tanneries, M-NM.
- The members' list is available, free of charge, M-NM.
- Web page: www.euroleather.com

COTREL

Committee of Associations of European Transformers Manufacturers

Comité des Associations de Constructeurs de Transformateurs dans la Communauté Européenne

EG-Zusammenarbeit der Fachverbände der Transformatorenhersteller

Agoria, Boulevard Reyers 80, 1030 Bruxelles, Belgium
Tel: +32 2/706 80 00
Fax: +32 2/706 80 09
E-mail: herman.looghe@agoria.be
Internet: http://www.cotrel.com

Founded: 1958
General meeting: May
Working languages: E
Secretariat: 2 members of staff

Information available:
- Directory of the Association.
- List of members available to the general public, free, on the internet.

CPE

European Farmers Coordination

Coordination Paysanne Européenne

Europäische Bauern Koordination

Rue de la Sablonnière, 18, 1000 Bruxelles, Belgium
Tel: +32 2/217 31 12
Fax: +32 2/218 45 09
E-mail: cpe@cpefarmers.org
Internet: www.cpefarmers.org

Contact: Mr. G. CHOPLIN

Founded: 1986
Working languages: F/E/D/Es/Ne/Po/It
Secretariat: 4 members of staff

Sectors of activity:
- European and international agricultural policies, food, environment, genetic technologies, territories.

Information available:
- Press releases.
- List of members available to the general public, free.

CPIV

Standing Committee of the European Glass Industries

Comité Permanent des Industries du Verre Européennes

Ständiger Ausschuss der europäischen Glasindustrien

Avenue Louise 89, 1050 Bruxelles, Belgium
Tel: +32 2/538 44 46
Fax: +32 2/537 84 69
E-mail: info@cpivglass.be
Internet: http://www.cpivglass.be

Pres.: J. DEMARTY
Sec.-Gen.: F. VAN HOUTE

Founded: 1967
General meeting: June
Working languages: E/F/D
Secretariat: 3 members of staff

Information available:
- A monthly "CPIV Info" – free (M) – E. Annual subscription of €185, NM – E/F.
- *Panorama of the EC glass industry, free, annual.
- *List of members, free.
- *List of glass manufacturers, website www.cpivglass.be.
- *=Available on web site.

CPIV

Permanent International Vinegar Committee

Comité Permanent International du Vinaigre

Ständiger Internationaler Ausschuss der Essighersteller – Gemeinsamer Markt

Reuterstrasse 151, 53113 Bonn, Germany
Tel: +49 228/21 20 17
Fax: +49 228/22 94 60
E-mail: info@verbaendeburo.de

Pres.: M. DOTHEY M.
Sec.-Gen.: Dr. MURAU

Founded: 1959
General meeting: October
Working languages: E
Secretariat: 2 members of staff

Information available:
- Research programme.
- Unified provisions for labelling, compositional requirements.

CPLOL

Standing Liaison Committee of EU Speech Therapists and Logopedists

Comité Permanent de Liaison des Orthophonistes-Logopèdes de l'UE

Rue des Deux Gares 2, 75010 Paris, France
Tel: +33 1/40 35 63 75
Fax: +33 1/40 37 41 42
E-mail: info@cplol.org
Internet: www.cplol.org

Pres.: L. SCHREY-DERN
Sec.-Gen.: B.E. KJAER

Founded: 1988
Working languages: E/F
Secretariat: 1 member of staff

Sectors of activity:
- "Evidence Based Practice: a challenge for Speech and Language Therapists", 05-07/09/2003, Edinburgh.

Information available:
- Database: summaries of the articles on speech and language therapy (CD-Rom).

CPME

Standing Committee of European Doctors

Comité Permanent des Médecins Européens

Rue de la Science 41 3e étage, 1040 Bruxelles, Belgium
Tel: +32 2/732 72 02
Fax: +32 2/732 73 44
E-mail: cpme@euronet.be
Internet: http://www.cpme.be

Pres.: Dr. B. GREVIN
Sec.-Gen.: Mrs. L. TIDDENS-ENGWIRDA

Founded: 1959
General meeting: November
Working languages: F/E
Secretariat: 5 members of staff

Sectors of activity:
- Improving public health for Europeans.

Information available:
- "Electronic News", on website.
- Databases: archives of documents adopted by CP.
- List of members available to the general public, free.

CRIET

The European Textile Finishers' Organisation

Comités Réunis de l'Industrie de l'Ennoblissement Textile dans les Communautés Européennes

Gesamtverbände der Textilveredlungsindustrien in den Europäischen Gemeinschaften

P.O. Box 518, 3900 AM Veenendaal, Netherlands
Tel: +31 318/56 44 88
Fax: +31 318/56 44 87

E-mail: criet@criet.org
Internet: http://www.criet.org

Pres.: K. BUYSE
Sec.-Gen.: C. LODIERS

Founded: 1956
General meeting: June
Working languages: F/E/D
Secretariat: 3 members of staff

Information available:
- Bulletin, quarterly, F/E/D, free, M.
- Members' list, free.

DHAEMAE-SIS

Disposable Hypodermic and Allied Equipment Manufacturers' Association of Europe

Association des Fabricants d'Aiguilles Hypodermiques et Produits Connexes en Europe

Vereinigung der Hersteller von Wegwerfbaren Subkutanspritzen und Verwandten Produkten in Europa

Place Saint Lambert 14, 1200 Bruxelles, Belgium
Tel: +32 2/772 22 12
Fax: +32 2/771 39 09
E-mail: richard.moore@eucomed.be
Internet: www.eucomed.org

Pres.: F. AERTS
Contact: R. MOORE

Founded: 1975
Working languages: E
Secretariat: 2 members of staff

Historical note:
- DHAEMAE became a special interest sector within the organisation of EUCOMED in 1995. Now DHAEMAE-SIS.

Sectors of activity:
- Liaison with CEN Technical Committees and ISO.
- Maintain quality standards throughout Europe; act as a non-competitive platform and spokesman for the manufacturers active in a specific market segment: high volume, sophisticated sterile products in the area of vascular access.

Information available:
- Position papers for statutory authorities.
- List of members, free.

DLC / CLD / ZAV

Dental Liaison Committee in the EU

Comité de Liaison des Praticiens de l'Art Dentaire des Pays de l'UE

Zahnärztlicher Verbindungsausschuss zur EU

Avenue de la Renaissance 1, 1000 Bruxelles, Belgium
Tel: +32 2/736 34 29
Fax: +32 2/735 56 79
E-mail: dlc@bzak.be

Pres.: Dr. W. DONEUS
Contact: Mrs. C. RITTER (Head of Office)

Founded: 1963
General meeting: May and November 2003
Working languages: E/F
Secretariat: 3 members of staff

EAA

European Aluminium Association

Association Européenne d'Aluminium

Avenue de Broqueville 12, 1150 Bruxelles, Belgium
Tel: +32 2/775 63 63
Fax: +32 2/779 05 31
Fax: +32 2/775 63 43
E-mail: eaa@eaa.be

Pres.: Chris BARK JONES
Sec.-Gen.: Patrick DE SCHRYN-MAKERS
Contact: Jaw TE BOS

Founded: 1981
Working languages: E
Secretariat: 16 members of staff

Sectors of activity:
- "Annual press conference", Brussels.

Information available:
- "Aluminium Quarterly Report", free, E/F/D.
- Press kit EAA Press Conference, E, F, G, free.
- Aluminium and Health fact sheets, E, F, G, free.
- EAA Guide: Ordering aluminium products according to EN standards, E, free.
- The implications of EU energy taxation for the European Aluminium Industry, E, free.
- Environmental issues in the Aluminium Industry, E, F, G.
- Aluminium in the Automotive Industry, E, F, G, I.
- Aluminium in the Construction Industry, E, F, I.
- Aluminium in Packaging, E, I.
- "Aluminium Packaging" (Vidéo 10 min.), E, F It, Esp.
- CD-Rom: "TALAT: Training in aluminium application technologies", €25, E.

EAAP / FEZ

European Association for Animal Production

Fédération Européenne de Zootechnie

Europäische Vereinigung für Tierproduktion

Via Nomentana 134, 00162 Roma, Italy
Tel: +39 06/86 32 91 41
Fax: +39 06/86 32 92 63
E-mail: eaap@eaap.org
Internet: www.eaap.org

Pres.: A. AUMAITRE
Sec.-Gen.: A. ROSATI

EACA

European Association of Communications Agencies

Boulevard Brand Whitlock 152, 1200 Bruxelles, Belgium
Tel: +32 2/740 07 10
Fax: +32 2/740 07 17
E-mail: info@eaca.be
Internet: www.eaca.be

Pres.: Mr. J. BEST
Sec.-Gen.: D. LYLE
Contact: Ms. A. WALGRAEF

Founded: 1959
General meeting: 03/10/2002
Working languages: E
Secretariat: 3 members of staff

Sectors of activity:
- "Brussels, the Face behind the Façade", 04/10/2002.

Information available:
- "The Communicator", E, M-NM.

EACB / GEBC

European Association of Cooperative Banks

Groupement Européen des Banques Coopératives

Europäische Vereinigung der Genossenschaftsbanken

Rue de l'industrie 26-38, 1040 Bruxelles, Belgium
Tel: +32 2/230 11 24
Fax: +32 2/230 06 49
E-mail: secretariat@eurocoopbanks.coop
Internet: http://www.eurocoopbanks.coop

Pres.: E. PFLIMLIN
Sec.-Gen.: H. GUIDER

Founded: 1970
Working languages: F/E/D
Secretariat: 8 members of staff

Information available:
- Information brochure, E/F/D, free, M-NM.
- Activity report, every 2 years, M-NM, E/F/D.
- List of members, free of charge.
- Key statistics, annual, free.

EADP

European Association of Directory and Database Publishers

Association Européenne des Editeurs d'Annuaires et de Bases de Données

Europäischer Verband der Adressbuch- und Datenbankverlegger

Avenue Franklin Roosevelt 127, 1050 Bruxelles, Belgium
Tel: +32 2/646 30 60
Fax: +32 2/646 36 37
E-mail: mailbox@eadp.org
Internet: http://www.eadp.org

Pres.: Mr. T. FENWICK
Sec.-Gen.: Ms. A. LERAT

Founded: 1966
Working languages: F/E/D
Secretariat: 4 members of staff

Information available:
- Internal documents, M.
- "Directories in Europe", F/E/D, M and NM, annual, free – CD-Rom Edition.
  1) List of members, classified per country, with their publications.
  2) List of professional groups and the directories published per group.
  3) List of publications classified by products or services.
  4) Code of Professional Practice of European Directory Publishers.
- Newsletter, 4/year, free, F/E/D.
- Survey of European based organizations providing directory products and services, F/E/D.
- Database: members and Directories which they publish.
- List of members available to the general public, free.
Publications:
- "Directories in Europe", free, F/E/D, yearly, September.
- The Internet site: http://www.eadp.org, contains: "Directories in Europe", direct access, English.

EADTU

European Association of Distance Teaching Universities

Association Européenne des Universités d'Enseignement à Distance

Europäischer Verband der Universitaten für Fernstudien

Valkenburgerweg 177, PO Box 2960, 6401 DL Heerlen, Netherlands
Tel: +31 45/567 22 14
Fax: +31 45/574 14 73
E-mail: secretariat@eadtu.nl
Internet: www.eadtu.nl

Pres.: J. BANG
Sec.-Gen.: P. HENDERIKX

Founded: 1987
General meeting: Various
Working languages: E
Secretariat: 7 members of staff

Information available:
- Directory, M – NM.
- Newsletter, M.
- Newsflash, M.
- Brochure, M – NM.
Database:
- member info.
- List of members available to the general public.

EAEVE

European Association of Establishments for Veterinary Education

Association Européenne des Etablissements d'Enseignement Vétérinaire

Europäischer Verband der Veterinarmedizinischen Ausbildungsstatten

Rue Leys 34, 1000 Bruxelles, Belgium
Tel: +32 2/736 80 29
Fax: +32 2/733 78 62
E-mail: eaeve@yahoo.co.uk
Internet: www.eaeve.org

Pres.: Prof. T.H. FERNANDES
Contacts: Prof. B. JONES (Secr.), S. ALLMAN (Exec. Com.)

Founded: 1988
General meeting: May, annually
Working languages: E

Sectors of activity:
- The EAEVE's main activity is running the European system of evaluation of veterinary training. This is now linked to the EAEVE's voluntary system of accreditation of veterinary teaching establishments.
- Stimulating concepts and planning for future developments in veterinary training in Europe.

Information available:
- A newsletter is produced periodically, M-NM.
- Each year since 1997, the EAEVE has published the proceedings of its annual symposium on veterinary education, in English and French. Titles vary according to the theme of the symposium, M-NM.
Database:
- A list of visiting experts. Internal use only.
CD-Rom:
- Member faculties produce such material on veterinary topics. No central list.
- EAEVE's members consist of the 50 veterinary faculties in Europe. All countries are covered, except Russia.
- List of members available to the general public. Free.

EAFE

European Association of Fisheries Economists

FOI, Rolighedsvej 25, 1958 Frederiksberg C, Denmark
Tel: +45/352 86 893
Fax: +45/352 86 80
E-mail: jl@foi.dk
Internet: http://www.eafe-fish.org/

Pres.: P. RODGERS
Contact: E. SABATENA (sec.)

Founded: 1989
General meeting: April
Working languages: E

Information available:
- "Conference Proceedings", annual, E.
- The members' list is available, free of charge.
- MEMBERS: More than 100 corporate, individual (qualified economists), and associate members (non-economists or economists working outside EEA).

EAHP / AEPH / EVKA

European Association of Hospital Pharmacists

Association Européenne des Pharmaciens des Hôpitaux

Europäische Vereinigung der Krankenhaus Apotheker

Walzegem 6, 9860 Oosterzele, Belgium
Tel: +32 9/360 37 89
Fax: +32 9/361 30 10
E-mail: lukcism@pandora.be
Internet: www.eahponline.org

Pres.: Mrs. J. SURUGUE

Founded: 1972
Working languages: E/F
Secretariat: 1 member of staff

Historical note:
- The Association is composed of representatives of the national hospital pharmacy associations in all EU Member States, plus Switzerland, Norway, Hungary and Slovakia.

Sectors of activity:
- To promote and further develop hospital pharmacy and to obtain and maintain general joint pharmaceutical principles and policy in the interest of public health.
- To promote cooperation with other organisations in the area of public health.
- To promote the position and function of the hospital pharmacist.
- To support and uphold the interests of hospital pharmacists from the member states of European Union and Council of Europe.

Information available:
- "European Journal of Hospital Pharmacists", 4/year.
- Database: names and addresses of delegates.

EALM / AEMB

European Association of Livestock Markets

Association Européenne des Marchés aux Bestiaux

Europäischer Viehmärkteverband

Rue de la Loi 81A Bte 9, 4ème étage, 1040 Bruxelles, Belgium
Tel: +32 2/230 46 03
Fax: +32 2/230 94 00
E-mail: uecbv@pophost.eunet.be
Internet: http://uecbv.eunet.be

Pres.: Harrison BOYD
Sec.-Gen.: Jesus LANCHAS
Contact: Jean Luc MERIAUX (UECBV Secretary General)

Founded: 1983
General meeting: May 2004, Spain
Working languages: F/E/D
Secretariat: 4 members of staff

Sectors of activity:
• Increasing the economic weight of livestock markets and their role in the organisation of the livestock and meat market, more specifically as regards price formation.
• Improving and modernising equipment and installations.
• Developing a European information and consultation network

Information available:
• Brochure of the Association, F/E, NM.
• The members' list is available, free of charge.

EANPC / AECNP

European Association of National Productivity Centres

Association Européenne des Centres Nationaux de Productivité

Rue de la Concorde 60, 1050 Bruxelles, Belgium
Tel: +32 2/511 71 00
Fax: +32 2/511 02 97
E-mail: eanpc@skynet.be
Internet: www.eanpc.org

Pres.: Mr. P. REHNSTRÖM
Sec.-Gen.: Mr. S. MOORES

Founded: 1966
General meeting: December
Working languages: E/F
Secretariat: 2 members of staff

Sectors of activity:
• Facilitate international cooperation between national and regional bi- and tripartite bodies focusing on raising productivity and job satisfaction.

Information available:
• "EPI", 3 times a year, E, M.
• The members' list is available, free.

EAPA

European Animal Protein Association

Association Européenne de Protéine Animale

Europäische Vereinigung für Tierprotein

Bd Baudouin 18 – 4th floor, 1000 Bruxelles, Belgium
Tel: +32 2/203 51 41
Fax: +32 2/203 32 44
E-mail: devries@skypro.be

Pres.: C. PENNING
Sec.-Gen.: D. DOBBELAERE
General meeting: November
Working languages: E
Secretariat: 2 members of staff

Information available:
• Members' list, free of charge.

EAPA

European Asphalt Pavement Association

Association Européenne des Producteurs des Enrobés

Europäische Asphalt Verband

Straatweg 68, 3621 BR Breukelen, Netherlands
Tel: +31 346/266 868
Fax: +31 346/263 505
E-mail: info@eapa.org
Internet: http://www.eapa.org

Pres.: H. GORMSEN
Sec.-Gen.: N. REMMER

Founded: 1973
Working languages: E/D/F
Secretariat: 2 members of staff

Sectors of activity:
• Working groups on Standardisation, Technical Developments, Health, Safety and Environment.

EAPO / AEOP

European Association of Fish Producers Organisations

Association Européenne des Organisations de Producteurs dans le secteur de la Pêche

Vereinigung von Erzeugergemeinschaften in der Europäischen Gemeinschaft

H. Baelskaai 25, 8400 Oostende, Belgium
Tel: +32 59/32 35 03
Tel: +32 59/33 22 31
Fax: +32 59/32 28 40
E-mail: rederscentrale@unicall.be
Internet: www.rederscentrale.be

Pres.: J. GOODLAD
Contact: Mr. CORBISIER

Founded: 1980
Working languages: E/F
Secretariat: 1 member of staff

EARTO

European Association of Research and Technology Organisations

Rue du Luxembourg 3, 1000 Bruxelles, Belgium
Tel: +32 2/502 86 98
Fax: +32 2/502 86 93
E-mail: info@earto.org
Internet: http://www.earto.org

Pres.: J. DEKKER
Sec.-Gen.: Dr. H. SCHLESING

Founded: 1999
General meeting: 20–21/03/2003
Working languages: E
Secretariat: 1 member of staff

Historical note:
• FEICRO merged, as of January 1, 1999, with EACRO to form EARTO.

Sectors of activity:
• Furtherance of research, development and technology diffusion for small and medium sized enterprises in Europe, based on its network of cooperative research centres.

Information available:
• "EARTO Newsletter", M-NM.
• List of members.

EAS

European Aquaculture Society

Société Européenne d'Aquaculture

Europäische Gesellschaft für Wasserlandwirtschaft

Slijkensesteenweg 4, 8400 Oostende, Belgium
Tel: +32 59/32 38 59
Fax: +32 59/32 10 05
E-mail: eas@aquaculture.cc
Internet: http://www.easonline.org

Pres.: M. NEW
Contact: A. LANE

Founded: 1976
Working languages: E
Secretariat: 5 members of staff

Information available:
• "Aquaculture International Journal", E, M-NM.
• Database: addresses of people involved/interested in aquaculture: researchers, universities, companies, farmers, etc.
• "Aquaculture Europe Magazine", M-NM.

EASA

European Advertising Standards Alliance

Alliance Européenne pour l'Ethique en Publicité

Rue de la Pépinière 10A, 1000 Bruxelles, Belgium
Tel: +32 2/513 78 06
Fax: +32 2/513 28 61
E-mail: library@easa-alliance.org
Internet: http://www.easa-alliance.org

Pres.: Chr. GRAHAM
Sec.-Gen.: Dr. O. GRAY

Founded: 1992
Working languages: E/F
Secretariat: 2 members of staff

Sectors of activity:
- The single voice for the promotion and support of effective advertising self-regulation in Europe.

Information available:
- "Alliance Update Newsletter", 2/year, E, M-NM.
- "Alliance Briefing", M, monthly, E.
- "EU Regulatory Brief", M, monthly, E.
- "EASA Ad-Alerts", M, E.
- "Cross border complaints report", quarterly, E, M-NM.
- "Cross border complaints leaflet", annual, E/F/D, M-NM.
- "EASA Leaflet", annual, E/F/D, M-NM.
- "Layman's Guide to Self-Regulation", E, M-NM.
- "The EASA Guide to Self-Regulation", E/F/Esp/Russ/Port, M-NM.
- "Advertising Self-Regulation in Europe", E, M-NM.
- EASA Surveys: "Children and Advertising", "Women & Men in Advertising", "Motor Vehicles", "Children's Compendium", "TV Advertising".
- The members' list is available, free of charge.
- Database: library documentation on self-regulation and self-regulatory codes in Europe.
- Information centre open on Mondays and Thursdays by appointment.

EATP

European Association for Textile Polyolefins

Association Européenne des Textiles Polyolefines

Europäischer Verband der Polyolefintextilien

Avenue E. Van Nieuwenhuyse 4, 1160 Bruxelles, Belgium
Tel: +32 2/676 74 72
Fax: +32 2/676 74 74
E-mail: info@eatp.org
Internet: http://www.eatp.org

Pres.: A. THOMSON
Sec.-Gen.: A. F. PRISSE
Contact: C. M. PURVIS (Dir. Gen.)

Founded: 1971
General meeting: November & May
Working languages: E
Secretariat: 4 members of staff

Sectors of activity:
- EATP works closely with a wide range of European organisations including the European Commission, Euratex, the European Standards Organisation, CEN and a number of other organisations who may influence the industry

Information available:
- "Polynews", twice a year, free of charge for members, €200 for non-members, E.
- "Market Study", regular updates, free for members, for sale for non-members, E.
- "Conference Proceedings", free for participants, for sale for non-participants, E.
- Members' list, for members use only.
- Databases: member company information + product info – non member company information.

EAZA

European Association of Zoos and Aquaria

Association Européenne des Zoos et des Aquariums

PO Box 20164, 1000 HD Amsterdam, Netherlands
Tel: +31 20/5200 753
Fax: +31 20/5200 754
E-mail: info@eaza.net
Internet: www.eaza.net

Pres.: Mr B. DE POER
Contact: K. BROUWER (Exec. Dir.)

EBA

European Borates Association

Bd S. Dupuis 233, 1070 Bruxelles, Belgium
Tel: +32 2/524 55 00
Fax: +32 2/524 45 75
E-mail: secretariat@ima-eu.org
Internet: http://www.ima-eu.org

Pres.: R. DOONE

EBC

European Brewery Convention

Convention Européenne de la Brasserie

Europäische Brauereikonvention

PO Box 510, 2380 BB Zoeterwoude, Netherlands
Tel: +31 71/545 60 47
Tel: +31 71/545 66 14
Fax: +31 71/541 00 13
E-mail: secretariat@ebc-nl.com

Pres.: J. VESELY
Sec.-Gen.: Mrs. M. VAN WIJNGAARDEN
Working languages: E/F/D
Secretariat: 3 members of staff

Sectors of activity:
- To initiate, promote and coordinate scientific research work within the malting and brewing industries, inside but also outside Europe. Congresses and symposia are organised, offering scientists, technologists and technicians the opportunity to share up-to-date knowledge and to discuss the results of their work. In addition, committees and working groups serve to facilitate the exchange of know-how and experience. The EBC contributes to the dissemination of research results through its publications.

Information available:
- "EBC Thesaurus", 2nd edition, €45.

EBC

European Builders Confederation

Confédération Européenne de l'Artisanat, des Petites et Moyennes Entreprises du Bâtiment

Europäische Konföderation des Handwerks und der Kleinen und Mittleren Bauunternehmen

Rue Jacques de Lalaing, 4, 1040 Bruxelles, Belgium
Tel: +32 2/514 23 23
Fax: +32 2/514 00 15
E-mail: secretariat@eubuilders.org
Internet: www.eubuilders.org

Pres.: Mr. C. DELGADO
Sec.-Gen.: Mrs. A. THIBAULT

Founded: 1990
General meeting: September/October
Working languages: E/F/Esp/It
Secretariat: 2 members of staff

Historical note:
- The E.B.C. (European Builders Confederation) is the European professional organisation that represents national associations of SMEs and craft enterprises working in the construction sector.
- EBC was established in 1990 and today is made up of twelve organisations representing eight countries (Belgium, France, Italy, Luxembourg, United Kingdom, Spain, Hungary and Slovenia). In total EBC groups together more than

The Directory of EU Information Sources

400.000 craftsmen and SMEs in the construction sector

Sectors of activity:
- Early warning of European legislative developments;
- the ability to influence legislative developments through campaigns;
- information on European standards and the opportunity to influence their development through NORMAPME (the European Association which defends the interests of Craft and SME in European Standardisation) of which EBC is member. NORMAPME sits on all European standardisation bodies (CEN, CENELEC...), and has, together with its members, established a network of fifteen experts including one from EBC;
- partnership with UEAPME (European Association of Craft and SME). EBC's membership of UEAPME enables it to leverage political influence and networking opportunities. EBC signed a partnership contract with UEAPME on November 18, 2003 and as a result benefits from: – UEAPME's political support – permanent access to UEAPME's network – the use of the UEAPME's media services;
- the opportunity to exchange experiences with craft and SME construction associations in other EU Member States. EBC members meet at least four times a year at the Board of Directors meetings, which are generally held in Brussels and which are translated into 4 languages (Fr, En, It, Es). The General Assembly takes place once a year. The host city rotates between EBC members;
- the opportunity to develop bids for collaborative projects co-financed by the European Union.
- Seminar, Brussels, spring 2005 for representatives of the craft and SME of the construction sector in the new member states

Information available:
- "EBC Newsletter", monthly, F/E.
- Annual report, free.
- The members' list is available, free of charge, please see the website

EBF / FEL

European Booksellers Federation
Fédération Européenne des Libraires

Chaussée de Charleroi 51b, 1060 Bruxelles, Belgium
Tel: +32 2/223 49 40
Fax: +32 2/223 49 38
E-mail: frandubruille.eurobooks@sky-net.be
Internet: http://www.ebf-eu.org

Pres.: Mrs. D. STOCKMANN
Contact: Ms. F. DUBRUILLE (Dir)

Founded: 1968
General meeting: May/June
Working languages: E
Secretariat: 2 members of staff

Historical note:
- Europe's bookselling associations have grouped together to resolve problems facing bookshops throughout Europe.

Sectors of activity:
- VAT on books.
- Postal services.
- Retail price maintenance in linguistic area.
- E-commerce.
- Training.

Information available:
- Newsletters, E – free, for members only.
- List of members available to the general public, free.

EBU / UER

European Broadcasting Union
Union Européenne de Radio-Télévision

Ancienne Route 17A,
1218 Grand-Saconnex / Genève, Switzerland
Tel: +41 22/717 21 11
Fax: +41 22/747 40 00
E-mail: ebu@ebu.ch
Internet: http://www.ebu.ch

Pres.: A. WESSBERG
Sec.-Gen.: J. STOCK

Office to the European institutions:
Rue Wiertz 50
B-1050 Bruxelles
Tel: +32 2/286 91 15
Fax: +32 2/286 91 10
E-mail: brux@ebu.ch

Founded: 1950
General meeting: July
Working languages: E/F
Secretariat: 250 members of staff

Historical note:
- Merger of the EBU, on 01/01/1993, with the International Radio & Television Organization (OIRT), the former association of Socialist bloc broadcasters.

Sectors of activity:
- The EBU assists its members in all areas of broadcasting: it briefs them on developments in the audiovisual sector and provides advice; it solves technical and legal problems; it develops news and programme exchanges; it manages the EUROVISION and EURORA.

Information available:
- "Diffusion", quarterly, E/F, M-NM.
- "EBU Review – Technical", published quarterly, E/F, M-NM.
- The EBU publishes technical documents, lists of European stations (broadcasting on long and medium wave, metric waves and television); technical standards, recommendations, statements, and information; special thematic brochures, M-NM.
- List of members, free, M-NM.
- Databases available only to members.
- EBU Yearbook, E/F, M-NM.

ECA

European Cockpit Association
Association Européenne du Cockpit
Europäischer Cockpitverband

Rue du Commerce 41, 1000 Bruxelles, Belgium
Tel: +32 2/705 32 93
Fax: +32 2/705 08 77
E-mail: eca@eca.skynet.be
Internet: http://www.eca-cockpit.com

Pres.: Mr. IVERSEM
Sec.-Gen.: Mr. D. SORENSON

Founded: 1990
General meeting: October each year
Working languages: E/F
Secretariat: 4 members of staff

Sectors of activity:
- To study scientific, technical, documentary and institutional problems of common interest to airline pilots and members of the cockpit crew of the civil aviation industry and the reinforcement of cooperation between those members.

ECA

European Carpet Association
Association Européenne du Tapis
Europäischer Teppichverband

Rue Montoyer 24, 1000 Bruxelles, Belgium
Tel: +32 2/280 18 13
Fax: +32 2/280 18 09

Pres.: M. MILLS
Sec.-Gen.: S. VAN DE VRANDE

Founded: 1994
General meeting: Various
Working languages: E
Secretariat: 2 members of staff

Sectors of activity:
- Standardisation.
- CEN.
- ISO.
- Environment.

ECA

European Chimney Association

Union Syndicale des Cheminées

Rue Louis Blanc 39-41, 92038 Paris La
　Défense Cedex, France
Tel: +33 1/47 17 62 92
Fax: +33 1/47 17 64 27
E-mail: eca@dial.oleane.com

Pres.: Mr. GODDEK
Sec.-Gen.: P. FOLEMPIN

ECA-PME

**European Confederation of
　Associations of Small and Medium-
　Sized Enterprises**

**Confédération Européenne des
　Associations de Petites et
　Moyennes Entreprises**

Avenue de la Renaissance 1, 1000
　Bruxelles, Belgium
Tel: +32 2/739 63 59
Fax: +32 2/736 05 71
E-mail: ceapme@skynet.be
Internet: www.ceapme.org

Pres.: Mr. OHOUEN
Sec.-Gen.: Mr. S. ZICKGRAF
Contact: W. GRUPP (Dir)

ECATRA

**European Car and Truck Rental
　Association**

**Association Européenne des
　Entreprises de Location de
　Véhicules**

Avenue de Tervuren 402, 1150 Bruxelles,
　Belgium
Tel: +32 2/761 66 14
Fax: +32 2/777 05 05
E-mail: do@interel.be
E-mail: do@ecatra.org
Internet: www.ecatra.org

Pres.: B. POLLAK
Sec.-Gen.: Mrs. D. OVERATH

Founded: 1964
General meeting: May or June
Working languages: E
Secretariat: 3 members of staff

Information available:
- The members' list is available, free of
　charge.

ECBP

**European Council for Building
　Professionals**

**Conseil Européen des
　Professionnels de la Construction**

Europäischer Rat für Baufachleute

Ny Vesergade 13, 3rd floor, 1471
　Copenhagen, Denmark
Tel: +45 3336 4150
Fax: +45 3336 4160
E-mail: ecbp@ecbp.org
Internet: www.ecbp.org

Pres.: K. SHERIDAN
Sec.-Gen.: D. GOODSIR

Founded: 1993
Working languages: E

ECBTA

**European Community Banana Trade
　Association**

**Association du Commerce de la
　Banane de la Communauté
　Européenne**

**Verband der Bananenhandler der
　Europäischen Gemeinschaft**

Avenue de Broqueville 272 Bte 17/B,
　1200 Bruxelles, Belgium
Tel: +32 2/777 15 85
Fax: +32 2/777 15 86
E-mail: secretariat@ecbta.com

Contacts: Mrs. AGUADO (Assistant of
　the General Delegate), Ph. BINARD
　(Gen. Del.)

ECCA

European Coil Coating Association

Rue du Luxembourg 19, 1000 Bruxelles,
　Belgium
Tel: +32 2/513 60 52
Fax: +32 2/511 43 61
E-mail: ecca@cybernet.be
Internet: http://www.eccacoil.com

Pres.: J. LAMESCH
Sec.-Gen.: P.J. FRANCK

Founded: 1967
General meeting: May
Working languages: F/E/D
Secretariat: 5 members of staff

Sectors of activity:
- "Autumn Congress", November,
　Brussels.

Information available:
- Brochure "Coil Coated Metal and the
　Automotive Industry", F/It/D.
- Brochure "Coil Coating and the
　Appliance Industry", F/D/Esp/E/It.
- Brochure "How to paint
　ecologically?", F/D/E.
- Brochure "Coil Coating and the
　Building Industry", F/D/Esp/Nl/E/It/
　Swe.
- Brochure "Roofing: the case for
　precoated metal", F/D/Esp/E/It/Nl.
- EURODES Brochure, F/D/E.
- Brochure "The Assembly of Coil
　Coating Metal", E.
- Brochure "Coil coating: Maintenance
　and Repairing", E.

- Binder "Building with coil coating –
　case book", E.
- ECCA Test Methods, E.
- Brochure "Coil Coating", E/F/D.
- Brochure "Saving you Money", E.

ECCA

**European Cable Communications
　Association**

Avenue des Arts 36 – 6th floor, 1040
　Bruxelles, Belgium
Tel: +32 2/521 17 63
Fax: +32 2/521 79 76
E-mail: ecca@ecca.be
Internet: http://www.ecca.be

Pres.: H. RIORDAN
Sec.-Gen.: P. KOKKEN
Contact: Ms. L. HEYLEN

Founded: 1955
Working languages: E
Secretariat: 4 members of staff

Sectors of activity:
- ECCA is the European cable
　television association grouping
　together cable associations and cable
　operators from 21 countries.

Information available:
- "Report of the Annual Meeting", free,
　M, E.
- "Newsletter", 5 a year, M, E.
- List of members available to the
　general public.

ECCO

**European Confederation of
　Conservators / Restorers
　Organizations**

**Confédération Européenne des
　Organisations de Conservateurs**

c/o Michael VAN GOMPEN, Rue
　Archimède 46, 1000 Bruxelles, Belgium
Tel: +32 2/230 72 91
Fax: +32 2/280 17 97
Internet: http://www.ecco-eu.org

Pres.: Y. PLAYER-DAHNSJÖ
Sec.-Gen.: Y. Van REEBUM
Contact: G. VAN GOMPEN

Founded: 1991
Working languages: E/F

Sectors of activity:
- Drafting ethical codes at European
　level.
- Helping to safeguard Europe's
　cultural heritage.

Information available:
- Official papers, M-NM.
- Newsletters, M-NM.
Database:
- Internal: legal articles, European
　legislation, conference proceedings,
　symposia, etc.

ECCS / CECM / EKS

European Convention for Constructional Steelwork

Convention Européenne de la Construction Métallique

Europäische Konvention für Stahlbau

Av. des Ombrages 32 Bte 20, 1200
  Bruxelles, Belgium
Tel: +32 2/762 04 29
Fax: +32 2/762 09 35
E-mail: eccs@steelconstruct.com
Internet: http://www.steelconstruct.com

Pres.: Mr. REMEC
Sec.-Gen.: G. GENDEBIEN

Founded: 1955
General meeting: September
Working languages: E/F/D
Secretariat: 3 members of staff

Sectors of activity:
- The European Convention for Constructional Steelwork has as main purpose the international promotion of the constructional steelwork industry as represented by the respective activities of the member companies of the National Associations. This promotion is realized in the following ways:
- by supporting the promotional activities of the National Associations:
  – exchange of experience in promotion work;
  – publication of promotional texts and marketing arguments to be used in the national promotion activities;
  – international symposia for engineers and architects;
  – public relations for constructional steelwork.
  – practical recommendations for the design and execution of steel structures;
  – building codes (Eurocodes, ...);
  – new applications for non-discrimination of constructional steel (fire and anti-corrosion protection, ...).
- by following the economic development of the constructional steelwork industry;
- by facilitating contacts between industrialists and opinion leaders of the industry.

Information available:
- The ECCS/CECM publishes a wide range of works covering: practical recommendations for the design and execution of steel structures; building codes (Eurocodes); multi-lingual lexicons; etc. For further details and publications list, contact the Brussels office.
- CD-Rom: Presentation of awards.
- List of members, publications and activities on web site.

ECCTO

European Community Cocoa Trade Organisation

Organisation Européenne pour le Commerce des Cacao

KaKao-Handelsorganisation der EG

Cannon Bridge, London EC4R 3XX,
  United Kingdom
Tel: +44 20/7379 2884
Fax: +44 20/7379 2389
E-mail: fcc@liffe.com
Internet: www.cocoafederation.com

Pres.: Sylvain OREBI
Sec.-Gen.: P.M. SIGLEY
Working languages: E
Secretariat: 2 members of staff

Sectors of activity:
- Cocoa Trade.

Information available:
- List of members available on the website.

ECED

European confederation of Equipment Distributors

Bld. De la Woluwe 46 b 14, , 1200
  Bruxelles, Belgium
Tel: +32 02 778 62 00
Fax: +32 02 778 62 62
E-mail: sigma@federauto.be
Internet: www.eced-association.org

Pres.: Leo LUBBERS
Sec.-Gen.: Philippe DECROCK

Historical note:
- A division of ILC; an independent association since 1999

Sectors of activity:
- represents over 2,300 rental operation and equipment distributors across Europe

ECETOC

European Centre for Ecotoxicology and Toxicology of Chemicals

Centre Européen d'Ecotoxicologie et de Toxicologie de Produits Chimiques

Europäisches Zentrum für Ökotoxikologie und Chemietoxikologie

Av. E. Van Nieuwenhuyse 4 Bte 6, 1160
  Bruxelles, Belgium
Tel: +32 2/675 36 00
Fax: +32 2/675 36 25
E-mail: info@ecetoc.org
Internet: http://www.ecetoc.org

Pres.: K.P. PESCHAK
Sec.-Gen.: Michael Y. GRIBBLE

Contact: Geneviève GERITS (Office Manager)

Founded: 1978
Working languages: E
Secretariat: 8 members of staff

Historical note:
- ECETOC was established in 1978 to provide a scientific forum through which the extensive specialist expertise in the European Chemical Industry can be harnessed to research, review, assess and publish studies on the ecotoxicology and toxicology of chemicals.

Sectors of activity:
- The Association's objective is to identify and evaluate, and through such knowledge help industry minimise any potentially adverse effects on health and the environment that may arise through the manufacture and use of chemicals. To achieve this mission, ECETOC facilitates the networking of suitably qualified scientists from its member companies and cooperates in a scientific context with intergovernmental agencies, health authorities, other public and professional institutions.

Information available:
- Numerous scientific reports – E – free for members, government organisations and academic institutions – €125 per copy for non-members.
- Publication list available on website, free to members, government organisations, academic institutions and libraries – €125 per copy for non-members.

ECF

European Coffee Federation

Fédération Européenne du Café

Tourniairestraat 3, P.O. BOX 90445,
  1006 BK Amsterdam, Netherlands
Tel: +31 20/511 38 15
Fax: +31 20/511 38 92
E-mail: ecf@coffee-associations.org
Internet: www.ecf-coffee.org

Pres.: J. VANHORICK
Sec.-Gen.: R. VAESEN

Founded: 1981
Working languages: E

Information available:
- "European Coffee Report", annual, free, E, M-NM.
- List of members available on the website.

ECMA

European Carton Makers Association

PO Box 85612, 2508 CH Den Haag, Netherlands
Tel: +31 70/312 39 11
Fax: +31 70/363 63 48
E-mail: mail@ecma.org
Internet: http://www.ecma.org

Pres.: G. WALL
Sec.-Gen.: J.H.M. LEJEUNE

Founded: 1973
Working languages: E/F/D
Secretariat: 3 members of staff

Sectors of activity:
Interests:
- Standardisation, statistics, promotion, networking.

Information available:
- "ECMA Carton News", 2x/year, E.
- "ECMA Code", 370 carton designs.
- "ECMA Dictionary", 1 700 pages, F/D/E/It/Esp.
- Databases: Code: €34, Dictionary: €16.

ECMA INTERNATIONAL

International Europe-based Industry Association for Standardizing Information and Communication Systems

Rue du Rhône 114, 1204 Genève, Switzerland
Tel: +41 22/849 60 12
Fax: +41 22/849 60 01
E-mail: helpdesk@ecma-international.org
Internet: http://www.ecma-international.org

Pres.: S. STATT
Sec.-Gen.: J. VAN DEN BELD

Founded: 1961
General meeting: June and December
Working languages: E
Secretariat: 6 members of staff

Historical note:
- Founded by computer industries.

Sectors of activity:
- The aims of the Association are: to develop, in co-operation with the appropriate national and international organizations, standards and technical reports in order to facilitate and standardise the use of information processing and telecommunication systems.

Information available:
- Free copies of the ECMA standards are available on written request, M-NM.
- Standards Mechanical Reports, as documents, paper or electronic (www), and on CD-Rom, all free of charge, M-NM.

- Memento, as documents, paper or electronic (www), and on CD-Rom, all free of charge, M-NM.
- 300+ standards and 80+ technical reports.
- List of members available to the general public, in Memento and on CD-Rom, free.
- Database: on www and on CD-Rom, Standards and full texts.
- CD-Rom: all standards and full texts of the last five years, on CD-Rom, free, M-NM.

ECNAIS

European Council of National Associations of Independent Schools

Conseil Européen d'Associations Nationales d'Ecoles Indépendantes

Europäischer Rat Nationaler Verbande von Freien Schulen

Sankt Kjelsgade 3, 2100 Copenhagen, Denmark
Tel: +45/70 20 26 42
Fax: +45/39 12 91 90
E-mail: secretariat@ecnais.org
Internet: www.ecnais.org

Pres.: C. DIAZ MUNIZ
Sec.-Gen.: P. KRISTENSEN

Founded: 1988
Working languages: E

Information available:
- List of members available to the general public: http://www.ecnais.org.

ECOO

European Council of Optometry and Optics

Conseil Européen de l'Optométrie et de l'Optique

Europäischer Rat für Optometrie und Optik

61 Southwark Street, London SE1 0HL, United Kingdom
Tel: +44 20/7207 2193
Fax: +44 20/7620 1140
E-mail: richardcarswell@aop.org.uk
Internet: http://www.europtom.com

Pres.: J. GOBER
Sec.-Gen.: R. CARSWELL
General meeting: May and October
Working languages: E/F/D
Secretariat: 4 members of staff

Information available:
- "Europnews", twice a year, E, free.
- List of members available to the general public, free.

ECPA

European Crop Protection Association

Association Européenne pour la Protection des Cultures

Europäischer Pflanzenschutzverband

Avenue E. Van Nieuwenhuyse 6, 1160 Bruxelles, Belgium
Tel: +32 2/663 15 50
Fax: +32 2/663 15 60
E-mail: ecpa@ecpa.be
Internet: http://www.ecpa.be

Contacts: Dr Friedhelm SCHMIDER (Director General), Ms. K. MATALONE

Founded: 1992
General meeting: November
Working languages: E
Secretariat: 15 members of staff

Sectors of activity:
- Food quality and consumer safety.
- Sustainable agriculture.
- Registration of crop protection products.
- Communications.

Information available:
All available to public on web site (www.ecpa.be):
- Various position papers, E, M-NM.
- Brochures and reports on various projects/subjects, E, M-NM.
- Annual report, M-NM.
- The members' list is available, free of charge.

ECPCI

Association of the European Cigarette Paper Converting Industry

Association Européenne de l'Industrie de Transformation du Papier à Cigarettes

Verband der Europäischen Zigaretten Papier Verarbeitenden Industrie

Rheinallee 25 B, 53173 Bonn, Germany
Tel: +49 228/93 44 60
Fax: +49 228/93 446 20
E-mail: info@verband-rauchtabak.de

Pres.: W. HINZ
Contact: F.P. MARX (Managing Director)

Founded: 1995

ECSA

European Community Shipowners' Associations

Rue Ducale 45, 1000 Bruxelles, Belgium
Tel: +32 2/511 39 40
Fax: +32 2/511 80 92
E-mail: mail@ecsa.be

Internet: www.ecsa.be

Pres.: E. GRIMALDI
Sec.-Gen.: G. DUNLOP

Founded: 1965
Working languages: E
Secretariat: 7 members of staff

Information available:
- Annual Report – M-NM – Free – E.
- Press releases on different policy issues, free, E.
- Newsletter.
- List of members available to the general public, free.

ECSLA

European Cold Storage and Logistics Association

Av. de Broqueville 272 – Bte 48, 1200 Bruxelles, Belgium
Tel: +32 2/762 77 80
Fax: +32 2/762 77 82
E-mail: info@ecsla.be
Internet: http://www.ecsla.be

Pres.: Dimitri VAMVACOPOULOS
Sec.-Gen.: Carole PRIER

Founded: 1967
General meeting: June
Working languages: D/E/Esp/F
Secretariat: 1 member of staff

ECTA

European Cutting Tools Association
Association Européenne d'Outillage Mécanique
Europäischer Verband der Hersteller für Ausrüstungen von Schneidewerkzeugen

Light Trades House, Melbourne Avenue 3, Sheffield S10 2QJ, United Kingdom
Tel: +49 69/66 03 12 51
E-mail: info@lighttradeshouse.uk
Internet: http://www.britishtools.com

Pres.: W. SENGERBUSCH
Working languages: F/E/D

ECTA

European Communities Trade Mark Association
Association Communautaire du Droit des Marques
Vereinigung für Warenzeichen der Europäischen Gemeinschaften

Bisschoppenhoflaan 286, Box 5, 2100 Deurne – Antwerpen, Belgium
Tel: +32 3/326 47 23
Fax: +32 3/326 76 13

E-mail: ecta@ecta.org
Internet: http://www.ecta.org

Pres.: Mr. HENRIKSEN
Sec.-Gen.: Mr. HAVELOCK
Contact: Jane MONTGOMERY

Founded: 1980
Working languages: E
Secretariat: 3 members of staff

Sectors of activity:
- Legal aspects of trade marks and industrial designs at EU level.
Conferences:
- "Twenty-third Annual Conference", June 2-5, 2004, Madeira:
- "Twenty-fourth Annual Conference", 2005, London

Information available:
- Special newsletter n° 30, "Seniority", E, £6.
- "Newsletters", M, twice a year, E.
- "Conference Books", annual, E.
- Special newsletter n° 34, "Comparative Advertising", E, £6.
- "Law Books II & III".
- The members' list can be purchased only with the special agreement of the association, £150.

ECTAA

Group of National Travel Agents' and Tour Operators' Associations within the EU
Groupement des Unions Nationales des Agences et Organisateurs de Voyages de l'UE

Rue Dautzenberg 36 box 6, 1050 Bruxelles, Belgium
Tel: +32 2/644 34 50
Fax: +32 2/644 24 21
E-mail: ectaa@skynet.be
Internet: http://www.ectaa.org

Pres.: W. KROMBACH
Sec.-Gen.: M. DE BLUST

Founded: 1961
General meeting: May
Working languages: F/E
Secretariat: 3 members of staff

Information available:
- "ECTAA report on the EU policies affecting the tourism industry", updated every year.

ECTP/CEU

European Council of Town Planners
Conseil Européen des Urbanistes
Europäischer Rat der Stadt-Regional- und Landesplaner

Chambre des urbanistes de Belgique, Avenue Louise 379 Bte 17, 1050 Bruxelles, Belgium

Tel: +32 2/639 63 00
Fax: +32 2/640 19 90
E-mail: cub@urbanistes.be
Internet: http://www.urbanistes.be

Pres.: Bruno CLERBAUX
Sec.-Gen.: R. UPTON

Founded: 1979
General meeting: Spring & Autumn
Working languages: F/E

Historical note:
- 1979: founding of the Liaison Committee of the National Associations and Institutes of Town Planners in the Member Countries of the EC.

Information available:
- "Reports of the Presidents" of the national associations members of the ECTP, annual, F/E.
- "ECTP Directory", M.
- List of members, free, M-NM.

ECYC

European Confederation of Youth Clubs Organisations
Confédération Européenne des Organisations des Centres de Jeunes

Ornevej 45, 2400 Copenhagen NV, Denmark
Tel: +45 38/10 80 38
Fax: +45 38/10 46 55
E-mail: ecycdk@centrum.dk
Internet: www.ecyc.org

Pres.: Ms. N. LEMOLA
Sec.-Gen.: A. CUMMINGS

ECYF4HC

European Committee for Young Farmers' and 4H Clubs

Schauflergasse 6, 1014 Wien, Austria
Tel: +45 1/53441 8600
Fax: +45 1/53441 8609
E-mail: ecyf4hc@pklwk.at
E-mail: europaeische@landjugend.at
Internet: www.ecyf4hc.org

Pres.: Ms Linda STEELE
Sec.-Gen.: Ms Sabine KLOCKER

Founded: 1957
General meeting: July
Working languages: E
Secretariat: 1 member of staff

Sectors of activity:
- Educate and train young people and create an awareness of the issues of the countryside
- Actively counteract rural depopulation
- Help to develop new rural youth organisations

- Take an active role in the development of environmental and agricultural issues and policies
- Network with other European NGOs
- Lobby and focus the attention of international and national bodies, as well as the general public, on the problems and needs of rural youth

Information available:
- Information for members and non-members is available through the website or on application to the secretariat at ecyf4hc@pklwk.at
- List of members available to the public on the website
- Image folder
- Project reports

EDA

European Decaffeinators Association

Association Européenne des Décaféineurs

Europäischer Verband der Entcoffeinierer

Rue de Copenhague 3, 75008 Paris, France
Tel: +33 1/53 42 13 38
Fax: +33 1/53 42 13 39
E-mail: eufed@cncafe.com

Pres.: B. BISCHEL
Sec.-Gen.: Dr. B. DUFRENE

Founded: 1969
Working languages: D/F/E
Secretariat: 2 members of staff

EDA

European Demolition Association

Association Européenne de Démolition

Europäischer Abbruchverband

PO Box 12, 3740 RC Baarn, Netherlands
Tel: +31 35/54 27 605
Fax: +31 30/68 99 905
E-mail: eda@eda-demolition.com
Internet: www.eda-demolition.com

Pres.: H.M. BUTTON
Contact: L. VAN DER GRIFT (sec)

Founded: 1976
General meeting: May/October
Working languages: E/F/D/Nl

Sectors of activity:
- To serve the interests of demolition contractors in Europe, especially on the issues of: standards, health & safety, research.

Information available:
- The magazine "DEMOVISION" – twice a year – in F/E/Nl/D.

EDA

European Dairy Association

Association Laitière Européenne

Europäischer Milchindustrieverband

Rue Montoyer 14, 1000 Bruxelles, Belgium
Tel: +32 2/549 50 40
Fax: +32 2/549 50 49
E-mail: eda@euromilk.org
Internet: http://eda.euromilk.org

Pres.: R. BRUZCZAK
Sec.-Gen.: J.F. KLEIBEUKER

Founded: 1995
General meeting: 01/11/2002
Working languages: E/F/D
Secretariat: 6 members of staff

Information available:
- Dairy Bulletin, bi-monthly, M, E/F/D.
- Annual report, M, E/F/D.
- List of members available free of charge.

EDANA

European Disposables and Nonwovens Association

Avenue E. Plasky 157, 1030 Bruxelles, Belgium
Tel: +32 2/734 93 10
Fax: +32 2/733 35 18
E-mail: info@edana.org
Internet: http://www.edana.org

Pres.: R. ALDORF

Founded: 1971
General meeting: June
Working languages: E
Secretariat: 11 members of staff

Sectors of activity:
- Nonwovens – Hygiene absorbent products – superabsorbents.
- EDANA organises workshops and symposia, and participates at fairs and congresses (Index Congress).
- EDANA sets and publishes test methods for various properties of nonwovens to be used as guidelines when establishing contractual specifications.
- EDANA's day-to-day work is carried out by a professional staff at the Association's offices in Brussels, and its main activities are dealt with by Committees and Task Forces which work on specific problems (e.g. Nonwoven Producers, Medical or Hygiene Converters and other specialised end-uses).

Information available:
- "GMP Summary for Health Care Nonwovens" – 7 pages – in E/F/D/It/Esp – minimum order of 5 copies – 25 CHF.

- "ERT – EDANA – Book of 23 recommended test methods" – 250 CHF.
- "Nonwovens" – minimum 5 copies: 70 CHF, or combined with another order – E/F/D.
- "Health benefits of diapers".

EDIG

European Defence Industries Group

Gulledelle 94 – B5, 1200 Bruxelles, Belgium
Tel: +32 2/775 81 10
Fax: +32 2/775 81 31
E-mail: edig@skynet.be
Internet: www.edig.org

Pres.: C. ANTONINI
Sec.-Gen.: J. WESENER

Founded: 1990
General meeting: May – December
Working languages: E
Secretariat: 3 members of staff

Historical note:
- 2004: Merger planned between AECMA, EDIG and EUROSPACE. Please refer to www.asd-europe.org for further information of the new association ASD

Information available:
- Database on European cooperative programmes and the companies and persons involved.
- List of members available to the general public, free.

EDiMA

European Digital Media Association

Association Européenne des Medias Numberiques

Friars House, Office 118, 157-168, Blackfriars Road, London SE1 8EZ, United Kingdom
Tel: +44 20/7401 2661
Fax: +44 20/7928 5850
E-mail: wes.himes@edima.org
Internet: www.edima.org

Contacts: Wes HIMES, Lucy CRONIN, Marco RUPP

Founded: 2000

Sectors of activity:
- Contributes to the creation of a business and legal environment in Europe that encourages new media companies to deploy innovative technologies that support the promotion, sale and protection of digital copyrighted content

EDMA

European Diagnostic Manufacturers Association

Place Saint Lambert 14, 1200 Bruxelles, Belgium
Tel: +32 2/772 22 25
Fax: +32 2/772 23 29
E-mail: edma@edma-ivd.be
Internet: www.edma-ivd.be

Pres.: C. TOBIN
Contacts: C. TARRAJAT (DG), Mrs. MOUNYA BAYA (Secr.)

Founded: 1991
General meeting: June
Working languages: E
Secretariat: 6 members of staff

Sectors of activity:
- to represent the in vitro diagnostics (IVD) industry active in Europe:
- to raise awareness and promote better use of laboratory testing;
- to work towards a realistic economic environment for healthcare;
- to support an appropriate regulatory system

Information available:
- Research statistics, website, M-NM.
- Minutes of meetings, EDMA documents, EDMA publications, EDMA News, EDMA Workshops, website, M

EDTNA/ERCA

European Dialysis and Transplant Nurses' Association / European Renal Care Association

Association Européenne du Personnel Soignant en Dialyse et Greffes / Association Européenne des Soins Rénaux

Verband des Europäischen Dialyse- und Transplantationspflegepersonals / Verband des Europäischen Nierenpflegepersonals

Pilatusstrasse 35 – Postfach 3052, 6002 Luzern, Switzerland
Tel: +41 41/766 05 80
Fax: +41 41/766 05 85
E-mail: info@edtna-erca.org
Internet: www.edtna-erca.org

Pres.: Georgia THANASA
Sec.-Gen.: Josefa FENSELAU

Founded: 1971
General meeting: The EDTNA/ERCA International Conference is held every year in September
Working languages: E/D/F/Esp/It/Gr
Secretariat: 7 members of staff

Information available:
- All available information, both for members and non-members may be found advertised on the website.

- List of members not available to the public.
- European Core Curriculum (Member: €13/Non-Member: €16).
- European Standards (Member: €13/Non-Member: €16).
- Psycho/social handbook (Member: 1st copy free, 2nd €13/Non-Member: €16).
- Monograph Acute Renal Failure (Member: €10/Non-Member: €15).
- Professional Nursing Portfolio (Member: 1st copy free, 2nd €10/Non-Member: €10).

EEA

European Elevator Association

Avenue L. Gribaumont 1 Bte 5, 1150 Bruxelles, Belgium
Tel: +32 2/772 10 93
Fax: +32 2/771 86 61
E-mail: info@eea-eeig.org
Internet: http://www.eea-eeig.org

Sec.-Gen.: L. RIVET
Contact: Stella BEDEUR (Office Manager)

Founded: 1990
General meeting: March
Working languages: E
Secretariat: 3 members of staff

Sectors of activity:
- The EEA seeks to promote the quality, safety and highest technical standards for installations and services relating to lifts, escalators and moving walkways in the European Union.

Information available:
- "EEA General Plaquette", M-NM.
- Guideline: "From the lift directive to the owner documentation", M.

EEA

European Express Association

Avenue de Cortenbergh 118, Box 8, 1000 Bruxelles, Belgium
Tel: +32 2/737 95 76
Fax: +32 2/737 95 01
E-mail: pblanchard@hillandknowlton.com
Internet: www.euroexpress.org

Pres.: J. MULDERS
Sec.-Gen.: P. BLANCHARD

Founded: 2000
General meeting: September
Working languages: E

Sectors of activity:
- Postal affairs.
- Customs.
- Indirect taxation.
- Transport.
- Security.
- Environment.

- The importance and impact of the express industry in Europe.
Conference:
- "Hermes Award".

Information available:
- Position papers.
- Databases: members and officials.

EECA

European Electronic Component Manufacturers' Association

Association Européenne des Fabricants de Composants Electroniques

Europäische Vereinigung der Elektronischen Komponentenhersteller

Diamant Building, Blvd Auguste Reyers 80, 1030 Bruxelles, Belgium
Tel: +32 2/706 86 00
Fax: +32 2/706 86 05
E-mail: secretariat.gen@eeca.be
Internet: http://www.eeca.org

Pres.: E. VILLA
Sec.-Gen.: M. SPÄT

Founded: 1973
General meeting: November
Working languages: E
Secretariat: 5 members of staff

Sectors of activity:
- The European Electronic Component Manufacturers' Association – EECA – exists to promote the harmonious development, viability and independence of the European electronic component manufacturing industry to enable it to function competitively and efficiently in the worldwide marketplace. EECA speaks for the various national groupings of European electronic components manufacturers, and is, in fact, the only international association representing them in Western Europe. All national associations of elcetronic components manufacturers from existing or potential EU member countries are eligible for membership. At present this membership includes EU component manufacturers industries and the industry associations of Belgium, France. Italy, the Netherlands, Spain, the UK, Austria, Sweden – together representing nearly 500 electronic components manufacturers with a total workforce of over a quarter of a million

Information available:
- "ESiA Newsletter"
- "EPCiA White Book"
- "EDiA Newsletter"
- "EPiA Folder"
- List of members avaialble through the website

EEPA

European Egg Processors Association

Association des Producteurs Européens d'Ovoproduits

Euro Eiprodukten Fabrikanten Verband

Bilkske 93, 8000 Brugge, Belgium
Tel: +32 50/44 00 70
Fax: +32 50/44 00 77
E-mail: filiepsr@eepa.org
Internet: www.eepa.org

Pres.: J.-Y. JUSTEAU
Sec.-Gen.: F. VAN BOSSTRAETEN

Founded: 1995
Working languages: Nl/F/E/D/Esp
Secretariat: 3 members of staff

Information available:
• List of members available to the general public, free.

EFA

European Driving Schools Association

Fédération Européenne des Auto Ecoles

Europäische Fahrlehrer Assoziation

Hofbrunnstrasse 13, 81479 München, Germany
Tel: +49 89/74 91 49 40
Fax: +49 89/74 91 49 44
E-mail: efa-eu@lbfmic.de
Internet: http://www.efa-eu.com

Pres.: G. VON BRESSENSDORF
Working languages: E/F/D
Secretariat: 1 member of staff

Sectors of activity:
• Bringing together professional driving school federations to harmonise the instruction of future drivers in Europe; harmonising driving tests; harmonising driving instructors' training.

Information available:
• "European road safety initiatives", free.
• The members' list is available, free of charge.

EFAA

European Federation of Accountants and Auditors for SMEs

Rue Newton 1, 1000 Bruxelles, Belgium
Tel: +32 2/736 88 86
Fax: +32 2/736 29 64
E-mail: info@efaa.com
Internet: http://www.efaa.com

Pres.: K.-E. HJORTH
Sec.-Gen.: P. POULSEN

Founded: 1994
Working languages: E
Secretariat: 1 member of staff

Information available:
• Newsletter, monthly, E.
• "Annual Report", E.
• Press Releases.
• List of members available to the general public, free.

EFAH / FEDESA

European Federation of Animal Health

Fédération Européenne de la Santé Animale

Europäische Föderation für Tiergesundheit

Rue Defacqz 1 Bte 8, 1000 Bruxelles, Belgium
Tel: +32 2/543 75 60
Fax: +32 2/537 00 49
E-mail: efah@efahsec.org
Internet: http://www.efahsec.org

Pres.: P. JAMES
Contact: B. WILLIAMS

Founded: 1987
Working languages: E/F
Secretariat: 11 members of staff

Sectors of activity:
• To inform the public of the animal health industry's research-based and innovative activities.
• To confirm its commitment to safeguarding the health of animals and ensuring the provision of healthy nutritious food products of animal origin.

Information available:
• Annual Report, F/E, M/NM.
• Dossier 11: "Sustainable Agriculture: Feeding more people, Safeguarding Wildlife and the Environment", M/NM.
• Dossier 15: "Veterinary Product Registration", M/NM.
• Dossier 13: "Companion Animals Today", M/NM.
• Dossier 14: "Facts and Figures about the European Animal Health Industry", M/NM.
• "Newsletter for the FEDESA members", F/E, M.
• "Fits News", M.
• "The Caruso Paper: Biotechnology in the European Union. Establishing a meaningful dialogue on biotechnology", free, M.
• "Economic effects of technology in agriculture: Do performance enhancers for animals benefit consumers?", M/NM.
• "The potential risk effects of antimicrobial residues on human gastro-intestinal microflora.", M/NM.
• "The Animal Health Care Industry in Europe", €400 for the first copy, €50 for additional copies, M/NM.
• "Responsible use of antimicrobials to control disease in farm animals", free, M/NM.
• "How to use the TRC – A briefing note for the membership of FEDESA", M.
• "A Survey of the Animal Health Industry in the Central and Eastern European Countries (CEESA Study)", €500, M/NM.
• "Benchmarking the competitiveness of the European Animal Health Industry", M/NM.
• The members' list is available, free of charge.
• Database: full coordinates of members, journalists and associations related to the FEDESA, EU members whose activities are related to the FEDESA.
• Members Reference Disk 2000 (CD-Rom), M.
• Veterinary Vaccinology, M/NM.
• "Full proceedings Forum V: Risk assessment & risk management for the food chain", E, M/NM.

EFAMRO

European Federation of Associations of Market Research Organisations

Fédération Européenne des Associations d'Instituts de Marketing

Europäische Föderation der Marktforschungs-institutsverbande

26 Chester Close North, Regent's Park, London NW1 4JE, United Kingdom
Tel: +44 20/7224 3873
Fax: +44 20/7224 3873
E-mail: efamro@aol.com
Internet: www.efamro.org

Pres.: V. RAVET
Contact: B. BATES (Dir. Gen.)

Founded: 1992
General meeting: Variable
Working languages: E

Information available:
• List of members available to the general public on web site

EFAPIT

European Federation of Animal Protein Importers and Traders

Fédération Européenne des Importateurs et Négociants en Protéine Animale

Europäische Föderation der Tierproteinimporteure und -Händler

Heer Bokelweg 157b, P.O. Box 202, 3000
   AE Rotterdam, Netherlands
Tel: +31 10/467 31 88
Fax: +31 10/467 87 61
E-mail: cvg@graan.com
Internet: http://www.graan.com

Pres.: Mr. O. DEROME
Contact: Mrs. M. S. STEGEHUIS
   (Secretary-Treasurer)

Founded: 1961
Working languages: E
Secretariat: 3 members of staff

Information available:
- EFAPIT does not publish any official
  documents.
- Informal information and statistics
  are available but solely for members.
- The members' list is available free of
  charge.

EFB

**European Federation of
   Biotechnology**

**Fédération Européenne de
   Biotechnologie**

**Europäische Föderation
   Biotechnologie**

Oude Delft 60, 2611 CD Delft,
   Netherlands
Tel: +31 15/21 27 800
Fax: +3115/ 21 27 111
E-mail: david@efbpublic.org
Internet: http://www.efbweb.org

Pres.: Prof. Børge DIDERICHSEN
Sec.-Gen.: Dr. David BENNETT

Founded: 1978
General meeting: General Assembly is
   always held together with the biannual
   European Congress on biotechnology
Working languages: E

Sectors of activity:
- The European Federation of
  Biotechnology is the association of
  scientific institutes, societies,
  companies, biotechnology
  associations and personal members
  active or interested in biotechnology
  and its safe and beneficial
  applications.

Main activities:
- EFB runs its scientific network
  within the rapidly developing field of
  biotechnology by performing a wide
  range of activities:
  – fostering collaboration between
  European biotechnologists from
  industry and academia and
  promoting biotechnology in a socially
  and ethically acceptable manner;
  – promoting international
  cooperation and networks in Europe
  and beyond;
  – initiating and/or organising
  specialised meetings & events, for
  example the biennial European
  Congress on Biotechnology;

– promoting education and training;
– promoting public understanding of
biotechnology;
– preparing position papers, reviews
and expertises on topical issues;
– publishing reports on new
developments in science;
– maintaining good contacts with the
European Commission's Research
Directorate-General and
collaborating as teams of experts in
research funding;
– disseminating information on
European Commission programmes
and policy.

Information available:
- Opinion papers (prepared by the
  Section on Applied Genome Research
  / former Working Party on Applied
  Molecular Genetics).
- Review papers: "Safe Biotechnology"
  Series (prepared by the Task Group
  on Safety in Biotechnology).
- "Made by Genetic Engineering"
  Series (prepared by the Section on
  Applied Genome Research / former
  Working Party on Applied Molecular
  Genetics).
- "Briefing Papers" (prepared by the
  Task Group on Public Perceptions in
  Biotechnology).
- Books, proceedings.
- Members registration database.
- The list of members is not available to
  the general public.

EFBS / FEECL / EuBV

**European Federation of Building
   Societies**

**Fédération Européenne d'Epargne
   et de Crédit pour le Logement**

**Europäische
   Bausparkassenvereinigung**

c/o Verband der Privaten Bausparkassen
   eV, Klingerhöfer Strasse 4, 10785
   Berlin, Germany
Tel: +32 2/231 03 71
Tel: +49 30/59 00 91 913
Fax: +32 2/ 230 82 45
Fax: +49 30/59 00 91 917
E-mail: info@efbs-bausparkassen.org
E-mail: info@efbs.org
Internet: www.efbs.org

Pres.: M. CAPELLA
Contact: Andreas J. ZEHNDER (Dir)

Founded: 1962
General meeting: 01–03/10/2002
Working languages: D/E/F
Secretariat: 3 members of staff

Sectors of activity:
- The Federation promotes the idea of
  home ownership.

Information available:
- "Annual Report", D/E/F, M-NM.
- "Newsletter", 4 times/year, D/E/F,
  M-NM.

- The members' list is available, free of
  charge.

EFBWW / FETBB / EFBH

**European Federation of Building
   and Woodworkers**

**Fédération Européenne des
   Travailleurs du Bâtiment et du
   Bois**

**Europäische Föderation der Bau-
   und Holzarbeiter**

Rue Royale 45 bte 3, 1000 Bruxelles,
   Belgium
Tel: +32 2/227 10 40
Fax: +32 2/219 82 28
E-mail: info@efbh.be
Internet: http://www.efbww.org

Pres.: A. JOHANSON
Sec.-Gen.: H. BIJEN

Founded: 1957
General meeting: Every 4 years – next:
   2007
Working languages: F/E/Nl/D
Secretariat: 8 members of staff

Sectors of activity:
- European umbrella-organisation for
  trade unions in the construction/wood
  and allied trades.
- Protection of interests of employees in
  the building, wood and woodworking
  sector.

Information available:
- Resolutions on different subjects (F/E/
  Nl/D/Esp/It/Dan), M-NM.

  – Public contracts.

  – European legislation (posting of
  workers,
  migration, health and safety).

  – Woodworking machines.

  – Building and woodworking
  environment, etc.
- Reports on specific subjects (in 4
  languages: F/E/Nl/D): published at
  conferences on building and
  woodworking, M-NM.
- Note on "Safety and health in the
  construction industry".
- Study on "The situation of workers in
  small and medium-sized enterprises
  in the building and woodworking
  sectors".
- Report on collective agreements in
  the furniture industry/construction
  industry/dredging, E.
- Information leaflets.
- "European Union: Posting of Workers
  in the Construction Industry", 13
  Ecus, Nl/D/E.
- "Construction Labour Research
  News", 4/year, free, E.
- "Multimessage", 6/year, free, E/F.
- List of members, free.

EFCA

European Federation of Engineering Consultancy Associations

Fédération Européenne des Associations d'Ingénieurs-Conseils

EuropäischeVereinigung der Verbände Beratender Ingenieure

Avenue des Arts 3-4-5, 1210 Bruxelles, Belgium
Tel: +32 2/209 07 70
Fax: +32 2/209 07 71
E-mail: efca@efca.be
Internet: http://www.efcanet.org

Pres.: Martin GÜLDNER
Sec.-Gen.: Jan VAN DER PUTTEN

Founded: 1992
General meeting: May
Working languages: E
Secretariat: 3 members of staff

Sectors of activity:
- The purpose of the association, which is a non-profit organisation, is, within and outside Europe, to further the scientific study and research concerning problems of engineering consultancy, to represent and promote European engineering consultancy and related services and to defend the interests of its members.
- Its general purpose is to further the principles, understanding, methods and practices of European engineering consultancy and related services and to provide a forum for exchange of information and experience in areas of interest to its members.

Information available:
- "EFCA Euro News", E, free, M-NM.
- The members' list is available on request and on the EFCA website, free of charge.
- "Panorama of EC Industry", by Eurostat, E/F.
- "Status Report on Quality Assurance for Engineering Consultancy Services in Europe", E.
- Bulletin, fortnightly, E, free, M (for NM on website).
- "Project Financing – Sustainable Solutions", E, M-NM, €20.

EFCE

European Federation of Chemical Engineering

Fédération Européenne du Génie Chimique

Europäische Föderation für Chemie-Ingenieurwesen

c/o DECHEMA, Theodor-Heuss-Allee 25, 60486 Frankfurt am Main, Germany
Tel: +49 69/75 64 143/209
Fax: +49 69/75 64 201
E-mail: efce@decherma.de
Internet: www.efce.info

Pres.: J.C. CHARPENTIER
Sec.-Gen.: G. KREYSA

c/o Institution of Chemical Engineers
Railway Terrace 165-189
UK-CV21 3HQ Rugby
Tel: +44 1788/57 82 14
Fax: +44 1788/56 08 33
SG: T. J. EVANS,

c/o Société de Chimie Industrielle
Rue St Dominique 28,
75007 Paris
Tel: +33 1/53 59 02 18
Fax: +33 1/45 55 40 33

Founded: 1953
Working languages: E

Sectors of activity:
- The Federation does not itself organize any events. All activities are carried out by its member societies, including technical and scientific events, and the Federation sponsors the events in the field of chemical engineering. The sponsored events are listed in a calandar of events which can be found on the internet at http: //www.efce.org/

Information available:
- "EFCE Newsletter", due to appear twice annually, free, E.

EFCEM

European Federation of Catering Equipment Manufacturers

Fédération Européenne des Constructeurs d'Equipement de Grandes Cuisines

Europäischer Verband der Hersteller von Grosskochanlagen

c/o ANIE, Via Gattamelata 34, 20149 Milano, Italy
Tel: +39 02/32 64 1
Fax: +39 02/32 64 327
E-mail: efcm@anie.it
Internet: www.efcem.org

Pres.: C. LOVISATTI
Sec.-Gen.: Mr. R. TARRANTO
Contact: A. GUERRINI

Founded: 1969
Working languages: E
Secretariat: 5 members of staff

Information available:
- "Membership List", annual, E, M-NM.
- "Std Listing", quarterly, free, E/F/ D, M.

EFCF

European Federation of City Farms

Schapenstraat 14, 1750 Lennik, Belgium
Tel: +32 2/532 01 90
Tel: +32 2/569 14 45
Fax: +32 2/532 23 22
E-mail: efcf@vgc.be

Internet: http://www.cityfarms.org

Pres.: M. DE STAERCKE

EFCI / FENI

European Federation of Cleaning Industries

Fédération Européenne du Nettoyage Industriel

Europäischer Dachverband der Gebäudereinigung

Rue de l'Association 27, 1000 Bruxelles, Belgium
Tel: +32 2/225 83 30
Fax: +32 2/225 83 39
E-mail: office@feni.be
Internet: www.feni.be

Pres.: I. FIEREMANS
Contact: O. RICHARD

Founded: 1988
Working languages: F/E
Secretariat: 3 members of staff

Sectors of activity:
- Representation of the profession before the EU Institutions.
- Analysis and dissemination of all EU information available concerning the cleaning industry sector.

Information available:
- "The Cleaning Industry in Europe", annual, M-NM, E/F, €125.
- "EFCI Booklet", F/E.
- "European Cleaning Journal", bimonthly, E.
- All information available on the sector in Europe (legislation, statistics, ...) on demand, free.
- The members' list is available, free of charge.

EFCLIN

European Federation of the Contact Lens Industry

Fédération Européenne des Industries de Lentilles de Contact

Waterwilg 1, 4761 WN Zeren Bergen, Netherlands
Tel: +31 16/83 29 308
Fax: +31 16/83 27 0 69
E-mail: info@etclin.com
Internet: http://www.etclin.com

Pres.: K. PAYNE

EFEMA

European Food Emulsifiers Manufacturers' Association

Association des Fabricants Européens d'Emulsifiants Alimentaires

Verband Europäischer Hersteller von Nahrungsmittelemulgatoren

Av. E. Van Nieuwenhuyse 4 Bte 2, 1160
  Bruxelles, Belgium
Tel: +32 2/676 73 96
Fax: +32 2/676 73 32
E-mail: efema@ecco.eu.com
Internet: http://www.emulsifiers.org

Sec.-Gen.: Mrs. M. VANOVERSTRATEN

Founded: 1973
General meeting: November
Working languages: E

Information available:
• List of member manufacturers, NM.

EFER

**European Federation of Electronics
  Retailers**

**Fédération Européenne des
  Commerçants en Electronique
  Domestique et Electroménager**

**Europäische Föderation der
  Einzelhändler für Elektronischen
  Hausgeräte**

Regentlaan 58, 1000 Bruxelles, Belgium
Tel: +32 2/550 17 14
Fax: +32 2/550 17 29
E-mail: dirk.rutten@nelectra.be

Pres.: W. VAN HOVE
Sec.-Gen.: D. RUTTEN

Founded: 1991
Working languages: E/F
Secretariat: 1 member of staff

Information available:
• Circular letter, 1 a week, F/E.
• Newsletter, bimonthly, free, F/E.
• List of members available to the
  general public, free.

EFF

European Franchise Federation

**Fédération Européenne de la
  Franchise**

Europäische Franchiseföderation

Avenue Louise 179 box14, 1050
  Bruxelles, Belgium
Tel: +32 2/520 16 07
Fax: +32 2/520 17 35
E-mail: info@eff.franchise.com
Internet: http://www.eff-franchise.com

Pres.: P. JEANMART
Contact: Mrs. C. CHOPRA (Exec. Dir.)

Founded: 1975
General meeting: Last quarter of each
  year
Working languages: E/F
Secretariat: 1 member of staff

Historical note:
• The EFF has had permanent offices in
  Brussels since 1998. The EFF has
  defined and upholds an auto-
  regulatory European Code of Ethics
  for Franchising (see web site).

Sectors of activity:
• Surveys on Franchising in Europe.
• Lobbying the Commission &
  European Parliament on specific
  legislation. The EFF has its own legal
  committee.
• Being at the heart of reflections on the
  evolution of franchising in Europe.
• Promoting inter-member
  benchmarking as a means of helping
  newer members become fully effective
  in their respective roles.

Information available:
• List of national franchise
  associations, EFF members – E – NM.
• Franchise statistics in Europe – NM.
• Text of the European code of ethics in
  the franchise sector, in language of
  each member, NM.
• "European Newsletter", 4/year, E, M.

EFFA

**European Flavour & Fragrance
  Association**

**Association des Industries d'Arômes
  et de Parfums**

Square Marie-Louise 49, 1000 Bruxelles,
  Belgium
Tel: +32 2/238 99 05
Fax: +32 2/230 02 65
E-mail: secretariat@effaorg.org
Internet: http://www.effa.be

Pres.: Mr. BODIFÉ
Sec.-Gen.: Mr. DILS

Founded: 1961
General meeting: April
Working languages: E
Secretariat: 3 members of staff

EFFAT

**European Federation of Trade
  Unions in the Food, Agriculture
  and Tourism sectors and allied
  branches**

**Fédération Européenne des
  Syndicats des Secteurs de
  l'Alimentation, de l'Agriculture et
  du Tourisme et des Branches
  Connexes**

**Europäische Föderation der
  Gewerkschaften des Lebens-,
  Genussmittel-, Landwirtschafts-
  und Tourismussektors und
  verwandter Branchen**

Rue Fossé-aux-Loups 38, 1000 Bruxelles,
  Belgium
Tel: +32 2/218 77 30
Fax: +32 2/218 30 18
E-mail: effat@effat.org
Internet: http://www.effat.org

Sec.-Gen.: H. WIEDENHOFER
Working languages: F/E/D/It
Secretariat: 10 members of staff

Historical note:
• Merger of EFA and ECF-IUF.

EFFC

**European Federation of Foundation
  Contractors**

**Fédération Européenne des
  Entreprises de Fondations**

**Europäischer Verband der
  Spezialtiefbauer**

Forum Court, Copers Cope Road 83,
  Beckenham BR3 INR, United Kingdom
Tel: +44 20/86 63 09 48
Fax: +44 20/86 63 09 49
E-mail: effc@effc.org
Internet: http://www.effc.org

Pres.: D.E. SHERWOOD
Contact: D. JENNINGS

Founded: 1988
Working languages: E

Sectors of activity:
• Development of European Technical
  Codes, improved conditions of
  contract for specialist activities.
• Safe working practices and good
  environment practice.

Information available:
• Annual Report, E.
• The members' list is available on the
  website.

EFFCA

**European Food and Feed Cultures
  Association**

**Association Européenne des
  Fabricants de Ferments à Usage
  Agro-alimentaire**

**Europäische Vereinigung der
  Fermenthersteller für
  Nahrungsmittelindustriegebrauch**

Bd Haussmann 85, 75008 Paris, France
Tel: +33 1/42 65 41 58
Fax: +33 1/42 65 02 05
E-mail: effca@effca.com
Internet: www.effca.com

Pres.: L. FREDICKSEN
Sec.-Gen.: N. VERGA (SG)

Founded: 1991
Working languages: E/F
Secretariat: 1 member of staff

Sectors of activity:
• Agri-food (ingredients and
  technological auxiliaries – processing
  aids).
• Lactic ferment – cultures.
• Human and animal foodstuffs.

Information available:
• The members' list is available, free of
  charge.

EFFCM / FEPF

European Federation of Fibre Cement Manufacturers

Fédération Européenne des Producteurs de Fibres-Ciment

Europäische Föderation der Faserzementindustrie

Av. de Tervueren 361, 1150 Bruxelles, Belgium
Tel: +32 2/778 12 11
Fax: +32 2/778 12 12

Pres.: M. VANDENBOSH
Sec.-Gen.: Mrs NOUS

Founded: 1984
General meeting: June
Working languages: E

Sectors of activity:
- The aim of the Federation is to encourage and promote international cooperation in the field of scientific research, and technical applications, and to represent the fibre-cement industry before the EU's institutions.

Information available:
- The members' list is available, free of charge.

EFFOST

European Federation of Food Science and Technology

Fédération Européenne de la Science et de la Technologie Alimentaire

Europäische Föderation der Nahrungsmittelwissenschaft und - Technologie

c/o Agrotechnology + Food Innovation, Bornsesteeg 59, PO Box 8129, 6700 EV Wageningen, Netherlands
Tel: +31 317/475 000
Fax: +31 317/475 347
E-mail: info@effost.org
Internet: http://www.effost.org

Contact: Mrs. N.M. SANDER

Founded: 1986
Working languages: E
Secretariat: 2 members of staff

Information available:
- Journal: "Trends in Food Science & Technology".
- Journal: "Innovative Food Science and Emerging Technologies (IFSET)".
- Yearbook: "Food Technology International".

EFFS

European Federation of Funeral Services

Fédération Européenne de Services Funéraires

Europäischer Vereinigung für Bestattungsdienste

Obere Donaustrasse 53, 1020 Wien, Austria
Tel: +43 171/737 62 36
Fax: +43 171/73 76 262
E-mail: office@effs.at
Internet: http://www.effs.at

Pres.: P. SKYBA

EFIA

European Fertilizer Import Association

Association Européenne des Importateurs d'Engrais

Europäischer Verband der Düngemittelimporteure

Rue de la Loi 62, 1040 Bruxelles, Belgium
Tel: +32 2/219 16 20
Fax: +32 2/219 16 26
E-mail: fvermeeren@whitecase.com

Pres.: O. GEYER
Contact: F. VERMEEREN

Founded: 1981
Working languages: E
Secretariat: 3 members of staff

Information available:
- List of members available upon request, free.

EFIP / FEPI / EVB

European Federation of Inland Ports

Fédération Européenne des Ports Intérieurs

Europäischer Verband der Binnenhafen

Place des Armateurs 6, 1000 Bruxelles, Belgium
Tel: +32 2/420 70 37
Fax: +32 2/420 03 71
E-mail: efip@skynet.be
Internet: www.inlandports.org

Sec.-Gen.: J. STURM

Founded: 1994
Working languages: E
Secretariat: 2 members of staff

Information available:
- Annual report.
- List of members available to the general public on website.

EFJ/IFJ / FEJ/FIJ / EJF/IJF

European Federation of Journalists

Fédération Européenne des Journalistes

Europaische Journalisten- Föderation

Résidence Palace – Bloc C, Rue de la Loi 155, 1040 Bruxelles, Belgium
Tel: +32 2/235 22 00
Fax: +32 2/235 22 19
E-mail: efj@ifj.org
Internet: http://www.ifj.org/regions/europe/idx.html

Pres.: Gustl GLATTFELDER
Sec.-Gen.: A. WHITE
Contact: R. SCHROEDER

Founded: 1989
General meeting: April
Working languages: E/F
Secretariat: 3 members of staff

Sectors of activity:
- The European Federation of Journalists works closely with the ETUC and other trade unions representing groups of workers in the mass media and cooperates in working out general principles and guidelines for common trade union policy in the field of mass media and cooperates in working out general principles and guidelines for common trade union policy in the field of mass media and information.
- The EFJ co-ordinates the activities of IFJ-affiliated unions in Europe and promotes the representation of common interests in the fields of economic, social and cultural policy within the EU and other European institutions.

Information available:
- "IFJ Euronews", 6x/year, E/F/D.
- "Direct Line", every month, E/F/Esp/D.
- "Handbook on Safety of Journalists", E/F/Esp.
- List of members available free (see website).

EFLA / AEDA

European Food Law Association

Association Européenne pour le Droit de l'Alimentation

Europäische Vereinigung für Lebensmittelrecht

c/o Coutrelis & Associés, Rue de la Loi 235, 1040 Bruxelles, Belgium
Tel: +32 2/230 48 45
Fax: +32 2/230 82 06
E-mail: efla_aeda@hotmail.com
Internet: http://www.efda-aeda.org

Pres.: C. COCKBILL
Sec.-Gen.: Mrs. N. COUTRELIS

Founded: 1973
General meeting: Every 2 years – September/October
Working languages: F/E

Sectors of activity:
- To develop the knowledge and European harmonisation of food law.

Conference:
- "Food Safety for Everybody", 19-20/09/2002, Budapest.
- Congrès AEDA: "Droit de l'Alimentation et Innovation" , Paris, 15-17 September, 2004.

Information available:
- EFLA Newsletter, quarterly, M, F/E.

EFLA / FEAP

European Foundation for Landscape Architecture

Fondation Européenne pour l'Architecture du Paysage

Rue de Washington 40, 1050 Bruxelles, Belgium
Tel: +32 2/346 38 62
Tel: +32 2/656 15 25
Fax: +32 2/346 98 76
E-mail: efla.feap@skynet.be
Internet: http://www.efla.org

Pres.: T. ANDREESSEN
Sec.-Gen.: T. SUNDT
Contact: Mrs. J. COLIN

Founded: 1989
General meeting: November
Working languages: F/E
Secretariat: 1 member of staff

Sectors of activity:
- To stimulate and promote educational exchange between the member countries.
- To promote study and research, the exchange of knowledge and technical information.
- To represent the landscape associations to the EU.
- To consult with the EU in the preparation of all directives relating to the natural and man-made environment.
- To coordinate and to promote professional practice and exchange between the member countries.
- To encourage the development of landscape architecture courses in the EU and to monitor and review their compatibility with the aims of the Foundation.
- Conferences: "Mobility for the Young Landscape Architecture Professional", 15/11/2002, Brussels.
- "Making today's landscapes a resource for the future", 17 & 18/11/2004, Brussels.

Information available:
- "Newsletter", 2/month, internet, M-NM.
- For consultation: European associations' books and reviews.
- Listing of schools, universities for architecture.
- List of members available to the general public, free.

EFMA

European Fertilizer Manufacturers Association

Association Européenne des Producteurs d'Engrais

Europäischer Verband der Düngemittelhersteller

Av. E. van Nieuwenhuyse 4, 1160 Bruxelles, Belgium
Tel: +32 2/675 35 50
Fax: +32 2/675 39 61
E-mail: main@efma.be
Internet: www.efma.org

Pres.: D. CLAUW
Sec.-Gen.: H. ALDINGER (Dir Gen)
Contact: Alison WILLIAMS (Communications Coordinator)

Founded: 1987
General meeting: October
Working languages: E
Secretariat: 10 members of staff

Historical note:
- Three organisations preceded EFMA. The first of these was the Centre d'Etude de l'Azote (CEA). It was established in Geneva in 1953, when competition in the existing export markets was beginning to grow and population growth in developing countries meant that new markets were emerging. The CEA's purpose was "...the scientific and practical study of methods capable of insuring a rational and increasing use of nitrogenous fertilizers throughout the world."
- In 1959, the producers decided to broaden the co-operation to include matters of general and economic interest: APEA (Association des Producteurs de l'Engrais Azoté), the first European producers' association with a European focus.
- In 1976, CMC Engrais, was formed exclusively by producers from the six EU countries at that time and its objective was to study the problems of the EU fertilizer producers in their dealings with the EU institutions.
- In 1988, APEA/CEA and CMC Engrais merged to form a single European fertilizer manufacturers' association: EFMA.

Sectors of activity:
- The mission of the European Fertilizer Industry is to respond to the needs of agriculture and society by providing, in accordance with the principles of Responsible Care, a dependable and competitive supply of high-quality mineral fertilizers.
- The industry encourages, moreover, the adoption of Best Agricultural Practices in the use of plant nutrients, thus stimulating farmers and growers to produce high-quality crops in an economically and environmentally sound manner.

Information available:
- Annual Review, M & NM.
- "The Fertilizer Industry of the European Union", M & NM.
- "Forecast of Fertilizer Consumption in EFMA Countries", annual, M & NM.
- Best available techniques booklets, M & NM.
- "Understanding Phosphorus and its use in Agriculture".
- "Codes of Best Agricultural Practice: Urea and Nitrogen", M & NM.
- "Sustainable Soil Management: an Achievable Goal", M & NM.
- "Guidelines for Transporting Nitric Acid in Tanks", M & NM.
- Database: Fertilizer Consumption database M & NM.
- List of members available on web site, free of charge

EFMD

European Foundation for Management Development

Fondation Européenne pour le Développement de la Gestion

Europäische Management-Entwicklungsstiftung

Rue Gachard 88, 1050 Bruxelles, Belgium
Tel: +32 2/629 08 10
Fax: +32 2/629 08 11
E-mail: info@efmd.be
Internet: www.efmd.be

Pres.: G. VAN SCHAIK
Contact: Mrs. M. PLOMPEN

EFOMP

European Federation of Organisations for Medical Physics

Fédération Européenne des Organisations pour la Physique Médicale

Europäische Föderation der Gesellschaften für Medizinische Physik

Centre G.-F. LECLERC, Service de Radiophysique, Rue Pr Marïon 1, BP 77 980, 21034 Dijon Cedex, France
Tel: +33 3/80 73 75 00
Fax: +33 3/80 67 19 15
E-mail: snaudy@dijon.fnclcc.fr
Internet: www.efomp.org

Pres.: I.L. LAMM
Contact: A. NOEL

Founded: 1980
Working languages: E
Secretariat: 7 members of staff

Sectors of activity:
- Harmonisation of education and training in medical physics within Europe.

- Proposing guidelines for accreditation programmes.
- Encouraging scholarships.

Information available:
- "European medical physics news", published on website.
- Database: officers of all member organisations.

EFPA

European Food Service and Packaging Association

Association Européenne d'Emballages Alimentaires à Usage Unique

Europäischer Verband für Lebensmittelverpackungen und Einweggeschirr

Avenue d'Auderghem 67, 1040 Bruxelles, Belgium
Tel: +32 2/286 94 96
Fax: +32 2/286 94 95
E-mail: efpa@eamonnbates.com
Internet: www.efpa.com

Pres.: D. SCHISLER
Sec.-Gen.: E. BATES
Contacts: J. KEY (Treasurer), O. SNADJE

Founded: 1974
Working languages: E
Secretariat: 3 members of staff

Sectors of activity:
Conference:
- "EFPA-FPI Joint Meeting", 24-25/04/2003, Roma.

Information available:
- List of members available on website.

EFPIA

European Federation of Pharmaceutical Industries and Associations

Fédération Européenne d'Associations et d'Industries Pharmaceutiques

Leopold Plaza Building (6th floor), Rue du Trône 108, 1050 Bruxelles, Belgium
Tel: +32 2/626 25 55
Fax: +32 2/626 25 66
E-mail: info@efpia.org
Internet: www.efpia.org

Pres.: F. HUMER
Contacts: B. AGER (Dir. Gen.), Ms. M.-C. PICKAERT (Deputy Dir. Gen.)

Founded: 1978
General meeting: May or June
Working languages: E/F
Secretariat: 35 members of staff

Sectors of activity:
- Pharmaceutical industries.
- Conference: Prague, 1-3 June 2005

Information available:
- Database: internal newsletters – members only
- List of members available to the general public and on the website.
- "EFPIA in figures", free, M, -NM
- "Annual Report", free, M, -NM

EFPRA

European Fat Processors and Renderers Association

Bd Baudouin 18 Bte 4, 1000 Bruxelles, Belgium
Tel: +32 2/203 51 41
Fax: +32 2/203 32 44
E-mail: devries@skypro.be

Sec.-Gen.: D. DOBBELAERE

Historical note:
- EFPRA = merger between UNEGA and EURA.

EFQM

European Foundation for Quality Management

Fondation Européenne du Contrôle de la Qualité

Avenue des Pléiades 15, 1200 Bruxelles, Belgium
Tel: +32 2/775 35 11
Fax: +32 2/775 35 35
E-mail: info@efqm.org
Internet: www.efqm.org

Contact: A. DE DOMMARTIN (Chief Exec.)

EFR

European Ferrous Recovery and Recycling Federation

Fédération Européenne de la Récupération et du Recyclage des Ferrailles

Europäischer Recycling-Verband für Eisen und Stahl

c/o BIR, Avenue Franklin Roosevelt 24, 1050 Bruxelles, Belgium
Tel: +32 2/627 57 71
Fax: +32 2/627 57 73
E-mail: bir@bir.org
Internet: http://www.efr2.org
Internet: http://www.bir.org

Pres.: A. RUBOCH
Contact: F. VEYS

Founded: 1972
General meeting: March
Working languages: E
Secretariat: 7 members of staff

Information available:
- Newsletter, E, M.
- Circulars, E, M.

EFTC

European Federation of Timber Construction

Fédération Européenne de la Construction Bois

Europäische Vereinigung des Holzbaus

Circuit de la Foire Internationale 2, 1347 Luxembourg-Kirchberg, Luxembourg
Tel: +352 42/45 11 33
Fax: +352 42/45 25
E-mail: contact@federation-des-artisans.lu
E-mail: j.franck@fda.lu
Internet: www.fda.lu

Pres.: G. KUENIG
Sec.-Gen.: J. FRANCK

EFWSID

European Federation of Wine and Spirit Importers and Distributors

Fédération Européenne des Importateurs et Distributeurs des Vins et Boissons Alcoolisées

Europäische Föderation der Wein- und Spirituosenimporteure und Grosshändler

King house 5, 1 Queen Street place, London EC4R 1XX, United Kingdom
Tel: +44 2072485377
Tel: +31 20/673 16 54
Fax: +31 20/664 54 66
E-mail: kvnw@xs4all.nl

Pres.: F. CLOTTU
Contact: Q. RAPPERT (Dir)

Founded: 1973
Working languages: E
Secretariat: 5 members of staff

EGA

European Generic Medicines Association

Association Européenne des Médicaments Génériques

Europäischer Verband der Generikaindustrie

Rue d'Arlon 15, 1050 Bruxelles, Belgium
Tel: +32 2/736 84 11
Fax: +32 2/736 74 38
E-mail: info@egagenerics.com
Internet: www.egagenerics.com

Pres.: R. O'RIORDAN
Sec.-Gen.: G. PERRY
Contact: Mrs. N. McCLAY

Founded: 1992
Working languages: E
Secretariat: 3 members of staff

Historical note:
- Originally established as the European Generics Forum and later as European Generics Association.

Sectors of activity:
- Consulted by EC Commission and EMEA on draft legislation and guidelines.
- Liaison with WHO and WTO.
- Participation in international conference on harmonisation and international generic pharmaceutical alliance.

Information available:
- All public information is on the website: www.egagenerics.com.
- The members' list is available on the website, free.

EGGA

European General Galvanizers Association

Association Européenne des Industries de Galvanisation d'Articles Divers

Europäische Vereinigung der Industrien für die Galvanisierung

Maybrook House, Godstone Road, Caterham CR3 6RE, United Kingdom
Tel: +44 1883/33 12 77
Fax: +44 1883/33 12 87
E-mail: mail@egga.com
Internet: http://www.egga.com

Pres.: J. VERSTAPPEN
Contact: M.G. BURCHER (Dir)

Founded: 1990
General meeting: Annual assembly for members only (June)
Working languages: E
Secretariat: 2 members of staff

Information available:
- "Proceedings of Intergalva Conferences", every 3 years, E.
- List of members available to the general public, free; also on website.
- Intergalva proceedings volumes (various prices).

EGOLF

European Group of Organisations for Fire Testing, Inspection and Certification

Ottergemsesteenweg 711, 9000 Gent, Belgium
Tel: +32 9/243 77 55
Fax: +32 9/243 77 51
E-mail: ruth.boughey@egolf.org.uk
Internet: http://www.egolf.org.uk

Pres.: Mr. L. TWILT
Contact: R. BOUGHEY

Founded: 1988
General meeting: March and September
Working languages: E
Secretariat: 1 member of staff

Sectors of activity:
- To improve collaboration between fire testing laboratories and inspection and certification bodies working in fire safety in Europe.
- To assist the creation, implementation and harmonisation of laboratory performance in use of European fire test standards.
- Training courses on the new European Fire Test Standards are available to both members and non-members

Information available:
- "EGOLF Standard Methods", €15.
- "EGOLF Technical Resolutions"."EGOLF Technical Recommendations".
- The members' list is available, free of charge.
- Database: test results and classifications of products tested to the new European Fire Test Standards, website.
- List of members available free of charge

EGTA

European Group of Television Advertising

Groupement Européen de la Publicité Télévisée

Europäische Gruppe für Fernsehwerbung

Rue Wiertz 50, 1050 Bruxelles, Belgium
Tel: +32 2/290 31 31
Fax: +32 2/290 31 39
E-mail: info@egta.com
Internet: http://www.egta.com

Pres.: W. NEUHAUSER
Sec.-Gen.: M. GREGOIRE
Contact: V. MARSCHNER (Office Manager)

Founded: 1974
General meeting: May
Working languages: F/E
Secretariat: 8 members of staff

Sectors of activity:
- Information on Council of Europe & EU Broadcasting Legislation.
- Training courses.
- Databases.
- Marketing.
- Audience measurement.
- Research.
- Interactivity and advertising around sporting events and sports sponsorship.
- Branding, Communication.
- Cross media advertising.

Information available:
- "EGTA News", M.
- "EGTA Positions", M-NM.
- Databases: "European Guide to TV Sponsorship", rules of TV sponsorship channel by channel.
- "General interest and political advertising", NM
- "Delcredere", M
- "The c/000 dataises" (radio & television), M
- "Teleshopping", NM
- "Barometer of TV and Radio advertising investments in Europe", M
- "Conditions for the TV advertising of pharmaceutical products", M
- "Conditions for the TV advertising of alcoholic beverages", M
- "Conditions for the TV advertising of cars"
- "EGTA study on TV advertising to children", M
- The members list is available, free of charge.

EHA/GEH

European Helicopter Association

Groupement Européen de l'Hélicoptère

Europäischer Hubschrauberverband

P.C. Hooftstraat 83 – 1, 1071 BP Amsterdam, Netherlands
Tel: +31 20/470 70 20
Fax: +31 20/470 70 21
E-mail: stuurman@eha.nl
Internet: http://www.eha.nl

Pres.: Lord GLENARTHUR
Contact: J.W. STUURMAN

Founded: 1981
General meeting: March and September
Working languages: E
Secretariat: 1 member of staff

Sectors of activity:
- Standardisation of regulations governing helicopter operations in Europe.

Information available:
- "EHA Information Handbook", annual, free, E.

EHI

Association of the European Heating Industry

Blvd Reyers 80, 1030 Bruxelles, Belgium
Tel: +32 2/706 79 62
Fax: +32 2/706 79 66
E-mail: felix.vaneyken@agoria.be

Pres.: G. CRIVELLI
Sec.-Gen.: F. VAN EYKEN

Founded: 2000

Historical note:
- Merger of AFECI and EHI

Sectors of activity:
- Energy.
- Environment.

Information available:
- List of members, free.

EHIA

European Herbal Infusions Association

Association Européenne des Infusions d'Herbe

Europäische Vereinigung Kräuter- und Früchtetee

Gotenstrasse 21, 20097 Hamburg, Germany
Tel: +49 40/23 60 16 33/14
Fax: +49 40/23 60 16 10
E-mail: ehia@wga-hh.de

Pres.: C. STUCCHI
Sec.-Gen.: Mrs. M. BEUTGEN

Founded: 1980
Working languages: E
Secretariat: 2 members of staff

Information available:
- Circular letters to members.

EHIMA

European Hearing Instruments Manufacturers Association

Association Européenne des Fabricants d'Audioprothèses

Europäische Vereinigung der Hörgerätehersteller

Bosch 135, 1780 Wemmel, Belgium
Tel: +32 2/461 37 52
Fax: +32 2/461 36 47
E-mail: ehima@skynet.be
Internet: http://www.ehima.com

Pres.: H. TÜRK
Sec.-Gen.: Mrs. A.M. WOLTERS

Founded: 1995
General meeting: November
Working languages: E
Secretariat: 2 members of staff

Sectors of activity:
- Developing the market.

Information available:
- The members' list is available, free of charge.

EHMA

European Health Management Association

Association Européenne de Gestion des Systèmes de Santé

Europäische Vereinigung für Management im Gesundheitswesen

Vergemount Hall, Clonskeagh, Dublin 6, Ireland
Tel: +353 1/283 92 99

Fax: +353 1/283 86 53
E-mail: marie@ehma.org

Pres.: Dr. Robert KONING
Contact: Ms. M. NI MHURCHU

Founded: 1966
General meeting: 25–27/06/2003
Working languages: E/F/D
Secretariat: 4 members of staff

Information available:
- "EHMA Newsletter", quarterly, E.
- "Eurobriefing", quarterly, newsletter.
- Database: full membership details.

EHPM

European Federation of Associations of Health Product Manufacturers

Groupement Européen des Associations des Fabricants de Produits de Réforme

Europäische Vereinigung der Verbände der Reformwaren- Hersteller

Rue de l'Association 50, 1000 Bruxelles, Belgium
Tel: +32 2/209 11 45
Fax: +32 2/223 30 64
E-mail: ehpm@eas.be
Internet: http://www.ehpm.org

Contact: A. BUSH (Chairman)

Founded: 1975
Working languages: E
Secretariat: 3 members of staff

EICTA / AEIIT

European Information, Communications and Consumer Electronics Technology Industry Association

Association européenne des Industries de l'Informatique et des Télécommunications et des Industries de Produits électroniques Grand Public

Blvd Reyers 80, 1030 Bruxelles, Belgium
Tel: +32 2/706 84 70
Tel: +32 2/706 84 80
Fax: +32 2/706 84 79
E-mail: info@eicta.org
Internet: http://www.eicta.org

Pres.: Andy MATTES
Sec.-Gen.: Mark MACGANN
Contact: M. MACGANN (Director General)

Founded: 1999
General meeting: Fall
Working languages: E/F
Secretariat: 8 members of staff

Historical note:
- Merger of ECTEL and EUROBIT.

Sectors of activity:
- ICT and Consumer Electronics

Information available:
- Databases: members, contacts, press.
- List of members available to the general public, free.
- Press releases and member list see website

EIGA

European Industrial Gases Association

Association Européenne des Gaz Industriels

Europäischer Verband für Technische Gase

Avenue des Arts 3-5, 1210 Bruxelles, Belgium
Tel: +32 2/217 70 98
Fax: +32 2/219 85 14
E-mail: info@eiga.org
Internet: www.eiga.org

Sec.-Gen.: F.H. FINGER

EIPG / GPIE

European Industrial Pharmacy Group

Groupe des Pharmaciens de l'Industrie en Europe

Délégation aux Affaires Extérieures, Rue du Zéphir 58B, 1200 Bruxelles, Belgium
Tel: +32 3/890 27 78
Fax: +32 3/890 29 35
E-mail: paul.nelis@alconlabs.com

Contact: P. NELIS
Working languages: F/E

Information available:
- Only available to the national associations which are members of the group or to official organisations.

EIRMA

European Industrial Research Management Association

Association Européenne pour l'Administration de la Recherche Industrielle

Rue Lauriston 46, 75116 Paris, France
Tel: +33 1/53 23 83 10
Fax: +33 1/47 20 05 30
E-mail: info@eirma.asso.fr
Internet: http://www.eirma.asso.fr

Pres.: H. DEWIT
Sec.-Gen.: A. DEARING

Founded: 1966
General meeting: May or June
Working languages: E
Secretariat: 5 members of staff

Historical note:
- Founded, following the OECD European/North American Conference on Research Management, by leading figures including Professor Hendrik Casimir, first EIRMA President and member of the Board of Management of Philips, and Dr Alexander King, Director of Science and Technology at the OECD and who subsequently become President of the Club of Rome

Sectors of activity:
- To increase the productivity and effectiveness of industrial research, development and innovation.
- Achieved through attention to three key areas: benchmarking and sharing insight into best practice; communicating that insight; and using the results to achieve improvement. Primarily a networking association, EIRMA positions itself also to be a natural first point of contact for governments and policy bodies seeking business insight into R&D.
- Benchmarking and networking activities organized in various formats (conferences, study groups, round tables) and cover the full spectrum of industrial research, development and innovation management. These activities provide the engine for generating published reports.
- Conferences: open to members and non-members, for details please see the website

Information available:
- Annual Report, free.
- The publications' list is available on, and all reports may be purchased through, the website: http://www.emrma.asso.fr.
- List of members available on the website, further information is not made available

EKA

European Kaolin Association

Boulevard S. Dupuis 233, 1070 Bruxelles, Belgium
Tel: +32 2/524 55 00
Fax: +32 2/524 45 75
E-mail: secretariat@ima-eu.org
Internet: http://www.ima-eu.org

Sec.-Gen.: Ms. WYART-REMY

ELA

European Logistics Association

Association Européenne de Logistiques

Europäische Logistikvereinigung

Avenue des Arts 19, 1210 Bruxelles, Belgium
Tel: +32 2/230 02 11
Fax: +32 2/230 81 23
E-mail: ela@elalog.org
Internet: www.elalog.org

Pres.: G. ROUX
Sec.-Gen.: M. FOURNY
Contact: Mrs. N. GEERKENS

Founded: 1985
General meeting: Once a year
Working languages: E
Secretariat: 1 member of staff

Information available:
- "Logistics Europe Journal", six times a year, free to members, E.
- Information Brochure: "What is ELA?", free to members, E.
- "Logistics Dictionary", annual, E.
- Conference Proceedings, every 2 years.
- Surveys, studies, etc.

ELA

European Lift Associations

Avenue Louis Gribaumont 1 bte 6, 1150 Bruxelles, Belgium
Tel: +32 2/779 50 82
Fax: +32 2/772 16 85
E-mail: info@ela-aisbl.org

Sec.-Gen.: S. LUTRIVET

Founded: 2000
General meeting: March
Working languages: E

ELA

European Association Logistics

Avenue des Arts 19, 1210 Bruxelles, Belgium
Tel: +32 2/230 02 11
Fax: +32 2/230 81 23
E-mail: ela@elalog.org
Internet: www.elalog.org

Pres.: G. ROUX
Sec.-Gen.: M. FOURNY

Founded: 1997
Working languages: E

Sectors of activity:
- Certification and assessment of European logistics diplomas.
- Education in logistics.

ELC

European Lighting Companies Federation

Fédération Européenne des Entreprises d'Eclairage

Europäische Föderation der Beleuchtungsunternehmen

Blvd A. Reyers 80, Diamond Building, 1030 Bruxelles, Belgium
Tel: +32 2/706 86 08
Fax: +32 2/706 86 09
E-mail: info@eicfed.org
Internet: http://www.elcfed.org

Pres.: J. DENNEMAN
Sec.-Gen.: g. STRICKLAND
Working languages: E
Secretariat: 2 members of staff

Information available:
- Position papers, E.

ELC

Federation of European Food Additives and Food Enzymes Industries

Fédération des Industries Européennes d'Additifs et d'Enzymes Alimentaires

Föderation der Europäischen Industrien für Nahrungszusätze und -Enzyme

Avenue des Gaulois 9, 1040 Bruxelles, Belgium
Tel: +32 2/736 53 54
Fax: +32 2/732 34 27
E-mail: elc@ecco-eu.com
Internet: http://www.elc-eu.org

Pres.: C. GUITTARD
Sec.-Gen.: Mrs. D. HEIJNEN
Working languages: E
Secretariat: 3 members of staff

Sectors of activity:
- European food additives and food enzymes legislation.

ELCA

European Landscape Contractors Association

Association des Entrepreneurs Paysagistes Européens

Gemeinschaft des Europäischen Garten-, Landschafts- und Sportplatzbaues

Alexander-von-Humboldt-Str. 4, 53604 Bad Honnef, Germany
Tel: +49 2224/77 07 20
Fax: +49 2224/77 07 77
E-mail: contact@elca.info
Internet: http://www.elca.info

Pres.: A. BERGER
Sec.-Gen.: Dr H. J. KURTH

Founded: 1963
General meeting: Spring and autumn
Working languages: E/D/F
Secretariat: 2 members of staff

Sectors of activity:
- Protection and representation of major interests of European landscape contractors.

- Promotion of co-operation with other organisations with similar aims. Promoting the mutual exchange of information and experience within the framework of congresses, seminars and meetings. Promotion of young people in the profession and mutual exchange of qualified young landscapers.

Information available:
- Annual Report.
- "ELCA-Newsletter", M-NM, E/D/F.
- "ELCA – 40 years", E/D.
- "ELCA Committee of Firms", D/E/F/ Nl.
- List of members available to the general public, free.

ELCDHyg

European Liaison Committee for Dental Hygiene

c/o Glasgow School of Dental Hygiene, Sauchiehall Street 378, Glasgow G2 3JZ, United Kingdom
Tel: +44 141/211 97 74
Fax: +44 141/211 98 00
E-mail: eagray.dief@virgin.net

Contact: Mrs. E.A. GRAY
Working languages: E

Information available:
- Database: part of a worldwide database regarding practice and education of dental hygienists.

ELF

European Locksmith Federation

Makalan-kata, c/o Safety set oy, 00500 Helsinki, Finland
Tel: +358 927/09 18 80
Fax: +358 973/973 68 50
E-mail: secretary@eurolockfed.com
Internet: http://www.eurolockfed.com

Pres.: P. ÖSMAN
Sec.-Gen.: T. KAJAN
Contact: O. LUOMALA

Founded: 1984

Information available:
- "Insight", 2-3 times annually.
- Members' list available to the public, free.

ELMA

European Association for Length Measuring Instruments and Machines

Forge House, 3 Summerleys Road, Princes Risborough HP27 9DT, United Kingdom
Tel: +44 1844/274222
Fax: +44 1844/274227

Founded: 1973
Working languages: E
Secretariat: 1 member of staff

Information available:
- Database: producers of length measuring instruments and machines in the Member countries, statistics on production, export and import.
- List of members, free.

ELVHIS

European Association of High Intensity Gas Infrared Heater Manufacturers

Association Européenne des Fabricants de Panneaux Infrarouges Lumineux à Gaz

Europäischer Leitverband der Hersteller von Gaz-Infrarot-Hellstrahlern e.V.

Bremerhavener Strasse 43, 50735 Köln, Germany
Tel: +49 221/7176 200
Fax: +49 221/7176 210
E-mail: figawa@t-online.de
Internet: http://www.elvhis.com

Pres.: B. H. SCHWANK
Sec.-Gen.: Dr. BURGER

Founded: 1993
General meeting: 4 meetings per year, changeable venue
Working languages: E

EMA / ASFE

European Midwives Association

Association des Sages-Femmes Européennes

c/o KNOV, Postbus 18, 3720 AA Bilthoven, Netherlands
Tel: +31 30/229 42 99
Fax: +31 30/229 41 62
E-mail: ema@knov.nl

Pres.: Ms. D. TAXBOL

Founded: 1968
Working languages: F/E

Information available:
- Report on the activities, responsibilities and independence of midwives in the European Union, £10.00, E/F.

EMA

European Medical Association

Boulevard Saint-Michel 89, 1030 Bruxelles, Belgium
Tel: +32 2/734 29 80
Fax: +32 2/734 20 23
E-mail: contact@EMAnet.org
Internet: http://www.EMAnet.org

Pres.: V. COSTIGLIOLA
Sec.-Gen.: P. KETTELAER

Founded: 1990
Working languages: F/E/It

Historical note:
- Association formed by doctors for doctors

Sectors of activity:
- Collaborate with the European Community on health projects.

Information available:
- EMA News.
Database:
- Contact details of + / – 10.000 doctors in Europe.
CD-Rom:
- CD-Rom for neuropsychiatrists, distributed free to doctors.
- Cancer site, GEDA site, ECHOP – June 2000 – electronic trade for medical equipment.

EMA

European Metallizers Association

Association Européenne de la Métallisation

Europäischer Metallisierungsverband

PO Box 85612, 2508 CH Den Haag, Netherlands
Tel: +31 70/312 39 17
Fax: +31 70/363 63 48
E-mail: mail@eurometallizers.org
Internet: www.eurometallizers.org

Pres.: L. ZAFS
Sec.-Gen.: Ms M. KIENJET
Contact: J.P. VAN HAIRINSEN

EMAA

European Management Accountants Association

Association Européenne de Comptables Agréés

Europäischer Verband der Bilanbuchhalter

Am Propsthof 15-17, 53121 Bonn, Germany
Tel: +49 228/63 93 18
Fax: +49 228/63 93 14
E-mail: kontakt@emaa.de
Internet: www.emaa.de

Pres.: U. BINIAS
Contacts: H. MATTLE (Vice-Pr), W. BUDAI (Vice-Pr), HORICKY (Vice-Pr)

Founded: 1994
General meeting: June
Working languages: D
Secretariat: 3 members of staff

Sectors of activity:
Functions and targets of the federation:
- Activities by EMMA and their members.

- Acknowledgment of comparable national certifications and diplomas.
- Harmonization of National Education Programmes and Exams within Europe.
- Lobbying.
- Membership Representation with authorities and Institutions of European Union.
- Foster Membership in other European Organizations.
- Events / Seminars.
- Publications.
- Cooperation with National Institutions of Industry and Commerce.

Information available:
- The available written informations are on our website, http://www.emaa.de, M-NM.
- List of members available to the general public

EMBO

European Molecular Biology Organization

Meyerhofstrasse 1, 69117 Heidelberg, Germany
Tel: +49 6221/88 91 0
Fax: +49 6221/88 91 200
E-mail: embo@embo.org
Internet: http://www.embo.org

Sec.-Gen.: Prof. Frank GANNON (Exec Dir)

Founded: 1964
General meeting: October
Working languages: E
Secretariat: 35 members of staff

Sectors of activity:
- Promoting biosciences in Europe.
- Numerous conferences and seminars, please see: http://www-db.embl-heidelberg.de/jss/servlet/de.embl.bk.embo.EmboSeminarlist

Information available:
- "EMBO Journal", 24/year, E.
- Lists of courses and workshops organized each year.
- "EMBO Reports", 12/year, E.
- List of members, not free.
- Annual report.
- Webpage: www.embo.org
- Newsletter (4-6/year mainly to members but also available on website).
- Programme leaflets, books and brochures.
- Film on teachers' workshop (DVD).
- Job database and Life Science Mobility Consultant

EMC

European Marketing Confederation

Place des Chasseurs Ardennais 20, 1030 Bruxelles, Belgium

Tel: +32 2/742 17 80
Fax: +32 2/742 17 85
E-mail: infodesk@emc.be
Internet: www.emc.be

Pres.: P. TOMKINS
Sec.-Gen.: Ms. J. RIDSDALE-JAW

Founded: 1992
Working languages: E
Secretariat: 3 members of staff

Information available:
- "Strategies Europe", M-NM, 10/year, E/F.
- "Annual Review", M-NM, E.
- Databases: expert speakers / EMC accredited students, etc., M-NM.
- "Read for You", M, 6/year, E.
- "European Fact File", M, 4/year, E.
- International Encyclopaedia of Marketing.

EMCEF

European Mine, Chemical and Energy Workers' Federation

Fédération Européenne des Syndicats des Mines, de la Chimie et de l'Energie

Europäische Föderation der Bergbare-, Chemie- und Energiegewerkschaften

Av. Emile de Béco 109, 1050 Bruxelles, Belgium
Tel: +32 2/626 21 80
Fax: +32 2/646 06 85
E-mail: info@emcef.org
Internet: www.emcef.org

Pres.: H. SCHMOLDT
Contact: R. REIBSCH (SG)

Founded: 1996
General meeting: Every year, at the end of April
Working languages: E/F/D
Secretariat: 9 members of staff

Historical note:
- Merger of FESCID and FME in 1996.

Sectors of activity:
- Gas and electricity.
- Chemistry / pharmaceutical.
- Energy.
- Mining.
- Oil.
- Cement.
- Paper / pulp.
- Rubber.
- Ceramics.
- Quarries.
- Waste processing.
- Environment and other related sectors.
- Plastics / PVC.
- Glass.
- Women.
- Collective bargaining and industrial relations.

Information available:
- List of members available to the general public.

EMF / FEM / EMB

European Metalworkers' Federation

Fédération Européenne des Métallurgistes

Europäischer Metallgewerkschaftsbund

Rue Royale 45 bte 2, 1000 Bruxelles, Belgium
Tel: +32 2/227 10 10
Fax: +32 2/217 59 63
E-mail: emf@emf-fem.org
Internet: www.emf-fem.org

Pres.: T. JANSSEN
Sec.-Gen.: R. KUHLMANN

Founded: 1971
General meeting: 2 Executive Committee meetings in the first and second semester of each year and a Congress every 4 years
Working languages: F/E/D
Secretariat: 14 members of staff

Sectors of activity:
- Cooperation between affiliates and coordination of the joint demands of the European metal unions.
- Creation of a trade union counterweight to European employers' associations and top multinational company management within the EU.

Information available:
- Official statements.
- List of members, free.

EMF / FHE / EHV

European Mortgage Federation

La Fédération Hypothécaire Européenne

Europäischer Hypothekenverband

Av. de la Joyeuse Entrée 14 Bte 2, 1040 Bruxelles, Belgium
Tel: +32 2/285 40 30
Fax: +32 2/285 40 31
E-mail: emfinfo@hypo.org
Internet: www.hypo.org

Pres.: M. SADOUN
Sec.-Gen.: Mrs. J. HARDT

Founded: 1967
Working languages: F/E/D
Secretariat: 9 members of staff

Sectors of activity:
- Studying measures which might be taken in respect of mortgage credit and disseminating the result of these studies.
- Promoting the interests of mortgage lenders in the EU.

Information available:
- "Hypostat (10 years statistical survey)".
- Annual Report.
- Extensive list of studies on mortgage credit in the EU.

EMO

European Mortar Industry Organization

Association de l'Industrie Européenne des Mortiers

Verband der Europäischen Mortelindustrie

Düsseldorfer Strasse 50, 47051 Duisburg, Germany
Tel: +49 203/99 23 9-0
Fax: +49 203/99 23 999
E-mail: hans-peter.braus@ baustoffverbaende.de
Internet: www.euromortar.de

Pres.: L. MOYNARD
Sec.-Gen.: H.P. BRAUS

Founded: 1999
Working languages: E
Secretariat: 10 members of staff

Sectors of activity:
- Technology.
- Standardisation.
- Environment.
Conference:
- EMO TEC, every two years.

Information available:
- The information is only available to members.

EMOTA/AEVPC

European Mail Order Traders' Association

Association Européenne de Vente par Correspondance

Europäische Vereinigung des Versandverkaufs

Rue Wiertz 50/28, 1050 Bruxelles, Belgium
Tel: +32 2/401 61 95
Fax: +32 2/401 68 68
E-mail: info@emota-aevpc.org
Internet: www.emota-aevpc.org

Pres.: J. MARTIN
Sec.-Gen.: A. WEENING

Founded: 1977
General meeting: May
Working languages: E/F
Secretariat: 2 members of staff

Information available:
- Statistics available on request, E/F, free, M-NM.
- Brochures in English and French, free, M-NM:
  1) Definition of mail order.
  2) Members' list.
  3) European Convention on cross-border mail order and distance selling.

EMU

European Metal Union

Union Européenne du Métal

Europäische Metall-Union

Einsteinbaan 1, 3430 GA Nieuwegein, Netherlands
Tel: +31 30/605 33 44
Fax: +31 30/605 31 22
E-mail: info@metaalunie.nl
Internet: http://www.metaalunie.nl

Sec.-Gen.: H. – J. KEIJER

ENERO

European Network of Environmental Research Organisations
E-mail: enero.secretary@issep.be
Internet: http://www.enero.dk

Pres.: B. DON
Sec.-Gen.: J.-C. MAQUINAY

Founded: 1992
General meeting: June and November
Working languages: E

Sectors of activity:
- Protection of man and the environment within the framework of industrial activities compatible with the notion of sustainable development.

Information available:
- List of members available to the general public, free.

ENGAGE

European Network of Engineering for Agriculture and Environment
MTT/vakola, Vakolantie 55, 03400 Vihti, Finland
Tel: +358 (9) 224 251
Fax: +358 (9) 224 6210
E-mail: hannu.haapala@mtt.fi
Internet: http://www.fal.de/engage/ index.htm

Pres.: Dr. Hannu HAPPALA
Sec.-Gen.: Kim KAUSTELL

Founded: 1988
General meeting: 2 meetings per year
Working languages: E

Sectors of activity:
- to identify and analyse opportunities for research and development in agricultural biosystems and environmental engineering to advance agriculture and associated industries;
- to explain, discuss and promote these opportunities both within EurAgEng in particular and to the European Union in general;
- to encourage and facilitate co-operation between appropriate

engineers and scientists within the European Union and in countries with scientific agreements with the European Union;
- to make readily available expert advice in the areas of agricultural, biosystems and environmental engineering.
- Participation in the activities of the Network is open to all institutions and organisations carrying out research and development in agricultural, biosystems and environmental engineering in the European Union and countries with scientific agreements with the European Union. A close working relationship with agriculture and associated countries enhances the links between science and practice and is therefore within the scope and goals of the Network.

Information available:
- Database: list of experts in agricultural engineering.
- List of members available to the general public.

ENGVA

European Natural Gas Vehicle Association

Kruisweg 813 A, 2132 NG Hoofddorp, Netherlands
Tel: +31 23/554 3050
Fax: +31 23/557 9065
E-mail: info@engva.nl
Internet: www.engva.org

Contact: J. SEISLER (Exec. Dir.)

Founded: 1994
General meeting: May
Working languages: E
Secretariat: 4 members of staff

Historical note:
- ENGVA was conceived in late 1992 by a small group of European gas companies interested in stimulating the market for natural gas vehicles (NGVs). More than two years in development, ENGVA was formed officially in January 1994 by a core group of 63 member companies from 17 countries. ENGVA became operational with a full time Executive Director in July 1994.

Sectors of activity:
- The mission of ENGVA is to develop a sustainable and profitable market for NGVs throughout Europe by creating a favourable political and economic environment that encourages the development of NGV technology as well as a European fuelling infrastructure.

Information available:

Communications & Research Reports:
- "ENGVA News", once every month, free, M-NM.
- "CompacFuels computer programme", M: €100, NM: €150.

Directories:
- "ENGVA Membership Business Guide", May 2000, free, M-NM.
- "ENGVA Membership Directory", May 2000, M: free, NM: not available.

Miscellaneous:
- "The Natural Gas Vehicle Book", M: €70, NM: €90.
- "The NGV Slide Show", M: €180, NM: €225.

ENPA

European Newspaper Publishers' Association

Association Européenne des Editeurs de Journaux

Europäische Zeitungs- Verleger- Vereinigung

Rue des Pierres 29/8, 1000 Bruxelles, Belgium
Tel: +32 2/551 01 90
Fax: +32 2/551 01 99
E-mail: wolff@enpa.be
Internet: http://www.enpa.be

Pres.: Mrs. D. ALDUY
Contact: D. WOLFF (Director)

Founded: 1961
General meeting: May and October
Working languages: F/E/D
Secretariat: 4 members of staff

Information available:
- Presentation brochures, M-NM.
- Position papers, M-NM.
- Monthly review, 11/year, M-NM.
- List of members, free.

ENS / SEEN

European Nuclear Society

Société Européenne de l'Energie Nucléaire

Europäische Kernenergie Gesellschaft

Rue Belliard 15-17, 1040 Bruxelles, Belgium
Tel: +32 2/505 30 50
Fax: +32 2/502 39 02
E-mail: ens@euronuclear.org
Internet: http://www.euronuclear.org

Pres.: Bertrand BARRE
Sec.-Gen.: Dr. Peter HAUG
Contact: Andrew TELLER (Society Manager)

Founded: 1975 / 2002
General meeting: May/June and November/December
Working languages: E
Secretariat: 3 members of staff

Sectors of activity:
- Founded in 1975 in Switzerland and transferred to Brussels in 2002, ENS has a membership of around 20 000 (engineers, scientists and electricity supply managers, ...). Its main aim is the fostering of the peaceful use of nuclear science and technology.
- Conferences: Nuclear Public Information in Practice, 13-16 February 2005, Paris
- Research Reactor Fuel Management, 10-13 March 2005, Budapest
- Nuclear Public Information in Practice. February 2006, Vienna

Information available:
- "ENS News" (e-Bulletin), 4 times a year, (NM), E.
- List of members available to the general public.

ENSCA

European Natural Sausage Casing Association

Association Européenne de la Boyauderie

Europäische Naturdarmverband

Gotenstrasse 21, 20097 Hamburg, Germany
Tel: +49 30/59 00 99 550
Fax: +49 40/2360 1610
E-mail: ensca@wga-hh.de

Pres.: B. LANDQUIST
Contacts: Ms. M. BEUTGEN, C. ANDRES

Founded: 1972
Working languages: E
Secretariat: 1 member of staff

Information available:
- Circulars, M, free, E.

EOQ

European Organization for Quality

Organisation Européenne pour la Qualité

Europäische Organisation für Qualität

Rue du Luxembourg 3, 1000 Bruxelles, Belgium
Tel: +32 2/501 07 35
Fax: +32 2/501 07 36
E-mail: shendrik@compuserve.com
E-mail: bjouslin@compuserve.com
Internet: http://www.eoq.org

Pres.: F. STEER
Sec.-Gen.: B. JOUSLIN DE NORAY

Founded: 1956
Working languages: E

Information available:
- "Congress Proceedings", annual, E/F, M-NM.
- "Seminar Proceedings", E/F, M-NM.

- "European Quality", 6x/year, E.
- The members' list is available, free of charge.

EOS / OES / EOS

European Organisation of the Sawmill Industry

Organisation Européenne des Scieries

Europäische Organisation der Sägewerke

Allée Hof-ter-Vleest 5 bte 4, 1070 Bruxelles, Belgium
Tel: +32 2/556 25 97
Fax: +32 2/556 25 95
E-mail: eos@cei-bois.org

Pres.: H.M. OFFNER
Sec.-Gen.: Filip DE JAEGER
Contact: Paula SERRANO (Adviser)

Founded: 1958
General meeting: May or June
Working languages: D/E/F
Secretariat: 2 members of staff

Sectors of activity:
- Conference: 20-23 October 2004: European Softwood Conference (Vienna)

Information available:
- Annual Report (May).
- List of members available to the general public free of charge

EOTA

European Organisation for Technical Approvals

Organisation Européenne pour l'Agrément Technique

Europäische Organisation für Technische Zulassungen

Avenue des Arts 40, 1040 Bruxelles, Belgium
Tel: +32 2/502 69 00
Fax: +32 2/502 38 14
E-mail: info@eota.be
Internet: www.eota.be

Pres.: C. SKJERNOV
Sec.-Gen.: P. CALUWAERTS

Founded: 1990
General meeting: Usually April and November
Working languages: E
Secretariat: 2 members of staff

Historical note:
- Recognised as an international non profit making organisation by Belgian Royal Decree of 23/03/1993.

Sectors of activity:
- EOTA is an organisation established under the provisions of the EC Council Directive of December 21, 1988 on the approximation of laws, regulations and administrative

provisions of the Member States relating to construction products (89/106/EEC), bringing together the bodies nominated by the EU Member States and the bodies nominated by those EFTA States, contracting Parties to the EEA Agreement, for the granting of the "European Technical Approvals – ETAs".

Information available:
- "Brochure on scope and content of EOTA in relation to the CPD", E, NM, free of charge.
- The members' list is available, free of charge.

EPA

European Association of Polyol Producers

Association Européenne des Producteurs de Polyols

Europäischer Verband der Polyol Hersteller

c/o ECCO, Avenue des Gaulois 9, 1040 Bruxelles, Belgium
Tel: +32 2/736 53 54
Fax: +32 2/732 34 27
E-mail: epa@ecco.be
Internet: http://www.ecco-eu.com

Sec.-Gen.: Mrs. D. HEIJNEN

Founded: 1991
Working languages: E
Secretariat: 1 member of staff

EPAG

European Property Agents Group

Avenue de Tervuren 36 bte 2, 1040 Bruxelles, Belgium
Tel: +32 2/735 49 90
Fax: +32 2/735 99 88
E-mail: cepi@cepi.be
Internet: www.cepi.be

Pres.: G. STELLER
Contact: Alexander BENEDETTI

Founded: 1990
General meeting: March and November
Working languages: F/E
Secretariat: 1 member of staff

Sectors of activity:
- Lobbying for the real estate professionals.
- Setting high standards for the code of ethics, education (meetings organised with Universities and Business schools in Europe to organise the best training possible), exchange of students, and exchange of data through a European website (Transeuropa)
- Study Day, together with CEAB and CEPI, Bruges, May 2005

Information available:
- "CEPI Info", available on website.
- Annual report on request, free, or see the website
- List of members available to the general public, free, see website.

EPBA

European Portable Battery Association

Association Européenne des Piles Portables

Europäische Vereinigung der Tragbaren Batterien

Avenue Marcel Thiry 204, 1200 Bruxelles, Belgium
Tel: +32 2/774 96 02
Fax: +32 2/774 96 90
E-mail: epba@eyam.be
Internet: http://www.epba-europe.org

Pres.: R. BUREL
Sec.-Gen.: R. BARLOW

Founded: 1958
Working languages: E
Secretariat: 5 members of staff

Information available:
- Position papers, NM.

EPC

European Publishers' Council

Conseil Européen des Editeurs

Europäischer Verlegerrat

49 Park Town, Oxford OX2 6SL, United Kingdom
Tel: +44 1865/31 07 32
Fax: +44 1865/31 07 39
E-mail: angelamills@epceurope.org
Internet: http://www.epceurope.org

Brussels office:
c/o Europe Analytica
Avenue Livingstone 26, bte 3
B-1000 Brussels
Tel: +32 2/231 12 99

Pres.: F. PINTO BALSEMA
Contact: Mrs. A. MILLS (Dir.)

Founded: 1991
Working languages: E/F

EPDCC

European Pressure Die Casting Committee

Comité Européen des Fondeurs

Europäisches Komitee der Metallgiessereien

Am Bonneshof 5, 40474 Düsseldorf, Germany
Tel: +49 211/47 96 154
Fax: +49 211/47 96 409

E-mail: gerghard.kluegge@gdm-metall-guss.de
Internet: http://www.gdm-metallguss.de

Sec.-Gen.: G. KLÜGGE
Working languages: E
Secretariat: 1 member of staff

Sectors of activity:
- Exchange of technical information on all aspects of pressure die casting.

Information available:
- Conference proceedings.
- List of members available to the general public, free.

EPEGA

European Poultry, Egg and Game Association

Hochkreuzallee 72, 51735 Bonn, Germany
Tel: +49 228/95 96 00
Fax: +49 228/95 96 050
E-mail: info@epega.org
Internet: www.epega.org

Pres.: Mr. BIEGI
Sec.-Gen.: C. VON DER CRONE

EPF

European Panel Federation

Fédération Européenne des Panneaux à Base de Bois

Europäischer Holswerkstoffverband

Allée Hof-ter-Vleest 5, Bte 5, 1070 Bruxelles, Belgium
Tel: +32 2/556 25 89
Fax: +32 2/556 25 94
E-mail: info@europales.org
Internet: http://www.europanels.org

Pres.: F. DE COCK
Sec.-Gen.: K. WIJNENDAELE

Founded: 1958
General meeting: June
Working languages: E
Secretariat: 5 members of staff

Sectors of activity:
- Promotion of wood as a renewable and recyclable raw material.

Information available:
- Annual report, E, €500, M-NM.
- Information brochure, M-NM.
- "EPF Newsletter", 10 times a year, M, E.
- CD-Rom: annual report, €1 000.
- List of members, free.

EPHA

European Public Health Alliance

Alliance Européenne de la Santé Publique

Europäische Allianz für öffentliche Gesundheit

Rue de Pascale 33, 1040 Bruxelles,
  Belgium
Tel: +32 2/230 30 56
Fax: +32 2/233 38 80
E-mail: epha@epha.org
Internet: www.epha.org

Pres.: A. HAYES
Sec.-Gen.: Mrs T. ROSE

Founded: 1994
Working languages: E/F
Secretariat: 5 members of staff

Sectors of activity:
- Advocating policies that support and promote health in all areas of EU activities.
- Providing information, commentary and analysis on EU public health policy and other health-relevant EU policies to members, decision-makers and the public.
- Strengthening the NGO network by involving members in policy developments and discussions in all EU institutions.
- Publishing the magazine "European Public Health Update" to ensure timely and relevant information exchange on public health developments in the European Union.
- Developing partnerships with European and national health organisations.

Information available:
- "European Public Health Update", bimonthly, E/F.
- Various position papers, free, E/F, M-NM.
- Database: members + other contacts, M.
- "European Health Directory", free, M-NM.
- List of members available to the general public, on Internet.

EPIA

European Photovoltaïc Industry Association

Avenue Charles Quint 124, 1083
  Bruxelles, Belgium
Tel: +32 2/465 38 84
Fax: +32 2/468 24 30
E-mail: epia@epia.org
Internet: www.epia.org

Pres.: E. MACIAS
Sec.-Gen.: Michel VIAUD

Founded: 1986
General meeting: May
Working languages: E

Sectors of activity:
- Promote PV entire sector.
- 19th European PV Conference, 7-11 June, 2004.
- Renewables 2004, Bonn, 1-4 June 2004.

EPMA

European Powder Metallurgy Association

Association Européenne de Poudre Métallurgique

Europäische Vereinigung des Metallpuders

Old Bank Buildings, Bellstone,
  Shrewsbury SY1 1HU, United
  Kingdom
Tel: +44 1743/24 88 99
Fax: +44 1743/362 968
E-mail: info@epma.com
Internet: http://www.epma.com

Contact: J. WROE (Exec. Dir.)

Founded: 1989
General meeting: April or May
Working languages: E
Secretariat: 8 members of staff

Sectors of activity:
- EPMA undertakes initiatives in the following areas: research, environmental safety, statistics, standards, education, promotion and publications, and conferences/ seminars/exhibitions.

Information available:
- "EPMA News", 4 times a year, E, free (M).
- "Quality Assurance Guidelines", Update Online at www.epma.com
- "Guide to EU Legislation on H&S", 2/ year, E, €100 (M) €200 (NM).
- Brochure "Powder Metallurgy – The Process – Its Products", 32pp, free.
- List of members searchable online database only at www.epma.com
- Database: list of members and product information

EPPF

European Profiles and Panels Producers Federation

Max-Planck-Strasse 4, 40237 Düsseldorf,
  Germany
Tel: +49 211/914 27 0
Fax: +49 211/67 20 34
Internet: http://www.eppf.com

Pres.: Mr. M. SPIES
Sec.-Gen.: Dr. R. PODLESCHNY

Founded: 1991
Working languages: E/F

Sectors of activity:
- First transformation of steel.

Information available:
- Dictionary of terms relative to the manufacture, marketing and applications of profiled steel sheets and sandwich panels in building and cold stores construction, first version.
- List of members available to the general public, free.

EPSU / FSESP / EGÖD

European Federation of Public Service Unions

Fédération Syndicale Européenne des Services Publics

Europäischer Gewerkschaftsverband für den Öffentlichen Dienst

Rue Royale 45 box 1, 1000 Bruxelles,
  Belgium
Tel: +32 2/250 10 80
Fax: +32 2/250 10 99
E-mail: epsu@epsu.org
Internet: www.epsu.org

Pres.: Ms. A. SALFI
Sec.-Gen.: Ms. C. FISCHBACH-PYTTEL

Founded: 1978
General meeting: June
Secretariat: 12 members of staff

Sectors of activity:
- Local and regional government.
- National and European administration.
- Public utilities.
- Health and social services.

Information available:
- Various publications, free.
- List of members available to the general public, free.

EPTA

European Power Tool Association

Association Européenne de l'Outillage Electrique

Verband der Europäischen Elektrowerkzeug- Hersteller

Postfach 701261, 60591 Frankfurt am
  Main, Germany
Tel: +49 69//6302 270
Fax: +49 69/6302 306
E-mail: werkzeuge@zvei.org

Pres.: U.E. RUEPP
Sec.-Gen.: K. greefe

Founded: 1984
General meeting: Every 2–3 years
Working languages: E/D
Secretariat: 2 members of staff

ERA

European Regions Airline Association

Association des Compagnies d'Aviation des Régions d'Europe

Verband der Fluglinien Europäischer Regionen

The Baker Suite, Fairoaks Airport,
  Chobham GU24 8HX, United Kingdom
Tel: +44 1276/85 64 95
Fax: +44 1276/85 70 38

E-mail: info@eraa.org
Internet: http://www.eraa.org

Pres.: J. RIBEIRO DA FONSECA
Contact: M. AMBROSE (Director-
General)

Founded: 1981
Working languages: E
Secretariat: 18 members of staff

Sectors of activity:
- ERA's mission is to be the principal body representing the interests of organisations involved in air transport in Europe's Regions.
- Environment; air safety; technical regulations; slot allocation; consumer rights; delays and capacity; user charges; flight time limitations.

Information available:
- "Regional Report", monthly, free.
- "Performance", quarterly, free.
- "ERA Yearbook", annual, free: M, GBP 75: NM, 2001, E.
- "Fly safely", quarterly.
- List of members available to the general public, on Internet.

ERA

European Rotogravure Association

Association Européenne de Héliogravure

Verband des Europäischen Tiefdruchindustrie

Swakopmunder Strasse 3, 81827 München, Germany
Tel: +49 89/439 50 51
Fax: +49 89/439 41 07
E-mail: info@era.eu.org
Internet: www.era.eu.org

Pres.: J. BORMANS
Sec.-Gen.: J. SIEVER

EREC / CEI

European Real Estate Confederation

Confédération Européenne de l'Immobilier

Europäische Makleronföderation

Sainctelette Square 11/12, 1000 Bruxelles, Belgium
Tel: +32 2/219 40 08
Fax: +32 2/217 88 41
E-mail: cei@web-cei.com
Internet: www.web-cei.com

Pres.: André S. GROOT
Sec.-Gen.: Mr. RUELENS

Founded: 1985
General meeting: January
Working languages: E
Secretariat: 1 member of staff

Sectors of activity:
- 22 October 2004, Congres/ Simposium, Brussels.

Information available:
- List of members available for purchase.

ERF

European Union Road Federation

Avenue Louise 106, 1050 Bruxelles, Belgium
Tel: +32 2/644 58 77
Fax: +32 2/647 59 34
E-mail: info@erf.be
Internet: http://www.erf.be

Pres.: A. ZARAGOZA
Sec.-Gen.: J. PAPI

Founded: 1998
General meeting: June
Working languages: E
Secretariat: 4 members of staff

Sectors of activity:
- To provide EU-wide policies and programmes designed to promote economic growth and trade relations, improve road safety, enhance environment, advance social conditions by improving European road networks.
- To initiate and support scientific studies aimed at improving the knowledge of the road system in the EU: road safety standards, environmental impact and network management.

Information available:
- Recent ERF Publications (NM):
- Voice of the European Road (Quarterly e-Newsletter).
- European Road Statistics 2002.
- The European Road Safety Manifesto.
- Guidelines to Black Spot Management.
- The European Road Users Charter.
- Recent ERF Position Papers (NM):
- The European Commission's Road Safety Action Programme.
- Road Restraint Systems – Passive Safety where it matters.
- Building and financing a Trans-European Network at the service of Europe's citizens (updated edition).
- The ERF's position on achieving a decoupling of transport growth and road deaths.
- Tunnel Safety Directive – the ERF's position.
- The ERF's vision of roads in 2020: placing the user at the heart of Transport policy.
- List of members freely available on the website.CD: Guidelines to Black Spot Management, October 2002, English (99 Euros).
- Voice of the European Road (Quarterly e-Newsletter by subscription)

ERMCO

European Ready-Mixed Concrete Organisation

Association Européenne du Béton Prêt à l'Emploi

Europäischer Transportbetonverband

Rue Volta 8, 1050 Bruxelles, Belgium
Tel: +32 2/645 52 12
Fax: +32 2/735 04 67
E-mail: secretariat@ermco.org
Internet: www.ermco.org

Pres.: Didier LEVY
Sec.-Gen.: Francesco BIASIOLI

Founded: 1967
General meeting: June
Working languages: E
Secretariat: 1 member of staff

Sectors of activity:
- conferences: Co-organises a tri-annual international conference, 14th ERMCO Congress was held in Helsinki, June 16–18 2004

Information available:
- Annual report containing 12 – 14 pp of statistics on production, number of depots and per capita consumption, M-NM, E.
- Members' activities (report), E. M – NM (as cited above)
- Relevant technical and/or environmental publications, as requested, free, M – NM
- Members' list , free, M – NM

ERPA

European Recovered Paper Association

Association Européenne pour la Récupération et le Recyclage des Papiers et Cartons

c/o BIR, Avenue Franklin Roosevelt 24, 1050 Bruxelles, Belgium
Tel: +32 2/627 57 70
Fax: +32 2/627 57 73
E-mail: bir@bir.org
Internet: www.bir.org
Internet: www.erpa.info

Pres.: M. KLEIWEG DE ZWAAN
Contact: F. VEYS

Founded: 1995
Working languages: E
Secretariat: 8 members of staff

Sectors of activity:
- Relations with board and paper manufacturers, with European Commission representatives, and with users of recycled paper and board.
- Conferences: Meetings during the BIR congress (2/year).

Information available:
- Minutes, market reports, statistics, position papers, technical papers published at the meetings, M.

ESA

European Spice Association

Association Européenne de l'Epice

Europäische Vereinigung des Gewürzes

Reuterstrasse 151, 53113 Bonn, Germany
Tel: +49 228/216 162
Fax: +49 228/22 94 60
E-mail: esa@verbaendeburo.de

Pres.: M. RENDLEN
Contact: S. LÜDTKE (Secr.)
Working languages: E
Secretariat: 2 members of staff

Information available:
- List of members, free.

ESA

European Sealing Association

Bowerham House, The Grove, Lancaster LA1 3AL, United Kingdom
Tel: +44 1524/844 222
Fax: +44 1524/844 222
E-mail: bse@europeansealing.com
Internet: http:// www.europeansealing.com

Pres.: M. WERNER
Contact: Dr. J. KOCH

Founded: 1992
General meeting: April or May
Working languages: E

Sectors of activity:
- Special focus on helping users to reduce fugitive emissions. For example, developing a Sealing Technology BAT Guidance Note for all industrial sectors covered by the EU's IPPC Directive. Latest draft is available for download from the ESA web site.

Information available:
- "ESA-Environmental News", quarterly, free, E, M.
- List of members available to the general public, free and see website.
- List of other publications, consult website.

ESA

European Snacks Association

6 Catherine Street, London WC2B 5JJ, United Kingdom
Tel: +44 20/7420 7220
Fax: +44 20/7420 7221
E-mail: esa@esa.org.uk

Internet: http://www.esa.org.uk

Pres.: A. SCHUBERT
Sec.-Gen.: S. CHANDLER

Founded: 1961
Working languages: E
Secretariat: 4 members of staff

Sectors of activity:
- Snackex 2005, 19-21/06/2005, Berlin, Germany

Information available:
- "The Snacks Magazine", quarterly, E, M-NM.
- Database: food additives and pesticides, M-NM.
- Database: market statistics.
- Database: EC legislation relevant to snacks.
- Video on potato chip processing.

ESBG / GECE / ESV

European Savings Banks Group

Groupement Européen des Caisses d'Epargne

Europäische Sparkassenvereinigung

Rue Marie-Thérèse 11, 1000 Bruxelles, Belgium
Tel: +32 2/211 11 11
Fax: +32 2/211 11 99
E-mail: info@savings-banks.com
Internet: http://www.savings-banks.com

Pres.: C. DE NOOSE

Founded: 1963
General meeting: June & December
Working languages: F/E/D
Secretariat: 30 members of staff

Sectors of activity:
- Monitoring of EU legislative and financial initiatives.
- Organisation of conferences, seminars and workshops.
- The ESBG participates in EU and other International Agencies' programmes to develop appropriate banking structures, strengthen institutions and provides training in the Central and Eastern European countries.

Information available:
- Annual report, F/E/D, M-NM.
- "Perspectives", monthly, E.
- "Newsletter", monthly, F/E/D/It/Esp.
- "Position papers", M.
- "Weekly Press Review", M.
- CD-Rom: "Business Directory", gratuit, E.
- Database: members + contact institutions.
- List of members available to the general public.

ESBO

European Solid Board Organisation

Laan Copes van Cattenburch 79, PO Box 85612, 2585 EW Den Haag, Netherlands
Tel: +31 70/312 39 18
Fax: +31 70/363 63 48
E-mail: mail@esbo.nl
Internet: www.esbo.nl

Pres.: D. SCHUT
Sec.-Gen.: H. A. VOSKAMP

Founded: 1961
General meeting: March
Working languages: E

Historical note:
- Formerly known as ASSCO

Information available:
- All available information, including list of members, via the website

ESDREMA

European Surgical Dressings Manufacturers' Association

c/o Dr. Massima Poretti, Via San Giovanni s/Muro 1, 20121 Milano, Italy
Tel: +39 2/86 75 21
Fax: +39 2/86 46 34 07

Pres.: Dr. Massima PORETTI

Founded: 1974
General meeting: Spring & Autumn
Working languages: E

Sectors of activity:
- Compilation of European wide statistics.
- The exchange of information on the general economic situation in each country.

Information available:
- The members' list is available publicly, free of charge.

ESF

European Safety Federation

Rue Gachard 88 Bte 4, 1050 Bruxelles, Belgium
Permanent Secretariat:
Binnensteenweg 180
2530 Boechout
Tel: +32 3/460 02 31
Fax: +32 3/460 02 13
E-mail: info@european-safety -federation.org
Internet: www.european-safety -federation.org

Pres.: Dr. David HARRIS
Sec.-Gen.: Henk VANHOUTTE
Contacts: G. VANDEPUTTE (Honorary President), Mrs. R. BOEL

Founded: 1991
General meeting: October/November

Working languages: E/D/F
Secretariat: 2 members of staff

Sectors of activity:
- "The newly amended PPE Directive 89/686. A step in safety in the workplace", November 2003, Düsseldorf.

Information available:
- "Brochure ESF", free, E/F/D.
- Database: PPE manufacturers and retailers.
- List of members available to the general public, free; see the website

ESF

European Spring Federation

Maison de la Mécanique, Rue Louis Blanc 39-41, 92400 Courbevoie, France
Tel: +33 1/47 17 64 10
Fax: +33 1/47 17 63 60
E-mail: info@esf-springs.com
Internet: www.esf-springs.com

Sec.-Gen.: Mr. DELMOTTE
Contact: M. GUILLEMET
Working languages: E

ESGG

European Seed Growers Group
Groupe Européen des Graines

Rue Jean-Jacques Rousseau 74, 75001 Paris, France
Tel: +33 1/44 82 73 33
Fax: +33 1/44 82 73 40
E-mail: esgg@wanadoo.fr

Pres.: G. MATTEUCCI
Contact: S. PRIN (Secr.)

Sectors of activity:
- Agriculture.
- Semences.

ESHA

European School Heads' Association
Association des Chefs d'Etablissements d'Enseignement
Europäische Schulleiter Vereinigung im Sekundarbereich II

c/o Ria van Peperstraten, Kromme Nieuwegracht 50, 3512 HK Utrecht, Netherlands
Tel: +31 30/234 9090
Fax: +31 30/234 9099
E-mail: r.vpeperstraten@vvo.nl
Internet: www.esha.org

Pres.: A. PETROLINO
Sec.-Gen.: J. LEMPINEN

Founded: 1988
General meeting: Spring and Autumn
Working languages: E

Information available:
- All general information about our activities is available through the website.
- List of members by arrangement only on application.
- A leaflet containing briefly main issues such as history, values, aims, means and how to contact. Free of charge.

ESHP

European Society of Handwriting Psychology
Société Européenne de Graphologie
Europäische Gesellschaft für Schriftpsychologie und Schriftexpertise

Klebestrasse 2077, 8040 Zürich, Switzerland
Tel: +41 1/493 32 62
Fax: +41 1/493 32 64
E-mail: egs-secretariat@web.de
Internet: www.egs-graphologie.ch

Pres.: P. RAINEREBRUTSCH
Contact: Mrs. I. SALZWEDEL (Admin.)

ESOMAR

The World Association of Research Professionals
Association Européenne pour les Etudes d'Opinion et de Marketing
Europäische Gesellschaft für Meinungs- und Marketing-Forschung

Vondelstraat 172, 1054 GJ Amsterdam, Netherlands
Tel: +31 20/664 21 41
Fax: +31 20/664 29 22
E-mail: email@esomar.org
Internet: http://www.esomar.org

Pres.: F. NAUCKHOFF
Sec.-Gen.: T. VONK
Contacts: M. VAN HAMERSVELD (Dir. Gen.), Ms. K. JOE

Founded: 1948
General meeting: September
Working languages: E/F/D
Secretariat: 25 members of staff

Sectors of activity:
- 4000 members working in marketing and market, social and opinion research in over 100 countries around the world.
- Organisation of 8 to 10 conferences (in Europe, the USA, South America and China) and 1 congress each year as well as regional conferences and workshops.
- Provision of professional codes,guidelines and reports on developments affecting marketing and market research as well as trend

information on the marketing research industry.
- Liaison with bodies such as the EC and the ICC (International Chamber of Commerce).
- Conferences: See http://www.esomar.org

Information available:
Publications (M-NM):
- "Excellence in International Research", €85 (NM), €68 (M).
- "Research World", free, M.
- "ESOMAR Conference and Seminar Books", €150 (NM), €120 (M).
- "The ESOMAR Handbook of Market and Opinion Research", €170 (NM), €135 (M).
- "Congress CD-Rom", €270 (NM), €215 (M).
- "ESOMAR Monograph Series: Collected papers for a concise state-of-the-art overview of various key research areas", €85 (NM), €68 (M).
- ESOMAR Reports: reports that cover several aspects of the market research industry, trying to find a balance between conciseness, quality of information and user-friendliness:
1. Annual Market Study on Market Statistics, E.
2. Prices Study 1997 – Worldwide, E.
3. Latin American Profile: Demographics and Socio-Economic level, E/Port/Esp, price for each report €68 (NM), €50 (M).

International Codes and Guidelines: the following Codes and Guidelines are free on request and available in E/F/D/Esp unless otherwise stated:
- "ICC/ESOMAR International Code of Marketing and Social Practice".
- "Guide to Opinion Polls. endorsed by ESOMAR/WAPOR".
- "ICC/ESOMAR Guideline on Maintaining the Distinctions between Marketing Research and Direct Marketing", E only.
- "Guidelines on Interviewing Children".
- "Guidelines on Mystery Shopping".
- "Guidelines on Tape and Video-Recording and Client Observation of Interviews and Group Discussions".
- "Guidelines on Pharmaceutical Marketing Research", E only.
- "The Arbitration Service".
- "Conducting Marketing and Opinion Research Using the Internet".
- "Standard Demographic Classification – A System of International Socio-Economic Classification of Respondents to Survey Research", E only.
- "Report on the Freedom to Publish Opinion Polls", E only.
- "ESOMAR Directory of Research Organisations", this directory lists 1500 major agencies and provides users and research suppliers with a major source of potential worldwide business partners. This is available

online to members and non-members. The printed version with research agencies contains Vol. I & II and costs €350 (NM), €175 (M). The listing of members is available only to members, and is not posted on the web.

ESPO

European Sea Ports Organisation

Organisation des Ports Maritimes Européens

Treurenberg 6, 1000 Bruxelles, Belgium
Tel: +32 2/736 34 63
Fax: +32 2/736 63 25
E-mail: mail@espo.be
Internet: http://www.espo.be

Pres.: D. WHITEHEAD
Sec.-Gen.: P. VERHOEVEN

Founded: 1993
Working languages: E
Secretariat: 3 members of staff

Sectors of activity:
- ESPO 2004 The European Sea Ports Conference, European Sea Ports in a Dynamic Market was held in Rotterdam, 17-18 June 2004

Information available:
- "ESPO News", free, E, M.
- "Annual Report", free, E, M-NM.
- "ESPO Environmental Code of Practice", free, E, M-NM.
- "ESPO Handbook", free, E, M-NM.
- "ESPO Environmental Review", free, E, M-NM.

ESRA

European Synthetic Rubber Association

Association des Caoutchoucs Synthétiques

Europäischer Synthesekeutschukverband

The Green 8, Richmond-on-Thames TW9 1PL, United Kingdom
Tel: +44 20/8332 11 13
Fax: +44 20/8332 92 92
E-mail: sue@iisrpes.stech.co.uk
Internet: www.cefic.org

Sec.-Gen.: Mrs. S. CAIN
Contact: Ms. N. SCHOUB

ESTA

European Security Transport Association

Association Européenne du Transport et Convoyage de Valeurs

Europäische Vereinigung für Geldtransport und -Begleitung

252 rue D. Lefevre, 1020 Bruxelles, Belgium
Tel: +32 2/467 02 83
Fax: +32 2/467 07 28
E-mail: francis.ravez@esta.biz

Pres.: R. MADDALONE
Sec.-Gen.: Francis RAVEZ
Contacts: B. D'HONDT (Vice-Pr), B. DUMOULIN (Vice-Pr), J. GODEFROIMONT

Founded: 1975
General meeting: May
Working languages: E/F
Secretariat: 1 member of staff

Sectors of activity:
- Continuing information on new technologies.
- EU coordination initiatives.

Information available:
- Database: statistics.

ESTA

European Steel Tube Association

Association Européenne du Tube d'Acier

Rue de Silly 130, 92100 Boulogne Billancourt, France
Tel: +33 1/41 31 56 40
Fax: +33 1/41 31 00 24
E-mail: esta.nb@wanadoo.fr

Sec.-Gen.: M. BODINEAU

Founded: ESTA: 1994 (formerly CDL: 1970)
Working languages: F/E
Secretariat: 3 members of staff

Sectors of activity:
- The association members of ESTA should be any EU national associations with membership principally involved in the manufacture of steel tubes.

Information available:
- List of members available to the general public, free.

ESTA

European Smoking Tobacco Association

Association Européenne de Tabac

Rond Point Schumann, 9 bte 1, 1040 Bruxelles, Belgium
Tel: +32 2/230 80 92
Fax: +32 2/230 82 14
E-mail: info@esta.be

Pres.: U. SLUITER
Contacts: F. P. MARKS (Gen. Man.), J. VAN DE MORTEL (Gen. Man.)

ESTA

European Surgical Trade Association

Buchenstrasse 76, 28211 Bremen, Germany
Tel: +49 421/34 78 608
Fax: +49 421/34 91 866
E-mail: esta@esta-office.com

Pres.: D. RIZZI
Sec.-Gen.: J. MARENZI

Founded: 1959
General meeting: August/September
Working languages: E

ESTOC

European Smokeless Tobacco Council

Conseil Européen du Tabac sans Fumée

Europäischer Rat für Rauchlosen Tabak

Streekbaan 100, 1800 Vilvoorde, Belgium
Tel: +32 2/732 22 04
Fax: +32 2/732 19 26
E-mail: mverhulst@compuserve.com
Internet: www.estoc.org

Pres.: S. LINDMARK
Contact: Mrs. VERHULST (Dir.)

ETA

European Tube Association

Association Européenne des Tubes Souples

Europäische Tuben Vereinigung

Am Bonneshof 5, 40474 Düsseldorf, Germany
Tel: +49 211/4796 144
Fax: +49 211/4796 408
E-mail: info@etna-online.org

Pres.: Dr. C. GRUPP
Contact: G. SPENGLER

Founded: 1959
General meeting: Every May/June
Working languages: F/E/D
Secretariat: 3 members of staff

Information available:
- List of members available to the general public.

ETAD

Ecological and Toxicological Association of Dyes and Organic Pigments Manufacturers

PO Box 99, 4005 Basel, Switzerland
Tel: +41 61/690 99 66
Fax: +41 61/691 42 78
E-mail: info@etad.com
Internet: http://www.etad.com

Pres.: Dr. F-M STÖHR
Contact: H. MOTSCHI

Founded: 1974
General meeting: May
Working languages: E
Secretariat: 4 members of staff

Information available:
- "Annual Report", free, E, M-NM.
- Various advisory brochures and information notices, E, M-NM.
- Database: health and environmental data on organic colorants
- Database: toxicological and ecotoxicological data for organic colorants and key intermediates, M.
- List of members available to the general public, free.

ETC / CET

European Tea Committee
Comité Européen du Thé
Europäisches Komitee des Tees

Rue de Copenhague 3, 75008 Paris, France
Tel: +33 1/53 42 13 38
Fax: +33 1/53 42 13 39
E-mail: enfed@eucafé.com

Pres.: Mr. T. KRAMER
Sec.-Gen.: Mrs. B. DUFRENE

Founded: 1960
Working languages: E
Secretariat: 2 members of staff

Information available:
- List of members available to the general public.

ETC / CET

European Travel Commission
Commission Européenne du Tourisme

Avenue Marnix 19a, PO Box 25, 1000 Bruxelles, Belgium
Tel: +32 2/502 01 13
Fax: +32 2/514 18 43
E-mail: info@etc-corporate.org
Internet: www.etc-corporate.org
Internet: www.visiteurope.com

Pres.: A. OBERASCHER
Contact: Robert FRANKLIN (Executive Director)

Founded: 1948
General meeting: Spring and autumn
Working languages: E/F
Secretariat: 2 members of staff

Sectors of activity:
- To promote Europe as a travel destination on major overseas markets (USA, Canada, Japan, Latin America).
- To foster the exchange of information between members and to carry out

research on topics of common interest to members.

Information available:
- "Europe's Senior Travel Market", E.
- Database: 1600 addresses of tourism sector organisations.
- List of members, free.

ETF

European Transport Workers' Federation
Fédération Européenne des Travailleurs des Transports
Europäische Transportarbeiter-Föderation

Rue du Midi 165, 1000 Bruxelles, Belgium
Tel: +32 2/285 46 60
Fax: +32 2/280 08 17
E-mail: etf@etf.skynet.be
Internet: http://www.itf.org.uk/etf

Pres.: W. HABERZETTL
Sec.-Gen.: Ms. D. ZINKE

Founded: 1999
Working languages: F/E/D
Secretariat: 7 members of staff

Sectors of activity:
- Transport and fisheries.
Conferences:
- 60 meetings a year.

Information available:
- Documentation and regulation of the European institutions.
- "News from Brussels".
- Database: members of the Joint Committees and members.
- List of members available to the general public, free.

ETNO

European Telecommunications Network Operators' Association

Avenue Louise 54, 1050 Bruxelles, Belgium
Tel: +32 2/219 32 42
Fax: +32 2/219 64 12
E-mail: etno@etno.be
Internet: http://www.etno.be/

Contact: M. BARTHOLOMEW (Dir)

Founded: 1992
General meeting: April – October
Working languages: E
Secretariat: 8 members of staff

Sectors of activity:
- Numerous seminars for members only.

Information available:
- Annual report, E, NM.
- List of members available to the general public, free.

ETRTO

European Tyre and Rim Technical Organisation
Organisation Technique Européenne du Pneu et de la Jante

Avenue Brugmann 32 bte 2, 1060 Bruxelles, Belgium
Tel: +32 2/344 40 59
Fax: +32 2/344 12 34
E-mail: info@etrto.org
Internet: http://www.etrto.org

Pres.: L. BERGOMI
Contact: J-Cl NOIRHOMME(CP)

Founded: 1964
General meeting: September
Working languages: E
Secretariat: 2 members of staff

Information available:
- "ETRTO: Standards Manual", free for members, E/F/D, annual, NM.
- "Recommendations on tyre care and maintenance", E/F/D, NM.
- "Engineering Design Information", E, published annually, NM.
- "Lexicon" (technical terms in F/E/D), NM.
- "Aircraft Tyre and Rim Data Book", annual, E.
- CD-Rom: €235 for 1 user, E/F/D.
- List of members, published in Standards Manual and available on the website

ETSA

European Telecommunication Services Association
Association Européenne des Entreprises de Service en Télécommunication

Rue de Spa 18, 1000 Bruxelles, Belgium
Tel: +32 2/285 06 18
Fax: +32 2/230 70 35
E-mail: diaz@masappartments.com
Internet: http://www.etsa.org

Pres.: P. PITSCH
Sec.-Gen.: Mrs. D. DE CONINCK DE MAERCKEM

Founded: 1988
Working languages: E/F
Secretariat: 1 member of staff

Sectors of activity:
- CTI Demonstration action: Thanks to financial support from the Information Society Project Office (European Commission), ETSA is currently organising an information campaign on Computer Telephony Integration, Telematic Applications and Teleteaching. In 10 countries, some 180 demonstration actions will be implemented reaching more than 3 500 participants.

- ETSA Employee Exchange:
  This programme allows SMEs' staff to gain new skills by working in a foreign country. This initiative was launched because SMEs can raise their competitiveness by investing in human resources.
- Qualif'Com:
  Qualif'Com is a Quality Management System for SMEs active in the field of telecommunication. Qualif'Com guarantees "Quality of Service" for the end-user. The Qualif'Com rating is voluntary and is given in three separate fields: cabling, service and maintenance; and engineering and consulting. In each country, an independent audit team assesses the companies on the basis of criteria such as organisation, business specific know-how, customer orientation. The Qualif'Com certificate is delivered for a period of 3 years.

Information available:
- List of members available to the general public, free.

ETSA

European Textile Services Association

Rue Montoyer 24 Box 7, 1000 Bruxelles, Belgium
Tel: +32 2/282 09 90
Fax: +32 2/282 09 99
E-mail: etsa@etsa-europe.org
Internet: www.etsa-europe.org

Pres.: T. KRAUTSCHNEIDER
Contact: R. LONG

Founded: 1994
Working languages: E
Secretariat: 3 members of staff

Sectors of activity:
- Textile services / textile rental.

Information available:
- "Why industrial laundering is better for the environment than domestic washing", E.
- "Professionally serviced dust control mats", E/F/D/Fin.
- "The clean way to cut costs", E/F/D/Fin.
- "Hand hygiene: recommendations for food business operators", E/F/D, free.
- "Horeca: market survey: hand hygiene", E/F/D.
- "The cotton story", F/D.
- "For cleaner hands", E/F/D.
- "Good hand hygiene", E/F/D.
- "Textile or paper?", E/F/D.
- "Why outsourcing can help you", E, free.
- "Reusable medical textiles", E/F/D.
- Database: scientific studies on hand hygiene.

ETTFA

European Tourism Trade Fairs Association

Association des Foires Touristiques Européennes

Europäischer Fremdenverkehrsmessenverband

PO Box 585, Richmond, Surrey TW9 1YQ, United Kingdom
Tel: +44 20/8948 66 56
Fax: +44 20/8948 80 97
E-mail: secretariat@ettfa.org
Internet: www.ettfa.org

Pres.: T. NUTLEY
Sec.-Gen.: Mrs. M. LAPTER

ETUC / CES / EGB

European Trade Union Confederation

Confédération Européenne des Syndicats

Europäischer Gewerkschaftsbund

Bd du Roi Albert II, 5, 1210 Bruxelles, Belgium
Tel: +32 2/224 04 11
Fax: +32 2/224 04 54/55
E-mail: etuc@etuc.org
Internet: http://www.etuc.org

Pres.: F. VERZETNITSCH
Sec.-Gen.: J.MONKS

Founded: 1973
Working languages: F/E/D/Nor
Secretariat: 45 members of staff

Sectors of activity:
- Several colloquia and seminars are organised throughout the year, covering primarily the internal market and the social dimension thereof (cfr website).

Information available:
- Various trade-union reports.

ETUCE / CSEE

European Trade Union Committee for Education

Comité Syndical Européen de l'Education

Europäisches Gewerkschaftskomitee für Bildung und Wissenschaft

Bd du Roi Albert II, 5 – 9th floor, 1210 Bruxelles, Belgium
Tel: +32 2/224 06 91/92
Fax: +32 2/224 06 94
E-mail: secretariat@csee-etuce.org

Sec.-Gen.: Martin ROMER
Contact: Mrs. D. VERSCHUEREN

Founded: 1975
General meeting: May (every 2 years)
Working languages: F/E

Secretariat: 2 members of staff

Information available:
- Bulletin, 3/year, F/E.
- Newsletter, F/E.
- "CSEE Info".
- Brochure: Equal opportunities.
- "Teacher Training in Europe".
- "Intercultural education against racism and xenophobia".
- "Health and health education".
- "Information and communication technologies in education".
- "Violence in schools".

ETUCO / ASE / EGA

European Trade Union College

Académie Syndicale Européenne

Europäische Gewerkschaftsakademie

Boulevard du Roi Albert II 5 bte 7, 1210 Bruxelles, Belgium
Tel: +32 2/224 05 30
Fax: +32 2/224 05 20
E-mail: etuco@etuc.org
Internet: www.etuc.org/etuco

Pres.: F. VERZETNITSCH
Contact: J. BRIDGFORD (Dir.)

Founded: 1990
Working languages: E/F/D
Secretariat: 14 members of staff

Sectors of activity:
- to organise courses for the ETUC and its organisations in areas concerning all questions relating to European integration as seen from the trade union point of view;
- to develop cooperation between the education officers in trade unions and in trade union colleges already operating at the national level and the College;
- to promote knowledge of economic, political and social developments at the European level, through the courses it runs;
- to intensify cooperation amongst European educational institutions.

ETUF: TCL / FSE: THC / EGV: TBL

European Trade Union Federation: Textiles, Clothing and Leather

Fédération Syndicale Européenne du Textile, de l'Habillement et du Cuir

Europäischer Gewerkschaftsverband Textil, Bekleidung und Leder

Rue J. Stevens 8, 1000 Bruxelles, Belgium
Tel: +32 2/511 54 77
Fax: +32 2/511 81 54
E-mail: fse.thc@skynet.be

Pres.: V. FEDELI
Sec.-Gen.: P. ITSCHERT

Founded: 1964
Working languages: F/E/D
Secretariat: 3 members of staff

Information available:
- List of members available to the general public, free.

ETV

European Tobacco Wholesalers Association

Association Européenne des Grossistes en Produits du Tabac

Europäischer Tabakwaren-Grosshandels-Verband E.V.

Stadtwaldgürtel 44, 50931 Köln, Germany
Tel: +49 221/40 07 00
Fax: +49 221/400 70 20
E-mail: lind@bdta.de
Internet: www.bdta.de

Pres.: E. SPENGLER
Sec.-Gen.: P. LIND

Founded: 1973
General meeting: June
Working languages: D/E
Secretariat: 1 member of staff

Information available:
- List of members available to the general public, free.

EUAC

European Union of Aquarium Curators

Union Européenne des Conservateurs d'Aquarium

c/o P. Van Den Sande, Eug. Fahylaan 34, 2100 Antwerpen, Belgium
Tel: +32 3/324 10 08
Fax: +32 3/275 69 13
E-mail: paul.vandensande@
antwerpen.be
Internet: www.euac.org

Pres.: J. LANGEN
Contact: P. VAN DEN SANDE (Dir. Exec.)

Founded: 1972
Working languages: E/F/D/Nl

Sectors of activity:
- Aquariology – public aquariums.

Information available:
- Proceedings of the congresses, E/Nl/D.
- Database: addresses of the majority of European Public Aquariums.
- The members' list is available upon request.

EUBA

European Bentonite Producers' Association

Boulevard S. Dupuis 233 Bte 124, 1070 Bruxelles, Belgium
Tel: +32 2/524 55 00
Fax: +32 2/524 45 75
E-mail: secretariat@ima-eu.org
Internet: http://www.ima-eu.org

Pres.: Mr.Chris WATKINS
Sec.-Gen.: Mr. Roger DOOME

EUCA

European Federation of Associations of Coffee Roasters

Fédération Européenne des Associations de Torréfacteurs de Café

Europäische Vereinigung der Rösterverbände

Tourniairestraat 3, P.O. Box 90445, 1006 BK Amsterdam, Netherlands
Tel: +31 20/511 38 14
Fax: +31 20/511 38 92
E-mail: euca@coffee-associations.org

Pres.: M. SERUTI
Sec.-Gen.: J.A.J.R. VAESSEN

Founded: 1967
Working languages: E
Secretariat: 2 members of staff

Information available:
- "European Coffee Report", annual, free, E, M-NM.

EUCAR

European Council for Automotive Research and Development

Rue du Noyer 211, 1000 Bruxelles, Belgium
Tel: +32 2/738 73 53
Fax: +32 2/738 73 12
E-mail: eucar@acea.be
Internet: www.eucar.be

Pres.: Mr. M REITZ
Sec.-Gen.: Mr. A. VANZYL

Founded: 1994
Working languages: E
Secretariat: 4 members of staff

Sectors of activity:
- The purpose of EUCAR is to encourage collaboration in R&D between its members and with relevant external bodies (suppliers, research institutes, ...).

Information available:
- List of members available to the general public, free.

EUCARPIA

European Association for Research on Plant Breeding

Association Européenne pour l'Amélioration des Plantes

Europäische Gesellschaft für Züchtungsforschung

University of Agricultural Sciences Vienna, Gregor Mendel Str 33, 1180 Wien, Austria
Tel: +43 1/47654-3309
Fax: +43 1/47654-3342
E-mail: hans.vollmann@eucarpia.org
Internet: http://www.eucarpia.org

Pres.: P. RUCKENBAUER
Sec.-Gen.: J. VOLLMANN

Founded: 1956
General meeting: General Congress / Assembly every 3 to 4 years
Working languages: E

Sectors of activity:
- EUCARPIA aims to promote scientific and technical co-operation in the field of plant breeding in order to foster its further development. Any activity in connection with a commercial interest is excluded.
- Conferences:
- See http://www.eucarpia.org

Information available:
- "EUCARPIA Bulletin", annual, €20, E, M-NM.
- Proceedings of Congress, triennial, E, M-NM.
- "Capsicum & eggplant newsletter", yearly, M-NM.
- "Cruciferae newsletter", yearly, M-NM.
- "Fruit breeding section newsletter", yearly, M-NM.
- Database: list of members, M.
- See http://www.eucarpia.org/03publications/recent_publ.html

EUCEPA

European Liaison Committee for Pulp and Paper

Comité Européen de Liaison pour la Cellulose et le Papier

Europäische Technische Vereinigung der Zellstoff- und Papierindustrie

Bd Haussmann 154, 75008 Paris, France
Tel: +33 1/45 62 11 91
Fax: +33 1/45 63 53 09
E-mail: eucepa@yahoo.fr
Internet: www.eucepa.com

Pres.: A. LOUREIRO
Contact: Mrs. BATAIS

Founded: 1956
Working languages: F/E/D

Sectors of activity:
- European paper-industry science and technology.

- EUCEPA: European Technical Association for the Pulp and Paper Industry.
- Development and promotion solely of scientific and technical knowledge in the pulp, paper and board industries through a free cooperation between the chemical and engineering association of the said industries from the various European countries. Organisation of discussions, conferences, congresses and symposia relating to these industries. Establishment of contacts with other international organisations to facilitate and encourage the exchange of knowledge and ideas.

Information available:
- "Preprints of events", M-NM.

EUCOLAIT

European Union of Dairy Trade

Union Européenne du Commerce des Produits Laitiers et Dérivés

Europäische Union des Handels mit Milcherzeugnissen

Avenue Livingstone 26 – Bte 5, 1000 Bruxelles, Belgium
Tel: +32 2/230 44 48
Fax: +32 2/230 40 44
E-mail: dairy.trade@eucolait.be
Internet: www.eucolait-dairytrade.org

Pres.: I. HAYES
Sec.-Gen.: Annelie GEHRING
Contact: Patricie PORTETEWE

Founded: 1959
General meeting: May
Working languages: F/E/D
Secretariat: 5 members of staff

Information available:
- "EUCOLAIT Information", monthly, E/D/F (only for members).
- Rapid information service by email (only for members).
- The members' list is available free of charge.

EUCOMED

European Association of Medical Technologies and Devices

Place St Lambert 14, 1200 Bruxelles, Belgium
Tel: +32 2/772 22 12
Fax: +32 2/771 39 09
E-mail: eucomed@eucomed.be
Internet: http://www.eucomed.be

Pres.: Mr. WILSON
Contacts: D. PIROYANO(CP), M. WAGNER (Dir. Gen.)

Founded: 1981
Working languages: E
Secretariat: 12 members of staff

Sectors of activity:
- EUCOMED organises seminars and conferences – reports on the conferences are published.

Information available:
- Publications:
  – "The Case against Reuse & Single Use Medical Devices", E/Esp/It/Port.
  – "CE-Marking – Protection, Performance and Safety First", Brochure, E.
  – "Good Distribution Practice (GDP)".
  – "Code of Business Practice".
  – "Long-Term Strategy".
- CD-Rom: "Industry fact file", E, €150, October 2000.

EUDA

European Dredging Association

Rue de Praetere 2-4, 1000 Bruxelles, Belgium
Tel: +32 2/646 81 83
Fax: +32 2/646 60 63
E-mail: info@euda.be
Internet: www.european-dredging.info/

Pres.: J. ALLAERT
Sec.-Gen.: F.J. MINK
Contact: Mrs. A.C.F. DE MEESTER (Assistant Secretary General)

Founded: 1993
General meeting: October
Working languages: E
Secretariat: 3 members of staff

Information available:
- List of members available to the general public.

EUFED

European Union Federation of Youth Hostel Associations

Fédération des Auberges de Jeunesse de l'Union Européenne

Jugendherbergsverband der Europäischen Union

Hoogstraat 25, rue Haute, 1000 Bruxelles, Belgium
Tel: +32 2/502 80 66
Fax: +32 2/502 55 78
E-mail: info@eufed.org
Internet: www.eufed.org

Pres.: Mr. P. KAISER
Sec.-Gen.: Ms S. CASSELL

Founded: 1987
General meeting: November
Working languages: E/F
Secretariat: 2 members of staff

Sectors of activity:
- Tourism.
- Youth.
- Environment.

- 23–24 April 2004 – Almada (Portugal) – EU funded Seminar: IOU Respect: Youth Hostels and Education through Sport for Young Fans and Players

Information available:
- EUFED e-bulletin, only in English (M / NM)
- Annual Report, only in English.
- List of members available to the general public free and on http://www.eufed.org.

EuLA

European Lime Association

Association Européenne de la Chaux

Europäischer Kalkverband

Rue du Trône 61, 1050 Bruxelles, Belgium
Tel: +32 2/511 31 28
Fax: +32 2/514 09 23
E-mail: secretariat@eula.be
Internet: www.eula.be

Pres.: R. GOFFIN
Contact: Y. DE LEFPINAY

Founded: 1990
General meeting: March – September
Working languages: D/E/F
Secretariat: 4 members of staff

Sectors of activity:
- Exchange of technical experience.
- Organisation of technical conferences.Conferences: 4th European Lime Conference Krakow 15-17.09.2004 "Lime for a cleaner Environment"

Information available:
- List of members available to the general public, free. (www.kalk.de/kalksite/dynamic/dyn.htm).
- Brochures and scientific publication on line, events, position papers.

EUMABOIS

European Federation of Woodworking Machinery Manufacturers

Centro Direzionale Milanofiori, 1a Strada Palazzo F3, 20090 Assago – Milano, Italy
Tel: +39 02/89210 253
Fax: +39 02/8259 009
E-mail: info@eumabois.com
Internet: http://www.eumabois.com

Pres.: G. BRUN
Sec.-Gen.: P. ZANIBON

Founded: 1960
Working languages: E
Secretariat: 5 members of staff

Information available:
- "Eumabois Directory", updated regularly, E.

- Database: fairs world-wide together with magazines related to specialised press for woodworking machinery.
- List of members available to the general public, free.

EUMAPRINT

European Committee of Printing and Paper Converting Machinery Manufacturers

Comité Européen des Constructeurs de Machines pour les Industries Graphiques et Papetières

Europäisches Komitee der Hersteller von Druck- und Papiermaschinen

c/o Swissmem, Kirchenweg 4,Postfach, 8032 Zürich, Switzerland
Tel: +041 138 44 111
Fax: +041 138 44 846
E-mail: eumaprint@swissmem.ch
Internet: http://www.eumaprint.org

Sec.-Gen.: L. SIGRIST

Founded: 1966
General meeting: June
Working languages: Esp
Secretariat: 10 members of staff

Information available:
- "Printing Industry Report", 4/year, Esp/E.
- "Packaging Industry Report", 2/year, Esp/E.
- EUMAPRINT (information brochure) available free from member associations.
- Database: several client lists.

EUMC

European Union for Small and Medium-Sized Enterprises

Union Européenne des Entreprises de Taille Moyenne

Europäischen Union Mittelständischer Unternehmen

Rue Posschier 2, 1040 Bruxelles, Belgium
Tel: +32 2/646 11 87
Fax: +32 2/649 87 62
E-mail: eumc@skynet.be
Internet: http://www.eumc.be

Pres.: J. KIERS
Sec.-Gen.: G. HAMMERSCHMIED

Founded: 1989
General meeting: December
Working languages: E/Nl/D/F
Secretariat: 5 members of staff

Sectors of activity:
- Seminars and conferences on the introduction of the European Single Currency.
- "Balkan Business Partnerships (focus on SMEs) Conference", Skopje.

- "Health Care Issues".
- "Business Incubator Centres".

Information available:
- "EUMC Business Briefing", M, monthly.
- Database: list of members.

EUMETSAT

European Organisation for the Exploitation of Meteorological Satellites

Organisation Européenne pour l'Exploitation de Satellites Météorologiques

Europäische Organisation für die Nutzung von Meteorologischen Satelliten

Am Kavalleriesand 31, 64295 Darmstadt, Germany
Tel: +49 6151/807 345
Fax: +49 6151/807 555
E-mail: press@eumetsat.de
Internet: http://www.eumetsat.de

Pres.: Dr. Lars PRAHVN
Contact: Ms. Livia BRIESE

Founded: 1986
General meeting: June/July + November/ December
Working languages: E/F

Sectors of activity:
- To establish, maintain and exploit European systems of operational meteorological satellites.
Conference:
- "2004 Meteorological Satellite Data Users' Conference", 31/05-04/06/2004, Prague

Information available:
- Annual Report, free, E/F.
- "IMAGE" Newsletter, bi-annual, free.
- "Proceedings of Scientific Meetings", annual, free, E.
- "Report of CGMS meeting", free, E.
- EPS, MTP & MSG leaflets, E and F
- Members: Intergovernmental organisation composed of 18 Member States and 7 cooperating states.
- List of members and information on publications and services are available at http://www.eumetsat.de

EuPC

European Plastics Converters

Confédération Européenne de la Plasturgie

Avenue de Cortenbergh 66, 1000 Bruxelles, Belgium
Tel: +32 2/732 41 24
Fax: +32 2/732 42 18
E-mail: info@eupc.org
Internet: http://www.eupc.org

Contact: Mr. DANGIS

Founded: 1990
Working languages: E
Secretariat: 4 members of staff

Information available:
- Newsletter.
- "EUPC Economic and Statistical Report", €200.
- Databases: members and contacts.
- The members' list is available free of charge.
- "General information in the field of plastics".

EURACOAL

European Association for Coal and Lignite

Association Européenne du Charbon et du Lignite

Av. de Tervueren 168 Bte 11, 1150 Bruxelles, Belgium
Tel: +32 2/771 99 74
Fax: +32 2/771 41 04
E-mail: eurocoal@eurocoal.org
Internet: http://www.eurocoal.org

Sec.-Gen.: L. JANSSENS
Working languages: F/E/D/Esp
Secretariat: 3 members of staff

Information available:
- Annual Report, M, E.
- List of members available to the general public, free.

EURADA

European Association of Development Agencies

Association Européenne des Agences de Développement

Avenue des Arts 12 Bte 7, 1210 Bruxelles, Belgium
Tel: +32 2/218 43 13
Fax: +32 2/218 45 83
E-mail: info@eurada.org
Internet: www.eurada.org

Pres.: G. EKSTRÖM
Contact: C. SAUBLENS

Founded: 1991
Working languages: E/F
Secretariat: 4 members of staff

Sectors of activity:
- Eurada manages a network of informal regional risk-capital organisations (Business Angels) and acts as the secretariat for a network of bodies interested in the benchmarking of regional competitiveness.

Information available:
- "EURADA News", bimontlhy, F/E, M.
- "Mini Guides", E/F, M.
- "Euro Rapport", E/F, M.

EURATEX

European Apparel and Textile Organisation

Organisation Européenne de l'Habillement et du Textile

Rue Montoyer 24, 1000 Bruxelles, Belgium
Tel: +32 2/285 48 80
Fax: +32 2/230 60 54
E-mail: info@euratex.org
E-mail: paulette.de.wilde@euratex.org
Internet: http://www.euratex.org

Pres.: Filiep LIBEERT (B)
Contact: W. LAKIN (Director General)

Founded: 1996
General meeting: June & November
Working languages: F/E/D
Secretariat: 12 members of staff

Historical note:
- Euratex founded after a merge between: Comitextil (The European Textile association) (founded in 1960)
- ECLA (The European Clothing Association) (founded in 1970)
- ELTAC (The European largest textile and clothing companies) (founded in 1989)

Sectors of activity:
- to define and defend vis-a-vis the institutions of the European Union external trade, industrial and social policies to the benefit of the enterprises in the sector;
- to contribute to the effective surveillance of the multilateral and bilateral agreements signed by the European Union, the objective being the establishment of fair international trading conditions;
- to develop alliances with upstream (equipment manufacturers, chemical industry...) and downstream (distribution, design...) sectors in order to maximize synergies between these various components;
- to foster innovation through technical research, technological transfer, vocational training ...;
- to promote the image of a dynamic and forward looking industry in an international environment to be improved, with public institutions the media and economic decision-makers in general;
- to provide the companies of the sector with relevant information on the economic environment, social, legislative and political developments in order to facilitate their decision-making.

Information available:
- Databases: statistics.
- Members' list, free of charge.
- Bulletin of Euratex: see webside: Publications

EUREAU

European Union of National Associations of Water Suppliers and Waste Water Services

Union Européenne des Associations Nationales de Distributeurs d'Eau et de Services d'Assainissement

Rue Colonel Bourg 127, 1140 Bruxelles, Belgium
Tel: +32 2/706 40 80
Fax: +32 2/706 40 81
E-mail: eureau@skynet.be
Internet: www.eureau.org

Pres.: M. PHILLIPS
Sec.-Gen.: F. RILLAERTS
Contact: F. RILLAERTS

Founded: 1975
Working languages: E/F
Secretariat: 2 members of staff

Information available:
- Brochures: EUREAU opinions to the EU on various Directives pertaining to water.
- Relation between asbestos and drinking water quality – F/E.
- Water services' needs of re-agents and additives for the treatment of drinking water – F/E.
- Proposal for a Council Directive relating to the quality of water for human consumption – F/E.
- Comments on the proposal for a Council Directive concerning the limit values for discharges of cadmium in the aquatic environment and quality objectives for cadmium in the aquatic environment – F/E.
- Experience with Directive 75/440/EEC concerning the quality required for the abstraction of drinking water in the Member States – F/E.
- Directive 79/869/EEC concerning the methods of measurement and frequencies of sampling and analysis of surface water intended for the production of drinking water in the Member States. Remarks on its application – F/E.
- Directive 80/778/EEC relating to the quality of water intended for human consumption. Remarks on its application – F/E.
- Directive 80/68/EEC on the protection of groundwater against pollution caused by certain dangerous substances – Remarks on its application – The problem of nitrates – F/E.
- EUREAU document on drinking water installations – Protection against backsiphonage – Method of risk analysis and choice of appropriate safety devices – F/E.
- Directive 75/440/EEC concerning the quality required of surface water intended for the abstraction of drinking water in the Member States – Proposal for a new approach – F/E.

- EUREAU notice about the problems water suppliers would have to face in the event of an accident happening in a nuclear power station – F/E.
- The nitrate problem – Declaration by EUREAU on solving the nitrate problem – F/E.
- EUREAU statement on proposals for a centralized water-savings policy – F/E.
- Advice of EUREAU on the respect of parameter 55 "pesticides and related products" of Directive 80/778 concerning the quality of water intended for human consumption – F/E.
- Updated comments by EUREAU on the revision of the Drinking Water Directive 80/778/EEC – E.
- EUREAU survey on artificial recharge, E.
- Implications to water suppliers and householders of the new WHO Guidelines for drinking water quality, E.
- "Management Systems of Drinking Water Production and Distribution Services", E/F.
- List of members, free.

EUREL

Convention of National Societies of Electrical Engineers of Europe

Fédération des Sociétés Nationales des Ingénieurs Electriciens de l'Europe

Föderation der Nationalen Elektrotechnischen Vereinigungen Europas

Avenue Roger Van Den Driesche 18, 1150 Bruxelles, Belgium
Tel: +32 2/646 76 00
Fax: +32 2/646 30 32
E-mail: eurel@eurel.org
Internet: http://www.eurel.org

Pres.: Prof. J. O' REILLY
Sec.-Gen.: M. LARSSON

Founded: 1972
General meeting: October
Working languages: E/F
Secretariat: 2 members of staff

Information available:
- "EUREL News" on website.
- "EUREL Handbook", E.
- Database: conferences organised by the most important member societies.
- List of members available to the general public, free.

EURELECTRIC

European Grouping of the Electricity Supply Industry

Groupement Européen des Entreprises d'Electricité

Europäische Vereinigung der Elektrizitätsversorgung

Boulevard de l'Impératrice 66, 1000 Bruxelles, Belgium
Tel: +32 2/515 10 00
Fax: +32 2/515 10 10
E-mail: eurelectric@eurelectric.org
Internet: www.eurelectric.org

Pres.: Mr. H. HAIDER
Sec.-Gen.: P. BULTEEL

EURIMA

European Insulation Manufacturers' Association

Avenue Louise 375 bte 4, 1050 Bruxelles, Belgium
Tel: +32 2/626 20 90
Fax: +32 2/626 20 99
E-mail: info@eurima.org
Internet: www.eurima.org

Pres.: J. SORENSEN

Founded: 1961
General meeting: June
Working languages: F/E/D
Secretariat: 6 members of staff

Sectors of activity:
• Thermal and acoustical building insulation.

Information available:
• "Acoustical Insulation and the Protection of Individuals".
• "Thermal Insulation means Environmental Protection".
• "Environment Protection needs Insulation needs Mineral Wool".
• "Mineral Wool Insulation and Climate Change".
• Database: Man-made-vitreous fibres.
• The members' list is available.

EURO CHLOR

Av E. Van Nieuwenhuyse 4 Bte 2, 1160 Bruxelles, Belgium
Tel: +32 2/676 73 50
Fax: +32 2/676 72 41
E-mail: eurochlor@cefic.be
Internet: www.eurochlor.org

Contact: Dr. B. S. GILLIATT (Executive Director)

Founded: 1991
General meeting: September
Working languages: E
Secretariat: 14 members of staff

Sectors of activity:
• Euro Chlor is an affiliate of the European Chemical Industry Council (CEFIC). It represents Western European chlorine producers and aims to promote the best safety, health and environmental practices; stimulate active dialogue with key influencers and provide balanced, science-based information.

Information available:
• A range of general and scientific/technical publications on chlorine-related issues is available. Check www.eurochlor.org.

EURO COOP

European Community of Consumer Cooperatives

Communauté Européenne des Coopératives de Consommateurs

Europäische Gemeinschaft der Verbrauchergenossenschaften

Rue Archimède 17 Bte 2, 1000 Bruxelles, Belgium
Tel: +32 2/285 00 70
Fax: +32 2/231 07 57
E-mail: info@eurocoop.coop
Internet: http://www.eurocoop.coop

Pres.: Mr. G. FABRITTI
Sec.-Gen.: Donal WALSHE

Founded: 1957
General meeting: May
Working languages: F/E
Secretariat: 4 members of staff

Historical note:
• Founded in 1957, Euro Coop, as the first consumer organisation in Europe, has made its expertise available to the European institutions for the promotion of consumer interests. An important part of Euro Coop's activity is the representation of consumers within the numerous advisory committees set up by the European Commission, and in particular the Consumer Committee.
• Euro Coop represents and upholds the structure and ethics of the cooperative undertaking at European level. This activity is achieved in particular, by its participation in different committees, such as the Committee on Commerce and Distribution set up by the European Commission, the Coordinating Committee of European Cooperative Associations and the Consultative Committee of Cooperatives, Mutual Societies, Associations and Foundations.

Sectors of activity:
• Consumer protection.
• To represent and promote consumer co-operatives.
• Contacts: EURO COOP is in close contact with the Economic and Social Committee and representatives of consumer cooperatives thereon as well as with other consumer representatives. The same applies for the European Parliament.
• Participation in numerous advisory committees of the European Commission and in particular the Consumers' Consultative Council.

Information available:
• "EUROFLASH", M, monthly, E/F.
• "Flash Food", M, monthly, E.
• "Info Environment", M, monthly, E.
• Position papers, M-NM, E/F.
• Circulars, M.
• List of members available to the general public, free.

EUROADSAFE

European Road Safety Equipment Federation

Fédération Européenne des Equipements Routiers de Sécurité

Europäische Föderation für Strassen Sicherheitsausrüstung

c/o SER, Rue de Picpus 152, 95012 Paris Cedex, France
Tel: +33 1/43 42 26 36
Fax: +33 1/43 42 47 71
Working languages: E
Secretariat: 3 members of staff

Information available:
• Database: Euroadsafe members.
• The members' list is available, free of charge.

EURO-AIR

European Association of Air Heater Manufacturers

Marienbürger Strasse 15, 50968 Köln, Germany
Tel: +49 221/376 48 30
Fax: +49 221/376 48 61
E-mail: info@figawa.com
Internet: www.figawa.be

Pres.: Mr. BROEX
Sec.-Gen.: N. BÜRGER

Founded: 1995
General meeting: March and September
Working languages: E
Secretariat: 5 members of staff

EUROALLIAGES

Comité de Liaison des Industries de Ferro-Alliages

Avenue de Broqueville 12, 1150 Bruxelles, Belgium
Tel: +32 2/775 63 01
Fax: +32 2/775 63 03
E-mail: euroalliages@skynet.be
Internet: www.euroalliages.com

Pres.: R. GAVIER DE PENARONDA
Sec.-Gen.: Mrs. I. VAN LIERDE

Founded: 1993
General meeting: November
Working languages: F/E
Secretariat: 2 members of staff

Information available:
- List of members available to the general public via website www.euroalliages.com.

EUROBAT

Association of European Storing Battery Manufacturers

Association de Fabricants Européens d'Accumulateurs

Vereinigung Europäischer Akkumulatoren-Hersteller

Avenue Marcel Thiry 204, 1200 Bruxelles, Belgium
Tel: +32 2/774 96 53
Fax: +32 2/774 96 90
E-mail: eurobat@eyam.be
Internet: http://www.eurobat.org

Pres.: W. WEVER
Contact: A.. WISTGEEST

Founded: 1968
Working languages: F/E/D
Secretariat: 3 members of staff

Information available:
- All information is available strictly to members only.

EUROCADRES

Council of European Professional Managerial Staff

Conseil des Cadres Européens

Rat der Europäischen Fach- und Führungskrafte

Boulevard du Roi Albert II, 5, 1210 Bruxelles, Belgium
Tel: +32 2/224 07 30
Fax: +32 2/224 07 33
E-mail: sat@eurocadres.org
Internet: http://www.eurocadres.org

Pres.: M. ROUSSELOT
Contact: Mrs. G. EBNER

EUROCAE

European Organisation for Civil Aviation Equipment

Organisation Européenne pour l'Equipement de l'Aviation Civile

Rue Hamelin 17, 75783 Paris Cedex 16, France
Tel: +33 1/45 05 71 88
Fax: +33 1/45 05 72 30
E-mail: eurocae@eurocae.com
Internet: http://www.eurocae.org

Pres.: T. KNIBBE
Contact: F. GRIMAL

Founded: 1963
Working languages: E
Secretariat: 5 members of staff

Sectors of activity:
- EUROCAE has been created to provide a regular forum where European administrations, airlines and industry can meet to discuss technical problems, and particularly develop minimum operational performance specifications for aviation systems.

Information available:
- "MASPS for Advanced Surface Movement Guidance and Control Systems", E, €75, January 2001.
- "Final Annual Report for Clarification of ED-12B – Software Considerations in Airborne Systems and Equipment", E, €80, October 2001.
- "User Requirement for Aerodrome Mapping Information", E, €110, October 2001.
- "MOPS for 1090 MHz Automatic Dependent Surveillance – Broadcast (ADS-B), E, CD-Rom only, €150, November 2001.
- "MOPS for Inflight Icing Detection Systems", E, €65, July 2001.
- "MOPS for Ground Ice Detection Systems", E, €70, November 2001.
- "DLASD for Oceanic Clearance Data Link Service", E, €70, May 2001.
- "Guide for the certification of Aircraft in a High Intensity Radiated Field (HIRF) Environment", E, €110, March 2001.
- "Interim MOPS for VDL Mode 4 Aircraft Transceiver for ADS-B", E, €100, July 2001.
- List of members available to the general public, free.

EURO-CASE

European Council of Applied Sciences Technology and Engineering

Rue Saint Dominique 28, 75007 Paris, France
Tel: +33 1/53 59 53 40
Fax: +33 1/53 59 53 41
E-mail: mail@euro-case.org
Internet: www.euro-case.org

Pres.: V. VAN DEN BALCK
Sec.-Gen.: P. FILLET
Contact: Ms. H. BONNET

Founded: 1992
General meeting: March and September
Working languages: E
Secretariat: 2 members of staff

Sectors of activity:
- The European Council of Applied Sciences, Technologies and Engineering is a European non-profit-making organisation of national Academies of Applied Sciences, Technologies and Engineering from eighteen European countries. Euro-CASE has access to top level European experience and provides impartial, independent and balanced advice on technological issues with a clear European dimension.
- Through its member Academies, Euro-CASE acts as a permanent forum for exchange and consultation between European Institutions, Industry and Research.
- The individual members of the Euro-CASE Academies are elected for their excellence and knowledge in specific fields and for their contributions to technologic, scientific, economic and social progress. This unique resource of experts, counting 5,200 individual Fellows of 18 national Academies, is the core of Euro-CASE.
- Euro-CASE organises the prestigious European IST Prize with the support and sponsorship of the IST Programme of the European Commission

Information available:
- All reports available on www.euro-case.org.
- The members' list is available to the general public.
- For details of meetings and seminars please see the website

EUROCHAMBRES

Association of European Chambers of Commerce and Industry

Association des Chambres de Commerce et d'Industrie Européennes

Vereinigung der Europäischen Industrien- und Handelskammern

Avenue des Ats 19 A-D, 1000 Bruxelles, Belgium
Tel: +32 2/282 08 50
Fax: +32 2/230 00 38
Fax: +32 2/280 01 91
E-mail: eurochambres@eurochambres.be
Internet: http://www.eurochambres.be

Pres.: Christoph LEITL
Sec.-Gen.: Arnaldo ABRUZZINI

Founded: 1958
General meeting: April – October
Working languages: F/E
Secretariat: 24 members of staff

Sectors of activity:
- takes part with its experts in the work of several European Commission advisory committees;
- exercises a real influence on the Economic & Social Committee due to the activities of some of its prominent representatives who are members of the ESC and to the work of the experts which it sends there;

- is invited to European Parliament hearings and to its specialist committees;
- is also represented within the Council of Europe where it enjoys the status of a non-governmental organisation (NGO);
- promotes information and training;
- promotes and organises colloquia, congresses and seminars on major economic policy issues which bring together experts, senior executives and political representatives;
- is establishing a vast information network in collaboration with the European Commission. The network is strengthened by the Euro-Info-Centres, many of which are located in Chambers of Commerce and Industry.

EUROCINEMA

Association de Producteurs de Cinéma et de Télévision

Rue Stévin 212, 1000 Bruxelles, Belgium
Tel: +32 2/732 58 30
Fax: +32 2/733 36 57
E-mail: eurocinema@eurocinema.be

Contact: Y. THIEC (Del Gen)

Founded: 1991
Working languages: F/E
Secretariat: 2 members of staff

EUROCOMMERCE

Avenue des Nerviens 9, 1040 Bruxelles, Belgium
Tel: +32 2/737 05 98
Fax: +32 2/230 00 78
E-mail: bastings@eurocommerce.be
Internet: http://www.eurocommerce.be

Pres.: Dr. P. BERNET
Sec.-Gen.: X.R. DURIEU
Contact: Fabienne BASTINGS (Asst. General Secretary)

Founded: 1993
General meeting: October
Working languages: F/E/D
Secretariat: 15 members of staff

Sectors of activity:
- Representation of the European retail, wholesale and international trades to the EU institutions.

Information available:
- "Newsletter", quarterly, F/E/D. M/NM
- Work programme. M
- "Newsfax". M
- Circulars. M
- Position papers. M/NM
- Information brochure. M/NM
- Annual report, F/E/D. M/NM
- Members' list, free. M/NM

- List of members freely available on the website

EUROCORD

Federation of European Rope, Twine and Netting Industries

Fédération Européenne des Industries de Corderie-Ficellerie et de Filets

EG-Verbindungsausschuss der Hartfaser- und Tauwerkindustrie

Rue de Monceau 47, 75008 Paris, France
Tel: +33 1/53 75 10 04
Fax: +33 1/53 75 10 02
E-mail: eurocord@eurocord.com
Internet: www.eurocord.com

Pres.: Mrs. L. GRAMAXO
Sec.-Gen.: Dr Anne JOURDAIN
Contact: Dr. A. JOURDAIN

Founded: 1959
General meeting: June
Working languages: E
Secretariat: 3 members of staff

Information available:
- Statistics (production, import/export), M. List of members available via the website

EUROCOTON

Committee of the European Cotton Textile Industry

Comité de l'Industrie Textile Cotonnière Européenne

Komitee der Baumwoll- und Verwandten Textilindustriën der EG

Rue Montoyer 24, bte 13, 1000 Bruxelles, Belgium
Tel: +32 2/230 32 39
Fax: +32 2/230 36 22
E-mail: michele.anselme@eurocoton.org

Pres.: J.F. GRIBOMONT
Sec.-Gen.: Mrs. M. ANSELME

Founded: 1954
General meeting: May or June each year
Working languages: F/E
Secretariat: 2 members of staff

Sectors of activity:
- To influence political decisions to help the industry adapt to the globalisation of markets and improve its international competition. EUROCOTON defends its members's trade interests as much on the community market (defensive aspect) as at export (offensive aspect) before private and public European and international institutions.
- System-cotton Textile Industry (cotton ginning, spinning and weaving of cotton and/or

discontinuous synthetic or artificial fibres, eventually integrated in textile finishing, simple confection of household textile) of which interests in European policy are: WTO trade negotiations, market access strategy, use of trade policy instruments, pan-euromediterranean strategy, custom and fiscal policy, entreprises industrial strategy, common agricultural policy, rural development policy.

Information available:
- Activity Statistics, annual, F/E, M-NM – fee on request and selection.
- Foreign trade statistics, half-yearly, F/E, M-NM, fee on request and selection.
- Economic survey and remarks, quarterly, F/E, M.
- Annual report, F/E, M-NM, fee on request and selection.
- Economic report per Member State, annual, F/E, M.
- The industry's position in respect of trade and industrial policy in the textile sector, F/E, M.
- Data base: foreign trade statistics and figures on the structure of the cotton industry at EU and international level, M.
- List of members – free on request (applications are selected however).

EUROFEDOP

European Federation of Personnel in Public Services

Fédération Européenne du Personnel des Services Publics

Europäische Föderation der Öffentlichbediensteten

Rue Montoyer 39, 1040 Bruxelles, Belgium
Tel: +32 2/230 38 65
Fax: +32 2/231 14 72
E-mail: info@infedop-eurofedop.com
Internet: www.eurofedop.org

Pres.: F. NEUGEBAUER
Sec.-Gen.: B. VAN CAELENBERG

Founded: 1966
Working languages: F/E/Nl/D/Esp
Secretariat: 5 members of staff

Sectors of activity:
- "Training".
- One of EUROFEDOP's activities is to set up professional councils and to organize conferences, seminars and training courses.
- Defend and promote the economic and social interests of European workers in public services taking into account their specific rights and purposes.

Information available:
- "BURNOUT in the health sector", F/E/D/Nl/Gr/Esp, M-NM.

- Reports from all the professional councils (Postal and Telecommunications Services – Finance – Ministries – Health Services – Women – Prison Services – Police – Local and Regional Authorities). Twice a year – F/E/Nl/D/Esp, M.
- Specialist studies for the sectors concerned (see above), M.
- Council of Europe, E.S.C., European Parliament, European Community brochures for the sectors concerned, M.
- "The efficacy of the Courts thanks to transboundary cooperation", Nl/F/D/E/Esp, M-NM.

EUROFEL

European Association of Feldspar Producers

Bd S. Dupuis 233 Bte 124, 1070 Bruxelles, Belgium
Tel: +32 2/524 55 00
Fax: +32 2/524 45 75
E-mail: secretariat@ima-eu.org
Internet: http://www.ima-eu.org

Pres.: Mr. R. DOOME
Sec.-Gen.: Mrs. M. WYART-REMI

EUROFER

European Confederation of Iron and Steel Industries

Association Européenne de la Sidérurgie

Europäische Wirtschaftsvereinigung der Eisen- und Stahlindustrie

Rue du Noyer 211, 1000 Bruxelles, Belgium
Tel: +32 2/738 79 20
Fax: +32 2/736 30 01
E-mail: mail@eurofer.be
Internet: http://www.eurofer.org

Pres.: G. DOLLE
Contact: D. VON HULSEN (Dir Gen)

Founded: 1976
Working languages: F/E/D/It/Nl
Secretariat: 23 members of staff

Information available:
- Publications, free of charge, see at http://www.eurofer.org/publications/index.htm
- List of members available to the general public, free.

EUROFEU

European Committee of the Manufacturers of Fire Protection Equipment and Fire Fighting Vehicles

Comité Européen des Constructeurs de Matériels d'Incendie et de Secours

Europäisches Komitee der Hersteller von Fahrzeugen, Geräten und Anlagen für den Brandschutz

Lyoner Strasse 18, 60528 Frankfurt am Main, Germany
Tel: +49 69/6603 1305
Fax: +49 69/6603 1464
E-mail: carmen.simon@vdma.org
E-mail: bernd.scherer@vdma.org
Internet: http://www.eurofeu.org

Pres.: K. HOFMANN
Sec.-Gen.: Mr. B. SCHERER
Contact: Mrs. C. SIMON

Founded: 1969
General meeting: September
Working languages: E/F/D
Secretariat: 2 members of staff

Information available:
- List of members available to the general public, free.

EUROFINAS

European Federation of Finance House Associations

Fédération Européenne des Instituts de Crédit

Europäische Vereinigung der Verbände von Finanzierungsbanken

Av. de Tervuren 267 Bte 10, 1150 Bruxelles, Belgium
Tel: +32 2/778 05 60
Fax: +32 2/778 05 79
E-mail: eurofinas@eurofinas.org
Internet: http://www.eurofinas.org

Pres.: Mr. A.F. MENEZES RODRIGUES
Sec.-Gen.: M. BAERT

Founded: 1960
Working languages: F/E/D
Secretariat: 7 members of staff

Information available:
- Newsletters, 3-4/year, F/E/D, M.
- Membership list, annual, free.

EUROFORGE

Liaison Committee for Forging Industries

Comité de Liaison des Industries Européennes de l'Estampage et de la Forge

Europaischer Schmiedeverband

Goldene Pforte 1, 58093 Hagen, Germany
Tel: +49 2331/95 88 12
Fax: +49 2331/51 04 62
E-mail: ltutmann@euroforge.org
Internet: www.euroforge.org

Pres.: P. SUNDSTRÖM
Sec.-Gen.: T.L. TUTMANN

Founded: 1953
Working languages: E
Secretariat: 9 members of staff

Information available:
- Euroforge Dictionary – Technical Terms in E/F/D.
- "Forging and Drop Forging" in F/E/D.

EUROGAS

European Union of the Natural Gas Industry

Union Européenne de l'Industrie du Gaz Naturel

Europäische Vereinigung der Erdgaswirtschaft

Avenue Palmerston 4, 1000 Bruxelles, Belgium
Tel: +32 2/237 11 11
Fax: +32 2/230 62 91
E-mail: eurogas@eurogas.org
Internet: www.eurogas.org

Pres.: P. GADONNEIX
Sec.-Gen.: Jean-Marie DEVOS

Founded: 1990
General meeting: June and December
Working languages: E/f/D
Secretariat: 5 members of staff

Sectors of activity:
- Studies and promotion of the European natural gas industry.
- Annual Stakeholders Conference

Information available:
- Annual report incorporating "Gas Statistics and Outlook", yearly, free, E.

EUROGIRO

Giro and Postbank Organisations in Europe

Eurogiro Network A/S, Carl Gustave Gade 3, 1th., 2630 Taastrup, Denmark
Tel: +45/43 71 27 72
Fax: +45/43 71 26 62
E-mail: eurogiro@eurogiro.com
Internet: www.eurogiro.com

Pres.: H. PARL
Contact: H. PARL (Manag. Dir.)

Founded: 1992
Working languages: E

Sectors of activity:
- Cross border payments.

Information available:
- List of members available to the general public, free.

EUROGLACES

Association of the Ice Cream Industries of the EEC

Association des Industries des Glaces Alimentaires de la CEE

Vereinigung der Speiseeisindustrie der EG

Rue de Copenhague 3, 75008 Paris, France
Tel: +33 1/53 42 13 38
Fax: +33 1/53 42 13 39
E-mail: b-dufrene@wanadoo.fr
Internet: www.euroglaces.com

Pres.: Mrs. M. MARTINEZ MADRID
Sec.-Gen.: B. DUFRENE

Founded: 1957
Working languages: E
Secretariat: 2 members of staff

Information available:
• List of members available to the general public.

EUROGYPSUM

Association of European Gypsum Industries

Association des Industries Européennes du Plâtre

Verband der Europäischen Gipsindustrien

Rue Gulledelle 98 Box 7, 1200 Bruxelles, Belgium
Tel: +32 2/775 84 90
Fax: +32 2/771 30 56
E-mail: info@eurogypsum.org
Internet: www.eurogypsum.org

Pres.: C. AIRAGHI
Sec.-Gen.: Ph. BENNETT

Founded: 1961
General meeting: October
Working languages: E/F/D
Secretariat: 2 members of staff

Information available:
• Databases: list of members and list of participants in committee meetings & task groups, M.
• List of members available to the general public, free, and on the website, NM.

EUROHEAT & POWER

Avenue du Diamant 26, 1030 Bruxelles, Belgium
Tel: +32 2/740 21 10
Fax: +32 2/740 21 19
E-mail: info@euroheat.org
Internet: www.euroheat.org

Pres.: T. BRUCE
Sec.-Gen.: Ms. S. FRONING
Contact: Ms. S. BASIU

Founded: 1954
Working languages: E

Secretariat: 3 members of staff

Historical note:
• The Association was created in 1954 in Paris under the name Unichal. Its main seat was moved in 1979 to Zurich and in 1998 to Brussels. Its new name Euroheat & Power, Unichal was adopted in 1995 in Stockholm and amended to simply Euroheat & Power in 2001.

Sectors of activity:
• Co-ordinating research in district heating in Europe.
Conference:
• "European district heating congress 2003", 08-10/06/2003, Helsinki.

Information available:
• "Brussels News", monthly, e-mail newsletter, M.
• "Euroheat & Power", M-NM, 10 a year + yearbook, D/E.
• CD-Rom on companies active in district heating.

EUROKOBRA

EUROKOBRA

Boulevard Poincaré 79, 1060 Bruxelles, Belgium
Tel: +32 2/655 77 11
Fax: +32 2/653 07 29
E-mail: eurokobra@bbri.be
Internet: www.eurokobra.org

Contacts: P. WOUTERS (Manager), J. SCHIETECAT (Secr.)

Founded: 1995
Working languages: E
Secretariat: 2 members of staff

Sectors of activity:
• Building physics and indoor climate.

EUROLAB

BAM-Bundesanstalt für Materialprüfung und Forschung, Unter den Eichen 87, 12205 Berlin, Germany
Tel: +49 30/81 04 37 62
Fax: +49 30/81 04 46 28
E-mail: eurolab@bam.de
E-mail: manfred.golze@bam.de
Internet: www.eurolab.org

Pres.: C.CIGANOPA
Sec.-Gen.: M.GOLZE

Founded: 1990
Working languages: E
Secretariat: 4 members of staff

Information available:
• "EUROLAB Newsletter", twice a year, free, E, M and NM.
• "EUROLAB reports", series.
• "EUROLAB Position Papers", series.
• "EUROLAB Annual Reports", free, E.
• The members' list is available to national delegations and is free.

EUROLATEX

Koningsbaan, 2560 Nijlen, Belgium
Tel: +32 3/410 13 00
Fax: +32 3/481 79 32
E-mail: arti@skynet.be

Sec.-Gen.: J. ROUCHAL

Founded: 1989
Working languages: E/F

EUROM

European Federation of Precision Mechanical and Optical Industries

Fédération Européenne de l'Industrie de l'Optique et de la Mécanique de Précision

Europäische Industrie-Vereinigung Feinmechanik und Optik

c/o ANFAO, Via pettiti 16, 20149 Milano, Italy
Tel: +39 02 32 48 46
Fax: +39 02 33 00 38 19
E-mail: pposso@worldcom.ch

Pres.: Mr. L. DEL VECCHIO

EUROM II

Optics Laser & Laboratory Instrumentation Group within European Federation of Precision Mechanical & Optical Industries

Rue L. Blanc 39, Courbevoie, 92038 Paris La Défense Cedex, France
Tel: +33 1/47 17 64 05
Fax: +33 1/47 17 64 81
E-mail: eurom2@blwa.co.uk

Pres.: M. LECLERCQ
Sec.-Gen.: F. PITHON
Working languages: F/D

EUROMAISIERS

EU Maize Millers Association

Groupement des Associations des Maïsiers des Pays de la EU

Arbeitsgemeinschaft der Maismühlenverbände der EG-Länder

Square de Meeûs 18, 1050 Bruxelles, Belgium
Tel: +32 2/502 08 08
Fax: +32 2/502 60 30
E-mail: euromaisiers@grainindustry.com

Pres.: Mr. VALLUIS
Sec.-Gen.: Ms. J. PEARSON

Founded: 1975
General meeting: May
Working languages: E

EUROMALT

Working Committee of the EU Malting Industry

Comité de Travail des Malteries de l'UE

Arbeitskomitee der Malzereien in der EG

Square de Meeûs 18, 1050 Bruxelles, Belgium
Tel: +32 2/502 08 08
Fax: +32 2/502 60 30
E-mail: euromalt@graininindustry.com

Pres.: H. RELANDER
Sec.-Gen.: J. PEARSON

Founded: 1959
General meeting: November
Working languages: E

EUROMAT

The European Federation of Coin Machine Associations

Fédération Européenne des Associations de l'Automatique

Europaische Vereinigung der Automaten-Verbände

haussée de wavre 214d, 1050 Bruxelles, Belgium
Tel: +32 2/626 19 93
Fax: +32 2/626 95 01
E-mail: secretariat@euromat.org
Internet: http://www.euromat.org

Pres.: E. ANTOJA

Founded: 1979
Working languages: F/E/D
Secretariat: 1 member of staff

Sectors of activity:
Objectives:
- Assisting the member associations in their efforts to adequately represent the national industries at national and international levels.
- Defending the industry interests by providing continued, accurate information to the citizens,tthe media and the administrations.
- Monitoring and influencing the European regulations on legal, commercial and technical aspects of the business to guarantee the best possible future for the industry.
- Supporting all member associations in their efforts to adopt, promote and enforce the appropriate code of conduct for themselves and their associates.

Information available:
- Information newsletter, free, F/D/E.
- "Rules and Standing Orders", free, F/E/D.
- List of members available to the general public, free.

EUROMETAL

European Federation of Associations of Steel, Tubes and Metal Merchants

Fédération Européenne des Associations de Négociants en Aciers, Tubes et Métaux

Bd de la Woluwe 46 bte 7, 1200 Bruxelles, Belgium
Tel: +32 2/771 53 40
Fax: +32 2/772 19 77
E-mail: grymafer@pi.be
Internet: www.eurometal.net

Pres.: J. VON RIEDERER
Sec.-Gen.: F. VAN REMOORTERE

Founded: 1964
General meeting: February
Working languages: D/E/F
Secretariat: 2 members of staff

Information available:
- The members' list is available, free of charge.

EUROMETAUX

European Association of Metals

Association Européenne des Métaux

Avenue de Broqueville 12, 1150 Bruxelles, Belgium
Tel: +32 2/775 63 10
Fax: +32 2/779 05 23
E-mail: eurometaux@eurometaux.be
Internet: www.eurometaux.org

Pres.: J.P. RODIER
Sec.-Gen.: Guy THIRAN

Founded: 1981
Working languages: F/E
Secretariat: 15 members of staff

Historical note:
- The Association was established pursuant to the Rome Treaty in 1957 when it was known as the "Comité de Liaison des Industries de Métaux Non Ferreux de la Communauté Economique Européenne". In 1988, it was constituted, under the name of EUROMETAUX, as an international association governed by Belgian law, due to the fact that the way in which Community legislation and its policies were developing was calling for an enlarged and reinforced industry presence at European level.

Sectors of activity:
- EUROMETAUX is the Brussels based organization representing the non-ferrous metals industries of the European Union and EFTA member countries. It is committed to achieving transparency and establishing dialogue with the EU authorities as well as ensuring early consultation in all fields of policy and legislation that may affect industry.

Information available:
- Position papers, M-NM.
- Studies.
- Annual report, free, E/F, M-NM.
- Database: details of working parties' members.
- List of members, free.

EUROMETREC

European Metal Trade and Recycling Federation

c/o BIR, Avenue Franklin Roosevelt 24, 1050 Bruxelles, Belgium
Tel: +32 2/627 57 72
Fax: +32 2/627 57 73
E-mail: bir@bir.org
Internet: http://www.eurometrec.org

Pres.: Mr. B. GRUFMAN
Sec.-Gen.: Francis VEYS

Founded: 1972
General meeting: March
Working languages: E/F/D
Secretariat: 6 members of staff

Sectors of activity:
- Professional organisation grouping together within the EU Member States national federations of companies responsible for the collection, trade, processing and recycling of recovered non-ferrous metals. More than a thousand companies.

Information available:
- Minutes of meetings for internal use, M, except the media.
- Press releases, M, except the media.
- Position papers, M, except the media.
- Statistics, M.
- Market reports, M.
- Study on the non-ferrous metals recycling industry.
- Databases: statistics – reports – members.

EUROMOL

European Organisation for the Manufacture of Leather Accessories, Travelware and Related Products

Calle Marques de la Ensainada 2, 4° planta, 28004 Madrid, Spain
Tel: +34 91/319 6252
Fax: +34 91/310 4954
E-mail: euromol@asefma.com

Pres.: O. MONTECCI
Sec.-Gen.: F. GUTIERREZ

Founded: 1962
Working languages: E/F

Historical note:
- Previously entitled CEDIM

Information available:
- List of members available to the general public, free.

EUROMOT

The European Association of Internal Combustion Engine Manufacturers

c/o VDMA e.V., Lyoner Strasse 18, 60528 Frankfurt am Main, Germany
Tel: +49 69/66 03 13 54
Fax: +49 69/66 03 23 54
E-mail: euromot@vdma.org
Internet: www.euromot.org

Pres.: H. DEKENA
Contact: H. MAYER

Founded: 1991
Working languages: E
Secretariat: 3 members of staff

Information available:
- Technical information on request.

EUROPABIO

European Association for Bioindustries

Avenue de l'Armée 6, 1040 Bruxelles, Belgium
Tel: +32 2/735 03 13
Fax: +32 2/735 49 60
E-mail: mail@europabio.org
Internet: http://www.europabio.org

Pres.: E. TAMBUYZER
Sec.-Gen.: H. SCHEPENS

Founded: 1996
Working languages: E
Secretariat: 9 members of staff

Historical note:
- Result of merging of SAGB (Senior Advisory Group on Biotechnology) and ESNBA (European Secretariat of National Biotechnology Associations).

Information available:
- Database: Members, journalists, MEPs, European Commission – M.

EUROPACABLE

European Confederation of Associations of Manufacturers of Insulated Wires and Cables

Confédération Européenne des Associations des Fabricants de Cables et Fils Isolés

Europäische Konföderation der Vereinigungen der Kabel- und Isolierdrahthersteller

Diamant Building, Boulevard Reyers 80, 1030 Bruxelles, Belgium
Tel: +32 2/702 61 25

Fax: +32 2/702 61 27
E-mail: ecable@aol.com
Internet: www.europacable.com

Pres.: Dr. V.BATTISTA
Sec.-Gen.: T. NEESEN

Founded: 1990
Working languages: E
Secretariat: 2 members of staff

EUROPARKS

European Federation of Leisure Parks

Federation Européenne des Parcs d'Attraction

Europäische Föderation der Freizeitparks

Rue Wiertz 50 bte 28, 1050 Bruxelles, Belgium
Tel: +32 2/401 61 62
Fax: +32 2/401 68 68
E-mail: j.bertus@wxs.nl
Internet: www.europarks.org

Pres.: M. WEDIN
Sec.-Gen.: J. BERTUS

Founded: 1981
Working languages: E

Sectors of activity:
Goals concerning industry lobby towards the European Union:
- Convince the European politicians and organisations of the economic and social importance of the industry.
- Further improve the safety reputation of the industry in any possible way.
- Actively pursue the harmonisation of rules and regulations.
- Actively try to reduce unfair competition.
- Maintain relationships with other leading organisations, which help to reach Europark's goals.
- Goals concerning the development of professionalism in the European park and leisure industry:
- Improve the information flow between the members.
- Intensify the exchange of knowledge and capabilities to improve the professionalism and management skills within the industry.
- Organise continuous trend watching in order to stay informed about trends and developments that are or may be of importance to the industry.
- Develop a complete and up to date database of economic information of all member parks.
- Improve the worldwide exchange of data of the industry and channel these though to the membership.
- Develop contacts with universities / educational institutions in Europe to exchange knowledge.

Information available:
- List of members available to the general public, free of charge.

EUROPATAT

European Union of the Potato Trade

Union Européenne du Commerce des Pommes de Terre

Europäische Union des Kartoffelhandels

Rue de Spa 8, 1000 Bruxelles, Belgium
Tel: +32 9/339 12 52
Fax: +32 9/339 12 51
E-mail: europatat@fvphouse.be
Internet: www.europatat.org

Pres.: Mr. J.STET
Sec.-Gen.: R. COOLS

Founded: 1953
General meeting: May–June
Working languages: F/E/D
Secretariat: 2 members of staff

Sectors of activity:
- EUROPATAT has its own quality regulations for potatoes and an arbitration and expertise system. These rules have been stipulated in the publication "Règles et Usages du Commerce Intereuropéen des Pommes de Terre".

Information available:
- List of arbitrators and experts, M-NM, free.
- List of members available to the general public, free, M-NM.
- R.U.C.I.P. regulations,F/E/D/Esp/Nl, M-NM.

EUROPEAN REGION OF WCPT

European Region of the World Confederation for Physical Therapy

Boulevard Louis Schmidt 119/2, 1040 Bruxelles, Belgium
Tel: +32 2/743 82 32
Fax: +32 2/736 82 51
E-mail: physio.europe@tiscali.be
Internet: www.physio-europe.org

Pres.: A. LOPES
Sec.-Gen.: David GORRIA

Founded: 1998
Working languages: F/E
Secretariat: 1 member of staff

Historical note:
- Current organisation established in 1998 following the merger of Standing Liaison Committee of Physiotherapists in the EU (1979) and WCPT Europe (1990).

Sectors of activity:

- To promote development of physiotherapy, reciprocity of qualifications and to improve the quality of physiotherapy education and practice in Europe.
- To promote physiotherapy in Europe and to oversee all matters dealing with physiotherapy.
- To promote free movement and the right of establishment of physiotherapists in Europe.
- To establish closer co-operation among the national physiotherapy associations of the Region in all professional matters in the interest of improved general health of the population of the region.
- To co-operate with international organisations in Europe to promote the European Region of WCPT aims and objectives.

Information available:

- "Post Basic Physiotherapy Education in the EU", E, €20.
- List of members available to the general public, free.

EUROPECHE

Association des Organisations Nationales d'Entreprises de Pêche de l'UE

Rue de la Science 23-25 bte 15, 1040 Bruxelles, Belgium
Tel: +32 2/230 48 48
Fax: +32 2/230 26 80
E-mail: europeche@skynet.be
E-mail: guy.vernaeve@copa-cogeca.be
Internet: www.europeche.org

Pres.: A. PARRES
Sec.-Gen.: G. VERNAEVE

Founded: 1962
General meeting: October
Working languages: F/E/D/Esp/It
Secretariat: 3 members of staff

Information available:

- Internal position papers.
- List of members available to the general public, free.

EUROPEN

European Organization for Packaging and the Environment

Organisation Européenne pour l'Emballage et l'Environnement

Europäische Vereinigung für Verpackung und Umwelt

Le Royal Tervuren, Avenue de l'Armée 6, 1040 Bruxelles, Belgium
Tel: +32 2/736 36 00
Fax: +32 2/736 35 21
E-mail: packaging@europen.be
Internet: www.europen.be

Pres.: H. JONGENEELEN
Contact: J. CARROLL (Manag. Dir.)

Founded: 1992
Working languages: E
Secretariat: 3 members of staff

Information available:

- "Understanding European and National Legislation on Packaging and the Environment", October 2001, €50.
- "Compliance with EU Packaging Law – A Practical Guide for Industry and Trade", includes CD-Rom version, 1999, €125 (Europe) – €135 (outside Europe).
- "Understanding the CEN Standards on Packaging and the Environment – Some Questions and Answers", December 2001, free, E.
- "Use of Lifecycle Assessment (LCA) as a Policy Tool in the Field of Sustainable Packaging Waste Management – A Discussion Paper".
- The members' list is available without addresses, free of charge.

EUROPGEN

European Generating Set Association

Comité de Coordination du Groupe Electrogène en Europe

Koordinierungskomitee der Kraftwerksfachverbände in Europa

c/o AMPS, Kirkby House, Smannell, Andover SP11 6JW, United Kingdom
Tel: +44 1264/365 367
Fax: +44 1264/362 304
E-mail: technical@amps.org.uk

Sec.-Gen.: R.A. WHEADON

Founded: 1989
Working languages: E/F
Secretariat: 3 members of staff

Sectors of activity:

- Energy.

Information available:

- "Statistics", M.
- The members' list is available, free of charge.

EUROPIA

European Petroleum Industry Association

Association de l'Industrie Pétrolière Européenne

Boulevard du Souverain 165, 1160 Bruxelles, Belgium
Tel: +32 2/566 91 00
Fax: +32 2/566 91 11
E-mail: info@europia.com
Internet: http://www.europia.com

Pres.: W. BONSE-GEUKING

Sec.-Gen.: P. TJAN

Founded: 1989
General meeting: May
Working languages: E
Secretariat: 12 members of staff

Sectors of activity:

- To contribute to the study and solution of issues arising from the manufacture, marketing and use of petroleum products in terms of quality control, environmental protection, health and safety.
- To promote the general public's and public authorities' understanding of the oil industry's contribution to economic, technological and social progress

Information available:

- Annual Activity Report, free, E, M-NM.
- Various "Position Papers", E, M-NM.

EUROPLANT

European Plantmakers Committee

Comité Européen des Ensembliers Industriels

Europäisches Komittee der Grossanlangen Bauwer

c/o VDMA, Lyonerstrasse 18, 60528 Frankfurt am Main, Germany
Tel: +49 69/6603 1275
Fax: +49 69/6603 2858
E-mail: agab@vdma.org
Internet: http://www.grossanlagerbau.vdma.org
Working languages: D/E/F
Secretariat: 1 member of staff

Sectors of activity:

- Contacts with the European authorities.
- Exchanges of experience about markets.
- Information to member associations.

EUROPUMP

European Association of Pump Manufacturers

Association Européenne des Constructeurs de Pompes

Europäische Vereinigung der Pumpenhersteller

Blvd Reyers 80, 1030 Bruxelles, Belgium
Tel: +32 2/706 82 30
Fax: +32 2/706 82 50
E-mail: guy.vandoorslaer@orgalime.org
Internet: www.europump.org

Pres.: Mr. P. MARINOVICH
Sec.-Gen.: G. VAN DOORSLAER

Founded: 1960
Working languages: E
Secretariat: 2 members of staff

EUROPUR

European Association of Flexible Polyurethane Foam Blocks Manufacturers

Association Européenne des Fabricants de Blocs de Mousse Souple de Polyuréthane

Verband der Europäischen Hersteller von Polyurethan Weichblockschann

Square Marie-Louise 49, 1000 Bruxelles, Belgium
Tel: +32 2/238 97 42
Fax: +32 2/230 19 89
E-mail: tspeeleveld@fedichem.br
Internet: http://www.europur.com

Pres.: W. DUPONT
Sec.-Gen.: T. SPEELEVELD

Founded: 1965
Working languages: E
Secretariat: 2 members of staff

Information available:
- "EUROPUR Newsletter", 4/year, E, M.
- The members' list is available, free of charge.

EURORAD

European Association of Manufacturers of Radiators

Association Européenne des Constructeurs de Corps de Chauffe

Europäische Vereinigung der Hersteller von Heizkörpern

c/o GFCC, 92038 Paris La Défense Cedex, France
Tel: +33 1/47 17 61 64
Fax: +33 1/47 17 60 03

Pres.: D. EITEL
Sec.-Gen.: P. TOLEDANO

Founded: 1964
General meeting: June
Working languages: E/F/D

EUROSAFE

European Committee of Safe Manufacturers Associations

Comité Européen des Associations de Fabricants de Coffres-Forts

Boerhavelaan 40, PO Box 190, 2700 AD Zoetermeer, Netherlands
Tel: +31 79/353 12 67
Fax: +31 79/353 13 65
E-mail: eurosafe@fme.nl

Pres.: P. LAECRAR
Sec.-Gen.: J. KAT

Founded: 1988
Working languages: E

Historical note:
- After preparatory consultations between representatives of the European safe-manufacturing industry from March 1988, it was decided to constitute EUROSAFE on 24 May 1988, in Paris.

EUROSEED

European Seed Association

Rue du Luxembourg 23 bp 15, 1000 Bruxelles, Belgium
Tel: +32 2/743 28 60
Fax: +32 2/743 28 69
E-mail: secretariat@euroseed.org
Internet: www.euroseed.org

Pres.: A. KEELING
Sec.-Gen.: J. WINTER

Founded: 2001
Working languages: F/E/D
Secretariat: 2 members of staff

Historical note:
- Merger of COMASSO, COSEMCO, AMUFOC and ASSOPOMOC

Information available:
- List of members available to the general public, free.

EUROSIL

European Association of Silica Producers

Bd. S. Dupuis 233 bte 124, 1070 Bruxelles, Belgium
Tel: +32 2/524 55 00
Fax: +32 2/524 45 75
E-mail: secretariat@ima-eu.org
Internet: http://www.ima-eu.org

Pres.: A. TALMANN
Sec.-Gen.: Mrs. M. WYART-REMY

EUROSMART

European Smart Card Association

Rue du Luxembourg 19-21, 1000 Bruxelles, Belgium
Tel: +32 2/506 88 38
Fax: +32 2/506 88 25
E-mail: info@eurosmart.com
Internet: www.eurosmart.com

Pres.: O. PIOU
Sec.-Gen.: B. DUPONT

Founded: 1994
General meeting: April
Working languages: E

Sectors of activity:
- The association is committed to expanding the world's smart card market, developing smart card standards and continuously improving quality and security applications.
- Promote smart cards and the smart card system.
- Standardise smart cards.
- Provide a forum for the exchange of marketing and technical data.
- Define a consistent range of quality and security levels.

Information available:
- "Smart Card Protection Profiles", M-NM.
- "RESET Smart card technology Roadmap", NM.
- "Position Papers on Identity applications, on security certification."
- "A to Z of Security Terms", M-NM.
- List of members available to the general public on website, free.

EUROSPACE

Organisation of the European Space Industry

Association de l'Industrie Spatiale Européenne

Avenue de Ségur 15-17, Staircase B, 2nd floor, 75007 Paris, France
Tel: +33 1/44 42 00 70
Fax: +33 1/44 42 00 79
E-mail: letterbox@eurospace.org
Internet: http://www.eurospace.org

Pres.: Mme P. SOURISSE
Sec.-Gen.: A. GAUBERT
Contact: A. GAUBERT

Founded: 1961
Working languages: F/E
Secretariat: 5 members of staff

Historical note:
- 2004: Merger planned between AECMA, EDIG and EUROSPACE. Please refer to www.asd-europe.org for further information of the new association ASD

EUROTALC

Scientific Association of the European Talc Industry

Bd. S. Dupuis 233 bte 124, 1070 Bruxelles, Belgium
Tel: +32 2/524 55 00
Fax: +32 2/524 45 75
E-mail: secretariat@ima-eu.org
Internet: http://www.ima-eu.org

Pres.: A. TALMANN
Sec.-Gen.: Mrs. M. WYART-REMY

EURO-TOQUES

Avenue des arts 43, 5 éme étage, 1040 Bruxelles, Belgium
Tel: +32 2/230 99 70

Fax: +32 2/230 80 95
Internet: www.euro-toques.org

Founded: 1986
Working languages: F/E
Secretariat: 1 member of staff

Sectors of activity:
- Catering – association grouping professionals from the Member States.
- Defending the trade's savoir-faire.
- Promoting trade in technologies and ideas.

Information available:
- "EURO TOQUES magazine", yearly, free, F.
- "France Info", quarterly, free, F.

EUROTRANS

European Committee of Associations of Manufacturers of Gears and Transmission Parts

Comité Européen des Associations de Constructeurs d'Engrenages et d'Eléments de Transmission

Europäisches Komitee der Fachverbände der Hersteller von Getrieben und Antriebselementen

Lyoner Strasse 18, 60528 Frankfurt am Main, Germany
Tel: +49 69/66 03 15 26
Fax: +49 69/66 03 14 59
E-mail: klaus.wuestenberg@vdma.org
Internet: www.euro-trans.org

Pres.: Mr. P. DULAEY
Sec.-Gen.: K. WÜSTENBERG

Founded: 1969
General meeting: May/June
Working languages: E

Information available:
- Economic Reports, quarterly, E.
- Technical Reports, quarterly, E.
- Economic studies, yearly, E.
- Statistics, yearly, E.
- The members' list is available, free of charge.

EUROVENT

European Committee of Air Handling and Air Conditioning Equipment Manufacturers

Comité Européen des Constructeurs de Matériel Aéraulique

c/o AGORIA, Diamant Building, Bd. Reyers 80, 1030 Bruxelles, Belgium
Tel: +32 2/706 79 85
Fax: +32 2/706 78 88
E-mail: info@eurovent-cecomaf.org
Internet: http://www.agoria.be

Pres.: G. ROBERTSSON
Sec.-Gen.: Ms.VANDERHORST
Working languages: E/F/D

Sectors of activity:
- Exhibition: "Expoclima".

Information available:
- A list of technical documents entitled "EUROVENT" is available on request.

EUROWATT

Room 8.4, Gresham House, 53 Clarendon Road, Watford WD17 1FR, United Kingdom
Tel: +44 1923/33 41 44
Fax: +44 1923/24 41 80

Contact: J.G. MORDUE

Founded: 1996
General meeting: January
Working languages: E/F/D
Secretariat: 3 members of staff

Historical note:
- EUROWATT was formed by a group of professional people associated with the power industries.

Sectors of activity:
- Reviewing technical and strategic policy decisions concerning the power generation industries (i.e. electricity, gas, nuclear, renewable energy sources etc...).

ESPA

European Salt Producers' Association

Association Européenne des Producteurs de Sel

Europäische Vereinigung der Salzhersteller

Avenue de l'Yser 4, 1050 Bruxelles, Belgium
Tel: +49 228/60 47 30
Internet: http://www.eu-salt.com

Pres.: R. SPEISER

Founded: 1957
Working languages: F/E/D
Secretariat: 2 members of staff

Sectors of activity:
- the technical committees,
- the documentation centre.

Information available:
- Economic information (salt worldwide) – M.
- Statistics (M).
- SALT ECHO (3 issues per year), M, free.
- Technical bulletins.
- Directory, M.
- Patents.
- Regulations.
- The members' list is available, free of charge, on website.

EUSIDIC

European Association of Information Services

Association Européenne des Services d'Information

Europäische Vereinigung der Informationsdienste

WG Plein 475, 1054 SH Amsterdam, Netherlands
Tel: +31 20/589 32 32
Fax: +31 20/589 32 30
E-mail: eusidic@caos.nl
Internet: http://www.eusidic.org

Pres.: J. VAN HALM
Contact: A. BRACKEL

Founded: 1970
Working languages: E
Secretariat: 2 members of staff

Information available:
- "Electricnewsidic", M.
- Database: membership data.
- Regular Fax/Email news service for members.

EUTECA

European Technical Caramel Association

Association Européenne de Caramels Colorants

Europäischer Verband der Hersteller von Farbstoffkaramel

c/o ECCO, Avenue des Gaulois 9, 1040 Bruxelles, Belgium
Tel: +32 2/736 53 54
Fax: +32 2/732 34 27
E-mail: euteca@ecco-eu.com

Pres.: M. KNOWLES
Sec.-Gen.: Dionne HEIJNEN

Founded: 1978
Working languages: E
Secretariat: 2 members of staff

Sectors of activity:
- European producers' association of caramel colours.

EUTECER

European Technical Ceramics Federation

Rue des Colonies 18-24 bte 17, 1000 Bruxelles, Belgium
Tel: +32 2/511 70 25
Tel: +32 2/511 30 12
Fax: +32 2/511 51 74
E-mail: sec@cerameunie.net
Internet: www.cerameunie. net

Pres.: J. HUBER
Sec.-Gen.: R. CHORUS

Founded: 1966
Working languages: F/E/D
Secretariat: 5 members of staff

Information available:
- "Courrier", quarterly, F/E/D, M.

EUTO

European Union of Tourist Officers

Union Européenne des Cadres du Tourisme

Europäischer Verband für Tourismusfachleute

2 Park House Drive, Heversham
LA7 7EG, United Kingdom
Tel: +44 1539/56 35 95
Fax: +44 1539/56 35 95
E-mail: euto@talk21.com
Internet: www.euto.org

Pres.: H. SCHÜLLER
Sec.-Gen.: J.T. OWEN

Founded: 1975
General meeting: September/October
Working languages: E
Secretariat: 1 member of staff

Information available:
- "EUTO bulletin", E, 3 per year, free.
- Information Leaflets.
- "EUTO-What is it? What does it do?", M-NM, free, E.

EUTS

European Union of Tapestries and Saddlers

Union Européenne des Tapissiers-Décorateurs et Selliers

Europäische Union der Tapeziere-Dekorateure und Sattler

Gurzelngasse 27, 4502 Solothurn, Switzerland
Tel: +41 32/623 86 70
Fax: +41 32/623 46 09
E-mail: info@interieursuisse.ch
Internet: www.interieursuisse.ch

Pres.: U. KERN
Sec.-Gen.: P. PLATZER
General meeting: November
Working languages: D/F/It/E

EUVEPRO

European Vegetable Protein Federation

Fédération Européenne des Protéines Végétales

Europäische Vereinigung für Pflanzliches Eiweiss

Avenue de Roodebeek 30, 1030 Bruxelles, Belgium
Tel: +32 2/743 87 30
Fax: +32 2/736 81 75
E-mail: euvepro@sia-dvi.be
Internet: www.euvepro.org

Pres.: Mr. GOEMANS
Sec.-Gen.: Mme. K. DE NEVE

Founded: 1977
Working languages: E
Secretariat: 2 members of staff

Information available:
- List of members available to the general public, free.

EUWEP

European Union of Wholesale with Eggs, Egg Products, Poultry and Game

Union Européenne du Commerce du Gros des Oeufs, Produits d'Oeufs, Volaille et Gibier

Europäische Union des Grosshandels mit Eiern, Eiprodukten, Geflügel und Wild

89 Charterhouse Street – 2nd floor, London EC1M 6HR, United Kingdom
Tel: +44 20/76 08 37 60
Fax: +44 20/76 08 38 60
E-mail: mark.williams@britishindustry-council.com

Pres.: P. KEMP
Sec.-Gen.: M. WILLIAMS

Founded: 1959
General meeting: May/june
Working languages: E/F/D

Sectors of activity:
- EUWEP is the umbrella organization for three trade associations: EEPTA – European Egg Packers and Traders Association; EEPA – European Egg Processors Association; EUWEP – Committee on Poultry & Game. The three organizations hope that this new structure will enable them to represent their interests vis-à-vis the European Commission in a more effective and more identifiable manner.

EVA

European Vending Association

Rue Van Eyck 44, 1050 Bruxelles, Belgium
Tel: +32 2/512 00 75
Fax: +32 2/502 23 42
E-mail: vending@eva.be
Internet: www.eva.be

Pres.: Mr. A. GARULLI
Contacts: Ms. C. PIANA (Director General), Nicole RYDEN (Information Officer & Cttee Coordinator)

Founded: 1976
General meeting: December
Working languages: E
Secretariat: 4 members of staff

Historical note:
- The association was founded in 1976 and changed to its present name in 1994.

Sectors of activity:
- Conference: 2nd Operators' Conference, Spring 2005, Prague

Information available:
- Information notes for members, E/F/D.
- Annual Report, NM, E/F/D/It.
- EVA Brochure, NM, E.
- HACCP guide (€8), M.
- Hygiene Awareness Booklet (€1), M.
- CD-ROM products: EVA-CVS, (€50, M-€200, NM)
- EVA-DTS (€50, M-€200, NM)
- Database: list of members and contacts.
- List of members: free of charge and on the website

EVCA

European Private Equity & Venture Capital Association

Association Européenne des Investissements en Capital à Risque

Europäischer Venture Capital Verband

Minervastraat 4, 1930 Zaventem, Belgium
Tel: +32 2/715 00 20
Fax: +32 2/725 07 04
E-mail: evca@evca.com
Internet: www.evca.com

Pres.: Herman DAEMS
Sec.-Gen.: J. ECHARRI
Contact: Ms. E. FAU-SEBASTIAN

Founded: 1983
General meeting: June
Working languages: E
Secretariat: 19 members of staff

Sectors of activity:
- The European Private Equity and Venture Capital Association (EVCA), established in 1983 and based in Brussels, promotes, facilitates and represents the needs and interests of the private equity and venture capital industry in Europe. EVCA has over 925 members in 50 countries, including the leading fund managers in the European private equity and venture capital industry. In 2003 (preliminary figures), the private equity industry raised €27,7 billion from institutional investors and invested €23.1 billion in Europe's growth companies. Conferences: EVCA Annual Symposium, Berlin, 2-4 June 2004.
- EVCA Technology Conference, Barcelona, 20-22 October 2004

Information available:
- Publications are available from www.evca.com.
- List of members available on the website

EVL

European Federation of Illuminated Signs

Fédération Européenne de la Publicité Lumineuse

Europäischer Verband der Lichtwerbung

5 Orton Enterprise Centre, Bakewell Road, Orton Southgate, Peterborough PE2 6XU, United Kingdom
Tel: +44 1733/23 00 33
Fax: +44 1733/23 09 93
E-mail: bevl@sign.u-net.com
Internet: www.evl-signs.com

Pres.: N. PEARCE
Contact: P.W. TIPTON

Founded: 1965
Working languages: E/F/D
Secretariat: 3 members of staff

Information available:
- Market and economic information available to members only.

EWA

European Welding Association

Association Européenne des Fabricants de Matériel de Soudage

Europäischer Verband der Hersteller von Schweisselektrodenapparaten

Washington Tower 3- Albert Embankment, London SE1 7SL, United Kingdom
Tel: +44 20/77933000
Fax: +44 20/77933003
E-mail: awillman@beama.org
E-mail: awillman@beama.uk

Pres.: M. MANN
Sec.-Gen.: A. WILLMAN
Working languages: F/E/D/Esp/Nl

Information available:
- Statistics, M.

EWA

European Water Association

Theodor-Heuss-Allee 17, 53773 Hennef, Germany
Tel: +49 2242/872 189
Fax: +49 2242/872 135
E-mail: overmann@atv.de
Internet: http://www.ewaonline.de

Pres.: H. THAULOW
Sec.-Gen.: Dr. SIGURD VAN RIESEN
Contact: Mrs. OVERMANN

Founded: 1981
Working languages: E/F/D

Sectors of activity:
- The conference list is available on request (*c.* 30 conferences).

Information available:
- "European Water Management", every two months, €9 (M), €35 (NM), €160 (companies, institutions, ...).
- Information package, free.

EWEA

European Wind Energy Association

The Renewable Energy House, Rue du Trône 26, 1000 Bruxelles, Belgium
Tel: +32 2/546 19 40
Fax: +32 2/546 19 44
E-mail: ewea@ewea.org
Internet: www.ewea.org

Pres.: Prof. Arthouros ZERVES
Contacts: Corin MAILLAIS (CEO), Ms Ann VAN DYCK (Office Administrator)
Working languages: D/E/F/Nl

Information available:
- List of members: links to over 200 members in 40 countries are listed on the website

EWPA

European Whey Products Association

Association Européenne des Produits de Lactosérum

Europäischer Whey-Produkte-Verband

Rue Montoyer 14, 1000 Bruxelles, Belgium
Tel: +32 2/549 50 40
Fax: +32 2/549 50 49
E-mail: ewpa@euromilk.org
Internet: ewpa.euromilk.org

Pres.: J. KLEIBEUKER
Sec.-Gen.: A. VAN DE VEN

Founded: 1996
Working languages: E/F/D
Secretariat: 6 members of staff

Sectors of activity:
- Research.
- Promotion.

Information available:
- Information is available to both members and non-members, depending on the subject.
- List of members available to the general public.

EWPM

European Wood Preservative Manufacturers Group

1 Gleneigles House, Vernon Gate, South Street, Derby DE1 1UP, United Kingdom
Tel: +44 13/32 22 51 04
Fax: +44 13/32 22 51 01

E-mail: sec-ewpm@bwpda.co.uk

Pres.: Dr.F. IMSGARD
Sec.-Gen.: Dr. C.R. COGGINS

Founded: 1977
General meeting: March
Working languages: E
Secretariat: 1 member of staff

Historical note:
- EWPM was formed from an informal grouping of wood manufacturers interested in environmental, health and safety and standardisation matters.

Information available:
- "Newsflash".
- List of members available to the general public, free.

EWRIS

European Wire Rope Information Service

Fédération Européenne des Industries de Câbles d'Acier

Europäische Informationsdienststelle für Drahtseil

Rue de Monceau 47, 75008 Paris, France
Tel: +33 1/53 75 10 04
Fax: +33 1/53 75 10 02
E-mail: ewris@ewris.com
Internet: www.ewris.com

Pres.: Mr. S. RUTHERFORD
Contact: Mrs. A. JOURDAIN

Founded: 1962
Working languages: E/F
Secretariat: 3 members of staff

FACE

Federation of Associations for Hunting and Conservation of the EU

Fédération des Associations de Chasse et Conservation de la Faune Sauvage de l'UE

Rue F. Pelletier 82, 1030 Bruxelles, Belgium
Tel: +32 2/732 69 00
Fax: +32 2/732 70 72
E-mail: administration@face-europe.org
Internet: http://www.face-europe.org

Pres.: G. de TURCKHEIM
Sec.-Gen.: Y. LECOCQ

Founded: 1977
General meeting: September
Working languages: D/E/F/Esp
Secretariat: 6 members of staff

Sectors of activity:
- Lobbying.

Information available:
- "Farming, Hunting and Biodiversity: a Win-win Scenario", E, free.

- The members' list is available on written request from FACE.

FACOGAZ

Association of European Gas Meter Manufacturers

Allée Broc à l'Aye 14, 1400 Nivelles, Belgium
Tel: +32 67/21 46 02
Fax: +32 67/21 46 02
E-mail: jsenave@skynet.be

Pres.: H. DOMBROWSKI
Sec.-Gen.: J. SENAVE
General meeting: June
Working languages: E

Sectors of activity:
- The objective of the association is to encourage technical and economic progress of the gas meter industry, especially to improve the production and to promote the exchange of information and of technical experience.
- The association does not pursue any commercial activities and cannot make decisions which influence the decision making authority of its members in economic matters.
- The association can also co-operate with other organisations concerned by the gas industry according to the agreements approved by the plenary meeting.
- Another target of the association is to discuss on a scientific basis all technical and economic questions which concern the gas meter industry, to inform its members about the collected documentation, if necessary to negotiate with all authorities, organisations or corporations in order to be helpful to all persons concerned by the gas meter industry and to intervene along the most favourable lines for the general interest of the manufacturers, distributors and gas consumers.
- The field of activities of the association is limited to gas meters alone, however of all types, systems and dimensions.

FAECF

Federation of European Window and Curtain Wall Manufacturers' Associations

Fédération des Associations Européennes des Constructeurs de Fenêtres et de Façades

Föderation der Europäischen Fenster- und Fassadenhersteller-Verbände

c/o UNCSAAL, Via Chieti 8, 20154 Milano, Italy
Tel: +39 02/31 92 061
Fax: +39 02/34 53 76 10
E-mail: generalsecretariat@faecf.org
E-mail: technicalsecretariat@faecf.org
Internet: http://www.faecf.org

Pres.: Panos KALLIAS
Sec.-Gen.: P. GIMELLI

Founded: 1968
Working languages: E
Secretariat: 3 members of staff

Information available:
- Statistics, M.
- Information supplied on request.
- List of members available on request of the General Secretariat or through the website

FAEP

European Federation of Magazine Publishers

Fédération Européenne d'Editeurs de Périodiques

Verband Europäischer Zeitschriftenverleger

Rue d'Arlon 15, 1050 Bruxelles, Belgium
Tel: +32 2/286 80 94
Fax: +32 2/286 80 95
E-mail: faep@eutop.com
Internet: www.faep.org

Pres.: P. LEIMIO
Contact: D. MAHON

Founded: 1974
General meeting: June
Working languages: F/E/Nl
Secretariat: 3 members of staff

Information available:
- A monthly newsletter on relevant EU matters, M.
- A quarterly magazine, M.
- Members' list, M.

FAFPAS

Federation of the Associations of the EU Frozen Food Producers

Fédération des Associations de Fabricants de Produits Alimentaires Surgelés de l'UE

Föderation der Tiefgefriernahrungs-mittelhersteller-Verbände der EG

Avenue de Roodebeek 30, 1030 Bruxelles, Belgium
Tel: +32 2/743 87 30
Fax: +32 2/736 81 75
E-mail: fafpas@sia-dvi.be

Sec.-Gen.: M. COENEN

Founded: 1962
Working languages: F/E
Secretariat: 2 members of staff

Information available:
- Consumption figures (tonnes).
- List of members available to the general public, free.

FAREGAZ

Union of European Manufacturers of Gas Pressure Controllers

Union des Fabricants Européens de Régulateurs de Pression de Gaz

c/o FIGAVA, Marienburger Strasse 15, 50968 Köln, Germany
Tel: +49 221/376 48 30
Fax: +49 221/376 48 61
E-mail: info@figawa.de
Internet: www.figawa.de

Pres.: H. ULMER
Contact: Mrs. B. BURGER

Founded: 1962
Working languages: E
Secretariat: 6 members of staff

FBE / EBF

Banking Federation of the European Union

Fédération Bancaire de l'Union Européenne

Rue Montoyer 10, 1000 Bruxelles, Belgium
Tel: +32 2/508 37 11
Fax: +32 2/511 23 28
E-mail: fbemail@fbe.be
Internet: www.fbe.be

Pres.: M. SELLA
Sec.-Gen.: N. BÖMCKE

Founded: 1960
Working languages: F/E
Secretariat: 18 members of staff

FEA

European Aerosol Federation

Fédération Européenne des Aérosols

Europäischer Aerosol Verband

Square Marie-Louise 49, 1000 Bruxelles, Belgium
Tel: +32 2/238 98 29
Fax: +32 2/280 09 29
E-mail: info@aerosol.org
Internet: www.aerosol.org

Pres.: K. COOL
Sec.-Gen.: A. D'HAESE

Founded: 1959
General meeting: Always in autumn.
Working languages: F/E
Secretariat: 2 members of staff

Sectors of activity:
- "Aerosols 2003 Congress and Exhibition", 2003, France.

Information available:
- Monthly: F.E.A. Aerosol-Bulletin – write to AEROSOL EUROPE, Postbox 1108 D-82323 Tutzing.
- "FEA Annual Report", E, free.
- "FEA Standards", E/F/D, €75.
- "Let's talk about ... aerosols", E/F/D, free.

- "Guidelines on Basic Safety Requirements in Aerosol Manufacturing", E, €37.
- "Guidelines on Basic Safety Requirements in Aerosol Storage", E, €37.
- "FEA Facts & Figures Leaflet", E, free.
- "FEA Statistics Report 2000", E, €85.
- List of members, €75.

FEACO

European Federation of Management Consulting Associations

Fédération Européenne des Associations de Conseil en Organisation

Europäische Föderation der Unternehmensberaterverbände

Avenue des Arts 3-5, 1210 Bruxelles, Belgium
Tel: +32 2/250 06 50
Fax: +32 2/250 06 51
E-mail: feaco@feaco.org
Internet: http://www.feaco.org

Pres.: R. REDLEY
Contact: Mrs. E. GROEN

Founded: 1960
General meeting: May + October
Working languages: E/F/Nl/Esp/D
Secretariat: 1 member of staff

Sectors of activity:

- Assist in promoting and developing the profession of management consultancy in Europe.
- Foster and maintain the highest standards of technical competence and professional practice.
- Create a link for the exchange of technical experience between members of the profession in the various national associations.
- Study, promote and protect the mutual professional interests of member associations.
- International Consultancy Conference, Athens, Greece 21-23 October 2004

Information available:

- Annual publication: "Survey of the European Management Consultancy Market", NM.
- Quarterly newsletter.
- List of national member firms, free and available via the website

FEAD

European Federation of Waste Management and Environmental Services

Fédération Européenne des Activités du Déchet et de l'Environnement

Europäische Föderation der Entsorgungswirtschaft

Avenue des Gaulois 19, 1040 Bruxelles, Belgium
Tel: +32 2/732 32 13
Fax: +32 2/734 95 92
E-mail: info@fead.be
Internet: http://www.fead.be

Pres.: Peter J. KNEISSL
Sec.-Gen.: Ms. V. VERAS

Founded: 1981
General meeting: February
Working languages: E/F/D
Secretariat: 4 members of staff

Sectors of activity:

- FEAD is the umbrella organisation of the national associations of private waste management companies which have a 50 percent share in the household waste sector and handle more than 80 percent of industrial waste in Europe. Founded in 1981, its principal missions are the representation of members' interests to the EU and worldwide exchange of information about the sector. FEAD maintains close links with numerous other international organisations. In addition, FEAD produces position papers on selected topics.
- Conference: FEAD Annual Conference 2005, Budapest, 30/9/05

Information available:

- Presentation brochure, F/E/D, free, (M-NM).
- List of members available to the general public, website, free.
- "FEAD Contact" (newsletter) – published 4 x year, M-NM, free.
- "FEAD Bulletin", updates on interesting issues, M.

FEANI

European Federation of National Engineering Associations

Fédération Européenne d'Associations Nationales d'Ingénieurs

Föderation Europäischer Nationaler Ingenieurverbände

Avenue Roger Van den Driesche 18, 1150 Bruxelles, Belgium
Tel: +32 2/639 03 90
Fax: +32 2/639 03 99
E-mail: philippe.wauters@feani.org
E-mail: isabelle.vandenberghe@feani.org
E-mail: francoise.declercq@feani.org
E-mail: rita.heissner@feani.org
Internet: www.feani.org

Pres.: Mr. ALEXOPOULOS
Sec.-Gen.: P. WAUTERS
Contacts: Mrs. I. VANDENBERGHE (Public Relations Secretary), Mrs. R. HEISSNER (Secr)

Founded: 1951
Working languages: D/E/F

Secretariat: 5 members of staff

Sectors of activity:

- FEANI is a federation of engineers that unites national engineering associations from 27 countries. Thus, FEANI represents the interests of over 2 million engineers in Europe. FEANI is striving for a single voice for the engineering profession in Europe and wants to affirm and develop the professional identity of engineers.
- Through its activities and services, especially with the attribution of the EUR ING professional designation, FEANI aims to facilitate the mutual recognition of engineering qualifications in Europe and to strengthen the position, role and responsibility of engineers in society.

Information available:

- "FEANI News", free, E, M.
- Guide of the FEANI register, M-NM, E.
- Databases: INDEX FEANI, E.
- List of members: www.feani.org.

FEAP

Federation of European Aquaculture Producers

Fédération Européenne des Producteurs Aquacoles

Rue Nicolas Fossoul 54, 4100 Boncelles, Belgium
Tel: +32 4/338 29 95
Fax: +32 4/337 98 46
E-mail: secretariat@feap.info
Internet: http://www.feap.info

Pres.: J. STEPHANIE
Sec.-Gen.: C. HOUGH

Founded: 1969
General meeting: May/June
Working languages: E/F
Secretariat: 2 members of staff

Sectors of activity:

- Development of appropriate research projects at European level.

Information available:

- "Production & Prices of Aquaculture Species in Europe", bi-annual, E, free of charge, only on the web.
- Database: addresses of member associations.
- The members' list is available, free of charge.

FEB

Fellowship of European Broadcasters

The Service Road 23, Potters Bar – Hertfordshire EN6 1QA, United Kingdom
Tel: +44 1707/64 99 10
Fax: +44 1707/66 26 53

E-mail: feb@feb.org
Internet: http://www.feb.org

Pres.: H. THOMAS

Sectors of activity:
- "Fellowship European Broadcasters Conference", 13-16/03/2003, Denmark.

FEBO

European Timber Trade Association

Fédération Européenne du Négoce du Bois

Europäischer Holzhandelsverband

Galerie du Centre, Bloc 1, 5è étage, Rue des Fripiers 15-17, 1000 Bruxelles, Belgium
Tel: +32 2/229 32 60
Fax: +32 2/229 32 64
E-mail: febo@fnn.be
Internet: www.febo.org

Pres.: Mrs. C. SWOBODA
Sec.-Gen.: P. STEENBERGHEN

Founded: 1998
Working languages: E/D/F
Secretariat: 4 members of staff

Sectors of activity:
- Information.
- Industrial law.
- Standards.
- Seminars.
- Business-help.
- Marketing.

Information available:
- The members' list is available, fee charged.

FEC

Federation of the European Cutlery Flatware Holloware and Cookware Industries

Fédération de l'Industrie Européenne de la Coutellerie et des Couverts de Table de l'Orfèvrerie et des Articles Culinaires

Föderation der Europäischen Schneidwaren-, Besteck-, Tafelgeräte-, Küchengeschirr und Haushaltgeräteindustrie

c/o UNITAM, 39-41 Rue Louis Blanc, 92400 Courbevoie, France
Tel: +33 1/47 17 64 60
Fax: +33 1/47 17 64 61
E-mail: unitam@mail.finema.com
Internet: www.fecinfo.org

Pres.: R. DESCOSSE
Contact: E. DESCHEEMAEKER

Founded: 1952
Working languages: E/D/F/It
Secretariat: 2 members of staff

Sectors of activity:
- The federation organises a congress every two years.

Information available:
- List of members available to the general public, free.

FECC

European Association of Chemical Distributors

Fédération Européenne du Commerce Chimique

Europäische Föderation des Chemischen Handels

Chaussée de Wavre 1519, 1160 Bruxelles, Belgium
Tel: +32 2/679 02 60
Fax: +32 2/672 73 55
E-mail: vle@fecc.org
Internet: http://www.fecc.org

Pres.: E. E. NORDMANN
Contact: Dr. H. HOUT (Dir Gen)
General meeting: June
Working languages: E/F/D/Nl
Secretariat: 3 members of staff

Information available:
- "The Bulletin", monthly, NM & M.
- Conference book for the Annual Congress.
- Databases: members and contacts of associated organisations

FECC

European Federation of Managers and Professionals in Building

Fédération Européenne des Cadres de la Construction

Rue de Londres 15, 75009 Paris, France
Tel: +33 1/55 31 76 76
Fax: +33 1/55 31 76 33/32
E-mail: president@cgcbtp.com

Pres.: R. JANERT
Sec.-Gen.: F. MARTINEAU

Founded: 1993
Working languages: E/F
Secretariat: 3 members of staff

Sectors of activity:
- Dissemination of social and professional information.
- Working parties looking at the questions of:
  – the standard of diplomas,
  – training,
  – mobility,
  – the employment of executives in the building sector, notably in respect of the decisions of the Edinburgh Summit aimed at launching a European growth initiative which will make it possible to finance large social infrastructure projects of Community interest,
  – pay,
  – pensions.

Information available:
- CEC Documents, free.

FECIMA

European Federation of International Trade in Agricultural Machines and Related Activities

Fédération Européenne du Commerce International des Machines Agricoles et Activités Connexes

Bd de la Woluwe 46 Bte 14, 1200 Bruxelles, Belgium
Tel: +32 2/778 62 00
Fax: +32 2/778 62 22
E-mail: mail@federauto.be
Internet: www.fecima.org

Pres.: Ph. LAGACHE
Sec.-Gen.: A. PONCELET
Contact: T. ANTONISSEN (Deputy Secretary General)

Founded: 1990
General meeting: June or July
Working languages: F/E
Secretariat: 3 members of staff

Sectors of activity:
- International trade of agricultural machines and related activities

Information available:
- Newsletters on European issues relating to trade, technical standards, etc., M
- List of members available to the general public, free of charge.
- Database: European Legislation concerning the sector/ Technical Harmonisation (on the website)

FECS

Federation of European Chemical Societies

Fédération des Sociétés Chimiques Européennes

Föderation Europäischer Chemiker Gesellschaften

c/o Royal Society of Chemistry, Burlington House, Piccadilly, London W1J 0BA, United Kingdom
Tel: +44 20/7440 3303
Fax: +44 20/7437 8883
E-mail: mcewane@rsc.org
Internet: www.fecs-chemistry.org

Contact: Ms. E. McEWAN

Founded: 1970
Working languages: E

Sectors of activity:
- Analytical chemistry.
- Food chemistry.
- Chemistry and the environment.
- Electrochemistry.
- Chemical education research.

TRADE AND PROFESSIONAL ASSOCIATIONS

The Directory of EU Information Sources

- Organometallic chemistry.
- Nuclear and radiochemistry.
- History of chemistry.
- Computational chemistry.

FECS

European Federation of Ceramic Sanitary Ware Manufacturers

Fédération Européenne des Fabricants de Céramiques Sanitaires

Europäische Föderation der Sanitär-Keramik-Hersteller

Rue La Boétie 3, 75008 Paris, France
Tel: +33 1/58 18 30 40
Fax: +33 1/42 66 09 00
E-mail: sanitaire@ceramique.org

Pres.: A. LORETI
Sec.-Gen.: F. de LA TOUR

Founded: 1954
Working languages: E/F
Secretariat: 3 members of staff

Sectors of activity:
- Standardisation.
- Environment policy.

FEDARENE

European Federation of Regional Energy and Environment Agencies

Fédération Européenne des Agences Régionales de l'Energie et de l'Environnement

Europäische Dachorganisation Regionale Energie- und Umweltbehorden

Rue du Beau-Site 11, 1000 Bruxelles, Belgium
Tel: +32 2/646 82 10
Fax: +32 2/646 89 75
E-mail: fedarene@euronet.be
Internet: www.fedarene.org

Pres.: R. LERON
Sec.-Gen.: M. GEISSLER

Founded: 1990
Working languages: E/F
Secretariat: 3 members of staff

Sectors of activity:
- Energy.
- Environment.

Information available:
- From sustainable development to local agenda 21.
- Vade-mecum of regional energy agencies.
- Fedarene info, …
Database:
- All energy and environment actors.
- List of members available to the general public, free of charge.

FEDEMAC

Federation of International Moving Associations

Schulstrasse 53, 65795 Hattersheim am Main, Germany
Tel: +49 6190/98 98 11
Fax: +49 6190/98 98 20
E-mail: troska@amoe.de
Internet: www.fedemac.de

Pres.: D. CAWLEFIELD
Sec.-Gen.: Dr. E. TROSKA
Working languages: E
Secretariat: 1 member of staff

Sectors of activity:
- FEDEMAC Congress, every two/three years.

Information available:
- "FEDEMAC Newsletter", 2/year, E, M.
- "FEDEMAC Directory" + CD-Rom, annual, F/E/Esp/D, M/NM.
- List of members available to the general public, free, M/NM.

FEDFA

Federation of European Deer Farmers Associations

Kuytegemstraat 66/2, 2890 Synt Amands, Belgium
Tel: +32 52/34 17 88
Fax: +32 50/500 667
E-mail: marc.peelman@skynet.be
Internet: www.fedfa.com

Pres.: T. SOLHEYM
Sec.-Gen.: M. PEELMAN

Founded: 1990
Working languages: E

Historical note:
- Represent 18 countries within Europe.

Sectors of activity:
- To safeguard the interests of the industry within the EU and third countries.
- To promote the science and practice of deer farming.
- To coordinate research and exchange of knowledge.
- To coordinate transport, welfare and disease control measures.

Information available:
- Information on FEDFA.
- Deer farming in different countries, quality assurance, recipes, photos and website links.
- List of members available to the general public, free of charge.

FEDIAF

European Pet Food Industry Federation

Fédération Européenne de l'Industrie des Aliments pour Animaux Familiers

Avenue Louise 89 Bte 2, 1050 Bruxelles, Belgium
Tel: +32 2/536 05 20
Fax: +32 2/537 84 69
E-mail: fediaf@fediaf.org
Internet: http://www.fediaf.org

Pres.: D. HAYMAN
Sec.-Gen.: T. MEYER

Founded: 1974
Working languages: F/E/D
Secretariat: 3 members of staff

Information available:
- Brochure on "The European Petfood Industry" – free, NM.
- List of members available to the general public, free.

FEDIMA

Federation of the European Union Manufacturers and Suppliers of Ingredients to the Bakery, Confectionery and Patisserie Industries

Nolet de Brauwerestraat 21A/12, 1800 Vilvoorde, Belgium
Tel: +32 2/306 79 34
Fax: +32 2/306 94 18
E-mail: fedima.vanhecke@pandora.be
Internet: www.fedima.org

Pres.: J. GILLESPIE
Sec.-Gen.: A. VAN HECKE

Founded: 1969
General meeting: September
Working languages: F/E
Secretariat: 2 members of staff

FEDIOL

EC Seed Crushers' and Oil Processors' Federation

Fédération de l'Industrie de l'Huilerie de la CE

Vereinigung der Ölmühlenindustrie der EG

Avenue de Tervueren 168 Box 12, 1150 Bruxelles, Belgium
Tel: +32 2/771 53 30
Fax: +32 2/771 38 17
E-mail: fediol@fediol.be
Internet: http://www.fediol.be

Pres.: R. PONT
Contact: P. COGELS

Founded: 1957
General meeting: September – rotation between member countries
Working languages: F/E
Secretariat: 6 members of staff

Information available:
- "Statistics", 1/year, F/E, free, M.
- List of members, free.

FEDMA

Federation of European Direct Marketing

Fédération Européenne du Marketing Direct

Avenue de Tervueren 439, 1150 Bruxelles, Belgium
Tel: +32 2 779 4268
Tel: +32 2/778 99 20
Fax: +32 2 779 4269
Fax: +32 2/778 99 24
E-mail: info@fedma.org
Internet: www.fedma.org

Pres.: Ara CINAR
Contacts: Alastair TEMPEST (Director General) Axel TANDBERG (Director Government Affairs), Andrea VREEKE (Manager Governemtn Affairs), Jørgen Nygaard ANDREASSEN (Membership Manager), Catherine BRETT (PR and Communications Manager)

Founded: 1997
General meeting: April
Working languages: E/F
Secretariat: 8 members of staff

Historical note:
- FEDMA was created in 1997 from the fusion of EDMA (est. 1976) and FEDIM (est. 1992).

Sectors of activity:
- Promoting the Direct Marketing Industry to consumers and businesses, especially in Central and Eastern Europe where we have helped to set up a number of new national Direct Marketing Associations;
- Improving the quality of Direct Marketing education via our education certification project;
- Promoting self-regulation;
- Participation in EC funded projects, such as CCform and ACTIN.
- Data Protection seminar to be held, December, Brussels

Information available:
- "Europe Direct Newsletter", M
- "FEDMA Membership News Newsletter", M
- "FEDMA Membership Directory", M
- "The International Handbook of Direct Marketing".
- Extensive information on European Direct Marketing legislation is available on our website which has a private members' section in addition to the public pages
- "FEDMA Legal Fact Pack", 80 pp., 2001. (free to members, NM price €250)
- Survey on Direct and Interactive Marketing Activities in Europe (published annually – free to members, €280 for non-members)
- Full details of the rest of our publications are available on our website

FEDOLIVE

Federation of the Olive Oil Industry of the EC

Fédération de l'Industrie de l'Huile d'Olive de la CE

Föderation der Olivenölindustrie in der EG

118 Avenue Achille Piretti, 92200 Neuilly sur Seine, France
Tel: +33 1/46 37 22 06
Fax: +33 1/46 37 15 60
E-mail: huiledolive@fncg.fr

Pres.: C. ROUSSE LA CORDERE
Sec.-Gen.: J. C. BARSACQ
General meeting: November
Working languages: F

Information available:
- Circulars sent out either by telex or telefax.

FEDSA

Federation of European Direct Selling Associations

Fédération des Associations Européennes de la Vente Directe

Europäische Föderation für Haustürverkauf und Dienstleistung

Avenue de Tervueren 14, 1040 Bruxelles, Belgium
Tel: +32 2/736 10 14
Fax: +32 2/736 34 97
E-mail: fedsa@fedsa.be
Internet: http://www.fedsa.be

Pres.: Dr. H. ADELMANN
Contact: Mrs. M. LA CROIX

Founded: 1968
General meeting: June + November
Working languages: E
Secretariat: 3 members of staff

Information available:
- "DS News", quarterly, M, E, free.
- The list of members is available, free.
- Annual Statistics.
- Database: books and reports + articles on direct selling.

FEE

Federation of European Accountants

Fédération des Experts Comptables Européens

Föderation der Europäischen Wirtschaftsprüfer

Rue de la Loi 83, 1040 Bruxelles, Belgium
Tel: +32 2/285 40 85
Fax: +32 2/231 11 12
E-mail: secretariat@fee.be
Internet: http://www.fee.be

Pres.: D. DEVLIN
Sec.-Gen.: H. OLIVIER

Founded: 1986
General meeting: Every 2 years : December
Working languages: E/F
Secretariat: 11 members of staff

Sectors of activity:
The Association is a non-profit association. Its objectives are:
- to work generally towards the enhancement and harmonisation of the practice of accountancy in the broadest sense in Europe in both the public and private sectors;
- to be the sole consultative organisation of the European accountancy profession in relation to the EU authorities;
- to arrange the holding of periodic congresses and seminars so as to:
  – enable members of the European accountancy profession to meet one another in an environment that facilitates discussion and the interchange of ideas concerning the profession,
  – direct attention to and inform members of the European profession about developments in relevant fields.

Information available:
- Activity Report, monthly, E/F, only for members and institutes.
- The FEE publishes other works and studies conducted by its different constituent committees. The list and prices of the publications may be obtained from the general secretariat.
- FEE Homepage on Internet: http://www.fee. be, free.
- FEE Europage on Internet: http://www.euro.fee.be, free.
- The members' list is available, free of charge.

FEEDM

Fédération Européenne des Emballeurs et Distributeurs de Miel

European Federation of Honey Packers and Distributors

Europäischer Verband der Honig Verpacker und Vertreiber

Grosse Baeckerstrasse 4, 20095 Hamburg, Germany
Tel: +49 40/37 47 19 13
Fax: +49 40/37 47 19 26
E-mail: feedm@waren-verein.de
Internet: www.feedm.com

Pres.: Vincent MICHAUD
Sec.-Gen.: Dr. Katrin LANGNER
Contact: Hanna LIEBIG

Founded: 1958
Working languages: E
Secretariat: 2 members of staff

FEEM

Federation of European Explosives Manufacturers

Avenue E. Van Nieuwenhuyse 4 bte 1, 1160 Bruxelles, Belgium
Tel: +32 2/676 72 02
Fax: +32 2/676 73 01
E-mail: bje@cefic.be
E-mail: pfu@cefic.be
Internet: http://www.cefic.org

Contact: P. VAN DER HOEVEN
Working languages: E

FEFAC

European Feed Manufacturers' Federation

Fédération Européenne des Fabricants d'Aliments Composés

Europäischer Verband der Mischfutterindustrie

Rue de la Loi 223 bte 3, 1040 Bruxelles, Belgium
Tel: +32 2/285 00 50
Fax: +32 2/230 57 22
E-mail: fefac@fefac.org
Internet: www.fefac.org

Pres.: Y. MONTECOT
Sec.-Gen.: A. DÖRING

Founded: 1959
General meeting: May
Working languages: F/E/D/(It)
Secretariat: 7 members of staff

FEFANA

European Federation of Animal Feed Additive Manufacturers

Fédération Européenne des Fabricants d'Adjuvants pour la Nutrition Animale

Europäischer Verband für Wirkstoffe in der Tierernährung

Avenue E. Van Nieuwenhuyse 4 box 1, 1160 Bruxelles, Belgium
Tel: +32 2/676 73 67
Fax: +32 2/676 74 05
E-mail: info@fefana.org
E-mail: pfu@cefic.be
E-mail: dja@cefic.be
Internet: www.fefana.org

Pres.: J-P. TENHOVE
Sec.-Gen.: D. JANS

Founded: 1963
Working languages: E/F/D
Secretariat: 2 members of staff

Information available:
- Internal information for member organizations, M.
- Extracts/abstracts of internal reports, M.
- Position papers from the "Ad hoc" working groups, M.

- Database: draft regulations and applications of EC regulations in respect of the use of animal feed additives, M.
- List of members, free, M-NM.
- Fact sheets giving information on the use of in-feed antibacterials, E, free.

FEFCO

European Federation of Corrugated Board Manufacturers

Fédération Européenne des Fabricants de Carton Ondulé

Europäische Föderation der Wellpappefabrikanten

Avenue Louise 250, 1050 Bruxelles, Belgium
Tel: +32 2/646 40 70
Fax: +32 2/646 64 60
E-mail: information@fefco.org
Internet: http://www.fefco.org

Pres.: V. BRUSAMARELLO
Sec.-Gen.: W. HOEBERT

Founded: 1952
General meeting: Twice a year.
Working languages: F/E/D
Secretariat: 9 members of staff

Information available:
- "Production Statistics", NM.
- "International Code", NM.
- "Classification of corrugated board qualities", NM.
- Members' address book, M.
- Annual report, free, D/E/F, M-NM.

FEFPEB

European Federation of Wooden Pallet and Packaging Manufacturers

Fédération Européenne des Fabricants de Palettes et Emballages en Bois

Europäischer Verband der Holzpackmittel und Palettenhersteller

PO Box 90154, 5000 LG Tilburg, Netherlands
Tel: +31 13/59 44 802
Fax: +31 13/ 59 44 749
E-mail: fefpeb@wispa.nl
Internet: www.fefpeb.org

Pres.: D.D.A. MOMKEL
Sec.-Gen.: A.J.M. CEELAERT

Founded: 1947
Working languages: E/F/D

Information available:
- List of members available to the general public, free.

FEFSI

Fédération Européenne des Fonds et Sociétés d'Investissement

Square de Meeûs 18 bte 3, 1050 Bruxelles, Belgium
Tel: +32 2/513 39 69
Fax: +32 2/513 26 43
E-mail: info@fefsi.be
Internet: www.fefsi.org

Pres.: W. MANSFELD
Sec.-Gen.: S. MATTHIAS

Founded: 1974
General meeting: June
Working languages: E/D/F
Secretariat: 7 members of staff

Sectors of activity:
- to maintain a high level of investor protection and encourage investor confidence;
- to preserve the integrity of the European investment funds industry;
- to promote the highest ethical standards in all areas of the the funds business;
- to contribute to the creation of a real European investment fund market and the opening of national markets;
- to be the competent and representative business partner of regulators, other associations, the press and the public in and outside Europe

Information available:
- "FEFSI Statistics", quarterly, €500, E, NM.
- Annual Report, M-NM, free.
- The members' list is available on FEFSI's website.

FEIBP

European Brushware Federation

Fédération Européenne de l'Industrie de la Brosserie et de la Pinceauterie

Europäische Föderation der Pinsel- und Burstenindustrie

Kaiserswerther Strasse 137, 40474 Düsseldorf, Germany
Tel: +49 211/6025 343-0
Fax: +49 211/6025 343-15
E-mail: info@euro-brush.de
Internet: http://www.eurobrush.com

Pres.: J. VEZIER
Contact: S. MIETH

Founded: 1958
Working languages: F/E/D
Secretariat: 2 members of staff

Information available:
- Statistical report (40 pages) – free, NM.
- Position papers, M.
- Sectoral documents, M.
- Annual report.

FEIC

Federation of the European Plywood Industry

Fédération Européenne de l'Industrie du Contreplaqué

Hof-ter-Vleestdreef 5 / 4, 1070 Bruxelles, Belgium
Tel: +32 2/556 25 84
Fax: +32 2/ 556 25 95
E-mail: info@europlywood.org
Internet: www.europlywood.org

Sec.-Gen.: K. WIJNENDAELE
Working languages: F/D/E
Secretariat: 1 member of staff

Sectors of activity:
• To facilitate contacts between the members.
• To organise joint research on problems facing its industry.

Information available:
• Annual report, M, F/D.

FEICA

Association of European Adhesives Manufacturers

Fédération Européenne des Industries de Colles et Adhésifs

Verband Europäischer Klebstoffindustrien

Ivo Beucker Strasse 43, 40237 Düsseldorf, Germany
Tel: +49 211/67931-10
Fax: +49 211/67931-88
E-mail: info@feica.com
Internet: www.feica.com

Pres.: L. BUSETTI
Sec.-Gen.: A. VAN HALTEREN

Founded: 1972
Working languages: E
Secretariat: 8 members of staff

Historical note:
• Founded in Rome.

Information available:
• "FEICA Handbook", yearly.
• "FEICA Focus", quarterly.

FEITIS

European Federation of Picture and Sound Technical Industries

Fédération Européenne des Industries Techniques de l'Image et du Son

Europäische Föderation der Bild- und Tontechnischen Industrien

Rue Hamelin 17, 75783 Paris Cedex 16, France
Tel: +33 1/45 05 72 55
Fax: +33 1/45 05 72 50
E-mail: davidcarr@m2tv.com

Pres.: D. CARR

Founded: 1990
General meeting: June
Working languages: F/E

Sectors of activity:
• Technical industries.
• Provision of film and video services.

Information available:
• Statistics/Comparative study on the potential of the EU's 15 Member States.

FELASA

Federation of European Laboratory Animal Science Associations

Fédération des Associations Européennes Scientifiques d'Expérimentation Animale

Föderation der Europäischen Versuchstierkundeverbände

58 Great Marlborough Street, London W1 1DD, United Kingdom
Tel: +44 20/74 05 04 63
Fax: +44 20/78 31 94 89
E-mail: jguillen@unav.es
Internet: www.felasa.org

Pres.: P. HARDY
Sec.-Gen.: J. GUILLEN

FEMB

Fédération Européenne du Mobilier de Bureau

Kaiserwerther Strasse 137, 40474 Düsseldorf, Germany
Tel: +49 211/6025 343-0
Fax: +49 211/6025 343-15
E-mail: info@femb.org
Internet: http://www.femb.org

Pres.: D. KRAUSE
Sec.-Gen.: S. MIETH

Founded: 1994
Working languages: D/E/F
Secretariat: 35 members of staff

Historical note:
• Formed over 30 years ago as part of the Business Equipment Trade Association.

Information available:
• The members' list is available, free of charge.

FEMFM

Federation of European Manufacturers of Friction Materials

Fédération Européenne des Fabricants de Matériaux de Friction

Europäischer Verband der Hersteller von Reibmaterialen

Rue Jean-Jacques Rousseau 79, 92158 Suresnes Cedex, France
Tel: +33 1/46 25 02 30
Fax: +33 1/46 97 00 80
E-mail: cboure@fiev.fr

Sec.-Gen.: G. VOSSKOETTER

Founded: 1971
Working languages: E
Secretariat: 3 members of staff

FEMGED

European Federation of Middle-Size and Major Retailers

Fédération Européenne des Moyennes et Grandes Entreprises de Distribution

Europäische Vereinigung der Mittel- und Grossunternehmen des Einzelhandels

Avenue des Vaillants 5, bte 7, 1200 Bruxelles, Belgium
Tel: +32 2/734 32 89
E-mail: femged@pi.be

Pres.: R. PANGELS
Contact: C. DROULANS

Founded: 1959
Working languages: F/D/E
Secretariat: 3 members of staff

Sectors of activity:
• Lobby.

Information available:
• "FEMGED European Newsletter", monthly, free, F/D/E.

FEMIB

Federation of the European Building Joinery Associations

Fédération Européenne des Syndicats de Menuiseries Industrielles du Bâtiment

Vereinigung der Europäischen Verbände der Holzindustrie im Baubereich

Walter-Kolb-Strasse 1-7, 60594 Frankfurt am Main, Germany
Tel: +49 69/95 50 54-13
Fax: +49 69/95 50 54-11
E-mail: femib@window.de
Internet: www.eurowindow.org

Pres.: J. RIBAS

Founded: 1958
General meeting: November
Working languages: F/E/D
Secretariat: 5 members of staff

Sectors of activity:
• Study tours.
• Congresses.
• Fairs.
• Workshops.

Information available:
• "Statistics", M.

- Information supplied after examination of request.
- "FEMIB News", E/D, 2 or 3 a year, free.
- List of members available to the general public, free.

FEMIN

European Federation of Manufacturers and Traders of Cleaning Machines, Material and Accessories

Square Gutenberg 13, 1000 Bruxelles, Belgium
Tel: +32 2/230 98 69
Fax: +32 2/231 16 44
Internet: pcosta@gmx.be

Contact: P.V. COSTA (EU Liaison Officer)

Founded: 1998
Working languages: F/E/D

FEP / FEE

Federation of European Publishers
Fédération des Editeurs Européens

Avenue de Tervueren 204, 1150 Bruxelles, Belgium
Tel: +32 2/770 11 10
Fax: +32 2/771 20 71
E-mail: malemann@fep-fee.be
Internet: www.fep-fee.be

Pres.: A.C. HILSCHER,

Pres.: A. BACH (from May 2004)
Contact: Ms. M. VON ALEMANN
General meeting: November – May
Working languages: E/F
Secretariat: 3 members of staff

Sectors of activity:
- Lobbying for the publishing world.

Information available:
- The members' list is available, free of charge.

FEPA

European Federation of Abrasive Manufacturers
Fédération Européenne des Fabricants de Produits Abrasifs
Vereinigung der Europäische Schleifmittel-Hersteller

Avenue Reille 20, 75014 Paris, France
Tel: +33 1/45 81 25 90
Fax: +33 1/45 81 62 94
E-mail: f.verguet@fepa-abrasives.org
Internet: www.fepa-abrasives.org

Pres.: G. SCOTTI
Contact: F. VERGUET

Founded: 1955
General meeting: May
Working languages: E/F/D

Secretariat: 2 members of staff

Sectors of activity:
- European standardisation.

Information available:
- Safety code for the use of grinders, D/F/E.
- List of standards for abrasives.

FEPD

European Federation of Perfume Retailers
Fédération Européenne des Parfumeurs Détaillants
Europäischer Parfümerie-Verband

An der Engelsburg 1, 45657 Recklinghausen, Germany
Tel: +49 2361/9248-0
Fax: +49 2361/9248-88
E-mail: info@parfuemerieverband.de
Internet: www.parfuemerieverband.de

Pres.: R.D. WOLF
Contact: W. HARIEGEL

Founded: 1960
Working languages: F/D/E
Secretariat: 2 members of staff

Sectors of activity:
- In addition to watching over members' interests, representing members before European and international institutions, and conducting market analysis, the FEPD promotes information exchanges and regularly convenes conferences so as to work out common principles and forms of action.
- Conference:
- "European Congress of Perfume Retailers", open to everyone, 4-5 days annual.

Information available:
- Circulars, 6-8 times/year, F/D/E.
- List of members, free.

FEPE

European Envelope Manufacturers' Association
Fédération Européenne des Fabricants d'Enveloppes
Europäische Vereinigung der Briefumschlagfabrikanten

Bergstrasse 110, 8032 Zürich, Switzerland
Tel: +41 1/266 99 22
Fax: +41 1/266 99 49
E-mail: info@fepe.de
Internet: www.fepe.de

Pres.: J. MADSEN MYGDAR
Sec.-Gen.: M. HABERLI
Working languages: E

FEPEDICA

Fédération Européenne du Personnel d'Encadrement des Productions, des Industries, des Commerces et des Organismes Agroalimentaires

Rue du Rocher 59-63, 75008 Paris, France
Tel: +33 1/55 30 13 30
Fax: +33 1/55 30 13 31
E-mail: agro@cfecgc.fr

Pres.: P. BROQUET
Sec.-Gen.: P. WEBER

Founded: 1990
Working languages: F
Secretariat: 3 members of staff

Information available:
- "Inforcadre", bimonthly, M, €3.70, F.
- "Vouloir Magazine", quarterly, M, €5.35, F.

FEPF

Common Market Committee of the European Federation of Porcelain and Earthenware Tableware and Ornamental Ware Industries
Fédération Européenne des Industries de Porcelaine et de Faïence de Table et d'Ornementation

Rue des Colonies 18-24 Bte 17, 1000 Bruxelles, Belgium
Tel: +32 2/511 70 25
Tel: +32 2/511 30 12
Fax: +32 2/511 51 74
E-mail: sec@cerameunie.net
Internet: www.cerameunie.net

Pres.: E. VON BOCH
Sec.-Gen.: R. CHORUS

Founded: 1958
Working languages: F/E/D
Secretariat: 5 members of staff

Information available:
- "Courrier", bimonthly, F/E/D, M.

FEPORT

Federation of European Private Port Operators
Fédération Européenne des Opérateurs Portuaires Privés
Vereinigung Europäischer Privater Hafenumschlag Betriebe

Avenue Michel Ange 68, 1000 Bruxelles, Belgium
Tel: +32 2/736 75 52
Fax: +32 2/732 31 49
E-mail: info@feport.be
Internet: www.feport.be

Pres.: Mr. VALKENIERS
Sec.-Gen.: Mrs. H. DE LEEUW

Founded: 1993
General meeting: March
Working languages: E
Secretariat: 2 members of staff

Information available:
- Newsletter, bi-monthly, E, M.
- Newsflash, E, M.
- The members' list is available, free of charge.

FEPPD

Fédération Européenne des Patrons Prothésistes Dentaires

Rue Jacques de Lalaing 4, 1040 Bruxelles, Belgium
Tel: +32 2/231 05 73
Fax: +32 2/230 50 27
E-mail: feppd@kmonet.org
Internet: www.feppd.org

Pres.: J. SCHWICHTENBERG
Sec.-Gen.: M. REY
Contact: Mrs. N. PAULUSSON

Founded: 1953
General meeting: May
Working languages: D/E/F
Secretariat: 2 members of staff

Information available:
- The members' list is available.

FERCO

European Federation of Contract Catering Organisations

Fédération Européenne de la Restauration Collective

Bastion Tower, Place du Champ de Mars 5, Bte 14, 1050 Bruxelles, Belgium
Tel: +32 2/550 36 76
Fax: +32 2/230 17 37
E-mail: ferco@online.be

Pres.: P. AUBERT
Sec.-Gen.: Mrs. M.-C. LEFEBVRE

Founded: 1990
General meeting: June – December
Working languages: F/E

Sectors of activity:
- Development of a social dialogue
- Development of a common system of VAT – Application of a reduced VAT rate for contract catering organisations.

Information available:
- List of members available to the general public, free.

FEROPA

European Federation of Fibre-Board Manufacturers

Fédération Européenne des Fabricants de Panneaux de Fibres

Europäische Föderation der Holzfaserplatten-Fabrikanten

Traverse des Rougons 724, 83510 Lorgues, France
Tel: +33 4/94 73 75 99
Fax: +33 4/94 67 67 07
E-mail: larsomdahl@wanadoo.fr
Internet: www.feropa.org

Pres.: V. SAIKOVSKI
Contact: L. OMDAHL

Founded: 1954
Working languages: E
Secretariat: 1 member of staff

Information available:
- List of members available through the website

FESE

Federation of European Securities Exchanges

Rue du Lombard 41, 1000 Bruxelles, Belgium
Tel: +32 2/551 01 80
Fax: +32 2/512 49 05
E-mail: detry@fese.be
Internet: http://www.fese.org

Pres.: M. GERONO
Sec.-Gen.: P. ARLMAN

Founded: 1974
Working languages: F/E/D/Nl
Secretariat: 5 members of staff

Sectors of activity:
- Cooperation amongst securities exchanges and Eastern Europe.
- Dialogue with European authorities.
- Information – statistics.
Conferences:
- General Assembly, 2/year.
- Working Group Meetings, M, 6/year.

Information available:
- Newsletter", E, M.
- Statistics – on EU Stock Exchanges, F/E, M-NM.
- List of members, free of charge.

FESI

European Federation of Associations of Insulation Contractors

Fédération Européenne des Syndicats d'Entreprises d'Isolation

Europäische Vereinigung der Verbände der Isolierunternehmen

c/o Hauptverband der Deutschen Bauindustrie e.V., Kurfurstenstrasse 129, 10785 Berlin, Germany
Tel: +49 30/212 86 163
Fax: +49 30/212 86 160
E-mail: bfa.wksb@bauindustrie.de

Pres.: K. VERSTEEGH
Contact: J. SCHMOLDT
Working languages: E
Secretariat: 2 members of staff

Information available:
- Specializzata – Edilizia, monthly, It, M-NM.
- "Isoliertechnik", every two months, M-NM.
- "Uiteuropoort Kringen", monthly, Nl, M-NM.
- "Technical lexicon", F/D/E/It/Esp/Nl/ Swe/Serbo-Croate.
- Document 01: "Insulation work on industrial plant – Ancillary work-calculation", F/E/It.
- Document 02: "Rules for carrying out thermal insulation work (working temperature higher than ambient temperature)", F/D/E/It/Esp/Swe.
- Document 03: "Rules for carrying out thermal insulation work (working temperature higher than ambient temperature)", F/D/E/It/Esp/Swe.
- Document 04: "Working Manual: System for measurement and recording for industrial insulation cladding", E.
- Document 05: "Problems associated with the Warranty of Specified Surface Temperatures", E.
- Document 06: "High profitability through ecologically based insulation thicknesses", E.
- Document 07: "Heat insulation of refrigerated premises and buildings – Technical clauses", E.

FESI

Federation of the European Sporting Goods Industry

Avenue de Janvier 3, 1200 Bruxelles, Belgium
Tel: +32 2/762 86 48
Fax: +32 2/771 87 46
E-mail: info@fesi-sport.org
Internet: http://www.fesi-sport.org

Pres.: K. UHL
Sec.-Gen.: A.S. BICHI

Founded: 1964
General meeting: September or November
Working languages: E
Secretariat: 2 members of staff

Sectors of activity:
- Protecting and promoting the joint interests of its members relating to all basic matters of the European market.
- Creating the conditions for supra-national co-operation of its members.
Conferences:
- Working Committees (Textile and Shoe Committee, Product Safety Committee, IPR Committee, Ski Committee, Contact with Sports Federations Committee, Supply Chain Committee)

Information available:
- Circulars, 2/month, E, M.

- Press releases are available on website, E, NM.
- The regular members' list is available on the website

FETFA

Federation of European Tile Fixers Associations

Union Européenne des Fédérations des Entreprises de Carrelage

Europäische Union der Fliesen Fachverbände

Kohlweg 18, 66123 Saarbruecken, Germany
Tel: +49 681/389 25 34
Fax: +49 681/389 46 134
E-mail: k.schaefer@bau-soar.de

Pres.: M. TOMAELLO
Sec.-Gen.: K. ZIEGLER

FETRATAB

European Federation of Tobacco Transformers

Fédération Européenne des Transformateurs de Tabac

Rue de Frémicourt 23, 75015 Paris, France
Tel: +33 1/45 66 86 43
Fax: +33 1/45 66 00 06

Pres.: Mr. CHIDICHIMO
Sec.-Gen.: M. FERAT
Working languages: E/F
Secretariat: 3 members of staff

FETSA

Federation of European Tank Storage Associations

Chaussée de Wavre 1519, 1160 Bruxelles, Belgium
Tel: +32 2/679 02 64
Fax: +32 2/672 73 55
Internet: www.fetsa.com

Pres.: Mr. KELLAWAY
Sec.-Gen.: H. STANDAAR

Founded: 1993
Working languages: E
Secretariat: 1 member of staff

Information available:
- "FETSA Flyer Brochure".

FEUGRES

European Federation for the Vitrified Clay Pipe Industry

Fédération Européenne des Fabricants de Tuyaux en Grès

Europäische Vereinigung der Steinzeugröhrenindustrie

Rue des Colonies 18-24, 1000 Bruxelles, Belgium
Tel: +32 2/511 30 12
Fax: +32 2/511 51 74
E-mail: sec@cerameunie.net

Pres.: R. SPOTTI
Sec.-Gen.: R. CHORUS
Working languages: E/F/D
Secretariat: 5 members of staff

FEUPF

European Federation of Professional Florists' Associations

Fédération Européenne des Unions Professionnelles de Fleuristes

Föderation der Europäischen Fachverbände der Floristen

Zandlaan 18, 6717 LP Ede, Netherlands
Tel: +31 318/52 75 68
Fax: +31 318/54 22 66
E-mail: info@vbw-groenplein.nl

Pres.: T. DUCHATEAU
Sec.-Gen.: A. ZWITSERLOOD

Founded: 1958
Working languages: E/D/F
Secretariat: 4 members of staff

Information available:
- Database: economic data.
- List of members available to the general public, free.

FEVE

Fédération Européenne du Verre d'Emballage

European Container Glass Federation

Europäischer Behälterglasindustrie-Verband

Avenue Louise 89, Bte 4, 1050 Bruxelles, Belgium
Tel: +32 2/539 34 34
Fax: +32 2/539 37 52
E-mail: info@feve.org

Pres.: C. PERALES
Sec.-Gen.: A. SOMOGYI
Contact: G. ROBYNS (Assistant Secretary General)

Founded: 1977
Working languages: F/E/D
Secretariat: 5 members of staff

Information available:
- "Directory of European Glass Containers Manufacturers", /E/F, M/ NM.
- Monthly: "Feve News" – F/E/D – monthly – subscription: €170 (M-NM).
- Glass Gazette – F/E/Esp – published once a year – free, M/NM.
- List of members available to the general public.

FFI

Freight Forward International

Avenue Marcel Thiry 204, 1200 Bruxelles, Belgium
Tel: +32 2/774 96 39
Fax: +32 2/774 96 90
E-mail: ffi@eyam.be
Internet: www.freightforwardinternational.org

Pres.: K. HERMS
Contact: M.T. SCARDIGLI

Founded: 1994
Working languages: E
Secretariat: 3 members of staff

Sectors of activity:
- FreightForward International (FFI) represents the interests of 9 of the largest global freight forwarders and logistics service providers which together employ more than 358,683 people, transporting volumes in excess of 325 million tons with a turnover of over 27.5 billion euro. The grouping focuses on policies of a non-competitive nature that enables forwarders and logistics service providers to offer and perform client oriented services and on policies that enable them to diversify the range and scope of their services as integrated-service providers.

Information available:
- List of members available to the general public, free.

FIC EUROPE

Federation of the Condiment Sauce Industries, Mustard and Fruit and Vegetables prepared in Oil and Vinegar of the European Union

Fédération des Industries des Sauces Condimentaires, de la Moutarde et des Fruits et Légumes préparés à l'Huile et au Vinaigre de l'Union Européenne

Avenue de Roodebeek 30, 1030 Bruxelles, Belgium
Tel: +32 2/743 87 30
Fax: +32 2/736 81 75
E-mail: fic.europe@sia-dvi.be

Sec.-Gen.: M. COENEN

Founded: 1960
Working languages: F/E/D
Secretariat: 2 members of staff

Historical note:
- Merger of three associations: AIFLV, CIMCEE and CIMSCEE

Information available:
- List of members available to the general public, free.

FIDE

International Federation for European Law

Fédération Internationale pour le Droit Européen

Internationale Föderation für Europarecht

c/o British Institute of International and Comparative Law, Charles Clore House, 17 Russell Square, London WC1B 5JP, United Kingdom
Tel: +44 20/7862 5151
Fax: +44 20/7862 5152
E-mail: m.andenas@biicl.org
Internet: www.biicl.org

Sec.-Gen.: M. ANDENAS
Working languages: D/F/E
Secretariat: 5 members of staff

Sectors of activity:
- Study and development of EU law and institutions.

FIDE

Federation of the European Dental Industry

Fédération de l'Industrie Dentaire en Europe

Vereinigung der Europäischen Dental-Industrie

Kirchweg 2, 50858 Köln, Germany
Tel: +49 221/50 06 87 12
Fax: +49 221/50 06 87 21
E-mail: info@fide-online.org
Internet: www.fide-online.org

Pres.: Dr A. GAMBERINI
Sec.-Gen.: H. RUSSEGGER
Contacts: Dr J. EBERLEIN (Vice-Pr.), Kim Sørensen, (Vice-Pr.)

Founded: 1957
General meeting: May & November
Working languages: E

FIEC

European Construction Industry Federation

Fédération de l'Industrie Européenne de la Construction

Verband der Europäischen Bauwirtschaft

Avenue Louise 66, 1050 Bruxelles, Belgium
Tel: +32 2/514 55 35
Fax: +32 2/511 02 76
E-mail: info@fiec.org
Internet: www.fiec.org

Pres.: W. KÜCHLER
Contact: U. PAETZOLD (Dir Gen)

Founded: 1905
General meeting: June
Working languages: F/E/D

Secretariat: 9 members of staff

Sectors of activity:
- to ensure, in an appropriate manner, the promotion and defence of the specific interests of its members to all institutions, all organisations or all persons and at all levels;
- to bring together its members, on an equal basis at international level, with a view to promoting and defending the interests of the Industry within the framework of the general interest of the Industry;
- to ensure adequate representation for the European Construction Industry and promote its image;
- to be a meeting place for its members and achieve mutual benefit through the exchange of experiences and information;
- to study and deal with all international problems relating to the construction industry, in accordance with the FIEC-EIC Protocol.
- Conference.
- FIEC Congress, 17 – 20/06/2004, Prague, Czech Republic

Information available:
- "Construction Activity in Europe", annual, F/E/D.
- Annual Report, E/F/D, free.
- "For a European Infrastructure Policy", free.
- In addition, information on practically all questions related to the construction industry can be obtained on request, free.
- FIEC News, 2 x /year, E/F/D, free.
- "FIEC Environmental Charter", E/F/D, free.
- "Transeuropean Transport Networks", E, free.
- "Key Figures", E/F/D, free.
- List of members, free.

FITCE

Federation of the Telecommunications Engineers of the European Community

Fédération des Ingénieurs des Télécommunications de la Communauté Européenne

c/o AGORIA, Diamant Building, Boulevard Reyers 80, 1030 Bruxelles, Belgium
Tel: +32 2/706 7805
Fax: +32 2/706 8009
E-mail: filip.geerts@agoria.be
Internet: www.fitce.org

Pres.: Carlos González MATEOS
Sec.-Gen.: Filip GEERTS

Founded: 1961
General meeting: September
Working languages: F/E

Information available:
- Publication – quarterly: "FITCE Review":

Predominantly in English but there are also articles written in all the EU's languages – annual subscription.
- "FITCE Forum", quarterly, E/F.

FORATOM

European Atomic Forum

Forum Atomique Européen

Europäisches Atomforum

Rue Belliard 15-17, 1040 Bruxelles, Belgium
Tel: +32 2/502 45 95
Fax: +32 2/502 39 02
E-mail: foratom@foratom.org
Internet: www.foratom.org

Sec.-Gen.: Dr. P. HAUG

Founded: 1960
General meeting: June + December
Working languages: E/F/D
Secretariat: 16 members of staff

Information available:
- "FORATOM Bulletin", /8 weeks, E/F/D, free, M-NM.
- "FORATOM Yearbook", free, E, M-NM.
- "FORATOM Flash", E, free, M.
- Databases: EP members, EC members, journalists Brussels, members and various industries, miscellaneous.
- List of members available to the general public, free.

FRESHFEL

Avenue de boqueville 272 bte 4, 1200 Bruxelles, Belgium
Tel: +32 2/777 15 80
Fax: +32 2/777 15 81
E-mail: info@freshfel.org
Internet: www.freshfel.org

Pres.: Mr. P BINARD

Founded: 1959
Working languages: F/E
Secretariat: 3 members of staff

Information available:
- Monthly information bulletin for members, F/E.

FRUCOM

European Federation of the Trade in Dried Fruit, Edible Nuts, Preserved Foods, Spices, Honey and Similar Foodstuffs

Fédération Européenne du Commerce en Fruits Secs, Conserves, Epices et Miel

Europäische Vereinigung des Handels mit Trockenfrüchten, Konserven, Gewürzen und Honig und verwandten Waren

Grosse Baeckerstrasse 4, 20095
  Hamburg, Germany
Tel: +49 40/37 47 19 13
Fax: +49 40/37 47 19 26
E-mail: frucom@waren-verein.de
Internet: www.frucom.org

Pres.: Jack TAILLIE
Sec.-Gen.: Dr. Katrin LANGNER
Contact: Hanna LIEBIG

Founded: 1959
Working languages: E
Secretariat: 2 members of staff

FTA

Foreign Trade Association

Avenue de Janvier 5, 1200 Bruxelles,
  Belgium
Tel: +32 2/762 05 51
Fax: +32 2/762 75 06
E-mail: info@fta-eu.org

Pres.: Mrs. J. PELTIER
Sec.-Gen.: J. EGGERT

Founded: 1977
Working languages: F/E/D
Secretariat: 5 members of staff

Information available:
- "FTA Report", D/E/F.
- "Newsletters", 12/month, F/E/D.
- The members' list is available.

FVE

Federation of Veterinarians of Europe

Fédération Vétérinaire Européenne

Europäische Föderation der Tierärtze

Rue Defacqz 1, 1000 Bruxelles, Belgium
Tel: +32 2/533 70 20
Fax: +32 2/537 28 28
E-mail: info@fve.org
Internet: http://www.fve.org

Contact: Mrs. N. DE BRIGNE (Acting
  Executive Director)

Founded: 1953
Working languages: E/F
Secretariat: 5 members of staff

Historical note:
- September 1961: Liaison Centre for Veterinarians.
- March 1993: Federation of the Veterinarians of Europe.

Information available:
- No publications but all information concerning EU veterinary legislation, veterinary training, future or present directives, diseases (rabies, etc.) is available.
- FVE newsletter, E, free.
- List of members, free.

GAFTA

Grain and Feed Trade Association

Gafta House, Chapel Place 6, Rivington
  Street, London EC2A 3SH, United
  Kingdom
Tel: +44 20/7814 9666
Fax: +44 20/7814 8383
E-mail: post@gafta.com
Internet: http://www.gafta.com

Pres.: B. VALLUIS
Contact: Mrs. P.KIRBY JOHNSON (Dir
  Gen)

Founded: 1878
General meeting: January
Working languages: E
Secretariat: 16 members of staff

Sectors of activity:
- Provision of Standard Forms of Contracts and arbitration and mediation facilities.
- Trade policy representation and dissemination of information.
- Training.
- Assurance Scheme – quality codes of good practice (HACCP)

Information available:
- "Newsletter", bi-monthly, M.
- CD-Rom: contacts CD, M, £ 20.

GAM

European Flour Milling Association

Groupement des Associations Meunières des Pays de l'UE

Arbeitsgemeinschaft der Handelsmühlenverbände in den EG-Ländern

c/o ECCO, Avenue des Gaulois 9, 1040
  Bruxelles, Belgium
Tel: +32 2/736 53 54
Fax: +32 2/732 34 27
E-mail: gam@ecco-eu.com

Pres.: H. FRANCOIS
Sec.-Gen.: L. REVERDY

Founded: 1959
Working languages: F/E
Secretariat: 3 members of staff

Sectors of activity:
- The object of the Association is the representation and the promotion of the interests of the milling industry of the European Community at European and international level.

Information available:
- List of members available to the general public, free.

GEGR

European Gas Research Group

Groupe Européen de Recherches Gazières

Avenue Palmerston 4, 1000 Bruxelles,
  Belgium
Tel: +32 2/230 80 17
Fax: +32 2/230 67 88
E-mail: gegr@arcadis.be
Internet: www.gegr.com

Pres.: L. GOROSPE
Contact: D. PENSHBECK

GEPVP

European Association of Flat Glass Manufacturers

Groupement Européen des Producteurs de Verre Plat

Europäische Vereinigung von Flachglashersteller

Avenue Louise 89, 1050 Bruxelles,
  Belgium
Tel: +32 2/538 43 77
Fax: +32 2/537 84 69
E-mail: info@gepvp.be
Internet: www.gepvp.be

Pres.: S. CHAMBERS
Sec.-Gen.: Ms. E. BULLEN

Founded: 1978
General meeting: March
Working languages: E/F/D/It
Secretariat: 2 members of staff

Sectors of activity:
- Activities concern the promotion as well as the scientific and technical study of glass properties.

Information available:
Brochures:
- The Association's activities – F/E/D/It – free – NM.
- Natural lighting in architecture – F/E/D/It – free – NM.
- A proposal for a standard for calculating the U value – F/E/D – free – M-NM.
Report:
- €80/69: "Flat glass in buildings" – free – M-NM.
- Thermie study on advantages of using high performance insulating glass, free, M/NM.

GERA – Europe

Global Entertainment Retail Association-Europe

Office 118, Friars House, 157-168
  Blackfriars Road, London SE1 8EZ,
  United Kingdom
Tel: +44 20/7620 2770
Fax: +44 20/7928 5850
E-mail: lucy.cronin@gera-europe.org
E-mail: ruben.schellingerhout@
  gera-europe.org
Internet: www.gera-europe.org

Founded: 2000

Historical note:
- created as the European arm of the Global Entertainment Retail Alliance

Sectors of activity:
- gives one voice to its members on commercial and legislative matters affecting their business. With the advent of internet distribution of music, film and other entertainment products, retailers are on the threshold of an exciting new developments, which will create new customer expectations and new commercial relationships. The association will make known the views of its members in the debate surrounding issues such as disintermediation, competition, and consumer privacy and choice. GERA-Europe also monitors and advises its members on other policy matters such as VAT, copyright and piracy

GIRP

European Association of Pharmaceutical Wholesalers

Groupement International de la Répartition Pharmaceutique

Internationaler Verband der Europäischen Pharmazeutischen Grosshandelsverbände

Avenue de Broqueville 40, 1200 Bruxelles, Belgium
Tel: +32 2/777 99 77
Fax: +32 2/770 36 01
E-mail: girp@girp.org
Internet: http://www.girp.org

Pres.: Jeffrey HARRIS
Sec.-Gen.: Monika DERECQUE-POIS
Contact: Lisa MCGOWN (Communication Manager)

Founded: 1960
Working languages: E
Secretariat: 3 members of staff

Information available:
- List of members, free."The Vital Link: Pharmaceutical Wholesalers in Europe".
- All information and publications available on the website

GISEMES – UNESEM

Groupement International et Union Européenne des Sources d'Eaux Minérales Naturelles

Rue de la Trémoille 10, 75008 Paris, France
Tel: +33 1/47 20 31 10
Fax: +34 1/47 20 27 62
E-mail: csem@wanadoo.fr

Pres.: T. FRIIS

Sec.-Gen.: Mrs. F. DE BUTTET
Working languages: E/F

GPRMC

European Composites Industry Association

Building Diamant, Avenue Reyerslaan 80, 1030 Bruxelles, Belgium
Tel: +32 2/706 79 60
Fax: +32 2/706 79 66
E-mail: gustaaf.bos@agoria.be
Internet: www.gprmc.be

Pres.: Gerd BUREICK
Sec.-Gen.: G. BOS

Founded: 1960; 2004
Working languages: E + (D/F/It/Esp/Nl)
Secretariat: 2 members of staff

Information available:
- "UP Resin Handling Guide", in 9 languages, M.
- GPRMC presentation leaflet, M.
- List of members available to the general public, free.

HOPE

Standing Committee of the Hospitals of the European Union

Comité Permanent des Hôpitaux de l'Union Européenne

Ständiger Ausschuss der Krankenhäuser der Europäischen Union

Boulevard Auguste Reyers 207-209, 1030 Bruxelles, Belgium
Tel: +32 2/742 13 20
Fax: +32 2/742 13 25
E-mail: sg@hope.be
Internet: www.hope.be

Pres.: Gérard VINCENT
Sec.-Gen.: Pascal GAREL

Founded: 1995
General meeting: June
Working languages: F/E/D
Secretariat: 3 members of staff

Information available:
- "Hospitals Healthcare Europe", 2003/2004, The Official Hope Reference Book, Campden Publishing, London, 2003, E/F/D, M/NM.

HOTREC

Hotels, Restaurants and Cafés in Europe

Bd Anspach 111, PO Box 4, 1000 Bruxelles, Belgium
Tel: +32 2/513 63 23
Fax: +32 2/502 41 73
E-mail: main@hotrec.org
Internet: http://www.hotrec.org

Pres.: Joaquim Cabrita NETO
Sec.-Gen.: Mrs. Marguerite SEQUARIS
General meeting: Twice a year
Working languages: E
Secretariat: 5 members of staff

Sectors of activity:
- Represents hotel and restaurant keepers and cafe owners in the EU.

Information available:
- List of members available on the website

IATM

International Association of Tour Managers

397 Walworth Road, London SE17 2AW, United Kingdom
Tel: +44 20/7703 9154
Fax: +44 20/7703 0358
E-mail: iatm@iatm.co.uk
Internet: http://www.iatm.co.uk

Pres.: Pauline GREY
Contact: R. JULIAN

Founded: 1962
General meeting: January
Working languages: E
Secretariat: 3 members of staff

Sectors of activity:
- To promote and maintain the highest standards of competence, integrity and professional conduct on the part of all Tour Managers.
- To promote, protect and improve the welfare and status of Tour Managers.
- Annual General Meeting, January 2005, Buenos Aires.

Information available:
- Memorandum of Association (Statutes), Ethics and Principles, in English.
- "IATM Newsletter", E, quarterly, M.

IBC / CIBC / IMV

International Butchers' Confederation

Confédération Internationale de la Boucherie et de la Charcuterie

Internationaler Metzgermeister Verband

Rue Jacques de Lalaing 4 Bte 10, 1040 Bruxelles, Belgium
Tel: +32 2/230 38 76
Fax: +32 2/230 34 51
E-mail: info@cibc.be

Pres.: B. KAMM
Sec.-Gen.: I. JAKOBI

Founded: 1907
Working languages: E/F/D
Secretariat: 2 members of staff

Historical note:
- In 1974, the general secretariat was transferred to Switzerland but

The Directory of EU Information Sources

afterwards it was transferred again to
Brussels due to the increase in the
lobbying activities.

Information available:
- "EU-INFO", 6 times a year, F/E/D.
- List of members, free.

IBFI

**International Business Forms
    Industries-European Operations**

**Industrie Internationale des
    Formulaires-Secrétariat Européen**

Mosstrasse 2, 3073 Gumligen-Berne,
    Switzerland
Tel: +41 31/952 61 12
Fax: +41 31/952 76 83
E-mail: uwannet@swissonline.ch

Sec.-Gen.: Dr. U. WANNER

Founded: 1952
Working languages: E/F/D
Secretariat: 1 member of staff

Sectors of activity:
- Economic survey.
- Market studies.
- Technical research.

Information available:
- Membership Directory – M.
- Newsletter – M.
- Perspective Europa – M/NM.

IDACE

**Association of the Food Industries
    for Particular Nutritional Uses of
    the European Union**

**Association des Industries des
    Aliments Diététiques de l'UE**

**Verband der Diätetischen
    Lebensmittelindustrie der EG**

Rue de Rivoli 194, 75001 Paris, France
Tel: +33 1/53 45 87 87
Fax: +33 1/53 45 87 80
E-mail: info@idaco.org
Internet: www.idaco.org

Pres.: P. CAULFIELD
Contact: A. BRONNER
General meeting: June
Working languages: E/F
Secretariat: 4 members of staff

Information available:
- List of members available to the
  general public, free.

IDF/FIL

International Dairy Federation

**Fédération Internationale de
    Laiterie**

Diamant Building, Blvd Reyers 80, 1030
    Bruxelles, Belgium
Tel: +32 2/733 98 88

Fax: +32 2/733 04 13
E-mail: info@fil-idf.org
Internet: http://www.fil-idf.org

Pres.: P. JACHNIK
Sec.-Gen.: E. HOPKIN

Founded: 1903
General meeting: September or October
Working languages: E/F
Secretariat: 9 members of staff

Information available:
- "Bulletin of the IDF", annual, E.
- Database: addresses – experts in
  dairying.
- List of members available to the
  general public, free.

IEACS

**Institute for Hunting and Sporting
    Firearms**

**Institut Européen des Armes de
    Chasse et de Sport**

Instituut für Jagd-, und Sportwaffen

Secretariat:
Cap de Bos 6, F-33430 Gajac, France
Tel: +33 5/56 25 24 46
Fax: +33 5/56 25 24 49
E-mail: eldwynn@aol.com

Pres.: C. PERONI
Contact: H. HEIDEBROEK

Social Headquarters:
Agoria – Groupe V
Bd Reyers 80
B-1030 Bruxelles

Founded: 1977
General meeting: March
Working languages: F/E

Sectors of activity:
- Development of scientific research in
  the field of sporting and hunting guns.
- Relations with the European
  institutions

Information available:
- Databases: industrial statistics,
  external trade, only for members.
- List of members available to the
  general public, free.
- European Union statistics on
  production, export, import of hunting
  and sport shooting firearms, number
  of hunters and sport shooters, only for
  members

IFAP/FIPA

**International Federation of
    Agricultural Producers**

**Fédération Internationale des
    Producteurs Agricoles**

Rue Saint Lazare 60, 75009 Paris, France
Tel: +33 1/45 26 05 53
Fax: +33 1/48 74 72 12
E-mail: ifap@ifap.org
Internet: www.ifap.org

Pres.: J. WILKINSON
Contact: D. KING

Founded: 1946
Working languages: F/E
Secretariat: 10 members of staff

Information available:
- IFAP newsletters: newsletter on
  IFAP's activities and its members – F/
  E – free – M-NM.
- Monographs and seminar reports on
  agriculture in developing countries.
- IFAP documentation and information
  service receives and analyses
  currently more than 300
  international periodicals from
  member organizations FAO, OSCD,
  etc. and other sources, covering such
  subjects as: agricultural policy, trade
  issues, commodity market trends and
  statistics, rural economy and
  sociology, farming systems, co-
  operatives, rural development issues.
- It also maintains an up-to-date
  collection of directories of agricultural
  information sources. A documentalist
  handles requests from member
  organizations and headquarters staff.

IFEAT

**International Federation of
    Essential Oils and Aroma Trades**

**Fédération Internationale des
    Huiles Essentielles et du
    Commerce des Arômes**

**Internationale Föderation der
    Ätherischen Öle und des
    Aromahandels**

6 Catherine Street, London WC2B 5JJ,
    United Kingdom
Tel: +44 20/7836 2460
Fax: +44 20/7836 0580
E-mail: ifeatadministrator@fdf.org.uk
Internet: www.ifeat.org

Contact: Mrs. J. YOUNG

Founded: 1977
Working languages: E
Secretariat: 1 member of staff

Sectors of activity:
- Organisation of international
  meetings and promotion of a
  constructive dialogue, among
  producers, dealers and users of
  fragrance and flavour materials.

Information available:
- Annual report (M).
- Annual conference documents, M/
  NM, £30.
- Information is available only to
  members; however, non-members
  may attend the annual conference but
  must pay a higher entrance free than
  members.
- "IFEAT Newsletter", 2-3/year, E,
  free, M.

IFSW

International Federation of Social Workers-European Region/EU Committee

Fédération Internationale des Assistants Sociaux-Réseau Européen

Please mark the envelope: PERSONAL, c/o Local Transport Group, Department for Education and Skills, Area 20, Sanctuary Buildings, Great Smith Street, Westminster, London SW1P 3BT, United Kingdom
Tel: +44 1604/414 345
Fax: +44 20/7925 5086
E-mail: vpeur@ifsw.org
Internet: www.ifsw.org

Pres.: D. N. JONES (IFSW Eur.)
Contact: Ana RADULESCU (Hon. Sec. Eur.)
General meeting: May/June
Working languages: E/F

Sectors of activity:
- IFSW in Europe has 35 member associations with a total of 165,600 social workers – the membership is representative as it covers all corners of Europe – over the last years a number of associations of social workers from the Central and Eastern European countries have been especially welcomed as new members of the Federation.
- IFSW in Europe brings together the knowledge and skills of European social workers and represents the experiences of social workers from all over Europe. It links the member organisations together for different projects and ensures communication on issues of interest to social workers such as social policy, partnership with service users, training and qualifications, working environment and development of the profession.
- IFSW undertakes projects on specific issues in close collaboration with the European Union, Council of Europe and others. IFSW in Europe has representatives in the IFSW global Human Rights Commission and the Permanent Ethical Committee.
- IFSW Europe co-operates with other organisations in Europe. It has a long standing tradition of working closely together with the "European Association of Schools of Social Work" and the "European Region of the International Council of Social Welfare".
- IFSW European Seminar – Social Work Challenges for Social Cohesion, 23-25 May 2005, Nicosia, Cyprus. Visit us at: www.socialwork2005.org

Information available:
- "European Social Worker", M, NM.
- Information available to M and NM. List of members available to the general public, please see the website

IMACE

International Margarine Association of the Countries of Europe

Avenue de Tervuren 168 bte 12, 1150 Bruxelles, Belgium
Tel: +32 2/772 33 53
Fax: +32 2/771 47 53
E-mail: imace.ifma@imace.org
Internet: www.imace.org

Pres.: D. DALLEMAGNE
Contact: Mrs. I. HERREMAN

Founded: 1958
General meeting: May
Working languages: E
Secretariat: 4 members of staff

Information available:
- Annual congress report – E – non-members may receive a copy on request.
- The members' list is available, free of charge and through the website

IMA-EUROPE

Industrial Minerals Association – Europe

Bd S. Dupuis 233 box 124, 1070 Bruxelles, Belgium
Tel: +32 2/524 55 00
Fax: +32 2/524 45 75
E-mail: secretariat@ima-eu.org
Internet: http://www.ima-eu.org

Pres.: G. MAJEWSKI
Sec.-Gen.: Mrs. M. WYART-REMY

Founded: 1993
Working languages: E
Secretariat: 5 members of staff

Sectors of activity:
- Sustainable development.
- Health and safety.
- Environment protection.
- Product legislation.

Information available:
- Minutes of meetings, free, E, M.
- Brochure, E, M/NM.
- List of members available to the general public, free.
- "IMA-Europe, an introduction".

INEC

European Institute of the Carob Gum Industries

Institut Européen des Industries de la Gomme de Caroube

Europäische Vereinigung der Johannisbrotkrenmehl-Hersteller

Swiss Federal Inst. of Technology, ETH-Zentrum LFO, 8092 Zürich, Switzerland
Tel: +41 1/632 53 68
Fax: +41 1/632 11 56
E-mail: zdenko.puhan@ilw.argl.ethz.ch

Sec.-Gen.: Z. PUHAN

Founded: 1971
General meeting: Each year in may.
Working languages: E
Secretariat: 1 member of staff

Sectors of activity:
- To concentrate at an international level on all scientific studies concerning research, production and application of carob bean gum, carob bean flour and all derivatives of carob kernels.
- Involved in defining standards.

INTERGRAF

International Confederation for Printing and Allied Industries a.i.s.b.l.

Square Marie-Louise 18 bte 27, 1000 Bruxelles, Belgium
Tel: +32 2/230 86 46
Fax: +32 2/231 14 64
E-mail: intergraf@intergraf.org
Internet: http://www.intergraf.org

Sec.-Gen.: Beatrice KLOSE
General meeting: June
Working languages: F/E/D
Secretariat: 6 members of staff

Sectors of activity:
- INTERGRAF organises:
  1) International conferences for specialist sectors like book-binding and print finishing, and security printing;
  2) The World Print and Communication Congress, every 3 years.
- Security Printers' Conference and Exhibition, 6-8 October 2004, Granda, Spain.
- World Print and Communication Congress, 24-28 January 2005, Cape Town, South Africa

Information available:
- Annual Statistical Report "InfoSECURA Newsletter"
- "Intergraf Co-operation Catalogue"
- "BAT Notes"
- "Proceedings of Comprint 2002"
- Studies and Surveys
- List of members available on the website

IPPA

International Pectin Producers Association

PO Box 151, Hereford HR4 8YZ, United Kingdom
Tel: +44 143/283 0529
Fax: +44 143/283 0716
E-mail: executive-secretary@ippa.info
Internet: www.ippa.info

Pres.: H. J. HJORTH

Sec.-Gen.: Hans-Ulrich ENDRESS
Contact: Colin D. MAY (Executive
Secretary)

Founded: 1969
General meeting: May
Working languages: E
Secretariat: 1 member of staff

Historical note:
- A founder member of ELC

Information available:
- List of members, free from website or
by email

IPTIC / CICILS

**EEC Standing Committee of the
International Pulse Trade and
Industry Confederation**

**Comité Permanent CEE de la
Confédération Internationale du
Commerce et des Industries des
Légumes Secs**

**Ständiger EG Ausschuss der
Internationalen Könferation des
Handels und der
Trockengemüseindustrien**

Bureau 273, Bourse de Commerce, Rue
de Viarmes 2, 75040 Paris Cedex 01,
France
Tel: +33 1/42 36 84 35
Fax: +33 1/42 36 44 93
E-mail: guy.coudert@cicilsiptic.org
Internet: www.cicilsiptic.org

Contact: G. COUDERT

Founded: 1964
General meeting: July
Working languages: F/E/Esp

Information available:
- Specific information available on
written request.

IRU

**Professional Road Passenger
Transport Liaison Committee to
the EU**

**Comité de Liaison du Transport
Professionnel Routier de
Personnes auprès de l'UE**

**Verbindungsausschuß für den
gewerblichen Strassen-
Personenverkehr bei der EU**

Avenue de Tervuren 32-34 bte 37, 4th
floor, 1040 Bruxelles, Belgium
Tel: +32 2/743 25 80
Fax: +32 2/743 25 99
E-mail: brussels@iru.org
Internet: www.iru.org

Sec.-Gen.: M. MARTIN

Founded: 1958
Working languages: F/E/D
Secretariat: 9 members of staff

Sectors of activity:
- The parent organisation – the
International Road Transport Union
(head-quarters in Geneva) – regularly
organises conferences, seminars, etc.
The IRU's liaison committees – which
comprise the IRU's member
professional organisations in the EU
– primarily organise working sessions
on dossiers which are either under
preparation or before the EU's
institutions.

Information available:
- List of members from the IRU (fee
charged).

ISA / AIE / ISV

**International Sweeteners
Association**

**Association Internationale pour les
Edulcorants**

Internationaler Süssstoff Verband

Avenue des Gaulois, 9, 1040 Bruxelles,
Belgium
Tel: +32 2/736 53 54
Fax: +32 2/732 3427
E-mail: isa@ecc-eu.com
Internet: www.sweeteners.org

Pres.: Dr. Chris GROENEVELD
Sec.-Gen.: Ms Margretae SAXEGAARD

Founded: 1972
General meeting: December
Working languages: E
Secretariat: 2 members of staff

Information available:
- "Fact Sheets on low-calorie
Sweeteners", E/F/D/Esp.
- Brochures: "Sweeteners and
Diabetes"
- Proceedings of conferences.

ISOPA

**European Isocyanates and Polyol
Producers Association**

Avenue E. Van Nieuwenhuyse 4, 1160
Bruxelles 190504, Belgium
Tel: +32 2/676 74 75
Fax: +32 2/676 74 79
E-mail: mike.jeffs@isopa.org
Internet: www.isopa.org

Pres.: R. LEPPKES
Sec.-Gen.: Mike JEFFS

Founded: 1987
General meeting: April and December
Working languages: E
Secretariat: 3 members of staff

Information available:
- All information is available from our
website

IUCAB

**International Union of Commercial
Agents and Brokers**

**Union Internationale des Agents
Commerciaux et des Courtiers**

De Lairessestraat 131-135, 1075 HJ
Amsterdam, Netherlands
Tel: +31 20/470 01 77
Fax: +31 20/671 09 74
E-mail: info@iucab.nl
Internet: www.iucab.nl

Pres.: W. HINDERER
Sec.-Gen.: J.W.B. VAN TILL

Founded: 1953
General meeting: May or June
Working languages: E
Secretariat: 2 members of staff

Information available:
- General information on all problems
of interest to commercial agents,
treated by the EU.
- Agency offers.
- IUCAB Info.
- Members' list, free.

IVTIP

In Vitro Testing Industrial Platform

PO Box 9143, 3007 AC Rotterdam,
Netherlands
Tel: +31 10/482 83 06
Fax: +31 10/482 77 50
E-mail: ivtip@ivtip.org
Internet: http://www.ivtip.org

Pres.: Dr. D. EIGLER
Contact: W.P. HERMANS

Founded: 1993
General meeting: 2 a year : in different
cities : April + November
Working languages: E
Secretariat: 2 members of staff

Information available:
- List of members, names only.

IWTO

**International Wool Textile
Organisation**

Rue de l'Industrie 4, 1000 Bruxelles,
Belgium
Tel: +32 2/505 40 10
Fax: +32 2/503 47 85
E-mail: info@iwto.org
Internet: http://www.iwto.org

Pres.: Mr. VOLLSTEDT
Contact: H. KUFFNER (Gen. Man.)

Founded: 1961
General meeting: 10–14/05/2003, Buenos
Aires
Working languages: F/E
Secretariat: 2 members of staff

Sectors of activity:
- IWTO is the international body representing the interests of the world's wool-textile trade and industry. As such, its membership covers the woolgrowers, traders, primary processors, spinners and weavers of wool and allied fibres in its member-countries, for whom it provides a forum for discussion of problems of joint concern and acts as their spokesman with all those bodies and authorities towards whom a common approach is deemed necessary.

Information available:
- Annual wool industry reports – F/E – M.
- Production capacity figures – F/E – M.
- General statistics – NM – F/E.
- List of members, free.

IZA

International Zinc Association

Avenue de Tervueren 168, bte 4, 1150 Bruxelles, Belgium
Tel: +32 2/776 00 70
Fax: +32 2/776 00 89
E-mail: info@iza.com
Internet: http://www.zincworld.org

Pres.: Mr. S. WILKINSON
Contact: Mr. B. WIRTHS (Project Leader, Communications, CP)

Founded: 1990
General meeting: October
Working languages: E
Secretariat: 4 members of staff

Sectors of activity:
- International association with scientific goals.

Information available:
- "Zinc Network", E, 12/year, M.
- "Zinc Protects", annual magazine, US$ 2.50.
- List of members available to the general public, free.

LANDOWNERS / PROPRIETE RURALE

European Landowners' Organisation

Organisation Européeene de la Propriété Rurale

Europäische Grundbesitzerorganisation

Avenue Pasteur 23, 1300 Wavre, Belgium
Tel: +32 10/232 902
Fax: +32 10/232 909
E-mail: ela@skynet.be
Internet: www.ela.org

Pres.: K. GROTENFELT
Sec.-Gen.: T. DE L'ESCAILLE
Contact: L. COURBOIS

Founded: 1972
Working languages: E/F
Secretariat: 7 members of staff

LEASEUROPE

European Federation of Equipment Leasing Company Associations

Fédération Européenne des Associations des Etablissements de Crédit-Bail

Europäische Vereinigung der Verbände von Leasing-Gesellschaften

Avenue de Tervuren 267, 1150 Bruxelles, Belgium
Tel: +32 2/778 05 60
Fax: +32 2/778 05 79
E-mail: leaseurope@leaseurope.org
Internet: www.leaseurope.org

Pres.: M. VERVAET
Sec.-Gen.: M. BAERT

Founded: 1972
Working languages: E
Secretariat: 7 members of staff

Sectors of activity:
- Conferences: for details please see the website

MAILLEUROP

Committee for the Knitting Industries in the EEC

Comité des Industries de la Maille de la CEE

Rue Montoyer 24 Bte 12, 1000 Bruxelles, Belgium
Tel: +32 2/285 48 92
Fax: +32 2/230 60 54
E-mail: francesco.marchi@euratex.org

Sec.-Gen.: F. MARCHI
Working languages: F/E

MAIZ' EUROP'

Confédération Européenne des Producteurs de Maïs

Headquarters:
Chemin de Pau 21, 64121 Montardon, France
Tel: +33 5/59 12 67 00
Fax: +33 5/59 12 67 10

Pres.: C. TERRAIN

Office in Paris:
Avenue du Président Wilson 8
F-75116 Paris
Tel: +33 1/47 23 48 32
Fax: +33 1/40 70 93 44

Founded: 1934
Working languages: F/Esp/E/D
Secretariat: 150 members of staff

MARCOGAZ

Technical Association of the European Natural Gas Industry

Avenue Palmerston 4, 1000 Bruxelles, Belgium
Tel: +32 2/237 11 11
Fax: +32 2/230 44 80
E-mail: marcogaz@marcogaz.org
Internet: www.marcogaz.org

Pres.: K. HOMANN
Sec.-Gen.: D. HEC

Founded: 1968
Working languages: E
Secretariat: 2 members of staff

Historical note:
- Created in 1968, Marcogaz has developed over the years an efficient reputation with the official bodies in the European Union and other influential partners.
- Marcogaz chief mission is to serve its members as the European window for any technical issue regarding natural gas.
- As the representative organisation of the European Natural Gas Industry, it aims at monitoring and taking influence when needed on European technical regulation, standardisation and certification with respect to safety and integrity of gas systems and equipment, and rational use of energy.
- Environment, Health and Safety issues related to natural gas systems and utilisation are also of great importance for Marcogaz.

Sectors of activity:
- Gas Infrastructure.
- Gas Utilisation.
- Environment Health and Safety

Information available:
- Upon request to the Secretariat.

MARINALG

Marinalg International

Boulevard Haussmann 85, 75008 Paris, France
Tel: +33 1/42 65 41 58
Fax: +33 1/42 65 02 05
E-mail: marinalg@marinalg.org
Internet: www.marinalg.org

Pres.: J-C. ATTALE
Contact: P. KIRSCH

Founded: 1973
Working languages: E/F
Secretariat: 1 member of staff

Sectors of activity:
- Maintaining permanent contacts with EU bodies responsible for making regulatory decisions on food industry additives.

Information available:
- Leaflet, free.

- List of members available to the general public, free.

NATCOL

Natural Food Colours Association

Association de Colorants Alimentaires Naturels

Natürliche Nahrungsmittel-farbstoffvereinigung

PO Box 3255, Boycestown, Carrigaline – Co Cork, Ireland
Tel: +353 21/491 9673
Fax: +353 21/491 9673
E-mail: secretariat@natcol.org
Internet: www.natcol.org

Pres.: Mr. B. S. HENRY
Sec.-Gen.: Dr. M. O'CALLAGHAN

Founded: 1979
General meeting: May
Working languages: E
Secretariat: 2 members of staff

Sectors of activity:
- NATCOL celebrates 25 years of service to the Colours manufacturing industry in 2004. To mark this achievement, NATCOL is organising a Legislation Forum for 7 May in Rome to coincide with its AGM. The theme for the Legislation Forum is the 'Impact of Changing (Global) Legislation on Food Additives, with special emphasis on colours'. The Forum will be addressed by speakers from JECFA (FAO & WHO Joint Secretariat), Food Additives Unit DG SANCO, the EFSA Food Additive Panel and ELC. The attendees are by invitation only and will include the current and applicant NATCOL members, IACM members and some special invited guests with past associations to NATCOL.

Information available:
- Information on natural food colours. (NM).
- The Association provides, where necessary, information to the general public and consumer associations in connection with health-political and health-legal aspects on matters pertaining to colours in food and related topics.
- Circulars, monthly, E, free, M.
- List of members, free.

OCE

Orthoptistes de la CE

Bierbeekstraat 14, 3001 Heverlee, Belgium
Tel: +32 16/23 95 24
Fax: +33 16/29 18 09
E-mail: maria.vanlammeren@ ur.kuleuven.ac.be
Internet: www.euro-orthoptistes.com

Pres.: Mrs. M. VAN LAMMEREN
Contact: Mrs. M.-H. ABADIE

Founded: 1989
Working languages: E/F
Secretariat: 1 member of staff

Sectors of activity:
- To share information on developments of the orthoptic profession in member countries (by updating the professional survey).
- To communicate to the European Commission information affecting orthoptics.
- Work in progress: to establish and make recommendations to be used by member countries on methods of assessing professional competence for incoming migrants and on harmonisation of orthoptic courses.

Information available:
- "Common appraisal criteria for accepting a migrant", F/E, M.
- List of members available to the general public, free.

OEA

Organisation of European Aluminium Refiners and Remelters

Am Bonneshof 5, 40474 Düsseldorf, Germany
Tel: +49 211/45 19 33
Fax: +49 211/43 10 09
E-mail: office@oea-alurecycling.org
Internet: www.oea-alurecycling.org

Pres.: J. MORRISON
Contact: G. KIRCHNER

Founded: 1960
Working languages: D/E/F?Esp
Secretariat: 3 members of staff

Sectors of activity:
- "OEA International Aluminium Recycling Congress".

Information available:
- "Aluminium Recycling Report", CD-ROM, annual, €30, NM.
- Statistics available for members only.
- List of members available to the general public, free.

OEB / ESO

Organisation Européenne des Bateliers

Europäische Schifferorganisation

Bd Bischoffsheim 36, 1000 Bruxelles, Belgium
Tel: +32 2/217 22 08
Fax: +32 2/219 54 86
E-mail: eso.oeb@skynet.be

Pres.: J. CONINGS

Founded: 1975
Working languages: Nl/F/D
Secretariat: 2 members of staff

OEICTO

European Organisation of Tomato Industries

Organisation Européenne des Industries de la Conserve de Tomates

Europäische Organisation der Tomatenkonservenindustrie

Avenue de Roodebeek 30, 1030 Bruxelles, Belgium
Tel: +32 2/743 87 30
Fax: +32 2/736 81 75
E-mail: oeit@sia.dvi.be

Pres.: D. NOMIKOS
Sec.-Gen.: Mrs. P. KEPPENNE
General meeting: In spring & autumn.
Working languages: F
Secretariat: 2 members of staff

Information available:
- Statistics, M (NM, at OEICTO's discretion).
- Members list, free.

OEITFL

Association of European Fruit and Vegetable Processing Industries

Organisation Européenne des Industries Transformatrices de Fruits et Légumes

Europäische Organisation der Obst- und Gemüseverarbeitenden Industrie

Avenue de Roodebeek 30, 1030 Bruxelles, Belgium
Tel: +32 2/743 87 30
Fax: +32 2/736 81 75
E-mail: oeiftl@sia-dvi.be
Internet: www.oeiftl.org

Sec.-Gen.: Mrs. P. KEPPENNE

Founded: 1978
Working languages: F/E
Secretariat: 2 members of staff

Information available:
- Statistics, M (NM, at OEITFL's discretion).
- Members'list, free.

ORGALIME

Liaison Group of the European Mechanical, Electrical, Electronic and Metalworking Industries

Organisme de Liaison des Industries Métalliques Européennes

Verbindungsstelle der Europäischen Maschinenbau-, Metall Verarbeitenden und Elektroindustrie

Diamant Building, Boulevard Auguste
  Reyers 80, 1030 Bruxelles, Belgium
Tel: +32 2/706 82 35
Fax: +32 2/706 82 50
E-mail: secretariat@orgalime.org
Internet: www.orgalime.org

Pres.: Mrs. CLEMENT
Sec.-Gen.: A. HARRIS

Founded: 1954
Working languages: D/E/F/It/Esp/Nl/Swe
Secretariat: 11 members of staff

Information available:
- "ORGALIME News", 3/year, free,
  M-NM, E.
- "Annual Report", free, M-NM, E.
- A large number of publications are
  available in English, French and
  German, M-NM, on request.
- Databases: contacts, EC, EP.
- List of members available to the
  general public, free.

PGEU / GPUE

Pharmaceutical Group of the EU

Groupement Pharmaceutique de
  l'UE

Rue du Luxembourg 19-21, 1040
  Bruxelles, Belgium
Tel: +32 2/238 08 18
Fax: +32 2/238 08 19
E-mail: pharmacy@pgeu.org
Internet: http://www.pgeu.org

Pres.: P. CAPILLA
Sec.-Gen.: F. GIORGIO

Founded: 1959
General meeting: March, June,
  November
Working languages: E/F
Secretariat: 4 members of staff

Sectors of activity:
- All pharmaceutical and allied
  problems in the EU Member States.
- Regular organisation of meetings
  (executive committee, general
  assembly, working parties,...)
  reserved to the Group's members and
  observer members from other
  countries (Switzerland, Norway,
  Cyprus, Hungary, Lithuania, Poland,
  Slovak Republic, Slovenia, Czech
  Republic, Latvia, Turkey, Croatia,
  Bulgaria, Malta); no commercial
  activities.

Information available:
- Brochure: "The Community
  Pharmacist at the Heart of
  Healthcare"
- Database: economic and statistical
  data. M.
- List of members available to the
  general public, free. NM. On website.

PLASTEUROPAC

European Association of Plastics
  Packing Manufacturers

Association Européenne des
  Fabricants d'Emballages
  Plastiques

Europäische Vereinigung der
  Plastik Verpackungshersteller

Rue de Chazelles 5, 75017 Paris, France
Tel: +33 1/46 22 33 66
Fax: +33 1/46 22 02 35
Internet: http://www.packplast.org

Contact: Mrs. F. GERARDI
Working languages: F/E

PNEUROP

European Committee of
  Manufacturers of Compressors,
  Vacuum Pumps and Pneumatic
  Tools

Comité Européen des Constructeurs
  de Compresseurs, Pompes à Vide et
  Outils à Air Comprimé

Europäisches Komitee der
  Hersteller von Kompressoren,
  Vakuumpumpen und
  Druckluftwerkzeugen

Diamant Building, Boulevard A. Reyers
  80, 1030 Bruxelles, Belgium
Tel: +32 2/706 82 30
Fax: +32 2/706 82 50
E-mail: guy.vandoorslaer@orgalime.org
Internet: www.pneurop.org

Pres.: P. SEROCZYNSKI
Sec.-Gen.: G. VAN DOORSLAER

Founded: 1960
Working languages: E
Secretariat: 2 members of staff

POSTEUROP

Association of European Public
  Postal Operators

Association des Opérateurs Postaux
  Publics Européens

Vereinigung der Öffentlichen
  Europäischen Postdienstbetreiber

44 avenue du Bourget, 1130 Bruxelles,
  Belgium
Tel: +32 2/724 72 80
Fax: +32 2/726 30 08
E-mail: posteurop@posteurop.org
Internet: http://www.posteurop.org

Pres.: Mr. J. DEMPSEY
Sec.-Gen.: Mr Marc POUW

Founded: 1993
General meeting: February 2004,
  September 2004
Working languages: F/E
Secretariat: 8 members of staff

Sectors of activity:
- The Association organises seminars
  and workshops on technical
  assistance for the Central and
  Eastern Countries (in Poland and
  Brussels), open to all PostEurop
  members and to a few non-members
  concerned by postal issues.

Information available:
- "Customer Newsletter", M/NM.
- Member Information Bulletin, every
  two months, F/E, free, M/NM.
- List of members available to the
  general public, free. M/NM.List of
  members available to the general
  public on the website.

POULTRY AND GAME /
VOLAILLE ET GIBIER

Confédération des Détaillants en
  Volaille et Gibier des Pays de la
  CEE

Rue Melsens, 28, 1000 Bruxelles,
  Belgium
Tel: +32 2/512 09 47
Fax: +32 2/512 03 74

Pres.: P. VAN GAEVER
Sec.-Gen.: Mr. VAN DER CRONE
Working languages: F
Secretariat: 2 members of staff

PPTA EUROPE

Plasma Protein Therapeutics
  Association Europe

Boulevard Brand Whitlock 114/5, 1200
  Bruxelles, Belgium
Tel: +32 2/705 58 11
Fax: +32 2/705 58 20
E-mail: pptaeu@pptaglobal.org
Internet: www.plasmatherapeutics.org

Pres.: C. WALLER

Founded: 1994
General meeting: September/October
Working languages: E
Secretariat: 9 members of staff

Historical note:
- The PPTA Europe is a non-profit
  trade association. It represents ten
  leading manufacturers of plasma-
  derived pharmaceutical products in
  Europe. Between them, the
  companies represented by this
  association meet more than 60 % of
  Europe's need for plasma based
  pharmaceuticals.

Sectors of activity:
- "IPDC International Plasma
  Derivatives Congress", 2003.

Information available:
- "The Source", monthly magazine,
  free, E, M.
- "Leadership Briefing", weekly, free,
  E, M

- PlasmaFax, M, free: PlasmaFax is a new way of identifying and receiving Plasma Products Industry documents. PlasmaFax is an around-the-clock service providing EAPPI Members with the ability to request documents to be faxed to them immediately, M.
- Bi-annual Report, NM.
- Database: documents system + directory, NM.
- List of members available to the general public, NM.

PRE

European Refractories Producers' Federation

Fédération Européenne des Fabricants de Produits Réfractaires

Europäische Industrieverband der Feuerfestkeramik

c/o Cerame-Unie, Rue des Colonies 18-24 bte 17, 1000 Bruxelles, Belgium
Tel: +32 2/511 30 12
Tel: +32 2/511 70 25
Fax: +32 2/511 51 74
E-mail: sec@cerameunie.net

Sec.-Gen.: R. CHORUS
Working languages: F/E/D
Secretariat: 5 members of staff

Information available:
- A glossary of technical terms – F/E/D/ It – €15
- A directory of products – D/E/F.

REHVA

Federation of European Heating and Airconditioning Associations

Fédération des Associations Européennes de Chauffage et Conditionnement d'Air

c/o SRBII, Rue Ravenstein 3, 1000 Bruxelles, Belgium
Tel: +32 2/514 11 71
Fax: +32 2/512 90 62
E-mail: rehva@srbii.be
Internet: www.rehva.com

Founded: 1963
Working languages: E
Secretariat: 1 member of staff

Sectors of activity:
- Heating and airconditioning.

Information available:
- "REHVA Journal", quarterly, free of charge, E.
- Database: list of members and delegates.
- The members' list is available to the public against administrative expenses.

RIAE

Recording Media Industry Association of Europe

Rue Notre Dame 42, 2951 Luxembourg, Luxembourg
Tel: +32 2/285 46 16
Fax: +32 2/280 39 36

Pres.: Dr. J. EICHER
Contact: Mrs. I. TONDEUR (Secr)
General meeting: 4–5 times a year
Working languages: E
Secretariat: 4 members of staff

Sectors of activity:
- Copyright legislation at EU and national level.
- Environmental legislation (packaging).

Information available:
- Databases: members, contacts.
- The members' list is available.

RICS EUROPE

European Society of Chartered Surveyors

Société Européenne Chartered Surveyors

Avenue de Cortenbergh 52, 1000 Bruxelles, Belgium
Tel: +32 2/733 10 19
Fax: +32 2/742 97 48
E-mail: ricseurope@rics.org
Internet: www.rics.org/europe

Contacts: Chris GRZESIK (Chairman), Catarina BOTELHO (RICS Europe Assistant)

Founded: 1993
General meeting: September or October
Working languages: E/F/Esp/Nl/Port/It/D
Secretariat: 9 members of staff

Sectors of activity:
- to promote the RICS qualifications worldwide by giving its members the highest standards of professionalism, skills and knowledge;
- to act in the public interest by monitoring and maintaining the quality and integrity of its members; and
- to influence policy makers by providing high profile research on the quality of the built and natural environments, with a committment to sustainability and by providing impartial, authoritative advice on major issues of global importance to communities, businesses and governments worldwide.

Information available:
- "European Alert", monthly, free, E, M-NM.
- "RICS Europe Brochure", free, M-NM.
- "Explore the Opportunities", free, M-NM.

- "RICS Business", free, M.
- Database: List of members

SCEPEA

Standing Committee of European Port Employers' Associations

Comité Permanent des Entreprises de Manutention dans les Ports Européens

Am Sandtorkai 2, 20457 Hamburg, Germany
Tel: +49 40/366 203
Fax: +49 40/366 377
E-mail: info@zds-seehaefen.de
E-mail: uta.ordemann@zds-seehaefen.de
Internet: www.zds-seehaefen.de

Contact: Mrs. U. ORDEMANN

SCOPE

Standing Committee of Police in Europe

Comité Permanent de la Police en Europe

Standiger Ausschuss der Polizei in Europa

Rue Leys 34, 1000 Bruxelles, Belgium
Tel: +32 2/736 80 29
Fax: +32 2/733 78 62
E-mail: scofpol@hotmail.com

Sec.-Gen.: P. WHITE

Founded: 1993
General meeting: No annual general meeting. Full committee meets in February and September annually.
Working languages: E

Sectors of activity:
- Policy and technical advice to European Commission.
- Scientific advice on, and development of, European norms for personal body protection against firearms and knife attack.

Information available:
- List of members available to the general public, on request, free.

SEFA

European Association of Steel Drum Manufacturers

Syndicat Européen de l'Industrie des Fûts en Acier

Verband der Europäischen Stahlfassindustrie

c/o Agoria, Diamant Building, Bd A. Reyers 80, 1030 Bruxelles, Belgium
Tel: +32 2/706 79 63
Fax: +32 2/706 79 66
E-mail: sefa@agoria.be
Internet: http://www.sefa.be

Pres.: F. DE MIGUEL
Sec.-Gen.: H. DEJONGHE

Founded: 1953
General meeting: May–June
Working languages: E
Secretariat: 1 member of staff

Sectors of activity:
- Promotion of drums worldwide through ICDM membership – website: www.icdm.org.

SEFEL

European Secretariat of Manufacturers of Light Metal Packaging

Secrétariat Européen des Fabricants d'Emballages Métalliques Légers

Europäisches Sekretariat der Hersteller von Leichten Metallverpackungen

Diamant Building, Boulevard Reyers 80, 1030 Bruxelles, Belgium
Tel: +32 2/706 79 58
Tel: +32 2/706 78 00 (switchboard)
Fax: +32 2/706 79 66
E-mail: sefel@agoria.be

Sec.-Gen.: P. DIEDERICH

Founded: 1959
Working languages: E

Information available:
- "Directory of European Light Metal Packaging Manufacturers", €85, E/F/D.
- Statistics on the light metal packaging industry, €60.
- A series of SEFEL recommendations.

SITS

Syndicat général des Industries de matériels et procédés pour les Traitements de Surfaces

Rue Louis Blanc 39/41, 92038 Paris La Défense Cedex, France
Tel: +33 1/47 17 63 73
Fax: +33 1/47 17 63 74
E-mail: info@sits.fr
Internet: http://www.sits.fr

Pres.: J. GALAND
Contact: Mrs F. LECLERC

Founded: 1963
General meeting: September
Working languages: E/F
Secretariat: 2 members of staff

Information available:
- "La Lettre du SITS", F.
- Database: manufacturers of surface treatment materials and processes.
- List of members.
- Library, M-NM.
- On Internet: keywords about surface treatment (linked to suppliers).

TBE

European Federation of Brick and Tile Manufacturers

Fédération Européenne des Fabricants de Tuiles et de Briques

Europäischer Verband der Mauerziegel- und Dachziegelhersteller

Rue des Colonies 18-24 Bte 17, 1000 Bruxelles, Belgium
Tel: +32 2/511 3012
Fax: +32 2/511 5174
E-mail: sec@ceramieunie.net
Internet: www.ceramieunie.net

Pres.: C. DAMEN
Sec.-Gen.: W.P. WELLER
Contact: R. CHORUS

Founded: 1952
Working languages: E/F/D/It
Secretariat: 5 members of staff

Information available:
- Database: Statistics.
- List of members available to the general public, free.

TEGOVA

The European Group of Valuers' Associations

3 Cadogan Gate, London SW1X OAS, United Kingdom
Tel: +44 20/7334 3728
Fax: +44 20/7695 1527
E-mail: rlowe@rics.org.uk
Internet: www.tegova.org

Pres.: D. FRANCOIS
Sec.-Gen.: P. CHAMPNESS
Contact: Ms. R. LOWE

Founded: 1977
General meeting: March
Working languages: E
Secretariat: 1 member of staff

Information available:
- The members' list is available, free of charge.
- "Approved European Property Valuation Standards".

TIE

Toy Industries of Europe

Rue des Deux Eglises 58, 1000 Bruxelles, Belgium
Tel: +32 2/227 53 01
Fax: +32 2/250 00 19
E-mail: tie@tietoy.org
Internet: http://www.tietoy.org

Pres.: A. MUNN
Contact: C. LESTER (SG)

Founded: 1997
Working languages: E/F/Nl/D/Esp
Secretariat: 4 members of staff

Historical note:
- The TME (Toy Manufacturers of Europe) and the FEJ (European Federation of Toy Industries) have decided to join forces and to form a single representative organisation to be known as TIE (Toy Industries of Europe).

Information available:
- "Toy Industry News", M-NM, free, E.
- "The Value of Toys and Play", M/NM, free, E/It.
- "The Toy Industry in Europe – Facts & Figures", M/NM, free, E.
- "Children and Advertising in Scandinavia", M/NM, free, E
- "Advertising Children and Adolescents", M/NM, free, E.

TII

European Association for the Transfer of Technologies, Innovation and Industrial Information

Association Européenne pour le Transfert des Technologies, de l'Innovation et de l'Information Industrielle

Europäische Vereinigung für den Transfer von Technologien, Innovation und Industrieller Information

Rue Aldringen 3, 1118 Luxembourg, Luxembourg
Tel: +352/46 30 35
Fax: +352/46 21 85
E-mail: tii@tii.org
Internet: http://www.tii.org

Pres.: G. OLLIVERE
Sec.-Gen.: Ms. C. ROBINSON

Founded: 1984
Working languages: E/F
Secretariat: 3 members of staff

Information available:
- "TII FOCUS", three times per year, M – free, NM – €100, E/F.
- Database: 2000 addresses from innovation support organisations.
- TII Members' Address Book, annual, E, free to members and €50 to non members.

TRANSBEUROP

European Federation of Butter and its Constituents Processing Industries

Fédération Européenne des Entreprises de Transformation du Beurre et de ses Composants

Europäischer Verband der Butter und dessen Bestandteile Verarbeitenden Unternehmen

Avenue Livingstone 26 box 5, 1000 Bruxelles, Belgium

Tel: +32 2/230 44 48
Fax: +32 2/230 40 44
E-mail: dairy.trade@eucolait.be
Internet: www.transbeurop.org

Pres.: L. MOLEWIJK
Sec.-Gen.: Mrs. A. GEHRING

Founded: 1982
Working languages: F/E/D
Secretariat: 4 members of staff

Information available:
- Information papers, M.
- Quick information service by fax, M.

TUTB/BTS

European Trade Union Technical Bureau for Health and Safety

Boulevard du Roi Albert II, 5, bte 5, 1210 Bruxelles, Belgium
Tel: +32 2/224 05 60
Fax: +32 2/224 05 61
E-mail: tutb@etuc.org
Internet: http://www.etuc.org/tutb

Contact: M. SAPIR (Dir)

Sectors of activity:
- provides expertise to the European Trade Union Confederation and the European Industry Federations on matters related to the working environment;
- co-ordinates trade union participation in European standardisation work;
- follows European policies on the assessment, classification and use of dangerous substances;
- supports trade unions in their dealings with European Works Councils;
- carries out studies and research, provides training and is building up a health and safety at work information system.

Information available:
- "TUTB – A European trade union initiative", free.
- "TUTB Newsletter", 3 issues a year, subscription, free.

UAE

European Lawyers' Union
Union des Avocats Européens
Europäischer Anwaltsverein

Grand-Rue 31 – 2nd floor, 2012 Luxembourg, Luxembourg
Tel: +352/46 73 46
Fax: +352/46 73 48
E-mail: jlemmer@pt.lu
Internet: www.uae.lu

Pres.: G. ABITBOL
Sec.-Gen.: J. LEMMER

UCBD

European Hardwood Federation
Union pour le Commerce des Bois Durs dans l'UE

Galerie du Centre – Bloc I – 5è étage, Rue des Fripiers 15/17, 1000 Bruxelles, Belgium
Tel: +32 2/219 43 73
Fax: +32 2/229 32 67
E-mail: ucbd@boisimport.be
Internet: www.boisimport.be

Pres.: Mats G. BÅÅTH
Sec.-Gen.: Mr. G. DAELMANS

UCTE

Union for the Coordination of Transmission of Electricity
Union pour la Coordination du Transport de l'Electricité
Union für die Koordinierung des Transportes elektrischer Energie

Boulevard Saint-Michel 15, 1040 Bruxelles, Belgium
Tel: +32 2/741 69 40
Fax: +32 2/741 69 49
E-mail: info@ucte.org
Internet: www.ucte.org

Pres.: M. FUCHS
Sec.-Gen.: M. BIAL

Founded: 1951
General meeting: May
Working languages: E
Secretariat: 8 members of staff

Sectors of activity:
- High-quality electricity at low cost.
- Conserving the environment.
- European integration.
- Future.

UEA

European Furniture Manufacturers Federation
Union Européenne de l'Ameublement
Verband der Europäischen Möbelindustrie

Chaussée de Haecht 35, 1210 Bruxelles, Belgium
Tel: +32 2/218 18 89
Fax: +32 2/219 27 01
E-mail: secretariat@uea.be
Internet: http://www.ueanet.com

Pres.: Calixto VALENTI
Sec.-Gen.: Bart DE TURCK

Founded: 1952
Working languages: F/E/D
Secretariat: 3 members of staff

Information available:
- "UEA Newsletter", bimonthly, E.
- "Statistics", annual, 100 EUR, E, M-NM.

UEAPME

European Association of Craft, Small and Medium-Sized Enterprises
Union Européenne de l'Artisanat et des Petites et Moyennes Entreprises
Europäische Union des Handwerks und der Klein- und Mittelbetriebe

Rue Jacques de Lalaing 4, 1040 Bruxelles, Belgium
Tel: +32 2/230 75 99
Fax: +32 2/230 78 61
E-mail: ueapme@euronet.be
Internet: http://www.ueapme.com

Pres.: Paul RECKINGER
Sec.-Gen.: H.-W. MÜLLER

Founded: 1979
Working languages: F/E/D/It
Secretariat: 22 members of staff

Historical note:
- Merged with EUROPMI

Sectors of activity:
- Everything concerning the interests of small and medium sized enterprises.

Information available:
- Circulars, 160/year, E/D/F/It, M-NM.
- The members' list is available, free of charge.

UEAtc

European Union of Agrement
Union Européenne pour l'Agrément Technique dans la Construction
Europäische Union für das Agrement im Bauwesen

PO Box 195, Bucknalls Lane, Garston, Watford WD25 9BA, United Kingdom
Tel: +44 1923/665 300
Fax: +44 1923/665 301
E-mail: mail@ueatc.com
Internet: www.ueatc.com

Pres.: A. MAUGARD
Sec.-Gen.: J. BLAISDALE

Founded: 1960
Working languages: D/E/F
Secretariat: 2 members of staff

Sectors of activity:
- Establishing technical reference documents for assessments (guides, technical reports).
- Promoting mutual recognition of national technical agreements.

Information available:
- "UEAtc Information", bi-annual, free of charge, D/E/F.
- "UEAtc Technical Guide", E/F.
- The members' list is available, free of charge.

UEC

Union Européenne de la Carrosserie

Bd de la Woluwe 46, 1200 Bruxelles,
 Belgium
Tel: +32 2/778 62 00
Fax: +32 2/778 62 22
E-mail: mail@federauto.be
Internet: http://www.federauto.be

Pres.: Mr. BLYWEERT
Contact: Mrs. H. VANDER STICHELE
Working languages: F/E/D/Nl
Secretariat: 5 members of staff

UECBV

**European Livestock and Meat
Trading Union**

**Union Européenne du Commerce du
Bétail et de la Viande**

**Europäische Vieh- und
Fleischhandelsunion**

Rue de la Loi 81A bte 9, 4ème étage, 1040
 Bruxelles, Belgium
Tel: +32 2/230 46 03
Fax: +32 2/230 94 00
E-mail: uecbv@pophost.eunet.be
Internet: http://uecbv.eunet.be

Pres.: L. SPANGHERO
Sec.-Gen.: J.L. MERIAUX

Founded: 1952
General meeting: April
Working languages: F/E/D
Secretariat: 6 members of staff

Information available:
- Brochure giving details of EU
  importers of cattle and meat, F/E,
  NM.
- List of members, free.

UEEIV

**Union of European Railway
Engineer Associations**

**Union des Associations Européennes
des Ingénieurs Ferroviaires**

**Union Europäischer Eisenbahn-
Ingenieur-Verbände**

Kaiserstrasse 61, 60329 Frankfurt am
 Main, Germany
Tel: +49 69/25 93 29
Fax: +49 69/25 92 20
E-mail: ueeiv@t-online.de
Internet: www.ueeiv.com

Pres.: Mr. SALZMANN
Contact: Mr. BRINKMANN
Working languages: D/E/F
Secretariat: 2 members of staff

Sectors of activity:
- Objectives of the Union:
  – high level of efficiency and of
  competitive strength of European
  railways;

– equal opportunities for railways in
comparison with other modes of
transport, equal governmental
outline conditions for European
railways, and in particular financial
responsibility of national
administrations for track
infrastructure;
– modern pan-European rail
infrastructure for high-performance
and high-speed lines.
- In its capacity as the EURAIL
FORUM, UEEIV is the lobby for all
European railways. First and
foremost, it supports the following
aims:
– EU Directive 91/440 must be
implemented for all railways in every
European country;
– government aid must be made
available for modernising the
railways;
– the railways must be offered the
same competitive conditions and tax
benefits as other transport operators.
This must also apply to infrastructure
charges in particular without any
restrictions;
– all transport operators must bear
the full burden of responsibility for
any environmental and other
external costs entailed by them,
including those resulting from an
accident. When it comes to price
formation, equal conditions must
apply.

Information available:
- Official Congress Documentation, D/
  E/F.
- Database: addresses.
- The members' list is available, free of
  charge.

UEIL

**European Union of Independent
Lubricant Manufacturers**

**Union Européenne des
Indépendants en Lubrifiants**

Rue Montesquieu 8, 75001 Paris, France
Tel: +33 1/42 44 26 20
Fax: +33 1/42 44 26 21
E-mail: ueil.paris@libertysurf.fr
Internet: www.ueil.org

Pres.: M. PEDENAUD
Sec.-Gen.: Mrs. BOURIENNE BAU-
TISTA

Founded: 1963
General meeting: October
Working languages: F/E
Secretariat: 3 members of staff

Information available:
- List of members available on website,
  free.

UEITP

**European Association of Potato
Processing Industry**

**Union Européenne des Industries de
Transformation de la Pomme de
Terre**

**Europäische Vereinigung der
Kartoffel Verarbeitenden
Industrie**

Von-der-Heydt-Strasse 9, 53177 Bonn,
 Germany
Tel: +49 228/932 91 11
Fax: +49 228/932 91 20
E-mail: demarriz@bogk.org

Sec.-Gen.: E. DEMARRIZ

UEMO

**European Union of General
Practitioners**

**Union Européenne des Médecins
Omnipraticiens**

**Europäische Vereinigung der
Omnipraktizierenden Ärzte**

PO Box 5610, Villagatan 5, 11486
 Stockholm, Sweden
Tel: +46 8/790 34 52
Fax: +46 8/20 57 18
E-mail: info@uemo.org
Internet: www.uemo.org

Pres.: C. FABIAN
Sec.-Gen.: C.-E. THORS
Working languages: E/F/D/Esp/It
Secretariat: 3 members of staff

Information available:
- A guide to the registration
  requirements for doctors of the
  European Union and information
  concerning access to medical practice
  in the social security systems.
- The position of the general medical
  practitioner in general practice in the
  health care system of the European
  Union.
- "UEMO criteria for General
  Practitioner Trainers".

UEMS

**European Union of Medical
Specialists**

**Union Européenne des Médecins
Spécialistes**

**Europäische Vereinigung der
Fachärzte**

Avenue de la Couronne 20, 1050
 Bruxelles, Belgium
Tel: +32 2/649 51 64
Fax: +32 2/640 37 30
E-mail: uems@skynet.be
Internet: www.uems.be

Pres.: H. HALILA

Founded: 1958
General meeting: October
Working languages: F/E
Secretariat: 3 members of staff

Information available:
- Database: specialised medical training.

UEMV

European Glaziers Association

Union Européenne des Miroitiers Vitriers

Europäischer Dachverband des Gläserhandwerks

PO Box 8049, 1180 LA Almstelveen, Netherlands
Tel: +31 20/45 32 655
Fax: +31 20/64 05 111
E-mail: info@uemv.com
Internet: http://www.uemv.com

Pres.: P. HUSMER
Contact: P.H.K. DE RIDDER

Founded: 1967
General meeting: Several dates and places a year
Working languages: D/E/F
Secretariat: 2 members of staff

UEPA

European Union of Alcohol Producers

Union Européenne des Producteurs d'Alcool

Europäische Union der Alkoholhersteller

Rue des Nerviens 65, 1040 Bruxelles, Belgium
Tel: +32 2/772 98 30
Fax: +32 2/772 98 24
E-mail: uepa@skynet.be

Pres.: A. DREUILLET
Sec.-Gen.: Ms. V. CORRE

Founded: 1993
General meeting: October
Working languages: E
Secretariat: 2 members of staff

Sectors of activity:
- The Association brings together producers of alcohol solely of agricultural origin.

Information available:
- Quarterly review, free, all EU languages.

UEPC

European Union of Developers and House Builders

Union Européenne des Promoteurs-Constructeurs

Europäische Union der Freien Wohnungsunternehmen

Rue de la Violette 43, 1000 Bruxelles, Belgium
Tel: +32 2/511 25 26
Fax: +32 2/219 71 99
E-mail: info@uepc.org
Internet: http://www.uepc.org

Pres.: G. PAVAN
Contact: L. WILLE (CRIVI BVBA) (Admin. Del.)

Founded: 1958
Working languages: D/E/F
Secretariat: 3 members of staff

Information available:
- "The legal position of the beneficiaries of a building permit".
- "A comparative study of property tax in Europe".
- List of members available to the general public, free.

UEPG

European Aggregates Association

Union Européenne des Producteurs de Granulats

Europäischer Verband der Kies-, Sand- und Schotterproduzenten

Travesia de Tellez 4, 28007 Madrid, Spain
Tel: +34 91/502 14 17
Fax: +34 91/433 91 55
E-mail: anefa@aridos.org
E-mail: rfernandezaller@aridos.org
Internet: www.uepg.org

Pres.: C. GOMEZ-CARRION
Sec.-Gen.: R. FERNANDEZ-ALLER

UEPS

European Union of the Social Pharmacies

Union Européenne des Pharmacies Sociales

Verband der Europäischen Sozialen Apotheken

Route de Lennik 900, 1070 Bruxelles, Belgium
Tel: +32 2/529 92 40
Fax: +32 2/529 93 76
E-mail: ueps@multipharma.be
E-mail: eusp@multipharma.be
Internet: www.eurosocialpharma.org

Pres.: W. JANSSENS
Sec.-Gen.: M.-H. CORNELY

Founded: 1961
Working languages: F/E/D/It/Nl
Secretariat: 2 members of staff

Sectors of activity:
- Distribution and dispensation of pharmaceuticals.

Information available:
- Presentation brochure.
- Annual report.
- "Flash", free, monthly, F/E/D/It.
- The members' list is available, free of charge.

UFE

Union of Potato Starch Factories of the European Union

Union des Féculeries de Pommes de Terre de l'Union Européenne

Vereinigung der Kartoffelstärken Betriebe der Europäischen Union

Rue d'Arlon 82, 1040 Bruxelles, Belgium
Tel: +32 2/282 46 77
Fax: +32 2/282 46 93
E-mail: ufe.brussels@worldonline.be

Pres.: P. KRIJNE
Sec.-Gen.: C. VISSER
General meeting: October
Working languages: E
Secretariat: 1 member of staff

UFEMAT

European Association of National Builders Merchants' Associations

Union Européenne des Fédérations Nationales des Négociants en Matériaux de Construction

Europäische Vereinigung der Nationalen Baustoffhändler-Verbände

A. De Deckerstraat 20, 1731 Zellik, Belgium
Tel: +32 2/466 24 83
Fax: +32 2/463 26 46
E-mail: info@batirencontre.be
Internet: http://www.fema.be

Pres.: Dr. L. HELBICH-POSCHACHER
Contact: C. LEUS

Founded: 1959
Working languages: F/E/D
Secretariat: 2 members of staff

Information available:
- The members' list is available to the general public, free of charge.

UGAL

Union of Groups of Independent Retailers of Europe

Union des Groupements de Détaillants Indépendants de l'Europe aisbl

Union der Verbundgruppen selbständiger Einzelhändler Europas

Avenue des Gaulois 3 bte 3, 1040 Bruxelles, Belgium
Tel: +32 2/732 46 60

Fax: +32 2/735 86 23
E-mail: info@ugal.org
Internet: www.ugal.org

Pres.: M. KARELSE
Sec.-Gen.: M. LABATUT

Founded: 1963
Working languages: F/D/E
Secretariat: 3 members of staff

Information available:
- Report on activities, yearly, F/D/E, M-NM.
- Technical information newsletters, M, F/D/E.

UITP – EuroTeam

International Association of Public Transport – EuroTeam

Union Internationale des Transports Publics

Internationaler Verband für Öffentliches Verkehrswesen

Rue Sainte Marie 6, 1080 Bruxelles, Belgium
Tel: +32 2/673 61 00
Fax: +32 2/660 10 72
E-mail: hans.rat@uitp.com
Internet: http://www.uitp.com

Sec.-Gen.: H. RAT

Founded: 1865
General meeting: 3 times a year
Working languages: F/E/D
Secretariat: 12 members of staff

Sectors of activity:
- Urban and regional public transport.

Information available:
- "EU Express", 12 a year, free, F/E/D, M-NM.
- "A report on the availability of EU funds for UITP members", E.
- Databases: list of members, of journalists, of people receiving publications.
- List of members available to the general public, free.

UNESDA – CISDA

Union of EU Soft Drinks Associations – Confederation of International Soft Drinks Associations

Blvd Saint Michel 79, 1040 Bruxelles, Belgium
Tel: +32 2/743 40 50
Fax: +32 2/732 51 02
E-mail: mail@unesda-cisda.org
Internet: http://www.unesda-cisda.org

Sec.-Gen.: A. BEAUMONT

Founded: 1959
Working languages: F/E/D
Secretariat: 4 members of staff

Information available:
- Database: European consumption / production statistics available on the website: www.unesda-cisda.org

UNICE

Union of Industrial and Employers' Confederations of Europe

Union des Confédérations de l'Industrie et des Employeurs d'Europe

Avenue de Cortenbergh, 168, 1000 Bruxelles, Belgium
Tel: +32 2/237 65 11
Fax: +32 2/231 14 45
E-mail: main@unice.be
Internet: www.unice.org

Pres.: Dr. Jürgen STRUBE
Sec.-Gen.: Philippe DE BUCK
Contacts: Maria Fernanda FAU (Director of Communications), Mr Peter KETTLEWELL (Documentalist)

Founded: 1958
General meeting: June
Working languages: E/F
Secretariat: 45 members of staff

Sectors of activity:
- UNICE was set up in 1958 and is recognised as the business world's official spokesman vis-à-vis the EU institutions. It is also the private-sector representative in the European Social Dialogue.

Information available:
- Monthly bulletin on UNICE activities distributed by e-mail, free.
- Individual position papers and press releases, M-NM, available on request, E/F.
- List of members available on the website

UNI-EUROPA

Regional European Organisation of Union Network International

Organisation Régionale Européenne d'Union Network International

Europäische Regionalorganisation von Union Network International

Rue de l'Hôpital 31, UNI (World in Nyon)
Avenue Reverdil 8-10
CH-1260 Nyon, 1000 Bruxelles, Belgium
Tel: +32 2/234 56 56
Fax: +32 2/235 08 70
E-mail: uni-europa@union-network.org
Internet: http://www.uni-europa.org

Pres.: Frank BSIRSKE
Sec.-Gen.: Philip JENNINGS
Contact: Mrs. B. TESCH-SEGOL (Regional Secretary)

Founded: 2000
General meeting: May 2004
Working languages: F/E/D/Esp/Swe

Historical note:
- Merger of EURO-FIET – MEI – FGI/FGE – CI.

Sectors of activity:
- Supply affiliates with information.
- Exchange of information and consultation with the EU institutions.
- Social dialogue at European level.

Information available:
- "UNI Info", monthly, F/E/D/Esp/Swe.

UNIFE

Union of European Railway Industries

Union des Industries Ferroviaires Européennes

Verband der Europäischen Eisenbahnindustrien

Avenue Louise 221 bte 11, 1050 Bruxelles, Belgium
Tel: +32 2/626 12 60
Fax: +32 2/626 12 61
E-mail: mail@unife.org
Internet: http://www.unife.org

Contact: D. NIEUWENHUIS (Gen. Manag.)

Founded: 1992
Working languages: E
Secretariat: 8 members of staff

Historical note:
- Established in Brussels in 1992, absorbing the previous activities of AICMR, CELTE and AFEDEF.

Information available:
- Statistics, M.
- Database: industrial and EU market information, M.
- Newsletter, free for members, E.
- Members' list available upon request.

UNISTOCK

Union of Professional Agribulk Warehouse Keepers

Union des Stockeurs Professionnels de Céréales dans l'UE

Vereinigung der Getreidelagerbetriebe der EG

Treurenberg 6, 1000 Bruxelles, Belgium
Tel: +32 2/736 75 52
Fax: +32 2/732 31 49
E-mail: info@feport.be
Internet: www.unistock.be

Sec.-Gen.: Mrs. H. DE LEEUW

Founded: 1969
General meeting: September
Working languages: E
Secretariat: 3 members of staff

UPEI

Union of European Petroleum Independents

Union Pétrolière Européenne Indépendante

Grosse Theater Strasse 1, 20354 Hamburg, Germany
Tel: +49 40/34 08 58
Fax: +49 40/34 42 00
E-mail: afm-verband.hamburg@t-online.de
Internet: www.upei.org

Pres.: H. WEISSER
Sec.-Gen.: B. SCHNITTLER

Founded: 1960
General meeting: April
Working languages: E
Secretariat: 2 members of staff

UPFE

Union of Welfare for EC Officials

Union de Prévoyance des Fonctionnaires Européens

Rue Stévin 202, 1000 Bruxelles, Belgium
Tel: +32 2/736 98 43
Fax: +32 2/736 70 19
E-mail: upfe@wanadoo.be

Pres.: A. PRATLEY
Sec.-Gen.: H. SMETS

Founded: 1965
Working languages: F/E/D

Information available:
- "Trait d'Union", 2 a year.

USSPE

Union Syndicale – European Public Service – Brussels

Avenue des Gaulois 36, 1040 Bruxelles, Belgium
Tel: +32 2/733 98 00
Fax: +32 2/733 05 33
E-mail: web@unionsyndicale.org
Internet: www.unionsyndicale.org

Pres.: A. HICK
Sec.-Gen.: P. BLANCHARD

Founded: 1974
General meeting: May
Working languages: F
Secretariat: 3 members of staff

Information available:
- "AGORA Magazine", 4x/year.
- Website: www.unionsyndicale.org.
- Databases: members.

WEI / IEO / WEI

Western European Institute for Wood Preservation

Institut de l'Europe Occidentale pour l'Imprégnation du Bois

West-Europäisches Institut für Holzimprägnierung

Allée Hof-ter-Vleest 5 bte 4, 1070 Bruxelles, Belgium
Tel: +32 2/556 25 86
Fax: +32 2/556 25 95
E-mail: info@wei-ieo.org
Internet: http://www.wei-ieo.org

Pres.: T. KARLSSON
Sec.-Gen.: Filip DE JAEGER
Contact: Frederik LAUWAERT

Founded: 1951
General meeting: March, September
Working languages: E/F/D
Secretariat: 3 members of staff

Sectors of activity:
- The overriding objective of the WEI is to establish, maintain and constantly improve the quality standards of the European wood preserving industry and to communicate the versatility and real benefits of pressure treated timber.
- The activities of WEI are based around wood preservatives, environmental and technical issues plus the marketing of finished wood products.
- WEI:
  – Provides technical, commercial and legal advice to its members;
  – Closely follows and contributes to European and national legislation affecting the production and use of pressure treated timber;
  – Develops quality standards for wood preservatives and treated timber and is heavily involved in the work of CEN, the European Committee for Standardisation;
  – Is involved in European R&D projects;
  – Serves as a focal point for consultation within and between the European wood preservation industries;
  – Produces a bimonthly newsletter and technical documents;
  – Organises technical meetings and congresses

Information available:
- "WEI Newsletter", 6/year, free for members, E/F/D.
- Members' list available on website.
- WEI brochure, free

WFA / FMA

World Federation of Advertisers

Fédération Mondiale des Annonceurs

Avenue Louise 120 Bte 6, 1050 Bruxelles, Belgium
Tel: +32 2/502 57 40
Fax: +32 2/502 56 66
E-mail: info@wfanet.org
Internet: www.wfanet.org

Pres.: R. KREINER
Contact: B. ADRIAENSENS

Founded: 1953
Working languages: F/E
Secretariat: 5 members of staff

Information available:
- Annual Report (M – NM) (E) – free.
- The News Report (M) (E) – 4 issues/year, free.
- "Annual Business Conferences Compilation", yearly, E.
- "Go International – your guide to marketing and business development" – by Keith V. Monk – published by McGraw Hill Gmbh (Germany) and on offer at a special price to WFA members. Obtainable via WFA Headquarters, Brussels.
- "Media Buying Groups".
- "Agency Contract Guidelines".
- "Compendium of Resolutions 1953-1990".
- "The NFA/EACA Guide to the Organization of TV Audience Research".
- "The Global Guidelines on Television Audience Measurement (GGTAMM)".
- Database: advertising and advertising legislation.
- Advertising Children and Adolescents (Study).
- List of members available to the general public, free.

WINDSCREEN / VITRIERS

European Car Windscreen Association

Association Européenne des Vitriers pour l'Automobile

Fahrzeugverglasung Europa

Van Santenlaan 20 – 7, 1700 AA Heerhugowaard, Netherlands
Tel: +31 72/544 09 53
Fax: +31 72/571 44 32

Pres.: P. S. BAIN
Sec.-Gen.: P. H. K. DE RIDDER

YES

Confederation of Young Entrepreneurs for Europe

Confédération des Jeunes Entrepreneurs pour l'Europe

Junge Unternehmer für Europa

Avenue de la Joyeuse Entrée 1, 1040 Bruxelles, Belgium

Tel: +32 2/280 34 25
Fax: +32 2/280 33 17
E-mail: secretariat@yes.be
Internet: www.yes.be

Pres.: T. DE LANGE
Sec.-Gen.: M. PEZZINI

Founded: 1990
General meeting: November
Working languages: E/F
Secretariat: 2 members of staff

Sectors of activity:
- Policies for SMEs in the EU.

Information available:
- "YES Newsletter", biannual.
- "YES Dispatches", quarterly.
- "Entrepreneurial-Mail", monthly, published on website, E, M-NM.

INDEX OF KEYWORDS

EUROPEAN INTEREST GROUPS AND NON-GOVERNMENTAL ORGANIZATIONS

ACA (Academic Cooperation Association): Rue d'Egmont 15, 1000 Brussels, Belgium; tel +32 2/513 22 41; fax +32 2/513 17 76; e-mail info@aca-secretariat.be; internet www.aca-secretariat.be; President: F. Mucke, Director-General: Wachter.

ACRR (Association of Cities and Regions for Recycling): Gulledelle 100, 1200 Brussels, Belgium; tel +32 2/775 77 01; fax +32 2/775 76 35; e-mail acrr@ibgebim.be; internet www.acrr.org; President: J.-P. Hannequart, Contact: Radermaker, Contact: F. Lesceu.

AEBR / ARFE / AGEG (Association of European Border Regions): Enscheder Strasse 362, 48599 Gronau, Germany; tel +49 2562/70 219; fax +49 2562/70 259; e-mail info@aebr.net; internet www.aebr.net; Secretary-General: J. Gabbe, Contact: Perou.

AECA (American European Community Association): Avenue de Messidor 208 bte 1, 1180 Brussels, Belgium; tel +32 2/344 59 49; fax +32 2/344 53 43; e-mail aeca@aeca-europe.org; President: De Veirman, Contact: Largent.

AECC (Association for Emissions Control by Catalyst): Avenue de Tervuren 100, 1040 Brussels, Belgium; tel +32 2/743 24 90; fax +32 2/743 24 99; e-mail info@aecc.be; internet www.aecc.be; Executive Director: D. Bosteels.

AEF (European Affairs): Avenue Livingstone 33, 1040 Brussels, Belgium; tel +32 2/230 04 10; fax +32 2/230 56 01; Managing Partner: M. van den Heuvel.

AEH (European Action of the Disabled): Wurzerstrasse 4a, 53175 Bonn, Germany; tel +49 228/820 93 0; fax +49 228/820 93 43; e-mail aeh.europe@t-online.de; internet www.vdk.de/aeh; President: W. Hirrlinger, Secretary-General: U. Laschet.

AEI (Action in Europe for Education, Invention and Innovation): Rue du Champ de Mars, 27, Espace Entreprise, 57200 Sarreguemines, France; tel +33 3/87 98 75 75; fax +33 3/87 98 27 27; President: G. Herrmann.

AEIDL (European Association for Information on Local Development): Chaussée St Pierre 260, 1040 Brussels, Belgium; tel +32 2/736 49 60; fax +32 2/736 04 34; e-mail aeidl@aiedl.be; internet www.aeidl.be; President: M.-L. Semblat, Director-General: Van Dingenen.

AEM (Association Européenne des Elus de Montagne): Avenue des Arts 1, bte 9, 1210 Brussels, Belgium; tel +32 2/221 04 39; fax +32 2/217 69 87; e-mail aem@promote-aem.org; internet www.promonte-aem.org; President: L. Caveri.

AEPL (European Anglers Alliance): Rue du Parnasse 42, 1030 Brussels, Belgium; tel +32 2/732 03 09; fax +32 2/732 03 09; e-mail eaa.aepl@skynet.be; internet www.eaa-europe.org; President: H. Minekus.

AER / ARE / VRE (Assembly of European Regions): Immeuble Europe, Place des Halles 20, 67054 Strasbourg Cedex, France; tel +33 3/88 22 07 07; fax +33 3/88 75 67 19; e-mail secretariat@are-regions-europe.org; internet www.are-regions-europe.org; President: L. Prokop.

AEUSCO (European Association of Schools and Colleges of Optometry): Route de Chartres 134, 91440 Bures-sur-Yvette, France; tel +33 1/64 86 12 13; fax +33 1/69 28 49 99; e-mail ico.direction@wanadoo.fr; internet http://ubista.ubi.pt/~aeusco; President: G. Rico.

AGE (European Older People's Platform): Rue Froissart 111, 1040 Brussels, Belgium; tel +32 2/280 14 70; fax +32 2/280 15 22; e-mail info@age-platform.be; internet www.age-platform.org/EN/index.htm; President: S. Langabaek, Director: C. Marking.

ALZHEIMER EUROPA / ALZHEIMER EUROPE: Route de Thionville 145, 2611 Luxembourg, Luxembourg; tel +352/46 35 25; fax +352/47 24 04; e-mail info@alzheimer-europe.org; internet www.alzheimer-europe.org; Contact: J. Krecke.

Amnesty International (Amnesty International EU Association): Rue d'Arlon 39-41 bte 10, 1000 Brussels, Belgium; tel +32 2/502 14 99; fax +32 2/502 56 86; e-mail amnesty-eu@aieu.be; internet www.amnesty-eu.org; Contact: D. Oosting.

AMRIE (Alliance des Intérêts Maritimes Régionaux en Europe): Rue du Commerce 20-22, 1000 Brussels, Belgium; tel +32 2/736 17 55; fax +32 2/735 22 98; e-mail info@amrie.org; e-mail jmazieres@amrie.org; Director: J. Mazières.

ANPED (Northern Alliance for Sustainability): PO Box 59030, 1040 KA Amsterdam, Netherlands; tel +31 20/475 17 42; fax +31 20/475 17 43; e-mail info@anped.org; internet www.anped.org; President: P. van der Gaag, Contact: Koffen.

ARTIS GEIE (Groupement Européen des Sociétés de Gestion Collective des Droits des Artistes Interprètes ou Exécutants): Rue d'Egmont 15, 1000 Brussels, Belgium; tel +32 2/512 30 17; fax +32 2/514 43 22; e-mail artisgeie.be@skynet.be; President: L. Cobos, Secretary-General: J.-C. Walter, Director: F. Greco.

ATD (International Movement ATD Fourth World): Avenue Victor Jacobs 12, 1040 Brussels, Belgium; tel +32 2/647 99 00; fax +32 2/640 73 84; e-mail atd.europe@tiscali.be; internet www.atd-fourthworld.org; Contact: S. Kenningham.

ATEE (Association for Teacher Education in Europe): Rue de la Concorde 60, 1050 Brussels, Belgium; tel +32 2/512 75 05; fax +32 2/512 84 25; e-mail atee@euronet.be; internet www.atee.org.

Autism-Europe / Autisme-Europe: Avenue E. Van Becelaere 26B bte 21, 1170 Brussels, Belgium; tel +32 2/675 75 05; fax +32 2/675 72 70; e-mail autisme.europe@arcadis.be; internet www.autismeurope.org; President: D. Vivanti.

BEUC (The European Consumers Organisation): Avenue de Tervueren 36 bte 4, 1040 Brussels, Belgium; tel +32 2/743 15 90; fax +32 2/740 28 02; e-mail consumers@beuc.org; internet www.beuc.org; Director: J. Murray.

CAN-Europe (Climate Action Network Europe): Rue de la Charité 48, 1210 Brussels, Belgium; tel +32 2/229 52 20; fax +32 2/229 52 29; e-mail info@climnet.org; internet www.climnet.org; President: K. Schoeters.

CAPITALES (Union des Capitales de l'Union Européenne): Plaza de la Villa, 28005 Madrid, Spain; tel +34 9/15 88 14 87; fax +34 9/15 88 16 06; e-mail internacionales@munimadrid.es; Contact: F. Deleau.

CARE FOR EUROPE (Christian Action Research & Education for Europe): Rue Archimède 55-57, 1000 Brussels, Belgium; 53 Romney Street, London SW1P 3RF, United Kingdom; tel +32 2/732 11 47; tel +44 207/233 04 55; fax +32 2/732 12 28; fax +44 207/233 09 83; e-mail mail@care.org.uk; e-mail info@careforeurope.org; internet www.care.org.uk; President: C. Colchester, Secretary-General: L. Browning.

CARE INTERNATIONAL: Boulevard du Régent 58/10, 1000 Brussels, Belgium; tel +32 2/502 43 33; fax +32 2/502 82 02; e-mail info@care-international.org; internet www.care-international.org.

CARITAS EUROPA: Rue de Pascale 4, 1040 Brussels, Belgium; tel +32 2/280 02 80; fax +32 2/230 16 58; e-mail info@caritas-europa.org; President: D. Vienot, Secretary-General: M. Wonders.

CECODHAS (European Liaison Committee for Social Housing): Rue Guillaume Tell 59b, 1060 Brussels, Belgium; tel +32 2/534 60 43; fax +32 2/534 58 52; e-mail ino@cecoshas.org; internet www.cecodhas.org; President: Roumet.

CEDAG (European Council for Voluntary Organisations): Rue Guillaume Tell 59 B, 1060 Brussels, Belgium; tel +32 2/542 63 13; fax +32 2/542 63 19; e-mail cedag@wanadoo.be; President: A. David.

CEDR (European Council for Agricultural Law): Avenue de la Toison d'Or 72, 1060 Brussels, Belgium; tel +32 2/543 72 08; fax +32 2/543 73 99; e-mail marc.heyerick@vlm.be; internet www.cedr.org; President: J. Hudault, Contact: M. Heyerick.

CEJI (European Jewish Information Centre): Avenue Brugman 319, 1180 Brussels, Belgium; tel +32 2/344 34 44; fax +32 2/344 67 35; e-mail Pascale.Charhon@ceji.org; internet www.ceji.org; Director: P. Charon.

CELSIG (European Liaison Committee on Services of General Interest): Rue de Rome 66, 75008 Paris, France; tel +33 1/43 71 20 28; fax +33 1/42 94 10 37; e-mail pierre.bauby@noos.fr; President: P. Bauby, Secretary-General: J.-C. Boual.

CEMR / CCRE (Council of European Municipalities and Regions): Rue d'Arlon 22, 1050 Brussels, Belgium; tel +32 2/511 74 77; fax +32 2/511 09 49; e-mail cemr@ccre.org; internet www.ccre.org; President: V. Giscard d'Estaing, Secretary-General: J. Smith.

CENPO (Centre for European Non-Profit Organisations): Rue de la Concorde 57, 1050 Brussels, Belgium; tel +32 2/740 00 00; e-mail info@cenpo.org; internet www.cenpo.org; President: Wedjwood, Contact: Carling.

CES (Confederation of European Scouts): Rue de la Margelle 5, 1341 Ottignies, Belgium; tel +32 10/61 42 78; e-mail pierredessy@belgacom.net; internet www.ces-scouts.com; internet www.sxb.nta.fr; Contact: B. Cockburn.

CESD (Centre for European Security and Disarmament): Rue Stévin 115, 1000 Brussels, Belgium; tel +32 2/230 07 32; fax +32 2/230 24 67; e-mail cesd@cesd.org; internet www.cesd.org; President: C. Riggle.

CESE (Planning Congresses): Via S. Stefano 97, 40126 Bologna, Italy; tel +39 051/300 100; fax +39 051/309 477; e-mail m.galantino@planning.it; internet www.planning.it; President: M. Galantino.

CIDSE (International Cooperation for Development and Solidarity): Rue Stévin 16, 1000 Brussels, Belgium; tel +32 2/230 77 22; fax +32 2/230 70 82; e-mail postmaster@cidse.org; internet www.cidse.org; Secretary-General: Chr. Overkamp.

CIFCA (Copenhagen Initiative for Central America): Rue de la Linière 11, 1060 Brussels, Belgium; tel +32 2/539 26 20; fax +32 2/539 13 43; e-mail andré.bogaert@ncos.ngonet.be; President: J. Van Eijck, Secretary-General: R. Rodriguez.

CITIZENSHIP / CIVISME (Centre Européen du Civisme): Avenue Franklin Roosevelt 17 (CP 108), 1050 Brussels, Belgium; tel +32 2/648 94 76; fax +32 2/640 93 93; internet www.europarl.eu.int; President: G. Haarsher, Secretary-General: M. Lambert.

CLONG (Liaison Committee of Development NGOs to the European Union): Square Ambiorix 10, 1000 Brussels, Belgium; tel +32 2/743 87 60; fax +32 2/732 19 34; e-mail sec@clong.be; e-mail rrichard@clong.be; Secretary-General: G. Dumon.

CLRAE / CPLRE / KGRE (Congress of Local and Regional Authorities of Europe): Conseil de l'Europe, 67075 Strasbourg Cedex, France; tel +33 3/88 41 20 00; fax +33 3/88 41 27 51; fax +33 3/88 41 37 47; e-mail rinaldo.locatelli@coe.int; internet www.coe.fr/cplre; President: L. Cuatrecasas, Contact: A. Schneider.

COFACE (Confederation of Family Organisations in the European Union): Rue de Londres 17, 1050 Brussels, Belgium; tel +32 2/511 41 79; fax +32 2/514 47 73; e-mail coface@email.mig.be; President: S.M. Lasson, Contact: W. Lay.

COIMBRA GROUP: Rue de Stassart 119, 1050 Brussels, Belgium; tel +32 2/513 83 32; fax +32 2/502 96 11; e-mail cguniv@coimbra-group.be; internet www.coimbra-group.be; Director: K. Delaere.

CONFLICT (Prevention of) / CONFLIT (Prévention) (European Platform on Conflict Prevention and Transformation): European Centre for Conflict Prevention, P.O. Box 14069, 3508 SC Utrecht, Netherlands; tel +31 30/242 77 77; fax +31 30/236 92 68; e-mail info@conflict-prevention.net; internet www.conflict-prevention.net; Executive Director: P. Van Tongeren, Contact: C. Bastiaansen.

CRED (Centre for Research on the Epidemiology of Disasters): Clos Chapelle-aux-Champs 30-94, 1200 Brussels, Belgium; tel +32 2/764 33 27; fax +32 2/764 34 41; e-mail cred@epid.ucl.ac.be; internet www.cred.be; President: Ph. Laurent, Executive Director: D. Sapir.

CREW (CREW scrl): Rue Capouillet 27, 1060 Brussels, Belgium; tel +32 2/534 90 85; fax +32 2/534 81 34; e-mail mail@crew.be; Director: R. Franciskides.

CRPM (Conférence des Régions Périphériques Maritimes): Rue St Martin 6, 35000 Rennes, France; tel +33 2/99 35 40 50; fax +33 2/99 35 09 19; e-mail secretariat@crpm.org; internet htt://

www.crpm.org; Secretary-General: X. Gizard.

CSREMB (Coopération Subrégionale des Etats de la Mer Baltique): Avenue Palmerston 20, 1000 Brussels, Belgium; tel +32 2/285 46 40; fax +32 2/285 46 57; e-mail guenther.schulz@hobru.landsh.de; Contact: G. Schulz.

CSW-EU (Christian Solidarity Worldwide EU Office): Rue Archimède 55-57, 1000 Brussels, Belgium; tel +32 2/742 20 82; fax +32 2/742 20 82; e-mail csw-eu@village.uunet.be; internet www.csw.org.uk; Director: A. Stangl.

CTA (Technical Centre for Agricultural and Rural Cooperation ACP-EU): Rue Montoyer, 39, 1000 Brussels, Belgium; tel +32 2/513 74 36; fax +32 2/580 86 8; e-mail cta@cta.nl; internet www.cta.nl; Secretary-General: Burguet, Director: C.B. Greenidge.

DEMYC (Democrat Youth Community of Europe): Danasvej 4-6, 1910 Frederiksberg C, Denmark; tel +45/33 23 40 95; fax +45/33 31 40 68; e-mail demyc@demyc.org; internet www.demyc.org; President: M. Friedl, Secretary-General: M. Loft.

EAEA (European Association for the Education of Adults): Rue Liedst 27, 1030 Brussels, Belgium; tel +32 2/513 52 05; fax +32 2/513 57 34; e-mail eaea-main@eaea.org; internet www.eaea.org; President: J. Toth, Secretary-General: E. Haase.

EAGLE (European Association for Grey Literature Exploitation): EAGLE Secretariat, c/o Fiz Karlsruhe, 76344 Eggenstein – Leopoldshafen, Germany; tel +49 7247/80 83 13; fax +49 7247/80 81 14; e-mail eagle@fiz-karlsruhe.de; internet www.kb.nl/eagle; President: A. Smith, Contact: E. Hellmann.

EAHIL / AEIBS (European Association for Health Information and Libraries): Secretariat:, c/o NVB Bureau, Nieuwegracht 15, 3512 LC Utrecht, Netherlands; tel +31 30/261 96 63; fax +31 30/231 18 30; e-mail eahil-secr@nic.surfnet.nl; internet www.eahil.org; Contact: S. Bakker. British Medical Association, 34A House, Library Tavistock Square, London WC1H 9JP, United Kingdom; tel +44 20/7383 6036; fax +44 20/7388 2544; e-mail tony.mcsean@bma.org.uk.

EAL / AEA (European Association of Lawyers): Avenue Louise 137 Bte 1, 1050 Brussels, Belgium; tel +32 2/543 02 00; fax +32 2/538 13 78; e-mail legal@vancutsem.be; President: J.P. van Cutsem.

EAMDA (European Alliance of Muscular Dystrophy Associations): Malta 4, Gzira Road, M-GZR O4 Gzira, Malta; tel +35 6/21 34 66 88; fax +35 6/21 31 80 24; e-mail eamda@hotmail.com; internet www.eamda.com; Executive Director: C. Cryna.

EAPN (European Anti Poverty Network): Rue du Congrès 37-41 Bte 2, 1000 Brussels, Belgium; tel +32 2/230 44 55; fax +32 2/230 97 33; e-mail team@ eapn.skynet.be; internet www.eapn.org; Director: F. Farrell.

EASE (European Association for Special Education): c/o Keith Bovair, 268 Cherry Hinton Road, Cambridge CB1 7AU, United Kingdom; tel +44 1223/413 348; e-mail kbovair@aol.com; internet www .media.uio.no; President: K. Bovair. Tuinwijk 63, 9870 Zulte, Belgium; tel +32 9/386 73 09; fax +32 9/380 14 80; L. de Cock.

EASSW (European Association of Schools of Social Work): Stenvej 4, 8270 Hoejberg, Denmark; tel +45/86 27 66 22; fax +45/86 27 74 76; e-mail dsh@dsh-ea .dk; internet www.eassw.org; President: C. Christensen.

EBAA (European Business Aviation Association): Brusselsesteenweg 2, 3080 Tervuren, Belgium; tel +32 2/766 00 70; fax +32 2/768 13 25; e-mail info@ebaa.org; internet www.ebaa.org; Chairman: B.M. Humphries, President: F.A. Chavatte, Contact: F.M. François.

EBCD (European Bureau for Conservation & Development): Rue de la Science 10, 1000 Brussels, Belgium; tel +32 2/230 30 70; fax +32 2/230 82 72; e-mail ebcd .info@ebcd.org; President: B. des Clers, Secretary-General: B. Des Clers, Director: D. Symons.

EBCO / BEOC / EBCO (European Bureau for Conscientious Objectors): Avenue Stobbaerts 81, 1030 Brussels, Belgium; tel +32 2/215 79 08; fax +32 2/ 245 62 97; e-mail ebcobrussels@ifias.net; internet http://teleline.terra.es/personal/ beoc.ebco/; President: H. Dijkman, Secretary-General: M. Schwärzel, Director: G. Greune.

EBCU (European Beer Consumers Union): c/o CAMRA, 230 Hatfield Road, St Albans, Herts AL1 4LW, United Kingdom; tel +44 1727/867201; fax +44 1727/ 867670; e-mail camra@camra.org.uk; internet www.camra.org.uk; President: D. Goodwin, Contact: I. Loe.

EBEN (Eibe – Institute of Responsible Business): Norwegian School of Management Bi, 2 P.O. Box 4636, 0506 Oslo, Norway; tel +47 22/98 50 56; fax +47 22/ 98 50 02; e-mail secretariaqt@eben.org; internet www.eben.org; President: Dr von Weltzien Hoivik, Contact: H.G. Vlam.

EBF (European Business Foundation): 39 Broughton Road, London W13 8QW, United Kingdom; tel +44 20/85 79 46 88; fax +44 20/88 40 73 45; President: A. Frodsham, Secretary-General: G. D'Angelo.

EBIS (European Brain Injury Society): Rue de Londres 17, 1050 Brussels, Belgium; tel +32 2/502 34 88; fax +32 2/502 20 46; e-mail ebis@euronet.be; internet www.ebissociety.org; President: Prof. A. Mazzucchi.

EBLIDA (European Bureau of Library, Information and Documentation Associations): PO Box 16359, 2500 The Hague, Netherlands; tel +31 70/309 05 50; fax +31 70/309 05 58; e-mail eblida@ deskbibliotheken.nl; internet www .eblida.org.

EBLUL (European Bureau for Lesser Used Languages): Avenue Bosquet 58, 75007 Paris, France; tel +33 1/47 05 38 20; fax +33 1/47 05 38 21; e-mail ebu_ vea@compuserve.com; internet www .eblul.org; President: B. Brezigar, Secretary-General: M. Warazin.

EBU (European Blind Union): Avenue des Arts 24 Bte 21, 1000 Brussels, Belgium; tel +32 2/280 33 28; fax +32 2/280 49 88; e-mail ebu.cleu@skynet.be; internet www.euroblind.org; President: J. A. Wall, Contact: E. Piccinni.

EC (Eurocities): Square de Meeûs 18, 1050 Brussels, Belgium; tel +32 2/552 08 88; fax +32 2/552 08 89; e-mail info@ eurocities.be; internet www.eurocities .org; President: C. Parmentier.

ECAS (Euro Citizen Action Service): Rue de la Concorde 53, 1050 Brussels, Belgium; tel +32 2/548 04 90; fax +32 2/548 04 91; e-mail admin@ecas.org; internet www.ecas.org; Director: T. Venables.

ECCE (European Council of Civil Engineers): 1 Great George Street, Westminster, London SW1P 3AA, United Kingdom; tel +44 20/7222 7722; fax +44 20/7222 7500; e-mail eccesecretariat@ hotmail.com; internet www.eccnet.org; Secretary-General: D. Maxwell.

ECCO (European Council of Conscripts Organisations): Sehlstedtsgatan 7, 11528 Stockholm, Sweden; tel +46 8/782 69 12; fax +46 8/782 67 66; e-mail ecco@home.sc; internet www.xs4all.nl/~ecco; President: A. Walmer.

ECCP (European Coordinating Committee for NGOs on the Question of Palestine): Quai du Commerce 9, 1000 Brussels, Belgium; tel +32 2/223 07 56; fax +32 2/250 12 63; e-mail abp.eccp@ euronet.be; President: P. Galand.

ECE (Eco-Counselling Europe): Mariahilferstrasse 89 / 22, 1060 Vienna, Austria; tel +43 1/581 13 28; fax +43 1/581 13 28-18; e-mail ecocounselling.europe@ nextra.at; internet www.ecocounselling-europe.org; President: C. Schrefel. Rue Van Elewijck 35, 1050 Brussels, Belgium; tel +32 2/644 96 66; fax +32 2/644 94 20; e-mail abece@skynet.be.

ECEAE (European Coalition to End Animal Experiments): c/o BUAV, 16a Crane Grove, London N7 8NN, United Kingdom; tel +44 20/77 00 48 88; fax +44 20/ 77 00 02 52; e-mail info@buav.org; President: M. Thew.

ECF (European Cyclists' Federation): Grünenstrasse 120, 28199 Bremen, Germany; tel +49 421/34 62 939; fax +49 421/346 29 50; e-mail office@ecf.com; internet www.ecf.com; President: H. Hahn-Kloeckner, Secretary-General: M. C. Coppieters.

ECL (Association of European Cancer Leagues): Rue de Pascale 33, 1040 Brussels, Belgium; tel +32 2/230 20 27; fax +32 2/231 18 58; e-mail hayes@globalmk.org; internet http://ecl.uicc.org; EU Liaison Officer: A. Hayes.

ECOSA (European Consumer Safety Association): P.O. Box: 75 169, 1070 AD Amsterdam, Netherlands; tel +31 20/511 45 13; fax +31 20/511 45 10; e-mail ecosa@ consafe.nl; internet www.ecosa.org; President: Rogmans.

ECPSA (European Committee for Promotion and Sponsoring of the Arts): Cala Tuset 8 – 1° Apt 2 A, 08006 Barcelona, Spain; tel +34 93/237 26 82; e-mail contact@cerec.org; internet www.cerec .org; President: C. Dweedy, Secretary-General: F. Minguella.

ECRE (European Council on Refugees & Exiles): Clifton Centre, Unit 22, 3rd floor, 110 Clifton Street, London EC2A 4HT, United Kingdom; tel +44 20/7729 5152; fax +44 20/7729 5141; e-mail ecre@ecre .org; internet www.ecre.org; Secretary-General: P. Baneke. Rue Belliard 205 Box 14, 1040 Brussels, Belgium; tel +32 2/514 59 39; fax +32 2/514 59 22; e-mail euecre@ecre.be.

ECTARC (European Centre for Traditional and Regional Cultures): Parade Street, Llangollen – Denbighshire LL20 8RB, United Kingdom; tel +44 1978/86 08 28; fax +44 1978/86 19 28; e-mail contact@llangollen.org.uk.

ECTU (European Council of Transport Users): Rue Ravenstein 4, 1000 Brussels, Belgium; tel +32 2/502 23 00; fax +32 2/502 32 42; President: B. Nielsen, Secretary-General: H. Baasch.

EDF (European Disability Forum): Rue du Commerce 39-41, 1000 Brussels, Belgium; tel +32 2/282 46 00; fax +32 2/282 46 09; e-mail info@edf-feph.org; internet www.edf-feph.org; Director: S. Trömel.

EDRC (Environment & Development Resource Centre): Boulevard Brand Whitlocklaan 146, 1200 Brussels, Belgium; tel +32 2/736 80 50; fax +32 2/733 57 08; President: R. A. Kingham, Director: W. J. Veening. Damrak 28-30, 1012 LJ Amsterdam, Netherlands; e-mail edrc@edrc.net.

EDUCATION (Restructuring) / ENSEIGNEMENT (Réorganisation) (International Restructuring Education Network Europe): Stationstraat 39, 5038 EC Tilburg, Netherlands; tel +31 13/535 15 23; fax +31 13/535 02 53; e-mail PeterPennartz@irene-network.nl;

internet www.irene-network.nl; Secretary: P. Pennartz.

EEB / BEE (European Environmental Bureau): Bd de Waterloo 34, 1000 Brussels, Belgium; tel +32 2/289 10 90; fax +32 2/289 10 99; e-mail info@eeb.org; internet www.eeb.org; Secretary-General: J. Hontelez.

EEE-YFU (European Educational Exchanges-Youth for Understanding): Regastraat 47/4, 3000 Leuven, Belgium; tel +32 16/29 08 55; fax +32 16/29 06 97; e-mail office@eee-yfu.org; internet www.eee-yfu.org; President: S. Himstedt, Contact: A. Nilsson.

EEIG EURODEVELOPPEMENT / GEIE EURODEVELOPPEMENT (European Economic Interest Group of Regional Financial Companies): Rue de Stassart 32, 1050 Brussels, Belgium; tel +32 2/548 22 11; fax +32 2/511 59 09; e-mail d.caron@europemail.com; internet www.eurodev.be; President: S. Vilain, Secretary-General: D. Caron, Contact: C. Smissaert.

EEOD (European Ecumenical Organization for Development): Rue Joseph II 174, 1000 Brussels, Belgium; tel +32 2/230 41 73; fax +32 2/231 14 13; Secretary-General: M. Clark.

EFA (European Federation of Asthma and Allergy Associations): Avenue Louise 327, 1050 Brussels, Belgium; tel +32 2/646 19 45; fax +32 2/646 41 16; e-mail efaoffice@skynet.be; internet www.efanet.org; President: E. Valovirta, Secretary-General: A. Heindal, Contact: S. Palkonen.

EFAD (European Federation of the Associations of Dietitians): Square Vergote 43, 1030 Brussels, Belgium; tel +32 478/48 20 48; e-mail cabinet.hazette@efad.org; internet www.efad.org; President: I.C.I. Mackay, Contact: J. Liddell.

EFAH / FEAP (European Forum for the Arts and Heritage): Rue des Sciences 10, 1060 Brussels, Belgium; tel +32 2/534 40 02; fax +32 2/534 11 50; e-mail efah@efah.org; internet www.efah.org; President: D. Klaic.

EFC (European Foundation Centre): Rue de la Concorde 51, 1050 Brussels, Belgium; tel +32 2/512 89 38; fax +32 2/512 32 65; e-mail efc@efc.be; internet www.efc.be; Chief Executive: J. Richardson.

EFCT / FEVC (European Federation of Conference Towns): BP 182, 1040 Brussels, Belgium; tel +32 2/732 69 54; fax +32 2/735 48 40; e-mail secretariate@efct.com; internet www.efct.com; President: P. Duran.

EFCW (European Forum for Child Welfare): Rue de la Concorde 53, 1050 Brussels, Belgium; tel +32 2/511 70 83; fax +32 2/511 72 98; e-mail info@efcw.org; internet www.efcw.org; President: Catriona Williams.

EFECOT (European Federation for the Education of Children of Occupational Travellers): Vooruitgangstraat 33/2, 1030 Brussels, Belgium; tel +32 2/227 40 60; fax +32 2/227 40 69; e-mail efecot@efecot.net; internet www.efecot.net; Contact: L. Knaepkens.

EFGP (European Federation of Green Parties): Rue Wiertz, Bureau PHS 2C85, 1047 Brussels, Belgium; tel +32 2/284 51 35; fax +32 2/284 91 35; e-mail efgp@europarl.eu.int; internet www.europeangreens.org; Secretary-General: A. Cassola.

EFIL (European Federation for Intercultural Learning): Rue des Colonies 18-24, 1000 Brussels, Belgium; tel +32 2/514 52 50; fax +32 2/514 29 29; e-mail info@efil.be; internet www.efil.afs.org; President: H. Garcea, Secretary-General: E. Hardt.

EFRP (European Federation for Retirement Provision): Rue Royale 97, 1000 Brussels, Belgium; tel +32 2/289 14 14; fax +32 2/289 14 15; e-mail efrp@efrp.org; internet www.efrp.org; President: A. Pickering.

EFTA (European Family Therapy Association): Rue du Bailli 9, 1000 Brussels, Belgium; tel +32 2/646 43 67; fax +32 2/646 43 67; e-mail melkaim@ulb.ac.be; internet www.efta-europeanfamilytherapy.com; President: M. Elkaim. Secretariat, Avenue Bois Williame 32, 5101 Erpent, Belgium; tel +32 81/31 04 39; fax +32 81/31 01 76.

EFTA (European Fair Trade Association): Rue de la Charité 43, 1210 Brussels, Belgium; tel +32 2/217 37 95; fax +32 2/217 37 98; e-mail efta@eftadvocacy.org; internet www.eftafairtrade.org; Contact: M. Iossa.

EGLEI / GEILE (European Group for Local Employment Initiatives): Square Ambiorix 45, 1000 Brussels, Belgium; tel +32 2/231 06 87; fax +32 2/280 02 84; e-mail eglei@eglei.be; President: H. Le Marois, Contact: C. Niarchos-Lentz.

EGMF (Euro Garden Forum): Boulevard A. Reyers 80, 1050 Brussels, Belgium; tel +32 2/7068230; fax +32 2/7068250; e-mail guy.vandoorslaer@orgalime.org; President: N. Stihl.

EHN (European Heart Network): Rue Montoyer 31, 1000 Brussels, Belgium; tel +32 2/512 91 74; fax +32 2/503 35 25; e-mail ehn@skynet.be; internet www.ehnheart.org; President: S. Logstrup.

EIA / AIE (European Information Association): Central Library, St Peter's Square, Manchester M2 5PD, United Kingdom; tel +44 161/228 36 91; fax +44 161/236 65 47; e-mail eia@libraries.manchester.gov.uk; internet www.eia.org.uk; President: I. Thomson.

EiB (European Information Bureau): 9 Bower Street, Stoke on Trent ST1 3BH, United Kingdom; tel +44 178/226 67 12; e-mail euro_bureau@hotmail.com; Director: J. Huff, Social Actions Director: Zenam Khan.

EIRA / ARIE (European Industrial Regions Association): Rue Joseph II 36-38, 1000 Brussels, Belgium; tel +32 2/230 91 07; fax +32 2/230 27 12; e-mail secretariat@eira.org; internet www.eira.org; President: R. Stone, Contact: B. Thiberge.

EISA (European Initiative for Sustainable Development in Agriculture): c/o FNL, Konstantinstrasse 90, 53179 Bonn, Germany; tel +49 228/979 93 33; fax +49 228/979 93 40; e-mail s.witsch@fnl.de; internet www.sustainable-agriculture.org; President: Breb, Secretary-General: S. Witsch, Contact: Dr Froehling.

ELEC / LECE (European League for Economic Co-operation): Place du Champ de Mars 2 bte 8, 1050 Brussels, Belgium; tel +32 2/219 82 50; fax +32 2/219 06 63; e-mail elec@easynet.be; internet www.elec.easynet.be; President: F. Chaffart, Secretary-General: J.-C. Koeune.

ELNI (Environmental Law Network International): Elisabethenstrasse 55-57, 64283 Darmstadt, Germany; tel +49 6151/81 91 31; fax +49 6151/81 91 33; e-mail h.unruh@oeko.de; internet www.oeko.de/elni; Contact: R. Barth.

ELSA (European Law Students' Association): Boulevard Général Jacques 239, 1050 Brussels, Belgium; tel +32 2/646 26 26; fax +32 2/646 29 23; e-mail elsa@brutele.be; internet www.elsa.org; President: R. Zarnauskaite, Secretary-General: L. Axrup.

EM (European Movement): 85 Frampton Street, London NW8 8NQ, United Kingdom; tel +44 20/7725 4300; fax +44 20/7725 4301; e-mail info@euromove.org.uk; internet www.euromove.org.uk; President: I. Taylor.

Emmaüs International: Rue Vaillant Couturier 183 bis, 94143 Alfortville, France; tel +33 1/48 93 29 50; fax +33 1/43 53 19 26; e-mail contact@emmaus-international.org; internet www.emmaus-international.org; President: R. Fior, Secretary-General: J.-M. Viennet.

ENAE (European Network on Ageing and Ethnicity): 113 Rose Street, Edinburgh EH2 3DT, United Kingdom; fax +44 131/220 27 79; e-mail enquiries@acscott.org.uk; internet www.ageconcernscotland.org.uk; Director: M. O'Neil.

ENAR (European Network Against Racism): Rue de la Charité 43, 1210 Brussels, Belgium; tel +32 2/229 35 70; fax +32 2/229 35 75; e-mail info@enar-eu.org; internet www.enar-eu.org; President: B. Quraishy, Secretary-General: V. Egenberge, Contact: P. Curzi.

ENOPF (European Network of One-Parent Families): c/o Gingerbread, 169 University Street, Belfast BT7 1HR, United Kingdom; tel +44 28/90 23 14 17; fax +44 28/90 24 07 40; e-mail enquiries@gingerbreadni.org; internet www.gingerbreadni.org; President: M. Cavanagh.

ENSP (European Network for Smoking Prevention): Chaussée d'Ixelles 144, 1050 Brussels, Belgium; tel +32 2/230 65 15; fax +32 2/230 75 07; e-mail info@ensp.org; internet www.ensp.org; President: Trudi-Prins.

ENU (European Network of the Unemployed): Araby House, 8 North Richmond Street, Dublin 1, Ireland; tel +353 1/856 00 88; fax +353 1/856 00 90; e-mail inou@iol.ie; internet www.multimania.com/enu/; Secretary-General: K. Kunnas.

EOEF / FEED (European Offender Employment Forum): Camelford House, 87–89 Albert Embankment, London SE1 7TP, United Kingdom; tel +44 20/75 82 72 21; fax +44 20/75 82 63 91; e-mail mikestewart; internet www.laborel.nl; President: C. Coppes, Secretary-General: De Jong, Contact: D. Dragtsma.

EORTC / OERTC (European Organisation for Research and Treatment of Cancer): Avenue E. Mounier 83 bte 11, 1200 Brussels, Belgium; tel +32 2/774 16 50; fax +32 2/772 35 45; e-mail eortc@eortc.be; internet www.eortc.be; Contact: F. Meunier.

EPA (European Parents Association): Rue du Champ de Mars 1a, 1050 Brussels, Belgium; tel +32 2/514 05 99; fax +32 2/514 47 67; e-mail infos@epa.be; internet www.epa-parents.org; Secretary-General: K. Schütz.

EPE (European Partners for the Environment): Avenue de la Toison d'Or 67, 1060 Brussels, Belgium; tel +32 2/771 15 34; fax +32 2/539 48 15; e-mail eupe@glo.be; internet www.epe.be; Executive Director: R. van Ermen.

ERDI (Consortium of European Research & Development Institutes for Adult Education): Kardinaal Mercierplein 1, 2800 Mechelen, Belgium; tel +32 15/ 44 65 00; fax +32 15/ 44 65 01; e-mail annemie.decrick@vocb.be; internet www.erdi.info; President: E. Nuissl von Rein, Secretary-General: J. Gomez.

ESAN (European Social Action Network): Rue Sainte Catherine 60, 59800 Lille, France; tel +33 3/20 55 10 99; fax +33 3/20 55 10 99; e-mail esan@nordnet.fr; internet www.esan.org; President: L. Dujardin.

ESCRS (European Society of Cataract and Refractive Surgeons): Temple House, Temple Road, Blackrock, Co. Dublin, Ireland; tel +353 1/209 11 00; fax +353 1/209 11 12; e-mail escrs@agenda-comm.ie; internet www.escrs.org;

President: Prof. J. Cunha-Viz, Secretary-General: L. Conroy.

ESED (European Society for Environment and Development): Rue de Meuse 47, 5541 Hastières-par-delà, Belgium; tel +32 82/64 45 80; fax +32 82/64 45 11; e-mail m.dubrulle@worldonline.be; President: M. Dubrulle, Secretary-General: Dr Halls.

ESF (European Science Foundation): Quai Lezay-Marnesia 1, 67080 Strasbourg Cedex, France; tel +33 3/88 76 71 00; fax +33 3/88 37 05 32; e-mail esf@esf.org; internet www.esf.org; President: R. van Duinen, Secretary-General: E. Banda, Contact: C. Quedrue.

ESIB (The National Unions of Students in Europe): Avenue de la Toison d'Or 17A Bte 80 – 5è étage, 1050 Brussels, Belgium; tel +32 2/502 23 62; fax +32 2/511 78 06; e-mail secretariat@esib.org; internet www.esib.org; Secretary-General: A. Bols.

ESIP (European Social Insurance Partners): Rue d'Arlon 50, 1000 Brussels, Belgium; tel +32 2/282 05 60; fax +32 2/230 77 73; e-mail esip@esip.org; internet www.esip.org; Director: F. Terwey.

ETS (European Tissue Symposium): Avenue des Arts 44, 1040 Brussels, Belgium; tel +32 2/549 52 30; fax +32 2/502 15 98; e-mail pbogaert@cov.com; internet www.europeantissue.com; President: P. Forlin, Contact: P. Bogaert, External Relations Advisor: R. van Lil.

ETSC (European Transport Safety Council): Rue du Cornet 34, 1040 Brussels, Belgium; tel +32 2/230 41 06; fax +32 2/230 42 15; e-mail info@etsc.be; internet www.etsc.be; Contact: J. Beckmann.

ETWELFARE (European Round Table of Charitable Social Welfare Associations): Rue de Pascale 4-6, 1040 Brussels, Belgium; tel +32 2/230 45 00; fax +32 2/230 57 04; e-mail euvertretung@bag-wohlfahrt.de; internet www.etwelfare.com; President: Kuper, Secretary-General: Geroms.

EUD (European Union for the Deaf): Coupure Rechts 314, 9000 Gent, Belgium; tel +32 9/225 08 33; fax +32 9/225 08 34; e-mail info@eudnet.org; internet www.eudnet.org; President: K. Sondergaard, Contact: H. Stevens.

EUFAMI (European Federation of Associations of Families of Mentally Ill People): Groeneweg 151, 3001 Hervelee, Belgium; tel +32 16/40 23 41; fax +32 16/40 23 41; e-mail info@eufami.net; internet www.eufami.org; President: B. Arino.

EUFORES (European Forum for Renewable Energy Sources): Rue du trône 26, 1000 Brussels, Belgium; tel +32 2/546 19 48; fax +32 2/546 19 47; e-mail eufores@eufores.org; internet www.eufores.org; President: E. McNally.

EUFORIC (Europe's Forum on International Cooperation): Wycker Grach Straat 38, 6221 CX Maastricht, Netherlands; tel +31 43/328 51 80; fax +31 43/328 51 85; e-mail info@euforic.org; internet www.euforic.org; President: S. Stocker.

EUJS (European Union of Jewish Students): Avenue A. Depage 3, 1000 Brussels, Belgium; tel +32 2/647 72 79; fax +32 2/648 24 31; e-mail info@eujs.org; internet www.eujs.org; President: J. Voloj, Secretary-General: M. Mucznik.

EURACOM (Action for Mining Communities): 9 Regent Street, Barnsley S70 2EG, United Kingdom; tel +44 12/2620 0768; fax +44 12/2629 6532; e-mail martincantor@ccc-alliance.demon.co.uk; Contact: M. Cantor.

EURAG (European Federation of the Elderly): Wielandgasse 9, 8010 Graz, Austria; tel +43 316/81 46 08; fax +43 316/81 47 67; e-mail eurag.europe@aon.at; internet www.eurag-europe.org; President: E. Mangers-Anen, Contact: G. Dayé.

EUROCASO (European Council of Aids Services Organisations): Rue Pierre-Fatio 17, 1204 Geneva, Switzerland; tel +41 22/700 15 00; fax +41 22/700 15 47; e-mail info@groupesida.ch; internet www.groupesida.ch; President: F. Hubner.

EURODAD (European Network on Debt and Development): Rue Dejoncker 46, 1060 Brussels, Belgium; tel +32 2/543 90 60; fax +32 2/544 05 59; e-mail info@eurodad.org; internet www.eurodad.org; President: T. van Hees.

EUROGROUP FOR ANIMAL WELFARE: Rue des Patriotes 6, 1000 Brussels, Belgium; tel +32 2/740 08 20; fax +32 2/740 08 29; e-mail info@eurogroupanimalwelfare.org; internet www.eurogroupanimalwelfare.org; Secretary-General: D. Wilkins.

EURONATUR (European Nature Heritage Fund): Konstanzer Strasse 22, 78315 Radolfzell, Germany; tel +49 7732/92 72 0; fax +49 7732/92 72 22; e-mail info@euronatur.org; internet www.euronatur.org; President: C.-P. Hutter.

EURO-ORIENTATION (European Association for Orientation, Vocational Guidance and Educational and Professional Information): Kortrijkstraat 343, 8870 Izegem, Belgium; tel +32 51/30 13 62; fax +32 51/32 04 56; e-mail gerard.wulleman@clb-net.be; President: G. Wulleman, Secretary-General: R. Stufkens.

EUROSTEP (European Solidarity Towards Equal Participation of People): Rue Stévin 115, 1000 Brussels, Belgium; tel +32 2/231 16 59; fax +32 2/230 37 80; e-mail admin@eurostep.org; internet www.eurostep.org; Director: S. Stocker.

EUROTEAM (European Action Committee for Public Transport): Rue Ste Marie 6, 1080 Brussels, Belgium; tel +32 2/673 61 00; fax +32 2/660 10 72; e-mail euroteam@uitp.com; Contact: Br. Ollier.

EVC / CEV (European Volunteer Centre): Rue de la Science 10, 1040 Brussels, Belgium; tel +32 2/511 75 01; fax +32 2/514 59 89; e-mail cev@cev.be; internet www.cev.be; President: C. Spence, Secretary-General: R. de Zutter.

EWL / LEF / EFL (European Women's Lobby): Rue Hydraulique 18, 1210 Brussels, Belgium; tel +32 2/217 90 20; fax +32 2/219 84 51; e-mail ewl@womenlobby.org; internet www.womenlobby.org; President: D. Fuchs, Secretary-General: M. McPhail.

EWMD (European Women's Management Development Network): Lichtenaverlaan 102-120, 3062 ME Rotterdam, Netherlands; tel +31 10/20 45 678; e-mail angelina.bucur@alliente.com; internet www.ewmd.org; President: A. Bucur.

EYCE (Ecumenical Youth Council in Europe): Rue du Champs de Mars 5, 1050 Brussels, Belgium; tel +32 2/ 510 61 87; fax +32 2/510 61 72; e-mail info@eyce.org; internet www.eyce.org; President: D. Thesenvitz, Secretary-General: D. Muller.

EYE Network (European Youth Exchange Network): Czerningasse 9, 1020 Vienna, Austria; tel +43 1/914 36 71; fax +43 1/914 36 71; e-mail eyenetwork@eyenetwork.org; internet www.eyenetwork.org; President: D. Bock, Secretary-General: A. Melnic.

FEANTSA (European Federation of National Organisations Working with the Homeless): Chaussée de Louvain 194, 1210 Brussels, Belgium; tel +32 2/538 66 69; fax +32 2/539 41 74; e-mail office@feantsa.org; internet www.feantsa.org; President: T. Specht-Kittler.

FEM (Female Europeans of Medium and Small Enterprises): Rue Jacques de Lalaing 4, 1040 Brussels, Belgium; tel +32 2/285 07 14; fax +32 2/230 78 61; e-mail d.rabetge@ueapme.com; internet www.fem-pme.com; President: M. Arnau, Contact: D. Rabetge.

FEM (Federation of European Motorcyclists Associations): Rue de Champs 62, 1040 Brussels, Belgium; tel +32 2/736 90 47; fax +32 2/736 94 01; e-mail fema@chello.be; internet www.fema.riderfrightf.org; President: E. Renette, Secretary-General: A. Perlot, Contact: C. Gesios.

FEPEDA (European Federation of Parents of Hearing Impaired Children): Tomstraat 47, 3800 Brustem, Belgium; tel +32 11/683 445; fax +32 11/683 445; e-mail fiapas@jet.es; internet www.fepeda.org; Contact: J. Stevens.

FERN (EU Forest Programme of the World Rainforest Movement): Avenue des Celtes 20, 1040 Brussels, Belgium; tel +32 2/742 24 36; tel +32 2/733 36 53; fax +32 2/736 80 54; e-mail FERN.belgium@wanadoo.be; Contact: C. Marijnissen, Contact: B. Muraille.

FERPA (European Federation of Retired and Elderly People): Boulevard du Roi Albert II 5, 1210 Brussels, Belgium; tel +32 2/224 04 11; fax +32 2/224 04 55; e-mail etuc@etuc.org; internet www.etuc.org; President: Debunne, Secretary-General: L. de Santis.

FOEE / CEAT (Friends of the Earth Europe): Rue Blanche 15, 1060 Brussels, Belgium; tel +32 2/542 01 80; fax +32 2/537 55 96; e-mail foee@foeeurope.org; internet www.foeeurope.org; President: V. Kotecky, Director: M. Rocholl.

FOOD BANKS / BANQUES ALIMENTAIRES (European Federation of Food Banks): Avenue du général Leclerc 53, 92340 Bourg-la-Reine, France; tel +33 1/45 36 05 45; fax +33 1/45 36 05 52; e-mail feba@eurofoodbank.org; internet www.eurofoodbank.org; Secretary-General: C. Vian.

FRERES DES HOMMES: Rue de Londres 18, 1050 Brussels, Belgium; tel +32 2/512 97 94; fax +32 2/511 47 61; e-mail fdhbel@skynet.be; internet www.france-fdh.org; Contact: C. Diaz.

FUEN / UFCE / FUEV (Federal Union of European Nationalities): Schiffbrücke 41, 24939 Flensburg, Germany; tel +49 461/128 55; fax +49 461/180 709; e-mail info@fuen.org; internet www.fuen.org; President: R. Arquint, Secretary-General: F. Nickelsen.

FYEG (Federation of Young European Greens): c/o European Parliament, ASP 8G138, 1047 Brussels, Belgium; tel +32 2/284 24 40; fax +32 2/284 92 73; e-mail office@fyeg.org; internet www.fyeg.org; Contact: A. Jovanovic.

GAIN (Graphic Arts Intelligence Network): Via Augusta 317, 08017 Barcelona, Spain; tel +34 93/204 65 63; fax +34 93/280 57 27; e-mail gaineurope@rccsa.org; internet www.gain-europe.com; President: R. Janssen.

GLOBEEU (Global Legislators Organisation for a Balanced Environment, European Union): Rue Boduognat 13, 1000 Brussels, Belgium; tel +32 2/230 65 89; fax +32 2/230 95 30; e-mail e.globe@innet.be; President: A. Mep.

GREENPEACE (Greenpeace International – European Unit): Chaussée de Haecht 159, 1030 Brussels, Belgium; tel +32 2/274 19 00; fax +32 2/274 19 10; e-mail european.unit@diala.greenpeace.org; internet www.greenpeace.org.

HANDICAP INTERNATIONAL: Rue de Spa 67, 1000 Brussels, Belgium; tel +32 2/28 0 16 01; fax +32 2/230 60 30; e-mail headoffice@handicap.be; internet www.handicapinternational.be.

HAR / RQH (Humanitarian Affairs Review): La Maison de l'Europe at the Bibliothèque Solvay, Parc Léopold, Rue Belliard 137, 1040 Brussels, Belgium; tel +32 2/738 75 92; fax +32 2/739 15 92; e-mail info@humanitarian-review.org; internet www.humanitarian-review.org; Contact: J. Bolle.

HE (Habitants d'Europe): Square Albert 1er 32, 1070 Brussels, Belgium; tel +32 2/522 98 69; fax +32 2/524 18 16; e-mail syndicatdeslocataires@swing.be; President: J. Garcia.

HRW (Human Rights Watch): Rue Van Campenhout 15, 1000 Brussels, Belgium; tel +32 2/732 20 09; fax +32 2/732 04 71; e-mail hrwatchen@skynet.be; internet www.hrw.org; President: K. Roth, Director: Eotteleicht, Contact: V. Saenen.

ICDA (International Coalition for Development Action): Rue Stévin 115, 1000 Brussels, Belgium; tel +32 2/230 04 30; fax +32 2/230 52 37; e-mail icda@icda.be; internet www.icda.be; President: J. Foerdegoodsen, Secretary-General: E. Bensah.

IEEP (Institute for European Environmental Policy): Avenue des Gaulois 18, 1040 Brussels, Belgium; tel +32 2/738 14 71; fax +32 2/732 40 04; e-mail central@ieeplondon.org.uk; internet www.ieep.org.uk; President: D. Baldock, Secretary-General: J. Taylor.

IFAW (International Fund for Animal Welfare): Rue Boduognat 13, 1000 Brussels, Belgium; tel +32 2/230 97 17; fax +32 2/231 04 02; e-mail info@ifaw.org; internet www.ifaw.org; President: L. Odonnel, Contact: Jones.

IFHOH-EUROPE (European Region of the International Federation of Hard of Hearing People): Drenikova 24, 1000 Ljubljana, Slovenia; tel +47 611/74 880; e-mail lillian.vicanek@c2i.net; internet www.ifhoh.org/members.htm; President: L. Vicanek, Secretary-General: S. Matinvesi.

IFIAS (Institute for International Assistance and Solidarity): Avenue J. Stobbaerts 81 A, 1030 Brussels, Belgium; tel +32 2/215 79 08; fax +32 2/245 62 97; e-mail ifias@ifias.net; internet www.ifias.net; Director: S. Drake.

IFIEC EUROPE (International Federation of Industrial Energy Consumers – European Section): Chaussée de Charleroi 119, 1060 Brussels, Belgium; tel +32 2/542 06 87; fax +32 2/542 06 92; e-mail roger.goffin@aventis.com; internet www.ifiec-europe.be; President: P. Claes, Secretary-General: R. Goffin.

IPPF (European Network of the International Planned Parenthood Federation): Rue Royale 146, 1000 Brussels, Belgium; tel +32 2/250 09 50; fax +32 2/250 09 69; e-mail info@ippfen.org; internet www.ippfen.org; President: V. Claeys.

IRIS (European Network on Women's Training): Rue Capouillet 27, 1060 Brussels, Belgium; tel +32 2/534 90 85; fax +32 2/534 81 34; e-mail mail@iris-asbl.org; internet www.iris-asbl.org; President: R. Franceskides.

ISCA-EU (International Save the Children Alliance-European Union): Rue Montoyer 39, 1000 Brussels, Belgium; tel +32 2/512 78 51; fax +32 2/513 49 03; e-mail savechildbru@skynet.be; President: D. Sutton.

IYCS-IMCS / JECI-MIEC (International Young Catholic Students-European Coordination-International Movement of Catholic Students): Rue du Marteau 19, 1000 Brussels, Belgium; tel +32 2/218 54 37; fax +32 2/218 54 37; e-mail jecimiec@skynet.be; internet www.users.skynet.be/jecimiec/index.htm; Secretary: M. van Damme.

JEF (Young European Federalists): Chaussée de Wavre 241D, 1050 Brussels, Belgium; tel +32 2/512 00 53; fax +32 2/512 66 73; e-mail jef.europe@euronet.be; internet www.jef-europe.net; President: A. Weston, Secretary-General: M. Bonnard.

JME (Jeunesses Musicales Europe): Palais des Beaux-Arts, Rue Royale 10, 1000 Brussels, Belgium; tel +32 2/513 97 74; fax +32 2/514 47 55; e-mail mail@jmi.net; internet www.jmi.net; President: B. Smileuski, Director: D. Franzen.

JRS (Jesuit Refugee Service – Europe): Résidence de Gesu, Haachtsesteenweg 8, 1210 Brussels, Belgium; tel +32 2/250 32 20; fax +32 2/250 32 29; e-mail europe@jesref.org; internet www.jrseurope.org; Contact: J. Dardis.

LIBER (European Research Libraries Organization): LIBER Secretariat, PO Box 2149, 1016 Copenhagen K, Denmark; tel +45/33 47 43 01; fax +45/33 32 98 46; e-mail ekn@kb.dk; internet www.kb.dk/liber/; President: E. K. Nielsen.

MHE-SME (Mental Health Europe – Santé Mentale Europe): (European Regional Council of the World Federation for Mental Health): Blvd Clovis 7, 1000 Brussels, Belgium; tel +32 2/280 04 68; fax +32 2/280 16 04; e-mail info@mhe-sme.org; internet www.mhe-sme.org; Contact: P. van den Heede.

MI (Mobility International): Boulevard Baudouin 18, 1000 Brussels, Belgium; tel +32 2/201 56 08; fax +32 2/201 57 63; e-mail mobint@arcadis.be; President: W. Tigges, Director: J. Pierre.

MULTIPLE SCLEROSIS / SCLEROSE EN PLAQUES (European Multiple Sclerosis Platform): Avenue Plasky 173 Bte 11, 1030 Brussels, Belgium; tel +32 2/305 80 12; fax +32 2/305 80 11; e-mail ms-in-europe@pandora.be; internet www.ms-in-europe.org; Secretary-General: C. Thalheim.

NIHIL (European Sustainable Cities & Towns Campaign): Rue de Trèves 49-51 box 3, 1040 Brussels, Belgium; tel +32 2/230 53 51; fax +32 2/230 88 50; e-mail campaign.office@skynet.be; internet www.sustainable-cities.org; Contact: A. Payne.

NORMAPME (European Office of Crafts, Trades and Small and Medium-Sized Enterprises for Standardisation): Rue Jacques de Lalaing 4, 1040 Brussels, Belgium; tel +32 2/282 05 30; fax +32 2/282 05 35; e-mail info@normapme.com; internet www.normapme.com; President: H.-W. Muller, Contact: L. Gourtsoyannis.

OBESSU (Organizing Bureau of European Schools Student Unions): Borrens 32, 1050 Brussels, Belgium; tel +32 2/647 23 90; fax +32 2/647 23 90; e-mail obessu@obessu.org; internet www.obessu.org; Secretary-General: S. Radu.

OCFE (Common Office for European Training): Rue Petite Aise 13, 6061 Charleroi, Belgium; tel +32 71/41 48 39; fax +32 71/41 47 39; e-mail ocfej@gate71.be; internet www.ocfe.org; Secretary-General: I. Zonta.

OSI (Open Society Institute): Rue des Minimes 26, 1000 Brussels, Belgium; tel +32 2/505 46 46; fax +32 2/502 46 46; e-mail osi@osi-brussels.be; Director: M. Wisse Smit.

PAEAC (Parliamentary Association for Euro-Arab Cooperation): Avenue de la Renaissance 10, 1000 Brussels, Belgium; tel +32 2/231 13 00; fax +32 2/231 06 46; e-mail medea@medea.be; internet www.medea.be; President: C.F. Nothomb, Secretary-General: J.-M. Dumont, Contact: J. Gezels.

PEACE / PAIX / FRIEDEN (Foundation for Peace): C/ Casp 31-2-1a A, 08010 Barcelona, Spain; tel +34 93/302 51 29; fax +34 93/301 75 62; e-mail info@fundacioperlapau.org; internet www.fundacioperlapau.org; President: A. Banda, Director: J. Armadans.

POETRY / POESIE (European Association for the Promotion of Poetry): Vrijdagmarkt 36, 9000 Gent, Belgium; tel +32 9/225 22 25; fax +32 9/225 90 54; e-mail info@poeziecentrum.be; internet www.poeziecentrum.be; President: W. Tibergien.

QCEA (Quaker Council for European Affairs): Square Ambiorix 50, 1040 Brussels, Belgium; tel +32 2/230 49 35; fax +32 2/230 63 70; e-mail info@qcea.org; internet www.quaker.org/qcea.

RC / EU Office (Red Cross / EU Office): Rue Belliard 65 box 7, 1000 Brussels, Belgium; tel +32 2/235 06 80; fax +32 2/230 54 64; e-mail infoboard@redcross-eu.net; internet www.redcross-eu.net.

SEFI (European Society for Engineering Education): Rue de Stassart, 1050 Brussels, Belgium; tel +32 2/502 36 09; fax +32 2/502 96 11; e-mail info@sefi.be; e-mail francoise.come@sefi.be; internet www.sefi.be; President: Prof. T.U. Weck, Secretary-General: F. Ma Come.

SOCIAL (Platform of European Social NGOs): Avenue des Arts 43, 1040 Brussels, Belgium; tel +32 2/503 16 30; fax +32 2/511 19 09; e-mail platform@socialplatform.org; internet www.socialplatform.org; President: S. Wilson.

SOLIDAR: Rue du Commerce 22, 1000 Brussels, Belgium; tel +32 2/500 10 20; fax +32 2/500 10 30; e-mail solidar@skynet.be; internet www.solidar.org; Secretary-General: G. Alhadeff.

T & E (European Federation for Transport and Environment): Boulevard de Waterloo 34, 1000 Brussels, Belgium; tel +32 2/502 99 09; fax +32 2/502 99 08; e-mail info@t-e.nu; internet www.t-e.nu; President: S. Klingberg, Director: B. Schell.

UEF (Union of European Federalists): Chaussée de Wavre 214 D, 1050 Brussels, Belgium; tel +32 2/508 30 30; fax +32 2/626 95 01; e-mail uef.european.federalists@skynet.be; internet www.federaleurope.org; President: Leinen, Secretary-General: Boissière, Contact: C. Hondrila.

UEPMD (European Union of Dentists): Aktienstreet 326, 45473 Mülheim-Ruhr, Germany; tel +49 208/763 095; fax +49 208/767 20 06; e-mail secgen@europeandentists.org; internet www.europeandentists.org; President: S. Nikolakakos, Secretary-General: A. Lupin.

UNITED (UNITED for Intercultural Action): Postbus 413, 1000 AK Amsterdam, Netherlands; tel +31 20/683 47 78; fax +31 20/683 45 82; e-mail info@unitedagainstracism.org; internet www.unitedagainstracism.org; Secretary-General: S. Daru, Contact: G. Ates.

UnitéE (Association pour l'Unité européennE): Rue du Dr Rocheford 7, 78400 Chatou, France; tel +33 1/30 53 07 93; fax +33 1/56 08 52 38; e-mail unitee@unitee.com; internet www.unitee.com.

WIDE (Women in Development, Europe): Rue de la Science 10, 1000 Brussels, Belgium; tel +32 2/545 90 70; fax +32 2/512 73 42; e-mail wide@gn-apc-org; internet www.eurosur.org/wide; Contact: Br. Holzner.

WORLD VISION EU Liaison Office: Rue de Toulouse 22, 1040 Brussels, Belgium; tel +32 2/230 16 21; fax +32 2/280

16 21; e-mail jane_backhurst@wvi.org; internet www.wvi.org; Director: J. Backhurst.

WOSM (World Organisation of the Scout Movement – European Region): Avenue Porte de Hal 39, 1060 Brussels, Belgium; tel +32 2/534 33 15; fax +32 2/706 52 67; e-mail eurobureau@euro.scout.org; internet www.scout.org; Secretary-General: Moreillon, Contact: Clayton.

WSCF EUROPE (World Student Christian Federation (Europe Region)): Prins Hendriklaan 37, 1075 BA Amsterdam, Netherlands; tel +31 20/662 79 56; fax +31 20/675 57 36; e-mail lss@xs4all.nl; internet www.wscfeurope.org; President: T. Helppi.

WWF (World Wide Fund for Nature, European Policy Office): Boulevard Emile Jacqmain 90, 1000 Brussels, Belgium; tel +32 2/340 09 99; fax +32 2/340 09 33; e-mail info@wwf.be; internet www.wwf.be; Director: T. Long, Contact: L. Devaux.

YAP (Youth Action for Peace): Avenue du Parc Royal 3, 1020 Brussels, Belgium; tel +32 2/478 94 10; fax +32 2/478 94 32; e-mail yapis@xs4all.be; internet www.yap.org; President: A. Pop.

YFJ (European Youth Forum): Rue Joseph II 120, 1000 Brussels, Belgium; tel +32 2/230 64 90; fax +32 2/230 21 23; e-mail youthforum@youthforum.org; internet www.youthforum.org; President: G. Filibeck, Contact: T. Flessenkemper.

APRODEV (Association of World Council of Churches and Related Development Organisations in Europe): Blvd Charlemagne 28, 1000 Brussels, Belgium; tel (+32) 2-2345660; fax (+32) 2-2345669; e-mail admin@aprodev.net; internet www.aprodev.net; Secretary-General: R.W.F. van Drimmelen.

CCME / CEME (Churches' Commission for Migrants in Europe / Commission des Eglises auprès des Migrants en Europe / Kommission der Kirchen für Migranten in Europa): 174 rue Joseph II, 1040 Brussels, Belgium; tel (+32) 2-2302011; fax (+32) 2-2311413; e-mail csc.bru@ece-kek .be; internet www.cec-kek.org; Secretary-General: D. Peschke.

CEC (Conference of European Churches): Route de Ferney, 150 PO Box 2100, 1211 Geneva 2, Switzerland; tel (+41) 227916111; fax (+4) 227916227; e-mail cec@cec-kek.org; internet www.cec-kek.org; President: J. Caligiorgis; Secretary-General: Rev. K. Clements.

CEEC (European Committee for Catholic Education / Comité Européen pour l'Enseignement Catholique / Europäisches Komitee für das Katholische Schulwesen): Avenue Marnix 19A, bte 6, 1000 Brussels, Belgium; tel (+32) 2-5114774; fax (+32) 2-5138694; e-mail ceec@skynet.be; internet http://ceec -edu.org; President: Can. A. de Wolf; Secretary-General: E. Verhack; Contact: M. Badart.

COMECE (Commission of the Bishops' Conferences of the EC / Commission des Episcopats de la CE / Kommission der Bischofskonferenzen der EG): Rue Stévin 42, 1000 Brussels, Belgium; tel (+32) 2-2350510; fax (+32) 2-2303334; e-mail comece@comece.org; President: Msgr J. Homeyer; Contact: Msgr N. Treanor.

OCIPE (Catholic European Study and Information Centre / Office Catholique d'Information et d'Initiative pour l'Europe / Katholisches Sekretariat für Europäische Fragen): Rue du Cornet 51, 1040 Brussels, Belgium; tel (+32) 2-7379720; fax (+32) 2-7379729; e-mail infos@ocipe.org; internet www.ocipe.org; President: L. Grégoire; Contact: J. Kerkhofs.

RCE (Rabbinical Centre of Europe): Rond-point Shuman 6, 1040 Brussels, Belgium; tel +32 2/234 77 22; fax +32 2/234 77 68; e-mail office@rce.eu.com; internet www.rce.eu.com; Executive Director: M. Garelik; Contact: L. Matusof.

MISCELLANEOUS

AUDIOVISUAL / AUDIOVISUEL (European Audiovisual Observatory / Observatoire Européen de l'Audiovisuel / Europäische Audiovisuelle Informationsstelle): Allée de la Robertsau 76, 67000 Strasbourg, France; tel (+33) 3-88-14-44-00; fax (+33) 3-88-14-44-19; e-mail obs@obs.coe.int; internet www.obs.coe.int; President: W. Closs; Contact: M. Booms.

EPO / OEB (European Patent Office / Office Européen des Brevets / Europäisches Patentamt): Erhardtstrasse 27, 80331 Munich, Germany; tel (+49 89) 2399-0; fax (+49 89) 2399-4560; internet www.european-patent-office.org.

EPPO / OEPP (European and Mediterranean Plant Protection Organization / Organisation Européenne et Méditerranéenne pour la Protection des Plantes / Europäische und Mediterranee Organisation für Pflanzenschutz): Rue le Nôtre 1, 75016 Paris, France; tel (+33) 1-45-20-77-94; fax (+33) 1-42-24-89-43; e-mail hq@eppo.fr; internet www.eppo.org; President: O. Felix; Contact: I.M. Smith; Contact: A.-S. Roy.

ETSI (European Telecommunications Standards Institute / Institut Européen des Normes de Télécommunication / Europäisches Institut für Telekommunikationsnormen): Route des Lucioles 650, 06921 Sophia Antipolis Cedex, France; tel (+33) 4-92-94-42-00; fax (+33) 4-93-65-47-16; e-mail etsi@etsi.fr; internet www.etsi.org; President: F. da Silva; Director-General: K.H. Rosenbroek; Deputy Director-General: J. Friis.

EUROCONTROL (European Organisation for the Safety of Air Navigation / Organisation Européenne pour la Sécurité de la Navigation Aérienne / Europäische Organisation für Flugsicherung): Rue de la Fusée 96, 1130 Brussels, Belgium; tel (+32) 2-7299011; fax (+32) 2-7299044; internet www.eurocontrol.int; President: V. Aguado; Contact: G. Stadler.

INDEX OF FULL NAMES

(Index entries have been extracted from the sections Trade and Professional Associations, European Interest Groups and Non-Governmental Organizations, European Church Associations, and Miscellaneous)

A

The Directory of EU Information Sources

G

The Directory of EU Information Sources

STUDIES IN EUROPEAN INTEGRATION

EU Member States

AUSTRIA

Krems

Donau-Universität Krems: Abteilung für Europäische Integration, Dr Karl-Dorrek-Strasse 30, 3500 Krems, Austria; tel (+43 2732) 893-24-01; fax (+43 2732) 893-44-00; e-mail eu@donau-uni.ac.at; internet www.donau-uni-ac.at/euro.
'EURO-JUS' Academic Expert in European Law (1)
'EURO-JUS' Master of Advanced Studies in European Law (2)
Duration: 2 semesters (1) and 4 semesters (2)
Language: German
In charge: Prof. Dr Manfred Straube, Dr Siegfried Fina
Contacts: Dr Siegfried Fina, Reinhold Lindner

Lochau

Schloss Hofen GmbH, Zentrum für Wissenschaft und Weiterbildung: Hoferstrasse 26, 6911 Lochau, Austria; tel (+43 5574) 4930-0; fax (+43 5574) 4930-22; e-mail schlosshofen.sh@schulen .vol.at; internet www.vol.at/schlosshofen
Master of Advanced Studies: European Law
Duration: 5 semesters
Language: German
In charge: Prof. Dr Waldemar Hummer (University of Innsbruck); Prof. Dr Michael Schzeitzer (University of Passau)
Contact: Dr Armin Paul

Schloss Hofen GmbH, Zentrum für Wissenschaft und Weiterbildung: Hoferstrasse 26, 6911 Lochau, Austria; tel (+43 5574) 4930-0; fax (+43 5574) 4930-22; e-mail schlosshofen.sh@schulen .vol.at; internet www.vol.at/schlosshofen
Academic Expert in European Law
Duration: 3 terms
Language: German
In charge: Prof. Dr Waldemar Hummer (University of Innsbruck); Prof. Dr Michael Schzeitzer (University of Passau); Dr Armin Paul

Vienna

Wirtschaftsuniversität Wien: Centre for International Studies, Wirtschaftsuniversität Wien, Augasse 2–6, 1090 Vienna, Austria; tel (+43 1) 313-36-4310; fax (+43 1) 313-36-752; e-mail zas@ wu-wien.ac.at; internet wu-wien.ac.at
Dr Rer. Soc. Oec.
Duration: 2 years
Language: German
Contact: Centre for International Studies

BELGIUM

Bruges

Collège d'Europe: Bureau d'Admission, 11 Dijver, 8000 Bruges, Belgium; tel (+32 50) 44-99-11; fax (+32 50) 44-99-00; e-mail info@coleurop.be; internet www .coleurop.be.
Master in European Studies
Duration: 1 year
Languages: French and English
Contact: Thierry Monforti (Academic Secretary)

Brussels

Université Libre de Bruxelles (ULB): Institut d'Études Européennes, Secrétariat des Affaires Étudiantes, 39 avenue F. D. Roosevelt, CP 172, 1050 Brussels, Belgium; tel (+32 2) 650-30-77; fax (+32 2) 650-30-68; e-mail iee@admin.ulb.ac.be; internet www.ulb.ac.be/iee.
DEA en Sciences Économiques
Duration: 1 year
Languages: French and English
In charge: G. Kurgan, J.-J. Heirwegh
Contact: M. Kuneben

Université Libre de Bruxelles (ULB): Institut d'Études Européennes, Secrétariat des Sciences Politiques, 50 avenue F. D. Roosevelt, CP 135, 1050 Brussels, Belgium; tel (+32 2) 650-39-04; fax (+32 2) 650-31-98; e-mail avanhoutvin@admin .ulb.ac.be; internet www.ulb.ac.be.
DEA en Sciences Politiques
Duration: 1 year
Languages: French and English
In charge: Pascal Delwit
Contact: Anne Vanhoutvin

Université Libre de Bruxelles (ULB): MBA–École de Commerce Solvay, 21 avenue F. D. Roosevelt, CP 145, 1050 Brussels, Belgium; tel (+32 2) 650-41-67; fax (+32 2) 650-41-99; e-mail mba@ulb.ac.be; internet www.ulb.ac.be/soco/solvay/mba.
Master of Business Administration
Duration: 1 year
Language: English
In charge: A. Farber
Contact: C. Leclercq

Université Libre de Bruxelles (ULB): Institut d'Études Européennes, Secrétariat des Affaires Étudiantes, 39 avenue F. D. Roosevelt, CP 172, 1050 Brussels, Belgium; tel (+32 2) 650-30-77; fax (+32 2) 650-30-68; e-mail iee@admin.ulb.ac.be; internet www.ulb.ac.be/iee.
DES en Droit Européen
Duration: 2 years (possible in 1 year)
Languages: French and English

In charge: G. Kurgan
Contact: M. Kuneben

Université Libre de Bruxelles (ULB): Institut d'Études Européennes, Secrétariat des Affaires Étudiantes, 39 avenue F. D. Roosevelt, CP 172, 1050 Brussels, Belgium; tel (+32 2) 650-30-77; fax (+32 2) 650-30-68; e-mail iee@admin.ulb.ac.be; internet www.ulb.ac.be/iee.
DES en Économie Européenne
Duration: 1 year
Languages: French and English
In charge: G. Kurgan
Contact: M. Kuneben

Université Libre de Bruxelles (ULB): Institut d'Études Européennes, Secrétariat des Affaires Étudiantes, 39 avenue F. D. Roosevelt, CP 172, 1050 Brussels, Belgium; tel (+32 2) 650-30-77; fax (+32 2) 650-30-68; e-mail iee@admin.ulb.ac.be; internet www.ulb.ac.be/iee.
DES en Politique Européenne
Duration: 2 years (possible in 1 year)
Languages: French and English
In charge: G. Kurgan
Contact: M. Kuneben

Université Libre de Bruxelles (ULB): Institut d'Études Européennes, Secrétariat des Affaires Étudiantes, 39 avenue F. D. Roosevelt, CP 172, 1050 Brussels, Belgium; tel (+32 2) 650-30-77; fax (+32 2) 650-30-68; e-mail iee@admin.ulb.ac.be; internet www.ulb.ac.be/iee.
DEC 2 en Études Européennes
Duration: 1 year
Languages: French and English
In charge: G. Kurgan
Contact: M. Kuneben

Vrije Universiteit Brussel (VUB): Fakulteit der Rechtsgeleerdheid, Program on International Legal Cooperation, Pleinlaan 2, 1050 Brussels, Belgium; tel (+32 2) 629-26-31; fax (+32 2) 629-26-62; e-mail secrpilc@vub.ac.be; internet www.vub.ac.be/pilc.
LL.M. in International Legal Co-operation
Duration: 1 year
Language: English
In charge: Prof. Dr B. De Schutter
Contact: A. Lodens

Ghent

Universiteit Gent: Faculteit der Rechtsgeleerdheid, Europees Instituut, Universiteitstraat 4, 9000 Ghent, Belgium; tel (+32 9) 264-69-02; fax (+32 9) 264-69-02; e-mail lode.vandenhende@ rug.ac.be; internet www.admin.rug.ac .be/acs/edu.html.
Specialisatieopleiding Europees Recht
Duration: 1 year
Language: Dutch
Contact: Lode Van Den Hende

Leuven

Katholieke Universiteit Leuven (KUL): Faculty of Law, Centre for Advanced Legal Studies, Tiensestraat 41, 3000 Leuven, Belgium; tel (+32 16) 32-52-08/32-53-12; fax (+32 16) 32-53-13; e-mail lut.herten@law.kuleuven.ac.be; e-mail jules.stuyck@law.kuleuven.ac.be.
Master of Laws
Duration: 1 year (possible in 2 years)
Language: English
In charge: Prof. Jules Stuyck (Director)
Contact: Lut Herten (Administrative Co-ordinator)

Katholieke Universiteit Leuven (KUL): European Studies, Blijde-Inkomststraat 5, 3000 Leuven, Belgium; tel (+32 16) 32-49-81; fax (+32 16) 32-53-44; e-mail arlet.hendrickx@arts.kuleuven.ac.be; internet www.kuleuven.ac.be/facdep/arts/onderw/eurstud.htm.
MA in European Studies
Duration: 1 year
Language: English
In charge: Prof. H. Van Gorp (Director)
Contact: A. Hendrickx

Liège

Université de Liège: Faculté de Droit, 7 boulevard du Rectorat, Bâtiment B31, 4000 Liège, Belgium; tel (+32 4) 366-30-38; fax (+32 4) 366-45-57; e-mail yrogister@ulg.ac.be.
DEA en Relations Internationales et Intégration Européenne
Duration: 1 year (or may be spread over a maximum period of 3 consecutive years)
Language: French
In charge: Jean Beaufays
Contact: Yves Rogister

Université de Liège: Institut d'Études Juridiques Européennes, 3 boulevard du Rectorat, Bâtiment B33, boîte 9, 4000 Liège, Belgium; tel (+32 4) 366-31-56; fax (+32 4) 366-31-55; e-mail ieje@ulg.ac.be; internet www.ulg.ac.be/ieje
DES en Droit Européen
Duration: 1 year
Language: French
In charge: Prof. Paul Demare
Contact: Nicolas Parisis (Assistant)

Louvain-la-Neuve

Université Catholique de Louvain (UCL): Institut d'Études Européennes, 1 place des Doyens, 1348 Louvain-la-Neuve, Belgium; tel (+32 10) 47-84-88; fax (+32 10) 47-85-49; e-mail gelinne@euro.ucl.ac.be; internet www.euro.ucl.ac.be/euro/home/iee.html.
Diplôme d'Études Complémentaires en Études Européennes
Duration: 1 year
Language: French
In charge: Prof. Michel Dumoulin
Contact: Nadine Gelinne

Université Catholique de Louvain (UCL): Institut d'Études Européennes, 1 place des Doyens, 1348 Louvain-la-Neuve, Belgium; tel (+32 10) 47-84-88; fax (+32 10) 47-85-49; e-mail gelinne@euro.ucl.ac.be; internet www.euro.ucl.ac.be/euro/home/iee.html.
Master in European Studies
Duration: 1 year
Language: English
In charge: Prof. Michel Dumoulin
Contact: Nadine Gelinne

Université Catholique de Louvain (UCL): Institut des Sciences du Travail, 1 place des Doyens, 1348 Louvain-la-Neuve, Belgium; tel (+32 10) 47-39-13/47-39-15; fax (+32 10) 47-39-14; e-mail gustin@trav.ucl.ac.be.
Master Européen en Sciences du Travail
Duration: 1 year (September–January in Belgium; February–June in another country)
Languages: French, English, German, Italian, Portuguese or Spanish
In charge: Prof. Armand Spineux
Contact: Marie-Louise Sacre-Gustin

Mons

Facultés Universitaires Catholiques de Mons (FUCAM): Faculté des Sciences Politiques, 151 chaussée de Binche, 7000 Mons, Belgium; tel (+32 651) 32-32-69/32-33-27; fax (+32 651) 32-33-63; e-mail leloup@fucam.ac.be; e-mail doison@fucam.ac.be; internet www.fucam.ac.be.
Diplôme d'Études Complémentaires en Relations Internationales et Européennes
Duration: 1 year
Language: French
In charge: Fabienne Leloup
Contact: Irène Doison

DENMARK

Aalborg

Aalborg Universitet: International Affairs, Fibigerstrade 2, 9220 Aalborg, Denmark; fax (+45) 98-15-11-26.
Diploma in European Studies
Duration: 1 year (courses start 1st February)
Language: English
In charge: Prof. S. Z. von Dosenrode
Contact: Jytte Kongstad

Aalborg Universitet: International Affairs, Fibigerstrade 2, 9220 Aalborg, Denmark; fax (+45) 98-15-11-26.
Master in European Studies
Duration: 2 years
Language: English
In charge: Prof. S. Z. von Dosenrode
Contact: Jytte Kongstad

Roskilde

Roskilde Universitet: Department of Social Sciences, POB 260, 4000 Roskilde, Denmark; tel (+45) 46-74-25-85; fax (+45) 46-74-30-80; e-mail bgr@ruc.dk.
European Labour Market Policy
Duration: 1 semester
Language: English
In charge: Dr Bent Greve

Roskilde Universitet: Department of Social Sciences, POB 260, 4000 Roskilde, Denmark; tel (+45) 46-74-25-85; fax (+45) 46-74-30-80; e-mail bgr@ruc.dk.
Master in European Social Policy Analysis
Duration: 1 year
Language: English
In charge: Dr Bent Greve

Roskilde Universitet: Jean Monnet Chair, POB 260, 4000 Roskilde, Denmark; tel (+45) 46-74-20-44; fax (+45) 46-74-30-83; e-mail amoroso@ruc.dk.
Master's Programme in European Society, Science and Technology (ESST)
Duration: 20 hours
Language: English
In charge: Prof. Bruno Amoroso
Contact: Danyi Wang

FINLAND

Helsinki

Helsinki School of Economics (HSE): Business Administration, Department of International Business, Runeberginkatu 22–24, 00100 Helsinki, Finland; tel (+358 9) 4313-8667; fax (+358 9) 4313-8511; fax (+358 9) 4313-8880; e-mail seristo@hkkk.fi; e-mail paajanen@hkkk.fi.
MSc in Economics
Language: English
In charge: Dr H. Seristo
Contact: M. Paajanen

University of Helsinki: LL.M. Steering Committee, Faculty of Law, POB 4, Yliopistonkatu 3, 00014 Helsinki, Finland; tel (+358 9) 1912-2148; fax (+358 9) 1912-2152; e-mail llm-programme@helsinki.fi.
LL.M.
Duration: 1 year
Language: English
In charge: Jan Klabbers
Contact: Laura Nyman

Tampere

University of Tampere: Department of Political Science and International Relations, International School of Social Sciences (ISSS), Faculty of Social Sciences, POB 607, 33101 Tampere, Finland; (+358 3) 1215-7284; fax (+358 3) 1215-7287; e-mail isss@uta.fi; internet www.uta.fi/laitokset/isss.
M.Soc.Sc. International Relations and European Studies
Duration: 2 years
Language: English
In charge: Osmo Apunen, Iyriki Kakonen
Contact: Marja Jukola-Aho (ISSS Administrator)

University of Tampere: Department of Political Science and International Relations, International School of Social Sciences (ISSS), Faculty of Social Sciences, POB 607, 33101 Tampere, Finland; tel (+358 3) 1215-7284; fax (+358 3) 1215-7287; e-mail isss@uta.fi; internet www.uta.fi/laitokset/isss.
Master of Social Sciences with European Studies
Duration: 2 years
Language: English
In charge: Harri Melin
Contact: Marja Jukola-Aho (ISSS Administrator)

University of Tampere: Department of Political Science and International Relations, International School of Social Sciences (ISSS), Faculty of Social Sciences, POB 607, 33101 Tampere, Finland; tel (+358 3) 1215-7284; fax (+358 3) 1215-7287; e-mail isss@uta.fi; internet www.uta.fi/laitokset/isss.
International Relations
In charge: Helena Rytövuori-Apunen
Contact: Marja Jukola-Aho (ISSS Administrator)

Turku

University of Turku: 20014 Turku, Finland; tel (+358 2) 333-53-87; fax (+358 2) 333-62-90; e-mail eantola@utu.fi; internet www.utu.fi/erill/jean-monnet.
Certificate of European Diplomatic Studies
Duration: 1 year
Language: English
In charge and contact: Esko Antola

FRANCE

Aix-en-Provence

Université d'Aix-Marseille III: Faculté de Droit et de Science Politique, 38 avenue de l'Europe, 13090 Aix-en-Provence, France; tel (+33 4) 42-52-72-50; fax (+33 4) 42-52-72-60; e-mail ceric@aix.pacwan.net; internet univ.u-3mrs.fr.
DEA Droit Communautaire
Duration: 1 year (possible in 2 years under certain conditions)
Language: French
In charge: Prof. L. Dubouis
Contact: Teyssot Castellan

Amiens

Université de Picardie Jules Verne: Faculté de Droit et des Sciences Politiques et Sociales, Pôle Universitaire Cathédrale, 10 Placette Lafleur, BP 2716, 80025 Amiens Cédex 01, France; tel (+33 3) 22-82-71-03; e-mail evelyne.mouton@u-picardie.fr; internet www.u-picardie.fr/~labocruc/e.
DEA de Droit Européen
Duration: 1 year (possible in 2 years)
Languages: French and other European languages used
Contact: Evelyne Mouton

Bordeaux

Université Montesquieu—Bordeaux IV: Avenue Léon Duguit, 33608 Pessac, France; tel (+33 5) 56-84-85-48; fax (+33 5) 56-84-29-25.
DEA de Droit Communautaire
Duration: 1 year
Language: French
In charge: Jean-Claude Gautron
Contact: Secrétariat CRDE

Cergy-Pontoise

University of Cergy-Pontoise: 8 avenue du Parc, Bâtiment L, 95000 Cergy-Pontoise, France; tel (+33 1) 34-25-49-09; fax (+33 1) 34-25-49-05; e-mail gbossuat@aol.com; e-mail bossuat@u-cergy.fr.
DEA Identité Européenne et Politique Française
Duration: 20 hours
Language: French
In charge: Gérard Bossuat
Contact: Nadine Poirou (Secrétariat, 3ème cycle)

Lille

Université de Lille II: 1 place Déliot, BP 629, 59024 Lille Cédex, France; tel (+33 3) 20-90-74-00; fax (+33 3) 20-90-74-03.
DEA de Droit
Duration: 1 year
Language: French
In charge and contact: Vincent Coussirat-Coustère

Université des Sciences et Technologies (Lille I): Faculté des Sciences Économiques et Sociales, Bâtiment SH2, 59655 Villeneuve d'Ascq Cédex, France; tel (+33 3) 20-43-67-52; fax (+33 3) 20-43-66-55; e-mail jayet@pop.univ-lille1.fr.
DEA Espace Européen Économique et Social
Duration: 1 year
Languages: French and English
In charge: Hubert Ayet, Philippe Rollet

Lyon

Université Jean Moulin (Lyon III): CDRE, 15 quai Claude Bernard, 69007 Lyon, France; tel (+33 4) 72-72-44-42; fax (+33 4) 72-72-44-66.
DEA de Droit Communautaire
Duration: 1 year (possible in 2 years)
Language: French
In charge: Christian Philip

Université Jean Moulin (Lyon III): Faculté de Droit, 15 quai Claude Bernard, 69003 Lyon, France; tel (+33 4) 72-72-45-93; fax (+33 4) 72-72-21-31.
DESS en Droit Communautaire
Duration: 1 year
Languages: French and English
In charge: Jean-Yves de Cara
Contact: Gémin Jacovidès

Montpellier

Université de Montpellier I: Faculté de Droit, 39 rue de l'Université, 34060 Montpellier Cédex, France; tel (+33 4) 67-61-54-58; fax (+33 4) 67-61-54-58; e-mail assidedh@imaginet.fr.
DEA en Droit Communautaire et Européen
Duration: 1 year
Language: French
In charge and contact: Prof. Frédéric Sudre (Jean Monnet Professor)

Nancy

Université de Nancy II: Centre Européen Universitaire, 15 place Carnot, CS 4219, 54042 Nancy Cédex, France; tel (+33 3) 83-36-52-84; fax (+33 3) 83-35-76-05.
DEA Droit Communautaire
Duration: 1 year
Language: French

Université de Nancy II: Centre Européen Universitaire, 15 place Carnot, CS 4219, 54042 Nancy Cédex, France; tel (+33 3) 83-36-52-84; fax (+33 3) 83-35-76-05; e-mail ceu@droit-eco.u-nancy.fr.
Diplôme d'Etudes Supérieures Européennes (DESE)
Duration: 1 year
Language: French
In charge: Prof. Alain Buzelay
Contact: C. Dumondel (Secretariat)

Université de Nancy II: Centre Européen Universitaire, 15 place Carnot, CS 4219, 54042 Nancy Cédex, France; tel (+33 3) 83-36-52-84; fax (+33 3) 83-35-76-05; e-mail ceu@droit-eco.u-nancy.fr.
DESE en Gestion Financière et Espace Européen
Duration: 1 year
Language: French
In charge: Prof. Alain Buzelay
Contact: C. Dumondel (Secretariat)

Paris

Institut d'Études Politiques de Paris: Secrétariat du Cycle supérieur d'études européennes, Pôle Européen de Sciences Po, 5 place Saint Thomas d'Aquin, 75007 Paris, France; tel (+33 1) 44-39-74-90; fax (+33 1) 44-39-74-91; e-mail europe@sciences-po.fr.
Cycle Supérieur d'Études Européennes
Duration: 2 years
Language: French
In charge: Prof. Jean Leca
Contact: Edith Regnault

Université de Paris I (Panthéon-Sorbonne): 12 place du Panthéon, 75231 Paris Cédex 05, France; tel (+33 1) 46-34-97-52; fax (+33 1) 46-34-98-69.
DESS Droit Européen
Duration: 1 year (October–October)
Language: French
In charge: Prof. Dominique Berlin
Contact: Mme de Perier

Université de Paris I (Panthéon–Sorbonne): 12 place du Panthéon, 75231 Paris Cédex 05, France; tel (+33 1) 46-34-97-52; fax (+33 1) 46-34-98-69.
DEA de Droit Communautaire et Européen
Duration: 1 year (October–October)
Language: French
In charge: Prof. Philippe Manin
Contact: Mme de Perier

Université de Paris I (Panthéon–Sorbonne): 12 place du Panthéon, 75231 Paris Cédex 05, France; tel (+33 1) 46-34-97-52; fax (+33 1) 44-07-08-33.
DESS en Droit du Marché Européen
Duration: 1 year (October–May)
Language: French
In charge: Prof. Dominique Berlin
Contact: Mme de Perier

Université de Paris II (Panthéon – Assas): Service des Inscriptions en 3ème cycle, 12 place du Panthéon, 75231 Paris Cédex 05, France; tel (+33 1) 44-41-56-64; fax (+33 1) 44-41-59-17.
DEA en Droit Communautaire
Duration: 1 year
Language: French
In charge: Prof. Jacqueline Dutheil de la Rochère, Prof. Hélène Gaudemet-Tallon

Université de Paris II (Panthéon – Assas): Service des Inscriptions en 3ème cycle, 12 place du Panthéon 12, 75231 Paris Cédex 05, France; tel (+33 1) 44-41-57-00; fax (+33 1) 44-41-55-13.
DESS de Droit Européen des Affaires
Duration: 1 year
Language: French
In charge: Prof. Louis Vogel
Contact: Mme Leleu

Université de Paris V (René Descartes): Faculté de Droit, 10 avenue Pierre Larousse, 92245 Malakoff Cédex, France; tel (+33 1) 41-17-30-00; fax (+33 1) 46-56-05-29; internet www.droit.univ-paris5.fr
DESS de Droit Européen des Affaires
Duration: 1 year
Languages: French and 1 foreign language of choice (English or German)
In charge: Prof. Patrick Lambaud
Contact: Service du 3ème cycle de la Faculté de Droit

Université de Paris X (Nanterre): 200 avenue de la République, 92001 Nanterre Cédex, France; tel (+33 1) 40-97-77-59
DEA Droit des Relations Économiques Internationales et Communautaire
Duration: 1 year
Language: French
In charge: Prof. Alain Pellet
Contact: Bureau du 3ème cycle

Université de Paris XI (Paris-Sud): Faculté de Droit Jean Monnet, Secrétariat du 3ème cycle, 54 boulevard Desgranges, 92330 Sceaux Cédex, France; tel (+33 1) 40-91-17-62; fax (+33 1) 40-91-17-15.
DESS en Droit de l'Union Européenne
Duration: 1 year

Language: French
In charge: Prof. Xavier Delcros
Contact: Mme Delaire

Université de Paris XI (Paris-Sud): Faculté de Droit Jean Monnet, 54 boulevard Desgranges, 92330 Sceaux Cédex, France; tel (+33 1) 40-91-17-63; tel (+33 1) 39-25-53-42; e-mail dormoy@jm.u-psud.fr.
DEA Droit Public International et Européen
Duration: 1 year
Languages French; fluent English is a requirement
Contact: Mme Delaire

Université de Marne-la-Vallée: Cité Descartes, 5 boulevard Descartes, Champs sur Marne, 77454 Marne-la-Vallée Cédex 2, France; tel (+33 1) 49-32-91-50; fax (+33 1) 49-32-91-53.
DESS de Géopolitique Européenne
Duration: 1 year
Languages: French, English, German and Spanish
In charge: Chantal Millon-Delsol
Contact: Odile Desarménien

Université de Paris Nord (Villetaneuse): UFR de Sciences Economiques et de Gestion, Avenue Jean-Baptiste Clément, 93430 Villetaneuse, France; tel (+33 1) 49-40-33-17; fax (+33 1) 49-40-33-34.
DESS Economie Européenne – Environnement, Information, Réglementation
Duration: 1 year
Language: French, with 1 course taught in English
In charge: Prof. Lysiane Cartelier (Professor, Economic Sciences), Mario Dehore (French Commissariat Général au Plan)
Contact: Prof. Lysiane Cartelier

Institut Catholique de Paris: Faculté Sciences Sociales et Économiques, 21 rue d'Assas, 75270 Paris Cédex 06, France; tel (+33 1) 44-39-52-89; fax (+33 1) 45-44-27-14.
DESS de Relations Publiques entre Groupements d'Intérêts et l'Union Européenne: Répresentation et Négociation
Duration: 1 year
Languages: French and English
In charge: Michel Clumen (Director)
Contact: Secretariat

Pôle Universitaire Léonard de Vinci: Direction Enseignement Affaires Européennes, 92916 Paris–La Défense Cédex, France; tel (+33 1) 41-16-72-52; fax (+33 1) 41-16-75-46; e-mail christine.delière-devinci.fr; internet web02.devinci.fr/mae
European Business Management and MA in European Public Policy (with South Bank University, London)
Duration: 34 weeks of lectures, 2 months business placement, 2 weeks based in European institutions in Brussels
Languages: French and English
In charge: Loïc Ernest (Law), Didier Schlacter (Industry, Enterprises), Josette

Peyrard (Finance), Michel Clamen (Lobbying)
Contacts: Eric Carlier (director), Christine Delière (Co-ordinator)

Poitiers

Université de Poitiers: Faculté de Droit, 93 avenue du Recteur Pineau, 86022 Poitiers Cédex, France; tel (+33 5) 49-50-71-51; tel: (+33 5) 49-45-31-35; fax (+33 5) 49-41-84-28; e-mail francois.herrouet@droit.univ-poitiers.fr; internet www.univ-poitiers.fr.
DEA Droit Public Général
Duration: 1 year
Language: French
In charge: J. Pierre Chevalier

Rennes

Université de Rennes 1: Faculté des Sciences Économiques, 7 place Hoche, 35065 Rennes Cédex, France; tel (+33 2) 99-25-35-75; fax (+33 2) 99-25-35-93; e-mail martine.levelu@univ-rennes1.fr.
DEA en Economie Industrielle
Duration: 1 year
Languages: French and English
Contact: Martine Levelu

Université de Rennes 1: Centre de Recherches Européennes (CEDRE), Faculté de Droit et de Science Politique, 9 rue Jean Macé, 35042 Rennes Cédex, France; tel (+33 2) 99-84-76-82; fax (+33 2) 99-84-77-40; e-mail cedre@univ-rennes1.fr; internet www.univ-rennes1.fr
DEA en Droit Communautaire
Duration: 1 year
Language: French
Contact: Gentiane Deslandes

Strasbourg

Université Robert Schuman (Strasbourg III): Secrétariat de l'Institut des Hautes Etudes Européennes, 10 rue Schiller, 67081 Strasbourg Cédex, France; tel (+33 3) 88-15-05-45; fax (+33 3) 88-36-86-11; e-mail ihee@urs.u-strasbg.fr.
Certificat d'Études Européennes
Duration: 1 year
Language: French
In charge: Prof. Flauss
Contact: Catherine Martineau (Secrétariat de la scolarité)

Université Robert Schuman (Strasbourg III): Secrétariat de l'Institut des Hautes Etudes Européennes, 10 rue Schiller, 67081 Strasbourg Cédex, France; tel (+33 3) 88-15-05-45; fax (+33 3) 88-36-86-11; e-mail ihee@urs.u-strasbg.fr.
DEA Droit Comparé des Droits de l'Homme: La Protection des Droits de l'Homme en Europe
Duration: 1 year
Language: French
Contact: Catherine Martineau (Secrétariat de la scolarité)

Université Robert Schuman (Strasbourg III): Secrétariat de l'Institut des Hautes Etudes Européennes, 10 rue Schiller, 67081 Strasbourg Cédex, France; tel (+33 3) 88-15-05-45; fax (+33 3) 88-36-86-11; e-mail ihee@urs.u-strasbg.fr.
DEA Histoire de l'Europe au XXème Siècle: Histoire des Relations Internationales et de l'Intégration Européenne
Duration: 1 year
Language: French
In charge: Prof. Nicole Pietri
Contact: Catherine Martineau (Secrétariat de la scolarité)

Université Robert Schuman (Strasbourg III): Secrétariat du DESS, Institut d'Etudes Politiques, 47 avenue de la Forêt Noire, 67081 Strasbourg Cédex, France; tel (+33 3) 88-41-77-25; e-mail maud.diebold@iep.u-strasbg.fr.
DESS Politiques Publiques en Europe
Duration: 1 year
Languages: French, German and English
In charge: Prof. Michel Devoluy, Damien Broussolle, Didier Georgakakis
Contact: Maud Diebold

Centre Universitaire d'Enseignement du Journalisme Robert Schuman (CUEJ): 11 rue du Maréchal Juin, BP 13, 67043 Strasbourg, France; tel (+33 3) 88-14-45-34; fax (+33 3) 88-14-45-35; e-mail admin@cuej.u-strasbg.fr; internet cuej.u-strasbg.fr.
DESS en Eurojournalisme
Duration: 1 year
Languages: French and 2 other community languages
Contact: Xavier Delcourt

Tours

Université de François Rabelais: Faculté de Droit, DEA Droit Public, 50 ave Jean Portalis, BP 607, 37206 Tours Cédex 3, France; tel (+33 2) 47-36-84-88; fax (+33 2) 47-36-84-87; e-mail iee@droit.univ-tours.fr.
DEA de Droit Public
Duration: 1 year
Language: French
Contact: Joëlle Tranchant

Université de François Rabelais: Faculté de Droit, DEA Droit Public, 50 ave Jean Portalis, BP 607, 37206 Tours Cédex 3, France; tel (+33 2) 47-36-84-88; fax (+33 2) 47-36-84-87; e-mail iee@droit.univ-tours.fr.
DESS de Juristes Européens
Duration: 1 year
Language: French
Contact: Joëlle Tranchant

Valenciennes

Université de Valenciennes: Faculté de Droit, d'Économie et de Gestion, 'Les Tertiales', Rue des Cent Têtes, BP 311, 59304 Valenciennes Cédex, France; tel (+33 3) 27-14-76-02; fax (+33 3) 27-14-

76-19; e-mail martine.feutry@univ-valenciennes.fr.
DESS Droit des Affaires Européennes et Internationales
Duration: 13 months
Language: French
In charge: Prof. Michel Defossez (Dean of the Faculty)
Contact: Martine Feutry

GERMANY

Aachen

Technische Hochschule Aachen: Faculty of Arts, Historisches Institut, RWTH Aachen, Kopernikusstrasse 16, 52056 Aachen, Germany; tel (+49 241) 80-60-30; fax (+49 241) 88-88-156; e-mail: lohrmann@rwth-aachen.de.
Master in European Studies
Duration: 2 years
Languages: German and 2 European languages
In charge: Prof. Armin Heinen
Contact: Hans Brückner

Rheinisch-Westfälische Technische Hochschule: RWTH Aachen, Koordinierungsstelle, Zusatzstudiengang Europastudien, Ahornstrasse 55-D, 52056 Aachen, Germany; tel (+49 241) 80-77-70/80-60-36; fax (+49 241) 888-83-57; e-mail armin.heinen@post.rwth-aachen.de; internet www.rwth-aachen.de/zentral/aaaguide-guide58.htm.
Magister in Europastudien (MES)
Duration: 2 years
Language: German
In charge: Prof. Armin Heinen
Contact: Dr Christian Bremen

Berlin

Freie Universität Berlin, Humboldt-Universität Berlin, Technische Universität Berlin: European Centre for Comparative Government and Public Policy, Rheinbabenallee 49, 14199 Berlin, Germany; internet www.eurozent.de
Postgraduate Programme in European Studies
Duration: 10 months
Languages: German, English and French

Bonn

Rheinische Friedrich-Wilhelmus-Universität: Universität Bonn, Juristische Fakultät, Adenauerallee 24–42, 53113 Bonn, Germany; tel (+49 228) 73-79-01; fax (+49 228) 73-91-00
Aufbaustudium zum LL.M. in Rahmen des European Consortium of Law
Duration: 2 years
Language: German
In charge: Dr Ulrike Dorn (Assistant to the Dean)

Rheinische Friedrich-Wilhelmus-Universität: Universität Bonn, Rechts- und Staatswissenschaftliche Fakultät, Adenauerallee 24–42, 53113 Bonn,

Germany; tel (+49 228) 73-92-61; fax (+49 228) 73-91-00; internet www.jura.uni-bonn.de.
Master in Comparative Law
Duration: 1 year
Language: German
Contact: Dr Ulrike Dorn (Assistant to the Dean)

Bremen

Universität Bremen: Fachbereich 06: Rechtswissenschaft, Postfach 330440, 28334 Bremen, Germany; tel (+49 421) 218-35-82; fax (+49 421) 218-45-88; e-mail llmeur@uni-bremen.de; internet www.uni-bremen.de.
LL.M. in European and International Law
Duration: 1 year (full-time); 2 years (part-time)
Languages: German, English and French
Contact: Gerlinde Thomann-Kreye (Secretariat)

University of Applied Sciences Bremen: Master of European Studies, Hochschule Bremen/Hochschule für Öffentliche Verwaltung, Doventorcontrescarpe 172, Block C, 28195 Bremen, Germany; tel (+49 421) 361-59-907; fax (+49 421) 361-51-73; e-mail mblaschke@hfoev.bremen.de; internet www.hs-bremen.de.
Master of European Studies
Duration: 1 year
Language: English
In charge and contact: Dr Monika Blaschke (Co-ordinator)

Freiburg

Albert-Ludwigs-Universität Freiburg: Abteilung Ausländerstudium, Rektorat, Fahnenbergplatz, 79085 Freiburg, Germany; tel (+49 761) 203-43-72; fax (+49 761) 203-43-77; e-mail wehof@rek2.ukl.uni-freiburg.de.
LL.M. Magister Aufbaustudiengang der Rechtswissenschaftlichen Fakultät
Duration: 2 semesters
Language: German
Contact: Mr Wehojsits

Hamburg

University of Hamburg: Europa-Kolleg Hamburg, Aufbaustudiengang Europawissenschaften, Windmühlenweg 27, 22607 Hamburg, Germany; tel (+49 40) 82-27-27-27/82-27-27-29; fax (+49 40) 82-14-65; e-mail EuropaKollegpublic@uni-hamburg.de; internet www.jura.uni-hamburg.de; internet www.europa-kolleg-hamburg.de.
Postgraduate Course in European Studies
Duration: 1 year
Languages: German and English
In charge: Prof. Dr Thomas Bruha
Contact: Dr Carsten Nowak

Europa-Kolleg Hamburg: Aufbaustudiengang Europawissenschaften, Windmühlenweg 27, 22607 Hamburg,

Germany; tel (+49 40) 82-27-27-27/82-27-27-26; fax (+49 40) 82-14-65; e-mail EuropaKollegpublic@uni-hamburg.de; internet www.jura.uni-hamburg.de; internet www.europa-kolleg-hamburg.de.
Master of European Studies
Duration: 1 year
Languages: German, English and French
In charge: Prof. Dr Thomas Bruha
Contacts: Dr Carsten Nowak, Wolfgang Wurmnest

Jena

Friedrich-Schiller-Universität Jena: Jean-Monnet-Lehrstuhl für Öffentliches Recht, Europarecht, Völkerrecht und Internationales Wirtschaftsrecht, Friedrich-Schiller-Universität Jena, Carl-Zeiss-Str. 3, 07740 Jena, Germany; tel (+49 3641) 94-22-65; fax (+49 3641) 94-22-62; e-mail bplecher@lawnet1.recht.uni-jena.de.
Doctoral Programme: The Scope for Private and Public Law Regulation in European and International Economic Law
Duration: 2-4 semesters
Languages: German, English and French
In charge: Prof. Dr Karl Meessen
Contact: Barbara Plecher

Konstanz

University of Konstanz: Faculty of Law, Fach D117, 78457 Konstanz, Germany; tel (+49 7531) 88-23-31/88-23-27; fax (+49 7531) 88-32-95; e-mail astrid.stadler@uni-konstanz.de.
EU LL.M.
Duration: 4½ years
Languages: German plus 2 other languages
In charge: Dr iur. Astrid Stadler (Dean)

Leipzig

Universität Leipzig: Institut für Sprach- und Übersetzungswissenschaft, Brühl 34–50, 04109 Leipzig, Germany; tel (+49 341) 97-37-600; fax (+49 341) 97-37-649; e-mail isuew@rz.uni-leipzig.de; e-mail steube@rz.uni-leipzig.de; e-mail herting@rz-uni-leipzig.de; internet www.uni-leipzig.de/philol/sprach/europa.htm.
Master in European Studies
Duration: 2 years
Languages: German, English, French or Spanish, either Russian or another East European language
In charge: Dr Anita Steube
Contact: Dr Beate Herting

Munich

Technische Universität München: Lehrstuhl Allg. und Ind. BWL, Leopoldstrasse 139, 80804 Munich, Germany; tel (+49 89) 360-78-252; fax (+49 89) 360-78-222; e-mail wagner@aib.wiso.tu-muenchen.de.

Arbeits- und Wirtschaftswissenschaftliches Aufbaustudium / Diplom-Wirtschaftsingenieur / MBA
Duration: 2-3 years
Language: German
Contact: Eckhard Wagner

Oldenburg

University of Oldenburg: Professor für Öffentliches Wirtschaftsrecht, Fachbereich 4: Wirtschafts-und Rechtswissenschaften, Postfach 2503, Birkenweg 5, 26111 Oldenburg, Germany; tel (+49 441) 798-83-38; fax (+49 441) 798-82-87; e-mail go-frank@mrza.uni-oldenburg.de.
Double Diploma with Le Havre
Duration: Five years
Languages: German and French
In charge: Prof. Dr Götz Frank
Contact: Claude Sdursto

Pforzheim

Fachhochschule Pforzheim: Akademisches Auslandsamt, Tiefenbronner Strasse 65, 75175 Pforzheim, Germany; tel (+49 7231) 28-61-41; fax (+49 7231) 28-61-40; e-mail wolfaaa@fh-pforzheim.de; e-mail kreuzer@fh-pforzheim.de; internet intl.fh-pforzheim.de; internet www.fh-pforzheim.de.
European Business Certificate (EBC)
Duration: 2 semesters
Languages: German and English
In charge: Prof. Dr Siegfried Kreuzer

Saarbrücken

Universität des Saarlandes: Europa-Institut, Sektion Wirtschaftswissenschaft, Abteilung BWL, Universität des Saarlandes, Gebäude 15, Postfach 151150, 66041 Saarbrücken, Germany; tel (+49 681) 302-25-53; fax (+49 681) 302-45-73; e-mail mbaadmission@europa-institut.uni-sb.de; internet www.europa-institut.uni-sb.de.
MBA Europe / Certificate in European Management
Duration: 2 semesters (certificate); 3 semesters (Master); 8 semesters (part-time)
Languages: German and English
In charge: Prof. Dr Christian Scholt, Prof. Dr Joachim Zentes
Contact: Andreas Johann

Universität des Saarlandes: Europa-Institut, Sektion Wirtschaftswissenschaft, Abteilung VWL, z. Hd Frau Dipl.-Vw. Gesa Miehe, Universität des Saarlandes, Gebäude 16, Postfach 151150, 66041 Saarbrücken, Germany; tel (+49 681) 302-45-41; fax (+49 681) 302-47-32; e-mail eiwiwivwl@rz-uni.sb.de; internet www.europa-institut.uni-sb.de.
Master of Economics—Europe
Duration: 3 semesters
Languages: German and English
In charge: Prof. Dr Robert Holzmann, Prof. Dr Ayuvo Brunetti

Contact: Steffen Schüle

Universität des Saarlandes: Institute of European Studies, Law Department, Universität des Saarlandes, Postfach 151150, 66041 Saarbrücken, Germany; tel (+49 681) 302-36-53; fax (+49 681) 302-43-69; e-mail llm@europainstitut.de; internet europainstitut.de.
Certificate of European Studies
Duration: 1 year
Language: German
Contact: Julia Legleitner (Executive Manager)

Trier

Universität Trier: Fachbereich Rechtswissenschaft, 54286 Trier, Germany; tel (+49 651) 201-25-27; fax (+49 651) 201-39-11; e-mail leich@uni-trier.de; internet www.uni-trier.de/uni/fb5/fb5.htm.
Magister der Rechte (LL.M.)
Duration: 1 year
Language: German
In charge: Dr Rolf Birk
Contact: Ulrike Leich

Würzburg

Julius-Maximilians-Universität Würzburg: Juristische Fakultät, Domerschulstrasse 16, 97070 Würzburg, Germany; tel (+49 931) 31-23-00/31-23-24; fax (+49 931) 31-23-24/31-23-17; e-mail L-rechtsvergleichung@jura.uni-wuerzburg.de; e-mail L-europarecht@jura.uni-wuerzburg.de; internet www.jura.uni-wuerzburg.de/studieninformationen/index.htm.
Master in European Law / Certificate of Advanced Studies in European Law
Duration: 1 to 2 years
Languages: German and English
In charge and contacts: Dr K. Kreuzer, Prof. Dr D.H. Scheuing

GREECE

Athens

National and Capodistrian University of Athens: Ippokratous 33, Athens, Greece; tel (+30 1) 361-75-08; fax (+30 1) 361-65-77; e-mail kremalis@ath.forthnet.gr; internet www.epikayp.edui.gr.
Postgraduate Degree of Public Law
Duration: 2 semesters
Language: Greek
In charge: Prof. Dr Konstantionos Kremalis
Contact: Athina Diakou

National and Capodistrian University of Athens: Xenophontos Street 4, 105 57 Athens, Greece; tel (+30 1) 324-05-21; fax (+30 1) 324-05-21.
Postgraduate Programme in European and International Studies
Duration: 2 years
Languages: Greek and English
In charge and contact: Panos Kazakos

Panteion University of Social and Political Sciences: Syngrou Ave 136, 176 71 Athens, Greece; tel (+30 1) 920-18-32; fax (+30 1) 922-36-90; e-mail gtsaltas@panteion.gr.
Postgraduate Certificate: European Union and Developing Countries
Duration: 1 year
Language: Greek
In charge: Grigoris Tsaltas
Contact: Secretariat

Thessaloniki

Aristotle University of Thessaloniki: Administration Building, University Box 491, 54006 Thessaloniki, Greece; tel (+30 31) 99-55-91; fax (+30 31) 99-55-92; e-mail kafkalas@estia.arch.auth.gr; internet estia.arch.auth.gr.
Doctorate in Spatial Development and Planning
Duration: 3 years (minimum)
Language: Greek
Contact: Grigoris Kafkalas

HUNGARY

Budapest

Budapest University of Economic Sciences: European Studies Centre, Fovám tér 8, 1093 Budapest, Hungary; tel (+36 1) 217-66-52; fax (+36 1) 218-07-96; e-mail hajnalorinc@eustudce.bke.hu; internet alpha.bke.hu/eu/index.html.
MA in European Studies
Duration: 2 years (4 semesters)
Languages: Hungarian and English
In charge: Hajna Istvánffy Lörinc
Contact: Monika Marton

Budapest University of Economics: Faculty of Social Sciences, Department of World Economics, Kinizsi u. 1–7, 1093 Budapest, Hungary; tel (+36 1) 218-23-13; fax (+36 1) 215-29-90; e-mail vg_blaho@pegasus.bke.hu.
Ph.D. in International Relations
Duration: 2 years' course work, 3 years' research
Language: English
In charge: Prof. Tamas Szentes
Contact: Dr Andras Blaho

Central European University: International Relations and European Studies, Nádor utca 9, 1051 Budapest, Hungary; tel (+36 1) 327-30-17; fax (+36 1) 327-32-43; e-mail ires@ceu.hu; internet www.ceu.hu.
MA in International Relations and European Studies
Duration: 1 year
Language: English
In charge: Stefano Guzzini
Contact: Paul Benjamin , Programme Coordinator

College for European Studies—Foreign Trade Centre: Diósy Lajos u. 22–24, 1631 Budapest, Hungary; tel (+36 1)

467-7843; fax (+36 1) 407-1563; e-mail emese@kkf.hu; internet www.kkf.hu.
Specialist in European Studies
Duration: 3 semesters
Language: Hungarian and English
In charge and contact: Prof. Fayne Peter Emese

Szeged

University Josef Attila: Tisza L. krt 54, 6720 Szeged, Hungary; tel (+36 62) 45-40-00; fax (+36 62) 45-42-15; e-mail varnay@juris.u-szeged.hu.
Specialist in European Law
Duration: 5 semesters
Language: Hungarian
In charge: Dr Ernö Va'rnay
Contacts: Mihály Pa'lfy, Krisztina Lehotay

IRELAND

Cork

University College Cork: Department of History, Cork, Ireland; tel (+353 21) 90-26-93; fax (+353 21) 27-33-69; e-mail n.buckley@ucc.ie.
Ph.D. in European Integration (1)
M.Phil. in European Integration (2)
Taught MA in European Integration (3)
Duration: by research (1); 2 years by research (2); 1 year (3)
Language: English
Contact: Norma Buckley

Dublin

University College Dublin: Postgraduate Studies Office, Faculty of Arts, Belfield, Dublin 4, Ireland; tel (+353 1) 706-8604; fax (+353 1) 269-8605; e-mail dallen@acadamh.ucd.ie.
MA in European Studies
Duration: 1 year
Language: English
In charge and contact: Bridget Laffan

University College Dublin: Faculty of Law, Roebuck Castle, Belfield, Dublin 4, Ireland; tel (+353 1) 706-8743; fax (+353 1) 269-2655
LL.M. in European Law
Duration: 1 year
Language: English
In charge: James Bergeron, Honora Ni Chriogain

Limerick

University of Limerick: Centre for European Studies, Department of Government and Society, Plassey Technological Park, Limerick, Ireland; tel (+353 61) 20-24-45; fax (+353 61) 20-25-69; e-mail annemccarthy@ul.ie; e-mail david.coombes@ul.ie.
MA in European Integration
Duration: 1 year
Language: English
In charge: David Coombes
Contact: Anne McCarthy

University of Limerick: Law Department , Limerick, Ireland; tel (+353 61) 20-23-44; fax (+353 61) 20-24-17; e-mail dermot.walsh@ul.ie.
Master's in European and Comparative Law
Duration: 1 year
Language: English
In charge and contact: Dermot Walsh

Maynooth

National University of Ireland—St Patrick's College: Maynooth, Ireland; tel (+353 1) 708-3664; fax (+353 1) 708-3314; e-mail denise.dunne@may.ie.
MA in European Union Studies
Duration: 1 year
Language: English
In charge and contact: Dr Denise Dunne

ITALY

Bologna

The Bologna Center of the Johns Hopkins University: Via Belmeloro 11, 40126 Bologna, Italy; tel (+39 051) 23-21-85; fax (+39 051) 22-85-05; e-mail admission@jhubc.it; internet www.jhubc.it.
Graduate Diploma or MA
Duration: 1 year for the Graduate Diploma; 2 years for the MA
Language: English
In charge and contact: Registrar

The Bologna Center of the Johns Hopkins University: Via Belmeloro 11, 40126 Bologna, Italy; tel (+39 051) 23-21-85; fax (+39 051) 22-85-05; e-mail admission@jhubc.it; internet www.jhubc.it.
Master of International Public Policy
Duration: 1 year
Language: English
Contact: Registrar

University of Bologna: Istituto giuridico A. Cicu, Via Zamboni 27/29, 40126 Bologna, Italy; tel (+39 051) 24-30-13; tel (+39 051) 35-42-50; fax (+39 051) 25-96-24; e-mail cirdce@biblio.cib.unibo.it.
Corso di Perfezionamento in Diritto delle Comunità Europee
Duration: 6 months (January–June)
Languages: Italian with additional seminars in French and English
In charge: Prof. Lucia Serena Rossi
Contact: Dr Chiara Cattabriga

Catania

Università degli Studi di Catania: Dipartimento Studi Politici, Via Vittorio Emanuele 49, 95124 Catania, Italy; tel (+39 095) 734-7209; fax (+39 095) 734-7209; e-mail attinaf@mbox.unict.it; www.fscpo.unict.it/vademec/department/dottri.htm.
Ph.D. Course in International Relations—Program of European Union Politics
Duration: 3 years
Languages: Italian, English and French
In charge and contact: Prof. Fulvio Attinà

Ferrara

Università degli Studi di Ferrara: Dipartimento di Scienze Giuridiche, Corso Ercole I d'Este 37, 44100 Ferrara, Italy; tel (+39 0532) 21-10-85; fax (+39 0532) 20-01-88; e-mail bln@ifeuniv.unife.it.
Dottorato in Diritto Comunitario e Comparato del Lavoro
Duration: 3 years
Languages: Italian, English and French
In charge: Prof. Gian Guido Balandi

Florence

European University Institute: Academic Service, Via dei Roccettini 9, 50016 San Domenico di Fiesole, Italy; tel (+39 0554) 68-53-73; fax (+39 0554) 68-54-44; e-mail applyres@datacomm.iue.it; internet www.iue.it.
Master in Law LL.M.
Duration: 1 year
Languages: English and French
In charge: Prof. Dr Patrick Masterson
Contact: Ken Hulley

European University Institute: Academic Service, Via dei Roccettini 9, 50016 San Domenico di Fiesole, Italy; tel (+39 0554) 68-53-73; fax (+39 0554) 68-54-44; e-mail applyres@datacomm.iue.it; internet www.iue.it.
Doctoral Program
Duration: 3 years
Languages: English and French
In charge: Prof. Dr Patrick Masterson
Contact: Ken Hulley

Università degli Studi di Firenze: Facoltà di Scienze Politiche 'C. Alfieri', Via Laura 48, 50121 Florence, Italy; tel (+39 055) 275-70-52; fax (+39 055) 275-70-29; e-mail varsori@ccs^6.scpol.unifi.it
MA in European Studies
Duration: 1 year
Language: English
In charge: Antonio Varsori
Contact: Cristina Panerai

Lecce

Università degli Studi di Lecce: Via per Monteroni, Complesso Ecotkne, 73100 Lecce, Italy; tel (+39 0832) 32-06-97; fax (+39 0832) 32-06-97; e-mail cmusillo@sesia.unile.it.
MA in EU Administrative Law
Duration: 4 months
Language: Italian
In charge: Ernesto Sticchi Damiano
Contact: Cristiano Musillo

Milan

Bocconi University Graduate School of Management (SDA Bocconi): Divisione Master, Via Balilla 18, 20136 Milan, Italy; tel (+39 02) 58-36-32-81; fax (+39 02) 58-36-32-75; e-mail antonella.carpani@sda.uni-bocconi.it; internet www.sda.uni-bocconi.it/miem.

Master of International Economics and Management (MIEM)
Duration: 1 year
Language: English
Contact: Antonella Carpani

Università degli Studi di Milano: Scuola di Specializzazione in Diritto ed Economia delle Comunità Europee, Presso Istituto di Diritto Internazionale, Via Festa del Perdono 7, 20122 Milan, Italy; tel (+39 02) 58-35-25-12; fax (+39 02) 58-30-68-26.
Diploma di Specialista in Diritto ed Economia della Comunità Europee
Duration: 2 years
Languages: knowledge of 2 EU languages, besides Italian and mother tongue
In charge: Fausto Pocar
Contact: Secretariat

Padua

Università degli Studi di Padova: Centre for Training and Research on Human Rights and the Rights of Peoples, Via Anghinoni 10, 35121 Padua, Italy; tel (+39 049) 827-44-35; fax (+39 049) 827-44-30; e-mail hrd-european.master@venis.it; e-mail a.papisca@cdu.cepadu.unipd.it; internet hrd-euromaster.venis.it.
European MA in Human Rights and Democratization
Duration: 1 year
Languages: English and French
In charge: Antonio Papisca
Contact: Dr Marco Mascia

Università degli Studi di Padova: Dipartimento di Studi Internazionali, Via del Santo 77, 35123 Padua, Italy; tel (+39 049) 827-43-61; fax (+39 049) 827-43-55; e-mail ardia@ux1.unipd.it; internet www.dsi.unipd.it/corsi/c4.html.
Diritto, Economia e Politica dell' Unione Europea
Duration: 1 year
Language: Italian
In charge: Prof. Gabriele Orcalli
Contact: Danilo Ardia

Parma

Collegio Europeo di Parma: Borgo Lalatta 14, 43100 Parma, Italy; tel (+39 0521) 20-75-25; fax (+39 0521) 38-46-53; e-mail ceuropeo@tin.it.
EU Law, Economics and Politics
Duration: 1 year
Languages: Italian and French
In charge and contact: Prof. Fausto Capelli (Director)

Pavia

Università degli Studi di Pavia: Dipartimento Storico Geografico, Strada Nuova 65, 27100 Pavia, Italy; tel (+39 0382) 30-35-77; fax (+39 0382) 30-38-42; e-mail eurofed@univp.it.

History of Federalism and European Unity
Duration: 3 years
Language: Italian
Contact: Cinzia Rognoni Vercelli

Pisa

Scuola Superiore di Studi Universitari e di Perfezionamento 'Sant' Anna': Via Carducci 40, 56127 Pisa, Italy; tel (+39 050) 88-32-20; fax (+39 050) 88-32-25; e-mail infostudenti@sssup.it; internet www.sssup.it.
Doctoral Degree in Law
Duration: 3 years
Language: Italian
In charge: Andrea de Guttry
Contact: Students' Office of Scuola Superiore Sant' Anna

Reggio di Calabria

University of Reggio di Calabria: Istituto Superiore Europeo di Studi Politici, via del Torrione 101/F, 89125 Reggio di Calabria, Italy; tel (+39 0965) 33-14-79; fax (+39 0965) 33-14-79; e-mail isespcde@tin.it; internet www.csii/unirc.it/elenco_ospiti.htm.
European Legal Culture
Duration: 6 months (100 hours of courses)
Language: Italian
In charge: Domenico Da Empoli
Contact: Maria Tripodi

Rome

Institute of European Studies 'Alcide de Gasperi': Via Poli 29, 00187 Rome, Italy; tel (+39 06) 678-42-62; fax (+39 06) 679-41-01.
Master in European Studies
Duration: 1 year
Language: Italian
In charge: Giuseppe Schiavone (President)
Contact: Cesare Selva

Institute of European Studies 'Alcide de Gasperi': Via Poli 29, 00187 Rome, Italy; tel (+39 06) 678-42-62; fax (+39 06) 679-41-01.
Diploma in European Studies
Duration: 1 year
Language: Italian
In charge: Giuseppe Schiavone (President)
Contact: Cesare Selva

Università degli Studi di Roma 'La Sapienza': Via del Castro Laurenziano 9, 00161 Rome, Italy; tel (+39 06) 49-76-69-77; fax (+39 06) 49-76-62-86; e-mail euspeinf@sce.eco.uniroma1.it.
Diploma of Specialization in Law and Economics of the European Union
Duration: 2 years
Language: Italian

Turin

University Institute of European Studies: Via Maria Vittoria 26, 10123

Turin, Italy; tel (+39 011) 562-5458; fax (+39 011) 53-02-35; e-mail iuse@arpnet .it; internet www.arpnet.it/iuse.
International Trade Law Post-Graduate Course
Duration: 3 months
Language: English
In charge: Gianmaria Ajani, Giuseppe Porro

LUXEMBOURG

Luxembourg

Institut Européen d'Administration Publique—Antenne de Luxembourg: 2 circuit de la Foire Internationale, 1347 Luxembourg, Luxembourg; tel (+352) 42-62-30; fax (+352) 42-62-37.
Maîtrise en Études Juridiques Euro-péennes (in co-operation with the universities of Nancy and Thessaloniki)
Duration: 1 year (October–June)
Languages: French and English
Contact: Mlle Schuller

MALTA

Msida

University of Malta: European Documentation and Research Centre, Msida MSD 06, Malta; tel (+356) 3290-2001; fax (+356) 33-76-24; e-mail cdrc@um.edu.mt; internet www.um.edu.mt.
MA in European Studies
Duration: 1 year (full-time); 2 years (part-time)
Language: English
In charge: Roderick Pace
Contact: Monica Cauchi (Communications Officer, EDRC)

University of Malta: European Documentation and Research Centre, Msida MSD 06, Malta; tel (+356) 3290-2001; fax (+356) 33-76-24; e-mail cdrc@um.edu.mt; internet www.um.edu.mt.
Magister Juris in European and Comparative Law
Duration: 1 year (full-time); 2 years (part-time)
Language: English
In charge: Prof. Peter G. Xuereb
Contact: Monica Cauchi (Communications Officer, EDRC)

NETHERLANDS

Amsterdam

University of Amsterdam: Amsterdam School of International Relations (ASIR), Rokin 84, 1012 KX Amsterdam, The Netherlands; tel (+31 20) 525-29-66; fax (+31 20) 638-79-26; e-mail asir@pscw.uva .nl; internet www.asir.nl.
Master in International and European Relations
Duration: 10 months
Language: English
Contact: Anne Marie Meijer

University of Amsterdam: Amsterdam School of International Relations (ASIR), Rokin 84, 1012 KX Amsterdam, The Netherlands; tel (+31 20) 525-29-66; fax (+31 20) 638-79-26; e-mail asir@pscw.uva .nl; internet www.asir.nl.
ASIR Postgraduate Degree in International and European Relations
Duration: 10 months
Language: English
Contact: Anne Marie Meijer

Groningen

Groningen University: Postbus 716, 9700 AS Groningen, The Netherlands; tel (+31 50) 363-57-48; fax (+31 50) 363-74-08; e-mail llm@rechten.rug.nl
LL.M.
Duration: 1 year
Language: English
Contact: H. A. Van der Meulen (Administrative Director, LL.M. programmes)

Leiden

Leiden University: Faculty of Law, Postbus 9520, 2300 RA Leiden, The Netherlands; Europa Institute, Hugo de Grootstraat 27, 2311 XK Leiden, The Netherlands; tel (+31 71) 527-77-38; fax (+31 71) 527-76-00; e-mail r.c.tobler@law .leidenuniv.nl; internet www.leidenuniv .nl.rechten.
LL.M. in European Community Law
Duration: 1 year (September–August)
Language: English
In charge: Prof. Piet Jan Slot (Programme Director)
Contact: Dr Christa Tobler (Programme Academic Co-ordinator)

Maastricht

Hogeschool Maastricht: Brusselseweg 150, 6217 HB Maastricht, The Netherlands; tel (+31 43) 346-66-30; fax (+31 43) 346-66-19; e-mail a.reverda@sph .hsmaastricht.nl; internet www.unl.ac .uk/socwork/eicss.
MA in Comparative European Social Studies
Duration: 1 year (full-time)
Language: English
In charge: A. Reverda
Contact: A. Reverda, A. Van den Berg

Universiteit Maastricht: Faculty of Law, International Affairs Office, Postbus 616, 6200 MD Maastricht, The Netherlands; tel (+31 43) 388-30-36; fax (+31 43) 325-65-38; e-mail mireya.serra-jner@ facburfdr.unimaas.nl; internet www .unimaas.ml~communis.
LL.M. in European and Community Law
Duration: 1 year
Language: English
In charge: Dr Hildegard Scheider (Director of Studies)
Contact: Mireya Serra-Janer (Co-ordinator)

Nijmegen

Katholieke Universiteit Nijmegen: CPO—Rechtenfaculteit, Postbus 10520, 6500 MB Nijmegen, The Netherlands, tel (+31 24) 361-30-90; fax (+31 24) 361-58-38; e-mail cpo@jur.kun.nl; internet www.jur.kun.nl/cpo.
LL.M. in European Business Law
Duration: 1 year
Language: English
Contact: M. Cornieltje (Co-ordinator, CPO/Pallas)

Rotterdam

Erasmus University: Faculty of Economics, Postbus 1738, 3000 DR Rotterdam, The Netherlands; tel (+31 10) 408-21-71; fax (+31 10) 408-91-43; e-mail kuijpers@few.eur.nl.
International Master's Programme on the Economics of European Integration
Duration: 1 year
Language: English
In charge: J. Kol
Contact: B. Kuijpers

The Hague

The Hague School of European Studies (HEBO): Postbus 16880, 2500 BW The Hague, The Netherlands; tel (+31 70) 445-86-61; fax (+31 70) 445-86-25; e-mail esjgerretsen@sost.hhs.nl.
MA in European Law and Policy
Duration: 1 year (full-time); 2 years (part-time)
Language: English
In charge: D. R. Verwey
Contact: Ms. C. Gerretsen

POLAND

Gdansk

Gdansk University: ul. Armii Krajowej 199/121, 81-824 Sopot, Poland; tel (+48 58) 551-1613; fax (+48 58) 551-1613; e-mail obie@panda.gb.univ.gda.pl; internet www.univ.gda.pl.
Postgraduate Diploma in European Integration
Duration: 2 semesters
Language: Polish
Contact: Krystyna Gawlikowska-Hueckel

Kraków

Uniwersytet Jagiellonski: Instytut Spraw Publicznych, Zaklad Integracji Europejskiej, Rynek Glowny 8, 31-042 Kraków, Poland; tel (+48 12) 411-4784; fax (+48 12) 422-5892; e-mail tkolodz@if .uj.edu.pl.
Business and Territorial Development in Poland's Integration Process to the European Union
Duration: 2 semesters
Language: Polish
In charge: Tadeusz Kolodziej
Contact: Anna Kosierkiewicz

Lódz

University of Lódz: Centre for European Studies, ul. Piotrkowska 262–264, 90-361 Lódz, Poland; tel (+48 42) 637-5047; fax (+48 42) 637-0586; e-mail obul@krysia.uni.lodz.pl.
Postgraduate Diploma in European Studies
Duration: 2 semesters
Language: Polish
In charge: Dr Maria Celina Blaszczyk
Contact: Dr Anna Borkowska

University of Lódz: Faculty of Law and Administration, ul. Uniwersytecka 3, 90-137 Lódz, Poland; tel (+48 42) 635-4038; fax (+48 42) 638-2732; e-mail mseweryn@krysia.uni.lodz.pl.
Postgraduate Studies in European Law
Duration: 1 year
Language: Polish
In charge: Anna Wyrozumska
Contact: Agnieszka Czernek

Szczecin

University of Szczecin: Faculty of Humanities, ul. Mickiewicza 18, 70-387 Szczecin, Poland; tel (+48 91) 484-4821; fax (+48 91) 484-2523.
MA/Certificate in Political Science on European Integration
Duration: 2 years for the certificate, 3 years for the MA
Language: Polish
In charge and contact: Dr hab. Andrzej Glowacki

Torun

Nicholas Copernicus University: Jean Monnet Centre for European Studies, ul. Gagarina 13A, 87-100 Torun, Poland; tel (+48 56) 611-4583; fax (+48 56) 611-4583; e-mail ncu-ces@econ.uni.torun.pl; internet www.cc.uni.torun.pl.
Diploma in European Studies
Duration: 4 semesters (2 years)
Languages: Polish and English
In charge and contacts: Prof. Dr hab. Janusz Justynski, Dr Shakir Mahmoud Amin

PORTUGAL

Coimbra

Universidade de Coimbra: Faculdade de Direito, Patio da Universidade, 3049 Coimbra, Portugal; tel (+351 239) 85-98-01; fax (+351 239) 82-33-53; e-mail apss@cygnus-ci.uc.pt.
Master in European Integration
Duration: 2 years
Language: Portuguese
In charge: Manuel Porto
Contact: Maria do Rosario Lucas

Universidade de Coimbra: Faculdade de Direito, Patio da Universidade, 3049 Coimbra, Portugal; tel (+351 239)

85-98-01; fax (+351 239) 82-33-53; e-mail apss@cygnus-ci.uc.pt.
Certificate and Diploma in European Studies
Duration: 1 year
Language: Portuguese
In charge: Manuel Lopes Porto
Contact: Clementina Ribeiro

Universidade de Coimbra: Faculdade de Economia, Av. Dias da Silva 165, 3004-512 Coimbra, Portugal; tel (+351 239) 79-05-35; fax (+351 239) 79-05-35; e-mail jasa@sonata.fe.uc.pt; internet www.fe.uc.pt/mestrado/economia/economia.html.
Master in Economics
Duration: 2 years
Language: Portuguese
Contact: João Sousa Andrade

Lisbon

Universidade Lusíada: Instituto Lusíada de Estudos Europeus, Rua da Junqueira 194, 1300 Lisbon, Portugal; tel (+351 21) 361-16-04; fax (+351 21) 363-83-07; e-mail hmachado@lis.ulusiada.pt.
Course in European Integration
Duration: 2 semesters
Languages: Portuguese, French and English
Contact: Júlia Motta Veiga

Universidade Técnica de Lisboa: Instituto Superior de Economia e Gestão, Rua do Quelhas 6, 1200 Lisbon, Portugal; tel (+351 21) 392-58-00; fax (+351 21) 395-31-55; e-mail romao@iseg.utl.pt.
Postgraduate course in European Studies
Duration: 200 hours
Language: Portuguese

SPAIN

Alcala

Universidad de Alcala: Centro de Estudios Europeos, Colegio de Trinitarios, C/ Trinidad No 1, 28801 Alcala de Henares (Madrid), Spain; tel (+34 91) 885-41-93/885-41-94; fax (+34 91) 885-40-95; e-mail cdecfmp@cdoc.alcala.es.
Master en Union Europea
Duration: 2 years
Language: Spanish

Barcelona

Universitat Autónoma de Barcelona: Edificio E1, 08193 Bellaterra (Barcelona), Spain; tel (+34 93) 581-20-16; fax (+34 93) 581-30-63; e-mail ineshumet@cc.uab.es; internet www.uab.es/iuee.
Master de Estudios Europeos Avanzados (Opción juridica)
Duration: 1 year or 2 years
Languages: Spanish, French and English
Contact: Inés Humet

Universitat de Barcelona: Facultad de Derecho, Biblioteca de Derecho, Avda Diagonal 684, 08034 Barcelona, Spain;

tel (+34 93) 402-44-60; fax (+34 93) 402-90-49; e-mail master@riscd2.ub.es.
Master en Estudios Internacionales
Duration: 2 years
Language: Spanish
In charge: Prof. Victoria Abellán
Contact: Prof. José Gómara

Bilbao

Universidad de Deusto: Avda de las Universidades 24, Apartado 1, 48080 Bilbao, Spain; tel (+34 94) 413-92-84; fax (+34 94) 413-92-84; e-mail bzubiaga@iee.deusto.es; internet www.deusto.es.
Diploma de Especialización en Estudios Europeos; Master en Estudios Europeos
Duration: 1 year, 2 years (Master)

Universidad del País Vasco: Apartado 644, 48080 Bilbao, Spain; tel (+34 94) 601-20-00; fax (+34 94) 464-82-99; e-mail zipderuj@lg.ehu.es.
Master Universitario en Integración Europea
Duration: 2 years
Language: Spanish
Contact: Dr José Luis de Castro Ruano

Universidad del País Vasco: Apartado 644, 48080 Bilbao, Spain; tel (+34 94) 601-20-00; fax (+34 94) 480-04-34; e-mail zibarsuo@lg.ehu.es; internet www.zi.lp.ehu.es.
Master in European Integration
Duration: 2 years
Language: Spanish
In charge: Prof. Dr Francisco Aldecoa Luzárraga
Contact: Oscar Arroyuelo

Universidad del País Vasco: Dep. de Relaciones Internacionales, Facultad de CCSS y de la Comunicación, Campus de Leioa, Apartado 644, 48080 Bilbao, Spain; tel (+34 94) 601-20-00 ext. 5278; fax (+34 94) 480-04-34; e-mail zibzalol@lg.ehu.es; internet www.zi.lp.ehu.es.
University Specialist in International Relations
Duration: 1 year
Language: Spanish
In charge: Prof. Dr Francisco Aldecoa Luzárraga
Contact: Lorena Zabala

Córdoba

Universidad de Córdoba: Facultad de Derecho, Puerta Nueva s/n, 14071 Córdoba, Spain; tel (+34 957) 25-49-62; fax (+34 957) 26-11-20; e-mail cde1cord@uco.es; internet www.uco.es.
European Union: Origins, Policies and Reforms
Duration: 2 years
Language: Spanish
Contacts: José Maria Cerezo López, Magdalena Reifs López

Universidad de Córdoba: Facultad de Derecho, Puerta Nueva s/n, 14071 Córdoba, Spain; tel (+34 957) 21-88-68; fax

(+34 957) 26 11 20; e-mail cde1cord@
uco.es; internet www.uco.es.
European Construction Process: Eco-
nomic and Monetary Union
Duration: 2 years
Language: Spanish
Contacts: José Maria Cerezo López, Mag-
dalena Reifs López

Granada

Universidad de Granada: Departa-
mento de Derecho Internacional Público
y Relaciones Internacionales, Plaza de la
Universidad s/n, 18001 Granada, Spain;
tel (+34 958) 24-34-59; fax (+34 958) 24-
34-58; internet www.ugr.es/~docto/
5114.htm.
International Legal Framework and
Development Prospects of the European
Union
Duration: 2 years
Language: Spanish
Contact: Concepción Martinez Soriano
(Administrator)

Jaén

Universidad de Jaén: Area de Derecho
Internacional Público y Relaciones Internacionales, Paraje Las Lagunillas s/n,
Edificio D-3, 23071 Jaén, Spain; tel (+34
953) 21-21-02; fax (+34 953) 21-22-22;
e-mail jmfarami@ujaen.es; internet www
.ujaen.es.
Doctorate in Economic and Legal Aspects
of the European Integration Process
Duration: 2 years
Language: Spanish
Contact: Prof. Juan Manuel de Farami-
ñán Gilbert

La Coruña

Universidada de La Coruña: Instituto
Universitario de Estudios Europeos
"Salvador de Madariaga", Casa de
Galeria, Campus Elviña s/n, 15071 La
Coruña, Spain; tel (+34 981) 16-70-00
ext. 1966; fax (+34 981) 16-70-13; e-mail
iuee@udc.es; internet www.udc.es/iuee.
Master in European Union Studies
Duration: 1 year (November–June)
Language: Spanish
Contact: Muriel Bouvier

León

Universidad de León: Facultad de
Ciencias Económicas y Empresariales,
Departamento de Economía, Campus de
Vegazana s/n, 24071 León, Spain; tel (+34
987) 29-17-30; fax (+34 987) 29-17-30;
e-mail deejma@isidoro.unileon.es.
Economy of European Integration
Duration: 2 years
Language: Spanish
Contact: J. M. Agüera Sirgo

Logroño

Universidad de La Rioja: Cátedra
Jean Monnet de Derecho Comunitario,
Departamento de Derecho, Universidad
de la Rioja, Cigüeña 60, 26004 Logroño,
Spain; tel (+34 941) 29-93-63/29-93-
46; fax (+34 941) 29-93-47; e-mail jose
.martin@dd.unirioja.es.
Diploma in European Studies
Duration: 3 months (March-May, 3 hours
weekly)
Language: Spanish
Contacts: José Martín y Pérez de
Nanclares, Mariola urrea Corres

Madrid

Universidad Autónoma de Madrid:
Departamento de Estructura Económica
y Economía del Desarrollo, Facultad de
Ciencias Económicas y Empresariales,
Ciudad Universitaria de Cantoblanco,
28049 Madrid, Spain; tel (+34 91) 397-
49-85; fax (+34 91) 397-49-71; e-mail
donato.fernandez@uam.es; internet www
.uam.es.
Doctorado en Integración y Desarrollo
Económico
Language: Spanish
In charge: Prof. Donato Fernández
Navarrete, Prof. Pablo Martín Urbano

Universidad Autónoma de Madrid:
Departamento de Análisis Económico,
Teoría Económica e Historia Económica,
Facultad de Ciencias Económicas y
Empresariales, Ciudad Universitaria de
Cantoblanco, 28049 Madrid, Spain; tel
(+34 91) 397-43-20; fax (+34 91) 397-
86-16; e-mail asamihi@uam.es; e-mail
alejandro.lorca@uam.es; internet www
.uam.es/deri.
Doctorate in Economics and International
Relations
Duration: 2 years
Language: Spanish
In charge: Cristina Muñoz Alonso,
Alejandro V. Lorca Corróns

Universidad Autónoma de Madrid:
Facultad de Derecho, Ciudad Universi-
taria de Cantoblanco, 28049 Madrid,
Spain; tel (+34 91) 397-81-61; fax (+34
91) 397-82-16; e-mail carmen.martinez@
uam.es.
Master de Derecho Comunitario Europeo
Duration: 8 months (October–June)
Language: Spanish
Contact: Prof. Carmen Martínez Capde-
vila

**Universidad Complutense de
Madrid:** Facultad de Ciencias de la
Información, Despacho 538, Avenida
Complutense s/n, 28040 Madrid, Spain;
tel (+34 91) 394-21-77; fax (+34 91) 394-
21-76.
Aspectos Rétoricos, Dialécticos y Estruc-
turales de la Información
Duration: 1 year (2 days per week)
Language: Spanish
In charge and contact: Prof. C. Antonio
Sánchez-Bravo

**Universidad Nacional de Educación
a Distancia (UNED):** Facultad de Cien-
cias Económicas y Empresariales, Depar-
tamento de Economía Aplicada e Historia
Económica, Planta 3-A, Despacho 327,
Calle Senda del Rey s/n, 28040 Madrid,
Spain; tel (+34 91) 398-63-78; fax (+34 91)
398-63-78; e-mail mcalvo@cee.uned.es;
internet www.deahe.es.
Doctorate in European Union Studies
Duration: 1 year
Language: Spanish
Contact: Antonia Calvo Hornero

**Universidad Nacional de Educación
a Distancia (UNED):** Facultad de Ciencias Políticas y Sociología, Obispo Trejo s/
n, 28040 Madrid, Spain; tel (+34 91) 398-
70-35; fax (+34 91) 398-70-03; e-mail
gpalomar@sr.uned.es.
Master in European Union Studies
Duration: 2 years
Languages: Spanish, English and knowledge of French
In charge and contact: D. Gustavo Palo-
mares Lerma

Salamanca

Universidad de Salamanca: Area de
Derecho Internacional Público, Facultad
de Derecho, Campus Miguel de Unamuno, 37007 Salamanca, Spain; tel (+34
923) 29-44-00; fax (+34 923) 29-45-16;
e-mail niju@gugu.usal.es; internet www
.usal.es/postgrado/fdoctorado.htm.
Law, Economy and Society in the Euro-
pean Union
Duration: 2 years
Language: Spanish
In charge: Araceli Mangas Martín
Contact: Nicolás Navarro Batista

Universidad de Salamanca: Facultad
de Economía, Campus Miguel de Una-
muno, 37007 Salamanca, Spain; tel (+34
923) 29-46-00 ext. 3123; fax (+34 923) 29-
44-77; e-mail rbonete@gugu.usal.es;
internet www.usal.es.
Curso Superior de Integración Económica
Europea
Duration: 80 hours
Language: Spanish
In charge and contact: Rafael Bonete
Perales

**Universidad Pontificia de Sala-
manca:** Instituto de Estudios Europeos
y Derechos Humanos, Calle Compañía 5,
37008 Salamanca, Spain; tel (+34 923)
21-72-36; fax (+34 923) 26-24-56; e-mail
j.r.flecha@upsa.es; internet www.upsa
.es/~/facultades/estudios%20europeos/
Estudios.html.
Master en Comunidades Europeas y Dere-
chos Humanos
Duration: 1 year
Language: Spanish
In charge: José R. Flecha
Contact: Oficina Información al Estu-
diante (+34 923) 21-89-04

San Sebastian

Universidad del Pais Vasco: Facultad
de Ciencias de la Educación, Avenida de
Tolosa 70, 20009 San Sebastian, Spain;

tel (+34 943) 44-80-00; fax (+34 943) 31-10-56; e-mail hdpetbaf@sc.ehu.es.
Diploma in European Studies
Duration: 2 years
Language: Spanish
In charge and contact: Felix Etxeberria

Santander

Universidad de Cantabria: Facultad de Derecho, Universidad de Cantabria, Avda. de los Castros s/n, 39005 Santander, Spain; tel (+34 942) 20-12-37; fax (+34 942) 20-12-13; e-mail escobar@ccaix3.unican.es.
EC Law and the European Union
Duration: 70 hours
Language: Spanish
In charge and contact: Concepción Escobar Hernández

Valencia

Universidad de Valencia: Campus de los Naranjos, Facultad de Derecho, Departamento Derecho Constitucional, Av. de los Naranjos, s/n, 46071 Valencia, Spain; tel (+34 96) 382-81-20; tel: (+34 96) 382-86-81; fax (+34 96) 382-81-19; e-mail roberto.viciano@uv.es; internet www.uv.es/cde/cursos/europa.
MA in EU Institutions and Politics
Diploma in EC Law
Diploma in EC Business Law
Duration: 550 hours for the MA, 170 hours for Diploma in EC Law, 260 hours for Diploma in EC Business Law
Languages: Spanish, English and French
In charge: Roberto Viciano Pastor, Javier Viciano Pastor
Contact: Roberto Viciano Pastor

Zaragoza

Real Instituto de Estudios Europeos: San Jorge 8, 1° piso, 50001 Zaragoza, Spain; tel (+34 976) 22-51-64; fax (+34 976) 233-95-80.
Master en Comunidades Europeas y Unión Europea
Duration: 1 year (October–June)
Language: Spanish
In charge: Dr Maximiliano Bernad (Universidad de Zaragoza), Dr J.A. Pastor Ridruejo (Judge, European Court of Human Rights)
Contact: Dr Maximiliano Bernad

SWEDEN

Lund

University of Lund: Department of Political Science, POB 52, 221 00 Lund, Sweden; tel (+46 46) 222-1144; fax (+46 46) 222-4006; e-mail mea@svet.lu.se; internet www.svet.lu.se.
MA in European Affairs
Duration: 1 year
Language: English
Contact: Carina Olsson

Stockholm

Stockholm University: European Law Dept, Faculty of Law, 106 91 Stockholm, Sweden; tel (+46 8) 16-32-83; fax (+46 8) 612-41-09; e-mail caroline.reuterskioeld@juridicum.su.se.
MA in European Law
Duration: 1 year
Language: English
Contact: Caroline Reuterskioeld

UNITED KINGDOM

Aberdeen

University of Aberdeen: Department of Politics and International Relations, Aberdeen AB24 3QY, United Kingdom; tel (+44 1224) 27-27-07; fax (+44 1224) 27-21-81; e-mail t.c.salmon@abdn.ac.uk.
M.Litt. in Applied European Studies
Duration: 12 months
Language: English
In charge and contact: Trevor C. Salmon

Aberystwyth

University of Wales Aberystwyth: Centre for European Studies, Department of International Politics, Aberystwyth SY23 3DA, United Kingdom; tel (+44 1970) 622702; fax (+44 1970) 622709; e-mail tmc@aber.ac.uk; e-mail jbt@aber.ac.uk; internet www.aber.ac.uk/~inpwww/eust/index.html.
MSc in the Politics of the European Union
Duration: 12 months
Language: English
Contacts: Thomas Christiansen and Ben Tonra

Bath

University of Bath: Department of European Studies, Claverton Down, Bath BA2 7AY, United Kingdom; tel (+44 1225) 826178; fax (+44 1225) 826987; e-mail j.m.howorth@bath.ac.uk; e-mail a.v.burge@bath.ac.uk; internet www.bath.ac.uk/departments/esml/em/main.htm.
MA in Contemporary European Political Culture
Duration: 12 months
Languages: English and at least 1 of French, German, Italian and Spanish
In charge: Prof. Jolyon Howorth
Contact: Ann Burge

University of Bath: Department of Social and Policy Sciences, Claverton Down, Bath BA2 7AY, United Kingdom; tel (+44 1225) 826090; fax (+44 1225) 826381; e-mail hssgjr@bath.ac.uk; internet www.bath.ac.uk/faculties/humsocsci/ifipa/taught.htm#mespa.
Master's in European Social Policy Analysis
Duration: 12 months
Language: English
Contact: Elaine Irvine (Postgraduate Administrator)

Belfast

Queen's University of Belfast: Institute of European Studies, Belfast BT7 1NN, United Kingdom; tel (+44 28) 9055-4433; fax (+44 28) 9068-3543; e-mail tom.wilson@qub.ac.uk; internet www.qub.ac.uk/ies.
MSSc in European Integration
Duration: 1 year (or 2 years part-time)
Language: English
In charge: Dr Robert Harmsen
Contact: Dr Thomas M. Wilson

Birmingham

Aston University: Postgraduate Programmes Administrator, School of Languages and European Studies, Birmingham B4 7ET, United Kingdom; tel (+44 121) 359-3611 ext. 4237; fax (+44 121) 359-6153; e-mail lespg@aston.ac.uk; internet www.les.aston.uk.
MSc in Comparative European Politics and Cultures
Duration: 12 months full-time; 24 months part-time
Language: English
Contacts: Dr Christina Schaeffner, Dr Georgios Varouxakis

University of Birmingham: Department of Political Science and International Studies, Edgbaston, Birmingham B15 2TT, United Kingdom; tel (+44 121) 414-6519; fax (+44 121) 414-3496; e-mail j.redmond@bham.ac.uk; internet www.bham.ac.uk.
Ph.D. in European Studies
Duration: 3 years
Language: English
In charge: Dr Judy Batt
Contact: Dr John Redmond

University of Birmingham: Institute for German Studies, Edgbaston, Birmingham B15 2TT, United Kingdom; tel (+44 121) 414-7182; fax (+44 121) 414-7329; e-mail a.g.hydeprice@bham.ac.uk; internet www.bham.ac.uk.
MA in European Studies
Duration: 1 year
Language: English
In charge: Dr Judy Batt
Contact: Adrian Hyde-Price

Bradford

University of Bradford: Department of European Studies, Bradford BD7 1DP, United Kingdom; tel (+44 1274) 233145; fax (+44 1274) 235550; e-mail m.haldane@bradford.ac.uk; internet www.brad.ac.uk/acad/euro-studies/webpage.htm.
MA in European Integration; MA in East European Studies; MA in European–Latin American Relations; MA in Modern European History
Duration: 1 year
Language: English
In charge: Dr C. Radaelli, J. Harrop
Contact: Margaret Haldane

Brighton

University of Sussex: Postgraduate Admissions, Sussex House, Falmer, Brighton BN1 9RH, United Kingdom; tel (+44 1273) 678412; fax (+44 1273) 678335; e-mail sei@sussex.ac.uk; internet www.sussex.ac.uk.
MA in Contemporary European Studies
Duration: 1 year
Language: English
In charge and contact: Paul Taggart

Bristol

University of Bristol: Department of Politics, 10 Priory Road, Bristol BS8 1TV, United Kingdom; tel (+44 117) 928-8829; fax (+44 117) 973-2133; e-mail michelle.cini@bris.ac.uk.
MPhil/Ph.D. in European Integration
Duration: 3 years
Language: English
In charge and contact: Dr Michelle Cini

University of Bristol: School for Policy Studies, 6 Priory Road, Bristol BS8 1TV, United Kingdom; tel (+44 117) 954-6737; fax (+44 117) 954-6738; e-mail kevin.doogan@bris.ac.uk; internet www.bris.ac.uk/depts/sps.
MSc in European Policy Studies
Duration: 2 years (part-time)
Language: English
In charge: Prof. Kevin Doogan
Contact: Andrea Osborne (Programme Secretary)

Cambridge

Anglia Polytechnic University: Anglia Law School, East Road, Cambridge CB1 1PT, United Kingdom; tel (+44 1223) 363271; fax (+44 1223) 352900; e-mail j.m.tiley@anglia.ac.uk.
LL.M./MA in International and European Business Law
Duration: 1 year (full-time); 2 years (part-time)
Language: English
In charge: J.M. Tiley
Contact: H. Ashman (Course Administrator)

University of Cambridge: Centre of International Studies, Fitzwilliam House, Trumpington Street, Cambridge CB2 1QY, United Kingdom; tel (+44 1223) 335333; fax (+44 1223) 331965; e-mail intstudies@lists.cam.ac.uk.
M. Phil in International Studies; M. Phil in European Studies
Duration: 1 year
Language: English
In charge: Clive Trebilcock
Contact: Secretary of M. Phil in European Studies

Canterbury

University of Kent at Canterbury: Rutherford College, Canterbury CT2 7NX, United Kingdom; tel (+44 1227) 823586; fax (+44 1227) 827033; e-mail c.h.church@ukc.ac.uk; internet www.ukc.ac.uk/international.
MA in International Relations and European Studies
Duration: 12 months (also available over 2 years)
Language: English
In charge and contact: Prof. Clive Church

Cardiff

Cardiff University: School of European Studies, POB 908, Cardiff CF1 3YQ, United Kingdom; tel (+44 29) 2087-4248; fax (+44 29) 2087-4946; e-mail jamesld@cardiff.ac.uk; internet www.cf.ac.uk/uwcc/euros/postgrad.html.
MSc (Econ.) in European Public Policy
Duration: 1 year (full-time); 2 years (part-time)
Language: English
In charge: Prof. Sean Loughlin
Contact: L. D. James (Postgraduate Secretary)

Cardiff University: School of European Studies, POB 908, Cardiff CF1 3YQ, United Kingdom; tel (+44 29) 2087-4564; fax (+44 29) 2087-4946; e-mail euros@cardiff.ac.uk; internet www.cf.ac.uk.
MSc (Econ) in the European Policy Process
Duration: 1 year (full-time) or 2 years (part-time)
Language: English
In charge: Prof. Sean Loughlin
Contact: Postgraduate Secretary

Colchester

University of Essex: Areas Office, Wivenhoe Park, Colchester CO4 3SQ, United Kingdom; tel (+44 1206) 872688; fax (+44 1206) 873965; e-mail daphne@essex.ac.uk; internet www.essex.ac.uk/centres/pei.
MA in European Integration
Duration: 1 year
Language: English
In charge: Emil Kirchner
Contact: Daphne Johnstone

University of Essex: Department of Government, Wivenhoe Park, Colchester CO4 3SQ, United Kingdom; tel (+44 1206) 872517; fax (+44 1206) 873598; e-mail elinor@essex.ac.uk; internet www.essex.ac.uk.
MA in European Politics
Duration: 1 year
Language: English
In charge and contact: Dr Elinor Scarbrought

Coventry

Coventry University: School of International Studies and Law, Priory Street, Coventry CV1 5FB, United Kingdom; tel (+44 24) 7688-8256; fax (+44 24) 7688-8679; e-mail isladmin@coventry.ac.uk; internet www.coventry.ac.uk/acad/isl.
MA in European Studies
Duration: 1 year (full-time), 2 years (part-time)
Language: English
Contact: Prof. Brian Hocking

Coventry Business School: Priory Street, Coventry CV1 5FB, United Kingdom; tel (+44 24) 7688-8492; fax (+44 24) 7683-8400; e-mail man.cbs@coventry.ac.uk; internet www.stile.coventry.ac.uk.
European Master of Business Administration
Duration: 1 year (full-time); 2 years (part-time)
Language: English
Contact: Dr David Morris

Coventry University: School of the Built Environment, Priory Street, Coventry CV1 5FB, United Kingdom; tel (+44 24) 7688-8485; fax (+44 24) 7688-8485; e-mail cbx103@coventry.ac.uk; internet www.coventry.ac.uk/acad/sb/building/ece.
MSc in European Construction Engineering
Duration: 1 year (full-time); 2 years (part-time)
Language: English
Contact: Keith Chapman

Dundee

University of Dundee: School of Contemporary European Studies, Perth Road, Dundee DD1 4HN, United Kingdom; tel (+44 1382) 344379; fax (+44 1382) 344802; e-mail c.m.lythe@dundee.ac.uk; internet www.dundee.ac.uk.
Ph.D. in Contemporary European Studies
Duration: 3 years
Language: English
In charge and contact: Charlotte M. Lythe

Durham

University of Durham: Postgraduate Admissions, Department of Politics, 48 Old Elvet, Durham DH1 3LZ, United Kingdom; tel (+44 191) 374-2810; fax (+44 191) 374-7630; e-mail j.m.richardson@durham.ac.uk; internet www.durham.ac.uk.
MA in European Political and Economic Integration
Duration: 1 year (October–September)
Language: English
In charge: Andrew MacMullen (MA Course Director)
Contact: J. Richardson (Administrative Officer)

University of Durham: Department of Law, 50 North Bailey, Durham DH1 3ET, United Kingdom; tel (+44 191) 334-2800; fax (+44 191) 334-2801; e-mail llm@durham.ac.uk; internet www.dur.ac.uk/law/llm/programme.htm.
LL.M. in European Legal Studies
Duration: 1 year
Language: English
In charge and contact: H.A. Cullen

Exeter

University of Exeter: School of Law, Amory Building, Rennes Drive, Exeter EX4 4RJ, United Kingdom; tel (+44 1392) 263380; fax (+44 1392) 263196; e-mail r.r.drury@exeter.ac.uk; e-mail n.l.symons@exeter.ac.uk; internet www.exeter.ac.uk/ead/extrel/pgp/law.htm.
LL.M. in European Legal Studies
Duration: 1 year
Language: English
In charge: R. R. Drury (Course Director for LL.M. in European Legal Studies)
Contact: N. L. Symons (Postgraduate Secretary)

University of Exeter: School of Business and Economics, Streatham Court, Rennes Drive, Exeter EX4 4PU, United Kingdom; tel (+44 1392) 263208; fax (+44 1392) 263242; e-mail m.j.j.macmillen@exeter.ac.uk; internet www.ex.ac.uk
MA in Economics of the European Union
Duration: 1 year (full-time); 2 years (part-time)
Language: English
In charge and contact: Malcolm Macmillen

Glamorgan

University of Glamorgan: The Law School, Treforest, Pontypridd CF37 1DL, United Kingdom; tel (+44 1443) 483004; fax (+44 1443) 483008; e-mail elu@Glamorgan.ac.uk.
LL.M. in EU Law by Distance Learning
Duration: 2 years
Language: English
Contact: Richard Owen

Glasgow

University of Glasgow: School of Law, The Stair Building, Glasgow G12 8QQ, United Kingdom; tel (+44 141) 330-4172; fax (+44 141) 330-5140; e-mail n.burrows@law.gla.ac.uk; internet www.law.gla.ac.uk.
LL.M. in European Studies
Duration: 1 year (full-time); 2 years (part-time)
Language: English
In charge and contact: Prof. Noreen Burrows

University of Strathclyde: Dept of Economics, 100 Cathedral Street, Glasgow G4 0LN, United Kingdom; tel (+44 141) 548-3581; fax (+44 141) 552-5589; e-mail economics@strath.ac.uk; internet www.strath.ac.uk.
MA in Business Economics
Duration: 1 year
Language: English
In charge: A. Hughes Hallet
Contact: R. Alpine

University of Strathclyde: The Law School, 173 Cathedral Street, Glasgow G4 0RQ, United Kingdom; tel (+44 141) 548-3481; fax (+44 141) 553-1546; e-mail carolh@law.strath.ac.uk; internet www.law-www-server.law.strath.ac.uk/teaching/llm/llm.html.
LL.M. in Information Technology and Telecommunications Law
Duration: 12/24 months
Language: English
Contact: Carol Hutton

Huddersfield

University of Huddersfield: Department of Law, Queensgate, Huddersfield HD1 3DH, United Kingdom; tel (+44 1484) 472192; fax (+44 1484) 472279; e-mail s.p.ware@hud.ac.uk.
LL.M in European Business Law
Duration: 1 year (full-time); 2 years (part-time)
Language: English
In charge: S. P. Ware (Course Director)

Hull

University of Hull: Department of Politics and Asian Studies, Hull HU6 7RX, United Kingdom; tel (+44 1482) 465808; fax (+44 1482) 466208; e-mail j.m.magone@pol-as.hull.ac.uk; internet www.hull.ac.uk/hull/css/ceushomepage.html.
MA in European Public Policy
Duration: 1 year (full time), 2 years (part-time)
Language: English
Contact: Dr José M. Magone

University of Hull: Institute of European Public Law, Hull HU6 7RX, United Kingdom; tel (+44 1482) 465857; fax (+44 1482) 466388; e-mail s.e.mcdonald@law.hull.ac.uk.
LL.M. in European Public Law
Duration: 1 year
Language: English
In charge: Prof. Patrick Birkinshaw
Contact: Sue McDonald

University of Hull: Centre for European Union Studies, Department of Politics and Asian Studies, Hull HU6 7RX, United Kingdom; tel (+44 1482) 465754; fax (+44 1482) 466208; e-mail m.d.burgess@pol-as.hull.ac.uk; internet www.hull.ac.uk/hull/css_web/ceushomepage.html.
MA in European Integration and Cooperation
Duration: 1 year (full time), 2 years (part-time)
Language: English
Contact: Dr Michael Burgess (Director)

Keele

University of Keele: Modern Languages Dept (French), Keele, Staffordshire ST5 5BG, United Kingdom; tel (+44 1782) 583277; fax (+44 1782) 584078; e-mail c.m.warne@keele.ac.uk; internet www.keele.ac.uk/depts/mlf/teach/maeuro.htm.
MA in European Studies
Duration: 1 year
Language: English
In charge and contact: Dr Chris Warne

University of Keele: Department of Politics, Keele, Staffordshire ST5 5BG, United Kingdom; tel (+44 1782) 583481; fax (+44 1782) 583452; internet www.keele.ac.uk/depts/po/pol/courses/ma/europema.htm
MA in European Politics
Duration: 1 year (full time), 2 years (part-time)
Language: English
In charge and contact: Prof. Michael Waller (Director of European Studies)

Lancaster

University of Lancaster: Department of Geography, Lancaster LA1 4YB, United Kingdom; tel (+44 1524) 593301/593736; fax (+44 1524) 847099; e-mail u.ite@lancs.ac.uk.
MSc European Environmental Policy and Regulation
Duration: 1 year (full-time), 2 years (part-time)
Language: English
In charge and contact: Dr Uwem Ite

Leeds

Leeds Metropolitan University: Leighton Hall, Beckett Park Campus, Headingley, Leeds LS6 3QS, United Kingdom; tel (+44 113) 283-2600; fax (+44 113) 283-7507.
MA in European Public Relations
Duration: 18 months
Language: English
In charge: Ralph Tench (Course Director)
Contact: Maureen James

University of Leeds: Department of Law, Leeds LS2 9JT, United Kingdom; tel (+44 113) 233-5009; fax (+44 113) 233-5056; e-mail lawawo@leeds.ac.uk.
MA in European Business Law by Open and Distance Learning
Duration: 2 years part-time
Language: English
Contact: A. Woods (Graduate Admissions)

University of Leeds: Centre for European Studies, Parkinson Building, Leeds LS2 9JT, United Kingdom; tel (+44 113) 233-4441; fax (+44 113) 233-6784; e-mail n.j.hey@leeds.ac.uk; internet www.leeds.ac.uk/ces.
MA in European Environmental Policy
Duration: 1 year
Language: English
Contact: Natalie Hey

University of Leeds: Centre for European Studies, Parkinson Building, Leeds LS2 9JT, United Kingdom; tel (+44 113) 233-4441; fax (+44 113) 233-6784; e-mail n.j.hey@leeds.ac.uk; internet www.leeds.ac.uk/ces.
MA in European Security Studies
Duration: 1 year
Language: English
Contact: Natalie Hey

University of Leeds: Department of Politics, Leeds LS2 9JT, United Kingdom; tel (+44 113) 233-4402; fax (+44 113) 233-4400; e-mail c.j.lord@leeds.ac.uk.
MA in European Union Politics by Open and Distance Learning
Duration: Normally 2 years part-time
Language: English
In charge and contact: Dr Christopher Lord

University of Leeds: Department of Politics, Leeds LS2 9JT, United Kingdom; tel (+44 113) 233-4402; fax (+44 113) 233-4400; e-mail c.j.lord@leeds.ac.uk.
MA in European Union and Developing Countries
Duration: 1 year (full-time), 2 years (part-time)
Language: English
In charge and contact: Dr Christopher Lord

University of Leeds: Centre for European Studies, Parkinson Building, Leeds LS2 9JT, United Kingdom; tel (+44 113) 233-4441; fax (+44 113) 233-6784; e-mail n.j.hey@leeds.ac.uk; internet www.leeds.ac.uk/ces.
MA in Law and Policy of the European Union
Duration: 1 year
Language: English
Contact: Natalie Hey

University of Leeds: Department of Law, Leeds LS2 9JT, United Kingdom; tel (+44 113) 233-5009; fax (+44 113) 233-5056; e-mail lawawo@leeds.ac.uk; internet www.leeds.ac.uk/law/csle.
MA in European Legal Studies
Duration: 1 year (full time), 2–3 years (part-time)
Language: English
Contact: Mandy Woods (Graduate Admissions)

University of Leeds: Centre for European Studies, Parkinson Building, Leeds LS2 9JT, United Kingdom; tel (+44 113) 233-4441; fax (+44 113) 233-6784; e-mail n.j.hey@leeds.ac.uk; internet www.leeds.ac.uk/ces.
MA in European Studies
Duration: 1 year
Language: English
Contact: Natalie Hey

University of Leeds: Centre for European Studies, Parkinson Building, Leeds LS2 9JT, United Kingdom; tel (+44 113) 233-4441; fax (+44 113) 233-6784; e-mail n.j.hey@leeds.ac.uk; internet www.leeds.ac.uk/ces.
MA in European Union Public Policy
Duration: 1 year
Language: English
Contact: Natalie Hey

Leicester

University of Leicester: Department of Economics, University Road, Leicester LE1 7RH, United Kingdom; tel (+44 116) 252-2886; fax (+44 116) 252-2908; e-mail rwa1@le.ac.uk; internet www.le.ac.uk/economics/teach/postgrad/ecpgee.html.
MSc in European Economic Studies
Duration: 1 year
Language: English
In charge and contact: Dr R.W. Ackrill

University of Leicester: Faculty of Law, University Road, Leicester LE1 7RH, United Kingdom; tel (+44 116) 252-2753; fax (+44 116) 252-5023; e-mail jmg16@le.ac.uk; internet www.le.ac.uk/law.
LL.M. in European and International Trade Law
Duration: 1 year (full-time), 2 years (part-time)
Language: English
In charge: Giorgio Monti
Contact: J. Goacher (Postgraduate Admissions Secretary)

University of Leicester: International Centre, Faculty of Law, University Road, Leicester LE1 7RH, United Kingdom; tel (+44 116) 252-2346; fax (+44 116) 252-2699; e-mail st22@le.ac.uk.
LL.M. or MA in European Union Law
Duration: 2 years (advance learning)
Language: English
In charge: Jeffrey Kenner
Contact: Susan Thornton (Course Administrator)

Liverpool

Liverpool John Moores University: School of Social Science, 15–21 Webster Street, Liverpool L3 2ET, United Kingdom; tel (+44 151) 231-4044; fax (+44 151) 231-4359; e-mail m.l.mannin@livjm.ac.uk.
European Studies and International Business
Duration: 1 year
Language: English
Contact: M. L. Mannin

Liverpool John Moores University: School of Social Science, 15–21 Webster Street, Liverpool L3 2ET, United Kingdom; tel (+44 151) 231-4044; fax (+44 151) 231-4359; e-mail m.l.mannin@livjm.ac.uk.
European Studies (MA) and Advanced Language Studies
Duration: 1 year
Language: English
Contact: M. L. Mannin

Liverpool John Moores University: School of Social Science, 15–21 Webster Street, Liverpool L3 2ET, United Kingdom; tel (+44 151) 231-4044; fax (+44 151) 231-4359; e-mail m.l.mannin@livjm.ac.uk.
MA European Studies and Policies
Duration: 1 year
Language: English
Contact: M. L. Mannin

University of Liverpool: Department of Politics, Roxby Building, Liverpool L69 3BX, United Kingdom; tel (+44 151) 794-2890; fax (+44 151) 794-3948; e-mail janv@liverpool.ac.uk; internet www.liv.ac.uk~polcomm/polmaeu.htm.
MA in European Union Politics
Duration: 1 year
Language: English
In charge: Dr Robert Geyer
Contact: Departmental Secretary

London

Birkbeck College, University of London: Department of Politics and Sociology, Malet Street, London WC1E 7HX, United Kingdom; tel (+44 20) 7631-6789; fax (+44 20) 7631-6787; e-mail j.tinkler@pol-soc.bbk.ac.uk; internet www.bbk.ac.uk/departments/polsoc/index.htm.
M. Phil/Ph.D. in Politics
Language: English
In charge: Dr Hussein Kassim
Contact: Jane Tinkler

Birkbeck College, University of London: Department of Politics and Sociology, Malet Street, London WC1E 7HX, United Kingdom; tel (+44 20) 7631-6789; fax (+44 20) 7631-6787; e-mail j.tinkler@pol-soc.bbk.ac.uk; internet www.bbk.ac.uk/departments/polsoc/index.htm.
MSc in European Politics
Duration: 1 year (full-time), 2 years (part-time)
Language: English
In charge: Dr Hussein Kassim
Contact: Jane Tinkler

South Bank University: 103 Borough Road, London SE1 0AA, United Kingdom; tel (+44 20) 7815-5744; fax (+44 20) 7815-5799; e-mail rookera@sbu.ac.uk.
MA in European Public Policy
Duration: 1 year
Languages: English and French
In charge: Dr Richard Rooke
Contact: Sue Mastel

University College London (UCL): School of Public Policy, Gower Street, London WC1E 6BT, United Kingdom; tel (+44 20) 7504-4992; fax (+44 20) 7504-4993; e-mail rachel.fagin@ucl.ac.uk; internet www.ucl.ac.uk/spp.
MSc in Public Policy
Duration: 12 months
Language: English
In charge: Prof. Stephen Smith (Jean Monnet Professor, Department of Economics)
Contact: Rachel Fagin (School of Public Policy)

University of Greenwich: Social Sciences, Avery Hill Road, London SE9 2UG, United Kingdom; tel (+44 20) 8331-8913; fax (+44 20) 8331-8905; e-mail m.ugur@greenwich.ac.uk; internet www.gre.ac.uk/~sd04/maeuro.html.

MA in European Public Policy
Duration: 1 year (full-time); 2 years (part-time)
Language: English
Contact: Dr Mehmet Ugur

Queen Mary and Westfield College, University of London: Centre for Commercial Law Studies, 339 Mile End Road, London E1 4NS, United Kingdom; tel (+44 20) 7975-5127; fax (+44 20) 7980-1079; e-mail admissions-ccls@qmw.ac.uk; internet www.ccls.edu.ac.uk.
LL.M. in European Community Law
Duration: 1 year
Language: English
In charge: Prof. Ian Fletcher (Director)
Contact: Jacqueline Wingard

University of North London: School of European and Language Studies, 166–220 Holloway Road, London N7 8DB, United Kingdom; tel (+44 20) 7753-3209; fax (+44 20) 7753-7069; e-mail d.edye@unl.ac.uk; internet www.unl.ac.uk.
MA in Modern European Studies
Duration: 1 year (full-time); 2 years (part-time)
Language: English
In charge and contact: Dave Edye

Thames Valley University: School of European, International and Social Studies, St Mary's Road, London W5 5RF, United Kingdom; tel (+44 20) 8231-2296; fax (+44 20) 8566-1353; e-mail jackie.gower@tun.ac.uk; internet www.tun.ac.uk.
MA in European Studies
Duration: 1 year (full time), 2 1/2 years (part-time)
Language: English
In charge and contact: Jackie Gower

Manchester

University of Manchester: Department of Government, Oxford Road, Manchester M13 9PL, United Kingdom; tel (+44 161) 275-4937; fax (+44 161) 275-4925; e-mail bernadette.mcloughlin@man.ac.uk; internet www.les.man.ac.uk/government.
MA (Econ.) in European Politics and Policy
Duration: 1 year (full-time); 2 years (part-time)
Language: English
In charge: Dr Peter Humphreys (Reader in Government)
Contact: Bernadette McLoughlin

Milton Keynes

De Montfort University: Department of Economics, Milton Keynes MK7 6HP, United Kingdom; tel (+44 1908) 834977; fax (+44 1908) 834879; e-mail priach@dmu.ac.uk
MA Economics and Politics
Duration: 12 months
Language: English
In charge and contact: Prof. A. Riach

Newcastle upon Tyne

University of Newcastle upon Tyne: Department of Politics, Newcastle upon Tyne NE1 7RU, United Kingdom; tel (+44 191) 222-7682; fax (+44 191) 222-5069; e-mail p.a.daniels@ncl.ac.uk; internet www.ncl.ac.uk/~npol.
MA in European Union Studies
Duration: 1 year (full-time); 2 years (part-time)
Language: English
Contact: Philip Daniels

University of Northumbria at Newcastle: Newcastle Business School, Ellison Place, Newcastle upon Tyne NE1 8ST, United Kingdom; tel (+44 191) 227-4433; fax (+44 191) 227-3893; e-mail nb.admissions@unn.ac.uk.
MA in European Business Administration
Duration: 1 year
Language: English
In charge and contact: Jan Shell

Newtownabbey

University of Ulster at Jordanstown: School of Public Policy, Economics and Law, Newtownabbey, Co Antrim, BT 37 0QB, United Kingdom; tel (+44 28) 9036-8872; fax (+44 28) 9036-6847; e-mail il.mcgowan@ulst.ac.uk
PGD European Law and Policy
LL.M. European Law and Policy
MSc European Law and Policy
Duration: 1 year full-time (or 2 years part-time)
Language: English
Contact: Dr Lee McGowan

Norwich

University of East Anglia: School of Law, Norwich NR4 1TJ, United Kingdom; tel (+44 1603) 592525; fax (+44 1603) 250245; e-mail dova.k@uea.ac.uk; internet www.uea.ac.uk.
MA in International Relations and European Studies
Duration: 1 year (full-time); 2 years (part-time)
Language: English
In charge: Dr A. Kempo-Welch, Dr T. Kastakopoulou
Contact: Dr T. Kastakopoulou

Nottingham

University of Nottingham School of Law: University Park, Nottingham NG7 2RD, United Kingdom; tel (+44 115) 951-5694; fax (+44 115) 951-5696; e-mail llmphd@nottingham.ac.uk; internet www.nottingham.ac.uk/law.
LL.M in International Law
Duration: 1 year
Language: English
In charge and contact: Prof. D.J. Harris

Portsmouth

University of Portsmouth: Faculty of Humanities and Social Sciences, School of Social and Historical Studies, Milldam, Burnaby Road, Portsmouth, Hants PO1 3AS, United Kingdom; tel (+44 23) 9284-2205; fax (+44 23) 9284-6040; e-mail humanities.admissions@port.ac.uk.
MA in European Studies
Duration: 1 year (full-time); 2 years (part-time)
Language: English
In charge: Dr Paul S. Flenley
Contact: Nadine Wilson

University of Portsmouth/Haagse Hogeschool: Faculty of Humanities and Social Sciences, School of Social and Historical Studies, Milldam, Burnaby Road, Portsmouth, Hants PO1 3AS, United Kingdom; tel (+44 23) 9284-2205 (UK); tel (+31 70) 445-8600 (Netherlands); fax (+44 23) 9284-6040 (UK); fax (+31 70) 445-8625 (Netherlands); e-mail humanities.admissions@port.ac.uk; e-mail esjgerretsen@sost.hhs.nl.
MA in European Law
Duration: 1 year (full-time); 2 years (part-time)
Language: English
In charge: Dr Paul S. Flenley
Contacts: Nadine Wilson, Cheryl Gerretsen

Reading

University of Reading: Graduate School for European and International Studies (GSEIS), Department of Politics, Whiteknights, POB 218, Reading RG6 2AA, United Kingdom; tel (+44 118) 931-8378; fax (+44 118) 975-5442; e-mail gseis@reading.ac.uk; internet www.rdg.ac.uk/eis.
MA in European and International Studies
Duration: 12 months
Language: English
In charge: Prof. C. Bluth
Contact: S. Smelt (Admissions Officer)

Salford

University of Salford: Department of Politics and Contemporary History, Salford M4 5WT, United Kingdom; tel (+44 161) 295-5000; fax (+44 161) 295-5077; e-mail s.j.ward@pch.salford.ac.uk.
MA in Contemporary European Studies
Duration: 1 year (full-time); 2 years (part-time)
Languages: All modules taught in English. Training in French, German, Spanish and Italian available.
In charge: Prof. Martin Bull
Contact: Dr Steven Ward

Sheffield

University of Sheffield: Department of Politics, Northumberland Road, Sheffield S10 2TU, United Kingdom; tel (+44 114) 222-1642; fax (+44 114) 273-9769; e-mail s.kelk@sheffield.ac.uk.

MA in Political Economy of the European Union
Duration: 1 year
Language: English
In charge: Prof. S.A. George
Contact: S. Kelk

Southampton

University of Southampton: Faculty of Law, Highfield, Southampton, SO17 1BJ; tel (+44 23) 8059-3551; fax (+44 23) 8059-3024; e-mail k.m.pack@soton.ac.uk; internet www.soton.ac.uk/~law/pg.html.
LL.M. in European Integration
Duration: 1 year
Language: English
Contact: PGCE Admissions Co-ordinator

Stoke-on-Trent

Staffordshire University Business School: Leek Road, Stoke-on-Trent ST4 2DF, United Kingdom; tel (+44 1782) 294092; tel: (+44 1782) 294065; fax (+44 1782) 747006; e-mail g.t.pugh@staffs.ac.uk; internet www.ruca.ua.ac.be/~eitei.
MA in Economics of International Trade and European Integration
Duration: 12 months
Language: English
Contact: Jenny Herbert

Swansea

University of Wales Swansea: Department of Politics, Singleton Park, Swansea SA2 8PP, United Kingdom; tel (+44 1792) 295302/295303; fax (+44 1792) 295716; e-mail r.j.bideleux@swansea.ac.uk.
MA or MSc(Econ.) in European Politics
Duration: 12 months
Language: English
In charge: Robert Bideleux (Senior Lecturer and Director)
Contact: Dr Jonathan Bradbury

Uxbridge

Brunel University: Department of Government, Brunel University, Uxbridge UB8 3PH, United Kingdom; tel (+44 1895) 274000 ext. 3510; fax (+44 1895) 812595; e-mail pgsec@brunel.ac.uk; internet www.brunel.ac.uk/depts/govn.
MA in European Politics
Duration: 12 months (full-time); 24 months (part-time)
Language: English
Contact: Pam Holloway

Brunel University: Department of Government, Brunel University, Uxbridge UB8 3PH, United Kingdom; tel (+44 1895) 274000 ext. 3510; fax (+44 1895) 812595; e-mail pgsec@brunel.ac.uk; internet www.brunel.ac.uk/depts/govn.
MA in European Policy Studies
Duration: 12 months (full-time); 24 months (part-time)
Language: English

Contact: Pam Holloway/Margaret Hunt (Postgraduate Secretaries)

Third Countries

BULGARIA
Sofia

University of Bulgaria—Centre for European Studies: bul. Dr G.M. Dimitrov 52-A, POB 28, 1125 Sofia, Bulgaria; tel (+359 2) 971-2411; tel: (+359 2) 707443; fax (+359 2) 971-2411; fax (+359 2) 707443; e-mail ces@mail.cesbg.org; internet www.cesbg.org.
MA in European Integration
Duration: 1 year
Languages: Bulgarian and English/French for visiting professors
In charge: Dr Ingrid Shikova (Executive Director, Centre for European Studies)
Contact: Iliana Eskenazi

CHINA
Shanghai

Fudan University: Centre for European Studies, 220 Handan Road, 200433 Shanghai, China; tel (+86 21) 6564-2668; fax (+86 21) 6564-6456; e-mail ces@fudan.edu.cn; internet www.fudan.edu.cn.
MA/Ph.D. in European Integration Studies
Duration: 3 years
Language: Chinese
Contact: Song Huiyi

ISRAEL
Jerusalem

Hebrew University of Jerusalem: Helmut Kohl Institute for European Studies, Faculty of Social Sciences, 91905 Jerusalem, Israel; tel (+972 2) 588-3286; fax (+972 2) 588-1535.
MA in European Studies
Duration: 1 year
Language: Hebrew
In charge: Alfred Tovias
Contact: Revital Goldberg

MACAU
Macau

University of Macau: Instituto de Estudos Europeus, Calçada do Gaio 6, Macau, Macau; tel (+82 853) 354325/6; fax (+82 853) 356155; e-mail ieem@macau.ctm.net; internet www.ieem.org.mo.
Master in European Studies
Duration: 2 years
Language: English
Contact: Sofia Marinho de Bastos

SWITZERLAND
Basle

University of Basle: Europa Institut, Gellerstrasse 27, 4052 Basle, Switzerland; tel (+41 61) 317-9767; fax (+41 61) 317-9766; e-mail europa@ubaclu.unibas.ch; internet www.unibas.ch/euro/index.html
Master of Advanced European Studies
Duration: 1 year (full-time); 2 years (part-time)
Languages: German, English and French
In charge and contact: Prof. Dr Georg Kreis

Geneva

University of Geneva: Institut Européen, 2 rue Daniel Colladon, 1204 Geneva, Switzerland; tel (+41 22) 705-7850; fax (+41 22) 705-7852; e-mail houze@uni2a.unige.ch; internet www.unige.ch/ieug
DES en Études Européennes
Duration: 2 semesters
Language: French
Contact: Marie-Hélène Houzé

Lausanne

University of Lausanne: Centre de Droit Comparé et Européen, BFSH 1, 1015 Lausanne-Dorigny, Switzerland; tel (+41 21) 692-2790; fax (+41 21) 692-2785; e-mail nicole.lagrotteria@cdce.unil.ch; internet www.unil.ch/droit.
LL.M. en Droit Européen et en Droit International Économique
Duration: 1 academic year
Languages: French and English
Contact: Nicole Lagrotteria

St Gallen

University of St Gallen (HSG): Dufourstrasse 59, 9000 St Gallen, Switzerland; tel (+41 71) 224-2616; fax (+41 71) 224-2611; e-mail mblhsg@unisg.ch; internet www.mbl.unisg.ch.
Master of European and International Business Law MBL—HSG
Duration: 16 months
Languages: German (65%) and English (35%)
Contact: Tobias Braegger

THAILAND
Bangkok

Chulalongkorn University: Vidyabhathana Building, 3rd floor, Phya Thai Road, 10330 Bangkok, Thailand; tel (+66 2) 218-3924; fax (+66 2) 218-3907; e-mail maeus@chula.ac.th; internet www.chula.ac.th/international/maeus/prog.html.
MA in European Studies
Duration: 1 year

Language: English
Contact: Prof. Apirat Petchsiri

TUNISIA

Tunis

University of Tunis: Faculté des Sciences Juridiques, Politiques et Sociales de Tunis, 1 rue Hédi Karray, 2049 Ariana (Tunis), Tunisia; tel (+216 1) 76-69-19; fax (+216 1) 71-72-55.
DEA en Droit Européen
Doctorat en Droit Européen
Duration: 2 years (DEA); 3 to 5 years (Doctorat)
Language: French
In charge and contact: Yadh Ben Achour (Dean of the Faculty of Social, Political and Legal Sciences)

TURKEY

Istanbul

Marmara University: European Community Institute, Jean Monnet Building, Goztepe Campus—Kadikoy, 81040 Istanbul, Turkey; tel (+90 216) 338-4196; fax (+90 216) 347-4543; e-mail acakir@ marun.edu.tr.
MA and Ph.D. in European Economics
Duration: 2 years (MA); 4 years (Ph.D.)
Language: English
In charge and contact: Prof. Dr Aslan Gündüz

Marmara University: European Community Institute, Jean Monnet Building, Goztepe Campus—Kadikoy, 81040 Istanbul, Turkey; tel (+90 216)

338-4196; fax (+90 216) 347-4543; e-mail acakir@marun.edu.tr.
LL.M. and Ph.D. in European Law
Duration: 2 years (LL.M.); 4 years (Ph.D.)
Language: English
In charge and contact: Prof. Dr Aslan Gündüz

Marmara University: European Community Institute, Jean Monnet Building, Goztepe Campus—Kadikoy, 81040 Istanbul, Turkey; tel (+90 216) 338-4196; fax (+90 216) 347-4543; e-mail acakir@ marun.edu.tr.
MA and Ph.D. in European Politics
Duration: 2 years (MA); 4 years (Ph.D.)
Language: English
In charge and contact: Prof. Dr Aslan Gündüz

EU GRANTS AND LOANS

EU FUNDING PROGRAMMES

THE STRUCTURAL FUNDS

European Regional Development Fund (ERDF)

Objectives. Over the years 2000–2006 the ERDF will endeavour to encourage competitiveness in the regions.
The Fund will contribute to Objectives 1 and 2 and to the INTERREG and URBAN Community Initiatives.

Directorate-General: Directorate-General for Regional Policy
Fax: (+32 2) 296-24-03
Internet: www.inforegio.cec.eu.int, www.europa.eu.int/comm/dgs/regional_policy/index_en.htm

European Social Fund (ESF)

Objectives. To support measures which aim to prevent and combat unemployment, develop human resources and foster social integration in the labour market, so as to promote a high level of employment, equal opportunities for men and women, sustainable development and economic and social cohesion.

Directorate-General: Directorate General for Social Policy
Fax: (+32 2) 296-97-69
Internet: www.europa.eu.int/comm/dgs/employment-social/index_en.htm

The European Agricultural Guidance and Guarantee Fund (EAGGF / FEOGA)

Objectives. To improve agricultural and rural structures.

Directorate-General: DG Agriculture
Tel: (+32 2) 296-59-64
Fax: (+32 2) 295-01-30
Internet: www.europa.eu.int/comm/dgs/agriculture/index_en.htm

The Financial Instrument for Guidance in the Fisheries Sector (FIFG)

Objectives. The objectives are: – to modernize and restructure fisheries and aquaculture;
– to assist the processing and marketing of fisheries and aquaculture products.

Directorate-General: Fisheries DG
Tel: (+32 2) 296-33-28
Fax: (+32 2) 296-30-33
Internet: www.europa.3eu.int/comm/dgs/fisheries/index_en.htm

THE COHESION FUND

The Cohesion Fund

Objectives. To enable the Member States in question (Spain, Greece, Portugal, Ireland) to catch up in economic terms in the fields of transport and the environment without damaging their integration into the Economic and Monetary Union (EMU).

Directorate-General: Regio
Internet: www.europa.eu.int/comm/dgs/regional_policy/index_en.htm

EUROPEAN UNION INITIATIVES

EQUAL

Objectives. The Equal Initiative aims to develop co-operation between the Member States and the Commission with view to promoting new ways of combating all forms of exclusion, discrimination and inequalities in the labour market.

Directorate-General: Directorate-General for Employment and Social Affairs
Fax: (+32 2) 296-51-84
Internet: www.europa.eu.int/comm/dgs/employment/index_en.htm

INTERREG III

Objectives. The objective of the new phase of INTERREG is to strengthen economic and social cohesion in the European Union by promoting cross-border, transnational and interregional co-operation and balanced development of the EU territory.
Particular priority needs to be given to the external borders of the European Union in view of enlargement as well as to insular and ultraperipheral regions.

Directorate-General: Directorate-General for Regional Policy
Responsible: Rudolf Niessler
Internet: www.europa.eu.int/comm/dgs/regional_policy/index_en.htm

LEADER +

Objectives. To continue to encourage the emergence and experimentation of rural territorial development strategies.

Directorate-General: Directorate-General Agriculture
Responsible: Catherine Combette
Tel: (+32 2) 295-62-26
Fax: (+32 2) 296-59-92
E-mail: catherine.combette@cec.eu.int
Internet: www.europa.eu.int/comm/dgs/agriculture/index.en.htm, www.rural-europe.aeidl.be

URBAN 2000-2006

Objectives. To help resolve problems of urban districts in difficulties.

Directorate-General: Directorate General for Regional Policy
Responsible: Elisabeth Helander
Fax: (+32 2) 296-60-03
E-mail: Elisabeth.helander@cec.eu.int
Internet: www.inforegio.cec.eu.int

LOANS

EURATOM

Objectives. Euratom loans are granted for the purpose of financing investment projects in the Member States relating to the industrial production of electricity in nuclear power stations and to industrial fuel cycle installations.

Directorate-General: Directorate-General Economic and Financial Affairs
Directorate-General: Financial Operations Service – ECFIN-SOF EURATOM Loans
Responsible: Peter Reichel
Tel: (+352) 4301-36-443
Fax: (+352) 4301-365-99
E-mail: peter.reichel@cec.eu.int

European Investment Bank (EIB)

Objectives. The EIB was primarily a source of loan finance for regional development, Trans-European networks infrastructure and environment projects.

Directorate-General: European Investment Bank
100 Bd Konrad Adenauer, 2950 Luxembourg, Luxembourg
Tel: (+352) 437-93-122
Fax: (+352) 437-93-189
E-mail: info@eib.org
Internet: www.eib.org

European Investment Fund (EIF)

Objectives. The EIF was created in 1994. It is the specialized financial institution for the support of the creation, growth and development of Small and Medium-sized Enterprises (SMEs).
The EIF intervenes through Venture Capital and Guarantee instruments.
The EIF does not finance directly SMEs, but always acts through financial intermediaries.
The EIF pursues Community objectives (Growth, Employment, Innovation) and at the same time must generate value for its shareholders.
The EIF always acts on a commercial basis.

The EIF is a tripartite structure, between the European Investment Bank (EIB), the European Commission and several banks and financial institutions. In June 2000, the EIB became the majority partner, thus reinforcing the role of the EIF as a leading venture capital investor in Europe.

The EIF may conduct its activities in the Member States of the European Union and in the accession countries.

Directorate-General: European Investment Fund
43 avenue J.F. Kennedy, 2968 Luxembourg, Luxembourg
Tel: (+352) 42-66-881
Fax: (+352) 42-66-800
E-mail: info@eif.org
Internet: www.eif.org

AGRICULTURE

Information measures relating to the Common Agricultural Policy

Objectives. Financing of information measures relating to the Common Agricultural Policy and aimed in particular at a) helping to explain, implement and develop that policy; b) promoting the European model of agriculture and helping people understand it; c) informing farmers and other parties active in rural areas; d) raising public awareness of the issues and objectives of the CAP

Directorate-General: Directorate-General for Agriculture
Responsible: Eugène Leguen de la Croix
E-mail: Eugene.Leguen-de-Lacroix@cec.eu.int@cec.eu.int
Internet: http://europa.eu.int/comm/dgagriculture/grants/capinfo/index_en.htm

Protection of the Community's forests against atmospheric pollution

Objectives. The objectives are:
– to provide increased protection for forests in the Community against atmospheric pollution; to establish, on the basis of a common network of observation plots;
– intensive and continuous monitoring of forest ecosystems on the basis of a network of permanent observation plots;
experiments in the field to improve understanding of atmospheric pollution in forests and its effects on forests;
– pilot projects to maintain damaged forests and to improve methods of observing and measuring damage to the forests.

Directorate-General: Directorate-General for Agriculture
Responsible: Robert Flies
E-mail: Robert.Flies@cec.eu.int
Internet: http://europa.eu.int/comm/agriculture/fore/index_en.htm

Rural development programmes 2000–06

Objectives. To improve agricultural structures, the diversification of production and activities, sustainable forest development, the social and economic development of rural areas, environmental protection and the promotion of equal opportunities for men and women.

Directorate-General: Directorate-General for Agriculture
Tel: (+32 2) 295-29-63
Fax: (+32 2) 299-17-61
Internet: http://europa.eu.int/comm/dgs/agriculture/index_en.htm

SAPARD – Community support for pre-accession measures for agriculture and rural development in the applicant countries of central and eastern Europe in the pre-accession period

Objectives. To provide Community support for agriculture and rural development during the pre-accession period in the applicant countries of central and eastern Europe (Bulgaria, the Czech Republic, Estonia, Hungary, Latvia, Lithuania, Poland, Romania, Slovakia and Slovenia).

Directorate-General: Directorate-General for Agriculture
Tel: (+32 2) 295-59-72
Fax: (+32 2) 295-17-46
Internet: http://europa.eu.int/comm/dgs/agriculture/index_en.htm

COMPETITION

Training of National Judges in EC Competition Law and Judicial Cooperation between National Judges

Objectives. To train national judges in the workings of EC competition law and in the necessity for judicial co-operation between national judges

Directorate-General: Directorate-General Competition
Responsible: Kris Dekeyser
E-mail: Kris.Dekeyser@cec.eu.int
Internet: http://europa.eu.int/comm/dgs/competition/proposals2

EDUCATION AND CULTURE

Community Action Programme for Youth

Objectives. To promote a greater sense of solidarity; active involvement in the European ideal; encouraging a spirit of initiative and enterprise.

Directorate-General: Directorate-General Education and Culture
Responsible: Pierre Mairesse
Tel: (+32 2) 296-20-09
Fax: (+32 2) 299-40-38

E-mail: Pierre.Mairesse@cec.eu.int
Internet: www.europa.eu.int/comm/education/youth/youthprogram.html

Cooperation with the United States and Canada in the field of higher education and vocational training

Objectives. To promote co-operation projects with the United States and Canada in the field of higher education and training.

Responsible: Nicole Versijp
E-mail: nicole.versijp@cec.eu.int
Internet: www.europa.eu.int/comm/education/progr.html, www.europa.eu.int/comm/education/ec-usa/usa.html, http://europa.eu.int/comm/education/canada/canada.html

CULTURE 2000

Objectives. To maintain:
– the mutual knowledge of the culture and history of the European people;
– the promotion of cultural heritage having European dimensions;
– the spread of European cultures into non-member countries and dialogue with other world cultures.

Directorate-General: Directorate-General for Education and Culture
Responsible: Antonios Kosmopoulos
Tel: (+32 2) 299-93-35
Fax: (+32 2) 299-92-83
E-mail: antonios.kosmopoulos@cec.eu.int
Internet: www.europa.eu.int/comm/culture/index_en.html

Jean Monnet Project – European integration in university studies

Objectives. To facilitate the introduction of European integration studies in universities by means of start-up subsidies

Directorate-General: Directorate-General for Education and Culture A2
Responsible: Belen Bernaldo-De-Quiros
Tel: (+32 2) 296-03-12
Fax: (+32 2) 299-92-05
E-mail: Belen.Bernaldo-De-Quiros@cec.eu.int
Internet: www.europa.eu.int/comm/education/ajm/index_en.html

LEONARDO DA VINCI II

Objectives. To improve the quality of continuous vocational training and the acquisition of aptitudes and skills throughout life through:
– mobility;
– developing innovation and quality;
– the promotion of linguistic skills;
– transnational networks;
– the development of reference tools.

Directorate-General: Directorate-General Education and Culture
Responsible: Marta Ferreira Lourenço
Tel: (+32 2) 296-26-58
Fax: (+32 2) 295-57-04
E-mail: Marta.Ferreira@cec.eu.int

Internet: www.europa.eu.int/comm/
education/leonardo_en.html

MEDIA Plus – development, distribution and promotion

Objectives. The objectives must work towards:
– an improvement in the competitiveness of the European audiovisual industry;
– the development of the audiovisual sector in countries or regions with a low capacity for audiovisual production and/or a restricted geographical and linguistic area.

Directorate-General: Directorate-General for Education and Culture
Responsible: Jacques Delmoly
Tel: (+32 2) 295-84-06
Fax: (+32 2) 296-66-84
E-mail: Jacques.Delmoly@cec.eu.int
Internet: www.europa.eu.int/comm/
avpolicy/media/index_en.html

SOCRATES

Objectives. The objectives are:
– to strengthen the European dimension of education;
– to promote a quantitative and qualitative improvement in knowledge of the languages of the European Union;
– to promote co-operation and mobility in the education field and to encourage innovation in teaching practices and materials.

Directorate-General: Education and Culture DG
Responsible: Sophie Poupe
Tel: (+32 2) 295-10-88
E-mail: sophie.poupe@cec.eu.int
Internet: www.europa.eu.int/comm/
education/socrates-en.html

TEMPUS

Objectives. To restructure higher education in the countries of Central and Eastern Europe and the Balkans

Directorate-General: Directorate-General Education and Culture
Responsible: Martin Westlake
Tel: (+32 2) 295-59-03
Fax: (+32 2)295-57-19
E-mail: Tempus@cec.eu.int
Internet: www.etf.eu.int/tempus.nsf,
www.europa.eu.int/comm/education/
tempus/index_en.html

INFORMATION SOCIETY

eContent Programme

Objectives. The eContent programme is aimed at supporting the production, dissemination and use of European digital content and to promote linguistic diversity on the global networks.

Directorate-General: DG INFSO
Responsible: Massimo Garriba
Fax: (+352) 4301-34959
E-mail: econtent@cec.eu.int
Internet: www.cordis.lu/econtent

EMPLOYMENT, SOCIAL AFFAIRS AND EQUAL OPPORTUNITIES

Community Action Programme on equal opportunities for men and women (2001-2005).

Objectives. The objectives are:
– to achieve gender mainstreaming;
– to mobilize all actors to achieve equality in a changing economy;
– to reconcile work and family life, to promote a gender balance in decision-making;
– to create optimum conditions for the exercise of equality rights.

Directorate-General: Directorate-General Employment, Social Affairs and Equal Opportunities
Responsible: Rosa Novo Cid-Fuentes
Tel: (+32 2) 295-84-80
Fax: (+32 2) 296-35-62
E-mail: eqop@cec.eu.int
Internet: http://europa.eu.int/comm/
employment_social/equ_opp/actprg_en
.html

Community Action Programme to combat discrimination 2001-2006

Objectives. To promote the fight against discrimination

Directorate-General: Directorate-General for Employment, Social Affairs and Equal Opportunities
Responsible: Anti-discrimination unit DG EMPL D4
E-mail: antidiscrimination@bxl.dg5
.cec.be
Internet: http://europa.eu.int/comm/dgs/
employment_social/tender_en.htm

Free movement of workers, coordination of social security systems and measures for migrant workers, including those from outside the Union

Objectives. This budget line could be used for the spontaneous co-financing of a few conferences relating to Regulation No 1408/71 and a few technological projects aimed at speeding up and simplifying administrative procedures in order to improve the system for acquiring rights and the calculation and payment of benefits pursuant to Regulations (EEC) No 1408/71 and (EEC) No 574/72.

Directorate-General: Directorate-General for Employment, Social Affairs and Equal Opportunities DIR. E
Responsible: Erwin Thomas
E-mail: Erwin.thomas@cec.eu.int

Innovative measures financed under Article 6 of the European Social Fund Regulation (Direction D)

Objectives. To develop innovative methods which can improve the efficiency of actions financed by the ESF

Directorate-General: Directorate-General for Employment and Social Affairs
Responsible: Dominique Be
Tel: (+32 2) 295-80-57
E-mail: Dominique.Be@cec.eu.int
Internet: http://europa.eu.int/comm/
employment_social/esf/en/index.htm

Community incentive measures in the field of employment (EIM)

Objectives. The objectives are: – to raise awareness of the European Employment Strategy;
– to contribute to the development of evaluation practice in the European Employment Strategy;
– mutual learning.

Directorate-General: Directorate-General for Employment, Social Affairs and Equal Opportunities

ENERGY AND TRANSPORT

Grants in the field of transport and for the organisation of conferences in the fields of energy and transport

Objectives. The objectives are:
– to award grants to promote the objectives of the transport policy;
– to organize conferences in the fields of energy and transport.

Directorate-General: Directorate-General for Energy and Transport
Responsible: M. J. Ferreira
Tel: (+32 2) 299-16-83
Fax: (+32 2) 299-39-06
Internet: http://europa.eu.int/comm/dgs/
energy_transport/home/calls/proposal_
en.htm

ECSC Steel RTD Programme

Objectives. To sustain and develop the Community steel industry's competitiveness in changing industrial, commercial and political contexts.

Directorate-General: Directorate-General XII for Science, Research and Development
Tel: (+32 2) 295-44-15 or 295-85-87
Fax: (+32 2) 296-59-87
Internet: www.cordis.lu/ecsc-steel/
home.html

The 5th Framework Programme

Objectives. The Fifth Framework Programme comprises four Community activities. The first Community activity relates to the following three themes:
1) unlocking the resources of the living world and the ecosystem;
2) creating a user-friendly information society;
3) promoting competitive and sustainable growth.

The second, third and fourth Community activities relate to the following three themes respectively:
a) confirming the international role of Community research;
b) innovation and participation of small and medium-sized enterprises;
c) improving human potential.

Directorate-General: Directorate-General XII
Internet: www.cordis.lu/fp5/

Transport of radioactive materials: safety, health protection and nuclear safety technologies (1st component of the SURE programme).

Objectives. To re-examine and harmonize safety practices in the transport of radioactive materials in the Community.

Directorate-General: Directorate-General for Energy and Transport
Responsible: Loris Rossi
Tel: (+32 2) 295-00-61
Fax: (+32 2) 295-58-52
E-mail: loris.rossi@cec.eu.int
Internet: http://europa.eu.int/comm/ energy/en/pfs_sure_en.html

ECONOMIC AND FINANCIAL AFFAIRS

EIF Start-up Facility

Objectives. The Facility supports the establishment and financing of SMEs in their start-up phase by investing in relevant specialized venture capital funds and by supporting the establishment and development of business incubators

Directorate-General: Directorate-General for Economic and Financial Affairs
Responsible: Dietmar Maass
Fax: (+352) 4301-36-609
E-mail: Dietmar.Maass@cec.eu.int
Internet: www.eif.org

Growth and environment

Objectives. To grant loans to SMEs in order to finance new investments in the environment

Directorate-General: Directorate-General Economic and Financial Affairs
Responsible: Pedro Monteiro-Carvalho
Fax: (+352) 4301-36609
E-mail: Pedro.Monteiro-Carvalho@ cec.eu.int
Internet: www.eif.org

Joint European Ventures (JEVs)

Objectives. The Community gives financial support to SMEs planning to launch new joint transnational ventures within the European Union.

Directorate-General: Directorate-General Economic and Financial Affairs
Responsible: Jeremy Heath
Fax: (+32 2) 295-21-54
E-mail: Jeremy.heath@cec.eu.int

Internet: www.europa.eu.int/comm .entreprise/entrepreneurship/financing/ jev.htm

Seed Capital Action

Objectives. The facility aims to stimulate the supply of capital for the creation of innovative new businesses with growth and job-creation potential, including those in the traditional economy, through support for seed funds, incubators or similar organizations in which the EIF participates

Directorate-General: Directorate-General Economic and Financial Affairs
Responsible: Dietmar Maass
Fax: (+352) 43013-6609
E-mail: Dietmar.Maass@cec.eu.int
Internet: www.eif.org

SME Finance Facility

Objectives. To encourage financial intermediaries, banks and investment funds in the Phare applicant countries to extend and maintain over the long term their loans to and capital investments in SMEs.

Directorate-General: Directorate-General for Economic and Financial Affairs
Responsible: Raul Gómez-Hernández
E-mail: Raul.gomez-hernandez@ cec.eu.int
Internet: www.ebrd.com

SME Guarantee Facility

Objectives. To encourage the granting of loans to SMEs by increasing the capacity of public or private guarantee systems in the Member States.

Directorate-General: Directorate-General for Economic and Financial Affairs
Responsible: Georges Floros
Fax: (+352) 4301-36-439
E-mail: Georgios.Floros@cec.eu.int
Internet: www.eif.org

ENLARGEMENT

PHARE

Objectives. Finance for economic development administrative reconfiguration, social change, legislative work to enable candidate countries to meet the criteria for membership of the EU.

Directorate-General: Directorate-General Enlargement
Internet: http://europa.eu.int/comm/ enlargement/pas/phare.htm

ENTERPRISE

Euro Info Centre Network

Objectives. To inform, advise and assist European enterprises in all EU-related questions.

Directorate-General: Directorate-General Enterprise

Responsible: Jacques McMillan
E-mail: Jacques.McMillan@cec.eu.int
Internet: http://europa.eu.int/comm/ enterprise/policy_en.htm

HRTP – Japan Industry Insight

Objectives. This 4-week or 11-week programme provides an integrated in-depth view of Japanese industrial structure and business practices: it provides the opportunity of a lifetime for EU executives to experience and understand both the cultural and economic elements which define and explain Japan's business and technological achievements. The knowledge gained during this programme will be extremely beneficial to companies who have or wish to have business relations with Japan.

Directorate-General: Directorate-General Enterprise A/2
Responsible: Philippe Jean
Tel: (+32 2) 299-11-11
Internet: www.eujapan.com

ENVIRONMENT

Community action programme in the field of civil protection

Objectives. The objectives are:
– to support efforts made by the Member States in the field of protection of persons and property;
– to facilitate co-operation, exchanges of experience and mutual assistance between the Member States.

Directorate-General: Directorate-General for the Environment
Responsible: Alessandro Barisich
E-mail: alessandro.barisich@cec.eu.int
Internet: http://europa.eu.int/comm/ environment/civil/index.htm

Community action programme promoting non-governmental organizations primarily active in the field of environmental protection

Objectives. To promote the activities of NGOs, which are primarily active in the field of environmental protection at a European level, by contributing to the development and implementation of Community environmental policy and legislation.

Directorate-General: Directorate-General for the Environment
Responsible: Saturnino Muñoz Gómez
Tel: (+32 2) 299-93-32
Fax: (+32 2) 296-95-60
E-mail: Saturnino.Munoz@cec.eu.int
Internet: http://europa.eu.int/comm/ environment/funding/intro_en.htm

Community cooperation framework for accidental or intentional marine pollution

Objectives. To support efforts made by the Member States at national, regional and local level to protect the marine environment, coasts and human health from the risk of accidental or intentional pollution at sea, with the exception of continuous pollution flows of telluric origin.

Directorate-General: Directorate-General for the Environment
Responsible: Alessandro Barisich
E-mail: alessandro.barisich@cec.eu.int
Internet: http://europa.eu.int/comm/environment/civil/index.htm

LIFE III2

Objectives. To contribute to the implementation, updating and development of Community policy and legislation relating to the environment.

Directorate-General: Directorate-General for the Environment
Responsible: Bruno Julien (LIFE-Nature)
Fax: (+32 2) 296-95-56 (LIFE-Nature)
E-mail: bruno.julien@cec.eu.int (LIFE-Nature)
E-mail: life-environment@cec.eu.int
Internet: http://europa.eu.int/comm/life/home.htm, http://europa.eu.int/comm/life/envir/natauto.htm

EUROPEAID

(at)lis (Alliance for the Information Society)

Objectives. To promote the information society and fight against the digital divide throughout Latin America with a view to stimulating co-operation with European counterparts and better serving the needs of local communities and citizens as part of sustainable development.

Directorate-General: EuropeAid Co-operation Office
Responsible: Adrianus Koetsenruijter
Head of Unit AIDCO E2, 200 Rue de la Loi, J 54 04/13, 1049 Brussels, Belgium
E-mail: europeaid-alis@cec.eu.int
Internet: www.ebusiness.com/funding/europeaid/aidco19_en.htm

AL-INVEST

Objectives. Internationalization of European and Latin American SMEs.

Directorate-General: Directorate-General for External Relations
Responsible: Pablo López-Herrerías
E-mail: Pablo.lopez-herrerias@cec.eu.int
Internet: http://europa.eu.int/comm/europeaid/projects/al-invest/network_en.cfm

ALURE

Objectives. Economic co-operation in the energy sector between Latin America and EU

Directorate-General: Commission Européenne

EuropeAid Office de Coopération – AIDCO, 200 Rue de la Loi (LOI 41 5/69), 1049 Brussels, Belgium
Responsible: Adrianus Koetsenruijter
Tel: (+32 2) 295-14-42
Fax: (+32 2) 299-39-41
E-mail: europeaid-alure@cec.eu.int
Internet: http://europa.eu.int:802/comm/europeaid/projects/alure/index_en.htm

Asia-Information and Communication Technology (Asia-IT & C)

Objectives. To support economic co-operation between the EU and South and South-East Asia. Asia IT & C aims to utilize the potential of European Information and Communications Technology for applications in the agriculture, education, health, transport, society, tourism, intelligent manufacturing and electronic commerce domains.

Directorate-General: Programme Management Office Europe
Directorate-General: Massimiliano Dragoni
Responsible: David McCormick, Xavier De Coninck
Tel: (+32 2) 298-48-73
Fax: (+32 2) 299-10-62
E-mail: info@asia-itc.org
Internet: www.asia-itc.org, http://europa.eu.int/comm/europeaid/tender/index_en.htm

ASIA-INVEST

Objectives. To encourage growth in two-way trade & investment flows and to promote the development of mutually beneficial trading relationships and investments between EU and South and South-East Asia.

Directorate-General: Asia-Invest Secretariat
200 Rue de la Loi, 1049 Brussels, Belgium
Responsible: Tamryn Barker
Tel: (+32 2) 299-69-69
Fax: (+32 2) 299-58-83
E-mail: europeaid-asia-invest@cec.eu.int
Internet: www.asia-invest.com

ASIA-URBS

Objectives. To strengthen the EU's participation in the socio-economic development of Asia, through support to local authorities

Directorate-General: Asia-Urbs Secretariat
44 1/20 Rue de la Loi, 1049 Brussels, Belgium
Responsible: Michael Pennington
Tel: (+32 2) 298-47-31
Fax: (+32 2) 299-10-62
E-mail: europeaid-asia-urbs@cec.eu.int
Internet: www.asia-urbs.com, http://europa.eu.int/comm/europeaid/projects/asia-urbs/index_en.htm

CARDS – Community Assistance for Reconstruction, Development and Stabilisation

Objectives. To support the participation of Albania, Bosnia and Herzegovina, Croatia, and the Former Yugoslav Republic of Macedonia in the stabilization and association process.

Directorate-General: Europeaid Co-operation Office
Responsible: Per Eklund
Tel: (+32 2) 299-57-94
Fax: (+32 2) 296-74-82
Internet: http://europa.eu.int/comm/europeaid/projects/cards/index_en.htm

Community Statistical Programme 2003–2007

Objectives. To have comparable, up-to-date, quality statistics throughout the Union, providing the necessary tools for the implementation of Community policies.

Directorate-General: Eurostat
Responsible: Petra Metzmeier-Weiss
Financial Unit A-3, BECH B4/392, 5 Rue Alphonse Weicker, 2721 Luxembourg–Kirchberg, Luxembourg
Tel: (+352) 4301-322-26
Fax: (+352) 4301-322-69
E-mail: Petra.Metzmeier-Weiss@cec.eu.int

EU-Asia Pro Eco

Objectives. The objectives are:
– improved environmental quality (a cleaner Asia, including a positive influence on global climate change) and health conditions;
– long-term sustainable investment and trade between EU and Asia;
– an improved environmental performance in economic sectors.

Directorate-General: Europeaid Co-operation Office
Responsible: Jaime García-Rodríguez
E-mail: Jaime.Garcia@cec.eu.int
Internet: http://europa.eu.int/comm/europeaid/projects/cards/index_en.htm

European initiative for democracy and human rights (EIDHR)

Objectives. To promote and support human rights and democracy in third countries.

European Programme for Food Aid and Food Security

Objectives. The objective is to implement an innovative food security policy to bring assistance to developing countries facing food deficit problems – temporary and mostly structural – linked to poverty. This programme is particularly active in post-crisis situations and implements the link that must exist between relief, rehabilitation and development.

Environment and forests in developing countries

Objectives. The objective is to support these countries in their efforts to integrate an environmental dimension into their development process. The objective of the forests programme is to support the conservation and sustainable management of tropical forests and other forests in these countries.

Fight against antipersonnel landmines (APL)

Objectives. The objective is to to help countries that suffer from the consequences of landmines and to restore the conditions necessary for their economic and social development.

Gender equality

Objectives. Promoting gender equality is crucial for development. Gender discrimination is a violation of human rights. It is also an obstacle to social and economic development. A disproportionate majority of the world's poor are women.

Industrial cooperation in the nuclear sector with Russia and Ukraine (second part of the Sure programme)

Objectives. To promote industrial co-operation, co-operation between regulatory bodies and those countries and the exchange of know-how within the nuclear industry to help the countries concerned achieve high safety standards.

Directorate-General: EuropeAid Cooperation Office
Responsible: Guy Doucet, Responsible: Nicola Main
Tel: (+32 2) 295-34-08
Fax: (+32 2) 299-52-06
E-mail: nicola.main@cec.eu.int

MEDA (Measures accompanying reforms of social and economic structures in non-member Mediterranean countries)

Objectives. The main aims are:
– to develop better socio-economic balance;
– to support economic transition;
– to foster regional integration;
– to gradually create a euro–Mediterranean free trade area.

Directorate-General: Directorate-General External Relations
Directorate-General: MEDA
E-mail: europeaid-info@cec.eu.int
Internet: http://europa.eu.int/comm/europeaid/index_en.htm, http://europa.eu.int/comm/europeaid/projects/meda/index_fr.htm

NGO co-financing and decentralized cooperation

Objectives. The objectives are:
– to promote development in favour of developing countries;
– to raise European public awareness of development issues;
– to strengthen the civil society of the South.

Promotion of the conservation and sustainable management of tropical forests and other forests in developing countries

Objectives. To promote the conservation and sustainable management of tropical forests and other forests in developing countries, so as to meet the economic, social and environmental demands placed on forests at local, national and global levels.

Directorate-General: Europeaid Cooperation Office
Responsible: Louis du Breil De Pontbriand
E-mail: louis.du-breil-de-pontbriand@cec.eu.int
Internet: http://europa.eu.int/comm/europeaid/index_en.htm, http://europa.eu.int/comm/europeaid/tender/index_en.htm

TACIS

Objectives. To support the process of transition to market economies and democratic societies in the partner countries of Armenia, Azerbaijan, Belarus, Georgia, Kazakhstan, Kyrgystan, Moldova, Mongolia, Russia, Tajikistan, Turkmenistan, Ukraine and Uzbekistan.

Directorate-General: Directorate-General External Relations
Responsible: Alistair MacDonald
Tel: (+32 2) 299-46-13
Fax: (+32 2) 299-38-06
E-mail: phare-tacis@cec.eu.int
Internet: http://europa.eu.int/comm/external_relations/index.htm

The EU Partnership for Peace Programme

Objectives. To help provide a solid foundation at the civil society level for a just and lasting peace in the Middle East. Priority is given to initiatives that have a potential to act as a bridge between Israeli and Arab societies in order to improve mutual understanding

Directorate-General: Europeaid Cooperation Office
Responsible: Andreas Havelka
Tel: (+32 2) 295-89-48

Fax: (+32 2) 295-56-65
E-mail: andreas.havelka@cec.eu.int
Internet: http://europa.eu.int/comm/europeaid/tender/gestion/pg/e03/index_en.htm

The European Development Fund

Objectives. To promote and expedite the economic, cultural and social development of African, Caribbean and Pacific countries

Directorate-General: Europeaid Cooperation Office
Responsible: Mikael Barfod
Internet: http://europa.eu.int/comm/europeaid/index_en.htm, http://europa.eu.int/comm/development/index_en.htm

EXTERNAL RELATIONS

ALFA

Objectives. Alfa supports joint co-operation projects between European and Latin American higher education institutions.

Directorate-General: Directorate-General Relex
Responsible: Cécilia Costa
Tel: (+32 2) 299-49-76
Fax: (+32 2) 299-10-47
E-mail: cecilia.costa@cec.eu.int
Internet: http://europa.eu.int/comm/europeaid/projects/alfa/index_fr.htm

EU Institute in Japan

Objectives. The objectives are:
– to develop as a centre of academic excellence with a view to broadening and deepening the base of European Union studies in Japan;
– to serve as a platform for better understanding and knowledge about the EU as a major stakeholder in the global political and economic system and in particular as a major partner in Japan's external relations;
– to implement EU-related outreach activities towards the broad public in Japan and provide accurate up-to-date and comprehensive information about the EU, its policies and institutions in order to enhance the visibility of the EU.

Directorate-General: Directorate-General for External Relations

Executive Training Programme in Japan/Korea

Objectives. The objective is to build up a pool of European business executives able to communicate and operate in the Japanese and Korean business environments.

Directorate-General: Directorate-General for External Relations

Pilot cooperation project in the field of higher education

Objectives. The objectives are:
– to set up a framework for two-way student mobility at postgraduate (Master) level. Australian and New Zealand students should study at universities in at least two EU Member States;
– to serve as a model for co-operation between other European and Australian institutions;
– to help to assess the appropriateness of a structured co-operation programme on the basis of a sectoral agreement.

Directorate-General: Directorate-General for External Relations

Projects promoting cooperation and commercial relations with countries of North America, the Far East and Australasia (USA, Canada, Japan, New Zealand, Korea)

Objectives. The objectives are to strengthen relations with the partner countries concerned in terms of:
– closer economic links;
– a better understanding of the EU;
– reinforcing education co-operation activities and academic links;
– developing a stronger political partnership.

Directorate-General: Directorate-General for External Relations
Internet: www.etp.org, http://jpn.cec.eu.int/english/index.htm, http://europa.eu.int/comm/external_relations/us/intro/ct.htm

Provision of assistance to the partner states in eastern Europe and central Asia

Objectives. The objectives are:
– to promote the transition to a market economy;
– to reinforce democracy and the rule of law in the partner states.

Directorate-General: Directorate-General for External Relations
Responsible: DG External Affairs Directorate E, 1049 Brussels, Belgium
Internet: http://europa.eu.int/comm/external_relations/ceeca/tacis/contacts.htm

URB-AL

Objectives. URB-AL is a horizontal decentralized co-operation programme that brings together cities, regions and other local bodies in the European Union and Latin America.

Directorate-General: Directorate-General for External Relations
E-mail: europeaid-urb-al@cec.eu.int

HUMANITARIAN AID OFFICE – ECHO

Financing Emergency Humanitarian Operations Lasting Six Months

Objectives. To provide assistance, relief and protection operations on a non-discriminatory basis to help people in third countries.
– to promote co-operation between national administrations responsible for implementing Community rules relevant to the fields of this action programme and to ensure that proper account is taken of the Community dimension in their actions;
– to promote the uniform application of the relevant Community law;
– to encourage transparency of actions taken by the national authorities and to improve the overall efficiency of national administrations in their tasks in the relevant fields

Directorate-General: Directorate-General Justice and Home Affairs
Responsible: Jean-Louis De Brouwer
E-mail: jai-argo@cec.eu.int
Internet: www.europa.eu.int/comm/justice_home/jai/prog_en.htm

DAPHNE

Objectives. The DAPHNE Initiative aims to contribute towards ensuring a high level of protection of physical and mental health by the protection of children, young people and women against violence, by prevention of violence and by the provision of support for the victims of violence, in order, in particular, to prevent future exposure to violence.

Directorate-General: Directorate-General Justice and Home Affairs
Responsible: Patrick Trousson
Fax: (+32 2) 299-67-11
E-mail: Patrick.Trousson@cec.eu.int
Internet: www.europa.eu.int/comm/justice_home/project/daphne/en/index.htm

European Refugee Fund

Objectives. The financing of projects and measures to provide practical support in relation to the reception and voluntary repatriation of refugees, displaced persons and asylum seekers, including emergency assistance to persons who have fled as a result of fighting in Kosovo.

Directorate-General: Directorate-General Justice and Home Affairs
Responsible: Fonds européen pour les réfugiés
DG JAI Unité A/2 – Immigration et Asile (LX46 6/54), 1049 Brussels, Belgium
Fax: (+32 2) 299-80-53

E-mail: jai-european-refugee-fund@cec.eu.int
Internet: http://europa.eu.int/comm/justice_home/jai/prog_fr.htm

Framework programme for judicial cooperation in civil matters

Objectives. The objectives are:
– to promote judicial co-operation in civil matters;
– to improve mutual knowledge of Member States' legal and judicial systems in civil matters;
– to ensure the sound implementation and application of Community instruments in the area of judicial co-operation in civil matters;
– to improve information to the public on access to justice, judicial co-operation and the legal systems of the Member States in civil matters.

Directorate-General: Directorate-General Justice and Home Affairs
Responsible: Anna Jansson
E-mail: jai-framework-civil@cec.eu.int
Internet: www.europa.eu.int/comm/justice_home/jai/prog_en.htm

FISHERIES

Structural operations in fisheries and aquaculture (by the Financial Instrument for Fisheries Guidance FIFG)

Objectives. The objectives are:
– to help achieve lasting balance between fish stocks and fishing;
– to strengthen competitiveness of operating stuctures and to develop economically viable firms in the sector;
– to improve supplies and enhance the commercial value of fishery and aquaculture products;
– to help revitalize areas dependent on fisheries and aquaculture

Directorate-General: Directorate-General for Fisheries
J99-0/37, Rue de la Loi, 1049 Brussels, Belgium
Internet: http://europa.eu.int/comm/dgs/fisheries/index_en.htm

RESEARCH

Research and Training on Nuclear Energy

Objectives. The European Atomic Energy Community (Euratom) Sixth Framework Programme for Research and Training activities is a collection of actions at EU level to fund and promote nuclear energy research. The aims in the area of management of radioactive waste are to establish a sound technical basis for demonstrating the safety of disposing spent fuel and long-lived radioactive wastes in geological formations, to study the practicability on an industrial scale of partitioning and transmutation techniques and to explore the potential of concepts that would produce less waste in nuclear energy generation.

Directorate-General: Directorate-General for Research
Responsible: Pablo Fernández-Ruiz (Director, DG Research
E-mail: pablo.fernandez-ruiz@cec.eu.int

Internet: www.cordis.lu/fp6

TRADE

Grant to an international organization to support organization of a workshop in Asia on trade facilitation

Objectives. The objectives are:
– to increase awareness of the importance of trade facilitation among Government officials, the business community and academics in Asia;
– to enhance the capacity of trade negotiators and decision-makers in Asian countries;
– to advance the EU's multilateral and bilateral trade facilitation objectives.

Directorate-General: Directorate-General for Trade

OTHER USEFUL SOURCES
OF INFORMATION

WEBSITES OF EUROPEAN UNION INSTITUTIONS

IMPORTANT SITES ON EUROPA

CELEX: internet http://europa.eu.int/celex/htm

RAPID: internet http://europa.eu.int/rapid/start/cgi/guesten.ksh

ECLAS: internet europa.eu.int/eclas

EUR-LEX: internet europa.eu.int/eur-lex

SCADPlus: internet http://europa.eu.int/scadplus

European Commission Personnel: internet http://europa.eu.int/idea/en/index.htm

Treaties: internet http://europa.eu.int/abc/treaties-en.htm

Official Documents of the EU: internet http://europa.eu.int/documents/index_en.htm

Official Documents of the Commission: internet http://europa.eu.int/documents/comm/index_en.htm

Green Papers: internet http://europa.eu.int/comm/off/green/index-en.htm

White Papers: internet http://europa.eu.int/comm/off/white/index-en.htm

Bulletin of the European Union: internet http://europa.eu.int/abc/doc/off/bull/en/welcome.htm

General Report on the Activities of the EU: internet http://europa.eu.int/abc/doc/off/rg/en/welcome.htm

Competition: internet http://europa.eu.int/comm/competition

Euro: internet http://europa.eu.int/euro/entry.html

Questions and Answers on the European Monetary Union: internet http://europa.eu.int/euro/quest/normal/entry.htm

EU INSTITUTIONS AND OTHER SITES

European Parliament: internet www.europarl.eu.int

European Ombudsman: internet www.euro-ombudsman.eu.int

Council of the European Union: internet http://ue.eu.int

European Commission: internet http://europa.eu.int

Court of Justice of the European Communities: internet www.curia.eu.int

European Court of Auditors: internet www.eca.eu.int

European Central Bank: internet www.ecb.int

European Economic and Social Committee: internet www.esc.eu.int

Committee of the Regions of the European Union: internet www.cor.eu.int

European Investment Bank: internet www.eib.org

EUR-OP: Office for Publications: internet http://publications.eu.int

Statistical Office of the European Communities: internet http://europa.eu.int/comm/eurostat

Cedefop: internet www.cedefop.gr

Community Plant Variety Office: internet www.cpvo.fr

European Agency for Safety and Health at Work: internet www.europe.osha.eu.int

European Agency for the Evaluation of Medicinal Products: internet http://eudraportal.eudra.org

European Environment Agency: internet www.eea.eu.int

European Foundation for the Improvement of Living and Working Conditions: internet www.eurofound.eu.int

European Monitoring Centre for Drugs and Drug Addiction: internet www.emcdda.org

European Training Foundation: internet www.etf.eu.it

Office for Harmonisation in the Internal Market: internet http://oami.eu.int

European Food Safety Authority: internet www.efsa.eu.int

European Maritime Safety Agency: internet www.emsa.eu.int

European Aviation Safety Agency: internet www.easa.eu,int/contactus_en.html

Dialogue with Citizens: internet http://europa.eu.int/citizensrights

EURODICAUTOM: internet http://europa.eu.int/eurodicautom/Controller

SYSTRAN (external): internet http://www.altavista.com

Interinstitutional Directory (Who's Who in the EU): internet http://europa.eu.int/idea/en.htm

CORDIS (Community Research and Development Information Service): internet www.cordis.lu

EUROPEAN COMMISSION'S DIRECTORATES-GENERAL AND SERVICES

internet http://europa.eu.int/comm/dgs_en.htm

Policies

Press and Communication: internet http://europa.eu.int/comm/dgs/press_communication/index_en.htm

Agriculture: internet http://europa.eu.int/comm/agriculture/index_en.htm

Competition: internet http://europa.eu/int/comm/dgs/competition/index_en.htm

Economic and Financial Affairs: internet http://europa.eu/int/comm/dgs/economy_finance/index_en.htm

Education and Culture: internet http://europa.eu/int/comm/dgs/education_culture/index_en.htm

Employment and Social Affairs: internet http://europa.eu/int/comm/employment_social/index_en.htm

Energy and Transport: internet http://europa.eu/int/comm/dgs/energy-transport/index_en.html

Enterprise: internet http://europa.eu/int/comm/dgs/enterprise/index_en.htm

Environment: internet http://europa.eu/int/comm/dgs/environment/index_en.htm

Fisheries: internet http://europa.eu/int/comm/dgs/fisheries/index_en.htm

Health and Consumer Protection: internet http://europa.eu/int/comm/dgs/health_consumer/index_en.htm

Information Society: internet http://europa.eu/int/comm/dgs/information_society/index_en.htm

Internal Market: internet http://europa.eu/int/comm/dgs/internal_market/index_en.htm

Joint Research Centre: internet www.jrc.cec.eu.int

Justice, Freedom and Security: internet http://europa.eu.int/comm/dgs/justice_home/index_en.htm

Regional Policy: internet http://europa .eu.int/comm/dgs/regional_policy/index_ en.htm

Research: internet http://europa.eu.int/ comm/dgs/research/index_en.html

Taxation and Customs Union: internet http://europa.eu.int/comm/dgs/ taxation_customs/index_en.htm

External Relations

Development: internet http://europa .eu.int/comm/dgs/development/index_ en.htm

Enlargement: internet http://europa .eu.int/comm/enlargement/index_en.htm

EuropeAid Co-operation Office: internet http://europa.eu.int/comm/dgs/ europeaid/index.htm

External Relations: internet http:// europa.eu.int/comm/dgs/external_ relations/index_en.htm

Humanitarian Aid Office - ECHO: internet http://europa.eu.int/comm/dgs/ humanitarian_aid/index_en.htm

Trade: internet http://europa.eu.int/ comm/trade/index_en.htm

Internal Services

Budget: internet http://europa.eu.int/ comm/dgs/budget/index_en.htm

European Anti-Fraud Office: internet http://europa.eu.int/comm/dgs/olaf

Eurostat: internet http://europa.eu.int/ comm/dgs/eurostat/index_en.htm

Financial Control: internet http:// europa.eu.int/comm/dgs/financial_ control/index_en.htm

Joint Interpreting and Conference Service: internet http://europa.eu.int/ comm/dgs/scic/index_en.htm

Legal Service: internet http://europa .eu.int/comm/dgs/legal_service/index_en .htm

Personnel and Administration: internet http://europa.eu.int/comm/dgs/ personnel_administration/index_en.htm

Translation Service: internet http:// europa.eu.int/comm/translation/index_ en.htm

NATIONAL STATISTICAL INSTITUTES

AUSTRIA

Österreichisches Statistisches Zentralamt: Hintere Zollamtsstrasse 2b, 1035 Vienna; tel (+43 1) 711 28 0; fax (+43 1) 711 28 77 28; e-mail info@statistik .gv.at; internet www.statistik.at.

BELGIUM

Institut National de Statistique: 44 Rue de Louvain, 1000 Brussels; tel (+32 02) 548 63 65/66; fax (+32 02) 548 63 67; e-mail info@statbel.mineco.fgov.be; internet www.statbel.fgov.be/info/contact_fr.htm.

CROATIA

Central Bureau of Statistics: Ilica 3 POB 671, 10000 Zagreb; tel (+385 1) 4814-791; fax (+385 1) 4806-148; e-mail belane.takacs@ksh.gov.hu; internet dzs .hr.

CYPRUS

Statistical Service of the Republic of Cyprus: Michalakis Karaolis Str., 1444 Nicosia; tel (+357) 22 60 21 30; fax (+357) 22 66 13 13; e-mail enquiries@cystat.mof .gov.cy; internet www.mof.gov.cy/cystat.

CZECH REPUBLIC

Czech Statistical Office: Na padesátem 81, 100 82 Prague 10; tel (+420) 274 052 304; e-mail infoservis@gw.czso .cz; internet www.czso.cz.

DENMARK

Danmarks Statistik: Sejrogade 11, 2100 Copenhagen; tel (+45) 39 17 39 17; fax (+45) 39 17 39 99; e-mail dst@dst.dk; internet www.dst.dk.

ESTONIA

Statistical Office of Estonia: Endla 15, 15174 Tallinn; tel (+372) 6259 300; fax (+372) 6259 370; e-mail stat@stat.ee; internet www.stat.ee.

FINLAND

Statistics Finland: Työpajankatu 13, 00022 Helsinki; tel (+358 9) 17341; fax (+358 9) 1734 2750; e-mail stat@stat.fi; internet www.stat.fi.

FRANCE

Institut National de la Statistique et des Etudes Economiques: 18 Boulevard Adolphe Pinard, 75675 Paris Cedex 14; tel (+33 1) 41 17 50 50; fax (+33 1) 41 17 66 66; internet www.insee.fr.

GERMANY

Statistisches Bundesamt: Gustav-Stresemann-Ring 11, 65189 Wiesbaden; tel (+49 611) 75 24 05; fax (+49 611) 75 33 30; e-mail info@destatis.de; internet www.destatis.de.

GREECE

National Statistical Service of Greece: Lycourgou Street 14-16, 101 66 Athens; tel (+30 1) 328 90 00; fax (+30 1) 523 36 10; e-mail info@statistics.gr; internet www.statistics.gr.

HUNGARY

Hungarian Central Statistical Office: POB 51, 1525 Budapest; tel (+36 1) 345 60 00; internet www.ksh.hu/pls/ksh/docs/ index_eng.html.

ICELAND

Statistics Iceland: Borgartúni 21a, 150 Reykjavik; tel (+354) 528 10 00; fax (+354) 528 10 99; e-mail information@statice.is; internet www.hagstofa.is.

IRELAND

Central Statistics Office: Skehard Road, Cork; tel (+353 21) 45 35 000; fax (+353 21) 45 35 555; e-mail webmaster@ cso.ie; internet www.cso.ie.

ITALY

Istituto Nazionale di Statistica: Via Cesare Balbo 16, 00184 Rome; tel (+39) 06 46 73 22 43; fax (+39) 06 46 73 22 44; e-mail redazioneweb@istat.it; internet www.istat.it.

LATVIA

Central Statistical Bureau of Latvia: Lāčplēša Street, 1301 Riga; tel (+371) 736 68 50; fax (+371) 783 01 37; e-mail csb@ csb.lv; internet www.csb.lv.

LIECHTENSTEIN

Amt für Volkswirtschaft: Gerberweg 5, 9490 Vaduz; tel (+423) 236 68 71; fax (+423) 236 68 89; e-mail info@avw.llv.li; internet www.llv.li.

LITHUANIA

Department of Statistics: Gedimino av. 29, 2600 Vilnius; tel (+370 5) 236 48 00; fax (+370 5) 236 48 45; e-mail statistika@std.lt; internet www.std.lt.

LUXEMBOURG

Service Central de la Statistique et des Etudes Economiques (STATEC): B.P. 304, 2013 Luxembourg; tel (+352) 478 42 52; fax (+352) 46 42 89; e-mail info@statec.etat.lu; internet www.statec .gouvernement.lu.

MACEDONIA

State Statistical Office: St. Dame Gruev 4, 1000 Skopje; tel (+389 2) 29 56 41; fax (+389 2) 11 13 36; e-mail info@stat .gov.mk; internet www.stat.gov.mk.

MALTA

National Statistics Office: Valletta; tel (+356) 2122 3221-5; fax (+356) 2124 8483; e-mail nso@gov.mt; internet www.nso .mt/stats_off.htm.

MOLDOVA

Département de la Statistique et Sociologie de la République de Moldova: Hincesti 53 highway, 2028 Chisinau; tel (+373 2) 73 37 74; fax (+373 2) 22 61 46; e-mail webmaster@statistica.md; internet www.statistica.md.

NETHERLANDS

Centraal Bureau voor de Statistiek: Prinses Beatrixlaan 428, 2273 XZ Voorburg; tel (+31 70) 337 38 00; fax (+31 70)

387 74 29; e-mail infoservice@cbs.nl; internet www.cbs.nl.

NORWAY

Statistics Norway: Kongens Gate 6, 0033 Oslo; tel (+47 21) 09 45 00; fax (+47 21) 09 45 73; e-mail ssb@ssb.no; internet www.ssb.no.

POLAND

Główny Urząd Statystyczny: al. Niedpodległości 208, 00-925 Warsaw; tel (+48 22) 608 30 00; e-mail dane@stat.gov.pl; internet www.stat.gov.pl.

PORTUGAL

Instituto Nacional de Estatística: Av. Antonio José de Almeida 2, 1000-043 Lisbon; tel (+351 21) 842 61 00; fax (+351 21) 847 63 80; e-mail drlvt@ine.pt; internet www.ine.pt.

ROMANIA

Institutul Naţional de Statistica: Bdul Libertaţii 16, Bucharest; tel (+40 1) 312 48 75; fax (+40 1) 312 48 73; e-mail romstat@insse.ro; internet insse.ro.

SLOVAKIA

Statistical Office of the Slovak Republic: tel (+421) 50 23 63 34; fax (+421) 55 42 45 87; e-mail peter.mach@statistics.sk; internet www.statistics.sk.

SLOVENIA

Statistical Office of the Republic of Slovenia: Vožarski pot 12, 1000 Ljubljana; tel (+386) 1 2415 104; fax (+386) 1 2415 344; e-mail info.stat@gov.si; internet www.stat.si/eng/kontakt.asp.

SPAIN

Instituto Nacional de Estadística: Paseo de la Castellana 183, 28071 Madrid; tel (+34) 91 583 91 00; fax (+34) 91 583 91 58; e-mail www.ine.es/infoine; internet www.ine.es.

SWEDEN

Statistics Sweden: Box 24 300, 10451 Stockholm; tel (+46 8) 506 940 00; fax (+46 8) 661 52 61; e-mail scb@scb.se; internet www.scb.se.

UNITED KINGDOM

Central Statistical Office: 1 Drummond Gate, London SW1V 2QQ; tel (+44) 84 56 01 30 34; fax (+44 16) 33 65 27 47; e-mail info@statistics.gov.uk; internet www.statistics.gov.uk.

EDUCATIONAL INSTITUTIONS AND EUROPEAN CITIES FOR CULTURE

European Schools

FOR GENERAL INFORMATION

Office of the Secretary-General of the Board of Governors of the European Schools: European Commission, Bât. Belliard 5/7 office 1/8, 1049 Brussels, Belgium; tel (+32 2) 295-37-46; fax (+32 2) 513-02-67; Secretary-General Michael Ryan.

BELGIUM

European School of Mol: Europawijk 100, 2400 Mol, Belgium; tel (+32 14) 56-31-01; fax (+32 14) 56-31-04; Director Richard Galvin.

European School of Brussels I / Uccle: 46 ave du Vert Chasseur, 1180 Brussels, Belgium; tel (+32 2) 373-89-11; fax (+32 2) 375-47-16; Director Kari Kivinen.

European School of Brussels II / Woluwé: 75 ave Oscar Jespers, 1200 Brussels, Belgium; tel (+32 2) 774-22-11; fax (+32 2) 774-22-43; Director Dimitri Sfingopoulos.

European School of Brussels III / Ixelles: 135 Blvd du Triomphe, 1050 Brussels, Belgium; tel (+32 2) 629-47-00; fax (+32 2) 629-47-92; Director Peter Hilmersson.

GERMANY

European School of Frankfurt-am-Main: Praunheimer Weg 126, 60439 Frankfurt-am-Main, Germany; tel (+49 69) 9288740; e-mail lshs@eursc.org; Director Hans-Arnold Loos.

European School of Karlsruhe: Albert-Schweitzer-Str. 1, 76139 Karlsruhe, Germany; tel (+49 721) 680090; fax (+49 721) 6800950; Director Tom Høyem.

European School of Munich: Elise-Aulinger-Str. 21, 81739 Munich, Germany; tel (+49 89) 6302290; fax (+49 89) 63022968; Director John Peryer.

ITALY

European School of Varese (Ispra): Via Montello 118, 21100 Varese, Italy; tel (+39) 0332-806111; fax (+39) 0332-806202; Director Marinus Jonkers.

LUXEMBOURG

European School of Luxembourg: Blvd Konrad Adenauer 23, 1115 Luxembourg – Kirchberg, Luxembourg; tel (+352) 4320821; fax (+352) 432082344; Director Harald Feix.

NETHERLANDS

European School of Bergen N.H. / Petten: Molenweidtje 5, Postbus 99, 1862 BC Bergen N.H., Netherlands; tel (+31) 725890109; fax (+31) 725896862; Director Sofia Gardeli.

SPAIN

European School of Alicante: Avenida Locutor Vicente Hipólito s/n, 03450 Playa de San Juan - Alicante; tel (+34) 965 15 56 10; fax (+34) 965 15 64 24; e-mail vlpr@eursc.org; Executive Secretary Beatriz Font.

UNITED KINGDOM

European School of Culham: Culham, Abingdon, Oxon., OX14 3DZ, United Kingdom; tel (+44 1235) 522621; fax (+44 1235) 554609; Director Mrs Bustorff-Silva.

European University Institute

ITALY

European University Institute: Badia Fiesolana, Via dei Roccettini 5, 50016 San Domenico di Fiesole, Florence, Italy; tel (+39) 055-4685228; fax (+39) 055-4685202.

Colleges of Europe

BELGIUM

College of Europe, Bruges: Dyver 11, 8000 Bruges, Belgium; tel (+32 50) 47-74-77; fax (+32 50) 47-71-10.

POLAND

College of Europe, Warsaw: ul. Nowoursynowska 84, 02-797 Warsaw, Poland; tel (+48 22) 545 94 00; fax (+48 22) 649 13 52; e-mail info@natolin.edu.pl.

Public Affairs Institutes

BELGIUM

European Centre for Public Affairs Brussels (ECPAB): 66 ave Adolphe Lacomblé, 1030 Brussels, Belgium; tel (+32 2) 737-77-46; fax (+32 2) 732-75-25; e-mail ecpab@ecpab.be; internet www.ecpab.be; founded 1996; ECPAB is a training institute dedicated to providing the best possible training in all fields related to EU public affairs; its objectives are: to run the Brussels based programmes in EU Institutional Relations and Public Affairs at the postgraduate level, to provide customized training opportunities for practitioners seeking a higher level of competence in their dealings with either the EU or their national government, to stimulate a better understanding of the role and practice of public affairs; programmes offered by ECPAB: intensive 7-day programme 'Working with the EU – Institutional Relations and Public Affairs', 2-day, hands-on seminar 'EU Funding at Your Fingertips' (how to apply for EU grants and loans, identify programmes and partners, and respond to tendering procedures), customized programmes in all European affairs-related fields focusing on the working of the EU institutions, policy-making and decision-making processes, lobbying techniques, information monitoring, management of public affairs, EU grants and loans, masterclass seminar; Executive Director Lucyna Gutman-Grauer; Development Manager Savina Tarsitano.

European Institute for Public Affairs and Lobbying (EIPAL): 214D chaussée de Wavre, 1050 Brussels, Belgium; tel (+32 2) 508-30-35; tel (+32 2) 358-11-89; fax (+32 2) 626-95-01; fax (+32 2) 358-45-66; e-mail info@eipal.be; internet www.eipal.be; founded 1994; the institute's objective is to provide European specialists with formal training in the functioning of the EU's institutions and in lobbying methods and practices; courses are given in cycles of 12 weeks (75 hours); during each cycle, 45 subjects are presented in the form of lectures, case studies and discussions; the courses are given each Monday and Thursday from 6.00 pm to 9.00 pm at IHECS (Institut des Hautes Etudes de Communications Sociales), 23 rue des Grandes Carmes, 1000 Brussels, Belgium; lectures are given by European officials and specialists, in English and in French; the number of students participating is limited to 35; Chairman Christian Le Clercq.

Management Institute

FRANCE

Institut Supérieur du Management Public et Politique (ISMAPP): 132 rue Perronet 132, 92200 Neuilly-sur-Seine, France; tel (+33) 1-46-24-61-61; fax (+33) 1-46-24-25-28; e-mail direction@ ismapp.com; internet www.ismpapp.com; founded 1997; offers two complementary courses: one in Paris, designed specifically for a professional career in France, the other in Brussels, with European speakers and teaching; the courses are open to students with a master's degree or equivalent; ISMAPP does not claim to offer a new-style political science course but seeks to complete the theoretical knowledge of the public institutions which young people have acquired during their formative years of study (students might learn, for example, how to draft a parliamentary amendment, how to handle the media, how to build a lobbying campaign and how to set up a partnership).

European Capitals of Culture

- 2005: Cork
- 2006: Patras

Contact: Mr Kosmopoulos, Culture 2000 Programme; tel: (+32 2) 299-93-35.